THE SOUND OF MUSIC A musical instrument is a device for creating pressure changes in the air. In the hands of a musician, these pressure changes can become the pleasing sounds of music. The transformation of these changes into our perception of sound begins when the changes in air pressure cause tiny hairs deep inside our ears to vibrate. (Chapters 11 and 12)

RICHARD HAMILTON SMITH /

Shilli Gabar
Ochn Snow
shili.gabr@
durham.ac.uk.
Sensation + perception
5th edition
£20.

PERCEIVING SIZE One way ... familiar objects, so in the ... estimate the height of the la... Thus, even though the lamp... are the same height in our fi... ther away and therefore mus...

THE SUBTLETIES OF SMELL The human sense of smell is often underestimated, but it is because of our ability to smell that we are able to enjoy the flavors of food. Trained experts can use smell to make fine discriminations between types of perfume or different vintages of wine. The chemist in this photo is using smell to research the properties of cork. (Chapter 15)

PERCEIVING THROUGH THE SKIN The ability of blind people to read by scanning the raised dots of Braille demonstrates humans' ability to take in information through the skin. To understand how we perceive through the skin, we need to consider not only the skin, but also thought processes such as those that guide the Braille reader's fingers over the page. (Chapter 14)

WHAT DO BABIES PERCEIVE Early psychologists thought that a young baby's perception of the world was incoherent, but modern researchers have shown that babies can perceive much more than originally thought. Perceptual psychologists have measured what babies can perceive and how their perceptual abilities improve as they get older. (Chapter 16)

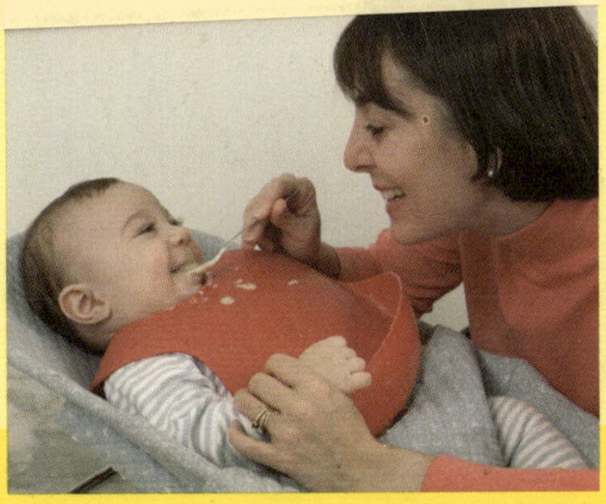

LAURA DWIGHT / CORBIS

HULTON-DEUTSCH COLLECTION / CORBIS

SENSATION AND PERCEPTION

FIFTH EDITION

E. BRUCE GOLDSTEIN
University of Pittsburgh

Brooks/Cole Publishing Company
I(T)P® An International Thomson Publishing Company

Pacific Grove • Albany • Belmont • Bonn • Boston • Cincinnati • Detroit • Johannesburg • London
Madrid • Melbourne • Mexico City • New York • Paris • Singapore • Tokyo • Toronto • Washington

15/8/01

Psychology Editor: *Marianne Taflinger*
Marketing Team: *Lauren Harp, Christine Davis*
Editorial Assistant: *Scott Brearton, Rachael Bruckman*
Production Coordinator: *Kirk Bomont*
Manuscript Editor: *Maryan Malone*
Permissions Editor: *Lillian Campobasso*
Cover Design: *Lisa Mirski Devenish, E. Kelly Shoemaker*
Interior Design: *Publications Development Company of Texas*
Interior Illustration: *Wayne Clark, Cyndie C. H. Wooley, Jon Clark*
Cover Image: *Damir Polić*
Art Editor: *Lisa Torri*
Typesetting: *Publications Development Company of Texas*
Printing and Binding: *R.R. Donnelley*

For more information, contact:

BROOKS/COLE PUBLISHING COMPANY
511 Forest Lodge Road
Pacific Grove, CA 93950
USA

International Thomson Publishing Europe
Berkshire House 168-173
High Holborn
London WC1V 7AA
England

Thomas Nelson Australia
102 Dodds Street
South Melbourne, 3205
Victoria, Australia

Nelson Canada
1120 Birchmount Road
Scarborough, Ontario
Canada M1K 5G4

International Thomson Editores
Seneca 53
Col. Polanco
11560 México, D. F., México

International Thomson Publishing GmbH
Königswinterer Strasse 418
53227 Bonn
Germany

International Thomson Publishing Asia
60 Albert Street
#15–10 Albert Complex
Singapore 189969

International Thomson Publishing Japan
Hirakawacho Kyowa Building, 3F
2-2-1 Hirakawacho
Chiyoda-ku, Tokyo 102
Japan

Printed in the United States of America

10 9 8 7 6 5

Library of Congress Cataloging-in-Publication Data
Goldstein, E. Bruce
Sensation and perception/E. Bruce Goldstein—5th ed.
p. cm.
Includes bibliographical references and index.
ISBN 0-534-34680-4 (alk. paper)
1. Senses and sensation. 2. Perception. I. Title
QP431.G64 1999
152.1—dc21 98-5846
CIP

THIS BOOK IS PRINTED ON ACID-FREE RECYCLED PAPER

To Barbara

About the Author

E. Bruce Goldstein is Associate Professor of Psychology and Director of Undergraduate Programs in Psychology at the University of Pittsburgh. He received his bachelor's degree in chemical engineering from Tufts University and his Ph.D. in experimental psychology from Brown University, and was a postdoctoral fellow in the biology department at Harvard University. Bruce has published numerous papers on visual physiology and visual perception and is the editor of the forthcoming *Handbook of Perception*. He teaches sensation and perception, introductory psychology as a natural science, the psychology of gender, and the psychology of art.

BRIEF CONTENTS

Contents

1

Introduction to Perception

2

Receptors and Neural Processing

5

PERCEIVING COLOR

6

PERCEPTUAL CONSTANCY

7

Perceiving Objects

8

Perceiving Visual Space

9

Size, Illusions, and Ecological Aspects of Perception

10

Perceiving Movement

11

Sound, the Auditory System, and Pitch Perception

12

Perceiving Loudness, Timbre, and the Auditory Scene

Something to Consider

Across the Senses

Preface

When I was a graduate student at Brown University I studied chemical reactions that occur in the visual receptors. In my youthful enthusiasm, I thought that understanding these chemical reactions was the key to understanding perception. I was not totally wrong, because the chemical reactions that occur when molecules in the receptors absorb light are an essential first step in the perceptual process. However, as I continued my study of perception, I soon realized that the perceptual process extends far beyond molecules in the receptors, stretching into the visual cortex and—as research was just beginning to suggest at the time—even into cortical areas beyond the primary sensory receiving areas. I also became aware that perception cannot be understood by studying physiology alone. I learned that psychophysics—the study of the relationships between stimuli and perception—is central to our understanding of perception.

My appreciation for both the psychophysics and physiology of perception has been reflected in each edition of *Sensation and Perception,* beginning with the first edition, which was published in 1980. As I wrote the first edition and the revisions that followed, I have been motivated by a desire to tell the story of perceptual research in a way that transmits the excitement of this fascinating topic. In each successive edition, I have made changes to reflect new developments in the field and to respond to feedback I've received from instructors and students. In this, the fifth edition, I have made numerous changes in both content and presentation while keeping the characteristics that so many people have appreciated in the previous editions. The following summarizes some of the features and changes in this fifth edition of *Sensation and Perception.*

Increased Clarity

One goal of this revision was to increase the clarity of the presentation. By listening to feedback from students and instructors who had used the fourth edition, and getting input from a student reviewer who flagged sections that were difficult, I was able to increase the readability of sections that students had found difficult in the last edition.

Cutting Edge Coverage

Another goal of this revision was to include new research. To this end, nearly 100 references to articles published in the last three years have been added. A few examples of cutting-edge topics that are new to this edition or are expanded from the last edition are the role of action in perception, the effects of brain damage on perception, modular processing of different perceptual qualities, the perception of ecologically valid stimuli, and the interplay between perception and attention.

"Bite-Sized" Chapters in a Logical Sequence

The chapters in this edition are shorter than in the fourth edition and the logical sequencing that has been a feature of earlier editions has been refined. The first four chapters introduce the basic idea behind the study of perception and establish the basic physiological principles that are needed to understand the rest of the text. The next six chapters build on these basic principles and consider the following topics in visual perception: color vision (Chapter 5), the perceptual constancies (Chapter 6), object perception (Chapter 7), space perception (Chapter 8), size, illusions, and the ecological approach (Chapter 9), and movement perception (Chapter 10).

Chapters 6 and 9 are new, serving two purposes: (1) they introduce new material, and (2) they contain material that was in chapters that were too long in the fourth edition and so help to shorten these chapters. For example, material on color and lightness constancy that was originally in the color vision chapter is now in Chapter 6. Although there are a greater number of chapters, the book is shorter than before. Thus, the chapters in this edition are more "bite-sized," and easier to digest.

Chapters 11 and 12, which cover basic mechanisms of hearing, represent a notable improvement in organization. The psychophysical and physiological approaches are no longer separated, as in previous editions, since these chapters are organized on the basis of perceptions rather than processes. Thus, Chapter 11 introduces the auditory system and focuses on pitch perception, and Chapter 12 focuses on auditory localization, loudness, and other auditory qualities.

The chapters on speech (Chapter 13), the cutaneous senses (Chapter 14), the chemical senses (Chapter 15), and clinical aspects of vision and hearing (Chapter 17) are updated versions of the corresponding chapters in the fourth edition, but the chapter on perceptual development (Chapter 16) is new. This chapter gathers together and integrates material from the *Developmental Dimensions* sections that appeared at the end of each chapter in the fourth edition. The result is a more coherent overview of perceptual development than was provided by the more piecemeal treatment in the previous edition.

Finally, the *Other Worlds of Perception* feature that appeared at the end of each chapter in the fourth edition has been eliminated as a separate section, but much of the material from these sections, which described how animals perceive, has been integrated into the text.

Underlying Principles and Commonalties Across the Senses

Short sections called *Underlying Principles* that appear after Chapters 4, 10, and 16 emphasize that although each of the senses has its own unique qualities, there are basic principles that cut across all of the senses. The first section introduces eight principles based on the material in Chapters 1–4. The second section applies theses principles to the material in Chapters 5–10 and adds three more principles. The third section applies all of the principles to the material in Chapters 11–16.

The idea that there are basic principles that hold across the senses is reinforced by a one-page section called *Across the Senses* that appears at the end of each chapter and which describes similar phenomena that occur across two or more senses. The topics in these sections are listed on page xviii.

Demonstrations

The *Demonstrations* have been a popular feature of previous editions, because they provide perceptual experiences that illustrate principles discussed in the text. The demonstrations are simple enough that students can easily do them and are integrated into the flow of the text so that they become part of the ongoing story. The demonstrations are listed on page xvii.

Thinking about the Material

A section called *Something to Consider* that appears at the end of each chapter discusses an especially important concept or a controversial issue, giving the student something open-ended to think about.

The Illustration Program

The extensive illustration program for which this text is known has been continued in this edition. There are over 600 diagrams, drawings, graphs, and photographs in this edition, with over 150 of these illustrations being new to this edition. Old illustrations were pruned and new ones added to reflect advances in research since the last edition.

Color Essays

As in the fourth edition, the color illustrations are contained in three short "color essays," which stand on their own but also illustrate phenomena described elsewhere in the text.

Study Questions

At the end of each chapter are study questions keyed to pages in the text. Beginning in Chapter 5, each set of questions begins with a special section designed to help students identify the "Underlying Principles" discussed in the chapter.

Glossary

As in the previous edition, all of the definitions of bold-faced terms are contained in a single glossary at the end of the book.

Help for the Instructor

A set of transparencies of some of the text's illustrations and a test bank are available to instructors. The instructor's manual contains a test bank and other material to help in teaching the course, including a chapter-by-chapter list correlating the interactions in the *Exploring Perception* CD-ROM (see below) with the book. The test bank, which is also available in computerized form, includes over 600 questions, many of which were "class tested."

Help for the Student

For the first time, a student's study guide is now available. This study guide supplements the study questions that are included in the book, with chapter outlines, expanded discussion of key terms and concepts, and practice test questions.

Web Site Links

A way to supplement the material in this book is to check perception-related sites on the World Wide Web. To find these sites, access the Brooks/Cole homepage at www.brookscole.com.

Exploring Perception CD-ROM

Exploring Perception, a CD-ROM for Macintosh and IBM Windows, is an exciting new ancillary available from Brooks/Cole. This interactive CD-ROM, which was developed by Colin Ryan of James Cook University, North Queensland, Australia, gives students an opportunity to actively explore many of the concepts described in the text, including psychophysics, physiological principles, and perception of color, form, motion, and depth. In addition, instructors can use *Exploring Perception* to demonstrate key principles in class by using the "organizer" function, which allows them to sequence material in the CD to fit their lecture. For further information about *Exploring Perception,* instructors can contact their local Brooks/Cole representative or inquire via e-mail to *info@brookscole.com.*

A Message to the Student

Although much of this preface has been directed to instructors, I want to close by addressing a few words to the students who will be using this book. As you read this book, you will see that it is a story about experiences that may initially seem simple, such as seeing a face or smelling a rose, but that turn out to be extremely complex. I hope that reading this book helps you appreciate both the complexity and the beauty of the mechanisms responsible for these experiences. I hope that as you gain an appreciation for the impressive advances that researchers have made toward understanding perception, you will also appreciate how much is still left to be discovered. But most important of all, I hope that reading this book will make you more aware of how perception affects you personally. After all, perception is something you experience all the time, and the study of perception can enhance this experience. I've found that studying perception has made me more observant of my environment, and more appreciative of the miraculous processes that transform energy falling on receptors into the richness of experience. I hope reading this book has the same effect on you. If you have questions, comments, or other feedback about this book, I invite you to communicate with me via e-mail at bruceg+@pitt.edu.

E. Bruce Goldstein

ACKNOWLEDGMENTS

Although I have been writing textbooks for more than two decades, I am still impressed by the extent to which creating a textbook is a group effort. One person who has played an indispensable role in creation of this book is Marianne Taflinger, my editor, who I thank for pushing me to write this revision even though I initially resisted. Marianne also supported my efforts by obtaining excellent reviews, making valuable suggestions regarding ways to improve the book, and approving the creation of many new illustrations for this edition.

My special thanks go to Nancy Marcus Land and all of the people at Publications Development Company in Crockett, Texas, who, with grace, creativity and extreme professionalism, turned my manuscript into this book. I thank Pam Blackmon at PDC for coordinating all parts of the production, and Kirk Bomont, who handled production liaison at Brooks/Cole, for his continued support.

I also wish to thank Lisa Torri, who again was a joy to work with on the art program, Kelly Shoemaker for her work toward creation of the cover design, Christine Davis for creating the brochure extolling the book's merits, and Jennifer Wilkinson for being patient with me as I worked on the study guide and instructor's manual. In addition, I thank my friends in Pittsburgh, who have finally become used to the fact that I am always writing "the book," and I especially thank my wife, Barbara, who has persevered with love and understanding through numerous book projects.

Thanks also to the following people who kindly provided new photographs for this edition: Velma Dobson, Kerry Green, Kelly Kaye, David Pisoni, Edmund Rolls, and Daniel Simons. Finally, I thank the following reviewers and colleagues who provided valuable feedback about the fourth edition and the manuscript for this edition:

Frank M. Bagrash
California State University, Fullerton

William P. Banks
Pomona College

Michael Biderman
University of Tennessee-Chattanooga

Bruce Bridgeman
University of California, Santa Cruz

Patrick Cavanagh
Harvard University

James C. Craig
Indiana University

W. Jay Dowling
University of Texas at Dallas

Susan E. Dutch
Westfield State College

Bradley Gibson
University of Notre Dame

Norma Graham
Columbia University

Donald Greenfield
Eye Institute of New Jersey

Timothy S. Klitz
University of Minesotta-Twin Cities

Harry Lawless
Cornell University

W. Trammell Neill
SUNY-Albany

Catherine Palmer
University of Pittsburgh

David B. Pisoni
Indiana University

Dennis Proffitt
University of Virginia

Lawrence D. Rosenblum
University of California at Riverside

Colin Ryan
James Cook University

H. A. Sedgwick
State University of New York

Kenneth R. Short
Creighton University

Steven M. Specht
Lebanon Valley College

Leslie Tolbert
University of Arizona

Robert G. Vautin
Wheaton College

William Yost
Loyola University of Chicago

1

Introduction to Perception

"You have been in Afghanistan, I perceive."

—Sherlock Holmes

Sherlock Holmes, the fictional detective created by Sir Arthur Conan Doyle, was famous for his ability to deduce startling conclusions from seemingly meager clues. One such example, in A *Study in Scarlet*, occurs when Holmes is introduced to his future sidekick, Dr. Watson, in London. Without prompting, Holmes immediately observes that Watson has just come from Afghanistan. Amazed that Holmes knows this fact about him, Watson naturally assumes that someone must have told Holmes that he had been an army doctor serving in Afghanistan. "Nothing of the sort," Holmes protests. He goes on to explain, "I *knew* you came from Afghanistan. From long habit the train of thoughts ran so swiftly through my mind that I arrived at the conclusion without being conscious of intermediate steps. There were such steps, however. The train of reasoning ran, 'Here is a gentleman of the medical type, but with the air of a military man. Certainly an army doctor, then. He has just come from the tropics, for his face is dark, and that is not the natural tint of his skin, for his wrists are fair. He has undergone hardship and sickness, as his haggard face says clearly. His left arm has been injured. He holds it in a stiff and unnatural manner. Where in the tropics could an English army doctor have seen much hardship and got his arm wounded? Clearly in Afghanistan.' The whole train of thought did not occupy a second. I then remarked that you came from Afghanistan, and you were astonished."

CHAPTER CONTENTS

SOME QUESTIONS WE WILL CONSIDER

- What is the difference between perceiving something and recognizing it? (4)
- How can we measure perception? (7)
- How are physiological processes involved in perception? (13)
- Why are we interested in studying perception? (23)

Doyle's readers are amused and entertained when Holmes claims that he performed such an elaborate chain of reasoning so instantaneously that he wasn't even "conscious of the intermediate steps." Only in fiction, we think, do detectives put theories together from such fragmentary clues. Yet this is just what you and I do every time we open our eyes or listen with our ears: Every waking moment, we are performing complex, instantaneous feats of organizing and integrating information and creating perceptions from it. As you will see in this book, the processes involved in perceiving our environment are as remarkable as the exploits of the greatest fictional detectives.

"But," you might say, "perception seems automatic to me. I don't really feel like there is anything very complex going on, or that I'm doing detective work. It feels as if my perceptions just happen." It makes sense to say this, because one of the great illusions in our lives is that perception is simple. We look across the street and see pedestrians dashing for the other side against a blinking "Don't Walk" sign. We walk through an open air market and smell the freshness of newly picked flowers. We turn on our radio and hear a voice proclaiming the latest news. Except for unusual conditions, such as dense fog that makes seeing difficult or a noisy environment that makes it hard to understand what someone else is saying, we easily experience most perceptions without expending any apparent effort. They just seem to happen.

But the ease with which we perceive things masks a multitude of complex processes that are occurring behind the scenes. We can draw an analogy between these hidden perceptual processes and what happens as we watch a play in the theater. As we sit comfortably in our seats watching a play, our attention is focused on the unfolding drama created by the characters in the play. But backstage, something entirely different is happening: An actress is rushing to complete her costume change; an actor is pacing back and forth to calm his nerves just before he goes on; the stage manager is checking to be sure the next scene change is ready to go; and high in the rafters, a stagehand is replacing a light bulb that blew out in the first act.

Just as the audience sees only a small part of what is actually happening during a play, your effortless perception of the world around you is also just a small part of what is happening as you perceive. This book is about both the perceptions of which you are aware and the backstage activity that is hidden from your view. One of the messages of this book is that perception does not just happen but is the end result of complex processes, many of which are not available to our awareness. To appreciate this hidden complexity of perception we will now look at some of the processes that are involved in perceiving.

The Perceptual Process

Consider the following situation: Ellen enters the billiard room in the Student Union and sees Bill standing across the room. As she walks toward Bill, she turns her head, sees him smile at her and returns his smile with one of her own. A simple encounter, effortlessly carried out. But behind this effortlessness lies the sequence of steps that we call the **perceptual process,** shown in Figure 1.1. We will describe each of these steps, beginning with Bill, our stimulus.

Distal Stimulus

Our starting point is the stimulus in the environment, which is called the **distal stimulus** (*Dist*al = stimulus

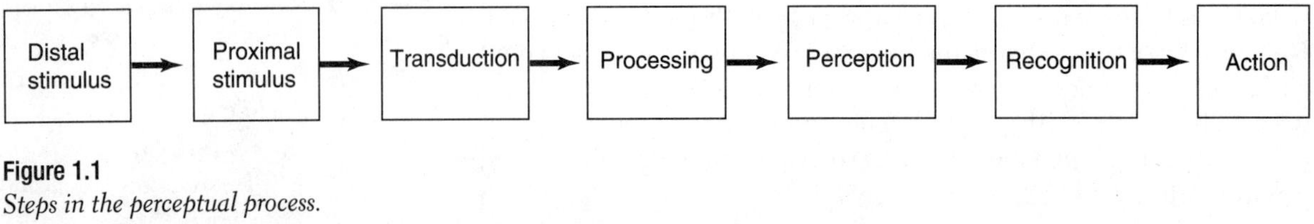

Figure 1.1
Steps in the perceptual process.

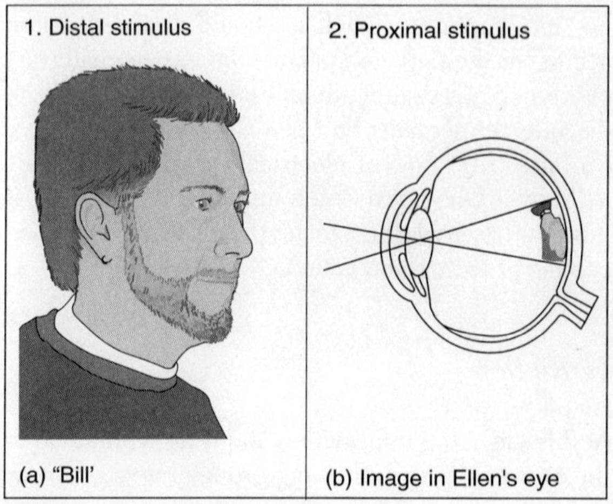

Figure 1.2
(a) We take Bill, the distal stimulus, as the starting point for our description of the perceptual process. (b) The proximal stimulus is Bill's image on Ellen's retina.

at a *dist*ance). In Figure 1.2a, Bill is the distal stimulus. The distal stimulus is specified in terms of its physical characteristics. Thus, a partial description of Bill as a distal stimulus would be that he has short dark hair, a neatly trimmed beard, and is 5′11″ tall.

Proximal Stimulus

The **proximal stimulus** is the stimulus that stimulates Ellen's visual receptors. (*Prox*imal = stimulus in *proximity* to the receptors). In the case of vision, the proximal stimulus is an *image* of Bill on the receptors that line the back of Ellen's eyes. This image is created when light is reflected from Bill into Ellen's eyes (Figure 1.2b).

It is important to understand the difference between the distal and proximal stimuli, because although the proximal stimulus (the image of Bill) is created from the distal stimulus (Bill), they are very different. Perhaps the most obvious difference is that while Bill is a muscular 5′11″ tall person, the proximal stimulus that he creates on Ellen's retina is a flat picture just a few millimeters in height. Another difference between Bill and the proximal stimulus is that the small two-dimensional proximal stimulus usually contains information about only part of the distal stimulus. For example, only light from the parts of Bill that are facing Ellen is reflected into her eyes, so she receives information about his face, but not the back of his head. Also, before the light reflected from Bill's face reaches Ellen's receptors, it must pass through the eye's focusing structures. If this focusing mechanism isn't working properly, the image may not be sharply focused on the receptors and so the proximal stimulus will be an out-of-focus image of Bill.

These changes that occur during creation of the proximal stimulus can have large effects on perception. Ellen can't see the back of Bill's head unless he turns around, and if Bill's image isn't focused properly, she would perceive him as being blurred. If you wear glasses and take them off for a moment, the distal stimulus is not affected, but the proximal stimulus becomes blurred, and perception becomes out-of-focus.

The transformation of the distal stimulus into the proximal stimulus is only the beginning of the perceptual process. Next comes another transformation, as the light illuminating the receptors is changed into electrical signals.

Transduction

Transduction is the transformation of one form of energy into another form of energy (Figure 1.3a). An example of transduction is the sequence of events that occurs when you touch the "Withdrawal" button on the screen of the money access machine at the bank. The pressure exerted by your finger is transduced into electrical energy, which is then transduced into mechanical energy to push your money out of the machine. In the nervous system, transduction occurs when environmental energy is transformed into electrical energy. In our example, the light of the proximal stimulus on Ellen's retina is transformed into electrical signals in tens of thousands of her visual receptors.

Neural Processing

Bill's image has now been transformed into electrical signals in Ellen's receptors, which then generate new

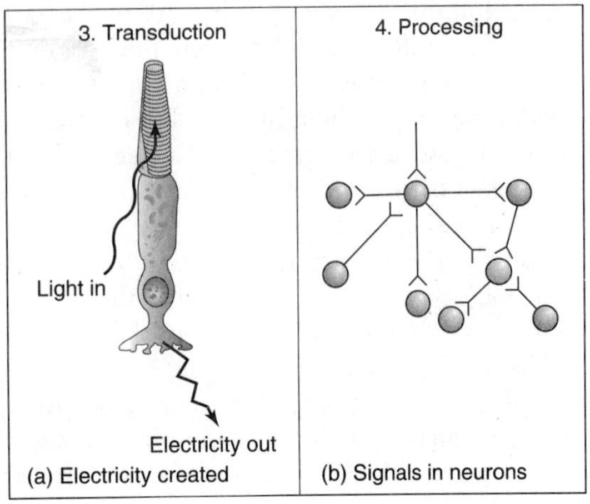

Figure 1.3
(a) Transduction occurs when light stimulates the receptors and the receptors create electrical energy. (b) This electrical energy is processed through networks of neurons.

signals in cells called *neurons* that we will describe shortly. These neurons create a series of interconnected pathways far more complex than the map that would be created if we could shrink the entire U.S. highway system down to the size of this page. It is along these pathways that electrical signals travel, first from the eye to the brain (with some stops in-between) and then within the brain itself. During their travels through this network of neurons, the electrical signals undergo neural processing. (Figure 1.3b).

Neural processing is the operations that transform the electrical signals in the networks of neurons. We will wait until Chapter 2 to describe exactly how these electrical signals are processed, but by returning to our analogy of the road map, we can understand processing on a simple level. Imagine that you are looking down on the traffic on a network of busy city streets at rush hour. You see one place where traffic from three or four other streets is flowing into a single street that has therefore become totally clogged and almost looks like a parking lot; another street has stop-and-go traffic because there are traffic lights at each intersection; and a third is a limited-access freeway that is flowing smoothly. Thus, the way different streets are laid out and the number of traffic signals can affect the flow of cars through the city.

In Chapter 2 we will see that a similar situation occurs for the nervous system. The way the pathways of the nervous system are laid out, and the nature of the interconnections between the various pathways, can affect the flow of electrical signals through the pathways. This is extremely important because it is this flow of signals that creates the next step in the perceptual process—perception.

Perception

At this stage, the information about Bill contained in the electrical signals flowing through nerve pathways in the brain is transformed into Ellen's perception of Bill (Figure 1.4a). She *sees* him smiling at her from across the room.

In the past, some accounts of the perceptual process have stopped at this stage. After all, once Ellen sees Bill, hasn't she perceived him? The answer to this question is yes, she has perceived him, but other things have happened as well—she has also recognized him as being her friend Bill and she has taken action to get closer to him. These two additional steps—recognition and action—are important outcomes of the perceptual process and also contribute to it.

Recognition

Recognition is our ability to place an object in a category that gives it meaning. For example, when Ellen sees Bill she also recognizes that she is seeing a male person she knows to be her friend Bill (Figure 1.4b). Although we might be tempted to group perception and recognition together, researchers have shown that they are separate processes. One way they have shown this is by demonstrating that some people with brain damage can see things well but have a very difficult time recognizing what they are. When we describe some of these people in Chapter 4, we will see that people who suffer from a condition called *prosopagnosia* can look directly at a close friend's face and *see* it clearly, without having an inkling that it is someone they know.

Figure 1.4
(a) Ellen has a conscious perception of Bill. (b) She recognizes Bill, and (c) takes action by turning her head and smiling.

Action

Action follows perception and recognition. Ellen perceives and recognizes Bill and begins to move toward him. She sees him smile and responds with a smile of her own (Figure 1.4c). Some researchers see action as being an important outcome of the perceptual process because of its importance for survival. David Milner and Melvyn Goodale (1995) propose that early in the evolution of animals the major emphasis of visual processing was not to create a conscious perception or "picture" of the environment, but to help the animal control navigation, catch prey, avoid obstacles, and detect predators—all crucial functions for the animal's survival.

The fact that perception often leads to action, whether it be an animal's increasing its vigilance when it hears a twig snapping in the forest, or Ellen moving toward Bill when she sees him standing across the room, means that perception is a continuously changing process. For example, as Ellen approaches Bill and looks at him from different vantage points, the image on her retina gets larger and changes shape, forming a new proximal stimulus.

When we look at the perceptual process in this way, we can appreciate that the *process* of perception doesn't really have a beginning or an ending point. It is a constantly changing, dynamic process. We can symbolize the changing nature of this process by rearranging the flow diagram of Figure 1.1 to form a circle, as in Figure 1.5. This arrangement captures the dynamic and continuously changing nature of the perceptual process and also enables us to see more easily how we might study it.

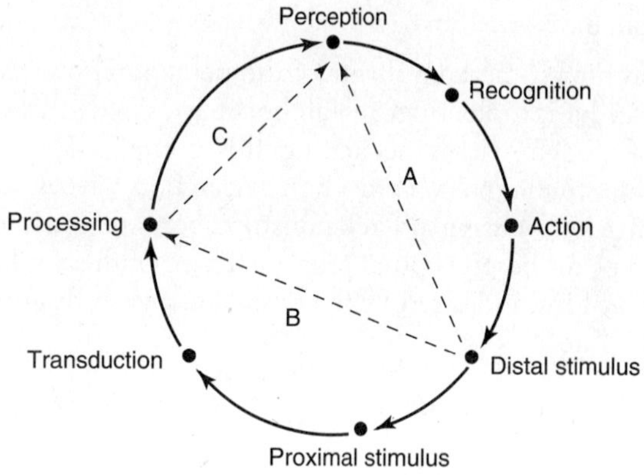

Figure 1.5
The perceptual cycle. This is the steps in the perceptual process from Figure 1.1, arranged in a circle. This emphasizes the fact that the perceptual process is dynamic and continually changing. The arrows represent the relationships between A: the stimulus and perception; B: the stimulus and processing; and C: processing and perception.

Figure 1.6
Studying perception by looking for relationships between the stimulus and perception has revealed a relationship between the converging lines in this scene and the perception of depth.

Studying the Perceptual Process

Although the complexity of the perceptual process can be intimidating, researchers have devised ways of studying it by separating this complex system into smaller parts. Perception researchers have done this by focusing on relationships between various steps in the perceptual process. Three of these relationships, indicated by the dashed arrows in Figure 1.5, are:

1. The stimulus–perception relationship (Arrow A).
2. The stimulus–physiology relationship (Arrow B).
3. The physiology–perception relationship (Arrow C).

Each of these relationships tells us something about perception. The **stimulus–perception relationship** defines the relationship between the physical stimuli in the world and what a person perceives. For example, the converging lines in the scene of Figure 1.6 lead to an impression of depth.

The **stimulus–physiology relationship** provides a window into the inner workings of the perceptual system by demonstrating the connection between stimuli and nerve firing. Through research on this relationship, which is carried out mainly on animals, we have learned a tremendous amount about the neural processing that occurs during the perceptual process. For example, this research has shown that different visual qualities, such as color, movement, and depth, activate different groups of neurons in the brain.

The **physiology–perception relationship** will be a central concern in this book because it provides information about how the inner workings of the brain result in perception. This relationship is, however, the most difficult of the three to measure because although physiological responding is relatively easy to measure in animals, it is practically and ethically difficult to measure in humans. Conversely, although perception is easy to measure in humans, it is more difficult to measure in animals. Despite these difficulties, we will see that researchers have devised ways to measure this relationship.[1]

The study of perception is largely the study of the three relationships in Figure 1.5 (although we will see that other relationships are also studied as well). To help you understand how these relationships are studied, we will now describe some basic principles and methods that have been used to study them. The stimulus–perception relationship has been studied by using the *behavioral approach to perception,* the stimulus–physiology relationship has been studied using the **physiological approach to perception,** and the physiology–perception relationship has been studied using a combination of these two approaches. We begin by considering the behavioral approach.

The Behavioral Approach: Linking Stimulation and Perception

The **behavioral approach to perception** focuses on the relationship between the physical properties of stimuli and the perceptual response to these stimuli. If you've taken other courses in psychology you might associate the term *behavioral* with things like learning (a rat pressing a bar in a Skinner box), thinking (a person solving a problem), or emotions (a person having an emotional reaction to a disturbing event). But just as learning, thinking, and emotions are all behaviors, perception is a behavior as well. Thus, in this book the behavioral approach refers not to learning, thinking, or emotions, but to the behavior we call perception. We call the techniques we use to measure perception *behavioral* techniques.

A number of behavioral techniques are used to measure the relationship between stimuli and perception. We will focus on two methods that are widely used—the *phenomenological method* and the *psychophysical method.*

The Phenomenological Method: Describing What Is Perceived

The **phenomenological method** simply involves asking subjects to describe what they perceive. For example, in a color-naming experiment, the experimenter presents a light and observers indicate the color they perceive. In experiments testing for the perceptual effects of brain damage, patients are asked to identify a common object or a picture of that object. Consider the following demonstration:

DEMONSTRATION

Perceiving a Picture

After looking at the drawing in Figure 1.7, close your eyes, turn to page 9, and open and shut your eyes rapidly to briefly expose the picture in Figure 1.10. Decide what the picture is, and then open your eyes and read the explanation below it. ●

Figure 1.7
Look at this drawing first, then close your eyes and turn the page, so you are looking at the same place on the page directly under this one. Then open and shut your eyes rapidly. (Adapted from Bugelski & Alampay, 1961.)

[1] Because a great deal of physiological research been done on cats and monkeys, students often express concerns about how these animals are treated. All animal research in the United States follows strict guidelines for the care of animals established by organizations such as the American Psychological Association and the Society for Neuroscience. The central tenet of these guidelines is that every effort should be made to ensure that animals are not subjected to pain or distress. Research on animals has provided essential information for developing aids to help people with sensory disabilities such as blindness and deafness and for helping develop techniques to ease severe pain.

Did you identify Figure 1.10 as a rat (or a mouse)? If you did, you were influenced by the clearly ratlike or mouselike figure you observed initially. But people who first observe Figure 1.13 on page 11 usually identify Figure 1.10 as a man. (Try this demonstration on some other people.) The **rat–man demonstration** shows that the subject's expectations about the meaning of a stimulus can influence their perception of the stimulus. We used the phenomenological method to show this because the data we needed was the subject's description of what he or she perceived.

Another example of an experiment in which subjects are asked to describe what they see is one by Steven Palmer (1975), which used the stimuli in Figure 1.18. Palmer first presented a context scene such as the one on the left and then briefly flashed one of the target pictures on the right. When Palmer asked subjects to identify the object in the target picture, they correctly identified an object like the loaf of bread (which is appropriate to the kitchen scene) 80 percent of the time, but correctly identified the mailbox or the drum (two objects that don't fit into the scene) only 40 percent of the time. As in the rat–man demonstration, this experiment also uses the phenomenological method to show how perception can be influenced by a person's expectations. We will see, as we study the relationship between stimuli in the world and perception, that asking people to describe what they perceive is an important tool for studying the perceptual process.

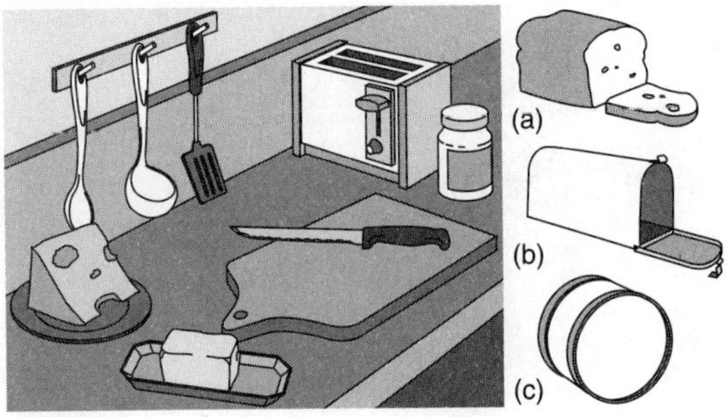

Figure 1.8
Stimuli used in Palmer's (1975) experiment. The scene at the left is presented first, and the observer is then asked to identify one of the objects on the right.

Although results from the phenomenological method can be valuable, they are usually qualitative in nature—they provide description but not precise measurement. Often, however, it is useful to be able to establish a quantitative relationship between the stimulus and perception. To achieve this, we look to the psychophysical methods. We begin by describing a group of methods called the "Classical" psychophysical methods because they were developed in the 19th century.

The Classical Psychophysical Methods: Measuring Thresholds

In the 19th century, the first scientific psychologists developed a number of methods called the **classical psychophysical methods** to measure thresholds—the smallest amount of stimulus energy necessary for an observer to detect a stimulus. Gustav Fechner (1801–1887) was a pioneer in developing the classical psychophysical methods. He proposed that it would be possible to demonstrate a relationship between the functioning of the body and experience by having people report their experiences as physical stimuli are systematically changed. Fechner cleverly picked an experience that was relatively easy to define—whether or not a person can detect a stimulus. In 1860, Fechner published his book *Elements of Psychophysics,* in which he focused on measuring a quantity called the absolute threshold.

The Absolute Threshold The **absolute threshold** is the smallest amount of stimulus energy necessary for an observer to detect a stimulus. Fechner described the following three methods for measuring the absolute threshold: the *method of limits,* the *method of adjustment,* and the *method of constant stimuli.*

To measure the threshold by using the **method of limits,** the experimenter presents stimuli in either ascending or descending order, as shown in Figure 1.9, which indicates the results of an experiment that measures a person's threshold for seeing a light.

On the first series of trials, the experimenter presents a light with an intensity of 105, and the observer

Intensity	(1) ↓	(2) ↑	(3) ↓	(4) ↑	(5) ↓	(6) ↑	(7) ↓	(8) ↑
105	Y						Y	
104	Y		Y		Y		Y	
103	Y		Y		Y		Y	
102	Y		Y		Y		Y	
101	Y		Y		Y		Y	Y
100	Y	Y	Y	Y	Y		Y	Y
99	Y	N	Y	N	Y	Y	Y	Y
98	N	N	Y	N	N	N	N	Y
97		N	N	N		N		N
96		N		N		N		N
95		N		N		N		N
Crossover values →	98.5	99.5	97.5	99.5	98.5	98.5	98.5	97.5

Threshold = Mean of crossovers = 98.5

Figure 1.9
The results of an experiment to determine the threshold using the method of limits. There are eight series of trials in this experiment, the descending trials alternating with the ascending trials. In the first series, the observer indicates by answering "no" at an intensity of 98 that he no longer sees the light. This change from "yes" at 99 to "no" at 98 is the crossover point, and the threshold value for this run is taken as the mean between 99 and 98, or 98.5. The procedure is then repeated in reverse, starting below the threshold and increasing the intensity until the subject says "yes." Both the descending and the ascending presentations are repeated a number of times, and the threshold is calculated as the mean of the crossover values for each run. The threshold is therefore 98.5 in this experiment.

indicates by a "yes" response that he sees the light. This response is indicated by a Y at an intensity of 105 on the table. The experimenter then decreases the intensity, and the observer makes a judgment at each intensity until he responds "no," that he did not see the light. This change from "yes" to "no" is the *crossover point* and the threshold for this series is taken as the mean between 99 and 98 or 98.5. By repeating this procedure a number of times, starting above the threshold half the time and starting below the threshold half the time, the threshold can be determined by calculating the average of all of the crossover points.

In the **method of adjustment,** the stimulus is slowly changed as either the observer or the experimenter adjusts the stimulus intensity in a continuous manner (as opposed to the stepwise presentation for the method of limits) until the observer can just barely detect the stimulus. This just barely detectable intensity is then taken as the absolute threshold. This procedure can be repeated several times and the threshold determined by taking the average setting. Having the observer adjust the stimuli has the advantage of giving the observer an active role in the process, thus maximizing the probability that he or she will stay awake during the entire experiment!

In the **method of constant stimuli,** five to nine stimuli are typically presented by the experimenter in random order. The results of a hypothetical determination of the threshold for seeing a light are shown in Figure 1.11. The data points in this graph were determined by presenting six light intensities 10 times each and determining the percentage of times that

Figure 1.10
Did you see a "rat" or a "man"? Looking at the more ratlike picture in Figure 1.7 increased the chances that you would see this one as a rat. But if you had first seen the man version (see Figure 1.13), you would have been more likely to perceive this figure as a man. (From Bugelski & Alampay, 1961.)

the subject perceives each intensity. The results indicate that the light with an intensity of 150 is never detected, the light with an intensity of 200 is always detected, and lights with intensities in between are sometimes detected and sometimes not detected. The threshold is usually taken as the intensity that results in detection on half the trials, so in this case the threshold is an intensity of 180.

The choice between the methods of limits, adjustment, and constant stimuli is usually determined by the accuracy that is needed and the amount of time available. The method of constant stimuli is the most accurate method but takes the longest time, whereas the method of adjustment is the least accurate but the fastest.

When Fechner published *Elements of Psychophysics,* he not only described his methods for measuring the absolute threshold, but also described the work of Ernst Weber (1795–1878), a physiologist, who, a few years before the publication of Fechner's book, measured another type of threshold, the *difference threshold.*

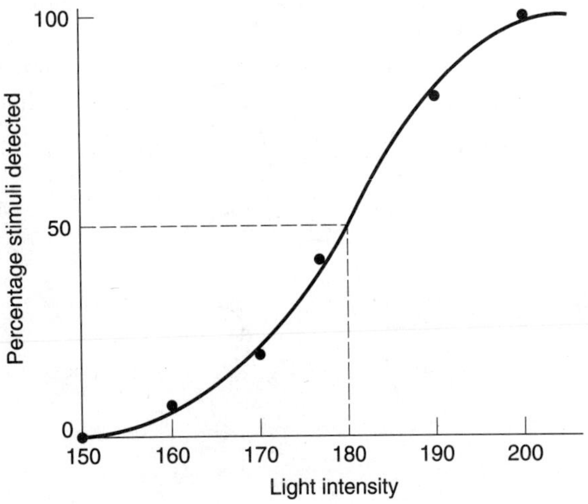

Figure 1.11
Results of a hypothetical experiment in which the threshold for seeing a light is measured by the method of constant stimuli. The threshold, the intensity at which the light is seen on half of its presentations (as indicated by the dashed line), is 180 in this experiment.

The Difference Threshold The **difference threshold,** which is also called the **just noticeable difference (JND),** is the smallest difference between two stimuli that a person can detect. To measure the difference threshold, Weber had subjects lift a small "standard" weight and then lift a slightly heavier "comparison" weight and judge which was heavier (Figure 1.12). When the difference between the standard and comparison weights was small, subjects found it difficult to detect the difference in the weights, but they easily detected larger differences. That much is not surprising, but Weber went further. He found that the size of the JND depended on the size of the standard weight. For example, the JND for a 100-gram weight is 5 grams (a subject could tell the difference between a 100- and 105-gram weight, but smaller differences remained undetected), and the JND for a 200-gram weight is 10 grams. Thus, as the magnitude of the stimulus increases, so does the size of the JND.

DEMONSTRATION

Measuring the JND

By doing a simple experiment with two boxes of wooden matches, you can demonstrate to yourself that the JND gets larger as the standard stimulus gets larger. Have a friend place 10 matches in one box (the standard) and 11 in the other (the comparison). Comparing the weights of the two boxes with your eyes closed, try to decide which box is heavier. After making this judgment, repeat this procedure; if you can't correctly judge which is heavier on three out of three trials, have your friend place another match in the comparison box, and try again. Continue this procedure until you can consistently judge which box is heavier. If, for example, you can consistently tell that the comparison box is heavier when it contains 12 matches, then the JND equals 2 matches. Now repeat the above procedures, but start with 20 matches in the standard box and 21 in the comparison. Since the JND gets larger as the weight of the standard gets larger, you should find that the JND for the 20-match standard is larger than the JND for the 10-match standard. ●

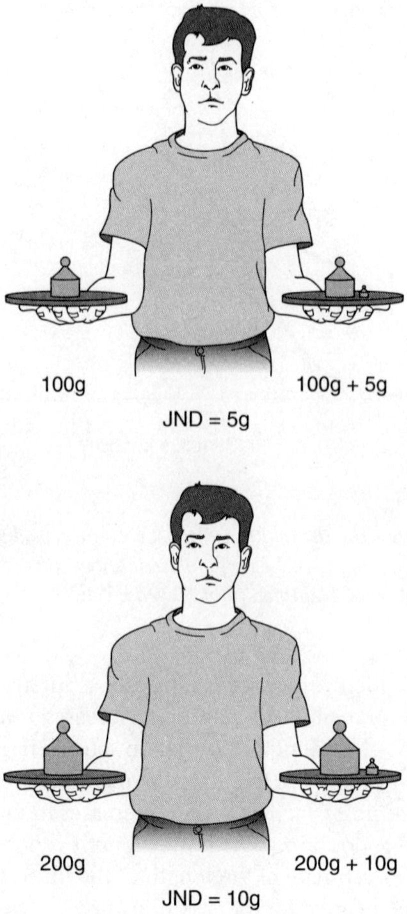

Figure 1.12
The just noticeable difference (JND). The person can detect the difference between a 100-gram weight and a 105-gram comparison weight but cannot detect a smaller difference, so the JND is 5 grams. With a 200-gram weight, the comparison weight must be 210 grams before the person can detect the difference, so the JND is 10 grams. Note that for both the 100- and 200-gram weights, the ratio of JND to weight is the same. This ratio is the Weber fraction.

Research on a number of senses has shown that the JND is larger for larger standard stimuli, and that, over a fairly large range of intensities, the ratio of the JND to the standard stimulus is constant. This relationship, which is based on Weber's research, was stated mathematically by Fechner as $JND/S = K$ and was called **Weber's law.** K is a constant called the *Weber fraction*, and S is the value of the standard stimulus. Applying this equation to our example of lifted weights, we find that, for the 100-gram standard, $K = 5/100 = 0.05$, and that, for the 200-gram standard, $K = 10/200 = 0.05$. Thus, in this example, Weber's fraction (K) is constant. In fact, numerous modern investigators have tested Weber's law and found that it is true for most senses, as long as the stimulus intensity is not too close to the threshold (Engen, 1972; Gescheider, 1976).

Fechner's proposal of three psychophysical methods for measuring the absolute threshold and his statement of Weber's law for the difference threshold were extremely important events in the history of scientific psychology because they demonstrated something that many people thought was impossible: the quantification of mental activity. This was a notable achievement at the time, and the methods developed in the 1800s are still used today to measure absolute and difference thresholds. In addition to being used to determine thresholds in research laboratories, simplified versions of the classical psychophysical methods have been used to measure people's detail vision when determining the prescription for glasses, or people's hearing when testing for possible hearing loss.

The classical psychophysical methods were developed to measure absolute and difference thresholds. But what about perceptions that occur above threshold? Most of our everyday experience consists of perceptions that are far above threshold, when we can easily see and hear what is happening around us.

Figure 1.13
Man version of the rat-man stimulus. (Adapted from Bugelski & Alampay, 1961.)

In order to measure these above-threshold perceptions, S.S. Stevens developed a technique called *magnitude estimation.*

Magnitude Estimation: Measuring Magnitude above Threshold

If we double the intensity of a light, does it look twice as bright? If we double the intensity of a tone, does it sound twice as loud? Although a number of researchers, including Fechner, proposed equations that related perceived magnitude and stimulus intensity, it wasn't until 1957 that S. S. Stevens developed a technique called *scaling* or **magnitude estimation** that accurately measured this relationship (Stevens, 1957, 1961, 1962).

Magnitude estimation is relatively simple: The experimenter first presents a "standard" stimulus to the observer (let's say a light of moderate intensity) and assigns it a value of, say, 10; he or she then presents lights of different intensities, and the observer is asked to assign a number to each of these lights that is proportional to the brightness of the light. If the light appears twice as bright as the standard, it gets a rating of 20; half as bright, a 5; and so on. Thus, each light intensity has a brightness assigned to it by the observer.

The results of a magnitude estimation experiment on brightness are plotted in Figure 1.14. This graph plots the means, for a number of observers, of the magnitude estimates of the brightness of a light versus the intensity of the light. You can see from the way this curve bends down that doubling the intensity does not double the perceived brightness. Doubling the intensity causes only a small change in perceived brightness, particularly at higher intensities. This result is called **response compression.** As intensity is increased, the responses increase, but not as rapidly as the intensity. To double the brightness, it is necessary to multiply the intensity by about 9.

Figure 1.14 also shows the results of magnitude estimation experiments for the length of a line, and for the sensation caused by an electric shock presented to the finger. The electric shock curve bends up, indicating that doubling the strength of a shock more than doubles the sensation of being shocked.

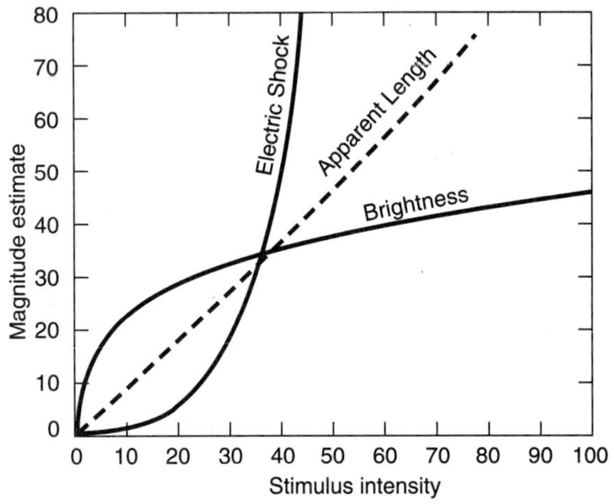

Figure 1.14
Curves showing the relationship between perceived magnitude and stimulus intensity for electric shock, line length, and brightness. (Adapted from Stevens, 1962.)

This is called **response expansion.** As intensity is increased, perceptual magnitude increases more than intensity. The length estimation curve is straight, with a slope of close to 1.0, so the magnitude of the response almost exactly matches increases in the stimulus (i.e., doubling the line length doubles the observer's estimate of the length of the line).

The beauty of the relationships derived from magnitude estimation is that the relationship between the intensity of a stimulus and our perception of its magnitude follows the same general equation for each sense. We show this by plotting the *logarithm* of the magnitude estimates versus the *logarithm* of the stimulus intensity, which causes all three curves to become straight lines (Figure 1.15). These functions are called **power functions** and are described by the equation $P = KS^n$. Perceived magnitude, P, equals a constant, K, times the stimulus intensity, S, raised to a power, n. This relationship is called **Stevens' power law.**

The power n, the exponent of the power law, indicates the slope of the lines in Figure 1.15. Remembering our discussion of the three types of curves in Figure 1.14, we can see that the curve that shows response compression has a slope of less than 1.0, the

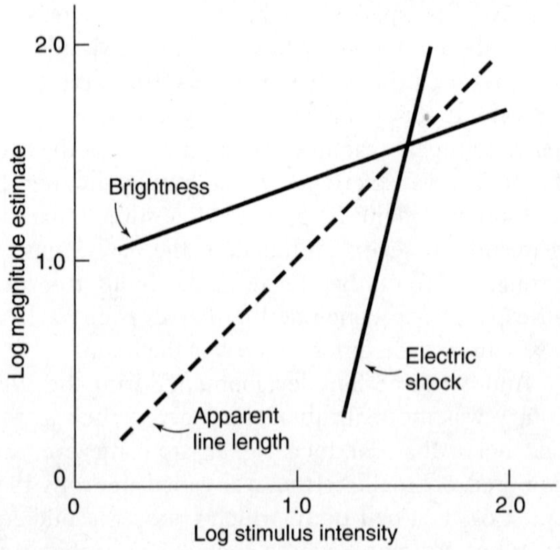

Figure 1.15
The three curves from Figure 1.14 plotted on log-log coordinates. Taking the logarithm of the magnitude estimates and the logarithm of the stimulus intensity turns the curves into straight lines. (Adapted from Stevens, 1962.)

straight line has a slope of about 1.0, and the curve that shows response expansion has a slope of greater than 1.0. Thus, the relationship between response magnitude and stimulus intensity is described by a power law for all senses, and the exponent of the power law indicates whether doubling the stimulus intensity causes more or less than a doubling of the response.

These exponents not only illustrate that all senses follow the same basic relationship, they also illustrate how the operation of each sense is adapted to how organisms function in their environment. Consider, for example, our experience of brightness. The light intensities present outside on a bright sunny day could be as high as 1,000 to 1 or greater if we compare, say, the sunlight reflected from the hood of a just polished car to the dark pavement underneath the car. If our perception of brightness spanned as large a range as the light intensities, we might be faced with such high contrasts and bright glare that looking at the scene would be difficult. However, the exponent for brightness is about 0.6, so changing intensity by a factor of about 9 or 10 just doubles the brightness, keeping our experience of contrasts within manageable limits.

The opposite situation occurs for electric shock, which has an exponent of 3.5 so that just small increases in shock intensity cause large increases in pain. This rapid increase in pain even to small increases in shock intensity serves to warn us of impending danger, and we therefore tend to withdraw even from weak shocks.

Using the techniques we have just described to determine relationships between stimuli and perception is one way to study perception. Another way is to use the physiological approach.

The Physiological Approach: Linking Stimulation and Neural Firing

What are the physiological mechanisms of perception? Modern research designed to answer this question has focused on determining the relationship between the stimulus and electrical signals called *nerve impulses,* and on determining the relationship between these nerve impulses and perception. Before describing the nature of these nerve impulses, let's look at some of the early history that led to this approach.

The Physiological Approach: Early History

Our modern ideas about the physiological basis of perception are descended from a long line of speculation and research regarding the physiological workings of the mind. Early research and speculations in this area focused on determining the anatomical structures involved in the operation of the mind. In the 4th century BC the philosopher Aristotle (384–322 BC) stated that the heart, not the brain, was the seat of the mind and the soul. Most of those following Aristotle did not repeat his error and correctly identified the brain as the seat of the mind.

It is interesting to note how speculations about how the brain works were influenced by the technology of the day (Bloom, Lazerson, & Hofstadter, 1985; Nelson & Bower, 1990). For example, the Greek physician Galen (ca. 130–200 AD) likened the functioning of the brain to the aqueducts and sewer systems of ancient Rome. Galen saw human health, thoughts, and emotions as being determined by four different fluids flowing from the cavities in the center of the brain, an idea that remained popular for 1,500 years.

Later ideas were also influenced by technology. Thus, the philosopher René Descartes (1596–1650) pictured the human body as operating like a machine that resembled the mechanical devices popular in the 17th century. His contemporary, the "father of astronomy" Johannes Kepler (1571–1630), thought the eye operated like an ordinary optical instrument that projected images onto the sensory nerves of the retina. This idea was partially true but did not explain the physiological processes that occur after the image is formed. Understanding these physiological processes had to await a better understanding of the nature of both electricity and the electrical signals that are conducted by these nerves.

Neurons and Electrical Signals

By the end of the 19th century, researchers had shown that a wave of electricity is transmitted down the nerve. To explain how these electrical signals result in different perceptions, Johannes Mueller in 1842 proposed the **doctrine of specific nerve energies,** which states that our perceptions depend on "nerve energies" reaching the brain and that the specific quality we experience depends on which nerves are stimulated. Thus he proposed that stimulating the eye results in seeing, stimulating the ear results in hearing, and so on. By the end of the 1800s, this idea had expanded to conclude that nerves from each of these senses reach different areas of the brain.

Another important development during the 19th century was the realization that **nerves,** such as the optic nerve that conducts signals from the eye, are composed of smaller structures called **neurons** that consist of (1) a **cell body,** which contains a nucleus and other structures whose metabolic mechanisms are needed to keep the cell alive; (2) **dendrites,** which branch out from the cell body to receive electrical signals from other neurons; and (3) an **axon,** or **nerve fiber,** a tube filled with fluid that conducts electrical signals (Figure 1.16).

When many neurons combine to create a nerve it is the axons of the neurons that form the individual components of the nerve, just as many individual wires travel within a telephone cable (Figure 1.17). Thus, the optic *nerve* contains about one million *axons* or *nerve fibers.*

There are variations on this basic neuron structure: Some neurons have long axons; others have short axons or none at all. Especially important for perception are neurons that are designed to receive signals from the environment through specialized structures called **receptors,** which are designed to receive environmental stimuli such as light or sound

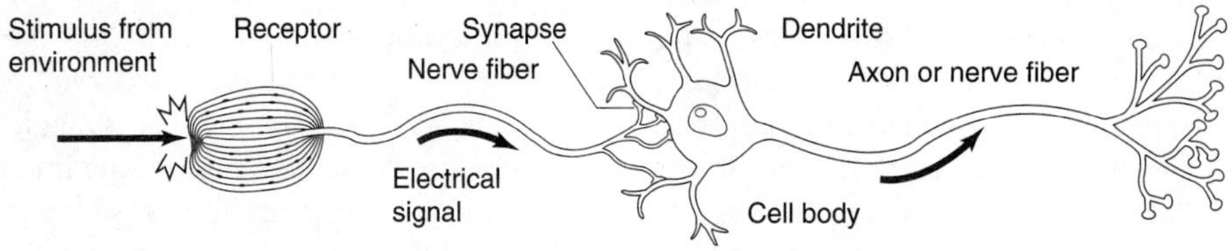

Figure 1.16
The neuron shown on the right consists of a cell body, dendrites, and an axon, or nerve fiber. A neuron that receives stimuli from the environment, shown on the left, has a receptor in place of the cell body.

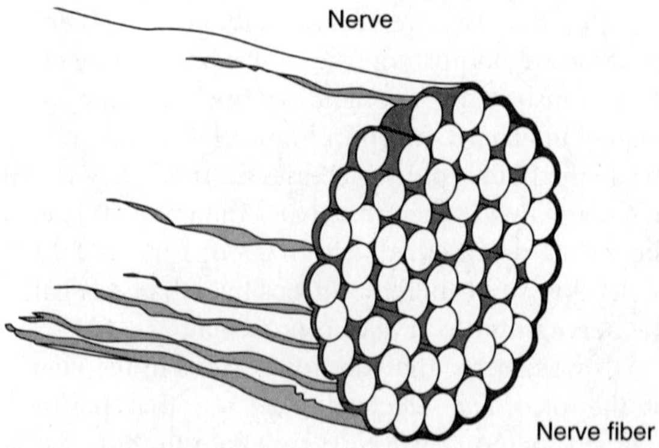

Figure 1.17
Nerves are made up of many nerve fibers. Most nerves contain many more fibers than are shown here. For example, the optic nerve, which conducts signals from the eye, contains about 1,000,000 nerve fibers.

waves and to transduce these stimuli into electrical signals.

By the beginning of the 20th century, researchers understood that receptors transduce environmental energy into electrical signals, which are transmitted along neurons to different areas of the brain for different senses. But an understanding of the nature of the electrical signals that are transmitted to the brain had to await the development of electronic amplifiers powerful enough to make visible the extremely small electrical signals generated by the neuron. When this equipment became available in the 1920s, researchers began recording these electrical signals, called *nerve impulses,* and began to understand the chemical basis of nerve signals (Adrian, 1928, 1932). Since nerve impulses form the essence of our understanding of the physiology of perception, we will look at some basic facts about these signals.

Recording Electrical Signals in Neurons

What kinds of electrical signals are transmitted by neurons? When most people think of electrical signals, they imagine signals conducted along electrical power lines or along the wires used for household appliances. Unlike the electrical wires of your television set, however, neurons are bathed in liquid. Some people find this fact disconcerting since we are taught that we should keep electricity and water separated. However, as we shall see, the body has devised ways to create electrical signals within a liquid environment.

The key to understanding the "wet" electrical signals transmitted by neurons is to understand the components of the neuron's liquid environment. Neurons are immersed in a solution rich in **ions,** molecules that carry an electrical charge. Ions are created when molecules gain or lose electrons, as happens when compounds are dissolved in water. For example, adding table salt (sodium chloride = NaCl) to water creates positively charged sodium ions (Na^+) and negatively charged chlorine ions (Cl^-). The solution *outside* the axon of a neuron is rich in positively charged sodium (Na^+) ions, while the solution *inside* the axon is rich in positively charged potassium (K^+) ions (Figure 1.18).

These and other ions create electrical signals in the neuron by flowing across the cell membrane of the axon. We can see how this works by observing the ion flow as electrical signals are conducted down the axon. To measure the electrical signals, we use two **microelectrodes,** small shafts of glass or metal with tips small enough to record the electrical signals from a single neuron.

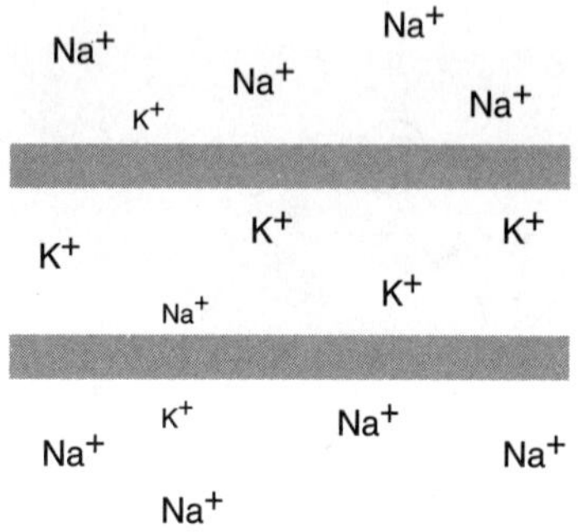

Figure 1.18
Cross section of a nerve fiber, showing the high concentration of sodium outside the fiber and potassium inside the fiber. Other ions, such as negatively charged chlorine, are not shown.

Figure 1.19a shows a pressure sensitive receptor and its nerve fiber with two microelectrodes positioned to record signals from the axon. The tip of the **recording electrode** is positioned inside the fiber and the tip of the *null electrode* is positioned outside the axon. The recording device that measures the difference in charge between these two electrodes indicates that the inside of the neurons has a charge that is 70 millivolts (mV; 1 mV = 1/1,000 volt) more negative than the outside of the neuron. This negative charge inside the neuron is called the neuron's **resting potential,** because it is the neuron's charge when it is at rest.

Now that we have measured the resting potential, we are ready to push on the axon's pressure receptor. If we push hard enough, we measure the rapid change in charge shown in Figure 1.19b. The charge inside the fiber rapidly increases from −70 mV to +40 mV compared to the outside and then returns back to the resting potential, all within about 1 msec (1/1,000 sec). This rapid increase in positive charge is called the nerve impulse or **action potential.**

If we observe the Na^+ and K^+ ions in the vicinity of the recording electrode, we see that positively charged sodium ions (Na^+) rush into the fiber at the beginning of the action potential, as the inside of

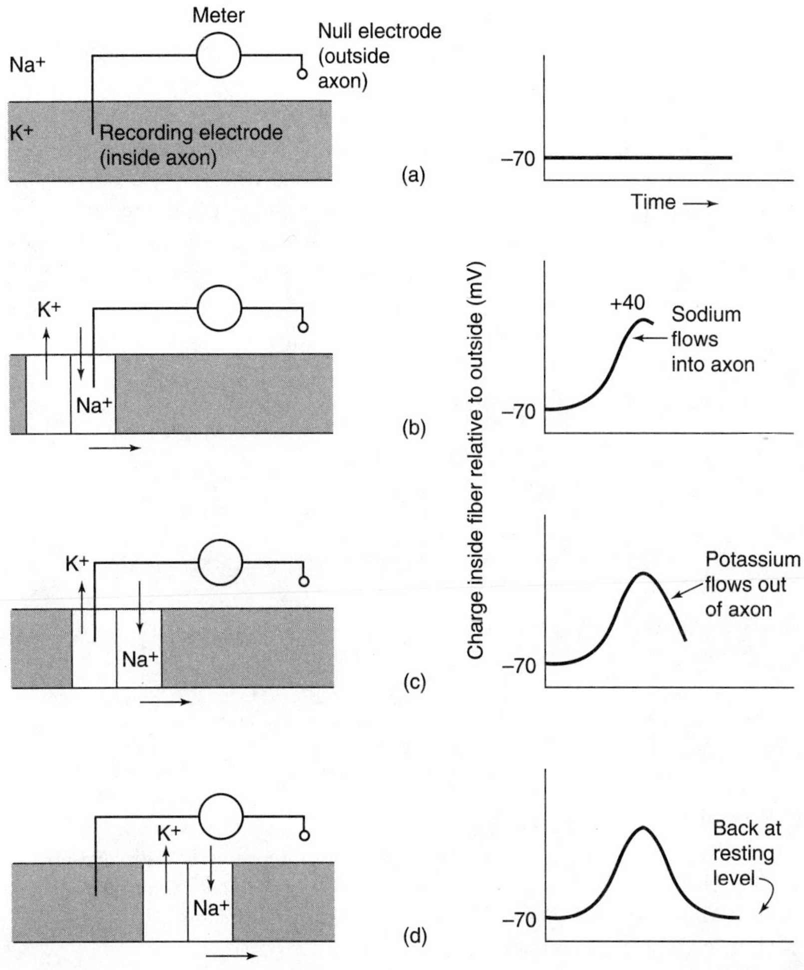

Figure 1.19
Effect of an action potential as it travels down a nerve fiber. As long as the fiber is at rest, there is a difference in charge of −70 mV between the inside and the outside of the fiber, as shown in (a). Events that occur once an action potential is generated are shown in (b), (c), and (d). The flow of sodium into the fiber and potassium out of the fiber is shown on the left, and the resulting change in the charge measured by the electrodes is shown on the right.

the fiber is becoming more positive. We also see that this inflow of Na^+ is followed by an outflow of positively charged potassium (K^+) that creates the downward phase of the action potential, causing the charge inside the axon to becomes more negative and eventually to return to its original level, as shown in Figures 1.19c and d.

These rapid changes in sodium and potassium flow that create the action potential are caused by changes in the fiber's permeability to sodium and potassium. **Permeability** is a property of the cell membrane that refers to the ease with which a molecule can pass through the membrane. Before the action potential occurs, the membrane's permeability to sodium and potassium is low, so there is little flow of these molecules across the membrane. The action potential begins when the membrane suddenly becomes permeable to sodium, which causes the sodium to pour across the membrane to the inside of the axon. After sodium flows into the axon for about 1/2,000 second, the membrane's permeability to sodium decreases and its permeability to potassium increases, causing the flow of potassium out of the axon for 1/2,000 of a second.

This process creates the rapid increase and then decrease in positive charge inside the axon that, from our vantage point at the recording electrode, lasts only 1/1,000 second. However, this rapid change in the axon's charge does not just occur at one place on the axon but travels down the axon to create our "wet" electrical signal—the action potential. Action potentials, therefore, are traveling positive charges created by the flow of charged molecules called *ions* across the walls of the axon.

After hearing this description of how Na^+ flows into the axon and K^+ flows out, students often wonder whether sodium would accumulate inside the axon and if potassium would accumulate outside the axon. This does not occur because a mechanism called the *sodium-potassium pump* in the axon continuously returns sodium to the outside of the axon and potassium to the inside, thereby maintaining sodium and potassium concentrations at their original levels so the axon can continue to generate nerve impulses. Let's now consider some basic properties of action potentials.

Basic Properties of Action Potentials

The action potential is a **propagated response:** Once it is triggered, it travels all the way down the axon. The action potential is also an **all-or-none response:** Once it is triggered, it stays the same size, no matter how far it has traveled down the axon and no matter how intense the stimulus is. We can show that it stays the same size no matter how intense the stimulus is by returning to our pressure sensitive receptor and increasing the intensity of the stimulus generating the action potential. The result of this demonstration is shown in Figure 1.20. Each action potential appears as a sharp spike because we have compressed the time scale so that we can display a number of action potentials.

The three records in Figure 1.20 represent the axon's response to three intensities of stimulation. Figure 1.20a shows how the axon responds to gentle stimulation applied to the skin, while Figures 1.20b and 1.20c show how the response changes as the

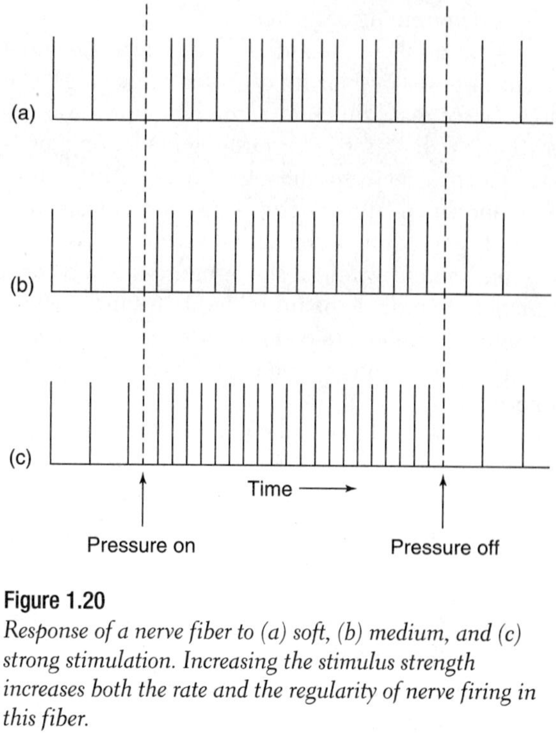

Figure 1.20
Response of a nerve fiber to (a) soft, (b) medium, and (c) strong stimulation. Increasing the stimulus strength increases both the rate and the regularity of nerve firing in this fiber.

stimulation is increased. Comparing these three records leads to an important conclusion: Changing the stimulus intensity does not affect the *size* of the action potentials, but does affect the *rate* of firing.

Although increasing the stimulus intensity can increase the rate of firing, there is an upper limit to the number of nerve impulses per second that can be conducted down an axon. This limit occurs because a neuron takes about 1 millisecond (1 msec = 1/1,000 sec) to recover from conducting an action potential before it can conduct another one. This interval is called the **refractory period,** and it sets the upper limit of the firing rate at about 500 to 800 impulses per second.

Another important property of action potentials is illustrated by the beginning of each of the records in Figure 1.20. Some action potentials occur even before the pressure stimulus is applied. In fact, many axons fire without any stimuli from the environment; this firing is called **spontaneous activity.** Although you may wonder why an axon would be designed to fire in the absence of outside stimulation, you will see later that this spontaneous activity plays an important role in determining our perceptions.

What do these properties of the action potential mean in terms of their function for perceiving? The action potential's function is to communicate information. We have seen that pushing harder on a pressure receptor increases the rate of nerve firing. Thus, these increased rates of nerve firing carry information about the intensity of the stimulus. But if this information remains within a single neuron, it serves no function. In order to be meaningful, this information must be transmitted to other neurons, and eventually to the brain or other organs that can react to this information.

The idea that the action potential in one neuron must be transmitted to other neurons poses the following problem: Once an action potential reaches the end of the axon, how is the message that the action potential carries transmitted to other neurons? One idea, put forth by the Italian anatomist Camillo Golgi (1844–1926), was that neurons make direct contact with each other, so that a signal reaching the end of one neuron passes directly to the next neuron. But the Spanish anatomist, Santiago Ramon y Cajal (1852–1934), showed that there is a very small space between the neurons, which is known as a **synapse** (Figure 1.21). Ramon y Cajal's discovery earned him the Nobel Prize in 1906. (He shared the prize with Golgi, who was recognized for his research on the structure of the neuron.)

The discovery of the synapse raised the question of how the electrical signals generated by one neuron are transmitted across the space separating the neu-

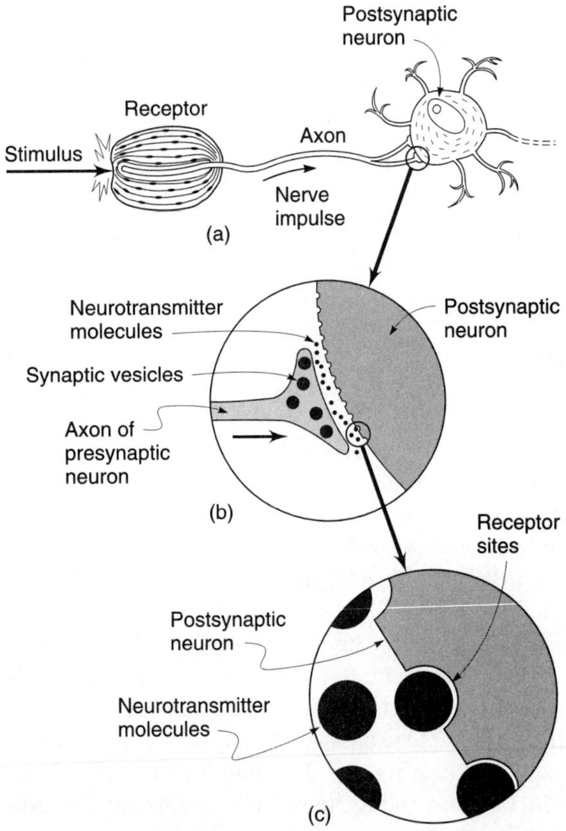

Figure 1.21
Synaptic transmission from one neuron to another. (a) A signal traveling down the axon of a neuron reaches the synapse at the end of the axon. (b) Close-up of the synapse showing the presynaptic neuron on the left and the postsynaptic neuron on the right. The nerve impulse reaching the synapse causes the release of neurotransmitter molecules from the synaptic vesicles of the presynaptic neuron. (c) The neurotransmitters fit into receptor sites and cause a voltage change in the postsynaptic neuron.

rons. As we will see, the answer lies in a remarkable chemical process that takes place at the synapse.

Chemical and Electrical Events at the Synapse

For neurons to communicate, the information carried by an action potential in one neuron (the **presynaptic neuron**) must cross the synapse and generate a signal in another neuron (the **postsynaptic neuron**). If this does not occur, the message will stop at the end of the presynaptic neuron, like a messenger who comes to a large body of water and lacks a boat to get across. How does information get across the synapse?

Early in the 1900s, it was discovered that the action potentials themselves do not travel across the synapse. Instead, they trigger a *chemical* process that bridges the gap between neurons. When the action potential reaches the end of the presynaptic neuron, it causes the release of chemicals called **neurotransmitters** that are stored in *synaptic vesicles* in the presynaptic neuron. As the name implies, neurotransmitters transmit neural information.

When the action potential reaches the synaptic vesicles at the end of the axon, the vesicles release their packets of neurotransmitters. The neurotransmitter molecules flow into the synapse to small areas called **receptor sites** on the postsynaptic neuron that are sensitive to specific neurotransmitters. These receptor sites exist in a variety of shapes that match the shapes of particular neurotransmitter molecules. When a neurotransmitter makes contact with a receptor site matching its shape, it activates the receptor site and triggers a voltage change in the postsynaptic neuron. Thus, a neurotransmitter is like a key that fits a specific lock. It has an effect on the postsynaptic neuron only if its shape matches that of the receptor site.

At the synapse, then, an electrical signal generates a chemical process that, in turn, triggers a change in voltage in the postsynaptic neuron. The neurotransmitter's action at the receptor site does not, however, automatically generate a new action potential in the postsynaptic neuron. Instead, when a neurotransmitter molecule makes contact with a receptor site that matches its shape, it has one of two effects depending on the type of transmitter and the nature of the cell body's membrane. It can cause **excitation,** which increases the rate of nerve firing, or it can cause **inhibition,** which decreases the rate of nerve firing.

Why does inhibition exist? If one of the purposes of the neuron is to transmit its information to other neurons why would the action potential trigger a process that stops further action potentials from being generated? The answer to this question is that the function of the neuron is to transmit information *and* to process it, and both excitation and inhibition are necessary for this processing. You will understand what processing is after we describe it in Chapter 2, but one way to look at it is to consider the synapse as being a control center, which controls the flow of information carried by action potentials. We will see in Chapter 2 that controlling the flow of information through neurons is an important part of neural processing.

A neuron usually receives many excitatory and inhibitory inputs, and in the brain, it is common for neurons to receive inputs from as many as a thousand other neurons. Figure 1.22 shows how the generation of action potentials depends on the interplay of the excitatory (E) and inhibitory (I) stimulation converging on the cell. When the neuron receives excitatory input, the rate of firing increases above the spontaneous level, as shown in Figure 1.22a, but as the amount of inhibition relative to excitation increases (Figure 1.22b through Figure 1.22e), the firing rate decreases. In Figure 1.22d and Figure 1.22e, the inhibition is so strong that the rate of nerve firing is decreased to below the level of spontaneous activity.

These facts about how neurons operate—especially the characteristics of their action potentials and the excitation and inhibition that occur at the synapse—provide the basis for much of the discussion of neurons and perception in the rest of this book. However, to complete our presentation of background information about the physiological approach to perception, we need to consider how these neurons work together in the brain.

Basic Structure of the Brain

One of the major concerns of this book is the human brain, a structure that, with its 100 billion neurons, has been called "the most complex structure in the

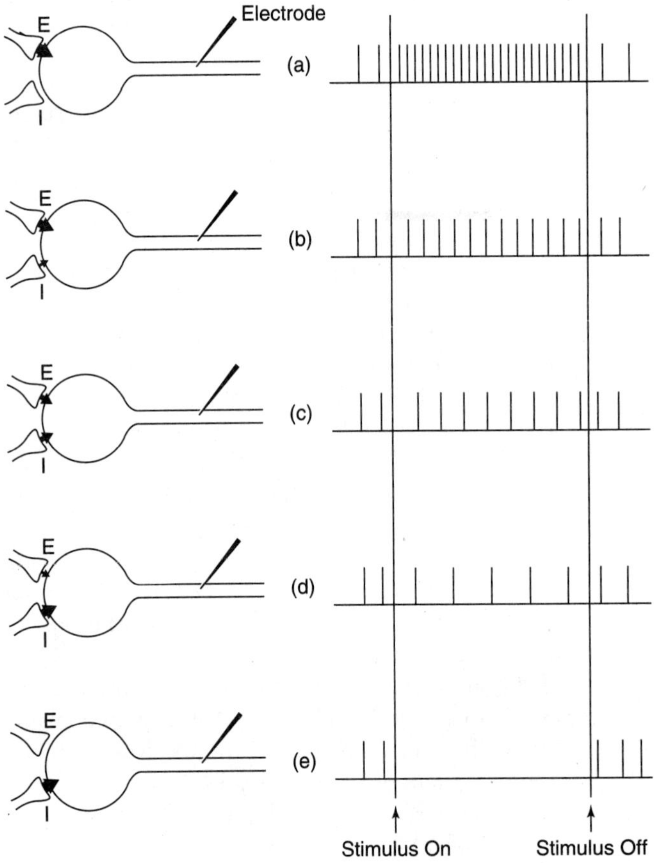

Figure 1.22
Effect of excitatory (E) and inhibitory (I) input on the firing rate of a neuron. The amount of excitatory and inhibitory input to the neuron is indicated by the size of the arrows at the synapse. The responses recorded by the electrode are indicated by the records on the right. The firing that occurs before the onset of the stimulus is spontaneous activity.

known universe" (Thompson, 1985). This complexity comes not just from the number of neurons, but from the vast number of interconnections between them, numbering in the thousands for many neurons.

Although we are far from understanding the vast complexity of how the brain operates, we have learned a tremendous amount in the last few decades about the connection between the brain and our perceptions. Much of the research on this connection has focused on activity in the **cerebral cortex,** the 2-mm-thick layer that covers the surface of the brain and which contains the brain's machinery for creating perception, as well as for other functions, such as language, memory, and thinking. A basic principle of cortical function is **modular organization**—the organization of specific functions into specific structures.

One example of modular organization is how the senses are organized into **primary receiving areas,** the first areas in the cerebral cortex to receive the signals initiated by that sense's receptors (Figure 1.23). The primary receiving area for vision is in the **occipital lobe,** for hearing it is in the **temporal lobe,** and for the skin senses—touch, temperature, and pain—it is in the **parietal lobe.** As we study each sense in detail, we will see that other areas in addition to the primary receiving areas are also associated with each sense. For example, in Chapter 4 we will see that within the cerebral cortex, there are structures called **nuclei** that are specialized for processing information about specific visual qualities. There is one nucleus concerned mainly with color perception, another with the perception of movement, and

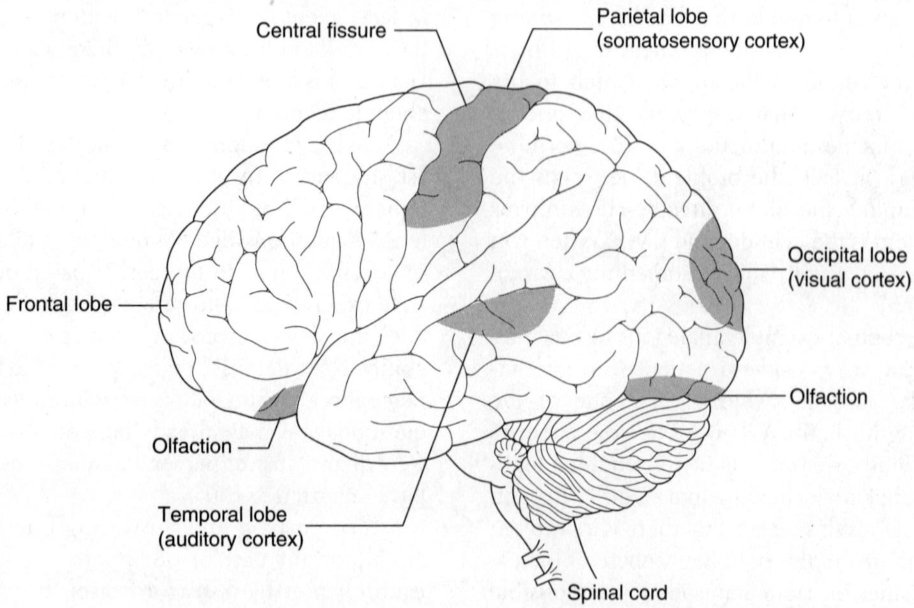

Figure 1.23
The human brain, showing the location of the primary receiving areas for the senses.

another with the perception of form. As we explore the physiological approach to perception in the chapters that follow, we will see that this approach offers a powerful way to understand how basic mechanisms that operate behind the scenes determine our experience.

The Approach in This Book

By looking in some detail at the processes that underlie our perceptions, this book celebrates the wonder of our ability to see, hear, taste, and smell and to feel qualities such as touch, temperature, and pain. We now describe the basic philosophy behind the approach in this book and consider some reasons for studying perception.

Achieving a Balance between Behavior and Physiology

To understand perception fully we need to study it by using both the behavioral and physiological approaches. The behavioral approach enables us to determine the relationship between perception and stimuli in the environment. The physiological approach enables us to uncover the physiological mechanisms that underlie these perceptions. Using both of these approaches together gives us a more complete picture of perceptual processes than using either of them alone.

In addition to helping us to understand all aspects of the perceptual process, using both behavioral and physiological approaches has another benefit: Studying a particular perception behaviorally can provide insights into underlying physiological processes. We can illustrate how this works by drawing an analogy between the operation of an automobile engine and the operation of the perceptual system. First, let's consider an automobile that has been running poorly. One clue as to what the problem might be is provided by the sound of the motor, which to the trained ear of our mechanic suggests that one of the cylinders may be malfunctioning. To determine whether this is, in fact, the problem, he opens the hood and examines the motor directly. He confirms that the problem is the cylinder and says, "When you hear that noise, it usually means something's wrong with a cylinder."

For a perceptual example analogous to our malfunctioning car, we consider a patient who has suffered a stroke caused by blockage of one of the arteries serving his brain. When we test the patient's vision behaviorally, we find that he has trouble identifying objects that are located in an area off to his left. This behavioral result suggests that there is a problem in a particular area in the right hemisphere of the patient's brain (since the right hemisphere is responsible for vision in the left visual field), a guess that we can then check by doing a brain scan that creates a picture of the brain's physiological operation. Thus in both of our examples, "perceptual" information—an abnormal sound for the car or a deficiency in perception for the patient—provides clues regarding the inner workings of both the car and our patient. Later in the book, we will have a number of opportunities to show how researchers have used perceptual information to provide important clues about what is going on physiologically, "under the hood," both for abnormal perception, as in our patient with brain damage, and for normal perception as well.

Answering Questions and Learning to Ask Them

We began this chapter by drawing an analogy between the perceptual process and a detective story. In addition to the detective work carried out by the perceptual system as it sifts through the information it receives in order to create perceptions of what is happening in our environment, there is another equally interesting detective story to tell: The story of how researchers have gone about studying perception. One of the basic tools used by perceptual researchers (and, in fact, scientists in general) is to pose questions and then work toward answering them. One of the major goals of this book is to involve you in asking questions about perception.

Asking questions is so important that I regularly ask students in my class to write questions about the topics we will be studying. I find that the students often ask questions like "Why does it take a while for my eyes to adjust to the dark?" based on things they have experienced, but rarely ask questions like "How does the way neurons are connected determine my ability to see details?" that require some knowledge of perception. In this book, we will answer perceptual questions you may already be wondering about and we will also answer perceptual questions that may not have occurred to you.

Since asking and answering questions is such an important part of our approach, we will open each chapter by posing a few of the questions that will be answered in the chapter. Some of these questions are similar to those that my students ask before they have read the chapter, and some are questions that students are able to ask only after they know something about the material in the chapter. One of my goals in this book is to teach you enough about perception so you can pose new questions of your own, that might never have occurred to you before reading this book.

In addition, you will find questions at the end of each chapter that will help you to review the material you have just read.

Filling in the Details and Learning Basic Principles

The purpose of this chapter has been to provide a brief introduction to the kinds of things we will be studying in the rest of the book. But the picture of perception we have presented so far is really only a rough sketch of what perception is. You know that perception is a complex process involving many steps, and you know some of the basic procedures and principles of the behavioral and physiological approaches to perception, but you don't yet know much about the specific details of the perceptual process.

Chapter 2 begins the story that is designed to fill in those details. As you read Chapter 2, you will begin getting a much better understanding of how an image is formed on the retina, what happens during transduction, and how neural processing works. But in addition to learning about these details, you will also be learning about something much bigger—basic perceptual principles that are true not only for vision but for senses such as hearing, touch, smell, and taste, as well.

To help you become aware of the "big picture" that is defined by these basic principles, we will summarize eight basic principles of perception in the "Underlying Principles" section that follows Chapter 4. (We will need Chapters 2, 3, and 4 to establish these principles, so we wait until then to summarize them.) Once you know what these principles are, you can then identify them as you read the remainder of the book, and as you answer the questions at the end of each chapter. What you will see as you do this is that these principles occur again and again. Thus, although you may be learning about different details in each chapter, these details are often governed by basic principles that hold across many different sensory qualities and sensory systems. You will see that a true understanding of the process of perception is just as much about understanding broad principles that hold across all of the senses as it is about learning facts that are specific to just one of the senses.

Another way to help you become aware of basic principles that hold across the senses, is a one-page section called "Across the Senses" that will appear at the end of each chapter, beginning in Chapter 2. This section will include information about senses in addition to the one we are considering in a particular chapter, focusing on similarities between the senses and on how the senses interact with one another.

The goals of Chapters 2, 3, and 4 are to give you both specific information that is important for understanding the visual system and the background you will need to understand the physiological approach to perception in the rest of the book. Although we focus on the sense of vision in these chapters, the material we will be discussing is also relevant to the other senses as well. Once you have completed Chapter 4, you will have the background that you can apply to the material in the other chapters in the book. Following Chapter 4, the book is organized as follows:

- Visual qualities (color, form, depth, size, movement): Chapters 5–10.
- Hearing (pitch, localizing sounds in space, perceiving speech): Chapters 11–13.
- Cutaneous senses (touch, pain): Chapter 14.
- Chemical senses (taste, smell): Chapter 15.
- Perceptual development: Chapter 16.
- Clinical aspects of vision and hearing: Chapter 17.

Why Do We Study Perception?

Before we begin answering questions about perception, let's consider why we are interested in studying it. From what you have read so far, you may be able to see that perception merits study simply because of the intellectual challenge it poses. The intellectual challenge of unraveling the complex processes involved in perception has motivated many thousands of researchers to spend their lives discovering the information presented in this book.

There are other reasons to study perception as well. Consider, for example, the importance of perception in our lives. To appreciate this, consider for a moment what life would be like without your senses. What would it be like to be without vision? Or without hearing? Or without touch? Most people who are missing just one of these senses learn to cope with their loss. But what if you were born lacking all three of these senses *plus* lacking the ability to taste and smell? The effect would be shattering because you would be isolated from everything in your environment. Consider for a moment what this would mean. If you survived infancy, would you ever become conscious of your isolation? Would you ever be able to develop language or the capacity to think? We can only speculate on the answers to these questions, but one thing is certain: Your experience would be barren, and your very survival would depend on others.

While satisfying intellectual curiosity and recognizing perception's importance in our lives may be strong motives to study perception, we also study it for more practical reasons. The study of perception has enabled us to begin to design devices to help blind people see and deaf people hear. We have learned to make precise measurements of perceptual capacities so that we can describe normal perception and, more important, so that we can specify the perceptual losses that occur because of aging, disease, or injury. We have applied our knowledge of perception to the acoustical design of concert halls and to the analysis of perfume fragrances. Our knowledge of perception has been essential to understanding the perceptual demands encountered when driving cars, piloting airplanes, and making observations from inside space vehicles (Figure 1.24).

Understanding perception is also important in appreciating the perceptual experience called *art*. Visiting an art museum or gallery can be an aesthetically satisfying and perhaps even an emotional experience even if you have never taken a course in perception. But students in my Psychology of Art class learn to ask questions about works of art that further enrich their experience of viewing art. For example, upon viewing the painting in Figure 1.25, Edward Hopper's *Sunlight in a Cafeteria* (1958), they might ask what perceptual devices Hopper has used to create the illusion that we are looking into a three-dimensional space even though this is a flat picture. Or they might ask how Hopper creates the impression of light shining through the window, or how he created the colors in this picture by mixing other colors together, or how people view this painting by rapidly moving their eyes from one part of the picture to the next.

The reasons to study perception range from a need to satisfy our intellectual curiosity about how the body works, to a need to develop practical solutions to perceptual problems, to the desire to better appreciate the perceptual aspects of art. But even if these reasons didn't exist, there is another reason for studying perception: *Perception is something you experience all the time*, and the study of perception can enhance this experience. Studying perception will make you more observant of your environment, more aware of your own perceptions, and more appreciative

Figure 1.24
Flying this airplane depends on a number of perceptual abilities, including the abilities to perceive form, depth, motion. (George Hall/Corbis)

Figure 1.25
The painting Sunlight in a Cafeteria (1958) by Edward Hopper illustrates a number of perceptual principles. It illustrates how perspective and other depth information can create the illusion that we are looking into a three-dimensional space even though this is a flat picture. It also illustrates the operation of cognition in perception, since most people would, based on their past experiences, interpret the two light areas on the walls to be light shining through the window rather than an interesting paint job (Yale University Art Gallery, New Haven, CN).

of the miraculous process that transforms energy falling on receptors into the richness of experience.

Something to Consider: The Complexity of Perception

In this chapter, we have introduced the idea that there is an underlying process to perception. But even though the sequence of steps that we have called the perceptual process may be more complex than you had imagined perception to be, the sequence we have described presents a very simplified picture of what is actually happening. As you read this book, you will come to appreciate the complex processes that lie behind each of the steps that we have described. For example, the physiological processing step involves the operation of complex circuits of neurons like the one shown in Figure 1.26, which is still an extremely simplified picture of the actual circuits.

We will also see that the steps in the perceptual process in Figure 1.6 may not always proceed in exactly the order shown. For example, although Figure 1.6 shows perception occurring first, followed by recognition, sometimes recognition can influence perception. We know this from some behavioral

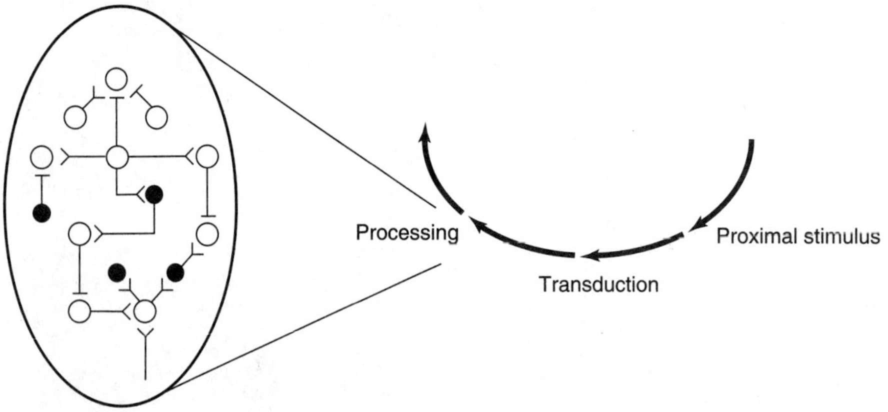

Figure 1.26
Each step of the perceptual cycle is extremely complex. For example, neural processing is carried out by hundreds of millions of interconnected neurons, symbolized here by the neural circuit.

experiments carried out by Mary Peterson (1994), who had people look at displays such as the one in Figure 1.27. This is a *figure-ground display* that can be perceived in at least two ways: (1) with a standing woman (the black part of the display) being seen as the figure on a white background; or (2) with the meaningless shape (the white part of the display) being seen as the figure, on a black background. When Peterson presented stimuli such as this for a fraction of a second and asked subjects which region seemed to be the figure, she found that her subjects were more likely to say that the meaningful part of the display (the woman in this example) was the figure.

Why were the subjects more likely to *perceive* the woman? One possibility is that they must have *recognized* that the black area was a familiar object. In fact, when Peterson turned the display upside down, so that it was more difficult to recognize the black area as a woman, subjects were less likely to see that area as being the figure. What this result means is that perception may not always occur before recognition. Perhaps some recognition occurs before a perception is completely formed, or perhaps perception and recognition can be occurring at about the same time. Figures 1.1 and 1.6 should, therefore, be taken not as being a complete picture, but as a reasonable, if somewhat simplified, starting point for our discussion.

Figure 1.27
Stimulus from Peterson's (1994) experiment.

STUDY QUESTIONS

1. What is the connection between what happens backstage at a theater and perception? (2)

The Perceptual Process

2. What is the distal stimulus? The proximal stimulus? What is the difference between the two? (2)
3. Describe all of the steps in the perceptual process, beginning with the distal stimulus and ending with action. (2)
4. Why can we say that the process of perception doesn't have a beginning or an ending point? (5)

Studying the Perceptual Process

5. What are the three relationships that perception researchers have focused on? What does each relationship tell us about perception? Which one is the most difficult to measure? (6)

The Behavioral Approach: Linking Stimulation and Perception

6. What relationship is the major concern of the behavioral approach to perception? (7)
7. What is the phenomenological method? Cite two examples of demonstrations or experiments in which the phenomenological method has been used. (7)
8. What relationship is measured by psychophysical methods? Who was the pioneer in developing the classical psychophysical methods? (8)
9. Define absolute threshold. Describe the three major psychophysical methods for measuring the absolute threshold. (8)
10. What is the difference threshold and who was the first to measure it? (10)
11. What is Weber's law and why was it especially important? (11)
12. Describe the magnitude estimation technique. When would you want to use it? (12)
13. What is response compression? response expansion? (12)
14. What is a power function? What is Stevens' power law? (12)
15. What does the exponent of the power function tell us? What is the functional significance of exponents of less than 1.0 and of more than 1.0? (12)

The Physiological Approach: Linking Stimulation and Neural Firing

16. Where did Aristotle place the location of the mind? (13)
17. What did the following people think about the operation of the mind or the brain: Galen, Descartes, Kepler. (14)
18. What is the doctrine of specific nerve energies? Who is associated with it? (14)
19. Describe the parts of a neuron. (14)
20. What is special about receptors? (14)
21. Define: ion, resting potential, action potential. What chemical are found inside and outside the nerve fiber? (15)
22. Describe the chemical events that occur in conjunction with the changes in charge that occur during conduction of an action potential. (16)
23. Describe the following: propagated response, all-or-none response, refractory period, spontaneous activity. (17)
24. What problem occurs when an action potential reaches the end of a neuron? (18)
25. What is a synapse and what happens at the synapse when the action potential gets there? (18)
26. What is excitation? inhibition? Describe how excitation and inhibition can interact at the synapse and how this interaction influences nerve firing. (19)

27. Where is the cerebral cortex? What is modular organization? What are the primary receiving areas and where are they located for each sense? (20)

The Approach in This Book

28. What is the point of the example in which a mechanic is able to tell what is wrong with a car's engine based on the sound of the engine? (21)

Why Do We Study Perception?

29. What are four reasons for studying perception? (23)

Something to Consider: The Complexity of Perception

30. Do the steps in the perceptual process always occur in the order shown in Figure 1.6? (25)
31. Describe Peterson's experiment and what it shows with regards to the question above. (26)

2

Receptors and Neural Processing

We begin our story of the perceptual process by looking at the operation of the visual system, focusing on the beginning of the process, as light enters the eye and stimulates the visual receptors. In this chapter, we are mainly interested in the eye, both because it is the site of the initial events in the perceptual process, and because it is within this initial outpost of vision that the processing begins that determines what we perceive. Basic visual abilities such as picking your friend's face out of a crowd or detecting objects that are illuminated only by moonlight can be traced directly to processing that occurs at the very beginning of the visual system. Thus, in this chapter we introduce one of the central themes of this book: Perception is constructed and shaped by the operation of our perceptual systems.

Introducing the Visual System: Transforming Objects into Electricity

The starting point for vision is light—the stimulus that activates the visual system and contains information about the nature of our visual world.

Chapter Contents

Some Questions We Will Consider

- How is the eye like a camera? (34)
- Why is it so difficult to pick one person's face out of a crowd? (55)
- How does the way receptors fire determine what we see? (58)

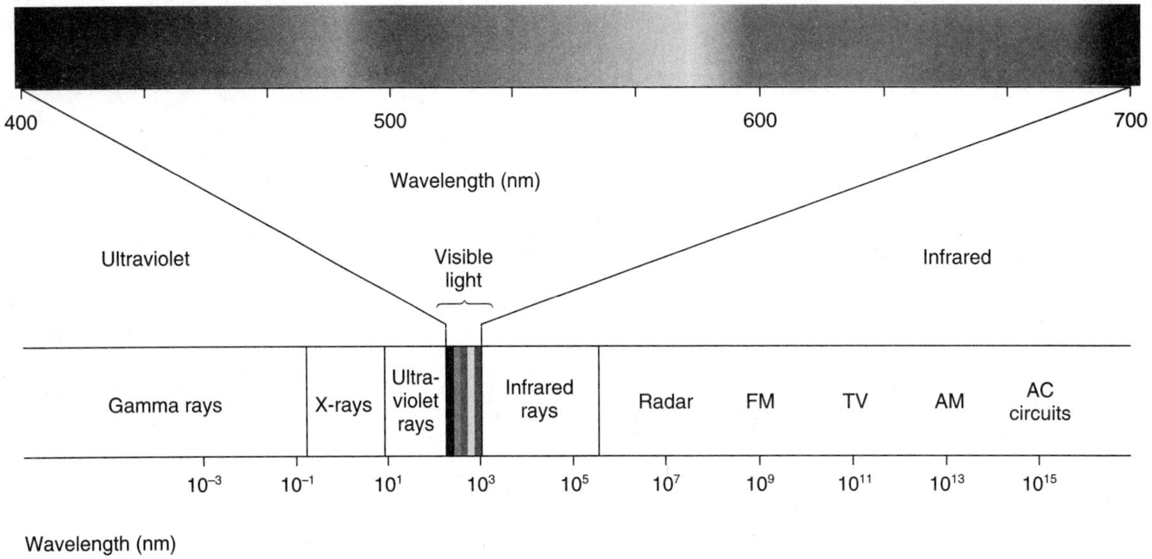

Figure 2.1
The electromagnetic spectrum, showing the wide range of electrical energy in the environment and the small range within this spectrum, called visible light, that we can see.

The Visual Stimulus: Visible Light Structured by the World

Visible light is a band of energy within the **electromagnetic spectrum,** which is a continuum of **electromagnetic energy**—energy radiated as waves that are produced by electric charges (Figure 2.1). The energy in this spectrum can be described by its **wavelength**—the distance between the peaks of the electromagnetic waves. The wavelengths in the electromagnetic spectrum range from extremely short-wavelength gamma rays (wavelength about 10^{-12} meters) to long-wavelength radio waves (about 10^4 meters).[1] Visible light, the energy within the electromagnetic spectrum that humans can perceive, has wavelengths ranging from 400 to 700 nanometers (nm), where 1 nanometer = 10^{-9} meters. For humans and some other animals, the wavelength of visible light is associated with the different colors of the spectrum (Color Plate 1.1).

[1] 10^{-12} meters is 0.00000000001 meters, or one ten-billionth of a meter; 10^{+4} meters is 10,000 meters.

Although we will usually specify light in terms of its wavelength, light can also be described as consisting of small packets of energy called *photons,* with one photon being the smallest possible packet of light energy. We will describe light in terms of photons when we consider the process of visual transduction later in this chapter.

Light energy entering the eyes causes us to perceive, and most of this energy is reflected into our eyes from objects. Thus we see the world around us—trees blowing in the breeze, a person across a crowded room, a highway stretching toward the horizon—because light is reflected from these things into our eyes. This process of reflection creates the **optic array**—the structured pattern of objects structures the light and we perceive this structured light as objects in our environment (Figure 2.2)

The light reflected into the eye is focused to create an image within the eye. This image causes electrical signals in the receptors, and these signals trigger the chain of events that eventually culminate in perception. We begin our description of this process by describing the structures in the visual system that make perception possible.

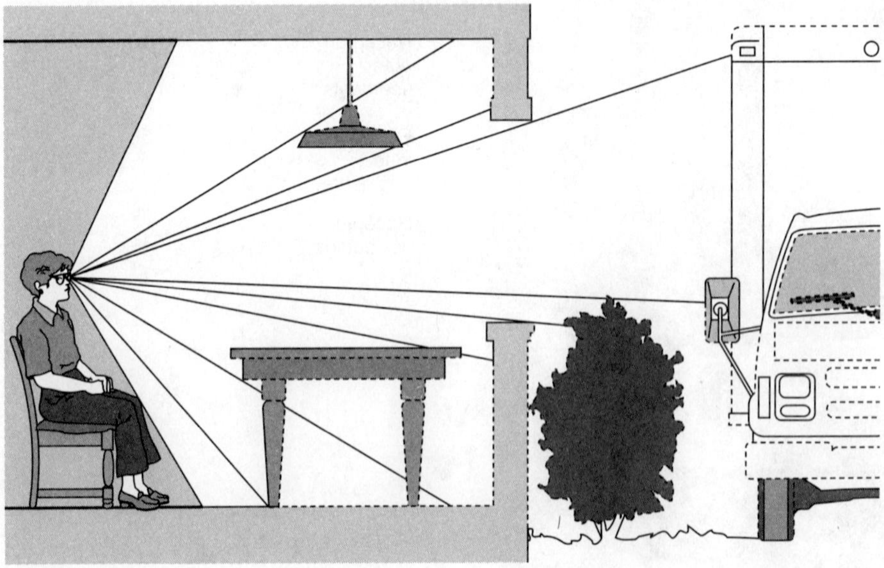

Figure 2.2
The optic array is the structured pattern of light reaching the observer's eye from the environment. Environmental surfaces visible to the observer are indicated by solid lines, invisible surfaces by dashed lines. Each visible surface structures the pattern of light entering the observer's eye. (Adapted from Gibson, 1979.)

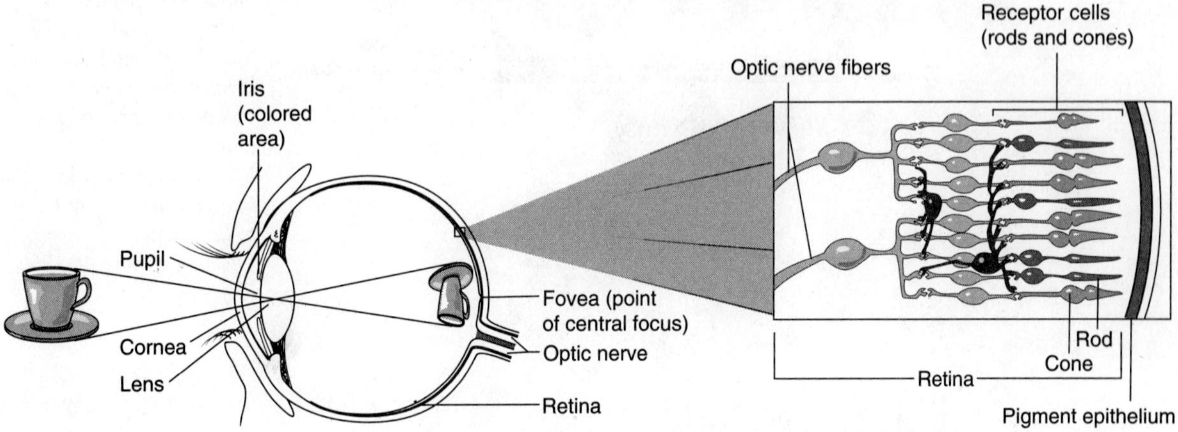

Figure 2.3
Cross sections of the human eye and retina. Structures we will be referring to in this chapter are the focusing elements (the lens and the cornea); the retina, which contains the receptors for vision as well as other neurons; the pigment epithelium, a layer containing nutrients and enzymes, upon which the retina rests; and the optic nerve, which contains the optic nerve fibers that transmit electrical energy out of the retina. The small depression in the retina, which is called the fovea, contains only cone receptors. The rest of the retina, which is called the peripheral retina, contains both rod and cone receptors.

Overall Structure of the Visual System

To orient our description of the visual system, let's first look at its overall layout (Figure 2.3). As light enters the eye it passes through the **cornea** (the transparent front of the eye), then through a hole called the **pupil,** and then through the **lens.** The cornea and the lens focus light onto the **retina,** a thin network of neurons which consists of the **rod** and **cone** receptors and four other types of neurons (Figure 2.4 and Color

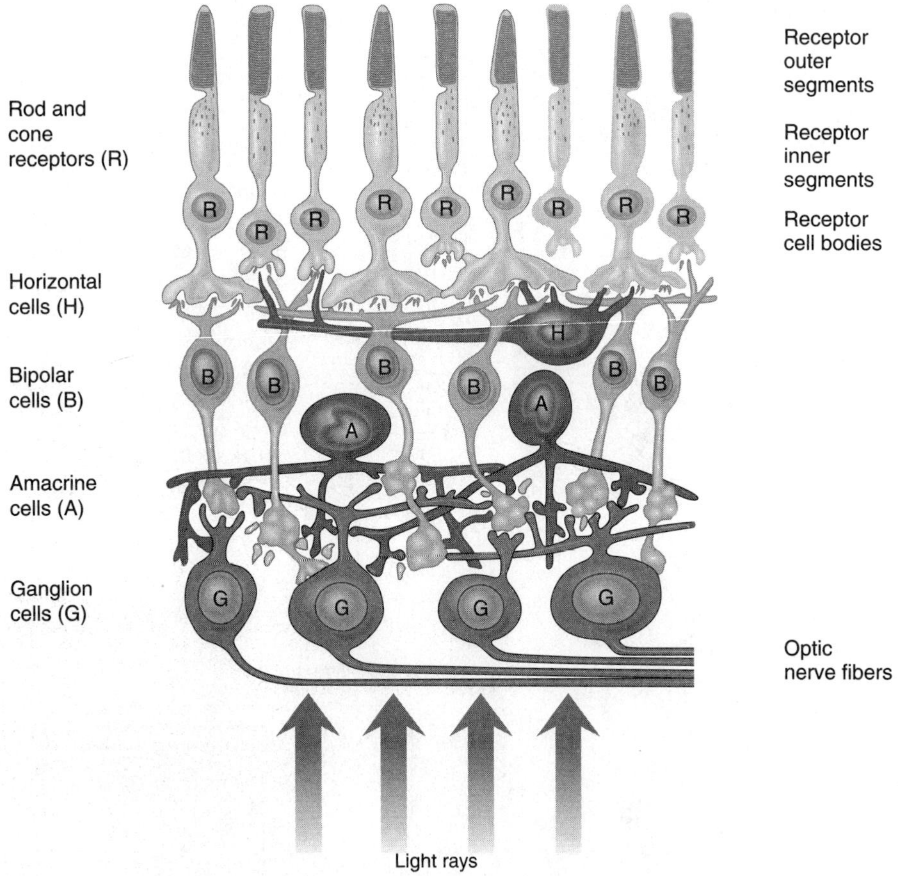

Figure 2.4
Cross section of the primate retina showing the five major cell types and their interconnections. Notice that the receptors are divided into inner segments and outer segments. The outer segments contain light-sensitive chemicals that trigger a signal in response to light. (Adapted from Dowling & Boycott, 1966.)

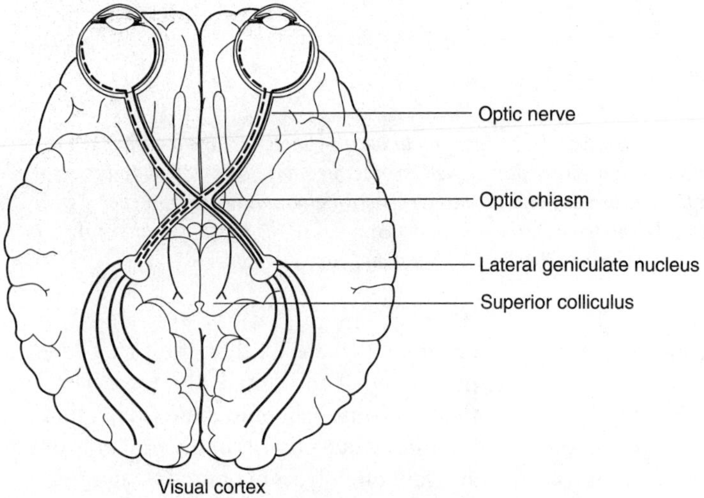

Figure 2.5
The visual system seen from underneath the brain showing how some of the nerve fibers from the retina cross over to the opposite side of the brain at the optic chiasm. A small proportion of optic nerve fibers goes to the superior colliculus. Most go to the lateral geniculate nucleus of the thalamus and then to the visual receiving area in the occipital lobe of the cortex.

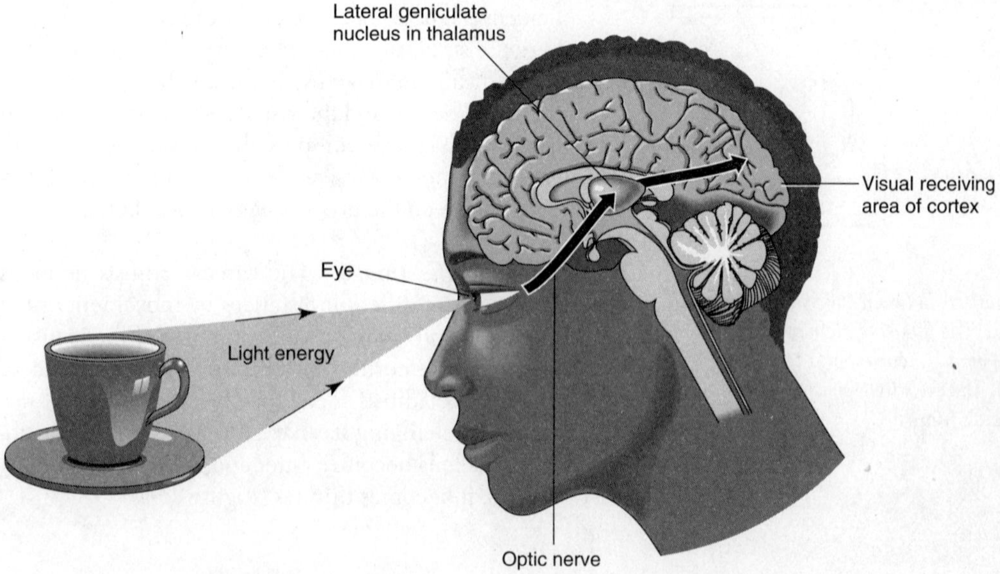

Figure 2.6
A side view of the brain, showing three major sites along the visual pathway: The eye, the lateral geniculate nucleus, and the visual receiving area of the cortex.

Plates 1.2 and 1.3). The rods and cones generate electrical signals in response to light. These signals are then transmitted through the other four kinds of neurons—the **bipolar cells, horizontal cells, amacrine cells,** and **ganglion cells.**

Electrical signals in the ganglion cells leave the back of the eye by way of the **optic nerve** (Figures 2.5 and 2.6). Most of the impulses in the optic nerve reach a nucleus in the **thalamus** called the **lateral geniculate nucleus (LGN)** and from there travel to the **visual receiving area** in the occipital lobe of the brain (also called the **visual cortex** or **striate cortex**). The journey of these nerve impulses does not, however, end in the occipital lobe. Signals from the visual receiving area travel to areas in the **extrastriate cortex** in two different pathways, the **ventral pathway** to the temporal lobe and the **dorsal pathway** to the parietal lobe (Figure 2.7).

Figure 2.7 shows that a large portion of the cerebral cortex is devoted to vision. We will describe the functioning of these cortical areas and the LGN in Chapters 3 and 4. In this chapter we consider how the eye focuses light and how the retina generates and processes electrical signals.

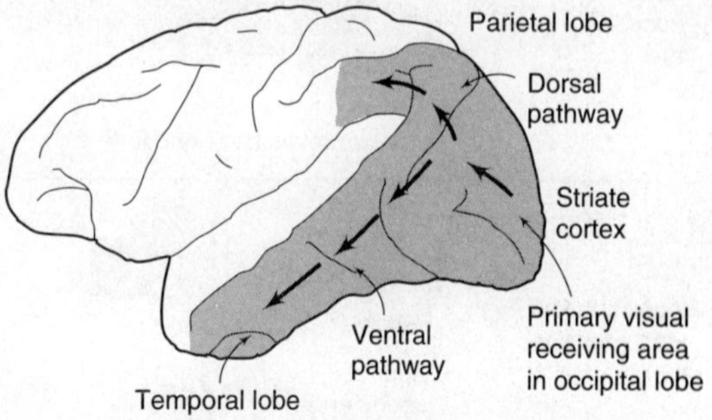

Figure 2.7
The monkey cortex, showing pathways from the primary visual receiving area, in the occipital lobe, to extrastriate visual areas in the parietal to the parietal and temporal lobes. The sequences of arrows indicate that there are a number of synapses along these pathways.

Is the Eye Like a Camera?

The eye has often been compared to a camera. There are similarities: Both are enclosures with a hole that admits light and both have a focusing mechanism that creates a sharp image on a light-sensitive surface

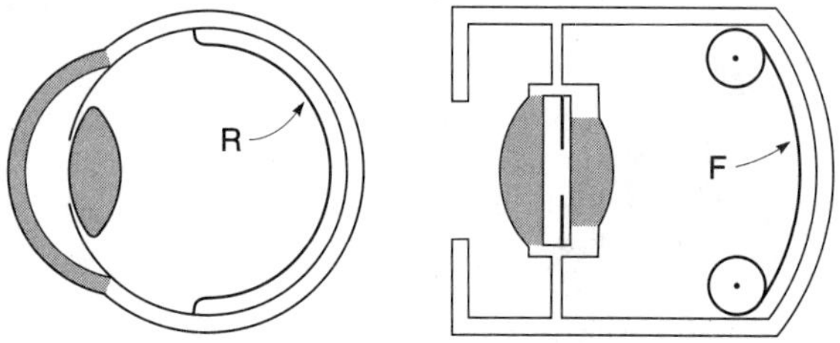

Figure 2.8
There are some similarities between the eye and this old-fashioned box camera. The focusing elements of the eye, the cornea and the lens (shaded), correspond to the two lenses of the camera (shaded). The eye's light sensitive retina (R) corresponds to the camera's film (F).

that covers the back of the enclosure (Figure 2.8). But here the similarity ends. The differences between the eye and camera make us appreciate the complexity of the eye. The eye and the visual system associated with it are vastly more complex than even the most advanced cameras. We can describe some of the differences between the eye and camera as follows:

Focusing the Image The camera adjusts its focus for objects at different distances by movement of the lens back and forth. For the eye, most of the focusing is done by the cornea, but the lens, directly in back of the cornea, adjusts focus for objects at different distances by changing its shape. To focus on nearby objects, the lens becomes fatter and to focus on far away objects, it becomes thinner (Figure 2.9a).

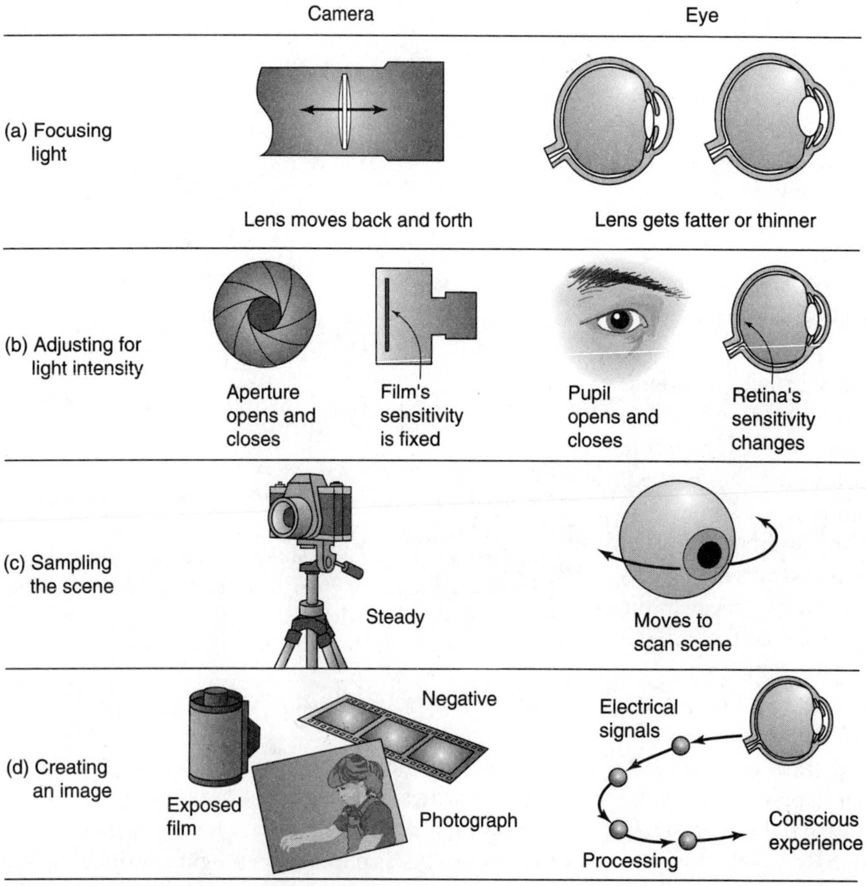

Figure 2.9
Comparison of the eye and the camera, emphasizing differences between the two. See text for details.

Adjusting for Light Intensity The camera adjusts for light intensity by opening and closing an aperture to admit more or less light. The eye also has an aperture, called the pupil, which gets smaller at high light intensities, to limit the amount of light that gets into the eye. But most of the eye's adjustment for intensity is accomplished through a complex mechanism that changes the sensitivity of the retina. In contrast, the camera's film has a fixed sensitivity, indicated by its ASA number (Figure 2.9b).

Sampling the Scene The cardinal rule for taking most photographs is "keep the camera steady." We aim the camera at the part of the scene we want to photograph, hold it still, and take the picture. One of the primary characteristics of the eye is that it is almost always moving. When we look at a scene our eye flits from one part of the scene to another, pausing momentarily on something that is interesting, and then moving on again. In spite of the eye's rapid movements, we perceive the world as being sharp and in focus (Figure 2.9c).

Creating the Image To create a photograph, the camera's exposed film is chemically treated to create a negative and this negative is then used to expose light-sensitive paper, which is chemically treated to create an image. To create perception, the electrical signals generated by the eye's receptors begin a long journey that extends through many neurons within the retina, the lateral geniculate nucleus, the striate cortex, and the extrastriate cortex (Figure 2.9d).

From this comparison, we can see that although the eye and visual system share certain superficial similarities with the camera, the eye is far more complex. Even today's computer-driven cameras can't rival the eye's complexity and versatility.

Adjusting Focus by Changing the Shape of the Lens

The visual process begins when light entering the eye is focused to form an image on the retina. This focusing is accomplished by the eye's two focusing elements, the cornea and the lens. The cornea, the transparent covering of the front of the eye, accounts for about 80 percent of the eye's focusing power. The lens adjusts focus for stimuli at different distances. To understand how the lens works, let's first consider what happens when we look at a light reflected from an object that is located more than 20 feet away. Light rays that reach the eye from this distance are

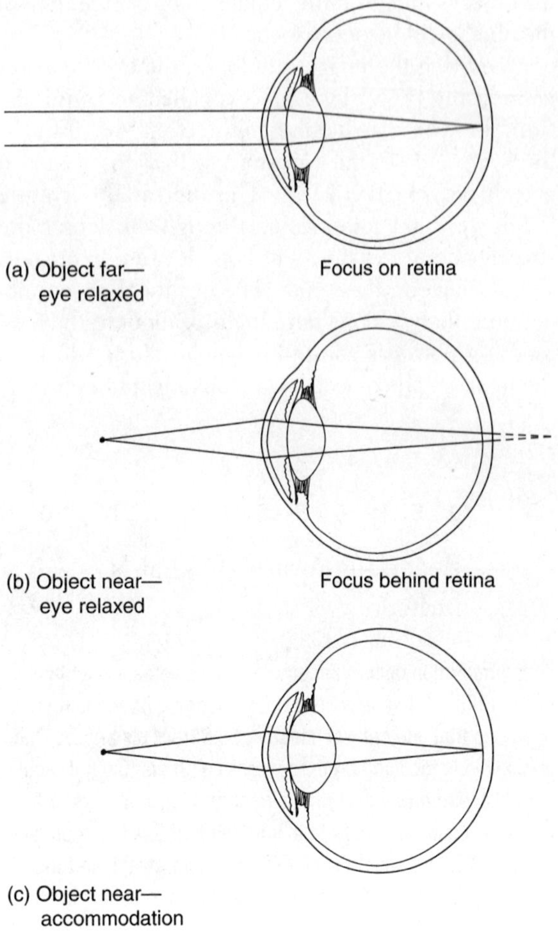

Figure 2.10
Focusing of light rays by the normal eye. (a) Parallel rays, from a spot of light farther away than 20 feet, are focused onto the retina. (b) When the spot of light is moved closer to the eye, the rays are no longer parallel, and the focus point of the light is pushed back behind the retina. (c) Accommodation, indicated by the fatter lens in this picture, pulls the focus point forward.

essentially parallel (Figure 2.10a), and these parallel rays are brought to a focus on the retina. If, however, we move the object closer to the eye, the rays that enter the eye are no longer parallel (Figure 2.10b), and the point at which light would come to a focus moves to a point behind the retina. Of course, the light never comes to a focus in this situation because it is stopped by the retina, and if things remain in this state, both the object's image on the retina and our perception of the object will be out of focus.

To bring the image into focus, the eye increases its **focusing power** by a process called **accommodation,** in which tightening muscles at the front of the eye increases the curvature of the lens so that it gets thicker (Figure 2.10c). This increased curvature bends the light rays passing through the lens more sharply and moves the focus point forward to create a sharp image on the retina. The beauty of accommodation is that we don't have to think about it; the lens' focusing power is constantly being adjusted to keep the image of the object we are looking at in focus.

DEMONSTRATION

Becoming Aware of What Is in Focus

Accommodation occurs unconsciously, so you are usually unaware that the lens is constantly changing its focusing power so that you can see clearly at different distances. This unconscious focusing process works so efficiently that most people assume that everything, near and far, is always in focus. You can demonstrate to yourself that this is not so by looking at a faraway object (at least 20 feet away), and then, while still looking at the far object, moving a pencil toward you while noticing the pencil point. (Don't focus on the point, just "notice" it.) As the pencil gets closer, you should notice that the point becomes blurred and is seen as double. When the pencil is about 12 inches away, focus on the point. You now see the point sharply, but the faraway object you were focusing on before has become blurred. Now, bring the pencil even closer until you can't see the point sharply no matter how hard you try. Notice the strain in your eyes as you try unsuccessfully to bring the point into focus. ●

The demonstration shows that accommodation enables you to bring both near and far objects into focus, but that objects at different distances are not in focus at the same time. You also saw that accommodation has its limits. When the pencil was too close, you couldn't see it clearly, even though you were straining to accommodate. The distance at which your lens can no longer adjust to bring close objects into focus is called the **near point.** We will see in Chapter 17 that the distance of the near point increases as a person gets older, a condition called **presbyopia** (for "old eye") that occurs because aging causes a loss in the ability to accommodate.

Once an image is focused on the retina, the next step in the visual process is stimulation of two kinds of visual receptors, the rods and the cones, that differ not only in shape but in the way they are distributed on the retina.

The Rod and Cone Receptors: Shape and Distribution

In 1865, Max Schultze saw the two different kinds of retinal receptors through his microscope: The rods, large and rod-shaped, and the cones, shorter and cone-shaped (Figures 2.11 and 2.12).

The rods and the cones differ not only in their shapes, but also in the way they are distributed on the retina (Figure 2.13). There is one small area in the retina, the **fovea** (see Figure 2.3), that contains only cones. The fovea is located directly on the line of sight, so anytime we look directly at an object, the center of its image falls on the fovea.

There are about 5 million cones in each retina, but since the fovea is so small, about the size of this "o," it contains only about 50,000 cones—one percent of the total number of cones in the retina (Tyler, 1997a, 1997b). Most of the cones are in the **peripheral retina,** the area surrounding the fovea that contains both rods and cones. However, in the peripheral retina the rods outnumber the cones by about a 20-to-1 ratio, since all 120 million rods in the retina are in the periphery. (See Color Plate 1.4.)

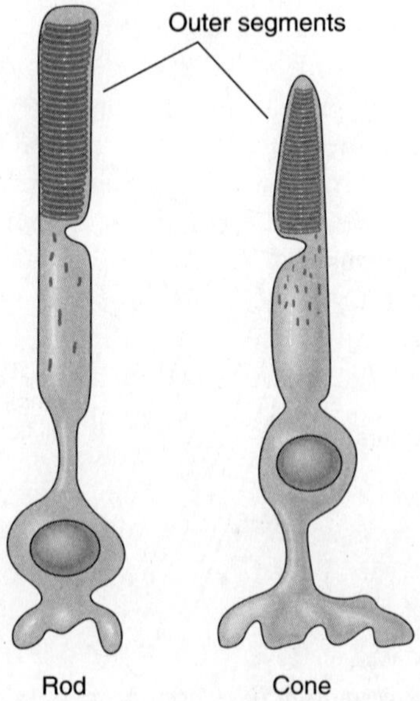

Figure 2.11
A drawing of the rod and cone receptors. The rod- and cone-shaped parts of the receptors are the outer segments, which contain light sensitive visual pigments.

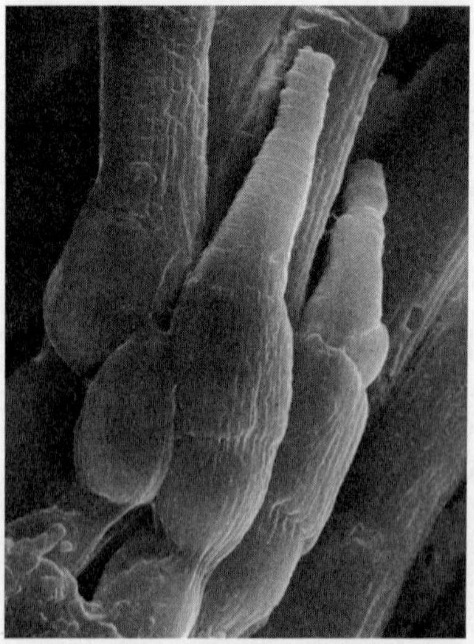

Figure 2.12
Scanning electron micrograph showing the rod and cone outer segments. The rod outer segment on the left is so large that it extends out of the picture, but the cylindrical shape of the rods and the tapered shape of the cones can be clearly seen in this picture (Lewis, Zeevi, & Werblin, 1969).

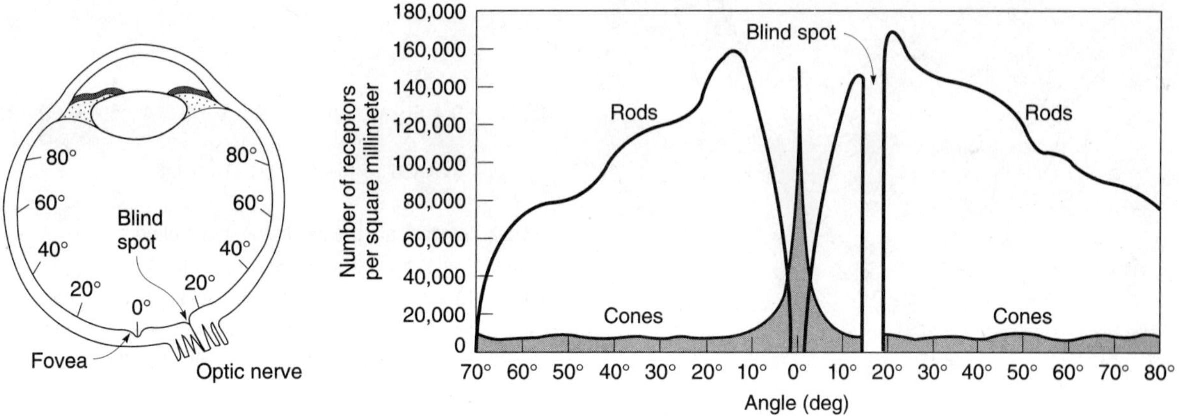

Figure 2.13
The distribution of rods and cones in the retina. The eye on the left indicates locations in degrees relative to the fovea, which are repeated along the bottom of the chart on the right. Notice in the distribution on the right that there are only cones at the fovea (0°) and that there are no receptors at all at the blind spot, the place where the ganglion cells leave the eye in the optic nerve. (Adapted from Lindsay & Norman, 1977.)

The cross section of the retina in Figure 2.4 shows that the rods and cones are facing away from the light, so the light passes through the other neurons in the retina before it reaches the receptors. One reason the receptors face away from the light is so they can be in contact with a layer of cells called the **pigment epithelium** (Figure 2.14), which contains nutrients and chemicals called *enzymes* that are vital to the receptors' functioning in ways we will describe later in this chapter. Backward-facing receptors pose little problem for vision, however, since the light easily passes through the transparent ganglion, amacrine, bipolar, and horizontal cells on its way to the receptors.

The backward-facing receptors do, however, create a problem for the ganglion cells: Since the receptors line the back of the eye, they seem to be blocking the ganglion cells from leaving the eye in the optic nerve. Figure 2.15 shows how the eye solves this problem. There is a small area with no receptors, where the eye's one million ganglion cell fibers stream out of the eye to form the optic nerve. Since there are no receptors in the place where the optic nerve leaves the eye, this area is called the **blind spot.** Although you are not normally aware of the blind spot, you can become aware of it by doing the following demonstration.

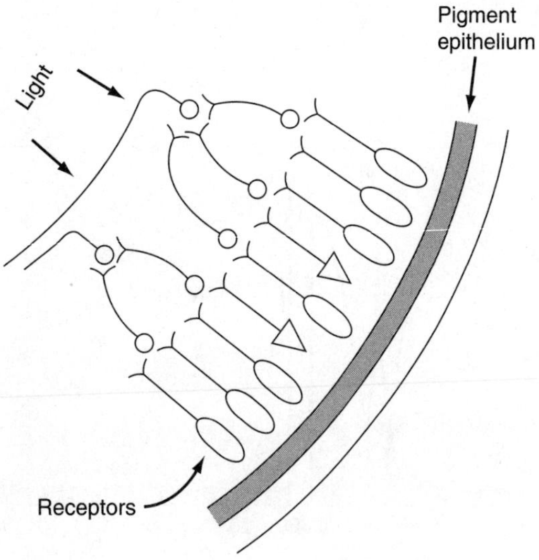

Figure 2.14
Close-up of the retina showing how the receptors face away from the light so the light must pass through other retinal neurons before reaching the receptors. Since these neurons are transparent, they do not prevent the light from reaching the receptors.

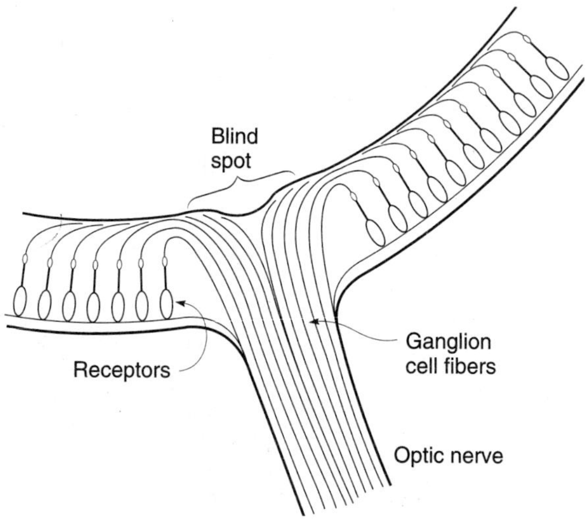

Figure 2.15
There are no receptors at the place where the optic nerve leaves the eye. This enables the receptor's ganglion cell fibers to flow into the optic nerve. The absence of receptors in this area creates the blind spot.

D E M O N S T R A T I O N

"Seeing" the Blind Spot

You can demonstrate the existence of the blind spot to yourself by closing your right eye and, with the cross in Figure 2.16 aligned with your left eye, looking at the cross while moving the book (or yourself) slowly back and forth. When the book is 6 to 12 inches from your eye, the circle disappears. At this point, the image of the circle falls on the blind spot. ●

Figure 2.16

Why aren't we usually aware of the blind spot? There are a number of reasons. First, we usually use two eyes, so when an image falls on the blind spot of one eye, it falls on the receptors of the other. But this explanation doesn't really answer our question, because we usually aren't aware of the blind spot even when we look with only one eye. One reason we aren't aware of it, even with one-eyed vision, is that the blind spot is located off to the side of our visual field, where objects are not in sharp focus. Because of this and because we don't know exactly where to look for it (as opposed to the demonstration, in which we are focusing our attention on the circle), the blind spot is hard to detect.

But perhaps the most important reason that we don't see the blind spot is that some mechanism located in the brain that we don't yet understand "fills in" the place where the image disappears (Churchland & Ramachandran, 1996). Think about what happened when the spot in the demonstration disappeared. The place where the spot used to be wasn't replaced by a "hole" or by "nothingness"—it was filled in by the white page.

DEMONSTRATION

Filling in the Blind Spot

To experience the blind spot's filling-in process in another way, close your right eye and, with the cross in Figure 2.17 lined up with your left eye, move the "wheel" toward you. When the center of the wheel falls on your blind spot, notice how the spokes of the wheel fill in the hole (Ramachandran, 1992). ●

The Rod and Cone Receptors: Transducing Light into Electricity

The place where the initial events of the visual process occur is the rod- or cone-shaped receptor outer segments, because this is where the light-sensitive visual pigments that are responsible for transduction are located. Looking inside the outer segment reveals discs stacked one on top of the other (Figure 2.18a),

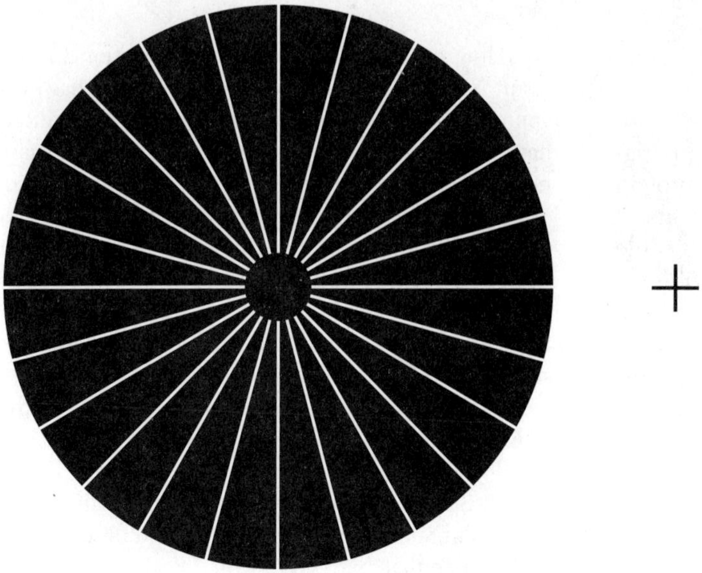

Figure 2.17
View this pattern as described in the text, and observe what happens when the center of the wheel falls on your blind spot (Ramachandran, 1992).

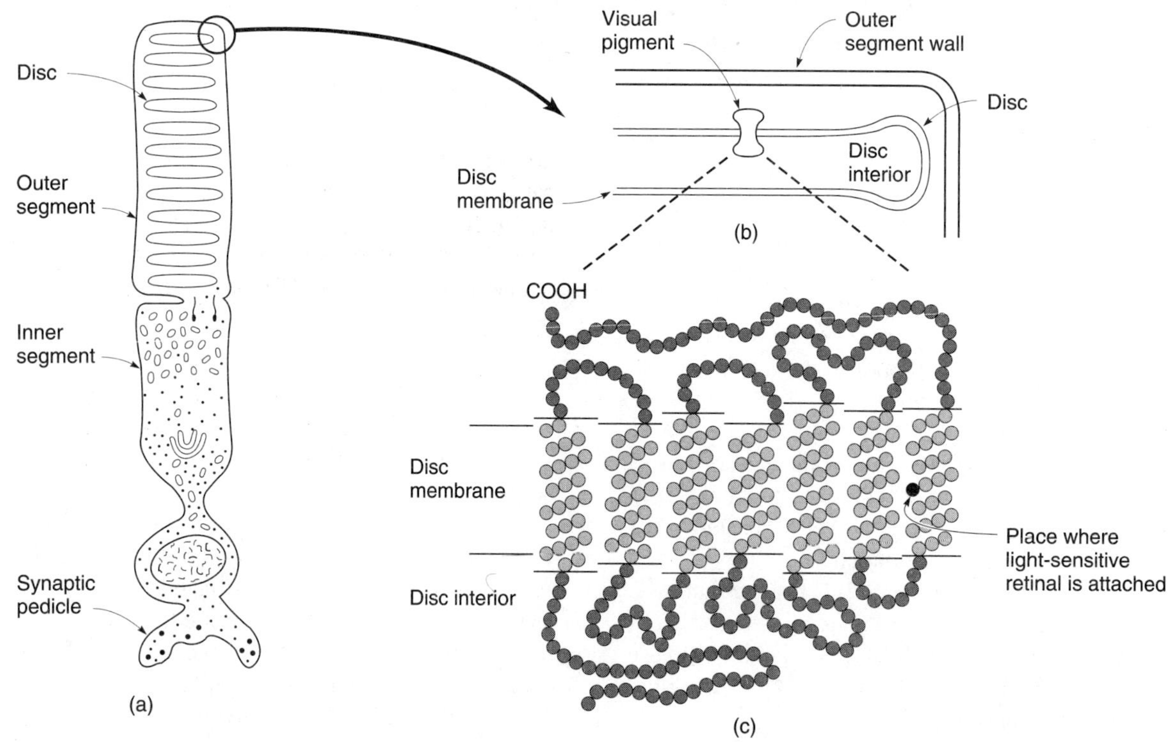

Figure 2.18

(a) Rod receptor showing discs in the outer segment. (b) Close-up of one disc showing one visual pigment molecule in the membrane. Notice how the molecule straddles the disc membrane. (c) Close-up showing how the protein opsin in the visual pigment molecule crosses the disc membrane seven times. The light-sensitive retinal molecule is attached at the place indicated.

which contain **visual pigment** molecules (Figure 2.18b) that loop back and forth across the disc membrane seven times (Figure 2.18c).

The visual pigment molecule shown in Figure 2.18c has two components: (1) a large protein called **opsin** with a molecular weight of about 40,000, and (2) a small light-sensitive molecule called **retinal,** with a molecular weight of only 268. The retinal, which is attached to the opsin at the point shown, reacts to light and is therefore responsible for **visual transduction**—the transformation of light energy into electrical energy. The transduction process begins when the light-sensitive retinal absorbs one photon of light. (Remember that a photon is the smallest possible packet of light energy.) When the retinal absorbs this photon it changes its shape (Figure 2.19), a process called **isomerization.**

How does the visual pigment's reaction to light result in an electrical signal? This question has been approached in two ways: Psychophysical experiments have shown that only one visual pigment molecule needs to be isomerized to excite a receptor, and physiological and biochemical experiments have uncovered the molecular mechanisms that make this excitation possible. We will describe the psychophysical experiment and the reasoning behind it in some detail since it is an excellent example of how psychophysical results can lead to physiological conclusions.

The psychophysical experiment that showed that only one visual pigment molecule needs to be activated to excite a rod was done in 1942 by Selig Hecht, Simon Shlaer, and Maurice Pirenne. By using a precisely calibrated light course, Hecht and his coworkers determined that an observer can detect a flash of light that contains only 100 photons. However, only about

THE VISUAL PROCESS

The stimulus for vision is visible light, a small band of energy contained within the electromagnetic spectrum. The electromagnetic spectrum stretches from X-rays, which have wavelengths as short as 10^{-12} meters, to radio waves, which have wavelengths as long as 10^{+4} meters (Plate 1.1). Visible light is located between these extremes with wavelengths on the order of 10^{-6} meters. Expanding this visible part of the electromagnetic spectrum reveals the familiar array of colors seen by humans with normal color vision (see text pages 46 and 136).

The visual process begins when visible light enters the eye and forms images on the retina, a thin layer of neurons lining the back of the eye (Plate 1.2). The magnified view of the retina shown to the right in Plate 1.2 reveals that the retina consists of a number of different types of neurons, including the rod and cone receptors, which transform light energy into electrical energy, and fibers that transmit electrical energy out of the retina in the optic nerve. (See Figure 2.4 on page 32 for a more detailed picture of the different retinal neurons.)

The cross section of the rhesus monkey retina in Plate 1.3 illustrates the layered nature of the retina. In this picture, light is coming from the top, and the receptors are facing the dark-colored pigment epithelium (shown in the lower-right corner) that lines the back of the retina. We can clearly see the layering by looking at the cell bodies of the retinal neurons. The red circles near the bottom of the picture are the cell bodies of the receptors (labeled R in Figure 2.4), the circles in the next layer are the cell bodies of the bipolar cells (labeled B in Figure 2.4), and the circles in the top, bluish layer are the cell bodies of the ganglion cells (labeled G in Figure 2.4) (page 32).

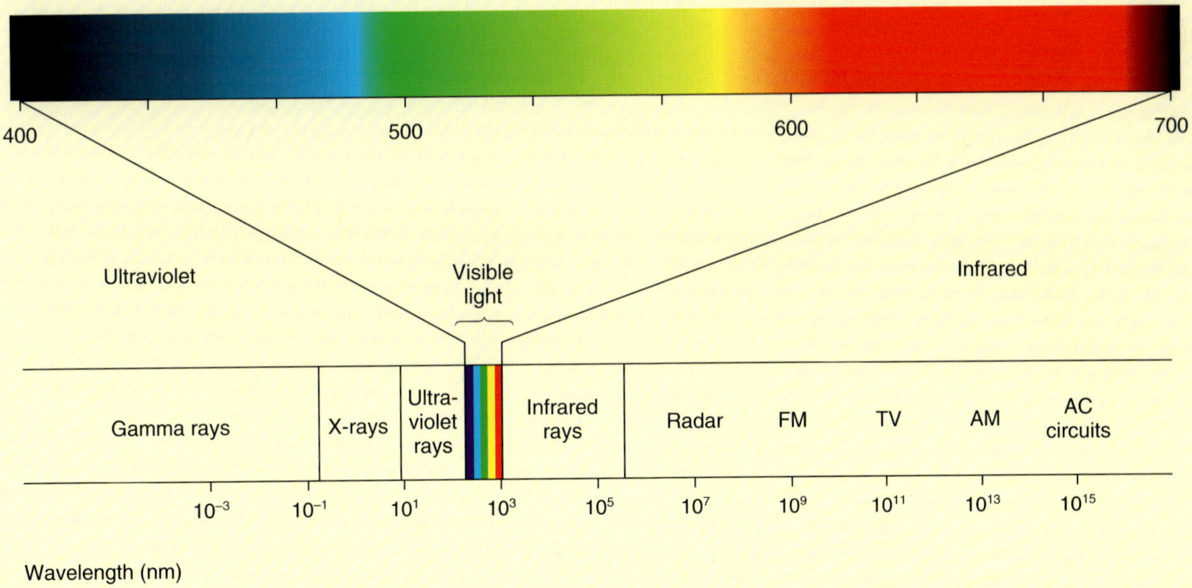

Plate 1.1

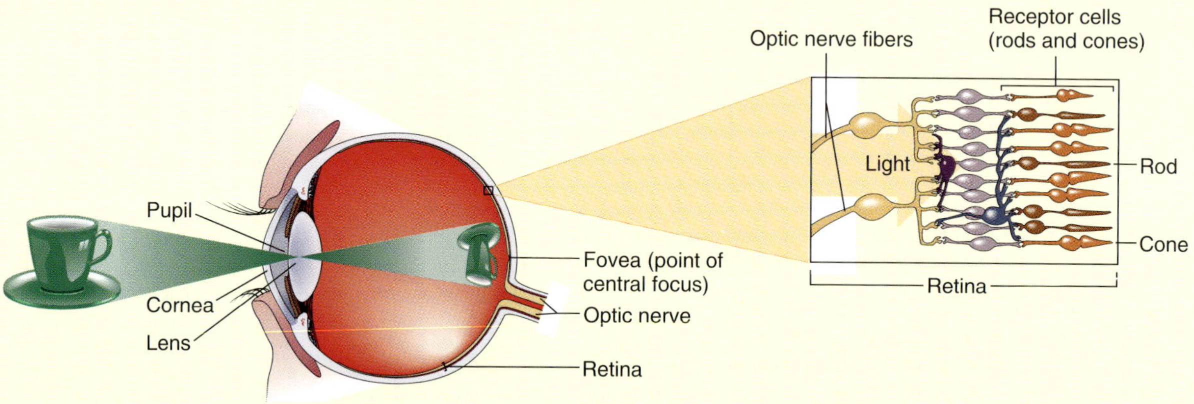

Plate 1.2

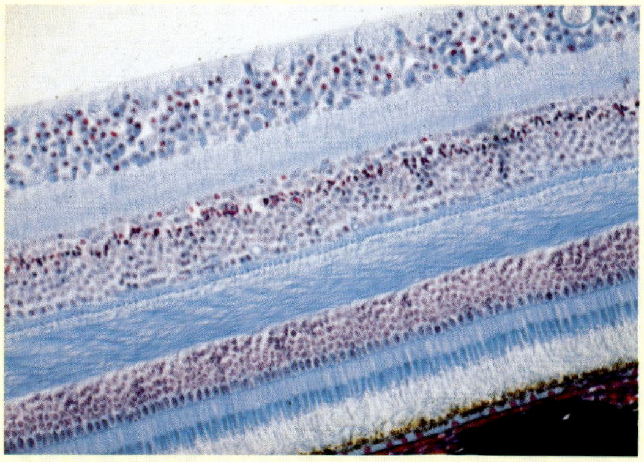

Plate 1.3

Looking down on the receptors, reveals the "mosaic" of rods and cones shown close up in Plate 1.4a and over a larger area in Plate 1.4b. In these pictures of the periphery of a monkey's retina, the rods are the small circles and the cones are the larger circles. The cones appear larger because the retina has been sliced across the receptors' inner segments (see Figure 2.4, page 32, and Figure 2.11, page 37), which are fatter in the cones than in the rods. Since this is the peripheral retina, there are many more rods than cones (page 37). A special dye, which affects only the cones that absorb light at the short-wavelength end of the spectrum, has stained them yellow. The orderly spacing of the cones reflects the highly organized nature of the visual system as a whole.

The rods and cones have different properties, with the rod system being more sensitive to shorter wavelengths than

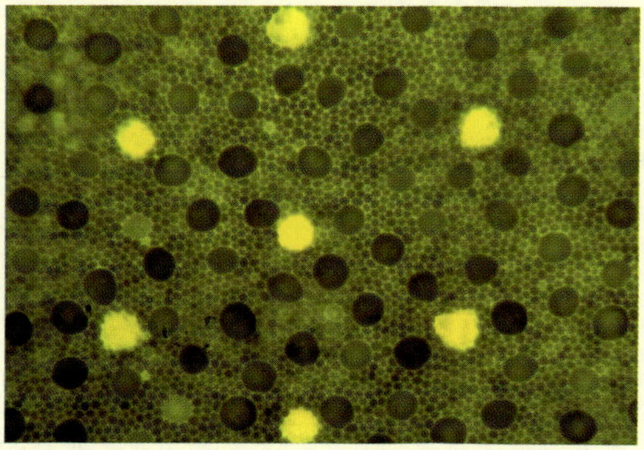

Plate 1.4a

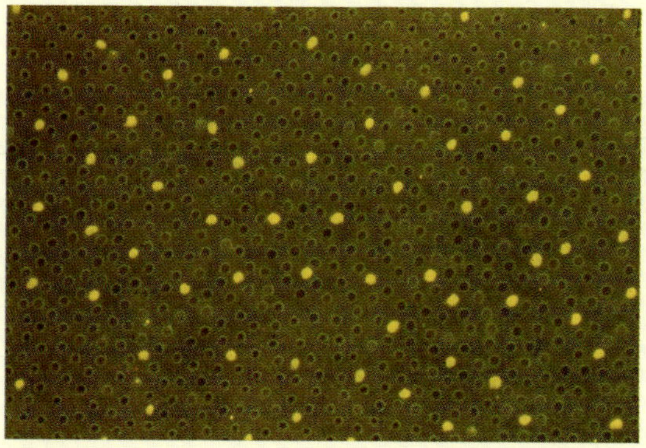

Plate 1.4b

Plate 1.5

the cone system. You can demonstrate this perceptually by following the Demonstration, "Experiencing the Shift from Cone Vision to Rod Vision, on page 46. If you close one eye to adapt it to the dark while leaving the other eye open, your perception of the brightness of the red and blue flowers in Plate 1.5 should change when you alternate eyes. When viewed with the dark-adapted eye, the blue flower should appear brighter compared to the red one than it does when viewed with the light-adapted eye. This shift in perception is caused by the shift from cone to rod vision that occurs during dark adaptation.

Both the rod and cone receptors contain light-sensitive visual pigment that reacts to light by changing shape and generating an electrical signal. This change in shape is accompanied by a change in the color of the pigment, which is called *bleaching.* In Plate 1.6, the left photograph shows a frog retina taken immediately after a light was turned on, so little bleaching has occurred and the retina appears red. When the retina is placed on a flat surface, as shown here, its edges bend over, causing a double layer of retina and a deeper red color around the edges. The black spots are small pieces of the pigment epithelium, the cell layer on which the retina rests when in the eye. The middle photograph was taken after some bleaching, so the retina is lighter red; in the right photograph, further bleaching has resulted in a light orange appearance. When bleaching is complete, the orange fades and the retina becomes transparent. If this retina were still in the frog's eye, the transparent retina would regain its red color as the pigment regenerated in the dark; however, little regeneration occurs when the retina is dissected from the eye, as in these photographs (pages 40 and 43).

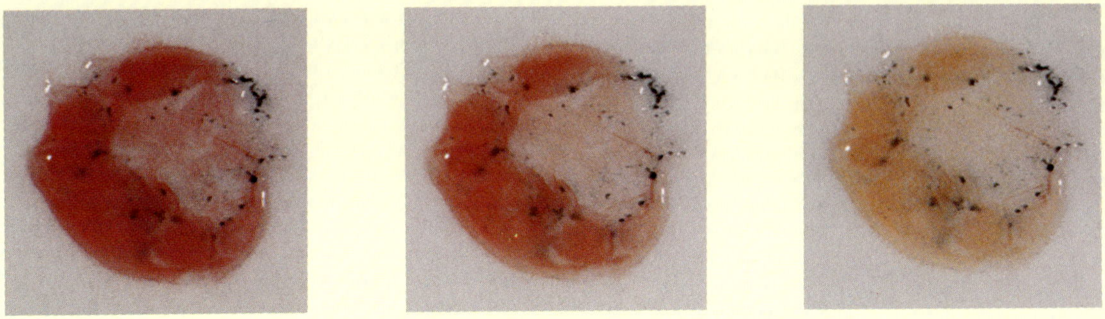

Plate 1.6

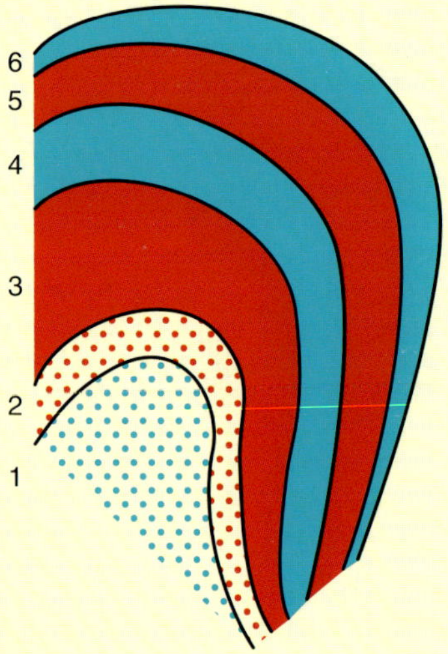

Plate 1.7

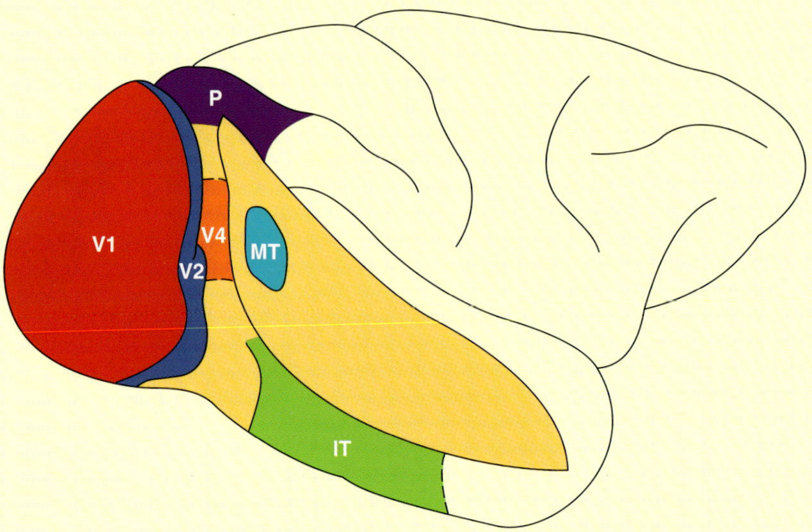

Plate 1.8

The signals generated in the receptors trigger electrical signals in the next layer of the retina, the bipolar cells, and these signals are transmitted through the various neurons in the retina, until eventually they are transmitted out of the eye by ganglion cell fibers. These ganglion cell fibers flow out of the back of the eye and become fibers in the optic nerve. Most of these optic nerve fibers reach the lateral geniculate nucleus (LGN), the first major way station on the way to the brain. The LGN is a bilateral nucleus, which means that there is an LGN on the left side of the brain, and also one on the right side.

Shown in cross section in Plate 1.7, the LGN has been colored to indicate two types of organization: (1) *Organization by eye.* Layers 2, 3, and 5 (red) receive inputs from the ipsilateral eye, the eye on the same side of the body as the LGN, and layers 1, 4, and 6 (blue) receive inputs from the contralateral eye, the eye on the opposite side of the body; (2) *Organization by type of ganglion cell.* Layers 1 and 2 (dots) called the *magnocellular* layer, receive inputs from the large M-ganglion cells; layers 3, 4, 5, and 6 (solid), called the *parvocellular* layer, receive inputs from the smaller P-ganglion cells (pages 74–75).

Fibers from the LGN stream to the primary visual receiving area, the striate cortex or V1, in the occipital lobe. Plate 1.8 shows the location of this area as well as a number of the major extrastriate areas that are involved in processing visual information. In this view of the monkey brain, part of the temporal lobe has been removed to show structures underneath. Areas that are labeled correspond to those described in Chapter 4 that are associated with the parietal and temporal extrastriate pathways (see Figures 4.1 and 4.4). IT stands for inferotemporal cortex; MT for medial temporal area; and P for the part of the parietal areas associated with vision. The yellow area represents other parts of the cortex that are also associated with vision. Area V3 is not visible, since it is hidden by a fold in the cortex.

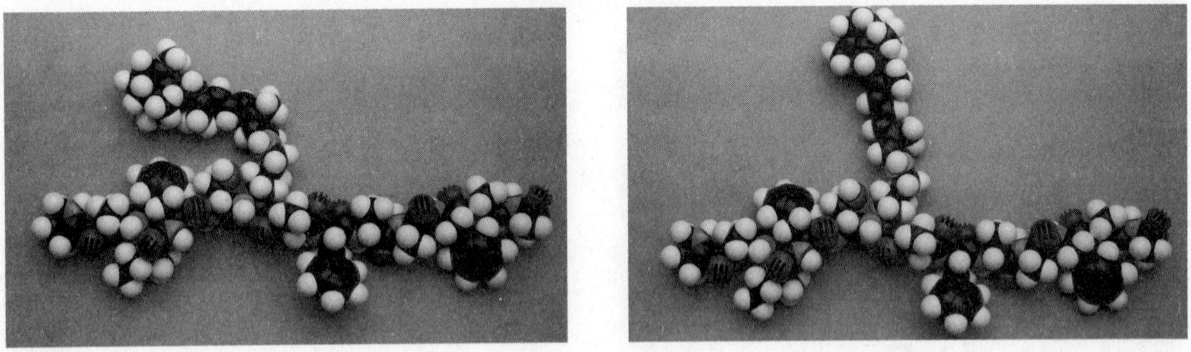

Figure 2.19
Model of a visual pigment molecule. The horizontal part of the model shows a tiny portion of the huge opsin molecule near where the retinal is attached. The smaller molecule on top of the opsin is the light-sensitive retinal. The model on the left shows the retinal molecule's shape before it absorbs light. The model on the right shows the retinal molecule's shape after it absorbs light. This change in shape is the isomerization process that triggers the generation of an electrical response in the receptor.

half of these photons actually reach the retina. The other half bounce off the surface of the cornea before entering the eye, or are reflected or absorbed by the lens, just inside the eye, or the jellylike vitreous humor that fills the inside of the eye. Of the 50 photons that do reach the retina, only about 7 are actually absorbed by visual pigment molecules. The rest either slip between the receptors or pass through a receptor without hitting the light sensitive part of a visual pigment molecule. Thus, Hecht's result indicated that the activation of only 7 visual pigment molecules results in the perception of a light—an impressive demonstration of the exquisite sensitivity of the visual system.

But Hecht wasn't satisfied just to show that 7 visual pigment molecules need to be activated for perception to occur. He reasoned that since the flash of light seen by the subject covered about 500 receptors, it is highly unlikely that more than one of the 7 activated visual pigment molecules would be in the same receptor. Look at it this way: You are in a helicopter flying over an array of 500 small cylinders. When you are directly above the cylinders, you release 7 ping-pong balls. What is the probability that 2 of these balls would end up in the same cylinder? The answer is "*very small*," and it is equally unlikely that 2 visual pigment molecules would be isomerized in the same receptor in Hecht's experiment. Hecht therefore concluded that only one visual pigment molecule needs to be isomerized in order to excite a rod receptor and when 7 receptors are activated simultaneously, we can see the light.

About 30 years after Hecht, Shlaer, and Pirenne concluded that a rod can be excited by the isomerization of only one visual pigment molecule, physiologists began uncovering the physiological mechanisms that make this amazing feat possible. What the physiologists found was that isomerization of one visual pigment molecule transforms it into an activated state that can trigger thousands of chemical reactions, which, in turn, trigger thousands more (Figure 2.20).

A biological chemical that in small amounts facilitates chemical reactions in this way is called an *enzyme*, and the sequence of reactions triggered by the activated visual pigment molecule is called the **enzyme cascade.** Just as pulling the plug covering the drain in your bathtub can empty the entire tub, isomerizing one visual pigment molecule can cause a chemical effect that is large enough to activate the entire rod receptor. For more specific details as to how this is accomplished see Baylor (1992), Ranganathan, Harris, and Zuker (1991), Stryer (1986), and Tessier-Lavigne (1991).

The visual pigments play an essential role in vision by triggering the electrical response in the receptors. In addition, the properties of visual pigments determine a number of the basic properties of vision. We can illustrate this by describing the *duplicity theory of vision.*

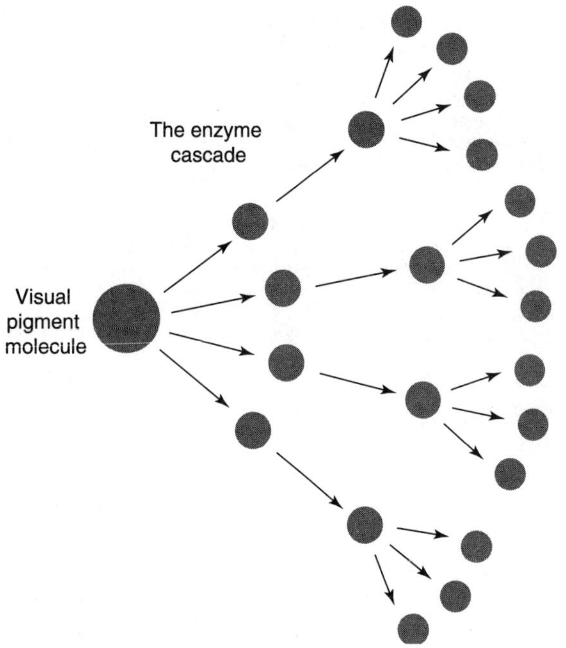

Figure 2.20
This sequence symbolizes the enzyme cascade that occurs when a single visual pigment molecule is activated by absorption of a quantum of light. In the actual sequence of events, each visual pigment molecule activates hundreds more molecules, which, in turn, each activate about a thousand more molecules. The net result is that isomerization of one visual pigment molecule activates about a million other molecules. This massive activation leads to generation of an electrical signal in the receptor.

Duplicity Theory: Different Receptors for Different Perceptions

In 1896, J. von Kries proposed the **duplicity theory of vision.** This theory states that the retina is composed of two types of receptors that not only look different, as was demonstrated by Max Schultze, but that also operate under different conditions and have different properties.

The existence of two receptor systems with different properties provides us with the opportunity to demonstrate how visual pigments determine some of the basic characteristics of visual perception. We will illustrate this by describing how properties of the rod and cone visual pigments determine the course of **dark adaptation**—the increase in the eye's sensitivity that occurs when illumination changes from light to darkness—and *spectral sensitivity*—the eye's sensitivity to specific parts of the visual spectrum. We first consider dark adaptation.

Dark Adaptation of the Rods and Cones

You are familiar with dark adaptation from your own experience: When you switch off the light in your bedroom at night, it may be difficult to see anything at first, but the longer you spend in the dark, the more your sensitivity increases, and eventually you can see things such as light coming in under the door, that you couldn't see at first.

DEMONSTRATION

Spending Some Time in Your Closet

You can experience the time course of dark adaptation by finding a dark place and making some observations as you adapt to the dark. A closet is a good place to do this, because it is possible to regulate the intensity of light inside the closet by opening or closing the door. The idea is to create an environment in which there is dim light (no light at all, as in a darkroom with the safelight out, is too dark).

Take this book into the closet. Have the book opened to this page. Close the closet door all the way so it is very dark, and then open the door slowly until you can just barely make out the white circle on the far left of Figure 2.21.

Your task is simple. Just sit in the dark and become aware that your sensitivity is increasing by noting how the circles to the right in Figure 2.21 slowly become visible over a period of about 20 minutes. Also note that once a circle

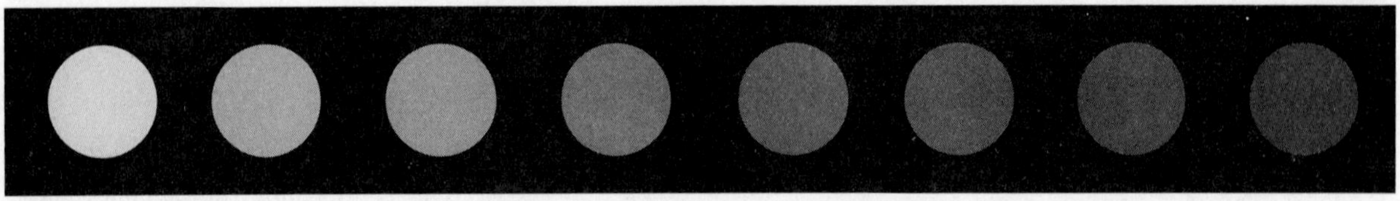

Figure 2.21

becomes visible, it gets easier to see as time passes. If you stare directly at the circles, they may fade, so move your eyes around every so often. Also, the circles will be easier to see if you don't look directly at them. Look slightly above the circles.

This demonstration demands patience, but remember that to become a Buddhist monk you would have to sit motionless in front of the temple door for two days! Sitting in a closet for 20 minutes is easy compared to that. As you sit there, also notice that other objects in the closet slowly become visible, but be careful not to look directly at the light coming through the door, because that will slow the process of dark adaptation. ●

Although it is easy to demonstrate that your sensitivity to light increases as you spend time in the dark, it is not obvious that this increase takes place in two distinct stages: an initial rapid stage and a later, slower stage. We will now describe three experiments that show that the initial rapid stage is due to adaptation of the cone receptors, and that the second slower stage is due to adaptation of the rod receptors. In our first experiment, we will describe how to measure a **dark adaptation curve,** a plot of sensitivity versus the time in the dark, which shows the two-stage process of dark adaptation. In our second experiment, we will measure the dark adaptation of the cones alone. And in our third experiment, we will measure the dark adaptation of the rods alone. Finally, we will see how the different adaptation rates of the rods and the cones can be explained by an important difference in a property of the receptors' visual pigments.

Experiment 1: Determining a Two-Stage Dark Adaptation Curve In all of our dark adaptation experiments, we ask our observer to adjust the intensity of a small, flashing test light so he or she can just barely see it. In the first experiment, our observer looks at a small fixation point while paying attention to a flashing test light that is off to the side. Since the observer is looking directly at the fixation point, its image falls on the fovea, and the image of the test light falls in the periphery (Figure 2.22). Thus, the test light stimulates both rods and cones, and any adaptation measured with this test light should reflect the activity of both the rod and the cone receptors. The procedure for measuring the dark adaptation curve is as follows:

- The observer is light-adapted by exposing him to an intense light.
- The observer's light-adapted sensitivity is measured by having him adjust the intensity of the test light so he can just barely see it. This is labeled light-adapted sensitivity in Figure 2.23.

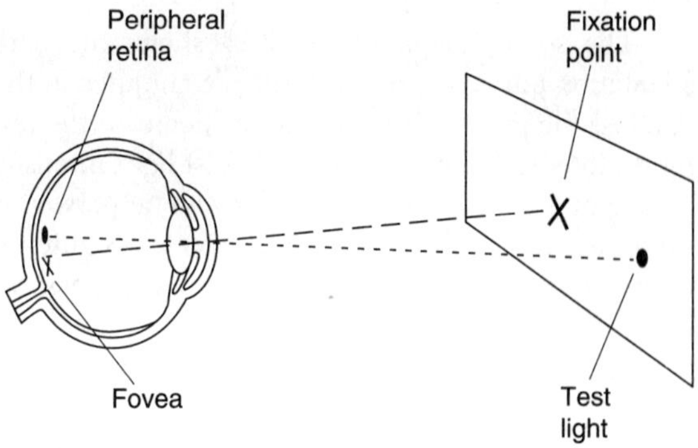

Figure 2.22
Viewing conditions for a dark adaptation experiment. The image of the fixation point falls on the fovea and the image of the test light falls in the peripheral retina.

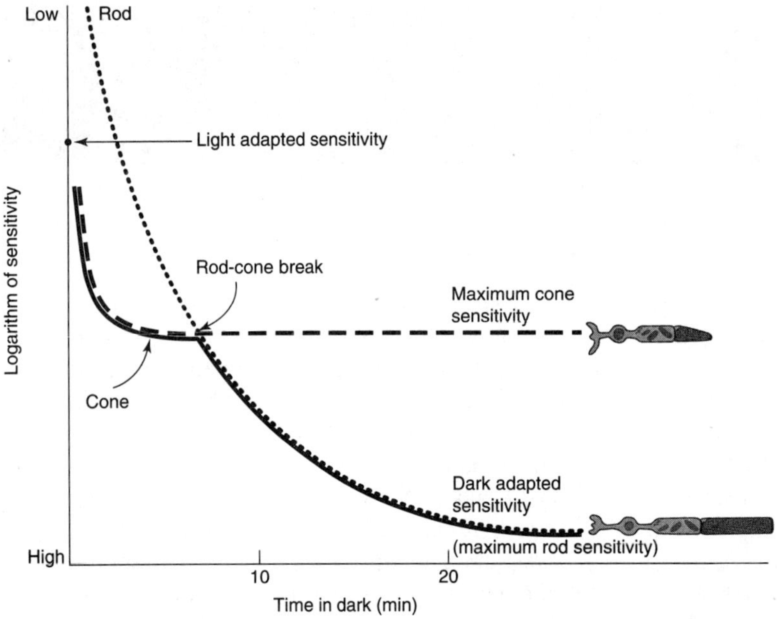

Figure 2.23
Dark adaptation curves. Actually, three curves are shown. The solid line shows the two-stage dark adaptation curve measured in experiment 1, with a cone branch at the beginning and a rod branch at the end. The dashed line shows the cone adaptation curve measured in experiment 2. The solid and dashed curves actually begin at the point marked "light adapted sensitivity," but there is a slight delay between the time the lights are turned off and the time the measurement of the curves begins. The dotted line shows the rod adaptation curve measured in experiment 3. Note that as these curves go down, sensitivity increases.

- The intense light is turned off.
- The course of dark adaptation is measured by having the observer continually adjust the intensity of the test light so it remains just barely detectable.

The solid line of Figure 2.23 shows the dark adaptation curve measured during 28 minutes in the dark. As the person dark adapts they decrease the test light's intensity. Since decreases in test light intensity correspond to increases in sensitivity (a person is more sensitive if he or she can detect less intense lights), we can describe dark adaptation as an *increase* in sensitivity with time.

The dark adaptation curve indicates that the observer's sensitivity increases in two phases. It first increases for about 3 to 4 minutes after the light is extinguished and then levels off; then, after about 7 to 10 minutes, the sensitivity begins to increase again and continues to do so for another 20 to 30 minutes. The sensitivity at the end of dark adaptation, labeled **dark adapted sensitivity,** is about 100,000 times greater than the **light adapted sensitivity** measured before dark adaptation began.

Experiment 2: Measuring Cone Adaptation To measure the adaptation of the cones, we repeat the first experiment but have the observer look directly at a test light so small that its entire image falls within the all-cone fovea. The resulting dark adaptation curve, indicated by the dashed curve in Figure 2.23, therefore reflects only the activity of the cones. This curve matches the initial phase of our original dark adaptation curve but does not include the second phase. Does this mean that the second part of the curve is due to the rods? We can show that the answer to this question is "yes" by doing another experiment.

Experiment 3: Measuring Rod Adaptation We know that the dashed curve of Figure 2.23 is due only to cone adaptation because our test light was focused on the all-cone fovea. To determine a pure rod dark-adaptation curve, we use a **rod monochromat**—a person who has a retina that, because of a genetic defect, contains *only* rods. (Students sometimes wonder why we can't simply place the test flash in the periphery, which contains mostly rods. The answer is that the few cones in the periphery will influence the beginning of the dark adaptation curve.)

The rod monochromat's dark adaptation curve shows that the light adapted sensitivity of the rods is much lower than that of the cones. Once dark adaptation begins, the rods increase their sensitivity and reach their final dark adapted level in about 25 minutes (Rushton, 1961). The fact that the rods begin adapting to the dark immediately after the light is extinguished means that they are adapting during the cone phase of a normal person's dark adaptation curve; however, we aren't aware of this early rod adaptation because of the greater sensitivity of the cones at the beginning of dark adaptation.

We can summarize the process of dark adaptation in a normal observer as follows: Both the rods and cones begin gaining in sensitivity as soon as the lights are extinguished, but since the cones are more sensitive at the beginning of dark adaptation, they determine the early part of the dark adaptation curve. When the cones finish their adaptation, after about 3 to 5 minutes, the dark adaptation curve levels off. However, at about 7 minutes after the beginning of dark adaptation, the rods (which have been increasing in sensitivity all along) become more sensitive than the cones, creating the **rod-cone break** (Figure 2.23). The dark adaptation curve then continues downward for another 15 minutes as the rods continue their increase in sensitivity.

The rods take 20 to 30 minutes to achieve their maximum sensitivity, compared to only 3 to 4 minutes for the cones. We will now show that these differences in the rate of adaptation can be traced to a process called *visual pigment regeneration* that occurs with different speeds in the rods and the cones.

Visual Pigment Regeneration When the visual pigment absorbs light, the light-sensitive retinal molecule changes shape and triggers the transduction process. It then separates from the larger opsin molecule and this separation causes the retina to change from its original red color to orange, then to yellow, and finally to transparent (Color Plate 1.6), a process called **pigment bleaching.** Before the visual pigment can again change light energy into electrical energy, the retinal and the opsin must be rejoined. This process, which is called **pigment regeneration,** occurs in the dark with the aid of enzymes supplied to the visual pigments by the nearby pigment epithelium (refer to Figure 2.14).

As the retinal and opsin components of the visual pigment recombine in the dark, the pigment changes from its transparent bleached state back to its darker unbleached state. William Rushton (1961) devised a procedure to measure the regeneration of visual pigment in humans by measuring the darkening of the visual pigment during dark adaptation. Rushton's measurements showed that cone pigment takes 6 minutes to regenerate completely, while rod pigment takes over 30 minutes. When he compared the course of pigment regeneration to the rate of psychophysical dark adaptation he found that the rate of cone dark adaptation matched the rate of cone pigment regeneration and the rate of rod dark adaptation matched the rate of rod pigment regeneration.

Rushton's result demonstrated two important connections between perception and physiology:

1. The increase in sensitivity of both rods and cones that occurs during dark adaptation is caused by visual pigment regeneration, and
2. The slow adaptation of the rods compared to the cones occurs because rod pigment regenerates more slowly than cone pigment.

So, the next time you enter a darkened room, remember that both the rod and the cone visual pigments begin regenerating immediately and that the regenerating pigments are what enable you, after 10 or 15 minutes in the dark, to see dimly illuminated objects that you couldn't see just after you turned out the light.

Another way to show that perception is determined by the properties of the visual pigments is to compare rod and cone **spectral sensitivity**—the receptor's sensitivity to light at each wavelength across the visible spectrum.

Spectral Sensitivity of the Rods and Cones

In our dark adaptation experiments, we used a white test light, which contains all wavelengths in the visible spectrum. To determine spectral sensitivity we use **monochromatic light,** light which contains only a single wavelength. We determine the threshold for seeing these monochromatic lights for wavelengths across the visible spectrum. For example, we might first determine the threshold for seeing a 420-nm light, then a 440-nm light, and so on, across the spectrum, using one of the psychophysical methods for measuring threshold described in Chapter 1. The result is the curve in Figure 2.24a, which shows that the threshold for seeing light is lowest in the middle of the spectrum; that is, less light is needed to see wavelengths in the middle of the spectrum than to see wavelengths at either the short- or long-wavelength ends of the spectrum.

We can change threshold to **sensitivity** by the formula, sensitivity = 1/threshold, and when we do this, our threshold curve of Figure 2.24a becomes the sensitivity curve of Figure 2.24b, which is called a **spectral sensitivity curve.**

Now that we know how to determine the spectral sensitivity curve, let's compare the curve for cone vision with the curve for rod vision. Figure 2.24b is the cone spectral sensitivity curve, which was determined as the person looked directly at the test light, so that it illuminated the fovea and stimulated only cone receptors.

To measure the spectral sensitivity of rod vision, we dark adapt the eye and present test lights to the peripheral retina. Since the rods are more sensitive than the cones in the fully dark adapted eye, adjusting the test flashes to threshold results in the **rod spectral sensitivity curve,** shown in Figure 2.25. Comparing this curve to the cone curve shows that the rods are more sensitive to short-wavelength light than are the cones, with the rods being most sensitive to light of 500 nm and the cones being most sensitive to light of 560 nm. This difference in the sensitivity of the rods and the cones to different wavelengths means that, as our vision shifts from our cones to our rods during dark adaptation, we become relatively more sensitive to short-wavelength light, that is, light nearer the blue and green end of the spectrum.

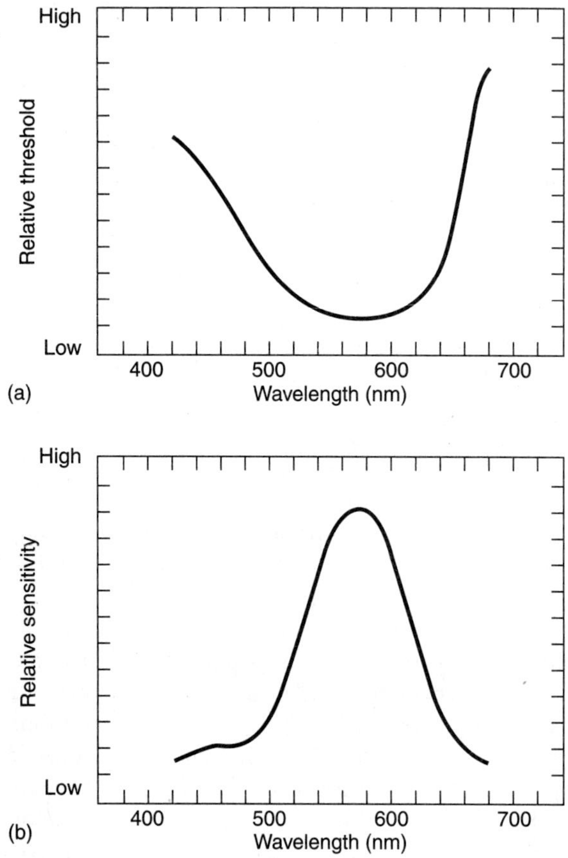

Figure 2.24
(a) The threshold for seeing a light versus wavelength. (b) If we take the reciprocal of the thresholds of the curve in (a) (reciprocal = 1/threshold), the curve turns over and becomes a plot of sensitivity versus wavelength, commonly known as a spectral sensitivity curve. (Adapted from Wald, 1964.)

You may have noticed an effect of this shift to short-wavelength sensitivity if you have observed how green foliage seems to stand out more near dusk. This shift from cone vision to rod vision that causes this enhanced perception of short-wavelengths during dark adaptation is called the **Purkinje** *(Pur-kin-jee)* **shift,** after Johann Purkinje, who described this effect in

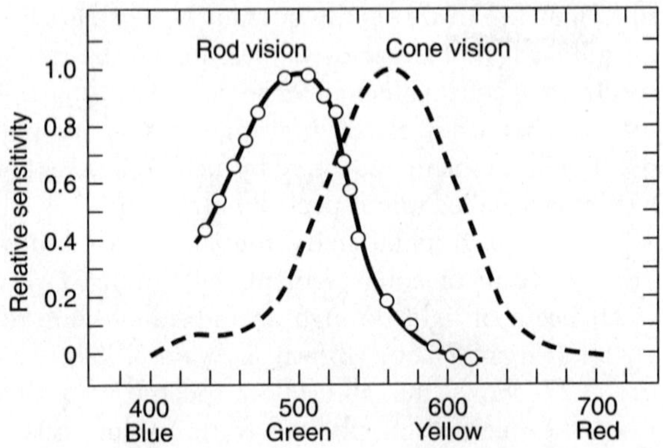

Figure 2.25
Spectral sensitivity curves for rod vision and cone vision. The maximum sensitivities of these two curves have been set equal to 1.0. However, as we saw in Figure 2.22, the relative sensitivities of the rods and the cones depend on the conditions of adaptation: The cones are more sensitive in the light, and the rods are more sensitive in the dark. The circles plotted on top of the rod curve represent the absorption spectrum of the rod visual pigment. (From Wald, 1964; Wald & Brown, 1958.)

1825. You can experience this shift from cone vision to rod vision by doing the following demonstration:

D E M O N S T R A T I O N

Experiencing the Shift from Cone Vision to Rod Vision

To experience the Purkinje shift, return to the closet (see Demonstration, "Spending Some Time in Your Closet") and make the following observations:

1. **Before entering the closet, adapt one eye to the dark by closing it for about 10 minutes. Do this in the light so that your opened eye stays adapted to the light while your closed eye is adapted to the dark.**
2. **After completing step 1, enter the closet, and with the door open, observe Color Plate 1.5 with your light-adapted eye, and compare the brightness of the blue and red flowers. When viewed with your light-adapted eye in daylight illumination, the two flowers should appear approximately equal in brightness.**
3. **Close the door so that it is completely dark. Close your light-adapted eye and open your dark-adapted eye.**
4. **Slowly crack open the door until enough light is present for you to just see the flowers with your dark-adapted eye. If you have kept the light intensity low enough, you will be seeing with your rods, and the flowers should appear gray rather than red and blue (since we perceive in black and white with our rods and in color with our cones, as we will see in Chapter 5). It is important to notice that the flowers' relative brightness should now be different from when you viewed them with your light-adapted eye. The flower on the left should now appear slightly brighter than the flower on the right. If you have forgotten how the flowers looked to your light-adapted eye, close your dark-adapted eye, open the door, and observe the flowers with your light-adapted eye again.** ●

The increased brightness of the blue flower compared to the red flower when you observed them with your dark-adapted eye is a demonstration of the Purkinje shift.

Pigment Absorption Spectra The difference we have described between the rod and cone spectral sensitivity curves can be explained by differences in the absorption spectra of the rod and cone visual pigments. An **absorption spectrum** is a plot of the amount of light absorbed by a substance versus the wavelength of the light. George Wald, who won the 1967 Nobel Prize in Physiology and Medicine for his research on visual pigments, determined the absorption spectrum of human rod pigment by using a procedure in which visual pigments are chemically extracted from the retinas of eyes donated to medical research (Wald & Brown, 1958). This extraction procedure produces a liquid solution that contains primarily rod pigment, since the rods contain about 99 percent of the visual pigment in the human retina.

(Remember that there are 20 times more rods than cones in the retina and that the cones are smaller than the rods.)

Wald and Paul Brown used a device called a **spectrophotometer,** which measured the amount of light absorbed by the pigment solution at wavelengths across the visible spectrum (Figure 2.26a), and obtained the absorption spectrum plotted as open circles in Figure 2.25. The match between the pigment absorption spectrum and the rod spectral sensitivity curve indicates that the spectral sensitivity of rod vision is due to the absorption of light by the rod visual pigment.

How does the spectral sensitivity curve for cone vision compare to the absorption spectrum of cone visual pigment? To answer this question we need to solve the following problem: How to measure the absorption spectrum of cone pigment if 99 percent of the pigment that we chemically extract from the retina is rod pigment? This problem was solved by the development of a technique called **microspectrophotometry.**

Microspectrophotometry measures the absorption spectrum of cone pigments by shining a very small beam of light through an individual cone receptor (Figure 2.26b) (Brown & Wald, 1964). Figure 2.27 shows the absorption spectra measured using the microspectrophotometry procedure (Dartnall, Bowmaker, & Mollon, 1983). There are three curves because there are three different cone pigments, each contained in its own receptor. The **short-wavelength pigment** absorbs light best at about 419 nm; the **medium-wavelength pigment** absorbs light best at about 531 nm; and the **long-wavelength pigment** absorbs light best at about 558 nm. (The differences in the absorption spectra are caused by differences in the structures of the large opsin part of the visual pigment molecule.)

How do short-, medium-, and long-wavelength cone pigments that absorb best at 419, 531, and 558 nm, respectively, result in a psychophysical spectral sensitivity curve that peaks at 560 nm? Apparently these three cone pigments combine to result in the spectral sensitivity curve. This result was demonstrated by comparing the three pigment absorption

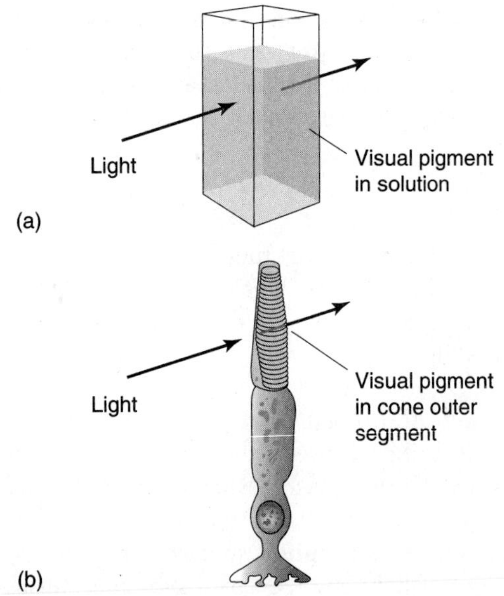

Figure 2.26
(a) A device called a spectrophotometer measures the absorption characteristics of rod visual pigments by shining lights ranging from short to long wavelengths into a liquid solution of visual pigment and then measuring how much light is transmitted through the solution for each wavelength. (b) The same procedure is used to measure the absorption characteristics of cone visual pigment, but the pigments are illuminated while still in the cone receptors. This technique is called microspectrophotometry, since it is spectrophotometry on a very small scale.

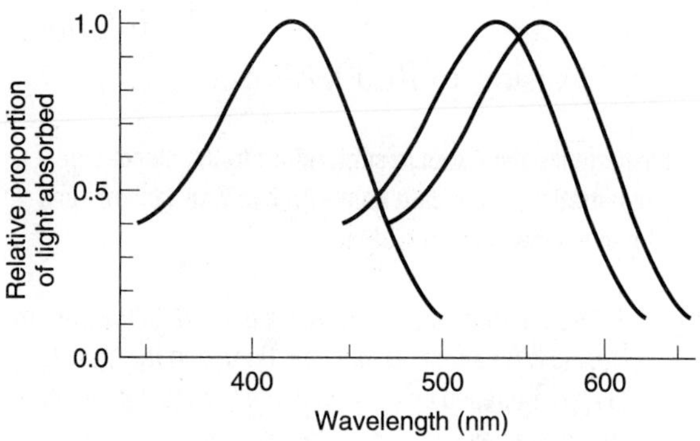

Figure 2.27
Absorption spectra of the three human cone pigments. (From Dartnall, Bowmaker, & Mollon, 1983.)

spectra to spectral sensitivity curves determined using the **two-color threshold method** introduced by W. S. Stiles (1953). In this method, a light that bleaches away two of the cone pigments and spares one pigment is presented to the retina (Figure 2.28). If the cone spectral sensitivity curve is determined by the combination of all three cone pigments, then measuring the spectral sensitivity while two of the pigments are gone should yield a curve that matches the pigment that remains. For [illegible] long-wavelength light that ble[illegible] long-wavelength pig[illegible]ngth pigment is p[illegible] should match the a[illegible]elength pigment. [illegible] spectral sensitivity cu[illegible] this method matched the absorpt[illegible] of the cone pigment that wasn't bleached. This result supports the idea that the spectral sensitivity curve of the cones is due to the combined action of the three cone pigments (Bowmaker & Dartnall, 1980).

From our description of rod and cone spectral sensitivity and dark adaptation, we can see that we can explain some perceptual phenomena in terms of the properties of the visual pigments. The idea that our perceptions are determined by physiological properties, such as the characteristics of the visual pigments, is a theme that continues throughout this book. We now consider the neural processing that occurs after signals are created in the receptors.

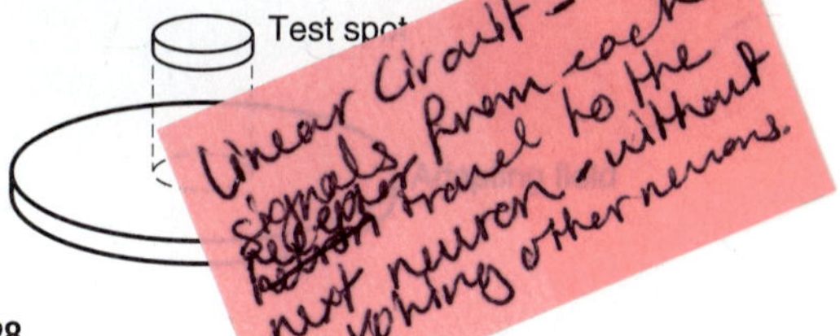

Figure 2.28
Stimulus arrangement for Stiles's two-color threshold method. The adapting field bleaches two of the three cone pigments. The small test spot is superimposed on the larger adapting field. The wavelength of the adapting field is kept constant, and the wavelength of the test spot is changed to measure the spectral sensitivity at wavelengths across the spectrum.

Neural Processing: Analysis and Transformation of Electrical Signals

How are the electrical signals generated in the receptors processed as they travel through complex networks of neurons? We are now ready to describe what we mean by neural processing.

Neural Circuits: The Basis of Processing

All sensory systems consist of networks of neurons which we will call **neural circuits.** The electrical signals generated in the receptors are processed as they travel through these neural circuits. To illustrate how this processing works, we will compare how three different neural circuits affect a neuron's response to a bar-shaped light stimulus of different lengths.

We begin with a simple neural circuit and then increase the complexity of this circuit in two stages, noting how this increased complexity affects the circuit's response to the stimulus. In these circuits we represent receptors by ellipses (⬭), cell bodies by circles (○), nerve fibers by straight lines (—), excitatory synapses by Y's (-<), and inhibitory synapses by T's (⊣). (See page 19 of Chapter 1 to review excitation and inhibition.) For this example, we will assume that the receptors respond to light, although the principles we will establish hold for any form of stimulation.

First, let's consider the circuit in Figure 2.29. We call this circuit a *linear circuit* because the signal generated by each receptor travels straight to the next neuron, and no other neurons are involved. Also, all 6 of the synapses in this circuit are excitatory. We stimulate the circuit by first illuminating receptor 4 with a spot of light. We then change this spot into a bar of light by adding light to illuminate receptors 3, 4, and 5 (3 through 5), then receptors 2 through 6, and finally receptors 1 through 7. When we measure the response of neuron B and plot this response in the

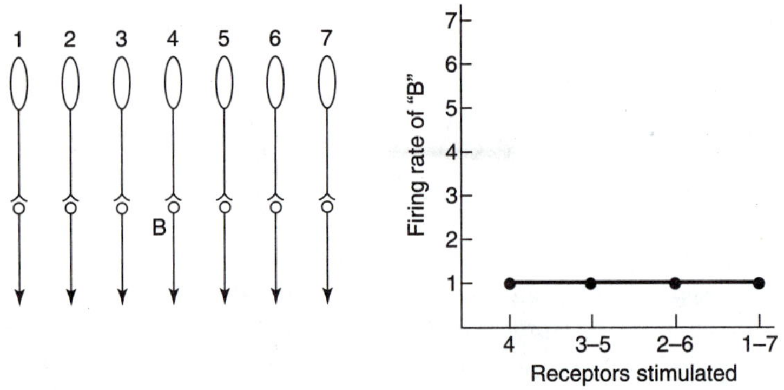

Figure 2.29
A linear circuit (left) and the responses of neuron B generated as we increase the number of receptors stimulated (right). Stimulating receptor 4 causes neuron B to fire, but stimulating the other neurons has no effect since they are not connected with neuron B.

graph to the right of the circuit, we find that neuron B fires when we stimulate receptor 4, but that stimulating the other receptors has no effect on neuron B, since it is still receiving exactly the same input from receptor 4. For the linear circuit, therefore, the firing of neuron B simply indicates that its receptor has been stimulated and doesn't provide any information about the length of the bar of light.

We now increase the complexity of the circuit by adding **convergence,** as shown in the circuit in Figure 2.30. Convergence occurs when two or more neurons synapse onto a single neuron. Thus, in this circuit, receptors 1 and 2 converge onto neuron A; 3, 4, and 5 converge onto B; 6 and 7 converge onto C; and A and C converge onto B. As in the previous circuit, all of the synapses are excitatory, but with the addition of convergence, one cell collects information from a number of other cells. We again focus our attention on neuron B, which, because of convergence, collects information from all of the receptors. When we monitor the firing rate of neuron B, we find that each time we increase the length of the stimulus, neuron B's firing rate increases, as shown in the graph in Figure 2.30. This occurs because stimulating more receptors increases the amount of excitatory transmitter released onto neuron B. Thus, in this circuit, neuron B's response provides information about the length of the stimulus.

We now increase the circuit's complexity further by adding two inhibitory synapses to create the circuit in Figure 2.31, in which neurons A and C inhibit neuron B. Now consider what happens as we increase the number of receptors stimulated. The spot of light stimulates receptor 4, which, through its excitatory connection, increases the firing rate of neuron B. Extending the illumination to include receptors 3 through 5 adds the output of two more excitatory synapses to B and increases its firing. So far, this circuit

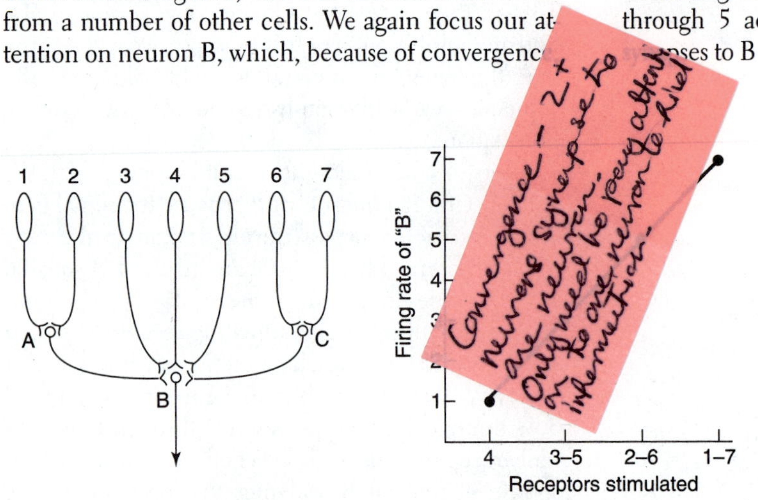

Figure 2.30
When we add convergence to the circuit, so that B receives inputs from all of the receptors, increasing the size of the stimulus increases the size of neuron B's response.

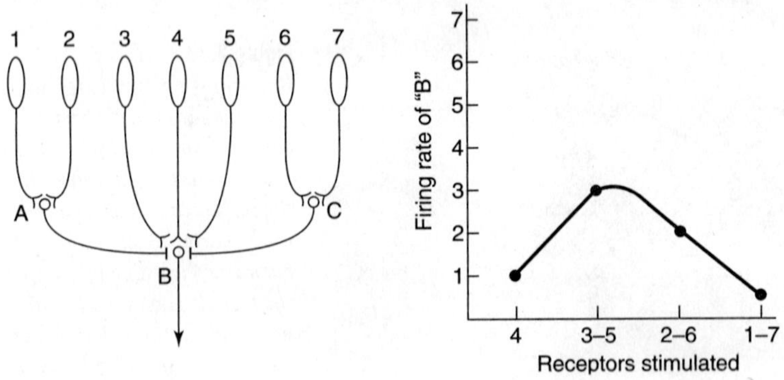

Figure 2.31
When we add inhibition to the circuit, so that stimulation of receptors 1, 2, 6, and 7 now inhibits B, neuron B responds best to stimulation of receptors 3 to 5.

is behaving similarly to the circuit in Figure 2.30. However, when we extend the illumination further to also include receptors 2 through 6, something different happens: Receptors 2 and 6 stimulate neurons A and C, which, in turn, inhibit neuron B, decreasing its firing rate. Increasing the size of the stimulus again to illuminate receptors 1 through 7 increases the inhibition and further decreases the response of neuron B.

In this circuit, neuron B fires weakly to small stimuli (a spot illuminating only receptor 4) or longer stimuli (illuminating receptors 1 through 7) and fires best to a stimulus of medium length (illuminating receptors 3 through 5). Convergence and inhibition has therefore created a neuron that responds best to a light stimulus of a specific size. The neurons that synapse with neuron B are therefore doing much more than simply transmitting electrical signals; they are acting as part of a neural circuit that processes the signals in a way that enables the firing of neuron B to indicate the size of the stimulus presented to the receptors. We will now see how the kind of neural processing shown in Figure 2.27 actually occurs in the retina.

Neural Processing in the Retina: Introduction to Receptive Fields

From Figure 2.4 we know that signals generated in the receptors travel through bipolar, horizontal, and amacrine cells to finally reach the ganglion cells, which then transmit these signals out of the back of the eye in the optic nerve. An important property of this network of retinal neurons is that signals from many receptors converge onto each ganglion cell (Figure 2.32). This convergence, combined with inhibition, mostly transmitted across the retina by the horizontal and amacrine cells, gives the retina properties like the circuit of Figure 2.31.

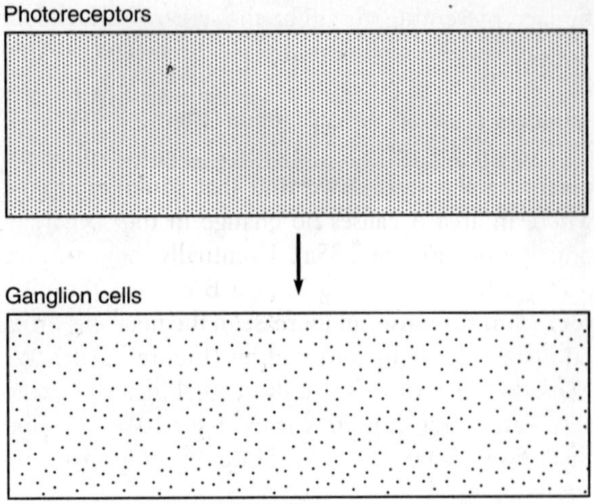

Figure 2.32
Convergence of receptors onto ganglion cells in the periphery of the rabbit retina. Each dot in the top panel represents three receptors, and each dot in the bottom panel represents one ganglion cell. The large difference between the number of receptors and the number of ganglion cells means that signals from many receptors converge onto each ganglion cell. (From Masland, 1988.)

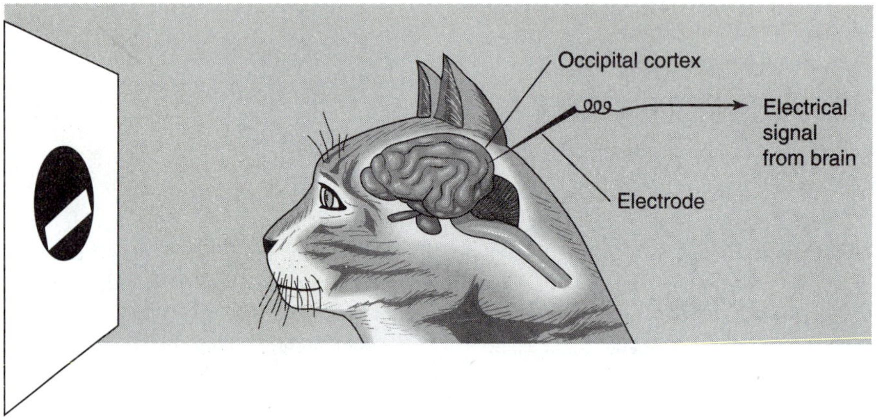

Figure 2.33

Recording electrical signals from a neuron in the visual cortex of an anaesthetized cat. The bar-shaped stimulus on the screen causes a nerve cell in the cortex to fire, and a recording electrode picks up the signals generated by this nerve cell. In an actual experiment, the cat is anesthetized and its head is held in place for accurate positioning.

To measure the results of the retina's convergence and inhibition we record from a ganglion cell fiber and determine how that fiber responds to stimulation of the receptors. Many experiments like this have been done on cats and monkeys, using a setup like the one shown in Figure 2.33, in which stimuli are presented on a screen at which the animal (a cat, in this case) is looking. Since the cat's eye is kept stationary, presenting stimuli on the screen is equivalent to shining lights on different places on the cat's retina, because for each point on the screen, there is a corresponding point on the cat's retina (Figure 2.34).

When we present the spot of light at different places on the screen, we find that stimulating anywhere in area A causes no change in the activity of our neuron (Figure 2.35a). Eventually, however, we discover that stimulating in area B causes an **excitatory** or **on-response**, an increase in the neuron's firing rate when the light is turned on (Figure 2.35b). We mark this area with +'s to indicate that the response to stimulation from this area is excitatory. We also find that stimulating in area C causes an **inhibitory response,** a decrease in nerve firing when the stimulus is turned on, plus an **off-response,** a burst of firing when the stimulus is turned off (Figure 2.35c) (Kuffler, 1953). We mark this area with –'s to indicate that responses from this area are inhibitory. Areas A, B, and C, together, are called the **receptive field** of the neuron—*the region of the retina that, when stimulated, influences the firing rate of the neuron.*

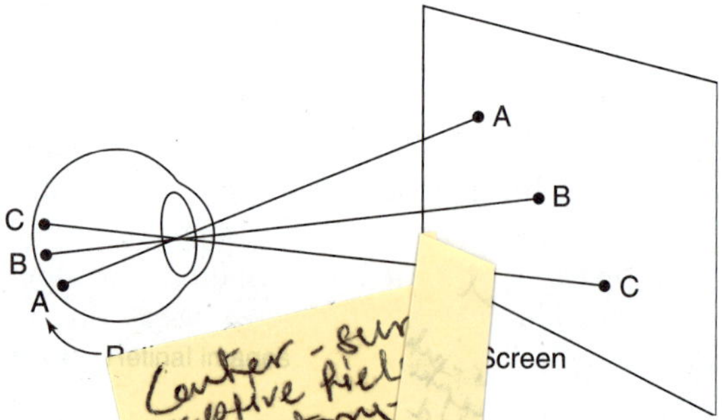

Figure 2.34

For every point on the screen where we present the stimuli, there is a corresponding point on the retina.

The receptive field in Figure 2.35 is called a **center-surround receptive field** because it responds one way to stimulation of the center area and another way to stimulation of the area surrounding this center area. This particular receptive field is an **excitatory-center-inhibitory-surround receptive field,** and there are also **inhibitory-center-excitatory-surround receptive fields.**

The fact that the center and the surround of the receptive field respond in opposite ways causes an effect called **center-surround antagonism.** This effect is illustrated in Figure 2.36, which shows what happens as we increase the size of a spot of light presented to the ganglion cell's receptive field. A small spot that is presented to the excitatory center of the

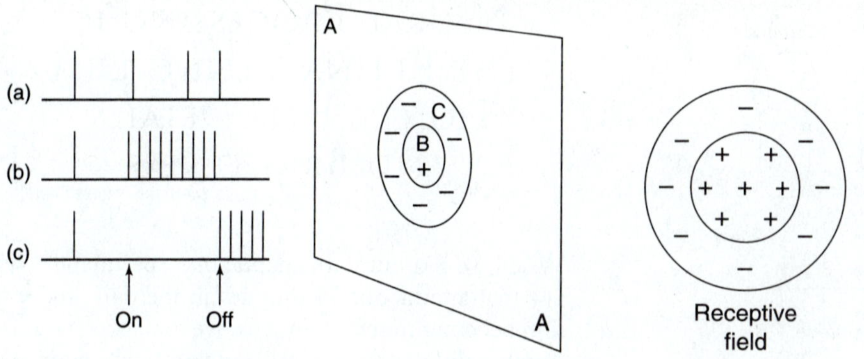

Figure 2.35
Response of a ganglion cell in the cat's retina to stimulation (a) outside the cell's receptive field (area A on the screen to the right); (b) inside the excitatory area of the cell's receptive field (area B); and (c) inside the inhibitory area of the cell's receptive field (area C). The excitatory-center-inhibitory-surround receptive field is shown on the far right without the screen.

receptive field causes a small increase in the rate of nerve firing (a), and increasing the light's size so that it covers the entire center of the receptive field increases the cell's response, as shown in (b). (Notice that we have used the term *cell* in place of *neuron* here. Since neurons are a type of cell, *cell* is often substituted for *neuron* in the research literature. In this book, we will often use these terms interchangeably.)

Center-surround antagonism comes into play when we increase the size of the spot of light, so that it begins to cover the inhibitory area, as in (c) and (d). Stimulation of the inhibitory surround counteracts the center's excitatory response, causing a decrease in the neuron's firing rate. Thus, this neuron responds best to a spot of light that is the size of the excitatory center of the receptive field.

This neuron fires similarly to the neuron in Figure 2.31c since it responds weakly to very small or very large stimuli and fires be[...] medium-sized stimuli. The circuit in Figur[...] [...]nilar to the circuit

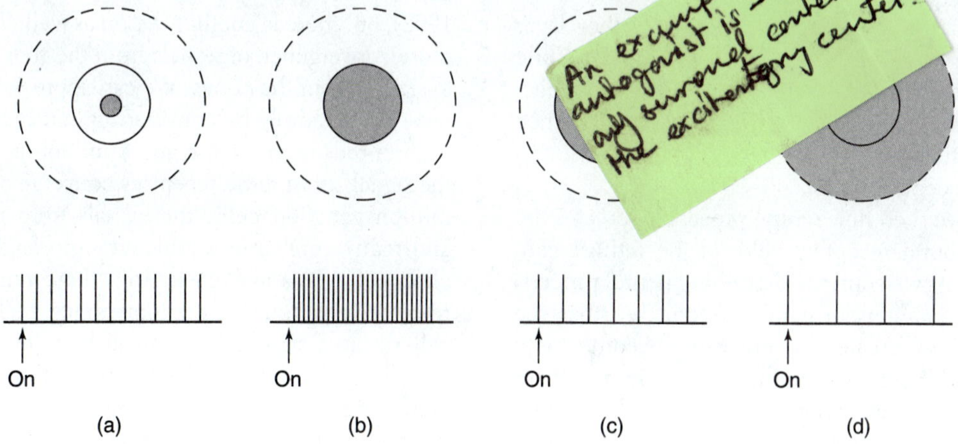

Figure 2.36
Response of an excitatory-center-inhibitory-surround receptive field. The area stimulated with light is indicated by the shading, and the response to the stimulus is indicated by the records below each receptive field. As the stimulus size increases inside the excitatory region of the receptive field in (a) and (b), the response increases. As the stimulus increases further, so that it covers the inhibitory region of the receptive field in (c) and (d), the response decreases. This cell responds best to stimulation that is the size of the receptive field center. (Adapted from Hubel & Wiesel, 1961.)

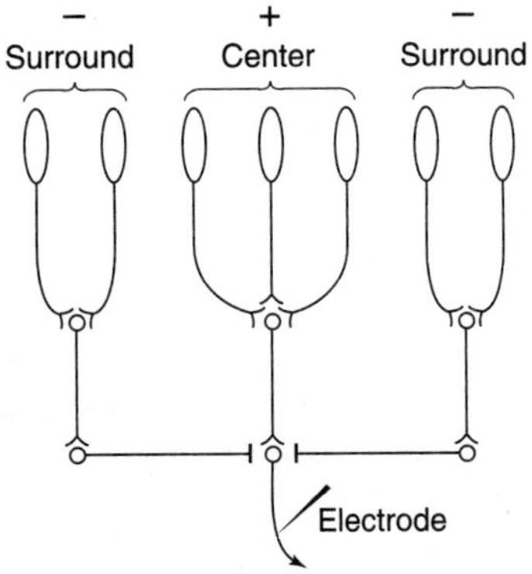

Figure 2.37
A neural circuit that would result in a center-surround receptive field. Signals from the surround receptors reach the cell from which we are recording via inhibitory synapses, while signals from the center receptors reach the cell via an excitatory synapse. Thus, stimulation of the center receptors increases the firing rate recorded by our electrode, and stimulation of the surround receptors decreases the firing rate. In the retina, these inhibitory signals are carried by horizontal and amacrine cells.

in Figure 2.31c, but we have added another layer of cells to make it more similar to the retina. While still vastly oversimplified compared to the retina's actual circuitry, Figure 2.37 illustrates the convergence and inhibition that, in the retina, produces center-surround receptive fields.

We have seen how neural processing creates the center-surround receptive fields of the retina's ganglion cells. As we continue describing neural processing in the chapters to come, we will see that the receptive fields created by processing become more complex at higher levels in the visual system so these higher-level neurons respond best to stimuli far more complex than a small spot of light. But we don't have to go to higher levels of the visual system to appreciate the effects of neural processing. Neural processing within the retina helps explain three basic properties of seeing—our sensitivity to light, our ability to see details, and our perception of brightness.

Neural Processing in the Retina: Seeing Dim Lights, Fine Details, and Brightness

When we did our dark adaptation experiments, we saw that after about 15 minutes in the dark, rod vision becomes much more sensitive than cone vision. Another difference between rod vision and cone vision is that we can see fine details much better with our cones. We will now ask two questions: "Why is rod vision more sensitive than cone vision?" and "Why can we see finer details with cone vision than with rod vision?"

Why Is Rod Vision More Sensitive Than Cone Vision?

One reason rod vision is more sensitive than cone vision is that it takes less light to generate a response from an individual rod receptor than from an individual cone receptor (Barlow & Mollon, 1982; Baylor, 1992), but there is another reason as well: There is far more convergence of signals from the rods compared to signals from the cones. We can appreciate that this must be so simply by considering that there are 120 million rods in the retina and 6 million cones. Since the signals from these receptors converge onto only 1 million ganglion cells, the signals from many rods and many cones must converge onto far fewer ganglion cells. It is also clear from these numbers that rods converge much more than cones; each ganglion cell receives signals from an average of about 120 rods, but from only about 6 cones. This difference between rod and cone convergence becomes even greater when we consider that many foveal cones have "private lines" to ganglion cells, so that each ganglion cell receives signals from only one cone—a complete lack of convergence.

How does the difference in rod and cone convergence translate into different dark adapted sensitivities

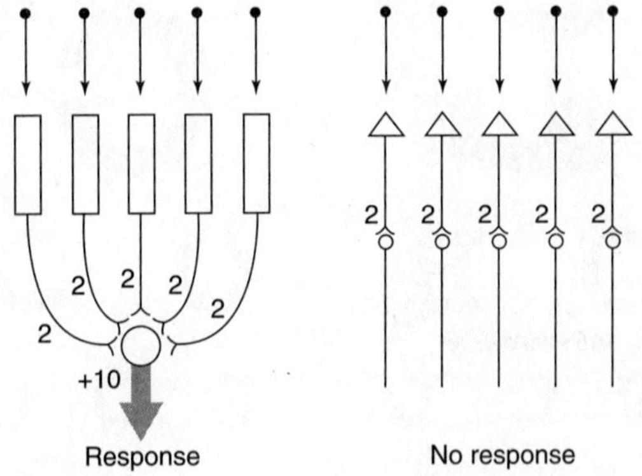

Figure 2.38
The wiring of the rods (left) and the cones (right). The dot and arrow above each receptor represents a "spot" of light that stimulates the receptor. The numbers represent the number of response units generated by the rods and the cones in response to a spot intensity of 2.0. At this intensity the rod ganglion cell receives 10 units of excitation and fires, but each cone ganglion cell receives only 2 units and therefore does not fire. Thus, the rods' greater spatial summation enables them to cause ganglion cell firing at lower stimulus intensities than the cones'.

of the cones and the rods? We can understand how neural wiring contributes to this difference in sensitivity by considering the two circuits in Figure 2.38, in which five rod receptors converge onto one ganglion cell and five cone receptors each synapse on their own ganglion cells. We have left out the bipolar, horizontal, and amacrine cells in these circuits for simplicity, but our conclusions will not be affected by these omissions.

For the purposes of our discussion, we will assume that we can present small spots of light to individual rods and cones. (Although it isn't possible to do this in the human retina because of the optics of the eye and the small sizes of the receptors, we will assume that we can do it for the purposes of our discussion.) We will also make the following additional assumptions:

1. One unit of light intensity causes one unit of response in a receptor.
2. A ganglion cell must receive ten "response units" to fire.
3. The ganglion cell must fire before perception of the light can occur.

When we present spots of light with an intensity of 1.0 to each receptor, the rod ganglion cell receives 5 response units, 1 from each of the 5 receptors, and each of the cone ganglion cells receives 1.0 response units, 1 from each receptor. Thus, when intensity = 1.0, neither the rod nor the cone ganglion cells fire. If, however, we increase the intensity to 2.0, the rod ganglion cell receives 2.0 response units from each of its 5 receptors, for a total of 10 response units. This total reaches the threshold for the rods' ganglion cell, it fires, and we see the light. Meanwhile, at the same intensity, the cones' ganglion cells are still below threshold, each receiving only 2 response units. For the cones' ganglion cells to fire, we must increase the intensity to 10.0.

These results demonstrate that one reason for the rods' high sensitivity compared to the cones' is the rods' greater **spatial summation**; that is, many rods summate their responses by feeding into the same ganglion cell. The cones, on the other hand, summate less, because only one or a few cones feed into a single ganglion cell. The greater spatial summation of the rods is reflected in the greater sizes of the receptive fields in the periphery of the retina, which contains mostly rods, compared to sizes of the receptive fields in the fovea, which contains only cones (Martin, 1991).

Why Can We See Finer Details with Cone Vision Than with Rod Vision?

The reason you often find it difficult to immediately see your friend's face in a crowded room is that, to recognize a face, you must look directly at it. Only all-cone foveal vision has good **visual acuity**—the ability to see details—so only the particular face at which you are looking is seen in enough detail to be recognized, while the rest of the faces in the crowd fall on the rod-rich peripheral retina and can't be recognized. You find your friend only after you move your eyes to bring the image of his or her face onto your foveas.

DEMONSTRATION

Foveal versus Peripheral Acuity

D I H C N R L A Z I F W N S M Q P Z K D **X**

You can demonstrate the superiority of foveal vision to peripheral vision by looking at the X in the line of letters and, without moving your eyes, seeing how many letters you can see to the left. If you do this without cheating (no fair moving your eyes!), you will find that you can read only a few letters. Because the cones are much more widely spaced in the periphery than in the densely packed fovea you cannot read letters that fall on the peripheral retina. ●

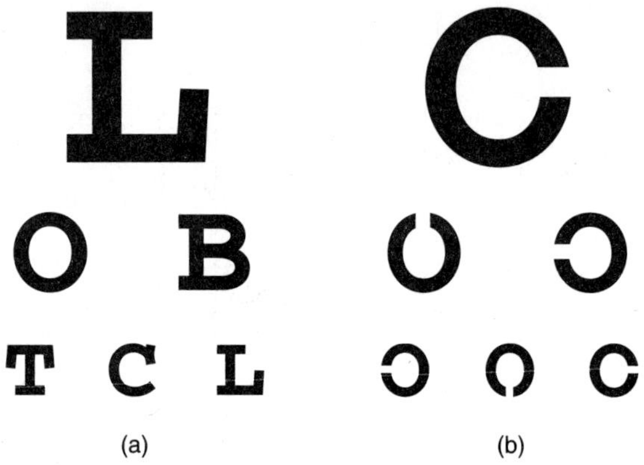

Figure 2.39
Snellen letters (a) and Landolt rings (b) used to test visual acuity.

Visual acuity can be measured in a number of ways, one of which is to determine how far apart two dots have to be before a space can be seen between them. We make this measurement by presenting a pair of closely spaced dots and asking whether there are one or two dots. We can also measure acuity by determining how large the elements of a checkerboard or a pattern of alternating black and white bars must be for the pattern to be detected. The letters of the Snellen chart (left) and the Landolt rings (right) in Figure 2.39 are perhaps the most familiar ways of measuring acuity. The observer's task is to identify the Snellen letters or to indicate the location of the gaps in the Landolt rings.

In the demonstration above, we showed that acuity is better in the fovea than in the periphery. Since you were light adapted, the comparison in this demonstration was between the foveal cones and the peripheral cones. Comparing the foveal cones to the rods results in even greater differences in acuity. We can make this comparison by measuring how acuity changes during dark adaptation. When we do this, we find that visual acuity drops (that is, details must be larger in order to be seen) as vision changes from cone function to rod function during dark adaptation.

We can understand how differences in rod and cone wiring explain the cones' greater acuity, by returning to our rod and cone neural circuits. As we stimulate the receptors in the circuits in Figure 2.40 with two spots of light, each with an intensity of 10, we will ask the following question: Under what conditions can we tell that there are two separate spots of light? We begin by presenting the two spots next to each other, as in Figure 2.40a. When we do this, the rod ganglion cell fires and the two adjacent cone ganglion cells fire. The firing of the single rod ganglion cell provides no hint that two separate spots were presented, and the firing of two adjacent cone ganglion cells could have been caused by a single large spot. However, when we spread the two spots apart, as in Figure 2.40b, the output of the cones signals two separate spots, because there is a silent ganglion cell between the two that are firing, but the output of the rods still provides no information that would enable us to say that there are two spots. Thus, the rods' convergence decreases its ability to resolve details (Teller, 1990).

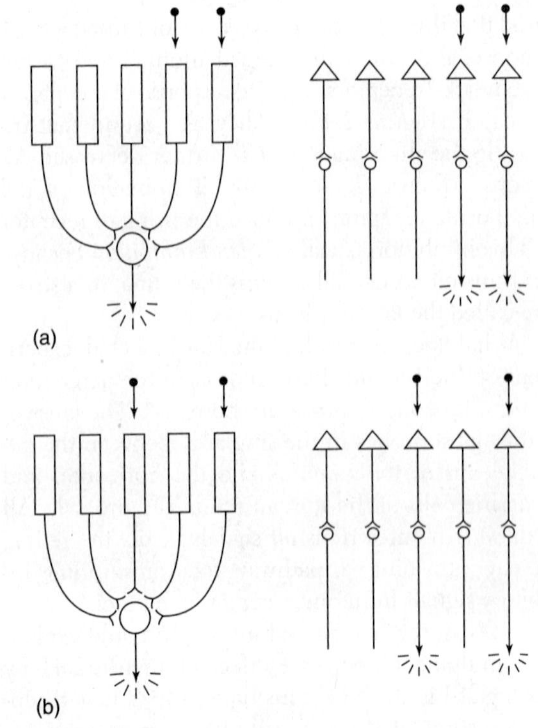

Figure 2.40
Neural circuits for the rods (left) and the cones (right). The receptors are being stimulated by two spots of light.

Neural Processing and the Perception of Brightness

We have seen how neural processing can explain our ability to detect dim lights and our ability to distinguish small details. Both of these cases involve perceptions that occur near threshold. But we can also show how neural processing influences perceptions, such as the brightness of a surface, that occur far above threshold.

DEMONSTRATION

Simultaneous Contrast

When you look at the two center squares in Figure 2.41, the one on the left appears much darker than the one on the right. Now, punch two holes 2 inches apart in a card or a piece of paper, place the two holes over the squares, and compare your perception of the squares as seen through the holes. ●

In this demonstration, you may have been surprised to see that the two squares look the same when

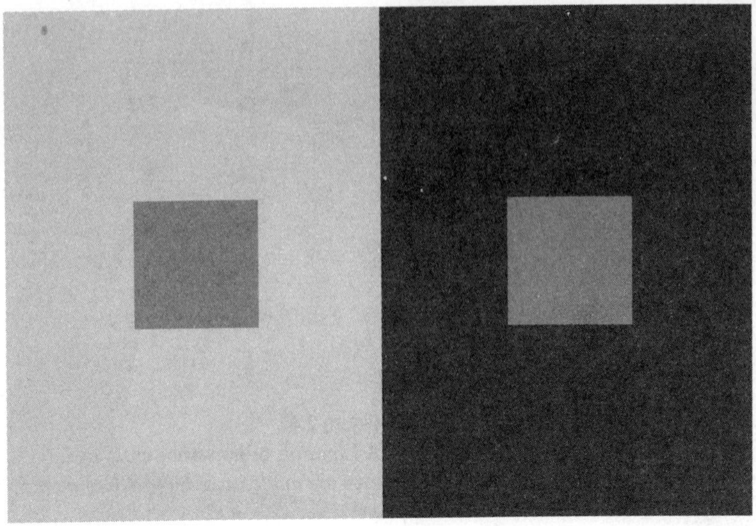

Figure 2.41
Simultaneous contrast. The two center squares reflect the same amount of light into your eyes but, because of the simultaneous contrast effect, look different.

their backgrounds are masked by … though they look very different whe… tern is visible. This effect is calle… **lightness contrast**—surrounding one … area that is either lighter or darker c… the appearance of the surrounded area. Based on what we know about the stimulus, we can say that simultaneous lightness contrast is caused by the difference in the backgrounds, but what is the physiological mechanism behind this effect?

This question was answered by Keffer Hartline, Henry Wagner, and Floyd Ratliff (1956), who used the creature in Figure 2.42—the horseshoe crab, or *Limulus*—to demonstrate an effect of neural processing called **lateral inhibition.** Hartline and his coworkers chose the *Limulus* because of the structure of its eye. The *Limulus* eye is made up of hundreds of tiny structures called *ommatidia*, and each **ommatidium** has a small lens on the eye's surface that is located directly over a single receptor. Since each lens and receptor is roughly the diameter of a pencil point (very large compared to human receptors), it is possible to illuminate and record from a single receptor without illuminating its neighboring receptors.

When Hartline et al. recorded from the nerve fiber of receptor A, as shown in Figure 2.43, they found that illumination of that receptor caused a large response. But when they added illumination to the three nearby receptors at B, the response of receptor A decreased (Figure 2.43b). They also found that increasing the illumination of B further decreased A's response (Figure 2.43c). Thus, illumination of the neighboring receptors *inhibited* the firing of receptor A. This inhibition is called *lateral inhibition* because it is transmitted laterally, across the retina, in a structure called the **lateral plexus.**

What does the result of the Hartline et al. experiment on the *Limulus* have to do with the perception of simultaneous contrast in humans? The answer to this question lies in the similarity between the lateral plexus of the *Limulus* and the horizontal and amacrine cells of the human retina (Figure 2.4). All of these structures transmit signals *across* the retina, thereby providing a pathway for transmitting inhibitory signals from one receptor to another.

We can see how lateral inhibition could explain the simultaneous contrast effect of Figure 2.41 by looking at Figure 2.44. This figure shows how receptors are stimulated by the simultaneous contrast display in Figure 2.41. Let's consider the left side of the display. The receptors under the small square on the left are simulated by the center square of the display,

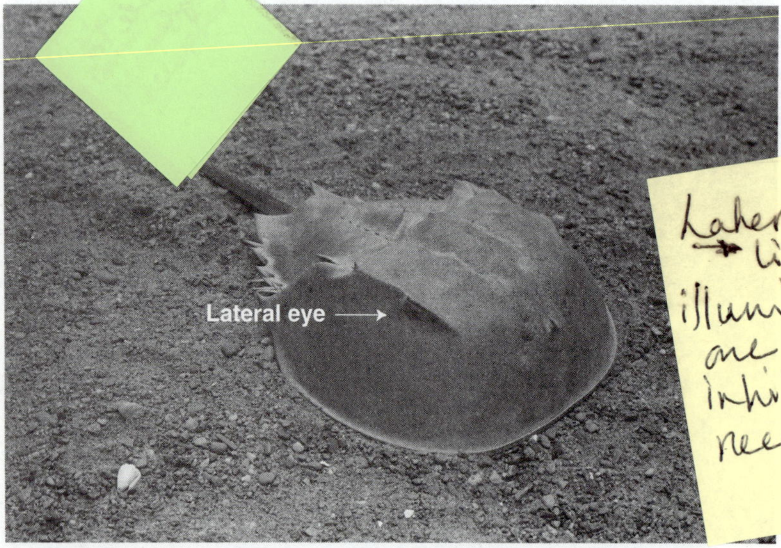

Lateral Inhibition
→ Limulus
illuminating one recepter inhibits near by recepters

…b. *Its large* … *up of hundreds of ommatidia, each containing a single receptor.*

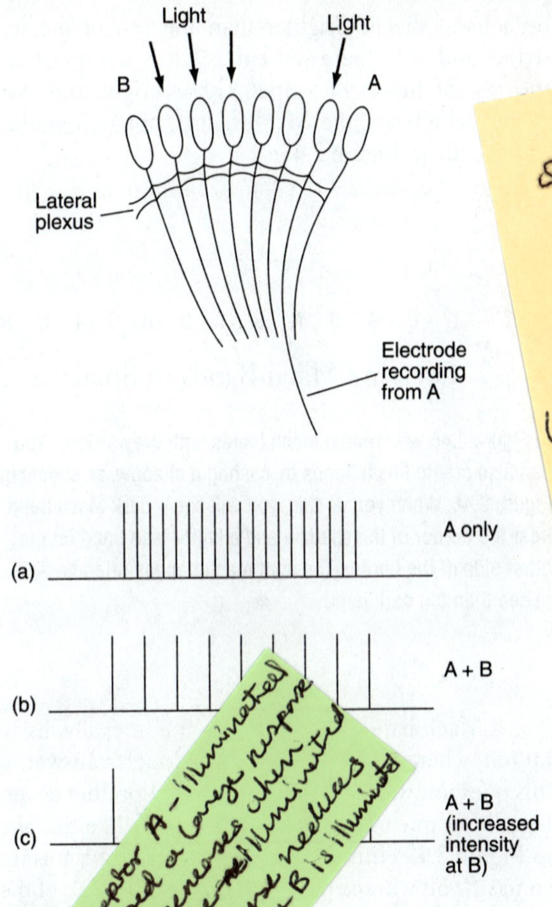

Figure [illegible]
A demo[illegible]*ibition in the Limulus. The records be*[illegible]*onse recorded by the electrode recording from* [illegible] *fiber of receptor A when receptor A is stimulated and* [illegible]*o other receptors are stimulated, (b) the receptors at B are stimulated simultaneously, and (c) the receptors at B are stimulated at an increased intensity. (Adapted from Ratliff, 1965.)*

[illegible] *con-* [illegible]

so they are illuminated by light of moderate intensity. The receptors under the left surround (the area that surrounds the small square) are stimulated by light of high intensity.

The amount of lateral inhibition sent from one area to another depends on how intensely the area is stimulated. Since the receptors under the left surround are intensely stimulated, they send a large [illegible] the cen-[illegible] arrows. The receptors in [illegible] also create inhibition, but much less. The net effect of this exchange of inhibition is that the response of the receptors under the small square are "turned down" by the inhibition received from the left surround and so we see that square as being dark.

If we apply the same reasoning to the right side of the display, we see that the right surround sends only a small amount of inhibition to the center square and so this square is "turned down" less than the left square and we see it as being light. Thus, even though the two squares reflect exactly the same amount of light into our eyes, the differences in the amount of inhibition they receive from their surrounds causes them to appear different.

Another effect that can be explained by lateral inhibition is the **Mach band** effect. This effect was studied in the 1880s by the German scientist Ernst Mach, who studied displays like the one in Figure 2.45a. If we measure the intensity across the stripes in Figure 2.45a with a light meter by starting at A and measuring the amount of light reflected by the stripes between A and D, we obtain the result shown in Figure 2.45b. We see that the intensity distribution between A and B is flat; that is, the same amount of light is reflected across the entire distance between A and B. Then, the intensity drops sharply at the border and stays at a constant lower level between C and D.

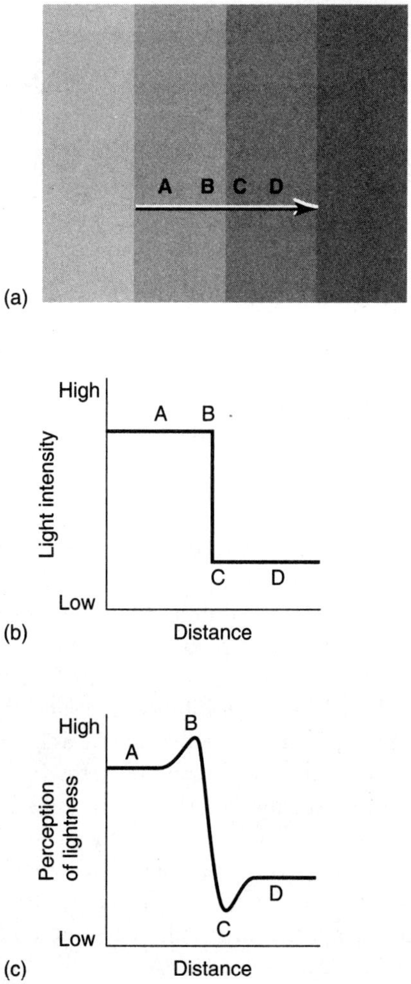

Figure 2.45
(a) Mach bands at a contour. Just to the left of the contour, near B, a faint light band can be perceived, and just to the right at C, a faint dark band can be perceived. (b) A plot showing the physical intensity distribution of the light, as measured with a light meter. (c) A plot showing the perceptual effect described in (a). The bump in the curve at B indicates the light Mach band, and the dip in the curve at C indicates the dark Mach band. Note that the bumps are not present in the physical intensity distribution (b).

Although our light meter tells us that the intensities remain constant across the two stripes, we *perceive* something very different. At B there appears to be a band that is brighter than the rest of the left stripe, and at C there is a band that is dimmer than the rest of the right stripe. These bright and dim bands, which are the Mach bands, are represented graphically in Figure 2.45c.

DEMONSTRATION

Creating Mach Bands in Shadows

In Figure 2.45 we created Mach bands with gray stripes. You can also create Mach bands by casting a shadow, as shown in Figure 2.46. When you do this, you will see a dark Mach band near the border of the shadow and a light Mach band on the other side of the border. The light Mach band is often harder to see than the dark band. ●

If Mach bands do not exist in the intensity distribution, where do they come from? Mach's answer to this question was based on his observation that covering all but one of the stripes in a display like the one in Figure 2.45 eliminates the bands. If you try this for yourself, you will see that without the influence of the adjacent stripes, the uncovered stripe appears the same all the way across, just as its intensity distribution indicates.

Based on this observation, Mach (1914) proposed that illumination of one area of the retina causes the receptors in that area to affect the response of receptors in another nearby area of the retina. This is exactly what lateral inhibition does, although Mach had no way of knowing about the physiology of lateral inhibition since he proposed his hypothesis in the late 1800s, long before Hartline's physiological research.

Thus, Mach used perceptual observations to propose a physiological hypothesis. It wasn't until many years later that Hartline's research demonstrated the actual physiological mechanism that Mach had predicted. Based on our modern physiological knowledge we can now propose a neural circuit to explain our perception of Mach bands.

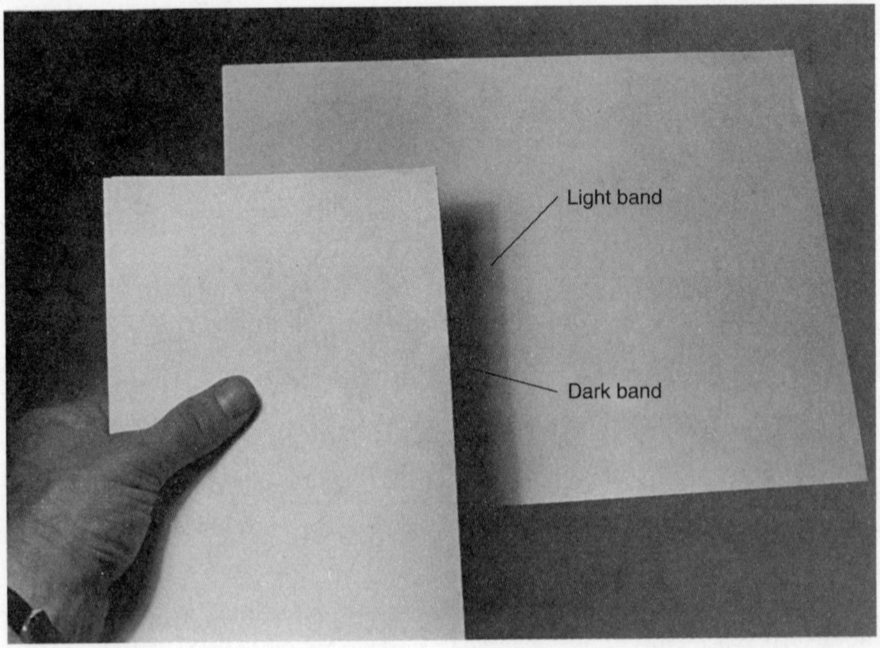

Figure 2.46
Shadow-casting technique for observing Mach bands. Illuminate a sheet of white paper with your desk lamp and then cast a shadow with another piece of paper.

A Neural Circuit for Mach Bands

We can see how lateral inhibition can lead to the perception of Mach bands by looking at the neural circuit in Figure 2.47, which shows six receptors, each of which sends lateral inhibition to its neighbors on both sides. To show how this circuit could cause the perception of Mach bands, let's illuminate these receptors so that A, B, and C receive intense illumination and D, E, and F receive dim illumination, analogous to the stimulus we would create by illuminating all six receptors equally and then casting a shadow on receptors D, E, and F.

Let's assume that receptors A, B, and C generate responses of 100, whereas D, E, and F generate responses of 20, as shown in Figure 2.47. Thus, without inhibition, A, B, and C generate equal responses, and D, E, and F generate equal responses. If perception were determined only by these responses we would, therefore, see a bright bar with equal intensity across its width in the area served by receptors A, B, and C

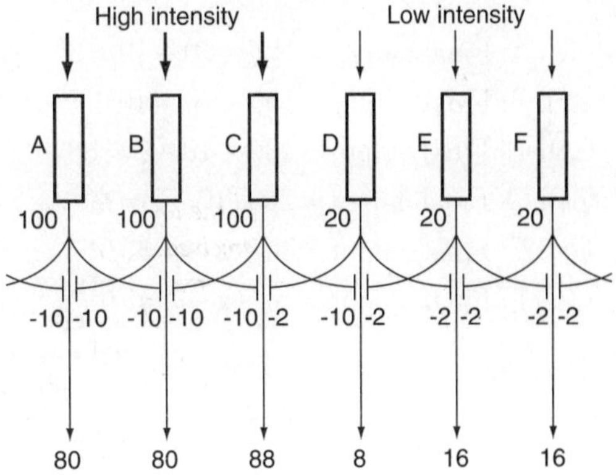

Figure 2.47
Six receptors that inhibit each other. If we know the initial output of each receptor and the amount of lateral inhibition, we can calculate the final output of the receptors. (See text for a description of this calculation.)

and a dim bar with equal intensity across its width in the area served by D, E, and F. We can show, however, by means of the following calculation, that lateral inhibition can modify the initial responses of these receptors to produce a physiological effect that mimics the perception of Mach bands:

1. Start with the initial response of each cell: 100 for A, B, and C and 20 for D, E, and F.
2. Determine the amount of inhibition that each cell receives from its neighbor on each side. For the purposes of our calculation, we will assume that each cell sends inhibition to its neighbor equal to one-tenth of that cell's initial output. Thus, cells A, B, and C will send $100 \times 0.1 = 10$ units of inhibition to their neighbors, and cells D, E, and F will send $20 \times 0.1 = 2$ units of inhibition to their neighbors.
3. Determine the final output of each cell by subtracting the amount of inhibition from the initial response. Remember that each cell receives inhibition from its neighbor on either side. (We assume here that receptor A receives 10 units of inhibition from an unseen receptor on its left and that F receives 2 units of inhibition from an unseen receptor on its right.) Here is the calculation for each cell in Figure 2.47:

   Cell A: Final output $= 100 - 10 - 10 = 80$
   Cell B: Final output $= 100 - 10 - 10 = 80$
   Cell C: Final output $= 100 - 10 - 2 = 88$
   Cell D: Final output $= 20 - 10 - 2 = 8$
   Cell E: Final output $= 20 - 2 - 2 = 16$
   Cell F: Final output $= 20 - 2 - 2 = 16$

The graph of these neural responses in Figure 2.48 looks similar to Figure 2.45c, where there is an increase in brightness on the light side of the border at C and a decrease in brightness on the dark side at D. The lateral inhibition in our circuit has therefore created "Mach bands" in the neural response. A circuit similar to this one, but of much greater complexity, is probably responsible for the Mach bands that we see.

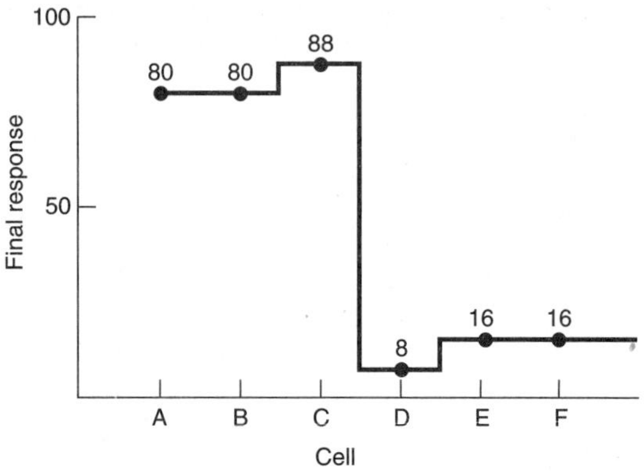

Figure 2.48
A plot showing the final receptor output calculated for the circuit of Figure 2.47. The bump at C and the dip at D correspond to the light and dark Mach bands, respectively.

Retinal Circuits: What They Can and Cannot Explain

As we have explored the physiology of the retina, we have been able to offer some physiological explanations for a few of our perceptions. However, we are just beginning to understand the physiological mechanisms responsible for most perceptual phenomena. We will now describe two cases that are noteworthy because the perceptions we experience pose a puzzle for explanations based on neural circuits in the retina. To experience the first example, try the following demonstration, which was originally proposed by Ernst Mach.

DEMONSTRATION

The Mach Card Demonstration

Fold a 3 × 5 or 4 × 6 card as shown in Figure 2.49, and orient it so that the left side is illuminated slightly less than the right

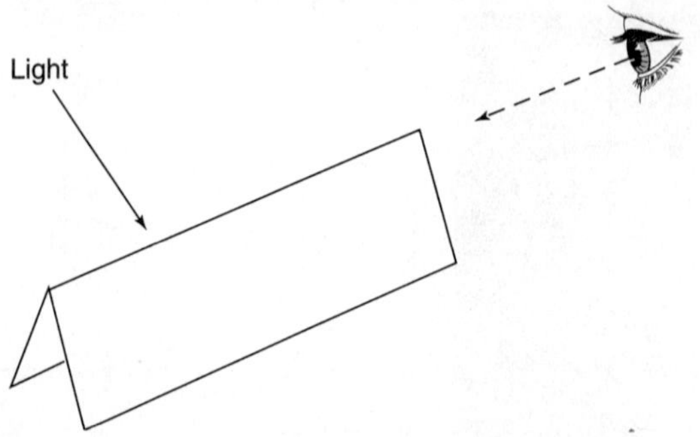

Figure 2.49
How to view the Mach card.

(the light should be coming from the right). When viewed with two eyes at about a 45-degree angle from above, both sides of the card look white, the left side appearing slightly shaded. Now, close one eye and view the card until your perception "flips" so that the card appears to stand on end like an open book with its inside toward you, as in Figure 2.50. When this happens, notice that something else also happens. The shadowed left side of the card gets much darker, and the illuminated right side may even appear luminous. ●

What's going on here? Consider what happens to the Mach card's image on the retina when it flips from one orientation to another. The key here is that the card never actually moves, so when the perceptual flip occurs there is no change in the pattern of light and dark on the retina and there would therefore be no change in the activity of the receptors or the amount of lateral inhibition. The change in brightness you perceive when the card flips cannot therefore be explained just by the activity of neural circuits in the retina. The next demonstration shows two patterns reported by David Knill and Daniel Kersten (1991) that also defy explanation in terms of receptor activity or lateral inhibition.

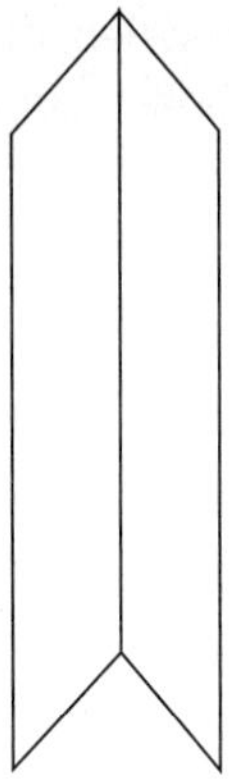

Figure 2.50
What the Mach card looks like when it perceptually "flips."

DEMONSTRATION

Surface Curvature and Lightness Perception

Compare the two displays in Figure 2.51. The one at (a) looks like a flat surface, and the one at (b) looks like two curved surfaces. In addition to their difference in surface curvature, they also appear to be shaded differently. The flat surface in (a) appears to be darker on the left than on the right, whereas the curved surfaces in (b) appear more evenly shaded. But now, take two pieces of paper and cover the top and bottom edges of (b) so it has straight edges as in (a). What do you see? ●

Perhaps you were surprised to see that when you turned the curved edges of (b) into straight lines, the left and right sides became much more like those in (a). This is actually not surprising because the intensity distributions of (a) and (b) are, in fact, identical. Since the intensities of the displays are identical, any explanation based only on stimulation of the receptors or on lateral inhibition would predict that the shading of the two patterns should look identical. But this does not occur. Apparently, the way we perceive the curvature of a surface can influence the way we perceive its shading. Exactly how this works is not clear, but it is clear that explanations based only on networks of retinal neurons cannot explain this effect (also see Adelson, 1993, for a similar demonstration).

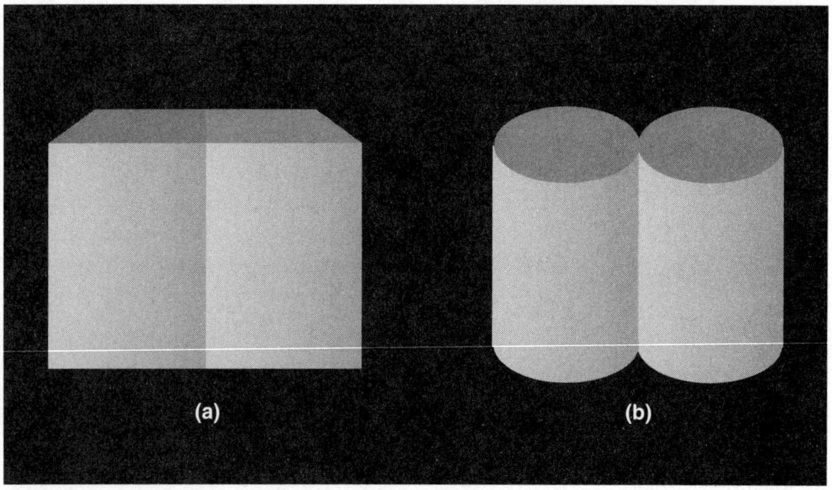

Figure 2.51
The light distribution is identical for (a) and (b), though it appears to be different. See text for further details. (Figure courtesy of David Knill & Daniel Kersten.)

The demonstrations we have presented show that we can't explain all perceptual phenomena by means of the interaction of neurons in the retina. This shouldn't surprise us because we know that although the perceptual process begins in the retina, a great deal of processing occurs in higher centers. In Chapters 3 and 4, we will describe what happens in these higher centers, focusing on the lateral geniculate nucleus and the striate and extrastriate areas of the cortex.

Something to Consider: The Difference between Physical and Perceptual

Throughout this chapter we have presented examples of situations in which there are differences between *physical stimuli* and the *perceptions arising from these stimuli*. A few examples from the chapter are:

- A light that remains the same intensity (physical) becomes brighter (perceptual) during dark adaptation.
- Two identical squares (physical) appear different (perceptual) when they are surrounded by different backgrounds. This is the simultaneous contrast effect.
- If we change a flat display in which the left side is less intense than the right side (physical) into one that has curved edges, as in Figure 2.51, the two sides look different for the flat display but almost the same for the curved display (perception).

Other examples from this chapter of differences between physical stimuli and perception are the stimulus that vanishes if it is on the blind spot (page 38), the stimuli that can be seen sharply and with more detail when viewed using the cones than the rods (page 55), the Mach band effect (page 59), and the Mach card effect (page 62). This mismatch between the physical and perceptual is not limited to vision, as you can see from the following Demonstration.

D E M O N S T R A T I O N

Sensing Points on the Skin

Hold two pencils side by side so their points are about half an inch apart. Close your eyes and touch both points simultaneously to your forearm. What do you feel? ●

Most people feel one point even though the physical stimulus is two points. Thus, the physical stimulus (2 points) and our perception (1 point) do not match.

Why does perception not always match the physical stimulus? The concepts we've introduced in this chapter provide the beginnings of an answer: Perception occurs indirectly—it is determined not by our direct contact with objects, but by indirect contact. Thus, even though the two pencil points may be in direct contact with your skin, your *perception* of these two points is based on the properties of the receptors that transduce stimuli into electricity and the way this electricity is processed in the nervous system.

This indirect property of perception sometimes causes a mismatch between the physical characteristics of stimuli and our perception of them, as in the examples we have presented above. In other cases, we often perceive physical properties accurately. In either case, it is important to distinguish between the physical properties of a stimulus and our perception of the stimulus, because they are not the same thing.

Sensing Environmental Energy by Humans and Animals

Humans can sense a number of different kinds of environmental energy. Table 2.1 lists the types of energy that can be sensed by humans and the action that takes place at the receptors that leads to transduction of this environmental energy into the electrical energy of the nervous system.

If we broaden our scope to include other animals, we find that some animals are sensitive to additional

Table 2.1

Sense	Stimulus Energy	Receptor Action
Vision	Visible light (electromagnetic energy)	Molecule in rod or cone receptor absorbs light 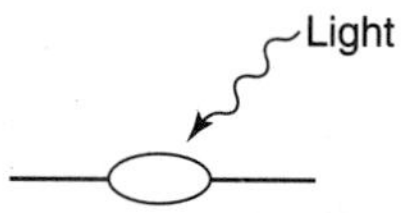
Audition	Pressure changes in air or water (mechanical energy)	Hair cell in ear bends 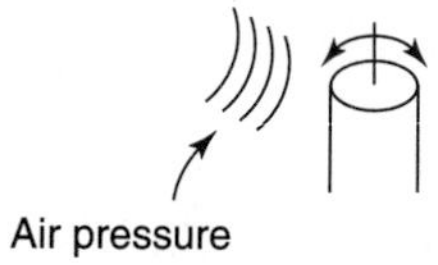
Skin senses (touch, pain)	Pressure on skin (mechanical energy)	Receptor in skin is deformed 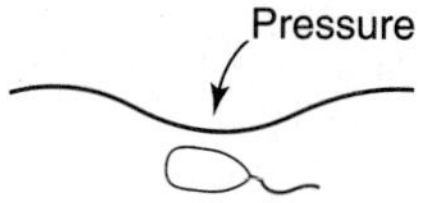
Olfaction and Taste	Chemicals in gas form (olfaction) and liquid form (taste) (chemical energy)	Receptor site in nose or on tongue is chemically stimulated 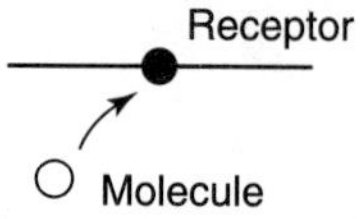

Figure 2.52
The python has heat-sensitive pits in the scales above and below its mouth.

types of energy. We know that bats can sense ultra high-frequency sound vibrations that are far above the human range of hearing, snakes can detect infrared radiation, some fish and amphibians can detect electrical fields, and birds can detect magnetic fields. A fascinating thing about each of these examples is the way detection of this energy is used by these animals to help them survive.

Bats use high frequency energy to detect prey such as moths. Bats emit bursts of high frequency energy, which hit the moth and are reflected back to the bat, who uses this reflected energy to determine the moth's location (Pollak & Casseday, 1989; Suga, 1990).

Snakes can detect a small mouse even in complete darkness by sensing the heat given off by the mouse's body with pit organs located in small cavities in the head between and in front of the eyes (Figure 2.52) (Newman & Hartline, 1982), and the duck- billed platypus can detect shrimp by sensing the electrical energy generated by action of the shrimp's muscles when the shrimps flick their tails. It senses this energy with receptors in its large bill, which it sweeps back and forth as it swims (Scheich et al., 1986).

Birds use their ability to detect magnetic fields to help them navigate over large distances, and although the exact mechanism responsible for the birds' sensitivity to magnetic fields is not fully known, it has been discovered that pigeons have small pieces of a magnetic substance called magnetite in their heads (Walcott, Gould, & Kirschvink, 1979), suggesting that birds may have small "compasses" in their heads. From these examples, we can see that the range of stimuli in the environment is matched by an impressive number of ways of detecting these stimuli.

Study Questions

1. What central theme of the book is stated at the beginning of this chapter? (29)

Introducing the Visual System: From Objects into Electricity

2. What is the electromagnetic spectrum and how does it relate to vision? (30)
3. What are two different ways that we can describe light? (30)
4. Why is the reflection of light important for perception? What is the optic array? (30)
5. Describe the eye, including the focusing structures, the receptors, and the other neurons that make up the retina. (31)
6. Describe the route that electrical signals follow from the eye to extrastriate areas of the cortex. (33)
7. Compare the eye to a camera by considering the operation of the following: (1) focusing the image; (2) adjusting for light intensity; (3) sampling the scene; and (4) creating the image. Based on this comparison what can we conclude about the complexity of the eye compared to a modern computer-driven camera? (33)
8. What are the eye's two focusing elements? How is light that is reflected from a far away object focused onto the retina? What happens when we move the object closer? (33)
9. How does the eye bring the image of a nearby object into focus? (33)
10. What is accommodation? When you accommodate, what happens to the shape of the lens? What is the near point? Presbyopia? (36)
11. How do the rods and cones differ in shape and distribution on the retina? (36)
12. What is the fovea? The peripheral retina? Which area of the retina contains only cones? Where are most of the cones? (36)
13. Why do the rods and cones face away from the light? What "problem" does the backward facing receptors create and how does the eye solve this problem? (38)
14. What is the blind spot? (38)
15. What are three reasons that we are usually not aware of the blind spot? (39)
16. Where are the visual pigments located in the visual receptors? (40)
17. Describe the structure of the visual pigment molecule. Which part of the molecule is sensitive to light? What happens when this part of the molecule absorbs light? (40)
18. Describe the Hecht, Shlaer, and Pirenne psychophysical experiment. What did they show about the sensitivity of the eye to light? Based on what they found, what can we conclude about the effect of isomerizing one visual pigment molecule? (40)
19. Describe the enzyme cascade and its role in transduction. (41)

Duplicity Theory: Different Receptors for Different Perceptions

20. What is the duplicity theory of vision? (42)
21. What is dark adaptation? Describe the dark adaptation curve. (42)
22. Describe how to measure the dark adaptation curve and how this procedure can be used to show (a) that the curve has two phases; (b) that the first part of the curve is due to adaptation of the cones; and (c) that the second part of the curve is due to adaptation of the rods. (43)
23. During the process of dark adaptation, when do the rods begin adapting? When do the cones begin adapting? When does the sensitivity of the rods surpass the sensitivity of the cones? (45)
24. What is visual pigment bleaching? visual pigment regeneration? What is needed in order for visual pigment regeneration to occur? (45)

25. Compare the rates of rod and cone visual pigment regeneration. How is this related to the dark adaptation curve? (45)

26. What is the spectral sensitivity curve? How is it determined using monochromatic lights? (46)

27. What is the relationship between sensitivity and threshold? (46)

28. How do we measure the cone spectral sensitivity curve? The rod spectral sensitivity curve? (46)

29. What is the Purkinje shift? Which wavelengths become more sensitive relative to the others when the Purkinje shift occurs as dusk approaches? (46)

30. What is plotted in an absorption spectrum? How is spectrophotometry used to determine the absorption spectrum of rod visual pigment? How does the absorption spectrum for rod visual pigment compare to the rod spectral sensitivity curve? (47)

31. What is microspectrophotometry and how is it used to determine the absorption spectrum of cone visual pigment? (48)

32. What are the three cone pigments? (48)

33. What is the two-color threshold method and what has it told us about how the cone pigments determine the cone spectral sensitivity curve? (49)

Neural Processing: Analysis and Transformation of Electrical Signals

34. What is a neural circuit? Compare how the following three types of circuits respond to a spot of light that is increased in length so it becomes a bar of light: (a) linear circuit; (b) circuit with convergence; (c) circuit with convergence and inhibition. (49)

35. What kind of information does circuit (c) above, with convergence and inhibition, provide about the properties of the stimulus? (51)

36. Presenting stimuli on a screen in front of a cat or monkey is equivalent to presenting the stimuli to __________. (52)

37. What is the receptive field of a neuron? Where is the receptive field of a retinal ganglion cell located and what does it look like? (52)

38. What is center-surround antagonism and how does it affect the firing of a cat's ganglion cell? (52)

Neural Processing in the Retina: Seeing Dim Lights, Fine Details, and Brightness

39. What are two reasons that rod vision is more sensitive than cone vision? (54)

40. Compare rod convergence and cone convergence. (54)

41. Describe how the differences in rod and cone convergence shown in Figure 2.38 can explain the rod's greater sensitivity. (55)

42. What is spatial summation? (55)

43. What is visual acuity? Which receptor system results in the best visual acuity, the rods or the cones? (55)

44. Describe how the differences in rod and cone visual acuity can be explained in terms of differences in rod and cone neural circuits. (56)

45. The rod's greater convergence __________ the rod's sensitivity and __________ the rod's acuity. (56)

46. What is simultaneous contrast and how does it affect our perception of brightness? (57)

47. Describe how Hartline and coworkers demonstrated the lateral inhibition effect in the Limulus. (58)

48. Describe how lateral inhibition can explain the simultaneous contrast effect in humans. (58)

49. What is the Mach band effect? Be sure you understand the difference between the intensity distribution across the Mach band display, and the person's perception of the display. (59)

50. Be able to calculate the output of the circuit in Figure 2.47 if you are given the initial output of the receptors and the amount of inhibition each receptor sends to its neighbors. (61)

Retinal Circuits: What They Can and Cannot Explain

51. What is the Mach card demonstration? What does it tell us about the ability of retinal circuits to explain brightness perception? (62)
52. How does surface curvature affect lightness perception in Figure 2.51 and what does this tell us about the ability of retinal circuits to explain brightness perception? (63)

Something to Consider: The Difference Between Physical and Perceptual

53. Describe at least five examples of situations in which there is a difference between the physical stimulus and the perception arising from that stimulus. (64)

Across the Senses: Sensing Environmental Energy in Humans and Animals

54. What kinds of environmental energy are associated with each of the senses in humans? (66)
55. What kinds of receptor action are associated with each kind of environmental energy above? (66)
56. What kinds of energy can be detected by bats, snakes, the platypus, and birds? (67)

3

Visual Processing: The Lateral Geniculate Nucleus and Striate Cortex

Chapter Contents

Some Questions We Will Consider

- The way the foveal cones are connected to other neurons in the retina is responsible for our ability to see details, but what happens in the brain, where this detail vision actually takes place? (89)
- Is there an electrical "picture" of an object in the brain that looks like the object's image on the retina? (93)
- How do electrical signals in neurons represent objects in the environment? (96)

In Chapter 1 we introduced the perceptual process by describing the sequence of events that took place when Ellen saw Bill and began walking toward him. As we look back on this process, taking into account what we learned about the retina in Chapter 2, we can describe the beginning of the process as follows:

> An image is formed on Ellen's retina. Light, in a pattern that illuminates some receptors intensely and some dimly, is absorbed by the visual pigment molecules that pack the rod and cone outer segments. Chemical reactions in the outer segments transduce the light into electrical signals. As these electrical signals travel through the retina toward the retinal ganglion cells, they combine, interact, excite, and inhibit. The ganglion cells send signals from the eye along the fibers of the optic nerve. Some of these signals travel to the superior colliculus, a structure involved in eye movements, but about 90 percent go to the lateral geniculate nucleus (LGN), a bean-shaped structure in the thalamus, which is the major way-station between the retina and the visual receiving area of the cortex.

Our purpose in this chapter and Chapter 4 is to begin answering the question: What happens in Ellen's LGN, visual cortex, and other areas of her cortex that enables her to perceive Bill? Since we will be taking a largely physiological approach to this question, we begin our search for the answer by doing a hypothetical experiment in which we create a picture of the activity in Ellen's brain that occurs as she perceives Bill. We use a device like a PET (positron emission tomography) scanner that creates images that show the biochemical activity in the brain.

As we monitor the activity in Ellen's brain, we see that our device indicates activity not only in the primary visual receiving area in the visual cortex, but in many other areas of the brain as well (Figure 3.1). We know from the results of experiments described in the coming chapters that a large number of brain areas, in the cerebral cortex, the outer layer of the brain responsible for perception, movement, and thinking, are activated in response to stimulation of the retina.

The end result of the activation of these many areas is Ellen's perception of Bill. In addition to showing that many areas of the brain are activated by a visual stimulus, our observation of the activated structures contains another important message: Since Ellen's perception of Bill is based on electrical activation of her brain, she perceives Bill *indirectly*. Her perception is based not on direct contact with Bill, but in the firing of nerve impulses in her brain. This means that there must be some information in the nerve firing that stands for "Bill."

What kinds of things must this nerve firing specify? Bill is about 5′ 11″ tall, has broad shoulders, and dark brown hair. As Ellen walks toward him, he moves slightly sideways and smiles at her. In this chapter and Chapter 4, we will describe the nature of the neural activity that stands for each of these properties. In doing this, we will establish basic principles that we will return to in later chapters when we consider not only visual qualities such as color, form, depth, and movement, but qualities in other senses such as pitch, loudness, pain, tastes, and odors.

In this chapter we are specifically interested in continuing the story we began in Chapter 2 in which we (1) described the anatomy and physiology of the visual system; and (2) began to relate this anatomy and physiology to perception. First we will consider what happens when signals traveling from the retina reach the LGN. Then we will focus on principles of neural processing in the primary visual receiving area in the occipital lobe of the brain. Our main goal is to understand how the visual system processes these signals and to understand what these processed signals mean. We begin by considering what happens to the signals in the LGN.

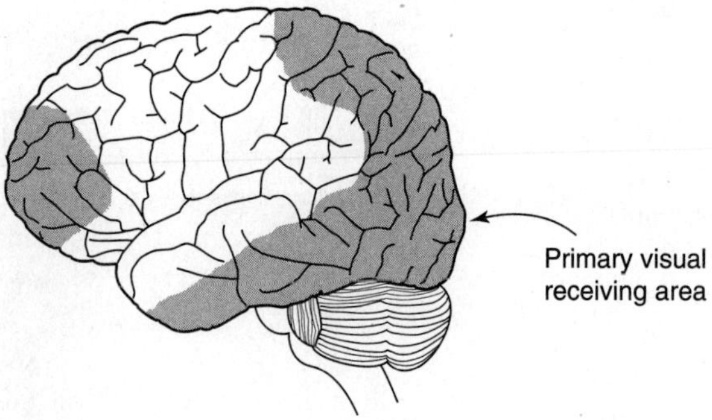

Figure 3.1
Shaded areas show some of the regions of the brain that may be activated by visual stimulation. In addition to the areas shown, other regions of the cortex, which are folded under and are therefore not visible in this view, are also activated.

The Lateral Geniculate Nucleus: Organization on the Way to the Cortex

One way to study how a sensory system processes information is to measure the receptive field properties of neurons at different levels of the system. We have seen that retinal neurons have center-surround receptive fields. Although we might expect that processing in the LGN might cause a change in this center-surround configuration, LGN neurons have the same center-surround configuration as retinal ganglion cells (refer to Figure 2.35).

The major function of the LGN is apparently not to modify the response of neurons, but to regulate neural information as it flows from the retina to the visual cortex (Casagrande & Norton, 1991; Humphrey & Saul, 1994).

Information Flow in the Lateral Geniculate Nucleus

The idea that one function of the LGN is to regulate the flow of information in the cortex is supported by the fact that, for every 10 nerve impulses that reach the LGN from the retina, only about 4 leave the LGN for the cortex. We can understand how this regulation of neural flow might occur by looking at the wiring diagram in Figure 3.2, which shows that LGN neurons are influenced not only by incoming signals from the retina, but by other neurons in the LGN, neurons elsewhere in the thalamus, and signals from the brainstem and the cortex. It has been determined that signals traveling "downward" from the visual cortex to the LGN, outnumber signals travelling "upward" from the retina to the LGN (Sherman & Koch, 1986; Wilson, Friedlander, & Sherman, 1984). We don't know the purpose of all of these signals that converge onto the LGN, but we can guess that the signals from the brainstem, which play an important role in regulating sleep, wakefulness, and attention, may be responsible for the fact that sleep slows down LGN firing, and heightened alertness increases its firing (Kaplan, Mukherjee, & Shapley, 1993).

Although regulating information flow may be an important function of the LGN, the most interesting property of the LGN for our purposes is not the way it may regulate the flow of neural information, but the way the information that flows into it is organized. Incoming signals are sorted to different areas of the LGN based on the eye they come from, the retinal receptors that generated them, and the type of ganglion cell transmitting the signal to the LGN.

Organization by Left and Right Eyes and Retinal Location

The lateral geniculate nucleus (LGN) is a bilateral structure, which means there is a nucleus in the left hemisphere of the brain and a nucleus in the right hemisphere. Viewing one of these nuclei in cross-section reveals 6 layers (Figure 3.3). Each of these layers receives signals from only one eye. The **ipsilateral**

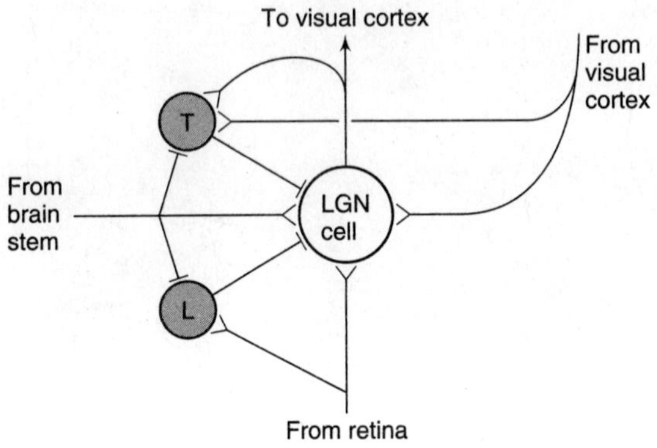

Figure 3.2
Inputs and outputs of an LGN neuron. In addition to the incoming signals carried in optic nerve fibers from the retina, this neuron is also receiving signals from the cortex, from a nucleus elsewhere in the thalamus (T), from another LGN neuron (L), and from the brain stem. Excitatory synapses are indicated by Ys and inhibitory ones by Ts. (Adapted from Kaplan, Mukherjee, & Shapley, 1993.)

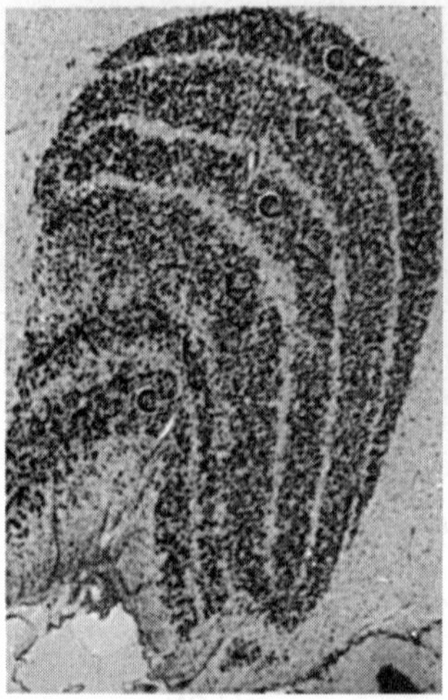

Figure 3.3
Cross section of the lateral geniculate nucleus. This is what the LGN looks like when treated with stain that darkens the cell bodies of the LGN neurons. This darkening shows that there are six layers of cell bodies, each separated by a light band. Layers 1, 4, and 6, marked C, receive input from the contralateral eye, and layers 2, 3, and 5, marked I, receive input from the ipsilateral eye. (From Livingstone & Hubel, 1988.)

eye (the eye on the same side of the body as the LGN) sends neurons to layers 2, 3, and 5 of the LGN. The **contralateral eye** (the eye on the opposite side of the body from the LGN) sends neurons to layers 1, 4, and 6. Thus, each eye sends half of its neurons to the LGN in the left hemisphere of the brain, and half to the LGN in the right hemisphere, and the LGN's layered structure keeps the signals from each eye separated.

Inputs to the LGN are also organized by the fact that the fibers entering the LGN arrange themselves so fibers coming from the same area of the retina reach the same area of the LGN. The result is a map of the retina on the LGN called a **retinotopic map.** This means that each location on the LGN corresponds to a location on the retina, and neighboring locations on the LGN correspond to neighboring locations on the retina. Thus, the receptive fields of neurons that are near to each other in the LGN, such as neurons A, B, C, and D in layer 6 (Figure 3.4), are adjacent to each other at A′, B′, C′, and D′ on the retina.

Retinotopic maps occur not only in layer 6, but in each of the other layers as well, and the maps of each of the layers are lined up with one another. Thus, if we lower an electrode through the LGN along the track indicated by the dashed line in Figure 3.4, we find that all of the neurons along that track have receptive fields in the same location on the retina. These aligned retinotopic maps caused the anatomist Gordon Walls (1953) to compare the LGN to a club sandwich, and to note that a toothpick piercing the LGN's "sandwich" layers would encounter neurons that all receive information from the same place on the retina (Mollon, 1990). This is an amazing feat of organization: One million ganglion cell fibers travel to each LGN, and on arriving there, each fiber goes to the correct LGN layer (remember that fibers from each eye go to different layers) and finds its way to a location next to other fibers that left from the same place on the retina. Meanwhile, all of the other fibers are doing the same thing in the other layers of the club sandwich!

Organization by Magno and Parvo Layers

There are two kinds of ganglion cells in the retina. **P-cells** have small or medium-sized cell bodies and respond to stimuli with sustained firing. **M-cells** have larger cell bodies and respond with brief bursts of firing. Distinguishing between these two types of ganglion cells is important because they process different

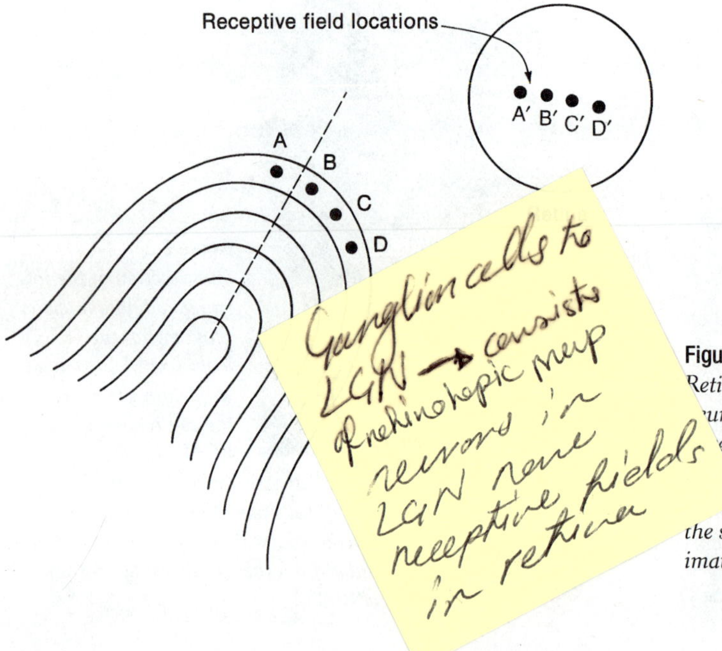

Figure 3.4
etinotopic mapping of neurons in the LGN. The urons at A, B, C, and D in layer 6 of the LGN e receptive fields located at positions A′, B′, C′, D′ on the retina. The receptive fields of neurons untered along an electrode track perpendicular to the surface of the LGN (dashed line) all have approximately the same location on the retina.

kinds of information about the environment, and they send this information to different areas in the LGN (Shapley, 1995).

M-cells synapse in layers 1 and 2, which are called the **magnocellular** (or **magno**) **layers**, and P-cells synapse in layers 3, 4, 5, and 6, which are called the **parvocellular** (or **parvo**) **layers** (Figure 3.4). By destroying either the magno or parvo layers of the monkey LGN and testing monkeys' ability to perceive various visual qualities, Peter Schiller, Nikos Logothetis, and Eliot Charles (1990) showed that the magno and parvo layers are specialized for the perception of different visual qualities.

Schiller and his co-workers first trained their monkeys behaviorally to determine their ability to perceive movement, pattern, shape, color, and depth. They then anesthetized the monkeys and injected a neurotoxin called ibotenic acid that destroyed part of the magno layers in some monkeys and part of the parvo layers in other monkeys (Figure 3.5). After recovering from the operation, the monkeys with lesions in the magnocellular layer had lost their ability to detect movement, and the monkeys with lesions in the parvocellular layer had lost their ability to detect color, fine textures and patterns, and the depth of small or finely detailed objects. Schiller and his co-workers therefore concluded that neurons in the magno and parvo layers represent two channels: The magno channel sends information about motion to the cortex, and the parvo channel sends information about color, texture, shape, and depth to the cortex. We will see in the next section that once this information reaches the cortex, it is processed further in separate pathways.

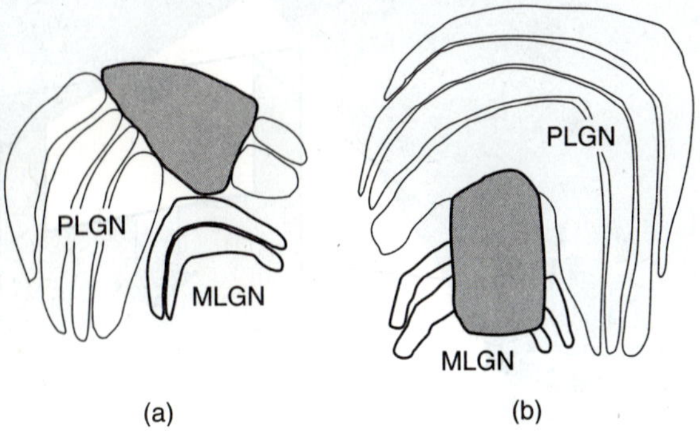

Figure 3.5
The areas of the LGN destroyed by Schiller and his coworkers are indicated by the shaded areas: (a) destruction of neurons in the parvocellular layers (PLGN); (b) destruction of neurons in the magnocellular layers (MLGN). (From Schiller, Logothetis, & Charles, 1990.)

The Striate Cortex: Response to Bars, Edges, and Orientation

One and a half million axons travel from each LGN to the visual receiving area of the brain, which is called the striate cortex because of the presence of white stripes (striate = striped) created by nerve fibers that run through it (Glickstein, 1988). The striate cortex is vastly more complex than the LGN, containing over 250 million neurons (Connolly & Van Essen, 1984). Like the LGN, the striate cortex is organized into layers (Figure 3.6) and we can divide the fibers entering the cortex into two streams corresponding to whether they are fibers from the magno or parvo layers of the LGN.

The signals in the fibers arriving from the LGN contain information that represents features of the visual scene ranging from simple changes in light intensity to complex patterns such as people's faces or the visual clutter of a busy city street. The task of the striate cortex is to process this incoming information so that various aspects of the visual scene become more clearly represented in the firing of individual neurons or groups of neurons. This process begins in the striate cortex and continues in the extrastriate cortex, which we will describe in the next chapter.

The story we have to tell of the striate cortex is an important one, because it establishes a number of important principles regarding how the nervous system responds to stimuli and how it is organized. We begin by describing the pioneering work of David Hubel and Torsten Wiesel, who, in research that began late

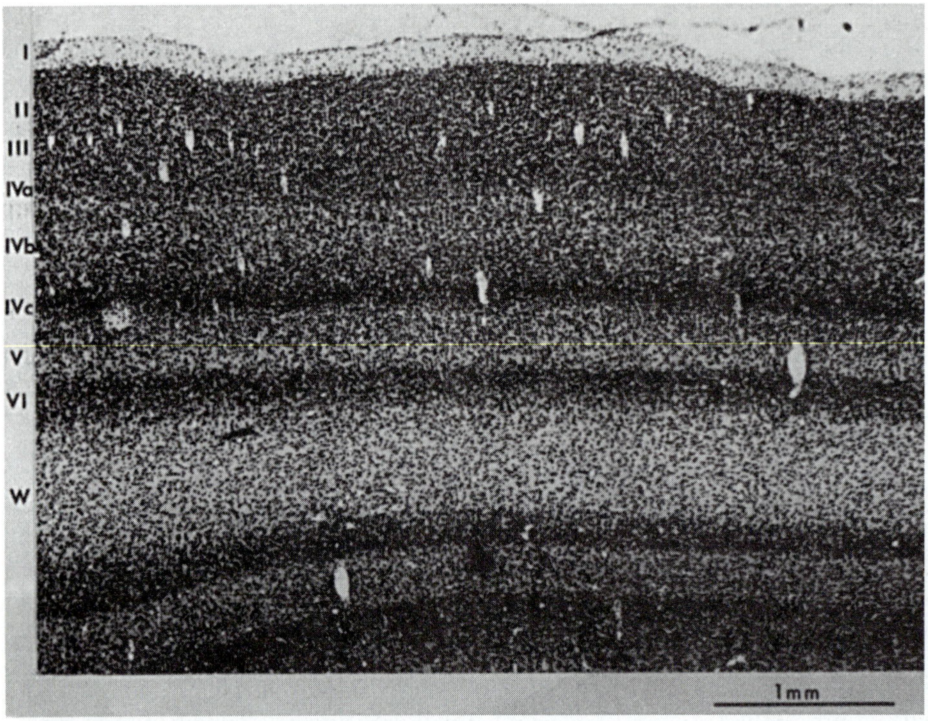

Figure 3.6
The layers of the visual cortex. Fibers from the LGN enter from the bottom, through the white matter (W) below layer VI, and synapse in layer IV. (From Hubel & Wiesel, 1977.)

in the 1950s and which culminated in a Nobel Prize in Physiology and Medicine in 1981, described receptive fields of neurons in the striate cortex and nearby areas of extrastriate cortex and showed how these neurons are organized.

When Hubel and Wiesel began their research, it was known that retinal ganglion cells had center-surround receptive fields and responded well to spots of light. But as they stimulated different areas of a cat's visual field with spots of light they were met with silence—the cortical neurons refused to respond. After attempting to elicit cortical responses for a number of hours, Hubel and Wiesel experienced something startling: As they inserted a glass slide containing a spot stimulus into their slide projector, a cortical neuron "went off like a machine gun" (Hubel, 1982). The neuron, as it turned out, was responding not to the spot at the center of the slide, but to the image of the slide's edge moving downward on the screen as the slide dropped into the projector (Figure 3.7). Upon realizing this, Hubel and Wiesel changed their stimuli from small spots to moving lines, and were then able to elicit responses from neurons in the cortex.

Figure 3.7
When Hubel and Wiesel dropped a slide in[illegible]ide projector, the image of the edge of the slide moving [illegible]wn unexpectedly triggered activity in a cortical neuron.

Receptive Fields of Neurons in the Striate Cortex

Once Hubel and Wiesel began stimulating the retina with moving lines while recording from neurons in the cortex, they discovered that most cortical neurons respond best to barlike stimuli with specific orientations. They distinguished three types of neurons based on the type of stimuli to which the neurons responded best (Hubel, 1982).

Simple Cortical Cells **Simple cells** have receptive fields that, like center-surround receptive fields, have excitatory and inhibitory areas. However, these areas are arranged side-by-side rather than in the center-surround configuration (Figure 3.8). This side-by-side arrangement means that a simple cell responds best to a bar of light with a particular orientation. The cell responds best when the bar is oriented along the length of the receptive field, as in Figure 3.8a and responds less and less as the bar is tilted away from this best orientation (Figure 3.8b and c) (Hubel & Wiesel, 1959).

This preference of simple cortical cells for bars with particular orientations is shown in the **orientation tuning curve** of Figure 3.9. This curve, which is determined by measuring the responses of a simple cortical cell to bars with different orientations, shows that the cell responds with 25 nerve impulses per second to a vertically oriented bar and that the cell's response decreases as the bar is tilted away from the vertical, until a bar tilted 20 degrees from the vertical elicits only a small response. (We can appreciate the narrowness of this tuning by noting that when a clock indicates that the time is 12:04, the angle between the hour hand and the minute hand is 24 degrees.) While this particular simple cell responds best to a bar with a vertical orientation, other simple cells respond best to bars with horizontal or diagonal orientations.

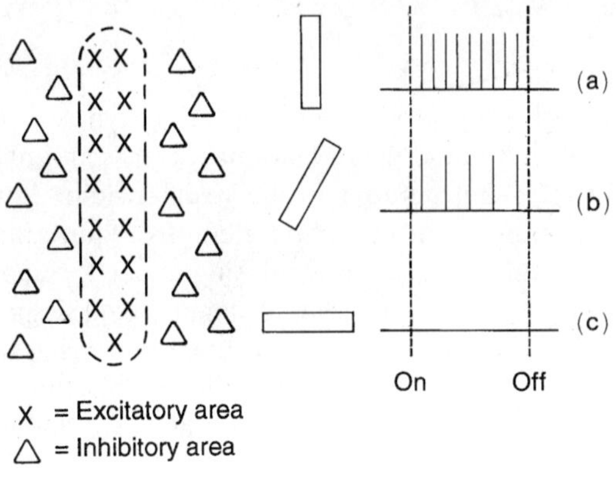

Figure 3.8
The receptive field of a simple cortical cell. This cell responds best to a vertical bar of light that covers the excitatory area of the receptive field (a) and responds less well as the bar is tilted so that it covers the inhibitory area (b and c). (Adapted from Hubel & Wiesel, 1959.)

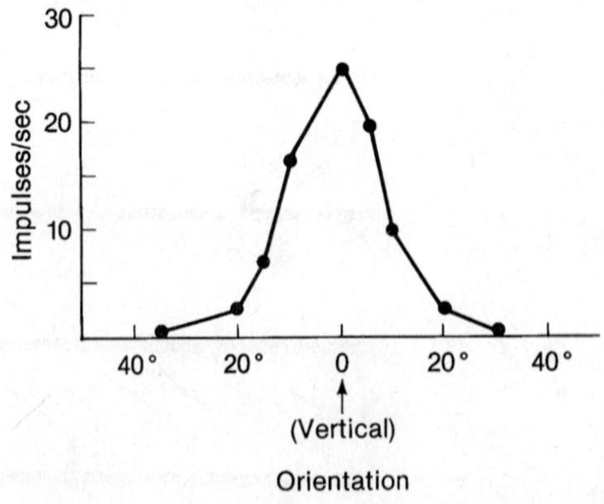

Figure 3.9
An orientation tuning curve of a simple cortical cell. This cell responds best to a vertical bar (orientation = 0) and responds less well as the bar is tilted in either direction.

Complex Cortical Cells **Complex cells,** like simple cells, respond best to bars of a particular orientation. However, while simple cells will respond to small spots of light or to stationary stimuli, most complex cells respond when a correctly oriented bar of light *moves* across the entire receptive field. Further, many complex cells respond best to a particular *direction* of movement (Figure 3.10).

End-Stopped Cells **End-stopped cells** fire to moving lines of a specific length or to moving corners or angles. The cell in Figure 3.11 responds best to a corner that is moving upward across the receptive field,

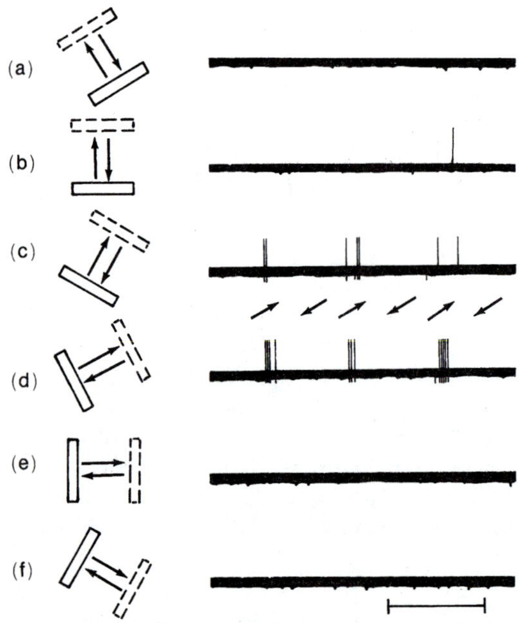

Figure 3.10
Response of a complex cell recorded from the visual cortex of the cat. The stimulus bar is moved back and forth across the receptive field. The records on the right indicate that the cell fires only when the bar is moved at a specific an… The cell does not respond when the bar is orien… (b), (e), and (f). A slight response oc… nse occurs in (d), bu… orientation, a resp… om left to right, a… . No response occur… e horizontal bar a… m Hubel & Wiesel,

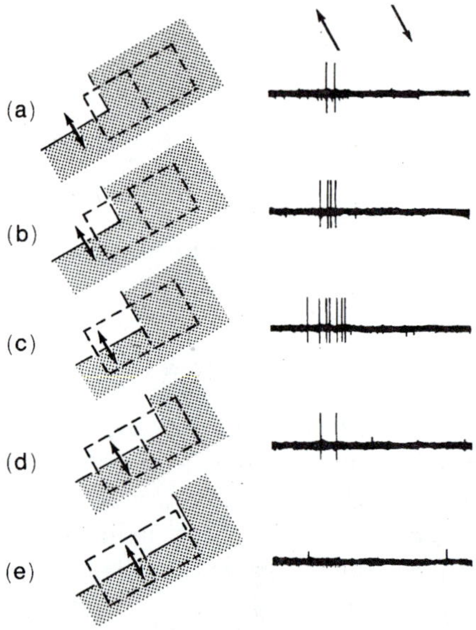

Figure 3.11
Response of an end-stopped cell recorded from the visual cortex of the cat. The stimulus is indicated by the light area on the left. This cell responds best to a light corner moving up (see the arrows above the records); there is no response when the corner moves down. Note that, as the corner is made longer as we progress from (a) to (b) to (c), the cell's firing rate increases, but that, when the length is increased further, as in (d) and (e), the firing rate decreases. (From Hubel & Wiesel, 1965a.)

as shown in Figu… fire if the stimulu… tend the length of this stimu… 3.11e, the cell no longer fires (Hubel & … iesel, 1965a).

From our vantage point in the striate cortex, we can see that the processing that occurs between the lateral geniculate nucleus and the cortex has created cortical neurons that fire in response to specific *features* of the stimulus, such as orientation or direction of movement. For this reason, these neurons are sometimes called **feature detectors.** Table 3.1, which summarizes the properties of the various types of neurons we have described so far, makes clear an important fact about neurons in the visual system: As we travel farther from the retina, neurons require more specific stimuli to fire. Retinal ganglion cells respond to many stimuli, whereas end-stopped cells respond only to bars of a certain length that are moving in a particular direction. Later, we will see that this specialization increases even further as we move into other visual areas of the cortex.

Hubel and Wiesel's demonstration of the existence of specialized orientation-selective neurons was a major advance in our understanding of visual physiology, because it provided a way to link the visual stimulus and neural activity. An object, according to this idea, causes numerous detectors with different

Table 3.1
Properties of neurons in retina, LGN and cortex.

Cell	Characteristics
Optic nerve fiber (ganglion cell)	Center–surround receptive field. Responds best to small spots but will also respond to other stimuli.
Lateral geniculate	Center–surround receptive fields very similar to the receptive fields of ganglion cells.
Simple cortical	Excitatory and inhibitory areas arranged side by side. Responds best to bars of a particular orientation.
Complex cortical	Responds best to movement of a correctly oriented bar across the receptive field. Many cells respond best to a particular direction of movement.
End-stopped cortical	Responds to corners, angles, or bars of a particular length moving in a particular direction.

orientations to fire, providing what might be the first step toward neural representation of the object.

But is there any evidence that these orientation detectors actually have any impact on perception? We can answer this question by looking at the results of some psychophysical experiments, which used a technique called selective adaptation to orientation.

Psychophysical Evidence for Orientation Detectors: Selective Adaptation to Orientation

The idea behind selective adaptation to orientation is that if a subject views a stimulus with a particular orientation, this viewing will fatigue neurons tuned to that orientation and this neural fatigue will cause a decrease in sensitivity to that orientation measured psychophysically.

We will describe an experiment in which subjects viewed stimuli called gratings (Figures 3.12 and 3.13). To understand the experiment, as well as others

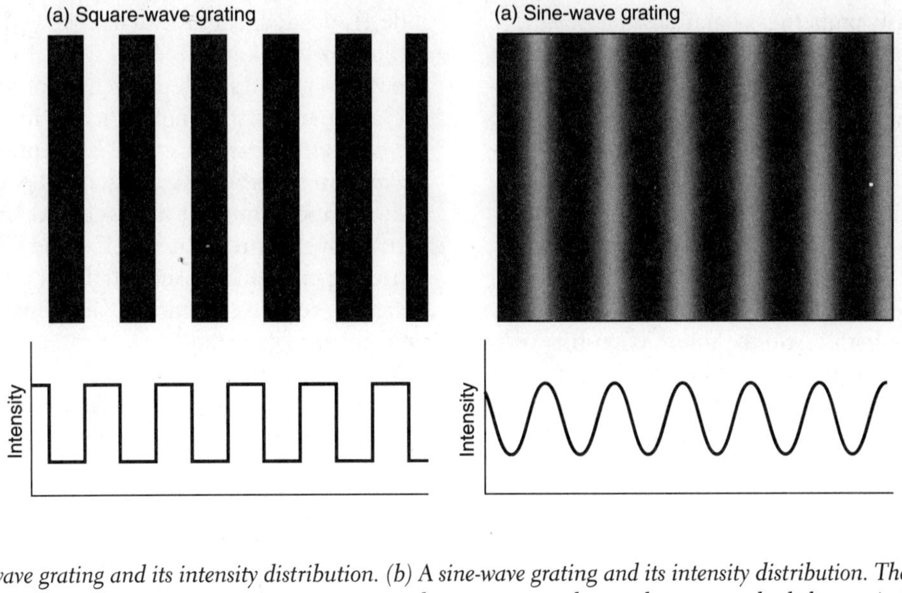

Figure 3.12
(a) A square-wave grating and its intensity distribution. (b) A sine-wave grating and its intensity distribution. The abrupt changes in intensity of the square-wave grating are seen as sharp contours, whereas the more gradual changes in intensity of the sine-wave grating are seen as fuzzy contours.

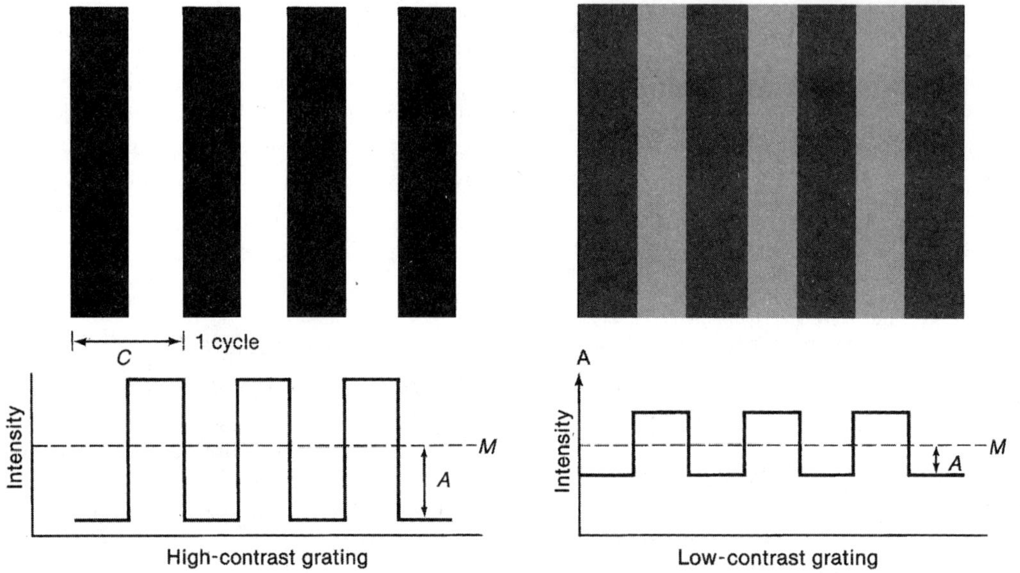

Figure 3.13
A high-contrast square-wave grating (left) and a low-contrast grating (right). Both gratings have the same mean intensity (M), indicated by the dashed line, but the grating on the left has a larger amplitude (A). The contrast of the gratings can be determined by dividing the amplitude of the grating by the mean intensity. The distance marked C on the grating on the left indicates the size of one cycle. Each of these gratings contains 3½ cycles.

that we will be describing later, we need to introduce some of the basic properties of gratings.

Gratings are alternating bars like those shown in Figures 3.12 and 3.13. We focus here on three properties of gratings: *waveform, contrast,* and *orientation.* The **waveform** of a grating refers to the grating's intensity profile—how the intensity changes as we move across the grating. The intensity profiles shown below each grating in Figure 3.12 indicate that the intensity of the bars of the grating in Figure 3.12a alternates abruptly between high (for each white bar) and low (for each black bar). Since the intensity profile looks like a series of squares or rectangles, this grating is called a **square-wave grating.** The intensity distribution for the grating in Figure 3.12b shows that this grating's intensity alternates more gradually between high and low. Since this curve follows a mathematical function called a *sine wave,* this grating is called a **sine-wave grating.** Much of the research using grating stimuli has used sine-wave gratings, for reasons that we will discuss soon.

The **contrast** of a grating is equal to its amplitude, A, divided by its mean intensity, M, which is indicated by the dashed line in Figure 3.13. This figure shows two gratings with different contrasts. In Figure 3.13a, the contrast is high, whereas in Figure 3.13b, the contrast is lower. A grating's **orientation** is its angle relative to vertical. Gratings may be oriented vertically or may be tilted at various angles (Figure 3.14).

We are now ready to describe the **selective adaptation** experiment that showed that it is likely that orientation selective neurons are involved in the perception of orientation.

Selective Adaptation to Orientation An experiment in which we selectively adapt to orientation is done as follows:

- *Measure the observer's contrast sensitivity to gratings with different orientations.*
  The **contrast sensitivity** to a grating is the sensitivity to the difference in light intensity of the

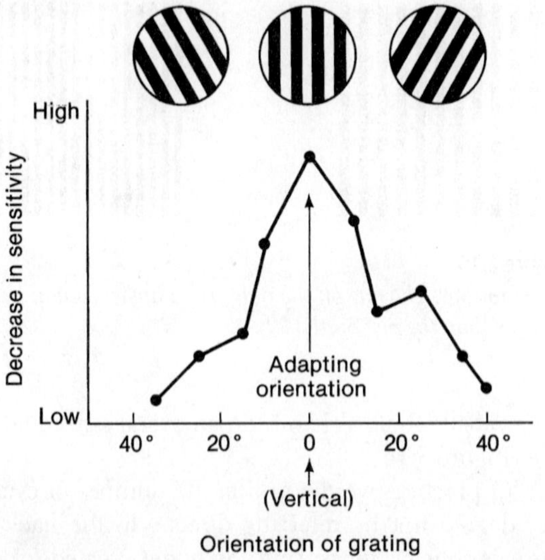

Figure 3.14
Top: Some of the grating stimuli used in the selective adaptation experiment. After measurement of the subject's contrast sensitivity to gratings with different orientations, the subject is adapted to the vertical grating (orientation = 0 degrees). The subject's contrast sensitivity to all of the gratings is then remeasured to determine the effect of the adaptation. Bottom: The curve in this graph shows that the subject's adaptation to the vertical grating causes a large decrease in her ability to detect the vertical grating when it is presented again, but that this adaptation has less effect on gratings that are tilted to either side of the vertical. Gratings tilted more than about 35 degrees from the vertical are essentially unaffected by adaptation to the vertical grating.

light and dark bars of the grating. To measure contrast sensitivity we decrease the intensity difference between the grating's light and dark bars until we reach the smallest difference at which the observer can just barely detect the bars, so decreasing the difference between the bars further would make the grating look like a homogeneous gray field. This intensity difference is the *contrast threshold*. We calculate the contrast sensitivity by the formula, contrast sensitivity = 1/contrast threshold. Thus, if a person has high contrast sensitivity, this means she can detect a grating in which there is only a small intensity difference between the light and dark bars.

- *Adapt the observer to a high-contrast grating.* In our example, we have our subject view a vertical grating like the one in the middle of Figure 3.14 for about one minute.
- *Remeasure the observer's contrast sensitivity to the same orientations that were measured before the adaptation.*

  When we remeasure the observer's contrast sensitivity we find that her sensitivity to the vertical grating has *decreased;* that is, she needs a greater intensity difference between the light and dark bars to see the vertical grating. Her sensitivity to the other gratings has also decreased, though not as much as to the vertical grating. This result is shown by the graph in Figure 3.14, which is the relationship between the orientation of the grating and the change in contrast sensitivity after adaptation.

To understand why contrast sensitivity decreases most to the vertical orientation, let's consider what is happening when our subject first views the vertical grating. Viewing this grating causes neurons that respond best to 0-degrees (vertical) to respond vigorously, and also causes some neurons that respond to orientations near 0-degrees to fire, although not as vigorously. This firing fatigues these neurons, with the 0-degree neurons being fatigued the most, ones near 0-degrees less, and ones far from 0-degrees, not at all.

When we then remeasure the contrast sensitivity to the gratings, the subject will have the most difficulty seeing the 0-degree gratings, because 0-degree neurons are the most fatigued. This decreases the contrast sensitivity to the 0-degree grating. The subject also has some trouble seeing gratings near 0-degrees since neurons that respond to these orientations are slightly fatigued, although not as much as for the 0-degree grating. Our psychophysical curve therefore shows the greatest decrease in sensitivity for the vertical orientation and less of a decrease in sensitivity for other orientations.

Our ability to explain the results of our psychophysical selective orientation adaptation experiment based on the response of orientation detectors supports the idea that orientation detectors do, in fact, play a role in perception. We will now describe research that has shown that neurons in the striate cortex also respond to a property of stimuli called *spatial frequency*.

Figure 3.15
Two gratings. The one on the right has a higher spatial frequency than the one on the left.

The Striate Cortex: Response to Spatial Frequency

We've seen that there are cortical neurons that respond best to bars with a specific orientation. Research has also shown that cortical neurons respond to gratings and that some neurons respond to gratings with a specific *spatial frequency*. To understand what this means, we need to understand what we mean by spatial frequency.

What Is Spatial Frequency?

Spatial frequency is how rapidly the stimulus changes across space. We can demonstrate spatial frequency by comparing the two gratings in Figure 3.15. The one on the right has a higher spatial frequency because it has more bars per unit distance than the one on the left. We specify a grating's spatial frequency in terms of *cycles per degree*—the number of cycles in the grating that fit within an angle of one degree on the retina. One cycle is a dark bar and a light bar and one degree is 1/360 of the circumference of the eyeball, about 0.3 mm on an average-sized adult eye (Figure 3.16).

In practice, we determine the number of cycles per degree not by referring directly to the back of the eye, but by measuring the angle created by extending lines from the eye out to the object. An easy way to apply this external method is to use the "thumb" method shown in Figure 3.17. You just have to remember that the image of a person's thumb held at arm's-length takes up about 2 degrees on the retina (O'Shea, 1991). Knowing this, you can use your thumb-at-arm's-length as a measuring device to determine the angle on the retina of any object in the environment.

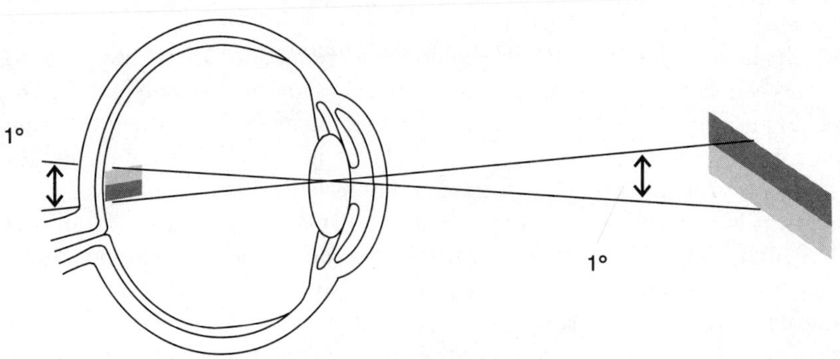

Figure 3.16
Stimuli in the environment cast images on the retina. One way to measure the size of the retinal image, is to measure the number of degrees on the back of the eyeball taken up by the image. An easier way to measure the angular size of an object is to extend rays from either side of the object back to the center of the lens. The angle between these two lines corresponds to the angle the object covers on the retina. In this example, one cycle of a grating (one dark bar and one light bar) covers about 1 degree on the retina, so the spatial frequency is 1 cycle per degree. (The size of one degree is exaggerated in this figure.)

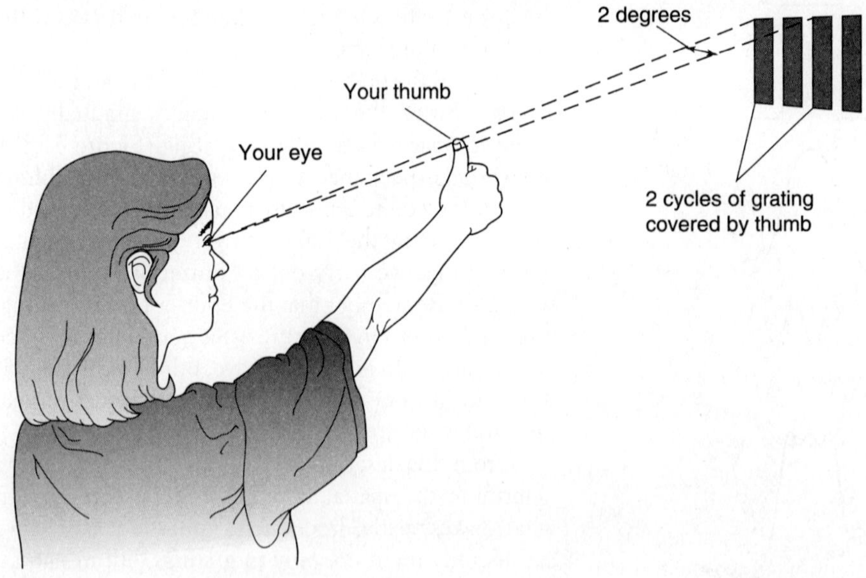

Figure 3.17
Procedure for viewing the grating in Figure 3.15a so its spatial frequency is about 1 cycle/degree. Holding your thumb at arm's length, position the grating so your thumb covers two pairs of black and white bars.

In Figure 3.17, the woman is using the thumb method to measure the spatial frequency of a grating. When she sights across the width of her thumb she finds that her thumb just covers two cycles of the grating (two pairs of dark and light bars). This means that these two cycles take up two degrees on the retina. Therefore, the angle for one cycle would be one degree and the spatial frequency of this grating would be one cycle per degree.

If a grating is a square-wave grating, it also contains spatial frequencies in addition to the ones we determine by measuring how many black and white bars occur within one degree. We can appreciate why this is so by zooming in on the grating to the border between a black bar and a white bar (Figure 3.18a). The abrupt change in intensity that occurs at this border contributes high spatial frequencies to the grating. (Remember that the definition of spatial frequency is *how rapidly the stimulus changes across space*. The fast change in intensity at the border is what causes these high spatial frequencies.)

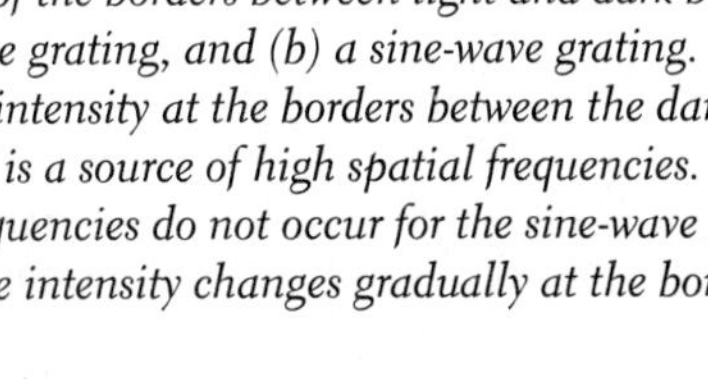

Figure 3.18
Close ups of the borders between light and dark bars of (a) a square-wave grating, and (b) a sine-wave grating. The sharp change in intensity at the borders between the dark and light bars in (a) is a source of high spatial frequencies. These high spatial frequencies do not occur for the sine-wave grating because the intensity changes gradually at the borders

To determine the spatial frequencies that are caused by changes at an edge, we use a procedure called Fourier analysis. **Fourier analysis** is a mathematical procedure that enables us to analyze any pattern of intensities into sine-wave components. Figure 3.19 shows the result of applying Fourier analysis to the square wave in Figure 3.19a and shows the following sine-wave components:

- A sine-wave with amplitude and frequency equal to that of the square wave. This is called the *fundamental* (Figure 3.19b).
- A sine-wave with amplitude equal to one-third of the square wave and frequency three times greater (Figure 3.19c). This is called the *third harmonic.*

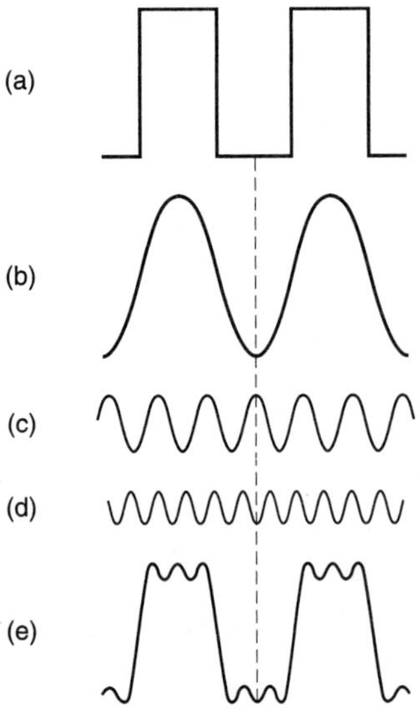

Figure 3.19
The sine-wave components for the square-wave grating at the top of the Figure, determined by Fourier analysis. When Fourier analysis is applied to the square-wave grating with the intensity distribution shown in (a), the sine waves shown in (b), (c), and (d) result. The dashed line is included to emphasize that the sine waves must be lined up correctly. See text for details.

- A sine-wave with amplitude equal to one-fifth of the square wave and frequency five times greater (Figure 3.19d). This is called the *fifth harmonic.*

When we add these sine waves together, we get the curve in Figure 3.19e, which looks something like a square wave. By adding the seventh and ninth harmonics and additional odd-numbered harmonics (according to Fourier's equations a square wave consists of only odd-numbered harmonics), the result gets closer and closer to our square wave. This shows that the square wave is, in fact, made up of a number of sine waves with different spatial frequencies. In this example, the fundamental frequency of the Fourier analysis (Figure 3.19b) indicates the spatial frequency determined by the way the grating repeats. The harmonics indicate the frequencies that occur because of the abrupt intensity change that occurs between the black and white bars.

What if the grating in Figure 3.17 was a sine-wave grating? Since the intensity changes gradually between the bars of a sine-wave grating (Figure 3.18b), we would expect that a sine-wave grating wouldn't contain the additional higher spatial frequencies that we observed in the square wave. To convince ourselves of this, we carry out a Fourier analysis on the sine wave. Remember that the Fourier procedure analyzes any pattern into its sine-wave components. Since our grating is already a sine wave, our Fourier analysis results in just one sine wave, identical to the original one, and without any higher-frequency components.

From this description, you can appreciate how to determine the spatial frequencies in a grating. But what makes spatial frequencies important is that we can identify them not only in gratings, but in natural scenes as well. Thus, in the house shown in Figure 3.20, we can identify the following spatial frequency components: Low spatial frequencies: The overall shape of the house (the large forms you would see if you viewed the house through a piece of frosted glass); Medium spatial frequencies: Medium-sized components such as the windows; High spatial frequencies: Smaller details such as the tiles on the roof and the pillars that support the railing on the front porch. In addition, high spatial frequencies also occur where abrupt intensity changes occur, such as the border between the dark roof tiles and the white masonry.

The spatial frequencies that occur in scenes are important because there are neurons in the striate cortex that respond to these spatial frequencies. We will show this by first considering physiological evidence for neurons that respond to spatial frequency, and then considering psychophysical evidence for these spatial-frequency-sensitive neurons.

Cortical Neurons as Spatial Frequency Detectors

When researchers have moved gratings across a screen, they have found some neurons that respond with higher firing to gratings than to bar stimuli (Albrecht, DeValois, & Thorell, 1980) and also neurons

Figure 3.20
This house, or any other natural scene, consists of many spatial frequencies. Cortical neurons that are tuned to respond to these spatial frequencies probably contribute to our perception of objects and scenes.

that are tuned to respond best to specific spatial frequencies. Figure 3.21, which shows turning curves for three simple cells, indicates that each cell responds best to a different spatial frequency and that each cell is tuned to respond to a narrow range of frequencies (Maffei & Fiorentini, 1973; cf. Robson et al., 1988). In addition, neurons have also been found that respond to the spatial frequencies that occur at sharp borders like the ones in Figure 3.18a (DeValois, DeValois, & Yund, 1979).

Thus, just as there are neurons tuned to respond to specific orientations, there are also neurons tuned to respond best to specific spatial frequencies. We will now see that researchers have obtained psychophysical evidence that the visual system responds to spatial frequencies.

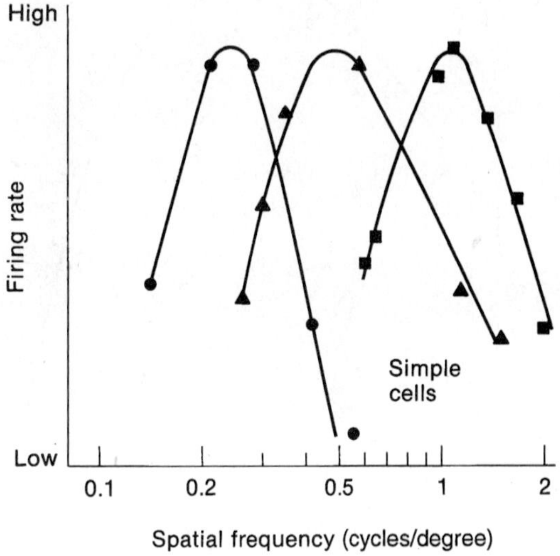

Figure 3.21
Tuning cures for three simple cortical cells to gratings moved across their receptive fields. Each cell requires gratings with a narrow range of frequencies. (Adapted from Maffei & Fiorentini, 1973.)

Psychophysical Evidence for Spatial Frequency Detectors: Selective Adaptation to Spatial Frequency

The psychophysical evidence that the visual system responds to spatial frequencies has been obtained using a technique called *selective adaptation to spatial frequency.* The starting point for this selective adaptation is measuring the **contrast sensitivity function (CSF),** which is a plot of contrast sensitivity (see page 80) versus spatial frequency.

We use sine-wave gratings to measure the CSF because, as we saw earlier, sine-wave gratings contain just the frequency indicated by the gratings' rate of repetition in cycles per degree. The additional high-frequency components that are present in a square-wave grating are not present in the sine wave grating.

We start with a sine-wave grating of very low frequency (wide bars) and determine the grating's contrast sensitivity by reducing the contrast until the grating appears to be a homogeneous gray field. If we repeat this measurement using gratings with higher and higher spatial frequencies, we get the solid curve in Figure 3.22, which is the contrast sensitivity function (Campbell & Robson, 1968).

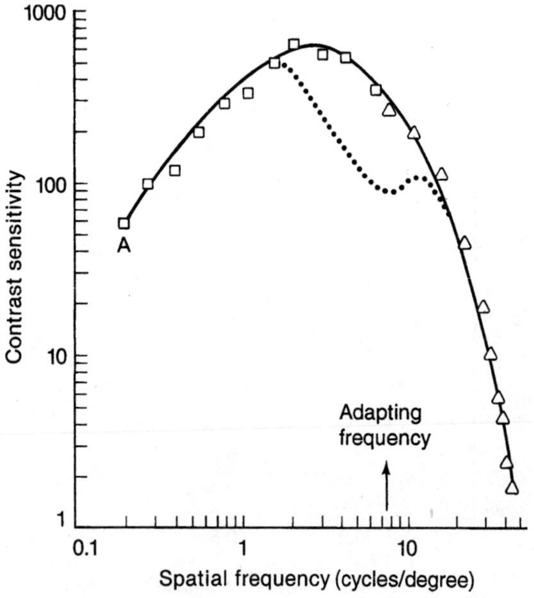

Figure 3.22

Squares and solid curve: Contrast sensitivity function for a sine-wave grating. (From Campbell & Robson, 1968.) Dotted curve: Contrast sensitivity measured after adaptation to a 7.5 cycles/degree grating.

This CSF tells us that the visual system is most sensitive to sine-wave gratings with frequencies between about two and four cycles per degree (observers can see these gratings even if the contrast between the bars is very low) and that sensitivity drops off at lower and higher frequencies. Thus, at low and high frequencies, the contrast must be much higher in order for an observer to see these gratings. You can verify that spatial frequency affects your perception by viewing the two gratings in Figure 3.15 from a distance of about 2 feet; the bars of the lower-spatial-frequency grating on the left will appear to have higher contrast than the bars of the grating on the right.

We are now ready to describe an experiment in which we selectively adapt for spatial frequency. This procedure is as follows:

- *Measure the observer's contrast sensitivity function (CSF).*
- *Adapt the observer to a grating.* In our example, we have the observer view a 7.5 cycle per degree sine-wave grating for 1 or 2 minutes.
- *Remeasure the CSF.* When we remeasure the CSF, we find that the sensitivity has deceased in the frequency range around the adapting frequency of 7.5 cycles/degree, as indicated by the dotted line in Figure 3.22. If we repeat this experiment using adapting gratings with different spatial frequencies, we get the same result, except that the CSF is decreased in sensitivity only near the frequency of the new adapting stimuli.

Apparently what is happening here is that the adapting grating causes neurons that are sensitive to the adapting grating's frequency to fire. This firing fatigues these neurons so they become less responsive. This decrease in responsiveness shows up as the decreased sensitivity in a band of frequencies around the adapting frequency. Results such as these have led researchers to conclude that the CSF is actually the sum of a number of separate channels, each of which is sensitive to a narrow range of spatial frequencies (Figure 3.23). You can actually experience how adaptation of **spatial frequency channels** can affect perception by doing the following demonstration.

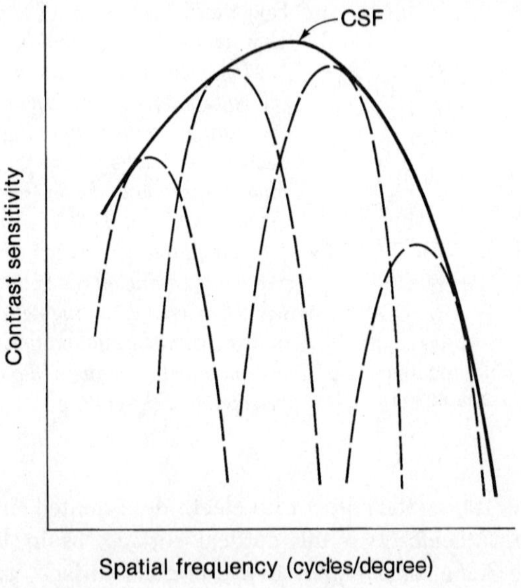

Figure 3.23
The contrast sensitivity function (solid line) and some of its underlying channels (dashed lines). These channels, each of which is sensitive to a narrow range of frequencies, add together to create the CSF.

DEMONSTRATION

Selective Adaptation of Spatial Frequency

Look at Figure 3.24 by moving your eyes back and forth along the horizontal line between the two gratings on the left, for about 60 seconds. This adapts you to the wide (low frequency) bars above the line and to the narrow (high frequency) bars below the line. After this adaptation, shift your gaze to the dot between the two gratings on the right and compare the spacing between the lines of the top and bottom gratings. ●

After adapting to the gratings on the left, the lines of the top grating on the right may appear more closely spaced than those of the bottom grating, even though the spatial frequencies of the gratings are actually the same. We can relate this perception back to the adaptation of neurons that respond to a narrow range of

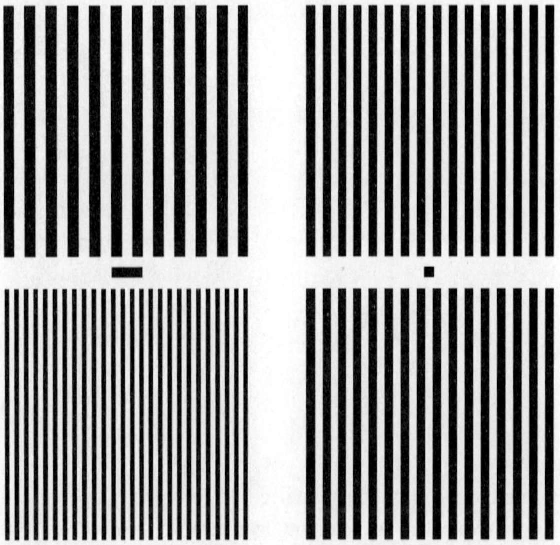

Figure 3.24
Stimuli for selective adaptation to spatial frequencies. See text for instructions.

spatial frequencies by considering the response generated by the two gratings on the right *before* the adaptation. These gratings generate a large response in neurons that are sensitive to the gratings' frequency, indicated by bar M in Figure 3.25a. These gratings also generate some response in neurons that respond best to lower (L) and higher (H) frequencies than the gratings.

When we adapt to the low-frequency grating (top left), neurons that respond best to low frequencies become fatigued. Then, when we shift our eyes to the grating on the right, we get the response shown in Figure 3.25b; the neurons tuned to low frequencies respond less than before they were adapted. Similarly, when we adapt to the high-frequency grating (bottom left), neurons that respond best to high frequencies become fatigued. Then, when we shift our eyes to the grating on the right, we get the response shown in Figure 3.25c; the neurons tuned to high frequencies respond less than before they were adapted.

Thus, adaptation to the gratings on the left changes the pattern of firing caused by the two gratings on the right. After adaptation, the pattern of firing to the top-right grating is weighted toward high frequencies (and we, therefore, see the bars as thinner),

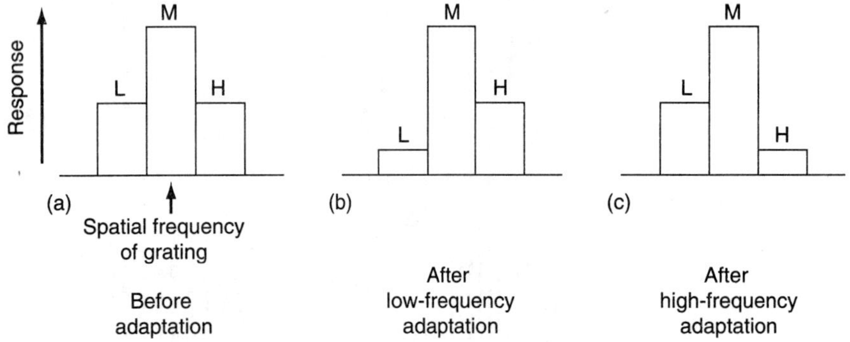

Figure 3.25
How neurons that respond best to low (L), medium (M), and high (H) spatial frequencies respond to the gratings on the right of Figure 3.24(a) before adaptation; (b) after adaptation to the low frequency grating at the top left; and (c) after adaptation to the high frequency grating on the bottom left. These changes in the pattern of firing caused by adaptation are accompanied by changes in our perception of the grating.

whereas the pattern of firing to the bottom-right grating is weighted toward low frequencies (so we see the bars as thicker).

We have seen that the idea that neurons in the visual system respond to specific spatial frequencies is supported by recordings from neurons, psychophysical selective adaptation experiments, and demonstrations like the one above. We have also seen that some cortical neurons respond selectively to specific orientations and to stimuli of specific lengths. When we compare the types of stimuli that cause cortical neurons to fire to the much simpler types of stimuli that cause neurons in the retina and LGN to fire, it is clear that a substantial amount of neural processing occurs in the cortex.

The sophisticated responses of cortical neurons are accompanied by sophisticated cortical organization. We will now describe this cortical organization by considering some experiments in which Hubel and Wiesel determined how neurons with common characteristics are organized in the cortex.

The Striate Cortex: Organization into Columns

To demonstrate how neurons are organized in the cortex, Hubel and Wiesel recorded from neurons by penetrating the cortex with electrodes oriented either *perpendicularly* to the cortical surface, as in Figure 3.26a, or *obliquely* to the cortical surface, as in Figure 3.26b. As they moved their electrode through the cortex, Hubel and Wiesel stopped at closely spaced intervals and recorded from neurons along the electrode track. The first question they asked was: Where are the receptive fields of these neurons located on the retina?

Location Columns and Retinal Maps

When Hubel and Wiesel lowered an electrode perpendicularly into a monkey's cortex, they found that the neurons they encountered had receptive fields either on top of each other or very close together on the

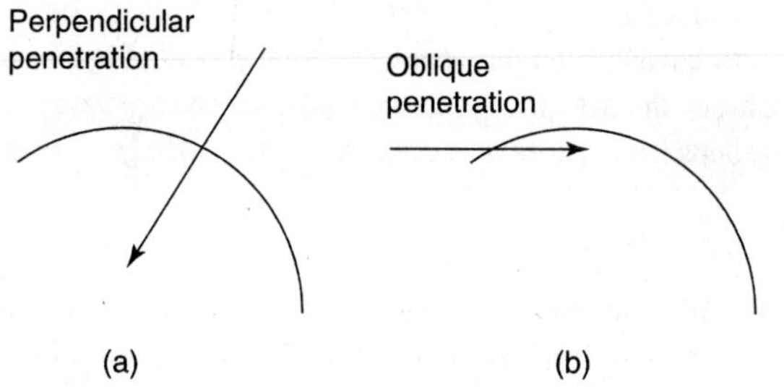

Figure 3.26
(a) Perpendicular and (b) oblique electrode penetrations of the cortex.

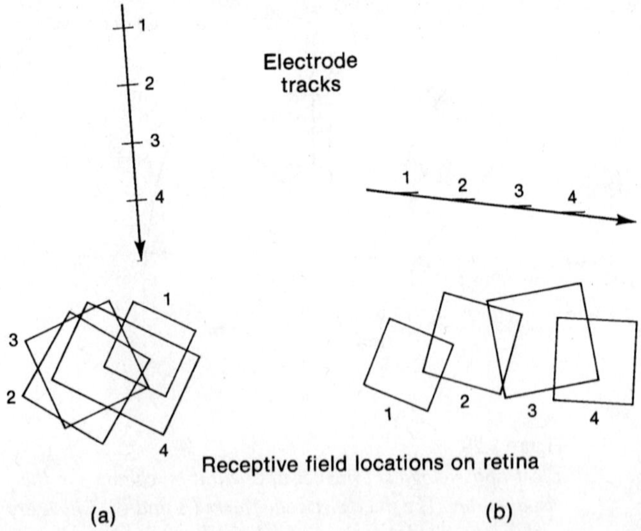

Figure 3.27
(a) When an electrode penetrates the cortex perpendicularly, the receptive fields of the neurons encountered along this track overlap. The receptive field recorded at each numbered position along the electrode track is indicated by a correspondingly numbered square.
(b) When the electrode penetrates obliquely, the receptive fields of neurons recorded from the numbered positions along the track are displaced, as indicated by the numbered receptive fields; neurons near each other in the cortex have receptive fields near each other on the retina.

retina, as shown in Figure 3.27a. They concluded from this result that the cortex is organized into **location columns,** and that the neurons within a location column have their receptive fields at the same location on the retina.

When Hubel and Wiesel penetrated the cortex obliquely (at an angle to the surface) and recorded from neurons separated by 1 mm along the electrode track, they found that the receptive fields were systematically displaced, and that neurons close to each other along the electrode track corresponded to receptive fields close to each other on the retina (Figure 3.27b). Thus, as in the LGN, there is a retinotopic map of the retina in the visual cortex, with each point on the retina being represented by a small area on the cortex.

An important feature of the map of the retina on the cortex is that neurons in and near the fovea are allotted extra space on the cortex compared to neurons from the peripheral retina. This effect is called the **magnification factor,** since although the fovea is only a small dot on the retina, accounting for only 0.01 percent of the retina's area, signals from the fovea reach an area that accounts for 8 percent of the area in the striate cortex.

We can understand why this magnification occurs by considering how neurons are packed in the retina and in the cortex. In the retina, the foveal receptors are packed very closely together, whereas the peripheral receptors are much more widely spaced. This packing of the receptors is mirrored by the ganglion cells that receive signals from these receptors: There are about 50,000 ganglion cells per square millimeter of retina near the fovea but fewer than 1,000 cells per square millimeter in the peripheral retina (Stone, 1965; Wassle et al., 1990).

When we move to the cortex, however, we see that cortical neurons are packed with the same density across all areas of the striate cortex. Thus, the large number of foveal neurons that are so closely packed together in the retina are spread out over a large area in the cortex (Figure 3.28). In contrast, the cells from the periphery, which are loosely packed in the retina, require less space in the cortex. The result is the magnification factor: More cortical space is allotted to parts of the retina that send more ganglion cell signals to the cortex. In fact, recent research shows that the magnification factor occurs both because the fovea sends more ganglion cell signals per unit area to the cortex than does the peripheral retina, and also because each foveal input is allotted extra cortical neurons. Thus, a ganglion cell situated near the fovea is allotted three to six times more cortical tissue than a ganglion cell from the periphery (Azzopardi & Cowey, 1993).

This magnified representation of the fovea in the cortex is related to perception. We know that the high

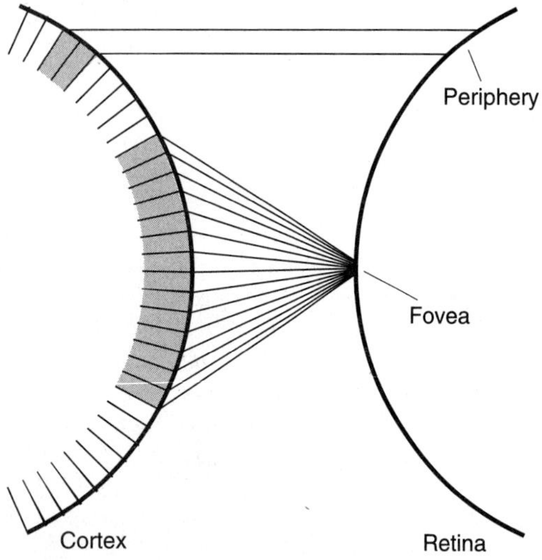

Figure 3.28
The principle behind the magnification factor, showing how ganglion cell fibers (indicated by the lines connecting the retina and cortex), which are closely packed in the fovea but sparsely packed in the peripheral retina, reach the striate cortex. At the cortex, all neurons are packed with the same density, so the input from the fovea needs to spread out over a larger area than the input from the periphery. The shaded areas represent the areas of cortex activated by stimulation of equal areas of the periphery and the fovea.

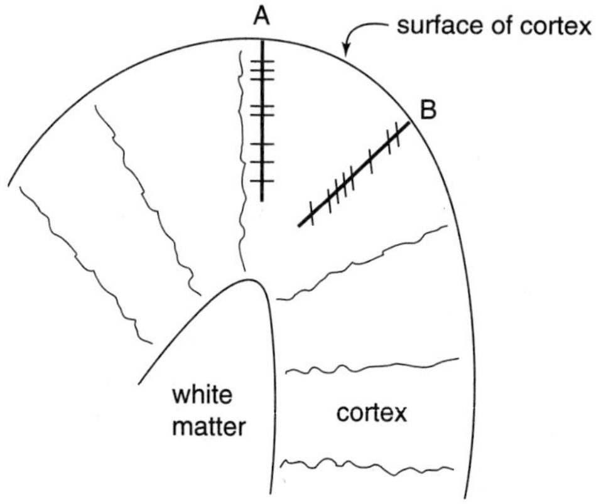

Figure 3.29
Electrophysiological evidence of orientation columns in the visual cortex. The microelectrode tracks (A and B), which are both perpendicular to the surface of the cortex, encounter simple, complex, and end-stopped cells along their paths, but all of these cells have the same preferred stimulus orientation (indicated by the lines cutting across each electrode track).

acuity of the cones occurs because of their lack of convergence (refer to Figure 2.40). We now see that this high cone acuity is achieved not only because of the way the cones are wired within the retina but also because the cones receive a large amount of space on the cortex. This extra cortical space is available for the extra neural processing needed to accomplish high-acuity tasks such as reading or identifying your friend's face in a crowd (Azzopardi & Cowey, 1993).

Orientation Columns

In the process of discovering simple, complex, and end-stopped cells in the cortex, Hubel and Wiesel observed that when they lowered their electrode so that its path was perpendicular to the surface of the cortex all of the neurons they encountered not only had receptive fields with the same location on the retina, but these neurons all preferred stimuli with the same orientations. Thus, all cells encountered along the electrode track at A in Figure 3.29 respond best to horizontal lines, whereas all those along electrode track B respond best to lines oriented at about 45 degrees. Based on this result, Hubel and Wiesel concluded that the cortex is organized into **orientation columns,** with each column containing cells that respond best to a particular orientation.

One of the interesting things about the discovery of orientation columns is that the proposal was based solely on electrophysiological responding. Looking at the cortex provides no clue that these columns exist because they are not normally visible. This problem was remedied by the development of a technique called the **2-deoxyglucose (2-DG) technique,** which made it possible to visualize these orientation columns. The 2-DG technique is based on the following facts:

1. Brain cells depend on glucose as a source of metabolic energy.
2. Cells that are more active use more glucose.

3. 2-Deoxyglucose (2-DG), a specialized form of glucose, can masquerade as glucose, so it is taken up by active cells as glucose is.

4. After 2-DG is taken up by the cell, it begins to be metabolized, but since the resultant metabolite can't cross the cell's wall, it accumulates inside the cell.

These properties of 2-DG enabled Hubel, Wiesel, and Michael Stryker (1978) to do the following experiment: After injecting a monkey with radioactively labeled 2-DG, they stimulated the monkey's visual system by moving black and white vertical stripes back and forth in front of the animal for 45 minutes. This stripe movement increased activity in the cells that prefer vertical orientations, causing them to increase their uptake of radioactive 2-DG. After this stimulation, the monkey was sacrificed, and when a slice of its visual cortex was placed in contact with a special photographic emulsion, the radioactive areas showed up as the dark stripes in Figure 3.30. These narrow bands, which were caused by the high activity of the cells that respond best to vertical stripes, confirmed what had previously been demonstrated electrophysiologically: The visual cortex consists of columns that contain cells with the same preferred orientation.

In addition to demonstrating that the visual cortex consists of columns of cells with the same preferred orientation, Hubel and Wiesel showed that adjacent columns have cells with slightly different preferred orientations. They showed this by moving an electrode through the cortex obliquely, as in Figure 3.26b, so that the electrode cut across orientation columns. When they did this, they found that the neurons' preferred orientations changed in an orderly fashion, and that, when they moved the electrode one millimeter across the cortex, they encountered cells that respond to the entire 180-degree range of orientations.

Ocular Dominance Columns

In addition to being organized for location and orientation, neurons in the cortex are also organized with respect to the eye to which they respond best. About 80 percent of the neurons in the cortex respond to stimulation of both the left and the right eyes. However, most cells respond *better* to one eye than to the other. This preferential response to one eye is called **ocular dominance,** and cells with the same ocular dominance are organized into **ocular dominance columns** in the cortex.

Hubel and Wiesel observed these columns during their oblique penetrations of the cortex. They found that a given area of cortex usually contains cells that all respond best to one of the eyes, but when the

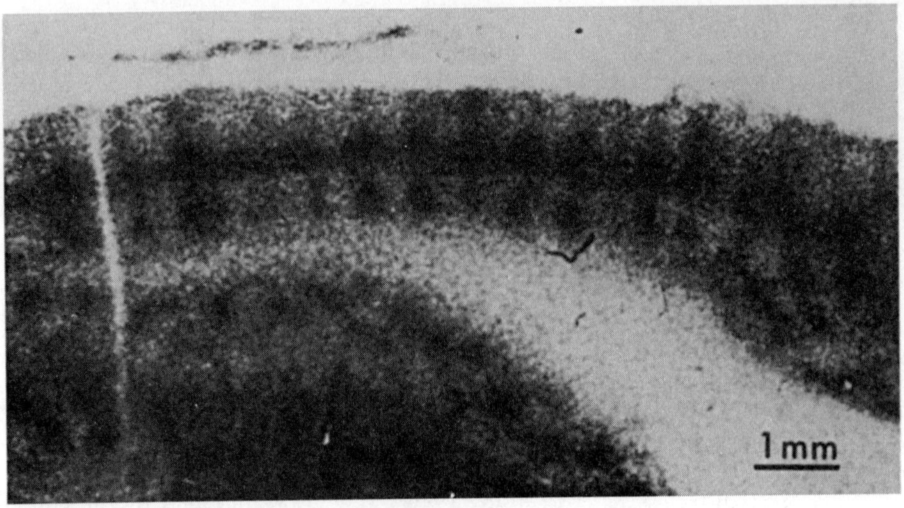

Figure 3.30
Magnified picture of a slice of visual cortex that has taken up radioactive 2-DG as described in the text. The dark vertical bands, produced by the radioactive 2-DG, are orientation columns. The dark horizontal band is layer 4 of the cortex. Neurons in this layer receive inputs from the LGN and respond to all orientations. (From Hubel, Wiesel, & Stryker, 1978.)

electrode was moved about 0.24–0.50 mm, the dominance pattern changes to the other eye. Thus, the cortex consists of a series of columns that alternate in ocular dominance in a left-right-left-right pattern.

Hypercolumns We have seen that the visual cortex is organized into columns that are based on location on the retina, orientation of the stimulus, and ocular dominance. A **hypercolumn** combines all three of these types of columns into a **processing module** that is equipped to processes information about any stimulus that falls within one small area of the retina. Figure 3.31 is a schematic diagram showing two side-by-side hypercolumns. Each hypercolumn contains a single location column (since it represents a particular place on the retina), left and right ocular dominance columns, and a complete set of orientation columns that cover all possible stimulus orientations from 0 to 180 degrees.

Figure 3.32 shows three hypercolumns, each of which processes information that falls within a small area on the retina. Area A on the retina is served by hypercolumn A in the cortex, Area B by hypercolumn B, and so on. There are over 2,500 hypercolumns in the striate cortex, so that each area on the retina has its own hypercolumn (Tovee, 1996).

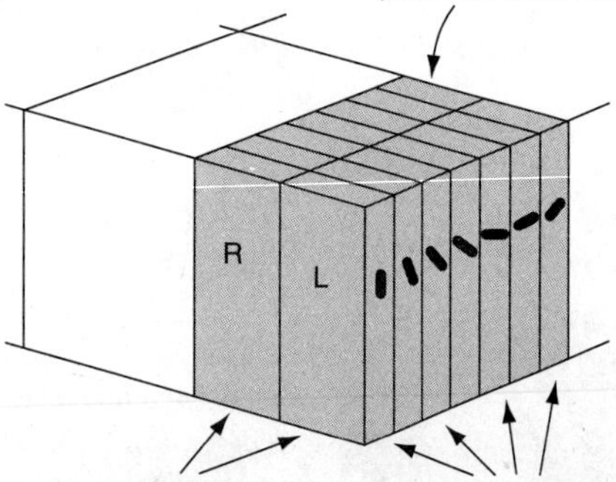

Figure 3.31
Schematic diagram of two hypercolumns. The light area on the left is one hypercolumn and the darkened area on the right is another hypercolumn. The darkened area is labelled to show that it consists of 1 location column, right and left ocular dominance columns, and a complete set of orientation columns.

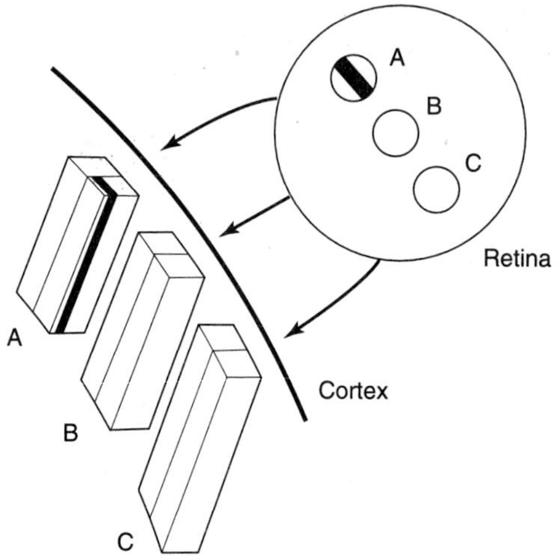

Figure 3.32
Three hypercolumns in the cortex that serve as "processing modules" for three areas on the retina. Note that the areas A, B, and C on the retina are not receptive fields. Since each neuron within a hypercolumn has its own receptive field on the retina and since there are thousands of neurons within a hypercolumn, there would be many receptive fields within each retinal location served by a hypercolumn. The dark bar falling within area A on the retina causes neurons in the darkened area of hypercolumn A to fire.

To appreciate how a hypercolumn works, let's present a small bar, orientated at 45 degrees to Area A of the retina of one eye (Figure 3.32). Since the bar falls within Area A, information about it will be processed within hypercolumn A. Most of the activity occurs within the ocular dominance column for the eye we are stimulating and since the stimulus is oriented at 45 degrees, most of the activity will occur within the 45-degree orientation column. The darkened area in hypercolumn A of Figure 3.32 indicates the area within the hypercolumn that is activated by this 45-degree bar.

Now let's consider what happens if we present a longer bar to the retina that extends across Areas A, B, and C. Figure 3.33 shows that since the bar covers all three areas on the retina, all three hypercolumns in the cortex will be activated. Since it is a 45-degree bar presented to one eye, one ocular dominance column and the 45-degree orientation column will be activated in each of these hypercolumns. From this pattern of activation, indicated by the darkened orientation columns in each hypercolumn, we can see that information that specifies "long-bar-shape" on the retina is translated into a pattern of cortical stimulation that differs greatly from the actual shape of the stimulus. Although this result may be surprising, it simply confirms a basic property of our perceptual system: Our perception is based on electrical signals that bear little actual resemblance to the environmental stimuli that they represent. Remember that the electrical signals in the visual system *represent* the environment, and that there is no particular reason that this representation must look like the distal stimulus.

Thus, the cortical representation of a stimulus presented to the retina does not have to resemble the stimulus; it just has to contain *information* that represents the stimulus. A long bar on the retina is represented by the information contained in the firings of

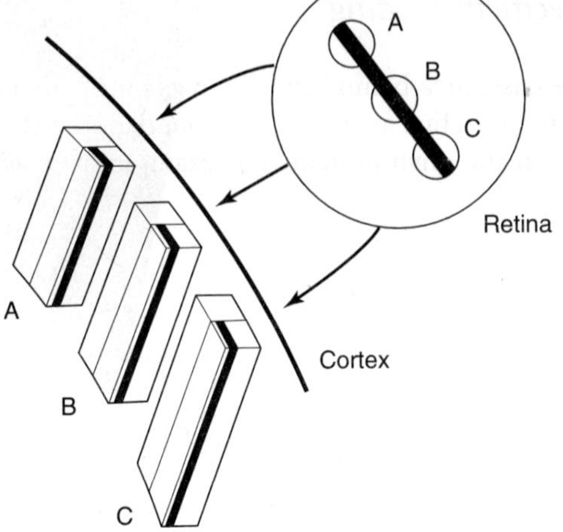

Figure 3.33
Same as Figure 3.32 except a longer bar that covers areas A, B, and C is presented to the retina. This bar activates neurons in the darkened regions of each of the hypercolumns.

neurons in different cortical columns. Before we perceive the bar, the information from these different columns must be combined, a process we will discuss in Chapter 4.

Our discussion until now has focused on how information is created by neural processing and how it is organized in the visual system. We have seen that neurons respond to specific stimuli and that they are organized into columns along with other neurons that respond to the same kinds of stimuli. We know that the neural signals in the cortex contain information that represents the things we see. We will now consider the form that this information takes and how it represents characteristics of the environment.

Sensory Coding: Making Sense of the Neural Information

At the end of the first chapter, I mentioned that I regularly ask my students to write down questions about perception. One of the best questions I have received was the following one, from Bernita Rabinowitz:

> A human perceives a stimulus (a sound, a taste, etc.). This is explained by the electrical impulses sent to the brain. This is so incomprehensible, so amazing. How can one electrical impulse be perceived as the taste of a sour lemon, another impulse as a jumble of brilliant blues and greens and reds, and still another as bitter, cold wind? Can our whole complex range of sensations be explained by just the electrical impulses stimulating the brain? How can all of these varied and very concrete sensations—the ranges of perceptions of heat and cold, colors, sounds, fragrances, and tastes—be merely and so abstractly explained by differing electrical impulses?

Bernita's question is an eloquent statement of the **problem of sensory coding:** *How does the firing of neurons represent various characteristics of the environment?* We have already begun working on this problem by describing neurons such as simple and complex cells that respond best to lines with specific orientations or that are moving in specific directions. But what about the reds, blues, and greens, and the tastes of a sour lemon that Bernita asks about? Can we answer Bernita by telling her that she perceives reds, blues, greens, and the taste of lemons because her brain contains neurons that respond specifically to these qualities? This idea, called **specificity coding,** is that different perceptions are signaled by activity in *specific neurons.* According to this idea, shown in Figure 3.34a, when Neuron B fires, we perceive blue, and when Neuron R fires, we perceive red.

Another idea, called **distributed coding,** is that different perceptions are signaled by the *pattern of activity* that is distributed across many neurons. According to this idea, the sensory code for blue might be the pattern of neural activity shown in Figure 3.34b, and the sensory code for red might be the pattern of neural activity in Figure 3.34c. When we discuss color vision in Chapter 5, we will see that the correct answer for color perception is closer to distributed coding. We will also see, in other chapters, examples of perceptions that are signaled by activity in specific neurons or by activity in small groups of neurons.

Describing sensory coding in this way may not, however, totally satisfy Bernita (since, as I found out during the term, she is a very inquisitive person). She might also inquire how electrical impulses, which are, after all, actually just sodium and potassium ions flowing across the nerve membrane, are *transformed* into the taste of a lemon or a jumble of blues and greens. When Bernita asks her question in this way, she is posing the **mind-body problem.** The mind-body problem asks how a physical event, such as molecules moving across membranes (the body part of the problem), can be transformed into the richness of perceptual experience (the mind part of the problem).

The mind-body problem is one of the great unsolved scientific and philosophical problems of our time. It is here that we have to tell Bernita that one of the true signs of scientific wisdom is realizing which problems we can potentially answer, and which problems might be beyond our present state of knowledge. Although some scientists have posed hypotheses about the origins of perceptual experience (e.g., Crick & Koch, 1995), the vast majority of research on the physiological mechanisms of perception has focused on looking for specific neurons or patterns of neural firing that represent specific perceptual qualities. Since sensory coding will be one of our central concerns as we discuss the physiological approach to perception throughout this book, we will now consider specificity coding and distributed coding in more detail, by considering how each of these methods of coding might represent a line with an orientation of 20 degrees.

S

... coding is that there ...nd to specific qual- ...mple, if specificity

Distributed coding—pattern of activity distributed across neurons.

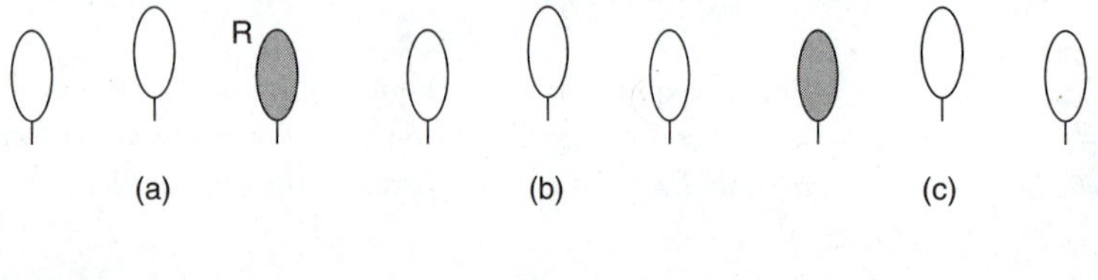

...gure 3.34
Possible solutions to the problem of sensory coding, using color vision as an example. Each symbol represents a neuron; activated neurons are shaded. (a) Specificity coding, where each color is signaled by activity in a specific neuron; (b) and (c) Distributed coding, where each color is signaled by the pattern of activity in a group of neurons.

coding were the mechanism used to represent the orientation of lines, each line would be signaled by a neuron that was tuned to fire only to that specific orientation. To evaluate this idea, let's consider how this would work for a 20-degree line. We know from Hubel and Wiesel's research that most cortical neurons respond best to specific orientations. However, the idea that the firing of one of these neurons can signal a 20-degree line runs into problems because these neurons also respond to orientations in addition to 20 degrees.

Figure 3.35a is a tuning curve for a neuron that responds with 30 impulses per second to a 20-degree line, but which also responds less strongly to a range of orientations on either side of 20 degrees. This response to a number of orientations might not be a problem if it weren't for the added complication that most neurons fire more rapidly to more intense stimuli. We can appreciate how this increase in firing rate to higher intensities might cause problems by considering the tuning curve in Figure 3.35b, which shows how increasing the intensity of the stimulus increases the neuron's firing rate. By following the dashed horizontal line in this figure, we can see that a response of 30 impulses per second could be caused by a low-intensity bar oriented at 20 degrees (Figure 3.35a) or by a high-intensity bar oriented at 10 or 30 degrees (Figure 3.35b). Thus, knowing the firing rate of this neuron doesn't indicate the orientation of the line.

Specificity coding also encounters problems when we consider the vast number of different stimuli we can perceive. Robert Erickson (1984) calculated that 100 billion possible figures can be produced with just half a dozen lines of differing location, length, orientation, and color. Thus, there are simply too many colors and forms, and tastes and smells as well, for most of our perceptions to be explained in terms of neurons that fire only to specific perceptual qualities. The mechanism for encoding most sensory qualities appears to be *distributed coding.*

Distributed Coding

The basic idea behind distributed coding is that different qualities are signaled by the *pattern* of activity that is distributed across many neurons. By looking at the tuning curves for the three neurons in Figure 3.36, we can see how distributed coding might work for perceiving orientation.

Neurons 1, 2, and 3 each respond best to different orientations. Let's consider how each of these neurons would respond to two different stimuli, a line oriented at 30 degrees and a line oriented at 60 degrees. The records on the right of Figure 3.36 show how neurons 1, 2, and 3 respond to the two orientations. For the 30-degree line, neuron 1 responds best, since 30 degrees is close to this neuron's best orientation. Neuron 2 responds less well, and neuron 3 responds hardly at all. For the 60-degree line, the pattern of firing is different, with neuron 3 responding best, neuron 2 responding less well, and neuron 1 responding hardly at all. These patterns are shown graphically in Figure 3.37.

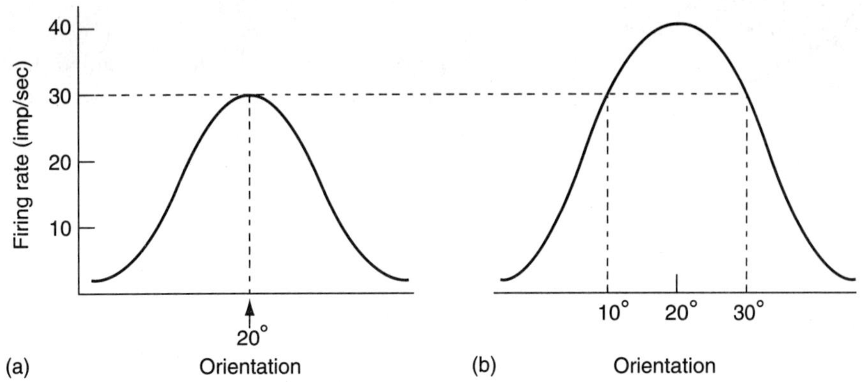

Figure 3.35
Tuning curves for a neuron that responds best to a line oriented at 20 degrees. (a) Tuning curve for a moderate intensity stimulus; (b) Tuning curve for a higher intensity stimulus.

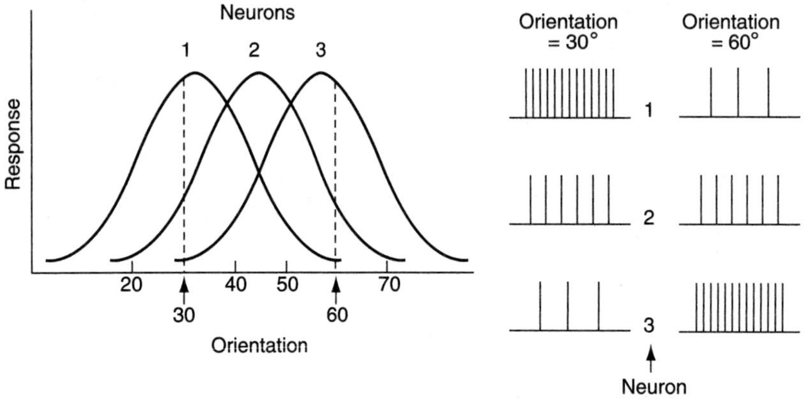

Figure 3.36
Left: Curve for three neurons that respond best to different orientations. By following the dashed line up and noting where they intersect with the curves, we can determine how each neuron responds to stimuli with different orientations. The records on the right show how the neurons respond to lines oriented at 30 degrees and at 60 degrees.

Thus, the brain can differentiate between the 30- and 60-degree orientations by registering the *pattern* of firing across a number of neurons. If we determine the patterns for many different orientations, we see that each orientation is signaled by its own pattern of responding. And most important, the pattern is unaffected, or affected only slightly, by changes in stimulus intensity. Increasing the intensity of each line increases the firing rate of all three neurons but leaves the *patterns* of response to the two stimuli unchanged.

Our description of sensory coding shows that distributed coding can be a powerful way to represent information in the nervous system. We will see that the pattern of firing of groups of neurons is a likely candidate for the sensory code for many different perceptual qualities. For example, in Chapter 5 we will see that our perception of different colors is signaled not by the firing of individual neurons for each color, but by the pattern of firing of many neurons.

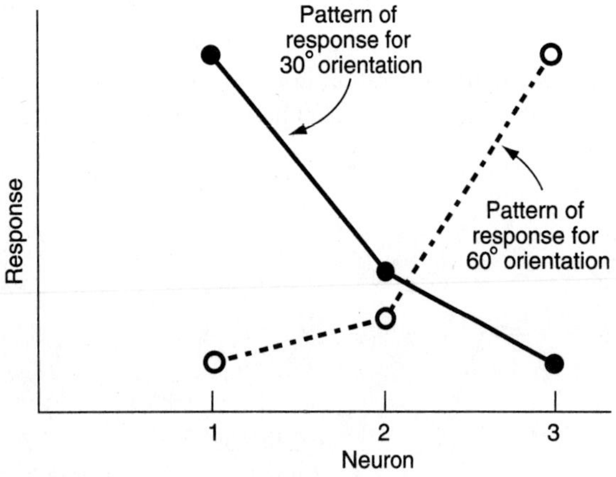

Figure 3.37
The patterns of response of neurons 1, 2, and 3 to the 30-degree orientation (solid line) and to the 60-degree orientation (dashed line). The curves are derived from the firing rates determined in Figure 3.36.

Something to Consider: Representing Bill

At the beginning of this chapter we noted that Ellen's perception of Bill is based not on direct contact with Bill, but on the firing of nerve impulses in her brain. We also noted that there must, therefore, be some information in the nerve firing that represents Bill. We have seen in this chapter that this representation looks nothing like Bill. The "Bill" represented in Ellen's brain is the firing of neurons that are responding to the orientations, line lengths, edges, and spatial frequency components that constitute Bill (Figure 3.38). Other neurons also fire to

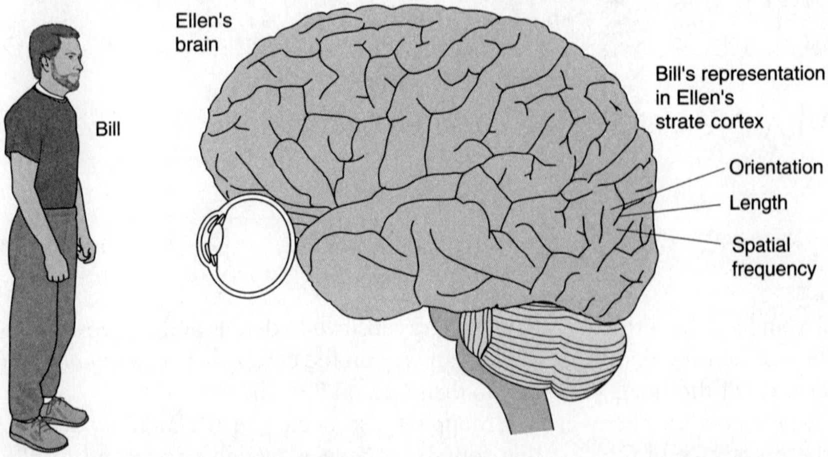

Figure 3.38
Bill is represented in Ellen's striate cortex by the firing of neurons sensitive to stimulus characteristics such as orientation, length, and spatial frequency. Other versions of this representation are created in neurons in the extrastriate cortex. One thing that all of these neural representations have in common is that they look nothing like Bill. They do, however, contain information that enables Ellen to perceive and recognize Bill.

represent Bill's movement, the color of his hair and clothing, and his distance from us.

But the activity we have observed in the striate cortex is just an early step in representing Bill. Further analysis that occurs in the extrastriate cortex creates more sophisticated neural representations from the basic characteristics signaled by the firing of the striate neurons. We will see in the next chapter that these representations involve neurons that respond best to more complex characteristics than the basic ones represented by the firing of neurons in the striate cortex.

Maps and Columns

The retinotopic maps on the LGN and striate cortex organize neural information in these structures along an important dimension—the location of the image on the retina. Similar mapping also occurs in other senses. For the sense of touch, there is a map of the body on the brain, so touching a particular place on the body activates a particular place on the somatosensory cortex in the parietal lobe (Figure 3.39). This map, which is arranged so that adjacent parts of the body are located adjacent to each other on the brain, is called a **somatotopic map.**

The maps for vision and touch are both distorted. Just as there is a magnification factor in vision in which the fovea is represented by a large area in the cortex, there is also a magnification factor in touch, so that parts of the body such as the tips of the fingers, that are very sensitive to details and fine textures, are allotted an area on the cortex that is far out of proportion to their area on the skin.

Mapping also occurs in the auditory system so that sound frequencies, which correspond to differ-

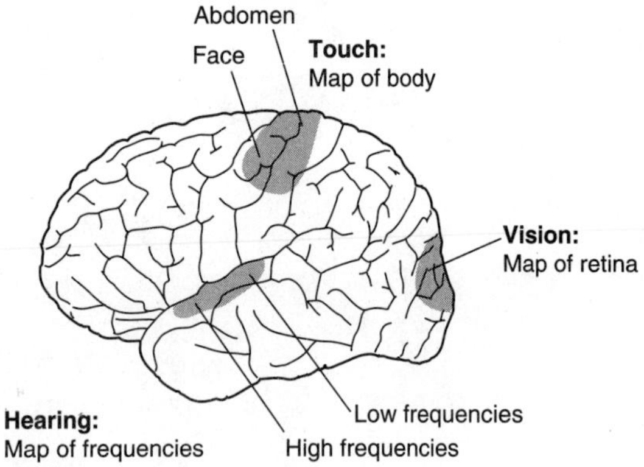

Figure 3.39
Each of the cortical receiving areas for hearing, vision, and touch (shaded areas) contain maps—neurons arranged in an orderly way that represents sound frequency, location on the retina, and places on the body.

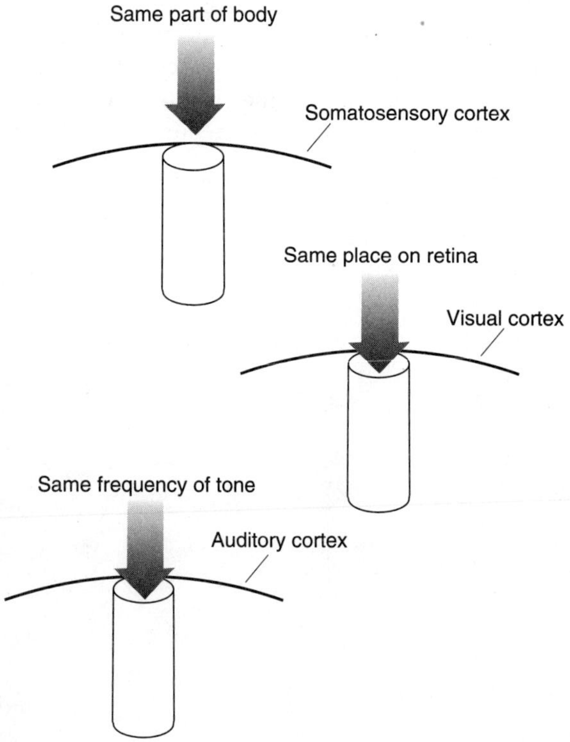

Figure 3.40
The cortical areas for touch, vision, and hearing all contain columns that process information about a specific location or property of the stimulus.

ently pitched tones, are arranged in an orderly way on the auditory cortex, with low frequencies represented by neurons at one end and high frequencies by neurons at the other end. This auditory map is called a **tonotopic map.**

In addition to having mapping in common, the visual, auditory, and somatosensory (touch) systems are also organized in columns (Figure 3.40). An electrode lowered perpendicularly to the cortical surface will encounter neurons that respond to the same location or orientation in the visual cortex; to the same location on the body in the somatosensory cortex, and to the same frequency in the auditory cortex.

This organization of these senses into maps and columns is probably an aid to further neural processing. For example, the fact that visual neurons with the same orientation preference are organized into columns might make it easier to construct complex cells from inputs from a number of simple cells with the same preferred orientation, and end-stopped cells from a number of complex cells with the same preferred orientation. It is not unreasonable to suspect that columnar organization may serve similar functions in the somatosensory and auditory systems.

Study Questions

1. Where do the signals that leave the retina go? (71)
2. What were the results of the hypothetical PET scan experiment? (72)
3. Why do we say that Ellen perceives Bill indirectly? (72)

The Lateral Geniculate Nucleus: Organization on the Way to the Cortex

4. How do the receptive fields of neurons in the LGN compare to the receptive fields of retinal ganglion cells? (72)
5. What is apparently a major function of the LGN? (73)
6. Inputs from which structures influence the firing of the LGN? (73)
7. What does it mean to say that the LGN is a bilateral structure? What is the ipsilateral eye? The contralateral eye? (73)
8. Describe how signals from each eye send signals to the 6 layers of the LGN. (73)
9. What is a retinotopic map? What does the existence of a retinotopic map say about the correspondence between neurons in the LGN and the retina? (74)
10. Why has the LGN been compared to a club sandwich? (74)
11. Describe the M- and P- ganglion cells in the retina and the magnocellular and parvocellular layers that they send their fibers to in the LGN. (74)
12. Describe Schiller's experiment in which the magno and parvo layers of the LGN were selectively destroyed. What did Schiller conclude from the results of this experiment about the functions of the magno and parvo layers? (75)

The Striate Cortex: Response to Bars, Edges, and Orientation

13. How many neurons reach the striate cortex from the LGN and how many neurons does the striate cortex contain? (75)
14. What is the task of the striate cortex? (75)
15. How did Hubel and Wiesel discover that neurons in the striate cortex fire to moving lines? (76)
16. Describe the properties of a simple cortical cell. What is an orientation tuning curve and what does it tell us about the response of a neuron? (77)
17. Describe the properties of complex cells and end-stopped cells. Why are these neurons sometimes called feature detectors? (78)
18. How do the stimuli required to cause neurons to fire change as we travel farther from the retina? (78)
19. What is the idea behind selective orientation adaptation? (79)
20. What is a grating? Understand what it means to say that a grating is a square-wave grating or a sine-wave grating. Understand what it means to say that a grating's contrast is high or low and understand how we measure a grating's orientation. (79)
21. What is contrast sensitivity and how is it measured? (80)
22. Describe the three steps that are involved in selectively adapting to orientation. (80)
23. What is the typical result that occurs after selective adaptation to orientation? What is the neural explanation of that result and what conclusion does that explanation support? (81)

The Striate Cortex: Response to Spatial Frequency

24. What is spatial frequency? Understand what it means to express spatial frequency in cycles per degree. (82)
25. What is the "thumb method" of determining the number of degrees that an object covers on the retina? (82)
26. An abrupt change in intensity at a border contains ___________ spatial frequency components. (83)
27. What is Fourier analysis and what does it accomplish? (83)
28. In the example in Figure 3.19, what does the fundamental frequency of the Fourier analysis indicate and what do the harmonics of the Fourier analysis indicate? (84)
29. Describe the kinds of objects in a scene that would have low spatial frequencies and the kinds would have high spatial frequencies. (84)
30. What is the evidence that there are neurons (a) that respond to gratings? and (b) that are tuned to respond to a narrow range of spatial frequencies? (c) that respond to the spatial frequencies that occur at sharp borders? (84)
31. What is the contrast sensitivity function (CSF)? (86)
32. Why do we use sine-wave gratings to measure the contrast sensitivity function? (86)
33. What does the CSF in Figure 3.22 tell us? (86)
34. What are the three steps in the procedure for selectively adapting to spatial frequency? (86)
35. What are the results of selective adaptation to spatial frequency and how can they be explained in terms of the fatiguing of neurons that are sensitive to spatial frequencies? (86)
36. What have researchers concluded about the CSF based on the results of selective adaptation to spatial frequency? (86)
37. Describe the result of the demonstration involving the gratings in Figure 3.24 and explain how the result of that demonstration could occur based on the fatiguing of neurons that respond to specific ranges of spatial frequencies. (87)

The Striate Cortex: Organization into Columns

38. How did Hubel and Wiesel show that the cortex is organized into location columns? (88)
39. What are location columns? If two neurons are in the same location column, what does that mean? (88)
40. Why do we say that there is a retinotopic map of the retina on the cortex? (88)
41. What is the magnification factor? (88)
42. Explain how the magnification factor occurs based on the relative densities of ganglion cell neurons in the fovea and the periphery and the way neurons are packed in the striate cortex. (88)
43. What is another reason for the magnification factor? (88)
44. How is the magnified representation of the fovea in the cortex related to perception? (88)
45. How did Hubel and Wiesel determine that there are orientation columns in the striate cortex? What does it mean to say that two neurons are in the same orientation column? (89)
46. What is the 2-deoxyglucose technique and what does it demonstrate? (89)
47. What is ocular dominance? What are ocular dominance columns? (91)
48. What is a hypercolumn and what do we mean when we say it is a processing module? (92)
49. Describe how parts of hypercolumns respond to stimulation of the retina with (a) a small bar, and (b) a longer bar. (92)
50. What do we mean when we say that the pattern of cortical stimulation caused by a stimulus differs greatly from the actual shape of the stimulus? (93)

Sensory Coding: Making Sense of the Neural Information

51. What is the problem of sensory coding? (93)
52. What is specificity coding? distributed coding? (94)

53. What is the mind-body problem and how does it differ from the problem of sensory coding? (94)

54. Describe why the way neural firing changes as intensity is increased makes it unlikely that the firing of a neuron that is tuned to orientation can signal the presence of a line with a particular orientation. (Understand Figure 3.35.) (95)

55. What is another argument against specificity coding? (95)

56. Understand how Figure 3.37 was determined and explain how the curves in this figure support the idea of distributed coding. (95)

Something to Consider: Representing Bill

57. How is Bill or any other person or object represented in the visual cortex? (96)

Across the Senses: Maps and Columns

58. Describe the maps on the somatosensory cortex and on the auditory cortex. How are these maps similar to maps on the visual cortex? (98)

59. Describe the columnar arrangement of neurons in the somatosensory and auditory cortices. (98)

60. How might the organization of the senses into maps and columns be an aid to neural processing? (99)

4

Higher-Level Visual Processing

What you have read so far has given you an idea of our understanding of what we knew about visual physiology in the 1970s. At that time, researchers thought that the striate cortex, with its various feature detectors, was the sole "perceptive center" in humans, and that the surrounding cortex was involved in higher-order processes such as visual memory (Zeki et al., 1991). In the 1970s, however, this view began to change, as researchers began discovering the extrastriate areas outside of the visual cortex, that respond to visual stimulation. Today we know that the extrastriate cortex consists of an extremely complex network of interconnected nuclei and that over half of the cortex can be activated by visual stimuli (Mishkin, 1986).

In this chapter, we bring our knowledge of visual processing up to date by asking questions such as: How do neurons in these extrastriate areas respond? How are the different areas organized? And, most important of all, what are their roles in perception? We will see that neurons in different areas respond to different features or qualities of the environment and that there is a rationale for how these areas are linked to one another. We begin by looking at how pathways in the extrastriate cortex are organized by describing two basic ideas: (1) Parallel streams: information in the extrastriate cortex is processed in two parallel streams that correspond roughly to the magnocellular and parvocellular streams of the LGN, and (2) Modularity: The function of specific structures in the extrastriate cortex is to process information about specific visual qualities.

Chapter Contents

Some Questions We Will Consider

- Are there separate brain areas that determine our perception of different qualities like color, depth, and form? (109)
- What happens to people's perceptions when they suffer brain damage? (115)
- Is there such a thing as unconscious perception? (116)
- How does the brain combine information about all of the qualities of an object into our perception of a whole object? (120)

Visual Processing Streams

To begin our description of parallel processing streams, we return to the research of Peter Schiller and his co-workers (1990) described in Chapter 3. Schiller showed that lesioning the magnocellular and parvocellular layers of the LGN caused different perceptual outcomes. Destroying neurons in the magnocellular layer affected movement perception; destroying neurons in the parvocellular layer affected the perception of color, form, and depth. When we follow the outputs of the magno and parvo layers of the LGN to the cortex we find that they synapse in different locations within area 4C of the striate cortex and they feed from layer 4C into separate streams that continue into the extrastriate cortex and which processes information about different aspects of the visual stimulus.

Streams for Perceiving What and Where

Figure 4.1 shows the two streams that transmit signals from the striate cortex into the extrastriate cortex. The stream reaching the parietal lobe, called the dorsal pathway, and the stream reaching the temporal lobe is called the ventral pathway. (*Dorsal* corresponds to the back or the upper surface of an organism. Thus, the *dorsal fin* of a shark or dolphin is the fin on the back that sticks out of the water. For upright walking animals such as humans, the dorsal part of the brain is the top of the brain (Figure 4.2). *Ventral* is the opposite of dorsal, so would be on the lower part of the brain.)

These two streams have different functions. The dorsal pathway is crucial for locating objects and has therefore been called the *where* pathway. The ventral pathway is important for identifying objects and has therefore been called the *what* pathway. (Mishkin, Ungerleider, & Macko, 1983; Ungerleider & Haxby,

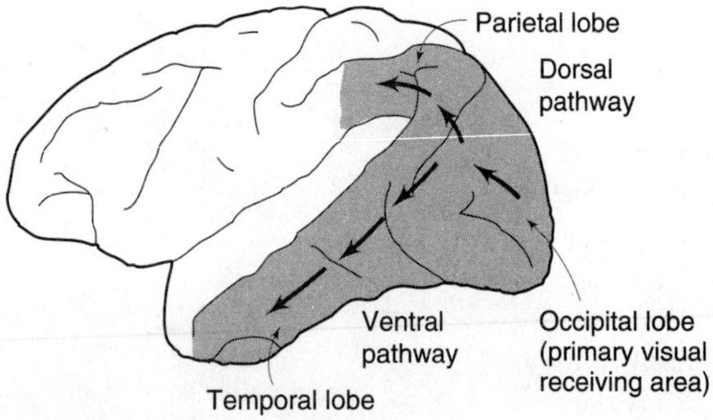

Figure 4.1
The monkey cortex, showing pathways from the primary visual receiving area, in the occipital lobe, to the parietal and temporal lobes. The pathway to the parietal lobe is called the dorsal pathway, because its destination is the dorsal (top) surface of the brain. The pathway to the temporal lobe is called the ventral pathway, because its destination is the ventral (bottom) surface of the brain (see Figure 4.2). The sequences of arrows indicate that there are a number of synapses along these pathways.

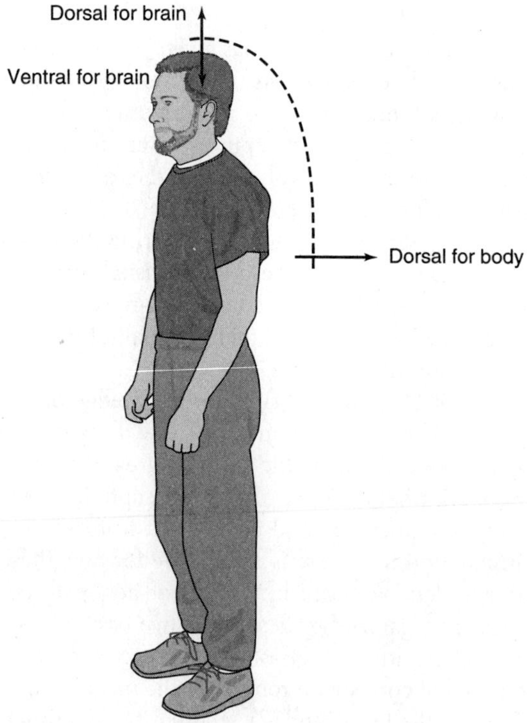

Figure 4.2
As described in the text, dorsal refers to the back surface of an organism. In upright standing animals such as humans, dorsal refers to the back of the body and to the top of the head, as indicated by the arrows and the curved dashed line. Ventral is the opposite to dorsal.

1994; Ungerleider & Mishkin, 1982). (Hint for remembering which of these terms go together: *Temporal* begins with a *t* and *what* and *ventral* contain *t*s. The remaining two terms, *where* and *dorsal*, go with *parietal*.)

We can understand the reasoning behind the conclusion that these two streams serve different functions by considering the results of experiments carried out by Leslie Ungerleider and Mortimer Mishkin (1982). These experiments presented monkeys with two different kinds of problem-solving tasks: (1) an *object discrimination* problem and (2) a *landmark discrimination* problem. Let's first consider the object discrimination problem. A monkey was familiarized with one object, like a rectangular solid, and was then presented with a two-choice task like the one shown in Figure 4.3a. To receive a reward, the monkey had to chose the "familiar" object, in this case the rectangular solid. Normal monkeys and monkeys with their parietal lobes removed accomplish this easily. However, monkeys with their temporal lobes removed found this task to be extremely difficult. Thus, the ventral pathway, reaching the temporal lobes is responsible for determining an object's *identity*, and is called the *what pathway*.

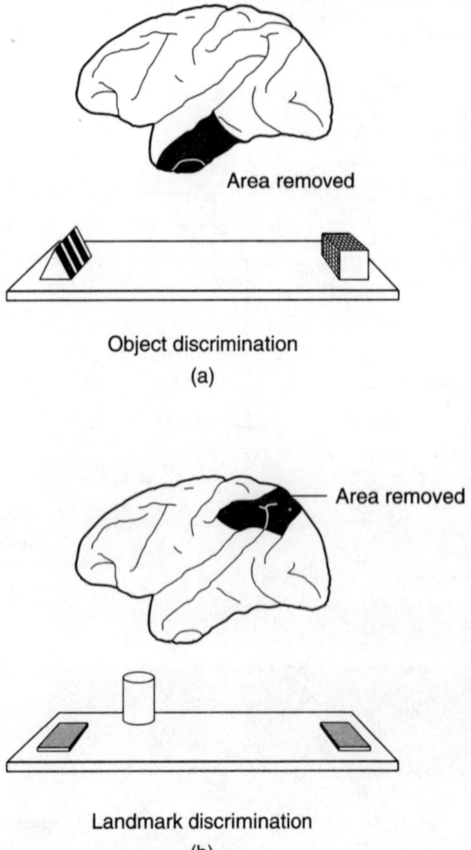

Figure 4.3
The two types of discrimination tasks used by Ungerleider and Mishkin. (a) In the object discrimination task the monkey had to pick the correct object. Monkeys with an area of their temporal lobes removed (shaded area of brain) had difficulty with this task. (b) For the landmark discrimination, the monkey had to pick the food well closer to the cylinder. Monkeys with an area of their parietal lobes removed found this task difficult. (From Mishkin, Ungerleider, & Macko, 1983.)

The landmark discrimination problem is shown in Figure 4.3b. Here, the monkey was rewarded for choosing the covered food well closer to the tall cylinder. This task was accomplished by normal monkeys or monkeys with their temporal lobes removed, but was difficult for monkeys lacking part of their parietal lobe. Thus, the dorsal pathway, reaching the parietal lobe, is responsible for determining an object's *location* and is called the *where pathway*.

Anatomists, physiologists, and psychologists have studied the dorsal and ventral pathways and the structures associated with them and have generally confirmed the idea of parallel pathways. Figure 4.4 is a simplified diagram that summarizes the general results of this research and that shows some of the main structures in the two pathways (also see Color Plate 1.8). Notice that the ventral (what) pathway begins with the retinal P ganglion cells and the LGN parvo layers and the dorsal (where) pathway begins with the retinal M ganglion cells and the LGN magno layers.

Most of the research supporting the idea of parallel pathways was done on monkeys, but research on humans, using **positron emission tomography** (PET), a technique that makes it possible to determine the areas of the brain that are activated by various types of tasks (Figure 4.5), has confirmed the idea that parallel pathways also exist in humans. For example, we would expect recognizing a face to activate the ventral (what) pathway, whereas locating a dot

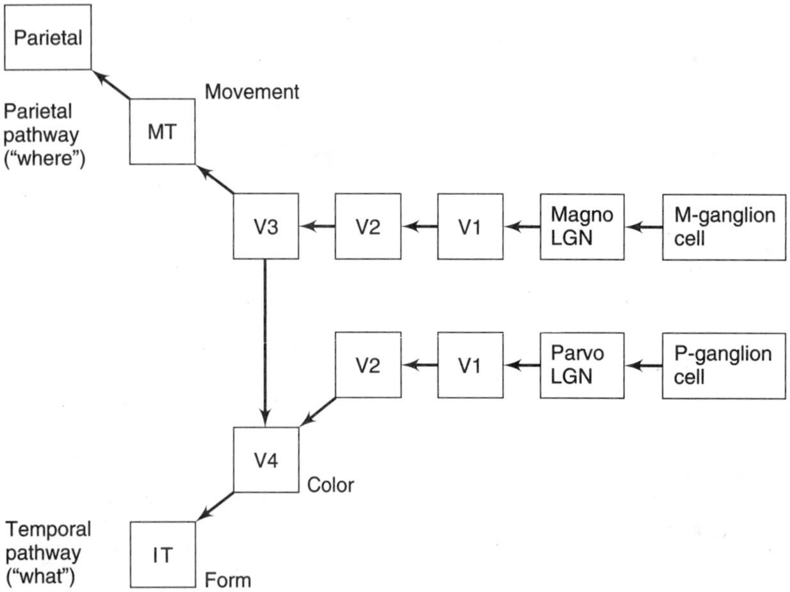

Figure 4.4
Simplified diagram of the visual pathways. Signals flow from right to left, starting with the M and P ganglion cells on the far right, which feed into the parietal and temporal pathways, respectively. V1 is the striate cortex, and V2, V3, and V4 are extrastriate visual areas; other extrastriate areas are IT, inferotemporal cortex; MT, medial temporal cortex; and Parietal, which refers to other areas in the parietal lobe. The visual qualities most strongly associated with areas MT, V4, and IT are indicated.

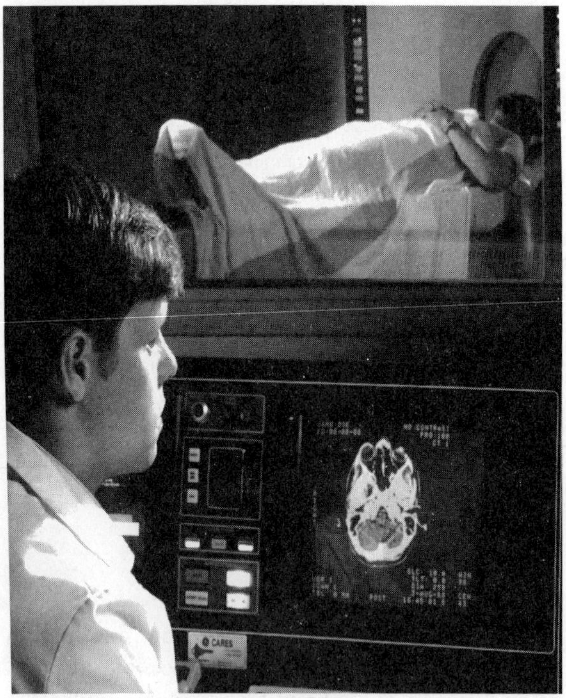

Figure 4.5
A person in PET scan apparatus in the background, with the control room in the foreground.

within a larger pattern would be expected to activate the dorsal (where) pathway. In general, the PET studies have obtained these predicted results (Haxby et al., 1991; Ungerleider & Haxby, 1994). We will also see below that research on people with cortical damage supports the idea of parallel pathways in humans.

Although we are describing the ventral and dorsal pathways as serving different functions, it is important to mention that the two pathways are not as separated as they may seem from Figure 4.4. The actual wiring diagram includes many anatomical connections that create "cross-talk" between the pathways (Boussourd, Ungerleider, & Desimone, 1990; Nakamura et al., 1993; Ungerleider & Haxby, 1994). For example, signals from both the magno and parvo layers of the LGN have been shown to reach area V4 in the ventral pathway (Maunsell, Nealey, & DePriest, 1990; Merigan & Maunsell, 1993). Thus, the picture we have been presenting of channels that serve specific functions is generally correct, but the idea of totally separate and independent channels for different qualities is an oversimplification.

Streams for What and How

While the idea of ventral and dorsal streams has been generally accepted, David Milner and Melvyn Goodale (1995) have suggested that rather than being called the what and where streams, they should be called the what and how streams. The ventral stream to the temporal cortex, they argue, is for perceiving objects, an idea that fits with the idea of "what." However, they propose that the dorsal stream to the parietal cortex is for taking action toward objects, such as picking up an object. Taking this action would involve knowing the location of the object, consistent with the idea of "where," but it also involves a physical reaction to the object. Thus, reaching to pick up a coffee cup involves information about the cup's location plus movement of the hand toward the cup. The dorsal stream, therefore, provides information about *how* to direct action with regard to a stimulus.

An example of evidence that supports the idea that the dorsal stream is involved in how to direct action is the existence of neurons in the parietal cortex that respond when a monkey looks at an object, and which also respond when it reaches toward the object (Sakata et al., 1992; also see Taira et al., 1990). But the most dramatic evidence supporting the idea of a dorsal "action" or "how" stream comes from the behavior of human patients with cortical damage.

Understanding the behavior of patients with cortical damage is the goal of a field called **neuropsychology,** which has taught us a great deal about the mechanisms underlying memory, thinking, language, and perception. The basic idea behind neuropsychology is that one of the best ways to understand how a system works is to study situations called **dissociations,** in which one function is absent while another is present.

To help us understand what dissociations tell us, we will consider the example of a broken television set (Parkin, 1996). One observation about broken television sets is that they can lose their color but still have a picture. This situation, when one function is absent and the other is present, is called a **single dissociation.** The existence of a single dissociation indicates that the two functions involve different mechanisms although they may not operate totally independently of one another.

Another observation about television sets is that they can lose their sound and have a picture or can lose their picture but still have sound. This situation, in which one function is absent (such as the sound) and the other is present (the picture) *and* when the opposite can also occur so the picture is absent and the sound is present, is called a **double dissociation** (Table 4.1). When a double dissociation occurs this means that the two functions—sound and picture in this example—involve different mechanisms that operate independently of one another. This makes sense for our television example when we consider that the television picture is created by its picture tube and the television's sound is created by its amplifier and speakers.

Neuropsychological research uses the same reasoning applied in this television example to observations of

Table 4.1
Double dissociations for TV sets (top) and people with brain damage (bottom). In both cases function 1 is present and function 2 is missing in one example, and the opposite occurs for the other example.

	Function 1 Sound	Function 2 Picture
Broken TV set #1	OK	No
Broken TV set #2	No	OK

	Function 1 Visual-Motor Orientation	Function 2 Judging Visual Orientation
Ventral stream damage	OK	No
Dorsal stream damage	No	OK

Milner + Goodale —
what - Temporal
How - Dorsal

what happens to people's abilities when they suffer brain damage. An example of how this approach has been applied to studying visual processing streams is provided by D.F., a 34-year-old woman studied by Milner and Goodale, who suffered damage to her ventral processing stream from CO_2 poisoning caused by a gas leak in her home. Her accident left her with good color and detail vision, but she was unable to recognize simple geometric forms and was unable to identify objects pictured in line drawings. For example, she identified a picture of a screwdriver as "long, black, thin" even though she knew what a screwdriver was, as indicated by the fact that she could easily identify a real screwdriver by feeling it with her hand. This inability to recognize common objects even though they can be seen is called **visual form agnosia.**

Another example of D.F.'s inability to recognize objects is shown by her response to the drawings in Figure 4.6. She was unable to recognize the apple or the book and was unable to copy these drawings. The drawings on the right, which she produced when she was asked to draw an apple and an open book from memory, indicate that her inability to recognize or draw the apple and the book wasn't due to a problem with her general knowledge about apples and books or a lack of drawing ability. Interestingly, however, when she was later shown the drawings she had produced, she had no idea what they were (Milner & Goodale, 1995).

D.F. also had difficulty matching the orientation of a card held in her hand to different orientations of a slot (Figure 4.7a). However, when she was asked to take action by "posting" this card through the slot, as you would when mailing a letter, she was able to orient the card and place it through the slot with great accuracy (Figure 4.7b). Thus, for D.F., with ventral stream damage, visual-motor orientation is intact (she could orient the card to push it through the slot) while judging visual orientation is absent (she couldn't match the card's orientation). D.F.'s result means that visual-motor coordination and judging visual orientation are different mechanisms, just as for the television set which has lost its color but still has a picture.

To show that these functions are not only served by different mechanisms, but are also independent, we have to demonstrate that a situation that is opposite to D.F.'s also occurs. In fact, this has been demonstrated in some patients with dorsal-stream damage who can judge visual orientation but who cannot accomplish the visual-motor orientation task.

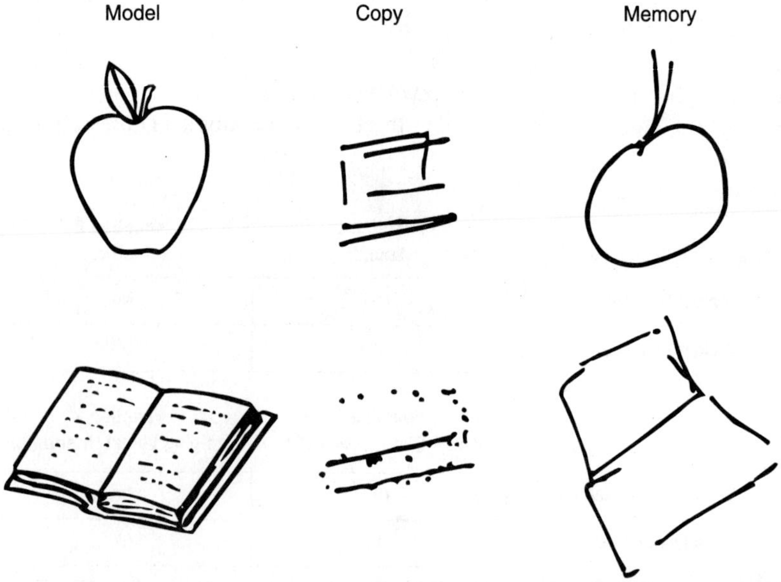

Figure 4.6
Patient D.F. could not recognize the apple or book drawings on the left and could not copy the drawings, as shown by her attempts in the middle column. The drawings on the right are ones she produced from memory. (From Milner & Goodale, 1995.)

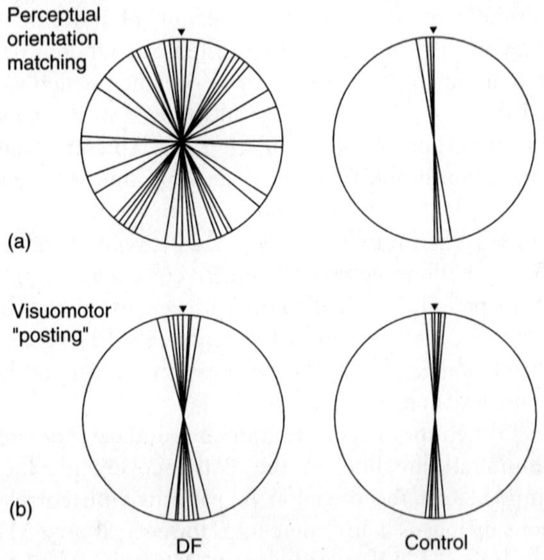

Figure 4.7
These plots indicate the orientation of the hand-held card in two tasks involving orientation. The top left plot shows patient D.F.'s attempts to match the orientation of the card to different orientations of a slot placed in front of her. Since correct performance for all orientations is indicated by a vertical line, this plot shows that D.F. was unable to accurately match the orientation of the card to the orientation of the slot. The bottom left plot shows patient D.F.'s performance when she was asked to place the card into the slot, as in mailing a letter. The nearly vertical lines in this plot indicate that she was able to accomplish this task. The plots on the right are for a normal control. (Adapted from Goodale et al., 1991.)

The combined results from D.F., with ventral stream damage, and these other patients, with dorsal stream damage, demonstrate a double dissociation and suggest that *perception* and *action* operate independently in the brain (Table 4.1).

Whether the most accurate description of the dorsal and ventral streams turns out to be *what* versus *where* or *what* versus *how* or some combination of the two, it is certain that there are structures in the extrastriate cortex that are specialized to serve specific functions. We will now describe research that supports this idea by showing that there are structures in the extrastriate cortex that are specialized to respond to specific types of stimuli.

Modularity Demonstrated by Specialized Neural Responding

One of the primary results of research on the extrastriate cortex has been the demonstration that certain cortical areas are processing information about specific visual qualities. We call this specialization **modularity.** Thus, if a particular structure contains a large proportion of neurons that respond selectively to a particular quality, we say that that structure is a **module** for that quality.[1]

An example of specialized modules is provided by the neurons of the medial temporal (MT) cortex and Area V4. Figure 4.8 shows that about 90 percent of neurons in Area MT respond selectively to an object's direction of movement, while less than 5 percent of the neurons in Area V4 are directionally selective (Merigan & Maunsell, 1993). In contrast, Figure 4.9, which compares V4 and MT for responses

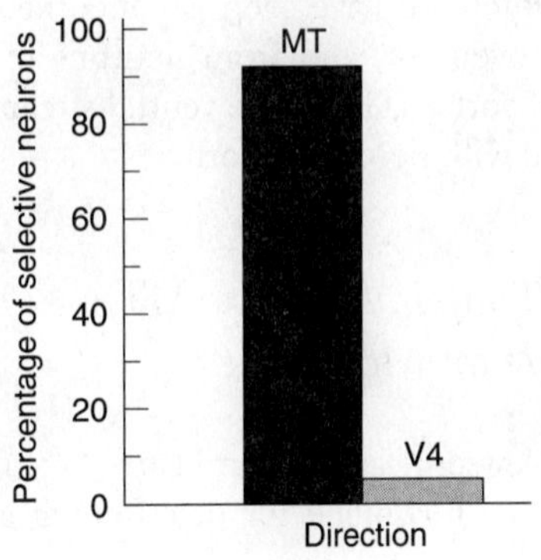

Figure 4.8
Most of the neurons in area MT (black bar) are directionally selective, whereas few in area V4 (shaded bar) are. (Adapted from Felleman & Van Essen, 1987.)

[1] See Fodor's (1983) book *The Modularity of Mind* for a detailed discourse on modularity, the properties of modules, and criteria for determining what a module is. Our definition of a module, which is somewhat different than Fodor's, is that a module is a structure that is specialized to process information about a specific perceptual quality.

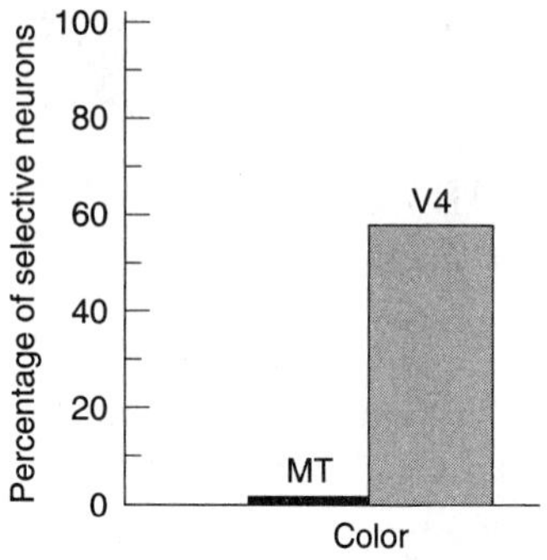

Figure 4.9
About 60% of the neurons in area V4 respond to color (shaded bar), whereas close to 0% in area MT respond to color. (Adapted from Felleman & Van Essen, 1987.)

to color, shows that about 60 percent of the neurons in Area V4 respond to color, compared to close to 0 percent in Area MT.

We will return to Area V4 in Chapter 5, when we discuss color vision. For now, we will look at further evidence for modularity by focusing on research that has recorded from neurons in Area MT, in the dorsal stream, which we have seen is concerned with perceiving movement, and from neurons in the inferotemporal cortex (IT), in the ventral stream, which is concerned with perceiving form.

Medial Temporal Cortex (MT): A Module for Movement

William Newsome and Edward Paré (1988) developed an ingenious technique for determining a monkey's threshold for detecting the direction of movement. They used a stimulus that consisted of a random pattern of moving dots created by a computer, which varied the degree to which the dots moved in the same direction. For example, Figure 4.10a represents zero correlation in the direction of the dots' movement, so that all dots moved randomly, much like the "snow" you see when your TV set is tuned between channels. Figure 4.10b represents 50 percent correlation, so that at any point in time half of the dots were moving in the same direction. Figure 4.10c represents 100 percent correlation, so that all of the dots were moving in the same direction.

When monkeys were trained to indicate the predominant direction of the dots' movement, they could detect the direction in patterns with correlations as low as 1 to 2 percent. However, if area MT was lesioned, the monkeys could detect the direction of movement only for patterns with correlations of 10 to 20 percent, so more of the dots were moving in the same direction. Thus, lesioning MT decreases the monkey's ability to detect the direction of movement (also see Movshon & Newsome, 1992; Pasternak & Merigan, 1994). We will consider further evidence that MT neurons are involved in motion perception in Chapter 10.

Inferotemporal Cortex (IT): A Module for Form

Neurons in the striate cortex respond to simple forms like bars or corners. As we move up the visual pathway into the extrastriate cortex, we encounter neurons that

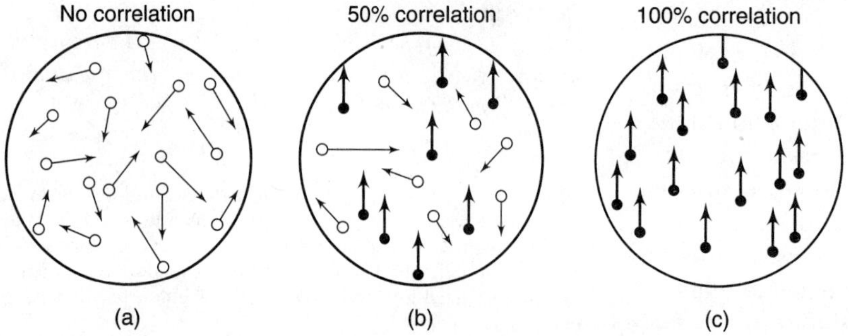

Figure 4.10
Stimuli used by Newsome and Paré. The dots on the left moved randomly, with no connection to one another. The ones in the center were partially correlated, half (the black dots) always moving in the same direction. The ones on the right were fully correlated, all moving in the same direction. (From Newsome & Pare, 1988.)

respond best to more and more complex stimuli, and when we reach the inferotemporal (IT) cortex, late in the ventral pathway, we find neurons that not only respond to complex forms, but also respond equally well when a particular form appears in different sizes and at different locations on the retina.

Neurons That Respond to Complex Forms The pioneering research on neurons in IT cortex was done by Charles Gross, David Bender, and Carlos Rocha-Miranda (1969) who found neurons in the monkey's IT cortex that responded best to brushlike shapes and to cutouts shaped like monkey hands. More recently, Keiji Tanaka and his coworkers (Ito et al., 1995; Kobatake & Tanaka, 1994; Tanaka, 1993; Tanaka et al., 1991) have found a number of different kinds of cells in IT cortex that respond to various kinds of shapes. Some, which they call **primary cells,** respond best to fairly simple stimuli like slits, spots, ellipses, and squares. But other cells, which they call **elaborate cells,** respond to more complex stimuli such as specific shapes or shapes combined with a color or a texture.

Figure 4.11 shows an example of how one of these elaborate cells responds to a number of similar stimuli. As they began testing this cell, Tanaka and his coworkers noticed that it responded well to a model of an apple, but that if they removed the apple's stem, the cell stopped responding. The way this cell responds to other shapes fits with this observation. The cell responds best to a circular disc with a thin bar (A), but responds poorly to the bar alone (B), the disc alone (C), the disc and a short bar (D), or the disc and a fat bar (E). The cell does respond to a square shape and the bar (F) or a star shape and the bar (G), but not as well as to the best stimulus—the circular disc and the bar.

Figure 4.12 shows some of the other shapes that elicited good responses from IT neurons and also shows that these cells are arranged in columns with cells responding to similar shapes in the same columns (also see Fujita et al., 1992). Tanaka proposed that a complex form stimulates a number of these neurons and that we perceive a particular form when the information from all of these neurons is combined.

While some of the cells studied by Tanaka responded only when the stimuli were located on a specific place on the retina or to a specific size of the stimulus, he also found **size-invariant neurons,** cells that responded equally well when the stimuli were varied in size, and **location-invariant neurons,** cells

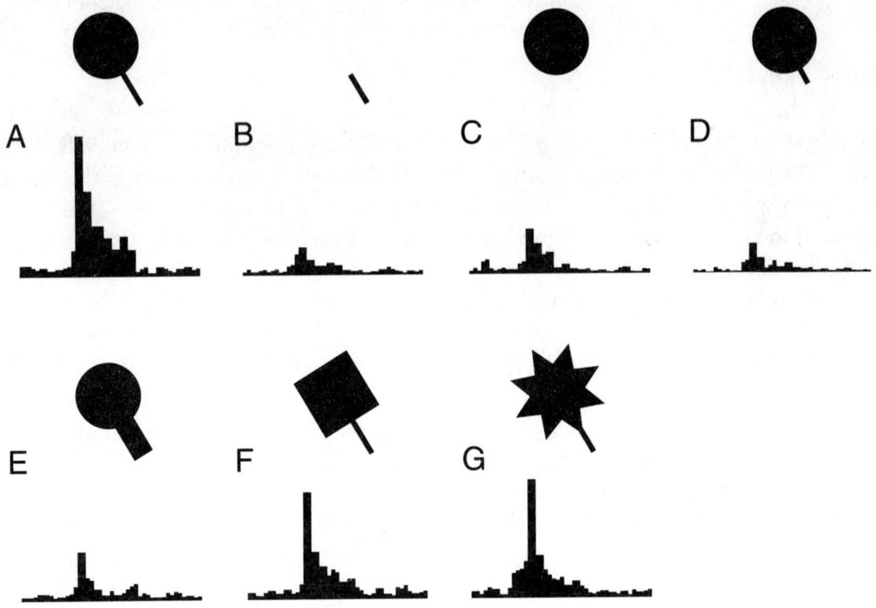

Figure 4.11
Responses of an elaborate cell to various stimuli. This cell responds best to stimulus A—a circular disc with a thin bar protruding from it (Tanaka et al., 1991).

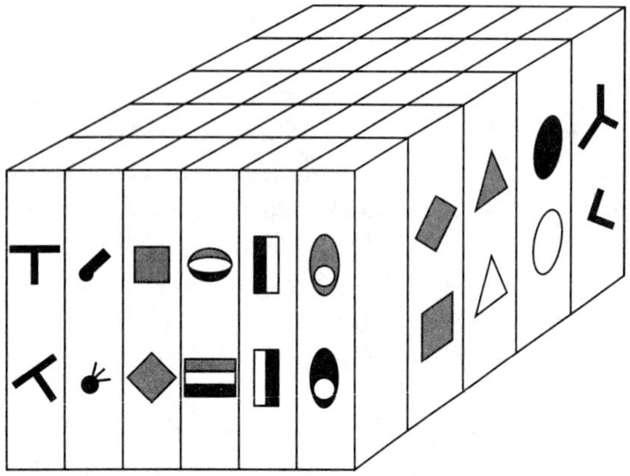

Figure 4.12
Neurons in the same column of IT cortex tend to respond to similar stimuli. This schematic diagram shows a number of columns in IT cortex and the kinds of shapes that cause neurons in each column to respond (M. Young, 1995).

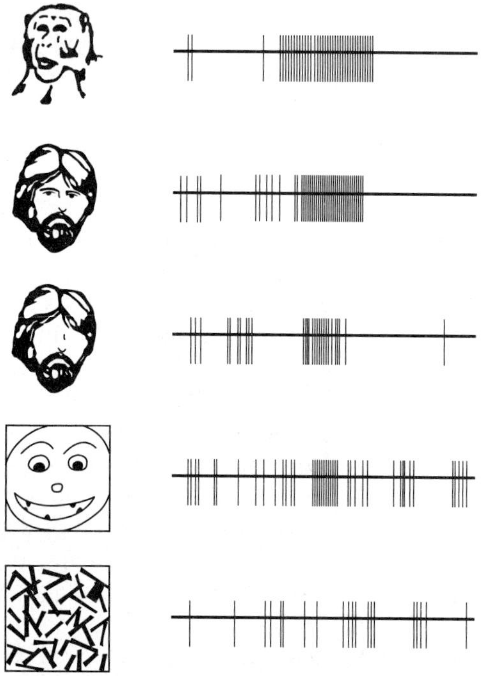

Figure 4.13
Responses of a neuron in a monkey's area IT to various stimuli. This neuron responds best to a full face, as shown by its response to monkey and human faces in the top two records. Removing the eyes or presenting a caricature of a face reduces the response. This neuron does not respond to a random arrangement of lines. (From Bruce, Desimone, & Gross, 1981.)

that continued to respond when stimuli were moved to different areas of the retina. Another property of many of these neurons is that they had large receptive fields, so the cell continued to fire even if the stimulus is moved some distance across the retina (also see Gross & Mishkin, 1977; Gross, Rocha-Miranda, & Bender, 1972; Lueschow, Miller, & Desimore, 1994; Perrett & Oram, 1993).

Neurons That Respond to Faces and Parts of the Body IT cells such as the one that responds as shown in Figure 4.13, respond best to pictures of faces (Gross, 1992, 1994; Rolls, 1992). Figure 4.14 shows the responses of a neuron that responds only to the head. Notice that it responds well to a photograph of a whole person, and to just the person's head, but stops responding when the head is covered up (Wachsmuth, Oram, & Perrett, 1994).

Other cells have been found in IT that respond best to faces that are seen in particular views. These neurons are called **view-specific cells** (Figure 4.15) (Perrett et al., 1992; Tanaka et al., 1991). There are also neurons called **view-invariant cells** that respond equally well to different views of the same face (Figure 4.16) (Perrett & Oram, 1993; Rolls, 1992; Tovee, Rolls, & Azzopardi, 1994).

What emerges from research on IT cells that respond to faces and other complex stimuli, is that there are two classes of cells: (1) size-, location-, and view-*invariant* neurons, which respond to a stimulus even when its size, location, or viewing angle is changed; and (2) size-, location-, and view-*specific* neurons that respond only to specific sizes, locations, and views. We don't know exactly which of these cells, or groups of cells, are responsible for our perception of faces and complex objects. However, most researchers believe that it is unlikely that a particular face or a particular complex object is signaled by the firing of just one highly specific cell, since even those "face cells" that respond best to a specific face also respond to some other faces as well. Apparently, our perception

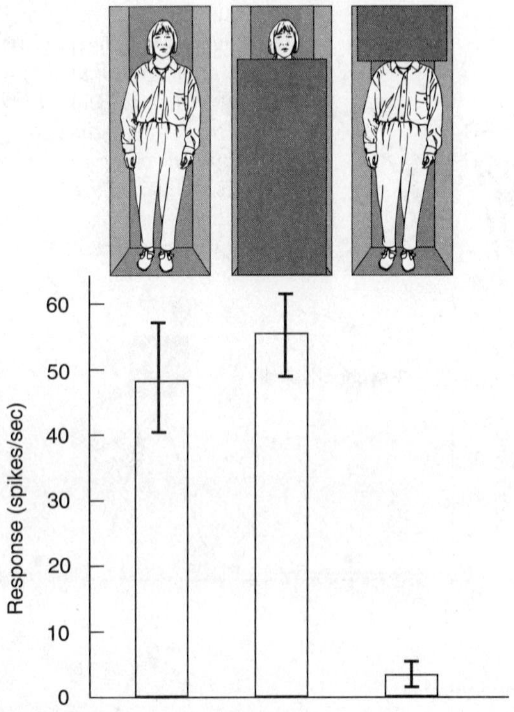

Figure 4.14
Response of a neuron in IT cortex that responds only to a picture of a person's head. Actual stimuli were photographs. (From Wachmuth, Oram, & Perrett, 1994.)

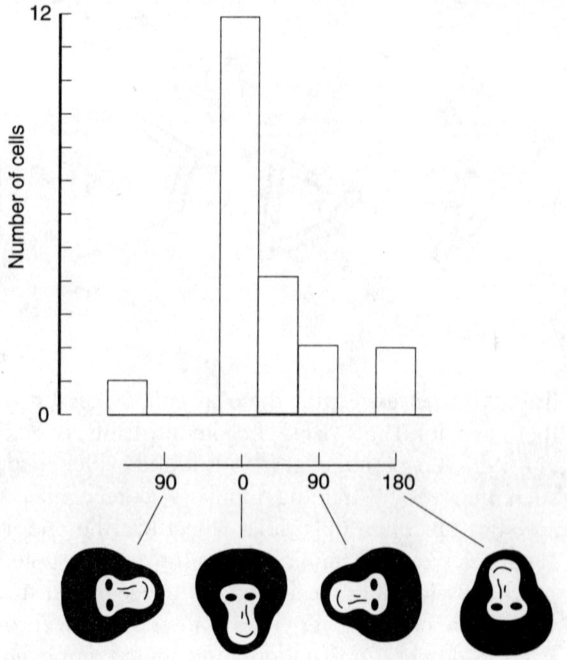

Figure 4.15
These are cells in IT cortex that respond best to a specific view of a face. This graph shows how many cells out of a group of 21 responded best to each of the four orientations of the monkey face shown. (From Tanaka et al., 1991.)

of faces is determined by the information provided by the firing of a number of neurons (Gross, 1992; Rolls, 1992; Rolls & Tovee, 1995; Young & Yamane, 1992).

Neurons That Fire Based on Past Experience with an Object The existence of the neurons in IT cortex that respond to faces and other complex objects raises some interesting questions: First, we can ask whether our visual system has evolved so that specialized neurons that respond to common and important stimuli like faces are automatically built into the system. The answer to this question may be yes, since neurons have been discovered in the cortex of 5-week-old infant monkeys that respond best to faces (Rodman, Scalaidhe, & Gross, 1993).

We can also ask whether there are neurons that gain their ability to respond to specific stimuli

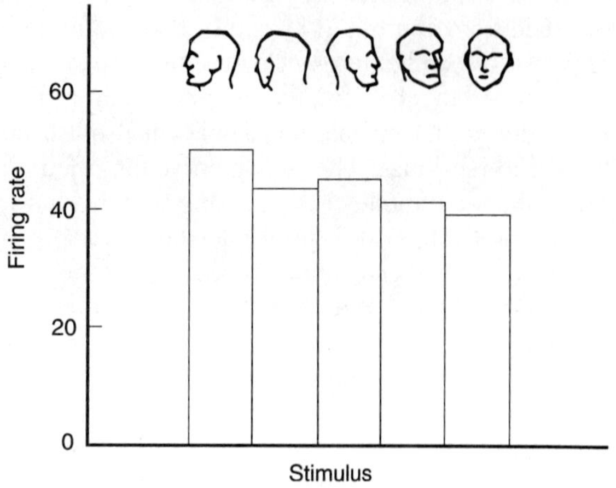

Figure 4.16
Response of a view-invariant neuron that responds with about the same firing rate to different views of a face. (From Perrett & Oram, 1993.)

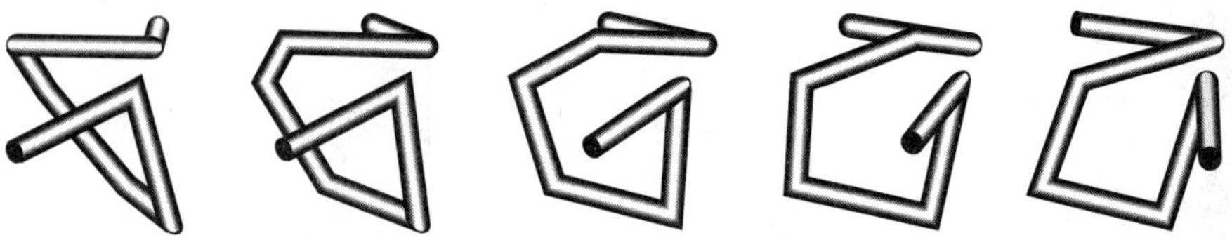

Figure 4.17
A number of different views of one of the stimuli used by Logothetis and Pauls (1995). Monkeys were trained to recognize one ot these views and were then tested to see how well they recognized the training view and others as well.

through experience with these stimuli. Nikos Logothetis and Jon Pauls (1995; Logothetis, Pauls, & Poggio, 1995; Logothetis et al., 1994) found evidence for such neurons by training monkeys to recognize a specific view of an unfamiliar object like the one in Figure 4.17. After training, the monkey was tested psychophysically to see how well it recognized this view of the object, other views of the same object rotated to different orientations, and some completely different objects. The results, shown in Figure 4.18a, indicate that the monkey recognized the view which it had been trained to recognize, and that recognition declined gradually as the object was rotated from this preferred view.

When Logothetis and Pauls repeated the same procedure, but instead of testing psychophysically, recorded from neurons in IT cortex, they found neurons that responded to objects that the monkey had been trained to recognize, but found no neurons that responded to objects that the monkey had not been trained to recognize. The tuning curve for a neuron that responded to one of the training stimuli, shown in Figure 4.18b, is very similar to the psychophysically determined recognition curve.

Logothetis and Pauls concluded that these neurons must have become "tuned" to the stimulus when it was seen during training. Thus, some cells in IT cortex can apparently "learn from experience" to fire to unusual objects like Logothetis and Paul's stimuli (or perhaps, in the monkey's natural environment, to configurations of tree branches), that the animal needs to recognize. Other cells in IT cortex, like the infant-monkey face cells, have a built-in preference for faces.

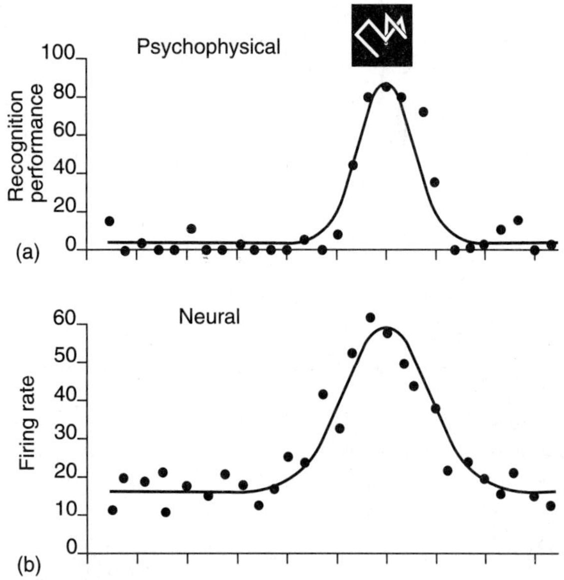

Figure 4.18
(a) A monkey's ability to recognize different views of an object. The monkey was trained on the view shown (0-degree orientation) and was then tested to see how well it recognized the object when it was shown in a number of different views. (b) Neural response of a neuron in a monkey's IT cortex to different views of the same object. The key result of this experiment is that the neural curve is similar to the curve for recognition performance. (From Logothetis & Pauls, 1995.)

The experiments we have described on MT and IT cortex support the idea that these structures are modules designed to serve different perceptions. It is also possible that smaller modules may exist within these structures that are specialized for seeing even more specific kinds of stimuli.

Modularity Demonstrated by the Effects of Cortical Damage in Humans

Another way to demonstrate modularity is by studying human patients who have suffered cortical damage. We've already seen in our description of patient D.F.'s visual form agnosia, how cortical damage can eliminate some functions while sparing others. Let's now look at some additional examples of dissociations caused by cortical damage.

Blindsight: Pointing to Something That Can't Be "Seen"

The behavior of patients with cortical damage can often reveal components of a system that are not obvious in the normal person (Parkin, 1996). For example, let's consider the case of D.B., a 34-year-old male who from an early age suffered from severe migraine headaches. These headaches eventually became so incapacitating that he had to have an operation to remove part of his striate cortex. The operation succeeded in reducing his migraines, but left D.B. with an area of blindness, called a **scotoma,** that covered about one-quarter of his field of vision. The extent of D.B.'s scotoma was measured by a technique called **perimetry,** in which a small spot of light is presented to different areas of the visual field, and the patient indicates whether he or she can see it. Figure 4.19 indicates the results of these perimetry measurements for D.B., with the black area indicating the extent of the scotoma.

When Lawrence Weiskrantz studied D.B.'s perception, he found that although D.B. claimed that he was unable to see anything in his scotoma, he was able to accomplish a number of tasks that indicated some residual vision (Weiskrantz, 1987; Weiskrantz et al., 1974). When Weiskrantz flashed a test spot in various areas of D.B.'s scotoma and told him to point to the light, D.B. claimed he could see no lights, yet he was able to point quite accurately to the light's location (Figures 4.20 and 4.21). When he saw the results, D.B. expressed surprise, because he said that he was just guessing. Upon further questioning about his perceptions, he said that he sometimes made his judgments based on a "feeling" he had on a particular trial, but that this feeling wasn't the same thing as seeing.

D.B. could also indicate whether an X or an O was presented within his scotoma. For this task, he reported that sometimes he experienced feelings like "jagged" or "smooth" that, again, were not the same thing as actually seeing an object. D.B's condition has been called **blindsight,** or "vision without awareness," because he is able to carry out certain perceptual tasks

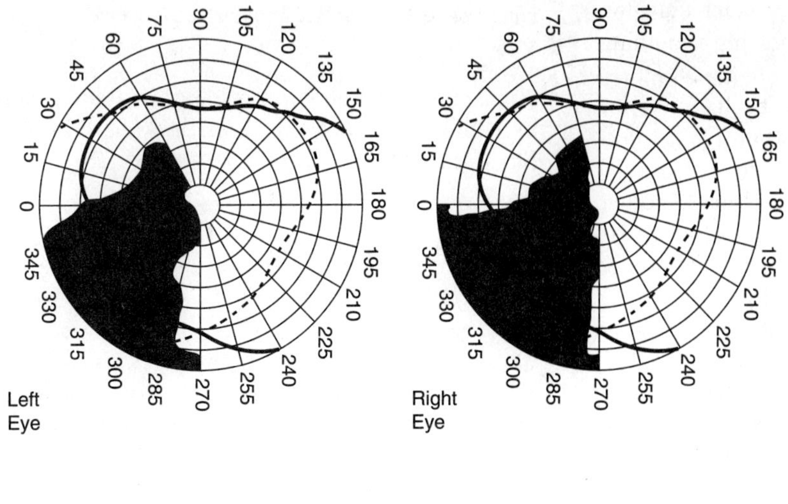

Figure 4.19
D.B.'s visual field defect as measured by perimetry. The dark areas indicate that D.B. did not report seeing the test light when it was presented to the lower left quadrant of the visual field for each eye. (From Weiskrantz, 1987.)

Figure 4.20
A person with blindsight pointing to a spot of light. Although the person claims he can't see the light, he is able to point to where it is. In an actual testing situation, the person would rest his or her head on a chin rest for more accurate positioning.

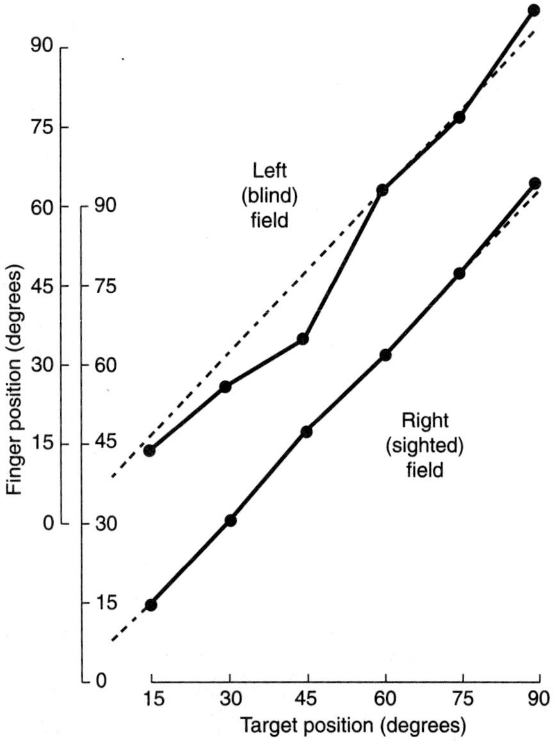

Figure 4.21
The top data points indicate where D.B. pointed when a target light was in different positions in the blind area of his visual field. Perfect accuracy is indicated by the dashed line. Although D.B.'s performance was not perfect, it was close to the dashed line over a wide range of orientations, even though he claimed he could not see the light. The bottom data points are for lights presented to the sighted area of D.B.'s visual field. In this case his pointing accuracy was almost perfect. (From Weiskrantz et al., 1974.)

even though he is blind as measured by perimetry. Blindsight is an example of **covert awareness,** an awareness about the stimulus that appears to be happening under the surface of conscious perception. The fact that D.B. had some awareness even in his "blind" areas, means that structures other than the striate cortex must be responsible for his remaining perceptual capacities.

One of these structures might be the superior colliculus, a structure that is important for controlling eye movements and which receives about 10 percent of the fibers that leave the retina. Another structure might be the extrastriate cortex, which receives some inputs directly from the retina (Milner & Goodale, 1995). Apparently the striate cortex is necessary for conscious awareness, but other visual areas also provide visual information. This becomes obvious in people like D.B. who have lost part of their striate cortex. It is likely, however, that these additional visual areas are probably providing visual information to people with normal vision as well (Cowey & Stoerig, 1991).

Visual Agnosia: Seeing without Recognizing

On page 108 we described how D.F.'s visual agnosia impaired her ability to recognize common objects and judge orientations. There are many different kinds of agnosia, all involving some deficiency in recognition, but differing in various details, depending on where the brain damage has occurred. The case of H.J.A. (Humphreys & Riddoch, 1987) illustrates another problem sometimes experienced by people with agnosia—they can perceive components of an object, but can't grasp the relation between the parts and integrate them into the perception of a whole object. For example, Figure 4.22 shows simple line drawings that H.J.A. described as follows:

> **Carrot:** "I have not the glimmerings of an idea. The bottom point seems solid and the other bits are feathery. It does not seem logical unless it is some sort of brush."
> **Nose:** "A soup ladle."
> **Onion:** "I'm completely lost at the moment. You don't put it on. It has sharp bits at the bottom like a fork. It could be a necklace of sorts."

These responses, plus the results of other tests, led Humphreys and Riddoch to conclude that D.B. sees objects in terms of their individual features but lacks the processing module that binds these individual features together into a coherent perception of a whole object.

Prosopagnosia: The Inability to Recognize Faces

People with a condition called **prosopagnosia** have difficulty recognizing faces of familiar people. Even very familiar faces are affected, so a person with prosopagnosia might not be able to recognize close friends, members of the family, and even the reflection of their own face in the a mirror (Burton et al., 1991; Hecaen & Angelerques, 1962; Parkin, 1996).

Does the existence of this disorder mean that there is a module that is specifically dedicated to the perception of faces? This is a controversial question, because although there are some cases in which the person's recognition problem seems restricted mainly to faces, like the farmer who was unable to recognize human faces, but who could accurately recognize the individual sheep in his flock (McNeil & Warrington, 1993), there are other cases in which the person's inability to recognize faces is accompanied by problems in recognizing other easily confused objects as well.

Whether or not there is a module that is specialized for recognizing faces, the existence of prosopagnosia supports the idea that there is a visual mechanism for recognizing complex objects, that operates separately from the mechanism responsible for basic sight. Prosopagnosia also provides evidence for the phenomenon of covert awareness. For example, when Tranel and Damasio (1985, 1988) showed a patient with prosopagnosia a series of familiar and unfamiliar faces, their skin resistance changed more in response to the familiar than to the unfamiliar faces, even though they consciously recognized none of the faces (also see Bauer, 1984).

Covert awareness in prosopagnosia has also been demonstrated behaviorally. For example, some patients learn to associate a name with a picture of a face more rapidly for faces of well-known people, such as politicians or film stars, than for faces of unfamiliar people, even though they can't recognize the well-known faces (DeHaan, Young, & Newcombe, 1987; Farah, 1992).

This covert awareness indicates that the prosopagnosic patients are processing some information about the faces, without being aware that they are doing so. They can see the faces, they possess some information about the identity of the faces, but can't access this information for the purposes of recognition. Thus,

Figure 4.22
Three of the line drawings that patient H.J.A. could not name. (From Humphreys & Riddoch, 1987.)

covert awareness in prosopagnosia provides further evidence of multiple perceptual mechanisms in the cortex.

Visual Attention: Visual and Neural Selectivity

The assumption behind our discussion so far has been that when a stimulus is imaged on the retina, it is processed through a sequence of structures and, if our visual system isn't damaged, at the end of this processing we perceive the stimulus. But this way of thinking about neural processing and perception doesn't tell the whole story, because people usually don't sit passively as stimuli are presented. Instead, they take an active role in their perception by seeking out stimuli that are of interest to them. This process of seeking out stimuli is called **attention.**

The Selectivity of Attention

Attention is important both because it directs our receptors to stimuli we want to perceive, and also because it influences the way information is processed once it stimulates the receptors (Wallace, 1994). The effect of attention on processing has perceptual consequences that in some cases enhances perception of the stimuli to which we are paying attention, and decreases our awareness of stimuli we are ignoring. Thus, when Ellen (from Chapter 1) selectively focuses her attention on Bill, she becomes not only more aware of him but she also becomes less aware of other objects or parts of the scene. She clearly sees Bill's smile and can detect subtle nuances in his facial expression, but even as she avoids bumping into other people as she negotiates her way toward him, she is hardly aware of most of the activity that is going on around her.

This selective property of attention is what William James (1890/1981) was referring to when he said that

> Millions of items . . . are present to my senses which never properly enter my experience. Why? Because they have no interest for me. My experience is what I agree to attend to. . . . Everyone knows what attention is. It is the taking possession by the mind, in clear and vivid form, of one out of what seem several simultaneously possible objects of trains of thought. . . . It implies withdrawal from some things in order to deal effectively with others.

Thus, normal attention, according to James, causes the things to which we attend to become clearer and more vivid and causes things to which we don't attend to never enter experience. An example of a situation in which an unattended item doesn't enter experience occurs when a person looks at something while thinking about something totally unrelated to what they are looking at. What often happens is that the person becomes unaware of the object at which they are looking. Have you ever realized, while reading a book, that your mind has been wandering and you can't remember the last few sentences you've read? This is essentially what William James was saying when he referred to unattended items that never enter experience.

This effect—taking in information about attended stimuli, but not about unattended stimuli—has been demonstrated in numerous experiments. When Irvin Rock and Daniel Gutman (1981) showed subjects two superimposed forms, one red and one green (Figure 4.23), and had them attend to just one of them, they found that subjects later recognized the one to which they were paying attention, but did not remember the one to which they were not attending (also see Goldstein & Fink, 1981). Paying attention is, therefore, more than just a way to orient the receptors toward stimuli that are interesting. In Rock and Gutman's experiment, the subjects were looking right at one of the objects, but in the absence of attention, they didn't remember seeing it just a short time later.

We are aware of the things toward which we direct our attention and may be unaware of the things we ignore. This perceptual phenomenon has been studied physiologically in experiments that show that there is a connection between paying attention and neural responding.

Figure 4.23
Two of the superimposed forms used by Rock and Gutman (1981). One was red and the other green.

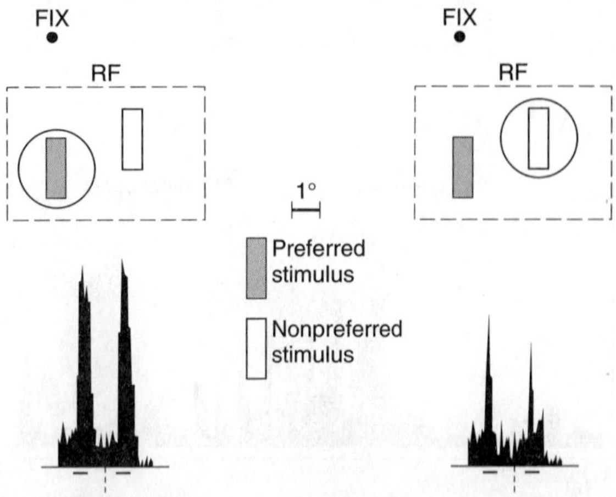

Figure 4.24
The effect of selective attention on the response of a neuron in area V4; the receptive field (RF) is indicated by the dashed line. The monkey kept its eyes fixed on the dot. When the monkey paid attention to the neuron's preferred stimulus, as indicated by the "spotlight" on the left display, the neuron fired (see records at the lower left). When the monkey paid attention to the nonpreferred stimulus, as indicated by the spotlight on the right display, the neuron fired less vigorously (see the record at the lower right). (Adapted from Moran & Desimone, 1985.)

Visual Attention and Neural Responding

In one of the early experiments demonstrating how attention affects neural responding, Jeffry Moran and Robert Desimone (1985) trained monkeys to keep their eyes fixated on a dot such as the one shown in Figure 4.24 and, as they recorded from a neuron in area V4, in the ventral stream, simultaneously presented two stimuli that fell within the neuron's receptive field. One of these stimuli, the preferred stimulus, was a color that caused the V4 neuron to fire vigorously, and the other, the nonpreferred stimulus, was a color that caused little or no response in the neuron.

While recording from this V4 neuron, Moran and Desimone signaled the monkey to pay attention to either the preferred or the nonpreferred stimulus on different trials. The results show that the stimulus to which the monkey attended had a large effect on the neuron's response (Figure 4.24): Attention to the preferred stimulus caused a strong response, and attention to the nonpreferred stimulus caused a weaker response. The important thing to remember about this experiment is that the monkey never moved its eyes, so the *stimulus always remained on the same place on the retina.* The larger response in the left record was therefore due solely to the monkey's attentional state. Moran and Desimone also obtained similar results for neurons in the IT cortex.

A more recent experiment by Carol Colby and coworkers (1995) shows that attention also affects the firing of neurons in the dorsal stream. The monkey keeps its eyes fixated on the dot marked FIX in the display in Figure 4.25a and a light is presented off to the right to the receptive field of a neuron in the parietal cortex. In the "fixation" condition, the monkey doesn't have to pay attention to the light, but in the "fixation and attention" condition the monkey has to pay attention to the light since it has to signal any time the light dims in intensity—an event that occurs every so often when the light is on.

The response of the parietal cortex neuron is shown for both conditions in Figures 4.25a and b. The difference is striking—even though the monkey is always looking at the fixation point and the stimuli flashed to the receptive field to the right are exactly

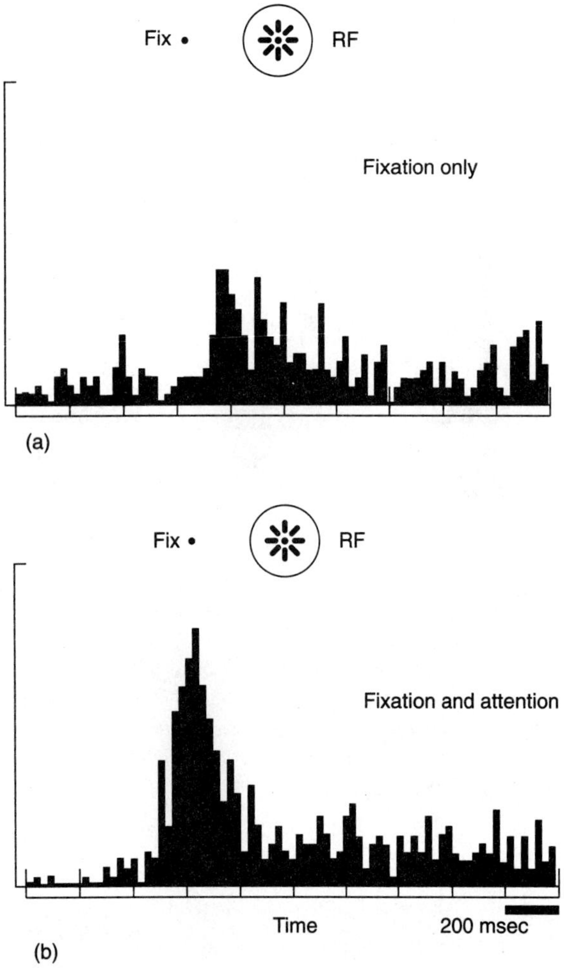

Figure 4.25
The results of Colby et al.'s (1995) experiment showing how attention affects the responding of a neuron in a monkey's parietal cortex. In (a) the monkey fixates on the fixation dot (FIX) while a light is flashed in the neuron's receptive field (RF) off to the right. In (b) the monkey fixates on the fixation dot and simultaneously pays attention to the light in the neuron's receptive field. The records below indicate that the neuron fired more when the monkey was paying attention.

the same for both conditions, the neuron's response is larger when the monkey is paying attention.

The results of these experiments, and many others, show that attention affects the processing of the stimulus in many different places in the visual system by creating a greater neural response to the attended stimulus compared to the unattended stimulus.

The Binding Problem: Combining Information from Different Areas

We have painted a picture of a perceptual process in which neural activity is simultaneously occurring in many areas of the brain. As Ellen looks at Bill, cells sensitive to faces and complex forms are firing in the IT cortex, cells sensitive to movement are firing in the MT cortex, and cells sensitive to color are firing in area V4. But Ellen does not perceive Bill as separated form, movement, and color perceptions. She experiences an integrated perception of Bill, with all of these components occurring together.

This raises an important question: How are Bill's various qualities combined, so that Ellen perceives a unified perception of him rather than separate, independent qualities? This problem of combining information that is being signaled in physically separated areas of the visual system is called the **binding problem.**

To begin dealing with the binding problem, we return to our discussion from Chapter 3 of how neurons in the striate cortex respond to a long bar with a particular orientation. We saw that presentation of the bar to the retina causes activity in each of the hypercolumns that process information from the receptors that the bar stimulates, so the electrical picture of a long bar oriented at 45 degrees might look like Figure 3.33. Three hypercolumns are activated and within each of these hypercolumns there is activity in the 45-degree orientation columns.

The way the bar is represented—split up into electrical activity in separated places in the cortex—raises an important question: How is the information in each of these areas combined to result in a perception of the whole bar? This is the binding problem for the bar because it asks how the separated areas of electrical signals generated by the bar are related to one another and combined (or bound together) to create a signal that stands for a single long bar.

One approach to solving the binding problem starts with evidence that these columns are connected with each other by a network of neurons (Gilbert & Wiesel, 1989). This communication between hypercolumns is a first step toward solving the problem, but we need to go a step further, by asking what kinds of messages might be shared between columns.

A description of the possible nature of the column-to-column messages has been proposed in a hypothesis by a number of German researchers (Engel et al., 1991; Engel, Konig, & Singer, 1991; Engel et al., 1992; Gray & Singer, 1989; Singer et al., 1993). Their hypothesis is that an object is represented in the visual system by a group of neurons called a **cell assembly.** An assembly becomes activated when the firing of the neurons in the assembly generates oscillatory responses (alternating bursts of high and low rates of firing) that become synchronized with one another. Evidence for this idea is provided by the results of an experiment described by Andreas Engel and his co-workers (1992).

Engel used two electrodes to simultaneously record activity from two neurons, separated by 7 mm in the striate cortex, that both responded best to vertically oriented bars. Figure 4.26 shows three different ways that stimuli were presented to the neurons'

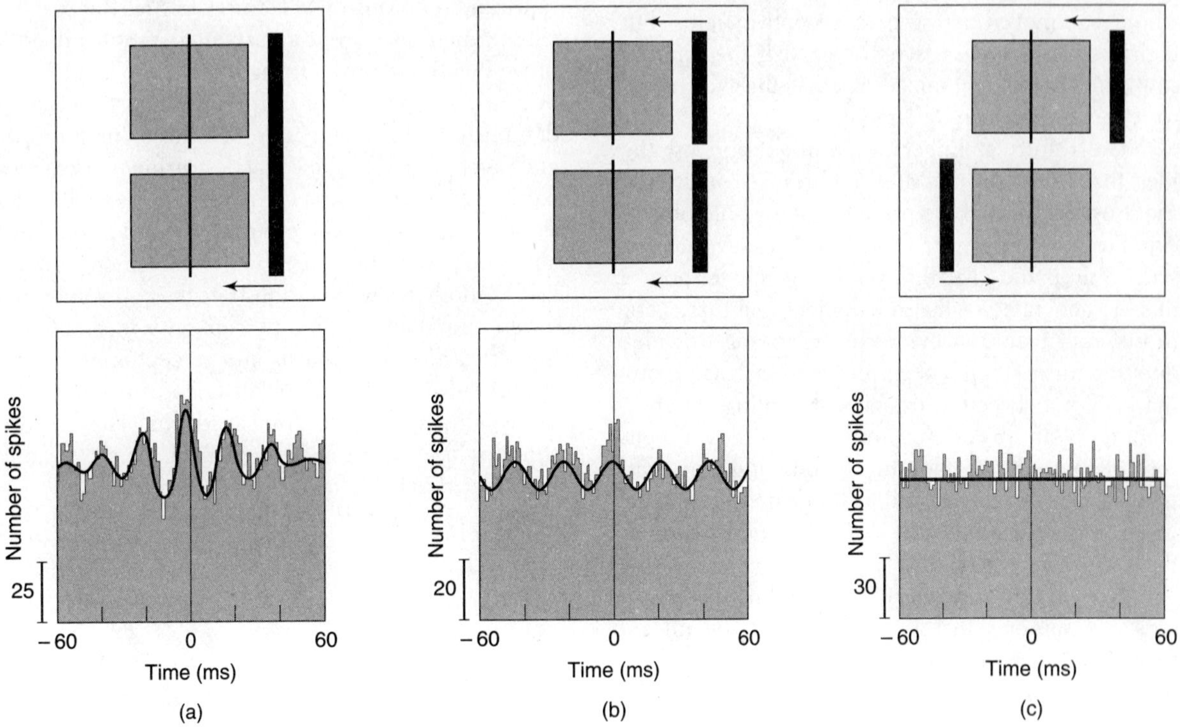

Figure 4.26
The top diagrams show the following three ways that a bar was swept across the receptive fields of two neurons in the cat's striate cortex: (a) the whole bar; (b) the bar split in two; and (c) the bar split and the parts moved in opposite directions. Each neuron responded with an oscillatory response (one that alternates between bursts of high and low firing). The bottom diagrams are cross-correlograms for each stimulus condition. Larger peaks and troughs, as in (a), indicate that the oscillating firing patterns generated by the two neurons were synchronized with each other. (Adapted from Engel et al., 1992.)

receptive fields (top records) and shows plots called cross-correlograms (bottom graphs) that indicate whether the neurons were firing in synchrony with each other.

Figure 4.26a shows the cross-correlogram when a single long bar was swept across the two receptive fields. The wavy record means that the neurons both fired in bursts separated by quieter periods (oscillatory responding) and that the two neurons' bursts were synchronized. When two smaller bars were swept across the receptive fields, as in Figure 4.26b, the synchronization of the two neurons' responses became weaker. When the two bars were moved in opposite directions, as in Figure 4.26c, the flatness of the cross-correlogram indicates that the synchronization had disappeared. In other words, the firing of these two neurons oscillated in a synchronized manner when a whole bar moved across their receptive fields, but their response was less synchronized if the bar was split, and not synchronized at all if the two halves were moving in opposite directions.

The results of Engel's experiment support the idea that responses that are synchronized in two or more neurons signal the presence of a whole object. Another way to describe this result is to say that this synchrony is the glue that binds together responses that are generated by the same object, but that occur in different places in the cortex. Carrying this idea one step further, it has been proposed that synchrony may occur between neurons representing different qualities of an object. According to this idea, if neurons that respond to color, movement, and shape fire in synchrony with each other, this synchronized firing would indicate that all three qualities belong to the same object (Stryker, 1989).

This idea that synchrony is a "binding" agent is a controversial one that is not accepted by all researchers, and while it is supported by a number of experiments (also see Brosch, Bauer, & Eckhorn, 1997; Neuenschwander & Singer, 1996), the final explanation of the binding problem may be quite different from this one. The important point is that any object causes activity in many places in the brain, so before we can say we understand the connection between neural responses and perception, we need to discover how all of these many separated signals somehow combine their information to create our perception of meaningful objects.

Something to Consider: Determining That Neural Responding Is Related to Perception

We have seen that neural responding is related to various kinds of *stimuli*—a face stimulus causes neurons in IT cortex to fire; dots moving in a particular direction cause neurons in MT cortex to fire. But just because a neuron fires to a particular stimulus doesn't prove that the neuron's firing is related to an animal's or a person's *perception* of the stimulus. One way to demonstrate this connection between neural activity and perception is to show that destroying neurons in a particular structure affects perception, as when lesioning neurons in MT cortex decreased a monkey's ability to perceive the direction of movement (Figure 4.10). Another way to demonstrate the connection between neural activity and perception is to simultaneously measure neural firing and perception.

David Leopold and Nikos Logothetis (1996) did an experiment that accomplished this. They used a stimulus like the one in Figure 4.27 in which a grating that slanted to the left was presented to a monkey's left eye and a grating slanted to the right was presented to

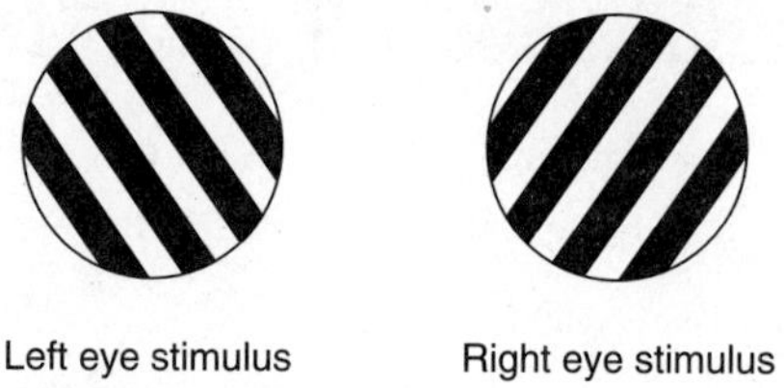

Figure 4.27
The types of grating stimuli that were simultaneously presented to the left and right eyes of the monkey in Leopold and Logothetis' (1996) binocular rivalry experiment.

the right eye. This situation, when two very different images are presented to the same places on the left and right eyes, causes **binocular rivalry**—the observer's perception alternates back and forth between the two images—so first one orientation is seen and then, a few seconds later, the other orientation is seen.

Leopold and Logothetis trained the monkeys to press a lever to indicate which orientation it was seeing, and then recorded from neurons in area V4. They found that about a third of the neurons they studied changed their firing in accord with what the monkey reported it was seeing. For example, a particular neuron might fire well when the left eye image was being perceived, but would respond poorly when the right eye image was perceived.

This demonstration of a connection between neural firing and perception is particularly interesting because at all times during the experiment the *stimulus did not change on the retina.* The image of the left grating remained steady on the left retina and the image of the right grating remained steady on the right retina. However, when the monkey's *perception* changed, the firing of the neurons changed as well.

This demonstration of a close relationship between neural firing and perception supports the idea of a connection between the firing of V4 neurons and the monkey's perception of the grating. This type of evidence—collected by measuring perception and neural responding simultaneously—enables us to be much more sure of a connection between physiology and perception than the usual situation in which physiological and perceptual responding are measured separately.

Neurons That Respond to Vision and Touch

In this chapter we have focused on neurons that respond to visual stimuli. Neurons have also been discovered that respond both to visual stimuli and to energy that stimulates other senses as well. These neurons are called **bimodal** (two senses) **neurons** or **multimodal** (many senses) **neurons.**

An example of bimodal neurons that respond to both visual and tactile stimuli is provided by an experiment in which Michael Graziano and Charles Gross (1995) recorded from neurons in an area of a monkey's parietal lobe that responds to tactile stimulation. They found a neuron that responded when they covered the animal's eyes and lightly stroked its face with a cotton swab (Figure 4.28). But this same neuron also responded to visual stimulation. Graziano and Gross discovered this when they uncovered the monkey's eyes and found that the neuron began responding as they moved the swab toward the face, beginning when the swab was about 10 cm away. Further study showed that this neuron responded when the swab was moving anywhere within a three-dimensional area attached to the tactile receptive field.

One of the interesting properties of this bimodal cell is that no matter where the monkey moved its head, the visual area moved with it. Cells like this were also found on the hand. Figure 4.29 shows the tactile receptive field of a cell that responded to touching the hand (shaded area). This cell's visual receptive field is in the circle surrounding the hand, and just as for the face neuron, when the monkey moved, the visual receptive field followed the body. So, when the hand is moved to the right (Figure 4.29b) the visual receptive field followed along.

This is a departure from the way visual cells usually respond. Remember that we defined a neuron's visual receptive field as the "area of retina which, when stimulated, affects the neuron's firing." But for

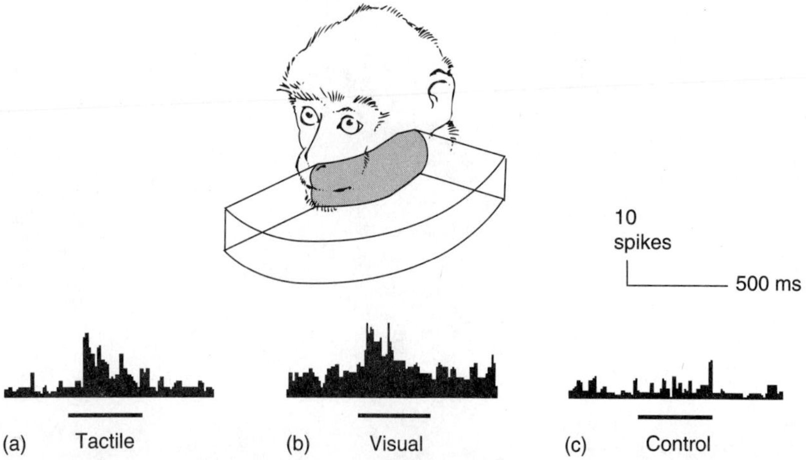

Figure 4.28
Responses of a neuron in the monkey's parietal cortex to (a) stroking of the shaded area of the monkey's face, (b) movement of an object toward the monkey's face within the area shown, and (c) movement of the object as in b, but with the monkey's eyes covered. (From Graziano & Gross, 1995.)

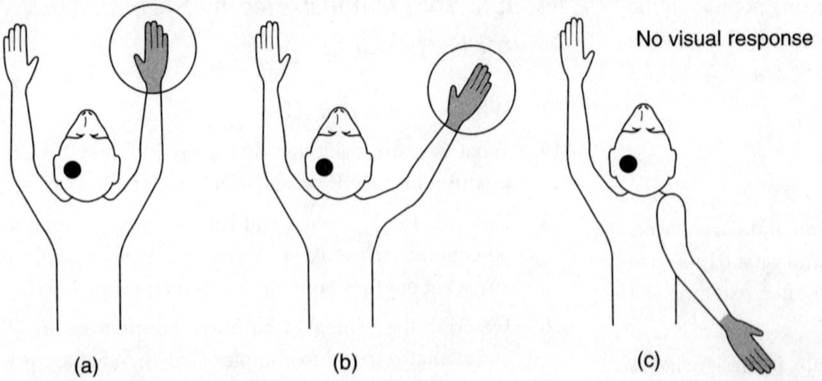

Figure 4.29
Graziano and Gross (1995) found a bimodal cell that responded both to tactile stimulation of the hand (indicated by shading) and visual stimulation of the area around the hand (indicated by the circle). If the hand was visible as in (a) and (b), the neuron responded to both tactile and visual stimulation. However, when the hand was not visible, the cell responded only to tactile stimulation.

this neuron the area of retina isn't what is important, because when the hand moves, the visual receptive field moves along with it and stimulates a different area of retina. In addition, when the hand moves out of the monkey's field of view, the visual response vanishes (Figure 4.29c). Since these visual receptive fields are based on the part of the body they are associated with, rather than with the area of retina stimulated, they are called **body-centered neurons.**

What do these neurons do? Graziano and Gross suggest that since the receptive fields move as the body moves, these cells could indicate the location of stimuli with respect to the body surface. These kinds of neurons would, therefore, provide useful information to a monkey interacting with the environment, with neurons like the hand neuron being particularly useful for coordinating vision and touch as an animal reaches for an object.

Study Questions

1. Compare the view of visual processing popular in the early 1970s to the conception of visual processing today. (103)

Visual Processing Streams

2. Where do neurons from the magno and parvo layers of the LGN synapse in the cortex and what happens to the signals from these two layers after reaching the cortex? (104)
3. What parts of the body and the brain are designated as "dorsal" and "ventral"? (104)
4. What are the "what" and "where" pathways? Describe both their anatomy and their functions. (104)
5. Describe Ungerleider and Mishkin's experiment that identified the "what" and "where" pathways or streams. (105)
6. What method has been used to confirm the idea of parallel pathways in humans? (105)
7. Are the dorsal and ventral pathways completely separated from one another? (106)
8. Describe Milner and Goodale's proposal that the two streams in the extrastriate cortex should be called the "what" and "how" streams. (107)
9. What is neuropsychology? (107)
10. What is a single dissociation? a double dissociation? What does the existence of each one tell us about the relationship between two functions? (107)
11. Describe the case of patient D.F. What was her condition called? What could she do perceptually? What was she unable to do perceptually? (108)
12. Describe the double dissociation that involves judgment of visual orientation and visual-motor orientation. What can we conclude from this double dissociation? (108)

Modularity Demonstrated by Specialized Neural Responding

13. What is modularity? (109)
14. What is some evidence that areas MT and V4 are modules for specific visual functions? (109)
15. Describe the Newsome and Paré research on motion perception in monkeys. What was their procedure and what did they conclude from their results? (110)
16. Describe the evidence that there are neurons in IT cortex that respond to complex shapes. What are primary cells? What are elaborate cells? (110)
17. What do we mean when we say that neurons in IT cortex are arranged in columns? (112)
18. What is a size-invariant neuron? a location-invariant neuron? (112)
19. What is the advantage of large receptive field size? (112)
20. Describe view-specific and view-invariant face cells. (112)
21. Are faces signaled by the firing of just one highly specific face cell? (112)
22. What conclusion might we draw from the fact that face-selective neurons have been recorded from 5-week-old monkeys? (113)
23. Describe Logothetis and Pauls' experiment, which provided evidence that cells can gain the ability to respond to specific stimuli through experience. Be sure to indicate how physiological and psychophysical data were combined to reach this conclusion. (114)

Modularity Demonstrated by the Effects of Cortical Damage in Humans

24. What is a scotoma? perimetry? (115)
25. What was unusual about D.B.'s perceptions? (115)
26. What is blindsight? covert awareness? (115)

27. Which structures might be responsible for D.B.'s blindsight? (116)

28. Describe the case of H.J.A. What kind of processing module is H.J.A. missing? (117)

29. What is prosopagnosia? What does the existence of prosopagnosia suggest? (117)

30. What is the evidence for covert awareness in prosopagnosia? What does the existence of this covert awareness mean? (117)

Visual Attention: Visual and Neural Selectivity

31. What is attention? What are two functions of attention? (118)

32. Describe Rock and Guttman's experiment. What does it tell us about the function of attention? (118)

33. Describe the Moran and Desimone and the Colby et al. experiments on the effects of attention on neural firing. Understand their procedures and what their results mean. (119)

The Binding Problem: Combining Information from Different Areas

34. What is the binding problem? (120)

35. Describe the solution to the binding problem involving cell assemblies and oscillatory responses proposed by Engel and coworkers. (121)

36. What is the evidence for Engel's proposal? (121)

Something to Consider: Determining That Neural Responding Is Related to Perception

37. If a neuron responds best to a particular stimulus such as a face, does that mean that the neuron's firing is related to an animal's perception of that stimulus? (122)

38. What is binocular rivalry? How was it used by Leopold and Logothetis to demonstrate a connection between neural responding and perception? (123)

Across the Senses: Neurons That Respond to Vision and Touch

39. What is a bimodal neuron? (124)

40. Describe the properties of the neurons that respond to both touch and vision that were studied by Graziano and Gross. (124)

41. What happens to the visual receptive field in Graziano and Gross' bimodal neurons, when the monkey moves different parts of its body? (124)

42. What property of these neurons leads to them being called body-centered neurons? (125)

43. What is a possible function of the monkey's body-centered neurons? (125)

CHAPTERS 1–4

UNDERLYING PRINCIPLES

The story about perception that you have read so far has taken you from the tips of the visual receptors, where visual pigment molecules react to light and trigger the first electrical signals in the visual system, to the extrastriate cortex, where neurons fire to specific shapes, colors, and other visual qualities. In describing the pathway from retina to extrastriate cortex, we have introduced characteristics of the visual system such as receptive fields, columns and maps in the cortex, and connections between physiology and perception. Since these characteristics occur not only in the visual system, but in the other senses as well, we have used them to create eight basic principles that hold across all of the senses. Although there are many differences between the senses, these principles highlight the many things they have in common. These principles are introduced here, both to review what we've done so far and to set the stage for the rest of the book.

THE EIGHT UNDERLYING PRINCIPLES

1. **Selective Receptors** Most individual receptors respond selectively to a restricted range of stimuli. An example of selective receptors:
   - Each type of cone receptor responds to a portion of the visible spectrum (Chapter 2). The cones illustrate that selectivity isn't necessarily narrow. Each cone responds to a range of wavelengths, but responds *best* to light from a particular region of the spectrum.

2. **Receptive Fields/Neural Selectivity** Most neurons (a) have a receptive field—an area on the receptor surface or in space which, when stimulated, influences the neuron's firing; and (b) fire

selectively to a restricted range of stimuli. Examples of receptive fields and neural selectivity:

- The receptive field of a retinal ganglion cell has a center-surround configuration on the surface of the retina. (2)
- Neurons in the striate cortex respond best to edges, movement in specific directions, and lines of specific lengths. (3)
- Some neurons in the parietal lobe have tactile receptive fields on the monkey's skin and visual receptive fields in the space extending outside of the body from this area of skin. (4)

3. **Distributed Response** Each stimulus causes a specific pattern of responding across a number of neurons. This is the distributed approach to sensory coding described in Chapter 3. Examples of distributed response:
   - The coding of line orientation described in Figures 3.36 and 3.37. (3)
   - The code for color vision (Figure 3.34), which we will describe in Chapter 5.
4. **Neural Maps** Neurons are arranged within a structure in an orderly way, based on a specific property. Examples of neural maps:
   - Maps of the retina on the lateral geniculate nucleus and striate cortex, called retinotopic maps. The property for a retinotopic map is location, so neurons that receive signals from adjacent locations in the retina are arranged adjacent to each other in the LGN and cortex. (3)
5. **Columnar Organization** Neurons that respond to specific stimulus properties are arranged in columns. These columns are usually perpendicular to the surface of the structure in which the neurons are located. Examples of columnar organization:
   - Location columns in the lateral geniculate nucleus (3)
   - Location, orientation, ocular dominance columns in striate cortex (3)
   - Columns in inferotemporal cortex that contain neurons that respond to specific types of shapes. (4)
6. **Parallel Pathways** Parallel neural pathways within a sense that are specialized to process information about specific stimulus characteristics. Examples of parallel pathways:
   - The magno and parvo pathways from the retina to the lateral geniculate nucleus and from the LGN to the cortex conduct information about motion (magno) and color, texture, shape, and depth (parvo) (3)
   - The ventral (what) and dorsal (where or how) pathways begin in the striate cortex and extend to the temporal and parietal lobes, respectively. (4)
7. **Physiological Connections with Perception** Physiological processes influence what we perceive. One of the major goals of research in perception is to demonstrate the connections that exist between physiology and perception. Examples of some of these connections:
   - The rates of rod and cone dark adaptation and the regeneration of rod and cone visual pigments (2).
   - Rod and cone spectral sensitivity and the absorption spectra of rod and cone visual pigments. (2)
   - Spatial summation of the rods and high rod sensitivity in the dark. (2)
   - Lack of cone convergence and high cone acuity. (2)
   - Lateral inhibition, Mach bands and simultaneous contrast. (2)
   - The magnification factor in the cortex and the high acuity of the foveal cones. (3)

- Enhanced neural response to attended stimuli. (4)
- Neural firing correlated with stimulus perceived during binocular rivalry. (4)

8. **Cognitive influences** The perceiver's thoughts, past experiences, and the meaning of the stimulus influence perception. Examples of cognitive influences:
   - The rat-man demonstration and Palmer's "kitchen" experiment. (1)
   - What an observer pays attention to is determined by factors such as the observer's interests and demands of the task. (4)

These eight principles were selected because we can find many examples of them within the sense of vision and in the other senses as well. Table 4.2 summarizes the occurence of these principles in the first four chapters.

Although these principles are the ones found most frequently in the first four chapters, there are other principles that could have been included as well. For example, the principle of perceptual organization—the process by which we organize stimuli into meaningful units—occurs in vision (when you organize smaller units, such as the letters in this sentence, into larger units, such as the words you are reading), or in hearing (when you hear certain notes as belonging together in a familiar melody), and in olfaction (when you perceptually group the hundreds of chemicals floating in the kitchen air into the separate smells of coffee and bacon). Thus, as we continue our survey of perception, we will supplement our eight principles with a few others.

Table 4.2
Shaded boxes in each column indicate that the chapter contains one or more examples of the principle on the left.

Principle	Chapter 2: Receptors	Chapter 3: LGN/Cortex	Chapter 4: Higher Processing
1. Selective receptors	■		
2. Receptive fields/ neural selectivity	■	■	■
3. Distributed code		■	■
4. Neural maps		■	
5. Columnar organization		■	■
6. Parallel pathways			■
7. Physiology and perception	■	■	■
8. Cognitive influence	■ Chapter 1		■

To help you identify the basic principles in the chapters that follow, you will be prompted to find examples of the principles by a question at the beginning of the "Study Questions" section at the end of each chapter beginning with Chapter 5. This *Underlying Principles* feature will be repeated following Chapters 10 and 16.

5

PERCEIVING COLOR

CHAPTER CONTENTS

SOME QUESTIONS WE WILL CONSIDER

- Why do blue dots appear after a flashbulb goes off? (139)
- What does someone who is color blind see? (148)
- Does everyone with normal color vision see colors in the same way? (152)

Color is one of the most obvious and pervasive qualities in our environment. We interact with it every time we note the color of a traffic light, when we choose clothes that are color-coordinated, or when we appreciate the lavishly colored brushstrokes of a painting. We pick favorite colors (blue being the most favored; Terwogt & Hoeksma, 1994). We react emotionally to colors (so, not coincidentally, colors are part of our emotional discourse, as in *purple with rage, green with envy,* or *feeling blue*; Terwogt & Hoeksma, 1994; Valdez & Mehribian, 1994), and we imbue colors with special meanings (for example, red meaning danger; purple, royalty; green, ecology). But for all of our involvement with color, we sometimes take it for granted, and just as with our other perceptual abilities, we may not fully appreciate color until we lose our ability to experience it. The depth of this loss for one person is illustrated by the case of Mr. I, a painter who became color blind at the age of 65 after suffering a concussion in an automobile accident:

> In March of 1986, the neurologist Oliver Sacks[1] received an anguished letter from Mr. I, who, identifying himself as a "rather successful artist," described how ever since he had been involved in an automobile accident, he had lost his ability to experience colors, exclaimed with some anguish, that "My dog is gray. Tomato juice is black. Color TV is a hodge-podge . . ."

[1] Dr. Sacks, well known for his elegant writings describing interesting neurological cases, came to public attention when he was played by Robin Williams in the 1995 film *Awakenings.*

In the days following his accident, Mr. I had became more and more depressed. His studio, normally awash with the brilliant colors of his abstract paintings, appeared drab to him, and his paintings, meaningless. Food, now gray, became difficult for him to look at while eating; and sunsets, once seen as rays of red, had become streaks of black against the sky.

Mr. I's color blindness was caused by cortical injury experienced after a lifetime of experiencing color, whereas most cases of total color blindness or of color deficiency (partial color blindness) occur at birth because of the genetic absence of one or more types of cone receptors. Most people who are born color blind are not disturbed by their lack of color perception since they have never known the perception of color, but some of their reports, such as the darkening of reds, are similar to Mr. I's. People with total color blindness often echo Mr. I's complaint that it is sometimes difficult to distinguish one object from another, as when his brown dog, which he could easily see when silhouetted against a light-colored road, became very difficult to perceive when seen against irregular foliage.

Eventually, Mr. I overcame his strong psychological reaction and began creating striking black and white pictures. But his account of his experiences upon losing his ability to perceive color provides an impressive testament to the central place of color in his life. (See Heywood, Cowey, & Newcombe, 1991; Nordby, 1990; Young, Fishman, & Chen, 1980; Zeki, 1990 for additional descriptions of cases of complete color blindness.)

Some Basic Properties of Color

To begin our discussion of color perception, we describe some of its basic properties, beginning with its functions.

Functions of Color Perception

What is color vision for? It certainly adds an aesthetic dimension to our lives, and color serves a signaling function by indicating whether a piece of fruit is ripe or spoiled, or the presence of human emotions such as fear (flushed skin) or embarrassment (a red blush). But perhaps its most important function is to help facilitate **perceptual organization**—the process by which of the world is organized into separated areas. The ability to tell one object from another and especially to see objects against a varied background, such as flowers in a field or individual people in a crowd, is greatly facilitated by the ability to see in color. In fact, this ability is crucial to the survival of many species. Consider, for example, a monkey foraging for fruit in the forest. A monkey with good color vision easily detects red fruit against a green background (Color Plate 2.1a), but a color-blind monkey would find it more difficult to find the fruit (Color Plate 2.1b).

Some researchers have even proposed that monkey and human color vision evolved for the express purpose of detecting fruit in the forest (Mollon, 1989; Walls, 1942). This suggestion sounds reasonable when we consider the difficulty color-blind human observers have when confronted with the seemingly simple task of picking berries. Knut Nordby (1990), a totally color-blind visual scientist who sees the world in shades of gray, described his experience as follows: "Picking berries has always been a big problem. I often have to grope around among the leaves with my fingers, feeling for the berries by their shape" (p. 308). If Nordby's experience, which is similar to Mr. I's difficulty in seeing his dog in foliage, is any indication, a color-blind monkey would have difficulty finding berries or fruit and might be less likely to survive than monkeys with color vision.

Although an inability to perceive color may make it difficult for an animal to obtain food, it is also important to acknowledge that large numbers of animals and a small percentage of people are either partially or totally blind to colors, yet this has not impaired their ability to survive. Looking at color perception in this way, we can conclude that while color endows us with useful abilities, it is also a luxury that may beautify our world, but is not essential for our survival.

Whatever the biological functions of color vision, it has been a topic that has fascinated psychologists and physiologists for centuries. The history of color vision research provides an excellent example of the detective work carried out by the perceptual researchers that we referred to at the beginning of Chapter 1. We will see, as we describe research on color vision, that one of the first questions that was asked was what aspects of the stimulus causes different objects to have different colors. Once researchers figured out that it was the wavelength of light, the next question was how these wavelengths are represented in the nervous system. Since this question was being asked in the middle of the 19th century, before we knew much about the details of neural functioning, answering this question was extremely difficult.

However, the best minds of the century were at work on the problem, including two of the leading scientists of the day, Hermann von Helmholtz and Ewald Hering, and they were able to predict the physiological mechanisms of color vision, based on the result of behavioral experiments. Thus, describing the research of Helmholtz, Hering, and those who followed them provides an excellent opportunity to illustrate how measuring perception can predict physiology. In addition, this chapter illustrates the operation of seven of the eight basic principles we introduced in the *Underlying Principles* section following Chapter 4 (page 128). This chapter, therefore, in addition to teaching the basic principle of color perception, also gives us an opportunity to apply the basic principles that appeared in Chapters 1 through 4.

Describing Color Experience

To describe our experience of color, we will first distinguish between the two types of color associated with the rods and the cones, and then ask two questions: (1) How many colors can we see? and (2) Are there "basic" colors?

Chromatic and Achromatic Color Imagine the following situation: You awaken early in the morning about 30 minutes before sunrise, and see only a hint of light in the sky. As you look out the window, you see only fuzzy, ill-defined grayish forms. Even though you know the trees outside are green and the flowers are red, yellow, lavender, and orange, you see none of these colors. Gray is your predominant perception (Color Plate 2.2a). However, as the sun rises and the sky lightens, your perceptions begin to shift from shades of gray to varied colors. The trees' leaves become green, and the flowers take on their familiar hues. In addition, another change occurs: Shapes that initially appeared fuzzy and ill-defined now have sharp outlines (Color Plate 2.2b).

This change in perception from fuzzy grays to sharply defined reds, greens, and yellows is caused by the shift from rod vision to cone vision that occurs as light intensity is increased. This perceptual shift illustrates distinction between achromatic colors and chromatic colors. White, black, and shades of gray are **achromatic colors.** Blue, red, green, and yellow are examples of **chromatic colors.** Another term for chromatic color is **hue,** but this term is rarely used in everyday language. We usually say, "The color of the fire engine is red" rather than "The hue (or chromatic color) of the fire engine is red." Therefore, throughout the rest of this book, we will use the word *color* to mean "chromatic color" or "hue," and we will use the term *achromatic color* to refer to white, gray, or black.

In addition to illustrating the difference between achromatic and chromatic color, the perceptual shift that occurs with the change from rod vision to cone vision raises an important question about the relationship between perception and neural processing: What is it about the neural processing in the rod and cone systems that accounts for the fact that our vision is achromatic with the rods and chromatic with the cones? We will return to this question later in the chapter.

How Many Colors Can We See? One approach to the question "How many colors can we see?" is to start at one end of the visible spectrum (Color Plate 1.1) and increase the wavelength until the observer indicates that he or she can discriminate a difference in color. When we do this, we find that observers can discriminate about 200 steps in the visible spectrum (Gouras, 1991a). We can multiply these 200 discriminable colors in two ways. First, we can vary the intensity of each step. Changing the intensity usually changes the brightness of the color, and if we slowly increase the intensity of one color, we can distinguish about 500 steps of brightness. Second, we can vary the *saturation* of each step. **Saturation** is inversely related to the amount of whiteness in a color—that is, the more saturated a color, the less whiteness it contains. Thus, if we start with a 640-nanometer (nm) light, which appears red, and then add white to it, we say that the resulting pink color is less saturated than the original red. Taking into account that each of the 200 discriminable colors has up to 500 values of brightness and 20 values of saturation, we calculate that we can discriminate about $200 \times 500 \times 20 = 2$ million different colors (Gouras, 1991a).

Another approach to determining the number of colors we can see is to determine how many names for colors there are. We are exposed to names such as "crushed strawberry," "azure blue," "Kelly green," and "Chinese red" by the worlds of advertising, paint manufacturing, and cosmetics. Although the ingenious names invented to describe different shades of paint, lipstick, floor tile, and fabric are far from 2 million, the number of such names is still impressively high. One compilation, published by the National Bureau of Standards, lists 7,500 different color names (Judd & Kelly, 1965). However, even 7,500 are far too many colors for us to deal with, so color vision researchers focus on just a few basic colors.

What Are the Basic Colors?

Research shows that we can describe all the colors we can discriminate by using the terms *red, yellow, green, blue,* and their combinations (Abramov & Gordon, 1994; Hurvich, 1981). When people are presented with many different colors and are asked to describe them, they can describe all of them if they are allowed to use all four terms, but they can't if one of these is omitted. Furthermore, other colors, such as orange, violet, purple, and brown, are not needed to achieve these descriptions (Fuld, Wooten, & Whalen, 1981; Quinn, Rosano, & Wooten, 1988). Thus, red, yellow, green, and blue are considered to be basic colors by color researchers.

Figure 5.1 and Color Plate 2.3 show the four basic colors arranged in a circle, so that each is perceptually similar to the one next to it. Red, yellow, green, and blue are considered basic not only because all of the colors in the color circle can be described in terms of these colors, but for other reasons as well. Cross-cultural studies show that, although different cultures vary in the number of terms used to describe colors, the sequence of color terms always enters the language in the sequence shown in Figure 5.2. All cultures use names that stand for the equivalent of black and white, and red, yellow, green, and blue are added before any others (Berlin & Kay, 1969; Boynton & Olson, 1987, 1990). After sifting through all of the evidence regarding the names people assign to different colors, researchers have concluded that only the terms in Figure 5.2 are used consistently by people, and that there must therefore be a universal,

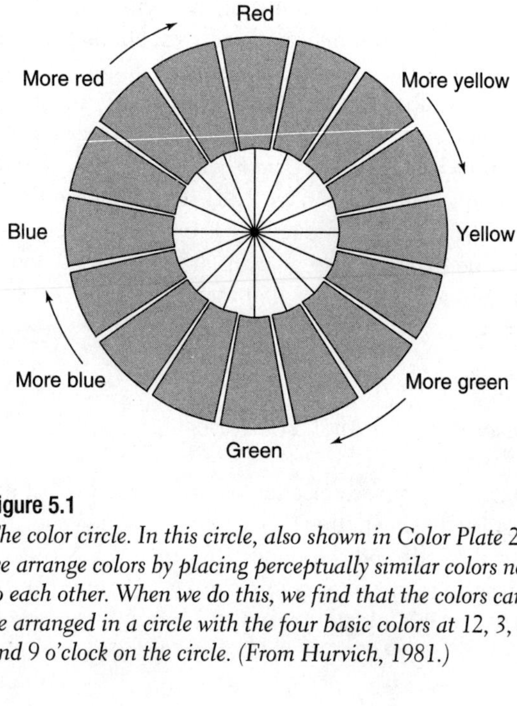

Figure 5.1
The color circle. In this circle, also shown in Color Plate 2.3, we arrange colors by placing perceptually similar colors next to each other. When we do this, we find that the colors can be arranged in a circle with the four basic colors at 12, 3, 6, and 9 o'clock on the circle. (From Hurvich, 1981.)

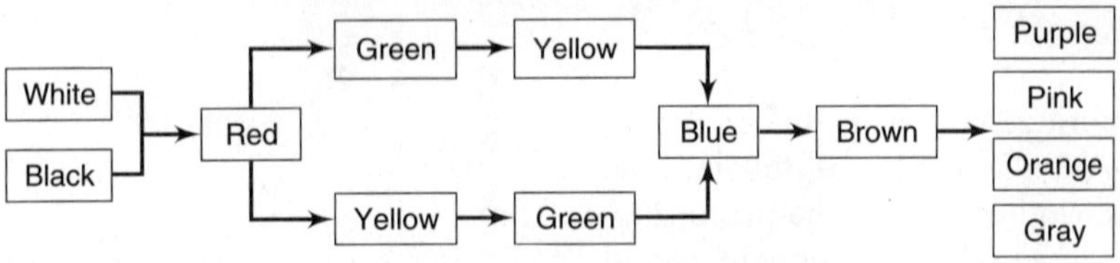

Figure 5.2
Colors named by different cultures follow the pattern shown here, the colors being added in the order shown. Thus, cultures with just two colors use black and white; cultures with three colors use black, white, and red; and cultures with four colors use black, white, and red, plus either green or yellow.

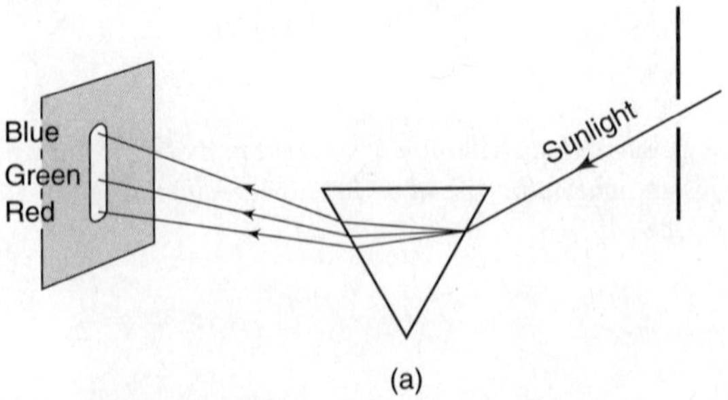

shared physiological basis for the experiences associated with these colors (Abramov & Gordon, 1994; Pokorny, Shevell, & Smith, 1991). In this chapter, we will focus on the nature of this physiological process. The first step is to answer the question: Which physical stimulus quality is most closely related to color perception? The answer to this question begins in Isaac Newton's room at Cambridge University in 1705.

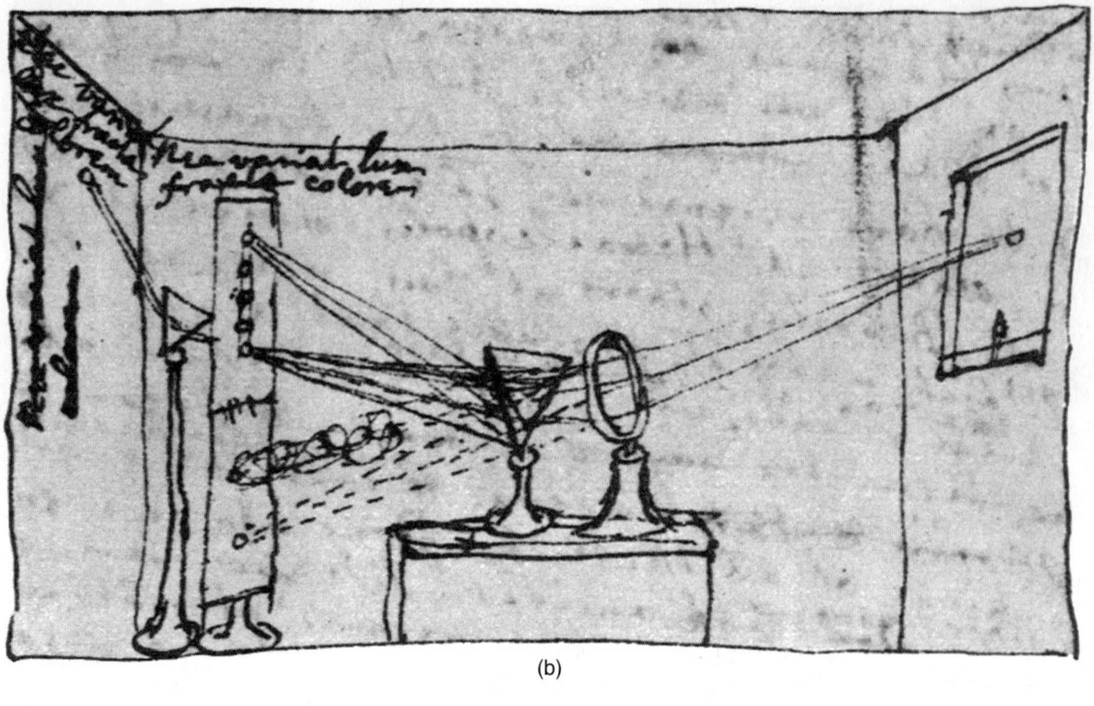

Figure 5.3
(a) When Isaac Newton passed sunlight through a prism he observed that the white sunlight was separated into the colors of the spectrum. (b) His original sketch of the experiment.

Color and Wavelength

In his room at Cambridge University, Isaac Newton placed a prism so that sunlight shining through a hole in the shutter of his window entered the prism (Figure 5.3). He observed that, as the sunlight passed through the prism, it was transformed into a spectrum of colors like the one in Color Plate 1.1. When Newton then recombined these spectral colors with a lens, he recreated the sunlight with which he started. On the basis of this and other experiments, Newton concluded that sunlight is made up of all of the spectral colors. Later work showed that these spectral colors differ in wavelength: Wavelengths between about 400 and 450 nm appear violet; 450–500 nm, blue; 500–570 nm, green; 570–590 nm, yellow; 590–620 nm, orange; and 620–700 nm, red. Thus, the wavelength of light is the physical property connected with color perception, and knowing the wavelength of a light gives us a good idea of its color.

In our everyday experience, however, we are rarely exposed to single wavelengths. Light sources that illuminate the objects in our environment give off many different wavelengths, and the objects reflect many wavelengths into our eyes. Let's first describe the wavelengths given off by two sources of light: the sun and incandescent light bulbs.

Figure 5.4 shows the **wavelength distributions** of two important light sources: **tungsten light,** the light emitted by incandescent light bulbs (named after the bulb's tungsten filament), and sunlight. The wavelength distribution of tungsten light contains much more intensity at long wavelengths than at short wavelengths, as indicated by the dashed line, and so appears yellow. The wavelength distribution of sunlight is relatively flat, indicating that sunlight contains an approximately equal intensity of each wavelength across the spectrum. Light that has equal intensity at all wavelengths in the spectrum is called **white light.**

Light from light bulbs or the sun can reach our eyes directly if we look at the light sources (not recommended in the case of the sun!), but most of the light we see is reflected from objects in the environment. We can understand why objects have different colors by looking at the reflectance curves of the objects themselves. **Reflectance** is the percentage

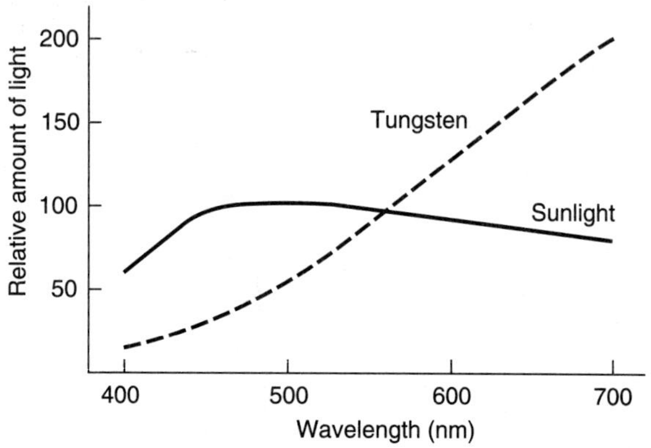

Figure 5.4
The wavelength distribution of sunlight and of light from a tungsten light bulb. (Based on Judd, MacAdam, & Wyszecki, 1964.)

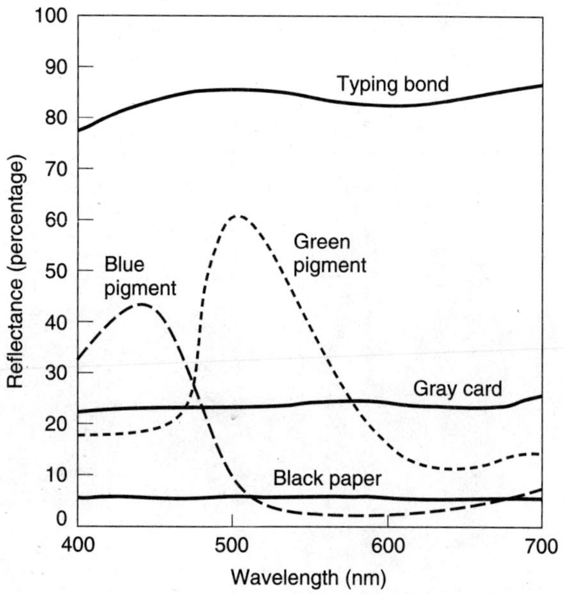

Figure 5.5
Reflectance curves for surfaces that appear white, gray, and black, and for blue and green pigments. (Adapted from Clulow, 1972.)

COLOR PERCEPTION AND COLOR MECHANISMS

The world of color is a world of yellow Miatas, brightly painted window shutters, orange-red sunsets, and multi-colored football jerseys. But what does color do for us in addition to creating aesthetic experiences, moods, and easier identification of opposing teams? For a monkey searching for food in the forest, color vision makes yellow or orange fruit easily visible against the green of the foliage (Plate 2.1a). In black and white, this fruit becomes more difficult to detect (Plate 2.1b) so a monkey without color vision would find food gathering difficult, a result which would have negative consequences for the monkey's survival (page 132).

Plate 2.2 shows the change in color perception that occurs as illumination changes from dawn to daylight. The view in (a) shows the scene as it would be perceived under the dim illumination of early dawn. The scene lacks color because the rods are responsible for vision under dim illumination. As the

Plate 2.1a

Plate 2.1b

Plate 2.2a

Plate 2.2b

Plate 2.3

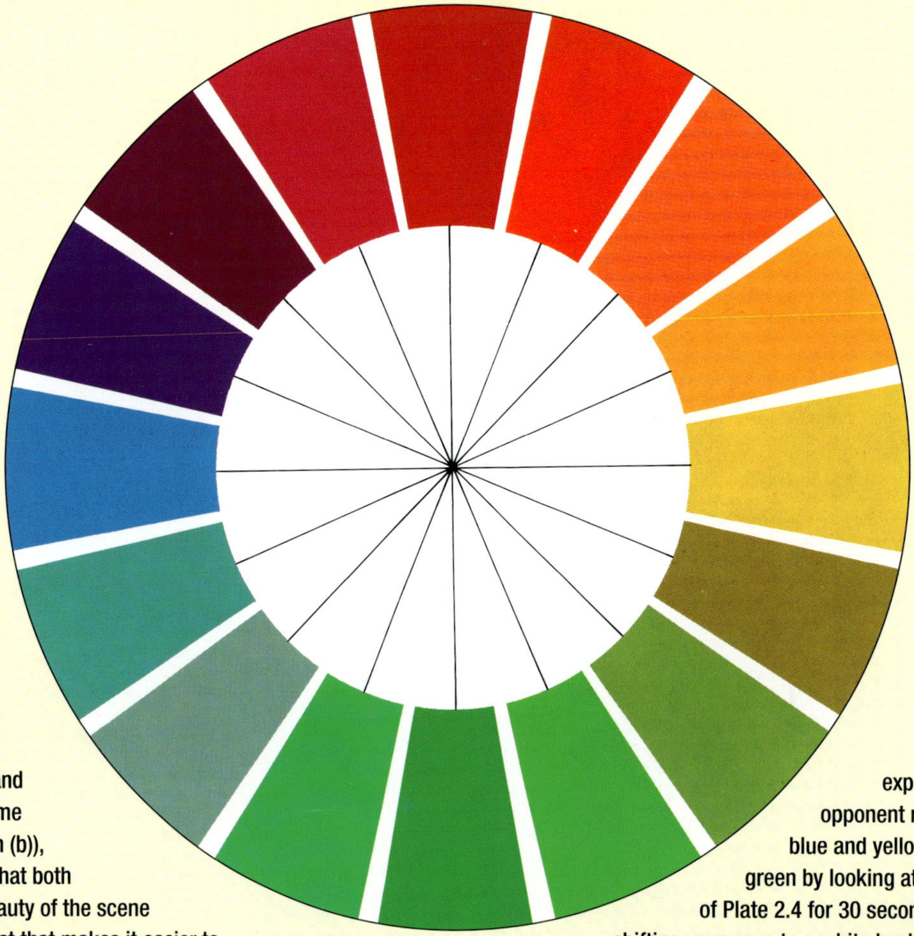

scene lightens and the cones become active (shown in (b)), colors emerge that both enhance the beauty of the scene and add contrast that makes it easier to decipher the scene's components. One of the many functions of color is to enhance the contrast between objects (page 133).

The experience we call color is closely linked to the spectral characteristics of light, as illustrated by the visible spectrum in Color Essay 1 (Plate 1.1). Another way to organize the perceptual experience of color is by using the color circle, which places colors in the same order as they appear in the spectrum, but arranges them in a circle (Plate 2.3). This arrangement helps show that all colors consist of various proportions of red, yellow, green, and blue—the colors that appear at 12, 3, 6, and 9 o'clock on the circle (page 134).

We can study some of the mechanisms of color vision by noting how our perception of color changes under different viewing conditions. For example, the cones synapse with other neurons in the retina to form opponent cells that fire in opposite ways to blue and yellow or red and green. You can experience the opponent responses of blue and yellow and red and green by looking at the center of Plate 2.4 for 30 seconds and then shifting your gaze to a white background. When you do this, observe how the blue and yellow and red and green panels reverse positions in the resulting afterimage (see "Opposing Afterimages" Demonstration, page 139).

Another way to demonstrate the opponent nature of the visual system is to place a small square of white paper within one of the squares in Plate 2.4, and follow the viewing instructions in the Demonstration, "Afterimages and Simultaneous Contrast" on page 140. You will observe an effect called *simultaneous contrast,* in which a surrounding field induces a color into the smaller, surrounded, area. The simultaneous contrast effect is also illustrated in Plate 2.5, which is a composition by Josef Albers, an artist who often used simultaneous contrast in his paintings (Courtesy of Yale University Press). Although one X looks yellow and the other looks gray, they are actually physically the same, as you can see by looking at the place where they are connected.

Plate 2.4

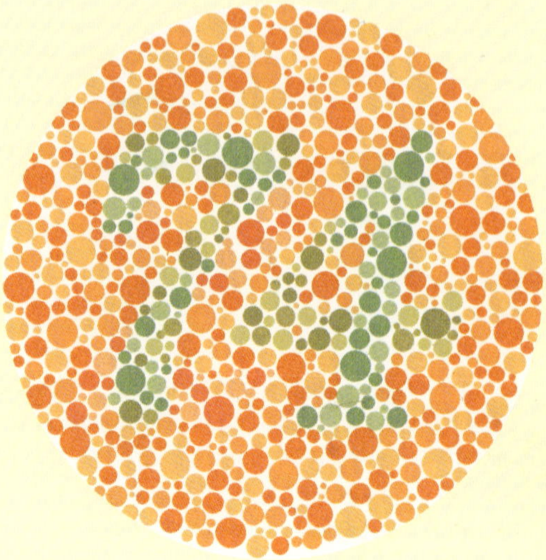

Plate 2.6

Plate 2.5

Plate 2.7

Plate 2.8

Color is by no means universally experienced. Many animals experience no colors and others perceive fewer colors than humans. Cats, dogs, and squirrels have color vision that is similar to the vision of color deficient humans (see page 148). Among humans, about 4 percent of males and a much smaller percentage of females are color deficient and therefore perceive a reduced palate of colors. One way to diagnose color deficiency is through a display such as the one in Plate 2.6, which is called an *Ishihara plate.* People with normal color vision see a 74, which is not seen by people with a form of red-green color deficiency. You can induce a mild (and temporary) form of color deficiency in yourself, by doing the following demonstration: Illuminate Plate 2.7 with bright sunlight or a desk lamp and view it with one eye open and the other closed for about one minute. Then blink back and forth and you will notice that reds viewed with the eye that was opened appear more washed out than reds viewed with the eye that was closed. The reason for this is that viewing the red field selectively bleached cone pigments sensitive to long wavelengths, making them less sensitive. People with red-green color deficiency are missing either their medium- or long-wave cone pigment (page 150).

Adapting the eye to one color, as you did when you looked at the red field, is called chromatic adaptation. For an explanation of how chromatic adaptation can partially explain color constancy see the "Adapting to Red" demonstration on page 159. Research has also shown that color constancy works best if an object or colored field is surrounded by many different colors. This research, that has investigated how color perception is influenced by complex visual displays, has used multicolored Mondrian displays like the one in Plate 2.8 as stimuli (page 161).

Creating Color by Subtraction or Addition

Newton's prism demonstration, in which he split white light from the sun into all of the colors of the spectrum, contains an important message regarding our perception of chromatic colors: We see white when we are stimulated by equal intensities of all wavelengths in the spectrum and we see chromatic colors when we are stimulated by only a portion of the spectrum.

Chromatic Color Created by Subtraction from White

One way to interpret Newton's result is that the perception of chromatic color occurs when some wavelengths are subtracted from white light. There are a number of ways that this subtraction can occur. One way, which we can observe in our natural environment, is by the scattering of light by the atmosphere. This is illustrated by the way light from the sun is scattered by particles in the air to create perceptions of the blue sky and yellow sun during the day, and of the red sun at sunset.

Sunlight entering the atmosphere encounters many small particles that scatter the light. When these particles are small in relation to the wavelength of the light, a condition known as **Rayleigh scattering** occurs, in which short wavelengths are scattered more than long wavelengths. As shown on the left side of Plate 3.1, this causes short wavelengths to be separated from the light entering the atmosphere, and it is these short wavelengths that cause us to see the sky as blue. The scattered light also causes objects in the distance to appear blue, since we must look through scattered short-wavelength light to see the object (Plate 3.2).

With short wavelengths scattered in the sky, the remaining light, which passes directly through the atmosphere, is rich in long wavelengths, so the sun appears yellow. This effect is exaggerated at sunset (Plate 3.1, right), when the light from the setting sun travels a greater distance through the atmosphere than it does at noon, thereby increasing the amount of short and medium wavelengths scattered and leaving only the longest wavelengths, which we perceive as the red setting sun.

Another way chromatic color is created by subtraction is illustrated by objects that appear colored because the substances they are made of subtract some wavelengths by a process called *absorption,* and reflect others by *selective reflection* (described on page 137). Thus, a ripe tomato appears red because the tomato absorbs short and medium wavelengths and reflects long wavelengths (Figure 5.6).

Plate 3.3 illustrates a situation in which complete reflection and selective reflection exist side-by-side. The white ice and snow in this close-up of an Alaskan glacier appears white because it reflects all wavelengths equally. Further inside the

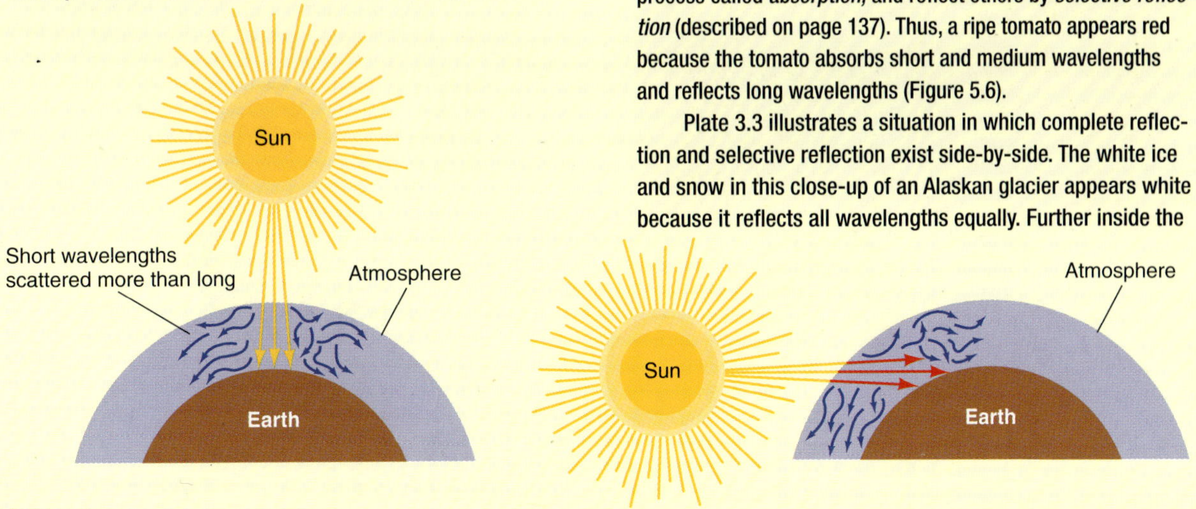

Plate 3.1

Plate 3.2

Plate 3.3

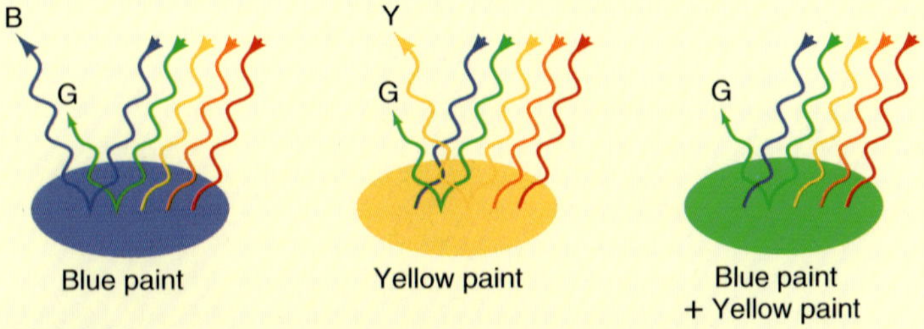

Plate 3.4

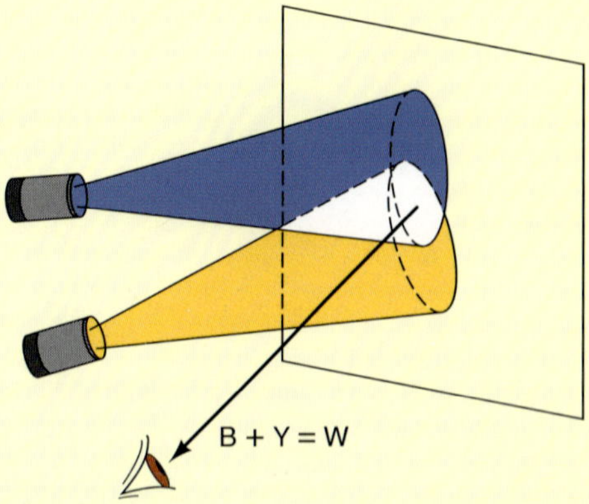

Plate 3.5

glacier, however, the ice has been subjected to intense pressure that has changed its properties. This highly compacted ice absorbs medium and long wavelengths and selectively reflects short wavelengths, thereby causing it to appear blue (see Figure 5.5, page 138).

The process of absorption also explains the colors we see when we mix paints - a process called **subtractive color mixture.** For example, many people have had the experience of mixing blue and yellow paints to create green (see page 142). We can understand how subtraction causes blue and yellow together to make green by first considering the wavelengths that are subtracted from white by the blue paint and the yellow paint separately (Plate 3.4 and Table 1).

Blue paint absorbs wavelengths associated with yellow, orange and red and some of the green, and reflects blue and a little green. Yellow paint absorbs blue, orange, red, and some of the green, and reflects yellow and a little green. When we mix the two paints together, both paints still absorb the same colors they absorbed when alone. From Table 1 we can see that the mixture of blue and yellow will therefore absorb all of the blue, yellow, orange, and red. What we perceive is the color that is reflected by both paints in common. From Table 1 we can see that green is the only color by both reflected by both paints. Therefore, blue plus yellow paints appears green.

The reason that our blue and yellow mixture resulted in green was that both paints reflected a little green. If our blue paint had reflected only blue and our yellow paint had reflected only yellow, these paints would reflect no color in common, so mixing them would result in little or no reflection across the spectrum, and the mixture would appear black. It is rare, however, for paints to reflect light in only one region of the spectrum. Most paints reflect a broad band of wavelengths. If paints didn't reflect a range of wavelengths, then many of the color mixing effects that painters take for granted would not occur.

Chromatic Color Created by Addition of Other Chromatic Colors

Chromatic colors can also be created by adding together two or more other chromatic colors. This process occurs when we superimpose two or more colored lights. Mixing lights is called **additive color mixture,** because all of the

Table 1

Parts of the spectrum that are absorbed and reflected by blue and yellow paint. The colors that are totally absorbed are indicated by shaded squares for each paint. Light that is usually seen as green is the only light that is reflected in common by both paints.

Wavelengths associated with . . .	Blue	Green	Yellow	Orange	Red
BLUE PAINT	Reflects all	Reflects some Absorbs some	Absorbs all	Absorbs all	Absorbs all
YELLOW PAINT	Absorbs all	Reflects some Absorbs some	Reflects all	Absorbs all	Absorbs all

Plate 3.6

Plate 3.7

wavelengths contained in each light still reach the eye when the lights are superimposed. Consider what happens when we look at blue and yellow lights that have been superimposed on a white projection screen (Plate 3.5). The short wavelengths of the blue light are reflected from the screen into our eyes, and the medium and long wavelengths of the yellow light are also reflected from the screen into our eyes. The result is that short, medium, and long wavelengths reach our eyes and we perceive white.

We can appreciate the difference between creating chromatic colors by addition (mixing lights) and by subtraction (mixing paints) by noting that every time we superimpose a *light* onto another light, we add to the amount of light reflected form the screen into the observer's eye. However, every time we add an additional glob of *paint* into a mixture of paints, we subtract from the amount of light reflected. The opposite nature of additive and subtractive color mixture is perhaps best illustrated by comparing the color that results from mixing blue, green, and red, *lights* to the color that results from mixing blue, green, and red *paints.* Mixing the lights results in white, while mixing the paints results in black (Plate 3.6).

Finally, there is another way that chromatic colors can be created by addition. This is a process called **optical color mixing,** in which colors add in the eye when small spots with different colors are viewed from a distance. You can experience this effect by propping up your book and slowly walking back from Plate 3.7. As you increase your distance, you are eventually unable to resolve the green and rod dots, which add in your eye just as if they were lights projected on top of one another to create a perception of yellow. This technique, which in painting is called **pointillism,** was used by French painters such as George Seurat and Paul Signac to create optical color mixing effects and to create shimmering effects often associated with natural light. An example of pointillism is illustrated by Signac's painting in Plate 3.8, in which the foreground is made up of tiny blue and orange dots. Move back from this picture and notice how the appearance of the foreground changes as it becomes more difficult to see the individual dots.

Plate 3.8

of the light falling on an object that is reflected from the object. A **reflectance curve** is a plot of reflectance versus wavelength. Figure 5.5 shows reflectance curves for white, gray, and black paper and for blue and green pigments. We can see from these curves that the region of the spectrum that is reflected determines an object's color. For the three achromatic colors, reflectance is approximately equal across the spectrum, but chromatic colors reflect some wavelengths and not others. This reflection of only some of the wavelengths in the spectrum—**selective reflection**—is shared by all objects that have chromatic color. Figure 5.6 shows reflectance curves for a few common foods, all of which selectively reflect light at the long-wavelength end of the spectrum and so appear yellow, orange, or red. Table 5.1 indicates the relationship between the color perceived and the wavelengths reflected.

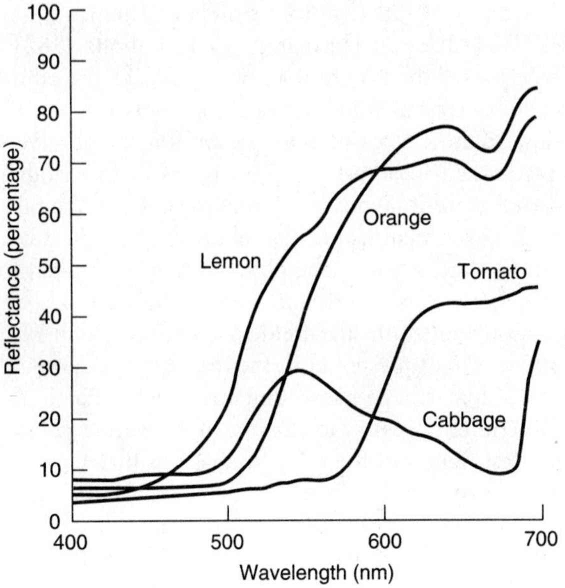

Figure 5.6
Reflectance curves of some common foods. Knowing which wavelengths are reflected enables us to roughly predict the pigment's color by consulting Table 5.1. Try this prediction for these foods and for the pigments in Figure 5.5. (Adapted from Clulow, 1972.)

Table 5.1
Relationship between predominant wavelengths reflected and color perceived

Wavelengths Reflected	Perceived Color
Short	Blue
Medium	Green
Long	Red
Long and medium	Yellow
Long and a little medium	Orange
Long and short	Purple
Long, medium, and short	White

An excellent example of the difference between achromatic colors, created by equal reflection of all wavelengths, and chromatic colors, created by selective reflection of only some wavelengths, is provided by the colors of some glaciers (Color Plate 3.3). Much of the snow on a glacier reflects all wavelengths equally, so appears white. But in some areas, extreme pressure packs the ice so tightly that it creates a crystalline structure that absorbs all medium and long wavelengths, leaving only the short wavelengths to be reflected to produce a deep blue color (Figure 5.7).

The objects we have described so far reflect some wavelengths and absorb the rest, but what about translucent things, such as liquids, plastics, and glass? The relationship between wavelength and color shown here also holds for these substances, except that they *transmit* rather than reflect light, and if they transmit certain wavelengths selectively, they appear colored. For example, cranberry juice selectively transmits long-wavelength light and appears red, while limeade selectively transmits medium-wavelength light and appears green.

Establishing the connection between wavelength and color is the first step in determining the sensory code for color. In Chapter 3, we saw that the sensory code is the characteristics of neural signals that represent various characteristics of the environment. Since we know that wavelength is the crucial physical property for determining color, the search for the sensory code for color has focused on answering the question:

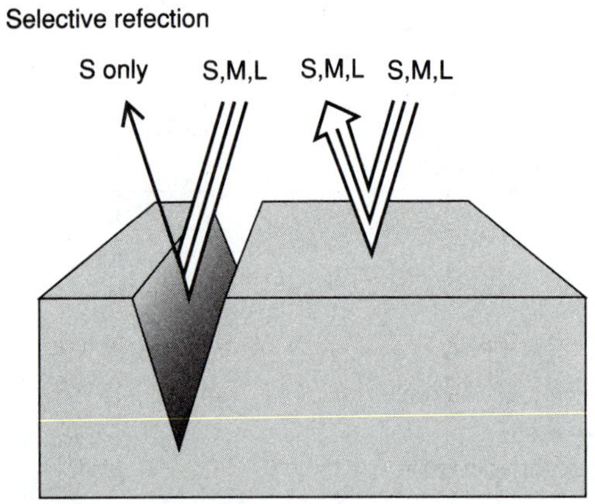

Figure 5.7
How light is reflected from two different areas of a glacier. On the right, short-, medium-, and long-wavelength light from the sun reaches the glacier and since all wavelengths are reflected equally, that area appears white. On the left, inside the crevice, the crystal structure of the tightly packed ice absorbs the medium and long wavelengths, leaving only the short wavelengths to be reflected. This area, therefore, appears blue. (See color plate 3.3)

How do nerve impulses in the visual system signal the wavelength of light?

Modern research on this question has been carried out in physiological laboratories. But our understanding of the physiology of color vision actually began with behavioral research that dates back to the 1800s.

Behavioral Research: Discovery of the Sensory Code for Color

In Chapter 1 we described a situation in which an auto mechanic predicted what was wrong with a car's engine based on listening to the engine's sound. In this example, observations of the car's sound were used to predict the mechanical problem that was happening under the hood. In the 1800s, an analogous tactic was used for color vision: observations of people's color perceptions were used to predict the physiological mechanisms responsible for these perceptions. The use of behavioral techniques to predict physiology was born of necessity, because researchers in the 1800s were not able to measure neural activity. They were clever enough, however, to realize that, by making the right behavioral observations, they could make educated guesses regarding the physiological mechanisms.

This story of how behavioral observations were used to predict the physiology of color vision is really two stories, each created by different people who looked at two different sets of behavioral evidence, and came to two different physiological conclusions. We will describe both of these conclusions, and we will then show how physiological research has proven that both are correct.

Trichromatic Theory: Color Matching

Two eminent 19th-century researchers, Thomas Young (1773–1829) and Hermann von Helmholtz (1821–1894), used the results of a psychophysical procedure called *color matching* to propose a theory of color vision. In these **color-matching experiments,** observers were asked to adjust the proportions of three other wavelengths in a mixture so that the color of the mixture looked identical to that of another, single wavelength. For example, the observer might be asked to mix 420-nm, 560-nm, and 640-nm lights in a comparison field until the field matched the color of a 500-nm light presented in the test field. They found that to make the test and comparison fields match it is sometimes necessary to add one of the wavelengths to the test field, but their key finding was that a person with normal color vision needs to be given at least three wavelengths to mix in order to make the test and comparison fields match. (Any three wavelengths can be used in the comparison field, as long as any one of them can't be matched by mixing the other two.) Most observers cannot, however, match all test wavelengths if they are provided with only two other wavelengths. For example, if they were given only the 420-nm and 640-nm lights to mix, the observers would be unable to match certain colors.

Based on the finding that at least three wavelengths are needed to match any wavelength in the test field, Thomas Young (1802) proposed the **trichromatic theory of color vision.** This theory, which was later championed by Helmholtz (1852; Figure 5.8) and is therefore also called the **Young-Helmholtz theory of color vision,** proposes that color vision depends on three receptor mechanisms, each with different spectral sensitivities. (Remember from Chapter 2 that spectral sensitivity indicates the sensitivity to wavelengths across the visible spectrum, as shown in curves like the ones in Figure 2.25.)

According to this theory, light of a particular wavelength stimulates the three receptor mechanisms to different degrees, and the pattern of activity in the three mechanisms results in the perception of a color. Each wavelength is therefore coded in the nervous system by its own pattern of activity in the three receptor mechanisms, an arrangement identical to the one we used to illustrate the distributed coding of orientation in Chapter 3 (see pages 95–96).

The way that Young and Helmholtz used the result of color matching experiments to conclude that color vision is based on three receptor mechanisms shows how psychophysics can predict physiology. However, before we consider the physiological data that support the Young-Helmholtz theory, let's look at another example of behavioral data predicting physiology. This example is provided by Ewald Hering's phenomenological approach to the study of color vision.

Figure 5.8
Hermann von Helmholtz (1821–1894), who championed the trichromatic theory of color vision.

Opponent-Process Theory: Phenomenological Observations

Although trichromatic theory explains a number of color vision phenomena, including color matching and **color mixing,** there are some color perceptions that it cannot explain. These color perceptions can be demonstrated through phenomenological observations, in which we present a stimulus and ask the observer what he or she perceives (see page 7). Ewald Hering (1834–1918; Figure 5.9), another eminent physiologist who was working at about the same time as Helmholtz, made a number of phenomenological observations, which showed that the colors red and green are perceptually paired with one another and the colors blue and yellow are paired with one another. This pairing of red and green and of blue and yellow is illustrated by the following three demonstrations.

D E M O N S T R A T I O N

"Opposing" Afterimages

Cover the blue and yellow squares in Color Plate 2.4 with a piece of white paper, and illuminate the red and green squares with your desk lamp. Pick a spot on the border between the two squares and look at it for about 30 seconds. If you then look at a piece of white paper and blink, the image you see, which is called an afterimage, is colored. Notice the position of the red and green areas in the afterimage. Then repeat this procedure for the blue and yellow squares. ●

Figure 5.9
Ewald Hering (1834–1918), who proposed the opponent-process theory of color vision.

Hering observed that viewing a red field generates a green afterimage, that viewing a green field generates a red afterimage, and that analogous results occur for blue and yellow.

DEMONSTRATION

Afterimages and Simultaneous Contrast

Cut out a ½-inch square of white paper and place it in the center of the green square in Color Plate 2.4. Cover the other squares with white paper, and stare at the center of the white square for about 30 seconds. Then look at a white background, and blink to observe the afterimage. What color is the outside area of the afterimage? What color is the small square in the center? Repeat your observations on the red, blue, and yellow squares in Color Plate 2.4. ●

When you made your observations using the green square, you probably confirmed your previous observation that green and red are paired, since the afterimage corresponding to the green area of the original square is red. But the color of the small square in the center also shows that green and red are paired: Most people see a green square inside the red afterimage. This green afterimage is due to **simultaneous color contrast,** an effect that occurs when surrounding an area with a color changes the appearance of the surrounded area. In this case, the red afterimage surrounds a white area and causes the white area to become green. (See Color Plate 2.5 for another demonstration of simultaneous contrast.) Table 5.2 indicates this result and the results that occur if we repeat this demonstration on the other squares. All of these results show a clear pairing of red and green, and of blue and yellow.

Table 5.2
Results of afterimage and simultaneous contrast demonstration

Original Square	Color of Outside Afterimage	Color of Inside Afterimage
Green	Red	Green
Red	Green	Red
Blue	Yellow	Blue
Yellow	Blue	Yellow

Another way to illustrate the pairing of red and green and of blue and yellow is by trying to visualize certain colors. Start by visualizing the color red. Attach this color to a specific object such as a fire engine if that makes your visualizing easier. Now visualize a reddish yellow and then a reddish green. Which of these two combinations is easiest to visualize? Now do the same thing for blue. Visualize a pure blue, then a bluish green and a bluish yellow. Again, which of the combinations is easiest to visualize?

Most people find it easy to visualize a bluish green or a reddish yellow but find it difficult (or impossible) to visualize a reddish green or a bluish-yellow. This inability to visualize red and green together or blue and yellow together was demonstrated using more quantitative methods in an experiment by James Gordon and Israel Abramov (1988; also see Abramov & Gordon, 1994). They presented single wavelengths and asked their observers to state the percentage of blue, green, yellow, and red they perceived at each wavelength. Whatever percentage they assigned, they had to be sure that the total added to 100 percent for all four colors at each wavelength.

The results of Gordon and Abramov's experiment showed that blue dominates at short wavelengths, green in the middle of the spectrum, and yellow and red at long wavelengths, just as we would expect from the visible spectrum (Figure 5.10). However, the important result for opponent-process theory is that there is very little overlap between the blue and yellow curves and the red and green curves—just as our visualization experiments would predict.[2]

These observations, plus Hering's observation that people who are color-blind to red are also blind to green, and that people who can't see blue also can't

[2] The small overlap between these curves that does exist, occurs because the curves represent the judgments of many observers. When we consider the perceptions of individual observers, there is no overlap between red and green and between blue and yellow.

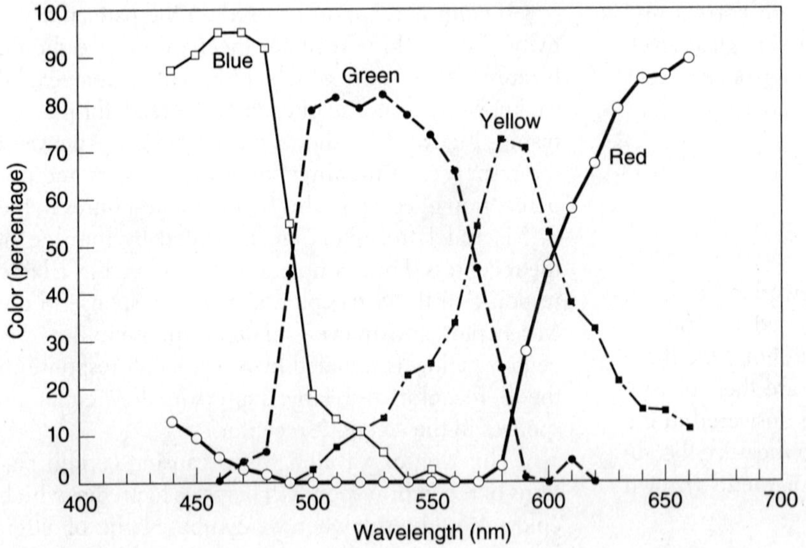

Figure 5.10
The results of a color-scaling experiment. After viewing each stimulus light, the subject rates her or his color sensation by assigning percentages to blue, green, yellow, or red so that they add up to 100 percent. These data, which are averages from a number of subjects, indicate very little overlap between blue and yellow and between red and green. Even this small amount of overlap decreases when we consider the results of individual subjects. (Adapted from Gordon & Abramov, 1988; also see Abramov & Gordon, 1994.)

see yellow, led him to the conclusion that red and green are paired and that blue and yellow are paired. Based on this conclusion, he proposed the **opponent-process theory of color vision** (Hering, 1878, 1905, 1964).

The basic idea underlying Hering's theory is shown in Figure 5.11. He proposed three mechanisms, each of which responds in opposite ways to different intensities or wavelengths of light. The Black (−) White (+) mechanism responds positively to white light and negatively to the absence of light. Red (+) Green (−) responds positively to red and negatively to green, and Blue (−) Yellow (+) responds negatively to blue and positively to yellow. Hering thought that these positive and negative responses were caused by the buildup and breakdown of chemicals in the retina, with white, yellow, and red causing a reaction that results in a buildup of the chemicals and black, green, and blue causing a reaction that results in a breakdown of the chemicals. Although this part of Hering's theory was not correct, modern physiological research showed that these colors do cause physiologically opposite responses.

We have seen that the proposal of the opponent-process and trichromatic mechanisms was based on behavioral observations made in the 1800s. We are now going to move ahead to the 1950s and 1960s to look at physiological results that show that color vision is based on the simultaneous operation of both the trichromatic and the opponent-process mechanisms.

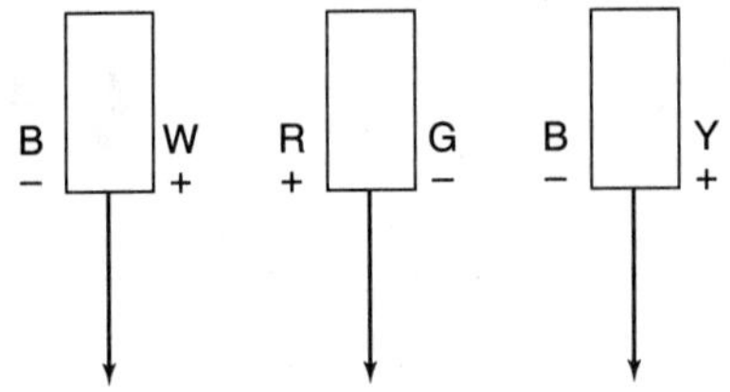

Figure 5.11
The three opponent mechanisms proposed by Hering.

Physiological Research on Color Vision

Over 70 years after the trichromatic and opponent-process theories were first proposed, physiological research showed that both theories are correct and that they can be combined at the physiological level. Before describing how this combining occurs, let's look at each line of physiological evidence separately.

Trichromatic Theory: Cone Pigments

Physiological researchers who were working to identify the receptor mechanisms proposed by trichromatic theory asked the following question: Are there three mechanisms, and, if so, what are their physiological properties? This question was answered in the 1960s, when researchers were able to measure the absorption spectra of the cone visual pigments (Brown & Wald, 1964).

Three Cone Pigments Dartnall et al. (1983) found human cone pigments with maximum absorption in the short- (419-nm), middle- (531-nm), and long-wavelength (558-nm) regions of the spectrum (S, M, and L in Figure 5.12). Schnapf, Kraft, and Baylor (1987) obtained similar results by electrophysiological recording from single middle- and long-wavelength human cones.

If color perception is based on the pattern of activity of these three receptor mechanisms, we should be able to determine which colors will be perceived if we know the response of each of the receptor mechanisms. Figure 5.13 shows the relationship between the responses of the three kinds of receptors and our perception of color. In this figure, the responses in the S, M, and L receptors are indicated by the size of the receptors. For example, blue is signaled by a large response in the S receptor, a smaller response in the M receptor, and an even smaller response in the L receptor. Yellow is signaled by a very small response in the S receptor and large, approximately equal responses in the M and L receptors.

Thinking of wavelengths as causing certain patterns of receptor responding helps us to predict which colors should result when we combine lights of different colors. For example, what color should result if we project a spot of blue light onto a spot of yellow light? The patterns of receptor activity in Figure 5.13 show that blue light causes high activity in the S receptors, and that yellow light causes high activity in the M and L receptors. Thus, combining both lights should stimulate all three receptors equally, and we should perceive white. This is exactly the result we achieve if we mix blue and yellow lights. (However, a different result occurs if we mix blue and yellow *paints.* The reason we achieve different results from lights and paints is explained in Color Essay 3.)

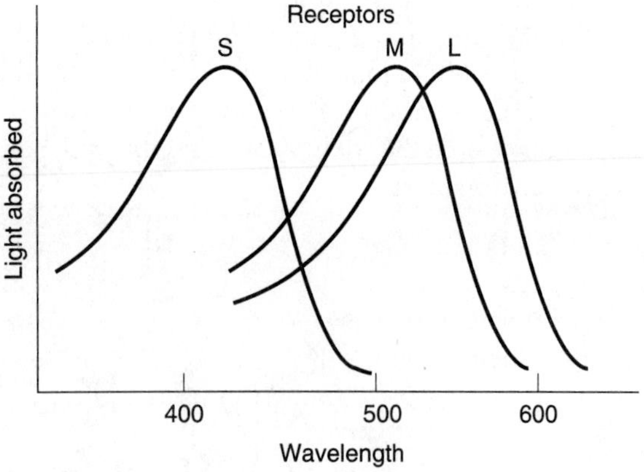

Figure 5.12
Absorption spectra of the three cone pigments. (From Dartnall, Bowmaker, & Mollon, 1983.)

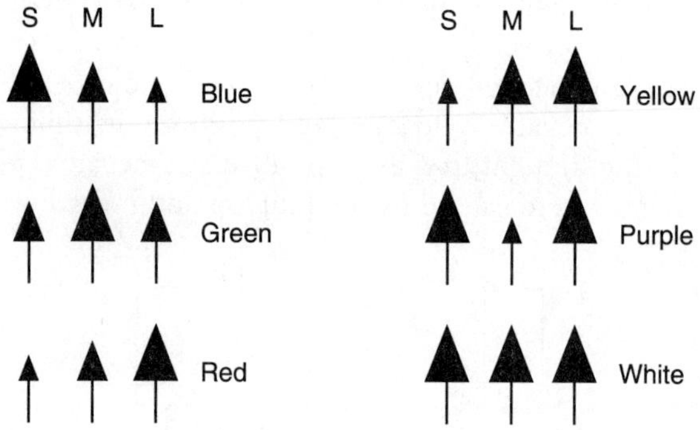

Figure 5.13
Patterns of firing of the three types of cones to different colors. The size of the cone symbolizes the size of the receptor's response.

The idea that our perception of colors is determined by the pattern of activity in different kinds of receptors says something important about the relation between neural responding and perception. Combining two or more wavelengths so they perceptually match a single wavelength creates two *physically different* fields that are *perceptually identical.* For example, when we mix a 620-nm red light and a 530-nm green light, we can create a yellow that matches the color associated with a 580-nm light (Figure 5.14). The 580-nm light and the mixture of the 620-nm and 530-nm lights appear identical because even though they are physically different, they create the same pattern of activity in the cone receptors. The 530-nm green light causes a large response in the M receptor, and the 620-nm red light causes a large response in the L receptor. Together, they result in a large response in the M and L receptors and a much smaller response in the S receptor. This is the pattern for yellow and is the same as the pattern generated by the 580-nm yellow light. Thus, as far as the visual system is concerned, these lights are identical.

Two lights that have different wavelength distributions but are perceptually identical are called **metamers.** The basic principle of metamers is as follows: *Two lights with different wavelength distributions appear to be the same color if they stimulate the receptors in the same ratios.* Putting this another way, we can say: *If two stimuli cause the same neural response, they will appear to be identical, even if they are physically different.*

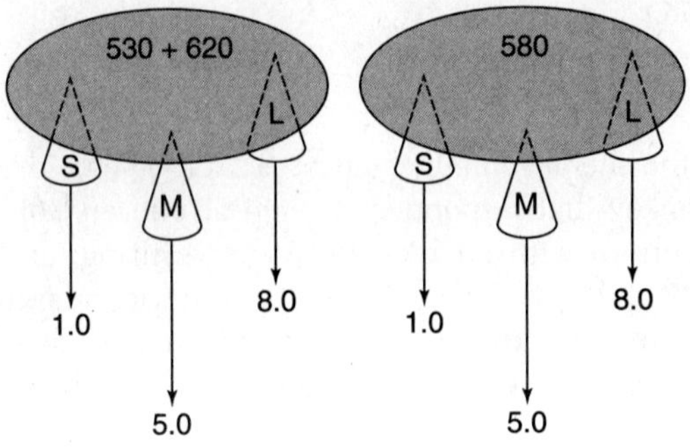

Figure 5.14
The proportions of 530- and 620-nm lights in the field on the left have been adjusted so that the mixed lights appear to be identical to the 580-nm light in the field on the right. The numbers, which indicate the responses of the short-, medium-, and long-wavelength receptors, show that there is no difference in the responses of the two sets of receptors. The identical neural responding causes the two fields to be perceptually indistinguishable.

The Molecular Structure of the Cone Pigments Another important advance in our understanding of the physiology of color vision came in the 1980s, when researchers determined the detailed structure of the visual pigment molecules (Mollon, 1989, 1993; Nathans, Thomas, & Hogness, 1986). We saw in Chapter 2 that the pigment molecule consists of a large protein, opsin, and a small, light-sensitive molecule, retinal (Figures 2.18 and 2.19). The retinal molecule is identical in all of the visual pigments, but different types of pigments have different sequences of the small molecular groups called amino acids that make up the protein. These differences in the amino acids are what cause different pigments to have different absorption spectra. Thus, the short- and middle-wavelength cones, which have only 44 percent of their amino acid sequences in common, have peak absorptions that are separated by 112 nm. In contrast, the middle- and long-wavelength cones, which have about 96 percent identical amino acid sequences, have peak absorptions that are separated by only 27 nm.

For the M and L pigments, a difference in one amino acid causes a shift of 5–7 nm in the peak of the absorption spectrum (Neitz, Neitz, & Jacobs, 1993). This means that changing just one amino acid could create new M and L cone pigments with absorption spectra shifted slightly from the "normal" M and L pigments. In fact, research has shown that some subjects with normal trichromatic vision have four different cone pigments: the three "standard" ones and an additional shifted one. For reasons we don't yet understand, their vision is still trichromatic, rather than tetrachromatic (based on four kinds of cones). Perhaps the responses of two cones with slightly different spectra are combined neurally by converging on the same neurons, so the psychophysical response appears to be from a single type of pigment (Dartnall et al., 1983; Neitz, Neitz, & Jacobs, 1993).

Opponent-Process Theory: Neural Responding

Although numerous phenomenological observations supported Hering's opponent-process theory, it has only recently been taken as seriously as trichromatic theory. One reason for its slow acceptance was that people couldn't imagine a physiological process that resulted in either the buildup or the breakdown of a chemical substance. This poor acceptance of opponent-process theory is illustrated by the amount of coverage given the theory in Yves LeGrand's 1957 book *Light, Color and Vision,* a standard reference on vision. Though 25 pages were devoted to trichromatic theory, opponent-process theory was dealt with in less than a page.

It wasn't until solid physiological evidence became available that opponent-process theory began to gain equal footing with trichromatic theory. This evidence took the form not of chemicals that were either broken down or built up by different wavelengths, as Hering proposed, but by neurons that respond in opposite ways to different wavelengths.

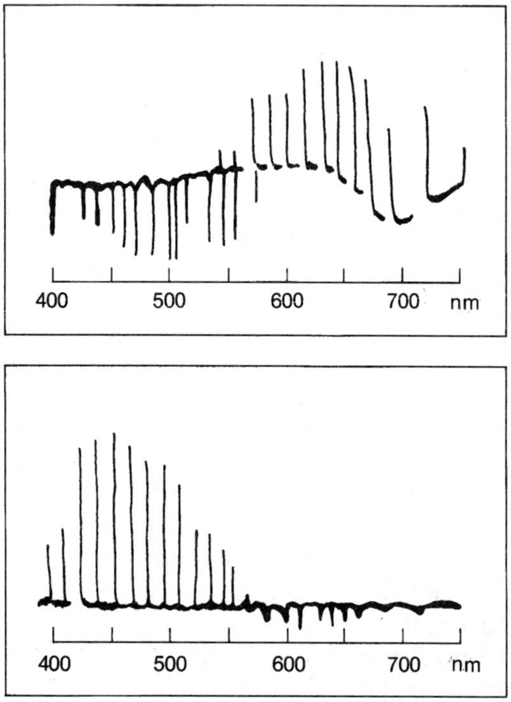

Figure 5.15
S-potentials recorded from the fish retina. The vertical lines are the responses generated by test flashes; the wavelengths are indicated on the horizontal scale. (From Svaetichin, 1956.)

Opponent Cells in the Retina and the Lateral Geniculate Nucleus Evidence for opposing electrical signals was provided by research on two animals with excellent color vision: the rhesus monkey and fish from the carp family. Gunnar Svaetichin (1956) discovered neurons in the fish retina that responded to light by slowly changing their electrical charge, a response he called the **S-potential.** This electrical response had a property that supported the opponent-process theory: The neurons responded positively (the inside of the neuron became more positive) to light at one end of the spectrum and negatively (the inside of the neuron became more negative) to light at the other end of the spectrum, as is illustrated in Figure 5.15. The top record is from a cell that responds negatively to short wavelengths and positively to long wavelengths. The bottom record is from a cell that responds positively to short wavelengths and very little to long wavelengths.

A few years after Svaetichin's discovery of opposing S-potentials, Russell DeValois (1960) found cells in the lateral geniculate nucleus (LGN) of the rhesus monkey that responded to light at one end of the spectrum with an increase in nerve firing, and to light at the other end of the spectrum with an inhibition of spontaneous activity. The firing of four such cells, which are called **opponent cells,** is shown in Figure 5.16. For each cell, spontaneous activity is indicated in the top record, and the responses to 450-nm (blue), 510-nm (green), 580-nm (yellow), and 660-nm (red) lights are shown in the other records. The B+Y− cell responds to the 450-nm light with an increase in firing and to the 580-nm light with an inhibition of spontaneous activity. The G+R− cell increases its firing to the 510-nm light and decreases its firing to the 660-nm light. The Y+B− and R+G− cells also show opponent responses, but they are

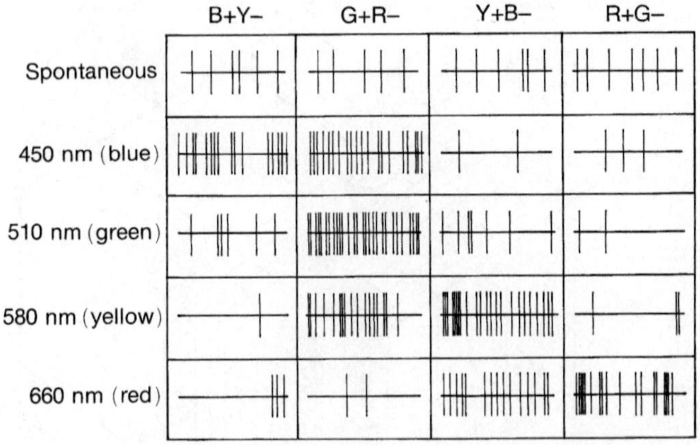

Figure 5.16
Responses of opponent cells in the monkey's lateral geniculate nucleus. These cells respond in opposite ways to blue and yellow (B+Y− or Y+B−) and to red and green (G+R− or R+G−). (From DeValois & Jacobs, 1968.)

inhibited by short wavelengths and are excited by long wavelengths.

The results of Svaetichin's and DeValois's experiments made believers of researchers who had doubted the physiological reality of opponent mechanisms in the visual system, and led other researchers to determine the detailed properties of these opponent mechanisms not only in the retina and the LGN, but also in the cortex.

Opponent Cells in the Cortex A number of types of opponent cells have been discovered in the monkey striate cortex (Derrington, Lennie, & Krauskopf, 1983; DeValois & Jacobs, 1984; Gouras, 1991a, 1991b; Hubel & Livingstone, 1990; Zrenner et al., 1990). Most of these cells have one thing in common: They are excited by wavelengths at one end of the spectrum and are inhibited by wavelengths at the other end of the spectrum. We will focus on two of these cortical opponent cells. The first, called a **type 1 color-opponent cell,** is like the LGN neuron: It is a center-surround cell that is inhibited by one band of wavelengths presented to the surround and is excited by another band presented to the center (or vice versa).

Another type of opponent cell found in the cortex is a **double color-opponent cell.** The receptive field of a double color-opponent cell recorded from layer IVc of the monkey's cortex is shown in Figure 5.17. The center of this cell's receptive field has an R+G− opponent response, and the surround has an R−G+ opponent response. The reason for the name *double color-opponent cell* is that the cell responds in an opponent fashion, but in opposite ways, depending on whether the center or the surround is stimulated.

Margaret Livingstone and David Hubel (1984) observed that these types of double color-opponent cells (R+G− center and R−G+ surround) are by far the most common types of color cells in the monkey, and they suggest that there may be a functional reason. In their natural habitat, monkeys need to perceive brightly colored fruit, usually red or orange, on a green leafy background. If the red fruit stimulates the R+ center of one of the monkey's double color-opponent cells and the green leaves stimulate the G+ surround, the cell will fire vigorously. Perhaps, suggested Livingstone and Hubel, the double color-opponent cells help create a high-contrast display that the monkey can see easily.

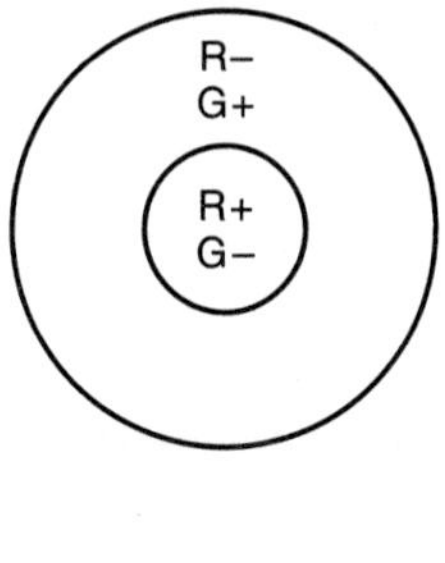

Figure 5.17
The receptive field of a double color-opponent cell in the monkey cortex. This neuron has an R−G+ response in the surround and an R+G− response in the center.

Livingstone and Hubel also observed that these double color-opponent cells are concentrated in cortical areas called **blobs** in the striate cortex, so called because these areas show up as bloblike shapes when the cortex is treated with a special stain. These blobs, which appear to receive inputs from the opponent cells in layer IVc (Michael, 1986), contain cells that respond to colors but not to orientation, unlike most other cells in the visual cortex, which prefer particular orientations. This segregation of color-sensitive cells within the blobs and orientation-sensitive cells outside the blobs is consistent with the idea of parallel processing in the visual system that we introduced in Chapters 3 and 4. Signals from the wavelength-sensitive neurons in the striate cortex travel to areas V2 and V4, all stations along the ventral stream that flows from the striate cortex to the temporal lobe (Figure 4.1).

Not only is color processed separately in the blob areas of the striate cortex, but within the blobs, opponent neurons are organized into columns, so only blue-yellow or red-green neurons are found within a particular column (Ts'o, 1989). This discovery of color columns in the cortex has led to a revision of the hypercolumn scheme we introduced in Figure 3.31, in which a hypercolumn was pictured as consisting of location, orientation, and ocular dominance columns. We now modify this scheme by adding color columns, as shown in Figure 5.18 (Livingstone & Hubel, 1984).

The existence of color-opponent cells raises two questions: (1) How do neural circuits result in opponent neurons? (2) Why are these neurons necessary for color vision? We will consider each of these questions in turn.

The How and the Why of Opponent Cells Figure 5.19 shows a neural circuit in the retina that creates opponent cells from the signals generated by the three types of cone receptors. Let's first focus on the R+G– cell. This cell receives inhibitory input from the M cone and excitatory input from the L cone. Thus, light in the middle of the spectrum, which preferentially stimulates the M cone, causes an inhibitory response in this cell. Similarly, light at the long-wavelength end of the spectrum, which preferentially stimulates the L cone, causes an excitatory response

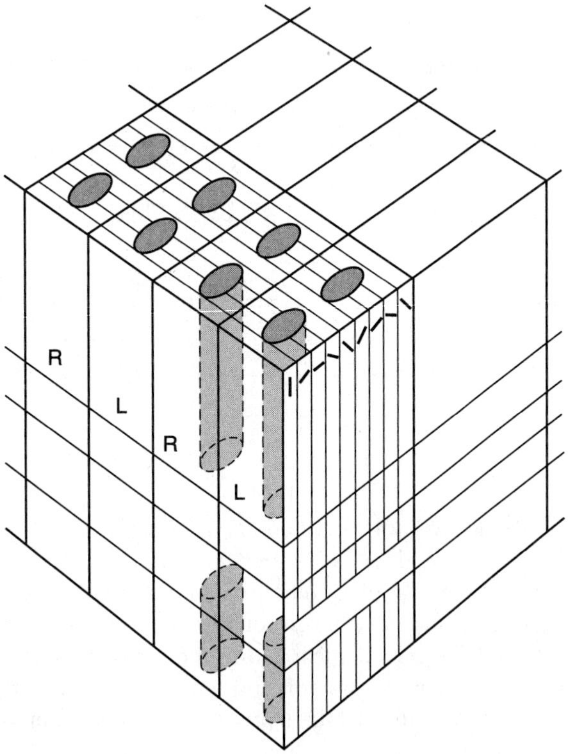

Figure 5.18
The hypercolumn organization of the cortex introduced in Chapter 3 (see Figure 3.31), with the addition of columns of color-opponent cells (shaded). These areas are called blobs because of their appearance when the cortex is stained. (Adapted from Livingstone & Hubel, 1984.)

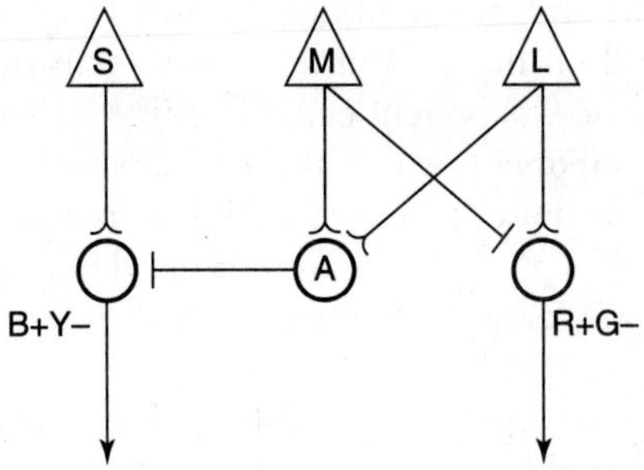

Figure 5.19
Neural circuit showing how the blue-yellow and red-green mechanisms can be created by excitatory and inhibitory inputs from the three types of cone receptors.

in this cell. The opponent response of the R+G– cell, therefore, occurs because it receives opposing inputs from the M and L cones.

The B+Y– cell receives an excitatory input from the S cone and an inhibitory input from cell A, which sums the inputs from the M and L cones. This arrangement makes sense if we remember that we perceive yellow when both the M and the L receptors are stimulated. Thus, cell A, which receives inputs from both of these receptors, causes the "yellow" response of the B+Y– mechanism.

Although this diagram is greatly simplified, it illustrates the basic principles of the neural circuitry for color coding in the retina. (See DeValois & DeValois, 1993, for examples of more complex neural circuits that have been proposed to explain opponent responding.) The important thing about this circuit is that its response is determined not only by the arrangement of inhibitory and excitatory synapses, but also by the properties of the receptors that send signals to these synapses. Processing in this circuit therefore takes place in two stages: First, the receptors respond with different patterns to different wavelengths, and then later neurons integrate the inhibitory and excitatory signals from the receptors.

Now that we know how opponent neurons are created, let's consider our second question: Why are opponent neurons necessary? Doesn't the firing pattern of the three types of cone receptors contain adequate information to signal which wavelength has been presented? The answer to this question is *yes*, but processing the receptor information further changes it into a form that signals specific wavelengths more clearly and efficiently.

To understand what this means, let's consider the response of the opponent R+G– cell in Figure 5.20b. To calculate this cell's response we refer to Figure 5.20a and subtract the M receptor's response curve from the L receptor's response curve. This transforms the M and L responses of Figure 5.20a into the opponent response of the R+G– cell of Figure 5.20b.

We can understand what subtracting the M receptor response from the L receptor response accomplishes by comparing the records in the right panels of Figure 5.20, which show how the receptors (top panel) and the opponent cell (bottom panel) respond

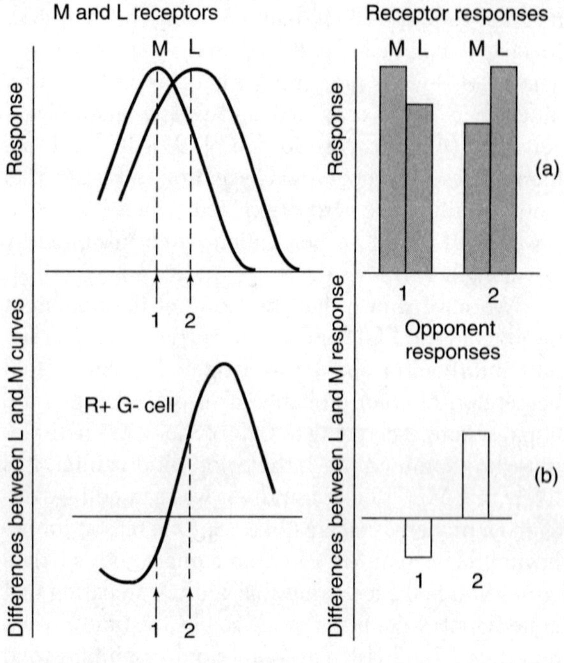

Figure 5.20
(a) Left: Response curves for the M and L receptors. Right: Bar graph indicating the size of the responses generated in the receptors by wavelengths 1 (left pair of bars) and 2 (right pair). (b) Left: Response of an R + G– cell that receives excitatory input from the L receptor and inhibitory input from the M receptor. Right: Bar graph showing the opponent response of the R + G– cell to wavelengths 1 and 2. The response to 1 is inhibitory, and the response to 2 is excitatory.

to two nearby wavelengths, labeled 1 and 2 in Figure 5.20. The top right panel shows that when wavelength 1 is presented, receptor M responds more than receptor L, and when wavelength 2 is presented, receptor L responds more than receptor M. But notice how much simpler this information becomes when we take the *differences* between the M and L responses and plot them in the lower right panel. Clearly, the opponent information in the bottom panel is simpler, and this simplicity makes it easier to tell the difference between the neural responses generated by each of the wavelengths.

Thus, the information contained in the firing of opponent cells transmits information about wavelength more efficiently than the information contained in the receptor response (Bucksbaum & Gottschach, 1983). In fact, it has been suggested that we perceive red when R+G– cells fire, green when G+R– cells fire, blue when B+Y– cells fire, and yellow when Y+B– cells fire (Abramov & Gordon, 1994). If this is so, then the response of our R+G– neuron in Figure 5.20 would result in the perception "red" when excited by wavelength 2 and no perception when inhibited by wavelength 1.

We have shown that the firing of the opponent neurons in the LGN and striate cortex (Area V1) signals information about wavelength. But our actual perception of color probably takes place later in the visual system. According to Oliver Sacks, the neurologist who examined Mr. I, the color blind painter, it is likely that Mr. I's color blindness was caused by damage to a higher visual area like V4. One reason for believing this is that Mr. I had no damage to his striate cortex and had excellent visual acuity, indicating that cone signals were being processed by the brain. Sacks describes Mr. I's vision as "V1 vision"—acuity is good and different wavelengths cause different shades of gray, but the actual perception of color has not yet been formed. That comes later.

Our description of the physiological mechanisms of color vision in the retina, the LGN, and the cortex verifies one of the major themes of this book: *Perception is shaped by neural processing.* We can now refine this statement by restating it as follows: *Visual perception is shaped by neural processing at all stages of the visual system.* Thus, something that happens right at the beginning of the process—light stimulating three different kinds of receptors—determines the way we mix colors to match other colors. Then a process that occurs later—the signals from the receptors forming opponent neurons—determine experiences such as the perception of afterimages and simultaneous contrast (Figure 5.21).

Thus, although the firing of the receptors in the retina and opponent neurons in the LGN and striate cortex occurs near the beginning of the perceptual process and may not *directly* cause color perception, this early processing leaves its imprint on our perceptions. To put this another way: Perception is determined both by what happens at the "end of the line" and by things that happen on the way there.

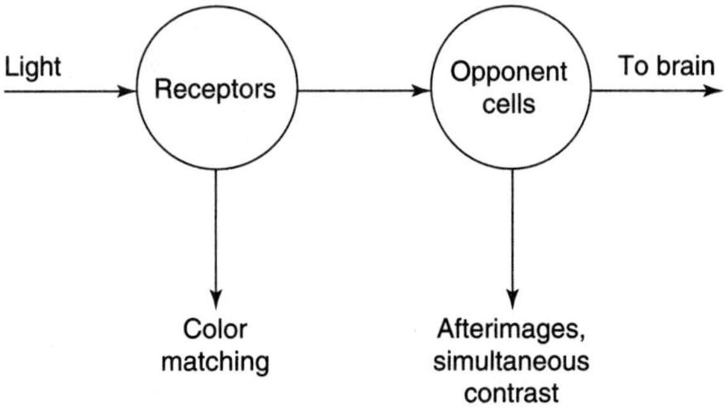

Figure 5.21
Our experience of color vision is shaped by physiological mechanisms both in the receptors and in the opponent neurons. The existence of three different kinds of cone receptors is responsible for the fact that we need a minimum of three wavelengths to match any wavelength in the spectrum. The opponent cells are responsible for perceptual experiences such as afterimages and simultaneous contrast. Note that, although the activity in the receptors and other neurons early in the visual system may shape our perception of color, color perception doesn't actually occur until sometime after the signals from these early neurons reach the brain.

Color Deficiency

It has long been known that some people have difficulty perceiving certain colors. Perhaps the most famous early report of **color deficiency,** an inability to perceive some of the colors that people with normal color vision can perceive, was provided by the well-known 19th-century chemist John Dalton (1798/1948), who described his own color perceptions as follows: "All crimsons appear to me to consist chiefly of dark blue: but many of them seem to have a tinge of dark brown. I have seen specimens of crimson, claret, and mud, which were very nearly alike" (p. 102).

Dalton's descriptions of his abnormal color perceptions led to the early use of the term *Daltonism* to describe color deficiency. We now know that there are a number of different types of color deficiency. This has been determined by color vision tests like the ones shown in Color Plate 2.6, which are called **Ishihara plates.** Subjects who are color deficient perceive either different numbers from a person with trichromatic vision or no numbers at all, as explained in the Color Essay. Another way to determine the presence of color deficiency is by using the color-matching procedure to determine the minimum number of wavelengths needed to match any other wavelength in the spectrum. This procedure has revealed the following three types of color deficiency:

1. A **monochromat** can match any wavelength in the spectrum by adjusting the intensity of any other wavelength. Thus, a monochromat needs only one wavelength to match any color in the spectrum.
2. A **dichromat** needs only two wavelengths to match all other wavelengths in the spectrum.
3. An **anomalous trichromat** needs three wavelengths to match any wavelength, just as a normal trichromat does. However, the anomalous trichromat mixes these wavelengths in different proportions from a trichromat, and an anomalous trichromat is not as good at discriminating between wavelengths that are close together.

Once we have determined whether a person's vision is color-deficient, we are still left with the question: What colors does a person with color deficiency see? When I pose this question in my class, someone inevitably suggests that we can answer this question by pointing to objects of various colors and asking a color-deficient person what he sees. This method does not, however, really tell us what the person perceives, because a color-deficient person may say "red" when we point to a strawberry simply because he has learned that people call strawberries "red." Mr. I was skilled at naming colors since he had color vision for the first 65 years of his life, but even people who have been color deficient from birth can learn to correctly label the colors of familiar objects. However, when a dichromat says a strawberry is red he may, for all we know, be having an experience similar to what a person with normal color vision would call "yellow."

To determine what a dichromat perceives we need to locate a **unilateral dichromat**—a person with trichromatic vision in one eye and dichromatic vision in the other eye. Since both of the unilateral dichromat's eyes are connected to the same brain, this person can look at a color with his dichromatic eye and then determine which color it corresponds to in his trichromatic eye. Although unilateral dichromats are extremely rare, the few who have been tested have helped us determine the nature of a dichromat's color experience (Alpern, Kitahara, & Krantz, 1983; Graham et al., 1961; Sloan & Wollach, 1948). Let's now look at the nature of the color experience of both monochromats and dichromats.

Monochromatism

Monochromatism is a rare form of color blindness that is usually hereditary and occurs in only about 10 people out of 1 million (LeGrand, 1957). Monochromats usually have no functioning cones; therefore their vision has the characteristics of rod vision in both dim and bright lights. Monochromats see everything in shades of lightness (white, gray, and black) and can therefore be called *color blind* (as opposed to dichromats, who see some chromatic colors and therefore should be called *color deficient*).

In addition to a loss of color vision, people with hereditary monochromatism have poor visual acuity and are so sensitive to bright lights that they often must protect their eyes with dark glasses during the day. The reason for this sensitivity is that the rod system is not designed to function in bright light and so becomes overloaded in strong illumination, creating a perception of glare.

Dichromatism

Dichromats experience some colors, though a lesser range than trichromats. There are three major forms of dichromatism: *protanopia*, *deuteranopia*, and *tritanopia*. The two most common kinds, protanopia and deuteranopia, are inherited through a gene located on the X chromosome (Nathans et al., 1986). Since males (XY) have only one X chromosome, a defect in the visual pigment gene on this chromosome causes color deficiency. Females (XX), on the other hand, with their two X chromosomes, are less likely to become color-deficient, since only one normal gene is required for normal color vision. These forms of color vision are therefore called *sex-linked* because women can carry the gene for color deficiency without being color-deficient themselves, and they can pass the condition to their male offspring. Thus, many more men than women are protanopes or deuteranopes.

- **Protanopia** affects 1 percent of males and 0.02 percent of females and results in the perception of colors across the spectrum indicated in Figure 5.22. A protanope perceives short-wavelength light as blue, and as wavelength is increased, the blue becomes less and less saturated until, at 492 nm, the protanope perceives gray. The wavelength at which the protanope perceives gray is called the **neutral point.** At wavelengths above the neutral point, the protanope perceives yellow, which becomes increasingly saturated as wavelength is increased, until at the long-wavelength end of the spectrum the protanope perceives a saturated yellow.
- **Deuteranopia** affects about 1 percent of males and 0.01 percent of females and results in the perception of colors across the spectrum as shown in Figure 5.22. A deuteranope perceives blue at short wavelengths, sees yellow at long wavelengths, and has a neutral point at about 498 nm (Boynton, 1979).
- **Tritanopia** is very rare, affecting only about 0.002 percent of males and 0.001 percent of females. As indicated in Figure 5.22, a tritanope sees blue at short wavelengths, sees red at long wavelengths, and has a neutral point at 570 nm (Alpern, Kitahara, & Krantz, 1983).

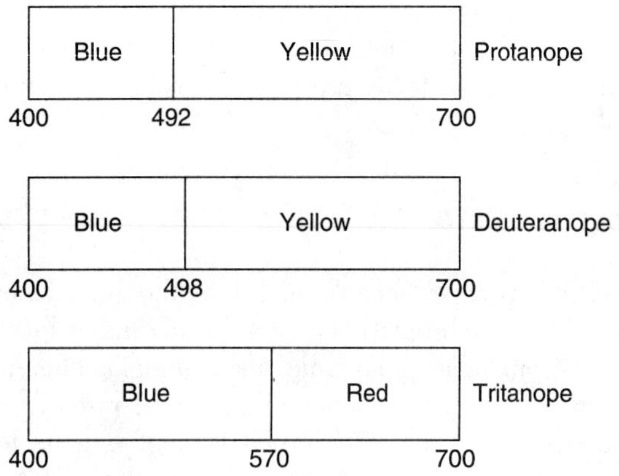

Figure 5.22
The color perceptions of the three kinds of dichromats. The number under the dividing line indicates the wavelength of the neutral point, the wavelength at which gray is perceived.

Physiological Mechanisms

What are the physiological mechanisms of color deficiency? Most monochromats have no color vision because they have just one type of cone or no cones. Dichromats are missing one visual pigment, with the protanope missing the long-wavelength pigment and the deuteranope missing the medium-wavelength pigment (Rushton, 1964). Because of the tritanope's rarity and because of the low number of short-wavelength cones, even in normal retinas, it has been difficult to determine which pigment tritanopes are missing, but they are probably missing the short-wavelength pigment.

More recent research has identified differences in the genes that determine visual pigment structure in trichromats and dichromats (Nathans et al., 1986). Based on this gene research, it has also been suggested that anomalous trichromats probably match colors differently from normal trichromats and have more difficulty discriminating between some wavelengths because their M and L pigment spectra have been shifted so they are closer together (Neitz, Neitz, & Jacobs, 1991).

Something to Consider: Colorless Wavelengths and Private Experiences

In addition to posing problems for us to solve, such as discovering the sensory code for wavelength, color perception also raises some interesting philosophical questions that apply not only to color perception but to other kinds of perception as well.

Are Wavelengths Colored?

Let's consider the question, "What makes a tomato red?" This might at first seem like an easy question, because we can answer that a tomato looks red because it reflects long-wavelength light. And this answer is correct, as far as it goes. Long wavelengths *are* usually associated with "redness."

But let's push our question further by asking, *why* do long wavelengths look red? Why don't long wavelengths look blue? or green? Although specific colors are related to specific wavelengths, the connection between wavelength and the experience we call "color" is an arbitrary one. There is nothing intrinsically "red" about long wavelengths or "blue" about short wavelengths. In fact, in his book *Opticks*, Isaac Newton made the following observation regarding the connection between wavelength and color:

> The Rays to speak properly are not coloured. In them there is nothing else than a certain Power and Disposition to stir up a Sensation of this or that Colour . . . So Colours in the Object are nothing but a Disposition to reflect this or that sort of Rays more copiously than the rest . . .

Newton was saying that the colors that we see in response to different wavelengths are not *contained* in the rays of light themselves. Rather, colors are *created* by our perceptual system, and although specific colors are related to specific wavelengths, the connection between wavelength and the experience we call color is an arbitrary one. There is nothing intrinsically "red" about long wavelengths or "blue" about short wavelengths. In fact, the light rays are simply energy and actually have no color at all.

We can find similar examples in the other senses. We hear in response to pressure changes in the air. But why do we perceive rapid pressure changes as high-pitched and slow pressure changes as low-pitched? Is there anything intrinsically "high-pitched" about rapid pressure changes? Or consider the sense of smell. We perceive some substances as "sweet" and others as "rancid," but where is the "sweetness" or "rancidity" in the molecular structure of the substances that enter the nose? Again, the answer is that these perceptions are not in the molecular structure. They are created by the action of the molecules on our nervous system.

The idea that our actual *experience* is created by our nervous system is hard for some people to understand. "After all," they say, "aren't we simply seeing what's out there?" It comes as a surprise to them that we experience things such as colors, sounds, tastes, or smells by a process in which our nervous system is stimulated by environmental energy and then adds the experience.

This idea becomes easier to appreciate when we ask the question: What do animals perceive? We find many examples of situations in which animals are capable of perceiving energy that humans can't perceive at all. Consider, for example, the honeybee. The honeybee has trichromatic vision, but its three kinds of receptors are spread out over more of the spectrum than are human receptors (Figure 5.23). Honeybees are sensitive to light in the ultraviolet region of the spectrum (very short wavelengths) that

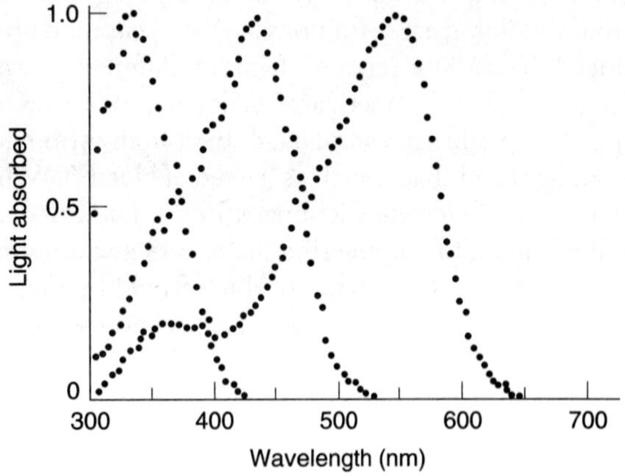

Figure 5.23
Absorption curves of the honeybee's three cone pigments. From these curves we can infer that the honeybee's vision extends into the ultraviolet (very-short-wavelength) region of the spectrum. (Adapted from Menzel et al., 1986.)

humans can't see, because one of the honeybee's receptors absorbs maximally at 335 nm (Menzel & Backhaus, 1989; Menzel et al., 1986). What "color" do you think bees perceive at these short wavelengths? You are free to guess, but you really have no way of knowing. Since, as Newton stated, "The rays are not colored," there is no color in the wavelengths, so the bee's nervous system creates its experience of color. For all we know, the honeybee's experience of color is quite different from ours, even for wavelengths that both humans and honeybees perceive.

The idea that the experience of color is a creation of the nervous system adds another dimension to the idea that our experience is shaped by physiology. Experience is not only *shaped* by physiology, but, in cases such as color vision, hearing, taste, and smell, the very nature of our experience is *created* by physiology.

Perception as a Private Experience

The colors assigned to different wavelengths are not only created by our physiology, but the experience of color is private for each person. One way to appreciate this is to think about how you might describe the experience of color to a person who is completely color blind. If you look in the dictionary for guidance, what you'll find are definitions like "the sensation produced by various rays of light of different wavelengths" (Oxford American Dictionary, 1980) or "a quality of visible phenomena, distinct from form and from light and shade, such as the red of blood." (Webster's New Collegiate Dictionary, 1956). The first definition doesn't help describe the experience and the second one uses an example which would be meaningless to a color blind person who has never seen the "red of blood."

If the only way we can describe color is by examples, it is impossible to make someone who is color blind understand what it is like to experience color. You can tell that person that you experience something called "blue" when you look at the sky, but that doesn't convey the *quality* of that experience. A similar situation exists for color-deficient people who see some colors but not as many as a person with normal color vision. Even if such a person says that the sky looks blue, it is quite likely that the color-deficient person is *experiencing* something quite different than a color-normal observer. (Remember from our earlier discussion that people who are color deficient can learn the names of common objects.)

We can generalize from our examples for color to perception as a whole, by saying that *perception is a private experience.* Just as we can't share the essence of experiencing blue with someone who has never experienced blue, we also can't share the essence of being touched or tickled, or smelling a rose, or tasting an apple, or hearing music, with someone who has never experienced those things.

Does this mean that each person perceives the world in different ways, so that you might perceive colors or sounds very differently than other people? We usually make the assumption that most people's perceptual experiences are generally similar, even though we have no way of knowing this for sure. But even though we assume approximate similarity of experience for "normal" observers, it is likely that small differences in experience do exist even for these observers, because of differences in people's perceptual systems, and also because of differences in people's expectations, past experiences, and culture. Later in this book, especially when we discuss pain perception, we will return to this idea that a person's expectations, past experiences, and culture influence what a person perceives.

How Color Affects Taste and Smell

If, when you were younger, you discovered the magic of your mother's food coloring, you may have created, as I once did, such exotic foods as green mashed potatoes or blue applesauce. If you then tried to interest someone in eating your concoctions, you probably found that people are not enthusiastic about trying strangely colored foods. The appearance of food plays an important role in people's attitudes about food, as evidenced by the large sums of money spent to produce appetizing looking pictures to put on the cans, jars, and boxes that package the food.

There is no question that the appearance of food influences its desirability, and research also indicates that people's ability to identify tastes and smells depends to some degree on color. For example, when Arnold Hyman (1983) asked subjects to identify the taste of samples of white birch beer, he found that subjects correctly identified it 70 percent of the time if the samples were colorless. However, when colored red, accuracy dropped to 25 percent, with various subjects stating that the red-colored birch beer tasted like cherry cough medicine, cherry soda, mint flavor, and dentist's mouthwash.

In Hyman's experiment, the presence of an extraneous color hampered taste identification, but other experiments have shown that when the color matches the taste (for example, red for cherry taste or yellow for lemon taste) people are much better at identifying the taste than if the color doesn't match the taste. Thus, C. N. DuBose and co-workers (1980) found that the taste of cherry, orange, and lime beverages were judged correctly an average of 67 percent of the time if the colors matched their beverages' taste, but were judged correctly only 37 percent of the time if the solutions were colorless or 28 percent if the colors didn't match the taste.

Research on how color affects the identification of odors has obtained essentially similar results—when colors and odors match, subjects are better at identifying the odor (Davis, 1981; Zellner, Bartoli, & Eckard, 1991). A possible explanation for the enhancing effect of color on odor identification is based on the idea that identifying odors appears to involve two processes: First the subject perceives the odor and then the subject must retrieve the odor's name from his or her memory—something people find very difficult to do. Thus, William Cain (1979, 1980) found that if a subject assigns a correct name to an odor the first time they smell it (for example, labeling an orange "orange"), they usually identify the object correctly the next time it is presented. If, however, they incorrectly label an object the first time they smell it (for example, labeling machine oil "cheese"), they usually misidentify it the next time it is presented. Cain concludes that people's difficulty in identifying odors occurs primarily because of their inability to retrieve the odor's name from their memory.

Thus, a color consistent with a substance's odor might aid in identification of that odor because it provides information that signals what the odor is likely to be. Sensing an orange leads us to expect the smell we associate with an orange, and when we actually smell that odor we can easily identify it. In addition to this cognitive effect on order perception there may also be a *perceptual* component operating as well. Cain reports such an effect when he notes that when subjects are told what an odor actually is, the odor becomes clearer to them. For example, when the experimenter tells a subject that a smell he had identified as "fishy-goaty-oily" actually comes from leather, the subject reports that his experience becomes *transformed* into the smell of leather. Thus, the effect of color on smell may involve a cognitive mechanism—thought processes such as expectations—but the ultimate outcome may be perceptual—the perceived smell changes.

Study Questions

Underlying Principles

Find examples of the following principles in this chapter:

- Selective receptors (142)
- Receptive fields/neural selectivity (144)
- Distributed response (142)
- Columnar organization (146)
- Parallel pathways (146)
- Physiological connections with perception (148)
- Cognitive influences (153)

See pages 128–130 for descriptions of these principles.

Some Basic Properties of Color

1. What is perceptual organization and how does color perception facilitate it? (132)
2. Why have some researchers proposed that monkey and human color vision evolved for the purpose of detecting fruit in the forest? (132)
3. Is color vision essential for human survival? (132)
4. What is the difference between chromatic and achromatic color? (133)
5. What is saturation? It has been estimated that we can discriminate about 2 million different colors. How was that estimate determined? (134)
6. How many color terms does it take to describe all colors we can discriminate? What are these terms? (134)
7. Describe the results of cross-cultural research on color naming. (134)
8. What did Newton discover about color in his room at Cambridge University? (136)
9. What is a wavelength distribution? What are the wavelength distributions of tungsten light and of white light? (136)
10. What is reflectance? a reflectance curve? selective reflection? (136)
11. What can we conclude about a color if it has the property of selective reflection? (137)
12. What is the relationship between the color perceived and the wavelengths reflected? (137)

Behavioral Research: Discovery of the Sensory Code for Color

13. What are color matching experiments? What result of color matching experiments led to the trichromatic theory of color vision? (138)
14. What is the trichromatic theory and who is associated with it? (139)
15. Describe observations about afterimages, simultaneous color contrast, color visualization, and color naming that support the idea that certain colors are opposites. What are these opposite pairs of colors? (139)
16. What is the opponent-process theory of color vision and who was associated with it? (141)

Physiological Research on Color Vision

17. What physiological research involving cone pigments supports the trichromatic theory of color vision? (142)
18. What is the connection between the pattern of cone receptor responding and color perception? (142)
19. Understand how to use the information in 18, above, to predict what colors will result from superimposing colored lights. (142)
20. What does it mean to say that two lights are metamers? (143)
21. Can lights that are physically different be perceptually identical? (143)
22. What structural feature is different in the different types of visual pigments? (143)
23. What is the relationship between the absorption spectrum of the visual pigments and the amino acid sequence of the protein opsin? (143)

24. A difference of one amino acid causes a shift of ______ nm in the peak of the pigments absorption spectrum. (143)

25. A person with normal color vision can have four different cone pigments. True or false? (143)

26. Describe the opponent responses of neurons in the fish retina and neurons in the monkey lateral geniculate body. (144)

27. Describe the receptive field layout and response to wavelength of type 1 color-opponent cells and double color-opponent cells. (145)

28. What is special about double color-opponent cells with an R+G– center, according to Livingstone and Hubel? (145)

29. What are blobs and what are the properties of neurons in these blobs? (146)

30. Information about color is processed in which stream in the extrastriate cortex? (146)

31. Describe the columnar organization of opponent neurons. (146)

32. Understand how the neural circuit in Figure 5.19 creates opponent cells from signals generated by the three types of cone receptors. (146)

33. What is the advantage of opponent neurons? (understand the point of Figure 5.20) (147)

34. Where does our perception of color probably occur in the visual system? Damage in which area of the cortex probably caused the color blindness of Mr. I, the painter described at the beginning of the chapter? (148)

35. What does it mean when we say that visual perception is shaped by neural processing at all stages of the visual system? (148)

Color Deficiency

36. What is color deficiency? (148)

37. What are two ways to determine color deficiency? (148)

38. What are the three different types of color deficiency? (149)

39. What do we need to do in order to determine what colors someone who is color deficient perceives? (149)

40. Why do we say that the color deficiency observed in two kinds of dichromats is sex-linked? (149)

41. What colors do monochromats and dichromats perceive? What are the three kinds of dichromats? What is the neutral point? (150)

42. What are the physiological mechanisms responsible for color deficiency? (150)

Something to Consider: Colorless Wavelengths and Private Experiences

43. What do we mean when we say that the wavelengths are not colored? (151)

44. How can the concept of colorless wavelengths be applied to some of the other senses? (151)

45. Can we tell what color a bee perceives from our knowledge of the absorption spectra of its visual pigments? (151)

46. What does it mean to say that experience is *created* by physiology? (152)

47. Why do we say that perception is a private experience? (152)

48. How likely is it that different people perceive the world in different ways? (152)

Across the Senses: How Color Affects Taste and Smell

49. How does adding extraneous color to a substance affect a person's ability to identify its taste? (153)

50. What is the effect of color on taste if an object's color matches its taste (for example, red for a cherry taste)? (153)

51. What are the two processes that appear to be involved in identifying odors? (153)

52. Why do people often find it difficult to identify odors? (153)

53. What is the relationship between cognition and perception in the identification of odors? (153)

6

PERCEPTUAL CONSTANCY

CHAPTER CONTENTS

Questions such as the ones on the lower right have fascinated psychologists since the beginning of scientific psychology. The reason these questions are intriguing is that each one of them describes a situation called **perceptual constancy,** in which the proximal stimulus (what happens on the retina) changes, but our distal stimulus and our perception remain constant.

We can appreciate the implications of perceptual constancy by considering what the world would be like if constancy didn't exist. If perception were based solely on the proximal stimulus, the world would be constantly changing. As your friend walks away from you, the size of his image on your retina gets smaller, so he would appear to get shorter and shorter with each step (Figure 6.1). As you walk from outdoors, where you are illuminated by the sun's light, with equal amounts of all wavelengths, to indoors, where you are illuminated by tungsten light, which is rich in long-wavelengths, your white shirt would turn yellow (Figure 6.2). As you view your watch from above, it looks circular but, glancing at it at an angle on your wrist, it would appear elliptical (Figure 6.3). In other words, without constancy you would be living in a confusing world, populated by constantly changing objects whose true sizes, shapes, and colors would be difficult to determine.

Fortunately, you are not subjected to the confusion of a world populated by objects with properties that are constantly changing. The situation is, in fact, quite the opposite. You perceive your friend as remaining 5′ 10″ tall as he walks away. Your shirt remains white whether it is illuminated by white light or long-wavelength rich tungsten light. Your watch remains circular no matter how you observe it. We begin

SOME QUESTIONS WE WILL CONSIDER

- Why doesn't a white shirt become yellow when the illumination changes from white light to artificial light that is rich in long wavelengths? (158)
- Why does the face of a wristwatch appear circular even when it is viewed at an angle? (167)
- Why don't people appear to shrink in size when they walk away? (168)

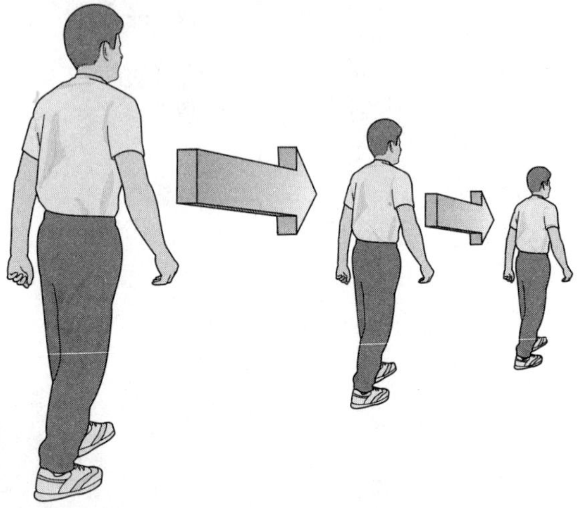

Figure 6.1
If size perception was based solely on the image on your retina, then a person would appear to get smaller as he walked away from you.

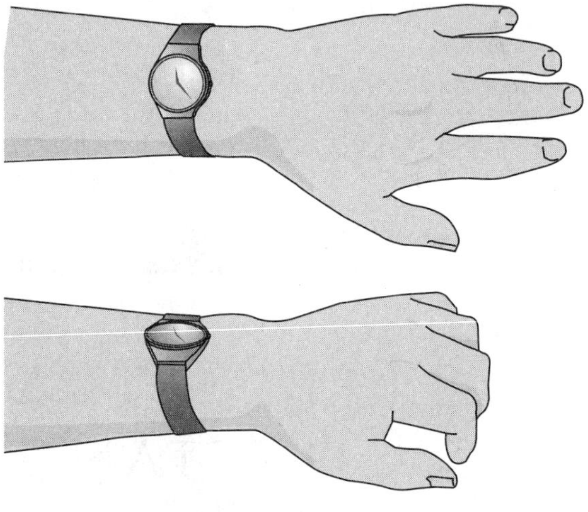

Figure 6.3
If shape perception was based solely on the image on your retina, then a circular watch would appear to have an elliptical shape when viewed from an angle.

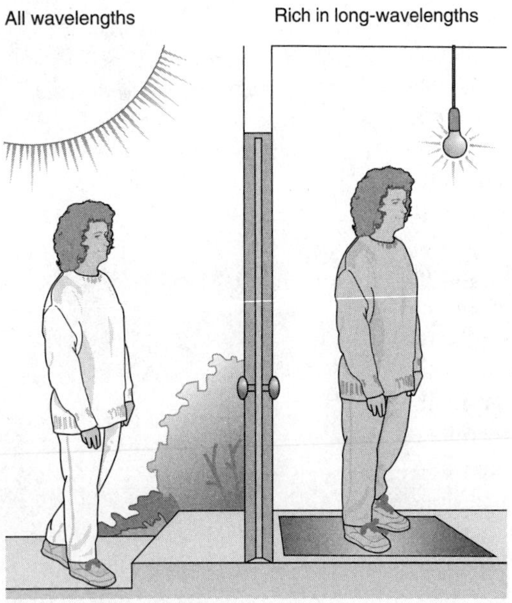

Figure 6.2
If color perception was based only on the wavelengths reaching your retina then clothes that appeared white in the sunlight (left) would change to a yellowish-red color when illuminated by a light bulb indoors (right).

our discussion of perceptual constancy by continuing our discussion of color vision from Chapter 5, and describing why our perception of chromatic colors like blue, red, and green remain relatively constant even when the illumination changes.

Color Constancy

Have you ever experienced changes in color under different illuminations? Experiments have shown that fluorescent lighting alters our perception of colors (Helson, Judd, & Wilson, 1956), and many people have found, unhappily, that their new clothes, which looked exactly right in the fluorescently lit store, did not appear the same color at home (Hurvich, 1981). Although small shifts of color perception sometimes do occur when the illumination changes, our overwhelming experience is that colors remain at least approximately constant under most natural conditions.[1] To experience the effects of color constancy do the following demonstration.

DEMONSTRATION

Color Perception under Changing Illumination

View Color Plates 2.3 and 2.4 so that they are illuminated by natural light by taking them outdoors or illuminating them with light from a window. Then illuminate them with the tungsten light bulb of your desk lamp. Notice whether the colors change and, if so, how much they change. ●

In this demonstration you may have noticed some change in color as you changed the illumination, but the change was probably much less than we would predict based on the change in the wavelength distribution of the light. Even though the wavelengths reflected from a blue object illuminated by long-wavelength rich tungsten light can match the wavelengths reflected by a yellow object illuminated by sunlight (Jameson, 1985), our perception of color remains relatively constant with changing illumination. As color-vision researcher Dorthea Jameson puts it, "A blue bird would not be mistaken for a goldfinch if it were brought indoors" (1985, p. 84).

Why does color constancy occur? We can point to a number of possible causes.

Chromatic Adaptation

One answer to why color constancy occurs lies in the results of the following demonstration.

[1]In some unnatural conditions like viewing colors under the sodium vapor lamps that sometimes illuminate highways or parking lots, the true colors of objects can become totally obscured. This occurs because the sodium illumination contains only a narrow band of wavelengths.

DEMONSTRATION

Adapting to Red

Illuminate the red field of Color Plate 2.7 with a bright light from your desk lamp; then, with your left eye near the page and your right eye closed, look at the field with your left eye for about 30 to 45 seconds. At the end of this time, look up and around, first with your left eye and then with your right. ●

This demonstration shows that color perception can be changed by **chromatic adaptation**—prolonged exposure to chromatic color. Adaptation to the red light selectively bleaches your long-wavelength cone pigment, which decreases your sensitivity to red light and causes you to see the reds and oranges viewed with your left (adapted) eye as less saturated and bright than those viewed with the right eye.

We can understand how chromatic adaptation contributes to color constancy by considering what happens when you walk into a room illuminated with tungsten light. The eye adapts to the long wavelengths that predominate in the tungsten light, decreasing your eye's sensitivity to long wavelengths. This decreased sensitivity causes the long-wavelength light reflected from objects to have less effect than before adaptation, and this compensates for the greater amount of long-wavelength "tungsten" light that is reflected from everything in the room. The result is a negligible change in your perception of color.

This idea that chromatic adaptation is responsible for color constancy has been tested in an experiment by Keiji Uchikawa, Hiromi Uchikawa, and Robert Boynton (1989) who had subjects view isolated patches of colored paper as shown in Figure 6.4, under three different conditions: Condition 1: Paper and observer illuminated by white light; Condition 2: Paper illuminated by red light, observer by white (the illumination of the object is changed but the observer is not chromatically adapted); and Condition 3: Both paper and observer illuminated by red

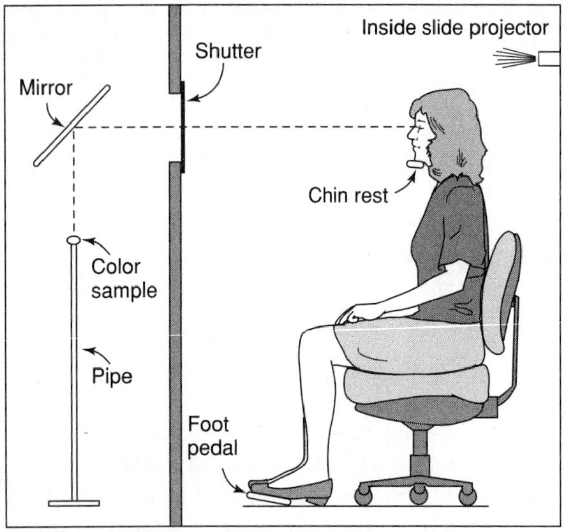

Figure 6.4
The experimental arrangement for Uchikawa et al.'s (1989) experiment. The subject viewed a patch of colored paper (color sample) located on the other side of a partition. The lighting of the color sample was changed by light from a slide projector in the left room (projector not shown). The lighting of the subject's environment was changed by light from a slide projector in the right room (inside slide projector).

light (the illumination of the object is changed and the observer is chromatically adapted).

The results from these three conditions are shown in Table 6.1. For Condition 1, the baseline condition, a green patch is perceived as green. In Condition 2, where the illumination on the object is changed but the observer experiences no chromatic adaptation, the observer perceives the patches of color as being shifted toward the red. Thus, color constancy did not occur in this condition. But in Condition 3, in which the observer did experience chromatic adaptation, perception was shifted only slightly to the red. Thus, the chromatic adaptation has created *partial* color constancy—the perception of the object is shifted but not as much as when there was no chromatic adaptation.

The Effect of the Surroundings

An object's perceived color is affected not only by the observer's state of adaptation, but also by the object's surroundings, as shown by the following demonstration.

DEMONSTRATION

Color and the Surroundings

Illuminate the green quadrant of Color Plate 2.4 with tungsten light. As you illuminate it, then look at the square through a small hole punched in a piece of paper, so that all you see through the hole is part of the green area. Now repeat this observation while illuminating the same area with daylight from your window. ●

When the surroundings are masked, most people perceive the green area to be slightly more yellow

Table 6.1
Results of Uchikawa et al.'s (1989) experiment

Condition	Paper Illumination	Observer Illumination	Perception of Normally Green Paper
1: Baseline	White	White	Green
2: No chromatic adaptation	Red	White	Shifted toward red
3: Chromatic adaptation	Red	Red	Shifted just slightly toward red

under the tungsten light than in daylight. The fact that color constancy works less well when we mask the surroundings has been studied by a number of investigators, who have shown that color constancy works best when an object is surrounded by objects of many different colors. Much of this research has used displays like the one in Color Plate 2.8, which is called a *Mondrian display*, because of its similarity to works created by the Dutch painter Piet Mondrian (Land, 1983, 1986; Land & McCann, 1971). For some theories about exactly how the presence of the surroundings enhances color constancy, see Brainard and Wandell (1986), Land (1983, 1986), and Pokorny, Shevall, and Smith (1991).

Memory Color

Although color constancy doesn't depend on prior knowledge about an object's color (it works with meaningless stimuli like colored squares), people's past knowledge can have a small effect on color perception through the operation of a phenomenon called **memory color,** in which an object's characteristic color influences our perception of its color. John Delk and Samuel Fillenbaum (1965) demonstrated memory color by showing observers shapes like the ones in Figure 6.5, all of which were cut from the same sheet of orange-red cardboard. Shapes such as the heart and the apple are characteristically red, while others, such as the bell and the mushroom, are not. The observer's task was to match the color of each object to that of a background field by adjusting the amount of redness in the background field. The result, in agreement with the idea of memory color, was that subjects matched characteristically red objects, such as the heart and the apple, with a redder background field than they used for nonred objects, such as the bell and the mushroom.

Figure 6.5
Some of the stimuli used in Delk and Fillenbaum's (1965) experiment on memory color. Although all of the stimuli were cut from the same orange-red paper, the apple and the heart were judged to appear slightly redder than the mushroom and the bell.

Physiological Mechanisms

So far we have taken a behavioral approach to color constancy, but we can consider color constancy from a physiological point of view as well. We have already seen that selective bleaching of visual pigments by chromatic adaptation is one physiological mechanism underlying color constancy, but we can also find a possible physiological basis for color constancy far from the receptors, in neurons of area V4 of the extrastriate cortex.

Semir Zeki (1983a, 1983b, 1984) studied neurons in area V4 by using Mondrian displays. In a typical experiment, Zeki positioned a square of this display that looked green and reflected predominantly medium-wavelength light onto the receptive field of a monkey's G+R– striate neuron and onto the receptive field of a V4 neuron. When Zeki illuminated the display with white light, he found that both the G+R– striate neuron and the V4 neuron fired. This makes sense, since the square reflects mostly medium-wavelengths when illuminated by white light. However, when he illuminated the display with long-wavelength light so now the green patch reflected more long-wavelength light than medium-wavelength light, the G+R– neuron's firing was inhibited, but the V4 neuron continued to respond (Table 6.2).

We can describe the difference between the response of V1 and V4 neurons as follows: The response of V1 neurons is correlated with the *wavelengths* reflected from the patch—it responds with excitation when short-wavelength light is present and with inhibition when long-wavelength light is present; the response of V4 neurons is correlated with the *color* that the patch appeared to the experimenter (and presumably also the monkey).

Because the patch was part of a complex display, it appeared green under both white and

Table 6.2
Results of Zeki experiments in which he illuminated a Mondrian display with white and long-wavelength lights and noted how V1 and V4 neurons responded to a square that looked green under both illuminations.

	Response of V1 Neuron (G+R–)	Response of V4 Neuron
White illumination	Excited	Excited
Long-Wavelength illumination	Inhibited	Excited

long-wavelength illumination, and the V4 neuron fired similarly in both cases. Zeki suggests that neurons such as this one represent the physiology behind color constancy and perhaps color perception in general. It is, however, unlikely that these V4 neurons are the final answer to color perception, because (1) they respond to white light, and (2) no receptive fields for V4 neurons are found outside the central 30 degrees of the visual field, but people experience color outside of this area (Abramov & Gordon, 1994). Thus, V4 is important for color vision, but additional areas are probably involved as well.

Lightness Constancy

We now focus on the property of objects called **lightness**—our perception of an object as being white, black, or shades of gray. When we are experiencing **lightness constancy** our perception of the whiteness, blackness, or grayness of objects remains constant no matter how the illumination is changed.

When we are experiencing lightness constancy, our perception of lightness is being determined by an object's **albedo**—the percentage of the light reflected from the object. Objects that look black have *low albedo;* they reflect about 5 percent of the light falling on them into your eye. Objects that look gray reflect about 10 to 70 percent of the light (depending on the shade of gray), and objects that look white, like the paper in this book, have *high albedo,* they reflect 80 to 90 percent of the light. Thus, our perception of an object's lightness is related not to the *amount* of light that is reflected from the object, which can change depending on the illumination, but on the *percentage* of light reflected from the object, which remains the same no matter what the illumination. We see a piece of white paper as white in a dimly lit room or in bright sunlight; and we see the black print on that paper as black, no matter what the illumination.

If lightness constancy didn't occur, the lightness of the objects around us would be constantly changing. Taking a piece of coal from inside to outside would change it from black to white! Without lightness constancy, it would become meaningless to say "this coal is black" or "this paper is white," because their lightness would change each time we changed the illumination.

What is responsible for lightness constancy? As for color constancy, we can point to a number of possible causes.

Intensity Relationships: The Ratio Principle

Evidence that relationships help cause lightness constancy is provided by the *simultaneous contrast effect,* illustrated in Figure 6.6. The two squares in this figure are physically different but appear the same, or nearly the same, because they are surrounded by different backgrounds. (To eliminate the effect of the backgrounds, view the small squares through two holes punched in a card.) The principle behind this effect is called the **ratio principle** (Jacobson & Gilchrist, 1988; Wallach, 1963). According to this principle, two areas that reflect different amounts of light will look the same if the ratios of their intensities to the intensities of the surrounds are kept constant (Figure 6.7). Thus, when you walk inside, out of the bright sunlight, the black letters on your T-shirt remain black and the white area remains white, because the *ratio* of intensities reflected from the two areas remains the same (Figure 6.8).

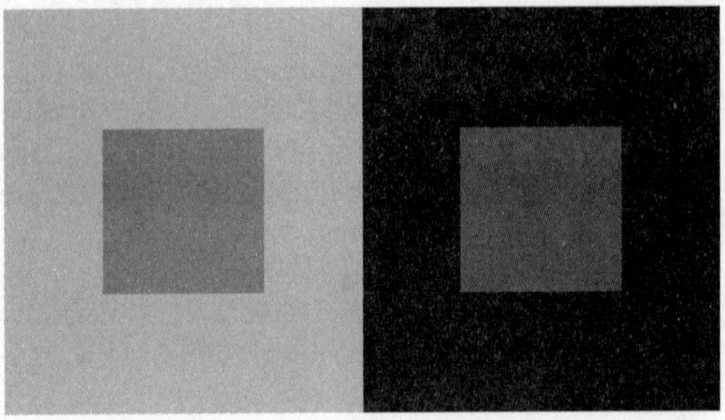

Figure 6.6
The two small squares reflect different amounts of light but appear close in lightness. To appreciate the actual physical difference between these squares, punch two holes 1½ inches apart in a card and look at the two squares with their backgrounds masked.

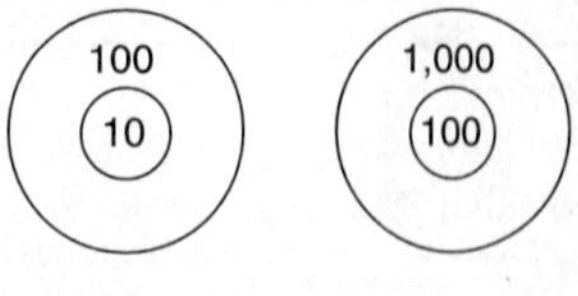

Figure 6.7
How simultaneous contrast can make two different disks appear identical. If light intensities were as indicated by the numbers in the outer rings and inner disks, the inner disks would appear identical because the ring-to-disk ratio is 10 to 1 in both cases. (Based on Wallach, 1963.)

An experiment by Gelb (1929) demonstrates that the subject must see a number of objects with different reflectances in order for the ratio principle to result in lightness constancy. Figure 6.9 shows the setup for Gelb's experiment: a disk of low reflectance was suspended in completely black surroundings and was illuminated by a hidden light that illuminated only the disk. When viewed from the observer's position, the disk, which would look black in your living room or outdoors, looked white. This result occurred because the only thing the disk could be compared to was the black background which was receiving no illumination at all. Since the black disk was reflecting far more light than anything else, it appeared white. But when Gelb placed a small piece of white paper partially in front of the illuminated black disk, the disk turned black! Introducing this piece of paper for comparison enabled the ratio principle to work and

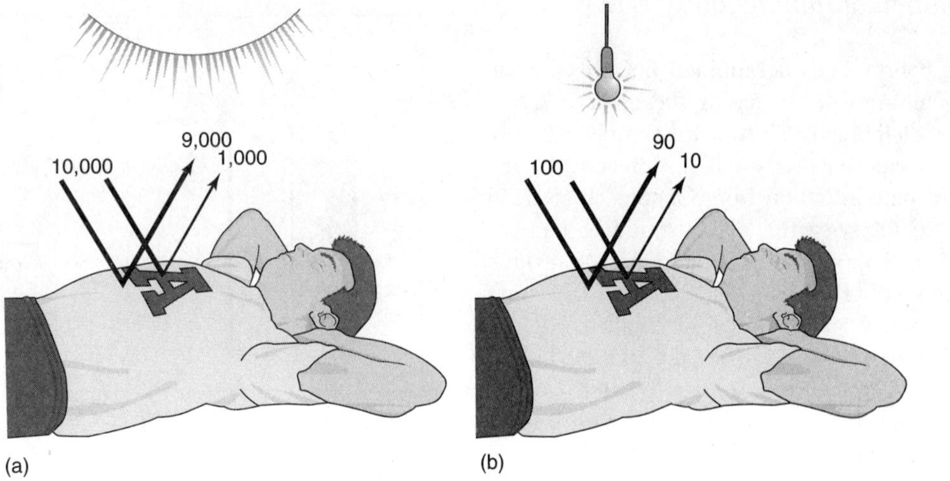

Figure 6.8
What happens to the amount of light reflected from the white and black parts of a T-shirt when viewed (a) outside so the illumination is high (intensity = 10,000), and (b) inside, so the illumination is low (intensity = 100). In both cases, the white area of the T-shirt reflects 90 percent of the light and the lettering reflects 10 percent, so that the ratio of the light intensities reflected from the white area and the letter remains at 9 to 1 under both levels of illumination and our perception of lightness remains constant.

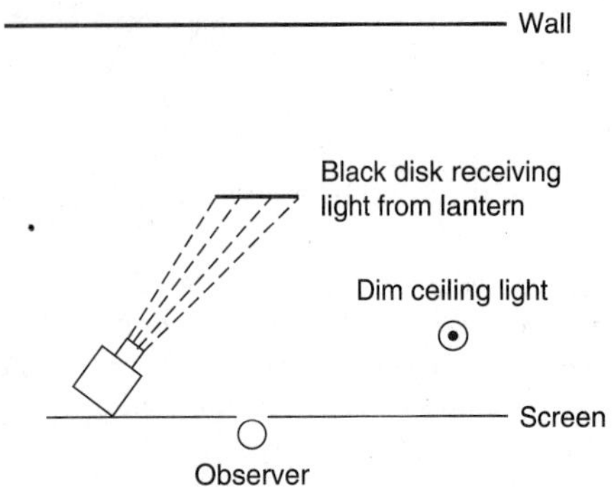

Figure 6.9
The setup of Gelb's concealed illumination experiment, seen from above. The observer could not see the light on the left, which was projected only onto the black disk. The background, which was also black, was dimly illuminated by the ceiling light. (Adapted from Hochberg, 1971.)

caused the black disk to look black. Thus, lightness constancy can break down when there are few objects in a display or when one of them (Gelb's black disk in this example) is the only one illuminated.

Interpretation of Illumination

Lightness constancy is determined not only by the pattern of illumination reaching the observer's eye, but also by the observer's *interpretation* of how an object is illuminated. For example, let's reconsider the Mach card demonstration from Chapter 2. (Reread pages 62–63 to review this demonstration.) The key result of this demonstration is that when the Mach card perceptually flips, your perception of the card's surfaces changes, so the previously shaded side appears darker than it did before the flip, and the lighter side appears lighter, even luminous. What is happening here is that the card's perceptual flip eliminates lightness constancy. Before the flip, sides of the card appear white, but afterward one side appears dark and the other appears light.

We can explain why our perception of the Mach card's lightness changes by considering how we register the illumination falling on the card. Before the card flips, we perceive edges of the card (shown as darker in the figure) as resting on the surface (indicated by the rectangle). This means that the right side of the card is illuminated and the left side is in shadow (Figure 6.10a). Our perceptual system apparently takes the illumination conditions into account, so both sides of the card appear white. Lightness constancy is working.

But when the card perceptually flips, the lower edges of the card (shown as darker) appear to be resting on the surface, and it appears that you are looking into an open book. This perceptual flip changes the apparent illumination conditions. Now the shaded left side appears to be illuminated and the illuminated right side appears to be facing away from the light (Figure 6.10b). This change creates the following problem for the perceptual system: The left side now *appears* to be illuminated but only a small amount of light is reflected from that side. However, the right side *appears* to be in the shade, but a lot of light is reflected from that side. To make sense of this situation the perceptual system concludes that the left side must be a low-reflectance material such as dark gray paper, and the right side must be a high-reflectance material

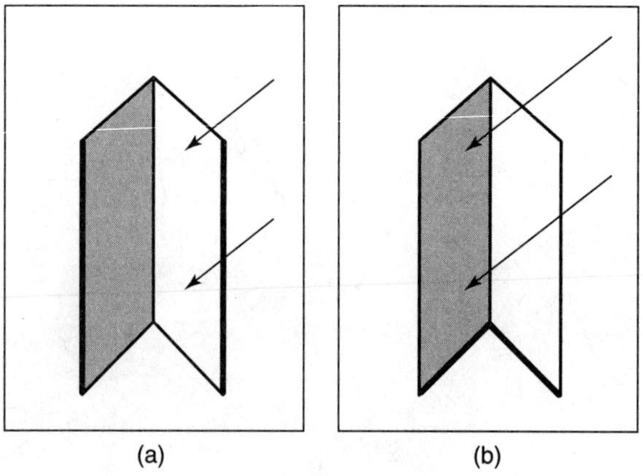

Figure 6.10
Why the Mach card changes in lightness when it perceptually "flips." (a) Initially, the two darkened edges are resting on the surface. (b) After the card flips, it appears to stand on end like an open book with its inside toward you. The darkened edges now appear to be resting on the surface. The arrows indicate the direction of the light.

such as white paper. Thus, lightness constancy breaks down and we see the two sides as being made of different kinds of paper.

The change in lightness perception we experience when the Mach card flips illustrates how our perception of illumination can affect our perception of lightness. We can also show this in another way in the following demonstration.

D E M O N S T R A T I O N

Lightness at a Corner

Stand a folded index card on end so that it resembles the outside corner of a room, and illuminate it so that one side is illuminated and the other is in shadow. When you look at the corner, you can easily tell that both sides of the corner are made of the same white material, but that the nonilluminated side is shadowed (Figure 6.11a). Now punch a hole in another card, and with the hole a few inches from the corner of the folded card, view the corner with one eye about a foot from the hole (Figure 6.11b). If, when viewing the corner through the hole, you perceive the corner as a flat surface, your perception of the left and right surfaces will change. ●

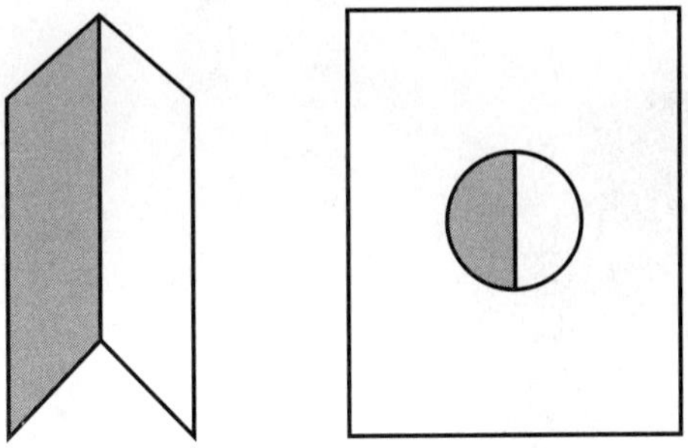

Figure 6.11
Viewing a shaded corner. (a) Illuminate the card so one side is illuminated and the other is in shadow. (b) View the card through a small hole so the two sides of the corner are visible, as shown.

Eliminating the perception of depth at the corner eliminates information about the conditions of illumination and eliminates lightness constancy, so that the light side appears lighter and the dark side appears darker. Some people even perceive the dark side as dark gray or black—a very different perception from when they saw the two sides as part of a three-dimensional corner. Thus, in both this demonstration and the Mach card demonstration, lightness constancy occurs when we interpret the illumination correctly, but it breaks down when we are unable to accurately judge the direction of the illumination.

Shadows

Lightness constancy occurs not only when we bring an object from the low illumination inside to the high illumination outside, but also when an object or surface is partially covered by a shadow. When you see a shadow on a red brick wall (Figure 6.12), you don't assume that the shadowed bricks are dark red and the bricks in sunlight are light red. Instead you assume that the shadowed and unshadowed areas are the same red all over, but that less light falls on some areas than on others.

What makes lightness constancy work in shadows? One reason is the shadow's meaningful shape. In this particular example, we know that the shadow was cast by some trees and a railing (especially since we can see the trees and railing), so we know it is the illumination that is changing, not the color of the bricks. Another clue that an illumination change is due to a shadow is provided by the nature of the shadow's contour, as illustrated by the following demonstration.

D E M O N S T R A T I O N

The Penumbra and Lightness Perception

Place an object, such as a cup, on a white piece of paper on your desk. Then illuminate the cup at an angle with your desk lamp and adjust the lamp's position to produce a shadow

Figure 6.12
The pattern created by shadows on a surface is usually interpreted as a change in the pattern of illumination, not as a change in the material making up the surface. The fact that we see all of the bricks on this wall as made of the same material, despite the illumination changes, is an example of lightness constancy.

with a slightly fuzzy border as in Figure 6.13a. (Generally, moving the lamp away from the cup makes the border get sharper.) The fuzzy border of a shadow is called the shadow's penumbra. Now take your marker and draw a thick line as shown in Figure 6.13b so you can no longer see the penumbra. What happens to your perception of the shadowed area inside the black line? ●

Covering the penumbra causes most people to perceive a change in the appearance of the shadowed area. Instead of looking like a shadow on a piece of white paper, it looks like a dark spot on the paper. Eliminating the penumbra has decreased lightness constancy so that a change in illumination is now perceived as a change in lightness.

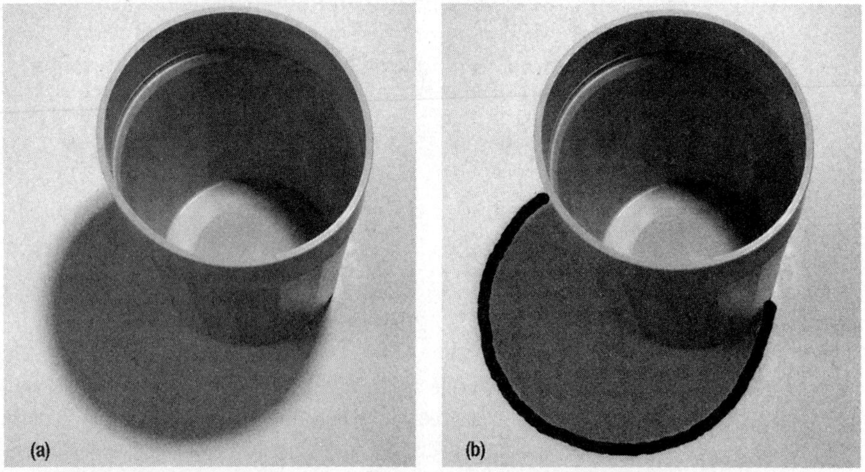

Figure 6.13
(a) A cup and its shadow. (b) The same cup and shadow with the penumbra covered by a black border.

The Physiology of Lightness Constancy

What is the physiological explanation of lightness constancy? Lateral inhibition is part of the answer, especially to explain the effect of the surround in Figure 6.6. Simply put, increasing the illumination increases the amount of light reflected from an area, but in also increasing the amount of illumination on the surroundings, it increases the lateral inhibition sent from the surroundings to that area (see page 59; Figure 2.44), it is unclear, however, what physiological mechanism explains the effects you have observed in the Mach card demonstration of Figure 6.10 and the "lightness-at-a-corner" demonstration. (Remember that we introduced the Mach card demonstration in Chapter 2 to demonstrate a phenomenon that could not be explained by lateral inhibition.) The physiological basis of lightness constancy is probably a combination of lateral inhibition and a higher order mechanism that remains to be determined.

Shape Constancy

Shape constancy is our perception of the shapes of objects as remaining constant even when we view them from different orientations that would change the shape of their image on our retina. To begin our discussion of shape constancy, do the following demonstration.

D E M O N S T R A T I O N

Viewing a Penny-at-an-Angle

Place a penny on your desk, then view it from a height of 5 inches and a distance of 20 inches, as shown in Figure 6.14. While viewing the penny, decide which shape in Figure 6.15 (viewed straight on, as shown in Figure 6.14) most closely matches your perception of the penny's shape at an angle. ●

To understand the rationale behind this demonstration, we need to realize that looking directly down on a penny, or any other circular object, creates a circular image on your retina, but when you look at these circular objects at an angle, they cast an elliptical image on your retina. If you picked stimulus number 1

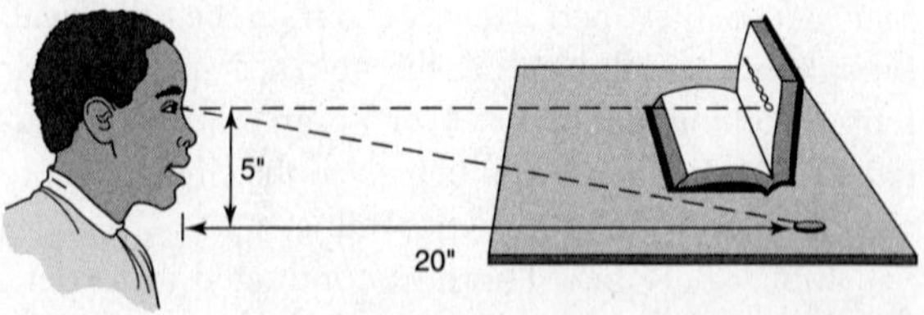

Figure 6.14
How to view the stimuli in Figure 6.15.

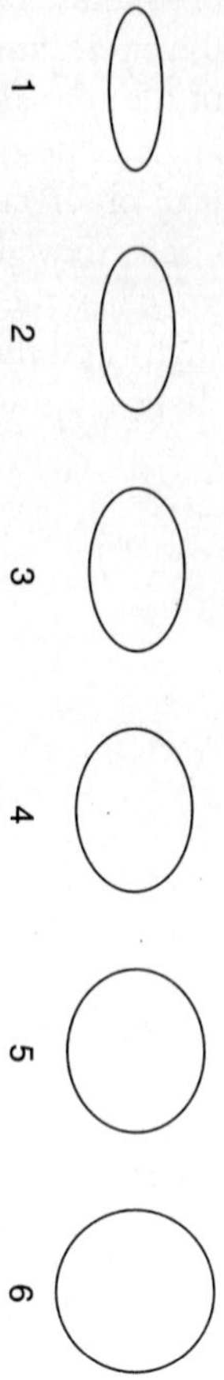

Figure 6.15

of Figure 6.15, then your perception matches the elliptical shape of the coin's image on your retina. If you picked number 6, then your perception matches the circular physical shape of the coin. Picking number 6 would be an example of perfect shape constancy—you perceived the circular coin as a circle no matter what the viewing angle. Most people pick numbers 3, 4, or 5, because they perceive the coin to be elliptical, though not as elliptical as the coin's shape on their retina. Picking numbers 3, 4, or 5 is an example of partial shape constancy—you perceived the circle as more circular than its image on your retina.

In 1931, Robert Thouless conducted an experiment similar to the demonstration above. His observers viewed a circle at a slant and picked the shape that most closely matched their perception. Figure 6.16 shows the results of one of Thouless' experiments. The circle represents the physical shape of the circle, and the shaded ellipse represents the shape of the retinal image when the circle is viewed at an angle. The dashed line shows the shape that Thouless' observers said matched their perception of the circle viewed at an angle. Since this judgment approaches the actual shape of the circle, but is still slightly elliptical, this would be an example of partial shape constancy.

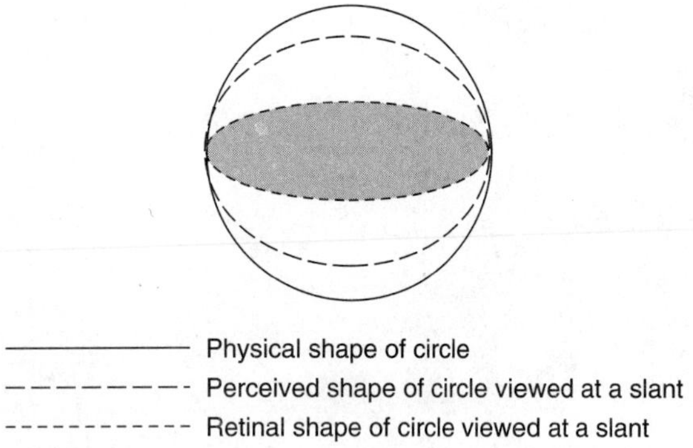

Figure 6.16
Results of Thouless' (1931) shape constancy experiment. Subjects viewed a circular shape (solid line) at an angle so the retinal image of the circle was a thin ellipse (shaded area). The dashed ellipse indicates their perception of the circle.

What determines shape constancy? Thouless found that eliminating a person's ability to see the object's orientation causes shape constancy to vanish and concluded that shape constancy involves a taking into account of the object's orientation in space. Under normal conditions, when orientation is easily perceived, shape constancy works and our perception is close to the object's physical shape. Thus, as you sit down to eat, your circular dinner plate doesn't deform to match the elliptical shape it is casting on your retina. Apparently, the visual system takes orientation into account to maintain a constant perception of shape.

Introduction to Size Constancy

We opened this chapter by contrasting what happens to the image on the retina when a person walks away from you (their image on your retina gets smaller) to your perception of that person's height (the person appears to stay the same height). In my Sensation and Perception class, I introduce the idea that our perception of size is not determined only by the size of the image on the retina, by standing about 3 feet from a person in the front row and asking them to estimate my height. They are usually pretty close, guessing around 5 feet 10 inches. I then take one large step back so I am now 6 feet away and ask the person to estimate my height again. If their perception of my height was governed by the size of my image on their retina, I would appear to be 2 feet 11 inches tall at the farther distance, since doubling my distance halves the size of my retinal image (Figure 6.17). But it probably doesn't surprise you that no one has ever said that I appear to shrink to just under three feet high when I take that step back. Rather, I appear to be about five foot ten inches no matter where I am standing.

The idea that we usually perceive objects as staying the same size even when they change their

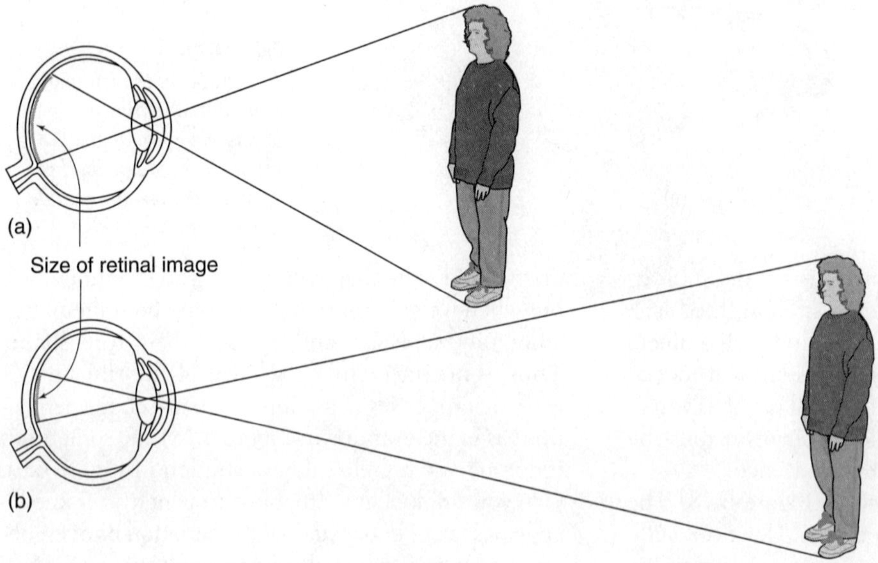

Figure 6.17
Doubling the distance from the eye halves the size of the retinal image.

distance is not a profound revelation, because it is a routine happening in our environment. Other than the rare expanding balloon, the sizes of objects remain constant, and that is how we perceive them, no matter what the distance. This perception of constant size in the face of changes in distance is called **size constancy,** and like color constancy, lightness constancy, and shape constancy, size constancy helps us to perceive a stable environment.

What causes size constancy? The following demonstration suggests an answer to this question.

DEMONSTRATION

Perceiving Size at a Distance

Hold a quarter between the fingertips of each hand so you can see the faces of both coins. Hold one coin about a foot from you and the other at arm's length. Observe the coins with both of your eyes open and note their size. Under these conditions, most people perceive the near and far coins as being approximately the same size. This is a demonstration of size constancy. Now close one eye, and holding the coins so they appear side-by-side, notice how your perception of the far coin has changed so that it now appears smaller than the near coin. ●

The key result of this demonstration is that eliminating a source of depth information by viewing the coins with just one eye decreases size constancy. (We will see in Chapter 8 that depth perception is worse with one eye than with two.) This result is consistent with the results of many experiments, which have concluded that size constancy depends on depth perception. We will describe these experiments as well as other explanations for size constancy and how size constancy may be involved in creating some visual illusions, in Chapter 9.

Something to Consider: Knowledge and Constancy

Does our knowledge of an object's real color, shape, or size influence our perception of constancy?

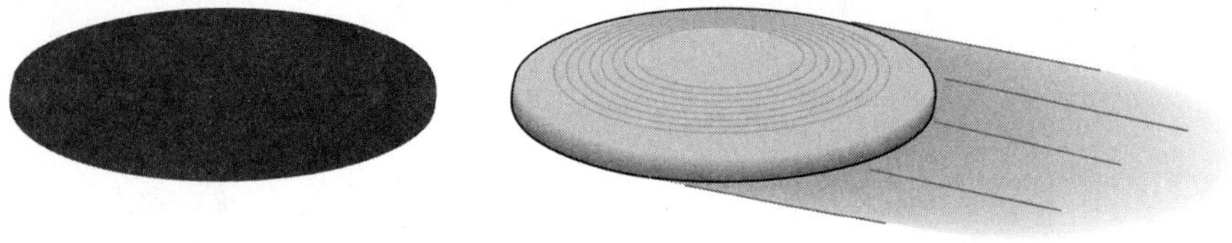

(a) (b)

Figure 6.18
The shape on the left might represent an elliptical object or a circle-at-an-angle. We interpret the shape on the right as a circle-at-an-angle.

Sometimes it does and sometimes it doesn't. In Gelb's lightness constancy demonstration, the black disk looked white if it was the only illuminated object in the field, and even if the subjects knew it looked black under normal lighting, they still saw it as white. In this situation, an automatic mechanism must be operating that is not affected by knowledge.

But what about the objects in Figure 6.18? The shape on the left looks like an ellipse. However, additional information transforms our perception of the same shape into a circular Frisbee seen at an angle, on the right. The shapes of objects can be ambiguous, but when we gain more information about them, this ambiguity vanishes, and we see their true shape. Thus, sometimes our knowledge of the situation or the true properties of an object can affect our perception (as in the example in Figure 6.18) and sometimes it doesn't (as in Gelb's demonstration in Figure 6.9). Can you think of any situations in which your knowledge or lack of knowledge of the situation or of an object's properties affected your perception?

Olfactory Constancy

Experiments in animals have shown that the flow rate of an odorant across the olfactory (smell) receptors causes an increase in the response of the olfactory nerve. This result is similar to the result in other senses. For example, increasing light intensity can increase the rate of firing of neurons in the optic nerve.

A similar result occurs psychophysically: When Rehn (1978) presented odorants with different rates of flow, and asked subjects to estimate the magnitude of the odor (see page 12 to review magnitude estimation), the subject's magnitude estimates of odor strength increased as the rate of flow was increased.

Rehn concluded that "the strength of a perceived odor is a function of the available odorant molecules for the olfactory receptors at a given time." (p. 204). However, in another experiment Robert Teghtsoonian and coworkers (1978) achieved two results—one that supported Rehn's conclusion, and one that doesn't.

When Teghtsoonian and co-workers presented subjects with different concentrations of odorants their subjects rated the higher concentrations as smelling stronger—a result consistent with Rehn's assertion that perceived odor is a function of the odorant molecules that are available to the receptors. However, when Teghtsoonian also instructed half of the subjects to sniff the chemical weakly and half of the subjects to sniff it strongly, they found that the sniff had no effect on the subject's magnitude estimates (Figure 6.19). Thus, for a given odorant concentration, subjects produced the same magnitude estimate for the weak sniff and for the strong sniff. That is, even though more odorant was delivered to the receptors for the strong sniffs compared to the weak sniffs, the magnitude estimates for both conditions was the same. Teghtsoonian considers the lack of effect of sniff intensity on odor judgments as being similar to the lack of effect of changing distance on size judgments (size constancy). He describes this result as an example of olfactory constancy, and suggests that just as subjects take distance into account when judging size, they also take the intensity of sniffing into account when judging odor intensity.

Olfactory constancy increases the chances that subjects will be able to accurately sense the concentration of an odorant, because they won't be misled by differences in odor intensity that could be caused by the different sniff intensities that they might use in different situations. Thus, if they sniff strongly to detect weak odorants and sniff weakly to sample strong, possibly toxic, odorants, they can still tell that one odorant is weak and the other is strong.

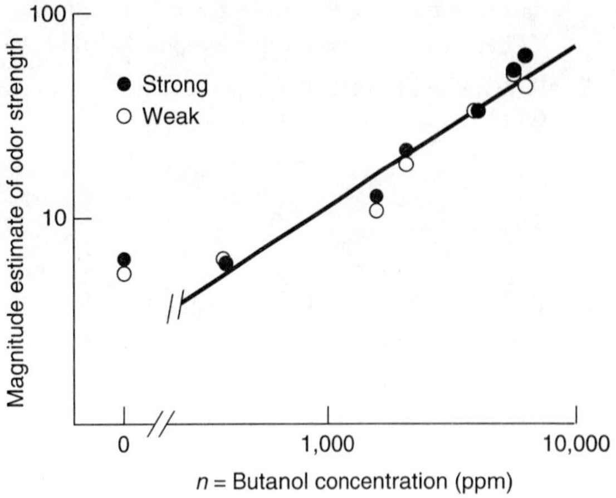

Figure 6.19
Magnitude estimates of odor strength for butanol. Odor strength increases at higher butanol concentrations, but is the same for strong sniffs (●) and weak sniffs (○). (Adapted from Teghtsoonian et al., 1978.)

Study Questions

Underlying Principles

Find examples of the following principles in this chapter:

- Physiological connections with perception (161)
- Cognitive influences (164)

1. What is perceptual constancy? (157)

Color Constancy

2. What is color constancy? (158)
3. Explain the following explanations of color constancy: chromatic adaptation (understand the Uchikawa et al. experiment), the effect of the surroundings, and memory color. (159)
4. What is the evidence that area V4 is important for color constancy? Compare the response of striate neurons and V4 neurons to changes in illumination. What do we mean when we say that the response of striate neurons is correlated with wavelength and the response of V4 neurons is correlated with perception? (161)
5. Why is it unlikely that the response of neurons in area V4 is the final answer to color perception? (162)

Lightness Constancy

6. What is lightness constancy? What is the relationship between lightness constancy and albedo? (162)
7. What is the simultaneous contrast effect? (162)
8. What is the ratio principle? (162)
9. Describe Gelb's experiment. What does it demonstrate about lightness perception? (163)
10. How does the Mach card demonstration show that lightness constancy is determined by the interpretation of how an object is illuminated? (164)
11. What does the lightness-at-a-corner demonstration show? (165)
12. What is a penumbra? How does it contribute to lightness constancy in shadows? How does identification of a shadow's shape contribute to lightness constancy in the shadow? (165)
13. What is the relationship between lightness perception and lateral inhibition? (167)

Shape Constancy

14. What is shape constancy? What is partial shape constancy? (167)
15. Describe Thouless' experiment. According to Thouless, what determines shape constancy? (167)

Introduction to Size Constancy

16. What is size constancy? (168)
17. What is the relationship between the size of an object's image on the retina and the perception of that object's size? (168)
18. What is the relationship between size constancy and depth perception? (169)

Something to Consider: Knowledge and Constancy

19. Describe a situation in which knowledge of the conditions of stimulation does not influence lightness constancy. (169)
20. Describe a situation in which knowledge of the situation or the conditions of stimulation influences shape constancy. (169)

Across the Senses: Olfactory Constancy

21. What did Rehn conclude about the major factor that determines the perceived strength of an odor? (171)

22. How did the results of Teghtsoonian's experiments contradict Rehn's conclusion by looking at how sniff intensity affects the perceived strength of an odor? (171)

23. What is olfactory constancy and how is it similar to size constancy? (171)

24. What is a possible beneficial effect of olfactory constancy? (171)

7

PERCEIVING OBJECTS

When you ask people what they see in a room, you will probably hear responses like "A chair, some books on the desk, pictures on the wall." Perception, for most people, is first and foremost the awareness of objects. We will see in this chapter that there are a number of ways to approach the study of object perception. These different approaches are reflected in the following questions that we can ask about how we perceive objects:

1. Why do some visual elements become grouped, so they seem to belong together and others so they appear separated from one another?
2. What is the nature of the *processing* that occurs between stimulation of the retina and perception? This question can be approached both physiologically and behaviorally.
3. How do we *recognize* what we see? That is once we perceive the various objects in the environment, how do we know that one is a person, one a tree, and so on?

We will consider each of these questions, beginning with the first one, which focuses on a process called perceptual organization.

CHAPTER CONTENTS

SOME QUESTIONS WE WILL CONSIDER

- Why haven't we been able to program a computer to see objects as well as people can? (176)
- What makes it possible to distinguish an object from its background? (186)
- How aware are we of objects that we aren't paying attention to? (199)

Organizing the Environment: Perceptual Organization

At this very moment you are carrying out feats of **perceptual organization**—organizing components of a scene to form perceptually separate objects. Perceptual organization is seeing each word on the page as separate from the others; it is seeing this book as separate from the surface on which it is resting; it is seeing your fingers as part of your hand; and it is perceiving some of the black blobs in Figure 7.1 as a Dalmatian.

Doing these things seems simple, just as most other aspects of perception. But we can appreciate the complexity of object perception by considering the fact that while a computer has defeated the human world champion chess player, it has proven difficult to program a computer to perceive even simple scenes. We can understand some reasons for this difficulty by considering a few of the problems that the computer must deal with in order to accurately perceive a scene:

1. Objects or scenes seen from one viewpoint are ambiguous. For example, you might think that the scene in Figure 7.2a is a circle of rocks, but viewing it from another angle reveals its true configuration (Figure 7.2b).
2. It is difficult to determine where one object ends and another begins. For example, in Figure 7.3 how do we know that the intersection at (a) is the corner of object 1, but the intersection at (b) is created by objects 1 and 2 together? Although computers have been programmed successfully to answer this kind of question for problems involving blocks, it is still difficult for a computer to answer it for more complex natural objects.
3. It is difficult to determine the shapes of objects that are partially hidden. Imagine, for example,

Figure 7.1
Some black and white shapes that become perceptually organized into a Dalmatian. (Photograph by R. C. James.)

Figure 7.2
An environmental sculpture by Thomas Macaulay. (a) When viewed from exactly the right vantage point (the second-floor balcony of the Blackhawk Mountain School of Art, Black Hawk, Colorado), the stones appear to be arranged in a circle. (b) Viewing the stones from the ground floor reveals a truer picture of their configuration.

how difficult it would be to program a computer to be able to identify the hidden object in Figure 7.4, something we can do with little effort.

4. In a scene such as the one in Figure 7.5, it is necessary to determine which changes in lightness and darkness are due to properties of objects in the scene and which are due to changes in the illumination. In this scene, changes in lightness and darkness are caused by the different reflectances of parts of the scene, such as the dark tree and roof tiles (low reflectance) and the white walls (high reflectance). Changes in lightness and darkness are also caused by the distribution of sunlight and shadows. It is difficult for a computer to determine which changes are due to the objects and which are due to changes in the illumination.

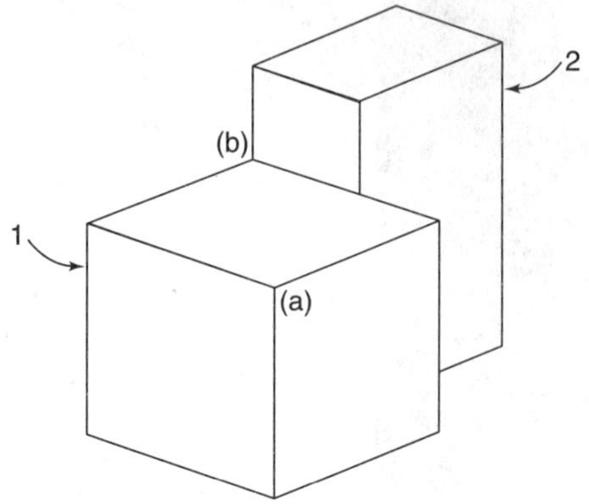

Figure 7.3

These are only a few of the problems facing computer vision. Things become even more complex when we consider the many varied shapes we see in the real world. (For more detailed discussions of the problems involved in computer vision, see Barrow & Tannenbaum, 1986; Beck, Hope, & Resenfeld, 1983; C. Brown, 1984; Hanson & Riseman, 1978; McArthur, 1982; Poggio, 1984; Winston, 1975.)

The reason for this brief foray into computer vision is to make the point that humans are presented with the same information as the computer, in the

Figure 7.4
"Mystery object" behind wall.

form of a two-dimensional image of the scene on our retina, yet we are able to solve the problems above and translate this image into a correct perception of the scene much more easily than even the most powerful computer. Although we are sometimes fooled (perhaps shape 2 in Figure 7.3 is not really a rectangular solid), most of the time we are able to solve effortlessly the complexities of object perception and to arrive at a correct perception of objects and the scenes within which these objects exist.

An early psychological approach to determining how humans perceive objects was proposed in the 1920s by a group of researchers known as the Gestalt psychologists.

The Beginnings of Gestalt Psychology

In the first decades of the 20th century, most psychologists explained perception in terms of an approach called **structuralism,** which stated that perceptions are created by combining tiny building blocks called *sensations*, just as each of the dots in the face in Figure 7.6 add together to create our perception of a face. However, Max Wertheimer, one of the founders of Gestalt psychology, disagreed with this idea. One of his arguments against structuralism involved the

Figure 7.5
For this scene it would be difficult for a computer to sort out which changes are due to properties of the objects in the scene and which are due to changes in illumination. In this scene it would be particularly difficult for a computer to determine what is happening in the shaded area just above the tile roof.

Figure 7.6
According to structuralism, a number of sensations (represented by the dots) adds up to create our perception of the face.

situation diagrammed in Figure 7.7. When the light at A is flashed on and off, and then after a dark interval of 50 msec (50/1,000 sec) the light at B is flashed on and off, it appears that the light has moved through the space between A and B. This is called **apparent movement**—*apparent* because in reality there is no movement, just one light flashing on and off followed by another light flashing on and off.

How, asked Wertheimer (1912), is it possible to explain the movement that appears to occur through the dark space separating the two lights in terms of sensations? Since there is no stimulation whatsoever in the space between the lights, no sensations are present to provide an explanation. With this demonstration and others, Wertheimer and the newly formed group of researchers, who called themselves **Gestalt psychologists,** rejected the structuralists' idea of perceptions being built from tiny sensations, and in its place proposed the idea that *the whole is different from the sum of its parts.*

Much of the evidence supporting the idea that the whole is different from the sum of its parts comes from pictures such as the ones in Figure 7.8, which show that our perception of one part of a stimulus depends on the presence of other parts of the stimulus.

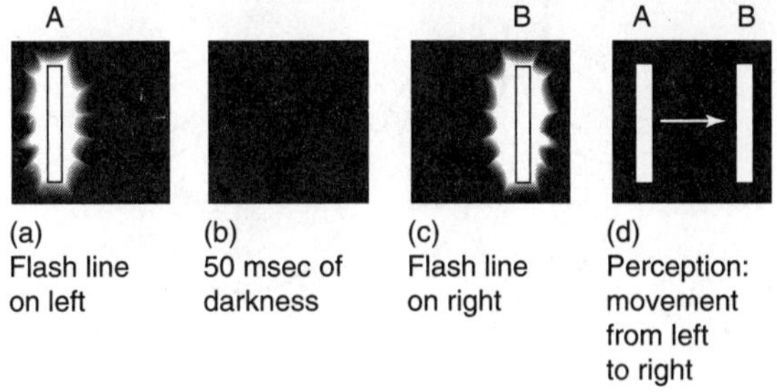

Figure 7.7
Wertheimer's (1912) experiment in movement perception.

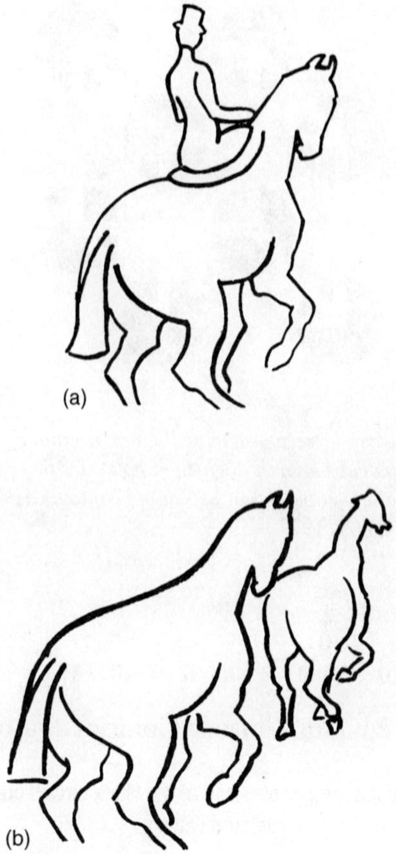

Figure 7.8
(a) A rearing horse. (b) One horse following another. (From Arnheim, 1974.)

We interpret the horse in Figure 7.8a as rearing back, but we interpret the identical horse in Figure 7.8b as moving forwa[illegible] The presence of the rider in one case and of th[illegible]orse in the other changes our interpretation [illegible] movement.

Or con[illegible] in Figure 7.9. If you see this as a c[illegible] in front of black circles, you [illegible]nt **illusory contours** that repre[illegible] (Bradley & Petry, 1977). T[illegible]*llusory* because they are[illegible]cal stimulus. You can[illegible] following demons[illegible]

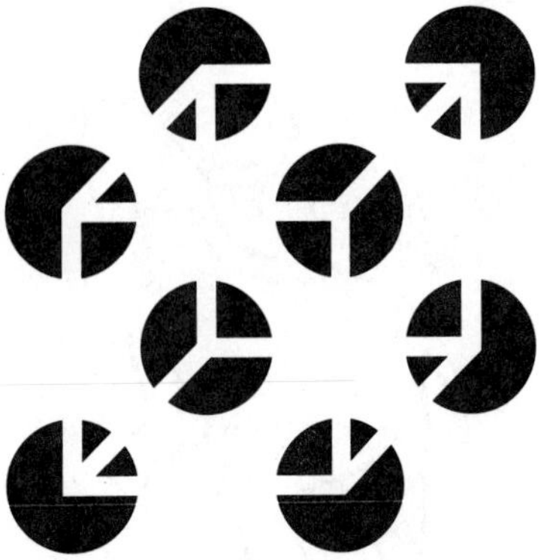

Figure 7.9
This figure can be seen as a cube floating in front of eight disks or as a cube seen through eight holes. In the first case, the edges of the cube appear as illusory contours. (From Bradley & Petry, 1977.)

DEMONSTRATION

Making Illusory Contours Vanish

1. **Place your finger over one of the black circles and notice how the illusory contours vanish.**
2. **Imagine that the black circles are holes and that you are looking at the cube through these holes. Notice how the illusory contours vanish in this case also.** ●

When you made the contours vanish by placing your finger over the black circle, you showed that the contour was illusory *and* that our perception of one part of the display (the contours) is [illegible]ffected by the presence of another part (the black c[illegible]le). The structuralists have a hard time explaining [illegible]ory contours because, just as in the apparent m[illegible]nt example, they can't identify the sensations [illegible]te our perception of the contour.

Making the contours vanis[illegible]ining that you are looking through black[illegible] a similar problem for the structuralists. [illegible]o explain this shift in perception in ter[illegible] that are present one moment and gone the next, especially since the stimulus on the page and the image it creates on your retina are exactly the same when you are perceiving the contours and when you are not perceiving them.

Examples such as these support the Gestalt idea that the whole is different than the sum of its parts, because we can't predict what perception of the whole display will be by considering each part separately. It is only by being present together that the individual parts combine to create our perception of the whole display.

The Gestalt idea that the whole is different than the sum of its parts was an important one, but the Gestalt psychologists were not satisfied to simply propose one principle. They were basically interested in perceptual organization—how we divide the world into separate objects—and they considered this important enough to formulate a number of rules they called the *laws of perceptual organization.*

(a)
(b)

Figure 7.10
(a) This is usually perceived as five circles, and not as the nine shapes in (b).

The Laws of Perceptual Organization

The **laws of perceptual organization** are a series of rules that specify how we organize small parts into wholes. Let's look at seven of the Gestalt laws.

Pragnanz *Pragnanz,* roughly translated from the German, means "good figure." The **law of Pragnanz**—the central law of Gestalt psychology (it is also called the **law of good figure** or the **law of simplicity**)—states: *Every stimulus pattern is seen in such a way that the resulting structure is as simple as possible.* The familiar Olympic symbol in Figure 7.10a is an example of the law of simplicity at work. We see this display as five circles, and not as other, more complicated, shapes such as the ones in Figure 7.10b.

Similarity Most people perceive Figure 7.11a as either horizontal rows of circles, vertical columns of circles, or both. But when we change some of the circles to squares, as in Figure 7.11b, most people perceive vertical columns of squares and circles. This perception illustrates the **law of similarity:** *Similar things appear to be grouped together.* This law causes the circles to be grouped with other circles and the squares to be grouped with other squares. Grouping can also occur because of similarity of lightness (Figure 7.12), hue, size, or orientation (Figures 7.13 and 7.14), or size.

Grouping also occurs for auditory stimuli. For example, notes that have similar pitches and that follow each other closely in time can become perceptually grouped to form a melody. We will consider this and

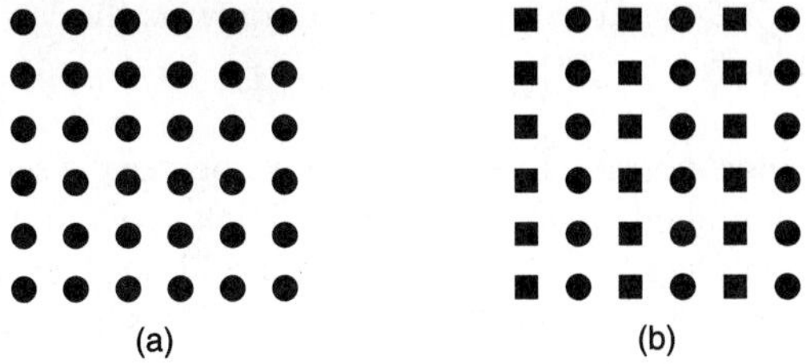

Figure 7.11
(a) Perceived as horizontal rows or vertical columns or both. (b) Perceived as vertical columns.

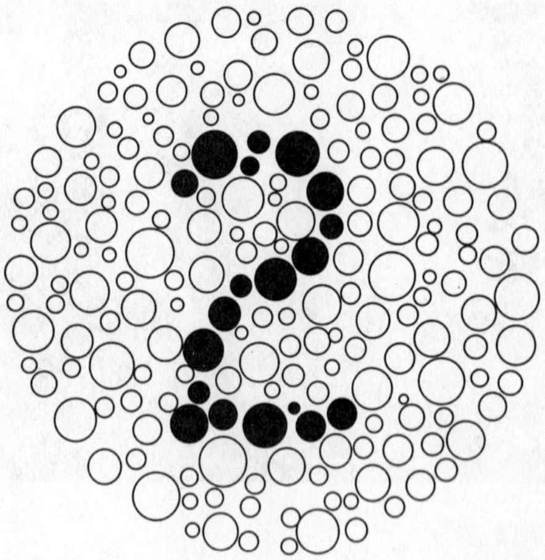

Figure 7.12
Grouping due to similarity of lightness. The light objects form one group, and the dark objects form another group.

Figure 7.13
Grouping due to similarity of orientation. In this pas de deux from The Nutcracker, *the perceptual unity of the two dancers is greatly enhanced by the similarity of their arm and body orientations. (Photograph by Randy Choura courtesy of the Pittsburgh Ballet Theater.)*

Figure 7.14
Grouping due to similarity. Our perception of the three women as one group occurs because of the similarity in the orientation of their bodies and arms, and the lightness of their costumes and legs. The male dancer is different in a number of respects including orientation, costuming, and movement, compared to the females, and so he is perceived as separated from them. (Photography courtesy of the Pittsburgh Ballet Theater.)

other auditory grouping effects when we describe the organizational processes in hearing in Chapter 12.

Good Continuation We see the electric cord starting at A in Figure 7.15 as flowing smoothly to B. It does not go to C or D, because that path would involve making sharp turns and would violate the **law of good continuation,** which states: *Points that, when connected, result in straight or smoothly curving lines, are seen as belonging together, and the lines tend to be seen in such a way as to follow the smoothest path.* Thus, even though the smoke in Camillo Pissarro's painting *The Great Bridge at Rouen* (Figure 7.16) cuts the bridge in two and the smokestack into three pieces, we assume, because of good continuation, that the various parts belong together, and the bridge and the smokestack, therefore, do not fall apart. Good continuation also came into play in helping us to perceive the smoothly curving circles in Figure 7.10.

Proximity or Nearness Our perception of Figure 7.17a as horizontal rows of circles illustrates the **law of proximity** or **nearness.** *Things that are near to each other appear to be grouped together.* And although every other circle is changed to a square in Figure 7.17b, we still perceive horizontal rows; in this case the law of proximity overpowers the law of similarity.

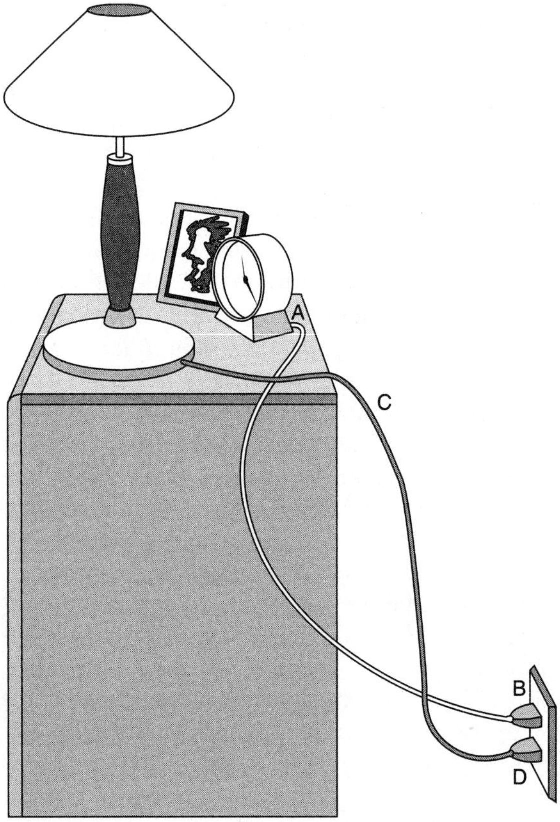

Figure 7.15
Good continuation. Both electric cords follow a smooth plan to the electrical outlet.

Connectedness In Figure 7.18 we perceive a series of "dumbbells" rather than pairs of dots, even though the dots separated by the spaces are closer together than the ones connected by the lines. This is the law of connectedness: *Things that are physically connected are perceived as a unit.* An interesting thing about this law of organization is that it was proposed by two modern perceptual psychologists, Irving Rock

Figure 7.16
The Great Bridge at Rouen *by Camille Pissarro (1896). (Museum of Art, Carnegie Institute, Pittsburgh.)*

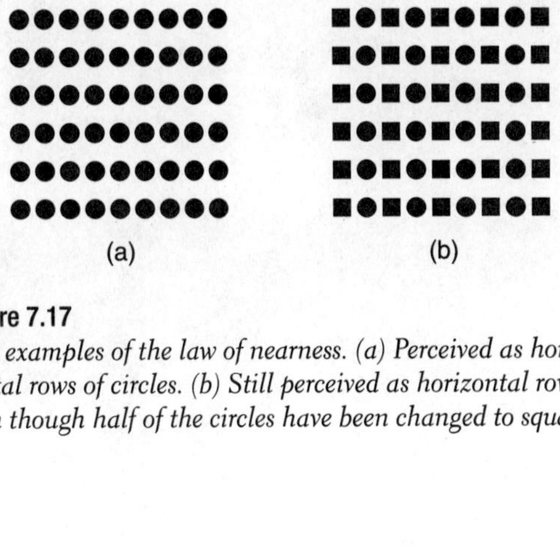

Figure 7.17
Two examples of the law of nearness. (a) Perceived as horizontal rows of circles. (b) Still perceived as horizontal rows, even though half of the circles have been changed to squares.

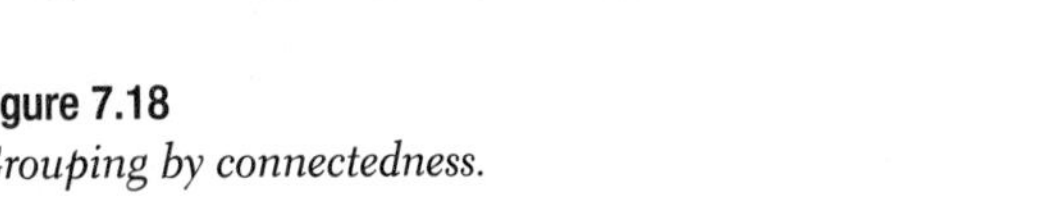

Figure 7.18
Grouping by connectedness.

and Stephen Palmer (1990). Thus, more than 70 years after its founding, Gestalt psychology is still influencing perceptual research. (Also see Pizlo, Salach-Golyska, & Rosenfeld, 1997, for a modern version of the law of good continuation.)

Common Fate The dancers in Figure 7.19 form a group by virtue of their nearness and similar orientation, but perhaps most important is their common fate—the fact that they are moving in the same direction. The **law of common fate** states: *Things that are moving in the same direction appear to be grouped together.* Although dance choreographers may not be familiar with the Gestalt laws, they are well aware that one way to create perceptual grouping is to choreograph groups of dancers moving together.

Meaningfulness or Familiarity The **law of familiarity** states: *Things are more likely to form groups if the groups appear familiar or meaningful* (Helson, 1933; Hochberg, 1971, p. 439). You can appreciate

Figure 7.19
Grouping due to common fate. The perceptual grouping of these dancers is enhanced both by their similarity of orientation and by their common fate, that is, the fact that they are all moving in the same direction at the same speed. (Photograph courtesy of the Pittsburgh Ballet Theater.)

how meaningfulness determines perceptual organization by doing the following demonstration.

DEMONSTRATION

Finding Faces in a Landscape

Consider the picture in Figure 7.20. At first glance this scene appears to contain mainly trees, rocks, and water. But on closer inspection you can see some faces in the trees in the background, and if you look more closely, you can see that a number of faces are formed by various groups of rocks. There are, in fact, 13 faces in this picture. If you have trouble seeing all of them, try looking at the picture from a few feet away. From this distance, previously unseen faces sometimes become visible. ●

Figure 7.20
The Forest Has Eyes *by Bev Doolittle (1985). Can you find 13 faces in this picture?*

In this demonstration some people find it difficult to perceive the faces at first, but once they succeed, they find it difficult to return to their previous perception of rocks and trees. The change that occurs when your perception changes from "rocks in a stream" or "trees in a forest" into "faces" is a change in the perceptual organization of the rocks and the trees. The two shapes that you at first perceive as two separate rocks in the stream become perceptually grouped together when they become the left and right eyes of a face. In fact, once you perceive a particular grouping of rocks as a face, it is often difficult *not* to perceive them in this way—they have become permanently organized into a face.

Meaningfulness also helps us separate the horses from their background in Figure 7.21. But there are other Gestalt laws at work here as well. Good continuation (the contours of the horses' backs and legs) and similarity (the similar shading of the horses' legs and bodies) also help us perceive the horses as separate from their background.

Aren't the Gestalt Laws Just Statements of the Obvious?

The "laws" we have been describing above often seem obvious. A typical comment to this effect might be something like, "Of course, we would expect to see the electrical cord in Figure 7.14 as extending smoothly from the lamp to the plug. I don't need a 'law of organization' to tell me that." This statement

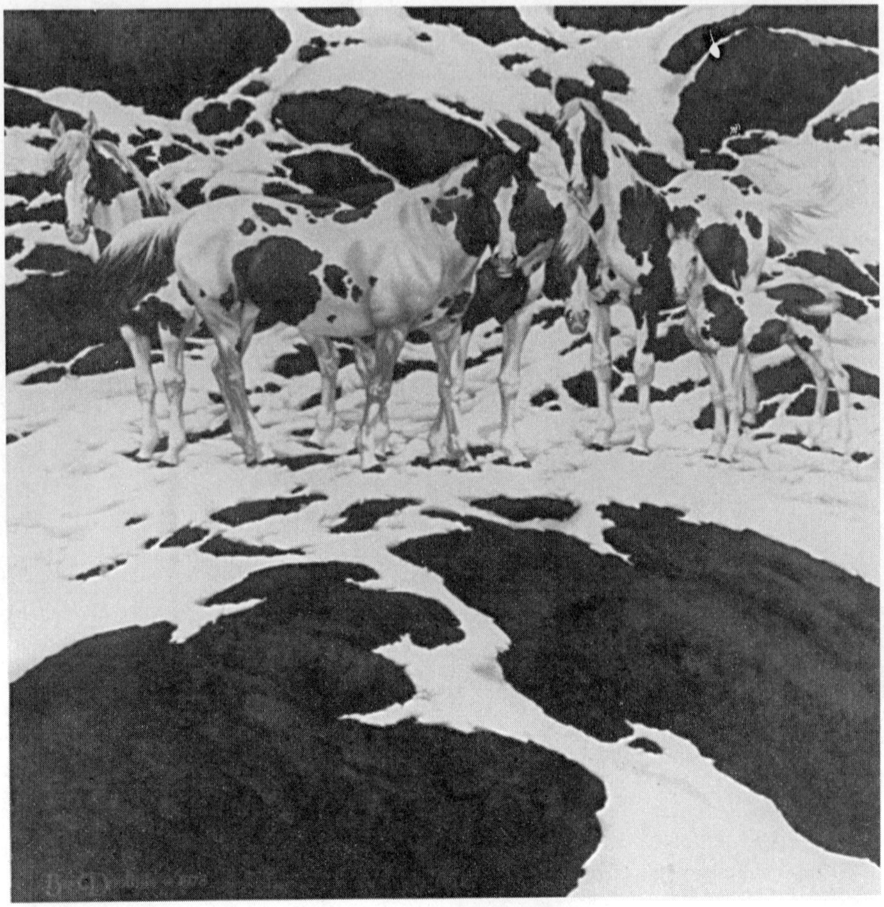

Figure 7.21
Pintos *by Bev Doolittle (1979).*

misses an important point. The Gestalt laws seem obvious because what they reflect are the day-to-day regularities of our environment. In our everyday experience, things do tend to follow along smooth paths rather than changing abruptly. (This is the basis of the law of good continuation.) Also, objects tend to be homogeneous, with changes in lightness or texture often being associated with different objects. (This is the basis of the law of similarity.)

What the Gestalt laws are saying is that we tend to perceive objects in the world according to rules that we have learned from observing the regularities of our environment. These rules seem obvious because we have become experts at perceiving these regularities. But the situation depicted in Figure 7.22a shows what happens in an unusual case when a regularity that usually occurs, breaks down. Based on the law of good continuation, we would perceive this as a single branch that is partially hidden by the tree. However, in this example, which occurs much more rarely, nature fools us. Most of the time, however, our perceptions help us reach correct conclusions about our environment. Although the Gestalt laws may seem simple and even obvious, they are important statements regarding how our perceptions usually match what we expect to find in our environment.

Another important principle related to perceptual organization is the idea of figure and ground. According to this idea, when we perceive something we are usually perceiving it as being in front of a background. Thus, I see the papers on my desk as figure, and the surface of the desk as ground. The Gestalt psychologists were interested in determining the properties of the figure and the ground and in determining what makes one area be perceived as figure and the other as ground.

Figure and Ground

One way the Gestalt psychologists studied the properties of figure and ground was by considering patterns like the one in Figure 7.23, which was introduced by Danish psychologist Edgar Rubin in 1915. This is called a **reversible figure-ground** pattern, because it can be perceived either as two black faces looking at each other, in front of a white background, or as a white vase on a black background.

Figure 7.22
(a) Is this a single branch behind the tree? It's most likely that it is, and this is what the law of good continuation would predict. However, it is also possible that two different branches could create this perception, as shown in (b).

Figure 7.23
A version of Rubin's reversible face-vase figure.

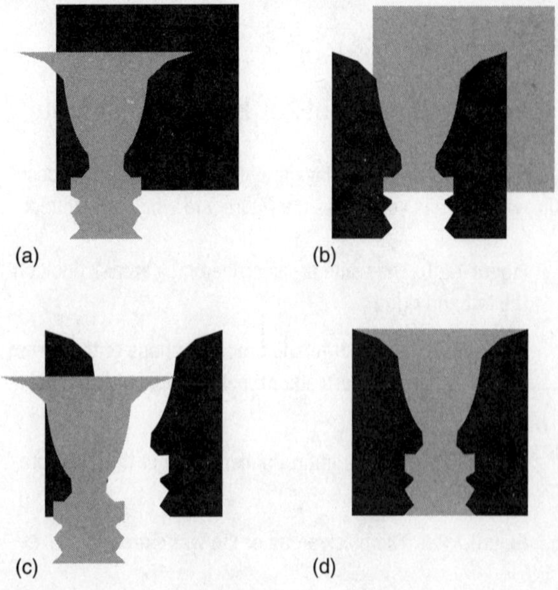

Figure 7.24
(a) When the vase is seen as figure, it is perceived in front of a homogeneous dark background; (b) When the faces are seen as figure, they are seen in front of a homogeneous light background; (c) It is unlikely that two objects in the world as shown here would have identical contours or (d) that these two objects would be viewed so their contours would exactly coincide. (Adapted from Bayliss and Driver, 1995.)

Some of the properties of the figure and ground are that: (1) The figure is more "thinglike" and more memorable than the ground; (2) The figure is seen as being in front of the ground. (3) The ground is seen as unformed material and seems to extend behind the figure; and (4) The contour separating the figure from the ground appears to belong to the figure.

You can demonstrate these four properties of figure and ground to yourself by noting that when the vase is seen as figure, it appears to be in front of the black background (Figure 7.24a), and when the faces are seen as figure, they are on top of the white background (Figure 7.24b). Also notice that, when you are perceiving the one pattern as figure, it is difficult, if not impossible, to simultaneously perceive the other one. Remember that the ground is seen as "unformed material," so as soon as you perceive the light area as figure, the vase is seen in front and the black area can't be two faces because it has become "unformed material" that extends behind the vase. Similarly, when the black area is seen as figure, the faces are seen in front and the light area is seen as unformed material.

The idea that it is impossible to perceive both the vases and the faces as figures simultaneously is another example of how our perception reflects the regularities in the environment. We can appreciate this by asking the following question: What is the likelihood that a vase and two faces would have exactly the same contours, as in Figure 7.24c, and would just happen to be viewed so their contours exactly coincided, as in Figure 7.23d? The answer is that although it is not impossible that this could happen, it is a highly unlikely occurrence. Since the visual system is tuned to regularities in our environment, it takes the unlikeliness of this occurrence into account, and any time an edge divides one object from another, it assigns the dividing edge to just one of the objects so that object is seen as figure and the other is seen as ground (Baylis & Driver, 1995).

DEMONSTRATION

Determinants of Figure and Ground

Look at the following displays and decide, as quickly as possible, which areas you see as the figure and which as ground:

Figure 7.25: The white areas or the black areas? (look on the left and right)

Figure 7.26: The wide-blade propeller shape of the "cross figure" or the narrow-blade propeller shape of the "plus figure"?

Figure 7.27: The upright propeller shape or the tilted propeller shape?

Figure 7.28: The black areas or the white areas? ●

There are no "correct" perceptions of these displays, but experiments have shown that certain properties of the stimulus influence which areas are seen as figure and which are seen as ground. Symmetrical areas tend to be seen as figure, so in Figure 7.25 the symmetrical black areas on the left and the symmetrical white areas on the right are seen as figure.

The Gestalt psychologists also found that stimuli with comparatively smaller areas are more likely to be seen as figure, so the plus figure in Figure 7.26 is more likely to be seen as figure than is the cross figure (Kunnapas, 1957; see also Oyama, 1960). Vertical or horizontal orientations are more likely to be seen as figure than are other orientations. Thus, the vertical-horizontal propeller shape in Figure 7.27 is more likely to be seen as figure than is the tilted propeller shape. Finally, as we saw in looking at Figures 7.20 and 7.21, meaningful objects are more likely to be seen as figure. Thus, the black areas in Figure 7.28, which include three arrows, tend to be seen as figure (the smaller size of the black areas compared to the

Figure 7.25
Symmetry and figure ground. Look to the left and to the right, and observe which colors become figure and which become ground. (Adapted from Hochberg, 1971.)

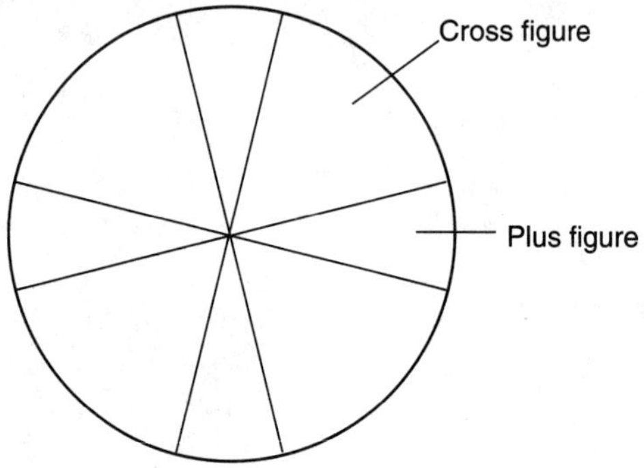

Figure 7.26
The effect of area on figure-ground perception. Which is more likely to be seen as figure, the wide-blade propeller shape of the cross figure or the narrow-blade propeller shape of the plus figure?

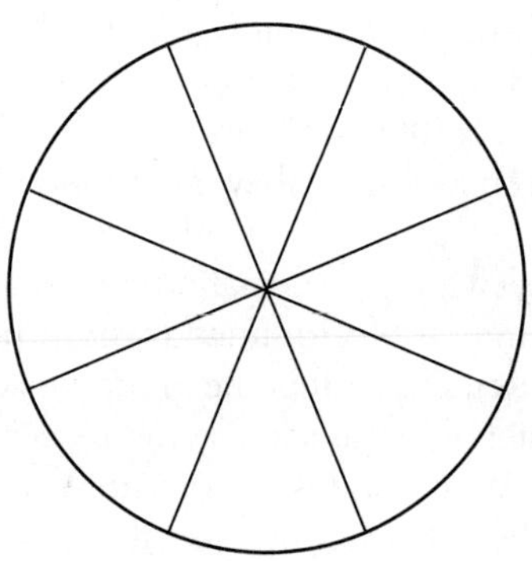

Figure 7.27
The effect of orientation on figure-ground perception. Which is easier to see as a figure, the vertical-horizontal propeller shape or the tilted propeller shape? What is your initial perception? Allow your perception to flip back and forth between the two alternatives. Which perception is present the longest?

Figure 7.28
Which do you see as figure, the black area or the white area? *After deciding, turn to Figure 7.31 on page 190.*

white areas also helps make the black into figures). However, adding two more black areas on either side, as in Figure 7.31, makes it easier to see that the white areas spell a word (WIN), so that these areas dominate our perception.

Evaluation of the Gestalt Approach

The Gestalt psychologists took a phenomenological approach to the study of perception. They described the phenomena they observed and gave some order to it through their laws of organization and by focusing attention on some of the factors that determine figure and ground. While the use of the phenomenological approach led the Gestalt psychologists to achieve some important insights into how perception operates, the Gestalt approach has also had problems dealing with the following:

It Is Difficult to Define Simplicity One of the most important of the Gestalt laws, the law of simplicity, is sometimes hard to apply because simplicity isn't precisely defined. We can see that it is not always easy to tell whether one pattern is simpler than another by considering the following demonstration.

D E M O N S T R A T I O N

Stimuli That Can Be Seen in More Than One Way

Many stimuli can be seen in more than one way. Look at Figure 7.29 and decide (1) how you perceive it initially and (2) which other perceptions are possible. ●

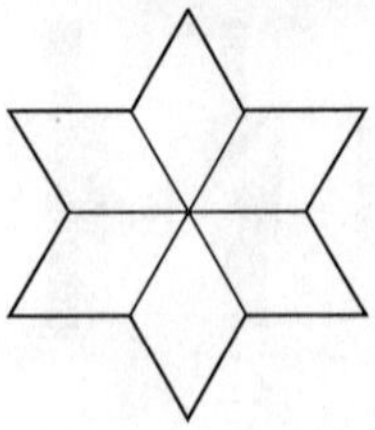

Figure 7.29
What is this?

Did you perceive Figure 7.29 as a flat, six-pointed star or as something else? It could also be two intersecting V's, one right side up and one upside down, as in Figure 7.30a (the upside-down V is shaded). Or perhaps it is a three-finned propeller on top of a triangle. (To see the propeller, try to perceive the shaded area of Figure 7.30a as the triangle and the light area as the three-finned propeller). Finally, look at 7.30b and imagine that the shaded areas on the left and right represent the pages of opened books. Clearly, Figure 7.31 can be perceived in a number of ways (also including, as my students have pointed out to me, two chairs, each with a missing leg).

Although we might expect the law of simplicity to predict that the simplest perception of Figure 7.29 would be the flat, symmetrical star, people often see the seemingly more complex perceptions suggested by Figure 7.30. In fact, many people find that their perceptions change between two or even three different objects as they continue to look at this display. Unfortunately, the law of simplicity can't explain why these changes occur or why some people even favor perceptions that may not seem very "simple" at all.

It Often Offers Only After-the-Fact Explanations The Gestalt approach proposes mainly after-the-fact explanations. For example, first comes the perception—we see Figure 7.29 as a flat star—and then

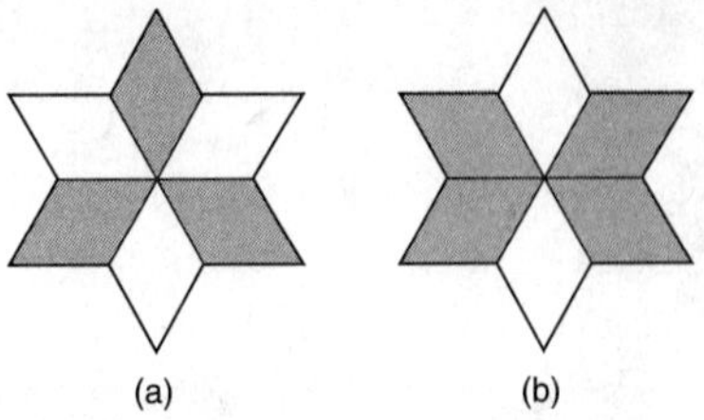

(a) (b)

Figure 7.30
Alternate perceptions of Figure 7.29.

Figure 7.31
In this version of Figure 7.28, which area is figure, white or black? Look for a three-letter word.

comes the explanation. In this case, a flat object is simpler than a three-dimensional one. A humorous example of this kind of after-the-fact explanation is provided by the "weather-forecasting stone" shown in Figure 7.32. If the stone is wet, the "forecast" is rain; if it is white on top, "snow"; and so on. What we need in both weather forecasting and perception are ways to *predict* what is going to happen before it happens, not simply descriptions of what has already happened (Pomerantz, 1981).

What Are the Mechanisms behind Gestalt Phenomena? This tendency of the Gestalt approach to *describe* rather than to *explain* reflects the Gestalt psychologist's failure to determine underlying mechanisms. What the Gestalt psychologists did was to provide us with the initial step in scientific research—they defined the basic phenomena to be studied. The next step is to investigate the mechanisms behind these phenomena, often using quantitative methods. A number of modern perceptual psychologists have done this (see Baylis & Driver, 1995; Peterson, 1994). One example of a modern experimental approach to Gestalt psychology is an experiment by Naomi Weisstein and Eva Wong (1986) designed to test the following idea: Analysis within the figure part of a figure-ground display is concerned with seeing fine details whereas analysis within the ground part is concerned with seeing larger areas.

Weisstein and Wong reasoned that if analysis within the figure concerns details, then we should see small details more easily when they are superimposed on the figure than when they are superimposed on the ground. Weisstein and Wong tested this idea by flashing vertical lines and slightly tilted lines onto a line drawing of Rubin's faces-vase reversible picture

Figure 7.32
A weather-forecasting stone that describes what has already happened rather than actually forecasting the weather.

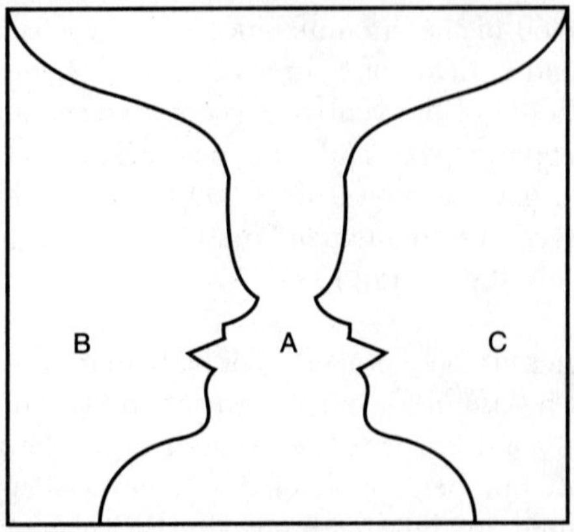

Figure 7.33
Rubin's face-vase figure used by Weisstein and Wong (1986). In their experiment, described in the text, vertical or tilted lines were flashed at locations A, B, or C. The lines' tilt, or lack of it, was more easily detecterd when the area on which the line was flashed was perceived as figure.

(Figure 7.33) and asking subjects to decide whether the line they saw was vertical or tilted. Since Rubin's figure is reversible, sometimes the faces (areas B and C) were seen as figure and sometimes the vase (area A) was seen as figure. On each trial, the subject indicated whether the vase or the faces were the figure, and the line was then flashed randomly on one of the areas. Subjects were three times more accurate in determining whether the line was tilted when it appeared on the figure. Thus, it does indeed appear that analysis of the figure involves processing information about detail.

The Gestalt psychologists explained perception by focusing on characteristics of the stimulus. Our perceptions, according to the Gestalt approach, can be explained in terms of factors such as the lightness, shape, color, size, and spacing of small units that create larger stimulus patterns. Modern psychologists have continued this stimulus-based approach to object perception by investigating some of the mechanisms behind the phenomena that the Gestalt psychologists described. This brings us to the second question about object perception we posed at the beginning of the chapter: What is the nature of the processing that occurs between stimulation of the retina and perception? As we will see, there are a number of ways to approach this question. We will start by considering neural processing.

Neural Processing: The Firing of Feature Detectors

What is the neural basis for object perception? One possible answer to this question is that object perception is based on the firing of highly specialized neurons that respond only to specific forms. In the early days of research on the neural mechanisms of object perception, such cells were rather fancifully named "grandmother cells," because presumably, if such specialized cells existed, there would be some that would fire only when you looked at your grandmother. Thus, the firing of this cell would signal "grandmother," another cell might signal "telephone," and so on (cf. Barlow, 1972).

Even when the idea of highly specialized neurons was first proposed, most researchers did not take the possibility of grandmother cells very seriously, primarily because there are so many different possible objects in the world that it would take an astronomical number of specialized neurons to perceive them all. Let's look at what we know about how neurons respond to forms to see what is reasonable.

The Neural Code for Objects

Our discussion of the neural code draws heavily on our description of neural processing in the extrastriate cortex in Chapter 4. In that chapter, we saw that the following occurs as we move toward higher levels in the visual system:

1. Neurons respond to more complex and specialized stimuli. For example, neurons in the retina respond best to small spots of light, whereas

neurons called *elaborate cells* in the IT cortex respond only to specific forms (Tanaka et al., 1991; see Figures 4.11 and 7.34). These cells are organized in columns, with neurons that respond to similar stimuli in the same column (see Figure 4.12).

2. Some neurons respond best to single views of objects (view-specific neurons) and others respond to many views of an object (view-invariant neurons). For example, in Chapter 4 we described a view-specific neuron in IT cortex that responds well to the vertical orientation of a monkey's head and poorly to other orientations (see Figure 4.15) and a view-invariant neuron that responds equally well to all views of a human face (see Figure 4.16).

3. Receptive fields get larger. Receptive fields in the retina can be as small as a degree or less. (Remember from page 82 that one degree would be 1/360 of the circumference of the eyeball.) Receptive fields of neurons in area V4, near the middle of the ventral pathway, average about 4 degrees in size, and some neurons in the IT cortex have receptive fields that can cover 150 degrees, which includes most of the visual field (Perrett & Oram, 1993).

Figure 7.34
Some of the stimuli that elicit the best response from neurons in the temporal lobe (Tanaka, 1993).

Each of these properties of higher order neurons would be useful for object perception. The neurons that respond to specialized stimuli would be necessary for our perception of the complex shapes we encounter in the environment. The view-invariant neurons would help us to perceive an object no matter what angle we viewed it from, and neurons that have large receptive fields would help us perceive objects no matter where they were in our visual field.

Does the fact that some neurons (such as the elaborate cells in IT cortex) respond to specialized stimuli mean that they are grandmother cells? Not exactly, because even though the elaborate cells respond to complex stimuli, there is a limit to how selective they are. A particular cell responds to one stimulus best, but also responds to other stimuli, as well. In addition, the different parts of a particular real-world object would cause many different kinds of elaborate cells to fire. Thus, when we present our object, thousands of elaborate cells fire.

If we could look at the activity in all of the IT cortex at once, as we are presenting an object, we might see that there is a large amount of activity in a particular column that contains neurons that respond best to a particular feature of our object. We would also see strong activity in other columns, that are activated by other features of the object. Since many of these neurons are view invariant, a similar pattern of firing will occur even if we view the object from a different angle or if we change position so it is in a different place in our visual field.

What we are describing here is a *distributed coding* of the object. This particular object is represented by the pattern of firing that is distributed over a large population of neurons in the IT cortex. Thus, even though individual neurons fire to fairly specific features, our object is represented by the firing of many neurons working together.

The Neural Code for Biologically Meaningful Objects

In addition to the elaborate cells that respond to geometrical features, many of the cells in the IT cortex respond best to a very important biologically meaningful object—the face (Rolls & Tovee, 1995; Tovee, 1995; Young & Yamane, 1992). To determine how specific these neurons are for faces, Edmund Rolls and Martin Tovee (1995) determined how neurons in the monkey's IT cortex responded to 68 different stimuli, some of which are shown in Figure 7.35. Twenty-three of these stimuli were faces and 45 were nonface stimuli, mostly landscapes and pictures of food.

The results for a typical neuron, shown in Figure 7.36, indicate that the neuron responds best to two or three of the faces, also responds to many of the other faces, but responds little to nonfaces. Thus, this neuron is selective for faces, so when it fires it means

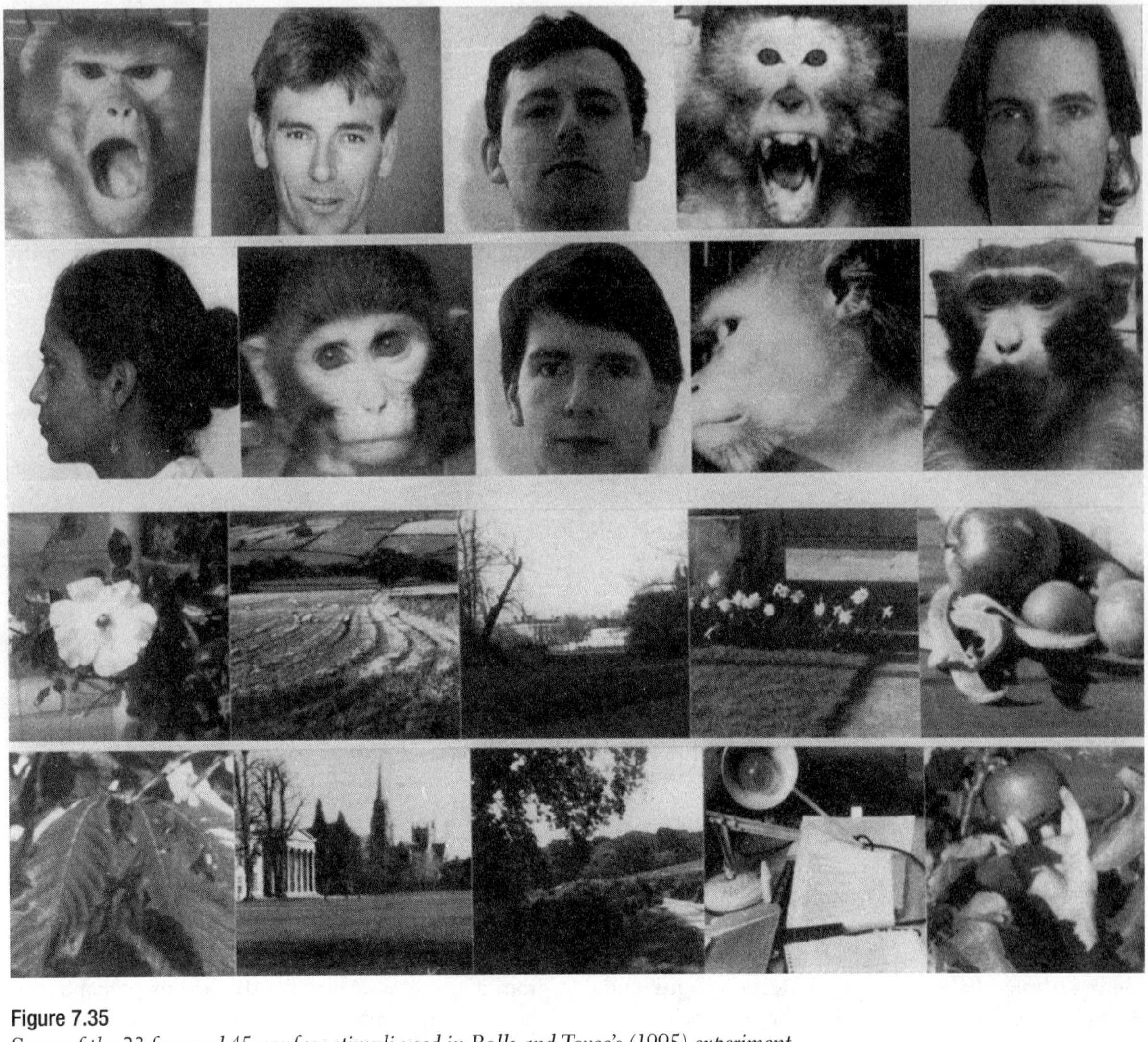

Figure 7.35
Some of the 23 face and 45 nonface stimuli used in Rolls and Tovee's (1995) experiment.

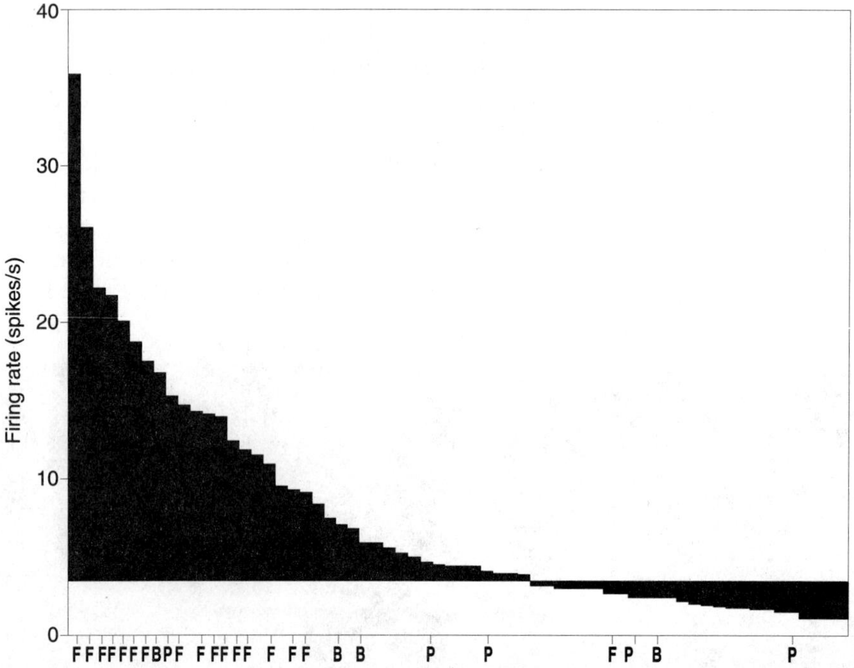

Figure 7.36
Firing rates of a single neuron to all 68 stimuli presented by Rolls and Tovee (1995). The bars marked F are the rates for pictures of faces. The bars marked P are the rates for pictures of faces in profile; the bars marked B were pictures of scenes that also contained a face; and the unmarked bars are the responses to the non-face stimuli. Bars that are below the line represent firing rates that are below the level of spontaneous activity.

that it is likely that the stimulus is a face. However, since this neuron, and others like it, do respond with varying degrees of intensity to many faces, the firing of just one of these neurons cannot indicate that a particular face—your grandmother or anyone else—is present.

The visual system represents different faces in much the same way that it represents different objects—by taking into account the pattern of response across the population of neurons that respond selectively to faces. Thus, for faces, the neural code is a combination of *selective coding* (neurons that respond selectively to faces) and *distributed coding* (the population of face-selective neurons responds with different patterns to different faces).

One of the messages of this book is that many of the causes of perception occur behind the scenes, outside of our conscious awareness (see page 2). The neural firing that occurs to complex stimuli and faces is an example of some of the behind-the-scenes activity that creates object perception. But while this physiological activity is occurring, *perceptual* processes are also occurring that we are also unaware of. Psychologists who have studied this behind-the-scenes activity using behavioral techniques have identified a number of perceptual features that we might call an "alphabet" of object perception.

Perceptual Processing: The Alphabet of Object Perception

In this section, we will consider two approaches that state that the visual system identifies basic features from a scene and then constructs our perception of the scene by combining these features. We begin with the *feature integration approach*.

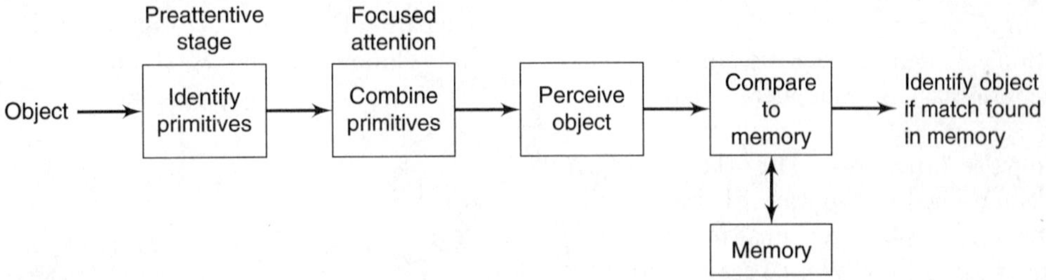

Figure 7.37
Flow diagram showing steps in Treisman's (1986, 1987, 1993) feature integration theory of object perception.

The Feature Integration Approach

The **feature integration approach** to object perception, or **feature integration theory** (which we will call FIT for short), proposes that object perception occurs according to the sequence of stages shown in Figure 7.37 (Treisman, 1987, 1993). In the first stage, called the **preattentive stage,** the visual system analyzes the image and determines the existence of basic features that are called **primitives**—simple, basic units of perception. Some examples of primitives are curvature, orientation, ends of lines, color, and movement (Figure 7.38).

In the second stage, called the **focused attention stage,** the primitives are combined to result in perception of the object. Thus, after the object is perceived, it is recognized by comparing this perception to information stored in memory. We will first consider why

Figure 7.38
Some of the primitives in this scene, indicated by the markings, are curvature, line orientation, and the ends of lines. In addition, the different colors of the objects are also primitives. According to feature integration theory, the first thing the visual system does upon being exposed to this scene, is to break it down into its primitives.

certain features have been identified as being the primitives, and will then describe the preattentive and focused attention stages in more detail.

Determining the Primitives The FIT's primitives have been determined in two ways: (1) by determining *pop-out boundaries* between areas made up of different elements, and (2) by a visual search procedure (Julesz, 1981; Treisman, 1987).

For the **pop-out boundary** method, two sets of elements are displayed next to each other to create textured fields, as in Figure 7.39. If the two areas either contain different primitives or have different values of the same primitive, then an immediately obvious boundary "pops out" between the two areas. For example, in Figure 7.39a the boundaries occur because the components have different orientations (different values of the same primitive). In Figure 7.39b, the boundary occurs because one component (the +'s) has "line crossings," two lines that cross each other, and the other (the L's) does not (there is a primitive in one of the fields but not in the other). However, no pop-out boundary occurs in Figure 7.39c, so no primitives can be identified.

In the **visual search** procedure for determining primitives, subjects are presented with a display that contains a number of elements and are told to find one particular element. To appreciate how this works, do the following demonstration.

D E M O N S T R A T I O N

Visual Search

Find the target in each of the displays in Figures 7.40 and 7.41. For each display, notice how difficult it is to find the target. ●

You probably identified the O in the first display as soon as you looked at it. It *pops out* because the O's property of curvature differs from the V's property of straight lines—that is, the O and the V have different primitives. It probably took you longer to find the R in the second display (unless by chance you happened to look at it right away), because the target letter, R, contains a vertical line and a curved line, like the P, and a slanted line and a curved line, like the Q. That is, the R shares some primitives with the P and the Q. In situations such as this, when primitives are shared,

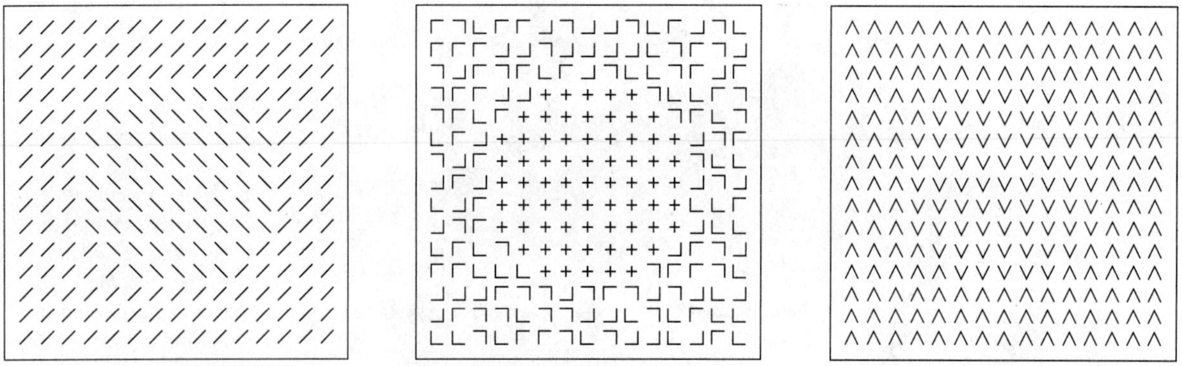

(a) (b) (c)

Figure 7.39

Texture segmentation based on differences in primitives. (a) Difference in orientation. (b) Difference in line crossings. In (c) no difference in primitives, so texture segregation doesn't occur. (From Nothdurft, 1990.)

The target in this display is an O.

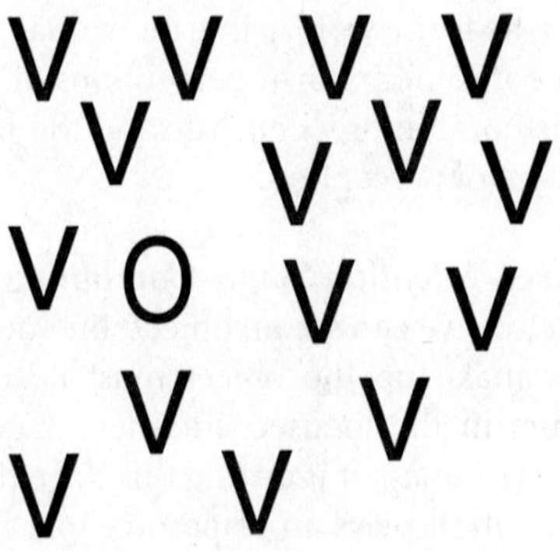

Figure 7.40
Visual search stimulus. You can find the O among the V's almost instantaneously.

visual search takes longer because we have to focus our attention on each of the elements in the display until we find the target.

By measuring the time subjects took to detect pop-out boundaries and to find target letters in search tasks, Treisman identified the following primitives: curvature, tilt, color, line ends, and movement. In addition, closed areas, contrast, and brightness have been identified as primitives (Beck, 1982; Julesz, 1984; Treisman, 1986). These primitives are detected during the preattentive stage of processing and during this stage they exist, not as part of the object, but independently of one another.

The target in this display is an R.

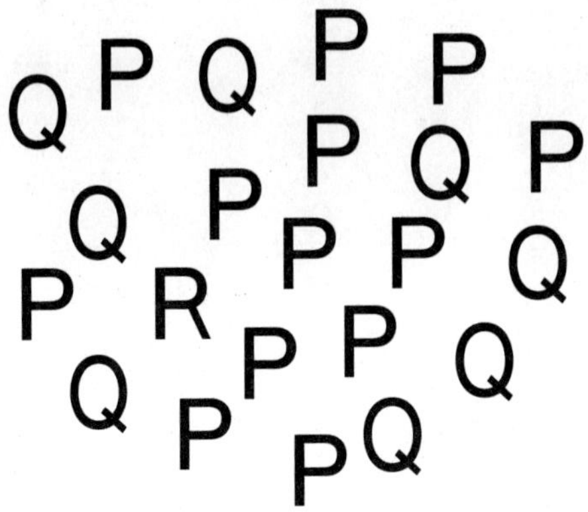

Figure 7.41
Visual search stimulus. Finding the R among the P's and Q's is not instantaneous unless, by chance, you happen to look at the R first.

The Preattentive Stage: Free Floating Primitives Treisman provided evidence that during the preattentive stage of processing, the primitives exist independently of one another, by doing an experiment like the following one: A display consisting of a red X, a blue S, and a green T is flashed onto a screen for one-fifth of a second, followed by a random dot pattern designed to eliminate any afterimage that may remain after the stimuli are turned off (Figure 7.42). When the subjects report what they have seen, they report seeing **illusory conjunctions,** like "red S" or "green X," on about a third of the trials. This result occurs even if the stimuli differ greatly in shape and size. For example, a subject who is presented with a small blue circle and a large green square might report that they perceived a large blue square.

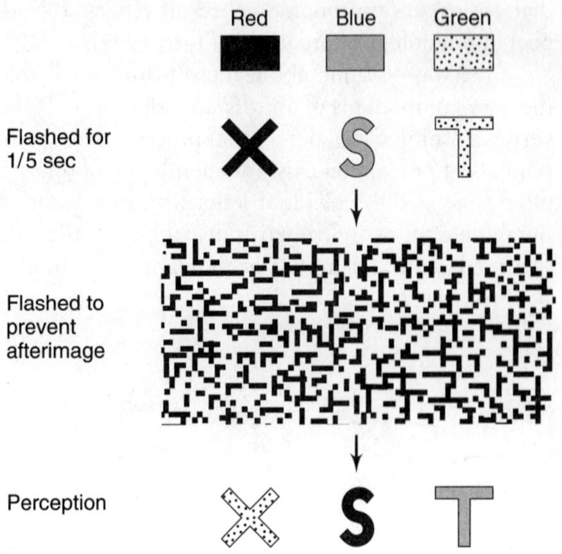

Figure 7.42
Treisman's experiment that illustrates illusory conjunctions. The X, S, and T are briefly flashed, followed by a random dot pattern flashed in the same location as the letters. On some trials observers report letters with colors different from the letter's actual color when it was presented. These changes in color are illusory conjunctions.

According to Treisman, these reports of illusory conjunctions mean that each primitive exists independently of the others during the preattentive stage. That is, primitives such as "redness," "curvature," or "tilted line" are not, at this early stage of processing, associated with a specific stimulus. They are, in Treisman's (1987) words, "free floating" and can therefore be incorrectly combined when stimuli are flashed briefly.

Although the fact that these qualities can exist independently of each other at an early stage of processing may at first seem surprising, this situation is actually what we might expect from what we know about visual physiology. Remember that properties such as color, form, and movement are processed in separate physiological streams, and that neurons that respond to different orientations and shapes are located in different columns in the cortex. Eventually all of these properties are combined to create a unified perception of an object, but before that happens, they exist independently of one another. It is possible that Treisman's psychophysical result reflects this aspect of physiological processing (Tarr, 1994).

One way to think about these primitives is that they are components of an *alphabet* of vision. At the very beginning of the perceptual process, these components of perception exist independently of one another, just as the individual letter tiles in a game of Scrabble exist as individual units when the tiles are scattered at the beginning of the game. Eventually, however, just as the individual Scrabble tiles are combined to form words, the individual primitives for vision combine to form perceptions of whole objects. This combining occurs during the focused attention stage of perception.

The Focused Attention Stage: Combining the Primitives Before we can see an object, the various primitives that make up the object must be combined. This occurs in the focused attention stage, and according to Treisman, it is during this stage that the observer's attention plays an important role in creating our perception of objects. Let's look at an experiment that supports the idea that attention is important during this "combining" stage.

A display consisting of one green X, many red O's, and many blue X's is briefly flashed and is immediately followed by a random dot pattern designed to eliminate any afterimage that may remain after the stimulus is turned off (Figure 7.43a). The subject's task is to indicate, based on this very brief exposure, whether there is a green X in the display and, if there is, to specify its location. Subjects easily detect the green X, because it is the only green object in the display, but they have difficulty specifying its location. The reason for this difficulty, according to Treisman, is that only one primitive is involved (the color green) so focused attention is not required, and the subject, therefore, does not pay attention to the object's location.

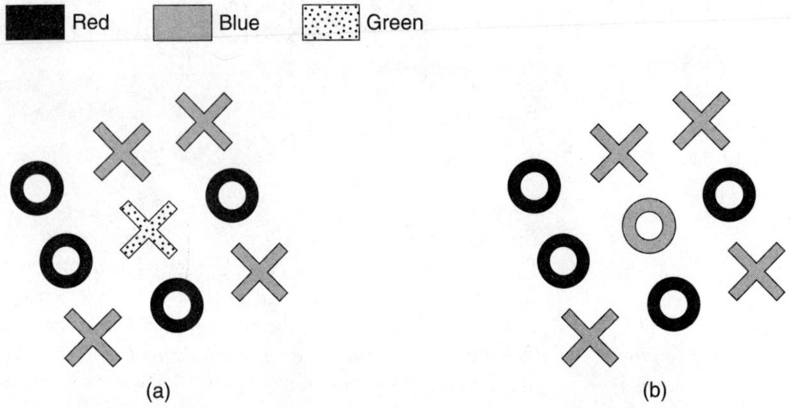

Figure 7.43
Two of Treisman's search patterns. In (a) the task is to find a green X; in (b) it is to find a blue O.

Consider, however, a task such as detecting a single blue O among many red O's and blue X's (Figure 7.43b). This task requires focused attention because to solve this problem the subject must locate an object that contains two properties: blueness *and* O-ness. To combine the two primitives, the subject must focus attention on a specific location. Thus, when subjects correctly identify the presence of the target in this task, they are also able to indicate its location. According to Treisman, a similar process takes place when we perceive everyday objects. Before we perceive the object it is broken down into primitives and then, with the aid of attention, the primitives are combined.

People sometimes wonder why the focused attention stage is necessary. After all, our general impression of our environment is that even though we are usually only paying attention to a small number of things at a time, we are generally aware of the rest of the scene that surrounds us. As Ellen, from Chapter 1, walks toward Bill in the Student Union, she manages to avoid the many potential obstacles that are in her way, even though she is focusing her attention on Bill.

We can deal with the question of why attention is a necessary part of the perceptual process physiologically by remembering that visual information is processed in two separated streams—the ventral stream, which flows toward the temporal cortex and processes information about "what" an object is, and the dorsal stream, which flows toward the parietal cortex and processes information about "where" the object is or "how" we interact with it. Eventually the information from these two pathways must be combined, and according to Treisman (1993), attention is the mechanism that accomplishes this combination. Attention is the "glue" that binds together the features at a location.

Another way to deal with the question of why attention is necessary is illustrated by an experiment by Daniel Levin and Daniel Simons (1997) that shows that we may not be as aware of things in our environment as we think. In this experiment, subjects viewed a video of a brief conversation between two women. Figure 7.44 shows a sequence of four frames from the video.

The noteworthy aspect of this video is that changes take place every time the camera angle changes. Thus, in Shot B, the woman's scarf has disappeared; in Shot C, the other woman's hand is on her chin, although moments later, in Shot D, her arms are on the table. Also, the plates change color from red in the initial views to white in Shot D.

Even though subjects were told to "pay close attention" to the film, only 1 of 10 subjects claimed to notice any changes. Even when the subjects were shown the video again and were warned that there would be changes in "objects, body position, or clothing," they noticed fewer than a quarter of the changes that occurred.

Although this may seem like a counter-intuitive result, it has been duplicated in a number of other experiments (Grimes, 1996; Rensink, O'Regan, & Clark, 1996; Wolfe, 1997). Apparently, we have a general awareness of our surroundings and the objects in it, but we are less aware of many of the details than we might think. Although more research needs to be done before we understand how attention works during the focused attention stage of processing, the results of many experiments do indicate that attention is an essential component of the perceptual process.

The Computational Approach

The basis of Treisman's feature integration theory is the idea that an object's primitives are determined in the beginning stage of the perceptual process. Another approach to object perception that relies on the identification of primitives is an approach called the **computational approach** because it treats the visual system as if it were a computer that has been programmed to perceive objects.

A person who is closely associated with the computational approach to object perception is David Marr, a vision researcher who, at the age of 32, discovered that he had leukemia and spent the last two years of his life writing a book titled *Vision* (1982). This book, along with a number of papers (Marr, 1976; Marr & Hildreth, 1980; Marr & Nishihara, 1978), set forth the basis of the computational approach.

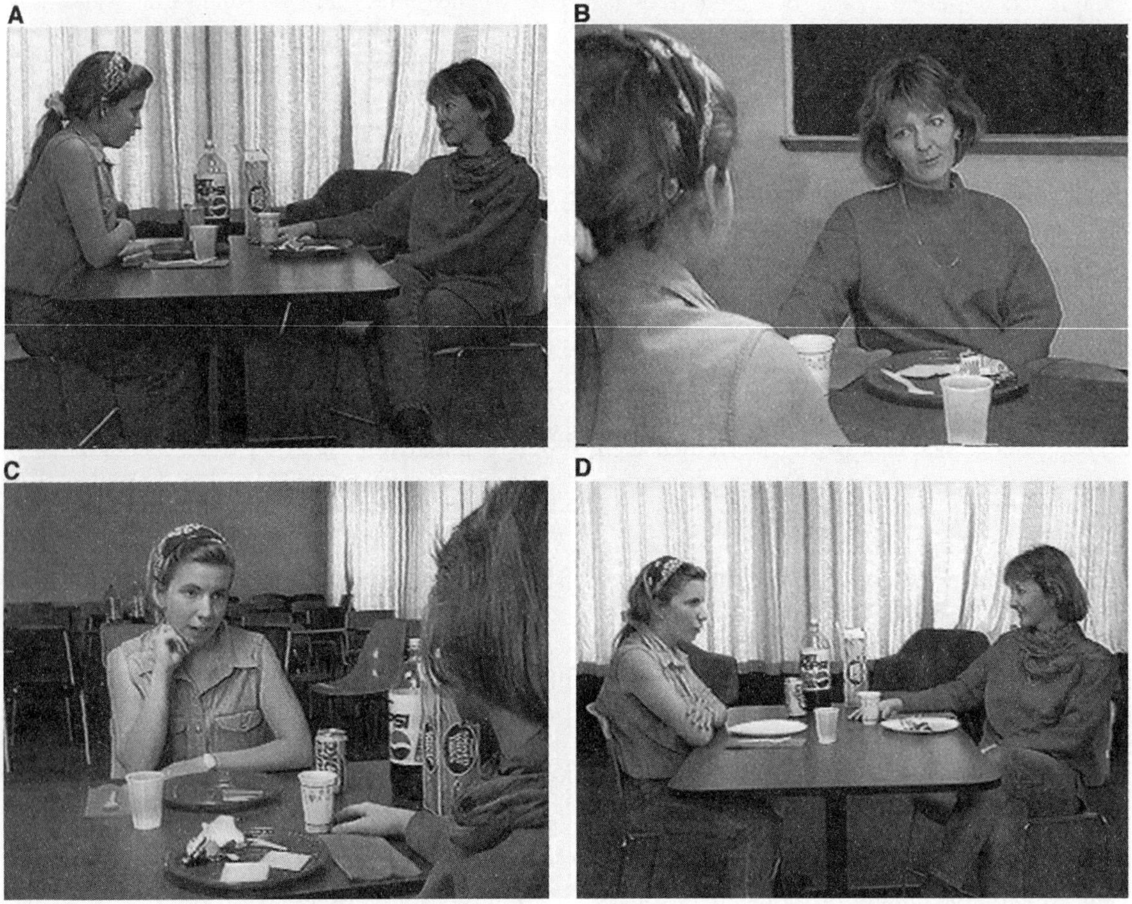

Figure 7.44
Series of shots from the video shown in the Levin and Simons (1997) experiment. Note that the woman on the right is wearing a scarf around her neck in Shots A, C, and D, but not in Shot B. Also, the color of the plates changes from red in the first three frames to white in frame D, and the hand position of the woman on the left changes between Shots C and D.

Marr's (1982) approach sees object perception as occurring in a number of different stages, just as Treisman's FIT does. What distinguishes Marr's approach is that he explains the perceptual process as if it were carried out by a computer that is programmed to analyze the image and determine what it is. We will describe how this "computer" is programmed by referring to the stages in the computational approach shown in Figure 7.45.

Our starting point is the image of the object or scene on the retina. This image is analyzed to determine areas of light and dark and where intensity changes occur. The purpose of this analysis is to determine the **raw primal sketch,** which is basically a collection of features. According to Marr, one of the visual system's main tasks at this stage is to identify an object's edges. We can appreciate the difficulty of doing this by looking at Figure 7.46. In this figure, intensity changes are caused by the edges of the object and by changes in illumination caused by the lighting conditions. To determine the shape of an object, the visual system must ignore shadows and

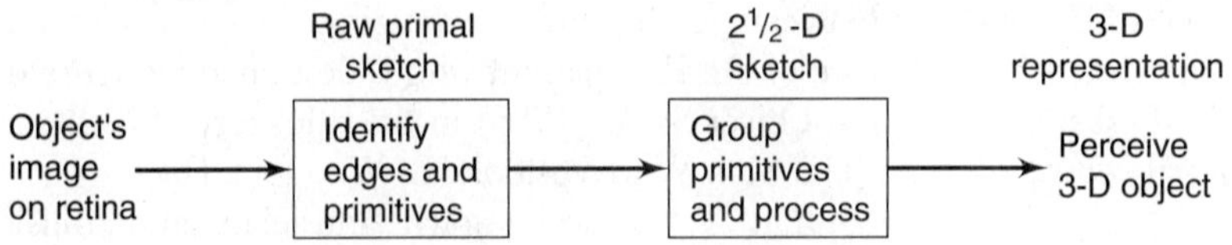

Figure 7.45
Flow diagram indicating the stages in Marr's computational approach to perception.

other changes in illumination, and locate the object's true edges.

How does the visual system accomplish this? Marr proposed that the visual system carries out a mathematical analysis of the intensity changes in the image and also takes into account what he calls **natural constraints** in the world. Natural constraints are basic properties of the environment, such as the fact that intensity usually changes gradually at borders created by shadows and highlights but changes more abruptly at borders created by an object's edges. According to Marr, the visual system takes this fact about the world into account and labels gradual borders as shadows and sharper intensity changes as borders between objects.

As the visual system analyzes the intensities of an object or scene to locate the edges, it also identifies a number of *primitives,* such as (1) blobs (closed loops), (2) segments of edges, (3) bars (open passages), and (4) terminations (the ends of edge segments). These primitives, plus the object's edges, make up the primal sketch.

The primal sketch is the result of the initial stage of computations, but we do not see it. Before conscious perception can occur, the visual system must process the information contained in the primal sketch. First, primitives that are similar in size and orientation are grouped, following Gestalt principles. These groups of primitives are then processed further, by procedures we will not describe here (see Marr,

Figure 7.46
Intensity changes occur both at the edges of this object and at the border created by the shadows and highlights on the surface of the object. To identify the object's shape, the visual system must identify the object's true edges.

1982, for details), to yield a representation of the object's surfaces and their layouts that Marr called the **2½-D sketch.** The information in the 2½-D sketch is then transformed into a three-dimensional representation that we actually see.

One way to look at Marr's system is to think of it as a computer that is programmed to take into account certain physical properties of the world (for example, the fact that shadows often have fuzzy borders). The data fed into this computer are the characteristics of the retinal image, particularly the pattern of light and dark areas in the image. The computer calculates the existence of objects in the environment based on these data and taking into account what it knows about the properties of images in the world. Our description of the way these calculations are carried out has been vague, because of the complexity of the calculations and also because Marr did not have time to work out many of the specific details of his system.

It is notable that even though there are differences between Marr's computational approach and Treisman's FIT approach (if you read Marr's book you will see that he uses a lot of mathematical description to explain how the visual "computer" analyzes the retinal image whereas Treisman's approach does not rely on this mathematical analysis of the image), they both propose that the first stage of object perception is the determination of the object's primitives. We will now look at an approach to object perception that focuses on how we *recognize* objects, and which also states that objects consist of basic units called primitives.

Recognizing Objects: Determining What Things Are

When we see an object, we usually go beyond "seeing" to "recognizing." To appreciate the difference between seeing and recognizing, let's consider the case of Dr. P., a patient who is described by neurologist Oliver Sacks (1985) in the title story of his book "The Man Who Mistook His Wife for a Hat."

Dr. P., a well-known musician and music teacher, first noticed a problem when he began having trouble recognizing his students visually, although he could immediately identify them by the sound of their voices. But when Dr. P. began misperceiving common objects, for example addressing a parking meter as if it were a person, or expecting a carved knob on a piece of furniture to engage him in conversation, it became clear that his problem was more serious than just a little forgetfulness. Was he blind, or perhaps crazy? It was clear from an eye examination that he could see well, so poor vision wasn't his problem. Also, by many other criteria, it was obvious that he was not crazy.

Dr. P's problem, which was eventually diagnosed as visual form agnosia caused by a brain tumor, made it impossible for him to recognize faces and other common objects. He perceived their *parts* but not the objects as a whole, so when Sacks presented him with a glove, Dr. P. described it as "a continuous surface unfolded on itself. It appears to have five outpouchings, if this is the word." When Sacks asked him what it was, Dr. P. hypothesized that it was "a container of some sort. . . . It could be a change purse, for example, for coins of five sizes."

The normally easy process of object recognition had, for Dr. P., been derailed by his brain tumor. He could see the object, and recognize parts of it but couldn't perceptually assemble the parts in a way that would enable him to recognize the object as a whole.

One approach that has been used to explain how object recognition occurs in people without brain damage is Irving Biederman's *recognition-by-components* approach. This approach proposes an "alphabet" of basic features as did Treisman's and Marr's, but instead of primitives such as color, form, and movement, the components are **volumetric primitives**—three-dimensional shapes that correspond to an object's parts, such as the fingers of the glove that Sachs showed to Dr. P.

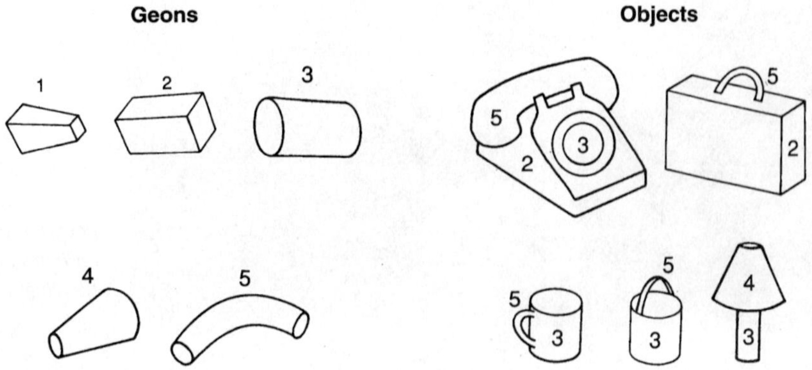

Figure 7.47
Left: Some geons. Right: Some objects created from the geons on the left. The numbers on the objects indicate which geons are present. Note that recognizable objects can be formed by combining just two or three geons. Also note that the relations between the geons matter, as illustrated by the cup and the pail. (From Biederman, 1987.)

The Recognition by Components Approach

Figure 7.47 shows the basic idea behind **recognition by components (RBC) theory.** According to RBC theory, an object or scene is analyzed into volumetric primitives, called **geons** (for geometric ions). These geons are three-dimensional shapes such as cylinders, rectangular solids, and pyramids. From the 36 different shapes in Biederman's system, it is possible to construct many thousands of objects by various arrangements of these components. According to Biederman, geons have the following basic properties:

1. They are view invariant. This means that their properties do not change when viewed from different angles. Geons are therefore easily recognizable from a wide range of viewpoints. For example, the rectangular solid in Figure 7.47 has three parallel edges from most viewing angles. Occasionally, however, we might view the rectangle from an angle that obscures its view-invariant properties. For example, if we look at the rectangular solid end-on, we cannot see its parallel edges. According to Biederman, these situations occur only rarely and when they do occur we find it difficult to recognize the object.
2. They are discriminable. Each of the geons can be distinguished from each of the others from all viewpoints.
3. They are resistant to visual noise: We can still perceive geons under less than ideal conditions. To illustrate this property, Biederman obscured parts of the geons that make up the object in Figure 7.48 but left enough of each geon so it could

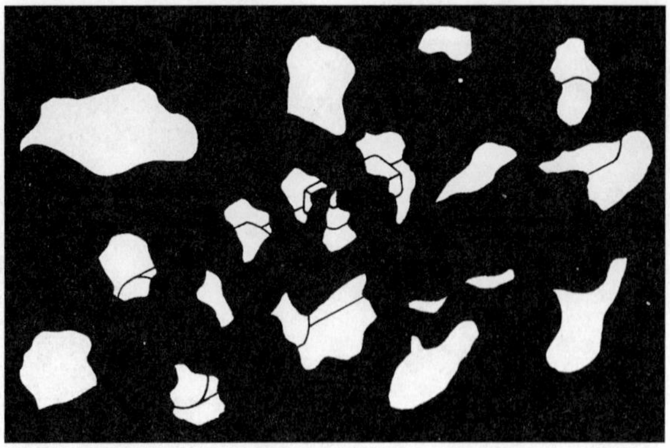

Figure 7.48
What is the object behind the mask? See the legend of Figure 7.49 for the answer. (From Biederman, 1987.)

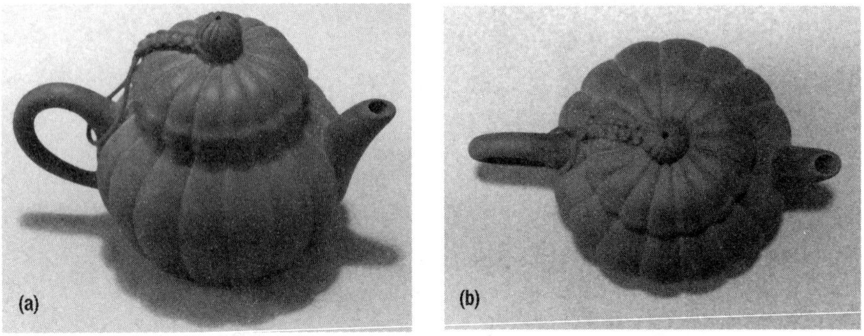

Figure 7.50
(a) A tea pot; (b) The same tea pot seen from a viewpoint that obscures most of its geons and therefore makes it difficult to recognize.

still be identified. The reason we can identify this object (what is it?), even though over half of its contour is obscured, is because we can still identify its geons. Our ability to identify an object if we can identify its geons is called the **principle of componential recovery.** If, however, we occlude the object's geons by obscuring their intersections (Figure 7.49), we can no longer identify the geons, and it becomes impossible to recognize the object.

Another way to make an object difficult to recognize is to view the object from an unusual viewpoint. For example, when we view the object in Figure 7.50a from the unusual perspective in Figure 7.50b we can't see its basic geons and, therefore, have difficulty identifying it.

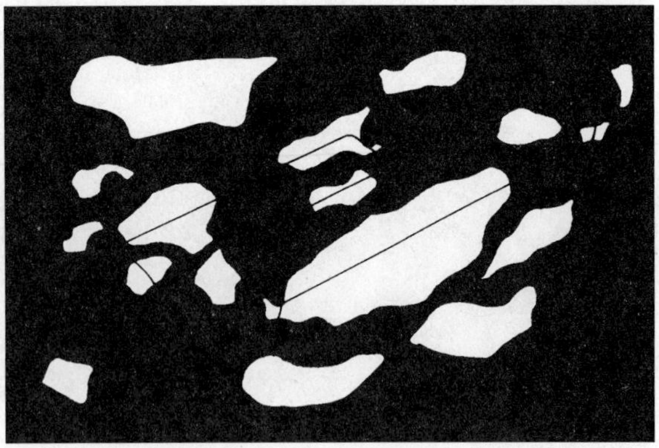

Figure 7.49
The same object as in Figure 7.48 (a flashlight) with the geons obscured. (From Biederman, 1987.)

The basic message of Biederman's theory is that, if enough information is available to enable us to identify an object's basic geons, we will be able to identify the object (also see Biederman & Cooper, 1991; Biederman et al., 1993). Biederman has also shown that it is possible to identify objects even if only a few of their geons are present. He demonstrated this by flashing line drawings like the ones in Figure 7.51 and asking subjects to name the object as rapidly as possible. The result of this experiment was that people could name most objects in less than a second based on only a few geons. For example, although the airplane consists of nine geons when complete (Figure 7.51c), it was identified correctly 80 percent of the time when only three geons were present (Figure 7.51a) and 90 percent of the time when four geons were present (Figure 7.51b).

One of the strengths of Biederman's theory is that it shows that we can recognize objects based on a relatively small number of basic shapes. However, some researchers have criticized it on the grounds that, while geons may enable us to distinguish between classes of objects (airplanes vs. toasters, for example), they do not always provide enough information to enable us to distinguish between different objects that have the same basic components. For example, many birds have tapered beaks, which would be described by the same geon, but there are differences in the rate of the beaks' taper in different birds. Thus, based on

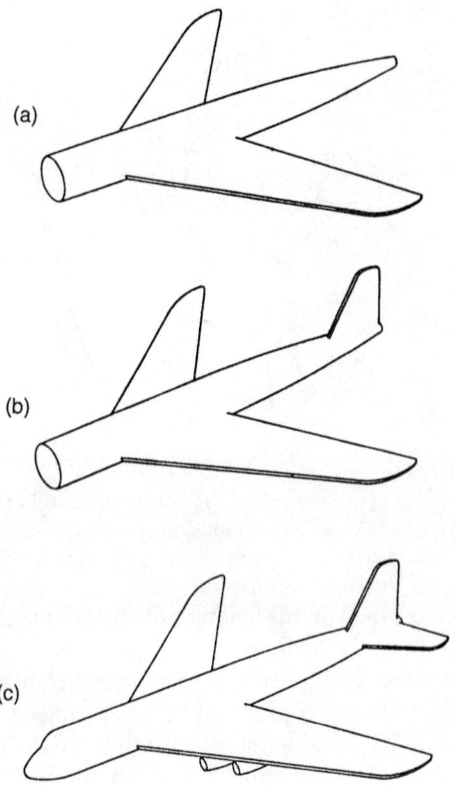

Figure 7.51
An airplane, as represented (a) by three geons, (b) by four geons, and (c) by nine geons. (From Biederman, 1987.)

geons, we might not be able to distinguish between two finches with slightly different beaks (Perrett & Oram, 1993).

Also, if we consider the physiology of neurons such as the elaborate cells (Figure 4.11) and other neurons that respond to complex shapes (Figure 7.34), we find that these neurons are tuned to respond to much smaller differences between shapes that exist between Biederman's geons. Thus, the RBC model succeeds in describing a way that we may recognize broad classes of objects, but it may need to be refined in order to explain how we can differentiate between objects that differ in detail, such as two types of birds or different models of automobiles, but which are constructed from the same basic components.

Knowledge, Experience, and Processing

All of the approaches we have considered, except the Gestalt approach, describe object perception as starting with the identification of small components called primitives. This initial analysis is determined largely by physical properties of the stimulus display such as areas of light and dark, changes in orientation, and the sizes and relationships between shapes in the image. But other factors in addition to the physical properties of the stimulus also influence perception. Perception can be influenced by knowledge that a person brings to the situation, and thought processes that are based on this knowledge. For example, subjects were able to identify the stimulus in Figure 7.48 as a flashlight and the one in Figure 7.51 as an airplane because of their previous knowledge of flashlights and airplanes.

The idea that knowledge and thought processes can influence perception is an old one in psychology that was originally proposed by Hermann von Helmholtz (of the trichromatic theory of color vision), in the form of his *likelihood principle.*

The Likelihood Principle and Hypothesis Testing

The idea that thought processes are involved in perception is not a new one. Remember that the Gestalt psychologists stated that the meaningfulness of a stimulus plays a role in determining perceptual organization. Even before the Gestalt psychologists, Herman von Helmholtz proposed the **likelihood principle:** *We will perceive the object that is most likely to be the cause of our sensory stimulation.* According to this principle, if a number of possible objects could have caused a particular pattern of light and dark on the retina, we will perceive the object that is *most likely* to occur *in that particular situation.* For example, consider the experiment we described in Chapter 1, in which subjects first see a kitchen scene and are then asked to identify three different objects (Figure 1.10). In this experiment the object that was most likely to appear in the kitchen scene (the loaf of bread) was most accurately identified.

A modern descendant of Helmholtz's likelihood principle is Richard Gregory's (1973) idea that perception is governed by a mechanism Gregory calls **hypothesis testing.** He states that "we may think of sensory stimulation as providing data for hypotheses concerning the state of the external world" (p. 61). Thus, you might hypothesize that the shadowy object in that dimly lit corner across the room is a small table. However, after looking at the corner more closely, you realize that this hypothesis is incorrect and, based on the new data garnered from your closer inspection, realize that the "table" is actually a toy drum.

Thus, we are not automatons that perceive in a totally automatic, nonthinking way. Our perceptions are determined by a combination of automatic processes that begin with properties of the stimulus, and individualistic processes that depend on a person's past experiences, knowledge, and expectations. Processing that starts with physical properties of stimuli such as primitives or patterns of light and dark is called **bottom-up processing.** Processing that depends on higher level information such as the person's knowledge and thought processes is called **top-down processing.** Let's consider some more examples of top-down processing.

Examples of Top-Down Processing

An experiment that illustrates top-down processing was done by Irving Biederman (1981), using the stimulus in Figure 7.52. Biederman flashed this scene on a screen and asked observers to identify an object located at a particular place in the scene (they were told where to look immediately before seeing the picture). When the observers were asked to identify the fire hydrant, Biederman found that they made more errors when the hydrant was in a strange location, such as on top of the mailbox, than when it was located where it belonged, on the sidewalk. The observers' knowledge of where fire hydrants belong influenced their ability to recognize the hydrant.

Figure 7.52
Stimulus used in Biederman's (1981) experiment. In this picture, observers were asked to identify the fire hydrant.

Another example of the possible operation of top-down processing is provided by what happens when observers are asked to report what they see in displays like the ones in Figure 7.53. When subjects are shown the single circle-with-a-break on the left, they tend to report that they see a circle. However, when

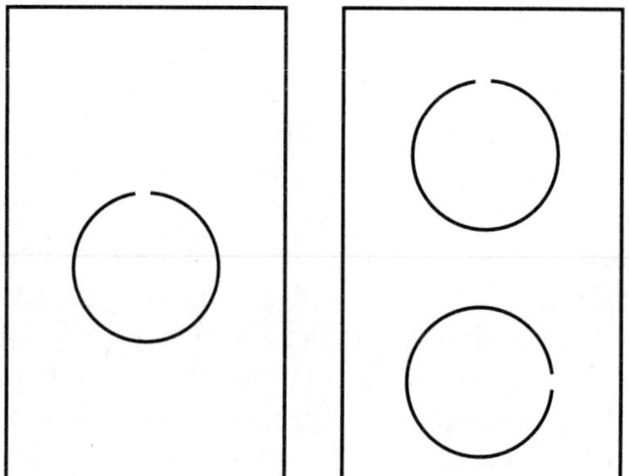

Figure 7.53
Stimuli used by Pomerantz and Lockhead (1991) to demonstrate cognitive effects in perception.

they are shown the two circles on the right, they tend to report that the circles contain exaggerated breaks, looking more like the letters C and U (Pomerantz & Lockhead, 1991).

Why does this result occur? One possible explanation is that since we often see circles with small breaks that are caused by unintended drawing mistakes, the observer assumes the single object on the left is a circle. However, when both circles have identical breaks in different positions, the observer infers that the breaks aren't accidental and, in fact, that they are the main thing that distinguishes between the two circles. The resulting exaggeration of the breaks occurs, therefore, because the observer's thought processes have intervened between the physical properties of the stimuli and perception of the stimuli.

Top-down processing is included in some of the theories of object perception we have described previously. For example, Treisman (FIT) states that the effect of meaning on perception first comes into play during the focused-attention stage, in which primitives are being combined. Our knowledge of the world allows us to rule out certain combinations of properties, so that it is unlikely that we would see blue bananas or furry eggs. Then after we perceive an object, knowledge comes into play again when we recognize a stimulus by comparing our perception of it to knowledge stored in memory (Figure 7.37). Thus, in many situations, bottom-up and top-down processing work together to determine perception (Figure 7.54).

In contrast to the important place that top-down processing plays in the later stages of Treisman's FIT approach and Biederman's RBC approach, David Marr's computational approach relies almost exclusively on bottom-up processing. His computational approach describes the perceptual process as operating like a computer that is programmed to extract information from the stimulus pattern and does not include the possibility that perception might be affected by the knowledge, expectations, or past experiences of the person doing the perceiving. However, the computational approach does say that the visual system is constructed to take into account the nature of the perceptual world (Marr's natural constraints). According to this idea, the *visual system*

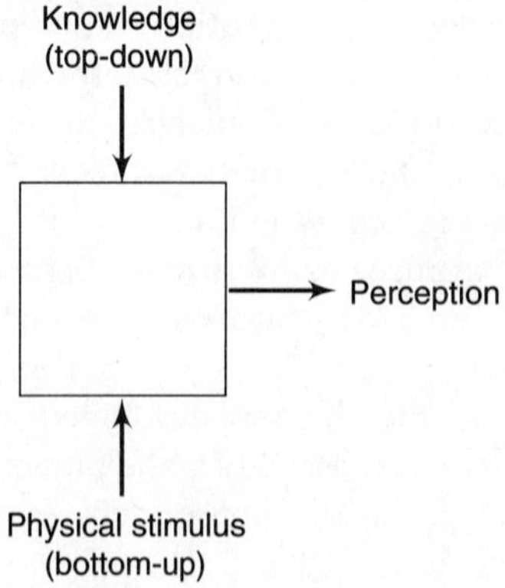

Figure 7.54
How both bottom-up and top-down processing contribute to perception.

brings some knowledge of the world into the perceptual situation. How did the visual system come to contain this knowledge? Most likely, through the process of evolution.

Evolution, Experience, and Neural Processing

One way that the visual system brings knowledge of the world into the perceptual situation is by possessing neural circuits that are tuned to respond best to stimuli that occur naturally in the environment. According to the theory of natural selection, genetically-based characteristics that enhance an animal's ability to survive, and therefore reproduce, will be passed on to the future generations. Thus a monkey whose visual system responds well to the movements, shapes, and colors of the jungle will be more likely to survive to pass on these characteristics than will a monkey with a visual system that is not as well adapted to respond to these characteristics of the environment. Through this evolutionary process, the visual system has been slowly shaped to fit the environment within which it functions (Goldstein, 1998).

In addition to the built-in knowledge of the world achieved through the process of evolution, the visual system also adapts to its environment through a process called **neural plasticity**, that operates on a much shorter time scale. Neural plasticity enables the visual system to undergo changes in its neural circuitry based on the stimulation it receives. In Chapter 4 we described experiments which show that experience in recognizing specific shapes can cause neurons in a monkey's cortex to become tuned to respond to those shapes (Logothetis & Pauls, 1995; see page 114). In the chapters that follow, we will describe similar examples of how the properties of neurons develop in response to environmental stimulation.

The visual system's functioning is, therefore, determined both by evolutionary processes that shape the basic structure of the system and neural plasticity that enables the system to further adapt to the actual stimuli it is receiving. It is through both of these mechanisms that the visual system receives its "knowledge" of the environment.

Something to Consider: Comparing the Ways of Explaining Object Perception

Our survey of ways to approach object perception might leave you wondering which of the explanations—Gestalt, neural feature detectors, feature integration theory, computational, or recognition-by-components—is "correct." All of them will undoubtedly be modified and refined in the years to come, as we learn more about both the physiological and behavioral mechanisms of object perception, but from what we know now it seems clear that each of these approaches has something to tell us about how we perceive objects.

These approaches each explain different aspects of object perception. The Gestalt approach describes how object perception depends on the stimulus configuration; the neural feature detector approach describes the connection between neural responding and perception, and the FIT, computational, and RBC approaches describe perceptual processes such as analyzing objects into primitives, attention, and recognition.

Although these approaches focus on different aspects of the perceptual process, they share a number of properties. The FIT, computational, RBC, and neural feature detector approaches all propose that at an early stage in object perception objects are analyzed into basic features or primitives. Another idea that occurs in a number of the approaches is that the mechanism for object perception is tailored to the environment, either through the use of top-down information provided by the observer's knowledge, or by built-in neural circuits, or by a combination of both.

Finally, most of the approaches are similar in that their workings are hidden from our conscious awareness. Whether we are describing the way neurons fire to specialized stimuli or how objects are perceptually analyzed into primitives, we are dealing with the behind-the scenes-activity that we first described in Chapter 1.

Shape Perception Through Vision and Touch

Have someone select a few objects for you to identify. Close your eyes and have the person place an object in your hand. Identify it, relying on touch alone, and then open your eyes and look at it. Based on this experience, how would you compare the process of perceiving shape through these two different senses? Touch, as a way to perceive shape, is more immediate—you are in direct contact with the object—but vision is faster and more accurate.

For someone who is blind, touch can serve as a substitute for vision—a process called **sensory substitution.** Paul Bach-y-Rita (1969, 1970, 1972) experimented with the possibility of substituting touch for vision using an array of 400 small vibrators that created patterns of vibration on a person's back corresponding to the pattern of light and dark in an image picked up by a television camera, with vibration being more intense for light areas and less intense for dark areas. Some highly trained subjects were able to use these vibrations to "see" remarkable details, as indicated by one subject's description: "That is Betty; she is wearing her hair down today and does not have her glasses on. Her mouth is open and she is moving her right hand from her left side to the back of her head."

A portable sensory substitution system, based on some of the principles studied by Bach-y-Rita, has been developed to enable blind people to read text or perceive graphic displays. This device, called the **Optacon,** transforms printed letters or graphic images into patterns of vibration that can be sensed through the fingers (Figure 7.55).

While touch can substitute for vision when vision is not available, touch is usually dominated by vision when they are placed in conflict with each other for shape perception tasks. This result, called **intersensory dominance,** was demonstrated in a classic paper

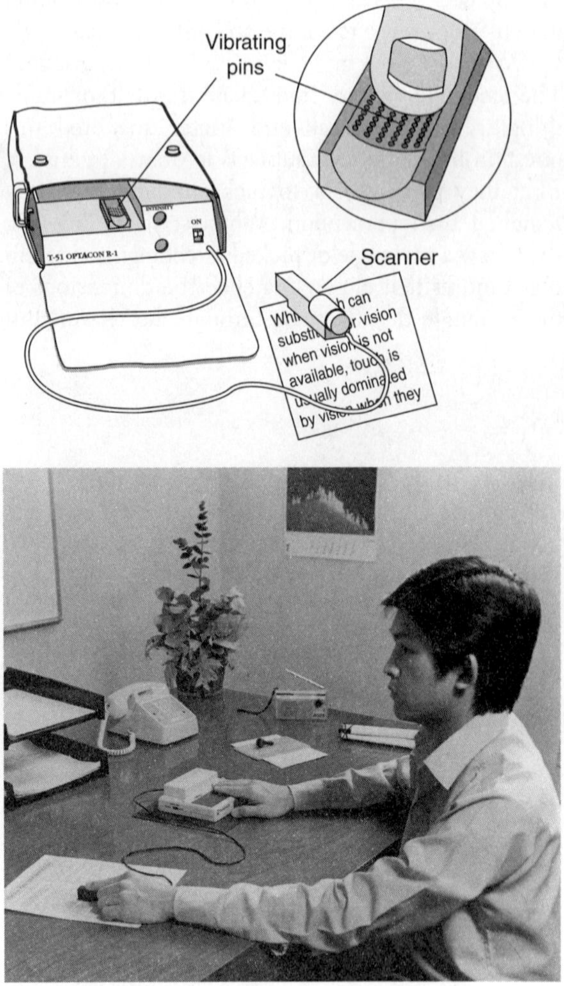

Figure 7.55
The Optacon, a device that translates printed words or pictures into patterns of vibrating pins that can be sensed by the finger. The person moves the scanner over the text and senses the vibrations by placing a finger on the pins.

by Irv Rock and Jack Victor (1964) who had subjects view small squares through distorting prisms that made the square look like a rectangle, with one side twice as long as the other. While looking at the square, the subject simultaneously felt it with their fingers through a silk cloth. Thus, the information the subjects received through the two senses didn't match—they *saw* a rectangle and *felt* a square.

What did Rock and Victor's subjects experience? The rectangle they saw, the square they felt, or something inbetween? Rock and Victor answered this question by asking their subjects to draw a picture of what they perceived or to pick another shape that matched their perception. When subjects did this, they drew a rectangle or picked a rectangular matching stimulus that closely matched the dimensions of the rectangle that they saw through the viewer. But not only did subjects base their judgment almost solely on the information they received through their visual system, over half of them reported that the stimulus they were feeling actually "felt" like a rectangular shape. For these subjects, the object *felt* the way it *looked!*

Many other experiments have confirmed that vision dominates touch for perceiving shape (Power, 1981; Warren & Rossano, 1991). This dominance of vision over touch makes sense when we consider that vision is the sense we habitually use for perceiving shape, and that it registers shape more accurately and rapidly than does touch. However, for a task in which vision is not the sense we habitually use, such as sensing the roughness of a surface, touch and vision influence a person's perception of roughness about equally (Lederman & Abbott, 1981).

Study Questions

Underlying Principles

Find examples of the following principles in this chapter:

- Receptive fields/neural selectivity (191)
- Distributed response (194)
- Columnar organization (192)
- Parallel pathways (197)
- Physiological connections with perception (202)
- Cognitive influences (205)

Organizing the Environment: Perceptual Organization

1. What is perceptual organization? (176)
2. What are four problems that a computer must deal with in order to accurately perceive a scene? (176)
3. How does the human ability to perceive objects compare to the ability of a powerful computer? (177)
4. What is structuralism? Why did Max Wertheimer disagree with the idea behind structuralism? (178)
5. What idea did the Gestalt psychologists propose in place of structuralism? (178)
6. What is an illusory contour? How does the existence of illusory contours in Figure 7.9 argue against structuralism? (179)
7. What are the laws of perceptual organization? (181)
8. Describe each of the following laws: Pragnanz, similarity, good continuation, proximity, connectedness, common fate, meaningfulness. (181)
9. Give an example of how a change in an object's meaning can cause a change in perceptual organization. (184)
10. Why do the Gestalt laws seem like statements of the obvious? (185)
11. What do we mean when we say that the Gestalt laws reflect regularities in the environment? (186)
12. What happens to our perception when the regularities that usually occur in the environment are violated? (186)
13. What is figure and ground? reversible figure-ground? (186)
14. What are four of the properties of the figure and the ground? (187)
15. What does the fact that we can't simultaneously perceive the vase and faces in a reversible figure-ground display as figure tell us about the idea that our perception reflects regularities in our environment? (187)
16. What are some of the determinants of figure and ground? (188)
17. Describe three things that cause problems for the Gestalt approach. (189)
18. Describe Weisstein and Wong's experiment. What does this experiment contribute to the Gestalt approach? (190)

Neural Processing: The Firing of Feature Detectors

19. What is a "grandmother" cell? (191)
20. Is it likely that the firing of grandmother cells is responsible for our perception of objects? (191)
21. What are three basic properties of higher-order neurons and what is their connection to object perception? (191)
22. Are elaborate cells in the IT cortex the same thing as grandmother cells? (192)
23. Is the neural basis of object perception probably selective or distributed? (192)
24. Describe the results of Rolls and Tovee's experiment, which determined how neurons in a monkey's IT cortex respond to a variety of different stimuli. (193)

25. What do we mean when we say that the neural code for faces is a combination of selective coding and distributed coding? (194)

Perceptual Processing: The Alphabet of Object Perception

26. What does feature integration theory propose about how object perception occurs? (195)
27. What are primitives? (195)
28. Describe the pop-out boundary and the visual search procedures for determining primitives. (196)
29. During what stage of processing are the primitives detected? (197)
30. Describe the experiment that demonstrated the existence of illusory conjunctions. What does the existence of illusory conjunctions mean? (197)
31. How does the idea that primitives can exist independently of one another at an early stage of processing fit with what we know about visual physiology? (198)
32. During what stage of processing are individual primitives for vision combined to form perceptions? (198)
33. What kinds of search tasks involve focused attention? (198)
34. According to Treisman, how is attention involved in everyday perception? (199)
35. What is a possible physiological reason that attention is a necessary part of the perceptual process? (199)
36. Describe the Levin and Simons experiment in which they had subjects watch a video of a brief conversation. What conclusion can we draw from this experiment? (199)
37. How does the computational approach conceive of the visual system? Who is the person most closely associated with the computational approach? (199)
38. What are the steps in the computational approach? (200)
39. What is the raw primal sketch? (200)
40. How does the visual system determine the raw primal sketch? What are natural constraints and how are they involved in determining the raw primal sketch? (201)
41. What must occur before conscious perception can occur, according to the computational approach to perception? What is the 2–1/2-D sketch? (201)
42. How are the FIT and computational approaches similar and different? (202)

Recognizing Objects: Determining What Things Are

43. How does the case of Dr. P. illustrate the difference between seeing and recognizing? (202)
44. What kind of "alphabet" of visual features (primitives) does the recognition-by-components approach to object perception propose? Who is the person most closely associated with this approach to object recognition? (202)
45. What are geons? What are the basic properties of geons? (203)
46. What is the principle of componential recovery? (204)
47. What is the basic message of the recognition by components theory? (204)
48. What is a strength of Biederman's theory? How has it been criticized? (204)

Knowledge, Experience, and Processing

49. What is the likelihood principle and who proposed it? (205)
50. What is hypothesis testing and who proposed it? (206)
51. What is bottom-up processing? top-down processing? (206)
52. Describe two examples of top-down processing. (206)
53. How is top-down processing included in some of the theories of object perception we have described? (207)
54. Does Marr's computational approach involve any top-down processing? (207)

55. What does it mean to say that the visual system brings some knowledge of the world into the perceptual situation? (207)

56. What does it mean to say that visual processing "evolved"? (207)

Something to Consider: Comparing the Ways of Explaining Perception

57. Which aspects of the perceptual process are addressed by each of the approaches to object perception that we have described? (208)

58. What do the various approaches we have described have in common? (208)

Across the Senses: Shape Perception Through Vision and Touch

59. Touch, as a way to perceive shape is ___________, but vision is ___________. (209)

60. What is sensory substitution? How was it used by Bach-y-Rita? How was it used in the Optacon system? (209)

61. What is intersensory dominance? Describe Rock and Victor's experiment. (209)

62. Which is more dominant when they are placed in conflict, vision or touch? (210)

63. Under what conditions do touch and vision influence a person's perception about equally? (210)

8

PERCEIVING VISUAL SPACE

CHAPTER CONTENTS

SOME QUESTIONS WE WILL CONSIDER

- How can we see far into the distance based on the flat image on the retina? (215)
- Why do we see depth better with two eyes, than with one eye? (222)
- Since bats sense their environment not with their eyes, but by sensing sound echoes, how do they experience the space that surrounds them? (240)

Imagine that you are standing on the hill overlooking the neighborhood of Figure 8.1. From this position, you effortlessly see one house as nearby, a hill as far in the distance, and the space between them as having "depth." But your three-dimensional perception of this scene is based on an image that exists in only two dimensions on the surface of your retinas.

Describing this process in terms of Figures 1.1 and 1.6, we would say that the distal stimulus, the three-dimensional environment, is transformed into the proximal stimulus, the two-dimensional image on the retina. Our visual system somehow uses this two-dimensional information to create a perception that matches the three-dimensionality of the environment. One way researchers have tried to understand this process is to ask what is it about this two-dimensional information on the retina that enables us to perceive the three-dimensional scene. One way of answering this question is called the *cue approach.*

THE CUE APPROACH

The **cue approach** to depth perception focuses on identifying information in the retinal image that is correlated with depth in the scene. For example, if one object partially covers another object, as the houses in the foreground of Figure 8.1 cover the houses in the background, the

Figure 8.1
A scene that contains many depth cues.

object that is partially covered must be at a greater distance than the object that is covering it. This situation, which is called *occlusion*, is a signal, or cue, that one object is in front of another. According to cue theory, we learn the connection between this cue and depth through our previous experience with the environment. After this learning has occurred, the association between particular cues and depth becomes automatic, and when these **depth cues** are present, we experience the world in three dimensions. A number of different types of cues have been identified that signal depth in the scene. We can divide these cues into the following groups:

1. **Oculomotor cues** are based on our ability to sense the position of our eyes and the tension in our eye muscles.
2. **Pictorial cues** are those that can be depicted in a still picture.
3. **Movement-produced cues** are created by movement of the observer or by movement of objects in the environment.
4. **Binocular disparity** creates depth perception by using the fact that our left and right eyes receive slightly different images because they are observing the scene from slightly different positions.

Oculomotor Cues

Oculomotor cues are based on feelings in the eyes that occur when the eyes move inward to point toward nearby objects, a process called **convergence,** and when the lens of the eyes change shape to focus on objects at different distances, the process of **accommodation** that we described in Chapter 2 (see page 36).

Convergence and Accommodation

You can experience the feelings in your eyes associated with convergence and accommodation by doing the following demonstration.

DEMONSTRATION

Feelings in Your Eyes

Look at your finger as you hold it at arm's length. Then, as you slowly move your finger toward your nose, notice how you feel your eyes looking inward and become aware of the increasing tension *inside* your eyes. ●

The feelings you experience as you move your finger closer are caused by (1) the **convergence angle** as your eye muscles cause your eyes to look inward, as in Figure 8.2a, and (2) **accommodation,** the change in the shape of the lens as it bulges to focus on a near object (see Figure 2.10). If you move your finger farther away, the lens flattens, and your eyes move sideways until they are both looking straight ahead, as in Figure 8.2b.

Convergence and accommodation serve as cues to depth because the position of the eyes and the shape of the lenses are related to the distance of the object we are observing. These cues are effective, however, only at distances closer than about 3 to 10 feet from the observer (see Cutting & Vishton, 1995; Liebowitz, Shina, & Hennessy, 1972).

Pictorial Cues

Pictorial cues are sources of depth information that can be depicted in a picture, such as the illustrations in this book or the picture formed on the retina. These cues are also called **monocular depth cues** because they work even if we use only one eye.

Occlusion

We have already described the depth cue of **occlusion.** When one object hides or partially hides another from view, the object that is hidden is seen as being farther away. Note that occlusion does not provide information about an object's distance from us; instead, it indicates relative depth—we know that the object that is partially covered is farther away than another object, but we don't know how much farther away it is.

Paul Signac's painting *Place des Lices, St. Tropez* (1893) (Figure 8.3) makes extensive use of occlusion. Place a piece of paper so that it covers everything below mark A, and notice how occlusion helps you determine the relative positions in depth of the tree branches in the top part of the picture. Then, move your paper up so that it covers everything below mark B. Since there is little occlusion within the upper left corner of the picture, it is difficult to tell which branches are in front and which are in back.

Relative Height

In addition to noticing that the tree branches in Signac's painting overlap one another, you can also see that the trees with bases that are higher in the picture

(a) (b)

Figure 8.2
(a) Convergence of the eyes occurs when a person looks at something very close. (b) The eyes look straight ahead when the person observes something far away.

Figure 8.3
Place des Lices, St. Tropez by Paul Signac (1893) (Museum of Art, Carnegie Institute, Pittsburgh, PA).

appear farther away. This is the cue of **relative height.** Objects with bases that are higher in your field of view, like the men in Figure 8.4, are usually seen as being more distant. But notice the clouds. The clouds that are *lower* in the picture appear farther away. We can therefore state the rule for relative height as follows: Objects with their bases below the horizon are seen as more distant if their bases are higher in the visual field. Objects above the horizon are seen as more distant if they are lower in the visual field.

Relative Size

If two objects are of equal size, the one that is farther away will take up less of your field of view than the one that is closer. The cue of **relative size** was demonstrated by Adelbert Ames, who had observers view illuminated balloons in a darkened room. When he increased the size of one balloon by pumping more air into it, the observers reported that the expanding balloon appeared to be moving closer. Other things being equal, larger size causes an object to appear closer.

Familiar Size

Look at the coins in Figure 8.5. If they were real coins, which would you say is closer? If you are influenced by your knowledge of the actual size of dimes, quarters, and half-dollars, you would probably say that the dime is closer. If you did, the cue of **familiar size** is influencing your judgment of depth. An experiment by William Epstein (1965) shows that, under certain conditions, our knowledge of an object's size influences our perception of that object's distance from us. The stimuli in Epstein's experiment were equal-sized photographs of a dime, a quarter, and a half-dollar, which were positioned the same distance from an observer. By placing these photographs in a darkened room, illuminating them with a spot of light, and having subjects view them with one eye, Epstein created the illusion that these pictures were real coins.

Figure 8.4
Relative height. Other things being equal, objects below the horizon that appear higher in the field of view are seen as being farther away. Objects above the horizon that appear lower in the field of view are seen as being farther away.

When the observers judged the distance of each of the coin photographs they estimated that the dime was closest, the quarter was farther than the dime, and the half-dollar was the farthest of them all. The observers' judgments were influenced by their knowledge

Figure 8.5
Line drawings of the stimuli used in Epstein's (1965) familiar-size experiment. The actual stimuli were photographs that were all the same size as a real quarter.

of the sizes of real dimes, quarters, and half-dollars. This result did not occur, however, when the observers viewed the scene with both eyes. When they did this, they were able to tell that all of the coins were at the same distance because, as we will see below, the use of two eyes provides important information for the perception of depth. Thus, when the observers in Epstein's experiment used two eyes, this extra information enabled them to disregard the effect of familiar size and correctly judge the distances of the coins. The cue of familiar size is therefore most effective when other information about depth is absent (see also Coltheart, 1970; Schiffman, 1967).

Atmospheric Perspective

Atmospheric perspective causes us to see distant objects as less sharp because, to observe these distant objects, we look through air that contains small particles such as dust, water droplets, and various forms of airborne pollution. The farther away an object is, the more air and particles we have to look through, making objects that are farther away look less sharp than close objects. Figure 8.6 illustrates atmospheric perspective. Compare the details visible in the mountains in the distance to the sharp details visible in the rock in the foreground.

If instead of viewing these California mountains you were standing on the moon, where there is no atmosphere, and hence no atmospheric perspective, far craters would look just as clear as near ones. But on earth, there is atmospheric perspective; the exact amount depends on the nature of the atmosphere. (Also see Color Plate 3.2.)

An example of how atmospheric perspective depends on the nature of the atmosphere occurred when one of my friends took a trip from Pittsburgh to Montana. He started walking toward a mountain that appeared to be perhaps a two- or three-hour hike away but found after three hours of hiking that he was still far from the mountain. Since my friend's perceptions were "calibrated" for Pittsburgh, he found it difficult to accurately estimate distances in the clearer air of Montana, so a mountain that would have looked a few hours away in Pittsburgh was much farther away in Montana.

Figure 8.6
This photograph of Moro Rock, Sequoia National Park, by Ansel Adams is an excellent example of atmospheric perspective, with the mountain ranges becoming less sharp with increasing distance (Ansel Adams © by the Trustees of the Ansel Adams Publishing Rights Trust).

Linear Perspective

How can we create a three-dimensional impression of depth on the two-dimensional surface of a canvas? This question has concerned artists since before the ancient Greeks, but it wasn't until 1435 that Leon Battista Alberti wrote *De Pictura,* the first book describing the principles of a drawing system called **linear perspective,** which made it possible to convincingly depict depth on a two-dimensional surface (see Hagen, 1979, 1986; Kubovy, 1986; White, 1968). Alberti's book describes a geometrical procedure for drawing a picture in linear perspective.

Another technique for creating perspective pictures, which is called **Alberti's window,** makes it possible for anyone to draw in perspective. You need only obtain a transparent surface such as a piece of glass or a rigid piece of transparent plastic; then, keeping your eye fixed in one place, look at a scene through the transparent surface and trace the contours of the scene onto the surface. This procedure is being used by the artist in Figure 8.7, but instead of drawing the picture directly on the window, he is using a grid on the window to transfer the scene to a canvas. This procedure results in a picture drawn in linear perspective that creates an impression of depth on the canvas. Another way to create a perspective picture is to take a photograph. The optical system of a camera accomplishes essentially the same thing as Alberti's window and records a perspective picture on film.

When a picture is drawn in linear perspective, lines that are actually parallel in the scene converge as they get farther away (Figure 8.8). The greater the distance, the greater the convergence, until, at a distance of infinity (very far away!), these lines meet at a vanishing point. This convergence that we see in perspective pictures also occurs in the environment, as we know from the familiar observation that railway tracks appear to converge as distance increases. This convergence, which provides information about depth, is referred to as the depth cue of **linear perspective.**

Figure 8.7
An artist drawing a picture in perspective using the method of Alberti's window.

Texture Gradient

Another source of depth information is the **texture gradient**—elements that are equally spaced in a scene appear to be packed closer and closer as distance increases, such as the squares in the Renaissance-era street of Figure 8.8. (Remember that according to the cue of relative size, more distant objects appear smaller. This is exactly what happens for the far-away elements in the texture gradient.) Texture gradients are important because they often extend over a large area. We will discuss them further in Chapter 9.

Movement-Produced Cues

All of the cues we have described so far work if the observer is stationary. If, however, we decide to take a walk, new cues emerge that further enhance our perception of depth. Hermann von Helmholtz (1866/1911) described the following situation in which movement enhances depth perception:

> Suppose, for instance, that a person is standing still in a thick woods, where it is impossible for him to distinguish, except vaguely and roughly, in the mass of foliage and branches all around him what belongs to one tree and what to another. . . . But the moment he begins to move forward, everything disentangles itself, and immediately he gets an apperception of the material contents of the woods and their relations to each other in space. (p. 296)

We will describe two different **movement-produced cues:** (1) motion parallax and (2) deletion and accretion.

Motion Parallax

Elaborating further on the effect of movement on depth perception, Helmholtz (1866/1911) described how, as we walk along, nearby objects appear to glide rapidly past us, but more distant objects appear to move more slowly. This effect becomes particularly striking when you look out the side window of a moving car or train. Nearby objects appear to speed by in a blur, while objects on the horizon may appear to be moving only slightly. This difference in the speed of movement for near and far objects is called **motion parallax,** which we can use as a cue to perceive the depths of objects based on how fast they move as we

Figure 8.8
A Street with Various Buildings, Colonnades, and an Arch (c. 1500); artist unknown (school of Donate Brumante). This is an example of a picture drawn in perspective so that lines that are parallel in the actual scene will converge to a vanishing point if extended into the distance (Museum of Art, Carnegie Institute, Pittsburgh, PA).

move: Far objects move slowly; near objects move rapidly.

We can understand why motion parallax occurs by looking at the eye in Figure 8.9. This figure shows what happens to the images of two objects, a near object at A and a far object at B, when a single eye moves from position 1 to position 2. First, consider how the image of the near object moves across the retina as the eye moves from 1 to 2. When the eye is at position 1, the image of object A is at A_1 on the retina, and when the eye has moved to position 2, the image of object A has moved all the way across the retina to A_2. Thus, when the eye moves from position 1 to position 2, the image of object A moves from one side of the observer's field of view to the other. The image of object B, on the other hand, moves only from B_1 to B_2 on the retina and therefore moves only a short distance across the observer's field of view. Thus, as the observer moves from left to right, the near object travels a large distance across the retina and therefore moves rapidly across the observer's field of view, but the far object travels a much smaller distance across the retina and therefore moves much more slowly across the observer's field of view.

Deletion and Accretion

When two surfaces are located at different distances, as in Figure 8.10a, any sideways movement of the observer causes the surfaces to appear to move relative to one another. The back surface is covered up, or **deleted,** by the one in front when the observer moves in one direction (Figure 8.10b), and the back surface is uncovered, or **accreted,** when the observer moves in the other direction (Figure 8.10c). These cues, which are related both to motion parallax and **overlap,** since they occur when overlapping surfaces appear to move relative to one another, are especially effective for detecting depth at an edge (Kaplan, 1969).

Binocular Disparity and Stereopsis

All of the cues we have discussed so far, with the exception of convergence, are monocular depth cues because they work even if we look through only one

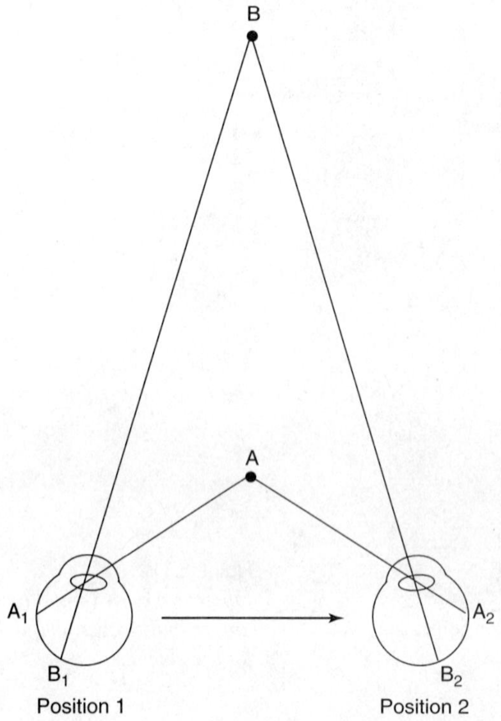

Figure 8.9
One eye, moving from left to right, showing how the images of two objects (A and B) change their position on the retina because of this movement. Notice that the image of the near object, A, moves farther on the retina than the image of the far object, B.

eye. We will now discuss **binocular disparity,** which is called a **binocular depth cue** because it involves both eyes. This cue is based on the fact that we see two slightly different views of the world because our eyes view the world from different positions.

Two Eyes: Two Viewpoints

The fact that we view the world from two different positions means that there are slightly different images in the two eyes. We can illustrate the existence of two images perceptually by the following demonstration.

DEMONSTRATION

Switch Eyes and the Image Changes

Hold your two index fingers vertically in front of you, about 6 inches from your face, with about an inch between them. With your right eye closed, position your fingers so that, between them, you can see an object that is a foot or more away (Figure 8.11a). Then, close your left eye and open your right eye, and notice how your fingers seem to move to the left, so that the object is no longer visible between them (Figure 8.11b). These two perceptions reflect the different views that are imaged on your left and right retinas (Figures 8.11c and 8.11d).

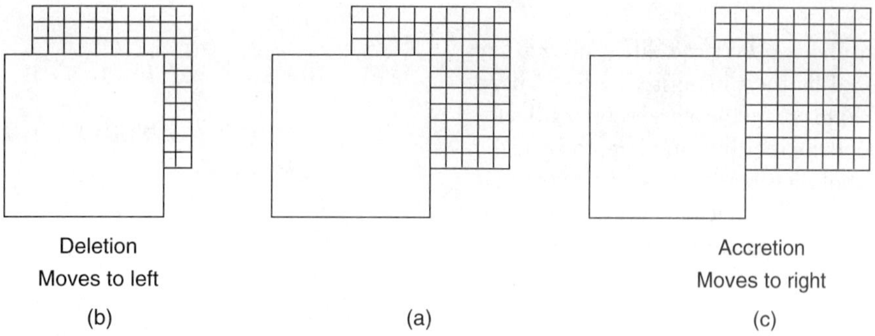

Figure 8.10
Deletion and accretion occur when an observer moves in a direction not perpendicular to two surfaces that are at different depths. If an observer perceives the two surfaces as in (a) and then moves to the left, deletion occurs so that the front object covers more of the back one, as in (b). If the observer starts at (a) and moves to the right, accretion occurs, so that the front object covers less of the back one, as in (c). Try this with two objects.

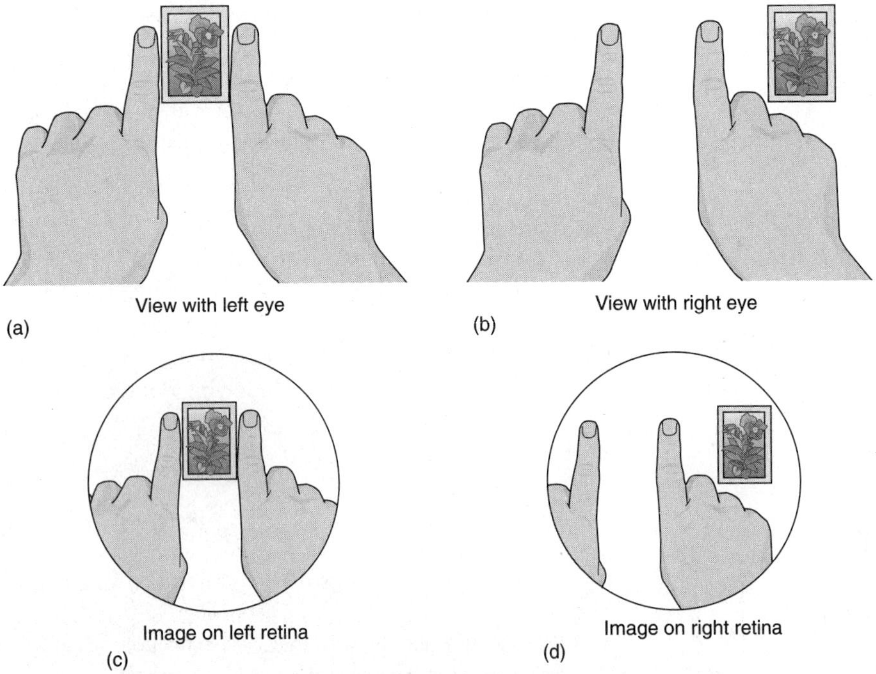

Figure 8.11
Observer's views (a and b) and retinal images (c and d) for the demonstration.

The fact that the two eyes see different views of the world was used by the physicist Charles Wheatstone (1802–1875) to create the **stereoscope,** a device that produces a convincing illusion of depth by using two slightly different pictures. This device, extremely popular in the 1800s and reinvented as the View Master in its modern form, presents two photographs that are made with a camera with two lenses separated by the same distance as the eyes. The result is two slightly different views, like those shown in Figure 8.12. The stereoscope presents the left picture to the left eye and the right picture to the right eye so that they combine to result in a convincing three-dimensional perception of the scene.

D E M O N S T R A T I O N

Binocular Depth from a Picture, without a Stereoscope

Place a 4″ x 6″ card vertically, long side up, between the stairs in Figure 8.13, and place your nose against the card so that you are seeing the left-hand drawing with just your left eye and the right-hand drawing with just your right eye. (Blink back and forth to confirm this separation.) Then relax and wait for the two drawings to merge. When the drawings form a single image, you should see the stairs in depth, just as you would if you looked at them through a stereoscope. ●

Figure 8.12
A stereoscopic photograph showing Tour de France winner Greg LeMond at a bicycle race in Ohio in 1989. The picture on the left is the view seen by the left eye, and the picture on the right is the view seen by the right eye. Although the two pictures may at first glance look the same, a closer look shows that the relationship between the foreground and the background is different in the two views. For example, compare the distance between Greg LeMond's helmet and the man seen over his shoulder. Also notice the relationship between Greg LeMond's head and the building in the far background. These displacements result in binocular disparity when a stereoscope presents these two views to each eye separately, and we experience a compelling perception of depth. (Stereogram by Mike Chikiris, Pittsburgh Stereogram Company, Pittsburgh, PA, 1990.)

The principle behind the stereoscope is also used in 3-D movies. To present different images to the left and right eyes in these movies, the film contains two slightly different images, which are separated into left and right eye images when viewed through special glasses (Figure 8.14). The separation of the images can be based on differences in color, in which case the glasses are green for one eye and red for the other, or differences in a property called *polarization*, in which case the glasses admit light that is polarized in different directions.

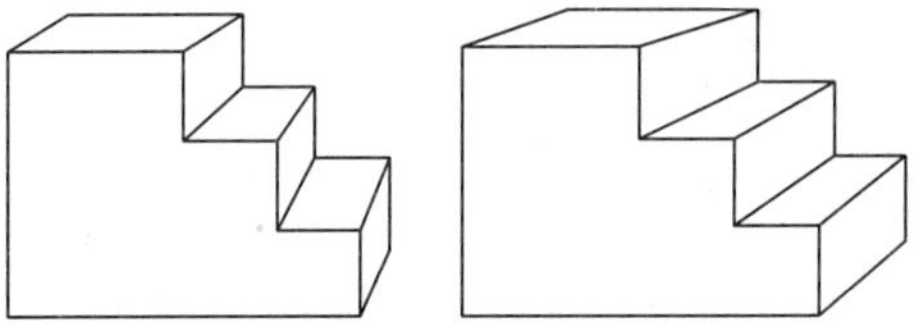

Figure 8.13

Three-dimensional movies became quite popular when introduced commercially in the 1950s and have occasionally appeared in movie theaters and at amusement parks since then. I still vividly remember a scene from a film called *The Maze,* in which a terrible froglike creature plummeted from a castle window directly toward me! Luckily, I survived to write this book.

Looking into a stereoscope shows that, when our two eyes receive slightly different images of the same scene, we experience an impression of depth. Wheatstone realized this and coined the term **stereopsis** to describe the impression of depth we experience from the two slightly displaced images on the retina. But what exactly is it about the differences between the images on the two retinas that creates stereopsis? To

Figure 8.14
A scene in a movie theater in the 1950s when three-dimensional movies were first introduced. The glasses create different images in the left and right eyes and the resulting disparity leads to a convincing impression of depth. (UPI/Corbis-Bettman)

this question, we need to introduce the concept of corresponding retinal points.

Corresponding Retinal Points

For every point on one retina, there is a corresponding point on the other. **Corresponding retinal points** are the places on each retina that connect to the same places in the visual cortex. We can determine approximately where these points are by locating where points on the retinas would overlap if one retina could be slid on top of the other. In Figure 8.15, we see that the two foveas, F and F′, fall on corresponding points, and that A and A′ and B and B′ also fall on corresponding points.

Figure 8.15
Corresponding points on the two retinas. To determine corresponding points, imagine that one eye is slid on top of the other one.

To apply our knowledge of corresponding points to depth perception, assume that the lifeguard in Figure 8.16 is looking directly at Ralph so his image falls on her foveas (F and F′), which are corresponding

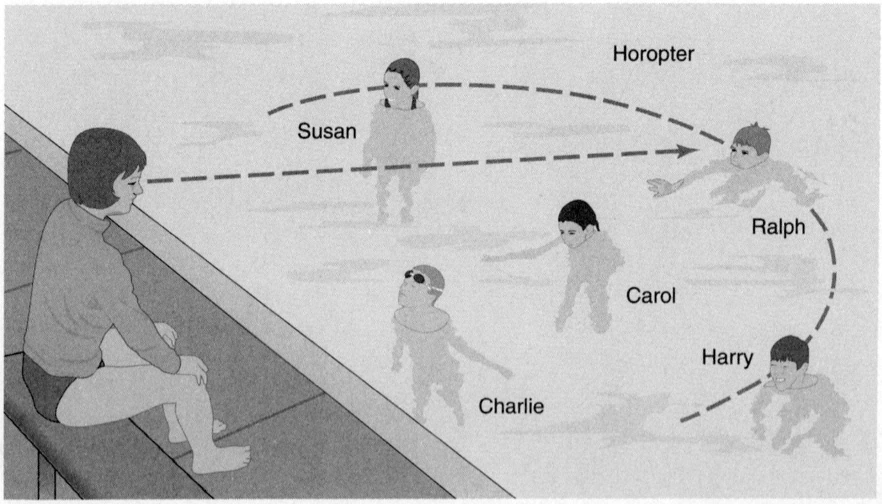

Figure 8.16
When the lifeguard looks at Ralph, the images of Ralph, Susan, and Harry fall on the horopter indicated by the dashed line. Thus, Ralph's, Susan's, and Harry's images fall on corresponding points on the lifeguard's retinas, and the images of all of the other swimmers fall on noncorresponding points.

points. However, Ralph is not the only person whose image falls on corresponding points.

There is an imaginary circle called the **horopter** that passes through the point of fixation (Figure 8.17). Any object that is on this circle falls on corresponding points on the two retinas. In our example, the horopter not only passes through Roger's head (the point of fixation) but also through the heads of Harry and Susan. Thus, Harry's and Susan's images fall on corresponding points on the lifeguard's retinas, as shown in Figure 8.18. (The situation we are describing here holds *only* if the lifeguard is looking at Ralph. If she changes her point of fixation, then a new horopter is created that passes through the new point of fixation.)

What does the horopter have to do with depth perception? To answer this question, let's consider where Carol's and Charlie's images fall on the lifeguard's retinas. Since their heads are not located on the horopter, their images fall on **noncorresponding** (or **disparate) points,** as indicated in Figure 8.19. For example, Carol's image falls on noncorresponding points B and G′. (Note that if you slid the retinas on top of each other, points B and G′ would not overlap.) The corresponding point to B is, in fact, located at B′, far from G′.

The angle between G′ and B′ is called the **angle of disparity,** and the key to binocular depth perception

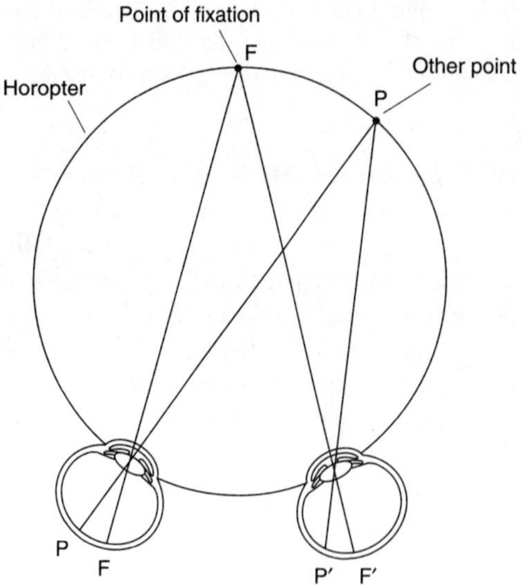

Figure 8.17
The horopter, showing how the images of two points on the horopter, F and P, fall on corresponding points F and F′ and P and P′ on the retina. (From Gillam, 1995.)

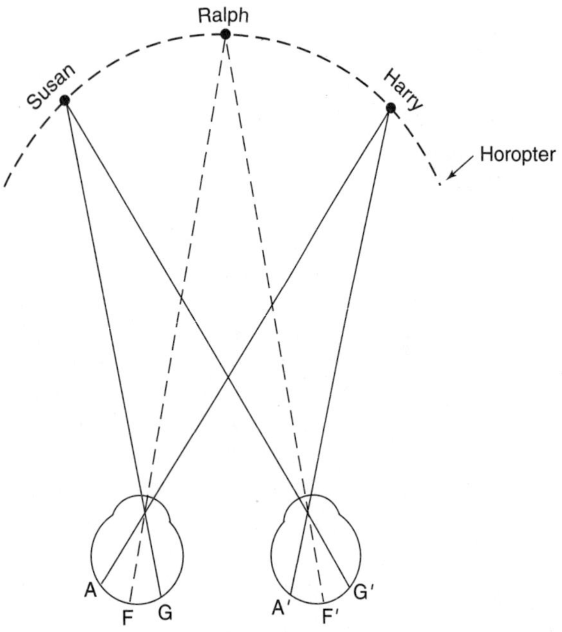

Figure 8.18
What's happening to the images of Susan, Ralph, and Harry inside the lifeguard's eyes? Susan's image falls on corresponding points G and G′; Ralph's image falls on the foveas, F and F′ (which are corresponding points); and Harry's image falls on corresponding points A and A′.

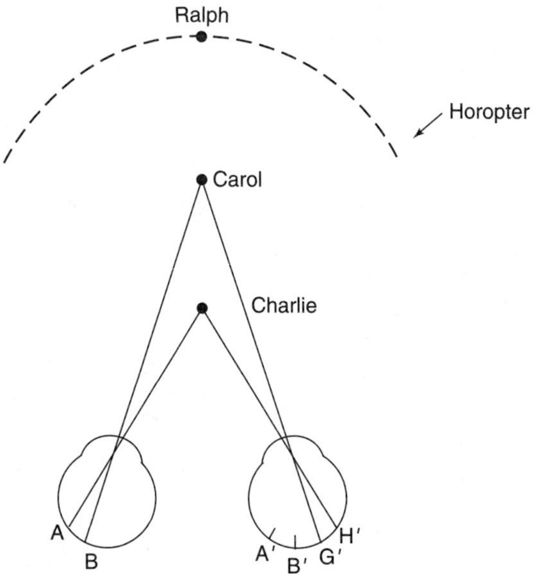

Figure 8.19
What's happening to the images of Carol and Charlie in the lifeguard's eyes? Since Carol and Charlie are not located on the horopter, their images fall on noncorresponding points.

is that *the farther the object is from the horopter, the greater is the angle of disparity.* You can understand this by noticing that Charlie's images, which fall on A and H′, are more disparate than Carol's images. Thus, the amount of disparity indicates how far Charlie and Carol are from where the lifeguard is looking. Since Charlie's angle of disparity is greater than Carol's, he must be located farther from the horopter and is therefore closer to the lifeguard.

When objects are located in front of the horopter, as Carol and Charlie are, their images move out to the sides of the retinas, and the resulting disparity is called **crossed disparity.** When objects are located beyond the horopter, as in Figure 8.20, their images move inward on the retinas, creating a condition called **uncrossed disparity.** The farther behind the horopter an object is, the more its images move inward on the retinas, and the greater is its disparity.

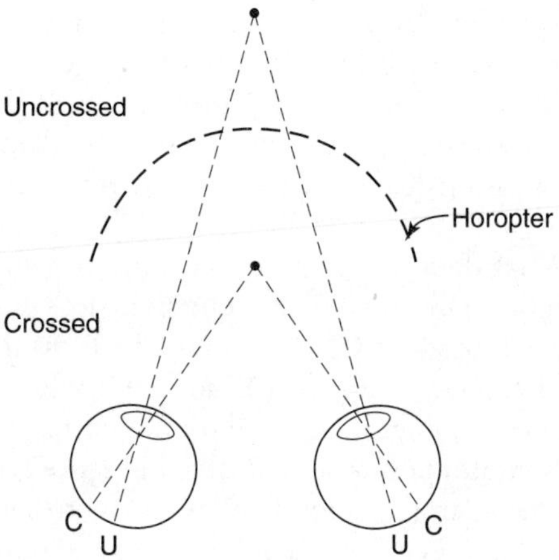

Figure 8.20
Crossed disparity occurs for objects in front of the horopter; uncrossed disparity occurs for objects behind the horopter. Notice how the retinal images move inward, toward the nose, as the object moves farther away.

Thus, crossed disparity indicates that an object is nearer than the horopter, and uncrossed disparity indicates that an object is farther than the horopter. (To remember which disparity is crossed and which is uncrossed, just remember that you have to cross your eyes to fixate on objects as they get nearer. Near objects create crossed disparity.)

We have seen that the disparity information contained in the images on the retinas provides information indicating an object's distance from where we are looking. Thus, when we look in a stereoscope or at a scene in the world, the different views we see with our left and right eyes create disparity, and this disparity generates the impression of depth called stereopsis (Figure 8.21).

Although our conclusion that disparity creates stereopsis may seem reasonable, showing that we perceive depth when two slightly displaced views are presented to the left and the right eyes doesn't prove that disparity is creating the depth we see. We can understand why this is so by realizing that scenes such as the one in Figure 8.12 may contain other depth cues, such as occlusion and relative size, that could be contributing to our perception of depth. How can we tell whether depth perception is caused by disparity, by pictorial cues, or by a combination of both? Bela Julesz answered this question by creating a stimulus that contained no pictorial cues, called the *random-dot stereogram.*

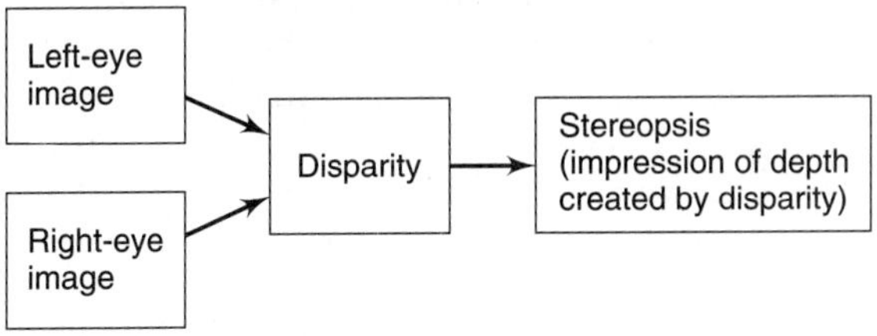

Figure 8.21
Disparity is created by the left-eye and right-eye images, and stereopsis occurs when an impression of depth is created by disparity.

Random-Dot Stereogram

By creating stereoscopic images of random-dot patterns, Julesz (1971) showed that subjects can perceive depth in displays that contain no depth information other than disparity. Two such random dot patterns, which constitute a **random-dot stereogram,** are shown in Figure 8.22. These patterns were constructed by first generating two identical random-dot patterns on a computer and then shifting a square-shaped section of the dots to the right, in the pattern on the right. This shift is too subtle to be seen in these dot patterns, but we can understand how it is accomplished by looking at the diagrams below the dot patterns. In these diagrams, the black dots are indicated by Zero's, A's, and X's and the white dots by 1's, B's, and Y's. The A's and B's indicate the square-shaped section where the shift is made in the pattern. Notice that the A's and B's are shifted one unit to the right in the right-hand pattern. The X's and Y's indicate areas uncovered by the shift that must be filled in with new black dots and white dots to complete the pattern.

The effect of shifting one section of the pattern in this way is to create disparity. When the two patterns are presented to the left and the right eyes in a stereoscope, we perceive a small square floating above the background. Since binocular disparity is the only depth information present in these stereograms, disparity alone causes stereopsis—the perception of depth.

With the identification of disparity information as an important source of depth information, it may appear that our understanding of binocular depth perception is complete. However, before we conclude our discussion of disparity, we need to consider an important step in the determination of stereopsis that we have so far ignored. To use disparity, the visual system needs to match points on one image with similar points on the other image. This is called the **correspondence problem.**

The Correspondence Problem

To help us understand the correspondence problem, let's return to the stereoscopic images of Figure 8.12.

1	0	1	0	1	0	0	1	0	1
1	0	0	1	0	1	0	1	0	0
0	0	1	1	0	1	1	0	1	0
0	1	0	A	A	B	B	1	0	1
1	1	1	B	A	B	A	0	0	1
0	0	1	A	A	B	A	0	1	0
1	1	1	B	B	A	B	1	0	1
1	0	0	1	1	0	1	1	0	1
1	1	0	0	1	1	0	1	1	1
0	1	0	0	0	1	1	1	1	0

1	0	1	0	1	0	0	1	0	1
1	0	0	1	0	1	0	1	0	0
0	0	1	1	0	1	1	0	1	0
0	1	0	Y	A	A	B	B	0	1
1	1	1	X	B	A	B	A	0	1
0	0	1	X	A	A	B	A	1	0
1	1	1	Y	B	B	A	B	0	1
1	0	0	1	1	0	1	1	0	1
1	1	0	0	1	1	0	1	1	1
0	1	0	0	0	1	1	1	1	0

Figure 8.22
Top: A random-dot stereogram. Bottom: The principle for constructing the stereogram. See text for an explanation.

When we view this image in a stereoscope, we see different parts of the image at different depths because of the disparity between images on the left and right retinas. Thus, Greg LeMond and the man on the right appear to be at different distances when viewed through the stereoscope, because they create different amounts of disparity. But in order for the visual system to calculate this disparity, it must compare the two images of Greg LeMond on the left and right retinas and the two images of the man on the left and right retinas.

How does the visual system compare the two Greg LeMonds? The answer to this question is that the visual system may match LeMond's images on the left and right retinas on the basis of the specific features of the images, matching his face on the left with his face on the right, and so on. Explained in this way, the solution to the correspondence problem seems simple: Since most things in the world are quite discriminable from each other, it is easy to match an image on the left retina with the image of the same thing on the right retina. However, as we have seen many times already in this book, things are often not as simple as they seem. The correspondence problem is a perfect example because it becomes more complex when we consider Julesz's random-dot stereograms.

You can appreciate the problem involved in matching similar parts of a stereogram by trying to match up the points in the left and right images of the stereogram in Figure 8.22. Most people find this to be a difficult task, involving switching their gaze back and forth between the two pictures and comparing small areas of the pictures one after another. Matching similar features on a random-dot stereogram is much more difficult and time-consuming than matching features in the real world, yet the visual system somehow matches similar parts of the two stereogram images, calculates their disparities, and creates a perception of depth. Although a number of proposals, all too complex to describe here, have been put forth to explain how the visual system solves the correspondence problem for random-dot stereograms, a totally satisfactory answer has yet to be proposed (Blake & Wilson, 1991).

Our discussion of depth perception has revealed that a number of cues contribute to our perception of depth, including binocular disparity, the pictorial cues, movement-based cues, and oculomotor cues. As shown in Figure 8.23, these cues work over different distances, some working only at close range (convergence and accommodation), some at close and medium ranges (relative height, motion parallax, binocular disparity), some at long range (atmospheric perspective), and some at the whole range of depth perception (occlusion and relative size) (Cutting & Vishton, 1995).

No one of these depth cues is crucial to our perception of depth. For example, we can eliminate binocular disparity by closing one eye, yet because of the remaining monocular cues we still see some depth. Depth cues, therefore, provide overlapping information, and working together, all contribute to our perception of depth, and increase our chances of accurately deducing the three dimensions of the world from the two-dimensional information on our retinas (Bruno & Cutting, 1988; Landy et al., 1995; Tittle & Braunstein, 1993).

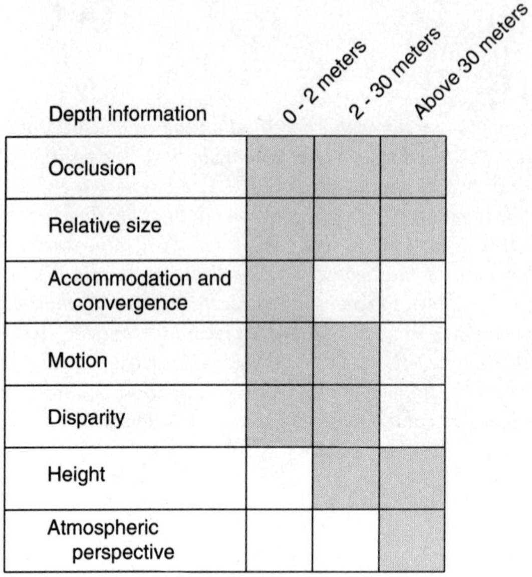

Figure 8.23
Range of effectiveness of different depth cues. Occlusion and relative size work over the entire range of vision, from close up to very far away. Accommodation is effective only at distances less than 2 meters, and atmospheric perspective provides the most useful depth information at distances above 30 meters. (Based on Cutting & Vishton, 1995.)

Binocular Vision: Physiology and Development

Psychophysical experiments, particularly those using Julesz's random dot stereograms, have shown that retinal disparity gives rise to a perception of depth. But how is this disparity information on the retinas translated into depth information in the brain? A number of researchers have shown that neurons in the visual cortex of the cat and the monkey respond to specific degrees of disparity.

Disparity Information in the Brain

Horace Barlow, Colin Blakemore, and John Pettigrew (1967) found cells in the visual cortex of the cat that respond best to stimuli that fall on points separated by a specific angle of disparity on the two retinas. Records from these cells in the visual cortex of the monkey, which David Hubel and Torsten Wiesel (1970) called **binocular depth cells** or **disparity detectors,** are shown in Figure 8.24. The record in Figure 8.24a shows that this cell does not respond when corresponding points (indicated by the overlap of the crosshairs to the left of the record) on the two eyes are simultaneously stimulated by a bar moving either from left to right or from right to left. Figures 8.24b, c, d, and e show that this cell does respond, however, when the disparity of the moving bar is increased, the

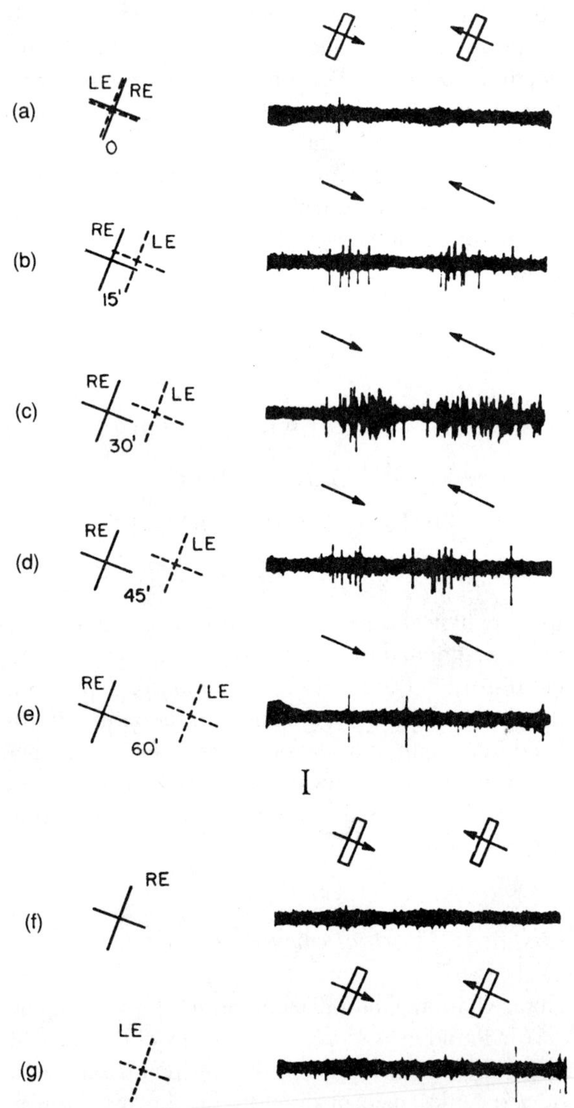

Figure 8.24
The response of a binocular depth cell in the visual cortex of the monkey. The positions of the crosshairs indicate the position of the bar in relation to the right eye (RE) and to the left eye (LE). This cell responds to movement of the bar in either direction (indicated by the arrows) and responds best when the two bars are presented simultaneously but are displaced 30 minutes in position, as shown in record (c). In records (f) and (g), bars are presented to the same positions as in record (c), but each bar is presented to the left and the right eyes separately. The cell does not respond in (f) and (g) because both eyes must be stimulated to cause a binocular depth cell to fire. (From Hubel & Wiesel, 1970.)

maximum response occurring in Figure 8.24c, at 30 minutes (half a degree) of disparity. Figures 8.24f and 8.24g indicate that no response occurs when each eye is *individually* stimulated by bars separated by 30 minutes of arc, even though a large response results when these same bars are presented to both eyes simultaneously, as in Figure 8.24c.

Do disparity-selective neurons cause stereopsis? Showing that these neurons exist does not prove that they have anything to do with perceiving depth. To show that these neurons are actually involved in depth perception, we need to do a behavioral experiment. Randolph Blake and Helmut Hirsch (1975) did such an experiment, in which they raised cats so that they experienced only monocular vision for the first six months of their lives. Their vision was alternated between the left and right eyes every other day during this period. When Blake and Hirsch recorded from neurons in the cortex, they found that these cats had few binocular neurons, and when they tested them behaviorally they found they were not able to use binocular disparity to perceive depth. Thus, Blake and Hirsch showed that eliminating binocular neurons eliminates stereopsis and confirmed what everyone suspected all along, that disparity-selective neurons are responsible for stereopsis. Thus, if an animal's convergence is fixed (that is, if its eyes are positioned to look at a particular point in space and don't move), the cells that fire best to different disparities will be excited by stimuli lying at different distances from the animal, and the animal will perceive these stimuli as being at different distances.

Other researchers have extended the initial work on disparity-sensitive neurons. For example, Simon LeVay and Thomas Voigt (1988) surveyed 272 neurons in areas V1 and V2 of the cat's cortex to create the distribution in Figure 8.25, which shows that some neurons respond to zero or near-zero disparity and many respond to either crossed (near) or uncrossed (far) disparity. Other researchers have found disparity-selective neurons all along the dorsal ("where" or "how") pathway, in areas V1, V2, and MT (Van Essen & DeYoe, 1995); and neurons involved in depth perception are also found in the ventral (or "what") pathway (Tyler, 1990). (Also see G. Poggio, 1990; Trotter et al., 1992, for more recent research describing how binocular depth cells have been recorded from the awake monkey.)

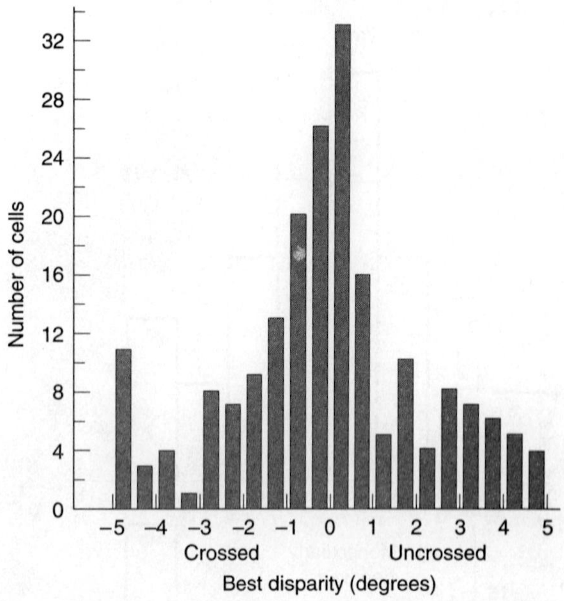

Figure 8.25
Histogram based on 272 neurons, which shows the number of cells that respond best to different angles of disparity. (From LeVay & Voigt, 1988.)

Sensitive Periods in the Development of Binocular Vision

About 80 percent of neurons in the cat's striate cortex are binocular neurons and most of these binocular neurons are disparity detectors. Research on binocular neurons has focused not only on how they operate in adult animals, but on how they develop in young animals. Research on this problem has yielded two important results: (1) Binocular neurons are present in very young cats and monkeys; and (2) These neurons need to receive *coordinated visual input from the left and right eyes* during a sensitive period early in the animal's life, in order for these neurons to be present in the adult animal.

The *sensitive period* for the development of binocular neurons is important because it means that normal development of the visual system depends on the information it receives from the environment and because of the practical implications of this conclusion—it is important for human children to be exposed to normal visual stimulation as they are developing. The research on both animals and humans has looked at how abnormal visual stimulation early in life affects the functioning of the visual system. The research on animals that we will describe now created this abnormal input in two ways: (1) by suturing one eye shut so the animal receives stimuli through only one eye, and (2) by using optical prisms to cause misalignment of the images in the left and right eyes.

The Effect of Monocular Rearing One way to deprive an animal of coordinated visual input to both eyes is to use a procedure called **monocular rearing,** in which one eye is sutured shut so the animal has the use of only one eye. The effect of monocular rearing on binocularity is illustrated by **ocular dominance histograms,** such as those in Figure 8.26. These histograms are determined by recording from a large number of cells and then rating each cell's ability to respond to stimulation of both the contralateral eye (the eye on the opposite side of the head from the cell) and the ipsilateral eye (the eye on the same side as the cell). Each cell is placed in one of seven categories according to the degree of ocular dominance, as listed in Table 8.1. The histograms in Figure 8.26 show the striking effect of monocular deprivation on the way the kitten's cortical cells responded to stimulation of each eye. Whereas most of the cells in the normal cat respond to both eyes, and therefore fall into categories 2 to 6 of the histogram, all the cells in the deprived kitten responded only to stimulation of the undeprived eye and are placed in category 7.

Hubel and Wiesel found that the longer kittens were monocularly reared, the greater were the abnormalities in their ocular dominance histograms; however, if the deprivation was postponed until the kittens became adult cats, even long periods of monocular

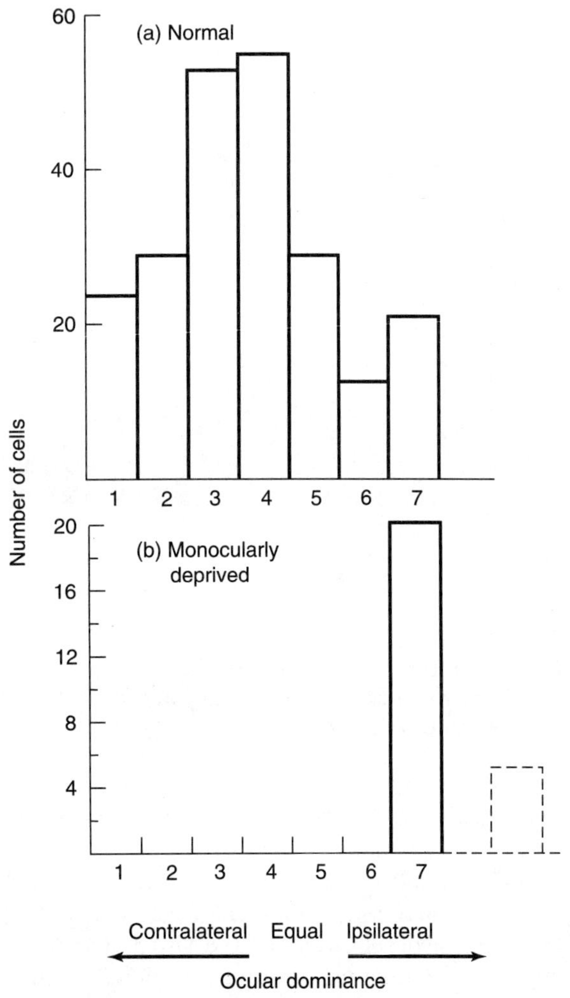

Figure 8.26
(a) An ocular dominance histogram of recordings from 223 neurons in the visual cortex of adult cats. Numbers refer to the categories described in Table 8.1. Note that a large number of cells respond to the stimulation of both eyes. (b) Ocular dominance histogram of 25 cells recorded from the visual cortex of a 2½-month-old kitten that was reared with its right eye occluded until the time of the experiment. The dashed bar on the right indicates that 5 cells did not respond to the stimulation of either eye. The solid bar indicates that all 20 cells that did respond to stimulation responded only in the eye that was opened during rearing (Wiesel & Hubel, 1963).

Table 8.1
Categories of binocular response

Category	Description
1	Cell responds only to stimulation of the contralateral eye. Thus, if the cell is in the right hemisphere, it responds only to stimulation of the left eye.
2	Cell responds much more to stimulation of the contralateral eye than to stimulation of the ipsilateral eye.
3	Cell responds slightly more to stimulation of the contralateral eye.
4	Cell responds equally to stimulation of each eye.
5	Cell responds slightly more to stimulation of the ipsilateral eye.
6	Cell responds much more to stimulation of the ipsilateral eye.
7	Cell responds only to stimulation of the ipsilateral eye.

rearing had no effect on their ocular dominance histograms. This finding led Hubel and Wiesel to propose a **sensitive period,** early in the kitten's life, during which monocular rearing has a large effect; once this period is past, however, rearing conditions have little effect.

To investigate this idea, Hubel and Wiesel (1970) monocularly reared kittens at various times after birth. They found that monocular rearing for only three days between the fourth and fifth weeks of life caused a large change in the ocular dominance histograms. But monocular rearing started after about the eighth week caused smaller effects. Hubel and Wiesel concluded that the sensitive period for susceptibility to monocular rearing in kittens begins in the fourth week and extends to about 4 months of age. Later research, using longer periods of monocular rearing and more sensitive tests of brain function, has shown that monocular rearing can cause effects as late as the sixth month in cats (Cynader, Timney, & Mitchell, 1980; Jones, Spear, & Tong, 1984; Olson & Freeman, 1980).

The Effect of Image Misalignment Misalignment of the images in the two eyes can be accomplished by either cutting the eye muscles, or fitting the animal with a helmet that contains small optical prisms. Cutting the eye muscles causes the eyes to become misaligned, as shown in Figure 8.27, and optical prisms, shown in Figure 8.28, change the direction of the light entering the eyes. Both procedures cause effects similar to those observed after monocular rearing. Whereas 80 percent of visual cortical cells in normal cats respond to stimulation of both eyes, only 20 percent of the cells in cats with cut eye muscles respond to stimulation of both eyes (Hubel & Wiesel, 1965b). Similarly, M. L. J. Crawford and G. K. von Noorden (1980) found that 70 percent of cortical cells in normal monkeys respond to stimulation of both eyes, but less than 10 percent of the cells in monkeys that had worn prism helmets for 60 days respond to stimulation of both eyes.

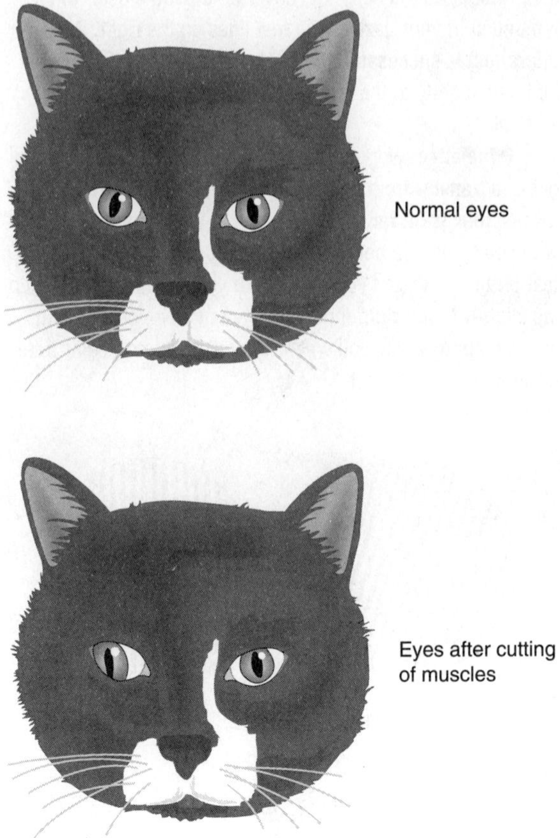

Figure 8.27
The appearance of a normal cat's eyes and the eyes of a cat that have been misaligned by cutting of the eye muscles.

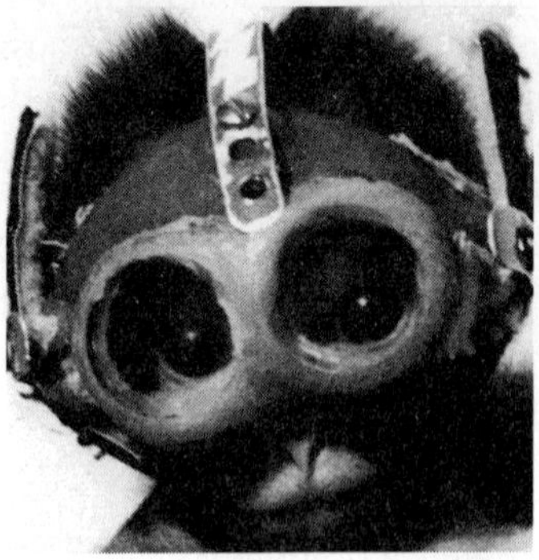

Figure 8.28
A monkey wearing an optical prism helmet, which causes a misalignment of the images in the two eyes (Crawford & von Noorden, 1980).

The loss of binocular cells has a large behavioral effect. Monkeys with few remaining binocular cells due to prism-rearing are unable to detect depth in random-dot stereograms, indicating that they have lost their ability to use binocular disparity to perceive depth (Crawford et al., 1984).

Deprivation Effects in Humans We've seen that the binocular vision of cats and monkeys is disrupted by early deprivation of binocular input (monocular rearing) or elimination of coordinated binocular input (image misalignment). Research studying people who, as young children had one of their eyes patched following an eye operation, suggests that similar effects also occur in humans.

Shinobu Awaya and coworkers (1973) investigated the histories of 19 people with a condition called **amblyopia,** in which one eye has poor vision that is not caused by a physical problem in the eye. They found that all of these people had their amblyopic (low visual acuity) eye closed early in life, following an eye operation, and that most of the closures had occurred during the first year after birth. This type of amblyopia has therefore been called **stimulus deprivation amblyopia,** a term that distinguishes it from amblyopia due to other causes (von Noorden & Maumanee, 1968).

Another cause of reduced vision in one eye is **strabismus,** an imbalance in the eye muscles that upsets the coordination between the two eyes. We have seen that upsetting the coordination between the eyes of kittens by cutting the eye muscles causes a loss of binocular neurons, just as in monocular deprivation. Numerous investigators have recently found evidence of a similar lack of binocular cells in people who had strabismus as young children. Strabismus can be corrected by a muscle operation that restores the balance between the two eyes. However, if this operation is not performed until the child is 4 to 5 years old, a loss of binocularly driven cells can occur similar to that observed in monocularly deprived cats or in cats with artificially produced strabismus.

How do we know that people who had early strabismus lack binocularly driven cells? Obviously, we can't record from single neurons in the human cortex. We can, however, make use of a perceptual effect called the *tilt aftereffect* to estimate the binocularity of a person's cortical neurons.

DEMONSTRATION

Interocular Transfer of the Tilt Aftereffect

You can experience the **tilt aftereffect** by covering up the pattern on the right in Figure 8.29 and staring at the adaptation lines on the left. As you stare, move your eyes around the small circle. Then, when you see the pattern begin to "shimmer," (about 30–60 seconds) cover up the left side of the figure and shift your gaze to the test lines on the right. If the aftereffect is successful, the lines on the right will appear to be tilted slightly to the right even though they are actually vertical.

If the effect worked you are now ready to see if you can get it to transfer from one eye to another—an outcome called **interocular transfer.** This time look at the adapting pattern with your right eye only (close your left eye) and then view the test pattern with just your left eye. If you see the test lines tilting slightly to the right (but probably not as much as when you used both eyes), you will have achieved intraocular transfer of the tilt aftereffect. ●

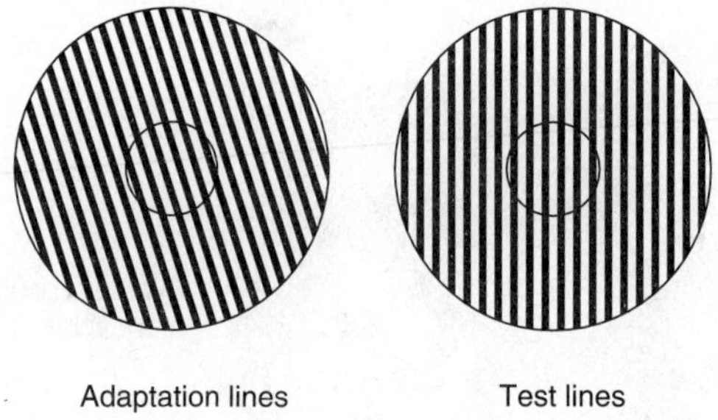

Figure 8.29
Stimuli for measuring the tilt aftereffect. Cover the test pattern on the right, and stare at the pattern on the left for about 60 seconds, moving your eyes around the circle in the middle. Then cover the left-hand pattern, and transfer your gaze to the test lines on the right. If you see the test lines as tilted to the right, you are experiencing the tilt aftereffect.

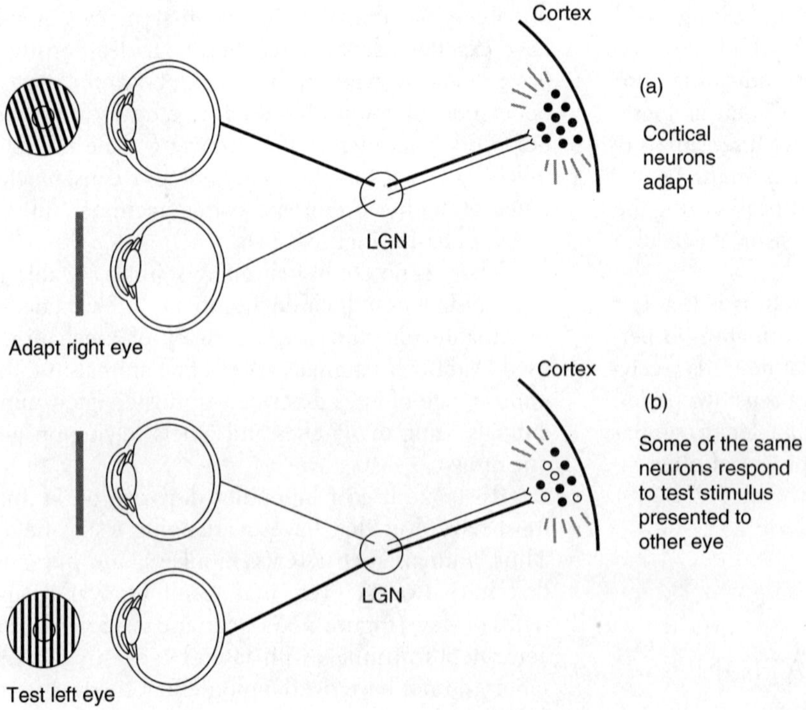

Figure 8.30
If the tilt aftereffect transfers from one eye to another, this means that some of the neurons that become fatigued by adaptation of the right eye (filled circles in a), are also stimulated by the test pattern presented to the left eye, as shown in (b).

The transfer of the tilt aftereffect from one eye to the other is evidence that there are binocular neurons in the cortex. We can understand why this is so, by considering that the basic physiological principle behind the tilt aftereffect is that exposing neurons to the adaptation pattern fatigues them so these neurons respond less when we look at the test pattern. This means that to achieve an adaptation effect, neurons that are affected by the adapting field must also be affected by the test field. Thus, if an effect occurs when we look at the adaptation pattern with the right eye and when we look at the test pattern with the left eye this means that there are neurons in the cortex that respond to stimulation of both the left and the right eyes. (Remember that the signals from the two eyes go to separated layers in the LGN and so the cortex is the first place they can meet (Figure 8.30).)

Martin Banks, Richard Aslin, and Robert Letson (1975) used the degree of transfer of the tilt aftereffect to assess the state of binocularly driven cells in the visual cortex in people who had strabismus early in life. Figure 8.31 plots the magnitude of interocular transfer as a function of the age at which 12 people born with strabismus had corrective surgery. When the surgery had been carried out early in the person's

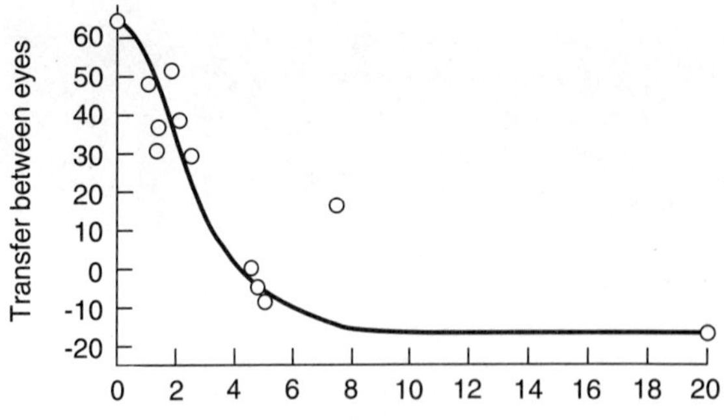

Figure 8.31
The degree of interocular transfer of the tilt aftereffect as a function of the age at which surgery had been performed to correct strabismus. (From Banks, Aslin, & Letson, 1975.)

life, interocular transfer was high, indicating good binocular function; but if the surgery had been delayed, interocular transfer was poor, indicating poor binocular function. Based on results such as these, Aslin and Banks (1978) concluded that a sensitive period for binocular development in humans begins during the first year of life, reaches a peak during the second year, and decreases by 4 to 8 years of age (also see Hohmann & Creutzfeldt, 1975).

What all of these experiments tell us is that our ability to use binocular disparity information to perceive depth depends on our binocular neurons receiving appropriate stimulation during a sensitive period early in our lives. As we will see in Chapter 16, similar principles also hold for the development of other visual qualities as well.

Depth Information across Species

We have seen that humans make use of a number of different sources of depth information in the environment. But what about other species? We know, based on observing animal behavior, that many animals have excellent depth perception. Cats leap on their prey; monkeys swing from one branch to the next; a pelican diving toward the water retracts its wings just before its beak pierces the surface; a male housefly follows a flying female, maintaining a constant distance of about 10 cm; and a frog accurately jumps across a chasm (Figure 8.32).

There is no doubt that many animals are able to judge distances in their environment, but what depth information do they use? A survey of mechanisms used by different animals reveals that animals use the entire range of cues described in this chapter, some animals using many cues and others relying on just one or two.

To make use of binocular disparity, an animal must have eyes that have overlapping visual fields. Thus, animals such as cats, monkeys, and humans, that have **frontal eyes,** that result in overlapping fields of view (Figure 8.33a), can use disparity to perceive depth. Animals with **lateral eyes,** such as the rabbit, do not have overlapping visual fields (Figure 8.33b) and therefore cannot use disparity to perceive depth.

The pigeon is an example of an animal with lateral eyes that are placed so the visual fields of the left and right eyes overlap only in a 35-degree area surrounding the pigeon's beak. This overlapping area,

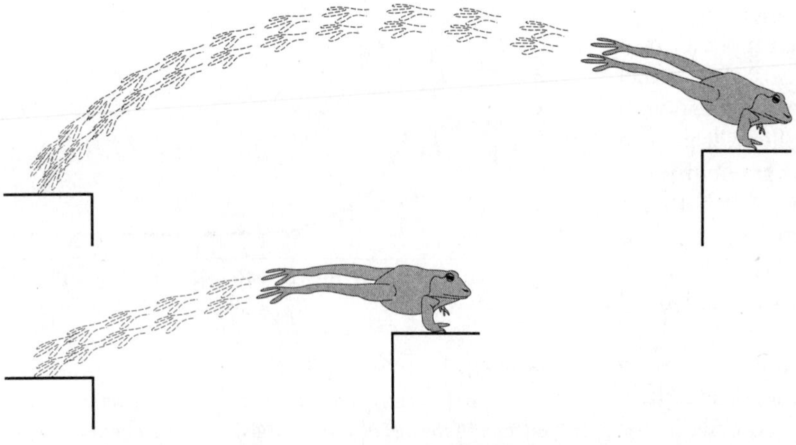

Figure 8.32
These drawings which are based on photographs of frogs jumping, show that the frog adjusts the angle of its jump based on its perception of the distance across the chasm, with steeper take-offs being associated with greater distances. (Adapted from Collett & Harkness, 1982.)

Figure 8.33
Frontal eyes such as those of the cat have overlapping fields of view that provide good depth perception. Lateral eyes such as those of the rabbit provide a panoramic view, but poorer depth perception.

however, happens to be exactly where pieces of grain would be located when the pigeon is pecking at them, and behavioral experiments have shown that pigeons do have a small area of binocular depth perception right in front of its beak (McFadden, 1987; McFadden & Wild, 1986).

Like humans, many animals use more than one type of depth cue in order to obtain the most accurate depth information possible. For example, frogs and toads use binocular vision to perceive depth, but if they are able to use only one eye, they can still use accommodation and other cues to judge how far they need to jump to capture prey (Collett & Harkness, 1982).

Many animals use information other than disparity to determine distances. Consider, for example, a rather strange water bug, the back swimmer *Notonecta*, which hangs upside down just below the surface of the water as it lies in wait for prey that may be approaching on the surface above it (Figure 8.34). *Notonecta* initially detects its prey by sensing vibrations and then makes a distance judgment based on the position of the prey's image on its retina. The image of distant prey falls on the part of the retina nearest the surface of the water, and as the prey approaches, its image moves down on the retina (Collett & Harkness, 1982; Schwind, 1978).

Movement parallax is probably insects' most important method of judging distance, and they use it in a number of different ways (Collett, 1978). For example, the locust makes a "peering" response—moving its body from side to side to create movement of its head—as it observes potential prey. T. S. Collett (1978) measured a locust's "peering amplitude"—the distance of this side-to-side sway—as it observed prey at different distances and found that the locust swayed more when targets were farther away. Since farther objects move less across the retina than nearer objects for a particular amount of observer movement (see Figure 8.9), a larger sway would be needed to cause the image of a far object to move the same distance across the retina as the

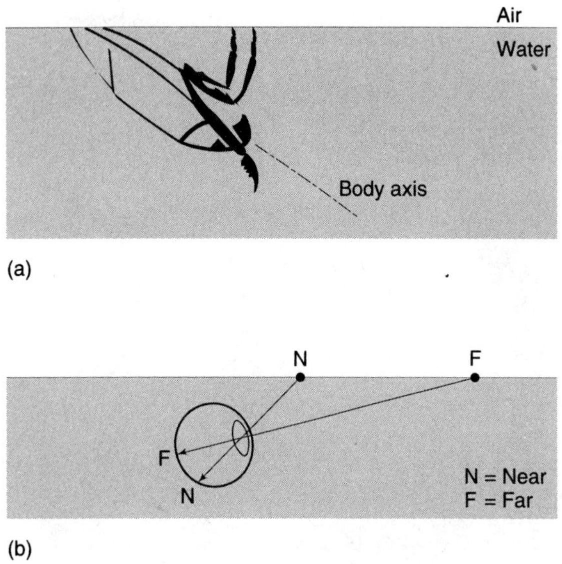

Figure 8.34
The backswimmer Notonecta awaits beneath the surface of the water. A faraway object located at F on the water creates an image at F on the retina, and as the object moves toward N on the water, its image moves toward N on the retina. Thus, the backswimmer can detect where its prey is on the surface of the water based on the position of its image on the retina. (From Schwind, 1978.)

image of a near object. The locust may therefore be judging distance by noting how much sway is needed to cause the image to move a particular distance across its retina. Another example of an animal that uses image movement to detect depth is the honeybee, which uses the information produced by the image movement that occurs as it flies across a field to determine the distances of nearby and faraway flowers (Lehrer et al., 1988).

From just the few examples described, we can see that animals use a number of different sources of depth information. The type of information used depends on the animal's specific needs and on its anatomy and physiological makeup. *Notonecta*, lying in wait for prey just under the waterline, needs only very rudimentary depth perception and has limited physical capabilities, so it uses a simple system to perceive its potential prey's distance. Humans, monkeys, and pigeons, which must negotiate their way through complex environments, need more precise depth perception that operates over a variety of distances. They therefore make use of a number of different depth cues that enable them to rapidly determine the locations of both nearby and faraway objects.

Something to Consider: How Do Bats Experience Space?

How do bats experience space? Of course, we have no way of knowing what any animal actually experiences, but bats present a particularly interesting comparison to humans, because humans' perception of space is based on reflected light, whereas bats' perception of space is based on reflected sound.

Bats sense objects by using a method similar to the *sonar* system used in World War II to detect underwater objects such as submarines and mines. *Sonar*, which stands for *so*und *na*vigation and *r*anging, works by sending out pulses of sound and using information contained in the echoes of this sound to determine the location of objects. Griffin (1944) coined the term **echolocation** to describe the biological sonar system used by bats to avoid objects in the dark.

Bats emit pulsed sounds that are far above the upper limit of human hearing, and they sense objects' distances by noting the interval between when they send out the pulse and when they receive the echo (Figure 8.35). Since they use sound echoes to sense objects, they can avoid obstacles even when it is totally dark.

How does the bat experience space based on these echoes? Remember that although a human's visual perception of a scene is based on the reflection of light energy from objects, we usually experience, not

Figure 8.35
When a bat sends out its pulses, it receives echoes from a number of objects in its environment. In this figure, which shows the echoes that are received by the bat, the bat is receiving echoes (a) from the moth, located about half a meter away; (b) from a tree, located about 2 meters away; and (c) from a house, located about 4 meters away. The echoes from each object return to the bat at different times, with echoes from more distant objects taking longer to return. The bat locates the positions of objects in the environment by sensing how long it takes the echoes to return.

"light," but the objects and surfaces of a scene. Does this mean that although the bat's perception of a scene is based on the reflection of sound energy from objects, that the bat experiences, not "sound," but the objects and surfaces of its scene? Or does the bat just experience sequences of echoes arriving at different times? Or is the bat's experience more like what we experience when we close our eyes and listen to sounds in our environment? These are questions that are fascinating to consider, but difficult, or impossible, to answer.

Visual and Auditory Space

Auditory space extends around your head in all directions, existing wherever there is a sound. The best way to experience auditory space is to close your eyes and notice the sounds around you, paying particular attention to the directions and distances of these sounds. Unless you are in an extremely quiet environment, you will probably get a feeling of objects (a computer humming, for example) and events (people talking, cars driving by) located at various positions in space. That is auditory space.

Auditory and visual space are similar in some ways and different in others. One of the most obvious similarities is the parallel between the cue of *binocular disparity* for vision and *binaural cues* for hearing. For vision, the depth cue of binocular disparity depends on differences in the images in the left and right eyes. For hearing, binaural cues depend on differences in the intensity and timing of sounds arriving at the left and right ears. (We will discuss binaural cues in more detail in Chapter 12.)

Another similarity between auditory and visual space is that they usually overlap. For example, when an orchestra conductor *hears* the oboe solo coming from directly in front of him, he also *sees* the oboe player seated directly in front of him. This overlap between auditory and visual space even occurs when orchestra conductors use a technique called the "inner audition" to practice without their orchestras by imagining a musical score in their minds. When they do this they not only imagine the sounds of the various instruments, but their locations relative to the podium, as well.

This overlap between where a sound seems to be coming from and where we see the source of this sound is also common in everyday situations far removed from the concert hall. You hear a conversation behind you and turn around to see two people talking at about the spot you would have predicted. But sometimes vision and hearing provide discrepant information, as when the sound is produced at one place but you see the apparent sound source somewhere else. A familiar example of this is occurs in movie theaters when an actor's dialogue is produced by a speaker located on the right side of the screen, while the actor who is talking is visually located in the center of the screen, many feet away. When this happens, we hear the sound coming from its *seen* location (the image at the center of the screen) rather than from where it is actually produced (the speaker to the right of the screen). This effect is called **visual capture** or the **ventriloquism effect.**

Visual and auditory space can differ in the amount of information that they provide. Under conditions of good visibility, visual space is more "filled," extending everywhere we can see (although we do have to turn around to see the visual space behind us). In very noisy environments such as a concert, a sporting event, or a noisy city street, auditory space might be "filled" in this way, but it more usually consists of isolated sounds at specific positions, with spaces between them. However, when visibility is poor, as occurs in the dark, visual space vanishes and auditory space becomes our major source of spatial perception. Blind people deal with this situation all the time, and consequently they pay close attention to what is happening in auditory space. So as people talk or automobiles whiz by, the blind person is taking in not only the meaning of the sounds, but also the locations of these sounds in auditory space.

Study Questions

Underlying Principles

Find examples of the following principles in this chapter:

- Receptive fields/neural selectivity (231)
- Parallel pathways (233)
- Physiological connections with perception (232)

The Cue Approach

1. What is the main focus of the cue approach? (215)
2. What are the four basic categories of depth cues? (216)

Oculomotor Cues

3. Describe convergence and accommodation. Over what distances are these cues effective for depth perception? (216)

Pictorial Cues

4. Why are pictorial cues also called monocular cues? (217)
5. Describe the following pictorial cues: occlusion, relative height, relative size, familiar size, atmospheric perspective, linear perspective, and texture gradients. (217)

Movement-Produced Cues

6. Describe the two movement-produced cues, motion parallax, and deletion and accretion. (221)

Binocular Disparity and Stereopsis

7. What is the basis of binocular disparity as a binocular depth cue? (222)
8. What is a stereoscope and what is the principle behind its operation? (224)
9. What is stereopsis and how is it related to disparity and to depth perception? (225, 229)
10. What are corresponding retinal points? (226)
11. What is the horopter? (227)
12. What is the angle of disparity and what information does it provide for depth perception? (227)
13. Define crossed disparity and uncrossed disparity. (228)
14. What is a random-dot stereogram and what does it tell us about the role of disparity in depth perception? (229)
15. What is the correspondence problem for depth perception? Has it been solved? (229)
16. Over what ranges of distance do the various depth cues provide information for depth perception? (231)

Binocular Vision: Physiology and Development

17. What is a binocular depth cell and what stimuli does it respond to? (231)
18. Describe Blake and Hirsch's experiment in which they raised cats so they experienced only monocular vision. What do the results of this experiment indicate? (232)
19. Are there disparity-neurons that respond to zero disparity? (232)
20. Which extrastriate pathways contain neurons that are involved in depth perception? (233)
21. What percentage of neurons in the cat's striate cortex are binocular neurons? (233)
22. What is an ocular dominance histogram? (233)
23. How does monocular rearing affect the binocular responding of cortical neurons as indicated by the ocular dominance histogram? (233)

24. What is the sensitive period for susceptibility to monocular rearing? (235)

25. What is the effect of monocular rearing on adult cats? (235)

26. What is the effect of image misalignment on binocularity? (235)

27. What are the behavioral effects of a loss of binocular cells? (236)

28. What is amblyopia? What is stimulus deprivation amblyopia and what causes it? (236)

29. What is strabismus and what effects does it cause on vision? (236)

30. Explain how the tilt aftereffect and interocular transfer has been used to determine whether people with early strabismus lack binocularly driven cells. (236)

Depth Information across Species

31. Are frontal eyes or lateral eyes better suited for using binocular disparity for the perception of depth? (238)

32. Describe the pigeon's use of binocular disparity. (239)

33. What kinds of information do the frog and the water bug *Notonecta* use to perceive depth? (239)

34. Describe how it was determined that the locust might use motion parallax to judge depth. (239)

Something to Consider: How Do Bats Experience Space?

35. What is echolocation? (240)

36. Compare the mechanisms of space perception in the bat and the human. (240)

37. What are some possible ways that bats might experience space on the location of objects in space? Is there any way we can determine what the bat actually experiences? (241)

Across the Senses: Visual and Auditory Space

38. How are visual space and auditory space similar and different? (242)

39. What happens when there is a discrepancy between visual and auditory space? (242)

40. When do visual stimuli provide more information about space than auditory stimuli? When do auditory stimuli provide more information? (242)

9

Size, Illusions, and Ecological Aspects of Perception

Chapter Contents

Some Questions We Will Consider

- Why do things look so small when viewed from an airplane or a tall building? (250)
- What enables me to tell how tall someone is, even if they are far away from me? (250)
- Why does the moon look so large when it is on the horizon, but appear tiny when it is higher in the sky? (256)
- Is it really true that the main purpose of perception is survival? (258)

> Whiteout—one of the most treacherous weather conditions possible for flying—can arise quickly and unexpectedly. As Frank pilots his helicopter across the Antarctic wastes, blinding light, reflected down from thick cloud cover above and up from the pure white blanket of snow below, makes it difficult to see the horizon, details on the surface of the snow, or even up from down. He knows the danger because he has seen pilots dealing with similar conditions fly at full power directly into the ice. He thinks he can make out a vehicle on the snow far below, and he drops a smoke grenade to check his altitude. To his horror, the grenade falls only three feet before hitting the ground. Realizing that what he thought was a truck was actually a discarded match box, Frank pulls back on the controls and soars up, his face drenched in sweat, as he comprehends how close he just came to becoming another whiteout fatality.

The fictional account above is based on actual descriptions of flying conditions at an Antarctic research base. It illustrates that our ability to perceive an object's size can sometimes be drastically affected by our ability to perceive the object's distance. A small matchbox seen closeup can, in the absence of accurate information about its distance, be misperceived as a large truck seen from far away.

We begin this chapter by looking at information that is important for the perception of size, and particularly at the connection between size perception and depth information. Our consideration of how depth perception affects size perception will lead us into a discussion of visual illusions, focusing on situations in which we misperceive size. A central message of this chapter is that illusions are created by the *context* in which objects are perceived, and that they often occur in situations in which there is ambiguous, inaccurate, or conflicting information. We will also see, however, that there is some disagreement among researchers as to why illusions occur. Our discussion of illusions will lead us into the third part of the chapter, perception in natural environments, which for purposes of survival, must be accurate most of the time.

The Information for Perceiving Size

Many experiments have shown that people are quite good at estimating the sizes of objects in natural scenes even if the objects are far away (Gibson, 1950; Sedgwick, 1986). One of the major questions researchers ask about size perception is, what information is involved in making these size judgments? Let's consider this question by referring to Figure 9.1a, which shows how Susan, standing near an observer, casts an image on the observer's retina.

We specify the size of Susan's image in terms of the angle it covers on the retina. (Remember from page 82 that the angle around the entire eyeball is 360 degrees; see Figure 3.16.) This angle is usually called the **visual angle.** From Figure 9.1b, we can see that if we replace Susan with her mother, who is taller, both the visual angle and size of the retinal image increase. Based on Figures 9.1a and 9.1b we might be tempted to say that our perception of size is determined by the size of an object's image on the retina. After all, the mother's retinal image and visual angle are larger than the child's and we perceive her as taller.

But if Susan begins to walk away, we see that this explanation can't be correct, because although her retinal image and visual angle become smaller as she walks away (Figure 9.1c) we continue to perceive her as the same size. Remember the demonstration described in the "Introduction to Size Constancy" on page 168 of Chapter 6: When I stand in front of someone in the front row of my class and then step back, doubling my distance and, therefore, halving the size of my image on the person's retina, they do not perceive me as shrinking to half my original size. In fact, they perceive me as staying about the same height. In Chapter 6, we introduced the principle of **size constancy**—our perception of size remains relatively constant even when an object's distance changes. In this chapter, we are going to continue the discussion we started there (read pages 168–169, if you haven't already).

Size constancy means that we correctly perceive an object's *physical size* no matter what its distance from us or what the size of its image on our retina, and like color constancy, lightness constancy, and

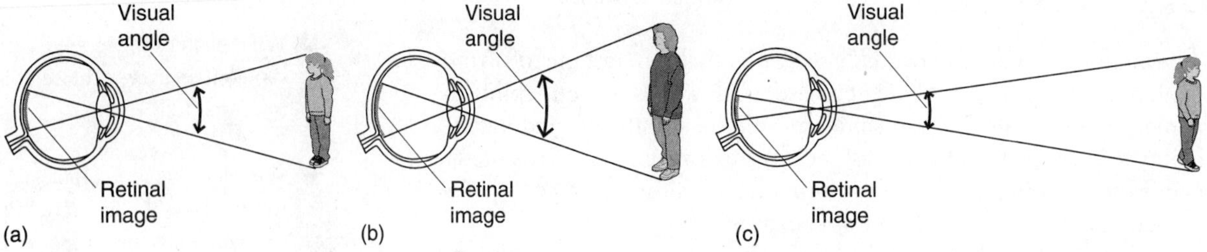

Figure 9.1
The size of an object's image on the retina depends on the object's size (compare a and b) and on the object's distance (compare a and c). Because of this effect of object distance, the size of the retinal image alone cannot provide accurate information about an object's actual size.

shape constancy, size constancy stabilizes our perceptual world by helping us correctly perceive the actual physical characteristics of objects.

What causes size constancy? When we ask that question, we are asking what enables us to accurately perceive the physical sizes of objects no matter what their distance. One answer is that we use **size cues** such as *familiar size* (we know the sizes of familiar objects such as people and automobiles) and *relative size.* (We can compare the size of an object to the size of a nearby object as shown in Figure 9.2.)

Another answer to this question refers back to the example of our helicopter pilot at the beginning of the chapter—our perception of size is influenced by our perception of distance. This was illustrated in a

Figure 9.2
The size of this wheel becomes apparent when it can be compared to an object of known size such as the person. If the wheel were seen in total isolation, it would be difficult to know that it is so large.

classic experiment by A. H. Holway and Edwin Boring (1941) in which they investigated the relationship between size perception and depth perception.

Size Constancy and Depth Perception

The setup for Holway and Boring's experiment is shown in Figure 9.3. The observer sits at the intersection of two hallways and sees a luminous *test circle* when looking down the right hallway and a luminous *comparison circle* when looking down the left hallway. The comparison circle is always 10 feet from the observer, but the test circles are presented at distances ranging from 10 feet to 120 feet. The observer's task on each trial is to adjust the diameter of the comparison circle to match that of the test circle.

An important feature of the test stimuli is that they all have the same visual angle (Figure 9.4) and so they all cast exactly the same-sized image on the retina (Figure 9.5). In the first part of Holway and Boring's experiment, many depth cues were available so the observer could easily judge the distance of the test circles. The results, indicated by line 1 in Figure 9.6, show that, even though all of the retinal images were the same size, the observers based their judgments on the physical sizes of the circles. When they viewed a large test circle that was located far away (such as F in Figure 9.4), they made the comparison circle large (Point F in Figure 9.6). If, however, they viewed a small test circle that was located nearby (such as N in Figure 9.4), they made the comparison circle small (Point N in Figure 9.6). The fact that they always adjusted the comparison circle to match the *physical size* of the test circle—even though all test circles had the same visual angle and therefore cast identical images on the retina—shows that their perception was based on size constancy.

Holway and Boring then asked whether size constancy would still hold if they began eliminating depth information from the hallway. They did this by having the observer view the test circles with one eye (line 2), then by having the observer view the test circles through a peephole (line 3), and finally by adding drapes to the hallway to eliminate reflections (line 4). The results of these experiments indicate that, as it became harder to determine the distance of the test

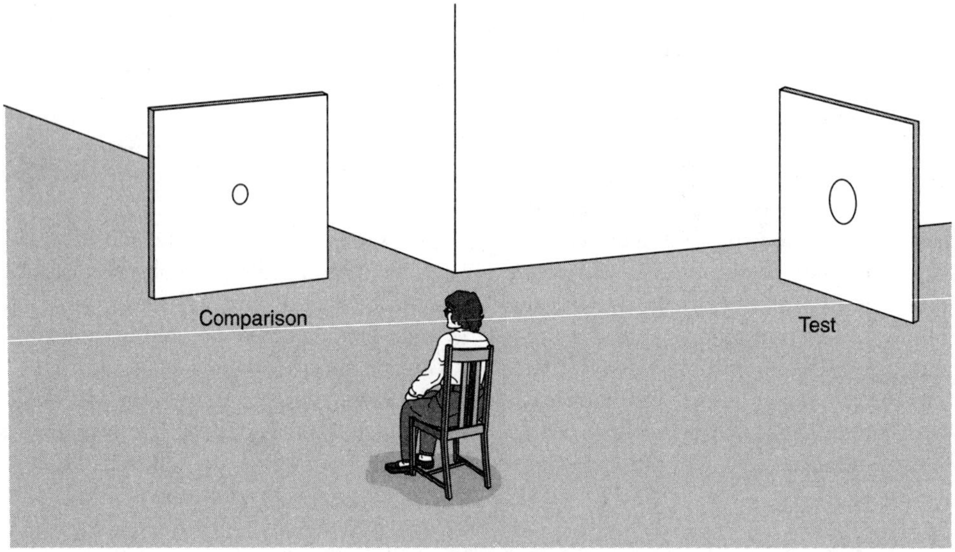

Figure 9.3
Setup of Holway and Boring's (1941) experiment. The observer changes the diameter of the comparison stimulus to match the size of the test stimulus.

circles, the observer's perception became more and more determined by the object's visual angle. This result is similar to the result of the Demonstration on page 169, in which we saw that eliminating depth information by closing one eye causes the coin with the smaller visual angle to appear smaller.

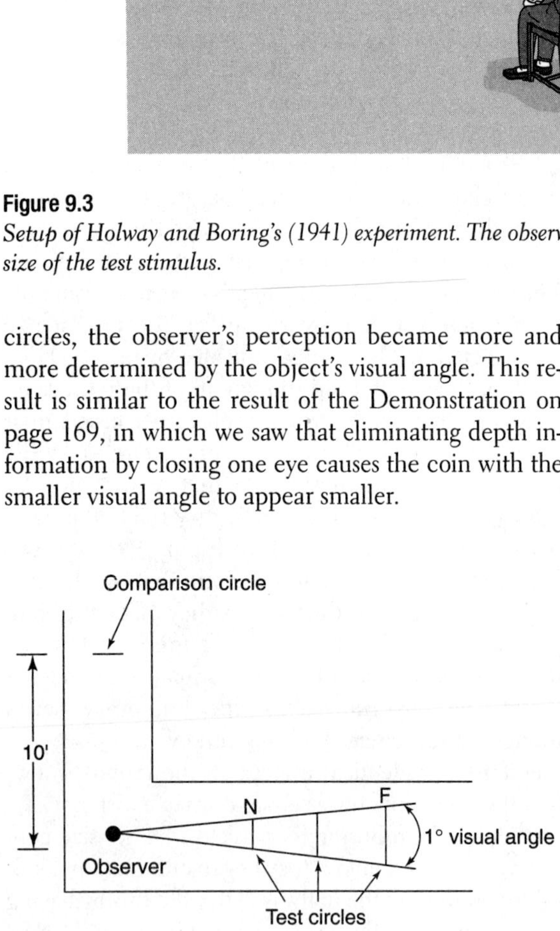

Figure 9.4
Top view of Holway and Boring's experiment. The key feature of this experiment is that the test circles all have the same visual angle and therefore cast the same image on the observer's retinas. (Adapted from Holway & Boring, 1941.)

Another example of size perception that is determined by visual angle is our perception of the sizes of the sun and the moon, which have the same visual angle. The fact that the sun and the moon have identical visual angles becomes most obvious during an eclipse of the sun. Although we can see the flaming corona of the sun surrounding the moon, as shown in Figure 9.7, the moon's disk almost exactly covers the disk of the sun.

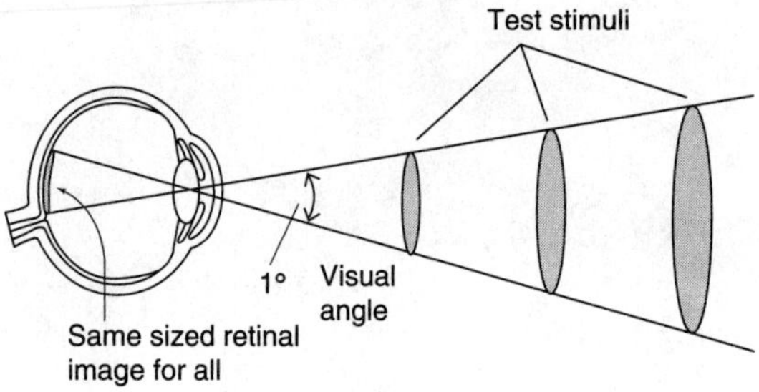

Figure 9.5
All of the test stimuli in the Holway and Boring experiment had the same visual angle. This means that they all cast the same sized image on the retina.

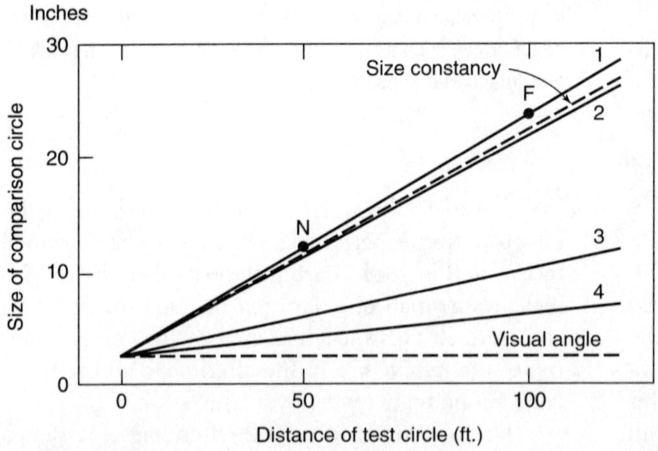

Figure 9.6
Results of Holway and Boring's experiment. The dashed line marked "size constancy" is the result that would be expected if the observers adjusted the diameter of the comparison circle to match the actual diameter of the test circle. The line marked "visual angle" is the result that would be expected if the observers adjusted the diameter of the comparison circle to match the visual angle of the test circle. Points N and F correspond to test stimuli N and F in Figure 9.5 for the condition when there was an abundance of depth cues. (Adapted from Holway & Boring, 1941.)

If we calculate the visual angles of the sun and the moon, the result is 0.5 degrees for both. As you can see in Figure 9.7, the moon is small (diameter 2,200 miles) but close (245,000 miles from earth), while the sun is large (diameter 865,400 miles) but far away (93 million miles from earth). Even though these two celestial bodies are vastly different in size, we perceive them to be the same size because as we are unable to perceive their distance, we base our judgment on their visual angles.

Yet another example of a situation in which visual angle determines our perception of size because

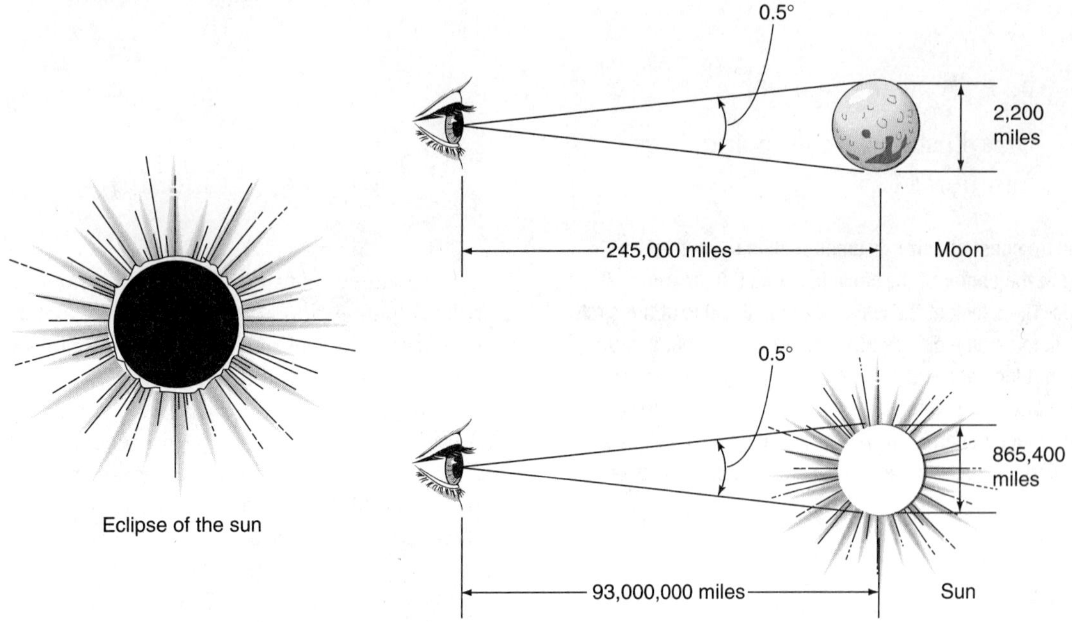

Figure 9.7
The moon's disk almost exactly covers the sun during an eclipse because the sun and the moon have the same visual angles.

inadequate depth information is available, is the way we perceive objects viewed from a high-flying airplane as being very small. Since we have no way of accurately estimating the distance from the airplane to the ground, we perceive size based on objects' visual angles, which are very small because we are so high up.

The link between depth perception and size perception has led to the proposal that when depth information is available, our perception of size is based on a *constancy-scaling mechanism* that supplements the information available on the retinas by taking an object's distance into account (Gregory, 1966). This constancy-scaling mechanism, which we will call **size-distance scaling,** operates according to the equation $S = K(R \times D)$, where S is the object's perceived size, K is a constant, R is the size of the retinal image, and D is the perceived distance of the object. Thus, as a person walks away from you, the size of her image on your retina, R, gets smaller, but your perception of her distance, D, gets larger. These two changes balance each other, and the net result is that you perceive her size, S, as remaining constant.

DEMONSTRATION

Size-Distance Scaling and Emmert's Law

You can demonstrate size-distance scaling to yourself by looking at the center of the circle in Figure 9.8 for about 60 seconds. Then, look at the white space to the side of the circle and blink to see the circle's afterimage. Now, repeat this procedure, but look at a wall far across the room. Blink to bring back the afterimage if it fades. You should see that the size of the afterimage depends on where you look. If you look at a distant surface such as the far wall of the room, you see a large afterimage that appears to be far away. If you look at a near surface such as the page of this book, you see a small afterimage that appears to be close.

Figure 9.8

Figure 9.9 illustrates the principle underlying the effect you just experienced, which was first described by Emmert in 1881. Staring at the circle in Figure 9.8 bleaches a small circular area of visual pigment on your retina. This bleached area of the retina determines the *retinal size* of the afterimage and remains constant no matter where you are looking.

The *perceived size* of the afterimage, as shown in Figure 9.9, is determined by the distance of the surface against which the afterimage is viewed. This relationship between the apparent distance of an afterimage and its perceived size is known as **Emmert's law:** The farther away an afterimage appears, the larger it will seem. This result follows from our size-distance scaling equation, $S = R \times D$. Since the size of the bleached area of pigment on the retina, R, always stays the same, increasing the afterimage's distance, D, increases the magnitude of $R \times D$ so we perceive the size of the afterimage, S, as larger when it is viewed against the far wall.

Visual Illusions

Size constancy contributes to our experience of **veridical perception**—perception that matches the actual physical situation. Veridical perception is most likely to occur in well-lit natural environments in which lots of information is available for perception. But if conditions are such that we receive inaccurate information as did our helicopter pilot in "whiteout" weather conditions, veridical perception breaks down and we experience an **illusion**—a non veridical perception such as mistaking a matchbox for a truck.

The size illusion experienced by our helicopter pilot is an example of an illusion occurring in the natural environment. However, most of the illusions that

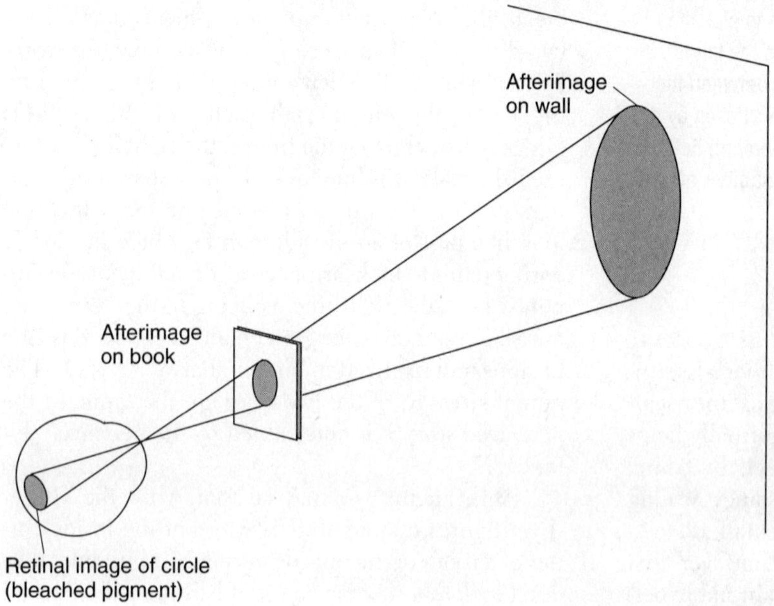

Figure 9.9
The principle behind the observation that the size of an afterimage increases as the afterimage is viewed against more distant surfaces.

psychologists have studied are ones that they have devised, like the **Müller-Lyer illusion** in Figure 9.10. The goal in constructing these illusions is to do experiments that will uncover the mechanism responsible for the illusion. As we consider some of these illusions, we will see that researchers do not always agree on what causes them.

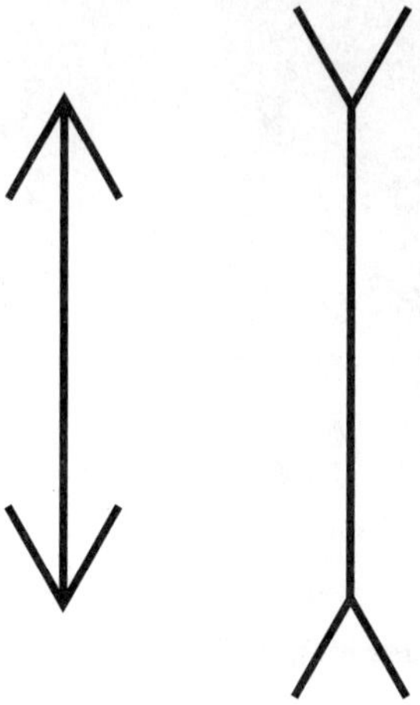

Figure 9.10
The Müller-Lyer illusion. Both lines are actually the same length.

The Müller-Lyer Illusion

In the Müller-Lyer illusion, the right vertical line appears to be longer than the left vertical line, even though they are both exactly the same length (measure them). The fact that one line appears longer than the other is obvious by just looking at these figures, but you can measure how much longer the right line appears by using the simple matching procedure described in the following demonstration.

D E M O N S T R A T I O N

Measuring the Müller-Lyer Illusion

The first step in measuring the Müller-Lyer illusion is to create some stimuli. Create a "standard stimulus" by drawing a line 30 millimeters long on an index card and adding outward-going fins, as in the right figure in Figure 9.10. Then, on separate cards, create "comparison stimuli" by drawing lines 28, 30, 32, 34, 36, 38, and 40 millimeters long with inward-going

fins, as in the left figure. Then, ask your subject to pick the comparison stimulus that most closely matches the length of the standard stimulus. The difference in length between the standard stimulus and the comparison stimulus chosen by the subject (typically between 10 percent and 30 percent) defines the size of the illusion. Try this procedure on a number of people to see how variable it is. ●

Why does this misperception of size occur? Richard Gregory (1966) explains the Müller -Lyer illusion on the basis of **misapplied size constancy scaling.** He points out that size constancy normally helps us maintain a stable perception of objects by taking distance into account. Thus, size constancy scaling causes a 6-foot-tall person to appear 6 feet tall, no matter what his distance. Gregory proposes, however, that the very mechanism that helps us maintain stable perceptions in the three-dimensional world sometimes create illusions when applied to objects drawn on a two-dimensional surface. We can see how this works by comparing the left and right lines in Figure 9.10 to the left and right pictures in Figure 9.11. Gregory suggests that the fins on the right line in Figure 9.11 make this line look like part of an inside corner, and that the fins on the left line make this line look like part of an outside corner. Since the inside corner tends to look farther away than the outside corner, we see the right line as being farther away, and our size-distance scaling mechanism causes this line to appear longer. (Remember that $S = R \times D$. The retinal sizes, R, of the two lines are the same, so the perceived size, S, is determined by the perceived distance, D.)

At this point, you may say that, while the Müller -Lyer figures may remind Gregory of the inside corner of a room or the outside corner of a building, they don't look that way to you (or at least they didn't until Gregory told you to see them that way). But according

Figure 9.11
According to Gregory (1973), the Müller-Lyer line on the left corresponds to an outside corner, and the line on the right corresponds to an inside corner.

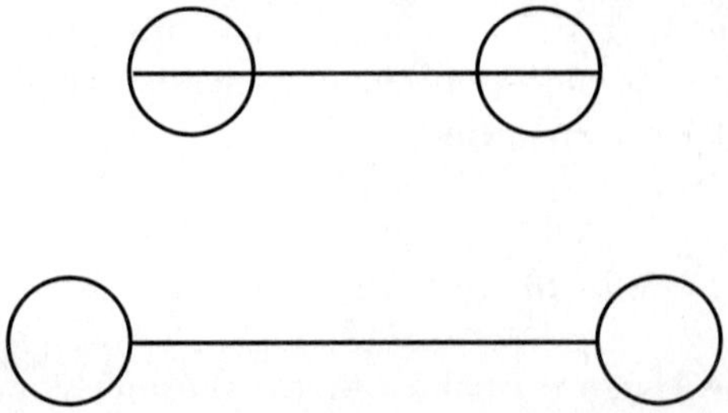

Figure 9.12
The "dumbbell" version of the Müller-Lyer illusion. As in the Müller-Lyer illusion, the two lines are actually the same length.

to Gregory, it is not necessary that you be consciously aware that the Müller -Lyer lines can represent three-dimensional structures; your perceptual system unconsciously takes the depth information contained in the Müller-Lyer figures into account, and your size-distance scaling mechanism adjusts the perceived sizes of the lines accordingly.

Gregory's theory of visual illusions has not, however, gone unchallenged. For example, figures like the dumbbell in Figure 9.12, which contain no obvious perspective or depth, still result in an illusion. And Patricia DeLucia and Julian Hochberg (1985, 1986, 1991; Hochberg, 1987) have shown that the Müller-Lyer illusion occurs for a three-dimensional display like the one in Figure 9.13, in which it is obvious that the spaces between the two sets of fins are not at different depths. You can experience this effect for yourself by doing the following demonstration.

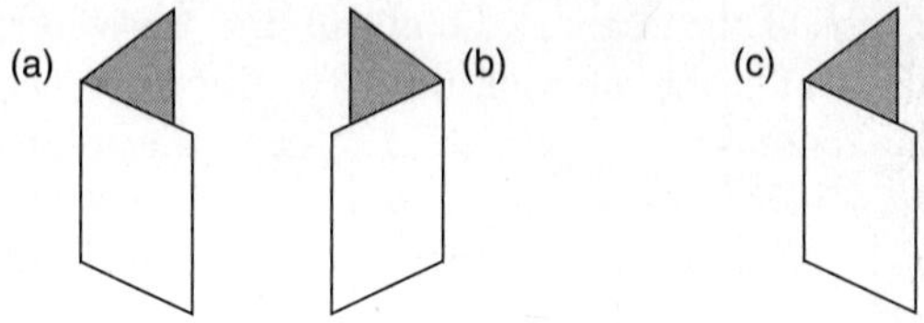

Figure 9.13
A three-dimensional Müller-Lyer illusion. The 2-foot-high wooden "fins" stand on the floor. Although the distance between edges (a) and (b) and between (b) and (c) are the same, the distance between (b) and (c) appears larger, just as in the two-dimensional Müller-Lyer illusion. Gregory's explanation of the illusion in terms of misapplied size constancy does not work in this case, since it is obvious that the spaces between the sets of fins are not at different depths.

D E M O N S T R A T I O N

The Müller-Lyer Illusion with Books

Pick three books that are the same size, and arrange two of them with their corners making a 90-degree angle and standing in positions A and B, as shown in Figure 9.14. Then, without using a ruler, position the third book at position C, so that distance b appears to be equal to distance a. Check your decision, looking down at the books from the top and from other angles as well. When you are satisfied that distances a and b appear about equal, measure the distances with a ruler. How do they compare? ●

If your perceptions were similar to those of the subjects in DeLucia and Hochberg's (1991) experiment, you set distance b so that it was smaller than distance a. This is exactly the result you would expect from the two-dimensional Müller-Lyer illusion, in which the distance between the outward-going fins appears enlarged compared to the distance between the inward-going fins. You can also duplicate the illusion

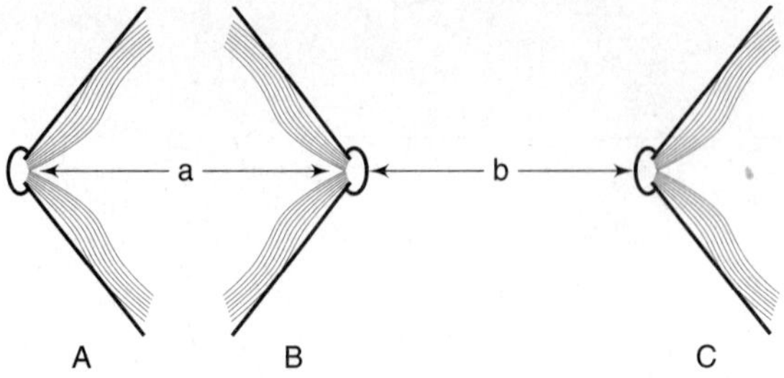

Figure 9.14
Creating a Müller-Lyer illusion with books (seen from the top).

shown in Figure 9.10 with your books, by using your ruler to make distances a and b equal. Then, notice how the distances actually appear. The fact that we can create the Müller-Lyer illusion by using three-dimensional stimuli such as these, as well as demonstrations like the dumbbell in Figure 9.12, is difficult for Gregory's theory to explain.

Another explanation of the Müller-Lyer illusion has been proposed by R. H. Day (1989, 1990), whose **conflicting cues theory** states that our perception of the length of the lines depends on two cues for length: (1) the actual length of the vertical lines, and (2) the overall length of the figure. According to Day, these two conflicting cues are integrated to form a compromise perception of length. Since the overall length of the right figure in Figure 9.10 is larger because of the outward-oriented fins, this length causes the vertical line to appear larger.

Another version of the Müller-Lyer illusion, shown in Figure 9.15, results in the perception that the space between the dots is greater in the lower figure than in the upper figure, even though the distances are actually the same. According to Day's conflicting cues theory, the space in the lower figure appears greater because the overall extent of the figure is greater. Thus, while Gregory feels that depth information is involved in determining illusions, Day rejects this idea and says that cues for length are what is important. Let's now look at some more examples of illusions, and the mechanisms that have been proposed to explain them.

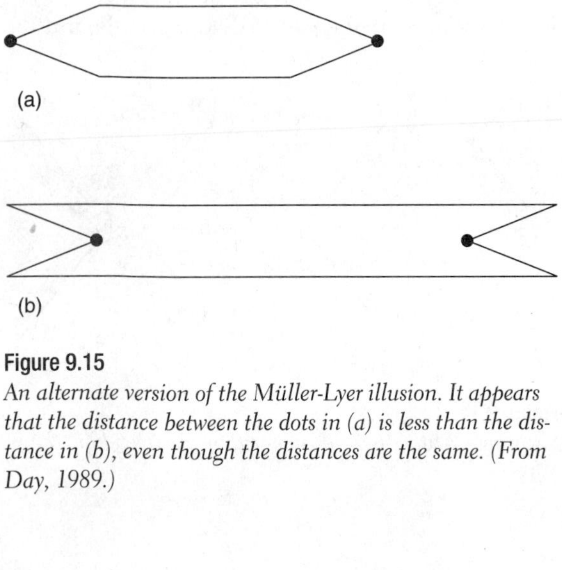

Figure 9.15
An alternate version of the Müller-Lyer illusion. It appears that the distance between the dots in (a) is less than the distance in (b), even though the distances are the same. (From Day, 1989.)

The Ponzo Illusion

In the **Ponzo** (or railroad track) **illusion,** shown in Figure 9.16, both horizontal lines are the same length and have the same visual angle, but the one on top appears longer. According to Gregory's misapplied scaling explanation, the top line appears longer, because of depth information that makes it appear farther away. Thus, just as for the Müller-Lyer illusion, the scaling mechanism corrects for this apparently increased depth (even though there isn't really any because the illusion is on a flat page) and we perceive the line to be larger.

The Ames Room

The **Ames room,** which was first constructed by Adelbert Ames, causes two people of equal size to appear very different in size (Ittleson, 1952). In the photograph of the observer's view of an Ames room in Figure 9.17, you can see that the boy, on the right, looks much taller than the woman, on the left. This perception occurs even though the boy is actually shorter than the woman. The reason for this erroneous perception of size lies in the construction of the room. Because of the shapes of the wall and the windows at the rear of the room, it looks like a normal rectangular room when viewed from a particular observation point; however, as shown in the diagram in Figure 9.18, the Ames room is, in fact, shaped so that the left corner of the room is almost twice as far away from the observer as the right corner.

What's happening in the Ames room? Because of the construction of the room, the woman has a much smaller visual angle than the boy. We think, however, that we are looking into a normal rectangular room, and since the boy and the woman appear to be at the same distance we perceive the one with the smaller visual angle as shorter. We can understand why this occurs by returning to our size-distance scaling equation,

Figure 9.16
The Ponzo (or railroad track) illusion. The two horizontal rectangles are the same length on the page (measure them), but the far one appears larger.

Figure 9.17
Ames room. The boy is actually shorter than the woman but he appears taller because of the distorted shape of the room.

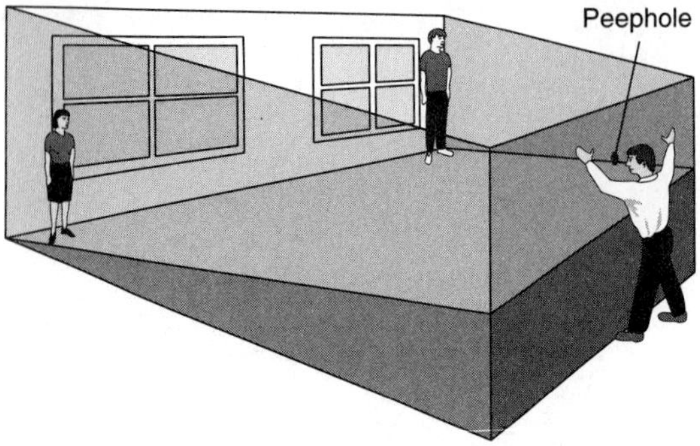

Figure 9.18
The Ames room, showing its true shape. The woman on the left is actually almost twice as far away from the observer as the man on the right; however, when the room is viewed through the peephole, this difference in distance is not seen. In order for the room to look normal when viewed through the peephole, it is necessary to enlarge the left side of the room.

$S = R \times D$. Since the perceived distance, *D*, is the same for the boy and the woman, but the size of the retinal image, *R*, is smaller for the woman, her perceived size, *S*, is smaller.

Here's another way to think about this: If you perceive two people to be the same distance from you, the one who has the smaller visual angle appears shorter. This is really a statement of the obvious: If a tall person and a short person stand next to each other, you perceive the short person as being shorter. The Ames room causes you to think that you are seeing two people at the same distance, which makes the farther one, with the smaller visual angle, appear to be shorter. (At the end of this chapter, when we discuss the ecological approach to perception, we will consider another explanation for our misperception of size in the Ames room.)

The Moon Illusion

You may have noticed that when the moon is on the horizon, it appears much larger than when it is higher in the sky. This enlargement of the horizon moon compared to the elevated moon, shown in Figure 9.19, is called the **moon illusion.** An explanation of the moon illusion that involves depth perception is called the **apparent-distance theory.** This theory is based on the idea that an object on the horizon, which is viewed across the filled space of the terrain, which contains depth information, should appear to be farther away than an object that is elevated in the sky and is viewed through empty space, which contains little depth information. The key to the moon illusion, according to apparent-distance theory, is that both the horizon and the elevated moons have the same visual angle, and that, if two objects have the same visual angle and one appears farther away, the one that appears more distant will appear larger (see the Ponzo illusion, Figure 9.16). The apparent-distance theory, therefore, states that, since the horizon moon and the elevated moon have the same visual angle, the farther-appearing horizon moon should appear larger.

Do the horizon and elevated moons really have the same visual angle? Since the moon's physical size (2,200 miles in diameter) and distance from the earth (245,000 miles) are constant throughout the night, the moon's visual angle must be constant. You can verify this in two ways: (1) Photograph the horizon and the elevated moons, and measure the resulting

Figure 9.19
An artist's conception of the moon illusion showing the moon on the horizon and high in the sky simultaneously.

photograph. You will find that the diameters in the resulting two pictures are identical. (2) View the moon through a ¼-inch-diameter hole (the size produced by most standard hole punches) held at arm's length. For most people, the moon will just fit inside this hole, and the fit will appear exactly the same wherever the moon is in the sky.

Evidence supporting a connection between the moon illusion and perceived distance has been provided by a series of experiments by Lloyd Kaufman and Irvin Rock (1962a, 1962b; Rock & Kaufman, 1962). For example, they showed that perception of the size of the horizon moon is strongly influenced by viewing the moon over the terrain, which causes it to appear farther away. They demonstrated this in a number of ways. They found that when the horizon moon was viewed over the terrain, it appeared 1.3 times larger than the elevated moon; however, when the terrain was masked off so that the horizon moon was viewed through a hole in a sheet of cardboard, the illusion vanished.

Kaufman and Rock also developed an apparatus that created artificial moons over different horizons. When their subjects used this apparatus to view the moon over horizons that were 2 miles away and 2,000 feet away, they saw the moon over the far horizon as larger than the moon over the near horizon. A number of other experiments in which Kaufman and Rock varied the apparent distance to the horizon also showed that, when the distance appeared greater, the moon appeared larger.

Another piece of evidence that has been proposed to support the apparent-distance theory is that, when people estimate the distance to the horizon and the distance to the sky directly overhead, they report that the horizon appears to be farther away. That is, the heavens appear "flattened" (Figure 9.20). If the horizon moon is seen as being on the surface of the sky, then the flattened heavens would cause the horizon moon to appear farther away, as the apparent-distance theory proposes. (However, some researchers have reported that subjects see the horizon moon as floating in space in front of the sky, a result that has caused them to question whether the "flattened heavens" can be used to explain the illusion; Plug & Ross, 1994.)

The principle involved in the apparent-distance explanation of the moon illusion is the same one that causes an afterimage to appear larger if it is viewed against a faraway surface. Just as the near and far afterimages created by viewing Figure 9.9 have the same visual angles, so do the horizon and the elevated moons. The afterimage that appears to be on the wall across the room simulates the horizon moon; the circle appears farther away, so your size-distance scaling mechanism makes it appear larger. The afterimage that appears to be on the page of the book simulates the elevated moon; the circle appears closer, so your scaling mechanism makes it appear smaller (King & Gruber, 1962).

Another theory of the moon illusion, the **angular size-contrast theory,** focuses not on the moon's apparent depth, but on the moon's visual angle compared to surrounding objects (Baird, Wagner, & Fuld, 1990). According to this idea, the moon appears smaller when it is surrounded by larger objects. Thus, when

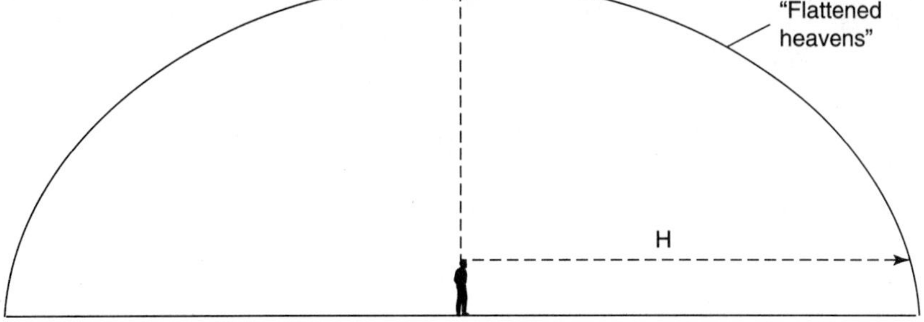

Figure 9.20
If observers are asked to consider that the sky is a surface and are asked to compare the distance to the horizon (H) and the distance to the top of the sky on a clear moonless night, they usually say that the horizon appears farther away. This results in the "flattened heavens" shown here.

the moon is elevated, the large expanse of sky surrounding it makes it appear smaller. However, when the moon is on the horizon, less sky surrounds it, so it appears larger.

The angular size-contrast theory explains Kaufman and Rock's finding that the moon appears larger when it is seen over horizons that appear farther away by pointing out that objects on the terrain, such as buildings, trees, or the texture of the ground, take up less of the field of view if they are farther away. Thus, when the moon is seen against a far horizon, it is compared to objects with small visual angles, and therefore, the moon appears larger.

Which theory of the moon illusion is correct? In a book devoted entirely to various explanations of the moon illusion, the editor concluded that most researchers do not yet agree on an explanation (Hershenson, 1989). According to Cornelis Plug and Helen Ross (1994), the moon illusion is best explained by a combination of factors, which in addition to the ones we have considered here, also include atmospheric perspective (looking through haze on the horizon can increase size perception), color (redness increases perceived size), and oculomotor factors (convergence of the eyes, which tends to occur when we look toward the horizon, can cause an increase in perceived size). Just as many different sources of depth information work together to create our impression of depth, many different factors may work together to create the moon illusion, and perhaps the other illusions as well.

Illusory Perception, Veridical Perception, and Conditions in the Environment

We have seen that not all researchers agree about the mechanism responsible for illusions. But whatever explanations turn out to be correct, everyone does agree that illusions are excellent examples of how context provided by the surrounding stimuli can affect perception of a stimulus. All of the illusions we have described, with the exception of the moon illusion, have been contrived by perception researchers by manipulating the context in which stimuli such as lines (Müller-Lyer and Ponzo illusions), spaces (modified Müller-Lyer illusion), and people (Ames room) appear.

But in our normal environment, illusions are rare, and in most circumstances we accurately perceive the things in our environment. It shouldn't really surprise us that we usually perceive things accurately, because the purpose of perception is to help us survive. Thus, in the larger evolutionary scheme of things, perceptual mechanisms of all organisms have evolved to help them do things such as move through the environment without injuring themselves, find food, and escape from predators. In the next section of this chapter, we will consider this way of looking at perception further, and we will also describe some other ways that perception researchers have considered perception in the natural environment.

The Ecology of Perception

We can approach our task in this section—to look at the way perception researchers have considered perception in the natural environment—on a number of different levels of analysis. We begin by taking a broad perspective, and looking at perception as a product of evolution. Doing this raises questions such as why did perception evolve, and why do the perceptual capacities of different species differ?

Evolutionary Aspects of Perception

Why did perception evolve? The answer to this question is that perception evolved for the purpose of survival, and that the variations in perceptual mechanisms we can observe across species reflect the specific survival needs of each animal. One of the best ways to draw a connection between perceptual mechanisms and survival is to consider the eye—a structure found throughout the animal kingdom, but in different forms that are designed to meet each animal's specific needs.

From our description of the human eye, we know that the fovea is the area of sharpest vision. This is so both because of the high density of cones and because of the lack of neural convergence, so that there is a high density of ganglion cells carrying messages from the fovea toward the brain. The eagle and the falcon provide an example of foveas with higher cone densities than those in humans; these higher cone densities increase acuity to two to three times that of humans—an asset for detecting small prey from a vantage point high in the sky (Fox, Lehmukuhle, & Westendorf, 1976; Reymond, 1985).

Humans, eagles, and falcons have small pit-shaped foveas, but some other animals have areas of high-detail vision that are spread out over a larger area. The red-eared turtle provides an example of such an arrangement: It has a horizontal area of high receptor density called the **area centralis** (K. Brown, 1969) (Figure 9.21). The linear area centralis has a property well suited to the turtle's view of the world since it is lined up with the horizon. This arrangement serves the turtle well because most of the visual stimuli that are important to the turtle, such as potential predators, appear on the horizon, where the turtle's vision is sharpest. Many other animals that live near to the ground have a linear area centralis, as well as some birds that also depend on the horizon for orientation as they are flying.

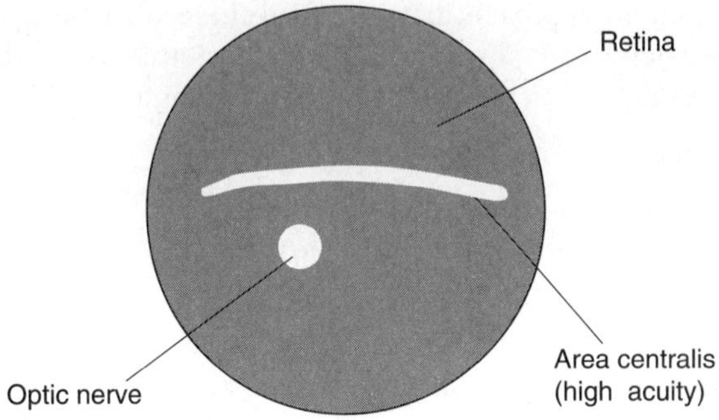

Figure 9.21
Looking down on the retina of the red-eyed turtle. The area centralis, which stretches across the retina to form a horizontal line, is the area of highest acuity.

Animals' eyes are adapted in other ways as well. For example, the wavelengths at which light-sensitive visual pigments absorb light are often shifted toward wavelengths that match the light environment. Thus, fish that live in murky water, in which longer wavelengths predominate, have pigments that are more sensitive at long wavelengths (Ali & Klyne, 1985; Lythgoe & Partridge, 1989).

Another adaptation is eye placement. Some animals, such as cats and humans, have frontal eyes with overlapping fields of view that provide good depth perception, and others, such as rabbits, birds, lizards, and rodents, have lateral eyes on the sides of their heads that provide a more panoramic view of the world, an especially important adaptation for monitoring the environment for the presence of predators (see Figure 8.33). When eyes see different areas of the environment, as in lateral-eyed animals, the eyes sometimes move independently, as in some birds and lizards, so that they can look for the most important objects on the left and the right simultaneously. In contrast, most frontal-eyed animals use "yoked" or coordinated eye movements to focus on one thing at a time.

Living in the water poses a focusing problem. For air-living animals, most of the focusing is done by the cornea; however, when the eye is submerged in water, which has physical properties similar to those of the cornea, the cornea loses most of its ability to bend light. Thus, fish and other animals that live in the water have rounded lenses that provide extra focusing power for seeing underwater.

The eyes of the "four-eyed" fish *Anableps* illustrate an ingenious solution to its visual environment. It swims along the surface of the water, so half of its eye sees through the air and half sees through the water. This fish has evolved an eye that is optically adapted to both air and water vision simultaneously (Figure 9.22). A horizontal pigmented stripe divides the eye into top and bottom halves, so the eye has two pupils: an upper one, which admits light from the air, and a lower one, which admits light from underwater. The secret of how the *Anableps* eye can focus light simultaneously from these two different environments is revealed by looking at the positioning of its lens. For light coming from the water, the lens is positioned so that it is elliptical, with greater focusing

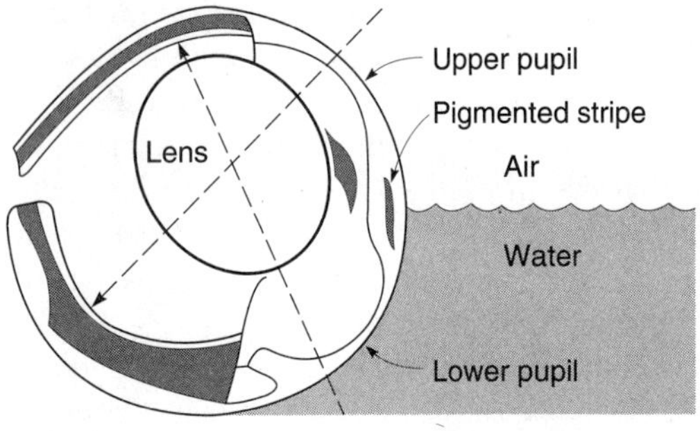

Figure 9.22
Eye of the Anableps. Light from the water passes through the lower pupil and is focused by the powerful elliptical axis of the lens. Light from the air passes through the upper pupil and is focused by the less-powerful flattened axis of the lens (Sivak, 1976).

power to compensate for the cornea's loss of focusing power underwater. For light coming from the air, the lens is flattened and has less focusing power, since the cornea can now help with the focusing.

We can also find examples of perceptual adaptations by considering some perceptual abilities of humans. Consider, for example, color constancy, which enables us to disregard the illumination conditions and perceive an object's true color. Imagine how confusing it would be if unripe green fruit on the vine appeared an edible red color when bathed by the long-wavelengths of the setting sun. Or imagine how hard it would be to deal with the environment if we lacked size constancy. Without this mechanism, far away objects, no matter how big, would appear small, and small nearby objects would appear large.

We have no way of knowing whether earlier animals lacked the constancy mechanism, but it is reasonable to suspect that without it, rapid and efficient perception of their environment would have been difficult and these animals may not have survived to reproduce more animals of their kind. Luckily, color and size constancy have been included in our tool box of perceptual capacities.

Or consider human achievements in sports. A quarterback arcs a football to an end far downfield; a figure skater lands a triple jump; a downhill skier negotiates a series of closely spaced gates with amazing speed. Of course, we didn't evolve for the purpose of playing football or excelling at winter sports, but the kinds of skills involved in sports are the same skills that enabled our early ancestors to be excellent hunters and to react quickly to danger.

We have so far restricted our examples to vision. But the other senses also evolved to serve survival mechanisms. Consider the sense of taste. Humans and other animals need salt to survive, and their taste systems are specialized to give salt a distinctive taste. Similarly sugar—an important source of energy—is signaled by a taste that is not only distinctively "sweet," but that has also been endowed with the important quality for most humans of being extremely pleasant.

One of the things that stands out about all of the perceptual adaptations that we have described is that they all have something to do with helping the animal act on its environment and react to conditions in the environment. In fact, the major force behind evolution is the way animals carry out this interaction with the environment. Animals that can interact successfully survive to reproduce, and the ones that are not adequately equipped for this interaction do not survive to reproduce, so their characteristics are not passed on to future generations.

J. J. Gibson was a perceptual psychologist who recognized the importance of studying perception in the natural environment. Over a period spanning more than 30 years, beginning with work in the 1940s and ending with his death in 1979, Gibson championed an approach that he called the **ecological approach to perception,** which considers how perception occurs in the natural environment.

J. J. Gibson's Ecological Approach to Perception

Gibson's approach is notable both because it differs in a number of ways from the way we have been describing perception in this book, and because it is based on Gibson's concern for studying perception as it occurs in the natural environment. For our brief description of Gibson's approach, which he described in three books (Gibson, 1950, 1966, 1979), we will focus on the following four principles:

1. The proper way to describe the stimulus is not in terms of the image on the retina, but in terms of information in the environment, called the optic array.
2. The important information for perception is created by movement of the observer.
3. The key information in the optic array that is created by this movement is invariant information—information that remains constant as the observer moves.
4. This invariant information leads directly to perception.

From these principles, we can draw the flow diagram in Figure 9.23, which is much simpler than the ones in Figure 1.1 and 1.6 that have been the basis of our discussion so far. To understand this diagram, we have to describe each of the four principles above.

Optic Array Gibson felt that when describing the stimulus it was not productive to consider the retinal image because our perceptions often do not correspond to what happens on the retina. Instead, Gibson proposed that the starting point of perception is the **optic array**—the structure of the light in the environment that is presented to the observer. We can illustrate what the optic array is by considering the stimulation reaching the person in Figure 9.24. This person perceives the objects, surfaces, and textures in the scene because of the way the light rays reaching the person are structured by these objects, surfaces, and textures. This structure, which is extremely complex because there are rays converging on the person from every part of the environment, is the optic array. However, the importance of the optic array lies not in the structure that it defines at any point in time, but in how this structure changes as the observer moves.

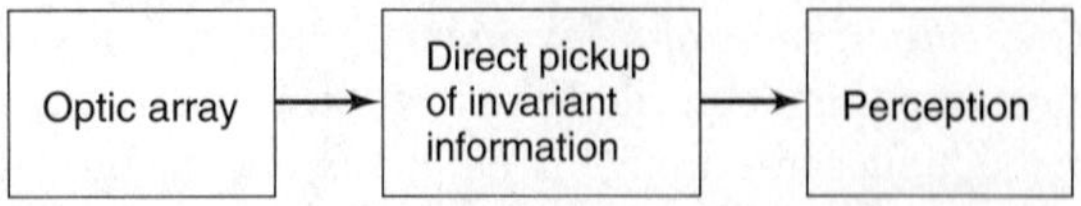

Figure 9.23
According to J.J. Gibson, perception can be explained based on the direct pickup of information from the optic array.

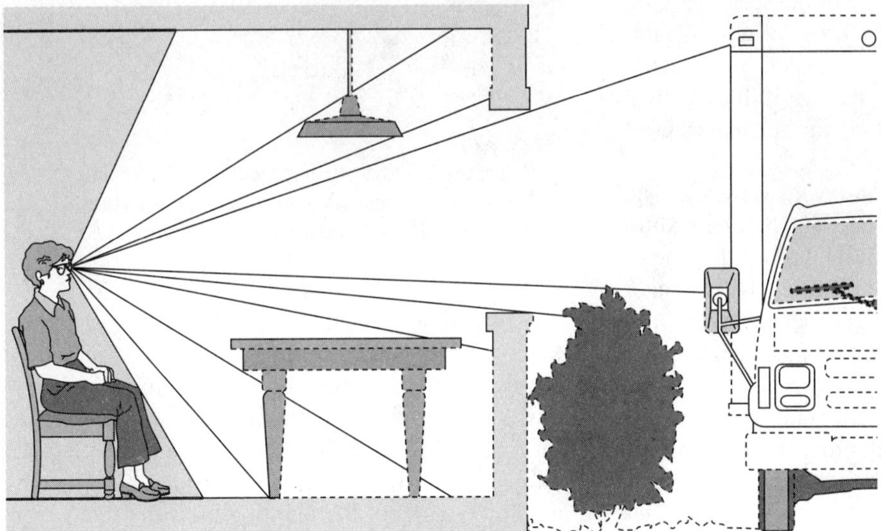

Figure 9.24
The optic array is the structured pattern of light reaching our observer's eye from the environment. Environmental surfaces visible to our observer are indicated by solid lines; invisible surfaces are indicated by dashed lines. Each of the visible surfaces structures the pattern of light entering the observer's eye.

The Importance of Movement One of Gibson's most important contributions to our understanding of perception came from his emphasis on the moving observer. After all, most of our perception occurs as we move relative to the environment—we walk, run, or drive through it, and even when we are sitting in one place, we move our eyes and heads to observe the scene around us.

Since movement is so important, Gibson focused his attention on identifying information in the optic array that transmits information about the environment as the observer is moving. One of the basic properties of this information is that it is **invariant information**—it remains constant even when the observer changes position or moves through the environment.

Invariant Information in the Environment Gibson identified a number of sources of invariant information. We will describe three of them: Texture gradients, flow patterns, and the horizon ratio.

A **texture gradient** occurs when a textured ground, such as the pattern in Figure 9.25, is viewed at an angle, so the individual elements of the gradient are seen as being packed closer and closer together as the distance from the observer increases. To appreciate what it means to say that texture gradients contain *invariant information*, lets consider the beach scene in Figure 9.26. In our first view of the scene (Figure 9.26a), we can identify four sources of depth information: (1) the texture gradient created by the sand; (2) the overlap of the two signs; (3) the relative heights of the two signs; and (4) the relative sizes of the signs.

Figure 9.26b shows the observer's view after she has walked a little way down the beach. The texture gradient information is still available, but the cue of overlap has vanished, since the two signs no longer overlap. Figure 9.26c shows the observer's view after she has walked past the signs. The signs are no longer visible, so they are no longer a source of depth information. Notice however, that the gradient, which extends across a large area, is still providing information about depth, and that this information is invariant—it remains the same as the observer changes her position.

Figure 9.25
Salt deposits in Death Valley, a pattern that forms a texture gradient since its elements appear smaller as distance increases. (W. Perry Company)

In addition to providing information about distance, texture gradients also indicate the orientations of surfaces. For example, the rapid changes in texture of the sides of the object represented in the painting in Figure 9.27 tell us that the sides are oriented at a steep angle, whereas the smaller change of texture along the edges of the painting indicates that we are looking at that surface almost straight on.

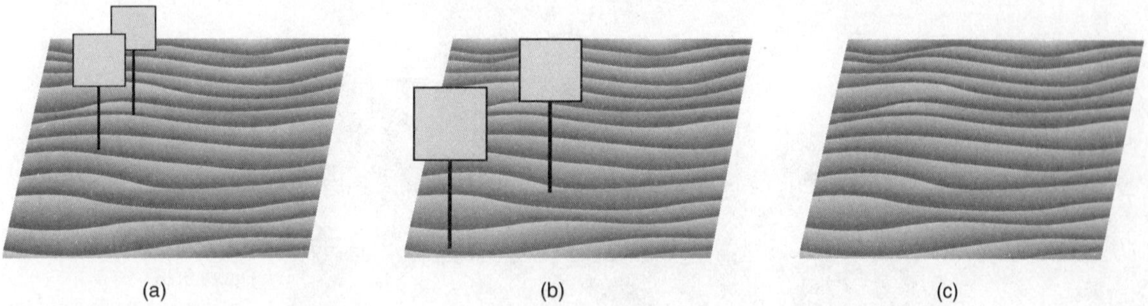

Figure 9.26
A person's views as she walks along the beach. In (a) she is walking toward two signs; in (b) she is near the signs; and in (c) she has passed them. Depth information can be obtained from the signs only from certain points of view, but it is available for the gradient as long as the person is on the beach.

A **flow pattern** is created as elements in the environment flow past a moving observer. For example, a moving observer looking to the side, like a person looking out the side window of a moving car, sees a **gradient of flow:** The speed of movement is rapid in the foreground and becomes slower as the distance from the observer increases (Figure 9.28). This is similar to the depth cue of motion parallax (see Figure 8.9) that we mentioned in Chapter 8, but Gibson emphasized the flow of the whole

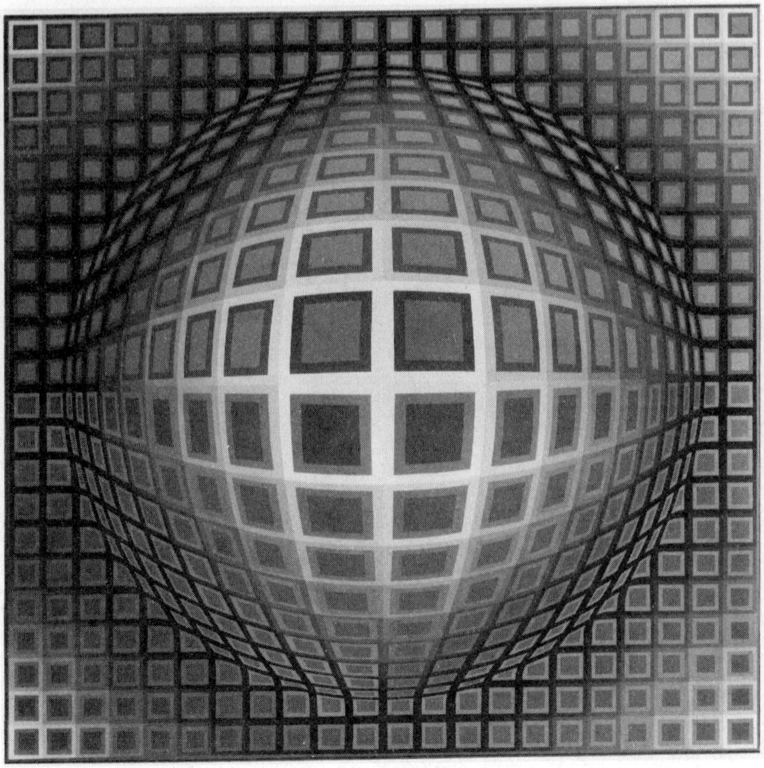

Figure 9.27
Vega-Nor by Victor Vasarely (1969). This painting creates an "object" with steeply sloping sides by using texture gradients. (Courtesy of the Albright-Knox Art Gallery, Buffalo, New York. Gift of Seymour H. Knox, 1969.)

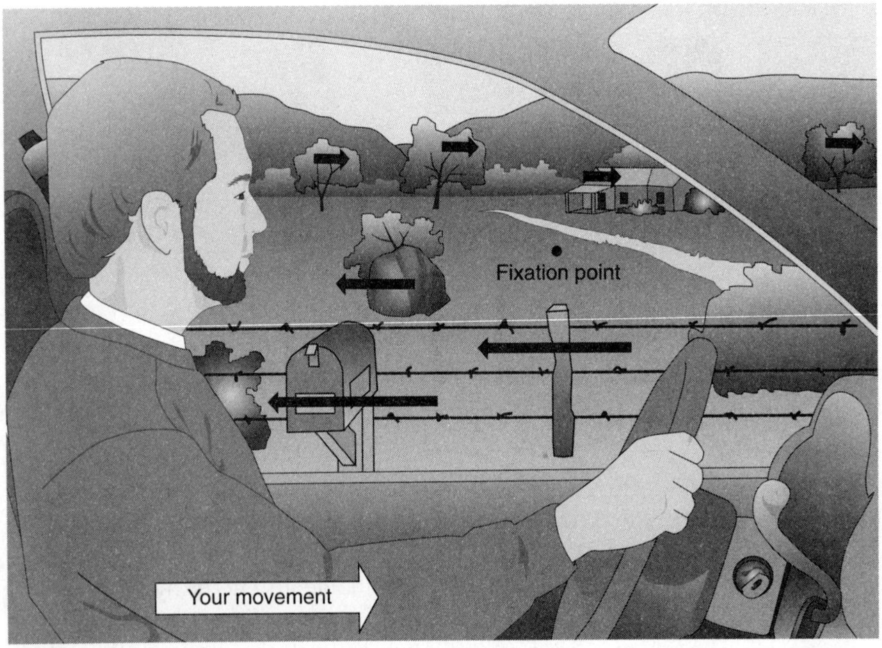

Figure 9.28
An observer looking out the side window of a car sees a gradient of flow in the environment. The sizes of the arrows indicate the speed of the optic flow (larger arrows mean greater speed) and the direction of the flow (the environment flows in opposite directions in front of and in back of the observer's fixation point).

field rather than the relative movement of just a few objects.

The deletion and accretion at edges that are at different depths (Figure 8.10) were also mentioned by Gibson as information that signals depth to the moving observer. Gibson also considered the flow that occurs as a person moves forward as providing information that helps the person negotiate his way through the environment. We will describe flow patterns created as the observer moves forward in the next chapter, when we discuss movement perception.

The **horizon ratio,** another source of invariant information, is the extent of an object that is above the horizon, divided by the extent of an object that is below the horizon (Gibson, 1950; Sedgwick, 1973, 1983). The **horizon ratio principle** states that if two objects standing on flat terrain that are in contact with the ground are the same size, their horizon ratios will be the same. Thus, since all of the telephone poles in Figure 9.29 have the same horizon ratio, we know they are the same size. We also know that the tree is larger than the telephone poles because the horizon ratio of the tree is greater than the ratio of the telephone poles (i.e., a greater proportion of the tree is above the horizon line). The horizon ratio is invariant

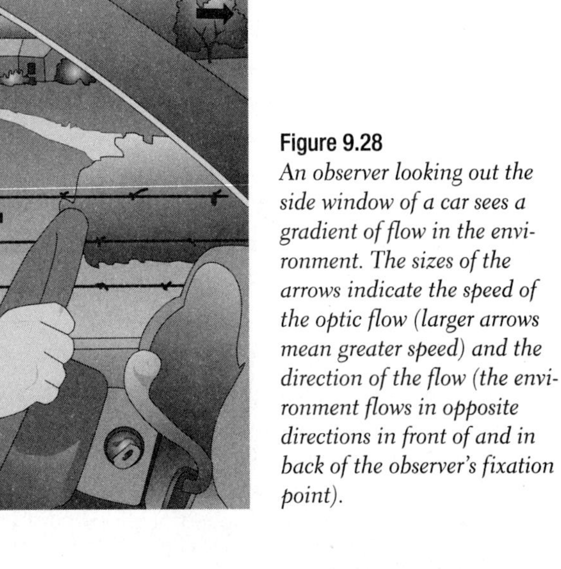

Figure 9.29
According to the horizon ratio principle, the horizon line intersects the telephone poles and the tree at a height equal to the viewer's eye level. Objects that are the same size, such as the three telephone poles, have the same horizon ratio. Since a larger proportion of the tree is above the horizon, we perceive it as being larger than the telephone poles.

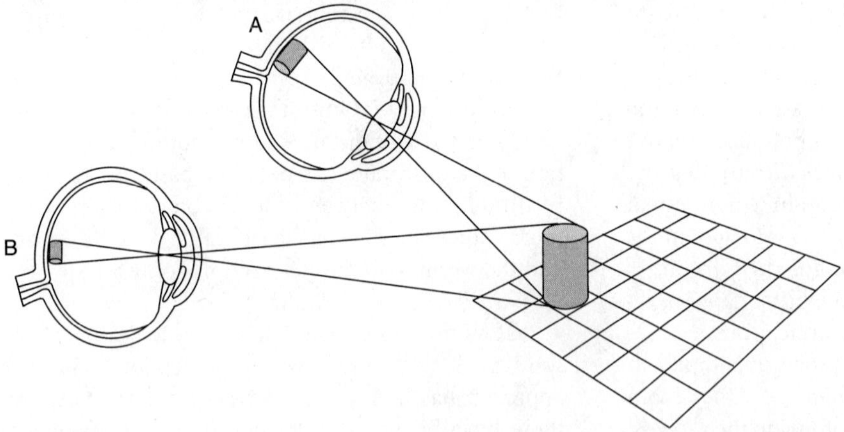

Figure 9.30
An observer, indicated by a single eyeball, looking at a cylinder on a checkerboard pattern from two different positions. The cylinder's image on the retina is larger when the observer is close (position A) than when the observer is far (position B).

with the observer's position in the scene, so although the size of a telephone pole may become larger in the field of view as an observer approaches, the proportion of the pole that is above and below the horizon line remains constant.

Direct Perception According to Gibson, the invariant information in the optic array is the information that leads *directly* to perception. This idea that perception happens directly from information picked up from the optic array is called **direct perception.** Gibson describes direct perception as follows:

> Saying perception of the environment is direct means it is not mediated by *retinal pictures, neural pictures,* or *mental pictures.* Direct perception is the activity of getting information from the ambient array of light. (Gibson, 1979, p. 147)

Gibson focused on how taking in information in the environment determines perception, *independently* of the retinal image and processing—two things that occupy such a central place in our diagram of Figures 1.1 and 1.6. To illustrate this idea, let's compare how the approach to perception we have been describing in this book, which we will call the *processing approach,* and Gibson's *direct approach* explain size constancy.

The processing approach we described at the beginning of this chapter says that since the size of an object's image on our retinas depends on its distance from us, our perception of that object's size must somehow involve a "taking into account" of its distance. Thus, as the observer in Figure 9.30 moves away from the cylinder, the cylinder's image on the retina becomes smaller, so the observer makes a calculation that takes distance into account to accurately perceive the cylinder's size.

Such a calculation is not necessary, according to Gibson, because an object's size can be determined directly by noting the number of units its base covers on a texture gradient. This principle is illustrated in Figure 9.31, which shows that, even as the observer moves away, he continues to perceive the cylinder's base as covering one unit on the texture gradient.

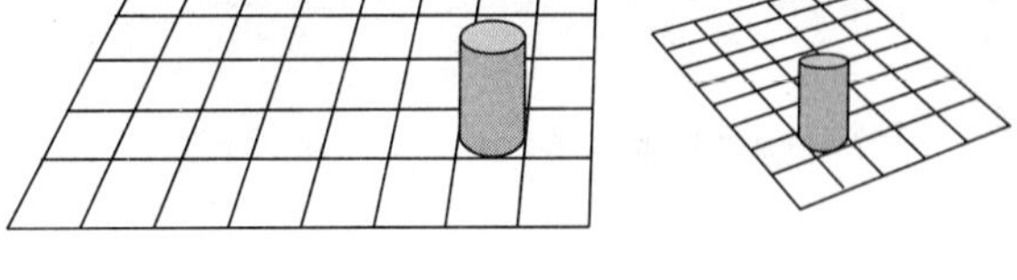

Figure 9.31
What the observer in Figure 9.30 sees from positions A and B. Athough moving from A to B decreases the size of the cylinder in the field of view and changes the angle of view, the cylinder still appears to cover one unit of the texture gradient in both situations.

Another way to illustrate how gradients help us to achieve the direct perception of size is shown in Figure 9.32, which shows two cylinders on the texture gradient formed by a cobblestone street. That the bases of the front and rear cylinders both cover about half a unit on the gradient indicates *directly* that the bases are the same size. A calculation in which retinal size and perceived distance are taken into account is not necessary. Perception, according to Gibson, is therefore not a matter of processing, but it happens *directly* from the information in the optic array.

Another way to compare the processing approach and direct perception is to consider the Ames room demonstration (Figure 9.17). According to the processing explanation, the visual system does a calculation that takes both the retinal size of the people in the room and their perceived distance into account (see the formula on page 250).

According to Gibson's approach, however, we don't need to take distance into account. Our perception of the size of the two people is based on how they fill the distance between the bottom and top of the room. Since the boy on the right fills the entire space and the woman on the left occupies only a little of it, we perceive the boy as taller.

How do perception researchers feel about Gibson's ecological approach to perception? Gibson's approach has had its supporters and detractors, and there have been lively debates about the ecological approach in the perception literature (Cutting, 1986; Epstein, 1977; Fodor & Pylyshyn, 1981; Gibson, 1979; Runeson, 1977; Ullman, 1980). Many researchers appreciate Gibson's emphasis on the moving observer, his focus on information contained on environmental surfaces, and his identification of invariant information in the optic array (Nakayama, 1994). However, others feel that information in addition to Gibson's invariants are involved in perception, and that perceptual processing is far too important a part of the perceptual process to ignore. In the next chapter, we will consider Gibson's ideas again as we describe how we perceive movement.

Figure 9.32
A texture gradient with two cylinders. According to Gibson, the fact that the bases of both cylinders cover the same number of units on the gradient provides direct information that the bases of the two cylinders are the same size.

The Physiology of Ecological Perception

One of the central premises of the ecological approach to perception is that we need to study perception as it occurs in natural conditions. Gibson did this by focusing on identifying stimulus information such as invariants, and he paid little attention to physiological mechanisms. However, physiology does play an indispensable role in perception, and present-day visual physiology researchers have taken very seriously the idea championed many years earlier by Gibson, that it is important to study perception as it occurs in the environment.

In Chapter 4 we presented numerous examples of how researchers used environmental stimuli to study neural responding. We saw that there are neurons in the extrastriate cortex that respond to complex stimuli such as faces. We also saw that there are neurons that "learn" from experience in perceiving specific forms, and that the dorsal stream is specialized to coordinate perception and actions such as picking up an object or mailing a letter.

There are also neurons that serve one of our most important adaptive abilities—the ability to perceive the properties of our environment as remaining constant even when we move or view stimuli under different conditions of illumination. We described *size-invariant neurons* in area IT that may help us achieve size constancy by responding to a particular form no matter what its size (Chapter 4) and color sensitive neurons in area V4 that may help us achieve color constancy by responding to an object's color under different conditions of illumination (Chapter 5).

The discovery of neurons that may serve higher level perceptual abilities, such as constancy, illustrates how we can study perception at different levels of analysis. Gibson studied perception at the stimulus level and made us aware of environmental stimuli such as texture gradients that help us achieve size constancy. The physiologists, studying perception at the neural level, have discovered neurons that may be responsible for some of the perceptions Gibson was concerned with. In the next chapter we will see how studying perception at different levels of analysis has helped us to understand how we perceive movement.

Something to Consider: Laboratory Research and Ecological Validity

Most of the research we have described in this book has been done under controlled laboratory conditions. Measuring a person's visual acuity or determining a neuron's receptive field requires conditions that enable us to accurately present a stimulus to a specific place on the retina. However, in this chapter we have introduced the idea that the study of perception should also take into account the way people perceive in their natural environment. Researchers who favor this approach to perception point out that people don't typically perceive with their heads kept still as they observe brief flashes of light. Instead, they take an active role in their own perception by selecting what they want to see, as they move freely through the environment.

Although researchers in the "laboratory control" camp and the "environmental stimuli" camp may disagree as to the most fruitful way to study perception, the view from outside these camps suggests that both approaches have something valuable to contribute to our understanding of the perceptual process. Most of what we know about the physiology of perception has come from laboratory experiments, and the control possible in the laboratory has enabled researchers to isolate and study specific information such as wavelength for color perception or depth cues for space perception. However, the environmental approach has shown researchers that they also need to study how people actually behave in their natural environment, and in doing this, the environmental approach has identified stimuli that were not obvious when perception research was restricted to the laboratory. What is happening now in perceptual research is a cross-fertilization of these two approaches, as physiological research (1) takes complex environmental stimuli into account, and (2) studies perception in animals as they actively interact with the environment.

This interaction between different approaches to perception returns us to the message we presented at the beginning of this book—we can't completely understand the perceptual process by focusing on just one part of it or by using just one approach. A broader view is needed to understand the vast complexity of perception.

Visual and Haptic Illusions

Although we are most familiar with visual illusions, the other senses also give rise to illusions. A class of illusions that are particularly interesting for our purpose of comparing perception across senses are *haptic illusions* that are direct counterparts to visual illusions such as the Müller-Lyer illusion (Figure 9.10), the vertical-horizontal illusion (Figure 9.33a) and the Bourdon illusion (Figure 9.33b). **Haptic perception** is perception based on exploration of an object with the hands and fingers, and the haptic versions of illusions are made by creating raised edges or three-dimensional models that a person can feel with their fingers such as the tactile version of the Bourdon illusion shown in Figure 9.34a. For example, in the visual version of the Bourdon illusion, subjects see line A, B, C, as being slightly bent, even though it is straight. In the haptic version, when a person feels the two opposite surfaces with their thumb and forefinger, they feel the upper surface as being slightly bent (Figure 9.34b) (Day, 1990).

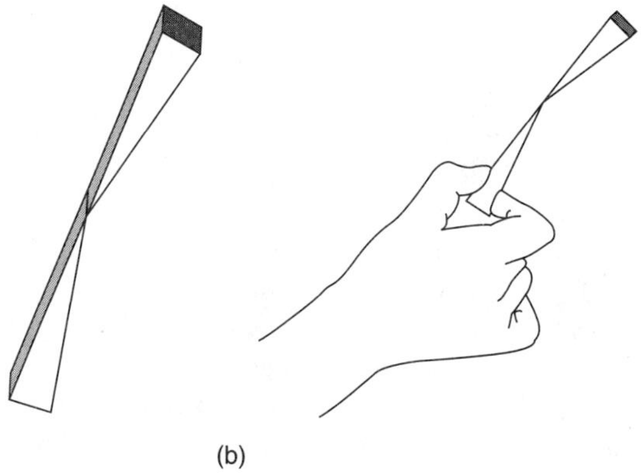

Figure 9.34
(a) Haptic version of the Bourdon illusion. (b) Person feeling the haptic Bourdon figure. The haptic illusion occurs when the person feels the upper surface as being slightly bent.

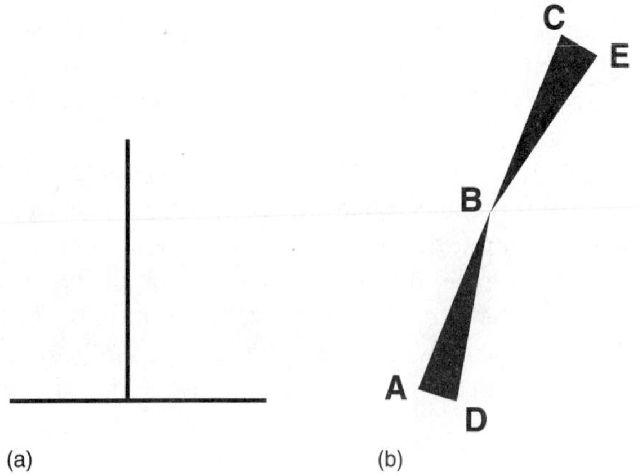

Figure 9.33
(a) Vertical-horizontal illusion; (b) Visual Bourdon illusion. (From Day, 1990.)

We don't know whether the same mechanisms are responsible for illusions that occur in two senses, but the similarities between them suggest that they may share mechanisms in common. For one thing, the sizes of the illusions are often similar in the two senses. For the visual Bourdon illusion, people see a bend of about 3.8 degrees, and in the haptic version, they feel a bend of about 3.5 degrees (Day, 1990). In addition, a decrease occurs in both visual and haptic versions of the same illusion as it is presented over many trials. Thus, Rita Rudel and Hans-Lukas Teuber (1963) found that when the visual Müller-Lyer illusion was viewed 80 times, its size decreased by about 33 percent, and when the haptic version was felt with the fingers for 80 trials, it decreased by about 45 percent. Rudel and Teuber also observed cross-adaptation between the two versions of the illusion. So if after presenting 80 trials of the haptic version of the Müller-Lyer illusion, they presented the visual version for the first time, the visual illusion was much smaller than it usually appears when a person views it for the first time, even though the subjects had not been adapted to the visual version. This cross-adaptation suggests that there may be some overlap in the mechanisms that cause these two illusions in the different senses.

Thus, although vision and touch differ greatly in terms of what we *experience*—a visual scene in one case and feelings on the skin in the other—they share many properties. When we study the skin senses in Chapter 14, we will see that these two senses have many physiological mechanisms in common.

Study Questions

Underlying Principles

Find examples of the following principles in this chapter:

- Receptive fields/Neural selectivity (266)
- Physiological connections with perception (259)

The Information for Perceiving Size

1. What is the visual angle? (246)
2. Why do we say that the perception of an object's size cannot be determined solely by the object's visual angle on the size of its image on the retina? (246)
3. What is size constancy? What does size constancy say about how we perceive an object's physical size? (246)
4. What are size cues? (247)
5. Describe Holway and Boring's experiment, including how the stimuli are arranged, the judgments made by the subjects, and the results. (247)
6. Under what conditions does size constancy hold, according to the results of the Holway and Boring experiment? (247)
7. What does our perception of the sizes of the sun and the moon demonstrate about size perception? (248)
8. Why do we perceive the sizes of objects viewed from an airplane as being very small? (250)
9. What is size-distance scaling? Know the equation and how to apply it. (250)
10. What is Emmert's law and how is it related to the equation for size-distance scaling? (250)

Visual Illusions

11. What is veridical perception? When is it most likely to occur? When is it most likely to break down? (250)
12. Describe the Müller-Lyer illusion and the misapplied size constancy explanation for this illusion. (251)
13. How does the dumbbell display in Figure 9.12 and the three-dimensional display in Figure 9.13 challenge the misapplied size constancy scaling explanation of the Müller-Lyer illusion? (253)
14. Describe the conflicting cues theory of the Müller-Lyer illusion. (254)
15. Describe the Ponzo illusion and how it has been explained. (254)
16. Describe the way people are perceived in the Ames room and how this perception is explained. (254)
17. Describe the moon illusion. (256)
18. What is the apparent distance explanation for the moon illusion? What evidence for this explanation was collected by Kaufman and Rock? (256)
19. Describe the parallel between the apparent distance explanation of the moon illusion and Emmert's law. (257)
20. Describe the angular size-contrast theory of the moon illusion. (257)
21. Which combination of factors are probably responsible for the moon illusion? (258)
22. What is the role of context in the illusions we have discussed? (258)

The Ecology of Perception

23. Describe the following adaptations of the eye: the fovea in the eagle and falcon; the area centralis in turtles; the wavelengths at which light-sensitive pigments absorb in fish; eye placement in animals with frontal eyes and lateral eyes; focusing by the *Anableps*. (259)
24. What are some examples of human perceptual adaptations in vision and taste? (260)
25. Who is most closely associated with the ecological approach to perception? (260)

26. What are four basic principles of the ecological approach? (261)
27. What is the optic array? (261)
28. What is invariant information? (262)
29. Describe the following three sources of invariant information: texture gradients, flow patterns, and the horizon ratio. What is an advantage of invariant information over traditional depth cues? (262)
30. What does Gibson mean when he says that perception is *direct*? (265)
31. Compare how Gibson's direct approach and the processing approach would describe size constancy. (265)
32. Compare how the direct approach and the processing approach describe how people are perceived in the Ames room. (266)
33. How have Gibson's ideas influenced present-day physiological researchers? (266)
34. How does a comparison of Gibson's approach to perception and the physiological approach illustrate how we can study perception at different levels of analysis? (267)

Something to Consider: Laboratory Research and Ecological Validity

35. What do the "laboratory control" and the "environmental stimuli" approaches each contribute to our understanding of perception? (267)

Across the Senses: Visual and Haptic Illusions

36. What is haptic perception? (268)
37. Describe the visual and haptic versions of the Bourdon illusion. (268)
38. What are some similarities between the visual and haptic versions of the Bourdon illusion and the Müller-Lyer illusion? What conclusions are suggested by the similarities? (268)

10

PERCEIVING MOVEMENT

CHAPTER CONTENTS

SOME QUESTIONS WE WILL CONSIDER

- How do films create motion from still pictures? (277)
- When scanning a room, the image of the room moves across the retina. Even though the image moves across the retina, why do we perceive the room and the objects in it as remaining stationary? (284)
- How do baseball outfielders position themselves at just the right place to catch a fly ball? (299)

How would it affect your life if you couldn't perceive movement? We can begin to answer this question by considering a patient who suffered from a condition called **motion agnosia,** in which the ability to perceive movement is impaired. This patient was admitted to the hospital after complaining of severe headaches, dizziness, and nausea (Zihl, von Cramon, & Mai, 1983; Zihl et al., 1991). A brain scan and other testing indicated damage to an area of the cerebral cortex around the border of the occipital and temporal lobes, in an area of the brain that roughly corresponds to the monkey's area MT, which is important for the perception of movement. The result of this damage, an inability to see movement in many situations, is described in the report of her case:

> The visual disorder complained of by the patient was a loss of movement vision in all three dimensions. She had difficulty, for example, in pouring tea or coffee into a cup because the fluid appeared to be frozen, like a glacier (see Figure 10.1). In addition, she could not stop pouring at the right time since she was unable to perceive the movement in the cup (or a pot) when the fluid rose. Furthermore the patient complained of difficulties in following a dialogue because she could not see the movements of the face, and, especially, the mouth of the speaker. In a room where more than two other people were walking she felt very insecure and unwell, and usually left the room immediately, because "people were suddenly here or there but I have not seen them moving." The patient experienced the same problem but to an even more marked extent in crowded streets or places, which she therefore avoided as much as possible. She could not cross the street because of her inability to judge

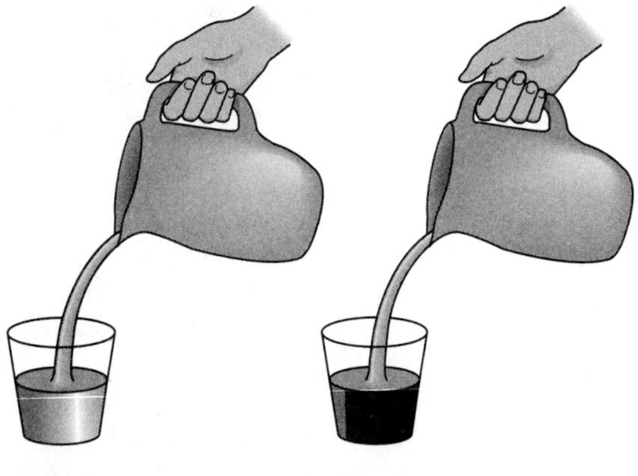

Figure 10.1
Zihl et al.'s patient, who had motion agnosia, perceived no change in the level of water being poured into a cup.

> the speed of a car, but she could identify the car itself without difficulty. "When I'm looking at the car [at] first, it seems far away. But then, when I want to cross the road, suddenly the car is very near." She gradually learned to "estimate" the distance of moving vehicles by means of the sound becoming louder. (Zihl et al., 1983, p. 315)

This patient's difficulty in perceiving movement was not simply a minor annoyance; she had difficulty doing things we take for granted and in some cases her safety was at risk. This woman's severe disability because of her lack of movement perception attests to the crucial role of movement perception in our day-to-day lives and to the fact that movement provides information that is necessary for normal and safe functioning.

The Information Provided by Movement

For many animals, movement provides information that is crucial for survival. By detecting the movement of potential prey, predators are more likely to catch that prey, and by detecting the movement of potential predators, the prey are more likely to survive. Thus, although some animals may have poor depth perception or rudimentary color vision, none lack the ability to perceive motion. Humans need movement perception to avoid cars and other moving objects in our environment and to take advantage of the following types of information provided by movement:

1. Movement provides information that attracts attention. If you are in a crowd and want to attract someone's attention, one of the best things you can do is wave your arms. Movement in our peripheral vision usually triggers an eye movement that brings the moving object's image onto our foveas so we can see it clearly.

2. Movement provides information about shape. The movement of an object provides information about the object's three-dimensional shape. We may not be sure of an unfamiliar object's shape if we see it from just one viewpoint, but if it moves relative to us or if we walk around it, its shape becomes obvious.

   One example of how movement can create an accurate perception of an object's three-dimensional shape is illustrated in Figure 7.2 (page 177). The rocks appear to be arranged in a circle when viewed from a particular position, but take on a totally different appearance when the observer moves to another position. Consider Figure 10.2a; we see what looks like two rectangles, one in front of the other. But moving to the position in Figure 10.2b, we see that the rectangle we thought was in front is actually in back, and that the rectangle we thought was in back isn't a rectangle at all. Thus, although what we see in Figure 10.2a looks reasonable, it is actually an ambiguous image that misleads us into the wrong conclusion about the shapes of the objects. By moving, we eliminate this ambiguity.

3. Movement provides information about figure and ground. To experience how movement can help us segregate figure from ground do the following demonstration.

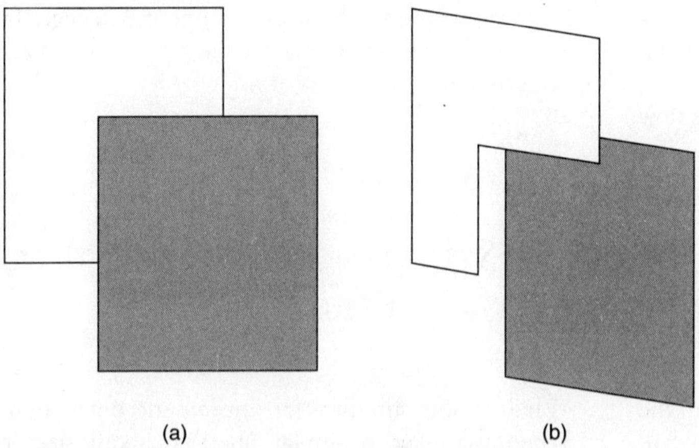

Figure 10.2
(a) At first this stimulus appears to be two rectangles, (b) but moving to another viewpoint reveals that the white shape is not a rectangle.

DEMONSTRATION
Perceiving a Camouflaged Bird

For this demonstration, you will need to prepare stimuli by Xeroxing the bird and the hatched-line pattern in Figure 10.3. Then cut out the bird and the hatched pattern so they are separated. Hold the picture of the bird up against a window during the day. Turn the copy of the hatched pattern over so the pattern is facing out the window (the white side of the paper should be facing you) and place it over the bird. If the window is adequately illuminated by the daylight you should be able to see the hatched pattern. Notice how the presence of the hatched pattern makes it more difficult to see the bird. Then slide the bird back and forth under the pattern and notice what happens to your perception fo the bird (from Regan, 1986). ●

Figure 10.3
The bird becomes camouflaged if the random lines are superimposed on the bird. When the bird is moved relative to the lines, it becomes visible, an example of how movement enhances the perception of form. (From Regan, 1986.)

The stationary bird is difficult to see when covered by the pattern, because the bird and the pattern are made up of similar lines. The way the bird becomes visible as soon as it begins moving shows how movement separates figure (the bird in this example) from ground (the pattern in this example).

4. Movement provides information that helps us interact with the environment. As we walk down the sidewalk or drive down the street, our movement causes objects to flow past us, and this flow provides information that keeps us on course and helps us avoid bumping into things. Our perception of movement is also crucial for doing things like hitting or catching a baseball, playing tennis, or playing a video game. In these situations, we both perceive an object's movement and coordinate our own movement with that of the moving object. A dramatic illustration of this coordination occurs every time a fly ball is hit toward the outfield in a baseball game. Even though the ball is traveling at over 100 miles per hour, the outfielder can run across the outfield and arrive at the place where the ball will land just when it gets there (McBeath et al., 1995; Todd, 1981).

In this chapter, we will explore the mechanisms responsible for our perception of movement and also consider a number of the ways that movement provides information that helps us perceive objects and make our way through the environment. We begin by looking at some of the ways movement perception has been studied.

Studying Movement Perception

What is the stimulus for movement perception? When we asked a similar question about size in Chapter 9 we at first suggested that our perception of an object's size might be determined by the size of the object's image on the retina. We soon discovered, however, that this can't be true, because as an object moves away from an observer, it is still perceived as having the same size even though the size of its image on the retina is becoming smaller. A similar situation occurs for movement perception. If an object moves across our field of view, and we keep our eyes station-

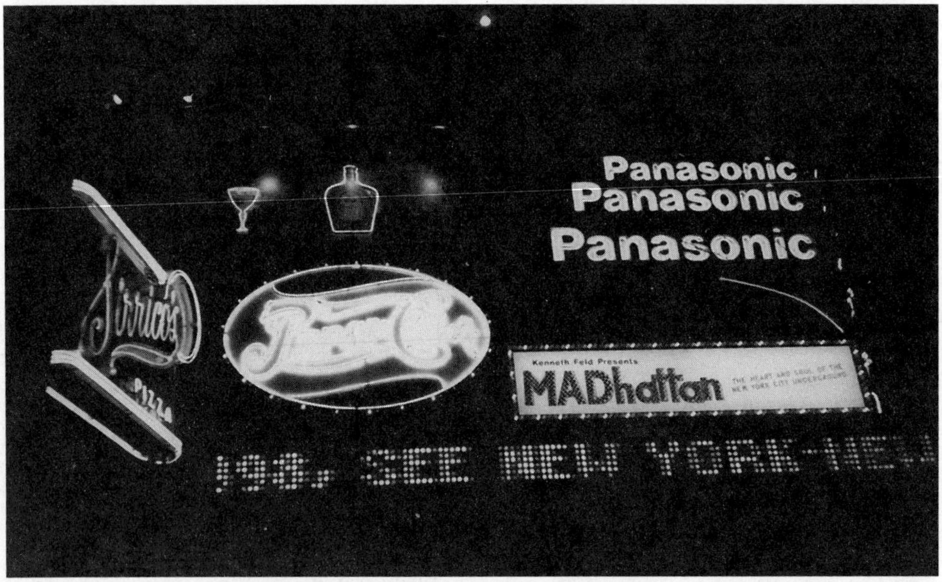

Figure 10.4
We see the message at the bottom of this sign move smoothly to the left, but this perception is created by stationary lights blinking on and off.

ary, then the object's image moves across the retina and we perceive the object as moving. However, there are a number of situations in which images move across the retina yet we perceive no movement, or the images remain stationary on the retina, yet we do perceive movement. Consider, for example, the following:

1. As you walk through the environment, the images of objects around you move across your retina and you see the objects in the environment move across your field of view. However, despite both the movement of the image across the retina and the perceived movement of the objects, you perceive the objects you are passing as stationary. That is, you realize you are moving, not the objects.
2. A series of lights on a sign flash one after another and you see a message moving across the electronic billboard (Figure 10.4). This is called **stroboscopic movement**, which is a type of **apparent movement.** Although the words *appear* to move, this perception is actually created by stationary lights that are flashing on and off. This is the kind of movement that creates motion from a sequence of still pictures in a film (Figure 10.5).
3. You look at a waterfall or a flowing stream and then look away and the ground appears to shift in the direction opposite to the movement of the waterfall. This example of apparent movement is called the **waterfall illusion**, or, more generally, a **movement aftereffect** (Figure 10.6).
4. You are sitting in your car at a stoplight and perceive your car rolling backward. You jam on the brakes, only to realize that your car is actually standing still and the car next to you is moving forward. This is called **induced movement,** because the movement of one object (usually the larger one) is *inducing* the perception of movement in another object. Examples of induced movement can be found in many places. For example, you are perceiving induced movement when you think you are perceiving a pigeon's head bobbing forward and backward as it walks

Figure 10.5
Eight frames from Edwin S. Porter's 1903 film The Great Train Robbery. This sequence lasts about 0.4 seconds when projected. The movement that results is an example of stroboscopic movement.

Figure 10.6
Looking at a waterfall, such as this one, can create an aftereffect of movement called the waterfall illusion, in which movement is perceived when the observer looks away from the waterfall. (Charles Mauzy/Corbis)

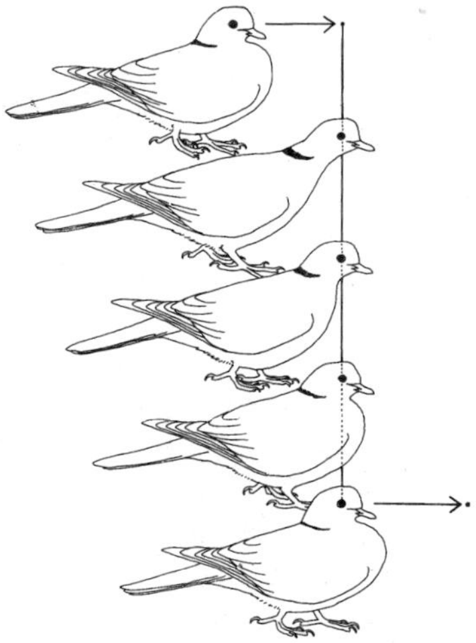

Figure 10.7
These pictures, taken from a film of a pigeon walking, show that a pigeon moves its head forward, then moves its body forward while keeping its head stationary. The phenomenon of induced movement causes the pigeon's head to appear to move backward, but it never actually does. (Figure courtesy of Mark Friedman; see Friedman, 1975.)

(it isn't—see Figure 10.7), or if it appears that the moon is racing through the clouds when it is the clouds that are moving and not the moon. You can demonstrate induced movement to yourself in the following demonstration.

DEMONSTRATION

Inducing Movement in a Dot

Stick a small dot of paper to the screen of your television set, as shown in Figure 10.8, and watch a program in which the television camera moves back and forth across a scene or follows a moving person or car (football, basketball, or hockey games are particularly good). These camera movements cause the entire television image to move across the screen, which will induce movement in your dot. ●

These examples should convince you that the study of movement perception is a complex undertaking. The first item on our list describes a situation in which movement is occurring across your field of view, but you perceive the moving stimuli as stationary, and items 2, 3, and 4 are **illusions of movement**—situations in which you perceive a stimulus as moving even though it is actually stationary. Even explaining our simplest case—a single object moving across your field of view—is more difficult than we might expect at first. In this chapter, we will not attempt to explain every situation in which movement perception occurs, but will focus on the basic principles of movement perception.

We begin our consideration of movement perception by going back in history to Exner's 1875 discovery that, when two electrical sparks are discharged next to each other, briefly separated in time, movement

Figure 10.8
As the camera follows these basketball players, the dot stuck to the center of the TV screen appears to move with them, an example of induced movement.

appears to occur across the space between them (Figure 10.9). This perception of movement across empty space, which corresponds to the examples of apparent movement in item 2 in our list, was put to practical use in the creation of the first motion pictures in the late 1800s.

Although by the early 1900s the motion picture industry was beginning to flourish, it wasn't until about 1912 that psychologists began to seriously study apparent movement. That was the year Max Wertheimer published his paper on apparent movement, which marked the beginnings of Gestalt psychology. Remember from Chapter 7 that Wertheimer used the existence of apparent movement in the empty space between two flashed stimuli to argue against the structuralists' idea that perceptions are created by the addition of sensations (see Figure 7.7). How, argued Wertheimer, can sensations explain a person's perception of movement through a space that is empty?

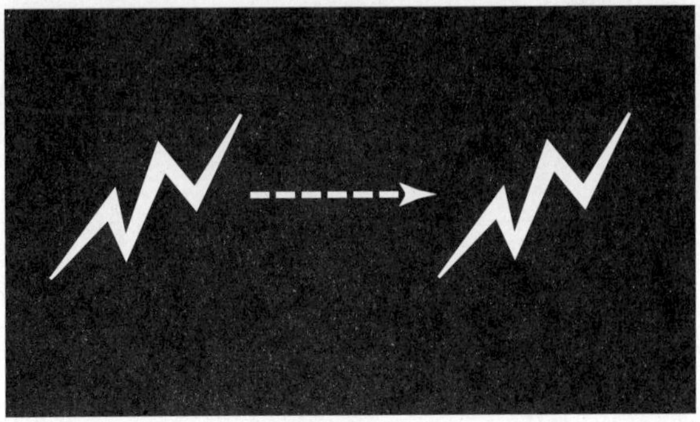

Figure 10.9
When Exner discharged two sparks, one after another, he perceived movement between them. This was one of the earliest scientific demonstrations of apparent movement.

Wertheimer and others began studying apparent movement psychophysically and found that the nature of the movement that occurs between two flashing lights depends on both the timing between the flashes and the distance between them. Figure 10.10 shows how our perception of two flashes of light changes as the time interval between the two flashes, the **interstimulus interval (ISI),** is increased (C. Graham, 1965). When the ISI is less than about 30 msec, the lights appear to flash on and off simultaneously. As the interval increases beyond 30 msec, partial movement is perceived between the two lights; and at a separation of about 60 msec, the lights appear to move continuously from one to the other. Finally, at time intervals above about 200–300 msec, no movement is perceived between the two lights; they appear successively, with first one flashing on and off, and then the other.

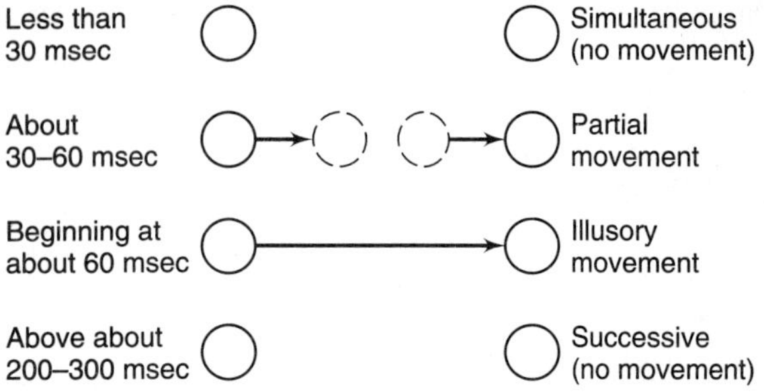

Figure 10.10
The perception of apparent movement depends on the time interval between the flashing of two lights. As the time interval is increased, the observer's perception goes through the stages shown.

The distance between the two lights also affects the perception of apparent movement. As the distance increases, either the time interval between the two flashes or the intensity of the flashes must be increased to maintain the same perception of movement.

D E M O N S T R A T I O N

A Demonstration of Apparent Movement

You can demonstrate some of the effects in Figure 10.10 to yourself, as follows: Place a dot on one side of a match as shown in Figure 10.11(a) and, slightly farther down, place a dot on the other side, as in (b). (This also works with a straw.) Then, with the match between your thumb and forefinger, as shown in (c), slowly begin to roll the match back and forth. Notice that at slow speeds (long ISIs) you see the dots one after another. Then, as you increase the speed, notice when movement occurs. At very high speeds (short ISIs), you will see both dots simultaneously, with no movement between them. ●

While some of the early movement researchers were studying the nature of apparent movement, oth-

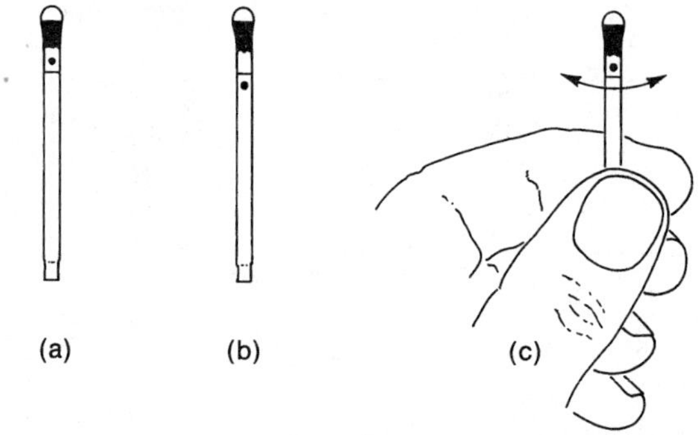

Figure 10.11
You can create apparent movement by drawing a dot on each side of a match (as shown in a and b), and by rolling the match back and forth between your fingers (as shown in c).

ers were focusing on **real movement**—the movement that occurs as an object actually moves through space. Early researchers showed that the threshold for perceiving movement in a homogeneous field is a velocity of about $\frac{1}{6}$ to $\frac{1}{3}$ of a degree of visual angle per second (Aubert, 1886). This means that you would just barely perceive the movement of the spot in Figure 10.12a if, when you view it from a distance of 1 foot, it takes about 14 seconds to travel from A to B. If, however, we add vertical lines to the space between A and B, as in Figure 10.12b, you would be able to perceive the spot's movement even at velocities as low as 1/60 of a degree of visual angle per second (which translates into a travel time of 280 seconds from A to B when Figure 10.12b is viewed from a distance of 1 foot). These results show that our perception of movement depends both on the velocity of the moving stimulus and on its surroundings.

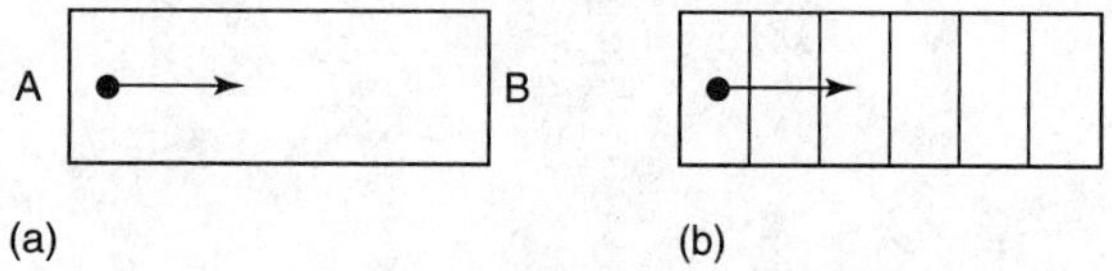

Figure 10.12
The context in which movement occurs, affects movement perception. It is easier to detect movement in (b) than in (a) because of the structure provided by the vertical lines in (b).

For many years, researchers continued to treat the apparent movement created by flashing lights and the real movement created by actual movement through space as if they were separate phenomena, governed by different mechanisms. However, today's researchers study both types of movement together and concentrate on discovering general mechanisms that apply to both real and apparent movement. In this chapter, we will follow this approach as we look for general mechanisms of movement perception. We begin with a fairly simple situation—a single spot or bar moving across the retina—and then introduce complexities like the ones we noted on page 277 We start by showing how neural movement detectors like the ones we described in Chapters 3 and 4 signal the direction of movement of a moving spot or bar stimulus.

Detecting Movement: Neural Firing and Environmental Information

How we detect movement has been studied physiologically by recording from neurons in the cortex that respond to movement, and psychophysically, by noting the environmental information associated with movement perception. We begin by considering the physiological research.

Directionally Selective Neurons in Movement Perception

Most of the neurons in the cortex respond best to a stimulus moving in a particular direction. The earliest place in the visual system in which these directionally selective neurons are found is the striate cortex. We begin by asking whether these directionally selective neurons actually play a role in movement perception. We can answer this question in much the same way that we answered a similar question in Chapter 8 about binocular depth cells. To determine whether binocular depth cells play a role in depth perception, we looked at the results of monocular rearing experiments in which kittens were allowed to see out of just one eye at a time. Since this monocular rearing eliminated the kittens' binocular depth cells and *also* eliminated their ability to use binocular disparity to see depth, we concluded that these neurons *are* needed to create the perception of depth from disparity.

Tatiana Pasternak (1990) used a similar tactic to determine whether directionally selective neurons are responsible for a cat's ability to perceive the direction of movement. To eliminate directionally selective neurons from a cat's cortex, she reared kittens in a dark room that was illuminated by light that constantly flickered eight times per second so that their vision consisted entirely of a series of still "snapshots" of their environment. Rearing the cats in this environment had two effects: (1) it eliminated over 90 percent of directionally selective neurons in the striate cortex, and (2) it almost totally eliminated the cats' ability to detect the *direction* of a moving stimulus, even though they were still able to detect the *presence* of the moving stimulus. Thus, directionally selective neurons in the striate cortex appear to be necessary for the perception of the direction of movement.

A Neural Mechanism for Directional Selectivity

When an image moves across the retina, it stimulates a series of receptors, one after the other. Werner Reichardt (1961) proposed the simple circuit in Figure 10.13 that results in a neuron that responds to movement in only one direction. To understand how this circuit works, let's look at what happens as we stimulate each receptor in turn, beginning with receptor A and moving toward the right. Receptor A synapses with G, so stimulation of A excites G, which then sends an inhibitory signal to H. (The X in Figure 10.14a indicates that H is being inhibited.) While this is occurring, the stimulus moves to receptor B

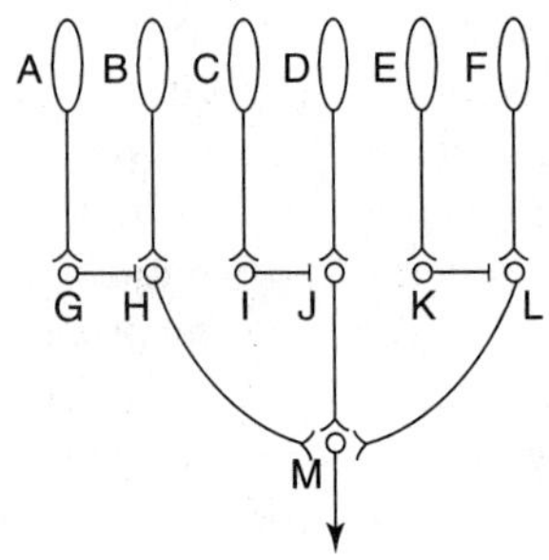

Figure 10.13
A neural circuit in which a neuron (M) responds to the movement of a stimulus across the receptors from right to left. The neuron does not, however, respond to movement from left to right.

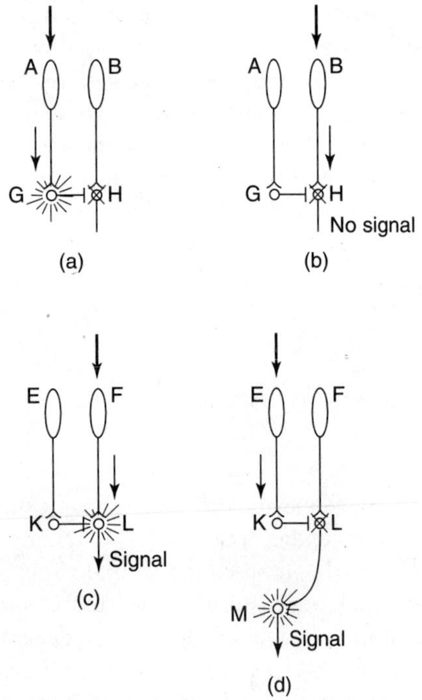

Figure 10.14
What happens as a light moves across the receptors of Figure 10.13. (a and b) Movement of a light from left to right. (c and d) movement from right to left.

and causes it to respond and to send an excitatory signal to H, but since H has been inhibited by G, it does not fire (Figure 10.14b). Thus, the signals from receptors A and B do not get past H and therefore never reach M, the neuron at the end of the circuit. This process is repeated as the stimulus moves across the remaining receptors. The net result is that M does not respond.

The outcome is different, however, if we begin at receptor F and move the stimulus to the left. Receptor F sends a signal to L, which causes it to fire (Figure 10.14c). The stimulus then moves to receptor E, which causes K to send inhibition to L. This inhibition, however, arrives too late. L has already fired and has stimulated M (Figure 10.14d). This process is repeated as the stimulus moves across the remaining receptors. The net result is that M fires. Thus, neuron M fires to movement to the left but does not fire to movement to the right.

Figure 10.15 is a tuning curve that shows how a complex cell in the cat's cortex responds to different directions of movement. The cell responds best to a moving bar oriented at about +20 degrees and responds less well to orientations on either side of 20 degrees. Based on this tuning curve, we might be tempted to propose that the firing of this neuron provides all the information necessary to indicate movement at +20 degrees. But if we remember the discussion of sensory coding in Chapter 3, we know that if the cell's firing rate is also affected by other properties, such as light intensity, the firing of a single neuron can't signal a specific property such as the direction of movement. (Review pages 95 to 96 and Figure 3.35 to refamiliarize yourself with the reasoning behind this conclusion.) Thus, knowing the rate at which this cell was firing does not tell us the direction of the bar's movement.

The brain probably deals with this problem by using distributed coding that takes into account the overall pattern of responses from a number of cells. Thus, as our +20-degree bar moves across the retina, it causes large bursts of firing in cells that prefer this orientation and smaller bursts in cells that prefer other orientations. The resulting pattern of response, which holds over a wide range of intensities, signals the bar's direction of movement.

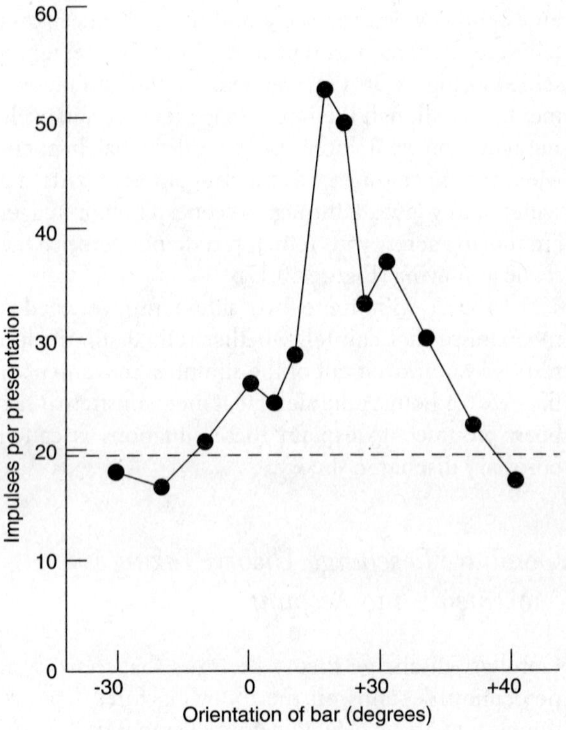

Figure 10.15
A directional tuning curve showing the relationship between the orientation of a moving bar and the response of a complex cell in the cat's cortex. The cell responds best when the bar is oriented at about 15 to 20 degrees. The dashed line indicates the rate of spontaneous firing. (Blakemore & Tobin, 1972)

The idea that movement perception is based on the pattern of firing of many directionally selective neurons in the striate cortex is a first step toward understanding the neural basis of motion perception. However, our perception of movement is probably determined not by activity in the striate cortex, but by activity further upstream, in the extrastriate cortex, which we will discuss next.

Neural Firing and Judging the Direction of Movement

Recent research on the neural basis of motion perception has focused on extrastriate areas, especially the medial temporal (MT) area. In Chapter 4 we noted that 90 percent of neurons in area MT are directionally selective and that lesioning area MT impairs a monkey's ability to detect the direction of movement, measured behaviorally.

We will now consider further evidence of a link between MT neurons and movement perception. William Newsome, Kenneth Britten, and Anthony Movshon (1989) demonstrated a connection between the firing of MT neurons and a monkey's ability to judge the direction of movement by presenting a moving-dot display like the one in Figure 10.16 to the receptive fields of neurons in the MT cortex. These displays are like the ones described in Chapter 4 in which the correlation between the dots' directions of movement can be varied from completely random

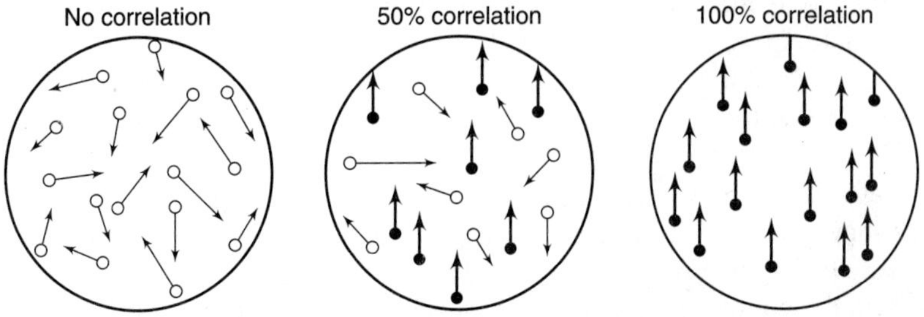

Figure 10.16
Moving-dot displays used by Newsome, Britten, and Movshon. These pictures represent moving-dot displays that were created by a computer. Each dot survives for a brief interval (20–30 microseconds), after which it disappears and is replaced by another randomly placed dot.

(as in Figure 10.16a) to 100 percent correlated (as in Figure 10.16c).

While the monkey was judging the direction in which the dots were moving, Newsome and his coworkers monitored the firing of an MT neuron stimulated by the moving-dot pattern. They found that as the dots' correlation increased, two things happened: (1) the MT neurons fired more rapidly and (2) the monkey judged the direction of movement more accurately. In fact, the firing of the MT neurons and the monkey's behavior were so closely related that the researchers could predict one from the other. For example, when the dots' correlation was 0.8 percent, the MT neuron response did not differ appreciably from the baseline firing rate on each trial, and the monkey judged the direction of movement with only chance accuracy. But at a correlation of 12.8 percent, the MT neurons always fired faster than their baseline rates, and the monkey judged the direction of movement correctly on virtually every trial.

This result and the results of the experiments we described in Chapter 4 support the idea that MT neurons are responsible for the perception of movement. However, the real significance of these results is that the connection between neural firing and the monkey's behavior is so close that it is possible to predict the monkey's ability to judge the direction of movement by monitoring the firing of only a few MT neurons. This means that although it may be correct to describe the neural code for the direction of movement as *distributed coding* (the information for direction is distributed over a number of neurons), only a small number of neurons are required. Since the firing of only a few neurons contains enough information to accurately signal the direction of movement, we can say that the code for movement perception begins to approach specificity coding at this level of the visual system (Britten et al., 1993; Movshon & Newsome, 1992; Newsome et al., 1995).

So far, the brain's detection of movement seems fairly straightforward: When a stimulus moves across the retina, movement detectors in the striate and extrastriate cortex that are sensitive to different directions of movement fire. But what happens if the eye moves, for example, when you see a bird flying overhead and follow its flight path with your eyes? In this case, represented in Figure 10.17a, you perceive the bird's movement, even though the bird's image remains relatively stationary on your fovea. Or consider what happens when you move your eyes to look at different parts of a scene or as you walk through a scene. Though images are moving across your retina, you do not perceive the scene as moving (Figure 10.17b).

To deal with these two situations, we need a mechanism that can tell whether retinal stimulation results from movement of the stimulus, movement of the eyes, or both. A physiological mechanism that has been proposed to explain these situations is called **corollary discharge theory.**

Corollary Discharge Theory: Taking Eye Movements into Account

Corollary discharge theory proposes that movement perception depends on the following three types of signals that are associated with movement of the eyes or images across the eyes: (1) A **motor signal** (MS), which is sent to the eye muscles when the observer moves or tries to move her eyes; (2) a **corollary discharge signal** (CDS), which is a copy of the motor

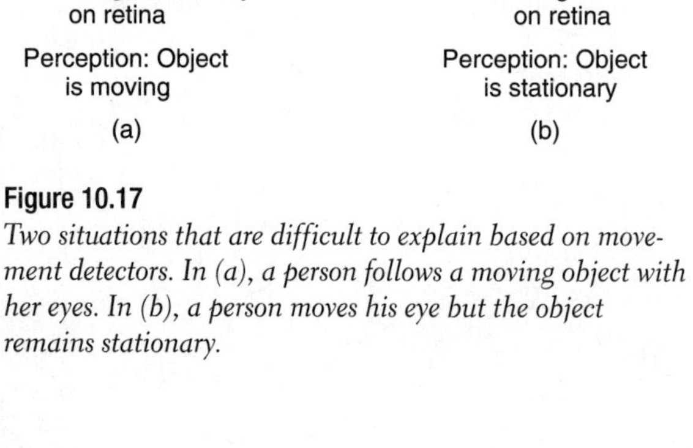

Figure 10.17
Two situations that are difficult to explain based on movement detectors. In (a), a person follows a moving object with her eyes. In (b), a person moves his eye but the object remains stationary.

signal; and (3) an **image movement signal** (IMS), which occurs when an image stimulates the receptors as it moves across the retina (Figure 10.18) (Gyr, 1972; Teuber, 1960; von Holst, 1954).

According to corollary discharge theory, our perception of movement is determined by whether the corollary discharge signal, the image movement signal, or both reach a structure called the **comparator,** which receives inputs from neurons that carry both of these signals. Movement is perceived when the comparator receives either the image movement signal or the corollary discharge signal separately (Figure 10.19a, b). However, when both signals reach the comparator simultaneously they cancel each other and movement is not perceived (Figure 10.19c).

The corollary discharge model has been tested behaviorally by determining whether movement perception does, in fact, occur when only the corollary discharge reaches the comparator. This has been accomplished in the following four ways, three of which you can experience for yourself:

1. By observing an afterimage as you move your eyes in a dark room (Figure 10.20a).

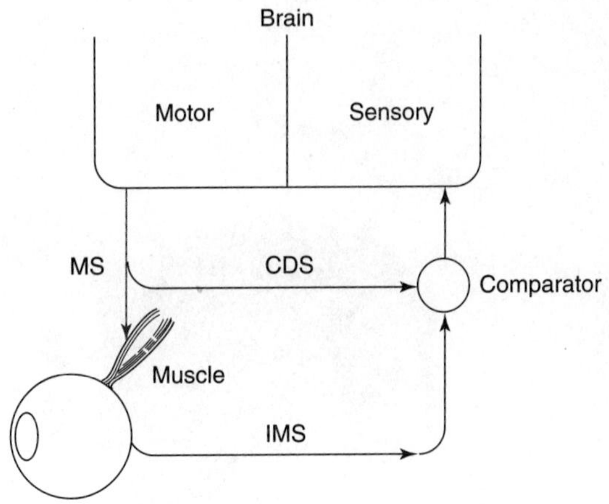

Figure 10.18
Diagram of the corollary discharge model. The motor area, sends the motor signal (MS) to move the eyes to the eye muscles, and sends the corollary discharge signal (CDS) to a structure called the comparator. Movement of a stimulus across the retina generates an image movement signal (IMS), which also goes to the comparator. The comparator sends its output to the visual cortex. (Adapted from Teuber, 1960.)

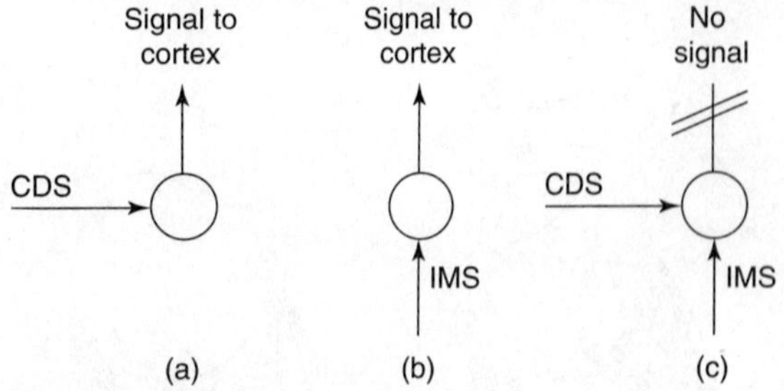

Figure 10.19
How inputs to the comparator (circle) affect movement perception. (a) Receiving the corollary discharge signal alone causes the comparator to send a movement signal to the cortex; (b) Receiving the image movement signal alone also causes the comparator to send a movement signal to the cortex; (c) When both the corollary discharge signal and the image movement signal reach the comparator at the same time, no movement signal is sent to the cortex.

DEMONSTRATION

Eliminating the Image Movement Signal with an Afterimage

Illuminate the circle in Figure 9.8 with your desk lamp and look at it for about 60 seconds. Then, go into your closet (or a completely dark room) and observe what happens to the circle's afterimage (blink to make it come back if it fades) as you look around. Notice that the afterimage moves in synchrony with your eye movements. ●

Why does the afterimage appear to move when you move your eyes? The answer cannot be that an image is moving across your retina, because the circle's image always remains at the same place on the

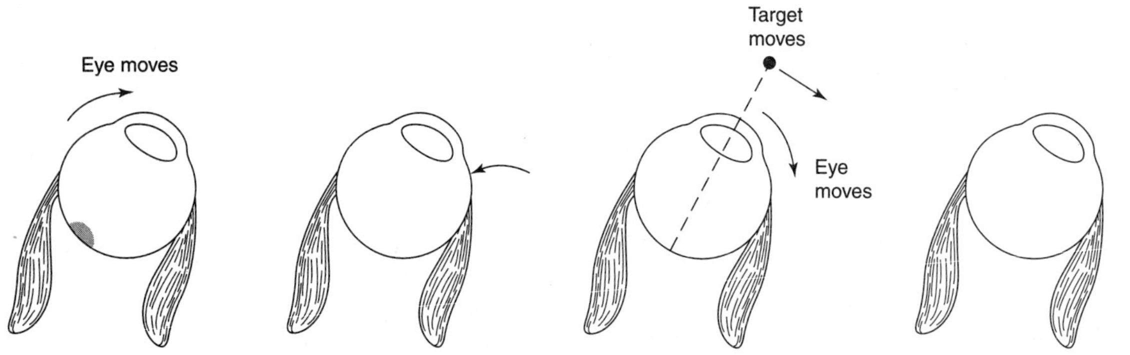

Figure 10.20

Voluntary movement of our eyes usually generates both a corollary discharge (because we send a signal to our eye muscles) and an image movement signal (because movement of the eyes usually causes movement of an image across the retina). There are, however, ways to create a corollary discharge without generating an image movement signal. In all four examples shown in the figure, a signal is sent to the eye muscles, and a corollary discharge is generated. No image movement signal is generated, because (a) staring at a spot for about 30 seconds bleaches a patch of retina, generating an afterimage, and the bleached spot stays at the same place on the retina as the eye moves; (b) when we push on the eyeball, we can send signals to the muscles to hold the eye steady; (c) the eye moves to track a moving object, so the object's image remains stationary on the retina; and (d) the eye is paralyzed so that the signal sent to the muscle cannot cause the eye to move.

retina. Without movement of the stimulus across the retina, there is no image movement signal. However, a corollary discharge signal accompanies the motor signals sent to your eye muscles. Thus, only the corollary discharge reaches the comparator, and you see the afterimage move.

2. By pushing on your eyeball while keeping your eye steady (Figure 10.20b).

D E M O N S T R A T I O N

Seeing Movement by Pushing on Your Eyeball

While looking steadily at one point, *gently* push back and forth on the side of your eyelid, as shown in Figure 10.21. As you do this, you will see the scene move. ●

Figure 10.21

Why is this man smiling? Because every time he pushes on his eyeball he sees the world jiggle.

Why do you see movement when you push on your eyeball? According to Lawrence Stark and Bruce Bridgeman (1983), when you push on your eyeball while keeping your eye fixed on a particular point, your eyes remain stationary because your eye muscles are pushing against the force of the finger so you can maintain steady fixation on the point. The motor signal sent to the eye muscles to hold the eye in place creates a corollary discharge, which occurs alone, since there is no **sensory movement signal.** We, therefore, see the scene move (also see Bridgeman & Stark, 1991; Ilg, Bridgeman, & Hoffmann, 1989).

3. By following a moving object such as a flying bird with your eyes (Figure 10.20c).

In this situation the eyes move to follow the bird, so the bird's image remains stationary on the observer's retina and there is no image movement signal. But since the eyes are moving, a corollary discharge occurs an the observer perceives the bird's movement. As to the rest of the scene, its image sweeps across the observer's retina as she tracks the bird's flight. This moving image generates an image movement signal for the scene, which reaches the comparator along with the corollary discharge. Since both signals reach the comparator together, the observer perceives the rest of the scene as stationary.

4. By paralyzing an observer's eye muscles and having the observer try to move his eyes.

In this situation, when the observer tries to move his eyes, a motor signal is sent to the eye muscles and causes a corollary discharge. But the paralyzed eye remains stationary, so there is no image movement signal. Since only the corollary discharge reaches the comparator, movement should be perceived. John Stevens (Stevens et al., 1976) showed that this is what occurs by volunteering to be temporarily immobilized by a paralytic drug. When he tried to move his eyes, the scene in front of him appeared to jump to a new position, just as predicted by the corollary discharge model. (Also see Matin et al., 1982, for another paralysis experiment.)

These four behavioral demonstrations support the central idea proposed by corollary discharge theory that there is a signal (the corollary discharge) that indicates when the observer moves, or tries to move, his or her eyes. When the theory was first proposed, there was little physiological evidence to support it, but now there is a great deal of research that supports the theory. For example, Claudio Galletti, Paolo Battaglini, and P. Fattori (1990) found neurons in area V3 of the monkey cortex (in the dorsal stream; see Figure 4.4) that respond strongly when the monkey holds its eyes stationary and a bar is swept across the cell's receptive field. However, this cell does not respond when the bar is held stationary and the monkey moves its eyes so the cell's receptive field sweeps across the bar (Figure 10.22). Galletti called this neuron a **real movement**

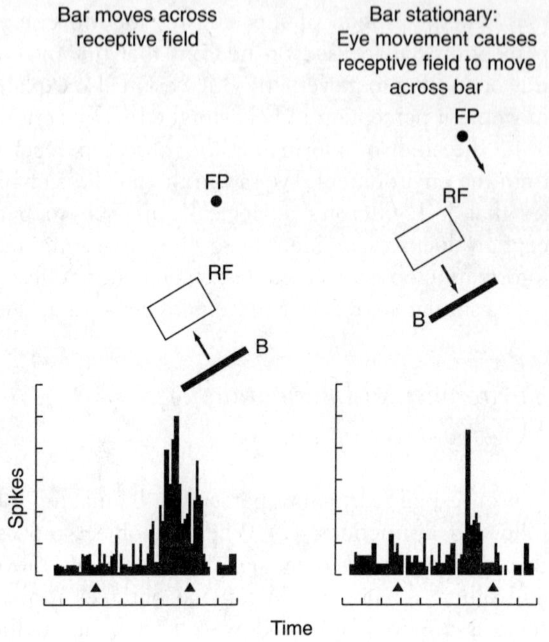

Figure 10.22
(a) When the monkey holds its eyes steady by looking at the fixation point (FP) and the bar stimulus (B) is swept across the receptive field (RF), this neuron responds briskly. (b) When the monkey moves its eyes by following the moving fixation point (FP), the receptive field sweeps across the bar stimulus. Although this creates the same effect on the retina as in (a), the neuron responds poorly. Apparently this real-movement neuron is taking the movement of the eyes into account in (b). (Adapted from Galletti, Battaglini, & Fattori, 1990.)

neuron because it responds only when the stimulus moves and doesn't respond when the eye moves, even though the stimulus on the retina is the same in both situations. (Also see Battaglini, Galletti, & Fattori, 1996; Robinson & Wurtz, 1976.)

These real movement neurons must be receiving information like the corollary discharge, which tells the neuron when the eye is moving. Corollary discharge theory is a good example of a theory that was originally based on psychophysical results and which later gained physiological support. Although neurons such as the real movement neurons behave in the way corollary discharge theory predicts, researchers have still not discovered the corollary discharge signal itself, where it originates, or where the hypothetical comparator might be.

Our description of mechanisms for movement perception has focused on neurons that fire in one way or another to movement. But we can also explain movement perception in behavioral terms by considering the kinds of information that observers receive from the environment. We saw in the previous chapter that J. J. Gibson's ecological approach to perception focuses on identifying the environmental information observers use for size perception. Gibson took a similar approach to movement perception.

Figure 10.23
Local movement: A person moving from left to right past a stationary observer who is looking at a spot straight ahead. In this situation, the person moves across the observer's field of view, as indicated by the arrows, but the background remains stationary.

Environmental Information for Movement Perception

Gibson explained motion perception by making the following distinctions: (1) When an object moves, there is a **local movement signal**—some things move and others do not. (2) When the observer moves, there is a **global optical flow**—all elements in the scene move.

A situation in which a local movement signal occurs is shown in Figure 10.23, in which the observer is looking straight ahead as a person walks by. This is the case most easily handled by movement detectors, since the image of the walking person moves across the retina. However, Gibson explains our perception of movement in this situation by simply pointing out that a local movement signal occurs as the person's movement covers and uncovers the stationary background. The important thing to remember about this explanation is that the *signal* that Gibson refers to comes not from the firing of a physiological detector, but from information that is contained in the environment.

A local movement signal also occurs when the observer moves her eyes to follow the person as he walks by (Figure 10.24). Even though the image of the walking person remains stationary on the observer's retina, the person's image still covers and uncovers the stationary background. Thus, in this example, like the previous one, the crucial information for movement perception is the local motion of the person relative to the background.

A situation in which global optical flow occurs is when the observer walks past the person, who is stationary (Figure 10.25). When the whole scene—both the stationary person and the background—sweeps across the observer's retina, this provides information that the observer is moving, and not the stationary person or the background.

Gibson's explanations work in an environment in which the background is visible, but they don't explain

Figure 10.24
Local movement: A person moves from left to right, as in Figure 10.23, but the observer follows the person with her eyes. The image of the moving person remains stationary on the observer's retina, while the background flows across the retina from right to left, as indicated by the arrows.

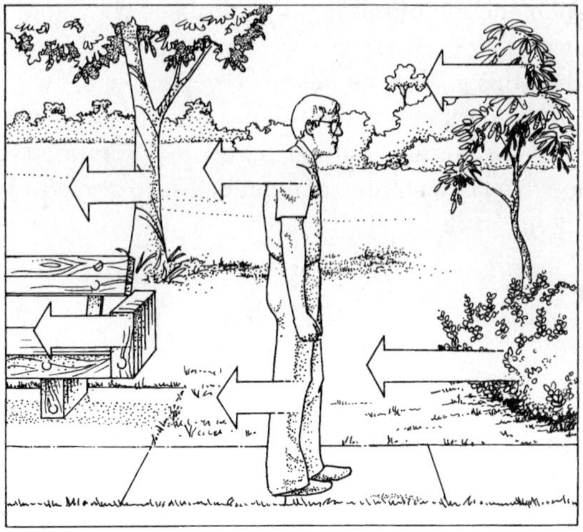

Figure 10.25
Global optical flow: The observer moves from left to right past a stationary person, and the images of the stationary person and the background flow across the observer's field of view, as indicated by the arrows.

how we perceive movement when the background is not visible, as occurs when a spot of light is seen in a dark room or when an object is seen against a completely textureless background. However, Gibson maintained that it was not necessary to explain artificial situations such as isolated spots of light moving in dark perception laboratories. His main concern was with the kind of stimulation described above, which is more typical of what we encounter in the environment.

In this section, we have considered two ways to explain how we perceive a stimulus move: (1) the physiological approach, which focuses on how the firing of neurons signals movement; and (2) the behavioral approach, which focuses on how environmental stimulation signals movement. But our perception of movement often depends on more than just the moving stimulus. Often the context within which the stimulus moves affects our perception of its movement. We now consider some examples of how this context affects movement perception.

The Effect of Context on Movement Perception

We can show how the arrangement of moving objects influences our perception in a number of ways.

A Framework Effect

The framework within which an object moves can affect how we perceive the direction of movement. For example, Figure 10.26a shows how a white dot moves back and forth along a diagonal path. When the dot moves alone, we perceive its movement as being diagonal. But when two black dots move horizontally, keeping aligned with the white dot's movement, as shown in Figure 10.26b, the white dot appears to bounce back and forth between the black dots. As the Gestalt psychologists point out, sometimes the perception of an overall pattern is different from the sum

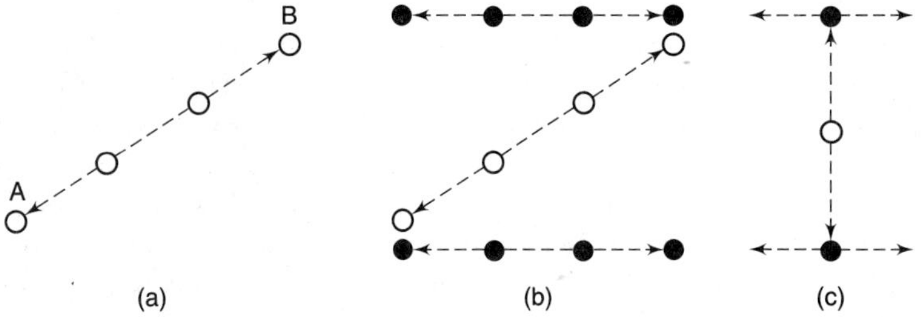

Figure 10.26
(a) The white dot moves back and forth on a diagonal path between A and B. (b) Two black dots are added that move horizontally to follow the white dot's movement. (c) The resulting perception: The white dot appears to bounce up and down between the moving black dots. Adding the black dots eliminates our perception of the white dot's diagonal motion.

of its parts. In this case, the presence of the black dots causes us to ignore the white dot's diagonal movement and to restructure our perception so that we see its movement relative to the black dots.

A Sequence Effect

When the two crosses in Figure 10.27a are presented rapidly, one after the other, subjects perceive the crosses as rotating either clockwise or counterclockwise. If, however, an initial cross is added to the series, as in Figure 10.27b, subjects perceive the movement as clockwise (Ramachandran & Anstis, 1986). This perception reflects the way movement usually occurs in the environment. Once movement starts in one direction it usually continues in that direction. Notice that this is similar to the Gestalt law of good continuation described in Chapter 7 for static stimuli, which stated that lines tend to be perceived as following the smoothest path.

Movement of the Human Form: Violating the Shortest-Path Constraint

When one stimulus is rapidly alternated with another, apparent movement occurs from one to the other. When this movement occurs, it generally follows the **shortest-path constraint**—movement tends to occur along the shortest path between two stimuli, even though a large number of other paths are also possible (Figure 10.28).

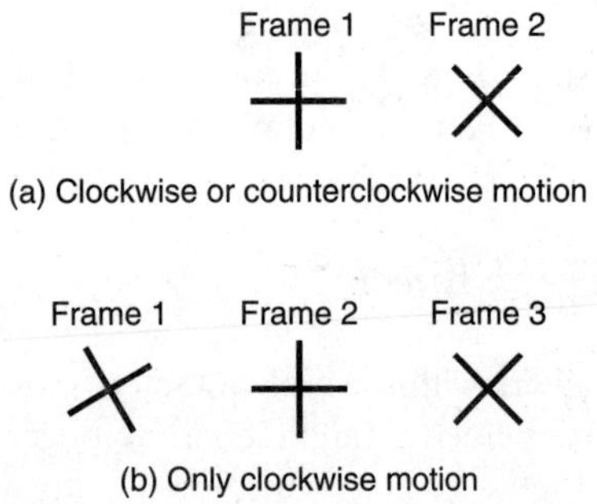

Figure 10.27
(a) Alternating an upright cross and a tilted one creates an ambiguous stimulus in which the rotation can be perceived as either clockwise or counterclockwise. (b) Adding the tilted cross on the left starts a clockwise movement, so that when the third cross is flashed, the movement is perceived as continuing in that direction. Note that the two stimuli in (a) and the final two in (b) are identical.

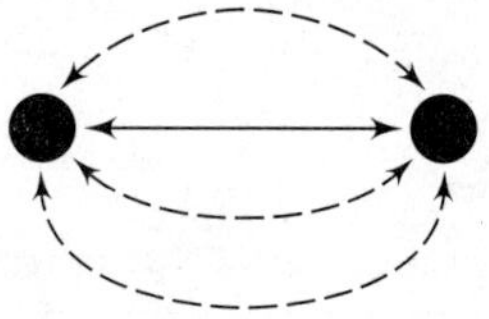

Figure 10.28
According to the shortest-path constraint, the apparent movement between the two rapidly alternating dots should occur along the shortest pathway (solid arrows) even though many other pathways are possible (dashed arrows).

But what happens if observers are shown two meaningful stimuli that would normally violate this constraint? An example of such a situation, shown in Figure 10.29, is two pictures of the same person with her right hand in different positions. Maggie Shiffrar and Jennifer Freyd (1990, 1993) asked the following question: When these pictures are alternated rapidly will observers perceive the woman's hand as moving through her left arm (this would follow the shortest-path constraint) or will they perceive her hand as moving around her arm (this would violate the shortest path constraint)?

The answer to this question depends on the length of time between the onset of the first and second pictures, called *stimulus onset asynchrony* (SOA). At SOAs below about 200 msec, the subjects' perceptions follow the shortest-path constraint. However, at SOAs longer than 200 msec, the subjects perceive movement along the longer path around the woman's arm, which violates the shortest-path constraint. These results are interesting for two reasons: (1) They show that the visual system needs time to process information in order to perceive the movement of complex meaningful stimuli (although 200 msec may seem like a short period of time, it is a long processing time by the nervous system's standards); (2) They suggest that there may be something special about the *meaning* of the stimulus—in this case, the human body—that influences the way movement is perceived. To test this idea, Shiffrar and coworkers showed that when objects such as boards are used as stimuli instead of humans, movement along the longer path doesn't increase with increasing SOA, as it does for pictures of humans (Chatterjee, Freyd, & Shiffrar, 1996).

Shiffrar (1994) suggests that these results reflect the visual system's separation into the ventral ("what") and the dorsal ("how" or "where") pathways that we described in Chapter 4. For subjects to perceive the biologically valid movement of the person's hand around (rather than through) her arm, they need to perceive both *what* the stimulus is and *where* it is located. This need to combine information, indicating both "what" and "where" a stimulus is, plus the long times involved, led Shiffrar to suggest that the perception of biological movement observed in her experiments occurs in a structure where information from the dorsal and ventral streams meet. One possible

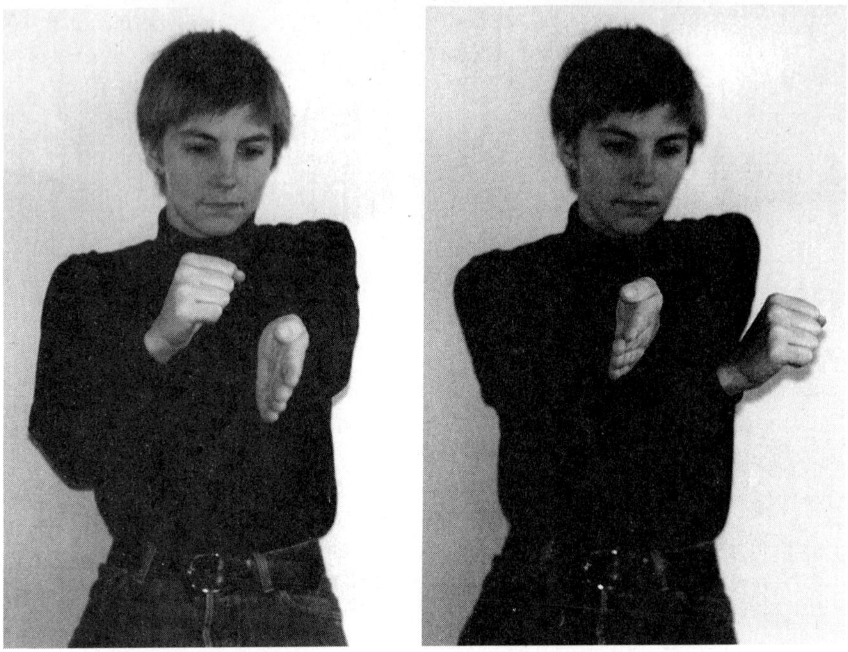

Figure 10.29
Photographs used to create the stimulus in the Shiffrar and Freyd (1990) experiment. When these pictures are alternated rapidly, the hand making a fist appears to move from one position to the other. The hand appears to go through the arm at short SOAs and around the arm at long SOAs. (Photographs courtesy of Maggie Shiffrar.)

candidate is the neurons in the superior temporal sulcus, which respond to images of human movement (Figure 10.30).

The research we have been describing so far in this chapter has focused on how we *perceive* movement. But other research on movement perception has been concerned with what movement tells us about our environment. We will now see that movement contributes to our perception of form and to our ability to interact with our environment.

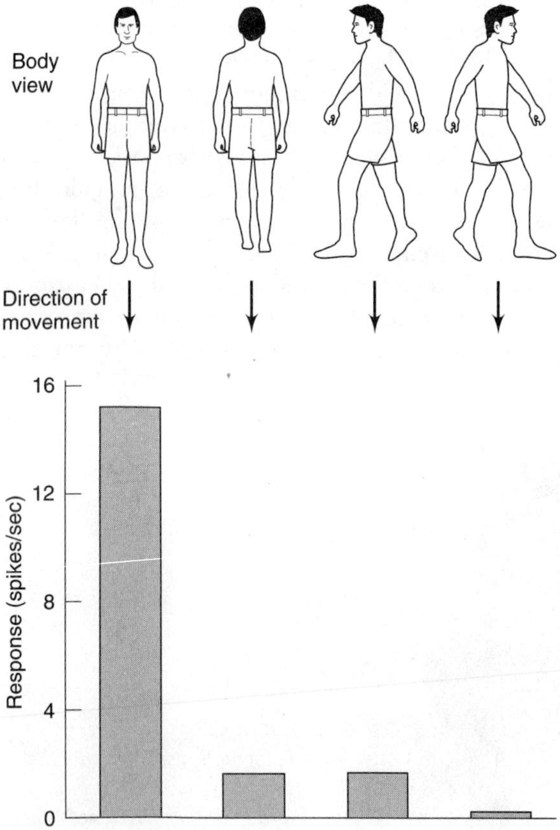

Figure 10.30
The response of a neuron in the macaque monkey's superior temporal sulcus that responded best to a frontal view of a person moving downward. Other views of the body generated little response even though they were moving in the same direction. (Adapted from Perrett et al., 1990.)

Movement Creates Structure

Movement can influence the forms we see and the way we perceptually organize elements in our environment. An example of how movement can influence our perception of form is a phenomenon called the *kinetic depth effect,* which creates three-dimensional structure from a moving shadow.

The Kinetic Depth Effect: Movement Creates Form Perception

In the **kinetic depth effect,** the three-dimensional structure of a stimulus is perceived from a moving two-dimensional image. Hans Wallach and D. N. O'Connell (1953) demonstrated this effect by casting a shadow of a cube on a transparent screen (Figure 10.31). When the shadow is stationary it looks flat, but when the cube is rotated, as indicated by the arrow, the shadow takes on a three-dimensional appearance, even though it is seen on a two-dimensional surface. Movement therefore creates the perception of three-dimensional structure on a two-dimensional surface.

DEMONSTRATION

The Kinetic Depth Effect with Pipe Cleaners

You can demonstrate the kinetic depth effect by bending a pipe cleaner so that it reproduces sides a, b, c, and d of the shape in Figure 10.31. Then, cast a shadow of the pipe cleaner on a piece of paper, as shown in Figure 10.32, and while viewing the shadow from the other side of the paper, rotate the pipe cleaner. The result should be a more three-dimensional perception than when the shadow was stationary. ●

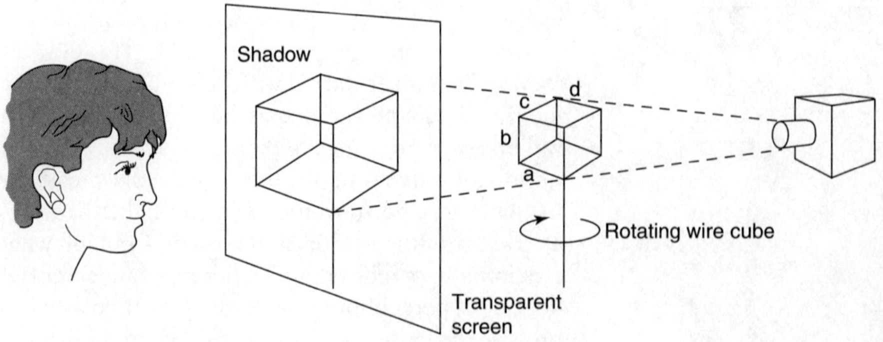

Figure 10.31
Setup similar to the one used by Wallach and O'Connell (1953) to demonstrate the kinetic depth effect.

In addition to creating three-dimensional structure from a two-dimensional image, as in the kinetic depth effect, movement also helps us perceptually organize elements in our environment into larger stimuli. One example of this is provided by how we perceive **biological motion**—the motion that occurs when humans or animals move.

Biological Motion: Movement Creates Perceptual Grouping

To appreciate the complexity of biological motions imagine what you would see if you placed small lights on a person's body, as in Figure 10.33, and viewed these lights as the person walked in a dark

Figure 10.32
Shadow-casting by a bent pipe cleaner. To achieve a sharp shadow, position the pipe cleaner about 2 feet from your desk lamp. (If it is too close to the lamp, the shadow will be fuzzy.) To perceive the kinetic depth effect, rotate the pipe cleaner between your fingers while observing the shadow from the other side of the paper.

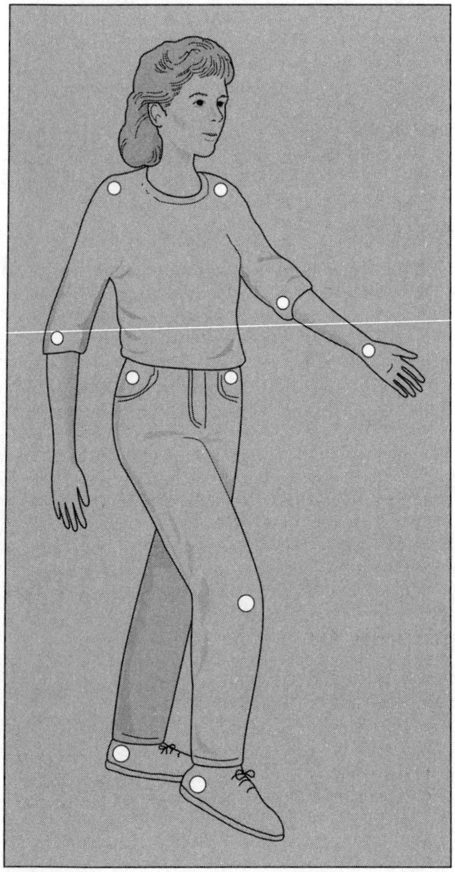

Figure 10.33
A person wearing lights for a biological motion experiment. In the actual experiment, the room is totally dark, and only the lights can be seen.

room. With the arms and legs swinging back and forth at the shoulders, elbows, hips, and knees, and the feet moving in flattened arcs, first one leaving the ground and touching down then the other, there is nothing simple about the movement of the lights.

Gunnar Johansson's (1975) pioneering studies of biological movement used this stimulus, which he called "point light walkers." He placed 10 to 12 small lights on a person, filmed them as they moved in the dark, and asked subjects viewing the films what they saw. He found that when the point-light walker stimulus was stationary, subjects reported seeing a meaningless pattern of lights. However, as soon as the walker started walking, subjects instantly identified the movement as being produced by a walking person. They didn't perceive a complex jumble of moving lights, but perceived a meaningful pattern. The movements of the lights had created a structure—a person walking—out of what was initially perceived as a random arrangement of dots. This perception of structure is particularly impressive because the movement of an individual light is not seen as the movement of a person (Figure 10.34). It is only when the dots move together that they become a person.

The perceptual grouping of point-light walker lights has also been studied physiologically, by recording from neurons in an area in the monkey's temporal cortex called the *superior temporal area.* Some cells in this area respond best to images of people walking. For example, Figure 10.30 shows the response of a neuron that responds best to images of a person walking forward. Some of the neurons that respond to people walking also respond to the movement of point-light walkers. M. W. Oram and David Perrett (1994) recorded from a neuron that responded well to a point light walker walking backward, but responded less well to forward movement or to the random movement of dots (Figure 10.35). This research on the monkey has also been extended to humans by monitoring human brain activity with

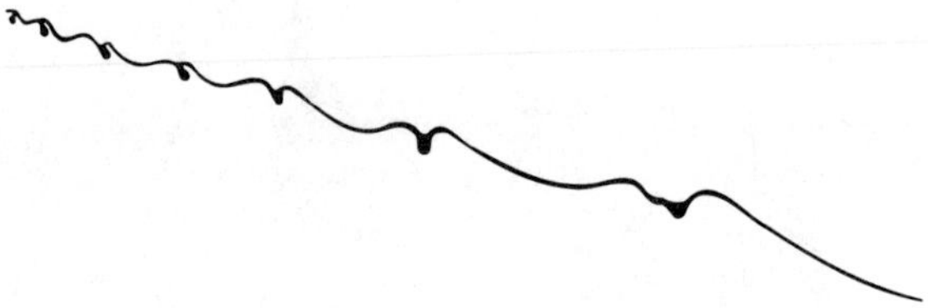

Figure 10.34
The path traced by one of the lights attached to the walking person's ankle. When viewing all of the lights moving together, the observer is unaware of these individual movements and perceives the entire configuration as a walking person.

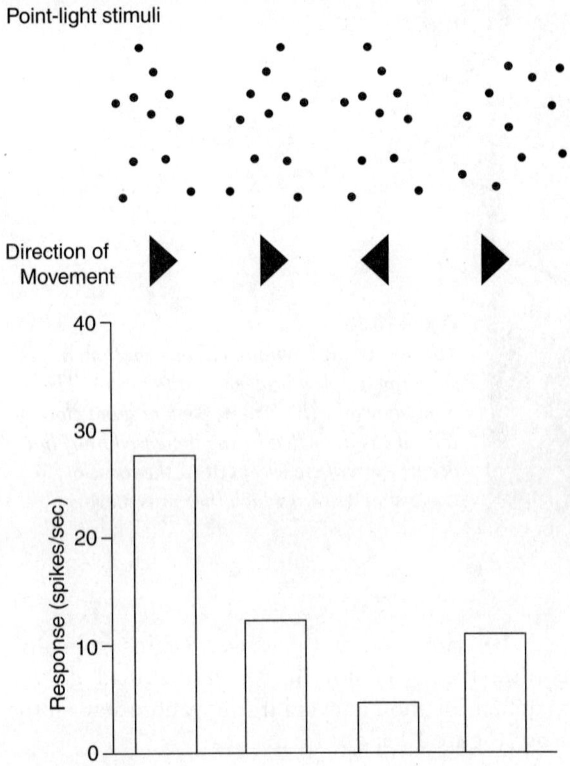

Figure 10.35
Response of a neuron in the superior temporal area of the monkey to point light walker stimuli (shown at the top) moving in various directions. This cell responds best to backward walking (a) and responds less well to walking forward to the right (b), walking forward to the left (c), and a jumbled motion stimulus moving to the right (d). (Adapted from Oram & Perrett, 1994.)

Positron Emission Tomography (PET). This research has shown that presenting moving point-light walkers causes an increase in activity in the human superior temporal sulcus (Bonda et al., 1996).

The kinetic depth effect and the perceptual organization that occurs with the point light walker stimuli show how movement helps us create perceptions that go beyond just perceiving movement. Movement also provides information, called *optic flow*, that helps us interact with our environment.

Optic Flow: Information from Action

How do we use information about motion to help us reach destinations in our environment? According to J. J. Gibson, we can answer this question by considering the information that is created by our movement through the environment. Gibson identified the crucial source of information for reaching our destination as being the **optic flow pattern**—the pattern created when our movement causes elements of the optic array (see page 261) to flow past us. For example, when we are looking out the front window of a moving car, or when we are walking down the street, elements flow past us on all sides, as illustrated in Figure 10.36, in which the size of the arrows indicate the rate of flow. Let's consider how this optic flow pattern helps us navigate through the environment.

Negotiating the Environment

Gibson emphasized an important property of the optic flow pattern: At greater distances, the rate of flow becomes less, until it reaches the **focus of expansion** (f.o.e.), the point in the distance where there is no movement. Gibson proposed that the f.o.e. always remains centered on the observer's destination and therefore provides invariant information indicating where the observer is heading. (See page 262 to review the idea of invariant information.) Thus, to reach a particular place, the moving person simply needs to keep that place centered on the f.o.e. of the optic flow pattern.

This idea works if the observer occasionally looks at his destination to be sure it is in the same place as the focus of expansion. However, this doesn't always occur. For example, automobile drivers tend to look at the center lines and the road's edge as they are driving (Schiff, 1980), especially when they are negotiating curves (Land & Lee, 1994). To deal with this situation, David Lee (1974, 1980) proposes that drivers use optic flow information other than the focus

Figure 10.36
The flow of the environment as seen from a car speeding across a bridge toward point A. The flow, shown by the arrows, is more rapid closer to the car (as indicated by the increased blur) but occurs everywhere except at A, the focus of expansion, toward which the car is moving.

of expansion to help them stay on course. Consider Figure 10.37a, which shows a straight stretch of road and a curve.

If the driver is on course on the straight stretch, the optic flow line that passes from view directly below the driver, which Lee calls the **locomotor flow line,** is centered on the road. This line indicates the course that the car will follow if no changes are made in steering. When the driver is on course, the optic flow lines and the edges of the road coincide (Figure 10.37a). When changes are made in steering, as might occur when negotiating a curve, the optic flow line changes, but stays lined up with the road as long as the driver is staying on course (Figure 10.37b). However, if the driver begins going off course, the optic flow line and the road do not match, a situation to avoid if you want to stay on the road (Figure 10.37c).

Not only do optic flow lines provide information that drivers are likely to pay attention to, but they are also useful when drivers negotiate curved roads, where the f.o.e. would be useless since the "destination point" is constantly changing throughout a curve. (See W. Warren, 1995; Warren et al., 1991; Warren, Morris, & Kalish, 1988, for additional information on optic flow.) In addition to helping a driver stay on course, optic flow information also informs the driver of the possibility of colliding with another vehicle.

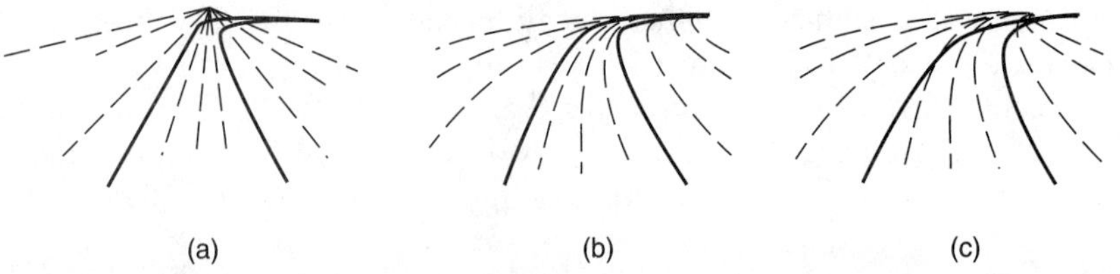

Figure 10.37
Optic flow lines for (a) movement along a straight stretch of road; (b) the correct negotiation of a curved stretch of road; and (c) the incorrect negotiation of a curved stretch of road. In (c) the car will go off the road unless a steering correction is made. (Lee, 1980)

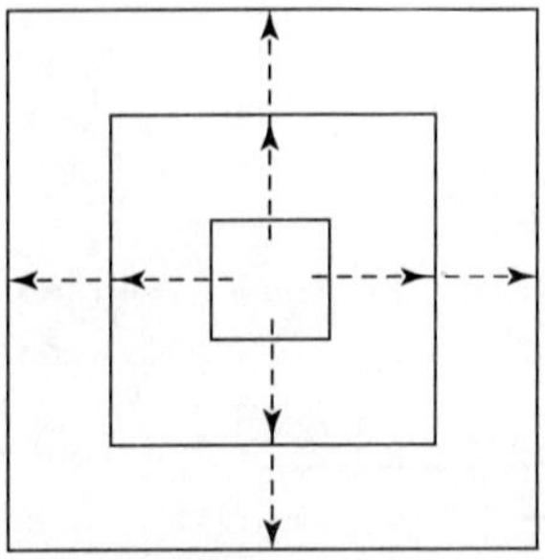

Figure 10.38
Three "snapshots" of a square as it moves directly toward an observer. The dashed arrows indicate that the square appears to be expanding outward as it moves closer.

Judging Time to Impact

Consider what occurs if you are following another car. If you stay at the same distance from this car, its visual angle (or size in your field of view) remains constant. But if you are gaining on the other car, its visual angle expands until, eventually (if you don't brake or change lanes to pass), you will collide with it. David Lee (1976) showed that the **rate of angular expansion** provides information that enables drivers to estimate when they will collide if they maintain the same speed and course. Lee's subjects viewed films of an object that was expanding as if it were on a collision course with the observer (Figure 10.38). The film was stopped before the "collision," and the observer was asked to estimate how long it would be before a collision would have occurred. Observers tend to underestimate the time to collision, but do estimate longer times for longer times to collision. It appears that the rate of angular expansion provides information that can be used to avoid colliding with other objects in the environment (McLeod & Ross, 1983; Schiff & Detwiler, 1979).

An example of physiological research using optic flow stimuli is a study by Michael Graziano, Richard Andersen, and Robert Snowden (1994). They found neurons in an extrastriate area called the *medial superior temporal area* (MST) that respond best to patterns of dots that are expanding outward, like the flow pattern in Figure 10.39a, and also neurons that respond best to circular motions and spiral motions (Figure 10.39b). Neurons such as these may provide the physiological mechanism that underlies our perception of environmental stimuli such as optic flow patterns (also see Duffy & Wurtz, 1991; Orban et al., 1992; Regan & Cynader, 1979).

The research we have described on optic flow was largely inspired by Gibson's ecological approach to perception, which emphasizes looking for links between environmental information and perception. Another example of how Gibson's ideas have provided a link between environmental stimulation and

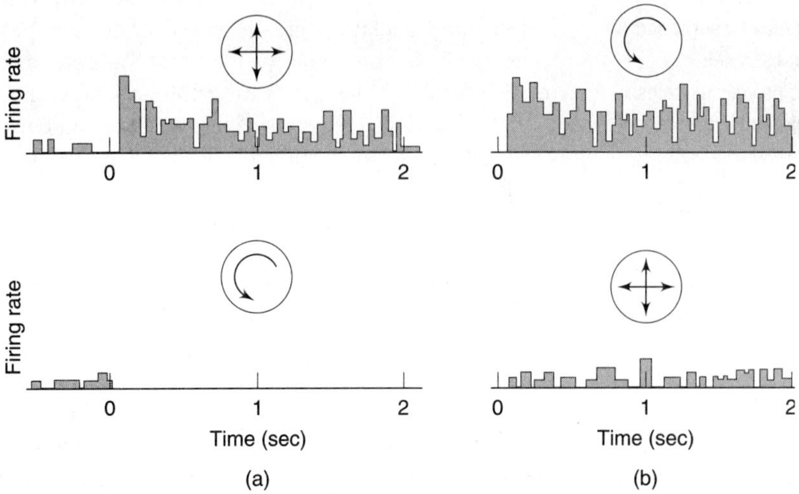

Figure 10.39
(a) Response of a neuron in the monkey's MST that responds with a high rate of firing to an expanding stimulus (top record), but that hardly fires to a stimulus that moves with a spiral motion (bottom record) or with other types of motion (not shown). (b) Another neuron that responds best to spiral movement (top) but does not respond well to an expanding pattern or other types of movement. (bottom) (From Graziano, Andersen, & Snowden, 1994.)

perception is his suggestion that vision is one of the proprioceptive senses—that is, one of the senses responsible for sensing the location, orientation, and movement of the body. This was an unconventional suggestion when it was made in 1966, because the senses usually identified as proprioceptive are the vestibular system of the inner ear, which is generally considered the major mechanism of balance, and the receptors in our muscles and joints, which help us sense the positions of our limbs. However, as we will see in the next section, it is possible to demonstrate a direct connection between vision and our ability to maintain our balance.

Maintaining Balance

We can appreciate Gibson's assertion that vision is one of the proprioceptive senses by doing the following demonstration.

D E M O N S T R A T I O N

Keeping Your Balance

Keeping your balance is something you probably take for granted. Even when standing on one foot, most people can keep their balance with little effort. Try it. Then, as you are balancing on one foot, close your eyes. You may be surprised by how difficult balance becomes when you can't see. Vision provides a frame of reference that helps your muscles constantly make adjustments to help you maintain your balance. ●

The importance of vision in maintaining balance was demonstrated in another way by David Lee and Eric Aronson (1974). Lee and Aronson placed 13- to 16-month-old toddlers in the "swinging room" in Figure 10.40. In this room, the floor is stationary, but the walls and ceiling of the room can swing forward and backward. The idea behind the swinging room was to duplicate the visual stimulation that normally occurs

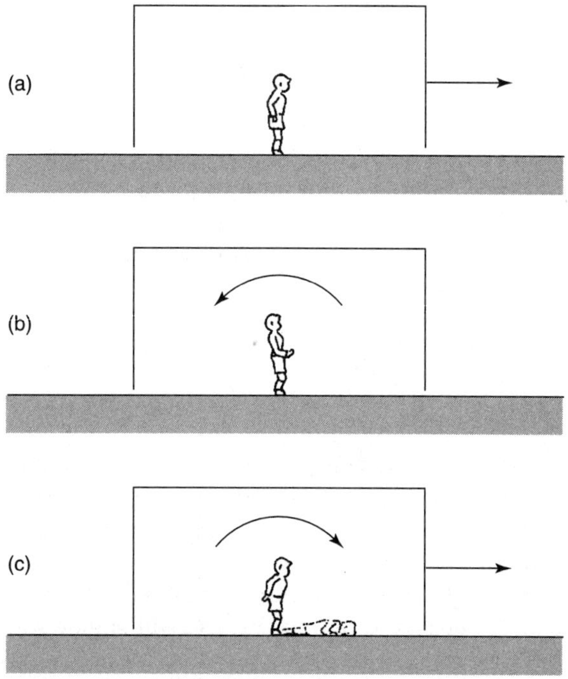

Figure 10.40
Lee and Aronson's swinging room. (a) Moving the room forward creates the same optic flow pattern (as in Figure 10.41b) that occurs when a person sways backward, as in (b). To compensate for this apparent sway, subjects sway forward, as in (c), and often lose their balance and fall down. (Based on Lee & Aronson, 1974.)

as our bodies sway forward and backward. Swaying forward and backward creates visual optic flow patterns as we see elements of the environment move relative to us. Swaying forward creates an expanding optic flow pattern (Figure 10.41a), and swaying backward creates a contracting optic flow pattern (Figure 10.41b).

These flow patterns provide information about body sway. Without realizing it, we are constantly using this information to make corrections for this sway so that we can stand upright. Lee and Aronson reasoned that if they created a flow pattern that made people think they were leaning forward or backward, they could cause them to lean in the opposite direction to compensate. They accomplished this by moving the room either toward or away from the standing children, and the children responded as predicted.

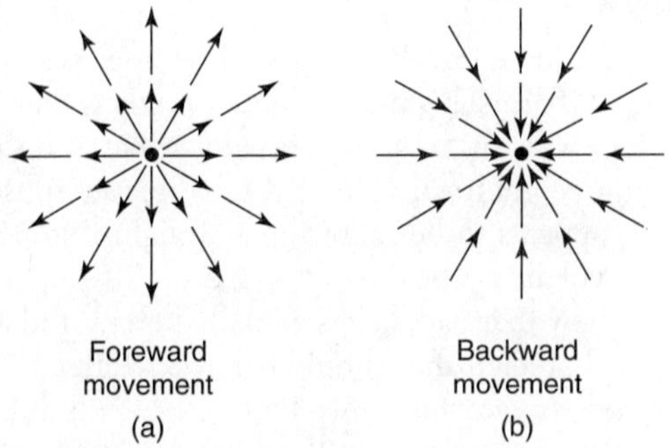

Figure 10.41
Flow patterns that occur (a) when we move forward and (b) when we move backward.

When the room moved toward them (creating the flow pattern for swaying forward), they leaned back, and when it moved away (creating the flow pattern for swaying backward), they leaned forward. In fact, many of the children did more than just lean: 26 percent swayed, 23 percent staggered, and 33 percent fell down!

Adults were also affected by the swinging room. If they braced themselves, "oscillating the experimental room through as little as 6 mm caused adult subjects to sway approximately in phase with this movement. The subjects were like puppets visually hooked to their surroundings and were unaware of the real cause of their disturbance" (Lee, 1980, p. 173). Adults who didn't brace themselves could, like the infants, be knocked over by their perception of the moving room. Thus, vision is such a powerful determinant of balance that it can override the traditional sources of balance information provided by the inner ear and the receptors in the muscles and joints (also see Fox, 1990).

The connection between movement perception and balance, as well as other functions of movement perception, such as helping us to stay on course, and keeping us from colliding with objects, emphasizes the fact that our perception of motion is often part of an interactive process. Sometimes we may sit passively and watch motion, as we do when we watch TV or a movie, but just as often we become active participants, as we simultaneously perceive motion and move through the environment ourselves.

Something to Consider: The Interactive Nature of Motion Perception

The occurrence of movement often indicates that something is happening. A person is approaching, a car door opens, a cat jumps onto the kitchen counter. When these things happen, we often not only perceive

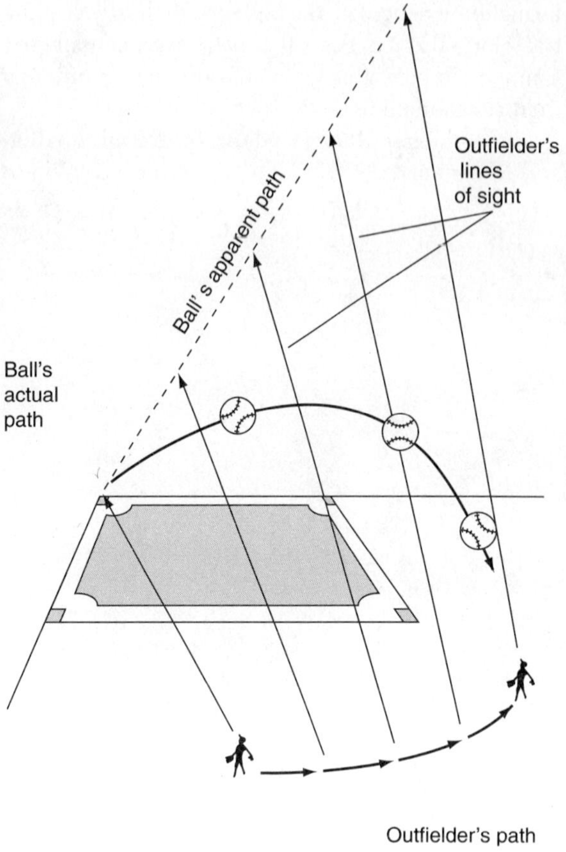

Figure 10.42
A fly ball travels along the path shown by the baseball. If the outfielder runs so the ball appears to follow a straight-line path (dashed line), his position will eventually intersect with the ball's position. (Adapted from McBeath, Shaffer, & Kaiser, 1995.)

the movement, but also interact with it in some way. We move toward the approaching person and extend our hand in greeting, we enter the car, we shoo the cat off the counter.

An example of the interactive nature of movement perception that has recently been studied experimentally is the process that occurs when a baseball player catches a fly ball hit high to the outfield. Although we know that ballplayers have the ability to run to where a fly ball is going to land so they can catch it, we haven't, until recently, known what information they use to accomplish this feat. One explanation suggested that the ballplayer perceives the initial trajectory and acceleration of the ball and uses this information to calculate the ball's parabolically curving trajectory. But it appears that ballplayers actually use a much simpler strategy, which doesn't require any mental calculations.

According to Michael McBeath, Dennis Shaffer, and Mary Kaiser (1995) all a ballplayer has to do to catch a fly ball is to run along a path that makes the ball appear to be traveling in a straight line, as shown in Figure 10.42. This model, which predicts that the outfielder will run in a curved path, is based on the following geometrical fact: If the ballplayer runs so the ball appears to be following a straight-line path, the ball will always be directly above.

To show that ballplayers actually behave the way the model predicts they should behave, McBeath and his coworkers videotaped two college students as they caught flies and found that they ran in curved paths, as predicted. They also had the fielders carry video cameras on their shoulders and aim them toward the ball as they ran to catch it. The resulting videotapes showed that the ball did, in fact, follow a straight-line trajectory as viewed by the camera.

McBeath's research emphasizes the idea that our perception of movement is often just the first step in a process which also includes our active reaction to the movement we perceive.

Apparent Movement on the Skin

The skin and retina have a great deal in common. There are center-surround receptive fields on the retina and center-surround receptive fields on the skin (see page 421). There are neurons in the visual cortex that respond selectively to specific directions of visual movement, and as we will see in Chapter 14, there are also neurons in the somatosensory cortex that respond selectively to specific directions of movement across the skin.

In addition to these physiological similarities, there are also perceptual parallels between these two senses. One of these parallels is that we can create the experience of apparent movement both by stimulating the retina and by stimulating the skin. When we stimulate one spot on the retina with a brief flash and then stimulate a nearby spot with another flash, we see movement between the two lights. Similarly, when we briefly vibrate one place on the skin, and then vibrate at another location, subjects feel movement from one place on the skin to the other (Sherrick & Rogers, 1966).

This apparent movement on the skin can't be caused by the spread of vibration into the area between the two places on the skin, because apparent movement can also occur across the space between the two arms. Subjects report that the movement appears to jump into the space between the arms, vanishes for a moment, and then jumps onto the other arm (Figure 10.43) (Sherrick, 1968).

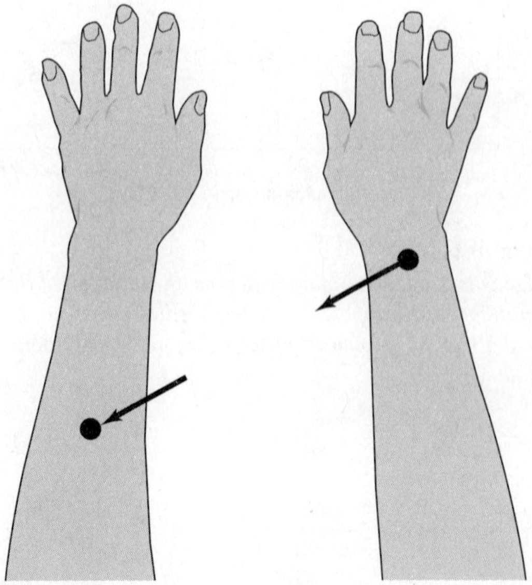

Figure 10.43
Tactile apparent movement that results when a point on the right arm is stimulated and then a point on the left arm is stimulated. The movement appears to jump from one arm to another, as shown.

An interesting similarity between visual and tactile apparent movement is shown in Figure 10.44, which plots subject's judgments of the goodness of movement on a scale of 1 to 100, versus the duration of each of the stimulus pulses. As the stimulus duration increases, the "goodness" of the perceived movement increases, both for visual and tactile movement. It is particularly impressive that the data for tactile apparent movement (Kirman, 1974) and visual apparent movement (Kolers, 1964) are almost exactly the same.

Returning to electrophysiological comparisons of vision and touch, a recent study has found that when adjacent areas of skin are stimulated rapidly enough to cause a perception of smooth apparent movement,

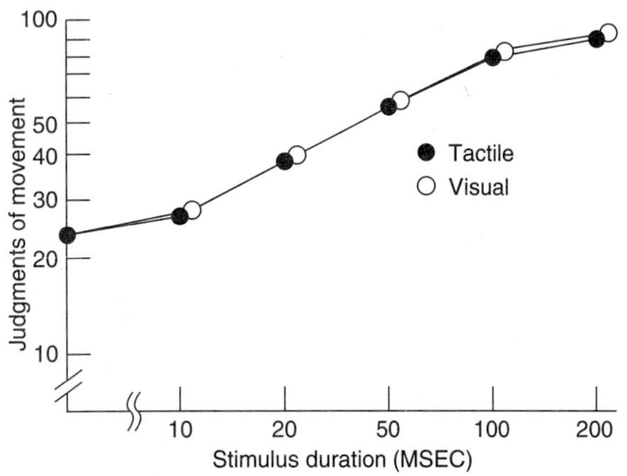

Figure 10.44
Judgments of goodness of movement vs. the duration of the stimuli for tactile apparent movement (filled circles) and visual apparent movement (open circles). (Adapted from Kirman, 1974.)

neurons in the somatosensory area of the cortex fire smoothly. However, when these same areas of skin are stimulated more slowly, so movement perception is absent (it feels like one point is stimulated and then the other), then these neurons fire in separated bursts (Gardner et al., 1992). Similar studies using visual stimuli have reported the same result: Rapid visual stimulation that results in apparent movement causes continuous firing of neurons in the striate cortex and area MT, but slower visual stimulation that does not cause the perception of apparent movement causes the same kind of firing in bursts that occurs in the somatosensory cortex (Mikami et al., 1986; Newsome et al., 1986). These parallels between movement in vision and touch led Esther Gardner and coworkers (1992) to conclude that "Linkage of successive stimuli appears to be a general property of cortical processing of sensory information" (p. 61).

Study Questions

Underlying Principles

Find examples of the following principles in this chapter:

- Receptive fields/neural selectivity (283)
- Distributed response (283)
- Parallel pathways (283)
- Physiology-perception connection (281)
- Cognition-perception connection (281)

The Information Provided by Movement

1. What four types of information are provided by movement? (274)

Movement: Studying Movement Perception

2. Why isn't movement across the retina sufficient as a stimulus for motion perception? (277)
3. In what situation does an object's image move across the retina, but we perceive the object as stationary? (277)
4. Describe the following situations in which we perceive movement even though there is no movement on the retina: stroboscopic movement, the waterfall illusion, induced movement. (277)
5. Which of the examples in 4 are illusions of movement? (277)
6. What was Exner's discovery? (278)
7. What was the significance of Wertheimer's work on apparent movement? (279)
8. What is the relationship between the interstimulus interval and the perception of apparent movement? (279)
9. What is the evidence that our perception of movement is affected by the context within which the moving stimulus exists? (280)

Detecting Movement: Neural Firing and Environmental Information

10. Where is the earliest place in the visual system where directionally selective neurons are found? (281)
11. How did Pasternak show that directionally selective neurons are responsible for the cat's ability to perceive the direction of movement? (281)
12. Describe Reichart's circuit that responds to movement in one direction. (281)
13. Many complex cells in the striate cortex are tuned to respond best to a particular direction of movement. Why is it unlikely that the response of one of these tuned neurons could provide enough information to indicate that movement is occurring in a particular direction? (282)
14. Which extrastriate area is important for movement perception? (283)
15. How did Newsome and coworkers demonstrate a connection between the firing of MT neurons and movement perception? (283)
16. Why would it be correct to describe the neural code for the direction of movement as distributed coding? Why can we say that the code approaches specificity coding? (283)
17. What is the basic idea behind corollary discharge theory? (284)
18. Describe what causes the motor signal to occur, the corollary discharge to occur, and the image movement signal to occur. (285)
19. What is the comparator? Which signals in 18, above, are received by the comparator according to corollary discharge theory? (285)
20. What perception occurs when the comparator receives either the image movement signal or the corollary discharge signal separately? What perception occurs when these two signals reach the comparator simultaneously? (285)
21. Explain what happens in the following situations and how these results are explained by corollary discharge

theory: (1) you observe an afterimage as you move your eyes in the dark; (2) you push on your eyeball while keeping your eye steady; (3) you follow a moving object with your eyes; (4) an observer with paralyzed eye muscles tries to move his eyes. (285)

22. What is a real movement neuron and how does the way it responds relate to corollary discharge theory? (287)
23. How did J. J. Gibson explain movement perception based on local motion signals and global optical flow? (288)
24. Can Gibson's approach to movement perception explain perception of an object's movement in an environment in which the background is not visible? How did Gibson feel about explaining perception in this kind of situation? (288)

The Effect of Context on Movement Perception

25. Describe how the framework within which an object moves can influence our perception of the direction in which it is moving. (289)
26. Describe how the sequence in which stimuli are presented can influence our perception of apparent movement. (290)
27. What is the shortest-path constraint? (290)
28. What happens if two meaningful stimuli such as a person's two arms are presented in a way that could violate the shortest-path constraint? (291)
29. Describe two things about the results in 28, above, that make them especially interesting. (291)
30. What is the possible relationship between the results in 28, above, and the visual system's separation into ventral and dorsal streams? (291)

Movement Creates Structure

31. What is the kinetic depth effect? (292)
32. What is biological motion? (293)
33. What is a point light walker? What do experiments using point light walker stimuli tell us about the relationship between movement and perceptual grouping? (294)
34. Describe the response of neurons in the monkey's temporal cortex that respond to images of people walking and to point light walker stimuli. How has this research been extended to humans? (294)

Optic Flow: Information from Action

35. According to Gibson, what is the crucial source of information for reaching our destination? (295)
36. What is the focus of expansion and how does it help us reach our destination, according to Gibson? (295)
37. Describe research that indicates the information that drivers use to stay on course. (295)
38. What is angular expansion and how is it related to judging time to impact? (297)
39. Describe neurons that respond to optic flow patterns. (297)
40. Why did Gibson suggest that vision is one of the proprioceptive senses? (298)
41. Describe Lee and Aronson's experiments on the relationship between optic flow and keeping one's balance. (298)

Something to Consider: The Interactive Nature of Motion Perception

42. Describe the perceptual information that a baseball outfielder uses to catch a fly ball. (299)

Across the Senses: Apparent Movement on the Skin

43. What are some similarities between receptive fields and neural responding in vision and the cutaneous (skin) senses? (301)
44. What are some similarities between apparent movement of tactile stimuli and apparent movement on the skin? (301)
45. What happens when points on the two arms are vibrated one after the other? (301)

CHAPTERS 5–10

Underlying Principles

This is the end of our description of the various visual qualities—color, shape, depth, size, and movement. We now look back at Chapters 5–10 to see how we have applied the Underlying Principles that we introduced on pages 128–130. Table 1 on page 306 shows which principles are relevant to each chapter. Specific examples of principles from each chapter are:

1. **Selective Receptors** Most individual receptors respond selectively to a restricted range of stimuli.
   - Three types of cone receptors (5)
2. **Receptive Fields/Neural Selectivity** Most neurons (a) have a receptive field—an area on the receptor surface or in space which, when stimulated, influences the neuron's firing; and (b) fire selectively to a restricted range of stimuli.
   - Opponent-process neurons that respond with excitation to some wavelengths and inhibition to other wavelengths. (5)
   - Double color-opponent center-surround receptive fields. (5)
   - Color-selective neurons in area V4 (5)
   - Neural feature detectors that respond to faces and other specific shapes. (7)
   - Binocular disparity detectors that respond to specific amounts of disparity. (8)
   - Neurons that respond to patterns of flow. (9)
   - Directionally selective neurons. (10)
   - Movement-selective neurons in MT cortex. (10)
   - Neurons in MST cortex that respond best to flow patterns, circular motion, and spiral motion. (10)
3. **Distributed Response** A stimulus causes a specific pattern of responding across a number of neurons. This is the distributed approach to sensory coding described in Chapter 3.
   - Wavelengths are indicated by the pattern of firing of the three types of cone receptors. (5)
   - Faces are identified by the pooling of responses of a number of face-selective neurons. (7)
   - Information about the direction of movement is provided by the pattern of firing of many directionally selective neurons in the striate cortex. (10)
   - The firing of small populations of neurons in MT has been linked to the perception of the direction of movement. (10)

Principle	Chapter: 5. Color	6. Constancy	7. Form	8. Space	9. Size, etc.	10. Motion
1. Selective receptors	■					
2. Receptive fields/ neural selectivity	■		■	■	■	■
3. Distributed response	■		■	■ *		■
4. Neural maps			■ *	■ *		■ *
5. Columnar organization	■		■			
6. Parallel pathways	■		■	■ *		■
7. Physiology–perception connection	■	■	■	■	■	■
8. Cognitive influences	■	■	■			■

■ Examples of these principles are described in the chapter (see examples).

■ * Examples of these principles are not described in the chapter, but are relevant. For example, neural maps are not discussed in Chapters 7, 8, and 10 but since they contain information about position on the retina, they would be important for the perception of form, space, and motion.

4. **Neural Maps** Neurons are arranged within a structure in an orderly way, based on a specific property.
   - The mapping of the retina onto the cortex was introduced in Chapter 3. There are no specific references to this mapping in Chapters 5–10, but this retinotopic mapping is essential for the coding of aspects of form, depth, and motion that involve location in space. This principle appears again in the chapters on hearing, and the somatic and chemical senses.

5. **Columnar Organization** Neurons that respond to specific stimulus properties are arranged in columns. These columns are usually perpendicular to the surface of the structure in which the neurons are located.
   - Columns of similar color-opponent neurons in the striate cortex. (5)
   - Orientation columns and columns of neurons that respond best to specific forms in the cortex and extrastriate cortex. (7)

6. **Parallel Pathways** There are parallel neural pathways within a sense that are specialized to process information about specific stimulus characteristics.
   - Color is processed in the ventral pathway. (5)
   - Form is processed in the ventral pathway. (7)
   - Motion is processed in the dorsal pathway. (10)

7. **Physiological Connections with Perception** Physiological processes influence what we

perceive. One of the major goals of research in perception is to demonstrate the connections that exist between physiology and perception.

- The following color phenomena have been connected to the properties of the cone receptors or the firing of opponent-process neurons: color mixing, afterimages, simultaneous contrast. (5)
- Visual pigment bleaching and color adaptation contribute to color constancy. (6)
- Neurons in area V4 respond to a light's perceived color rather than to its wavelength, and therefore may contribute to color constancy. (6)
- Cortical damage affects the ability to recognize forms. (7)
- Rearing kittens so they experience only monocular stimulation eliminates binocular neurons and the ability to use the cue of binocular disparity to perceive depth. (8)
- Size-invariant neurons in area IT may be involved in size constancy. (9)
- Rearing kittens in an environment without movement eliminates directionally selective neurons and the ability to perceive the direction of movement. (10)
- A neural signal—perhaps the "corollary discharge"—stabilizes our perception of the world when we move or move our eyes. (10)
- The firing of movement-sensitive neurons in MT cortex has been linked to the perception of the direction of movement. (10)

8. **Cognitive Influences** The perceiver's thoughts, past experiences, and the meaning of the stimulus influences perception.

- Color affects the perception of taste and smell. (5)
- Memory color influences color perceptions. (6)
- Interpretation of the direction of illumination influences lightness perception. (6)
- The likelihood principle and hypothesis testing, as well as other top-down processes, are involved in form perception. (7)
- The perception of apparent movement is influenced by the sequence of apparent movement stimuli and by knowledge that the moving stimulus is a person. (10)

From all of these examples, we can conclude that our eight principles have some generality, since, with the exception of neural maps, each principle appears in at least one chapter, and some appear in many chapters. We can also see that receptive fields and neural selectivity are principles that hold across all of the visual qualities. This makes sense when we consider that receptive fields are important for locating an object in space, and neural selectivity is the mechanism by which the nervous system creates distinctive patterns of firing that represent specific qualities of experience.

While all of the entries in the table make a case for the idea that there are basic principles that hold across the various visual qualities, we also need to consider what the open cells in the table are telling us. One thing that the open cells indicate is that every principle does not hold for all of the visual qualities. Not every quality is organized in columns or is mapped onto the cortex in an orderly way and not all perceptions depend on specialized receptors. For example, our perception of forms is created not by receptors that respond to specific forms but by the neural processing that occurs in the cortex.

We can also propose other principles in addition to the eight that we established after Chapter 4. The fact that seven of our eight principles are physiological reflects the fact that these principles were based on the physiologically-oriented material in Chapters 2–4. Now, based on what we have learned in Chapters 5–10 we can also propose a number of nonphysiological principles. Three additional principles, that hold across a number of visual qualities and which are also relevant to the chapters on hearing, the cutaneous senses and the chemical senses are as follows:

Perceptual Constancy We tend to perceive the properties of objects as being constant even when the proximal stimulus changes, as when we look at an object from different distances or viewpoints. Examples: color, lightness, shape, size, and smell constancy (6); size constancy (9).

Perceptual Grouping Small elements are often perceptually grouped into larger units. Examples: Gestalt grouping principles (7); Perceptual organization of point-light walkers (10).

Context and Perception Our perception of a stimulus often depends on the context within which the stimulus is perceived. Examples: Simultaneous color contrast (5); lightness contrast (6); the Gestalt principle that the whole is different than the sum of its parts (7); The perception of size as dependent on depth cues or the surroundings (6, 9); visual illusions (9); effect of context on movement perception (10).

In the chapters that follow, we move on to consider the senses of audition, the cutaneous senses, and the chemical senses. We will again encounter many of our eight basic principles as well as examples of the three additional principles we have added above. We will summarize principles relevant to Chapters 11–16 in the next *Underlying Principles* section, which follows Chapter 16.

11

SOUND, THE AUDITORY SYSTEM, AND PITCH PERCEPTION

Hearing has an extremely important function in my life. I was born legally blind, so although I can see, my vision is highly impaired and is not correctable. Even though I am not usually shy or embarrassed, sometimes I do not want to call attention to myself and my disability. . . . There are many methods that I can use to improve my sight in class like sitting close to the board, or copying from a friend, but sometimes these things are impossible. Then I use my hearing to take notes. . . . My hearing is very strong. While I do not need my hearing to identify people who are very close to me, it is definitely necessary when someone is calling my name from a distance. I can recognize their voice, even if I cannot see them.

Jill Robbins

As a competitive gymnast I have found hearing to be extremely important. On an apparatus such as the balance beam, I have to do tricks such as jumping forward or backward onto my hands and then back to my feet. Because I'm flipping so fast, it's impossible to always see where I'm landing, but I can hear it. If the time between my takeoff and hearing my hands hit the beam is equal to the time between when my hands hit and when my feet hit, I know that I am going to land the trick OK and stay on the beam. But if I flip onto my hands and then I hear my feet hit the beam

CHAPTER CONTENTS

SOME QUESTIONS WE WILL CONSIDER

- If a tree falls in the forest and no one is there to hear it, is there a sound? (311)
- What is it that makes sounds high pitched or low pitched? (315)
- How do sound vibrations inside the ear lead to the perception of different pitches? (325)

too quickly, I know that I'm off balance and am going to fall off. Hearing [sound] is always the first clue that lets me know that I am off balance.

Jennifer Steinback

These statements were written by two of my students to illustrate a special effect hearing has had on their lives. The next statement illustrates a student's reaction to losing her hearing.

In an experiment I did for my sign language class, I bandaged up my ears so I couldn't hear a sound. I had a signing interpreter with me to translate spoken language. The two hours that I was "deaf" gave me a great appreciation for deaf people and their culture. I found it extremely difficult to communicate, because even though I could read the signing, I couldn't keep up with the pace of the conversation. . . . Also, it was uncomfortable for me to be in that much silence. Knowing what a crowded cafeteria sounds like and not being able to hear the background noise was an uncomfortable feeling. I couldn't hear the buzzing of the florescent light, the murmur of the crowd, or the slurping of my friend's Coke (which I usually object to, but which I missed when I couldn't hear it). I saw a man drop his tray and I heard nothing. I could handle the signing, but not the silence.

Eileen Lusk

You don't have to bandage up your ears for two hours to appreciate what hearing adds to your life. Just close your eyes for a few minutes, observe the sounds you hear and notice what they tell you about your environment. What most people experience is that by listening closely they become aware of many events in the environment that without hearing they would not be aware of at all (Figure 11.1). Let's consider this function of hearing, as well as others, in more detail.

The Functions of Hearing

Our ability to hear events that we can't see serves an important *signaling* function for both animals and humans. For an animal living in the forest, the rustle of leaves or the snap of a twig may signal the approach

Figure 11.1
The auditory world of the people sitting on the bench includes a large number of stimuli that are hidden from the visual system but that can be sensed through hearing.

of a predator. Or consider the many signaling functions that hearing serves for humans, among them the warning sound of a smoke alarm or an ambulance siren, the distinctive high-pitched cry of babies who are distressed, or tell-tale noises that signal problems in a car engine that is not running smoothly.

But hearing also has functions in addition to signaling. On the first day of my perception class, I ask my students which sense they would choose to keep if they had to pick between hearing and vision. There are arguments in favor of keeping each of these senses, but two of the strongest arguments for keeping hearing instead of vision are music and speech. Many of my students hesitate to consider giving up hearing because of the pleasure they derive from listening to music, and they also realize that speech is important because it facilities communication between people.

Helen Keller, who was both deaf and blind, stated that she felt being deaf was worse than being blind, because blindness isolates you from *things*, but deafness isolates you from *people*. Being unable to hear people talking creates an isolation that makes it difficult to relate to others and sometimes makes it difficult even to know what is going on. To appreciate the importance of hearing for knowing what is going on, try watching a dramatic program on television with the sound turned off. You will be surprised at how little, beyond physical actions and perhaps some intense emotions, you can understand about the story.

Our goal in this chapter is to describe the basic mechanisms responsible for our ability to hear. We will describe the nature of sound and the anatomy of the auditory system, and then will focus on the physiological mechanisms for our perception of pitch. In the next chapter, we will ask questions such as: How do we perceptually organize the sounds in our environment so we can tell one from another? How do we tell where a sound source is located? What gives different musical instruments their distinctive tonal qualities? The starting point both for understanding our perception of pitch and for answering these questions is to consider exactly what we mean by the word "sound." One way to do this is to consider the following riddle:

> If a tree falls in the forest and no one is there to hear it, would there be a sound?

This question is useful because it is based on the fact that we can use the word "sound" in two different ways. Sometimes "sound" refers to a *physical stimulus* and sometimes it refers to a *perceptual response*. The answer to the question about the tree depends on which definition of sound we use (Figure 11.2).

We can define sound physically as *rapid pressure changes* in the air or other medium. By this definition the answer to the question about the tree is "yes," because the falling tree causes pressure changes whether or not someone is there to hear them.

We can define sound perceptually as the *experience of hearing*. By this definition the answer to the question is "no," because if no one is in the forest, there would be no experience.

This difference between physical and perceptual is an extremely important one and is a difference that we need to keep clear as we discuss hearing in this chapter and the next two. (Also see "Something to Consider: The Difference Between Physical and Perceptual" on page 64 of Chapter 2.) One way to avoid confusing the *physical* sound stimulus and our *experience* of sound is to use the term **acoustic stimulus** or **sound stimulus** to refer to the *physical pressure changes* and **sound** to refer to our *experience of hearing*. We will first describe sound as a physical stimulus and will then describe sound as a perceptual experience.

Sound as a Physical Stimulus: Pressure Changes in the Air

Our perception of sound depends on the vibrations of objects. But we don't perceive an object's vibrations directly. We perceive the object's effect on the air, water, or any other elastic medium that surrounds it. Let's begin by considering your radio or stereo system's loudspeaker, which is really a device for producing vibrations to be transmitted to the surrounding air.

Figure 11.2
When this tree falls, will there be a sound if no one is there to listen? The answer to this question depends on whether we define sound as a physical stimulus or as an experience.

The Sound Stimulus Produced by a Loudspeaker

People have been known to turn up their stereos loud enough so that these vibrations can be felt through a neighbor's wall, but even at softer levels, these vibrations are there. (Turn on your radio or stereo and feel the vibrations by placing your hand gently on the speaker. This technique is sometimes used by deaf people to "listen" to music. An even better way to feel this vibration is to place your hands on an inflated balloon that is positioned in front of a loud speaker.)

The vibrations you feel when you place your hand on the speaker affect the surrounding air, as shown in Figure 11.3. When the diaphragm of the speaker moves out, it pushes the surrounding air molecules together, increasing the density of molecules near the diaphragm. This increased density increases the air pressure. When the speaker diaphragm moves back in, it decreases the density of molecules near the diaphragm, decreasing the air pressure. By repeating this process many hundreds or even thousands of times a second, the speaker creates a pattern of alternating high- and low-pressure regions in the air as neighboring air molecules affect each other. This pattern of air pressure changes, which travels through air from its source at 340 meters per second (and through water at 1,500 meters per second), is called a **sound wave.** The qualities of the sounds we hear, particularly the pitch and loudness of a tone, are related to two properties of this

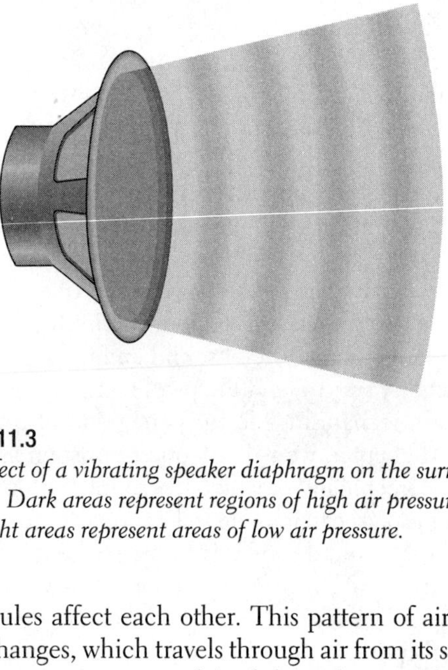

Figure 11.3
The effect of a vibrating speaker diaphragm on the surrounding air. Dark areas represent regions of high air pressure, and light areas represent areas of low air pressure.

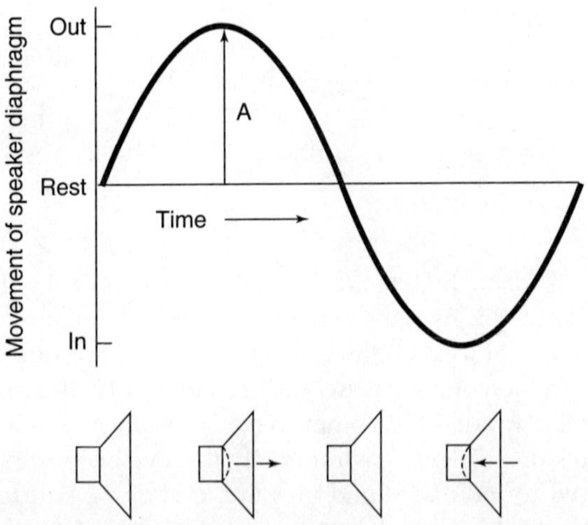

Figure 11.4
In response to a sine-wave stimulus from a computer, a speaker diaphragm moves out and then back in, as shown in the pictures in the figure. The time course of this motion is indicated by the sine-wave curve, which indicates the amount that the diaphragm has moved as a function of time. The amplitude (A) represents the maximum deflection of the speaker diaphragm from its rest position.

sound wave, its frequency and its amplitude. We introduce frequency and amplitude by focusing on a simple kind of sound wave, called a **pure tone,** in which pressure changes occur in a pattern described by a mathematical function called a *sine wave,* as shown in Figure 11.4. Tones with this pattern of pressure changes are found occasionally in the environment. A person whistling or the high-pitched notes produced by a flute are examples of sounds that are close to pure tones. Pure tones for laboratory studies of hearing are generated by computers, which can cause our speaker diaphragm to vibrate in and out with a sine-wave motion with a particular **amplitude**—the distance the diaphragm moves from its rest position (labeled A in Figure 11.4) and **frequency**—the number of times per second that the speaker diaphragm goes through the cycle of moving out, back in, and then out again.

The diaphragm's sine-wave motion is transferred to the air, creating the pure tone stimulus shown in Figure 11.5. The tone's frequency is indicated in units called **Hertz** (Hz), where one Hertz is one cycle per second. Thus, a 1,000-Hz tone is a pure tone that goes through 1,000 cycles per second. Humans can hear frequencies between about 20 and 20,000 Hz.

Specifying the Amplitude of a Sound Stimulus

One way to specify a tone's amplitude would be to indicate the difference in pressure between the high and low peaks of the sound wave. But this method of specifying amplitude runs into difficulty when we consider the wide range of pressure changes humans can hear. For example, if the pressure change caused

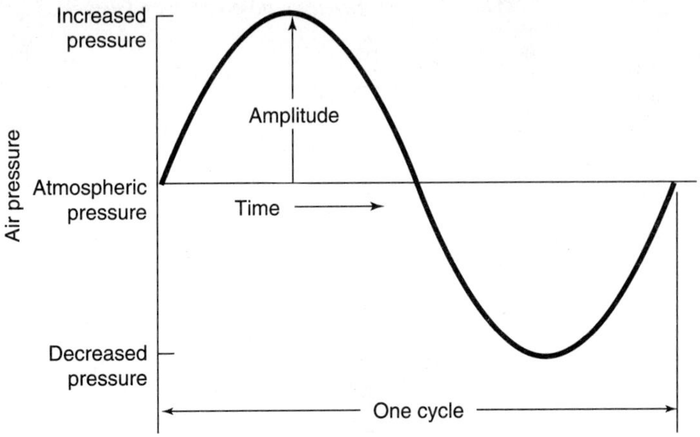

Figure 11.5
The sinusoidal vibration of the speaker diaphragm results in a sinusoidal change in the air pressure, as shown in the figure.

by a near-threshold sound, such as a barely audible whisper, is set equal to 1, then the sound pressure of loud radio music would be about 10 thousand and the sound pressure of a jet engine at takeoff would be about 10 million.

To compress this large range into a more manageable scale, auditory researchers use a unit of sound called the **decibel,** which is named after Alexander Graham Bell, the inventor of the telephone. The following equation is used to convert sound pressure into decibels:

$$\text{dB} = 20 \text{ logarithm } \frac{p}{p_0}$$

where dB stands for decibels, p is the sound pressure of the stimulus, and p_o is a standard sound pressure that is usually set at 20 micropascals, an extremely small pressure.

The zero point of the decibel scale is the pressure of a 1,000-Hz tone at threshold, since the sound pressure for this tone is 20 micropascals. We can use the equation above to calculate the decibels for this 1,000-Hz tone as follows:

If pressure = 20 micropascals

$$\text{dB} = 20 \times \log \frac{p}{p_0}$$

$$= 20 \times \log \frac{20}{20} = 20 \times \log 1.0$$

$$= 20 \times 0 \text{ (the logarithm of 1.0 equals 0)}$$

$$= 0 \text{ dB SPL}$$

Adding the notation SPL, which stands for **sound pressure level,** indicates that we have used the standard pressure of 20 micropascals in our calculation. Let's now repeat this calculation for two higher pressure levels:

If pressure = 200

$$\text{dB} = 20 \times \log \frac{200}{20} = 20 \times \log 10.0$$

$$= 20 \times 1 \text{ (the logarithm of 10 equals 1)}$$

$$= 20 \text{ dB SPL}$$

If pressure = 2,000

$$\text{dB} = 20 \times \log \frac{2{,}000}{20} = 20 \times \log 100.0$$

$$= 20 \times 2 \text{ (the logarithm of 100 equals 2)}$$

$$= 40 \text{ dB SPL}$$

Notice that *multiplying* sound pressure by 10 *adds* 20 dB. As you can see from Table 11.1, continuing this process all the way up to a sound pressure of 10 million only increases the decibels to 140. Because of the way decibels compress the large range of sound pressures in our environment, the decibel scale is used to indicate sound pressure, and as we will see shortly, this *physical property* of sound is related to the *perceptual property* of loudness.

Specifying the Frequency of a Sound Stimulus

We have seen that we can specify the frequency of a pure tone stimulus by indicating how many times per second the sine-wave repeats itself. Our auditory experience is dominated, however, not by pure tones, but by more complex stimuli such as music, speech, and the various sounds produced by nature and machines. These complex stimuli usually contain many frequencies.

Table 11.1
The relation between sound pressure and decibels

Pressure (p/p_0)	dB SPL
1	0
10	20
100	40
1,000	60
10,000	80
100,000	100
1,000,000	120
10,000,000	140

To understand how complex stimuli are made up of many frequencies, let's consider the musical tones produced by striking the keys on the piano keyboard (Figure 11.6). As we move from left to right on the keyboard, the frequency of the notes increases from 27.5 Hz for the lowest note on the keyboard to 4,186 Hz for the highest note. Although each note on the keyboard is associated with a single frequency, each tone produced by the piano and other musical instruments actually contains a large number of frequencies.

As we strike a key on the piano, we set one of the piano's strings into vibration, and this vibration produces pressure changes like the one shown in Figure 11.7. Although these pressure changes are more complex than the sine-wave pressure change of a pure tone, they have something in common with the pure tone. Both the pure tone and the note on the piano create *periodic pressure changes*—changes that repeat in a regular pattern. This property of regular repetition of the pressure changes, which is called **periodicity,**

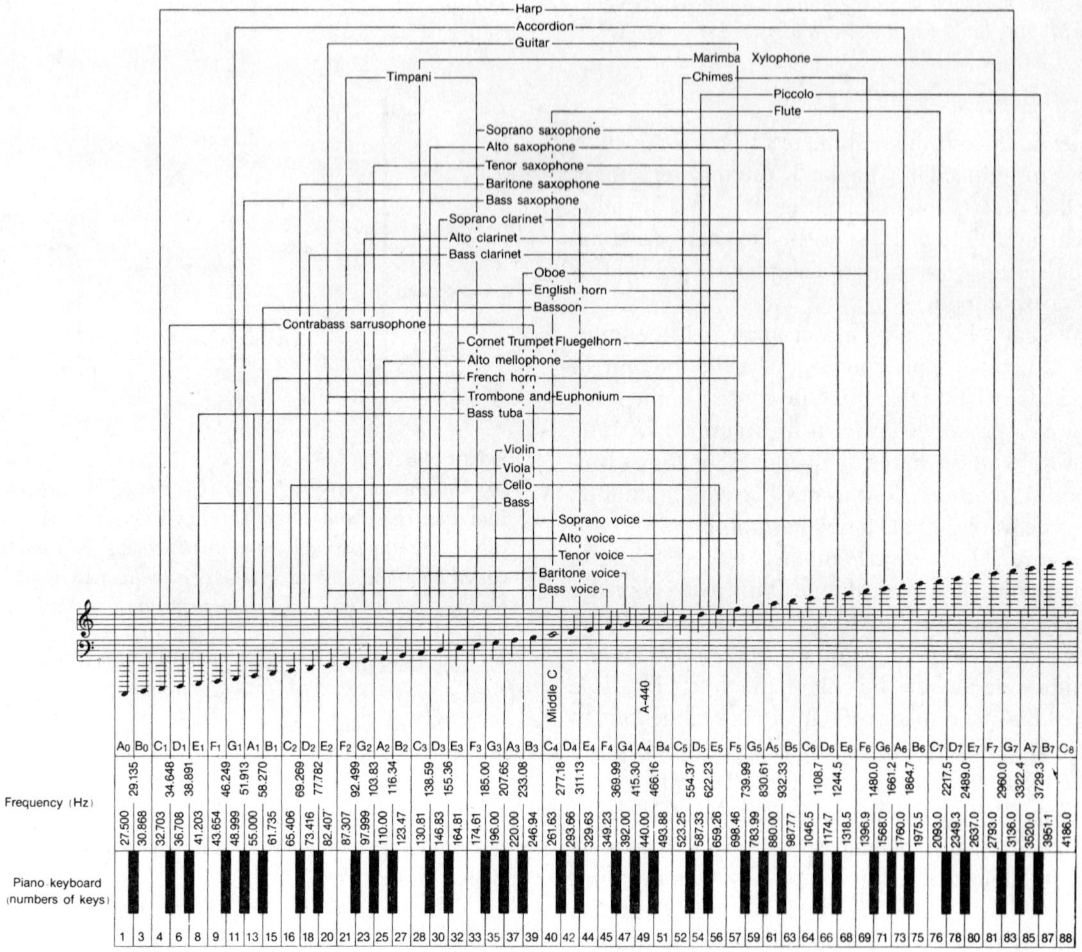

Figure 11.6
The piano keyboard, showing the frequencies associated with each note and the ranges of various other instruments. (Adapted from Conn, Ltd.)

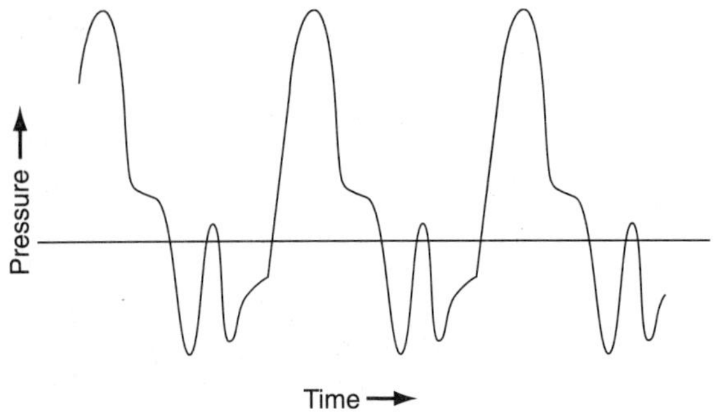

Figure 11.7
Pressure changes as a function of time for a musical tone. This waveform is more complex than the sine wave associated with pure tones like the one in Figures 11.3 and 11.4.

enables us to use the technique of Fourier analysis that we introduced in Chapter 3. You may remember from that description that Fourier analysis is a mathematical procedure that can be used to analyze a visual grating stimulus (or a more complex scene) into its sine-wave components.

We can also apply Fourier analysis to complex tones. When we apply Fourier analysis to the tone in Figure 11.7 we find that this tone consists of the three sine-wave components shown in Figure 11.8a. The sine wave with the lowest frequency is the tone's **fundamental frequency** (or the first harmonic), and the other sine waves are the tone's **harmonics.**

Figure 11.8b shows another way to indicate the properties of a musical tone. This plot, a **Fourier frequency spectrum,** indicates each harmonic's frequency by a line's position on the horizontal axis and its amplitude by the height of the line. The line marked F is the fundamental frequency of the tone in Figure 11.7 and corresponds to the frequency marked on the piano keyboard (in this case, the 440 Hz of A above middle C). The harmonics are all multiples of the fundamental frequency, so the second harmonic has a frequency of $440 \times 2 = 880$ Hz and the third harmonic has a frequency of $440 \times 3 = 1{,}320$ Hz. As we will see in Chapter 12, the tones of most musical instruments have many harmonics, and these harmonics create the distinctive sounds of different instruments. For now, the important point is that this

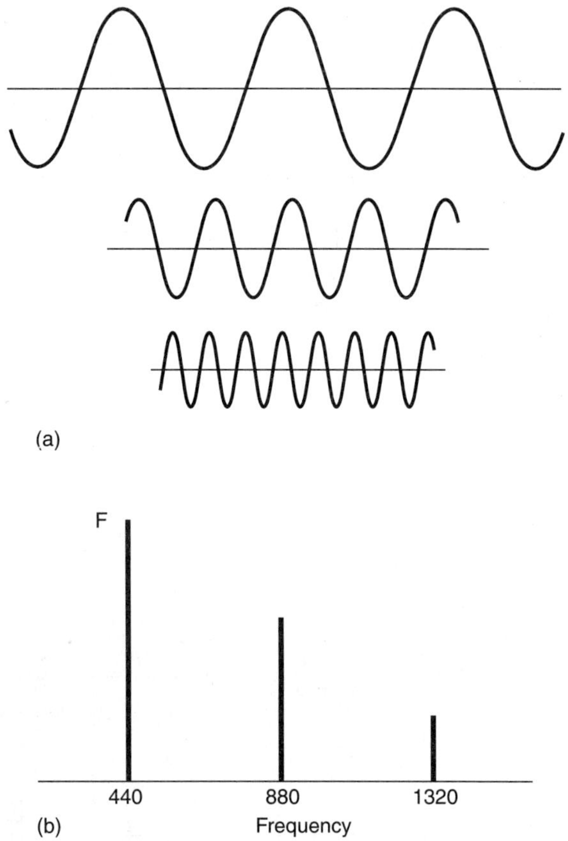

Figure 11.8
(a) The musical tone in Figure 11.7 can be broken down into these three sine waves. This breakdown can be accomplished for any periodic waveform by the use of a procedure called Fourier analysis. (b) The Fourier frequency spectrum for the tone in Figure 11.7. The spectrum indicates that the tone is made up of one component with a frequency of 440 Hz, another with a frequency of 880 Hz and a third with a frequency of 1,320. The heights of the lines indicates the amplitude at each frequency.

complex musical tone is actually composed of a number of frequencies.

There are many sounds in our environment in addition to pure tones and musical tones. As I sit in my office writing, I hear water gurgling in the small fountain to the right of my desk, the humming of my computer on the left, birds chirping outside, and the start-up noises of a car on the street below. Sounds such as these, plus human speech, are more complex than musical tones, but many of these sounds can also be analyzed into their frequency components. We will describe speech perception in detail in Chapter 13. In the remainder of this chapter we will focus on pure tones and musical tones, because these sounds are the ones that have been used in most of the basic research on the operation of the auditory system.

Table 11.2
Some common sound pressure levels (in decibels)

Sound	SPL (dB)
Barely audible sound (threshold)	0
Leaves rustling	20
Quiet residential community	40
Average speaking voice	60
Loud music from radio/heavy traffic	80
Express subway train	100
Propeller plane at takeoff	120
Jet engine at takeoff (pain threshold)	140
Spacecraft launch at close range	180

Sound as a Perceptual Response: The Experience of Hearing

The sound stimuli we have been describing give rise to three types of perceptual experience—loudness, pitch, and timbre.

Loudness

Loudness is the aspect of sound that is most closely associated with the amplitude of the acoustic stimulus (Table 11.1). It has also been defined as the *magnitude* of auditory sensation. Table 11.2 lists some environmental sounds, ranging from ones that aren't very loud, such as a barely audible whisper or leaves rustling, to those that are extremely loud, such as a jet engine at takeoff. From the amplitudes, stated in decibels, that are associated with these sound experiences, you can see that increasing the amplitude of the stimulus increases its loudness. We will consider loudness in more detail in Chapter 12.

Pitch

Pitch is how high or low a tone sounds. The pitch of a pure tone is related to its frequency: low frequencies cause low pitches and high frequencies cause high pitches. **Tone height** is the property of increasing pitch that accompanies increases in a tone's frequency. Thus, if we start at the left end of a piano keyboard and move toward the right, the fundamental frequency, the pitch, and the tone height all increase.

In addition to the increase in tone height that occurs as we move toward higher frequencies on the piano keyboard, something else happens: The letters of the notes A, B, C, D, E, F, and G repeat themselves. This repetition of notes reflects a quality called **tone chroma.** Notes with the same letters sound similar, even though they have different fundamental frequencies. These similar-sounding tones are separated by intervals of one or more **octaves,** so that a tone one octave above another tone has a fundamental frequency twice that of the lower tone. Thus, A_4 on the piano keyboard has a fundamental frequency of 220 Hz, A_5 has a fundamental frequency of 440 Hz, A_6 has a frequency of 880 Hz and so on. Tones in this octave relation to one another have the same chroma.

The concepts of tone height and tone chroma can be illustrated by arranging tones in a spiral like the one in Figure 11.9. Tones higher up on the spiral have more tone height (i.e., their pitch is higher), and tones directly above or below each other (see vertical line) have the same tone chroma (i.e., these tones are indicated by the same letter). Tone chroma is important because two notes with the same

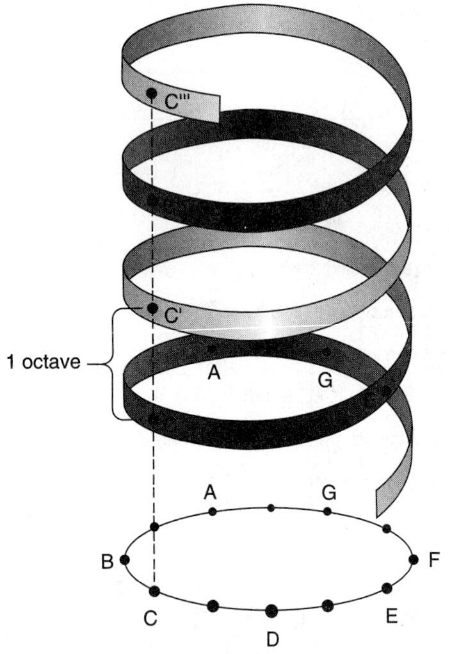

Figure 11.9
Representing the notes of the scale on an ascending spiral graphically depicts the perceptions of tone height and tone chroma. As we move up along a vertical line, we encounter notes with the same letter. These notes, which are separated by octaves and therefore sound similar to each other, have the same tone chroma. As we move from one note to another in ascending the spiral, each note sounds higher than the note preceding it. This property is called tone height. Thus, two C's separated by an octave or more would have different tone heights but the same tone chroma.

chroma are *psychologically* similar. Thus, a male and a female can be regarded as singing "in unison" even if their voices are separated by an octave or more. This similarity between the same notes in different octaves also makes it possible for a singer on the verge of overreaching his or her voice range to shift the melody down to a lower octave.

Timbre

If two tones have the same loudness, pitch, and duration, but sound different, this difference is a difference in **timbre** (pronounced tim'-ber or tam'-bre). For example, a flute and a bassoon playing the same note sound very different. The flute sounds "clear" or "mellow" and the bassoon sounds "nasal" or "reedy." We will see in Chapter 12 that these differences in timbre are caused by a number of factors, including differences in the energy of the harmonics created by different musical instruments.

Auditory System: Structure and Function

The auditory system must accomplish three basic tasks before we can hear. First, it must deliver the acoustic stimulus to the receptors. Second, it must transduce this stimulus from pressure changes into electrical signals, and third, it must process these electrical signals so they can efficiently indicate qualities of the sound source such as pitch, loudness, timbre, and location.

We begin our description of how the auditory system accomplishes these tasks by describing the basic structure of the system. Our first question, "How does energy from the environment reach the receptors?" was easy to answer for vision since light enters the eye through the pupil and travels to the back of the eyeball, where it reaches the rods and cones. However, the auditory system is much more complicated. We begin our description as the sound stimulus enters the outer ear.

The Outer Ear

When we talk about the "ears" in everyday conversation, we are usually referring to the *pinnae*, the structures that stick out from the sides of the head. While this most obvious part of the ear is of some importance in helping us determine the location of sounds and is of great importance for those who wear eyeglasses, it is the part of the ear we could most easily do without. The major workings of the ear are found inside the head, hidden from view.

Sound waves first pass through the **outer ear,** which consists of the **pinna** and the **auditory canal** (Figure 11.10). The auditory canal is a tubelike structure about 3 cm long that protects the delicate structures of the middle ear from the hazards of the outside world. The auditory canal's 3-cm recess, along with its wax, which has an unpleasant effect on curious insects (Schubert, 1980), protects the delicate **tympanic membrane,** or **eardrum,** at the end of the canal and helps keep this membrane and the structures in the middle ear at a relatively constant temperature.

In addition to its protective function, the outer ear has another role: to enhance the intensities of some sounds by means of the physical principle of **resonance.** Resonance occurs when sound waves near the **resonant frequency** of the auditory canal are reflected from the closed end of the canal and, on their way back out, reinforce the incoming sound waves of the same frequency. The resonant frequency of the auditory canal, which is determined by the length of the canal, is about 3,400 Hz, and measurements of the sound pressures inside the ear indicate that the resonance that occurs in the auditory canal has a slight amplifying effect on frequencies between about 2,000 and 5,000 Hz.

The Middle Ear

When airborne sound waves reach the tympanic membrane at the end of the auditory canal, they set it into vibration, and this vibration is transmitted to structures in the middle ear, on the other side of the tympanic membrane. The **middle ear** is a small cavity, about 2 cm^2 in volume, which separates the outer and inner ears (Figure 11.11). This cavity contains the **ossicles,** the three smallest bones in the body, which are suspended by four ligaments. The first of these bones, the **malleus,** is set into vibration by the tympanic membrane, to which it is attached, and transmits its vibrations to the **incus,** which, in turn, transmits its vibrations to the **stapes.** The stapes then transmits its vibrations to the inner ear by pushing on the membrane covering the **oval window.**

Why are the ossicles necessary? We can answer this question by noting that both the outer ear and middle ear are filled with air, but the inner ear contains a watery liquid called *cochlear fluid,* which is much denser than the air (Figure 11.12). The mismatch between the low density of the air and the high density of the cochlear fluid creates a problem: Pressure changes in the air are transmitted poorly to the

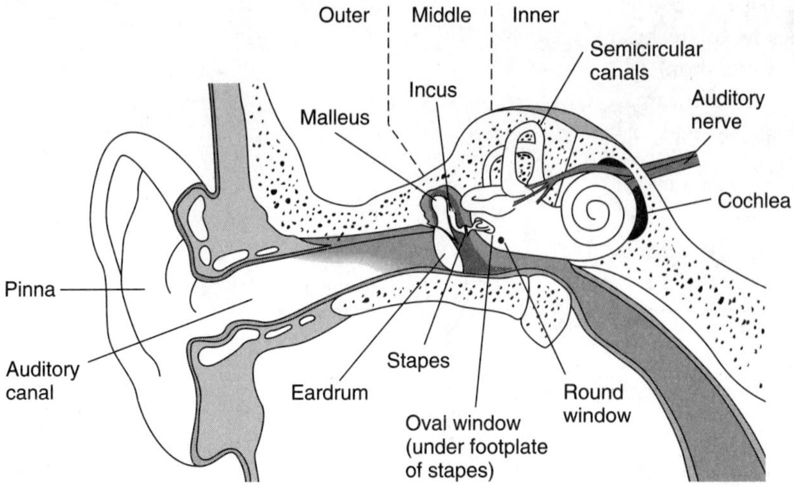

Figure 11.10
The ear, showing its three subdivisions—outer, middle, and inner.

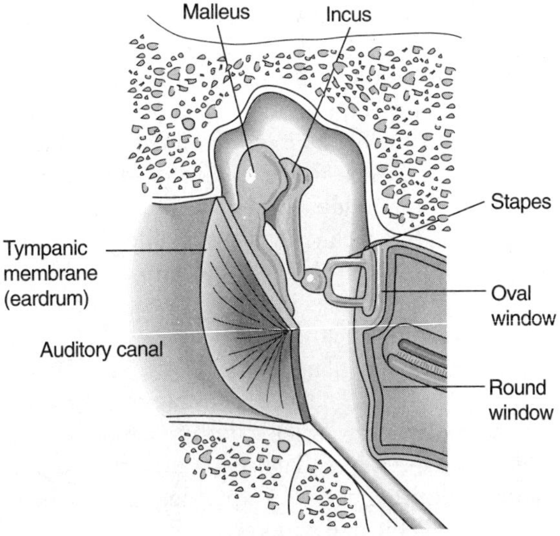

Figure 11.11
The middle ear. The three bones of the middle ear transmit the vibrations of the tympanic membrane to the inner ear.

much denser cochlear fluid. If these vibrations had to pass directly from the air to the fluid, only about 3 percent of the vibrations would be transmitted (Durrant & Lovrinic, 1977). The ossicles help solve this problem in two ways:

1. The ossicles concentrate the vibration of the large tympanic membrane onto the smaller stapes. The tympanic membrane has an area of about 0.6 cm^2, whereas the stapes footplate has an area of about 0.032 cm^2—a ratio of about 17 to 1. Concentrating the vibration of the large tympanic membrane onto the smaller stapes, as shown in Figure 11.13, increases the pressure per unit area in the same way that a 110-lb woman wearing shoes with 1-cm diameter spiked heels can generate a pressure of 110,000 pounds per square foot by standing on one heel.

2. The ossicles act according to the lever principle. Figure 11.14 illustrates this principle. If a board is balanced on a fulcrum, a small weight on the long end of the board can overcome a larger weight on the short end of the board. Though it is not obvious from looking at the ossicles, they are hinged so that they increase the vibration by a factor of about 1.3 by means of this lever principle.

These two mechanisms increase the strength of the vibrations by a factor of at least 22 ($1.3 \times 17 = 22.1$); (Durrant & Lovrinic, 1977), with some calculations setting this value as high as a factor of 100 (Schubert, 1980). Without the ossicles of the middle ear, it would be much more difficult for us to hear. When the effect of losing the ossicles is measured in patients whose ossicles have been damaged beyond surgical repair, it has been found that the sound pressure must be increased by a factor of 10 to 50 for the person to achieve the same hearing ability as when the ossicles were functioning.

The middle ear also contains the **middle ear muscles,** the smallest skeletal muscles in the body.

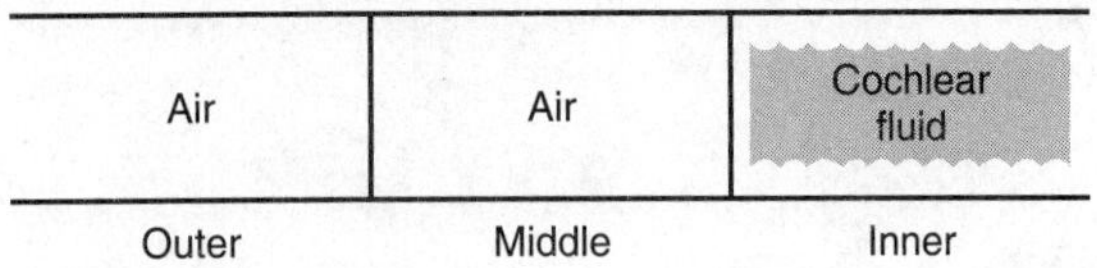

Figure 11.12
Environments inside the outer, middle, and inner ears. The fact that liquid fills the inner ear poses a problem for the transmission of sound vibrations from the air of the middle ear.

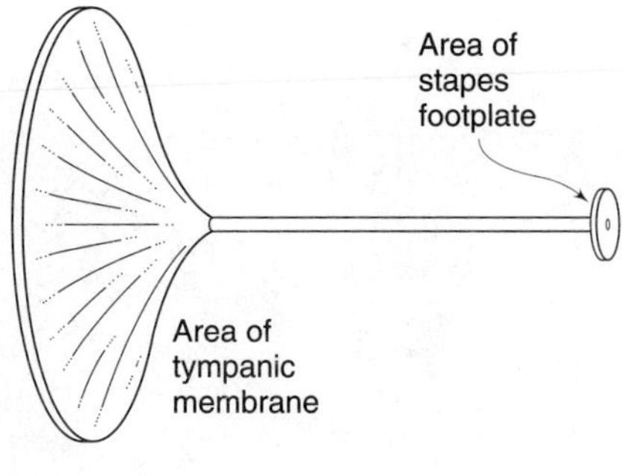

Figure 11.13
A diagrammatic representation of the tympanic membrane and the stapes, showing the difference in size between the two. (From Schubert, 1980.)

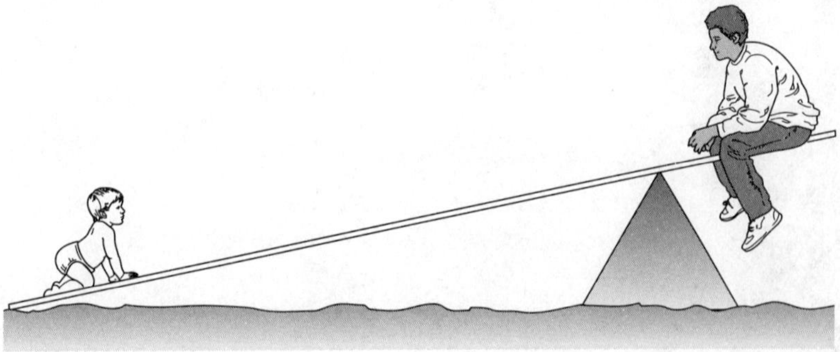

Figure 11.14
The lever principle. The baby on the long end of the board can overcome the weight of the man on the short end. (The baby will, however, be in for a surprise if it crawls very far toward the man.)

These muscles are attached to the ossicles, and at very high sound intensities they contract to dampen the ossicle's vibration, thereby protecting the structures of the inner ear against potentially painful and damaging stimuli.

The Inner Ear

The main structure of the **inner ear** is the liquid-filled **cochlea.** The liquid inside the cochlea vibrates because of the vibration of the stapes against the oval window. The cochlea, which is a bony snail-like structure, is difficult to visualize because it is rolled into 2¾ turns. But we can see the structure inside more clearly by imagining how the cochlea would appear if uncoiled to form a long straight tube (Figure 11.15). The most obvious feature of the uncoiled cochlea is that the upper half, called the *scala vestibuli,* and the lower half, called the *scala tympani,* are separated by a structure called the **cochlear partition,** which extends almost the entire length of the cochlea. Note that this diagram is not drawn to scale and so doesn't show the cochlea's true shape. In reality, the uncoiled cochlea would be a cylinder 2 mm in diameter and 35 mm long.

We can best see the structures within the cochlear partition by looking at the cochlea end-on and in cross section, as in Figure 11.16. When we look at the cochlea in this way, we see that the cochlear partition contains a large structure called the **organ of Corti.** Details of the organ of Corti are shown in Figure 11.17. From these figures, we can see that (1) the organ of Corti contains the *inner and outer hair cells;* (2) it sits on top of the **basilar membrane;** and (3) it is covered on top by the **tectorial membrane.**

The **hair cells** are shown in Figure 11.18. There are two types of hair cells, the **inner hair cells** and the **outer hair cells.** A key component of both of these types of hair cells are the fine **cilia,** which protrude from the top of the hair cell. These cilia give the hair cells their name.

One of the most important events in the auditory process is the bending of the cilia, because this bending leads to *transduction*—the changing of the sound stimulus into electrical signals. What causes the cilia to bend? To answer this question let's return to the oval window, where the stapes is vibrating. When the stapes pushes in on the oval window, it transmits pressure to the liquid inside the cochlea. From Figure 11.15b, we might think that this pressure would be transmitted down the scala vestibuli, around the opening at the end of the cochlear partition, and down the scala tympani to the **round window.** However, this is not what happens.

Very little pressure is transmitted around the end of the cochlear partition; the opening joining the scala tympani and the scala vestibuli functions almost as if it were closed. Rather than transmit pressure through the opening, the liquid in the scala vestibuli pushes on the cochlear partition. This push causes the elastic basilar membrane to move downward. Then, when the stapes pulls back from the oval window the process is reversed and the basilar membrane moves upward.

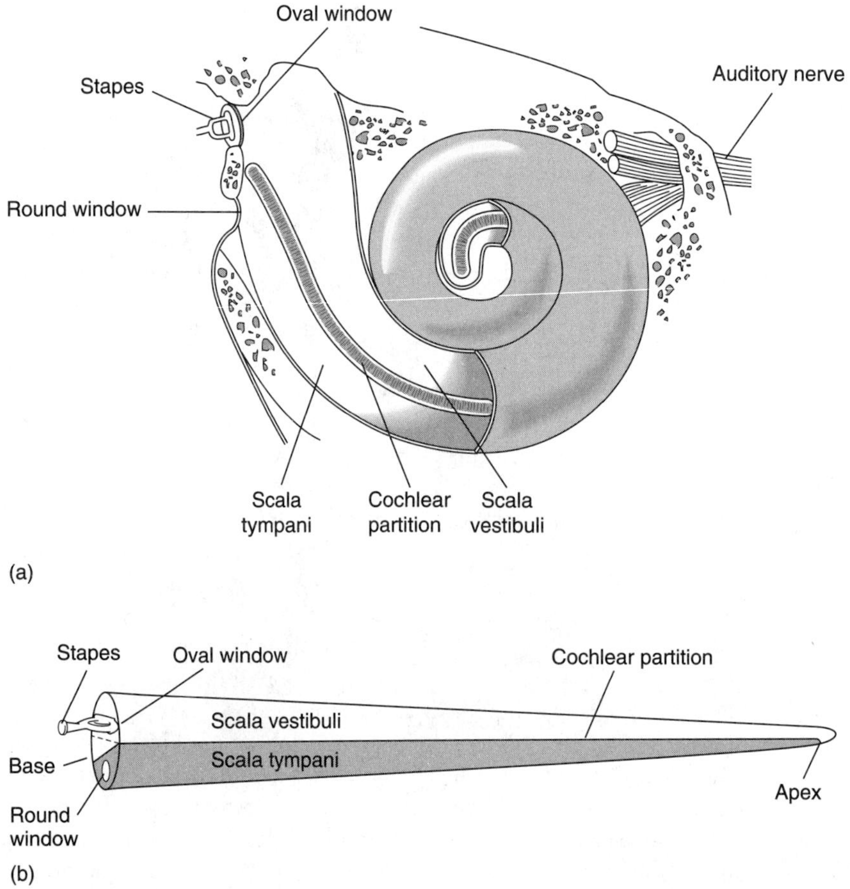

Figure 11.15
(a) A partially uncoiled cochlea. (b) A fully uncoiled cochlea. The cochlear partition, which is indicated here by a line, actually contains the basilar membrane and the organ of Corti, which are shown in Figures 11.16 and 11.17.

This up and down motion of the basilar membrane causes two effects (1) the organ of Corti, which rests on the basilar membrane, also vibrates with an up-and-down motion and (2) the tectorial membrane, which covers the organ of Corti, moves with a back-and-forth motion relative to the cilia of the hair cells (Figure 11.19). These two motions cause the cilia of the inner hair cells to bend because of their movement against the surrounding liquid and the cilia of the outer hair cells to bend because they are embedded in the tectorial membrane (Dallos, 1996).

The bending of the cilia of the inner hair cells generates the electrical signal that is transmitted to fibers in the auditory nerve. (We will describe the function of the outer hair cells later in the chapter.) When the inner hair cells' cilia bend in one direction, the hair cells depolarize (their charge decreases as does that of the nerve fiber in Figure 1.19), and when the cilia bend in the other direction, the hair cells hyperpolarize (their charge increases). This alternation between increases and decreases in charge every time the basilar membrane vibrates causes the hair cells to

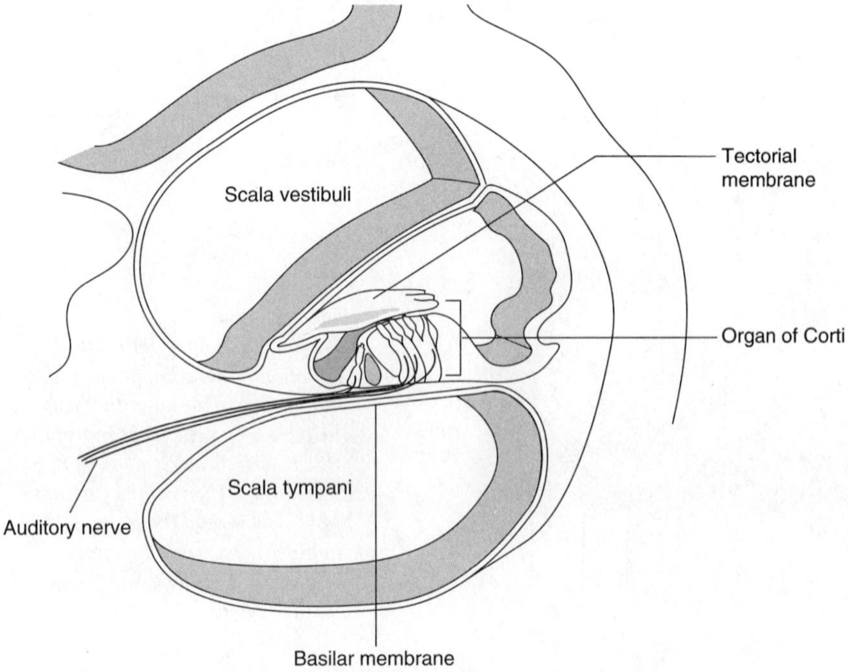

Figure 11.16
A cross section of the cochlea.

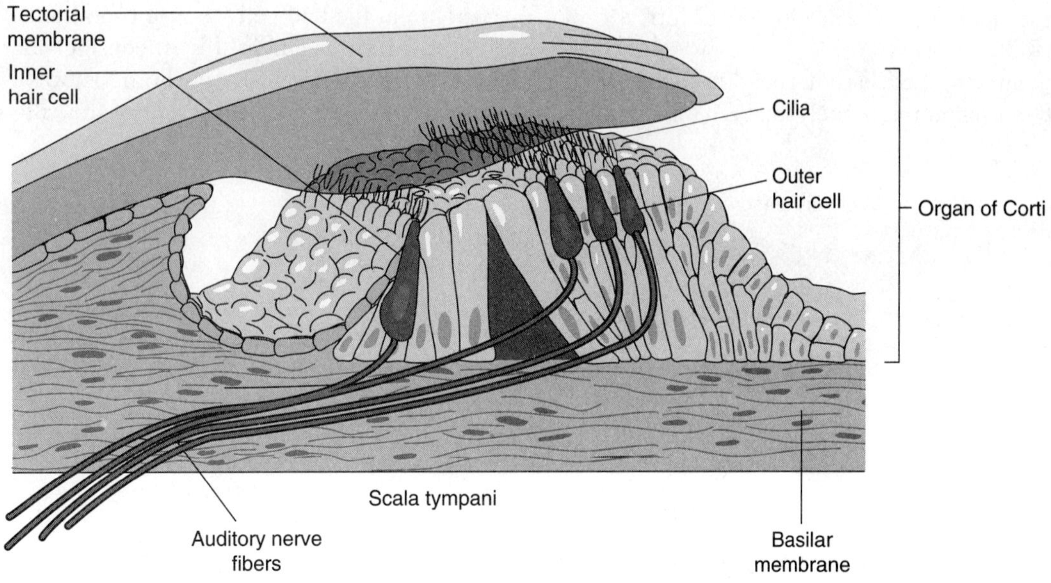

Figure 11.17
A cross-section of the organ of Corti, showing how it rests upon the basilar membrane and how the tectorial membrane is positioned over the hair cells. (Adapted from Denes and Pinson.)

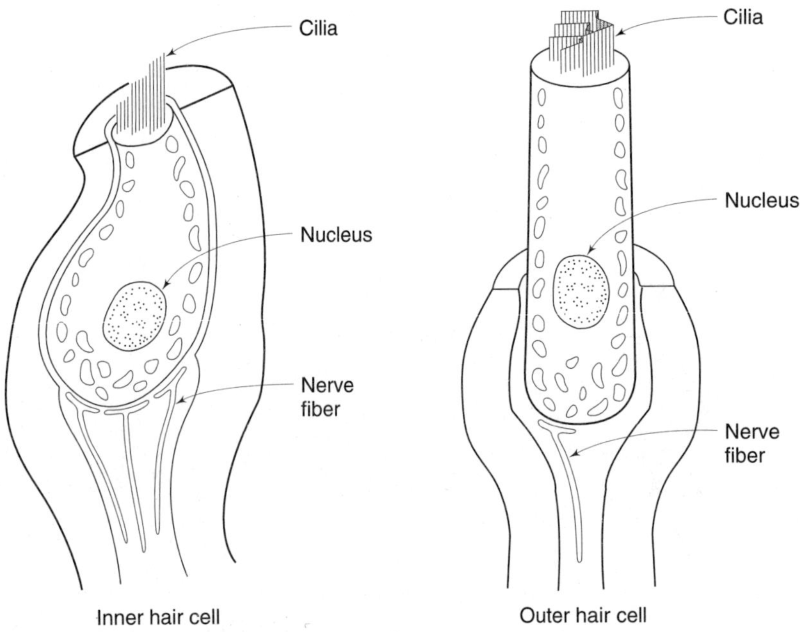

Figure 11.18
The inner and outer hair cells. Vibration of the cilia, or hairs, generates an electrical signal that causes the release of a chemical transmitter, which generates a response in nerve fibers, which then conduct signals that travel toward the brain in the auditory nerve. (Adapted from Gulick, 1971; Gulick, Gescheider, & Frisina, 1989.)

release a burst of neurotransmitter, and this transmitter causes bursts of firing that sends a neural message along the auditory nerve about the occurrence of sound (Kelly, 1991).

The amount the cilia must bend to cause the release of transmitter is extremely small. At the threshold for hearing, cilia movements as small as 100 trillionths of a meter (100 picometers) can generate a response in the hair cell. To give you an idea of just how small a movement this is, consider that if we were to increase the size of a cilium so it was as big as the Eiffel Tower, the movement of the cilia would

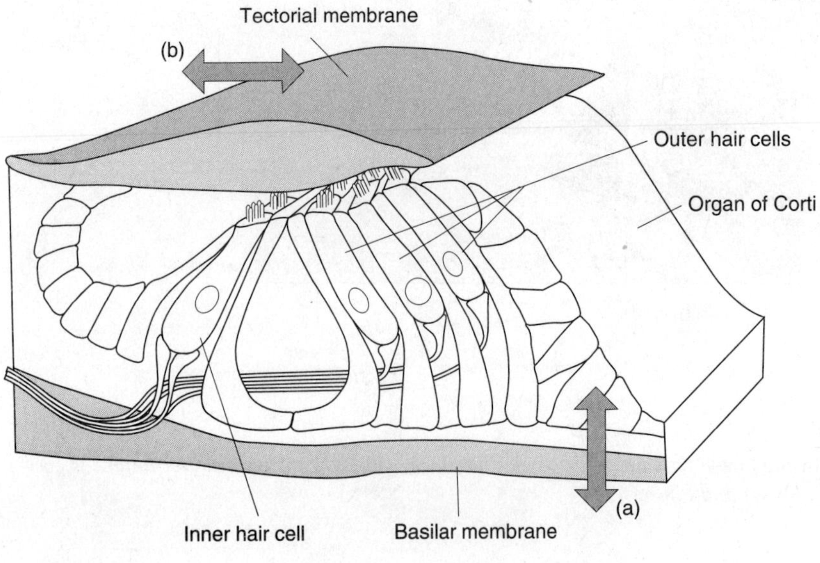

Figure 11.19
Vibration of the basilar membrane causes (a) the organ of Corti to vibrate up and down and (b) the tectorial membrane to move with a complex back-and-forth motion relative to the hair cells.

translate into a movement of the pinnacle of the Eiffel Tower of only 10-mm(Figure 11.20). (Hudspeth, 1983, 1989)

The Auditory Pathways

The auditory nerve carries the signals generated by the inner hair cells as these signals begin their journey toward the auditory receiving area in the cortex. Figure 11.21 shows the pathway the auditory signals follow from the cochlea to the auditory cortex. After auditory nerve fibers from the cochlea synapse in the **cochlear nucleus**, they then synapse in the **superior olivary nucleus** in the brain stem, the **inferior colliculus** of the midbrain, and the **medial geniculate nucleus** of the thalamus. (Remember that signals from the retina synapse in a nearby area of the thalamus, the lateral geniculate nucleus.)

From the medial geniculate nucleus, fibers go to the primary **auditory receiving area,** in the temporal lobe of the cortex (Figure 11.22). If you have trouble remembering this sequence of structures, remember the acronym SONIC MG (a very fast sports car), which represents the three structures between the cochlear nucleus and the auditory cortex, as follows: SON = Superior Olivary Nucleus; IC = Inferior Colliculus; MG = Medial Geniculate Nucleus.

The primary auditory receiving area is also called A1, since it is the first place signals are received in the cortex. Just as in the visual system, there are numerous other cortical areas beyond the primary receiving area. The **secondary auditory cortex,** or A2, lies just below A1, and numerous other auditory areas surround A1 and A2, mainly in the temporal lobe (Brugge & Reale, 1985).

In addition to the pathways shown in Figure 11.21, there are also fibers that connect structures on the opposite sides of the brain, and *efferent fibers* that send signals from the brain back toward the cochlea. We will discuss efferent fibers at the end of the chapter.

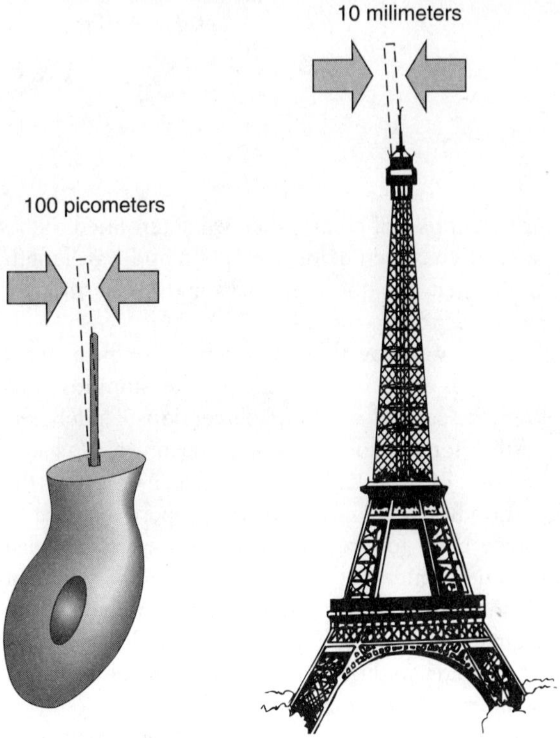

Figure 11.20
The distance the cilia of a hair cell moves at the threshold for hearing is so small, that if the volume of an individual cilium is scaled up to that of the Eiffel Tower, the equivalent movement of the Eiffel tower would be about 10-mm.

The Place Code for Pitch: Traveling Waves, Tuning Curves, and Maps

Now that we have seen how pressure changes entering the outer ear become transformed into bursts of firing in the auditory nerve, we will ask one of the central questions of auditory research: *How does the firing of these neurons signal different pitches?* This question is analogous to one we considered in the chapter on color vision, when we asked: *How does the firing of neurons signal different colors?* We saw that the first step in answering this question about color vision was to identify wavelength as the characteristic of the stimulus most closely associated with

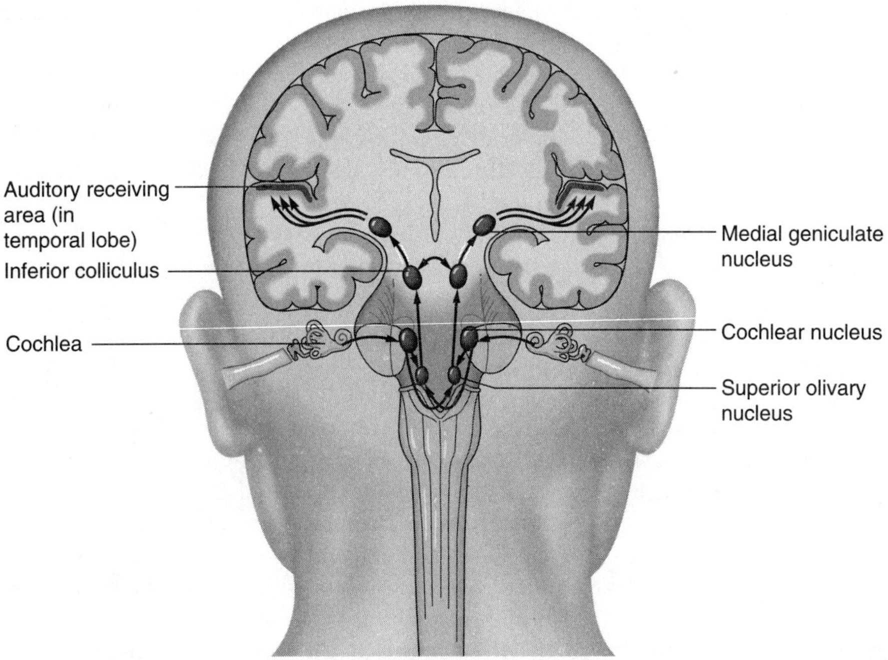

Figure 11.21
Diagram of the auditory pathways. This diagram is greatly simplified, as numerous connections between the structures are not shown. Note that auditory structures are bilateral—they exist on both the left and right sides of the body—and that messages can cross over between the two sides. (Adapted from Wever, 1949.)

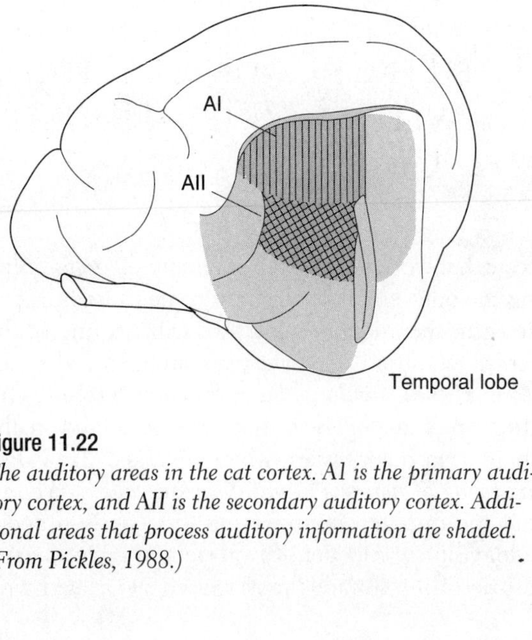

Figure 11.22
The auditory areas in the cat cortex. AI is the primary auditory cortex, and AII is the secondary auditory cortex. Additional areas that process auditory information are shaded. (From Pickles, 1988.)

our perception of color. Once we determined the relationship between color perception and wavelength, we changed our question to: *How does the firing of neurons signal wavelength?*

Since we know that the frequency of the acoustic stimulus is the characteristic of the stimulus most closely associated with our perception of pitch, our question for the auditory system becomes, *How does the firing of neurons signal frequency?* One way this question has been answered is to propose that there is a **place code for frequency.** According to this idea, different frequencies are signaled by activity in neurons that are located at different *places* in the auditory system. This process begins in the cochlea, with hair cell receptors in different places in the cochlea signaling different frequencies (Figure 11.23).

We will first describe an early version of place theory proposed by Hermann von Helmholtz, and will then describe the modern version of place theory proposed by Georg von Bekesy, and recent research that has built on Bekesy's discoveries.

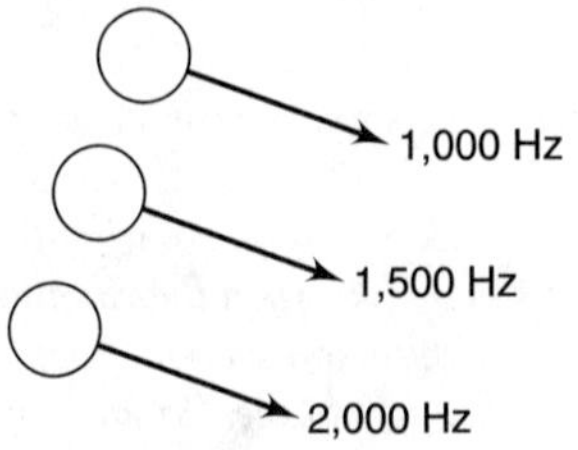

Figure 11.23
The idea behind a place code for frequency is that different frequencies are signaled by neurons located in different places in the auditory system. This drawing, which doesn't represent any particular structure in the auditory system, shows three different neurons located in different places that fire best to different frequencies.

Helmholtz' Resonance Theory

An early place theory was proposed by Hermann von Helmholtz (1863/1954), who also championed the trichromatic theory of color vision. Helmholtz' proposal was called **resonance theory.** This theory proposed that the basilar membrane is made up of a series of loosely connected transverse fibers, as shown in Figure 11.24, each tuned to resonate to a specific frequency. Helmholtz knew that the basilar membrane was wider at one end than at the other, so he hypothesized that low frequencies would set the longer fibers into vibration and high frequencies would set the shorter fibers into vibration, just as long strings on the harp or piano correspond to low pitches and short strings to high pitches.

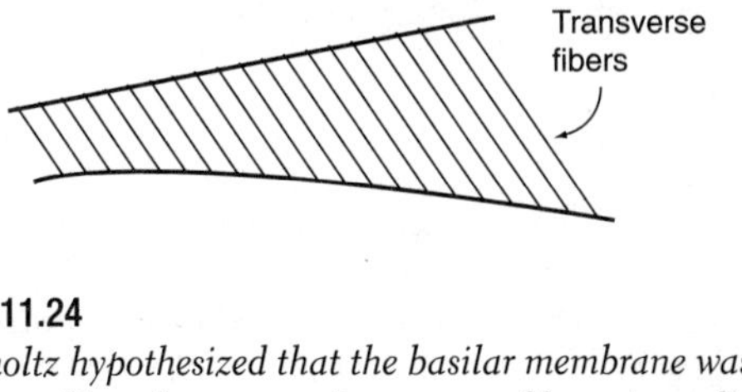

Figure 11.24
Helmholtz hypothesized that the basilar membrane was made up of loosely connected transverse fibers. According to Helmholtz, vibration of long fibers signaled low frequencies and vibration of short fibers signaled high frequencies.

According to this idea, a particular frequency would stimulate only the basilar membrane fiber sensitive to this frequency, and this fiber's vibration would cause the hair cells at this location on the basilar membrane to fire. Resonance theory has been rejected, however, because we now know that the basilar membrane's fibers are connected to each other so that one cannot resonate independently of the others, as Helmholtz proposed. As we will see next, large portions of the basilar membrane vibrate in response to sound.

Békésy's Discovery: The Basilar Membrane Vibrates in a Traveling Wave

Georg von Békésy established the modern era of research on the ear with a series of studies begun in 1928, which culminated in Békésy's being awarded the Nobel Prize in physiology and medicine in 1961. Békésy focused his attention on the basilar membrane—the structure that stretches from one end of the cochlea to the other and that supports the organ of Corti. His major concern was determining how the basilar membrane vibrated in response to different frequencies. He determined this in two ways: (1) by actually observing the vibration of the basilar membrane, and (2) by building a model of the cochlea that took into account the physical properties of the basilar membrane.

Békésy observed the vibration of the basilar membrane by boring a hole in the ear of a human cadaver, stimulating it with sound, and observing the membrane's vibration with a microscope (Békésy, 1960). He found that the vibrating motion of the basilar membrane is similar to the motion that occurs when one person holds the end of a rope and "snaps" it, sending a wave traveling down the rope. This **traveling wave** motion of the basilar membrane is shown in Figure 11.25.

Békésy also determined how the basilar membrane vibrates by analyzing its structure, taking note of two important facts: (1) The **base of the basilar membrane** (the end located nearest the oval window and the stapes) is three or four times narrower than that of the **apex of the basilar membrane** (the end of

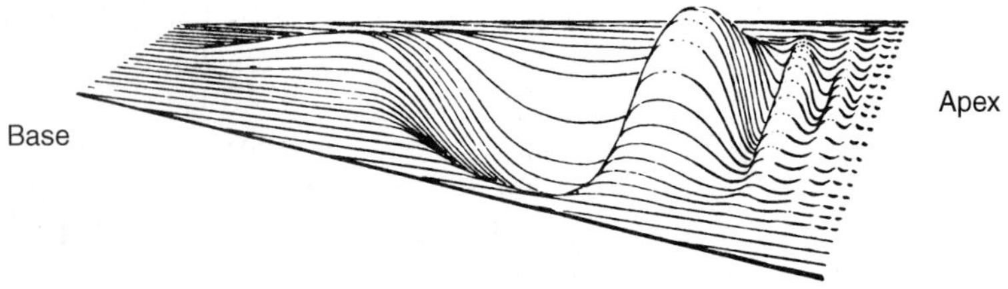

Figure 11.25
A perspective view showing the traveling wave motion of the basilar membrane. This picture shows what the membrane looks like when the vibration is "frozen" with the wave about ⅔ of the way down the membrane. (From Tonndorf, 1960.)

the membrane located at the far end of the cochlea; Figure 11.26), and (2) the basilar membrane is about 100 times stiffer at its base than at its apex. Using this information, Békésy constructed models of the cochlea which revealed that the basilar membrane vibrates in a traveling wave in response to the pressure changes caused by vibration of the cochlear fluid.

Figure 11.27 shows what a traveling wave looks like at three successive moments in time. The solid horizontal line represents the basilar membrane at rest. Curve 1 shows the position of the basilar membrane at one moment during its vibration, and curves 2 and 3 show the positions of the membrane at two later moments. Since the shape of the traveling wave changes at each point in time, it is difficult to visualize the wave's overall effect on the basilar membrane. We can, however, visualize its overall effect more easily by determining the maximum displacement that the wave causes at each point along the membrane. This maximum displacement, which is indicated by the dashed line, is called the **envelope of the traveling wave.** The envelope is important because it tells us which hair cells along the basilar membrane will be affected the most by the membrane's vibration. Since the amount that the cilia bend depends on the amount that the basilar membrane is displaced, hair cells located near the place where the basilar membrane vibrates the most will be stimulated the most strongly.

Békésy's (1960) observations of the basilar membrane's vibrations led him to conclude that the envelope of the traveling wave of the basilar membrane has two important properties:

1. The envelope is peaked at one point on the basilar membrane. The envelope of Figure 11.27 indicates that point P on the basilar membrane is displaced the most by the traveling wave. Thus, the hair cells near point P will send out stronger signals than those near other parts of the membrane.

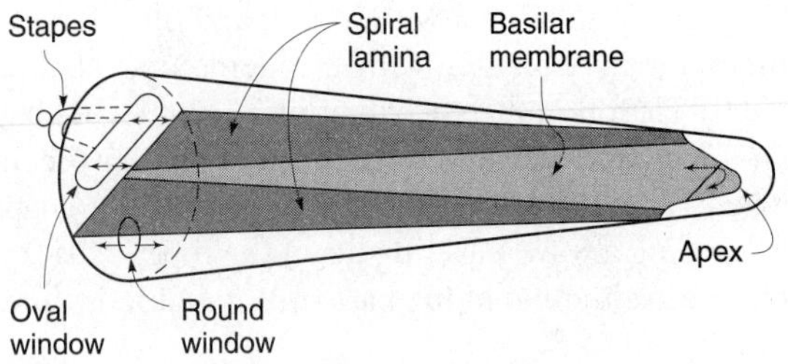

Figure 11.26
A perspective view of an uncoiled cochlea, showing how the basilar membrane gets wider at the apex end of the cochlea. The spiral lamina is a supporting structure that makes up for the basilar membrane's difference in width at the stapes and the apex ends of the cochlea. (From Schubert, 1980.)

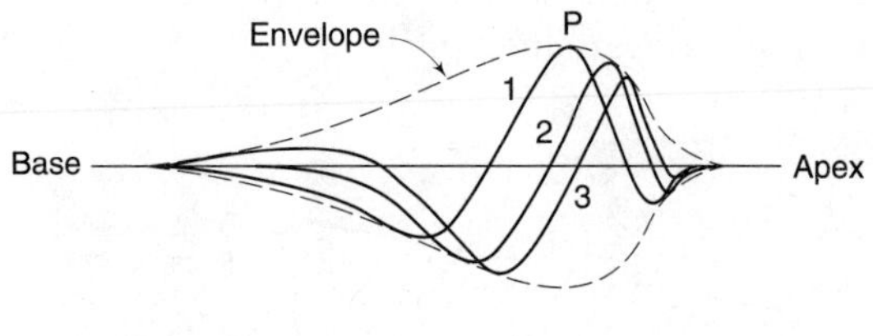

Figure 11.27
Vibration of the basilar membrane, showing the position of the membrane at three instants in time, indicated by the solid lines, and the envelope of the vibration, indicated by the dashed lines. P indicates the peak of the basilar membrane vibration. Hair cells located at this position on the membrane are maximally stimulated by the membrane's vibration. (Adapted from Bekesy, 1960.)

2. The position of this peak on the basilar membrane is a function of the frequency of the sound. We can see in Figure 11.28, which shows the envelopes of vibration for stimuli ranging from 25 to 1,600 Hz, that low frequencies cause maximum vibration near the apex. High frequencies cause more of the membrane to vibrate and the maximum vibration is near the base. (One way to remember this relationship is to imagine low frequency waves as being long waves that reach farther.)

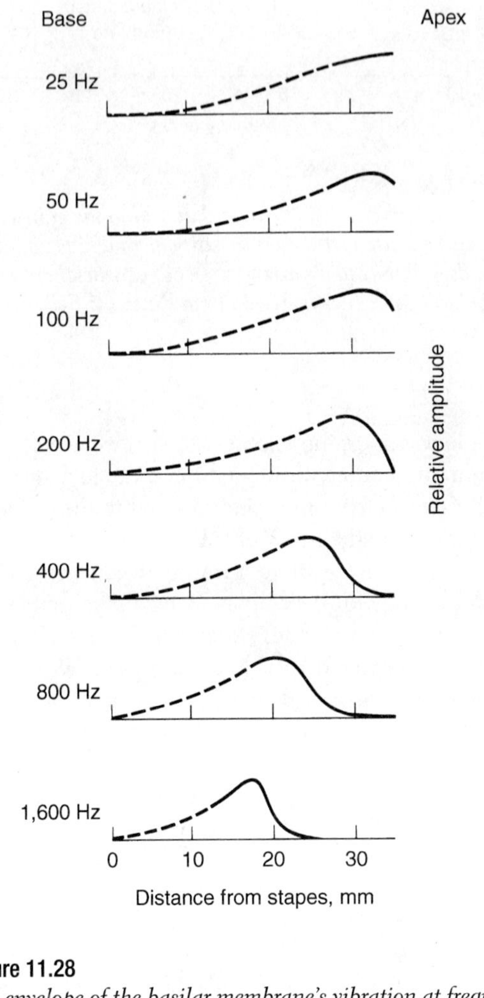

Figure 11.28
The envelope of the basilar membrane's vibration at frequencies ranging from 25 to 1,600 Hz, as measured by Bekesy (1960).

These observations of how the vibration of the basilar membrane depends on frequency have been repeated by other researchers using techniques more sensitive than the ones available when Bekesy was making his observations. These new observations confirmed that the place of maximum basilar membrane vibration depends on frequency and showed that the peak vibration for a particular frequency is even more sharply localized than Békésy had observed (Johnstone & Boyle, 1967; Khanna & Leonard, 1982). In addition, other research has confirmed Békésy's place theory in other ways. We will now consider some physiological evidence for place coding.

Physiological Evidence for Place Coding

Békésy's linking of the place on the cochlea with the frequency of the tone has also been confirmed by measuring the electrical response of the cochlea and of individual hair cells and auditory nerve fibers.

Tonotopic Maps on the Cochlea Early electrophysiological evidence for place coding was provided by placing disc electrodes at different places along the length of the cochlea and measuring the electrical response to different frequencies. The result is a **tonotopic map**—an orderly map of frequencies along the length of the cochlea (Culler et al., 1943). This result, shown in Figure 11.29, confirms the idea that the apex of the cochlea responds best to low frequencies and the base to high frequencies.

Hair Cell and Auditory Nerve Fiber Tuning More precise electrophysiological evidence for place coding is provided by microelectrode recording from individual hair cells and auditory nerve fibers. Measuring the intensity in dB SPL necessary to elicit a small response at each frequency yields a curve called a **frequency tuning curve.** The curve in Figure 11.30 is from a single hair cell in the guinea pig's cochlea that is most sensitive at about 18,000 Hz (Russell & Sellick, 1977). The frequency to which

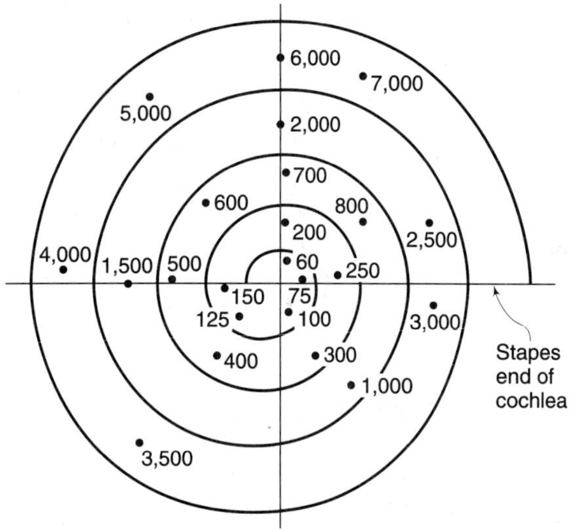

Figure 11.29
Tonotopic map of the cochlea. Numbers indicate the location of the maximum electrical response for each frequency. Low frequencies cause the largest response near the apex end of the spiral, and high frequencies cause the largest response at the base, at the stapes end of the cochlea. (From Culler et al., 1943.)

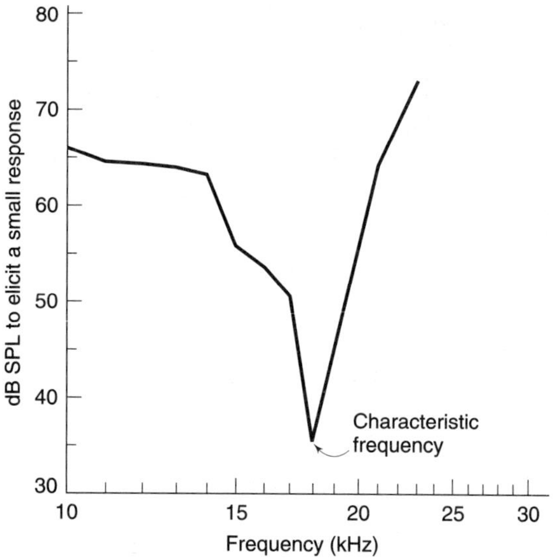

Figure 11.30
The tuning curve of a single inner hair cell in the guinea pig cochlea. This hair cell is most sensitive at 18,000 Hz and responds well only to a narrow range of frequencies above and below this frequency. (Data from Russell & Sellick, 1977.)

the hair cell is most sensitive is called the **characteristic frequency** of the neuron. Auditory nerve fibers have tuning curves that are similar to hair-cell tuning curves. Figure 11.31 shows curves for cat auditory nerve fibers with characteristic frequencies at about 680 Hz, 4,000 Hz, and 12,000 Hz.

It is clear from the physiological evidence, that specific frequencies are signaled by activity at specific places along the cochlea and in the auditory nerve fibers that transmit these signals from the cochlea. We can also demonstrate this separation of frequencies along the cochlea psychophysically by using a procedure called *masking.*

Psychophysical Evidence for Place Coding

One of the principles we established when we studied color vision was that perceptual observations can provide information about a system's underlying physiology. For example, observing that we need to mix a minimum of three wavelengths in order to match any other wavelength in the spectrum, led to the proposal of the trichromatic theory of color vision.

We can demonstrate a link between perception and physiology for hearing by using a psychophysical technique called **auditory masking.** The basic principle behind masking is that one tone, if intense enough, can *mask* or decrease our perception of another tone that is occurring at the same time.

A Masking Experiment The procedure for a masking experiment is shown in Figure 11.32. First, the threshold for hearing is determined across a range of frequencies, by determining the lowest intensity at each frequency that can just be heard (Figure 11.32a). Then, a masking stimulus is presented at a particular place along the frequency scale, and while the masking stimulus is sounding, the thresholds for all frequencies are redetermined (Figure 11.32b).

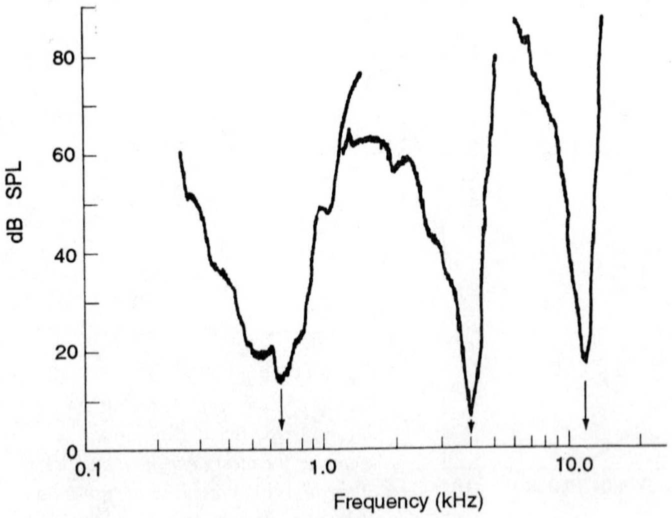

Figure 11.31
The tuning curves of three auditory nerve fibers in one animal. The characteristic frequency of each fiber is indicated by the arrows along the frequency axis. (From Kiang, 1975.)

We will describe an experiment by J. P. Egan and H. W. Hake (1950) in which they used a **white noise** masking stimulus. A white noise stimulus is one that contains a band of frequencies with equal sound pressure at each frequency. Such a combination of frequencies sounds something like the "shhhhhh" sound you can make by separating your teeth slightly and blowing air across your lower teeth. Egan and Hake's noise stimulus was a band of frequencies 90 Hz wide centered on 410 Hz. Thus, it contained frequencies ranging from 365 to 455 Hz.

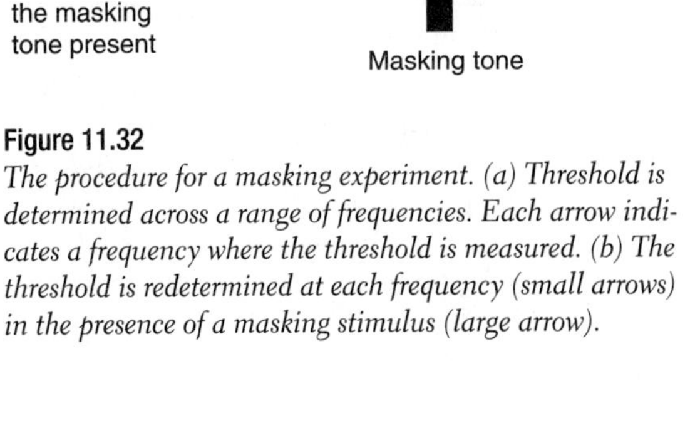

Figure 11.32
The procedure for a masking experiment. (a) Threshold is determined across a range of frequencies. Each arrow indicates a frequency where the threshold is measured. (b) The threshold is redetermined at each frequency (small arrows) in the presence of a masking stimulus (large arrow).

When Egan and Hake measured the thresholds in the presence of this masking noise, they observed the result shown in Figure 11.33, which indicates the amount that the masking noise increased the original threshold at each frequency. Notice that the threshold increases the most for frequencies near the frequencies in the masking tone. Also, notice that this curve is not symmetrical. That is, the masking effect spreads more to high frequencies than to low frequencies.

We can relate this asymmetrical effect of the masking tone to the vibration of the basilar membrane, as shown in Figure 11.34, which reproduces the vibration patterns from Figure 11.27 caused by 200-Hz, 400-Hz, and 800-Hz tones. We can see how a 400-Hz masking tone would affect the 200- and 800-Hz tones by noting how their vibration patterns overlap. Notice that the pattern for the 400-Hz tone, which is shaded, almost totally overlaps the pattern for the higher-frequency 800-Hz tone, but that it does not overlap the place of peak vibration of the lower-frequency 200-Hz tone. We would therefore expect the masking tone to have a large effect on the 800-Hz tone but a smaller effect on the 200-Hz tone. This is exactly what happened in Egan and Hake's masking experiment. Thus, the asymmetrical masking function in

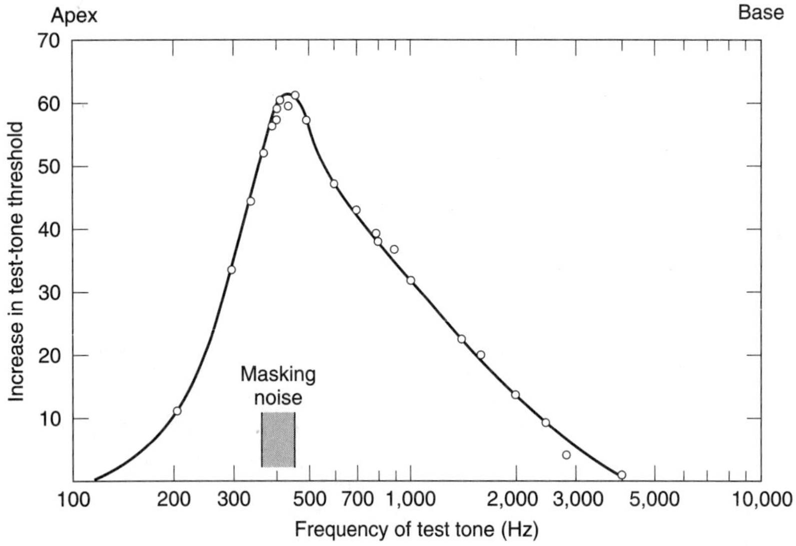

Figure 11.33
Results of Egan and Hake's (1950) masking experiment. The threshold increases the most near the frequencies of the masking noise and the masking effect spreads more to high frequencies.

Figure 11.33 is consistent with Bekesy's description of the way the basilar membrane vibrates.

Masking has also been used in another way to determine a function called the *psychophysical tuning curve,* which is also consistent with the place mechanism.

Psychophysical Tuning Curves The procedure for determining a **psychophysical tuning curve** is shown in Figure 11.35. We present a low-intensity (10-dB-SPL) pure tone called the *test tone,* with a frequency that remains constant throughout the experiment. We then present a series of masking tones that are pure tones—one with the same frequency as the test tone and others with lower and higher frequencies—and determine the sound pressure level for each masking tone that is needed to reduce the loudness of the low-intensity tone so that it is just barely detectable.

We can understand the rationale behind this procedure by imagining that the horizontal line in Figure 11.35 is the basilar membrane. If the test tone

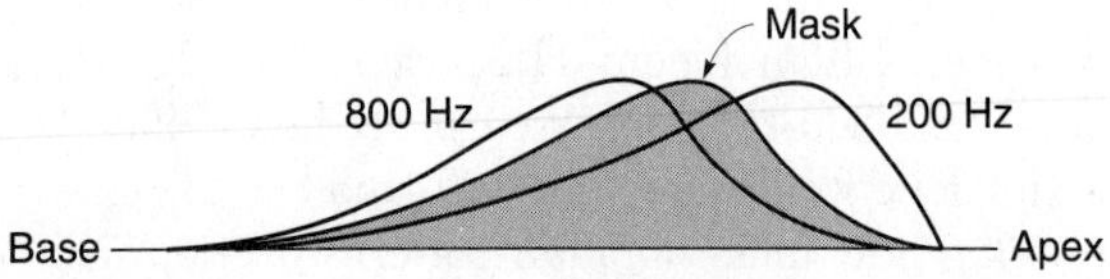

Figure 11.34
Vibration patterns caused by 200- and 800-Hz test tones, and the 410-Hz mask, taken from basilar membrane vibration patterns in Figure 11.28. The pattern for a 400-Hz tone is used for the masking pattern (shaded). Since the mask actually contains a band of frequencies, the actual pattern would be wider than is shown here. It would, however, still be asymmetrical and would overlap the 800-Hz vibration more than the 200-Hz vibration.

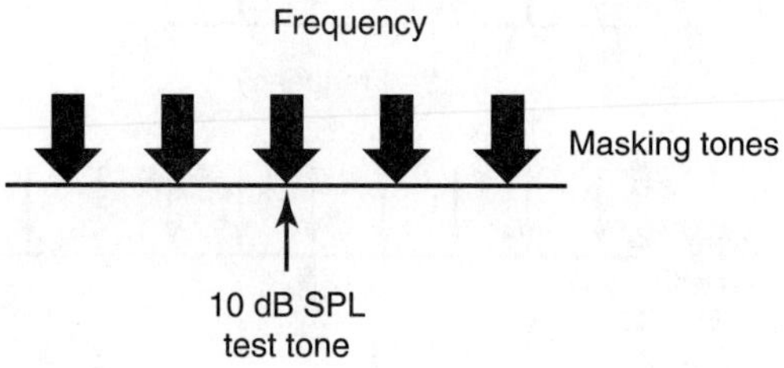

Figure 11.35
The procedure for measuring a psychophysical tuning curve. A 10-dB SPL test tone (small arrow) is presented and then a series of masking tones (wider arrows) are presented at each frequency. The psychophysical tuning curve is the sound pressure of the masking tones needed to reduce the perception of the test tone to threshold.

causes vibration mainly at one place on the membrane, then masking tones that are far away will be affecting other areas of the basilar membrane and will not affect our perception of the test tone. In contrast, masking tones closer to the frequency of the test tone will affect the same area of basilar membrane and will affect perception of the test tone.

The results of this experiment, shown in Figure 11.36a, indicate that this is exactly what happens. When the masking tone has the same frequency as the test tone, it doesn't need to be very intense in order to mask the test tone. However, when the masking tone has a lower or higher frequency than the test tone, higher intensities are required to achieve masking. For comparison, tuning curves for auditory nerve fibers (see Figure 11.31) are plotted on the right (Figure 11.36b). The close match between the psychophysical and neural tuning curves occurs because both reflect the same process—the peaked traveling wave of the basilar membrane.

Bekesy's pioneering research, combined with the physiological and psychophysical research we have just described, left no doubt that the basilar membrane's traveling wave causes inner hair cells located at different places along the cochlea to fire to specific frequencies. But what about the outer hair cells? Even though they outnumber the inner hair cells by 3 to 1, researchers have been uncertain about their function, since only about 5 percent of the signals reaching the auditory nerve are from outer hair cells. However, it has recently become apparent that the outer hair cells serve an important function: they act as "electromechanical amplifiers" that sharpen the vibration pattern of the basilar membrane.

The Outer Hair Cells: Electromechanical Amplifiers

One of the findings that had puzzled auditory researchers was the difference they observed between the vibration pattern of the basilar membrane measured in live animals compared to the pattern measured in deceased animals or isolated cochleas. For both the live and deceased preparations, the pattern showed peaks for different frequencies, as Bekesy found. But in the live animals, the peaks were much

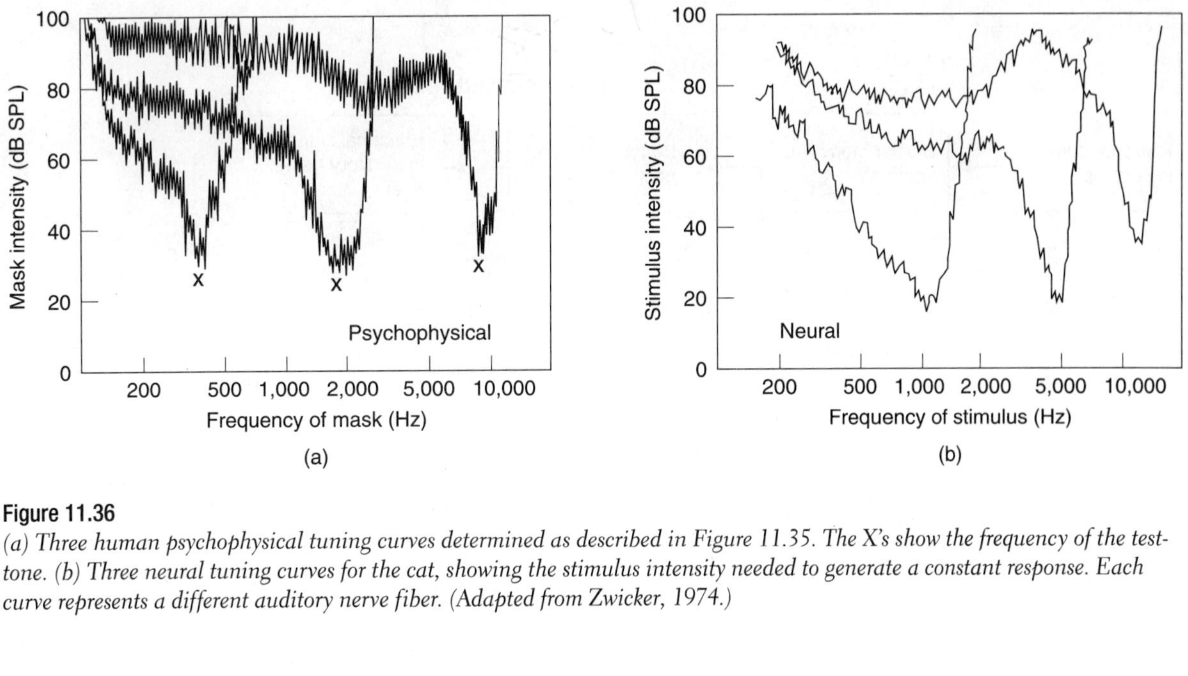

Figure 11.36
(a) Three human psychophysical tuning curves determined as described in Figure 11.35. The X's show the frequency of the test-tone. (b) Three neural tuning curves for the cat, showing the stimulus intensity needed to generate a constant response. Each curve represents a different auditory nerve fiber. (Adapted from Zwicker, 1974.)

sharper, resembling the hair cell and auditory nerve fiber tuning curves of Figures 11.30 and 11.31 (Johnstone, Patuzzi, & Yates, 1986). It appeared that something else must be influencing the basilar membrane's vibration in the live animal, but what could it be?

The answer to this question appears to be that sound triggers a **motile response** in the outer hair cells. A motile response is a movement, and the outer hair cells move in response to sound by tilting slightly and getting longer (Brownell et al., 1985; Dallos, 1996; Patuzzi, 1996; Zenner, 1986). Even more interesting, this motile response is tuned to frequency, so outer hair cells near the base of the basilar membrane have a larger motile response to high frequency sounds and outer hair cells near the apex of the basilar membrane have a larger motile response to low-frequency sounds.

The discovery that outer hair cells get longer and tilt in response to sound led to the suggestion that this motile response sharpens the vibration of the basilar membrane and amplifies its motion. The idea that this mechanical response amplifies the basilar membrane's vibration is supported by the finding that destruction of the outer hair cells causes a large decrease in the response of the inner hair cells (Dallos, 1996; Ryan & Dallos, 1975). Thus, the inner hair cells and outer hair cells work together, along with the vibration of the basilar membrane, to create maximum activity at a specific place along the cochlea for each frequency. Figure 11.37 summarizes the way the inner and outer hair cells and basilar membrane work together to accomplish this.

The Cochlea as Frequency Analyzer

The physiological and psychophysical evidence that individual frequencies are represented by activity at a particular place along the basilar membrane means that we can think of the cochlea as a frequency analyzer. Thus, when we present a tone with a particular frequency, the basilar membrane acts as a frequency analyzer by causing activity for that frequency to occur at a particular place along the cochlea.

This frequency analysis also occurs for complex tones like the one in Figure 11.7. When we applied Fourier analysis to this pattern of pressure changes, we found that this tone consists of three frequency components, one at 440 Hz, one at 880 Hz, and one at 1,320 Hz (Figure 11.8). When we look at the basilar

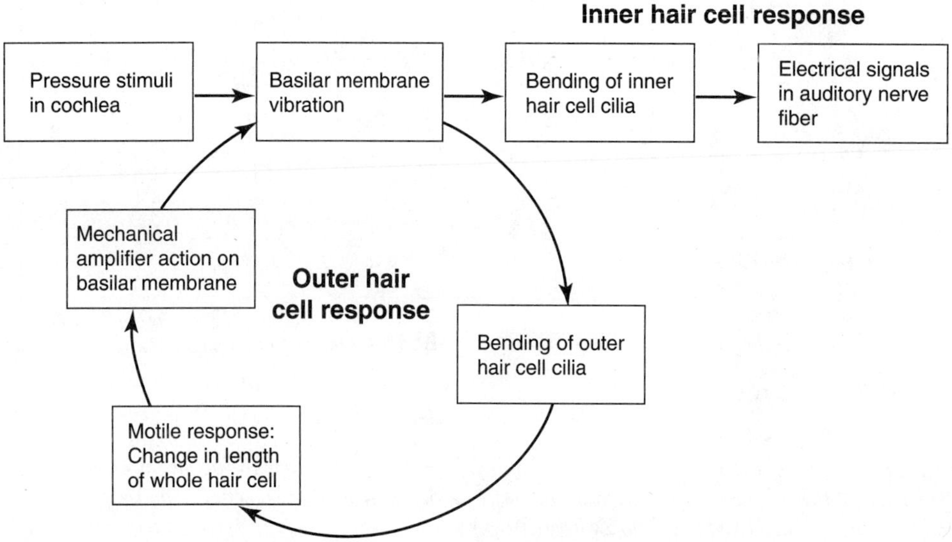

Figure 11.37
Cooperation between the inner and outer hair cells: The basilar membrane's vibration is sharpened by the motile response of the outer hair cells. This vibration stimulates the inner hair cells, which send their signals to fibers in the auditory nerve.

membrane's response to this complex tone, we see that the cochlea performs this same analysis, creating peaks in the basilar membrane vibration at the places corresponding to 440, 880, and 1,320 Hz (Hudspeth, 1989). The basilar membrane, therefore, sorts out the frequencies that make up complex tones, and for the tone in Figure 11.7 we observe the most neural activity in auditory nerve fibers with characteristic frequencies of 440, 880, and 1,320 Hz. (Figure 11.38). This activity in these fibers is then transmitted through the various structures of the auditory pathway, to the auditory receiving area of the cortex.

Representation of Frequencies in the Auditory Cortex

The result of the journey from cochlea to cortex is the formation of a tonotopic map in the cortex, like the one in Figure 11.39. This map indicates that neurons with the same characteristic frequencies are arranged in an orderly way in the cat's auditory cortex (Reale & Imig, 1980; Schreiner & Mendelson, 1990). Neurons that respond best to high frequencies are located to the left, and neurons that respond best to lower frequencies are located to the right. In addition to the surface map shown in Figure 11.39, there is also a **columnar arrangement** similar to that observed in the visual system. Neurons recorded along an electrode track that is perpendicular to the surface of the cortex all have the same characteristic frequency (Abeles & Goldstein, 1970). This type of tonotopic map, which has been found in neurons all along the pathway from the cochlea to the cortex, mirrors the frequency analysis that began in the cochlea with vibration of the basilar membrane and activation of the hair cells.

The Timing Code for Pitch

We have presented a large amount of evidence that indicates information about frequency is represented by the firing of specific hair cells, auditory nerve fibers, and neurons in the central auditory system. But frequency can also be represented in the auditory system by the timing or rate of neural firing.

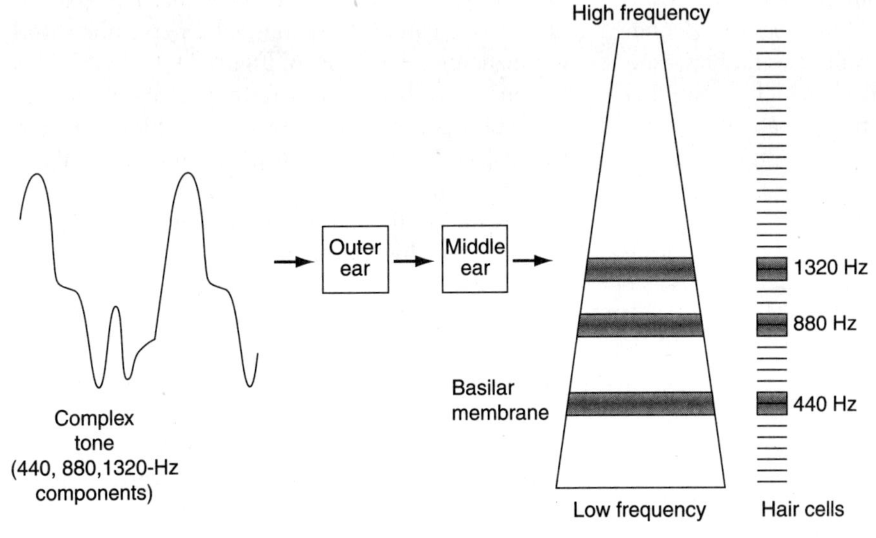

Figure 11.38
The cochlea is called a frequency analyzer because it analyzes incoming sound into its frequency components and translates the components into separated areas of excitation along its length. In this example, the complex tone from Figure 11.6, which consists of frequency components at 440, 880, and 1,320 Hz, enters the outer ear. The shaded areas on the basilar membrane represent places of peak vibration for the tone's three components, and the darkened hair cells represent the hair cells that will be most active in response to this tone.

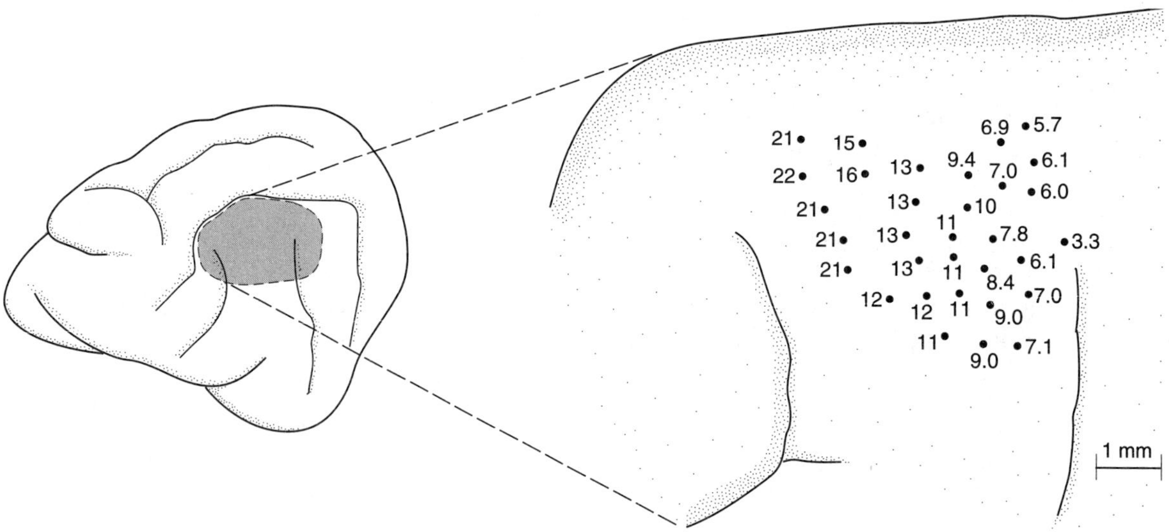

Figure 11.39
Left: The cat's brain, showing the location of the auditory receiving area (shaded). Right: A close-up of the auditory receiving area, showing the tonotopic map on the cortical surface. Each large dot represents a single neuron, and the number beside each dot represents the characteristic frequency of that neuron in thousands of Hz. (From Abeles & Goldstein, 1970; Gulick, Gescheider, & Frisina, 1989.)

An early proposal linking the rate of nerve firing and the frequency of the stimulus was Rutherford's (1886) idea that the frequency of the stimulus is signaled by the frequency of nerve firing. According to this idea, a 3,000-Hz tone would be signaled by an auditory nerve fiber firing 3,000 impulses per second (Figure 11.40). This proposal cannot work, however, because of the refractory period, which limits the nerve fibers' maximum rate of firing to about 500 impulses per second (see Chapter 1). Thus, a single nerve fiber cannot fire at 3,000 impulses per second.

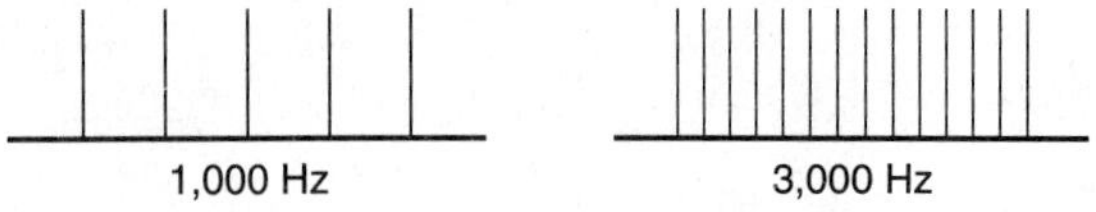

Figure 11.40
The idea behind the timing code for frequency proposed by Rutherferd is that different frequencies are signaled by the rate or pattern of nerve firing. Here, the rate of firing to a 3,000-Hz tone is higher than the rate of firing to a 1,000-Hz tone.

To deal with this problem with Rutherford's proposal, E. Glen Wever and C. W. Bray (1937) proposed the **volley principle,** which states that high rates of nerve firing can be accomplished if nerve fibers work in the manner illustrated in Figure 11.41. In this illustration, five fibers work together, each fiber firing every fifth period of the sound wave. Fiber a fires to the first period and then becomes refractory. While fiber a is refractory, fibers b, c, d, and e fire to the second, third, fourth, and fifth periods, respectively, and then fiber a, which has now recovered from its refractory period, fires to the sixth period, and so on. Thus, although the rate of firing of each individual fiber is limited by its refractory period, the information from groups of fibers can signal high frequencies of stimulation, as indicated by the bottom record.

Thirty years after Wever and Bray proposed the volley principle, Jerzey Rose and coworkers (1967) found evidence that stimulus frequency can, in fact,

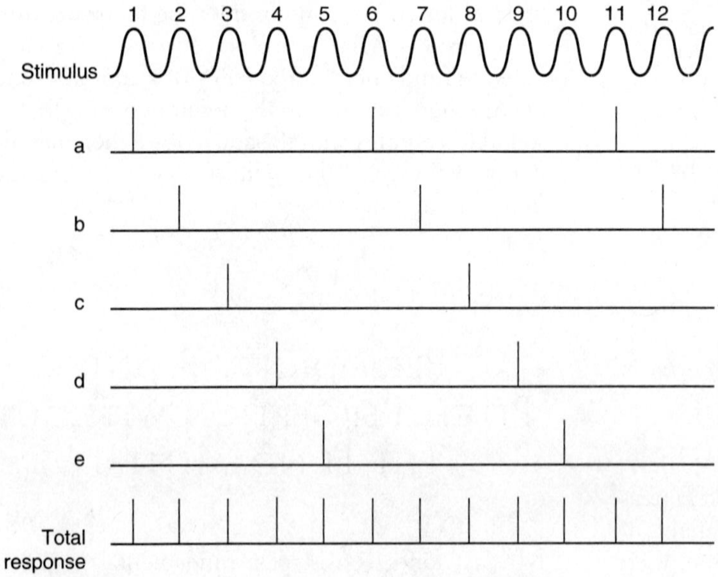

Figure 11.41
How a number of nerve fibers work together, according to Wever and Bray's volley principle.

be signaled by the firing of groups of nerve fibers. Rose described a phenomenon called **phase locking** in which neurons fire in synchrony with the phase of a stimulus. This synchronous firing is illustrated in Figure 11.42 which shows the relationship between a pure tone stimulus and the firing of three auditory nerve fibers. We can see that fiber *a* fires irregularly, but that when it does fire, it always fires at the peak of the sine-wave stimulus. Similar results for two more fibers are also shown in this figure. Note that although the rates and patterns of firing are different for each fiber, the firing of all three is phase-locked to the stimulus.

When large groups of fibers are phase-locked to a stimulus, they create a firing pattern like the one shown in Figure 11.43. This figure shows that when a large number of fibers fire in response to a tone of a particular frequency, the fibers fire in bursts separated by silent intervals, and that the timing of these bursts depends on the frequency of the stimulus. Thus, the timing of firing in the auditory nerve can indicate the frequency of the stimulus.

Is the timing information contained in auditory nerve fibers transmitted to the auditory cortex? The answer to this question is that as we reach higher and higher stations in the auditory system, phase locking

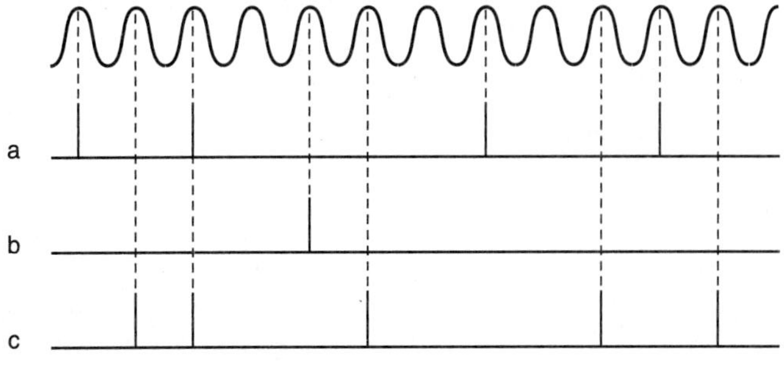

Figure 11.42
The response of three nerve fibers (a, b, and c) that are phase-locked to the stimulus. Notice that the fibers don't fire on every cycle of the stimulus, but when they do fire, they fire only when the stimulus is at its peak.

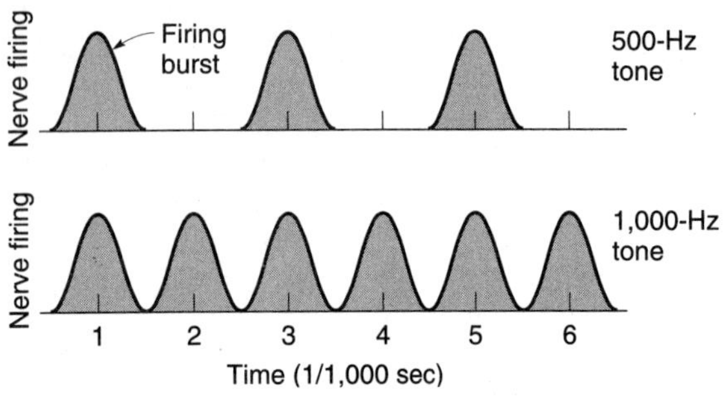

Figure 11.43
Phase locking causes large numbers of nerve fibers to fire in bursts separated by silent intervals.

becomes weaker, until in the auditory cortex, phase locking occurs only at frequencies below about 500 Hz (Ribaupierre, 1997). Timing information, therefore, plays only a minor role in coding frequency at the cortex, but does provide information about frequency to nuclei earlier in the auditory pathways.

From the research we have described so far, we can conclude that our perception of pitch depends on the place code, with timing playing some role at low frequencies and in structures below the auditory cortex. We will now consider some questions which have challenged auditory researchers to go beyond the problems posed by pure tones or even complex musical tones. We will consider the following three questions: (1) What do we perceive when we eliminate the fundamental frequency of a complex tone? (2) Are there neurons in the auditory system that respond to complex stimuli? and (3) Are there parallel neural pathways in the auditory system like the ones in the visual system?

Periodicity Pitch: Pitch Perception without the Fundamental

Musical tones consist of a fundamental frequency plus harmonics that are multiples of the fundamental frequency. Since the tone's pitch is associated with the fundamental frequency, the tone in Figure 11.44a with a 400-Hz fundamental frequency sounds lower than the tone in Figure 11.44b with an 800-Hz fundamental frequency. But what happens if we eliminate the 400-Hz tone's fundamental frequency and leave the 800-, 1,200-, and 1,600-Hz harmonics, as in Figure 11.44c? You might guess that the tone's pitch would now correspond to the pitch of the 800-Hz

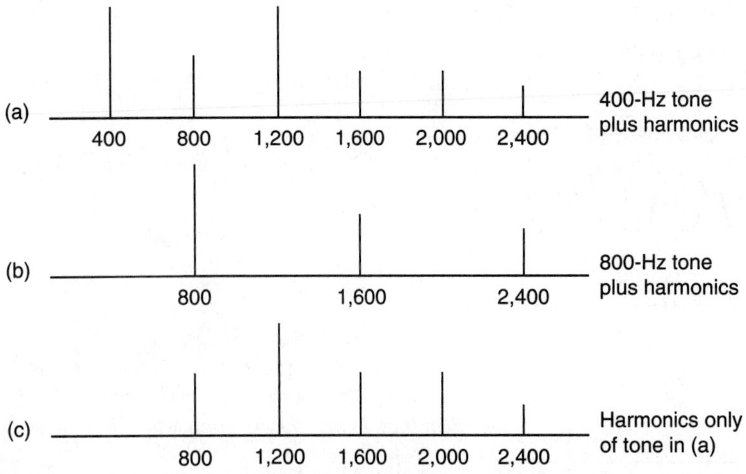

Figure 11.44
Fourier spectra of (a) a 400-Hz tone plus its harmonics, (b) an 800-Hz tone plus its harmonics, and (c) the 400-Hz tone in (a) without its 400-Hz fundamental.

tone, since the tone's lowest frequency component is now 800 Hz. This is not, however, what happens. Removing the 400-Hz fundamental changes the tone's timbre slightly but has no effect on the tone's pitch. The fact that pitch does not change when we remove the fundamental is called **periodicity pitch** or the **effect of the missing fundamental.**

The fact that tones with different frequency components can have the same pitch poses problems for the place theory of pitch perception, because even though the acoustic stimuli in Figures 11.44a and 11.44c cause different patterns of vibration on the basilar membrane, they are perceived as having the same pitch. Periodicity pitch is therefore explained by looking to activity in more central structures of the auditory system.

One piece of evidence that periodicity pitch is determined centrally is the finding that periodicity pitch is perceived even if two tones are presented to different ears. For example, presenting a 1,600-Hz tone to the left ear and a 1,700-Hz tone to the right ear results in a perception of pitch that corresponds to 100 Hz (Houtsma & Goldstein, 1972). (Remember that since harmonics are always multiples of the fundamental frequency, the *difference* between two adjacent harmonics corresponds to the fundamental frequency.) The perception of periodicity pitch when the tones are presented to separate ears means that periodicity pitch must be determined somewhere in the auditory system where signals from both ears are combined. The first place this occurs is the superior olivary nucleus (see Figure 11.21).

Further evidence that periodicity pitch is determined centrally is the finding that patients with damage to a specific area of the auditory cortex in the right hemisphere are not able to hear the pitch of the missing fundamental (Zatorre, 1988). These results and others have led to the proposal that periodicity pitch is the result of a **central pitch processor**—a central mechanism that analyzes the *pattern* of harmonics and selects the fundamental frequency that is most likely to have been part of that pattern (see Evans, 1978; Getty & Howard, 1981; Goldstein, 1978; Meddis & Hewitt, 1991; Srulovicz & Goldstein, 1983; Wightman, 1973, for details of various central processor models).

Thus, periodicity pitch suggests the following possibility about how the auditory system analyzes the sound stimulus: The firing of auditory nerve fibers contains place and timing information about the various frequency components in the auditory stimulus. However, we perceive a sound's pitch only after the firing caused by these components has been analyzed by more central mechanisms. Thus, the same pitch can be signaled by a large amount of activity in neurons that respond to a tone's fundamental frequency, or by the pattern of neural activity in neurons that fire to a number of different frequencies.

The phenomenon of periodicity pitch not only gives us some insight into how the auditory system may operate physiologically, but also has a number of practical consequences. Consider, for example, what happens as you listen to music on a cheap radio that can't reproduce frequencies below 300 Hz. If you are listening to music that contains a tone with a fundamental frequency of 100 Hz, your radio can't reproduce the fundamental frequency of the 100-Hz tone or of the 200-Hz second harmonic of that tone. Even though the radio reproduces only the third (300-Hz) and higher (400, 500, 600, etc.) harmonics of this tone, periodicity pitch comes to the rescue and causes you to perceive a pitch equivalent to that produced by a 100-Hz tone. Similarly, even though the telephone doesn't reproduce the fundamental frequency of the human voice, we are usually able to identify people's voices on the phone (Truax, 1984).

Periodicity pitch has also been used to overcome the following problem in the construction of pipe organs: An organ designer wants to produce a pitch corresponding to a 55-Hz tone. However, the longest organ pipe he can use is 1.5 m long, a length that produces a pitch with a 110-Hz fundamental frequency. A longer pipe would be needed to produce the 55-Hz tone. The solution: Use the 1.5-m pipe, with its 110-Hz fundamental and a 1.0-m pipe, which produces a 165-Hz fundamental. Since 110 Hz and 165 Hz are the second and third harmonics of a 55-Hz tone ($55 \times 2 = 110$; $55 \times 3 = 165$), these two pipes, when sounded together, produce a tone with a pitch corresponding to 55 Hz (Dowling & Harwood, 1986).

Neural Response to Complex Stimuli

When we described the workings of the visual system, we saw that there are neurons in the striate cortex and the extrastriate cortex that respond to specialized stimuli such as faces or complex geometrical forms. This specialization also occurs in the auditory system, although so far nothing as dramatic as the visual neurons that respond to faces has been discovered. For example, cells have been found in the auditory cortex that respond neither to pure tones nor to combinations of tones but that do respond to noises like keys jingling or paper tearing (Whitfield & Evans, 1965). There are also cortical cells in the cat that respond only to smooth changes in the frequency of a tone: Some cells respond only when the tone is changed smoothly from low to high frequencies, and others respond only when the tonal frequency is changed smoothly from high to low. These cells have been called **frequency sweep detectors,** because they respond well to changes in frequency but poorly or not at all to steady tones of a single frequency (Mendelson & Cynader, 1985; Phillips et al., 1985; Whitfield & Evans, 1965).

Thomas McKenna and coworkers (1989) have also recorded from neurons in areas A1 and A2 of the cat's cortex that respond poorly to single tones, but respond well if these same tones are part of a five-tone sequence. Other neurons have been found in auditory areas outside of A1 or A2 that respond poorly to pure tone stimuli but respond vigorously to noise stimuli that contain many frequencies (Rauschecker, Tian, & Hauser, 1995) (Figure 11.45). Some neurons in this area respond best to recordings of rhesus monkey calls. This result is particularly interesting because these *monkey call neurons* are found in an area in the monkey's cortex that is analogous to the human area involved in speech. This finding raises the interesting, but as yet unproved, possibility that there could be neurons in the human auditory system that respond to specialized speech sounds.

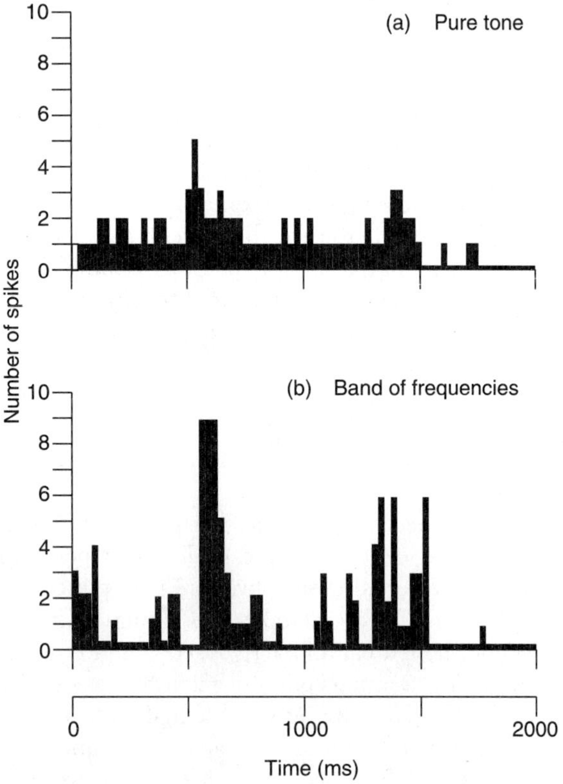

Figure 11.45
Response of a neuron in the monkey cortex that (a) responds poorly to a pure tone; but (b) responds well to a noise stimulus that contains many frequencies. (Adapted from Reschecker, Tian, & Hauser, 1995.)

Although we don't know whether there are actually neurons in the human auditory cortex that respond to specific speech sounds, we do know that specific areas in the human auditory cortex are activated by melodies of sequences of tones. Albert Zatorre, Alan Evans, and Ernst Meyer (1994) identified these areas by using positron emission tomography (PET) to measure the blood flow in the cortex as people listened to simple 8-note melodies played on a synthesizer keyboard. They found specific areas in the frontal and temporal lobes of the right hemisphere that respond to these melodies. They also found that when people had to decide whether the last tone in the sequence was higher or lower in pitch than the first tone, a number of additional regions in the right hemisphere were activated. This task, which involves holding the pitch of the first tone in memory until the last tone is presented, involves higher level auditory processing. Evidence such as this supports the idea that areas of the auditory cortex in addition to A1 are involved in our perception of complex auditory stimuli.

Parallel Pathways in the Auditory System

When we described the visual system, we noted that researchers have, in the last few decades, discovered many visual areas that respond to specific kinds of stimuli, and that information is processed in parallel pathways such as the ventral and dorsal pathways. A similar situation may exist for the auditory system, although the evidence is still preliminary. We know that anatomically there are parallel pathways carrying signals toward the auditory cortex. Based on these pathways and the fact that some auditory neurons respond to specific types of stimuli, some researchers have suggested that, just as the parallel pathways in the visual system are associated with different aspects of the visual stimulus, these auditory pathways might be associated with different aspects of the auditory stimulus (Aitkin, 1990; Ribaupierre, 1997; Rouiller, 1997).

The observation that the cortex receives signals from neurons that are traveling in separate pathways has also led some researchers to propose that different areas of the auditory cortex may be specialized to respond best to particular features of the sound stimulus (Ribaupierre, 1997). However, currently this is just a hypothesis that is not supported by much hard evidence.

In addition to the pathways carrying signals from the cochlea toward the cortex, the auditory system also contains many pathways that send signals *back* from the cortex and other structures, toward the cochlea, a phenomenon called **efferent feedback** (Guinan, 1996). One example of efferent feedback is a pathway that carries signals from the superior olivary nucleus back to the hair cells.

What does this efferent feedback accomplish? One hint at the answer to this question is that electrically stimulating the superior olivary nucleus decreases the sensitivity of the inner hair cells (Brown & Nuttall, 1984). These efferent signals keep the hair cells from reaching their maximum response rate too quickly as sound intensity increases. Other functions that have been proposed for efferent feedback are to make hearing easier by reducing the effect of background noise (Kawase, Delgutte, & Liberman, 1993), and to help a person focus attention on one stimulus by reducing the response to stimuli that the person is ignoring (Guinan, 1996).

Something to Consider: Are Frequencies Really High Pitched or Low Pitched?

In the chapter on color vision, we saw that the visual system causes different wavelengths to be perceived as different colors, even though there is actually no color in the wavelengths (see page 151). Just as we can say for vision that "the wavelengths of light rays do not contain any color," we can also say for hearing that "the frequencies of sound vibrations do not contain different pitches."

Another way to state this is to say that experience is not necessarily contained in the stimulus. A rock, a building, the vibrations of your stereo's speakers, and heat from the sun are just physical stimuli. Nothing says that they must create a particular kind of experience in the organisms that are able to sense them. The important thing for humans and other animals is that they receive enough information about these stimuli to enable them to survive to "sense another day." Sound provides important information about events in the environment that disturb the air (or water, if you are a fish), and the auditory system arbitrarily assigns low pitches to low frequencies and high pitches to high frequencies, so we can tell the different frequencies of vibration apart.

We can take this idea one step farther by wondering what animals that are sensitive to frequencies far beyond our range of hearing, experience. In the next chapter, we will see that dogs can hear stimuli up to 50,000 Hz and bats and dolphins are sensitive to acoustic signals beyond 100,000 Hz. How do you think dogs, bats, and dolphins experience these extremely high frequencies? Do they experience a pitch that corresponds to the high pitches we perceive, do they perceive pitches higher than we can even imagine, or perhaps something that is completely different than what humans call pitch? We have no way of knowing what these animals experience, but we do know that whatever their experience, it is not contained in the stimulus, but is created by the nervous system's response to the stimulus.

Cross-Modality Experience: Bright Tones and Colored Words

> Presented with a tone pitched at 2,000 cycles per second and having an amplitude of 113 decibels, S said, "It looks something like fireworks tinged with a pink-red hue. The strip of color feels rough and unpleasant and it has an ugly taste-rather like that of a briny pickle." (Luria, 1968, p. 46)

Subject S, whose reaction to a tone is described above, is describing his experience of **synesthesia**—stimulation of one modality that leads to perceptual experience in another. This phenomenon is rare, occurring in less than one percent of people, but has been described in hundreds of published reports since the eighteenth century (Marks, 1974).

The idea of seeing a colored light in response to a sound stimulus might be viewed as strange and idiosyncratic, but in surveying many accounts of synesthetic experience, Lawrence Marks (1975) concluded that many of the associations between sound and color are often systematic and constant from one person to another. The strongest associations have been reported between vowel sounds and colors, with the vowel *a* causing sensations of blue and red; *e*, yellow and white; *i*, yellow and white; *o*, yellow, red, and black; and *u*, blue or black.

What is the mechanism responsible for these cross-modality experiences? E. Paulesu and coworkers (1995) approached this question physiologically by measuring brain activity of six women with color-word synesthesia using positron emission tomography (PET). When they presented pure tones to these subjects, they observed activation only in auditory areas, in line with the fact that these subjects did not experience synesthesia to tones. But when words were presented, the subjects experienced visual sensations, and brain activation occurred in the language area *and* in a number of higher order visual areas. Based on these results, Paulesu concluded that color-word synesthesias are generated by an interaction between brain areas for language and vision.

If we think about synesthesia in terms of interactions between brain areas, then the phenomenon shares a similarity with many of the perceptions we have described in this book, in which interactions between brain areas is a normal part of the perceptual process. In fact, even people without synesthesia can draw associations between sensations in different

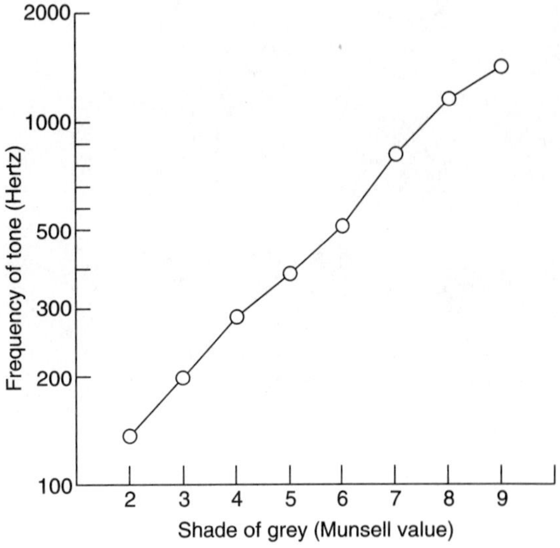

Figure 11.46
Average results for a group of subjects who matched sound frequencies (Hertz) to shades of grey (Munsell value). Higher Munsell values are lighter shades of grey. (From Marks, 1974.)

modalities. This has been demonstrated using a technique called **cross-modality matching** in which a subject is presented with a stimulus in one modality and is asked to adjust a stimulus in another modality to match it. When Marks (1974) presented subjects with squares of paper ranging from black to white and asked them to indicate the sound of tone that matched them, he found that the people associated lighter squares with higher pitches (Figure 11.46). Or when subjects were asked to rate the brightness and pitch of color words like "blue" and "red," Marks found that red, white, and yellow are rated brighter and higher in pitch, and black and brown are rated as less bright and lower in pitch (Figure 11.47).

Thus, while people with synesthesia may actually experience colored sounds, people without it can also draw relationships between colors, tones, and brightness. Although the senses are separated in many ways, they also share commonalties of experience.

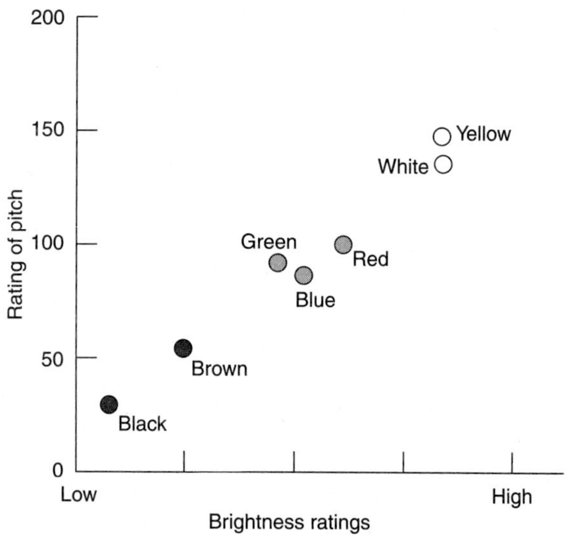

Figure 11.47
Average results for a group of subjects who rated the brightness and pitch of color words. Dark colors such as black and brown were given low pitch and brightness ratings. Light colors such as yellow and white were given high pitch and brightness ratings. (Adapted from Marks, 1974.)

Study Questions

Underlying Principles

Find examples of the following principles in this chapter:

- Selective receptors (330)
- Receptive fields/neural selectivity (330)
- Neural maps (335)
- Columnar organization (335)
- Parallel pathways (341)
- Physiology-perception connection (330)

The Functions of Hearing

1. Describe the signaling function of hearing. (310)
2. What was Helen Keller's argument in favor of the idea that being deaf was worse than being blind? (311)
3. What are the two answers to the question: If a tree falls in the forest and no one is there to hear it, is there a sound? Explain why each of these answers could be correct by comparing the physical and perceptual difficulties of sound. (311)

Sound as a Physical Stimulus: Pressure Changes in the Air

4. What is the physical stimulus for the perception of sound? (311)
5. What is a sound wave? (312)
6. What is a pure tone? What pure tones are found in the environment? What is amplitude? frequency? (313)
7. What units are used to measure a tone's frequency? What is the frequency range of human hearing? (313)
8. Describe the decibel scale that is used to specify the amplitude of a tone. How is the zero point of the decibel scale determined? What property of the decibel scale enables it to compress the large range of sound pressures in the environment into a small range of decibels? (313)
9. How is a complex tone different than a pure tone? What do complex musical tones have in common with pure tones? (315)
10. What do we find when we apply Fourier analysis to a complex tone? (316)
11. What is the fundamental frequency of a tone? What is the second harmonic? What is the relationship between the various harmonics? (316)
12. What is a Fourier frequency spectrum? (316)

Perceptual Responses: The Experience of Sound

13. Define loudness. What is the relationship between decibels and loudness? Is the decibel scale a scale for loudness? (317)
14. Define pitch, tone height; tone chroma. (317)
15. What is the relationship between the fundamental frequencies of tones separated by an octave? What is the perceptual relationship between tones separated by octaves? (317)
16. Define timbre. (318)

Auditory System: Structure and Function

17. What are the structures of the outer ear? (318)
18. What is resonance? What effect does it have on the sound stimulus in the outer ear? (319)
19. What are the structures of the middle ear? (319)
20. Why are the ossicles necessary? (319)
21. What are two ways that the ossicles increase the strength of the sound stimulus? (320)
22. How does severe damage to the ossicles affect hearing? (320)

23. What is the function of the middle ear muscles? (320)

24. What is the main structure of the inner ear? (321)

25. Describe the cochlear partition and the organ of Corti. What are the main structures within the organ of Corti and what two membranes are closely associated with it? (321)

26. Describe the two kinds of hair cells. What do they have in common? What causes transduction? (321)

27. How is the vibration of the stapes transmitted through the liquid in the cochlea? What is the effect of this vibration on the organ of Corti and the hair cells? (321)

28. How much must the hair cells bend in order to generate an electrical signal that results in a sound that is near the threshold for hearing? (324)

29. Describe the auditory pathways that extend from the auditory nerve to the auditory cortex. (325)

The Place Code for Pitch: Traveling Waves, Tuning Curves, and Maps

30. What is the key question that we ask about the neural code for pitch perception? (325)

31. What is the basic idea behind the place code for frequency? (326)

32. Describe Helmholtz' resonance theory. Why was it incorrect? (327)

33. Describe the traveling wave motion of the basilar membrane that was discovered by Békésy. (327)

34. How did Békésy discover the basilar membrane's traveling wave motion? (327)

35. What is the envelope of the traveling wave and how does it change as a function of a tone's frequency? (328)

36. Describe the following physiological evidence for place coding: Tonotopic maps on the cochlea, hair cell tuning, and auditory nerve fiber tuning. Be sure you understand what is being plotted in a frequency tuning curve. (329)

37. What is auditory masking? Describe Egan and Hake's masking experiment. How can the results of that experiment be related to the vibration of the basilar membrane? (330)

38. What is the procedure for determining a psychophysical tuning curve? How do psychophysical tuning curves compare to neural tuning curves, and what does this mean? (332)

39. What is the basis for saying that the outer hair cells are electromechanical amplifiers? (333)

40. How do the inner and outer hair cells work together to create maximum activity at particular places along the cochlea for each frequency? (334)

41. What do we mean when we say that the cochlea is a frequency analyzer? How does this frequency analysis work for pure tones and for complex tones? (334)

42. How is frequency represented in the auditory cortex? Describe the columnar arrangement of the auditory cortex. (335)

The Timing Code for Pitch

43. Describe Rutherford's proposal of a timing code for pitch. What was the flaw in his proposal? (336)

44. Describe the volley principle. (336)

45. Describe how phase locking transmits information about the frequency of a tone. In what auditory structures is phase locking the strongest? (337)

Periodicity Pitch: Pitch Perception without the Fundamental

46. What must we do to a complex tone stimulus to demonstrate periodicity pitch (also called the effect of the missing fundamental)? (338)

47. What is the evidence that periodicity pitch is determined centrally? (339)

48. What is the central pitch processor? What does periodicity pitch suggest about the way the auditory system analyzes the sound stimulus? (339)

49. What are some practical applications of periodicity pitch? (339)

Neural Response to Complex Stimuli

50. Describe the response of neurons in the auditory cortex that respond best to complex tones. (340)
51. What have experiments using PET scans told us about the human cortical response to complex tones? (340)

Parallel Pathways in the Auditory System

52. What is the evidence for parallel pathways in the auditory system? (341)
53. What is efferent feedback? What is the function of efferent feedback? (341)

Something to Consider: Are Frequencies Really High Pitched or Low Pitched?

54. What do we mean when we ask whether frequencies are really high pitched or low pitched? (341)

Across the Senses: Cross-Modality Experience: Bright Tones and Colored Words

55. What is synesthesia? (343)
56. What is the strongest association between sounds and colors? (343)
57. What is the result of PET scan experiments on subjects who experience color-word synesthesia? What does this result tell us about the possible mechanism of synesthesia? (343)
58. What is cross-modality matching? What happens when subjects are asked to match sounds to the shades of paper squares? When they are asked to match the brightness and pitch of color words? (344)
59. What is the significance of the results in 58, above, with regards to synesthesia? (344)

12

Perceiving Loudness, Timbre, and the Auditory Scene

CHAPTER CONTENTS

SOME QUESTIONS WE WILL CONSIDER

- Why do saxophones and trumpets sound different, even when they are playing the same note? (354)
- What makes it possible to tell where a sound is coming from in space? (364)
- Does loss of vision result in better hearing? (377)

Albert Bregman (1990) begins his book *Auditory Scene Analysis* by posing the following problem (Figure 12.1):

> Imagine that you are on the edge of a lake and a friend challenges you to play a game. The game is this: Your friend digs two narrow channels up from the side of the lake. Each is a few feet long and a few inches wide and they are spaced a few feet apart. Halfway up each one, your friend stretches a handkerchief and fastens it to the sides of the channel. As waves reach the side of the lake, they travel up the channels and cause the two handkerchiefs to go into motion. You are allowed to look only at the handkerchiefs and from their motions to answer a series of questions: How many boats are there on the lake and where are they? Which is the most powerful one? Which one is closer? Is the wind blowing? Has any large object been dropped suddenly into the lake? (pp. 5–6)

This seems like an impossible problem. How can we determine how many boats there are, where they are located, and which one is the most powerful simply by observing the motions of the handkerchiefs? Although Bregman's boat problem is an extremely difficult one, our auditory system routinely solves a problem that is equally complex, when, based on the motions of the two tympanic membranes, it enables us to tell how many people are talking in a room, where they are located, and which one is the loudest.

Figure 12.1
Is it possible to determine what is happening on the lake by watching how the handkerchiefs react to the waves? Since we are able to make judgments about the identities and locations of people talking in a room based on vibrations of our eardrums, perhaps it isn't so far fetched to suggest that we can determine information about the boats based on how the handkerchiefs move in response to water waves.

Bregman's clever analogy between the moving handkerchiefs and our vibrating eardrums helps us appreciate how amazing it is that the information from these vibrations is transformed into information about the identities and locations of sounds in our environment. But what is even more amazing is that the vibrations of our tympanic membranes not only inform us about the identities and locations of sounds but also help create auditory experiences as varied as hearing music, people's voices, and the rustle of leaves in the wind.

In this chapter, we will describe how we perceive some of the more complex acoustic stimuli in our environment and will consider how we perceive a sound's loudness, timbre, and location. We begin by considering the psychophysics of two characteristics of hearing: detecting sounds near threshold and perceiving the loudness of sounds that are above threshold.

Sensitivity and Loudness: Exquisite Sensitivity, but Frequency Matters

Our senses are exquisitely sensitive. The visual system can detect a flash of light that contains as few as seven photons of light energy, and the ear's sensitivity is equally impressive. The auditory system can detect pressure changes so small that they cause the eardrum to move only 10^{-11} cm, a dimension that is less than the diameter of a hydrogen atom (Tonndorf & Khanna, 1968), and is so sensitive that the air pressure at threshold in the most sensitive range of hearing is only 10 to 15 dB above the air pressure generated by the random movement of air molecules. This means that if our hearing were much more sensitive than it is now, we would hear the background hiss of colliding air molecules!

Although the ear can detect extremely small pressure changes, it is more sensitive to some frequencies than to others. The function that indicates how our sensitivity to sound pressure varies with frequency is called the *audibility curve.*

The Audibility Curve

The **audibility curve** is analogous to the spectral sensitivity curve for vision, which we described in Chapter 2. The spectral sensitivity curve indicates the light intensity necessary to detect a light at wavelengths across the visible spectrum. The audibility curve indicates the intensity, measured in dB, necessary to just hear a tone, at frequencies across the range of hearing. We can see from Figure 12.2 that our threshold is lowest (that is, we are most sensitive) at frequencies between about 2,000 and 4,000 Hz, the range of frequencies that is most important for understanding speech.

The U-shape of the audibility curve means that we need higher stimulus intensities to hear frequencies higher and lower than our "best hearing" range of 2,000 to 4,000 Hz. For example, a 20-Hz tone must have an intensity of 75 dB before we can hear it, and a 20,000-Hz tone must have an intensity of 20 dB for us to hear it. The range of human hearing is usually regarded as being between 20 and 20,000 Hz, since frequencies below or above this range can be heard only at extremely high pressures or can't be heard at all.

The **auditory response area** includes all sounds between the audibility curve and the upper curve in Figure 12.2, which defines the threshold for feeling. At intensities below the audibility curve, we can't hear a tone, and at intensities above the threshold for feeling, tones become painful. Thus, the useful range of hearing is contained within the auditory response area between these two curves.

Although the useful range of hearing for humans extends between about 20 and 20,000 Hz, we can see from the audibility curves in Figure 12.3 that other animals have different "windows" on the auditory

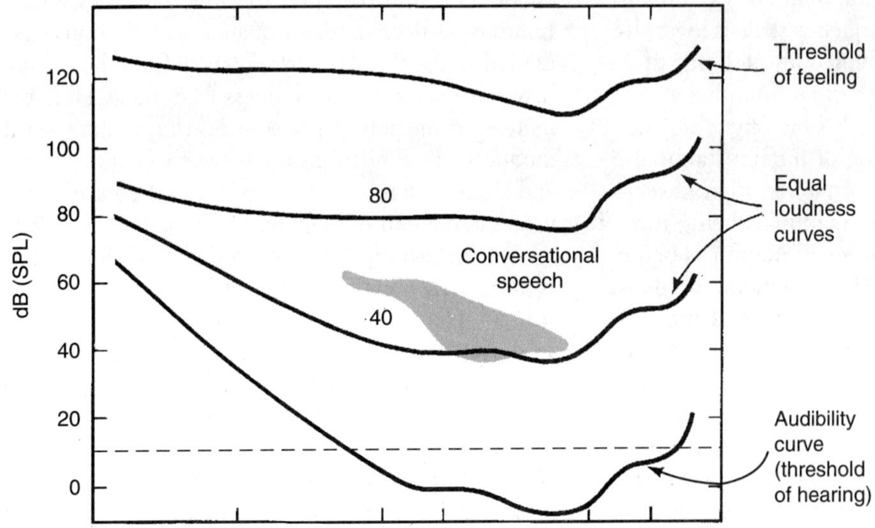

Figure 12.2
The audibility curve and the auditory response area. Hearing occurs between the audibility curve (the threshold for hearing) and the upper curve (the threshold for feeling). Tones with SPLs below the threshold for hearing cannot be heard; tones with SPLs above the threshold of feeling result in pain and eventually cause damage to the ear. The shaded area indicates the frequency and intensity range of conversational speech. The places where the dashed line at 10 dB crosses the audibility function indicates which frequencies can be heard at 10 dB SPL.(From Fletcher & Munson, 1933.)

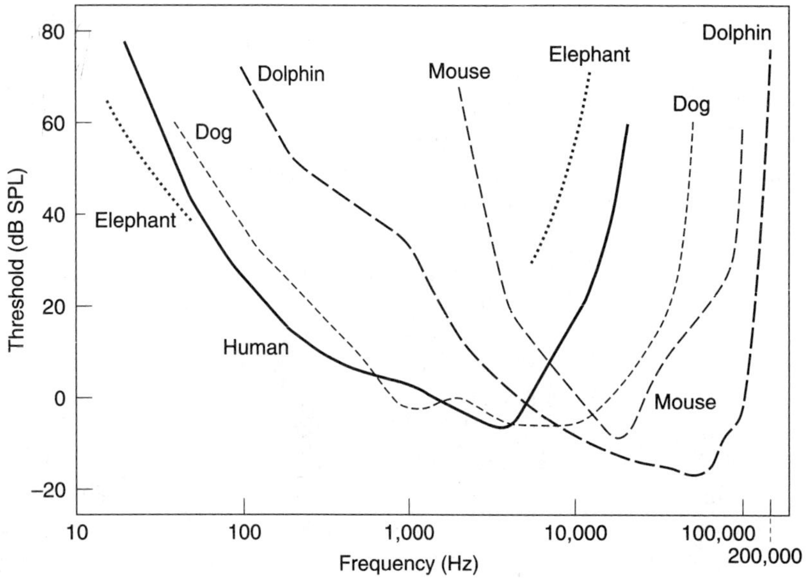

Figure 12.3
Audibility curves for a few animals. Notice that the frequency scale is logarithmic, so high frequencies are allotted less distance than low frequencies. Only the low and high ends of the elephant curve are shown to prevent overlap with the other curves. (Based on data from Au, Eong, Tau, & Lim, 1993; Heffner, 1983; Heffner & Heffner, 1980, 1985; Heffner & Masterton, 1980.)

world. Elephants can hear stimuli below 20 Hz, the homing pigeon can detect frequencies as low as 0.05 Hz and dogs, mice, and dolphins are able to hear at frequencies far above the highest frequencies humans can detect. Notice that the frequency scale is logarithmic so high frequencies are allotted less distance than low frequencies.

We don't understand exactly how physiology determines the ranges of hearing of different animals, but we do know that there is a relationship between size and sensitivity, with large mammals being most sensitive below 10,000 Hz and small mammals being most sensitive above 10,000 Hz. In general, animals that hear best at high frequencies have small and stiff outer and middle ear structures and those that hear best at low frequencies have large tympanic membranes and compliant middle ear structures (Rosowski, 1996). One way to estimate the high-frequency limit of an animal's hearing is to note the size of its head, since animals with smaller heads generally have better high-frequency hearing (Heffner & Heffner, 1985).

Loudness, Sound Pressure, and Frequency

When we hold a tone's frequency constant and increase its sound pressure, the tone becomes louder. **Loudness** is the *magnitude* of auditory sensation (Plack & Carlyon, 1995). We already know from the relation between decibels and loudness (see Table 11.2) that increasing the sound pressure of a tone increases its loudness. This relationship between sound pressure and loudness has been measured by S. S. Stevens, who used the method of magnitude estimation (see Chapter 1) to determine the curve in Figure 12.4. Loudness is plotted, in units called the **sone,** versus sound pressure, in decibels (where one sone is the loudness of a 1,000-Hz tone at 40 dB). This curve indicates that increasing the sound pressure by a factor of 10 (which is the same as increasing the SPL by 20 dB) increases the loudness by a factor of about 4.0.

Loudness is a function not only of sound pressure, but also of frequency. Thus, saying, "The tone is 40 dB SPL" tells us nothing about how loud it is unless we also know its frequency. From the audibility

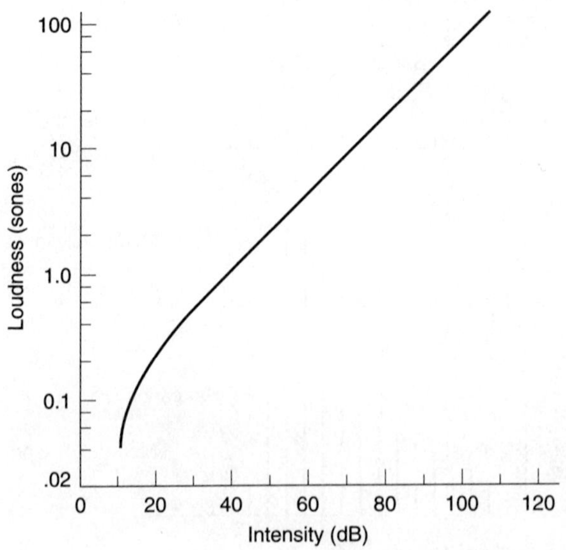

Figure 12.4
The growth in loudness in sones for a 100-Hz tone as a function of intensity. Above about 25 dB SPL, the growth of loudness with intensity is a power function with an exponent of 0.6. (Adapted from Gulick, Gescheider, & Frisina, 1989.)

curve, we can see that a 40-dB SPL tone is just above threshold if its frequency is 100 Hz, but is well above threshold if its frequency is 1,000 Hz. Another way to understand the relationship between loudness and frequency is by measuring equal loudness curves.

Equal Loudness Curves

The curves marked **equal loudness curves** in Figure 12.2 indicate the number of decibels that create the same perception of loudness at frequencies across the range of hearing. We measure an equal loudness curve by designating one tone as a standard and matching the loudness of all other tones to it. For example, the curve marked 40 in Figure 12.2 was determined by matching the loudness of frequencies across the range of hearing to a 1,000-Hz 40-dB SPL tone. Similarly, the curve marked 80 was determined by matching the loudness of different frequencies to a 1,000-Hz 80-dB SPL tone.

Notice that the audibility curve and the equal loudness curve marked 40 curves up at high and low frequencies, but the equal loudness curve marked 80 is more flattened. This means that at 80 dB SPL all tones from 30 to 5,000 Hz have about the same loudness. The difference between the flat 80 curve and the upward-curving audibility function explains something that happens as you adjust the volume control on your stereo system. If you are playing music at a fairly loud level—say, 80 dB SPL—you should be able to easily hear each of the frequencies in the music because, as the equal loudness curve for 80 indicates, all frequencies between about 20 Hz and 5,000 Hz sound equally loud at this intensity.

However, when you turn the intensity down to 10 dB SPL all frequencies don't sound equally loud. In fact, from the audibility curve in Figure 12.2 we can see that frequencies below about 400 Hz (the bass notes) and above about 10,000 Hz (the treble notes) are inaudible at 10 dB. (To determine the frequencies below and above which a 10-dB tone is inaudible, notice that the dashed 10-dB line crosses the audibility curve at about 400 Hz and 12,000 Hz. This means that frequencies lower than 400 Hz and higher than 12,000 Hz are not audible at 10 dB.)

Being unable to hear very low and very high frequencies creates a bad situation, because it means that when you play music softly you won't hear the very low or very high pitches. To compensate for this, most stereo receivers have a button labeled "loudness" that selectively boosts the level of very high and very low frequencies so that you can hear them, even when you are playing your stereo very softly.

Physiological Aspects of Loudness

What is the physiological mechanism for loudness? One possibility is that increasing sound pressure increases the rate of nerve firing and this greater rate of nerve firing signals louder tones. However, the fact that loudness increases over a pressure range of nearly 120 dB for frequencies in the middle of the range of hearing, poses a problem for this explanation because most nerve fibers increase their firing rate over only about a 40-dB range of sound pressures. At about 40 dB, they reach **saturation:** that is, their rate of firing stops increasing with further increases in sound pressure. One way the auditory system may deal with this problem is with fibers that begin firing at about 40 or 50 dB and continue to increase their firing at high pressures (Lieberman, 1978; Palmer & Evans, 1979).

Another solution to the problem of the neural coding of loudness is based on place theory: the fact that a pure tone causes maximum neural activity at a particular place on the basilar membrane. As shown in Figure 12.5, most of the neural response to low intensities of a particular frequency is centered on one place on the basilar membrane. However, at higher intensities, two things happen: (1) Neurons that were already firing rapidly begin to saturate, and (2) neurons at other places on the basilar membrane begin to fire. Perhaps the broadness in the pattern of auditory firing provides the neural information that signals loudness (Gulick, Gescheider, & Frisina, 1989).

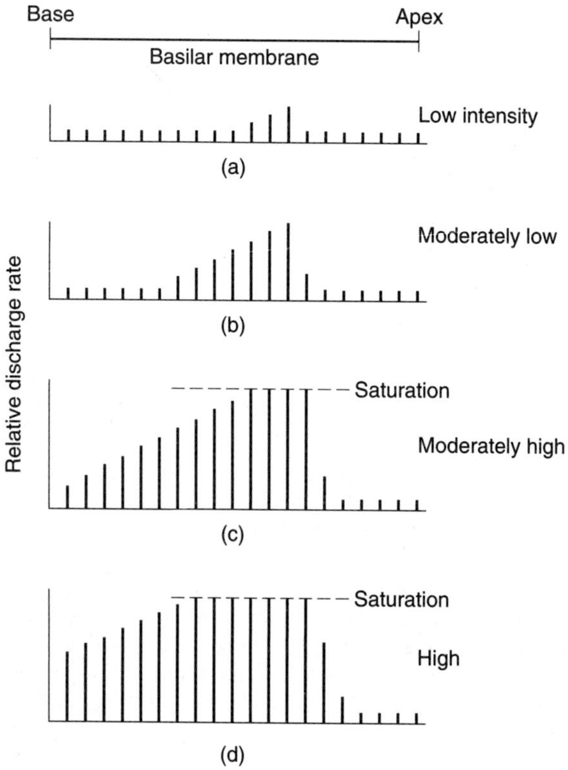

Figure 12.5
How increasing stimulus intensity affects the discharge rate of neurons along the basilar membrane. (a) At low intensity, firing is low and is localized at one place on the membrane; (b) increasing intensity increases firing at that place, and fibers some distance away begin firing; (c) at moderately high intensities, some fibers begin to saturate; (d) more saturation occurs at high intensities. It is possible that the broader pattern of basilar membrane excitation that occurs at high intensities provides information regarding the intensity of the stimulus. (Adapted from Gulick et al., 1989.)

Sound Quality: What a Stimulus Sounds Like

One of the things we learn as children is how to recognize different musical instruments. One particularly delightful way this has been taught is through Prokofief's musical version of *Peter and the Wolf,* which uses the distinctive sounds of each instrument to represent different animals. The flute represents the bird, the French horns represents the wolf, the bassoon represents the grandfather, and the violins and string quartet represent Peter. One thing that differentiates the sounds of these instruments from one another is their pitch—the flute is high-pitched and the bassoon is low-pitched. But even when two instruments play the same note with the same loudness, we can still tell them apart, because they differ in a quality called *timbre.* We noted in Chapter 11 that when we hear a flute and a bassoon play the same note, we might describe the sound of the flute as *clear* or *mellow* and the sound of the bassoon as *nasal* or *reedy.* These differences in timbre illustrate that sounds can have different qualities in addition to pitch and loudness. Sounds can differ in other qualities as well. For example, we can describe sounds as *flat* or *resonant,* or one tone can sound as if it is reaching us directly from one location, whereas another tone can appear to surround us. We will now consider why some of these differences in sound quality occur.

Timbre

A number of different characteristics of the sound stimulus act together to produce an instrument's timbre—the quality that makes two musical instruments playing the same note with the same loudness and duration sound different (Handel, 1995). One factor that causes differences in timbre is the relative strengths of the harmonics that occur for all complex musical tones. (Remember from Chapter 11 that complex musical tones contain a fundamental frequency plus harmonics which are multiples of the fundamental frequency.)

Figure 12.6 compares the harmonics of the guitar, the bassoon, and the alto saxophone playing the note G_3 with a fundamental frequency of 196 Hz. Both the relative heights of the harmonics and the number of harmonics are different in these instruments. For example, the guitar has more high-frequency harmonics than either the bassoon or the alto saxophone. Although the frequencies of the harmonics are always multiples of the fundamental frequency, harmonics may be absent, as is true of some of the high-frequency harmonics of the bassoon and the alto saxophone.

The best example of an instrument that produces a tone with few harmonics is the flute. You can see from Figure 12.7 that for a 1,568-Hz tone (G_6) the flute has only one harmonic in addition to the fundamental, and this harmonic has very little energy. Because the fundamental contains most of the energy of this tone, the flute has the thinnest and purest tone of all of the musical instruments. At the other extreme, instruments like the guitar and the lower notes on the

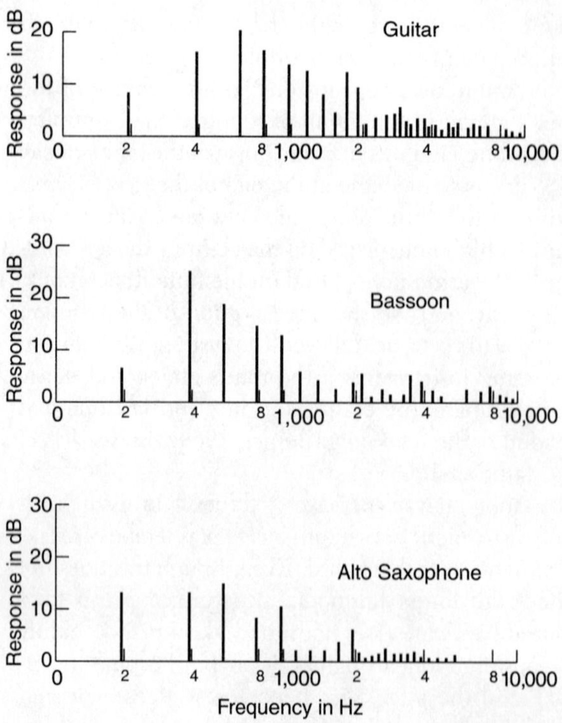

Figure 12.6
Fourier spectra for a guitar, a bassoon, and an alto saxophone playing a tone with a fundamental frequency of 196 Hz. The position of the lines on the horizontal axis indicates the frequencies of the harmonics and their height indicates their intensities. (Olson, 1967)

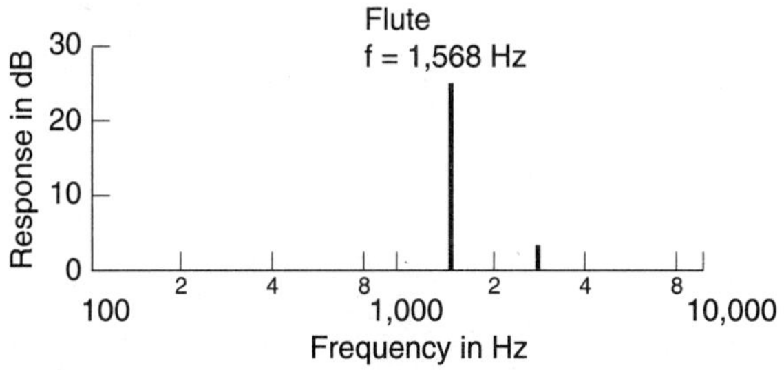

Figure 12.7
Fourier spectrum of a flute playing a tone with a fundamental frequency of 1,568 Hz. (Olson, 1967)

piano, which have many harmonics, have much fuller, richer tones than the flute.

Timbre also depends on the time course of the tone's **attack** (the buildup of sound at the beginning of the tone) and by the time course of the tone's **decay** (the decrease in sound at the end of the tone). Thus, it is easy to tell the difference between a tape recording of a high note played on the clarinet and a recording of the same note played on the flute if the attack, the decay, and the sustained portion of the tone are heard. However, it is difficult to distinguish between the same instruments if the tone's attack and decay are eliminated by erasing the first and last one-half second of the recording (Berger, 1964; also see Risset & Mathews, 1969).

Another way to make it difficult to distinguish one instrument from another is to play a tape of an instrument's tone backward. Even though this does not affect the tone's harmonic structure, a piano tone played backward does not sound like a piano, mainly because the tone's original decay has become the attack and the attack has become the decay (Berger, 1964; Erickson, 1975). Thus, timbre depends both on the tone's steady-state harmonic structure and on the time course of the attack and decay of the tone's harmonics.

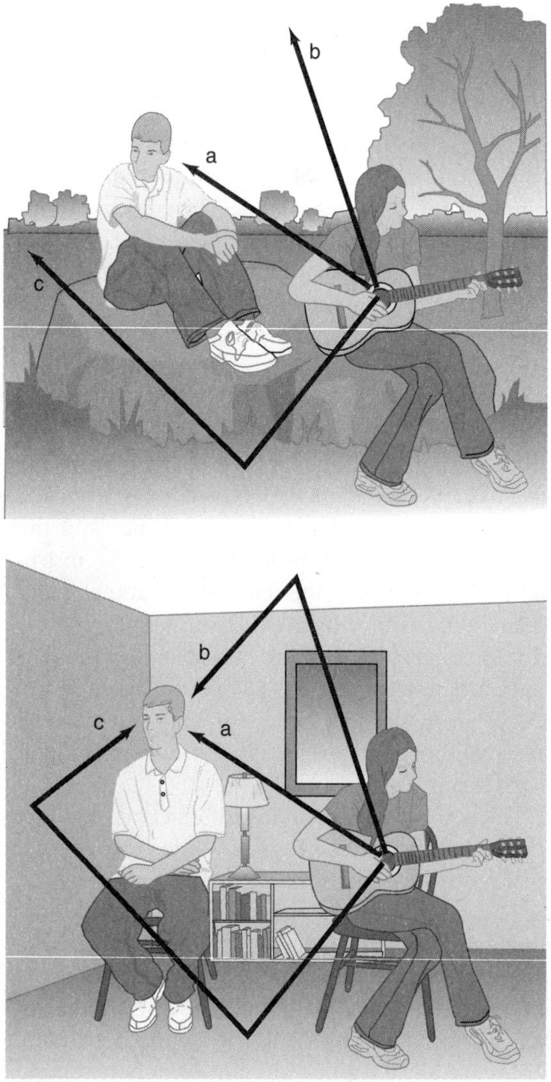

Figure 12.8
Top: When you hear a sound outside, you hear mainly direct sound (path a). Bottom: When you hear a sound inside a room, you hear both direct sound (a) and indirect sound (b and c) that is reflected from the walls, floor, and ceiling of the room.

Direct and Indirect Sound

When we studied vision, we saw that our perception of light depends not only on the nature of the light source but also on what happens to the light between the time it leaves its source and the time it enters our eyes. If light passes through haze on its way from an object to our eyes, the object may seem bluer or fuzzier than it would if the haze were not there. Similarly, our perception of sound also depends not only on the sound produced at the source, but also on what happens to the sound between the time it leaves the source and the time it enters our ears.

Figure 12.8 illustrates how the nature of the sound reaching your ears depends on the environment in which you hear the sound. If you are sitting outdoors next to someone playing a guitar, some of the sound you hear reaches your ears after being reflected from the ground or objects like trees, but most of the sound travels directly from the sound source to your ears. If, however, you are listening to the same guitar in an enclosed room, then most of the sound bounces off of the room's walls, ceiling, and floor before reaching your ears. The sound reaching your ears directly, along path a, is called **direct sound,** and the sound reaching your ears later, along paths like b and c, is called **indirect sound.**

The science of *architectural acoustics* is largely concerned with how this indirect sound changes the quality of the sounds we hear in rooms. The major factor affecting indirect sound is the amount of sound absorbed by the walls, ceiling, and floor of the room. If most of the sound is absorbed, then there are few sound reflections, and we hear little indirect sound. If little of the sound is absorbed there are many sound reflections, and we hear much indirect sound. The amount of indirect sound produced by a room is expressed as the **reverberation time** of the room—the time it takes for the sound to decrease to one-thousandth its original pressure.

What is the relationship between reverberation time and our perception of music? If the reverberation time is short, music will sound "dead," because most of the sound is absorbed by the room and it is difficult to produce sounds of very high intensity. If the reverberation time is long, music sounds "muddled," because the sound reflected by the room causes the sounds to overlap each other. Thus, the acoustical engineer tries to design a room in which the reverberation time is optimal for the sounds that will occur in the room. The optimal reverberation time for hearing music depends on the size of the room, with most average-sized concert halls needing a reverberation time of about 1.5 to 2.0 seconds.

However, reverberation time is not the only factor that affects our perception of music in concert halls. This is illustrated by the problems associated with the design of New York's Philharmonic Hall. When it opened in 1962, Philharmonic Hall had a reverberation time of close to 2.0 seconds, a value comparable to the reverberation times of many of the most successful concert halls in the world. Even so, the hall was criticized for sounding as though it had a short reverberation time, and musicians in the orchestra complained that they could not hear each other. These criticisms resulted in a series of alterations to the hall, made over many years, until eventually, when none of the alterations proved satisfactory, the entire interior of the hall was destroyed and the hall was completely rebuilt. The new hall, renamed Avery Fisher Hall, was reopened in 1976, 14 years after Philharmonic Hall's original opening, but this time with good acoustics. Based on experiences like this one, it is safe to say that determining the optimal acoustics of concert halls is not an exact science (Backus, 1977).

The Precedence Effect

Another aspect of the reverberation that occurs when you listen to music or to someone talking in an enclosed room is that the direct sound reaches your ears before the indirect sound. Since your ears receive a sequence of sounds coming from many directions, why do you perceive the sound as coming from only one location? The answer to this question is that, for reasons still not completely understood, perception of the sound's location depends on the sound that reaches the ears first. This effect, which is called the **precedence effect,** was extensively studied by Wallach, Newman, and Rosenzweig (1949).

Wallach et al. demonstrated the precedence effect by having a subject listen to music coming from two speakers located an equal distance away. When the music came from both speakers simultaneously, the subject heard the music coming from a point between the two speakers. However, if Wallach caused the sound from one speaker to precede the sound from the other by a fraction of a second, the subject reported that the sound appeared to come only from the speaker that had first produced the sound. Wallach eventually concluded that the first sound reaching our ears is heard, and that sounds arriving within about 70 msec of this first sound are suppressed. Since Wallach proposed this hypothesis, other researchers have suggested that a mechanism other than suppression is responsible for the auditory system's favoring initial sounds over later ones. One reason for this suggestion is that the later sounds do have some effect on perception, as we will see below (Perrott, 1989; Yost & Guzman, 1996).

DEMONSTRATION

Experiencing the Precedence Effect

To demonstrate the precedence effect, turn your stereo system to monaural (or "mixed"), so that both speakers play the same sounds, and position yourself between the speakers, so that you hear the sound coming from both speakers at a point between them. Then move a small distance to the left or right. When you do this, the sound appears to be coming from only the nearer speaker. ●

You might think that the precedence effect occurs because moving toward one speaker makes the sound from that speaker louder. However, Wallach showed that the small increase in loudness that would occur from moving slightly closer to one speaker cannot cause you to hear only that speaker; you hear only the nearer speaker because the sound from that speaker reaches your ears first.

When you hear the sound coming from the near speaker, do you no longer hear the far speaker? You can answer this question by positioning yourself closer to one speaker and having a friend disconnect the other speaker. When this happens, you will notice a difference in the quality of the sound. Even when you think you are listening to only the near speaker, because that is where the sound appears to originate, sounds from the far speaker are also affecting your perception, giving the sound a fuller, more expansive quality. Your perception of a sound's location is usually determined by the sound that reaches the ears first, but its quality is influenced by sounds reaching the ears later (Green, 1976).

Auditory Scene Analysis: Identifying Sound Sources

So far we have focused on how we perceive individual pure tones or musical tones. But we rarely encounter either single pure tones or single musical tones in our environment. Consider, for example, what you might hear in a crowded restaurant. Two people at a nearby table are talking quietly to one another. At the same time, the person in back of you is talking in a loud voice about his summer vacation, which you would really rather not hear about. In the background, you hear dishes clanking in the kitchen, music from speakers high in the ceiling, and the hum of the restaurant's air conditioning unit. What you are hearing in the restaurant is the **auditory scene.** The auditory scene is the array of sound sources in the environment, where a **sound source** is anything that creates sound stimuli. The process by which you separate the stimuli produced by each of the sources in the scene into separate perceptions is called **auditory scene analysis** (Bregman, 1990, 1993).

It might seem as if analyzing an auditory scene into its separate components would be relatively simple. After all, different sources sound different and are located at different places, so it should be easy to tell one source from another. But just as for the other perceptions we have discussed in this book, what seems simple often involves unanticipated complexities.

We can appreciate why auditory scene analysis is complicated by comparing the process of perceiving our auditory scene to seeing a visual scene. In the restaurant, we see objects such as chairs, people, and tables, that are located at different places in the room. One of the things that helps us to separate these objects from one another is that each one is imaged on a different part of the retina (Figure 12.9a). But as we listen to the sounds in the restaurant, the pressure changes created by all of the sound sources—the people, the clanking plates, the music, and the air conditioner—all enter our ears simultaneously and create overlapping patterns of

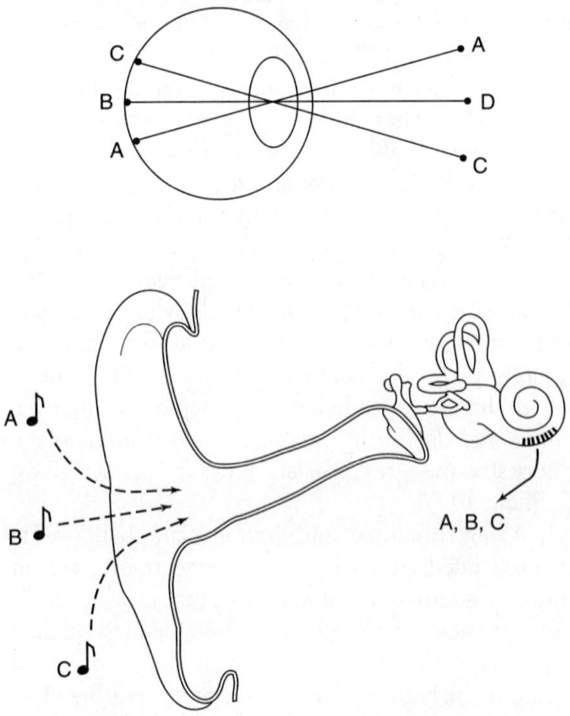

Figure 12.9
Comparing scene perception in vision and hearing. (a) Vision: Three objects, A, B, & C that are located in different places are imaged on three different places on the retina; (b) Hearing: Three sound sources A, B, and C, with the same or overlapping frequencies, that are located at different places can stimulate the same hair cells in the organ of Corti.

vibration on the basilar membrane. This result is, therefore, quite different from the situation for vision, because different sound sources can simultaneously affect the same place on the basilar membrane, and the information from these different sources can therefore be carried in the same auditory nerve fibers (Figure 12.9b).

Despite this difficulty, the auditory system somehow separates these overlapping vibrations into our perception of individual sound sources. Although it has proven to be extremely difficult to understand how our auditory system accomplishes scene analysis physiologically, a number of principles of auditory grouping have been proposed, based on psychophysical research, that help us to differentiate one sound source from another.

Principles of Auditory Grouping

Just as visual stimuli are perceptually organized so that certain elements of a scene appear to belong together, so are sound stimuli. This perceptual organization occurs according to rules that are based on how sounds originate in the environment. For example, tones that originate from a single source usually come from one point in space. Thus, one factor that helps us separate one source from another is its location—we can differentiate quiet talking on our left from the loud talking behind us partially because they are located in different places. Let's now consider some of these principles of auditory grouping. As we describe them, notice that some are similar to the Gestalt laws we described in Chapter 7 for the grouping of visual stimuli.

Location *Sounds created by a particular source usually come from one position in space or from a slowly changing place.* Any time two sounds are separated in space, the cue of location helps us separate them perceptually. In addition, when a source moves, it typically follows a continuous path rather than jumping erratically from one place to another. This continuous movement of sound helps us perceive the sound from a passing car as originating from a single source.

Similarity of Timbre *Sounds that have the same timbre are often produced by the same source.* This principle simply means that we tend to group stimuli that sound similar together. We can illustrate this by considering an effect created by David Wessel (1979), who presented listeners with sequences of tones shown in Figure 12.10a. In this figure the filled circles are tones with one timbre and the open circles are tones with a different timbre. When the tones are played slowly they sound like three repeated notes that are increasing in pitch and that change in timbre, as would occur if a clarinet alternated notes with

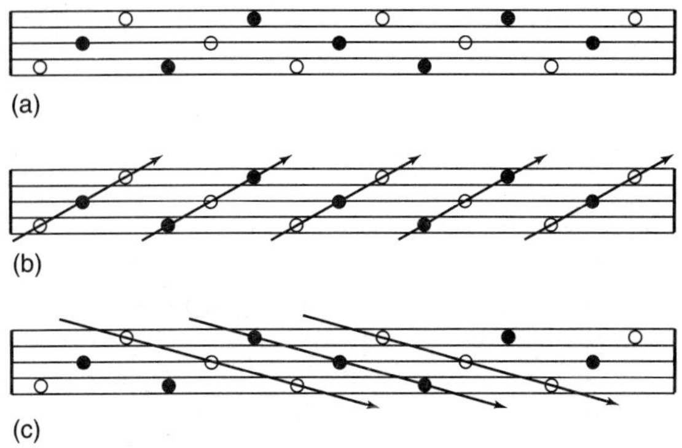

Figure 12.10
(a) The repeating series of three notes presented by Wessell (1979). The O's stand for a tone with one timbre, the ●'s for a tone with a different timbre. (b) When the tones are presented slowly they are perceived as ascending sequences with alternating timbres. (c) When the tones are presented rapidly, they are perceived as descending sequences with the same timbre. This is Wessel's timbre illusion.

a trumpet (Figure 12.10b). However, when they are played rapidly, the notes with different timbres are heard as separate descending streams with different timbres, as would occur if the clarinet and trumpet each played separate three-note sequences (Figure 12.10c). This is an example of **auditory stream segregation**—the separation of the acoustic stimuli entering the ear into different perceptual streams (also see Bregman & Pinker, 1978).

Similarity of Pitch *Sounds with similar frequencies are often produced by the same source.* This principle means that tones that have similar pitches tend to be perceived as belonging together. Composers made use of grouping by similarity of pitch long before psychologists began studying it. Composers in the Baroque period (1600–1750) knew that, if a single instrument plays notes that alternate rapidly between high and low tones, the listener perceives two separate melodies, with the high tones perceived as being played by one instrument and the low tones as being played by another. An excerpt from a composition by J. S. Bach that uses this device is shown in Figure 12.11. When this passage is played rapidly, the low notes sound as if they are a melody played by one instrument, and the high notes sound like a different melody played by another instrument. This effect, which has been called *implied polyphony* or *compound melodic line* by musicians, is an example of auditory stream segregation (see Jones & Yee, 1993; Yost & Sheft, 1993).

Albert Bregman and Jeffrey Campbell (1971) demonstrated auditory stream segregation based on pitch by alternating high and low tones, as shown in the sequence in Figure 12.12. When the high-pitched tones were slowly alternated with the low-pitched tones, as in Figure 12.12a, the tones were heard in one stream, one after another: hi-lo-hi-lo-hi-lo, as indicated by the dashed line. But when the tones were alternated very rapidly, the high and low tones became perceptually grouped into two auditory streams so that the listener perceived two separate streams of sound, one high-pitched and one low-pitched, occurring simultaneously (Figure 12.12b) (see Heise & Miller 1951; Miller & Heise, 1950 for an early demonstration of auditory stream segregation).

This grouping of tones into streams by similarity of pitch is also demonstrated by an experiment done by Bregman and Alexander Rudnicky (1975). The listener is first presented with two standard tones, X and Y (Figure 12.13a). When these tones are presented alone, it is easy to perceive their order (XY or YX).

Figure 12.11
Four measures of a composition by J. S. Bach (Choral Prelude on Jesus Christus unser Heiland, 1739). When played rapidly, the upper notes become perceptually grouped and the lower notes become perceptually grouped, a phenomenon called auditory stream segregation.

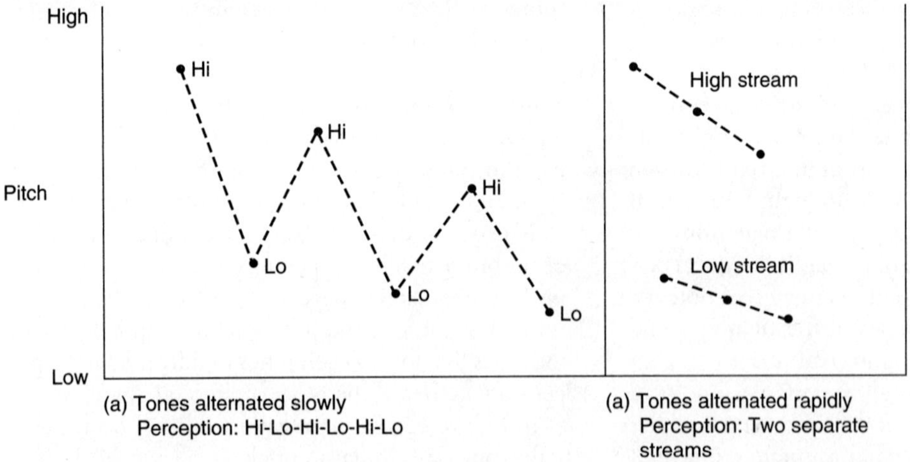

Figure 12.12
(a) When high and low tones are alternated slowly, auditory stream segregation does not occur, so the listener perceives alternating high and low tones. (b) Faster alternation results in segregation into high and low streams.

However, when these tones are sandwiched between two distractor (D) tones (Figure 12.13b), it becomes very hard to judge their order. The name *distractor tones* is well taken: They distract the listener, making it difficult to judge the order of tones X and Y.

But the distracting effect of the D tones can be eliminated by adding a series of "captor" tones (C) (Figure 12.13c). Since these captor tones have the same pitch as the distractors, they capture the distractors and form a stream that separates the distractors from tones A and B. The result is that X and Y are perceived as belonging to a separate stream, and it is much easier to perceive the order of X and Y.

A final example of how similarity of pitch causes grouping is an effect called the **scale illusion** or **melodic channeling.** Diana Deutsch (1975, 1996)

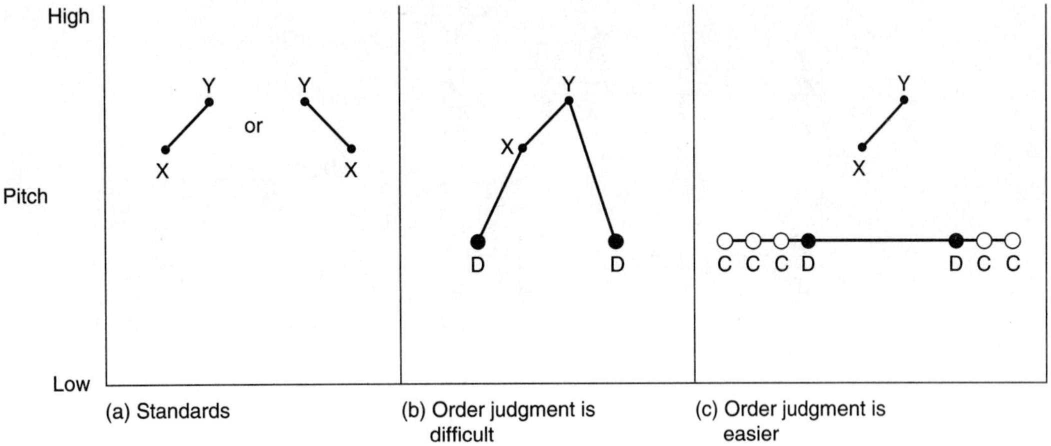

Figure 12.13
Bregman and Rudnicky's (1975) experiment. (a) The standard tones X and Y have different pitches. (b) Test 1: The distractor (D) tones group with X and Y, making it difficult to judge the order of X and Y. (c) Test 2: The addition of captor (C) tones with the same pitch as the distractor tones causes the distractor tones to form a separate stream (law of similarity) and makes it easier to judge the order of tones X and Y. (Based on Bregman & Rudnicky, 1975.)

demonstrated this effect by presenting two scales simultaneously, one ascending and one descending (Figure 12.14a). The subjects listened to these scales through earphones that presented successive notes from each scale alternately to the left and right ears (Figure 12.14b). If we focus just on the right ear, the notes alternate from high to low to high. Similarly, if we focus on the left ear, the notes alternate from low to high to low. But this was not what the subjects perceived. They perceived smooth sequences of notes in each ear with the higher notes in the right ear, and lower ones in the left ear (Figure 12.14c).

This illusion highlights an important property of perceptual grouping. Most of the time the principles of auditory grouping help us to accurately interpret what is happening in the environment. It is most effective to perceive similar sounds as coming from the same source, because this is what usually happens in the environment. When the perceptual system applies the principle of grouping by similarity to the artificial stimuli presented through earphones, it makes the mistake of assigning similar pitches to the same ear. But most of the time, when psychologists aren't controlling the stimuli, the fact that sounds with similar frequencies often are produced by the same sound source helps the auditory system to correctly determine where sounds are coming from.

Temporal Proximity *Sounds that occur in rapid progression tend to be produced by the same source.* We can illustrate the importance of timing in stream segregation by returning to our examples of grouping by similarity. Before stream segregation due to similarity of timbre or pitch can occur, tones with similar timbres or frequencies have to occur close together in time. According to the principle of temporal proximity, tones that follow each other rapidly tend to be perceived together. If the tones are too far apart in time, as in Figure 12.12a, segregation will not occur, even if the tones are similar in pitch.

Onset and Offset *Sounds that stop and start at different times tend to be produced by different sources.* If you are listening to one instrument playing and then another one joins in later, you know that two sources are present.

Good Continuation *Sounds that stay constant or that change smoothly are often produced by the same source.* This property of sounds leads to a principle

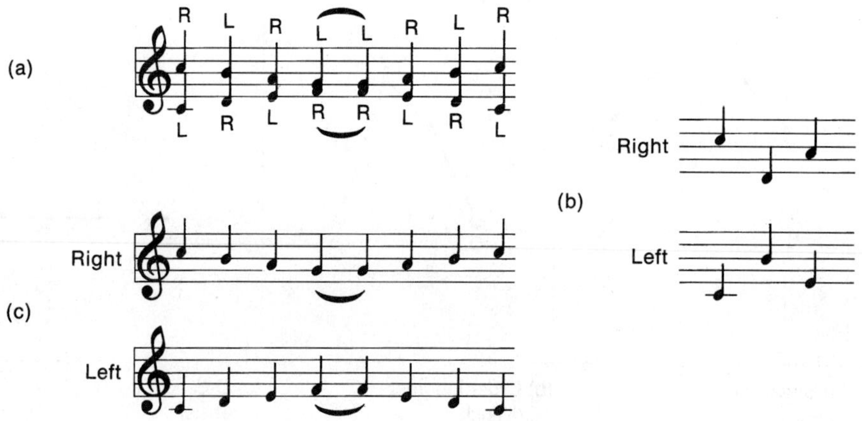

Figure 12.14
(a) These stimuli were presented to the subject's left and right ears in Deutsch's (1975) "scale illusion" experiment. (b) The first three notes presented to the left and right ears in Deutsch's experiment. The notes presented to each ear do not form a scale; they jump up and down. (c) What the subject hears. Although the notes in each ear jump up and down, the subject perceives a smooth sequence of notes in each ear. This effect is called the scale illusion or melodic channeling. (Based on Deutsch, 1975.)

analogous to the principle of good continuation for vision (see page 182). Sound stimuli with the same frequency or smoothly changing frequencies are perceived as continuous even if they are interrupted by another stimulus.

A musical example of this principle is shown in Figure 12.15a (Deutsch, 1996). This musical excerpt consists of one series of identical repeated notes (top) and another sequence that rises and then falls in pitch (bottom). Even though the pitches of the two musical streams cross (Figure 12.15b), they are perceived as two separate streams.

Richard Warren, C. J. Obuseck, and J. M. Acroff (1972) illustrated good continuation in a different way by presenting the stimuli shown in Figure 12.16. When bursts of tone were interrupted by gaps of silence (Figure 12.16a), listeners perceived the tones as stopping during the silence. If, however, the silent gaps were filled in with noise (Figure 12.16b), the listeners perceived the tone as continuing behind the noise (Figure 12.16c). This demonstration is analogous to the demonstration of visual good continuation in Pissarro's painting in Figure 7.16. Just as the smokestack in the painting is perceived as continuous even though it is twice interrupted by smoke, an interrupted tone can be perceived as continuous even though it is interrupted by bursts of noise.

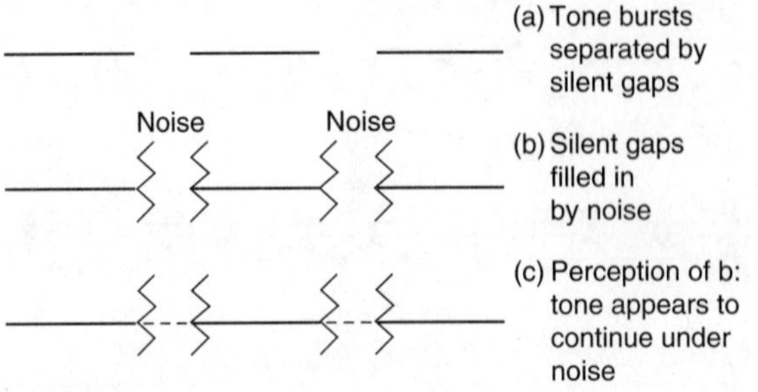

Figure 12.16
A demonstration of good continuation, using tones.

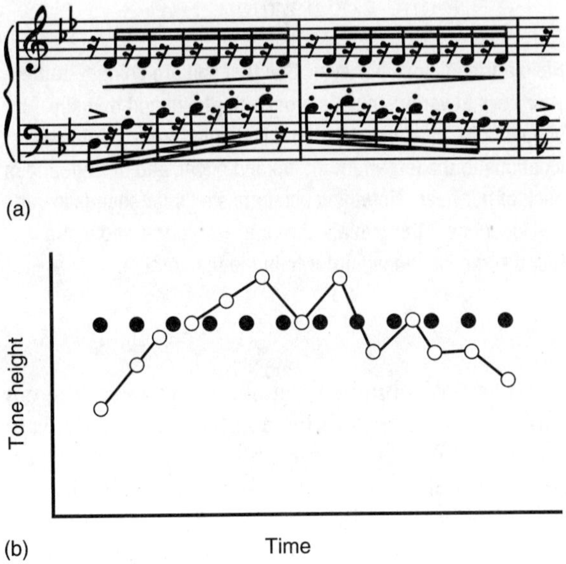

Figure 12.15
Top: A selection from Leyenda *by Albinez, showing the two musical lines, one of repeating notes and the other a sequence of changing notes. Bottom: The listeners perceive the repeating notes as one stream (filled circles) and the changing tones as another stream even though the notes overlap. (Adapted from Deutsch, 1996.)*

Experience An example of how past experience can affect the perceptual grouping of auditory stimuli is provided by W. Jay Dowling (1973), who had his subjects listen to two *interleaved melodies* by alternating notes of "Three Blind Mice" with notes of "Mary Had a Little Lamb" (Figure 12.17a). When the subjects listened to these combined melodies, they reported hearing a meaningless jumble of notes. However, when they were told the names of the songs, they were able to hear the melody, to which they were paying attention.

What the listeners were doing, according to Dowling and Dane Harwood (1986), was applying a **melody schema** to the interleaved melodies. A melody schema is a representation of a familiar melody that is stored in a person's memory. When people don't know that a melody is present, they have no access to the schema and therefore have nothing with which to compare the unknown melody. But if they are told which melody is present, they compare what they hear to their stored "Three Blind Mice" or

Figure 12.17
(a) "Three Blind Mice," (b) "Mary Had a Little Lamb," and (c) the two melodies interleaved ("Three Blind Mice": stems up; "Mary Had a Little Lamb": stems down).

"Mary Had a Little Lamb" schemas and perceive the melodies.

I demonstrate to my classes how schemas affect hearing words by playing a Rolling Stones recording and asking the class to try to identify the lyrics. This task is extremely difficult, because of both the loud instrumental backing and Mick Jagger's sloppy enunciation. But when I play the song a second time, and project the words onto a screen, the previously difficult-to-understand words become easy to perceive.

Each of the principles of auditory grouping that we have described provide information about the number and identity of sources in the auditory environment. But each principle alone is not foolproof, and basing our perceptions on just one principle can lead to error, as in the case of the scale illusion, which is purposely arranged so similarity of pitch dominates our perception. Thus, in most naturalistic situations, we base our perceptions on a number of these cues working together. This is similar to the situation we described for visual perception in which we saw that our perception of objects depends on a number of Gestalt laws of organization working together and our perception of depth depends on a number of depth cues working together.

Auditory Localization: Determining Where Sound Sources Are Located

We have described how our perception of the auditory scene involves auditory stream segregation—perceiving the individual sources as separate. Perceiving the auditory scene also involves **auditory localization**—the perception of the location of these sources. To get a feel for how well people can localize sounds, do the following demonstration.

D E M O N S T R A T I O N

Sound Localization

Have a friend close her eyes. Say that you are going to rattle your keys at various places around her head and that she should point to where the sound is coming from. Do this at locations to the left and right, up and down, and in front and in back of her head. Note how accurate she is for sounds in various locations. After you are through, ask your friend if she found some locations harder to judge than others. ●

There is substantial variability between different subjects' sound localization ability (so you might want to try this on a few people), but when measurements from a number of people are averaged, results like those in Figure 12.18 are obtained. This figure indicates, on an imaginary sphere that surrounds a listener's head, how well listeners can localize sounds that are in different positions in space (Makous & Middlebrooks, 1990; Middlebrooks & Green, 1991). Listeners can localize sounds that are directly in front of them most accurately (localization errors average 2 to 3.5 degrees) and sounds behind their head least accurately (localization errors are as high as 20 degrees).

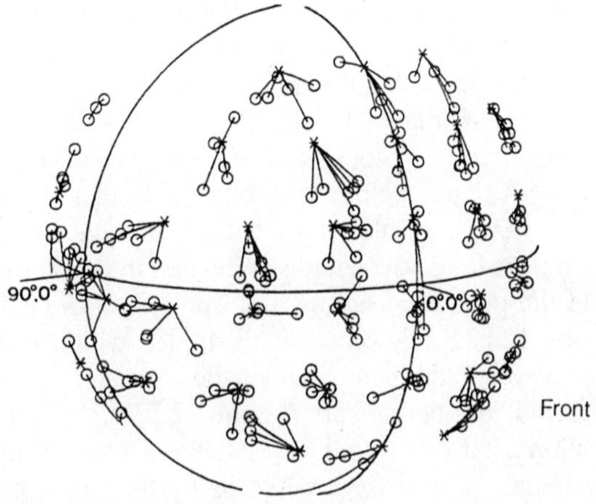

Figure 12.18
Subjects' ability to localize sounds. The asterisks are the actual sound locations, and the circles are the subject's estimates of their location. Longer lines connecting the asterisks and circles indicate less accurate localization. (From Makous & Middlebrooks, 1990.)

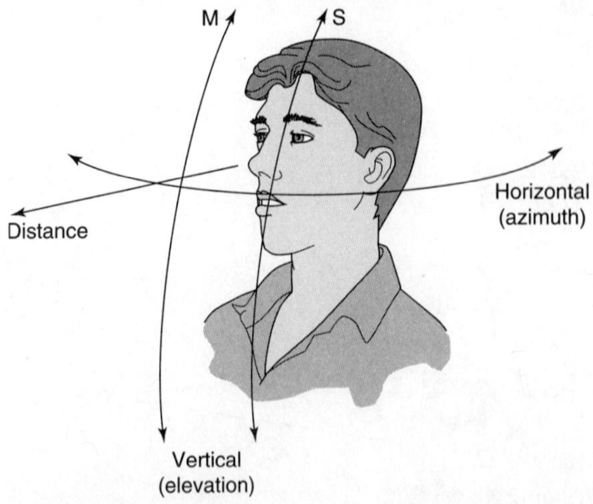

Figure 12.19
Horizontal, vertical and distance coordinate systems for localization. Two vertical coordinates are shown, one (M) in which the vertical coordinate is positioned on the subject's midline. The other vertical coordinate (S) in which vertical position is varied off to the side.

Auditory location is commonly described using the following three coordinate systems (Figure 12.19):

1. The horizontal (or azimuth) coordinate specifies locations that vary from left to right relative to the listener.
2. The vertical (or elevation) coordinate specifies locations that are up and down relative to the listener.
3. The distance coordinate specifies how far the sound source is from the listener.

Research on auditory location has focused on determining the kinds of information that listeners use to judge the location of sounds. This information is provided by **localization cues,** with different cues being associated with different coordinate systems.

Interaural Differences

Interaural differences refer to differences in the stimuli reaching the left and right ears. These cues are called **binaural cues** since they involve both ears. These cues are analogous to the binocular cues for depth perception, that involve both eyes. The two major interaural cues, *interaural time difference* and *interaural intensity difference,* provide information primarily about localization along the azimuth coordinate.

Interaural Time Difference Sounds originating from many locations in space reach one ear before the other. The difference between the time that the sound reaches the left and right ears is called the **interaural time difference.** The basis for the idea that there is a difference in the time that a sound reaches the left and right ears is illustrated in Figure 12.20. When the source is located at A, directly in front of the listener, the distance to each ear is the same, and the sound reaches the left and right ears simultaneously. However, if a source is located at B, off to the side, the sound reaches the right ear before it reaches the left ear. Since the interaural time difference is

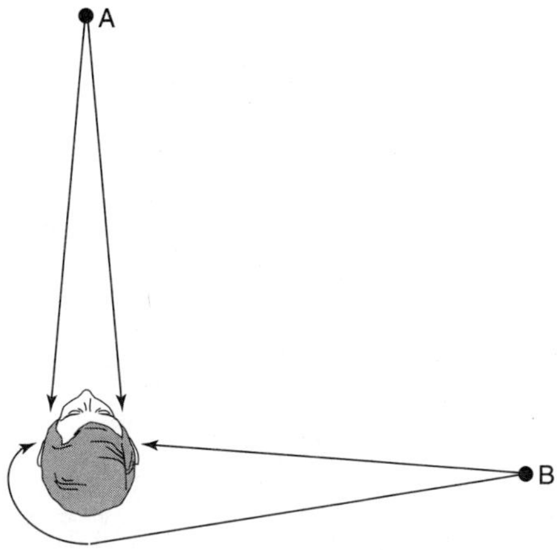

Figure 12.20
The principle behind interaural time difference. The tone directly in front of the listener, at A, *reaches the left and the right ears at the same time. However, if the tone is off to the side, at* B, *it reaches the listener's right ear before it reaches the left ear.*

larger for sounds that are located more to the side, the size of the interaural time difference can be used as a cue to determine a sound's location.

The way interaural time difference changes with a sound's location has been measured by placing microphones in a person's ears and determining the arrival time of sound stimuli originating from different positions in space. The results of these measurements indicate that the interaural time difference is zero when the source is directly in front of or directly behind the listener. As the source is moved to the side, the delay between the time the sound reaches the near ear and the time it reaches the far ear approaches a maximum of about 600 microseconds (6/10,000 sec) when the sound is located directly opposite one of the ears, as in B of Figure 12.19 (Feddersen et al., 1957). Although time differences on the order of microseconds are very small, it has been shown psychophysically that we can detect differences in arrival time as short as 10 microseconds (Durlach & Colburn, 1978).

Interaural Intensity Difference The other binaural cue is the **interaural intensity difference,** the difference in the intensity of the sound reaching the two ears. This interaural intensity difference occurs because the head creates a barrier that cases an **acoustic shadow** that keeps high-frequency sounds from reaching the far ear (Figure 12.21). We can appreciate why only high frequency sounds are affected, by imagining water waves approaching a wooden pole that is protruding from the water (Figure 12.22). Large waves, which have long wavelengths compared to the diameter of the pole, proceed, uninterrupted, past the pole (Figure 12.22a). However, small ripples, which have short wavelengths compared to the diameter of the pole, hit it and bounce off. (Figure 12.22b). A similar situation occurs for sound waves. Low frequency (long wavelength) waves are unaffected by the head, but high frequency (short wavelength) waves bounce off of the head, creating the acoustic shadow.

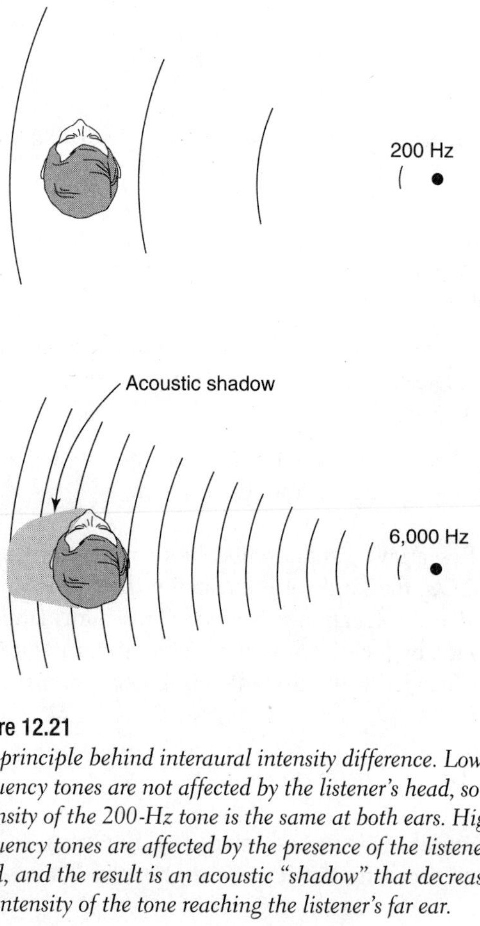

Figure 12.21
The principle behind interaural intensity difference. Low-frequency tones are not affected by the listener's head, so the intensity of the 200-Hz tone is the same at both ears. High-frequency tones are affected by the presence of the listener's head, and the result is an acoustic "shadow" that decreases the intensity of the tone reaching the listener's far ear.

Figure 12.22
Top: The low frequency water waves are hardly affected by one pole, so continue uninterrupted past the pole. Bottom: the high frequency ripples bounce off of the pole, which changes the motion of the ripples. This is similar to the way low and high frequency sounds interact with a person's head.

This effect of frequency on the interaural intensity difference has been measured by using small microphones to record the intensity of the sound reaching each ear in response to a moveable sound source. The results show that there is little difference in intensity for frequencies below approximately 1,000 Hz, but that quite sizable differences in intensity occur for higher frequencies (Figure 12.23).

Both interaural time difference and interaural intensity difference provide information about the azimuth (left-right position) of a sound source, but are not as well suited for providing information about the vertical position of the source, especially when the sounds are located midway between the two ears. We can see why this is so by looking at coordinate M in Figure 12.19. When sounds are located directly in front of a listener, moving the sound source along the elevation coordinate causes no change in the interaural time or intensity differences because the distance between the left and right ears remains the same. Thus, some other information must be involved in judging elevation. This information is provided by pinnae cues.

Pinnae Cues

The pinnae (Figure 12.24) provide a **monaural cue** to localization—information that requires only one ear. The pinnae's effect on sound localization was demonstrated in an experiment by Gardner and Gardner (1973), who inserted plugs of various shapes

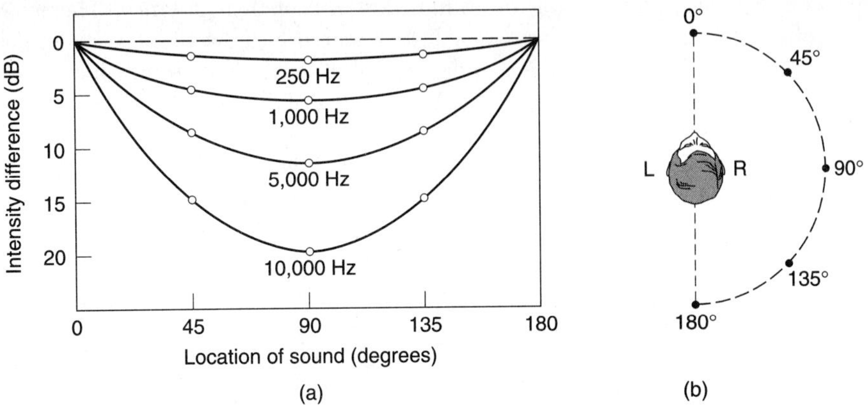

Figure 12.23
(a) The difference in intensity between the two ears for a 70-dB-SPL tone of different frequencies located at different places around the head. (From Gulick, Gescheider, & Frisina, 1989.) (b) The dots indicate the locations of the tones used for the intensity measurement in the graph in (a). The tones were located 2 m from the center of the head.

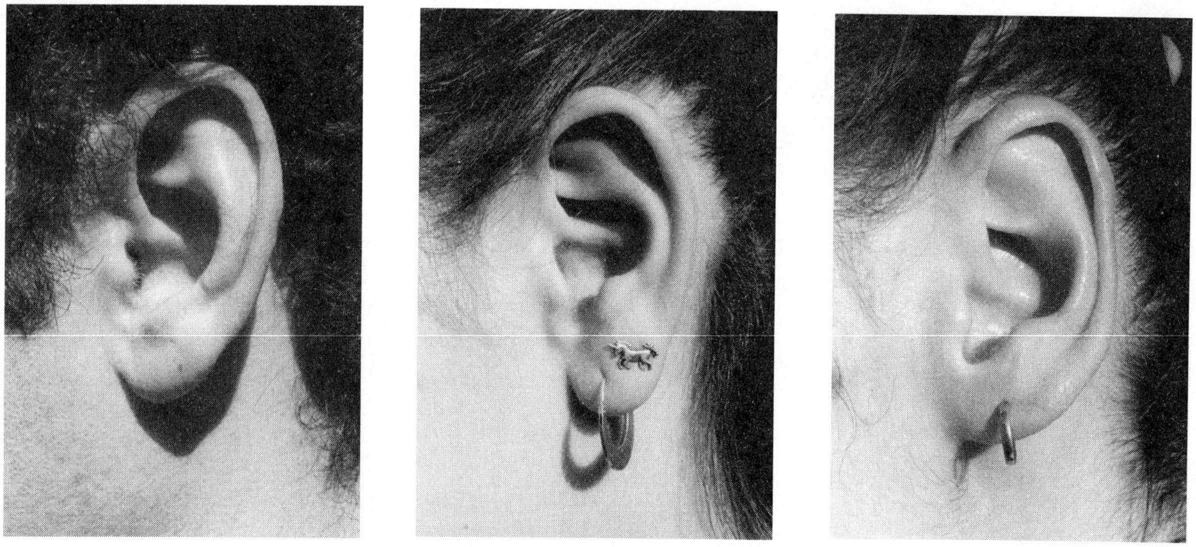

Figure 12.24
Different people have pinnae with very different shapes. These shapes affect how the sound bounces around in the pinna. This "bouncing" provides information for sound localization by changing the frequency composition of the sounds.

into people's ears. As they increasingly made the pinnae smoother by inserting different plugs, the listeners had more and more difficulty localizing sounds. You can demonstrate how the pinnae affect localization by placing earphones over your ears that still enable you to hear sounds in the environment. When you do this, you will notice that sounds become more difficult to localize than when you are wearing no earphones. This effect becomes particularly evident when you try to localize sounds with your eyes closed.

What is the nature of the localization information provided by the pinnae? The answer appears to be that various frequency components of the complex sounds in our environment are reflected back and forth within the various folds of the pinnae and these reflections add a distinctive pattern of echoes to each sound.

When a sound moves to a different position relative to a listener's head, these reflections decrease the intensity of some frequency components and amplify others. These different patterns of frequencies then become cues to the location of the sound (Batteau, 1967; Butler & Belendiuk, 1977; Oldfield & Parker, 1984; Scharf, 1975; Wightman & Kistler, 1993).

Pinnae cues are very important for localizing sounds on the vertical coordinate that are positioned on the head's midline (line M of Figure 12.19). When sounds are off to one side (curves) pinnae cues work together with the binaural cues to determine localization (Butler & Humanski, 1992).

Distance Cues

Close your eyes and listen to the sounds around you. You are aware not only of the azimuth and elevation of the sounds, but also of their distance. There has been very little research on how we make these distance judgments, but a number of cues have been suggested. We will describe four of them.

Sound Pressure Doubling the distance of a sound source decreases the sound pressure reaching the listener by about 6 dB (Wightman & Jenison, 1995). It has, therefore, been suggested that sound pressure provides a cue for distance, with lower pressures indicating greater distance. Daniel Ashmead, LeRoy DeFord, and Richard Odom (1990) had subjects judge which of two tones, presented at different distances, were closer. They found that when the pressures at the sound source were the same (so a lower sound pressure would reach the subject's ears for the far tone), subjects could judge differences in distance of about 6 percent. However, when the pressures were adjusted so that no matter where the sound source moved, the same sound pressure reached the subjects' ears, the subjects were still able to judge distance, although their accuracy decreased to about 16 percent. Thus, sound pressure provided information about distance, but since subjects were still able to make distance judgments even in the absence of sound pressure differences other distance cues must also be providing information about distance.

Frequency When we described the visual depth cue of atmospheric perspective, we saw that light is affected by the atmosphere through which it passes on its way from an object to the observer. A similar thing happens to sound, since high frequencies are absorbed by the atmosphere more than low frequencies. Thus, sounds that are farther away tend to be richer in low frequencies and therefore have a lower pitch.

Movement Parallax This cue parallels the visual depth cue of movement parallax, in which near objects appear to move across the field of view faster than far objects. A similar effect occurs when we move relative to continuous sounds. Sounds that are nearby will shift their location faster than sounds that are far away.

Reverberation As the distance of a sound source increases, the amount of reverberant (indirect) sound increases compared to the amount of direct sound, since greater distances provide more opportunities for sounds to be reflected from objects in the environment. Thus, the amount of reverberation can be used as information for the perception of a sound's distance (Mershon & Bowers, 1979).

Each of these distance cues, plus others we have not mentioned, provide information about a sound's distance. Just as a number of cues for visual depth work together to determine a person's perception of depth, these cues for sound distance also work together to determine a person's perception of a sound's distance.

The Physiological Basis for Localization

One thing about the physiological basis of localization is clear: The primary auditory cortex (A1) is necessary for localization. We will first look at evidence for this and then at research that has investigated how single neurons respond to sound sources that are located at different positions in space.

Role of the Primary Auditory Cortex (A1) The evidence that the primary auditory cortex is necessary for localization is straightforward: Removal of all or part of A1 degrades auditory localization. William Jenkins and Michael Merzenich (1984) took advantage of the fact that there is a tonotopic map in the auditory cortex (see Figure 11.29) and placed lesions in parts of a cat's area A1 that represented a small band of frequencies. When they tested the cat's ability to localize sounds, they found that their ability to localize was impaired just for the tones with frequencies represented in the band that was lesioned.

Interaural Time Difference Detectors By recording from single neurons in A1, researchers have identified some neurons, called **interaural time difference detectors,** that respond to specific interaural time differences. For example, in a monkey one of these cells fires best when a sound reaches the left ear 800 microseconds before it reaches the right ear (Brugge & Merzenich, 1973). This cell is similar to the binocular depth cells, described in Chapter 8 (Figure 8.24), that respond best to specific angles of disparity between the two eyes. These interaural time difference cells have been recorded not only from the auditory cortex but also from nuclei as early in the auditory system as the superior olivary nucleus, the first nucleus in the system to receive inputs from both ears (Hall, 1965).

Directionally Selective and Azimuth Sensitive Neurons There are **directionally sensitive neurons** in the auditory cortex of the monkey that respond to

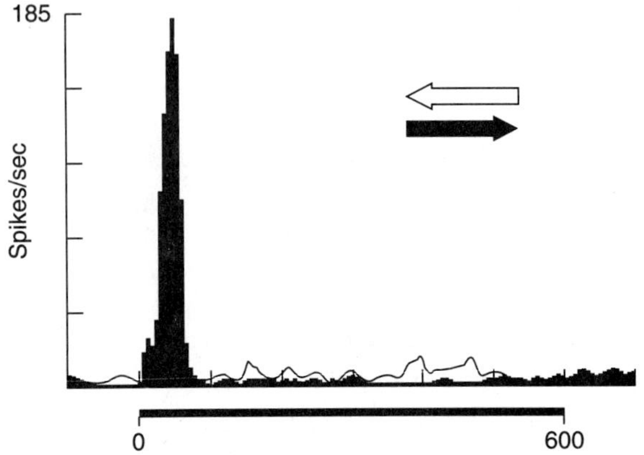

Figure 12.25
Directionally selective neuron. Record from a neuron in the auditory cortex that responds with a large burst of firing to movement of a sound to the right (black record), but doesn't respond to movement of the sound to the left (white record). (From Ahissar et al., 1992).

the direction that a sound stimulus is moving (Figure 12.25) and neurons called **azimuth sensitive neurons,** that respond best to a sound source's left-right position in space (Ahissar et al., 1992). Figure 12.26 shows the response of one of these azimuth-sensitive neurons that fires well to a broad area of stimulation on the left and responds poorly when the stimulus is presented to the right.

The firing of just one of these azimuth-sensitive neurons provides only rough information about where a sound stimulus is located because it responds to a broad area in space. More precise localization of the stimulus would require the pooling of information from a number of these neurons (Ahissar et al., 1992), or using additional information such as the timing of nerve firing (Brugge, Reale, & Hind, 1996). One example of how the timing of nerve firing might provide information about sound localization is provided by neurons called *panoramic neurons* that have been discovered in an area outside of A1 in the cat.

Panoramic Neurons Some neurons appear to signal location by the timing of their neural discharges (Middlebrooks et al., 1994). The way location is signaled by these neurons is illustrated in Figure 12.27, which shows the pattern of firing of one cortical neuron to sounds coming from a number of directions. Notice that the neuron fires to sounds coming from all directions, but that the pattern of impulses is different for different directions. That's why this neuron is called a **panoramic neuron**—it fires to sounds originating in any direction and indicates each location by its pattern of firing. Since a large number of neurons fire to a particular tone, information from a number of these neurons could help to precisely locate a sound (Barinaga, 1994).

Although neurons have been discovered in the cat and monkey that respond best to sounds presented in particular areas in space, the tuning of these neurons is not very precise. Most respond to

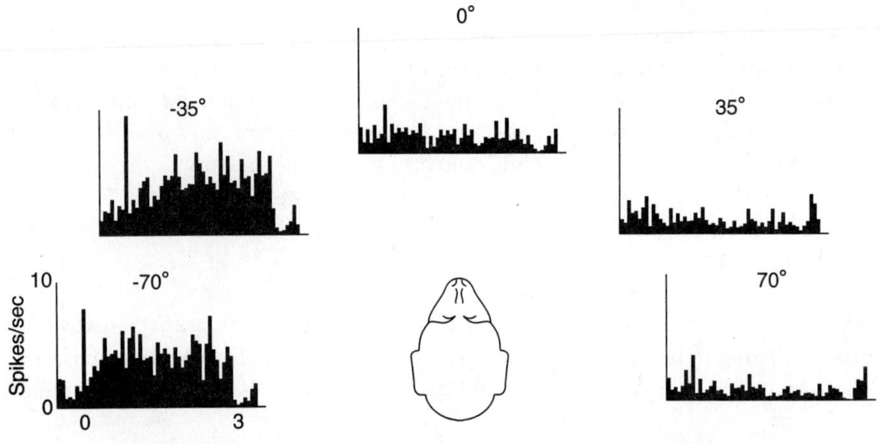

Figure 12.26
Azimuth-sensitive neuron. Records from a neuron that responds to sounds on the monkey's left (-70 and -35 degree records), but which responds poorly to sounds located on the right (35 and 70 degrees). Firing at 0, 35 and 70 degrees is not significantly above the spontaneous firing level. (Ahissar et al., 1992)

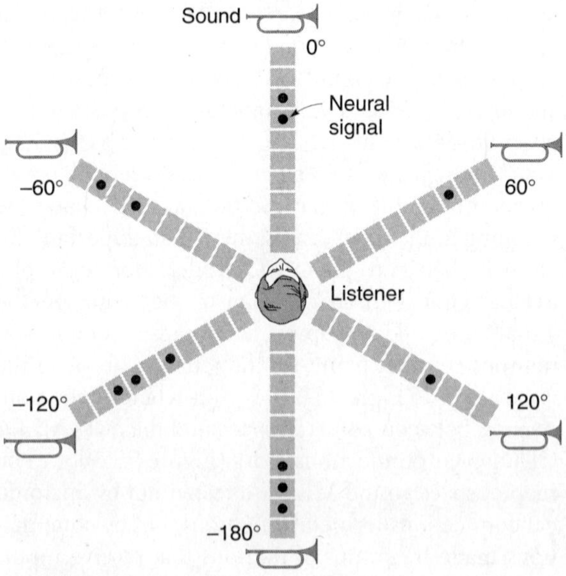

Figure 12.27
Panoramic neuron. How one neuron can indicate the location of a sound based on its pattern of firing. When the sound is directly in front of the listener, at 0 degrees, the nerve fires two impulses in quick succession, as indicated by the dots on the line. However, when the sound is at –60 degrees, there is a slight pause between the two impulses. Other directions cause other patterns of firing. Thus, this neuron has a different timing code for each direction. (Based on data from Middlebrooks et al., 1994.)

sounds located within a fairly broad area in space. The barn owl provides an example of neurons that respond to precise positions in space and which are arranged in a topographic map.

The Barn Owl's Topographic Map of Space

Research on the neural basis of sound localization in the owl has focused on a structure called the *mesencephalicus lateralus dorsalis* (MLD), which is roughly equivalent to the inferior colliculus of mammals. By presenting stimuli with the apparatus shown in Figure 12.28. Eric Knudsen and Masakazu Konishi (1978a, 1978b) found neurons that respond only when the sound stimulus originated from a small elliptical area in space, the receptive field of the cell. Furthermore, they found that some of these receptive fields have excitatory centers and inhibitory surrounds, so that an excitatory response that was elicited by a sound in the center of the receptive field could be inhibited by another sound presented to the side of or above or below the center. This property of the MLD cells means that center-surround receptive fields exist not only on the retina (Figure 2.35), but also in auditory space.

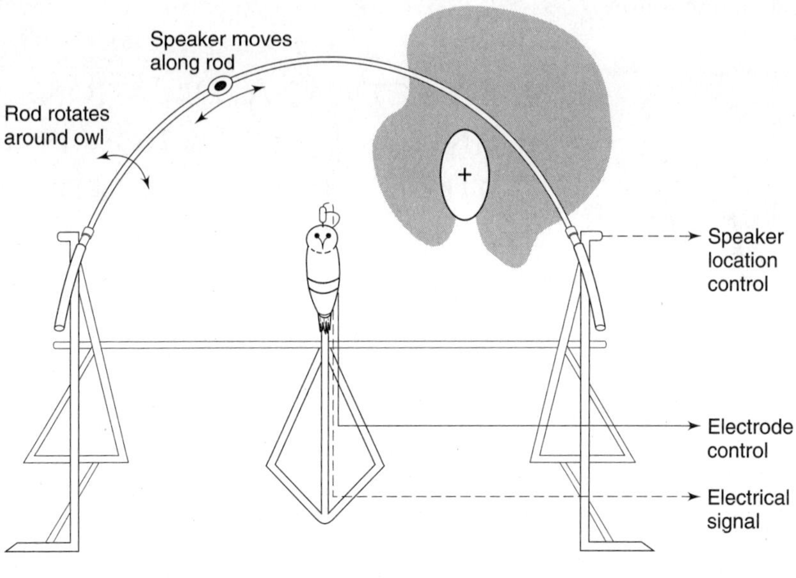

Figure 12.28
The apparatus used by Knudsen and Konishi (1978a, b) to map auditory receptive fields in space. The sound was moved to different positions in space by sliding the speaker along the curved rod, and by moving the rod around the owl. The elliptical area marked with a "+" is the excitatory area of a typical receptive field, and the shaded area is the inhibitory area.

Knudsen and Konishi not only found cells with receptive fields at particular locations in space, but also discovered that these cells are arranged so there is a map of auditory space on the MLD. That is, each cell on the MLD responds to a specific area in space (relative to the position of the head), and adjacent cells respond to adjacent areas of space (Figure 12.29).

We can compare this mapping of space on the MLD to other maps in the nervous system: for example, just as each point on the MLD corresponds to a particular area in space, each point on the retina is represented by a small area on the visual cortex (page 89). Similar point-by-point mapping also occurs in the auditory system and the somatosensory system (see pages 98–99).

Although we can see parallels between the point-by-point mapping of space in the owl's MLD and the mapping in the other senses, there is an important difference between them. Consider, for example, the principle behind the map of the retina on the visual cortex. This map occurs because sequences of neurons connect points on the retina to areas on the visual cortex (Figure 12.30a). But where is the connection between points in space and the owl's MLD? Clearly, no connections exist (Figure 12.30b). The map of space in the MLD is created not by anatomical connections formed by neurons, but by computations made by groups of neurons that receive inputs from both left and right ears.

The fact that the owl's receptive fields in space depend on inputs from both ears is supported by a simple experiment: Plugging one of the owl's ears eliminates the receptive fields in space. And partially plugging one ear, so that it receives less sound than it ordinarily would, shifts the location of the receptive field, so that the sound source must be moved to a new location to cause the neuron to fire (Konishi, 1984).

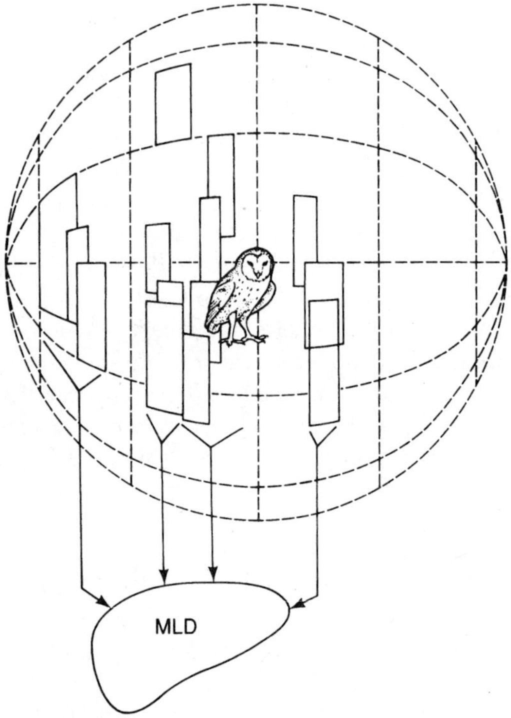

Figure 12.29
The top of this figure shows the owl surrounded by the locations of a number of receptive fields. The receptive fields are indicated by rectangles, although in reality they are shaped more like the one in Figure 12.28. The arrows point to the MLD location from which the bracketed receptive fields were recorded. The three receptive fields to the left of the figure were recorded from the left side of the MLD, whereas the group of receptive fields to the right were recorded from the lower right of the MLD. Thus, there is a map on the MLD that corresponds to the positions of its neurons' receptive fields in space. (Adapted from Knudsen & Konishi, 1978.)

A Practical Application: Sound as Information for the Visually Impaired

For people who have poor vision or are totally blind, sound provides an important source of information about the environment. Sound can provide information about the locations of objects in two ways: (1) The person can create sounds and note the echo created by objects that reflect the sound, or (2) when objects create sounds, the person can use sound cues like those described above to locate the object.

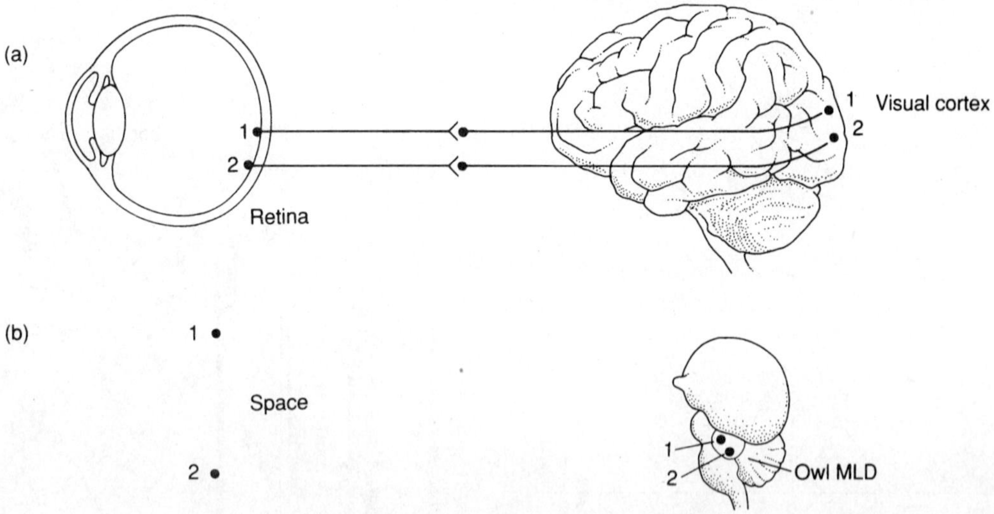

Figure 12.30
(a) The map of retinal locations in the visual cortex (b) and the map of locations in space in the owl's MLD are constructed according to different principles. The retinal map on the visual cortex occurs because there are neural connections linking points on the retina with neurons in the cortex. There is, however, no such anatomical connection between neurons in the owl's MLD and its receptive fields in space. The map in the MLD is constructed from information received by the left and right ears rather than from anatomical connections.

Using Echoes to Locate Objects

One way that sound provides information about the environment is through echoes, which can indicate the distance of objects. This effect has been demonstrated in experiments showing that sightless people can judge the distance of objects by noting how the sounds of their footsteps or vocalizations change as they approach these objects. For example, C. Ammons, P. Worchel, and K. Dallenbach (1953) asked blindfolded subjects to walk toward an obstacle positioned at a distance of 6, 12, 18, 24, or 30 feet, until they perceived it (and stopped) or collided with it. With some practice, all subjects were able to stop before colliding with the obstacle; however, if they wore earplugs in addition to being blindfolded, they collided with the object more frequently.

Perhaps the most impressive demonstration of how sound can be used to detect objects is an experiment that was inspired by the way bats and dolphins use echo-ranging, in which they determine the distances and sizes of objects by emitting a sound and then sensing the echo reflected from the object. Two blind college students were asked to judge which of two objects was farther away. They were told that, while making this judgment, they could produce any sound they wished. The subjects produced sounds in a variety of ways. They snapped their fingers, hissed, whistled, and, most often, repeated words, such as "now, now, now . . . " By judging the echo produced by these sounds, they were able to tell which of the two objects was closer. In fact, their performance was so impressive that it was possible to vary the separation between the two objects and to use the method of constant stimuli (see Chapter 1) to determine the psychophysical function shown in Figure 12.31 (Kellogg, 1962; also see Rice, 1967).

Using echoes to estimate the distance of objects is an impressive feat, but it is not very accurate and is often not useful in the everyday environment because of the presence of so many distracting sounds. However, a system called the Personal Guidance System is

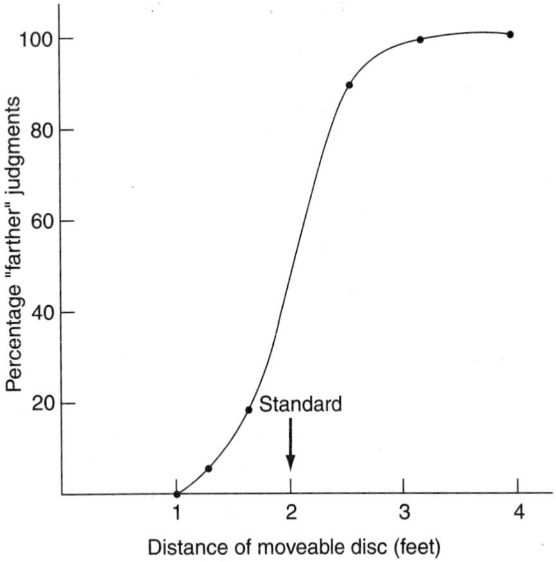

Figure 12.31
The results of an experiment in which a blind observer was presented with two 1-foot-diameter plywood disks, a standard disk that was always 2 feet away and a moveable disk that was either closer or farther than the standard. The observer judged whether each moveable disk was closer or farther than the standard, making 100 judgments for each disk. That this blind observer was able to judge distance based on echo ranging is indicated by the fact that changing the distance of the variable by less than a foot (from 1.59 to 2.55 feet) resulted in a change from 19 to 89 percent "farther" responses. (Data from Kellogg, 1962.)

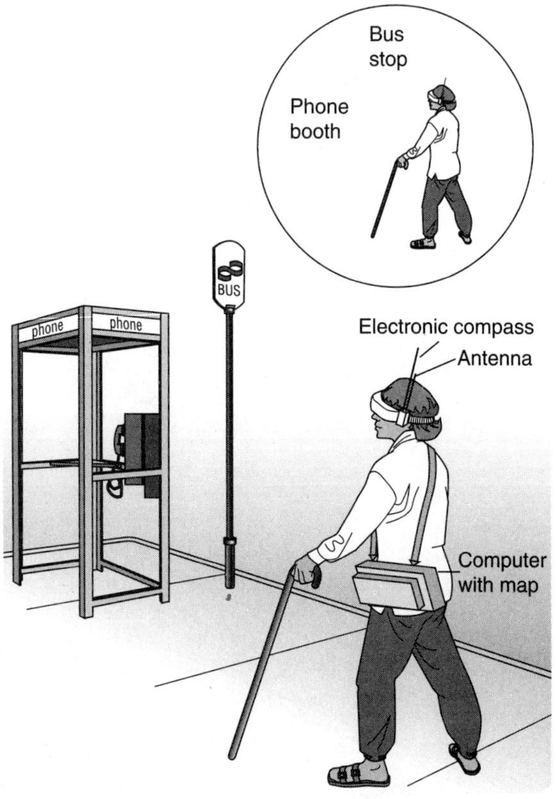

Figure 12.32
A blind person using an electronic navigation system. As the person walks through the environment, her position relative to the objects in the environment is determined by communication with Global Positioning Satellites combined with information provided by the computer, which contains a map of the area within which the person is walking. The circle indicates that the person hears the words bus stop and phone booth, and that these sounds appear to originate from the position in auditory space where these objects are located. The system shown here is a proposed miniaturized version of a larger system that is now being tested. (Adapted from Loomis et al., 1994.)

being developed that makes use of advanced technology and the binaural cues we discussed above.

Personal Guidance System Based on Binaural Cues

The Personal Guidance System is being developed by researchers at the University of California at Santa Barbara and Carnegie-Mellon University (Figure 12.32) (Loomis et al., 1994; Loomis, Hebert, & Cicinelli, 1990). The blind person is fitted with an electronic compass and a transmitter and receiver that communicate with Global Positioning Satellites that are orbiting the earth. Signals from these satellites determine the person's location, within 1 meter, relative to a map that has been programmed into the computer and that indicates the locations of objects in the scene such as the telephone booth and bus stop. Based on this information, a computer generates messages, such as "Telephone booth here" or "Bus stop 20 feet ahead," that the person hears through earphones. These messages are presented to the earphones so that the loudness and timing of the sounds reaching the left and right ears corresponds to how the sound would be perceived if the objects themselves were making the sounds. Thus, not only does the person hear "Telephone booth here," but the sound appears to come from the location of the telephone booth.

This system has been successfully tested in a prototype that is quite a bit bulkier than the one shown in Figure 12.32. Note that this system will work only when an accurate map of the environment can be fed into the computer, so this system can't locate objects, such as cars and people, that are not on the map. Although the availability of actual models of this system is at least a decade away, even the creation of the prototypes that now exist is an impressive demonstration of how basic knowledge about hearing mechanisms can be used for practical applications.

The Ecology of Auditory Perception: Two Kinds of Listening

How would you describe the sounds in your environment? When most people are asked to describe what they are hearing, they refer to the source that is creating the sound. Thus, I would describe the sounds I'm hearing in my office as "the air conditioner blowing" and "a squeaky chair next door." However, an auditory researcher might describe the air conditioner sound as "a continuous high-to-medium-pitched white noise sound" and the chair as "a sequence of short high-pitched sounds."

William Gaver (1993a, 1993b) suggests these two ways of describing sounds represent two kinds of listening. **Musical listening** focuses on the *perceptual qualities* of sounds—things such as the sounds' pitch and timbre. **Everyday listening** focuses on listening to *events* such as an air conditioner blowing or a chair squeaking.

In this chapter and Chapter 11 we have been primarily concerned with musical listening, because most auditory research has focused on basic perceptual qualities such as pitch, loudness, and timbre. This way of approaching the study of hearing has been extremely productive, because it has taught us a great deal about the basic operation of the auditory system.

Although everyday listening comes much closer to describing our everyday experience, little research has been done on this type of listening. Recently, however, some researchers have taken the first steps toward considering everyday listening. These researchers are interested in studying natural sounds, as they occur in the environment, and in taking an *ecological approach* to auditory perception that is analogous to J. J. Gibson's ecological approach to visual perception that we discussed in Chapters 8 through 10.

The first step in studying everyday listening is to describe the types of sounds in our environment. Gaver distinguishes the following three types of sounds: (1) vibrating solids (sounds like footsteps, a ringing bell, a can opener); (2) aerodynamic events (sounds like the air conditioner or the wind blowing through the trees; and (3) liquid sounds (water pouring or an object being dropped into the water).

Everyday listening has also been studied by determining how well people can identify sounds. When Gaver played taped sounds, he found that subjects could identify whether a person was running up and down stairs, the size of an object dropped into the water, and a cup being filled. Subjects can also tell whether a walker is male or female based on the sounds of their footsteps (Li, Logan, & Pastore, 1991).

How do subjects make these judgments? Some clues can be found in the mistakes they make. For example, subjects often identify the sound made by opening and closing a file drawer as a bowling alley. The reason for this confusion is apparently that both the file drawer and the bowling alley create a rolling sound followed by an impact. Other research has systematically looked at the relationship between physical properties of stimuli and their perceptual effects.

For example, Lynn Halpern, Randolph Blake, and James Hillenbrand (1986) wondered what makes a sound unpleasant. They found that sounds like scraping a garden tool across slate (which mimics the sound of fingernails scraping across a blackboard) are extremely unpleasant. They then asked what component of the scraped-slate sound was mainly responsible for its unpleasantness. Although they thought that the high-frequency components of the sound would be the culprit, when they presented the low- and high-frequency components of the sound separately, they found that the low frequencies in the sound were responsible for the unpleasantness.

Research like this on everyday sounds represents just the beginnings of attempts to understand how people perceive complex auditory stimuli. The problems involved are difficult, since the stimuli are so complicated, but just as researchers have become more interested in complex visual stimuli like faces and complex forms (see Chapters 4 and 7), they are also becoming more interested in the complexities of everyday auditory stimuli.

Something to Consider: Recognizing Sounds

Although we can hear sounds without thinking about them, our *recognition* of the sources that create these sounds involves past experiences and thought processes. Imagine, for example, that you are walking through an Amazonian rainforest. You hear a melange of sounds that are strange, beautiful, and scary all at the same time. As you listen to these sounds, you wonder what kinds of events might be producing them. (What was that splashing sound? A fish jumping or an alligator? Was that screech a bird or a monkey?)

Meanwhile your guide, who is receiving the same acoustic stimulation you are receiving, experiences not a cacophony of unknown sounds, but a series of familiar events—an alligator plopping into the water, the wind causing vine-covered trees to scrape together, a monkey screeching. The guide's familiarity with the sounds of the rainforest has enabled him to identify sounds that are unfamiliar to you and to more easily make sense of what is happening in the auditory scene.

A more familiar example of the effect of past experience on perception is the sound of a number of ceramic dinner plates crashing to the floor and breaking, with one surviving plate twirling more and more rapidly before finally coming to rest (McAdams, 1993). Because of their past experiences with crashing or twirling plates, most people hearing these noises would know what had happened. Imagine, however, how a person from a culture that had no ceramic plates or hard floors might react to this stimulus.

Thus hearing, like vision, involves both bottom-up processes such as activation of receptors, neurons, and various areas of the brain, and top-down processes that depend on matching the sounds we hear with what we have learned from our past experiences.

Blindness Leads to Improved Hearing and Cortical Changes

Does the loss of one sense enhance the senses that remain? This question has been hotly debated for many years, with proponents on both sides. Recent experiments by Josef Rauschecker and Martin Korte (1993; also Korte & Rauschecker, 1993; Rauschecker, 1995) provide evidence that cats that have been deprived of pattern vision have enhanced ability to localize sounds. Rauschecker and Korte deprived kittens of pattern vision in both eyes, a condition called **binocular deprivation,** by suturing their eyelids shut at birth, so they could perceive only diffuse light. When the cats were grown, they were trained to walk toward the location of a sound source presented at one of seven different locations (Figure 12.33). When they compared the performance of these deprived cats to the performance of sighted cats on the same task, they found that the deprived cats localized the sounds more accurately than the sighted cats.

What is the physiological basis for the deprived cats' superior localization ability? To answer this question, Rauschecker and Korte recorded from neurons in the *anterior ectosylvian nucleus,* which contains an area that is specialized for sound localization and also areas that respond to somatosensory (touch) and visual stimuli (Figure 12.34). Comparing this area in the deprived and sighted cats yielded an extremely interesting result: The deprived cats had expanded auditory and somatosensory areas and a diminished visual area. In addition, the neurons in the expanded auditory area were more sharply tuned to detect sound location.

Analogous results have been obtained in deaf humans, who can respond more quickly and accurately than hearing subjects to moving visual targets (Neville, 1990). In addition, when a physiological response called the *event related potential* is measured from the

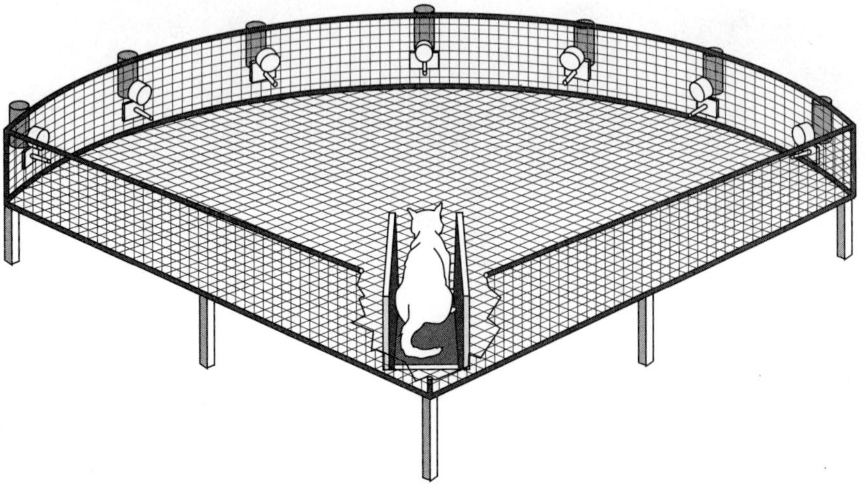

Figure 12.33
Apparatus used to test cats' sound localization. The cat is shown in the start position. There are seven speakers. The cats were trained to walk towards the location of the sound, which came from one of the speakers on each trial. (From Rauschecker & Korte, 1993.)

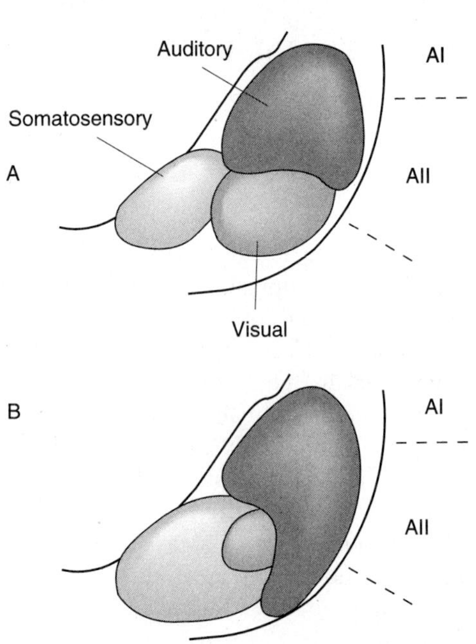

Figure 12.34
The anterior ectosylvian nucleus, which is located near auditory areas A1 and A11 and which contains auditory, visual and somatosensory areas. A: Sizes of the three areas for a normal cat; B: Sizes of the three area for a cat that had been deprived of pattern vision in both eyes as a kitten. The auditory and somatosensory areas have increased in size at the expense of the visual area. (From Rauschecker & Korte, 1993.)

parietal lobe, the response to light stimulation is larger in deaf subjects than in hearing subjects. Thus, in Rauschecker's study, blindness in cats improved auditory performance and physiological representation of audition in the cortex, and in Neville's study, deafness in humans improved visual performance and physiological responding to visual stimuli. The overall message of these studies, plus other similar ones, is that the brain is able to change its structure and functioning to adapt to long-term changes in an animal's sensory environment.

Study Questions

Underlying Principles

Find examples of the following principles in this chapter:

- Receptive fields/neural selectivity (370)
- Distributed response (370)
- Neural maps (372)
- Physiology-perception connector (369)
- Cognition-perception connection (363)
- Receptual grouping (359)

1. Describe the analogy between handkerchiefs at the edge of a lake and the process of hearing. What is the point of this analogy? (349)

Sensitivity and Loudness: Exquisite Sensitivity, but Frequency Matters

2. Why do we say that the ear is exquisitely sensitive? (350)
3. What is the audibility curve? The auditory response area? How does the human range of hearing and audibility curve compare to the animal range of hearing and audibility curves? (351)
4. What is the relationship between sound pressure and loudness? What is the sone? (352)
5. Why does saying "The tone is 40-dB SPL" not really tell us how loud the tone will sound? (352)
6. What is an equal loudness curve? Compare the shapes of equal loudness curves for 40-dB SPL and 80-dB SPL. (353)
7. What happens perceptually if you play music at a loud level and then turn the intensity down? (353)
8. What is a problem in explaining the physiological basis of loudness? What are two possible solutions to this problem? (353)

Sound Quality: What a Stimulus Sounds Like

9. What is timbre? Describe how the harmonic structure of a tone influences timbre. What other characteristics of a tone influence timbre? (354)
10. What is direct sound? indirect sound? reverberation time? How does the sound of music in a concert hall depend on reverberation time? (356)
11. What is the precedence effect? What did Wallach conclude about the mechanism responsible for the precedence effect? What do modern researchers say about Wallach's proposal? (357)

Auditory Scene Analysis: Identifying Sound Sources

12. What is a sound auditory source? The auditory scene? Auditory scene analysis? (358)
13. Why is auditory scene analysis a problem? (358)
14. Describe the following principles of auditory grouping: location, similarity of timbre, similarity of pitch, temporal proximity, onset and offset, good continuation, experience. (359)
15. What is auditory stream segregation? (360)
16. Describe the experiments on similarity of pitch that were carried out by Bregman and Campbell and by Bregman and Rudnicky. (360)
17. What is the scale illusion? Describe Deutsch's experiment that demonstrates this illusion. (361)

Auditory Localization: Determining Where Sound Sources Are Located

18. What is auditory localization? (364)
19. Describe the three coordinates used to describe auditory localization. (365)

20. What are the two major interaural cues? Why are they called binaural cues? (365)

21. Describe the principle behind interaural time difference. (365)

22. Describe the principle behind interaural intensity difference. What is the principle behind the acoustic shadow, and why does it occur more for some frequencies than for others? (366)

23. What are pinnae cues? Why are they called a monaural cue to localization? What is the nature of the information for location that is provided by the pinnae? Which cues provide information about location when sounds along the midline move along the vertical coordinate? Which cues provide information about location when sounds located off to the side move along the vertical coordinate? (367)

24. Describe the following cues for distance: sound pressure, frequency, movement parallax, reverberation. (368)

25. What is the physiological basis for localization? Describe the role of the auditory cortex, interaural time difference detectors, directionally selective neurons, azimuth sensitive neurons, and panoramic neurons. (369)

26. Describe the barn owl's topographic map of space. (371)

27. What are the parallels between the point-by-point mapping of space in the owl's MLD and mapping in the visual cortex? (372)

28. What is a major difference between mapping of space in hearing and in vision? What do we mean when we say that the physiology of localization is a computational process? (372)

29. What happens if we plug an owl's ear? if we partially plug the ear? (372)

A Practical Application: Sound as Information for the Visually Impaired

30. What is the idea behind using echoes to locate objects? What is the experimental evidence that it can be done? (372)

31. Describe the principle behind the Personal Guidance System. (374)

The Ecology of Auditory Perception: Two Kinds of Listening

32. What is the difference between musical listening and everyday listening? (375)

33. What is the ecological approach to auditory perception? (375)

34. What is the first step in studying everyday listening? (375)

35. How well can people identify everyday sounds? (375)

36. What makes the sound of fingernails scratching a blackboard unpleasant? (376)

Something to Consider: Recognizing Sounds

37. What is the connection between experience and recognizing sounds? (376)

Across the Senses: Blindness Leads to Improved Hearing and Cortical Changes

38. What effect does depriving cats of pattern vision have on their ability to localize sounds? (377)

39. What is the physiological basis for the superior localization ability of binocularly deprived cats? (377)

40. What effect does deafness in humans have on their ability to respond to moving targets? On the event related potential that is elicited by light stimulation? (377)

13

Speech Perception

Speech, like other sounds, is a disturbance of the air. Speech sounds are produced when air pushed from the lungs into the mouth is shaped into patterns of air pressure changes by actions of the various structures in the vocal tract (Figure 13.1).

Although we perceive speech easily under most conditions, beneath this ease lurks processes as complex as those involved in perceiving the most complicated visual scenes. One way to appreciate this complexity is to consider attempts to use computers to recognize speech. After decades of research into computer speech recognition, useful computer speech recognition systems are only now becoming available. The phone company uses computer speech recognition to identify simple messages such as telephone numbers or phrases such as "I want to make a credit card call." There are dictation machines that can translate speech that is spoken clearly and in a quiet environment into printed text. Software programs are available that make it possible for personal computers to respond to spoken commands (Markowitz, 1996).

As impressive as these feats of machine intelligence are, they pale in comparison to the ability of humans to understand the speech produced by a wide variety of speakers, under conditions that include the presence of various background noises, sloppy pronunciation, and the often chaotic give-and-take that routinely occurs when people talk with one another.

This chapter will help you appreciate the complex perceptual problems posed by speech and will describe research that has helped us begin to understand how the human speech perception system has solved

CHAPTER CONTENTS

SOME QUESTIONS WE WILL CONSIDER

- Can computers perceive speech as well as humans? (381)
- Why does an unfamiliar foreign language often sound like a continuous stream of sound, with no breaks between words? (384)
- Does each word that we hear have a characteristic pattern of air pressure changes associated with it? (385)

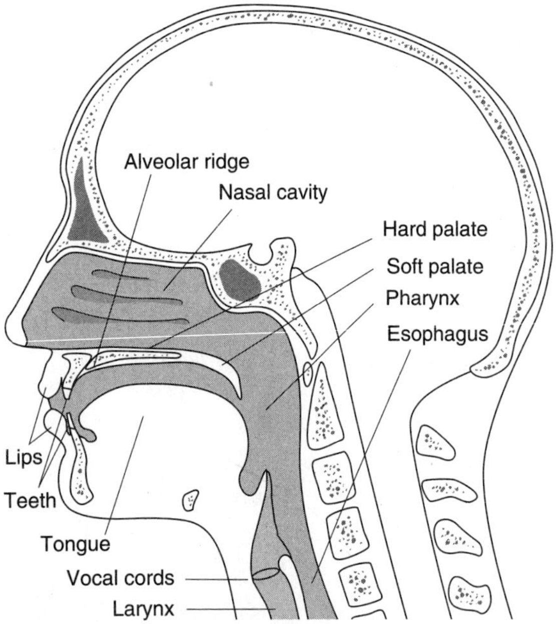

Figure 13.1
The vocal tract includes the nasal and oral cavities and the pharynx, as well as components that move, such as the tongue, lips, and vocal chords.

some of these problems. We begin by describing the nature of the vibrations produced by our vocal apparatus.

The Speech Stimulus

Think about what you hear when someone speaks to you. You perceive a series of sounds called *syllables*, which create words, and these syllables and words appear strung together one after another like beads on a string. For example, we perceive the phrase "perception is easy" as the sequence of units: "per-cep-shon—is—e-z." But although our perception of speech may be easy and the sounds we hear may appear to be discrete sounds that are lined up one after another, the actual situation is quite different.

Rather than following each other in an orderly sequence, neighboring sounds overlap one another. In addition, the pattern of air pressure changes for a particular word can vary greatly depending on how fast someone is talking, whether the speaker is male or female, young or old, or speaks with a regional accent. To understand why speech sounds overlap and why the same sound can be represented by many different patterns of pressure changes, we need to describe the speech stimulus and how it is produced. We will do this in two ways: (1) in terms of short segments of sound, called **phonemes,** and (2) in terms of the patterns of frequencies and intensities of the pressure changes in the air, called the *acoustic signal.*

Phonemes: Sounds and Meanings

Our first task in studying speech perception is to separate speech sounds into manageable units. What are these units? The flow of a sentence? A particular word? A syllable? The sound of a letter? A sentence is too large a unit for easy analysis, and some letters have no sounds at all. Although there are arguments for the idea that the syllable is the basic unit of speech (Mehler, 1981; Segui, 1984), most speech research has been based on a unit called the **phoneme.** The phoneme is the shortest segment of speech that, if changed, changes the meaning of a word. Consider the word *bit,* which contains the phonemes /b/, /I/, and /t/. (We indicate phonemes and other speech sounds by setting them off with slashes.) We know that /b/, /I/, and /t/ are phonemes, because we can change the meaning of the word by changing each phoneme individually. Thus, *bit* becomes *pit* if /b/ is changed to /p/, it becomes *bat* if /I/ is changed to /a/, and it becomes *bid* if /t/ is changed to /d/.

The phonemes of English, listed in Table 13.1, are represented by phonetic symbols that stand for speech sounds; 13 phonemes have vowel sounds and 24 phonemes have consonant sounds. Your first reaction to this table may be that there are more vowels than the standard set you learned in grade school (*a, e, i, o,* and *u*). The reason is that some vowels can have more than one pronunciation, so there are more vowel sounds than vowel letters. For example, the

Table 13.1
Major consonants and vowels of English and their phonetic symbols

Consonants				Vowels	
p	*pull*	s	*sip*	i	*heed*
b	*bull*	z	*zip*	I	*hid*
m	*man*	r	*rip*	e	*bait*
w	*will*	š	*should*	ε	*head*
f	*fill*	ž	*pleasure*	æ	*had*
v	*vet*	č	*chop*	*u*	*who'd*
θ	*thigh*	ǰ	*gyp*	U	*put*
ð	*thy*	y	*yip*	ʌ	*but*
t	*tie*	k	*kale*	o	*boat*
d	*die*	g	*gale*	ɔ	*bought*
n	*near*	h	*hail*	a	*hot*
l	*lear*	ŋ	*sing*	ə	*sofa*
				ɨ	*many*

such as the tongue, lips, teeth, jaw, and soft palate (Figure 13.1).

Let's first consider the production of vowels. Vowels are produced by vibration of the vocal cords, and the specific sounds of each vowel are created by changing the overall shape of the vocal tract. This change in shape changes the resonant frequency of the vocal tract and produces peaks of pressure change at a number of different frequencies (Figure 13.2). The frequencies at which these peaks occur are called **formants.**

Each vowel sound has a characteristic series of formants. The first formant has the lowest frequency. The second formant is the next highest, and so on. The formants for the vowel /ae/ are shown on a display called a **sound spectrogram** in Figure 13.3. The sound spectrogram indicates the pattern of frequencies and intensities over time that make up the

vowel *o* sounds different in *boat* and *hot* and the vowel *e* sounds different in *heed* and *head.* Phonemes, therefore, refer not to letters but to *speech sounds* that serve to distinguish meaning.

Because different languages use different sounds, the number of phonemes varies in different languages. While there are only 11 phonemes in Hawaiian, there are 48 in English, and as many as 60 in some African dialects. Thus, phonemes are defined in terms of the sounds that create meaning in a specific language. Each phoneme is produced by movements of structures within the vocal apparatus, and these movements produce patterns of pressure changes in the air which are called the **acoustic stimulus** or the **acoustic signal.**

The Acoustic Signal: Patterns of Pressure Changes

The acoustic signal for speech is created by air that is pushed up from the lungs past the vocal cords and into the vocal tract. The sound that is produced depends on the shape of the vocal tract as air is pushed through it. The shape of the vocal tract is altered by moving the **articulators,** which include structures

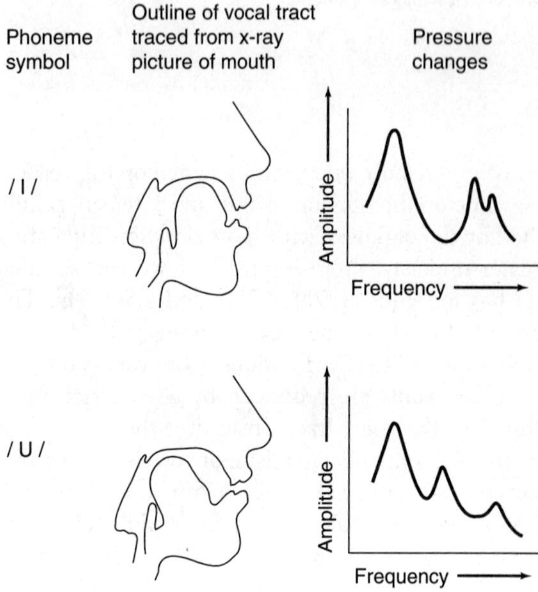

Figure 13.2
Left: The shape of the vocal tract for the vowels /I/ and /u/. Right: The amplitude of the pressure changes produced for each vowel. The peaks in the pressure changes are the formants. Each vowel sound has a characteristic pattern of formants which is determined by the shape of the vocal tract for that vowel. (Adapted from Denes & Pinson, 1993.)

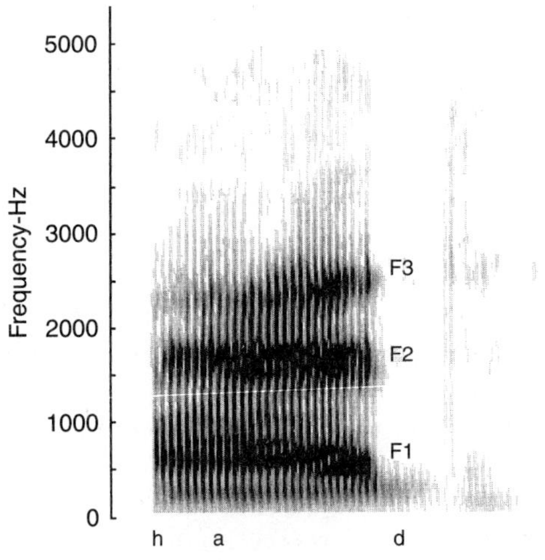

Figure 13.3
Spectrogram of the word had *showing the first (F1), second (F2), and third (F3) formants for the vowel /ae/. (Spectrogram courtesy of Kerry Green.)*

acoustic signal. Frequency is indicated on the vertical axis, time on the horizontal axis, and intensity is indicated by the darkness, with more darkness indicating greater intensity. From Figure 13.3 we can see that /ae/ has formants at 500, 1,700, and 2,500 Hz. The vertical lines in the spectrogram are pressure oscillations caused by vibrations of the vocal cord.

Consonants are produced by a constriction or closing of the vocal tract. Instead of the continuous stream of energy characteristic of vowels (notice that you can hold a vowel until you run out of breath), consonants are characterized by rapidly changing bursts of energy and periods of silence. To illustrate how different consonants are produced, let's focus on the sounds /d/ and /f/. Make these sounds and notice what your tongue, lips, and teeth are doing. As you produce the sound /d/, you place your tongue against the ridge above your upper teeth (the alveolar ridge of Figure 13.1) and then release a slight rush of air as you move your tongue away from the alveolar ridge (try it). As you produce the sound /f/, you place your bottom lip against your upper front teeth and then push air between the lips and the teeth.

These movements of the tongue, lips, and other articulators create patterns of energy in the acoustic signal that we can observe on the sound spectrograph. For example, the spectrogram for the sentence "Roy read the will" shown in Figure 13.4 shows aspects of the signal associated with vowels and consonants. For example, the three horizontal bands marked F1, F2, and F3 are the three formants associated with the /e/ sound of *read.* Rapid shifts in frequency preceding or following formants are called **formant transitions** and are associated with consonants. For example, T2 and T3 are formant transitions associated with /r/ of *read.*

Now that we know how speech is produced and how it is represented on a speech spectrograph, we are ready to look at some of the problems that we must solve in order to understand speech perception.

Problems Posed by the Speech Stimulus

The main problem facing researchers who are trying to understand speech perception is that the relationships between the acoustic signal and the sounds we hear are extremely complex. One reason for this complexity is that the acoustic signal is not neatly separated into individual words. This lack of separation between the signal for each word creates the *segmentation problem.*

The Segmentation Problem

When we listen to someone speak, we hear individual words. But when we look at the speech spectrograph, we see that the acoustic signal is continuous, with either no physical breaks in the signal, or breaks that don't necessarily correspond to the breaks we perceive between words (Figure 13.5). The fact that

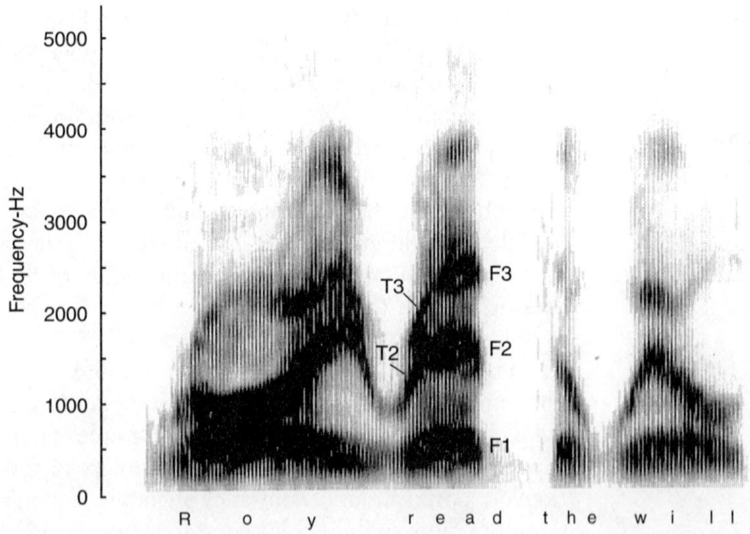

Figure 13.4
Spectrogram of the sentence, "Roy read the will," showing formants such as F1, F2, and F3, and formant transitions such as T2 and T3. (Spectrogram courtesy of Kerry Green.)

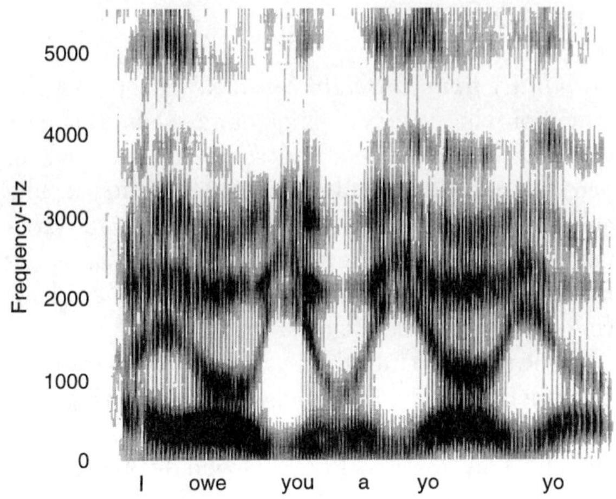

Figure 13.5
Spectrogram of "I owe you a yo-yo." This spectrogram does not contain pauses or breaks that correspond to the words that we hear. This absence of breaks in the acoustic signal creates the segmentation problem. (Spectrogram courtesy of David Pisoni.)

there are usually no spaces between words becomes obvious when you listen to someone speaking a foreign language. To someone who is unfamiliar with that language, the words seem to speed by in an unbroken string. However, to a speaker of that language, the words seem separated, just as the words of your native language seem separated to you. To solve the segmentation problem, we must determine how we divide the continuous stream of the acoustic signal into a series of individual words.

The Variability Problem

Another problem posed by the speech stimulus is that the acoustic signal is so variable that there is no simple correspondence between the acoustic signal and individual phonemes. This variability comes from the following sources.

Variability from a Phoneme's Context The acoustic signal associated with a phoneme changes depending

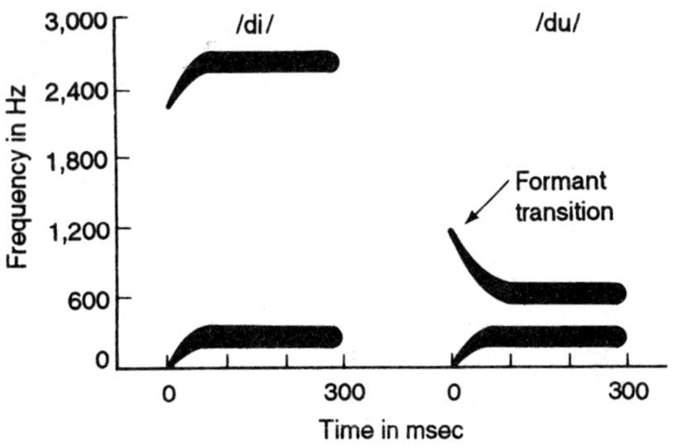

Figure 13.6
Hand-drawn spectrograms for /di/ and /du/. (From Liberman et al., 1967.)

on its context. For example, look at Figure 13.6, which shows spectrograms for the sounds /di/ and /du/. These are smoothed hand-drawn spectrograms that show the two most important characteristics of the sounds: the formants and the **formant transitions.** The formants for /di/ are the horizontal bands of energy at about 200 and 2,600 Hz and the formants for /du/ are at 200 and 600 Hz. Since formants are associated with vowels, we know that the formants at 200 and 2,600 Hz are the acoustic signal for the vowel /i/ in /di/, and that the formants at 200 and 600 Hz are the acoustic signal for the vowel /u/ in /du/.

Having identified the formants as the acoustic signals for the vowels, we know that the signals for the consonant /d/ must be the formant transitions that precede the formants. But notice that the formant transitions for the second (higher frequency) formants of /di/ and /du/ are different. For /di/, the formant transition starts at about 2,200 Hz and rises to meet the second formant. For /du/, the first transition starts at about 1,100 Hz and falls to meet the second formant. Thus, even though we *perceive* the same /d/ sound in /di/ and /du/, the acoustic signals associated with these sounds are different.

This effect of context occurs because of the way speech is produced. The articulators are constantly moving as we talk, so the shape of the vocal tract for a particular phoneme is influenced by the shapes for the phonemes that precede and follow it. This overlap between the articulation of neighboring phonemes is called **coarticulation.** Notice how you produce phonemes in different contexts. For example, say *bat* and *boot.* When you say *bat,* your lips are unrounded, but when you say *boot,* your lips are rounded, even during the initial /b/ sound. Thus, even though the /b/ is the same in both words, you articulate them differently. In this example, the articulation of /oo/ in *boot* overlaps the articulation of /b/, causing the lips to be rounded even before the /oo/ sound is actually produced.

The fact that we perceive the sound of a phoneme as the same, even though the acoustic signal is changed by coarticulation, is an example of perceptual constancy. This term may be familiar to you from our observations of constancy phenomena in the sense of vision, such as color constancy (we perceive an object's chromatic color as constant even when the wavelength distribution of the illumination changes) and size constancy (we perceive an object's size as constant even when the size of its image changes on our retina). Perceptual constancy in speech perception is similar. We perceive the sound of a particular phoneme as constant even when the phoneme appears in different contexts that change its acoustic signal.

Variability from Different Speakers People say the same words in a variety of different ways. Some people's voices are high pitched, and some are low pitched; people speak with accents; some talk extremely rapidly and others speak extremely slowly. These wide variations in speech in different speakers means that for different speakers a particular phoneme or word can have very different acoustic signals.

Speakers also introduce variability by their sloppy pronunciation. For example, say the following sentence at the speed you would use in talking to a friend: "This was a best buy." How did you say "best buy"? Did you pronounce the /t/ of *best,* or did you say "bes buy"? What about "She is a bad girl"? While saying this rapidly, notice whether your tongue hits the top of your mouth as you say the /d/ in *bad.* Many people omit the /d/ and say "ba girl." Finally, what about "Did you go to the store?" Did you say "did you" or "dijoo"? You have your own ways of producing various words and phonemes and other people have theirs. Analysis of how people actually speak, has determined that there are 50 different ways to produce the word "the" (Waldrop, 1988).

That people do not usually articulate each word individually in conversational speech is reflected in the spectrograms in Figure 13.7. The spectrogram in Figure 13.7a is for the question "What are you doing?" spoken slowly and distinctly, whereas the spectrogram in Figure 13.7b is for the same question taken from conversational speech, in which "What are you doing?" becomes "Whad'aya doin?" This difference shows up clearly in the spectrogram, which indicates that, although the first and last words *(what*

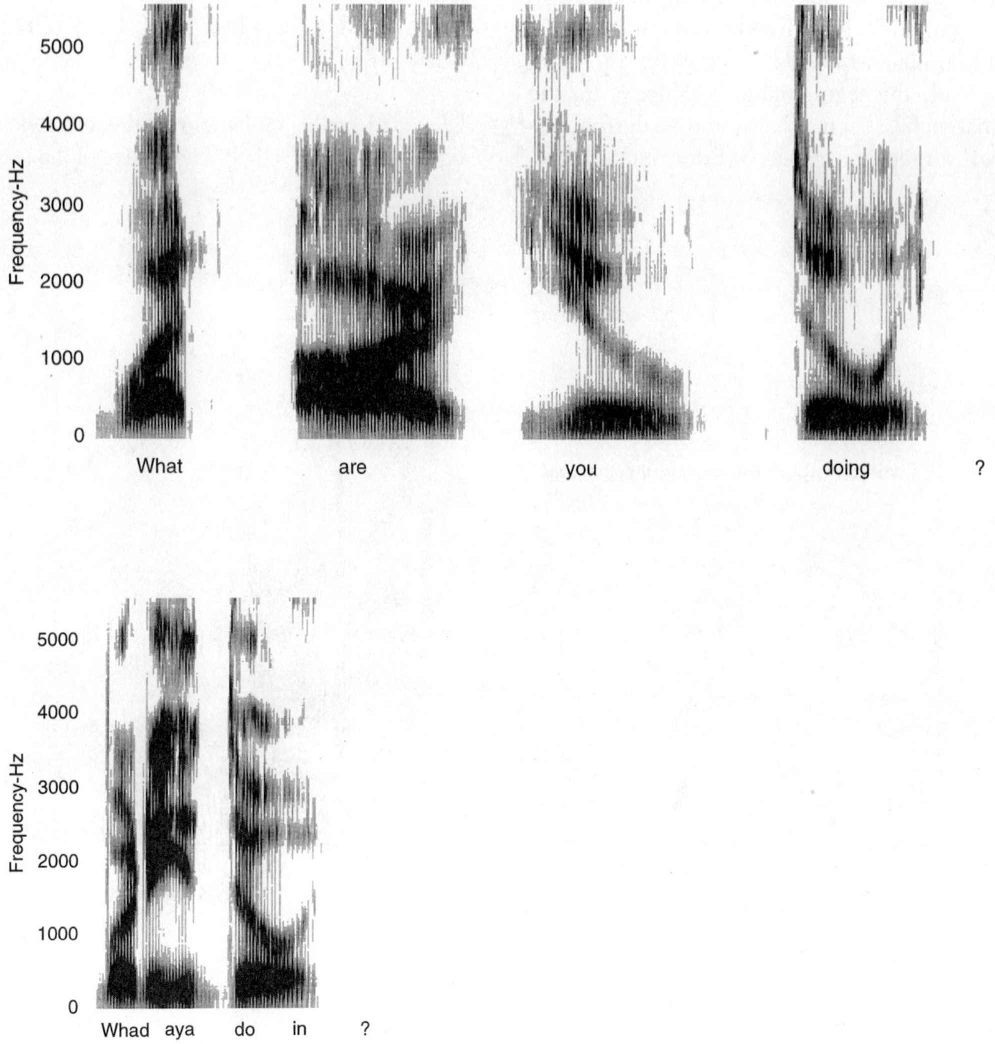

Figure 13.7
(top) Spectrogram of "What are you doing?" pronounced slowly and distinctly. (bottom) Spectrogram of "What are you doing?" as pronounced in conversational speech. (Spectrograms courtesy of David Pisoni.)

and *doing)* create similar patterns in the two spectrograms, the pauses between words are absent or are much less obvious in the spectrogram of Figure 13.7b, and the middle of this spectrogram is completely changed, with a number of speech sounds missing.

The variability in the acoustic signal that is caused by coarticulation, by different speakers, and by sloppy pronunciation creates a problem for the listener: He or she must somehow transform the information contained in this highly variable acoustic signal into familiar words. This variability problem, combined with the segmentation problem, are the reasons that it has been so difficult to design machines that can recognize speech. But humans somehow recognize speech even in the face of what might seem to be extreme difficulties. Although we don't yet know exactly how they do it, research conducted over the past 50 years has begun to unravel the mystery of how humans perceive speech.

Stimulus Dimensions of Speech Perception

Our goal in the remainder of this chapter is to highlight our current state of knowledge of the mechanisms

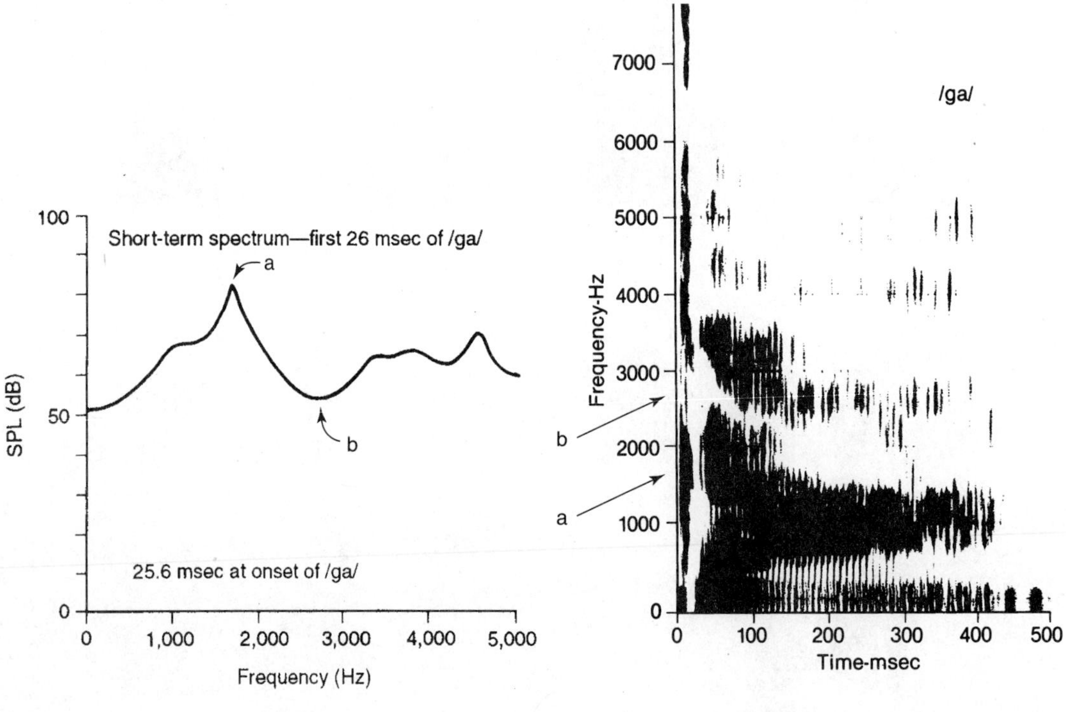

Figure 13.8
Left: A short-term spectrum of the acoustic energy in the first 26 msec of the phoneme /ga/. Right: Sound spectrogram of the same phoneme. The peak in the short-term spectrum marked a corresponds to the dark band of energy marked a in the spectrogram. The minimum in the short-term spectrum marked b corresponds to the light area marked b in the spectrogram. Note that the spectrogram on the right shows the energy for the entire 500 msec duration of the sound, whereas the short-term spectrum only shows the first 26 msec at the beginning of this signal. (Courtesy of James Sawusch.)

involved in speech perception. First, we focus on how speech perception researchers have studied relationships between the acoustic stimulus and the perception of speech.

The Search for Invariant Acoustic Cues: Matching Physical Energy and Phonemes

One of the ongoing projects of speech perception research has been to identify invariant **acoustic cues** in the acoustic signal. An **invariant acoustic cue** is a feature of the acoustic signal that is associated with a particular phoneme and that remains constant even when phonemes appear in different contexts or are spoken by different speakers. Since invariant acoustic cues are not that obvious from the normal speech spectrogram, researchers searching for these invariant cues have devised new ways of displaying and analyzing the acoustic signal.

One way of displaying the acoustic signal is called the **short-term spectrum.** A short-term spectrum creates a detailed picture of the frequencies that occur within a short segment of time. For example, the short-term spectrum on the left of Figure 13.8 shows the frequencies that occur during the first 26 msec of the sound /ga/ along with the regular spectrogram for /ga/, on the right. The peak in the short-term spectrum labeled *a*, and the minimum, labeled *b*, correspond to the dark and light energy bands *a* and *b* at the very beginning of the spectrogram. The advantage of the short-term spectrum is that it provides a precise and detailed picture of the acoustic signal. A sequence of short-term spectra can be combined to create a **running spectral display** that shows how the frequencies in the auditory signal change over time (Figure 13.9).

Researchers have identified some invariant acoustic cues in these running spectral displays. The invariance of these cues has been demonstrated by showing that people can identify characteristics of phonemes based on these cues, even in different contexts (Blumstein & Stevens, 1979; Kewley-Port, 1983; Kewley-Port & Luce, 1984; Searle, Jacobson, & Rayment, 1979; Stevens & Blumstein, 1978, 1981). For example, a low-frequency peak that continues in succeeding frames (marked with V in Figure 13.9) indicates that the vocal cords are vibrating. Notice that it occurs for /da/ but not for /pi/. The listener can, therefore, use this information to help differentiate between these two sounds.

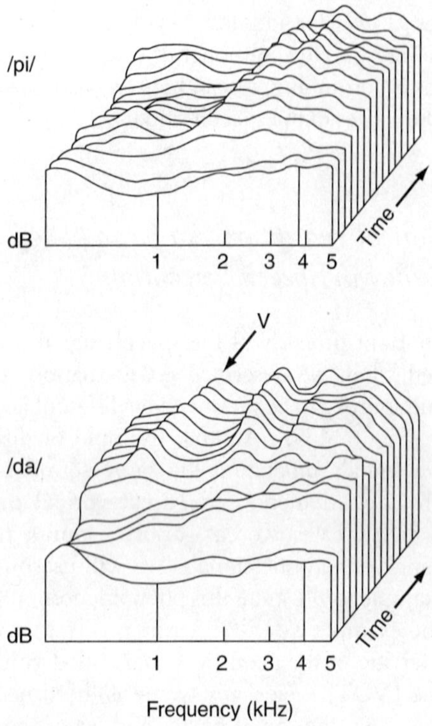

Figure 13.9
Running spectral displays for /pi/ and /da/. These displays are made up of a sequence of short-term spectra like the one in Figure 13.8. Each of these spectra is displaced 5 msec on the time axis, so that each step we move along this axis indicates the frequencies present in the next 5 msec. The low-frequency peak (V) in the /da/ display is a cue for vibration of the vocal cords. (From Kewley-Port & Luce, 1984.)

Although the search for invariant acoustic cues has yielded some encouraging results, it hasn't been possible to identify invariant cues for all of the speech sounds (Nygaard & Pisoni, 1995). (Also see Sussman, Hoemeke & Ahmed, 1993; Sussman, McCaffrey, &

Matthews, 1991 for additional evidence for invariant acoustic cues.) Thus, although the search for invariant cues is continuing, researchers are also looking at other properties of the speech signal.

Categorical Perception: An Example of Constancy in Speech Perception

An important property of the speech signal, that we observed when we described coarticulation, is that the same sound can be produced by different acoustic signals (Figure 13.6). Another example of different acoustic signals producing the same sound is provided by a phenomenon called **categorical perception,** which creates two categories of sounds from a wide range of acoustic signals. We will use one specific example to illustrate this phenomenon.

The example we will describe involves varying a characteristic of the acoustic signal called **voice onset time (VOT).** Voice onset time is the time delay between when the sound begins and when the vocal cords begin vibrating. We can illustrate this delay by comparing the spectrograms for the sounds /da/ and /ta/ in Figure 13.10. We can see from these spectrograms that the time between the beginning of the sound /da/ and the beginning of the vocal cord vibrations (indicated by the presence of vertical striations in the spectrogram) is 17 msec for /da/ and 91 msec for /ta/. Thus, /da/ has a short VOT and /ta/ has a long VOT.

We will describe a categorical perception experiment that uses these two sounds, /da/ and /ta/. We begin the experiment by presenting a computer-generated sound with VOT = 0 msec that is perceived as /da/. We then increase the VOT in small steps and ask listeners to indicate whether they hear a /da/ or a /ta/ at each step. The results of such an experiment are shown in Figure 13.11 (Eimas & Corbit, 1973). All of the stimuli with VOT = 0 are heard as /da/, and listeners continue to hear /da/ until the VOT reaches about 35 msec. At that point, listeners suddenly begin hearing /ta/, and when the VOT is increased to 40 msec or above, most of the stimuli are identified as /ta/. The VOT when the perception changes from

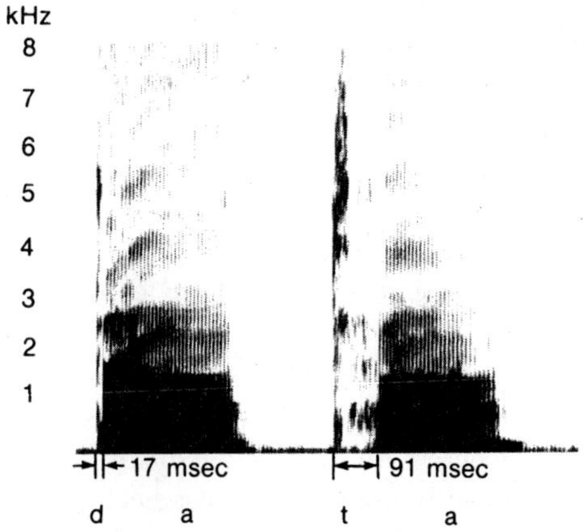

Figure 13.10
Spectrograms for /da/ and /ta/. The voice onset time—the time between the beginning of the sound and the onset of voicing—is indicated at the beginning of the spectrogram for each sound. (Spectrogram courtesy of Ron Cole.)

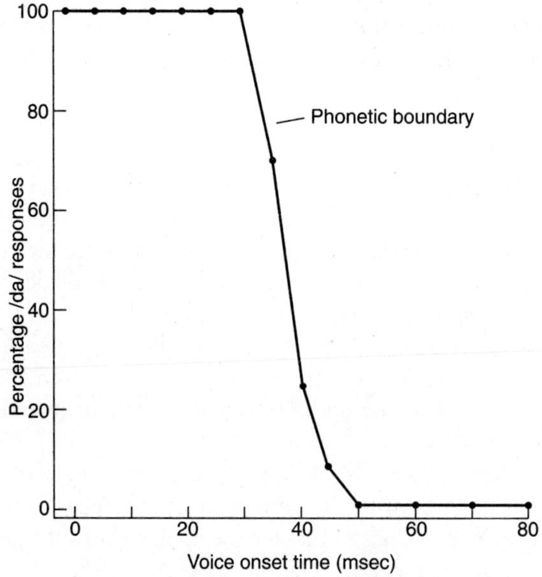

Figure 13.11
The results of a categorical perception experiment indicate that /da/ is perceived for VOTs to the left of the phonetic boundary, and that /ta/ is perceived at VOTs to the right of the phonetic boundary. (From Eimas & Corbit, 1973.)

/da/ to /ta/ is called the **phonetic boundary.** The key result of the categorical perception experiment is that, even though the VOT is changed across a wide range, the listener perceives only two categories: /da/ on one side of the phonetic boundary and /ta/ on the other side.

Once we have demonstrated categorical perception using the procedure above, we can further confirm the existence of just two categories across the range of VOTs, by running a discrimination test, in which we present two stimuli with different VOTs and ask the subject whether they sound the same or different. When we present two stimuli that are on the same side of the phonetic boundary, such as 10 and 30 msec VOTs, the listener says they sound the same (Figure 13.12). However, when we present two stimuli that are on opposite sides of the phonetic boundary, such as 30 and 50 msec VOTs, the listener says they sound different. The fact that all stimuli on the same side of the phonetic boundary are perceived as identical is an example of perceptual constancy (Figure 13.13). If this constancy did not exist, we would perceive different sounds every time we changed the VOT. Instead, we experience one sound on each side of the phonetic boundary. This simplifies our perception of phonemes and helps us more easily perceive the wide variety of sounds in our environment.

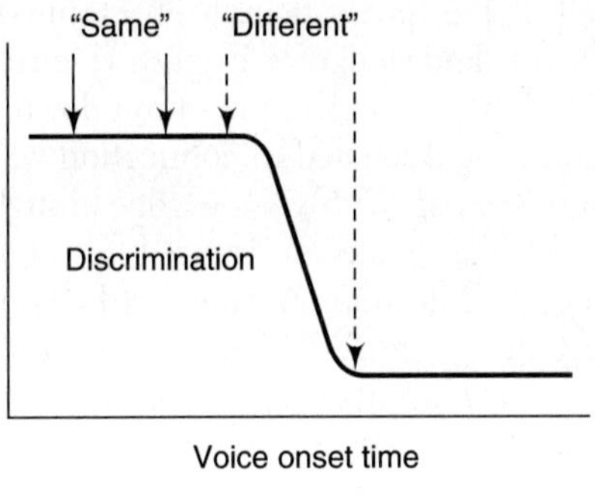

Figure 13.12
In the discrimination part of a categorical perception experiment, two stimuli are presented, and the subject is asked to indicate whether they are the same or different. The typical result is that two stimuli with VOTs on the same side of the phonetic boundary (solid arrows) are judged to be the same, and that two stimuli on different sides of the phonetic boundary (dashed arrows) are judged to be different.

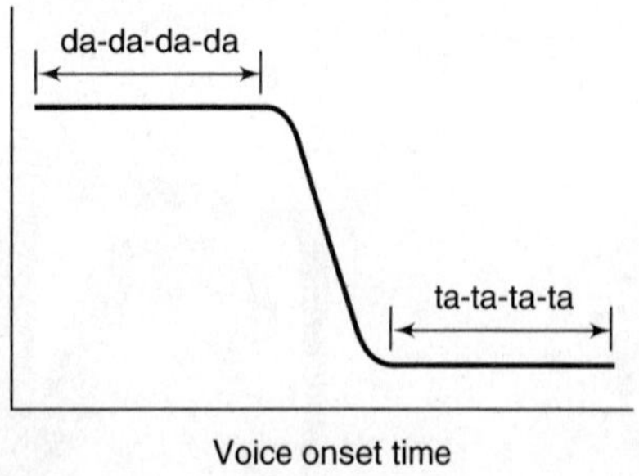

Figure 13.13
Perceptual constancy occurs when all stimuli on one side of the phonetic boundary are perceived to be in the same category even though their VOT is changed over a substantial range. This diagram symbolizes the constancy observed in the Eimas and Corbit (1973) experiment, in which /da/ was heard on one side of the boundary and /ta/ on the other side.

The Multimodal Nature of Speech Perception: Information from Hearing and Vision

Another property of speech perception is that it is **multimodal.** That is, our perception of speech can be influenced by information from a number of different senses. *Across the Senses* at the end of the chapter describes how speech can be perceived through touch using the Tadoma method. Speech perception can also be influenced by visual information, as demonstrated by an effect called **audio-visual speech perception** or the **McGurk effect,** after the man who first described it (McGurk & MacDonald, 1976).

The procedure for achieving audio-visual speech perception is illustrated in Figure 13.14. A subject observes a videotape showing a person making the lip movements for the sounds /ga-ga/. But as he receives this visual information, he simultaneously receives an auditory sound track, which is the acoustic signal that is usually heard as /ba-ba/. Despite the fact that the

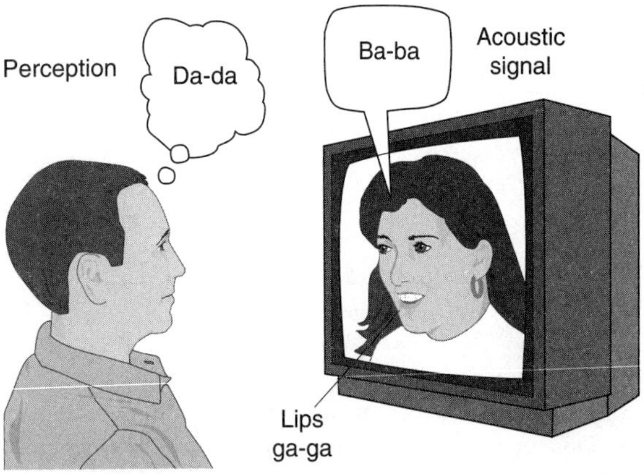

Figure 13.14
Audio-visual speech perception. The woman's lips are moving as if she is saying /ga-ga/, but the actual sound being presented is /ba-ba/. The listener, however, reports hearing the sound /da-da/. If the listener closes his eyes, so that he no longer sees the woman's lips, he hears /ba-ba/. Thus, seeing the lips moving influences what the listener hears.

subject is receiving the acoustic signal for /ba-ba/, he actually *hears* the sounds /da-da/. This misperception is a striking perceptual effect in which subjects are convinced that the woman in the videotape is saying /da-da/ even though that stimulus is never actually present. If they close their eyes, they hear /ba-ba/. If they open them, they hear /da-da/. Thus, although auditory energy is the major source of information for speech perception, visual information can also exert a strong influence on what we hear.

Cognitive Dimensions of Speech Perception

Our discussion so far in this chapter has emphasized the relationship between speech perception and the stimuli we receive. But our perception of speech depends on more than just the energy that reaches our receptors. There is a cognitive dimension to speech perception as well, that depends on information stored in the listener's memory about the nature of language and the voice characteristics of specific speakers. The following demonstration illustrates how our knowledge of the meanings of words enables us to perceive these words even when the stimulus is incomplete.

D E M O N S T R A T I O N

Perceiving Degraded Sentences

Read the following sentences:

(1) M*R* H*D * L*TTL* L*MB H*R FLC* W*S WH*T* *S SN*W**

(2) TH* S*N *S N*T SH*N*NG T*D**

(3) S*M* WDS *R* EA*I*R T* U*D*R*T*N* T*A* *T*E*S** ●

Your ability to read the sentences, even though up to half of the letters have been eliminated, was aided by your knowledge of English (Denes & Pinson, 1993). This is an example of top-down processing that we have discussed in connection with visual perception (see page 206): Knowledge brought to the situation by the perceiver is used to supplement the bottom-up information provided by stimulation of the receptors (Figure 13.15). One example of the effect of top-down processing in speech perception is provided by the process of segmentation, in which the speaker breaks the continuous acoustic signal into individual words.

Meaning and Segmentation

To help you appreciate the role of meaning in achieving segmentation, do the following demonstration.

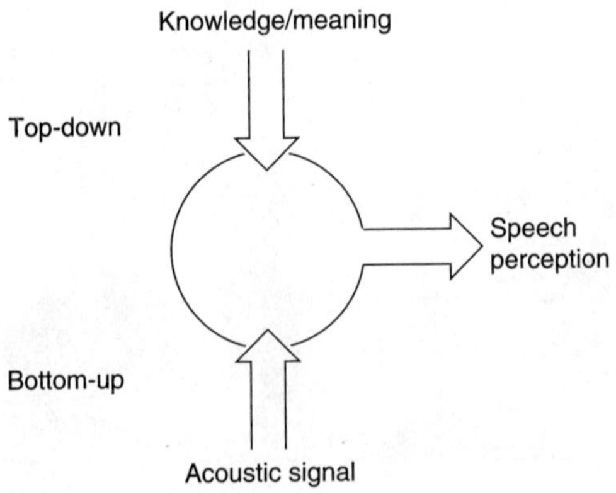

Figure 13.15
Speech perception is the result of top-down processing (based on knowledge and meaning) and bottom-up processing (based on the acoustic signal) working together.

DEMONSTRATION

Segmenting Strings of Sounds

1. **Read the following words: *Anna Mary Candy Lights Since Imp Pulp Lay Things.* Now that you've read the words, what do they mean? If you think that this is a list of unconnected words beginning with the names of two women, Anna and Mary, you're right; but if you read this series of words a little faster, ignoring the spaces between the words on the page, you may hear a connected sentence that does not begin with the names Anna and Mary. (For the answer see the bottom of page 404—but don't peek until you've tried reading the words rapidly.)**
2. **Read the following phrase fairly rapidly to a few people: "In mud eels are, in clay none are," and ask them to write the phrase.** ●

If you succeeded in creating a new sentence from the series of words in the first demonstration, you did so by changing the segmentation, and this change was achieved by your knowledge of the meaning of the sounds. When Raj Reddy (1976) asked subjects to write their perception of "In mud eels are, in clay none are," he obtained responses like "In muddies, sar, in clay nanar"; "In may deals are, en clainanar"; and "In madel sar, in claynanar." In the absence of any context, Reddy's listeners clearly had difficulty figuring out what the phrase meant and therefore forced their own interpretation on the sounds they heard. Had the listeners known that the passage was taken from a book about where amphibians live, their knowledge about possible meanings of the words would have facilitated segmentation and increased probability of their decoding the sentence correctly.

Pairs of words that flow together in speech also exemplify how segmentation results from meaning: "Big girl" can be interpreted as "big Earl," and the interpretation you pick will probably depend on the overall meaning of the sentence in which these words appear. This example is similar to the familiar "I scream, you scream, we all scream for ice cream" that many people learn as children. The acoustic stimuli for "I scream" and "ice cream" are identical, so the different segmentations must be achieved by the meaning of the sentence in which these words appear (Figure 13.16).

Top-down processing not only helps us to segment the acoustic signal, but also helps us to recognize phonemes and words. We will now describe some experiments that show how meaningful contexts can enhance a listener's ability to recognize phonemes and words.

Meaning and Phoneme Perception

A large amount of research has shown that it is easier to perceive phonemes if they are part of a meaningful context. Philip Rubin, M. T. Turvey, and Peter Van Gelder (1976) showed that meaning enhances a listener's ability to recognize phonemes by presenting a series of short words like SIN, BAT, and LEG, or non-words like JUM, BAF, and TEG, and asking subjects to respond by pressing a key as rapidly as possible whenever they heard a sound that began

Figure 13.16
Archie is experiencing a problem in speech segmentation. (TM © ACP 1988 Archie Comic Publications, Inc.)

with /b/. On the average, subjects took 631 milliseconds to respond to the nonwords and 580 msecs to respond to the real words. Thus, when a phoneme is at the beginning of a real word it is identified about 8 percent faster than if it is at the beginning of a meaningless syllable.

The effect of meaning on the perception of phonemes was demonstrated in another way by Richard Warren (1970), who had subjects listen to a recording of the sentence: "The state governors met with their respective legislatures convening in the capital city." Warren replaced the first /s/ in "legislatures" with the sound of a cough and told his subjects that they should indicate where in the sentence the cough occurred. No subject identified the correct position of the cough, and even more significantly, none of the subjects noticed that the /s/ in "legislatures" was missing. This effect, which Warren called the **phonemic restoration effect,** was experienced even by students and staff in the psychology department who knew that the /s/ was missing.

Warren not only demonstrated the phonemic restoration effect but also showed that it can be influenced by the meaning of words *following* the missing phoneme. For example, the last word of the phrase "There was time to *ave . . ." (where the * indicates the presence of a cough or some other sound) could be *shave, save, wave,* or *rave,* but subjects heard the word *wave* if the remainder of the sentence had to do with saying goodbye to a departing friend.

The phonemic restoration effect was used by Arthur Samuel (1981) to show that speech perception is determined both by a context that produces expectations in the listener (top-down processing) and also by the nature of the acoustic signal (bottom-up processing). To demonstrate the role of top-down processing, Samuel masked various phonemes in sentences with a "white-noise" masker like the sound produced by a television set tuned to a nonbroadcasting channel, and found that the phonemic restoration effect is more likely to occur when the phoneme appears in a long word. Apparently, subjects are able to use the additional context provided by the long word to help identify the masked phoneme. Further evidence for the importance of context is Samuel's finding that more restoration occurs for a real word like *prOgress* (where the capital letter indicates the masked phoneme) than for a similar "pseudoword" like *crOgress* (Samuel, 1990).

To demonstrate the role of bottom-up processing, Samuel found that restoration is better if the masking sound and the masked phoneme sound similar. Thus, phonemic restoration is more likely to occur for a phoneme such as /s/, which is rich in high-frequency acoustic energy, if the mask also contains a large proportion of high-frequency energy.

What's happening in phonemic restoration, according to Samuel, is that we use the context to develop some expectation of what a sound will be. But before we actually perceive the sound, its presence must be *confirmed* by the presence of a sound that is similar to it. If the white noise mask contains frequencies that make it sound similar to the phoneme we are expecting, phonemic restoration occurs, and we are likely to hear the phoneme. If the mask does not sound similar, phonemic restoration is less likely to occur (Samuel, 1990).

Meaning and Word Perception

Meaningfulness also makes it easier to perceive whole words. An early demonstration of this effect by George Miller and Steven Isard (1963) showed that words are more intelligible when heard in the context of a grammatical sentence than when presented as items in a list of unconnected words. They demonstrated this by creating three kinds of stimuli: (1) normal grammatical sentences, such as *Gadgets simplify work around the house*; (2) anomalous sentences, that follow the rules of grammar but make no sense, such as *Gadgets kill passengers from the eyes*; and (3) ungrammatical strings of words, such as *Between gadgets highways passengers the steal.*

Miller and Isard used a technique called **shadowing,** in which they presented these sentences to subjects through earphones and asked them to repeat aloud what they were hearing. The subjects reported normal sentences with an accuracy of 89 percent, but their accuracy fell to 79 percent for the anomalous sentences, and 56 percent for the ungrammatical strings.

The differences among the three types of stimuli became even greater when the subjects heard the stimuli in the presence of a background noise. For example, at a moderately high level of background noise, accuracy was 63 percent for the normal sentences, 22 percent for the anomalous sentences, and only 3 percent for the ungrammatical strings of words.

This result is telling us that when words are arranged in a meaningful pattern, we can perceive them more easily. But most people don't realize that it is their knowledge of the nature of their language that helps them fill in sounds and words that might be difficult to hear. For example, our knowledge of permissible word structures tells us that ANT, TAN, and NAT are all permissible sequences of letters in English, but that TQN or NQT cannot be English words.

At the level of the sentence, our knowledge of the rules of grammar tells us that *the cat is weird* is a permissible sentence, but *is weird cat the* is not a permissible sentence. Since most of our everyday experience is with meaningful words and grammatically correct sentences, we are continually using our knowledge of what is permissible in our language to help us understand what is being said. This becomes particularly important when listening under less than ideal conditions such as in noisy environments or if the speaker's voice quality or accent is difficult to understand.

The way meaningfulness enhances our perception of words that are difficult to understand because of noise has also been demonstrated by Aita Salasoo and David Pisoni (1985). They asked subjects to write down what they heard after hearing meaningful sentences, anomalous sentences, and words presented alone. They were primarily interested in how well the subjects could identify target words in which part of the word was replaced by electronic noise.

Salasoo and Pisoni varied the percentage of the word that was obscured by noise and whether the beginning of the word or the end of the word was obscured. When they determined the percentage of the word that had to be present before it could be identified, they found that (1) Less of a word needs to be present if it is in a meaningful sentence. Most of an isolated word needs to be present for correct identification, but only about half of the word needs to be present if it is heard within a meaningful sentence (Figure 13.17); (2) Less of a word needs to be present if just the beginning of the word is heard, than if just the end of the word is heard. The information at the beginning of the word is apparently more important for word identification than the information at the end of the word.

All of these results support the idea that the knowledge a listener brings to a situation helps the listener decode the acoustic signal into phonemes and meaningful words and sentences. In addition, there is also evidence that a listener's experience in listening to specific speakers can enhance their ability to perceive what is being said.

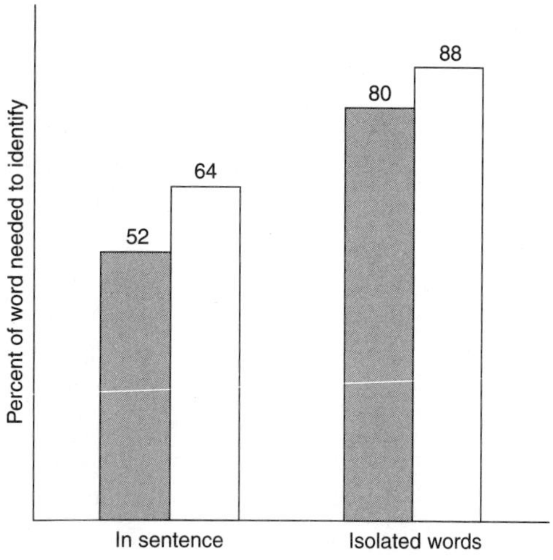

Figure 13.17
The results of Salasoo and Pisoni's (1985) experiment. The height of the bars represents the percentage of a word that had to be present in order for it to be accurately identified. Shaded bars: only the beginning of the word is present; Open bars: only the end of the word is present. The bars on the left are for when a word appears within the context of a sentence. The bars on the right are for when a word appears in isolation. Words are perceived more easily if the word appears in a sentence, and if the beginning of the word is present.

Speaker Characteristics

When you're having a conversation, or hearing a lecture, or listening to dialogue in a movie, you usually focus on determining the meaning of what is being said. But as you are taking in these messages, you are also, perhaps without realizing it, taking in characteristics of the speaker's voice. These characteristics, which are called **indexical characteristics,** carry information about speakers such as their age, gender, where they are from, their emotional state, and whether they are being sarcastic or serious. Consider, for example, the following joke:

> A linguistics professor was lecturing to his class one day. "In English," he said, "A double negative forms a positive. In some languages, though, such as Russian, a double negative is still a negative. However, there is no language wherein a double positive can form a negative."
>
> A voice from the back of the room piped up, "Yeah, right."

This joke is humorous because "Yeah, right" contains two positive words which, despite the linguistic professor's statement, produce a negative statement that most people who are aware of contemporary English usage would interpret as "I disagree." (or "No way," to use a more colloquial expression.) The point of this example is not just that "Yeah, right" can mean "I disagree," but that the meaning of this phrase is determined by our knowledge of current English usage and also (if we were actually listening to the student's remark) by the speaker's tone of voice, which in this case would be highly sarcastic.

Indexical characteristics of a person's speech are important not only because they help convey meaning, as in the example above, but because they are used by the perceptual system as an aid to recognition. This was demonstrated by Thomas Palmeri, Stephen Goldinger, and David Pisoni (1993) who had subjects listen to a sequence of words. After each word, the subject indicated whether the word was a new word (this was the first time it appeared) or an old word (it had appeared previously in the sequence). They found that subjects reacted more rapidly and judged whether the word was new or old more accurately when the same speaker said all of the words, than if different speakers said the words. What this means, according to Palmeri and his coworkers, is that the listeners are taking in two levels of information about the word: (1) its meaning, and (2) characteristics of the speaker's voice.

In another experiment that demonstrates the importance of the speaker's voice for speech perception, subjects listened to the voices of 10 different speakers. Following this training, the listeners were given a word intelligibility test to determine how well they could identify words spoken by the speakers. When the results of this test were compared to the performance of a control group who were also trained to recognize the same 10 speakers but who heard unfamiliar speakers for the intelligibility test, it was found that those hearing the familiar speakers performed better on the test (Nygaard, Sommers, & Pisoni, 1994).

In order for performance to be better with the familiar speakers, the voice characteristics of these speakers would have to be stored in the listener's long-term memory. When presented with the word intelligibility test, listeners retrieve this information about the familiar speakers from their memory and use it to help them identify the words.

From the results of this experiment and the others we have discussed, we can conclude that speech perception depends both on the bottom-up information provided by the acoustic signal and on the top-down information provided by the meanings of words and sentences, the listener's knowledge of the rules of grammar, and information that the listener has about characteristics of the speaker's voice.

We can appreciate the interdependence of the acoustical and meaningful units of speech when we realize that, although we use the meaning to help us to understand the acoustic signal, the acoustic signal is the starting point for determining the meaning. Look at it this way: There may be enough information in my sloppy handwriting so that a person using bottom-up processing can decipher it solely on the basis of the squiggles on the page, but my handwriting is much easier to decipher if, by using top-down processing, the person takes the meanings of the words into account. Speech perception apparently works in a similar way. Although most of the information is contained in the acoustic signal, taking meaning into account makes understanding speech much easier.

The Physiology of Speech Perception

Researchers have investigated the physiology of speech perception in a number of different ways: (1) By recording neural responses to both natural speech stimuli and stimuli resembling parts of the speech signal; (2) by studying patients who, because of brain damage, have difficulty understanding or producing speech; and (3) by recording the change in blood flow in different parts of the brain during speech perception.

Neural Responses to Speech and Complex Sounds

Most of the research explaining the neural response to speech stimuli has focused on how neurons in the auditory nerve respond to speech sounds. For example, Figure 13.18 shows the short-term spectrum for the sound /da/ and the firing pattern for a representative population of cat auditory nerve fibers with low, medium, and high characteristic frequencies. (Remember from

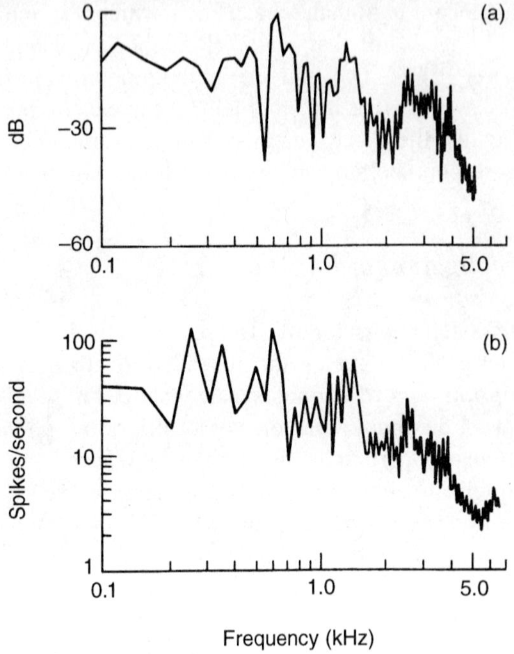

Figure 13.18
(a) Short-term spectrum for /da/. This curve indicates the energy distribution in /da/ between 20 and 40 msec after the beginning of the signal. (b) Nerve firing of a population of cat auditory nerve fibers to the same stimulus. (From Sachs, Young, & Miller, 1981.)

Chapter 11 that the neuron's characteristic frequency is the frequency to which this neuron responds best.) The match between the speech stimulus and the firing of a number of neurons in the auditory nerve indicates that information in the speech stimulus is represented by the pattern of firing of auditory nerve fibers (also see Delgutte & Kiang, 1984a, 1984b).

Another approach to studying the relation between neural responding and speech perception is to look for neurons that respond to parts of the speech stimulus, such as the formant transitions and formants shown in Figure 13.4. Neurons have been found in a number of animals, including bats, birds, frogs, and cats, that respond best to combinations of tones that, like speech stimuli, have specific timing and frequencies (Fuzessery & Feng, 1983; Margoliash, 1983; Nelson, Erulkar, & Bryan, 1966; Olsen & Suga, 1991a, 1991b). Most significantly, neurons have been found in an area of the monkey cortex that is analogous to human speech areas, which respond to recordings of monkey "calls" (Rauschecker, Tian, & Hauser, 1995). The existence of these neurons in the monkey as well as the other animals, opens the possibility that there may be neurons in the human cortex that respond best to complex, speechlike stimuli.

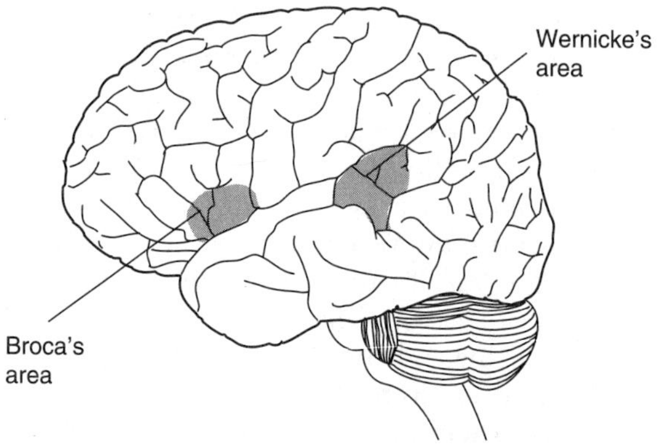

Figure 13.19
Broca's and Wernicke's areas, which are specialized for language production and comprehension, are located in the left hemisphere of the brain in most people.

Localization of Function

It has been known for over 150 years that the brain operates according to a principle called **localization of function**—specific functions are localized in specific areas of the brain. One form of localization is *lateralization*—a particular function is processed more strongly in either the left hemisphere or the right hemisphere. For most people, speech is processed in specific areas in the left hemisphere of the brain (Figure 13.19). Damage to Broca's area, in the frontal lobe, causes difficulty in speaking, and damage to Wernicke's area, in the temporal lobe, causes difficulty in understanding speech (Geschwind, 1979). These difficulties in speaking and understanding are forms of **aphasia** (Kolb & Whishaw, 1985).

There are numerous forms of aphasia, with the specific symptoms depending on the area and extent of the damage. The form that involves speech perception is called **Wernicke's aphasia**—an inability to comprehend words or arrange sounds into coherent speech. Wernicke's aphasia is a form of *fluent aphasia*, so called because people with this disorder can produce fluent speech, although their production often consists of meaningless strings of words and words in which phonemes are confused, that has been described as "word salad."

We can understand the basis of the problem in Wernicke's aphasia by considering the problem native Japanese speakers have in discriminating between /l/ and /r/. Native Japanese speakers are not able to distinguish /l/ from /r/ when they hear English, because the Japanese they heard spoken when they were infants, did not distinguish between the sounds /l/ and /r/. Thus, the necessary templates for these two sounds did not develop in their brains, and as adults they lack the physiological mechanisms to distinguish between these two sounds. It has been suggested that people with Wernicke's aphasia have a similar problem—because of their brain damage, they cannot isolate phonemes or classify them into known phonemic systems (Kolb & Whishaw, 1985).

Research using the PET (positron emission tomography) scan on humans, which measures changes in blood flow in the brain during the perception of pitches and the perception of speech stimuli, shows that pitch stimuli activate areas in the right hemisphere, but that speech stimuli activate areas in the left hemisphere (Zatorre et al., 1992). In addition to physiological evidence of the lateralization of speech perception, psychophysical experiments indicate that speech stimuli are more easily processed when presented through earphones to the right ear than when they are presented through earphones to the left ear. Since signals from the right ear are sent preferentially to the left hemisphere, this right-ear preference indicates that speech stimuli are processed in the left hemisphere (Kimura, 1961).

Something to Consider: Is Speech "Special"?

Some researchers working in the field of speech perception think that there is something special about speech perception that sets it apart from the perception of other auditory stimuli. The idea of a mechanism that is specialized for the perception of speech has its appeal, especially when we remember how the visual system operates. We know that there are nuclei in the visual system that are specialized to process information about different qualities, such as color, depth, and movement (Casagrande, 1994). In addition, there are neurons that are specialized to respond to complex visual stimuli such as faces (Perrett, Hietanen, Oram, & Benson, 1992). This evidence from vision, along with the fact that language is processed in specific areas of the cortex, makes it seem reasonable that there could be a specialized mechanism that exists especially to process speech stimuli.

The idea that there is a specialized mechanism for speech is, however, not universally accepted by all speech perception researchers. Some researchers feel that while the speech signal may be extremely complex, the perception of this signal can be explained by regular auditory mechanisms.

The question of whether speech is "special" or if it is served by the same auditory mechanism that serves other auditory stimuli, has generated a voluminous amount of research over the more than 30-years since the idea of a special speech mechanism was proposed (Liberman et al., 1967). To illustrate the kinds of evidence that have been presented on both sides of this question, we will consider a phenomenon called **duplex perception** that was originally introduced to support the idea that speech is special.

Duplex perception is created by splitting the acoustic signal for a sound into two parts and presenting one part to each ear. For example, Figure 13.20a shows the speech spectrogram for the sound /da/, which consists of three formant transitions and their formants. Alvin Liberman and Ignatius Mattingly (1989) created duplex perception by presenting just the transition for the third formant to the left ear (Figure 13.20b), and the rest of the signal, which is called the

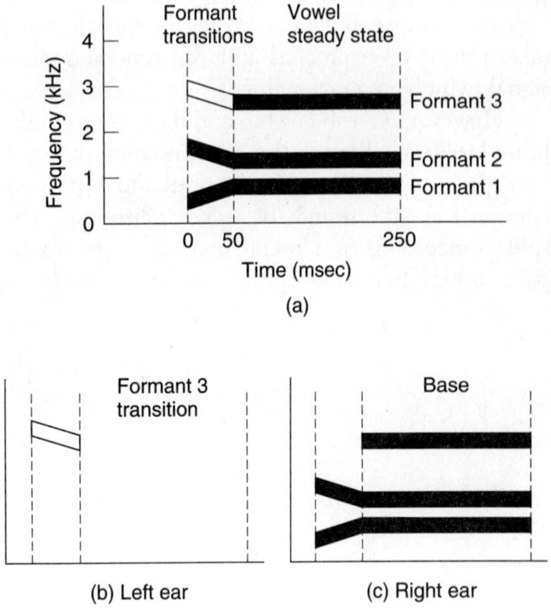

Figure 13.20
(a) The spectrogram for the sound /da/. Duplex perception occurs when the transition for the third formant (b) is presented to the left ear and the rest of the signal, called the base (c), is presented to the right ear. The listener perceives the sound /da/ in the right ear and a "chirp" in the left ear. See text for further details.

base, to the right ear (Figure 13.20c). What the listener hears is the speech sound /da/, from the combined acoustic signal from the left and right ears, and a nonspeech "chirp," from the third formant transition from the left ear.

According to proponents of the special speech mechanism, this experiment illustrates two kinds of perception: (1) a special speech mode, which combines the formant transition presented to the left ear and the base presented to the right ear to create the speech sound /da/, and (2) the auditory mode, which creates the nonspeech "chirp" sound from the high-frequency formant transition presented to the left ear.

Whalen and Liberman (1987) point out that when the left ear formant transition has a low intensity, the listener hears only the speech sound. The intensity of the left ear signal must be increased to a higher level, before the listener hears the nonspeech chirp sound, as well. They concluded that this result confirms the special nature of speech, since processing the formant transition as speech (which creates the speech sound) takes priority over processing it as a general auditory signal (which creates the chirp).

However, Carol Fowler and Lawrence Rosenblum (1990) challenged this interpretation of duplex perception by creating an effect similar to duplex perception from the sounds of a door slamming. They split a recording of a metal door closing into two parts, a high-frequency component at the beginning of the sound and a lower frequency component at the end of the sound. These two components are similar to the formant transition and the base of the speech sound used by Liberman and Mattingly. When Fowler and Rosenblum presented the high-frequency component to the left ear and the low-frequency component to the right ear, subjects heard the sound of a metal door slamming (the combination of the left- and right-ear stimuli) plus a "shaking" sound like the sound made by sand or small pellets being shaken in a cup (the high-frequency left-ear stimulus). According to Fowler and Rosenblum this demonstration of duplex perception with nonspeech stimuli means that duplex perception can occur for environmental stimuli in general, which includes speech, slamming doors, and other stimuli as well (see Hall & Pastore, 1992 for a musical example).

Which interpretation of duplex perception is correct? Is speech perception served by a mechanism that is specialized for the perception of speech or by a mechanism similar to the ones that help us perceive environmental sounds in general? There are many more experiments in addition to our duplex perception example that present evidence on either side of this issue (Mattingly & Studdert-Kennedy, 1991). This debate, which is still unresolved, is a good example of how researchers can approach the same problem from different perspectives.

TADOMA: "HEARING" WITH TOUCH

How can people who are both deaf and blind know what someone is saying? One way they can accomplish this is to place their hand on the speaker's face and neck and their thumb lightly on the speakers lips. They determine what the speaker is saying by feeling the vibrations and positions of the mouth, lips, and tongue (Figure 13.21). This tactile method of speech perception was introduced in Norway in the 1890s. Later, in the United States, two children, Tad Chapman and Oma Simpson, were taught to use their tactile sense to perceive speech, and gave tactile speech perception its name—**Tadoma.**

Figure 13.21
The Tadoma method of speech perception. The thumb is placed on the lips and the fingers fan out across the left side of the face. There is also a two-handed version of the Tadoma method.

To appreciate what kind of information can be perceived using the Tadoma method, place your hand on your own face, as shown in Figure 13.21, and, while talking, notice how your fingers can sense the vibrations of the vocal cords on the neck, the shape of the lips, and the air flow through the mouth. When you try this, you will see that the information available using this method is incomplete at best, because movements such as the positioning of the tongue in the mouth can't be sensed by this method. Nonetheless, the Tadoma method has proven to be a surprisingly successful way to perceive speech, for the few people who have learned to use it.

One experienced Tadoma user was able to correctly identify 56 percent of consonant-vowel sounds such as coo, fa, and me, which is an impressive performance since many of these combinations do not form meaningful words (Reed et al., 1982). In fact, when subjects are tested using meaningful speech, their performance increases into the 80 percent range (Norton et al., 1977). Thus, just as for the normal mode of perceiving speech, meaningfulness increases comprehension.

The success of the Tadoma method adds to the evidence that speech is a multimodal sense. Speech information can be transmitted through a number of different channels, including not only auditory and visual (see page 75), but tactile as well.

Study Questions

Underlying Principles

Find examples of the following principles in this chapter:

- Cognition-perception connection (392)
- Perceptual constancy (386)
- Perceptual grouping (393)
- The effect of context on perception (394)

1. How do the speech recognition capabilities of modern computers compare to the speech recognition ability of humans? (381)

The Speech Stimulus

2. What unit of analysis is most speech perception research based on? (382)
3. What is the definition of a phoneme? (382)
4. Why are there different numbers of phonemes in different languages? (383)
5. What is the acoustic signal and how is it produced? (383)
6. How are vowels produced and what causes different vowels to have different frequencies? (383)
7. What is a formant? (383)
8. How is the acoustic stimulus displayed on the sound spectrograph? (384)
9. How are consonants produced? How does this differ from the production of vowels? (384)
10. How come the energy bands for formants aren't always horizontal during natural speech? What is a formant transition? (384)

Problems Posed by the Speech Stimulus

11. What is the segmentation problem? Why do sounds of an unfamiliar foreign language sometimes appear to be an unbroken string of sound? (384)
12. How does variability occur in the acoustic signal because of a phoneme's context? Be sure you understand how the spectrograms in Figure 13.6 show this. (385)
13. What is coarticulation? (386)
14. How does the perception of phonemes provide evidence for perceptual constancy? (386)
15. How does variability occur in the acoustic signal because of different speakers? (386)
16. How is the articulation of conversational speech different than the articulation of individual words? (387)
17. Why has it been so difficult to design machines that can recognize speech? (388)

Stimulus Dimensions of Speech Perception

18. What is an invariant acoustic cue? (389)
19. What is a short-term spectrum? A running spectral display? Why are these ways of displaying the acoustic stimulus valuable? (389)
20. Has it been possible to identify invariant acoustic cues for all speech sounds? (389)
21. What is achieved when categorical perception occurs? (390)
22. What is voice onset time? (390)
23. Describe a categorical perception experiment in which voice onset time is varied. (390)

24. What is the phonetic boundary? How do listeners discriminate between sounds that are on the same side of the phonetic boundary? On different sides? (391)

25. What is the relation between categorical perception and constancy for speech sounds? What is the advantage of the existence of constancy? (391)

26. What do we mean when we say that speech perception is multimodal? (391)

27. What is audio-visual speech perception? What does the existence of audio-visual speech perception illustrate? (391)

Cognitive Dimensions of Speech Perception

28. What do we mean when we say that there is a cognitive dimension to speech perception? (392)

29. How come you can read sentences in which half of the words are removed? (392)

30. Describe Reddy's demonstration in which subjects misperceived speech. What is the point of this demonstration? What is a major factor that helps us to achieve segmentation? (393)

31. How do the acoustic stimuli for "I scream" and "ice cream" compare? What causes us to perceive these words as different from one another? (393)

32. Describe Rubin and coworkers' phoneme-identification experiment. What do the results of this experiment demonstrate? (394)

33. What is the phonemic restoration effect? What does it demonstrate about the perception of phonemes? (394)

34. What do Samuel's experiments on the phonemic restoration effect demonstrate? (395)

35. Describe Miller and Isard's experiment on the relationship between meaningfulness and the perception of words. (395)

36. Why are words recognized more accurately when they are in a meaningful context? (395)

37. What do the results of Salasoo and Pisoni's experiment tell us about the relationship between the context in which a word appears and a person's ability to recognize the word? (395)

38. What are indexical characteristics? What is the point of the joke about the student's response to the linguistics professor? (396)

39. Why are indexical characteristics important? What did Palmeri conclude from the results of his experiment? (396)

40. What was the result of the Nygaard, Sommers, and Pisoni experiment which used familiar and unfamiliar speakers? What was the possible mechanism behind it? (396)

41. What can we conclude from the results of the above experiments with regard to the roles of bottom-up and top-down processing in speech perception? (397)

The Physiology of Speech Perception

42. What is the relationship between the firing of populations of auditory nerve fibers and the acoustic stimulus for speech? (397)

43. In addition to looking for correspondences between the speech stimulus and neural firing, what other approach has been taken to studying the relationship between neural responding and speech perception? (398)

44. Define localization of function and lateralization. Speech is lateralized on what side of the brain for most people? (390)

45. What are two areas that are specialized for producing and perceiving speech? (398)

46. What is aphasia? What form of aphasia involves problems in perceiving speech? (398)

47. Describe the basis of the problem people with Wernicke's aphasia have in understanding speech. (398)

48. What does research using PET scans tell us about the lateralization of speech perception? (398)

Something to Consider: Is Speech "Special"?

49. Why might it be reasonable to suggest that there is a specialized mechanism for speech perception? (399)
50. What is duplex perception and how has the existence of duplex perception been interpreted to support the idea that speech is special? (399)
51. Describe Fowler and Rosenblum's duplex perception experiment. How did they interpret their results? (400)
52. Has the debate about whether or not speech is special been resolved? (400)

Across the Senses: Tadoma: "Hearing" with Touch

53. Describe how the Tadoma method of tactile speech perception came into being. (401)
54. What is the procedure for Tadoma? What kind of information can it transmit about speech? (401)
55. How well can an experienced Tadoma user identify consonant-vowel sounds? How does performance change for meaningful speech? (401)

[**Answer:** An American delights in simple playthings.]

14

The Cutaneous Senses

Chapter Contents

Some Questions We Will Consider

- What is the most sensitive part of the body? (418)
- Is it possible to reduce pain with our thoughts? (428)
- Do all people experience pain in the same way? (431)

Geerat Vermeij, blind since the age of 4 from a childhood eye disease, had come with his parents from his boyhood home in the Netherlands to live in the United States. After being educated in residential schools for the blind and in the regular school system, he attended Princeton University. During his senior year at Princeton, he applied to a number of graduate schools to study evolutionary biology, with a specialty in mollusks. He was rejected by a number of schools, who said his blindness would make it impossible for him to study biology, but he was granted an interview by Edgar Boell, the director of graduate study in the biology department at Yale. Boell took Vermeij to the museum, introduced him to the curator, and handed him a shell. Here is what happened next, as told by Vermeij (1997):

> "Here's something. Do you know what it is?" Boell asked as he handed me a specimen.
>
> My fingers and mind raced. Widely separated ribs parallel to outer lip; large aperture; low spire; glossy; ribs reflected backward. "It's a *Harpa*," I replied tentatively. "It must be *Harpa major*." Right so far.
>
> "How about this one?" inquired Boell, as another fine shell changed hands. Smooth, sleek, channeled suture, narrow opening; could be any olive. "Its an olive. I'm pretty sure it's *Oliva sayana*, the common one from Florida, but they all look alike."
>
> Both men were momentarily speechless. They had planned this little exercise all along to call my bluff. Now that I had passed, Boell had undergone an instant metamorphosis. Beaming with enthusiasm and warmth, he promised me his full support. (Vermeij, 1997, pp. 79–80)

Vermeij was admitted to graduate study at Yale, graduated with a PhD in evolutionary biology and is presently Professor of Geology at the University of California at Davis and editor of the scientific journal *Evolution.* He does all of his work with his hands, using his exquisitely trained sense of touch to identify the mollusks he studies. It has, for him, provided a window into the world of shells that has enabled him to surpass many of his sighted colleagues, partially because he, of necessity, ignores extraneous visual details and focuses on the physical characteristics that he can feel.

Geerat Vermeij's abilities illustrate the amazing capabilities of touch. Another example of the capabilities of touch is provided by braille, the system of raised dots that enables blind people to read with their fingertips (Figure 14.1). A braille *character* consists of a *cell* made up of from one to six dots. Different arrangements of dots and blank spaces are used to represent the alphabet, as shown, and in addition to characters for each letter of the alphabet, there are also characters for numbers, punctuation marks, and common speech sounds and words.

The blind Frenchman Louis Braille introduced his first version of this raised dot system to students at the Paris School for the Young Blind in 1824. At that time, the only reading materials available to blind people were a few books that were printed by embossing the shapes of conventional letters onto the page. These books, however, were rarely read, because each letter had to be tediously scanned in order to determine its complete shape. The dots of braille eliminated this problem and, although many sighted educators argued that it was absurd to teach the blind an alphabet that was so different from the standard alphabet, students enthusiastically adopted the raised dot system. In 1854, 30 years after Braille had first introduced his system, it was given official recognition in France (American Foundation for the Blind, 1969).

Experienced braille readers can read at a rate of about 100 words per minute, slower than the rate for visual reading, which averages about 250 to 300 words per minute, but impressive nonetheless, when we consider that the sensations experienced as a braille reader's fingertips skim over an array of raised dots are transformed into vast amounts of information that go far beyond simply sensations on the skin.

But the importance of the sense of touch and the other sensations we feel through the skin extends beyond its usefulness as a way to take in information. Imagine how your ability to write might change if your hand were anesthetized. Would you know how firmly to grasp your pen if you had no feeling in your hand? Consider all of the other things you do with your hands. How would losing feeling in your hands affect your ability to do these things? We know that a

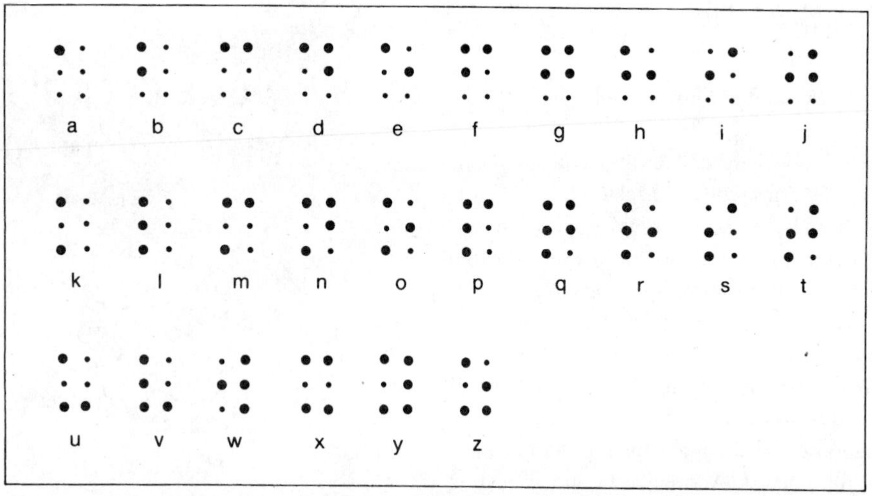

Figure 14.1
The braille alphabet consists of raised dots in a 2×3 matrix. The large dots in this alphabet indicate the location of the raised dot for each letter. Blind people read these dots by scanning them with their fingertips.

complete loss of our ability to feel with the skin is dangerous, as demonstrated by people who, because they can't feel touch or pain, suffer constant bruises, burns, and broken bones in the absence of the warnings provided by touch and pain (Melzack & Wall, 1983; Rollman, 1991; Wall & Melzack, 1994). And consider for a moment what sex would be like without the sense of touch. Or perhaps a better way to put this is to ask if sex without the sense of touch is something people would be capable of or care about at all.

When we recognize that the perceptions we experience through our skin are crucial for protecting ourselves from injury and for motivating sexual activity, we can see that these perceptions are crucial to our survival, and to the survival of our species. We could, in fact, make a good case for the idea that perceptions felt through the skin are more important for survival than those provided by vision and hearing.

In this chapter, we will be considering the **cutaneous sensations**—sensations based on the stimulation of receptors in the skin. Our main focus will be on the following cutaneous sensations: (1) tactile perception, the term we will use to refer to all perceptions, except pain, that are caused by mechanical displacement of the skin; (2) the perception of temperature, caused by heating or cooling of the skin; and (3) the perception of pain, caused by stimuli that are potentially damaging to the skin.

Anatomy of the Somatosensory System

The cutaneous senses are served by the **somatosensory system,** which also includes **proprioception,** the sense of position of the limbs, and **kinesthesis,** the sense of movement of the limbs. In this chapter we will focus our attention primarily on touch and pain. As we look at the anatomy of the somatosensory system by first focusing on the skin, where the receptors for touch and pain are located, we will notice an important parallel with the visual system: The skin, like the retina, contains a number of different kinds of receptors.

The Skin and Its Receptors

Comel (1953) called the skin the "monumental façade of the human body" for good reason. It is the heaviest organ in the human body, and if not the largest (the surface areas of the gastrointestinal tract or of the alveoli of the lungs exceed the surface area of the skin), it is certainly the most obvious, especially in humans, whose skin is not obscured by fur or large amounts of hair (Montagna & Parakkal, 1974).

In addition to its warning function, the skin also prevents body fluids from escaping and at the same time protects us by keeping bacteria, chemical agents, and dirt from penetrating our bodies. Skin maintains

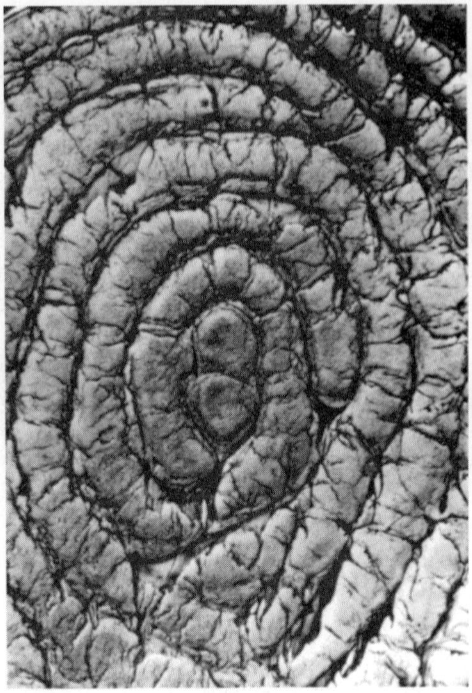

Figure 14.2
A scanning electron micrograph of the glabrous (hairless) skin on the tip of the finger, magnified 27 times. (From Shih & Kessell, 1982.)

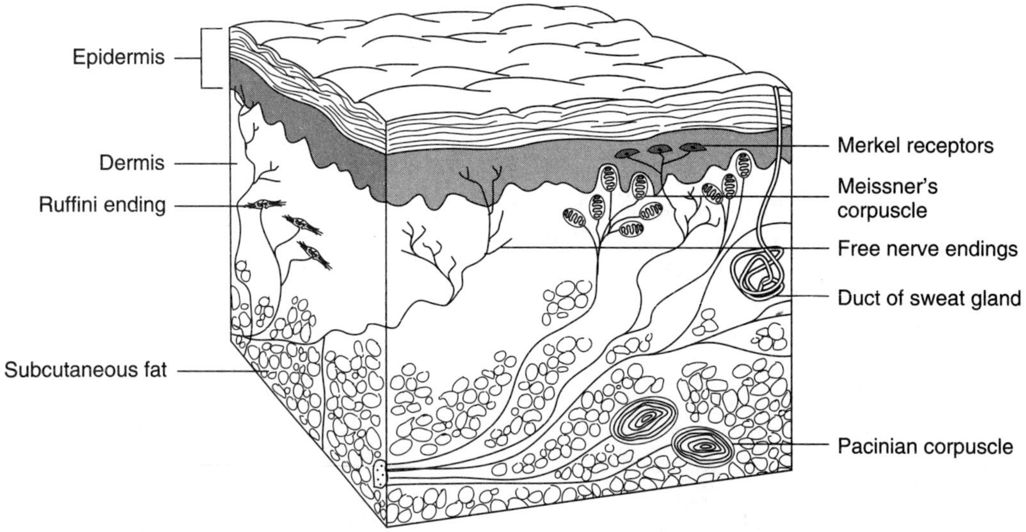

Figure 14.3
A cross section of glabrous skin, showing the layers of the skin and some of its receptors.

the integrity of what's inside and protects us from what's outside, but it also provides us with information about the various stimuli that contact it. The sun's rays heat our skin and we feel warmth; a pinprick is painful, and when someone touches us, we experience pressure or other sensations.

The staging ground for the creation of these experiences is the outer layer of the skin, the **epidermis,** which is actually several layers of cells, the outermost one (the surface of the skin) being tough dead skin cells. (Stick a piece of cellophane tape onto your palm and pull it off. The material that sticks to the tape is dead skin cells.) Hairy skin covers most of the body, but hairless (glabrous) skin is found on the fingers and palms of the hands, and on the toes and soles of the feet (Figure 14.2).

Receptors are located in the epidermis and the layer directly under the epidermis, the **dermis** (Figures 14.3 and 14.4). The four receptor structures each respond to specific kinds of stimulation and each is associated with specific perceptions:

- **Merkel receptor**—a disk-shaped receptor located near the border between the epidermis and the dermis.

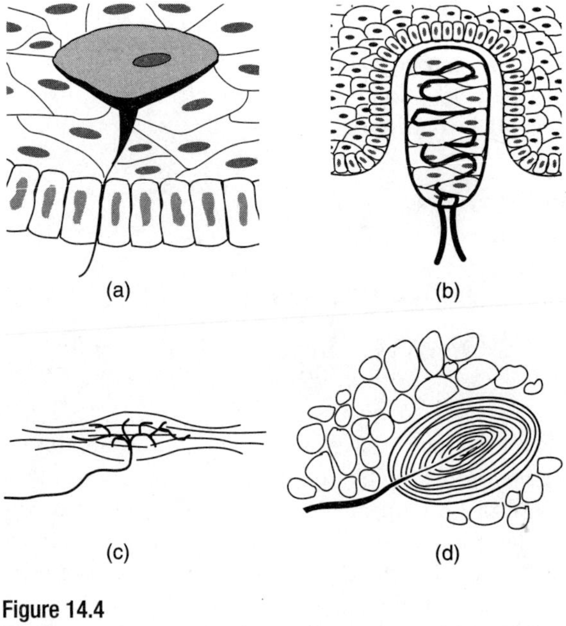

Figure 14.4
The four major receptors for tactile perception: (a) Merkel receptor; (b) Meissner corpuscle; (c) Ruffini cylinder; and (d) Pacinian corpuscle.

- **Meissner corpuscle**—a stack of flattened cells located in the dermis just below the epidermis; a nerve fiber wends its way through these cells.
- **Ruffini cylinder**—many-branched fibers inside a roughly cylindrical capsule.
- **Pacinian corpuscle**—a layered, onionlike capsule that surrounds a nerve fiber; located deep in the skin, the Pacinian corpuscle can also be found in many other places, including the intestines and the joints.

The physical properties of these receptors, as well as their location in the skin and the sizes of their receptive fields, cause the fibers associated with them to respond to different types of stimuli and therefore to result in different cutaneous perceptions.

Central Structures

Modern anatomical studies have identified a complex web of connections that transmit signals from the skin to the brain that appears to rival those of the visual and auditory systems. We will focus on a few of the basic characteristics of the system. Nerve fibers from receptors in the skin travel in bundles called *peripheral nerves* that enter the spinal cord through the **dorsal root** (Figure 14.5).

Once they enter the spinal cord, the nerve fibers go up the spinal cord in two major pathways: the **medial lemniscal pathway** and the **spinothalamic pathway.** Just as parallel pathways in the visual and auditory systems serve different perceptual functions, so it is with the cutaneous system. The lemniscal pathway has large fibers that carry signals related to

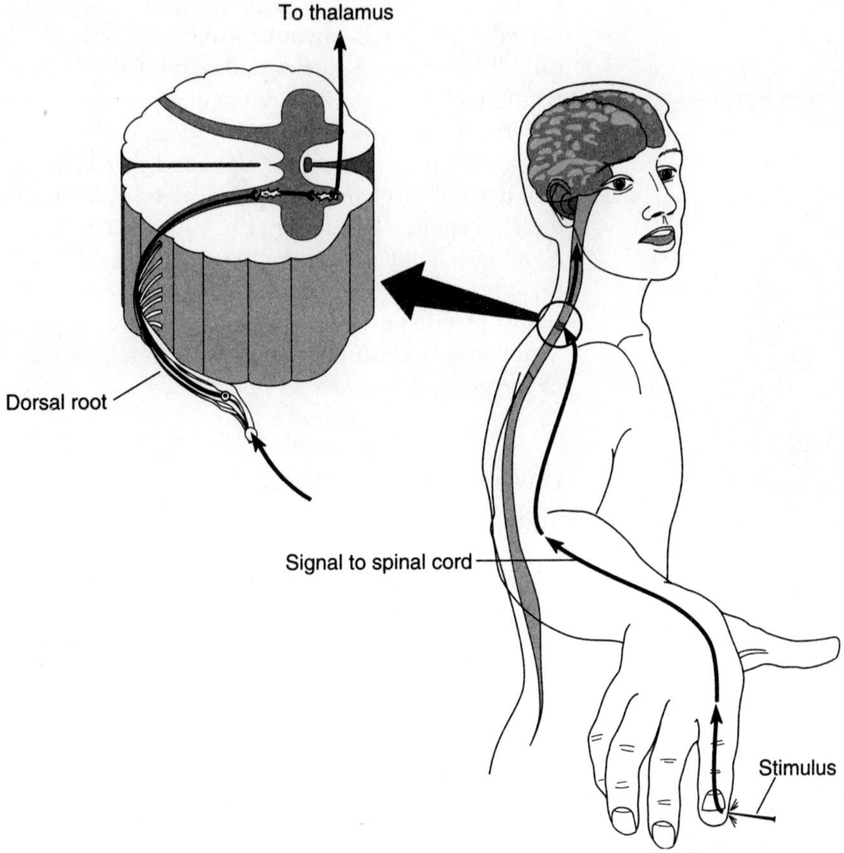

Figure 14.5
The pathway from receptors in the skin to the spinal cord. The fiber carrying signals from a receptor in the finger enters the spinal cord through the dorsal root and then travels up the spinal cord toward the thalamus. This picture is greatly simplified, since there are a number of somatosensory pathways traveling up the spinal cord, and some of them cross over to the opposite side at various points along the way.

sensing the positions of the limbs (proprioception) and perceiving touch. The spinothalamic pathway consists of smaller fibers that transmit signals related to temperature and pain.

Fibers from both pathways cross over to the other side of the body during their upward journey to the thalamus. Most of these fibers synapse in the **ventral posterior nucleus** in the thalamus, but some synapse in other thalamic nuclei. From the thalamus, signals travel to the **somatosensory receiving area (SI)** in the parietal lobe of the cortex and from there to the **secondary somatosensory cortex (SII)** and other higher order areas (Figure 14.6). Since these signals have crossed over to the opposite side of the body on their way to the thalamus, signals originating from the left side of the body reach the right hemisphere of the brain, and signals from the right side of the body reach the left hemisphere.

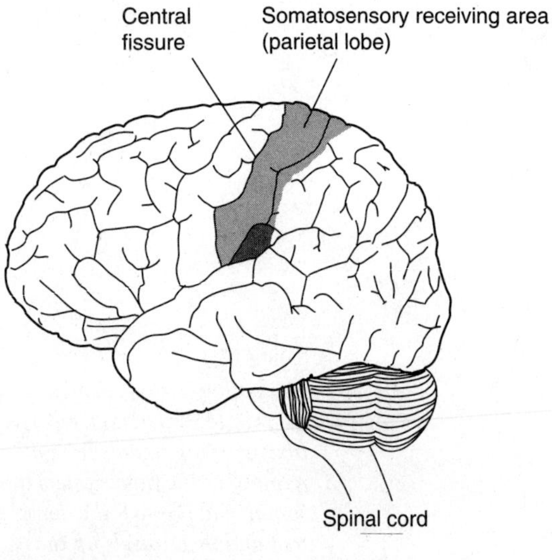

Figure 14.6
The somatosensory cortex in the parietal lobe. The somatosensory system, like the visual and auditory systems, has a number of different areas. The primary somatosensory area, S I (light shading), receives inputs from the ventral lateral posterior nucleus of the thalamus and then sends fibers to the secondary somatosensory area, S II (dark shading), part of which is hidden behind the temporal lobe.

Having described the overall layout of the cutaneous system, we will focus our attention on how information about various tactile qualities is transmitted from the receptors to the brain. We do this by first looking at psychophysical evidence that indicates that there are four channels for tactile information, each of which corresponds to one of the receptors in Figure 14.4.

The Psychophysics and Physiology of Tactile Perception

We sense stimuli that mechanically displace the skin through the operation of separate channels that have been described both physiologically and psychophysically. These channels are described physiologically by noting that there are four different types of receptor structures that are sensitive to specific aspects of the stimuli presented to the skin, and that there are four types of mechanoreceptive *fibers* associated with these receptors. We can describe these channels psychophysically by noting that each channel responds to different frequencies of tactile stimulation and results in different tactile perceptions. We begin by considering what psychophysics has to tell us about tactile perception.

Psychophysical Channels for Tactile Perception

When we described the functioning of the visual system in Chapter 2, we saw that there are two different types of receptors: rods and cones. We were able to tell the difference between them because they were distributed differently on the retina, with the fovea containing only cones and the peripheral retina containing both rods and cones. We can also distinguish between different receptors in the skin, but it is more difficult to separate them topographically because there is no area of the skin, analogous to the fovea, that contains only one type of receptor. The various receptors in the skin are, however, sensitive to different frequencies of vibration, and based on these differences, S. J. Bolanowski and his coworkers (1988, 1994) were able to differentiate four different channels for information about tactile perception in glabrous skin and three channels in hairy skin.

In their research on glabrous (nonhairy) skin, Bolanowski and his coworkers isolated the different channels by using a number of methods, including cooling the skin (some channels are sensitive to temperature and some are not) and presenting masking vibrations that selectively decreased the sensitivity of one tactile channel so another one could be studied. Table 14.1 summarizes the results of their research, noting (1) the names of the channels; (2) the frequency range over which each channel responds; (3) the receptor associated with each channel; and (4) the perception associated with each channel.

From Table 14.1 we can see that, among them, the four channels respond to frequencies ranging from 0.3 Hz, which would correspond to someone slowly pushing and releasing your skin with their finger about once every three seconds, to over 500 Hz, which corresponds to an extremely rapid vibration that might be created by machinery. Each channel is associated with a particular type of tactile perception. For example, the NP III channel responds to low frequencies and is associated with the perception of *pressure*, while the PC channel responds to high frequencies and is associated with the perception of *vibration*. We can also see that each of these channels is associated with one of the receptors in Figure 14.4.

Table 14.1
Psychophysical channels for tactile perception

Channel	Best Frequencies	Receptor Structure	Perception
NP III	0.3–3 Hz	Merkel receptors	Pressure
NP I	3–40 Hz	Meissner corpuscle	Flutter
NP II	15–400 Hz	Ruffini cylinder	Buzzing
PC	10 > 500 Hz	Pacinian corpuscle	Vibration

PC stands for "Pacinian corpuscle"; NP stands for "non-Pacinian."

Four Neural Channels for Tactile Perception

Physiological research has shown that there are four neural channels for tactile perception, each of which corresponds to one of the psychophysical channels. The four neural channels have been described by recording from nerve fibers in the skin of both animals and humans; human recording has been accomplished by the use of a technique called **microneurography**, in which a very fine recording electrode is inserted under the skin to record from a single nerve fiber in a person's hand (Vallbo & Hagbarth, 1967). The four types of fibers that have been identified are called **mechanoreceptive fibers** because they respond to mechanical displacement of the skin.

These mechanoreceptive fibers are described in Table 14.2 noting (1) the name of the fiber, which indicates whether its response adapts rapidly (RA = **rapidly adapting fiber**) or slowly (SA = **slowly adapting fiber**); (2) the size of the fiber's receptive fields; (3) the receptors that are associated with each type of fiber; and (4) the stimuli to which each type of fiber

Table 14.2
Types of mechanoreceptive fibers

Type of Fiber	Receptive Field Size	Receptor Structure	Best Stimulus
SA I (slowly adapting)	Small	Merkel receptors	Pressure
RA I (rapidly adapting)	Small	Meissner corpuscle	Taps on skin
SA II (slowly adapting)	Large	Ruffini cylinder	Stretching of skin or movements of joints
PC (rapidly adapting)	Large	Pacinian corpuscle	Rapid vibration

responds. There are two types of rapidly adapting fibers (RA I and PC). These fibers fire when stimulation is applied and then the response drops rapidly to zero, even if the stimulus continues. There are two types of slowly adapting fibers (SA I and SA II). These fibers fire when a stimulus is applied and continue responding as long as the stimulus continues. To appreciate the connection between the psychophysical and physiological channels, note the similarities between the last two columns of Tables 14.1 and 14.2, and also look at Figure 14.7, which combines much of the information in these two tables.

The PC Channel: Response to High Frequencies Caused by Its Receptor Ending Why does each type of fiber respond to a different type of stimulation? One thing that determines their response is the type of receptor ending, which can modify the pressure reaching the fiber. This modification of the response by a receptor ending has been most thoroughly studied for the Pacinian corpuscle (Figure 14.8), because of its distinctive elliptical shape (which makes it easy to identify), its large size (about 1 mm long and 0.6 mm thick), and its accessibility (it is found in the skin, muscles, tendons, and joints, and also in the cat's mesentery, a readily accessible membrane attached to the intestine, from which Pacinian corpuscles can easily be removed).

To determine how the PC receptor affects the responding of its nerve fiber, Werner Lowenstein and R. Skalak (1966) measured the response of a Pacinian corpuscle's nerve fiber under two conditions: (1) when the corpuscle was partially dissected away, so that pressure could be applied closer to the nerve fiber, and (2) when the corpuscle remained, so that pressure could be applied to it. Their result showed that when most of the corpuscle was removed, so the stimulus was presented near the nerve fiber as shown at B in Figure 14.8, the fiber responded when the pressure was first applied, as the pressure continued, and when the pressure was removed. However, when pressure was applied at A, to the intact corpuscle, the fiber responded only when the pressure was first applied and when it was removed. Thus, the presence of the Pacinian corpuscle gives its nerve fiber the properties of a PC fiber, so that it rapidly adapts to constant stimulation such as sustained pressure but responds well to changes in stimulation that occur at the onset and offset of pressure and to rapidly changing stimulation, such as vibration.

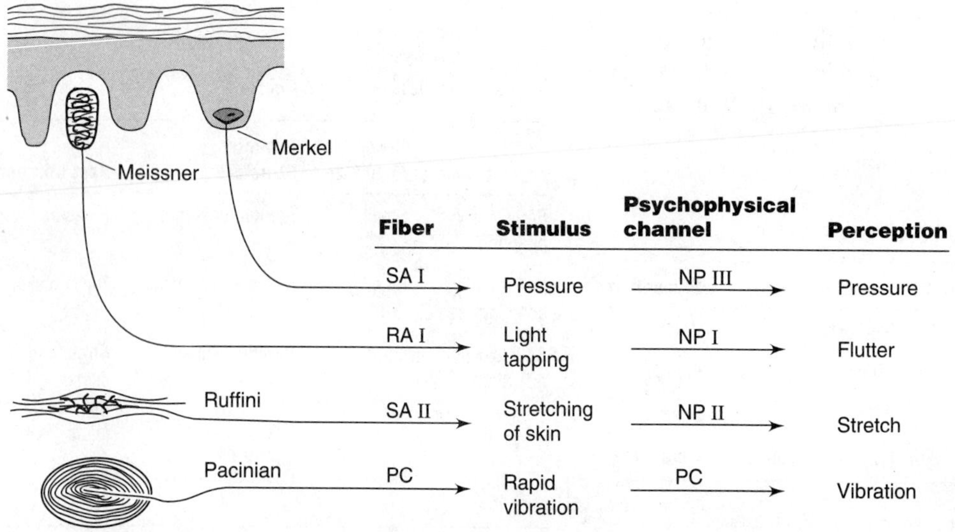

Figure 14.7 *The relationship between the four receptor endings (left), the four types of mechanoreceptive fibers (center), and the four psychophysical channels (right). Also note the relationship between the stimulus that best excites each fiber and the perception associated with each psychophysical channel.*

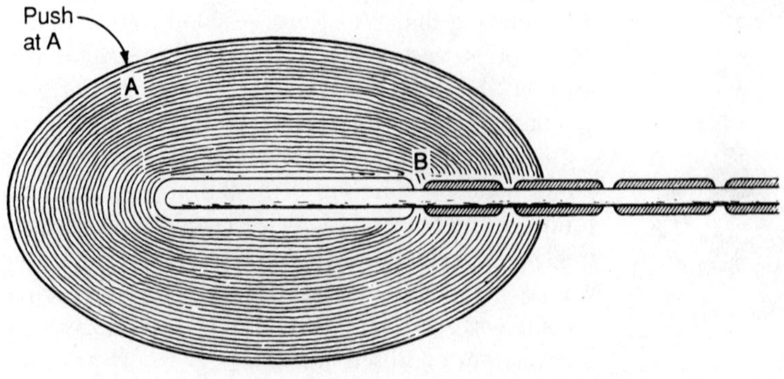

Figure 14.8
A Pacinian corpuscle. (From Lowenstein, 1960.)

The SA1 Channel: Response to Details While the PC channel is specialized to respond to changes in stimulation, the SA1 channel is specialized to respond to details. Two clues that this would be the case is that these neurons have small receptive fields and are located near the surface of the skin (see Table 14.1). The sensitivity of the SA1 channel to details has been demonstrated more directly by recording the neural response to raised-dot patterns rolled across the skin. Kenneth Johnson and Graham Lamb (1981) recorded firing from single fibers in the monkey's finger as raised-dot patterns were presented on a rotating drum (Figure 14.9). By rolling the dots over a fiber's receptive field a number of times, and moving the drum down slightly after each scan, Johnson and Lamb were able to create displays called **spatial event plots,** which indicate how well the fibers respond to small details. (See Figure 14.9 for a description of how these spatial event plots are determined.)

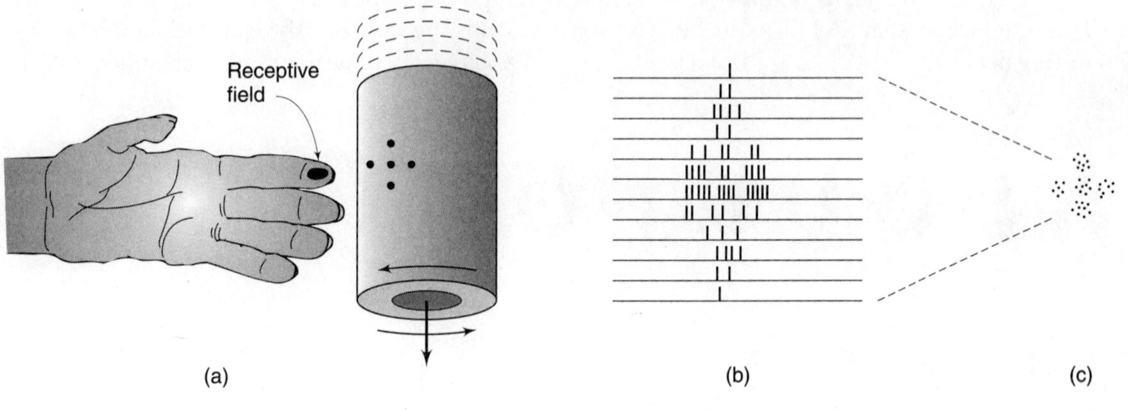

Figure 14.9
(a) Raised-dot stimuli are rolled across the receptive field of a mechanoreceptive fiber on a monkey's fingertip. (b) Sweeping the stimulus across the receptive field generates nerve impulses in the fiber. These nerve impulses are shown on the horizontal lines. Each line represents the impulses generated by one sweep across the receptive field. After each sweep, the drum is moved down slightly, the stimulus is presented again, and a new response is recorded. This process is repeated for a number of positions of the drum. (c) A spatial event plot is created when each nerve impulse is represented by a dot, and the dots are compressed vertically and horizontally so that the pattern of dots has about the same dimensions as the raised-dot stimulus. (Adapted from Martin & Jessell, 1991.)

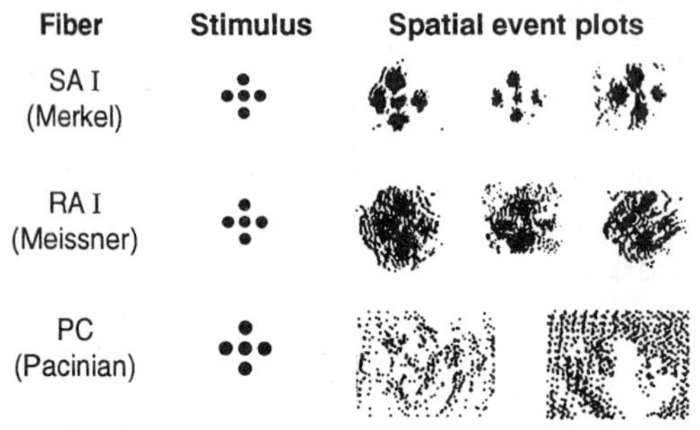

Figure 14.10
Left: Raised-dot stimulus presented as shown in Figure 14.9 to a monkey's fingertip. Right: Some typical spatial event plots generated by this pattern for SA I, RA I, and PC fibers that are associated with Merkel receptors, Meissner corpuscles, and Pacinian corpuscles, respectively. The SA II fiber, which is associated with the Ruffini cylinder, generates only a small response to this type of stimulation. (Adapted from Johnson & Lamb, 1981.)

Figure 14.10 shows how the spatial event plots for three types of fibers compare to the original raised-dot pattern. We can see that the plot for the SA I fiber looks similar to the dot pattern, whereas the plots for the RA I and PC fibers do not look like the pattern. (S II fibers respond poorly to this type of stimulus.) This result means that SA I fibers are best suited for resolving details.

Showing that SA I fibers respond well to details does not prove that they are actually used for perception. To show a connection between the fiber's response and perception, we need to compare the responses of these fibers to psychophysically measured performance. Francisco Vega-Bermudez, Kenneth Johnson, and Steven Hsiao (1991) did this by measuring how well subjects could identify raised letters that were scanned across their fingertips. They found that the subjects identified some of the letters accurately, but that they confused others.

Why were some letters identified accurately and others not? We can answer this question by looking at the spatial event plots in Figure 14.11 for the responses of monkey SA I fibers to the same letters that were used in the psychophysical experiments. First, consider the following psychophysical result: Subjects often identified C's as O's but only rarely said an O was a C. Now consider the physiological result shown in Figure 14.11. The SA I fiber's response to C and O both look very much like an O. Thus, misidentifying a C as an O appears to be caused by the fact that the physiological response to a C looks similar to the letter O. This parallel between people's psychophysical judgments and physiological responding supports the idea that SA I fibers are important for identifying details. (Also consider the following psychophysical result: *B* was often identified as *D*, but *D*

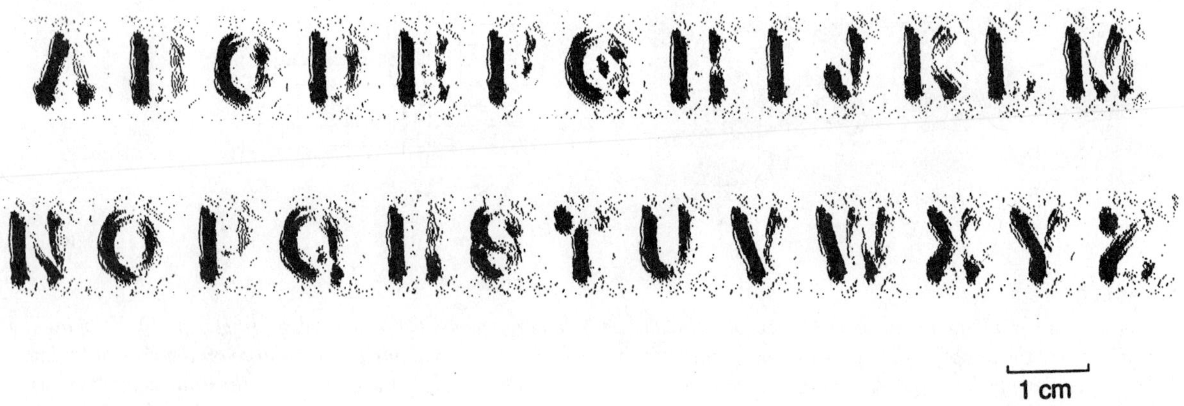

Figure 14.11
Spatial event plots generated by rolling raised letters across the receptive fields of SA I fibers. (From Vega-Bermudez, Johnson, & Hsiao, 1991.)

was rarely identified as *B*. Look at the *B* and *D* responses of the SA I fiber to see the neural parallel to this psychophysical result.)

These results indicate that SA I fibers are probably important for detail perception. Keep in mind, however, that stimulating the skin usually activates a number of tactile channels, some more strongly than others, depending on the stimulus. Thus, as you run your fingers over a textured surface, the SA1 fibers fire to small ridges and indentations and you feel the fine texture. Meanwhile, the PC fibers are responding to the rapid changes in pressure that are occurring as your finger moves. The response of each of these fibers contributes to our perceptual experience. RA1 fibers are probably also stimulated as well, and all of these fibers together create your overall experience (Roland, 1992).

We can draw a parallel between this description of how a number of kinds of tactile information are combined and our description of the process in vision, in which qualities such as form, color, and motion are processed in separate streams and are then combined to create a coherent perception of an object. We don't know if the process for touch is the same as this, but the idea of different qualities being combined is similar. And in addition to the tactile qualities transmitted in the four tactile channels, another important quality is also involved in our perceptual experience of the textured surface. As we perceive the texture, we also perceive its temperature. This perception of temperature occurs because of the stimulation of thermoreceptors in the skin.

Thermoreceptors: The Neural Response to Temperature

Thermoreceptors respond to specific temperatures and to changes in temperature. There are separate thermoreceptors for warm and cold. Figure 14.12 shows how a **warm fiber** responds to increases in temperature. The response of this neuron illustrates the following properties of a warm fiber: (1) It increases its firing rate when the temperature is increased; (2) it continues to fire as long as the higher temperature continues; (3) it decreases its firing rate when the temperature is decreased; and (4) it does not respond to mechanical stimulation (Duclaux & Kenshalo, 1980; Kenshalo, 1976). **Cold fibers,** on the other hand, increase their firing rate when the temperature is decreased and continue to fire at low temperatures. The different ways that cold and warm fibers respond to steady temperatures are shown in Figure 14.13. Cold fibers respond in the 20°C to 45°C range, with the best response at about 30°. Warm fibers respond in the 30° to 48° range, with the best response at about 44°. (Note that body temperature is 37°C.)

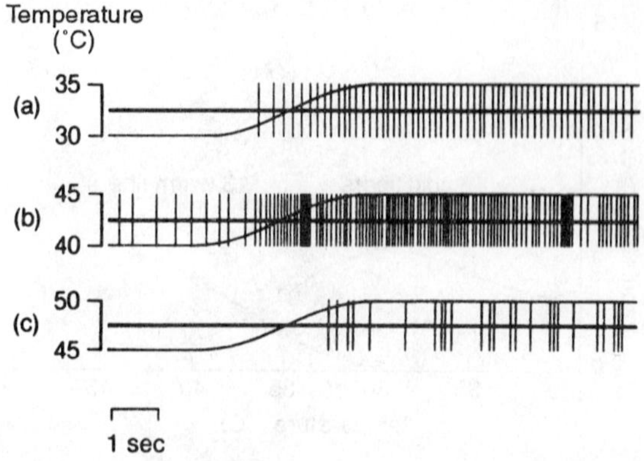

Figure 14.12
The response of a "warm" fiber in the monkey. At the beginning of each record the firing rate is low because the fiber has been at the same temperature for a while. The fiber fires, however, when the temperature is increased (indicated by the sloping line) and continues to fire for a period of time immediately after the increase. Record (b) indicates that this fiber fires best when the temperature is increased from 40°C to 45°C. (From Duclaux & Kenshalo, 1980.)

It is clear that receptors and fibers at the very beginning of the somatosensory system have a large influence on what we perceive. The importance of receptors in the skin for perceiving different qualities parallels the situation in the visual system, where properties of the rod and cone receptors determine our sensitivity to light and our ability to see details and colors. When we studied the visual system, we also saw that the cones in the fovea, which are responsible for the high acuity that enables us to see details, are represented by a disproportionately large area on

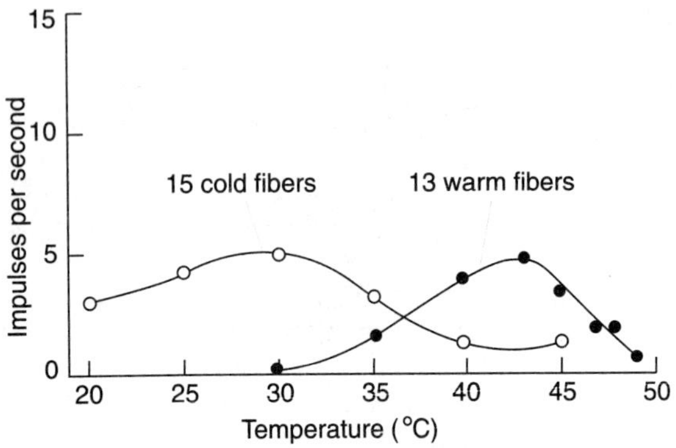

Figure 14.13
Responses of temperature-sensitive fibers in the monkey to constant temperatures. The curve on the left (open circles) shows the average response of a group of 15 "cold" fibers that respond best at about 30°C. The curve on the right (filled circles) shows the average response of a group of 13 "warm" fibers that respond best at about 44°C. (From Kenshalo, 1976.)

the visual cortex. We will now see that neural processing creates a similar result in the cutaneous system.

NEURAL PROCESSING OF TACTILE STIMULI

We will demonstrate a connection between neural processing and cutaneous perception by making use of the basic fact that tactile acuity is better on some parts of the body, such as the hands and the fingertips, than on others, such as the limbs, the back, and the trunk. Let's consider this finding and how it is related to neural processing.

Measuring Tactile Acuity: The Two-Point Threshold

One way to determine tactile acuity is to measure the **two-point threshold**—the smallest separation between two points on the skin that is perceived as two points rather than one. When the two-point threshold is measured on different parts of the body, we find that there are areas on the skin that have higher acuity than others.

D E M O N S T R A T I O N

Comparing Two-Point Thresholds

To measure two-point thresholds on different parts of the body, hold two pencils side by side (or better yet, use a drawing compass) so that their points are about 12 mm (0.5 in.) apart; then touch both points simultaneously to the tip of your thumb and determine whether you feel two points. If you feel only one, increase the distance between the pencil points until you feel two; then note the distance between the points. Now move the pencil points to the underside of your forearm. With the points about 12 mm apart (or at the smallest separation you felt as two points on your thumb), touch them to your forearm and note whether you feel one point or two. If you feel only one, how much must you increase the separation before you feel two? ●

If your results from this demonstration match those from the laboratory, you will find that the two-point threshold on your forearm is much larger than the two-point threshold on your thumb. Figure 14.14, which shows how the two-point threshold varies on different parts of the body, indicates that the two-point threshold is over 10 times larger on the forearm than on the thumb. This result is analogous to the results for the visual system. Areas that are responsible for making fine spatial discriminations—the fovea for vision and the fingers for touch—have high acuity, whereas other areas have lower acuity. One way to relate these acuity differences to physiology is to compare the sizes of the receptive fields on different parts of the body.

Receptive Fields and Tactile Acuity

We would expect that areas with high tactile acuity would have small receptive fields. The reason for this

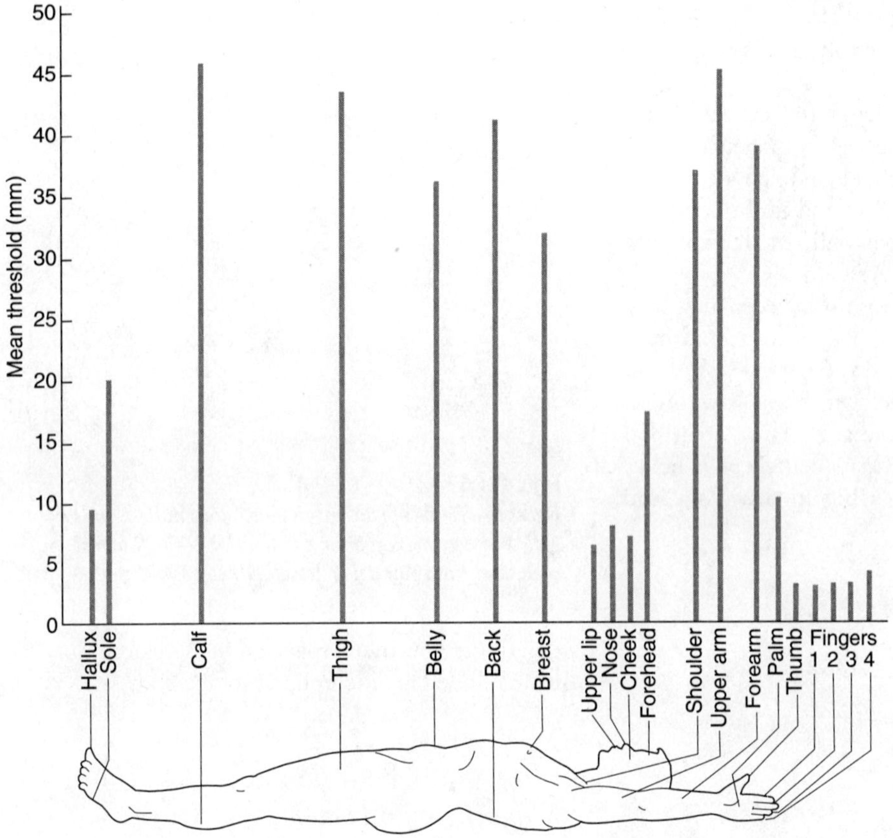

Figure 14.14
Two-point thresholds for males. Two-point thresholds for females follow the same pattern. (From Weinstein, 1968.)

expectation is shown in Figure 14.15. Figure 14.15a shows the receptive fields of two neurons with large receptive fields and two points stimulating the skin within one of these receptive fields. Since the stimulation falls within just one of the receptive fields, just one neuron fires and we have no information that two points were stimulated.

Figure 14.15b shows the receptive fields of two neurons with small receptive fields being stimulated at two points with exactly the same separation as in Figure 14.15a. Since the receptive fields of these neurons are small, the two points stimulate both neurons, thereby increasing the chances that we would perceive the two stimulations as two separate points. (See page 57 of Chapter 2 for the same reasoning, as applied to the rod and cone visual receptors.)

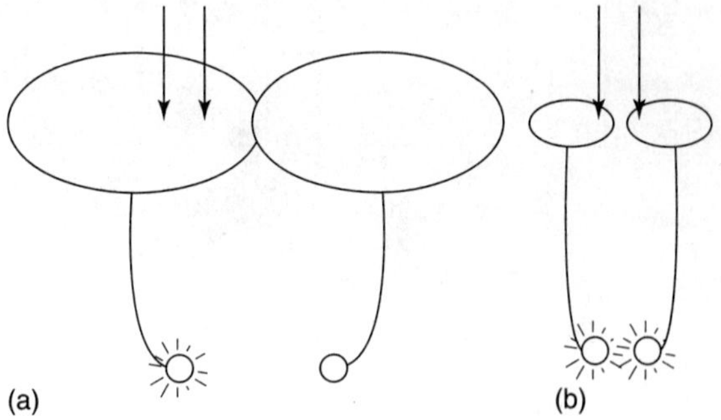

Figure 14.15
The reason for the relation between acuity and receptive field size. (a) Two stimuli cause only one neuron to fire when the receptive fields are large; (b) The same two stimuli cause two neurons to fire when the receptive fields are small. The finer-grained analysis provided by the small receptive fields result in smaller two-point thresholds.

In line with this prediction, Vallbo and Johansson (1978) found that the density of RA1 and SA1 fibers, which have small receptive fields, was higher on the fingertips than on the hand. In fact, Vallbo and Johansson found a direct relationship between the size of the two-point threshold and the density of the small receptive fields of RA I and SA I fibers (Figure 14.16). Parts of the body with small two-point thresholds have small receptive fields.

We get the same relationship between receptive field size and the area on the body if we record from neurons in the monkey's cortex. Figure 14.17 shows that the sizes of receptive fields increase as we move from the fingertips toward the arm. Thus, areas that have higher tactile acuity have smaller receptive fields. Another way to relate tactile acuity to physiology is to determine how much space on the somatosensory cortex is allotted to different parts of the body.

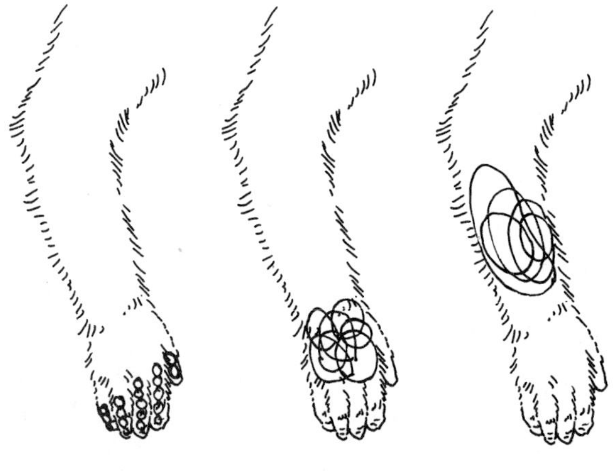

Figure 14.17
Receptive fields of cortical neurons are smallest on the fingers and become larger on the hand and the forearm. (Adapted from Kandel & Jessell, 1991.)

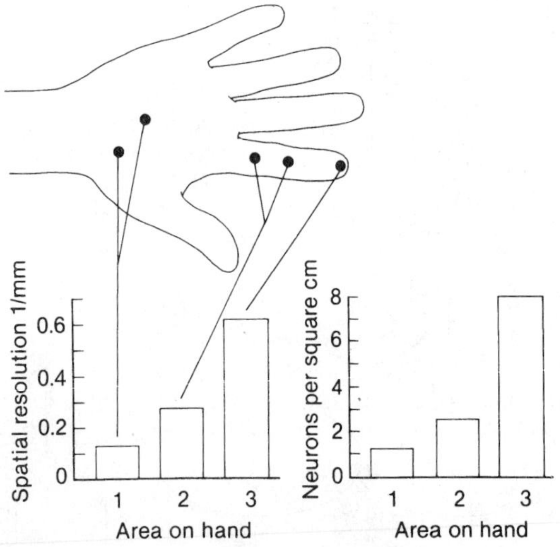

Figure 14.16
Left: The bar graph shows the spatial resolution at one place on the hand and two places on a finger. Spatial resolution, which is determined by taking the inverse of the two-point threshold (so that a small two-point threshold results in high spatial resolution), increases as we move from the hand to the fingertip. Right: The density of small receptive field neurons (RA I and SA I fibers) at the same three locations. These data indicate that areas that have high spatial resolution have high densities of small receptive field neurons. (From Vallbo & Johansson, 1978.)

Maps of the Body on the Cortex: The Magnification Factor

We can extend the relation between tactile acuity and physiology to the cortex by showing that parts of the body with high acuity are allotted larger areas on the cortex. This relation between acuity and space on the cortex is similar to the *magnification factor* that we described in Chapter 3 for the visual system. We saw that the fovea, with its densely packed cone receptors and excellent detail vision, is represented by a cortical area far out of proportion to its size relative to other areas on the retina. The fovea's cortical area is *magnified* to provide the extra neural processing needed to perceive the fine details of objects imaged on the fovea.

We can show that a similar situation exists in the cutaneous system by measuring the area on the cortex that corresponds to different areas of the body. When we do this, we see that, for each area on the skin, there is a corresponding area on the surface of the somatosensory cortex, as shown in Figure 14.18. The strangely shaped cortical representation that results is called a **homunculus,** Latin for "little man."

The homunculus shows that some areas on the skin are represented by a disproportionately large area of the brain. The area devoted to the thumb, for example, is as large as the area devoted to the entire forearm. As with the magnification factor for foveal vision, the apparent over-representation of various body parts on the sensory cortex is related to the functioning of these areas. By comparing Figures 14.14 and 14.18, we can note the close relationship between the two-point threshold on the skin and the cortical representation of the skin: Areas on the skin with small two-point thresholds are represented by large areas on the cortex. Thus, the map of the body on the brain may look distorted, but the distortions represent the extra neural processing that enables us to accurately sense fine details with our fingers and other parts of the body.

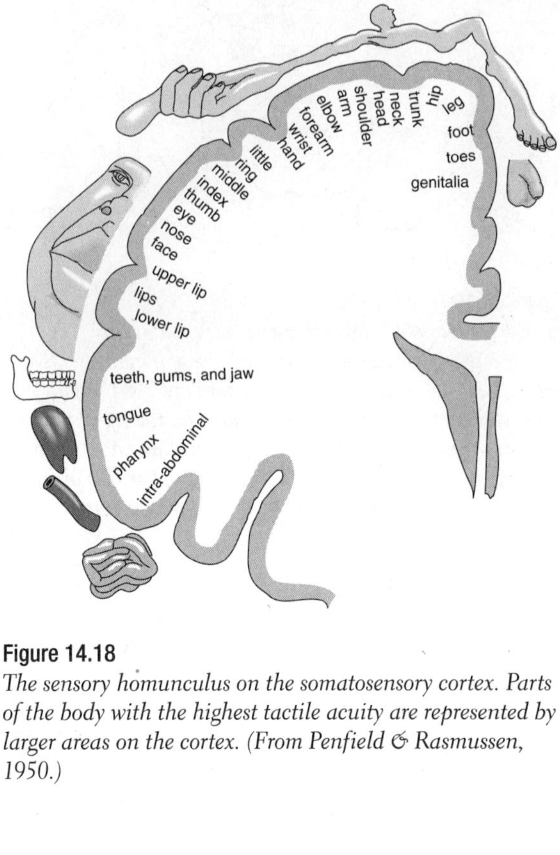

Figure 14.18
The sensory homunculus on the somatosensory cortex. Parts of the body with the highest tactile acuity are represented by larger areas on the cortex. (From Penfield & Rasmussen, 1950.)

Two additional facts about this map are important. First, the somatosensory cortex is arranged in columns. This means that when an electrode oriented perpendicular to the surface of the cortex is lowered into the cortex, all of the neurons it encounters have receptive fields from the same area of the skin. Thus, like the visual cortex and the auditory cortex, these columns process information from a particular area of the body (Kandel & Jessell, 1991).

Second, there are at least 10 separate maps of the monkey's body in its brain (Kaas & Pons, 1988; Kandel & Jessell, 1991; Nelson et al., 1980). The apparent reason for these multiple representations is that different areas within the somatosensory area have different functions. For example, one area may be specialized for the discrimination of forms and another for the discrimination of textures. Whatever their function, these multiple maps of the body on the brain exhibit the same distortions as our simple homunculus in Figure 14.18: Areas of the body that discriminate fine details are allotted large areas on the cortex.

Changing the Maps on the Brain: Plasticity of the Somatosensory Cortex

The fact that the size of different parts of the map is related to how sensitive the body part is to tactile stimulation, shows that the brain's functioning is adapted to an organism's needs. Further evidence for this adaptation is provided by experiments which show that the map changes when signals from a particular part of the body are prevented from reaching the cortex. For example, if receptor signals are prevented from reaching the monkey's somatosensory cortex by loss of a finger or by damage to the peripheral nerves conducting impulses from the skin, this reduces the area on the cortex that is devoted to that part of the body (Kaas, 1991; Kaas, Merzenich, & Killackey, 1983; Pettit & Schwark, 1993; Pons et al., 1991).

Maps in the somatosensory cortex can also be changed by *increasing* the stimulation reaching the cortex. William Jenkins and Michael Merzenich (1987) showed that increasing stimulation of a specific area of the skin causes an expansion of the cortical area receiving signals from that area of skin. They demonstrated this effect by training monkeys to complete a task that involved the extensive use of a particular location on one fingertip. Comparison of the cortical maps of the fingertip measured just before the training and three months later shows that the area representing the stimulated fingertip was greatly expanded after the training (Figure 14.19). Thus, the cortical area representing part of the fingertip, which is large to begin with, becomes even larger when the area receives a large amount of stimulation. The sensory homunculus of Figure 14.18 is not, therefore, a permanent, static map but can be changed by experience. This ability of the nervous system to change in response to experience is called **neural plasticity.** For an example of neural plasticity in the visual system, see page 233 of Chapter 8, which describes how restricting a young monkey's vision to a single eye eliminates cortical neurons that respond to binocular (two-eyed) stimulation. (Also see Chapter 12, page 377.)

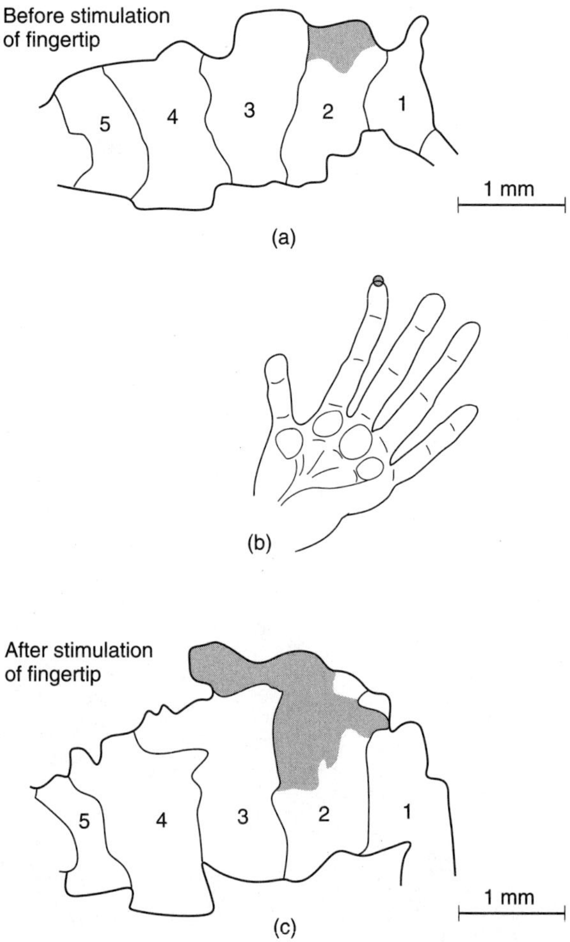

Figure 14.19
(a) Each numbered zone represents the area in the somatosensory cortex that represents one of a monkey's five digits. The shaded area on the zone for digit 2 is the part of the cortex that represents the small area on the tip of the digit shown in (b). (c) The shaded region shows how the area representing the fingertip increased in size after this area was heavily stimulated over a two-month period (From Merzenich et al., 1988.)

Neurons That Respond to Specialized Stimuli

Neural processing in the cutaneous system is reflected not only by the expanded space in the cortex for certain areas of the body, but by changes in the neurons' receptive fields as we move from the receptors toward the cortex. Early in the system, neurons have center-surround receptive fields, like the one in Figure 14.20, which shows the receptive field of a neuron in the monkey's thalamus that receives signals from receptors in the skin of the monkey's arm. This is an excitatory-center-inhibitory-surround receptive field similar to the center-surround receptive fields of visual neurons in the retina and lateral geniculate nucleus (Mountcastle & Powell, 1959).

When we move to the cortex, we find some neurons with center-surround receptive fields, and also others that respond to more specialized stimulation of the skin. Figures 14.21 and 14.22 show the receptive fields of neurons in the monkey's somatosensory cortex that are quite similar to the receptive fields of simple and complex cells in the visual cortex. The cell in Figure 14.22 responds to an edge oriented horizontally but responds less well to other orientations. Figure 14.21 shows a cell that responds to movement across the skin in a specified direction (Hyvarinin & Poranen, 1978; see also Costanzo & Gardner, 1980;

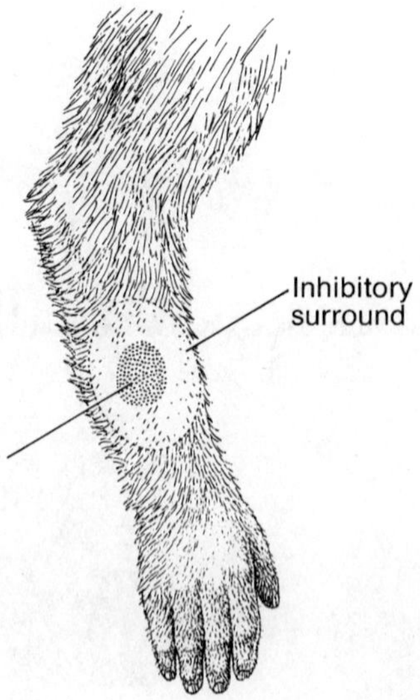

Figure 14.20
An excitatory-center-inhibitory-surround receptive field of a neuron in a monkey's thalamus.

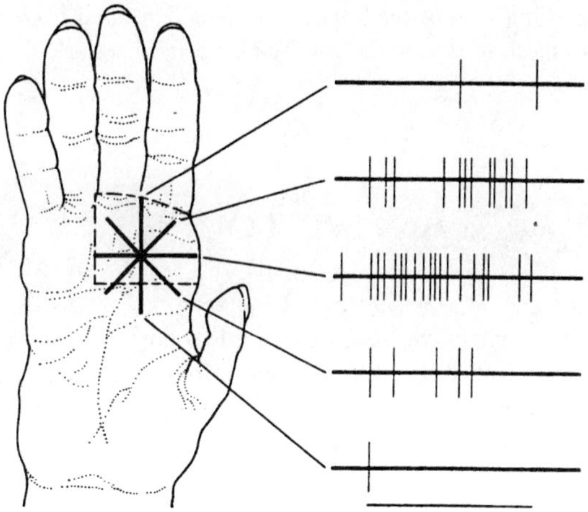

Figure 14.21
The receptive field of a neuron in the monkey's somatosensory cortex that responds when an edge is placed on the hand. This cell responds well when the edge is oriented horizontally but responds less well to other orientations. (From Hyvarinin & Poranen, 1978.)

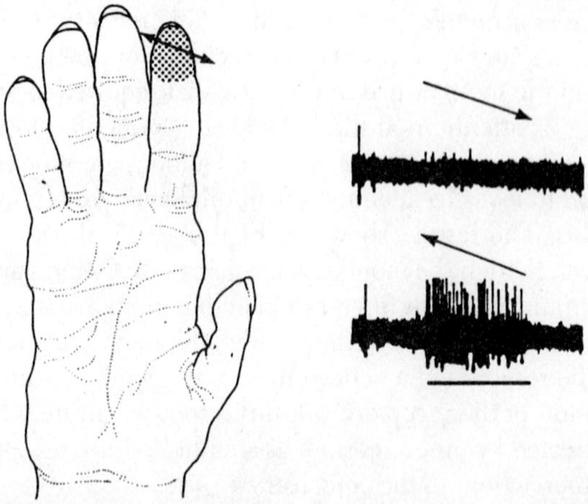

Figure 14.22
The receptive field of a neuron in the monkey's somatosensory cortex that responds to movement across the fingertip from right to left but does not respond to movement from left to right. (From Hyvarinin & Poranen, 1978.)

Warren, Hamalainen, & Gardner, 1986; Whitsel, Roppolo, & Werner, 1972. Also see Edin, et al., 1995; Essick & Edin, 1995 for data on humans).

In Chapter 10, we proposed a neural circuit to explain how visual neurons could respond selectively to movement in one direction (see Figure 10.13). It is likely that a similar type of circuit is behind the directional selectivity of cutaneous neurons like the one in Figure 14.22 (Gardner & Costanzo, 1980).

The similarity between these neurons and neurons in the visual system is striking. In both vision and touch, neurons near the receptors respond to a wide range of stimuli, whereas neurons in the cortex respond only to more specific stimuli. Another parallel between touch and vision is that at higher cortical levels in each system there are neurons that are affected by attention.

We saw in Chapter 4 that the firing of some neurons in the extrastriate cortex is influenced by whether or not the monkey is paying attention to a stimulus (see page 119). Steven Hsiao and coworkers (1993, 1996) have demonstrated a similar effect for neurons sensitive to touch in areas SI and SII. They recorded the response to raised letters that were rolled across a monkey's finger using a rotating drum like the one in Figure 14.9. In the tactile-attention condition the monkey had to do a task that required focusing its attention on the letters being presented to its fingers. In the visual-attention condition, the monkey had to focus its attention on an unrelated visual stimulus. The results, shown in Figure 14.23, show that even though the monkey is receiving exactly the same stimulation on its fingertips in both conditions, the response is larger for the tactile-attention condition. The response of a neuron may be triggered by stimulation of the receptors, but this response can then be affected by processes such as attention, thinking, and other actions of the perceiver.

An example of how actions of the perceiver can affect neural responding is provided by the neural firing shown in Figure 14.24. This neuron does not respond when the experimenter stimulates the skin, but does respond when the monkey grasps certain objects. It responds when the monkey grasps a ruler, but does not respond when the monkey grasps a cylinder. Neurons like these probably play an important role in a process called active touch.

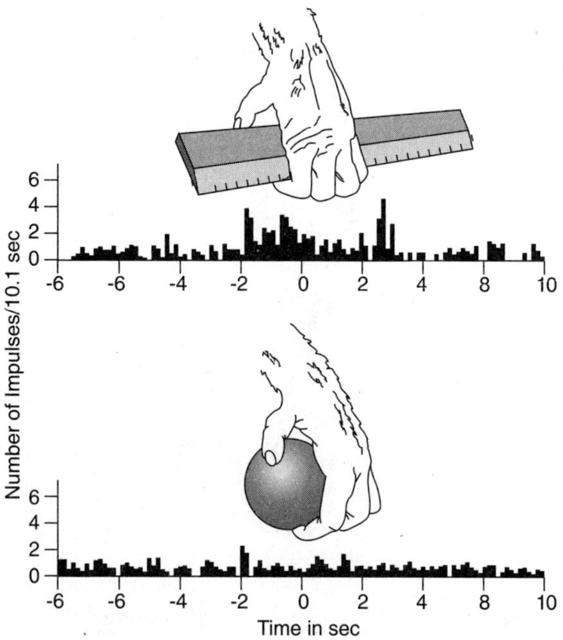

Figure 14.24
The response of a neuron in a monkey's parietal cortex that fires when the monkey grasps a ruler, but that does not fire when the monkey grasps a cylinder. The neuron's rate of firing is indicated by the height of the bars. The monkey grasps the objects at time = 0. (From Sakata & Iwamura, 1978.)

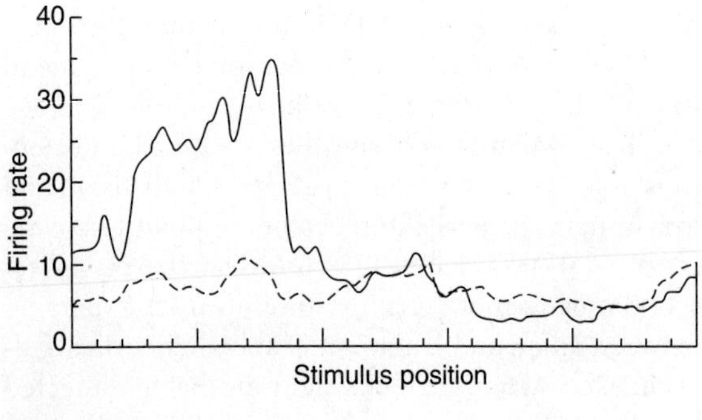

Figure 14.23
Firing rate for a neuron in area S1 of a monkey's cortex that is responding to a raised letter being rolled across the monkey's fingertips. A large response occurs in the tactile-attention condition (solid line) and a small response occurs in the visual-attention condition (dashed line) even though the stimulation on the fingertips was the same in both conditions. (Adapted from Hsiao et al., 1996.)

Active Touch

The research we have described so far has described stimulation of the skin in ways quite unlike what usually happens in everyday experience. We don't normally have our skin touched by two separated pencil tips or stimulated by dots or letters pressed onto our skin with a rolling drum. In these situations, stimuli are applied to the skin of a passive subject. But in our experience, touch is usually active. We run our fingers across the smooth surface of a table, rhythmically hit the keys of our computer, or feel a baseball leave our fingers as we throw it. This kind of touch, which is called **active touch,** has a number of qualities that distinguish it from passive touch. To appreciate these differences, do the following demonstration.

DEMONSTRATION

Comparing Active and Passive Touch

Ask another person to select five or six small objects for you to identify. Close your eyes and have the person place each object in your hand. Your job is to identify the object by touch alone. As you do this, be aware of what you are experiencing: your finger and hand movements, the sensations you are feeling, and what you are thinking. Do this for three objects. Then hold out your hand, keeping it still, with fingers outstretched, and let the person move each of the remaining objects around on your hand, moving their surfaces and contours across your skin. Your task is the same as before: to identify the object and to pay attention to what you are experiencing as the object is moved across your hand. ●

In this demonstration, you experienced both active and passive touch. According to J. J. Gibson (1962), who championed the importance of movement in perception (Chapters 9 and 10), this distinction is important because of differences in both what we experience in the two cases and the kinds of information we receive. Gibson and others compared the experience of active and passive touch by noting that we tend to relate active touch to the *object* being touched, whereas we tend to relate passive touch to the *sensation* experienced in the skin. For example, if someone pushes a pointed object into your skin, you might say, "I feel a pricking sensation on my skin"; however, if you push on the tip of the pointed object yourself, you might say, "I feel a pointed object" (Kruger, 1970). Another example of a difference between active and passive touch is that, when you move your hand over the edges and surfaces of an object (active touch), you do not perceive the object as moving, even though it is moving relative to the skin. If, however, someone moves an object across your skin (passive touch), you perceive the object moving across your skin.

Though we do not completely understand why these two types of touch result in different experiences, we do know that a number of properties differentiate active from passive touch. An important property of active touch, according to Gibson, is that it is *purposive:* that is, when you feel something, especially an object with which you are unfamiliar, your purpose is to determine its shape. Just as you visually scan a scene by looking at its most interesting or important areas, you feel an object by touching the parts that contain information about its shape. This purposiveness may be important in determining the experience of active touch.

In addition to its purposive aspect, active touch includes other properties absent from passive touch. As you feel something, you stimulate receptors not only in the skin but also in the joints and tendons that are activated as you move your fingers or hands over an object, whereas passive touch stimulates only the receptors in the skin. Furthermore, moving your fingers over an object enables you to perceive not only the tactile sensations that occur when a stimulus is applied to passive skin but also the sounds that occur when skin moves actively over a surface (Taylor, Lederman, & Gibson, 1973).

Using Active Touch to Identify Objects

Gibson (1962) proposed that active touch is superior to passive touch for gathering information about objects in our environment. He demonstrated this superiority by showing that, when subjects actively felt cookie cutters of various shapes, they were able to identify the shape correctly 95 percent of the time, but, when the cookie cutters were pushed onto the skin by someone else, the subjects could identify the shape only 49 percent of the time.

However, others have argued that the thing that is important for identifying objects is not active touch, but *movement* of the stimulus across the skin. When Gibson's cookie cutter experiment was repeated with an additional passive condition in which the experimenter moved the edges of the cookie cutters across the subjects' fingers, subjects correctly identified the shape 93 percent of the time (Schwartz, Perez, & Azulaz, 1975). This result suggests that movement across the skin, not purposiveness, is what is important in discriminating shapes.

Although some studies in addition to Schwartz's have found that passive touch based on moving stimuli can produce identification equal to active touch (Vega-Bermudez et al., 1991), other studies have shown that active touch is superior. For example, Morton Heller (1986) had subjects identify braille dot patterns (Figure 14.1) under three different conditions: The subjects moved their fingers over the dots (active); the experimenters moved the dots over the subjects' stationary fingertips (passive with movement); or the experimenters pushed the dots into the subjects' stationary fingertips (passive with no movement). The results, shown in Figure 14.25, indicate that active touch is better than both types of passive touch. However, in another experiment using braille characters, Grunwald (1965) found that subjects who were experienced braille readers recognized braille characters equally well using passive or active touch. Thus, depending on the conditions and the subjects, active touch is sometimes better than passive touch, and sometimes there is no difference between them. However, when it comes to identifying three-dimensional objects by touch, it seems clear that active touch is the superior mode. This ability to identify three-dimensional objects based on touch is called *haptic perception*.

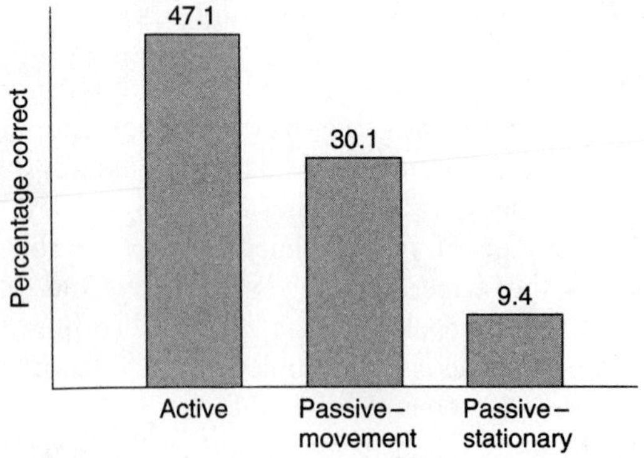

Figure 14.25
The results of Heller's (1986) experiment, in which he had subjects identify braille dot patterns under three different conditions.

Haptic Perception: Tactile Perception of Three-Dimensional Objects

If you did the Demonstration in which someone gave you objects to identify, you were engaging in **haptic perception**, perception in which three-dimensional objects are explored with the hand. Haptic perception provides a particularly good example of a situation in which a number of different systems are interacting with each other. As you manipulated the objects that you were trying to identify, you were using three distinct systems: (1) sensory—sensing the cutaneous sensations such as touch, temperature, and texture and the movements and positions of your fingers and hands; (2) motor—moving your fingers and hands; and (3) cognitive—thinking about the information provided by the sensory and motor systems, in order to identify the object. This is an extremely complex process (although, just as in the rest of perception, the complexity is not always apparent when it is happening) because these three systems must all be coordinated with one another. For example, the motor system's control of finger and hand movements is guided by cutaneous feelings in the fingers and the hands, by the person's sense of the positions of the fingers and hands, and by thought processes that determine what information is needed about the object in order to identify it.

We know from the example of Geerat Vermeij, the biologist, that shells can be identified with a high level of accuracy by touch alone, and psychophysical research on this process has shown that people can accurately identify most common objects within one or two seconds (Klatzky, Lederman, & Metzger, 1985). When Susan Lederman and Roberta Klatzky (1987, 1990) observed subjects' hand movements as they made these identifications, they found that people use a number of distinctive movements, which they called **exploratory procedures (EPs)**, and that the types of EPs used depend on the object qualities the subjects are asked to judge.

Four of the EPs observed by Lederman and Klatzky are shown in Figure 14.26, and the frequency with which they are used to judge different object qualities are shown in Figure 14.27. Subjects tend to use just one or two EPs to determine a particular quality. For example, people use mainly *lateral motion* and *contour following* to judge texture, and they use *enclosure* and *contour following* to judge exact shape.

One of the themes of this book is that our perceptions are influenced by the neural activity generated at the beginning of the sensory process, when the receptors are stimulated. But in our brief description of active touch, we have seen that there is more to perception than just the stimulation of receptors. For example, we saw that inexperienced braille readers identify braille characters more accurately by using active touch than by using passive touch, but experienced readers identify characters equally well by using either method. It is likely that the difference between inexperienced and experienced readers has to do both with how they scan the characters and with enhanced cognitive processing in the experienced readers (Foulke, 1991; Kruger, 1982; Pick, Thomas, & Pick, 1966).

You may also have noticed, in doing the demonstration, that it was easier to identify familiar objects than unfamiliar objects, and that, if you had trouble identifying a particular object, you were engaging in a good deal of cognitive activity as you were attempting to determine what the object was. Thus, although

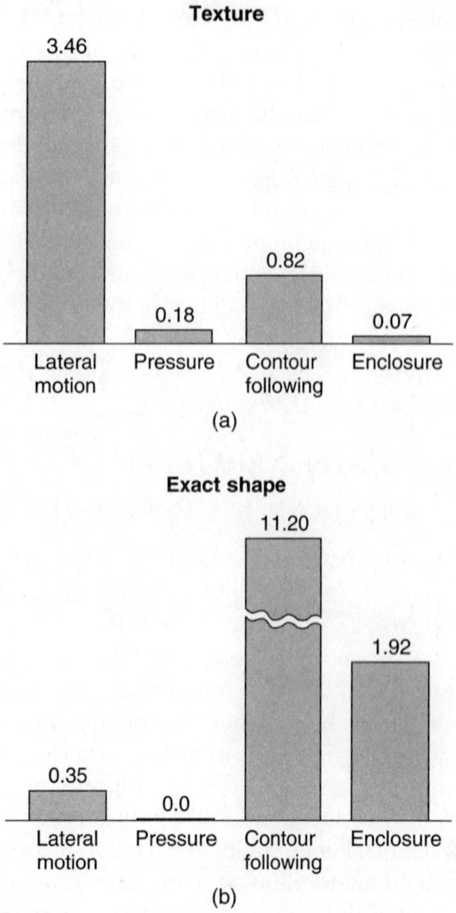

Figure 14.27
Average duration in seconds that subjects used various exploratory procedures (a) to judge texture and (b) to judge an object's exact shape. Subjects use lateral motion and contour following to judge texture. Contour following is the major exploratory procedure used to judge exact shape. (Based on data in Lederman & Klatzky, 1987.)

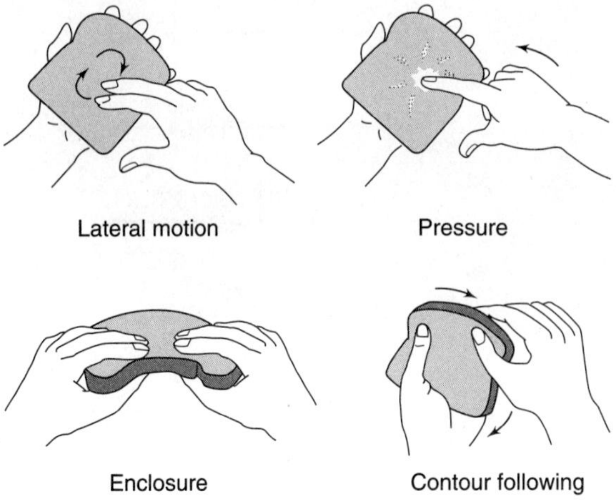

Figure 14.26
Some of the exploratory procedures (EPs) observed by Lederman and Klatzky as subjects identified objects. (From Lederman & Klatzky, 1987.)

our perceptions begin with the stimulation of receptors, they are often influenced by higher order cognitive factors. To end this chapter, we consider some examples of how people's perceptions are determined not only by signals generated by receptors in the skin but also by higher level activity, which includes thoughts, emotions, and cultural influences. We will focus our attention on pain perception, since there is a great deal of evidence that pain is affected by factors in addition to stimulation of the receptors.

Pain Perception: Neural Firing and Cognitive Influences

One of the recurring themes in this book has been the interaction between bottom-up and top-down processing. We have emphasized bottom-up processing, which begins with stimulation of the receptors. However, we have also seen that perception can be affected by factors in addition to the stimulation of the receptors. For example, in Chapter 1 we used the rat-man demonstration to show how prior experiences can influence our perceptions. First seeing Figure 1.7 causes people to perceive Figure 1.8 as a rat, whereas first seeing Figure 1.9 causes people to perceive the same stimulus as a man (page 9). For hearing we described an experiment in which observers' knowledge of a melody such as *Mary Had a Little Lamb* enabled them to perceptually separate this melody from another one that was being played simultaneously (page 363). These demonstrations plus others, which show how attentional processes can affect neural firing in vision (Figures 4.24 and 4.25) and touch (Figure 14.23) show that our perceptions can be affected by more than simply how our receptors are stimulated.

In this section, we will consider the role of both bottom-up and top-down processing in the perception of pain. We first consider the receptors in the skin that trigger pain signals and then describe examples of how cognitive activity can influence both our perception of pain and the neural signals that reach the brain.

Neural Responding and Pain Perception

Nociceptors respond to stimulation such as intense pressure, extreme temperature, or burning chemicals that can damage the skin. Figure 14.28 shows the response of a cat's nociceptor, which begins firing when the temperature reaches about 45°C, the same temperature at which a human begins to feel pain (Beck, Handwerker, & Zimmerman, 1974; Zimmerman, 1979).

The correspondence between the firing of cortical neurons that respond to pain stimuli and the animal's behavior was demonstrated by Willie Dong and coworkers (1994). They recorded from neurons in area 7b of the monkey's cortex, an area that receives inputs from the primary and secondary somatosensory

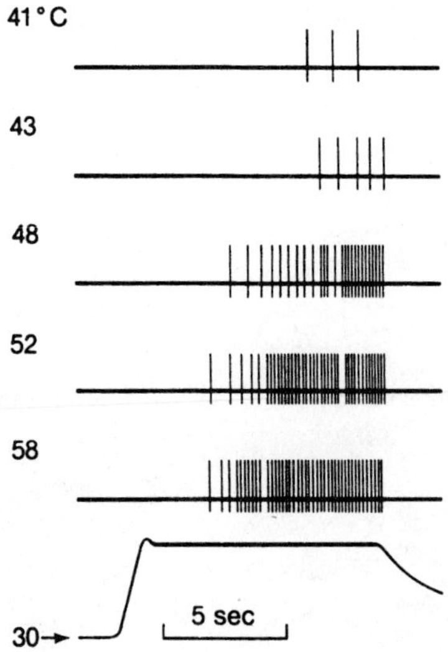

Figure 14.28
The response of a nociceptor in the cat to heating of the skin. This fiber begins firing at temperatures above about 45°C and reaches maximum firing rates above about 55°C. (From Beck, Handwerker, & Zimmerman, 1974.)

areas (SI and SII) and which contains some neurons that respond to pain stimuli.

As they heated an area on the monkey's skin, they measured how likely the monkey was to press a button that turned off the heat. The results for one monkey, shown in Figure 14.29, indicate that this neuron fired more rapidly at higher temperatures (open circles and solid line). Also, the curve for the percentage of trials on which the monkey pushed the button to turn off the heat (filled circles and dashed line) is similar to the curve for nerve firing. This correspondence between the two curves demonstrates a close relationship between the firing of neurons in the brain and the perception of pain.

We are just beginning to understand the connection between neural responding and pain perception, a connection that is made more complicated by the fact that our perception of pain depends not only on stimulation of neurons in the skin, but on more central influences, as well.

Culture, Experience, and Pain Perception

Pain provides an excellent example of a cutaneous sense that is influenced by central factors. In this section, we will show how a subject's culture and past experiences can affect their perception of pain. The effect of culture on pain perception is graphically demonstrated by rituals such as the hook-swinging ceremony practiced in some parts of India (Kosambi, 1967). This ritual is described as follows:

> The ceremony derives from an ancient practice in which a member of a social group is chosen to represent the power of the gods. The role of the chosen man (or "celebrant") is to bless the children and crops in a series of neighboring villages during a particular period of the year. What is remarkable about the ritual is that steel hooks, which are attached by strong ropes to the top of a special cart, are shoved under his skin and muscles on both sides of his back [Figure 14.30]. The cart is then moved from village to village. Usually the man hangs onto the ropes as the cart is moved about. But at the climax of the ceremony in each village, he swings free, hanging only from the hooks embedded in his back, to bless the children and crops. Astonishingly, there is no

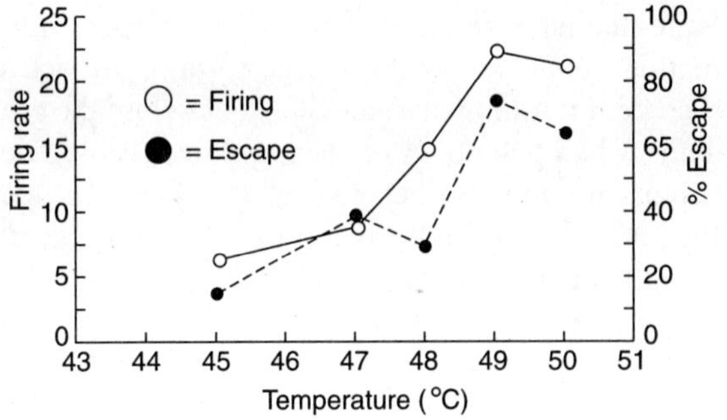

Figure 14.29
Open circles and solid line: Firing rate (left axis) of a neuron in area 7b of a monkey's cortex to heating of the skin. The firing rate increases as temperature increases. Filled circles, dashed line: Percentage of trials (right axis) on which the monkey pushed a button to escape from the stimulus. (Adapted from Dong et al., 1994.)

Figure 14.30
The "celebrant" of the Indian hook-swinging ceremony is suspended by ropes that are attached to steel hooks that pierce his back. Here, the celebrant hangs onto the ropes as a cart takes him from village to village. After he blesses each child and farm field in the village, he swings freely, suspended by the hooks in his back. (From Kosambi, 1967.)

> evidence that the man is in pain during the ritual; rather, he appears to be in a "state of exaltation." (Melzack & Wall, 1983, p. 28)

It seems unbelievable that a person could feel little or no pain while hanging from steel hooks embedded in his back, but this is apparently what happens during the hook-swinging ceremony. Perhaps the ceremony has some effect on the celebrant's mental state that prevents him from feeling pain. There are, in fact, many examples of situations in which a person's mental state affects pain perception. For example, H. K. Beecher (1972) found that morphine reduces pain that is due to pathology, such as cancer, that is often accompanied by anxiety, but doesn't reduce pain that is produced under controlled laboratory conditions, that is not accompanied by anxiety. Results such as these led Beecher to state that "Some agents are effective only in the presence of a required mental state."

Further evidence that a person's mental state affects his or her perception of pain is provided by Beecher's observation that only 25 percent of men seriously wounded in battle requested a narcotic for pain relief, whereas over 80 percent of civilians about to undergo major surgery requested pain relief. One reason for these percentages is the mental states of the patients. The civilians were upset about their surgical wounds because they associated these wounds with disturbing health problems. For the soldiers, on the other hand, their wounds had a positive aspect: they provided escape from a hazardous battlefield to the safety of a behind-the-lines hospital. In addition, the stress of the combat from which they were escaping may have also added to their apparent insensitivity to pain. We will consider why this might occur shortly.

In a hospital study, when surgical patients were told what to expect and were instructed to relax to alleviate their pain, they requested fewer painkillers following surgery and were sent home 2.7 days earlier than patients who were not provided with this information. Studies have also shown that up to 35 percent of patients with pathological pain get relief from taking a **placebo,** a pill that they believe contains painkillers but that, in fact, contains no active ingredients (Weisenberg, 1977). These examples indicate that pain perception is affected by central influences. One explanation of how this might occur is called *gate control theory.*

Gate Control Theory

Gate control theory was proposed by Ronald Melzack and Patrick Wall (1965, 1988) to explain how pain perception can be affected both by central influences, such as those described above, and by tactile stimuli, as when rubbing the skin causes a decrease in the perception of pain. The gate control system consists of cells in an area of the dorsal horn of the spinal cord called the **substantia gelatanosa,** and **transmission cells** (T-cells) located in the dorsal horn near the substantia gelatanosa (Figure 14.31a). The neural circuit containing these cells is shown in Figure 14.31b. The output of the gate control system determines pain perception, with greater activity causing greater pain. The output of the gate control system, which flows through the T-cells, is controlled by two kinds of substantia gelatanosa cells: one (SG+), which opens the pain gate by sending excitation to the T-cells, and one (SG−), which closes the pain gate by sending inhibition to the T-cells.

If only **small-diameter fibers** (S-fibers), the nociceptors we discussed earlier, are active, then pain occurs, since SG+ cells open the gate. However, when **large-diameter fibers** (L-fibers), which carry information about nonpainful tactile stimuli, are active, then pain is inhibited, since SG− cells close the gate. Thus, when potentially damaging stimuli cause nociceptors and their S-fibers to fire, the SG+ cells open the gate and pain increases. But when more gentle stimuli, such as massage, rubbing, and gentle vibration, cause activity in L-fibers, the SG− cells close the gate and pain decreases. Another way to close the gate is by sending signals from the structure labeled "Central control," which represents the brain or other higher order structures. As indicated in the circuit, signals from central control close the gate by activating SG−cells.

The idea that signals from the brain can reduce the perception of pain is supported by the results of an experiment conducted by David Reynolds (1969).

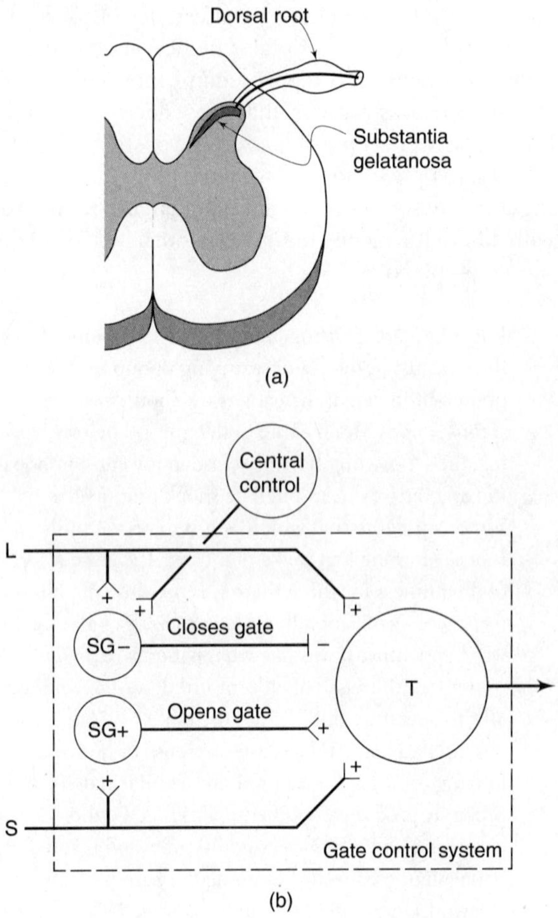

Figure 14.31
(a) Cross section of the spinal cord showing fibers entering through the dorsal root and the substantial gelatinosa (shaded) where some of the cells of Melzack and Wall's (1988) proposed gate control circuit are located. (b) The circuit proposed by Melzack and Wall for their gate control theory of pain perception.

Reynolds first showed that a rat responds vigorously then its tail or paw is pinched. He then electrically stimulated a specific area in the rat's midbrain and showed that, while the stimulation was on, the animal no longer seemed to mind having its tail or paw pinched. In fact, Reynolds was even able to perform abdominal surgery on rats with no anesthesia other than the electrical stimulation. This effect of brain stimulation, which has been confirmed in many experiments, is called **stimulation-produced analgesia** (SPA).

Gate control theory can also be applied to the pain reduction achieved by **acupuncture.** Acupuncture is the procedure practiced in China in which fine needles are inserted into the skin at certain points in the body. Twirling these needles, or passing electrical current through them, can produce **analgesia** (the elimination of pain without loss of consciousness), which makes it possible to perform major surgery in a totally awake patient (Melzack, 1973). Although the exact mechanism by which acupuncture works is still unknown, gate control theory offers the general explanation that the stimulating needles close the gate by activating L fibers or fibers descending from the brain.

Although the specific neural circuit proposed by gate control theory is not accepted by everyone (Nathan, 1976; Perl & Kruger, 1996), the idea that our perception of pain depends not only on input from nociceptors, but also on input from fibers usually not concerned with pain, and from central influences, is supported by a large amount of research. Another important development in our understanding of how central factors influence pain perception is the discovery that the nervous system contains endorphins, chemicals produced by the brain that have properties closely related to those of opiates such as morphine.

Endorphins

A family of substances called **endorphins,** endogenous (naturally occurring in the body) morphinelike substances, have been found in the nervous system, and these substances have powerful analgesic effects (Mayer, 1979; Watkins & Mayer, 1982). We can link the discovery of these naturally occurring substances to research on opiate drugs such as opium and heroin, which have been used since the dawn of recorded history to reduce pain and induce feelings of euphoria.

By the 1970s researchers had discovered that the opiate drugs acted on individual receptors in the brain, which respond to stimulation by molecules with specific structures. The importance of structure for exciting these "opiate receptors" explains why a drug called **naloxone** can have such powerful effects in counteracting the effects of heroin. Injecting a small dose of naloxone into an overdosed heroin addict can almost immediately revive the victim. The reason for this is that naloxone has a similar structure to heroin and apparently blocks the action of heroin by attaching itself to the same receptor sites as heroin.

The discovery of opiate receptors posed an important question. What were these opiate receptor sites doing in the brain? After all, they most certainly evolved long before people started taking heroin. Researchers concluded that there must be naturally occurring substances in the body that act on these sites, and in 1975 neurotransmitters were discovered that act on the same receptors that are activated by opium and heroin and are blocked by naloxone. One group of these transmitters are the pain-reducing endorphins.

Since the discovery of endorphins, researchers have accumulated a large amount of evidence linking endorphins to pain reduction. For example, stimulation-produced analgesia works best when these endorphin sites are stimulated, a finding suggesting that SPA works by releasing endorphins into the nervous system.

Further evidence linking endorphins with pain relief is provided by the fact that injection of naloxone decreases the effect of pain-reducing procedures such as acupuncture and SPA. This decreased effect would occur if naloxone were inhibiting the activity of the endorphins responsible for the effects of acupuncture and SPA. This evidence strongly suggests that the brain uses endorphins to control pain.

In addition to decreasing the effect of acupuncture and SPA, naloxone decreases the analgesic effect of placebos. Since placebos contain no active chemicals, their effects have always been thought to be "psychological." Now endorphins provide a physiological explanation of the psychological effect of placebos and, presumably, of some of the other psychological effects we have discussed.

Finally, let's consider another effect that may involve endorphins: **stress-induced analgesia,** a decrease in sensitivity to pain that occurs in stressful situations. There is experimental evidence that animals' pain thresholds are raised by stress (Jessell & Kelly, 1991), and there is anecdotal evidence, such as the reports of soldiers who report feeling little pain in response to serious wounds, that stress decreases pain in humans as well. A possible example of stress-induced analgesia is provided by African explorer David Livingstone's description of a dramatic encounter he had with a lion during one of his early journeys to find the source of the Nile:

> I hear a shout. Starting, and looking half round, I saw the lion just in the act of springing upon me. I was upon a little height; he caught my shoulder as he sprang, and we both came to the ground below together. Growling horribly close to my ear, he shook me as a terrier does a rat. The shock produced a stupor similar to that which seems to be felt by a mouse after the first shake of the cat. It caused a sort of dreaminess in which there was no sense of pain nor feeling of terror, though quite conscious of all that was happening. It was like what patients partially under the influence of chloroform describe, who see all the operation but feel not the knife. . . . The shake annihilated fear, and allowed no sense of horror in looking round at the beast. This peculiar state is probably produced in all animals killed by the carnivora; and if so, is a merciful provision by our benevolent creator for lessening the pain of death. (David Livingstone, *Missionary Travels,* 1857; quoted in Jessell & Kelly, 1991, p. 398)

This example of a possible central influence on pain perception emphasizes the complexity of the processes involved in the perception of pain. In this chapter, we have only scratched the surface of this complexity, both for pain and for the other cutaneous senses. We know quite a bit about how receptors are stimulated, how they respond, and how they send their signals along various pathways on their way to the brain. However, we know much less about processes that occur later in the system, such as the neural processing that occurs in the somatosensory cortex. As we consider the chemical senses of olfaction and taste in the next chapter, we will experience an analogous situation, as we see that we know far more about responses that occur near the beginning of the system than we do about responses that occur as we move toward the cortex.

Something to Consider: Do All People Experience Pain in the Same Way?

People often wonder how their perceptions compare to other people's perceptions. In this section we consider the idea that there may be differences between different people's perceptual experiences, but since all perceptual experience is private, we have no way of really knowing what other people are experiencing.

From what we have learned about perception so far, we know that it is likely that different people perceive things differently. We know, for example, that some people's vision is color-deficient, because they are missing a cone visual pigment (page 150), that even people with normal color vision may perceive colors differently because of subtle differences in the absorption spectra of their visual pigments (page 143), and that people with disabilities such as deafness or blindness may have enhanced powers of perception in their remaining senses (page 377).

But while evidence such as this allows us to conclude that two people may have different perceptual experiences to the same stimuli, can we ever know whether two people are having exactly the *same* perceptual experience? The answer to this question is that we have no way to tell whether two people are having identical perceptual experiences, because perception is a private experience (see page 152).

The idea that perceptions are private experiences is true of all of the senses but is particularly true of pain. We can appreciate why this is so by returning to color vision. If someone says "That looks blue to me" and both you and the other person have trichromatic color vision, you have at least an approximate idea of what seeing "blue" probably means to the other person. If, however, the person says, "That hurts a lot," what do you know about their experience? "Hurting a lot" can describe a wide variety of experiences even for yourself, so how can you begin to know what it means for someone else? Let's consider some of the reasons that people find it difficult to relate to other people's reported pain experiences.

1. *Pain can occur in the absence of outward stimulation.* Although outward stimulation is sometimes present, as when a person hits their finger with a hammer, pain can occur even if no external stimulus is present. Headaches, the ache of a bad back, and the pain of terminal cancer all come from within. One of the most dramatic examples of pain from within is provided by the **phantom limb** phenomenon, which is reported by people who have had a limb amputated. These people not only experience the missing limb as still being present but may also report feeling pain in the phantom limb (Melzack, 1992).
2. *Pain is influenced by factors other than tissue damage.* We have already seen that pain can be influenced by factors such as a person's emotions, expectations, and level of stress. Thus, when two people are exposed to exactly the same external stimulus, it is possible for one person to experience intense pain while the other experiences little or no pain.
3. *People describe the same stimulus differently.* To show that different people describe the same stimulus differently, Clark and Clark (1980) presented electric shocks to a group of Western subjects and to a group of Nepalese subjects and asked them to indicate the intensities at which they experienced "faint pain" and "extreme pain." Although the Westerners and the Nepalese began detecting the shocks at the same intensity, the Nepalese subjects required much higher stimulus intensities before they said they experienced "faint pain" and "extreme pain" (Figure 14.32). Was this result due to the Nepalese subjects' lower sensitivity to the shocks, or did it simply mean that the Nepalese were more conservative responders?

   Analyzing these results by means of a procedure based on signal detection theory (see

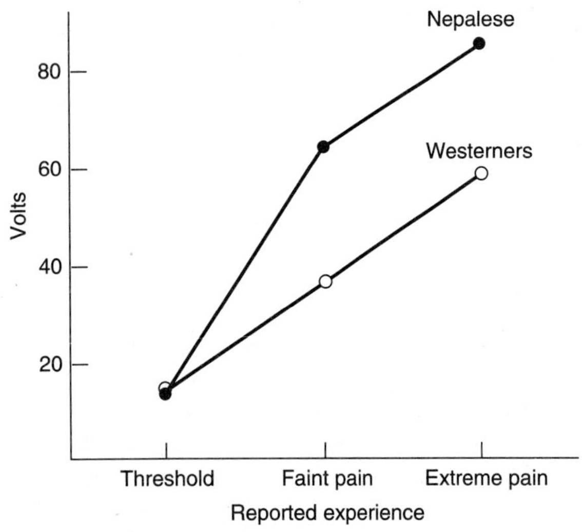

Figure 14.32
Results of the Clark and Clark (1980) experiment, which shows that the threshold for detecting a shock was the same for the Western subjects and the Nepalese subjects, but that the Nepalese subjects took much higher levels of shock before reporting "faint pain" or "extreme pain."

Appendix) indicated that there was probably no difference in the way both groups of subjects experienced the intensity of the shocks. Apparently the Nepalese subjects withstood higher levels of pain before reaching what they considered faint pain or extreme pain. It may be that Nepalese culture teaches people to withstand pain without complaining. A similar result was obtained by Evelyn Hall and Simon Davies (1991), who had female varsity track athletes and female nonathletes rate their level of pain in response to immersion of their hands in freezing ice water. Although both groups were exposed to the same stimulus, the athletes rated their pain as less intense (their average rating was 76 on a 150-point pain scale) than the nonathletes (whose average was 130). Perhaps the athletes had learned, during painful training workouts, to withstand higher levels of pain.

4. *Pain may mean different things to different people.* The idea that "pain" may signify different perceptual qualities to different people is supported by the following statement by Katherine Foley, Director of Pain Services at Memorial Sloan-Kettering Cancer Center in New York: "I believe that when a person tells you there is pain, they are telling you there is discomfort. But it may not be a physical pain; it may be a metaphor for anxiety or depression or spiritual suffering. We use 'pain' for physical and emotional distress, and sometimes people don't make the distinction very well" (quoted in Rosenthal, 1992, p. B6).

All of these examples illustrate why pain is so difficult to describe or to compare between people, and why it is therefore perhaps the most private of our senses. But remember that we have no way of knowing exactly what other people are experiencing, not only for pain, but for all of the other senses, as well.

PICTURE PERCEPTION BY TOUCH

How do people who have been blind from birth relate to drawings? John M. Kennedy (1993, 1997) and Morton Heller (1989) have researched this question by considering how blind people draw and how they interpret raised-line drawings that they sense by touch. They report that some people who have been blind from a young age can draw depictions of objects in the environment and that some blind people can be quite skilled at identifying raised-line outline drawings.

Heller had subjects who were congenitally blind (blind from birth), late blind (blind after having some visual experience), and sighted (normal vision but wearing a blindfold) feel raised line drawings like the ones in Figure 14.33. The congenitally blind and sighted subjects performed poorly, but the late-blind subjects identified a third of the pictures correctly (Figure 14.34a). The performance of the late-blind subjects indicates that some information about pictures can be taken in by touch.

When Heller presented the names of objects and asked the same subjects to try to figure out which name best described each picture, their performance improved dramatically, with the late blind subjects identifying almost all of the pictures correctly (Figure 14.34b). The superior performance of

Figure 14.33
Pictures of the raised-line drawings that Heller presented to blind and sighted subjects. (From Heller, 1989.)

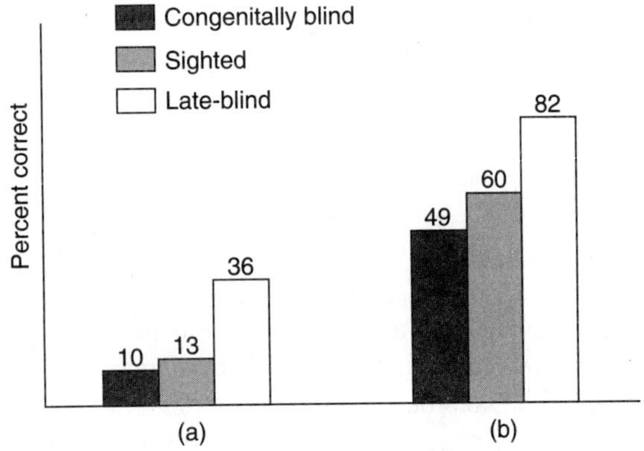

Figure 14.34
The results of Heller's experiments. (a) Performance when subjects were asked to identify raised line drawings by touch. (b) Performance when subjects were asked to match the picture to a description.

the late-blind subjects illustrates the benefits of combining visual experience with significant experience with tactile pattern perception. Based on the results of his experiments, Heller suggests that spatial perception may not be inherently visual or tactual. He suggests that perhaps spatial understanding is *amodal*—it involves general perceptual skills rather than ones that are specifically visual or tactile.

Kennedy (1997) came to a similar conclusion based on the results of experiments in which he tested blind subjects' ability to sense pictures tactually. In one of these experiments, he had blind subjects feel the series of contours in Figure 14.35. The subjects interpreted the raised edges that were near one another (the ones on the left) as being a single boundary between two surfaces, but they interpreted the edges that were far apart (the ones on the right), as being two separate surfaces. The significance of this result is that it corresponds to the perception most sighted people experience with their sense of vision.

Perhaps, suggests Kennedy, there is an amodal region of the brain that receives inputs from both vision and touch and which interprets contours in the same way, whether they are generated by a visual stimulus or a tactile stimulus. The function of this region would be to help people coordinate incoming information from both senses.

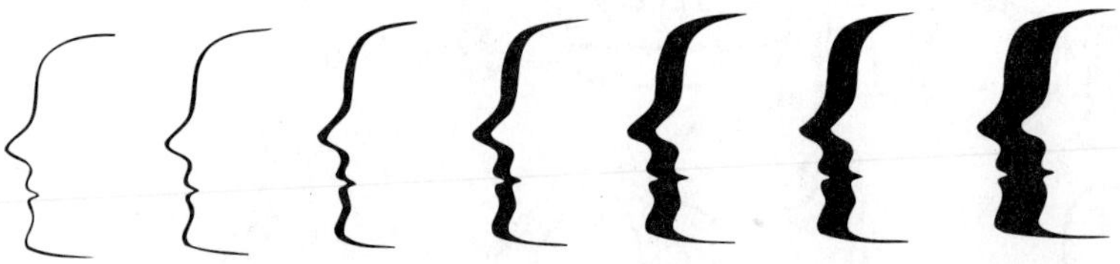

Figure 14.35
Pictures of raised-line contours presented to blind subjects. (From Kennedy, 1997.)

Study Questions

Underlying Principles

Find examples of the following principles in this chapter:

- Selective receptors (411)
- Receptive fields/neural selectivity (422)
- Distributed response (415)
- Neural maps (419)
- Columnar organization (419)
- Parallel pathways (409)
- Physiology-perception connection (426)
- Cognition-perception connection (427)
- Perceptual grouping (406)
- Effect of context on perception (428)

1. Describe the braille system of reading. How fast can experienced braille readers read compared to the average visual reader? (406)
2. What would be some of the consequences of losing the ability to feel sensations through the skin? (406)

Anatomy of the Somatosensory System

3. What is the somatosensory system? (407)
4. What is one of the main functions of the skin? (407)
5. Describe the layers of the skin and the four major receptor structures found in the skin. (408)
6. Describe the pathway that nerve fibers follow from the time they leave the receptors until they reach the cortex. (409)

The Psychophysics and Physiology of Tactile Perception

7. Describe the four psychophysical channels for tactile perception. What stimulus dimension is used to differentiate between them and what perceptions are associated with them? (410)
8. Describe the four neural channels for tactile perception. What receptors are associated with each channel and what stimuli do they respond to? (411)
9. What is the connection between the psychophysical and the neural channels for tactile perception? (412)
10. How does the Pacinian corpuscle determine the type of stimulation to which its fiber responds? The PC channel is specialized to respond to what type of stimulation? (412)
11. The SA1 channel is specialized to respond to what type of stimulation? Describe the experiments using raised-dot patterns rolled over the fingers that demonstrated this. (413)
12. What is a spatial event plot? What do spatial event plots tell us about why some letters can be identified accurately and others not? (413)
13. Which types of fibers would fire in response to running the fingers over a textured surface? (415)
14. What is a thermoreceptor? A warm fiber? A cold fiber? (415)

Neural Processing of Tactile Stimuli

15. What is the two point threshold? How does it differ on different parts of the body? (416)

16. What is the relationship between the size of the two-point threshold and the size of receptive fields of RA1 and SA1 fibers? The density of RA1 and SA1 fibers? (418)

17. What is the relationship between the size of the two-point threshold and the size of receptive fields of cortical neurons? (418)

18. What is the relationship between tactile acuity for different parts of the body and the amount of space allotted to those parts of the body in the cortex? (418)

19. Compare the magnification factor for tactile perception to the magnification factor for visual perception. What is the homunculus? (418)

20. What do we mean when we say that there are columns in the somatosensory cortex and that there are multiple maps of the body in the somatosensory cortex? Why would these multiple maps exist? (419)

21. How does (a) reducing stimulation of the skin and (b) increasing stimulation of the skin affect cortical maps? What does this tell us about the sensory homunculus? (419)

22. Compare the receptive fields of neurons in the skin to the receptive fields of neurons in the cortex. (421)

23. Compare cutaneous receptive fields and visual receptive fields. (421)

24. Describe Hsiao's experiment that showed that the response of neurons in the monkey's somatosensory cortex is influenced by the monkey's attentional state. (421)

25. Describe the neuron that responds when stimulation results from an animal's own actions but does not respond to stimulation by the experimenter. (422)

Active Touch

26. What are some differences in the *experience* of active and passive touch? (423)

27. What other differences are there between active and passive touch? (423)

28. What is the evidence that active touch is better than passive touch for identifying objects? What are the results of experiments comparing active and passive touch as used by experienced braille readers? (423)

29. What is haptic perception? What three systems come into play when an object is being identified using haptic perception? (424)

30. What are exploratory procedures and how do they differ for different object qualities? (424)

Pain Perception: Neural Firing and Cognitive Influences

31. What is a nociceptor? Under what conditions does a nociceptor fire? (426)

32. Describe neurons in the monkey's cortex that respond to heating the skin. How did Dong relate the firing of these neurons to the monkey's perception of pain? (426)

33. What are some examples of situations in which the perception of pain is determined by factors in addition to stimulation of receptors in the skin? (427)

34. Describe gate control theory. Which types of fibers are responsible for opening the gate? For closing the gate? What stimuli are responsible for opening and closing the gate? (428)

35. What is stimulation-produced analgesia and why is it important? (429)

36. How would gate control theory explain analgesia achieved through acupuncture? (429)

37. What are endorphins? Under what conditions would they affect the perception of pain? (429)

38. What is stress-induced analgesia? (430)

Something to Consider: Do All People Experience Pain in the Same Way?

39. What do we mean when we say that perception is a private experience? (431)

40. What are some reasons that people find it difficult to relate to other people's reported pain experiences? (431)

41. Describe the experiments comparing how Western subjects and Nepalese subjects report their experience of pain, and how athletes and nonathletes report their experience of pain. (431)

Across the Senses: Picture Perception by Touch

42. Is it possible for people who are blind from birth to draw pictures of objects in the environment? (433)
43. How well do congenitally blind, late blind and sighted subjects identify raised line drawings by touch? What does this result mean? (433)
44. What did Heller do that increased the performance of the subjects in 43, above? What does the superior performance of the late-blind subjects indicate? What does Heller conclude about the nature of spatial perception? (433)
45. Describe Kennedy's experiment in which he had blind subjects feel raised-edge contours. What is the significance of his result? What does Kennedy suggest about a possible brain mechanism for vision and touch? (434)

15

The Chemical Senses

Chapter Contents

Some Questions We Will Consider

- Why is a dog's sense of smell so much better than a human's? (441)
- Why does a cold inhibit the ability to taste? (451)
- Why is ammonia irritating and why do chili peppers burn? (463)

This chapter introduces olfaction (smell) and taste, two senses that respond to chemical stimuli. The sense of smell creates perceptions in response to gaseous molecules that contact receptors in the nose; the sense of taste creates perceptions in response to liquid molecules that contact receptors in the mouth. These senses have been called *molecule detectors* because they endow these gas and liquid molecules with distinctive smells and tastes (Cain, 1988; Kauer, 1987).

In this chapter, as in the ones preceding it, we are interested in examining commonalties between the senses. But we are also interested in what is unique about olfaction and taste. One of their most unique properties is that the stimuli responsible for tasting and smelling are on the verge of being assimilated into the body, solids or liquids through the mouth and gasses through the nose (Scott & Giza, 1995). As a result, taste and smell are often seen as "gatekeepers," which function (1) to detect things that would be bad for the body and that should therefore be rejected, and (2) to identify things that the body needs for survival and that should therefore be consumed.

This gatekeeper function is aided by the large affective, or emotional, component of taste and smell, since things that are bad for us often taste or smell unpleasant, and things that are good for us generally taste good. In addition to assigning "good" and "bad" affect, smelling an odor associated with a past place or event can trigger memories, which in turn may create emotional reactions.

A unique property of olfactory and taste systems that is related to the fact that they are constantly exposed not only to the chemicals that they are designed to sense, but also to irritants such as bacteria and dirt, is that the receptors in the olfactory and taste systems undergo a cycle of birth, development, and death over a 5 to 7 week period (Figure 15.1). This constant renewal of the receptors, which is called **neurogenesis,** is unique to the senses. In vision, hearing, and the cutaneous senses, the receptors are safely protected inside structures such as the eye, the inner ear, and under the skin, however, the receptors for taste and smell are relatively unprotected and need a mechanism for renewal.

Olfaction and taste are served by two separate systems and appear to operate according to different principles.

We treat olfaction first and then taste. Although we will be considering olfaction and taste separately, we will see that they often interact. Thus, as you savor the "taste" of something you are eating, you probably, in fact, are experiencing a combination of taste and smell. We will have more to say about this combined experience, which is called *flavor,* when we begin our discussion of taste in the second part of the chapter.

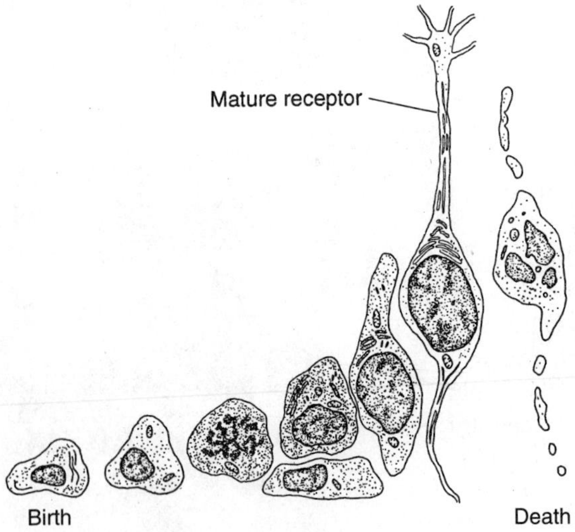

Figure 15.1
Neurogenesis of an olfactory receptor. A unique feature of smell and taste, compared to the other senses, is the way the receptors for smell and taste develop and then die over a 5 to 7 week period. The mature receptor develops from the cell on the left and then dies, as shown on the right. (From Graziadei, 1976.)

Olfaction: Uses and Facts

Olfaction is extremely important in the lives of many species, since it is often their primary window to the environment (Ache, 1991). One important contrast between humans and other species is that many animals are **macrosmatic** (having a keen sense of smell that is important to their survival), whereas humans are **microsmatic** (having a less keen sense of smell that is not crucial to their survival). The survival value of olfaction for many animals lies in their use of olfaction to provide cues to orient themselves in space, to mark territory, and to guide them to specific places, other animals, and food sources (Holley, 1991). Olfaction is also extremely important in sexual reproduction, since it triggers mating behavior in many species (Doty, 1976; Pfeiffer & Johnston, 1994).

Although smell may not be crucial to the survival of humans, the vast sums of money spent yearly on perfumes and deodorants, as well as the emergence of a new billion-dollar-a-year industry called *environmental fragrancing,* which offers products to add pleasing scents to the air in both homes and businesses, attests to the fact that the role of smell in our daily lives is not inconsequential (Owens, 1994).

But perhaps the most convincing argument for the importance of smell to humans comes from those who suffer from **anosmia,** the loss of the ability to smell due to injury or infection. People suffering from anosmia describe the great void created by their inability to taste many foods because of the close connection between smell and flavor. One woman who suffered from anosmia and then briefly regained her sense of smell stated, "I always thought I would sacrifice smell to taste if I had to choose between the two, but I suddenly realized how much I had missed. We take it for granted and are unaware that *everything* smells: people, the air, my house, my skin" (Birnberg, 1988; quoted in Ackerman, 1990, p. 42). Olfaction is more important in our lives than most of us realize, and while it may not be essential to our survival, life is often enhanced by our ability to smell and becomes a little more dangerous if we lose the olfactory warning system that alerts us to spoiled food, leaking gas, or smoke from a fire.

The powers of the human olfactory system have often been underrated, especially when human olfactory capabilities are compared to the olfactory powers of other animals. Let's consider some facts that put our olfactory abilities into perspective:

- Fact 1: *Although humans are less sensitive than many other animals to odors, our olfactory receptors are exquisitely sensitive.* Rats are 8 to 50 times more sensitive to odors than humans, and dogs are from 300 to 10,000 times more sensitive, depending on the odorant (Laing, Doty, & Breipohl, 1991). But even though other animals can detect odors that humans are unaware of, the human's *individual* olfactory receptors are as sensitive as any animals'. H. deVries and M. Stuiver (1961) demonstrated this by showing that human olfactory receptors can be excited by the action of just one molecule of odorant. Nothing can be more sensitive than one molecule per receptor, so the human's lower sensitivity to odors compared to that of other animals must be due to something else. That something else is the *number* of receptors: only about 10 million in humans compared to about 1 billion in dogs (Dodd & Squirrell, 1980; Moulton, 1977).

- Fact 2: *Humans are capable of detecting small differences in odor intensity.* The ability to detect differences in intensity is indicated by the difference threshold—the smallest difference in intensity between two stimuli that can just be detected (see Chapter 1). In the past, olfaction has been reputed to have the largest difference threshold of all the senses, with typical values ranging from about 25 to 33 percent (Gamble, 1898; Stone & Bosley, 1965). That is, the concentration of an odorant must be increased by 25 to 33 percent before a person can detect an increase in odor intensity.

  When William Cain (1977) carefully measured the difference threshold by placing two odorants of different concentrations on absorbent cotton balls and asking subjects to judge which was more intense, his results were better than those of most other studies, with an average difference threshold of 19 percent and a relatively low difference threshold of 7 percent for *n*-butyl alcohol. But Cain didn't stop with these measurements, because an average difference threshold of 19 percent still seemed high to him. He next analyzed the stimuli he had presented to his human subjects using a **gas chromatograph,** a device that accurately measures the concentration of the vapor emitted by each stimulus. Cain found what he had suspected: Stimuli that were supposed to have the same concentration actually varied considerably, apparently because of differences in the airflow pattern through the cotton in different samples.

  By eliminating this variability in stimulus concentration, Cain was able to demonstrate that the difference threshold was smaller than had been previously measured. When he presented stimuli to subjects by using an **olfactometer,** a device that presents olfactory stimuli with much greater precision than cotton balls, Cain found an average difference threshold of 11 percent, with *n*-butyl alcohol having an impressively low threshold of only 5 percent. These figures, which begin to approach the difference thresholds for vision and hearing, show that our ability to detect differences in smell intensity is, in fact, not that poor compared to the other senses.

- Fact 3: *Although it is often difficult to recognize some odors, the ability to do this improves with training.* Although humans can tell the difference between approximately 10,000 different odors (Axel, 1995), early research on odor identification seemed to indicate that our ability to name specific odors is poor, because when asked to identify odors people were typically successful only about half the time (Engen & Pfaffmann, 1960). However, later experiments showed that, under the right conditions, our ability to identify odors is actually quite a bit better than that. For example, J. A. Desor and Gary K. Beauchamp (1974) found that subjects could identify only about half of the smells of familiar substances like coffee, bananas, and motor oil. But when Desor and Beauchamp named the substances when they were first presented and then reminded their subjects of the correct names when they failed to respond correctly on subsequent trials, the subjects could, after some practice, correctly identify 98 percent of the substances.

According to Cain (1979, 1980), the key to the good performance in Desor and Beauchamp's experiment is that their subjects were provided with the correct names, or labels, at the beginning of the experiment. In his own experiments, Cain showed that when subjects assign a correct label to a familiar object the first time they smell it (for example, labeling an orange "orange"), or when the experimenter provides the correct labels, the subjects usually identify the object correctly the next time it is presented. When, however, subjects assign an incorrect label to an object the first time they smell it (for example, labeling machine oil as "cheese"), they usually misidentify it the next time it is presented. Thus, according to Cain, when we have trouble identifying odors, this trouble results not from a deficiency in our olfactory system, but from an inability to retrieve the odor's name from our memory.

The amazing thing about the role that memory plays in odor identification is that knowing the correct label for the odor actually seems to transform our perception into that odor. Cain (1980) gives the example of an object initially identified by the subject as "fishy-goaty-oily." When the experimenter tells the subject that the fishy-goaty-oily smell actually comes from leather, the smell is then transformed into that of leather. I recently had a similar experience when a friend gave me a bottle of Aquavit, a Danish drink with a very interesting smell. As I was sampling this drink with some friends, we tried to identify its smell. Many odors were proposed ("anise," "orange," "lemon"), but it wasn't until someone turned the bottle around and read the label on the back that the truth became known: "Aquavit (Water of Life) is the Danish national drink—a delicious, crystal-clear spirit distilled from grain, with a slight taste of caraway." When we heard the word *caraway*, the previous hypotheses of anise, orange, and lemon were instantly transformed into caraway. Thus, the olfactory system has the information needed to identify specific odors, but needs assistance from memory to apply that information to the actual naming of these odors.

DEMONSTRATION

Naming and Odor Identification

To demonstrate the effect of naming substances on odor identification, have a friend collect a number of familiar objects for you, and without looking, try to identify the odors. You will find that you can identify some but not others, and when your friend tells you the correct answer for the ones you identified incorrectly, you will wonder how you could have failed to identify such a familiar smell. But don't blame your mistakes on your nose; blame them on your memory. ●

- Fact 4: *Human olfaction has the potential to provide information about other people.* Many animals use their sense of smell to recognize other animals. As McKenzie (1923) remarked about the dog, "He can recognize his master by sight, no doubt, yet, as we know, he is never perfectly satisfied until he has taken stock also of the scent, the more precisely to do so bringing his snout into actual contact with the person he is examining. It is as if his eyes might deceive him, but never his nose." Humans, however, are socially constrained from behaving like dogs. Except in the most intimate situations, it is considered poor form to smell other people at close range. However, what if we lived in a society that condoned this kind of behavior? Could we identify other people based on their smell? A recent experiment suggests that the answer to this question may be "yes."

Michael Russell (1976) had subjects wear undershirts for 24 hours, without showering or using deodorant or perfume. The undershirts were then sealed in a bag and given to the experimenter, who, in turn, presented each subject with three undershirts to smell: One was the subject's own shirt, one was a male's, and one was a female's. About three-quarters of the subjects succeeded in identifying their own undershirt, based on its odor, and also correctly identified which of the other shirts had been worn by males or females (see also McBurney, Levine, & Cavanaugh, 1977). Similar results have also been reported for breath odors, which subjects can identify as being produced by a male or a female (Doty et al., 1982). It has also been shown that young infants can identify the smell of their mother's breast or armpits (Cernoch & Porter, 1985; Macfarlane, 1975). These results don't suggest that people can identify other people solely by their smell, but they do show that our ability to use smell in such situations may be underrated.

The phenomenon of **menstrual synchrony** also suggests a role for smell in interpersonal relations. Martha McClintock (1971) noted that women who live or work together often report that their menstrual periods begin at about the same time. For example, one group of seven female lifeguards had widely scattered menstrual periods at the beginning of the summer, but by the end of the summer, all were beginning their periods within four days of each other. To investigate this phenomenon, McClintock asked 135 females, aged 17 to 22, living in a college dormitory, to indicate when their periods began throughout the school year. She found that women who saw each other often (roommates or close friends) tended to have synchronous periods by the end of the school year. After eliminating other explanations such as awareness of the other person's period, McClintock concluded that "there is some interpersonal physiological process which affects the menstrual cycle" (p. 246).

What might this physiological process be? Michael Russell, G. M. Switz, and K. Thompson (1980) conducted an experiment that suggests that smell has something to do with this process. He had a "donor" woman wear cotton pads in her armpits for 24 hours, three times a week. The sweat extracted from these pads was then rubbed onto the upper lip of a woman in the experimental group. A control group of women received the same treatment, but without the sweat. The results for the experimental group showed that, before the experiment there had been an average of 9.3 days between the onset of the donor's and the subject's periods, but after five months, the average time between onsets was reduced to 3.4 days. The control group showed no such synchrony. Since the donors and the subjects in the experimental group never saw each other, Russell concluded that odor must be the factor that causes menstrual synchrony (also see Preti et al., 1986).

From these facts about olfaction, it is clear that the human olfactory system has capacities that are more impressive than often believed. We will now describe some of the physiological properties of olfaction.

The Olfactory System

To introduce the olfactory system, we will describe the anatomy of the receptors that generate electrical signals from olfactory stimuli and the central destination of these signals.

The Olfactory Mucosa

The picture in Figure 15.2 is not an underwater coral reef or vegetation on the forest floor. It is a picture of the surface of the **olfactory mucosa,** the dime-sized region located high in the nasal cavity which contains the receptors for olfaction and is therefore where transduction occurs. Figure 15.3a shows the location of the mucosa, on the roof of the nasal cavity and just below the **olfactory bulb,** which is actually

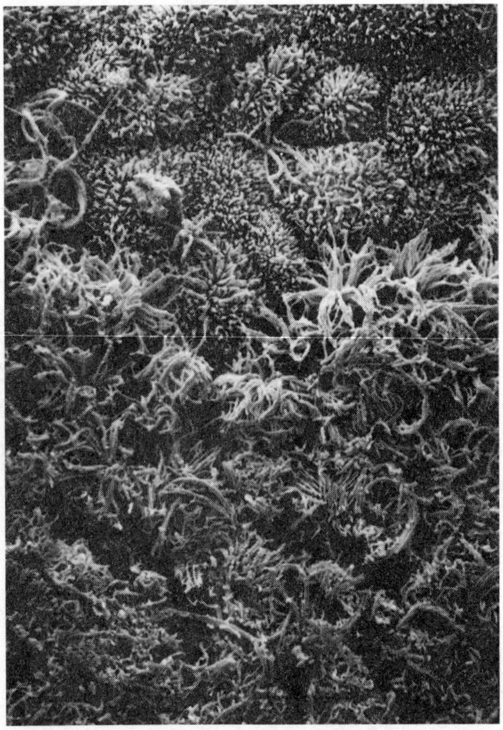

Figure 15.2
A scanning electron micrograph of the surface of the olfactory mucosa. The region in the foreground is densely covered with the cilia of olfactory receptors. (From Morrison & Moran, 1995.)

an outcropping of the brain. (Figures 15.3a and b). If we zoom in on the mucosa, we can see that it contains **olfactory receptor neurons** and supporting cells (Figure 15.3c), and looking at the ends of the neurons reveals cilia. Figure 15.3d shows a close-up of just two cilia, although each receptor neuron contains many more than that.

The cilia are the place where the odorant molecules contact the receptor neurons. The cilia contain **olfactory receptor proteins,** which are the active sites for olfaction. Odorant molecules reach these active sites in two ways: (1) by flowing directly to the site in inhaled air; and (2) by binding to molecules called **olfactory binding proteins (OBP)** that are secreted into the nasal cavity and which transport the odorant molecules to the receptor sites (Figure 15.3d) (Pevsner et al., 1985, 1990).

When the odorants reach the active sites, the olfactory receptor protein triggers a series of reactions that lead to the opening of ion channels in the membrane. This process is shown schematically in Figure 15.3e. When the ion channels open, ion flow occurs across the membrane and the flow of ions across the membrane causes an electrical signal in the cilium (Firestein, 1992; Lancet, 1992; Reed et al., 1992; Shepherd, 1992a, 1992b). This signal is transmitted to the rest of the olfactory receptor neurons and into its axon, which transmits the signal toward the olfactory bulb of the brain in the olfactory nerve.

A closeup of the olfactory receptor protein is shown in Figure 15.3f. This protein molecule consists of strings of amino acids (circles) that cross the membrane of the olfactory receptor neuron seven times. There are many different types of receptor proteins, each made up of different sequences of amino acids. You may remember that the visual pigment molecule in the visual receptors also crosses the membrane seven times (see Figure 2.18). Olfaction and vision both have active molecules in their receptors that come from the same molecular family (Buck & Axel, 1991; Shepherd, 1994).

Receptor Proteins, Receptor Neurons, and Glomeruli

What happens to the electrical signals that are generated in the olfactory receptor neuron? Figure 15.4 shows how the receptor neurons are organized in relation to the olfactory bulb. Our knowledge of the way these receptor neurons and their associated receptor proteins are organized in the olfactory system has recently benefited from new genetic techniques that make use of the fact that olfactory receptor proteins are created from instructions coded in genes. By combining these new genetic techniques with conventional anatomical techniques, it has been possible to show that there are a large number of different types of receptor proteins and receptor neurons. It has also been possible to show that the olfactory system is organized so that (1) each receptor neuron contains

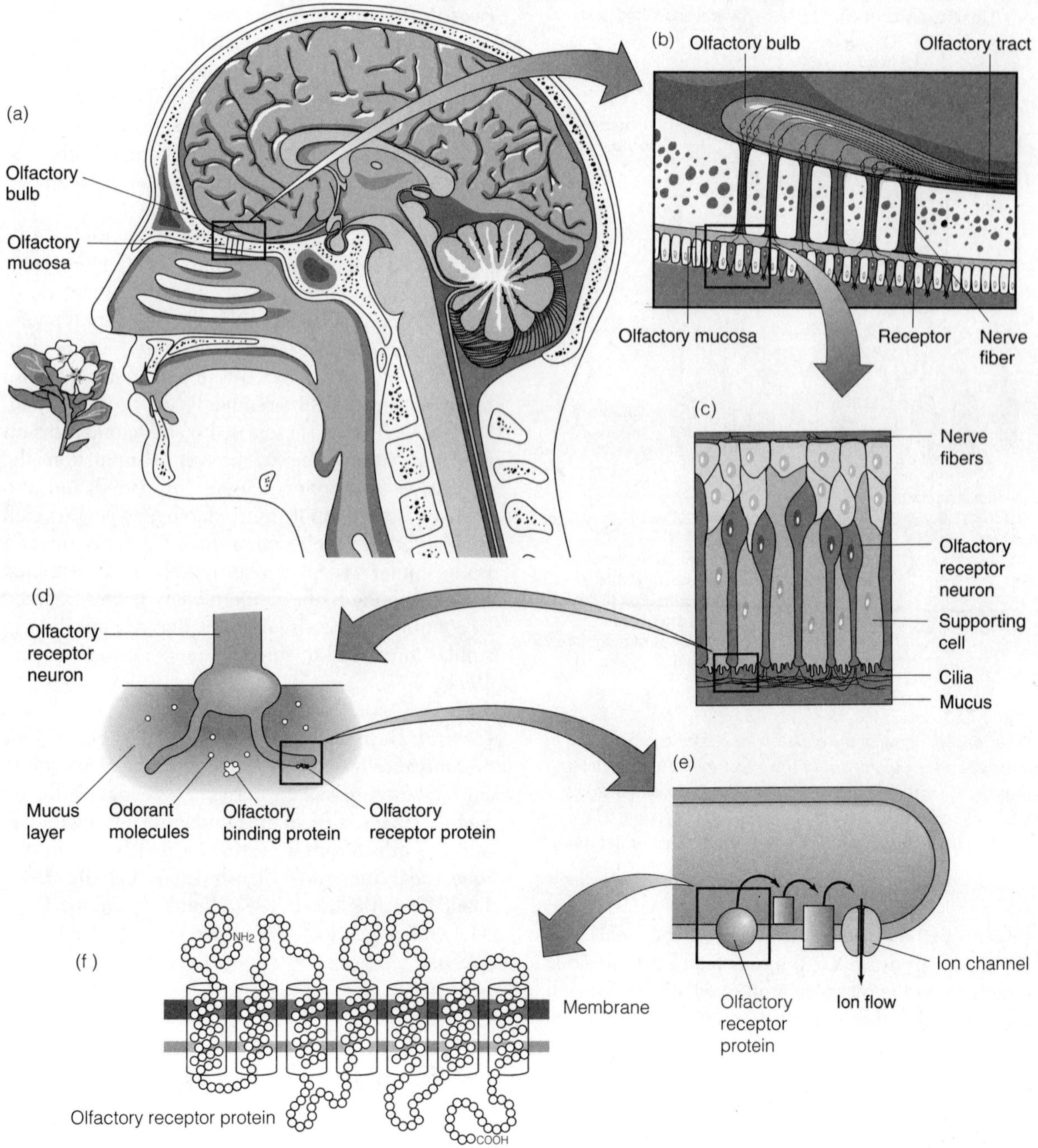

Figure 15.3
Zooming in from the olfactory mucosa to the olfactory receptor proteins.

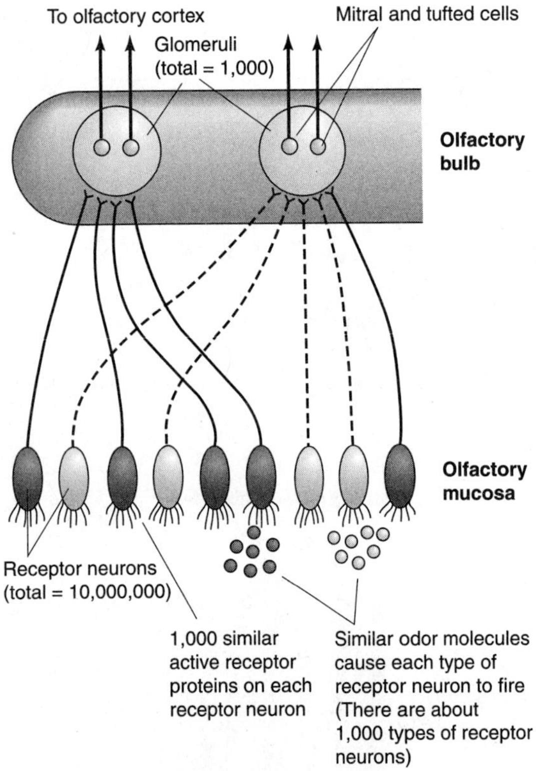

Figure 15.4
Relationship between the olfactory receptor neurons in the mucosa and the glomeruli in the olfactory bulb. The fact that there are different types of receptor neurons is symbolized by shaded and unshaded neurons in the figure. There are actually about 1,000 different types of receptor neurons.

proteins that react to the same type of chemicals, and (2) signals from similar neurons feed into the same structures in the olfactory bulb (Axel, 1995). We will now describe this organization, starting with the smallest units, the receptor proteins.

Receptor Proteins Using gene cloning techniques, it has been possible to identify about 1,000 different genes, each of which specifies a type of receptor protein. This genetic research has led to the conclusion that there are 1,000 different types of receptor proteins, each of which responds to a small group of odorants (Axel, 1995).

Receptor Neurons There are about 10,000,000 receptor neurons in the olfactory system. There are about 1,000 different types of these receptor neurons, with each type containing about 1,000 similar receptor proteins. (Compare this to the visual system, which contains 3 different types of cones with each type containing millions of similar cone pigments.)

Glomeruli There are about 1,000 structures called glomeruli in the olfactory bulb. Each glomerulus receives inputs mainly from one particular type of receptor neuron. For example, all of the inputs reaching the glomerulus on the left in Figure 15.4 are identical receptor neurons. But many glomeruli also receive some inputs from other types of receptor neurons, as well. This is indicated by the glomerulus on the right, which receives most of its input from the same type of receptor neurons (unshaded) but also receives some input from another type, as well (shaded). Since each glomerulus collects information from similar receptor neurons about a restricted group of odorants, the glomeruli have been compared to columns in the visual cortex that respond best to similar forms and to similar orientations (Shepherd, 1994).

Central Destinations Neurons called *mitral cells* and *tufted cells* transmit signals from the glomeruli to the olfactory areas of the cortex. These include the **olfactory cortex,** a small area under the temporal lobe, and the **orbitofrontal cortex,** located in the frontal lobe, near the eyes (Figure 15.5) (Cinelli, 1993; Dodd & Castellucci, 1991; Frank & Rabin, 1989; McLean & Shipley, 1992; Price et al., 1991; Takagi, 1980).

Odor: Stimulus and Quality

The stimuli for olfaction are molecules in the air. Thus, smelling any object or substance is based on molecules that have traveled from the object or

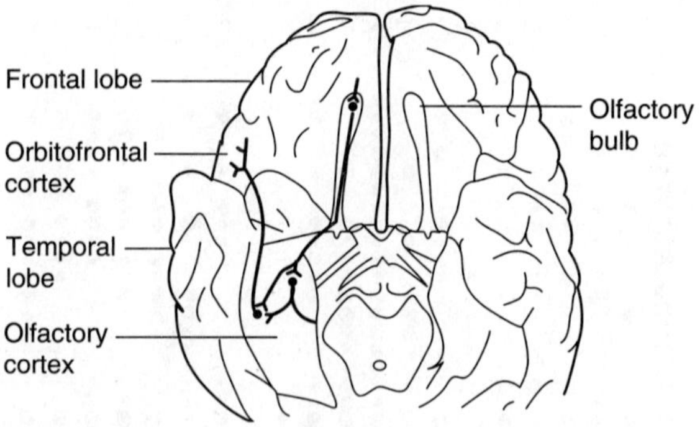

Figure 15.5
The underside of the brain, showing the neural pathways for olfaction. On the left side, the temporal lobe has been deflected to expose the olfactory cortex. (From Frank & Rabin, 1989.)

substance, through the air, and into your nose. One of the most persistent problems in the study of smell has been identifying which properties of these molecules are associated with specific smells.

We can appreciate why it is important to determine a relationship between molecular properties and smells by remembering how researchers approached the study of color vision. The key initial discovery was the realization that color perception is related to the wavelength of light. Establishing this relationship enabled researchers to concentrate on wavelength in searching for the sensory code for color. Thus, as we saw in the chapter on color vision, the question "What is the sensory code for color?" became "What is the sensory code for wavelength?" Similarly, by establishing that pitch is related to the frequency of the sound stimulus, hearing researchers searching for the sensory code for pitch were able to pose the question, "What is the sensory code for frequency?"

Unfortunately, it has not been possible to use similar tactics to determine the sensory code for olfaction, because we have not been able to link specific properties of odorant molecules to perceptions of specific odors. Thus, while researchers have found that odor quality is affected by physical and chemical properties, such as chemical reactivity and the electrical charge of the elements in a molecule, a simple relationship between these properties and perception has not yet emerged. For example, some molecules, that are very similar, can smell very different (Figure 15.6a) where other molecules, that are very different, can smell similar (Figure 15.6b). Thus, we are far from being able to specify a physical property for odor that is analogous to wavelength for color and frequency for pitch (Kauer, 1987).

The Neural Code for Odor Molecules

How does the brain know what the nose detects? This is the problem of neural coding for olfaction. Since researchers have not been able to link odors to specific properties of odorants, they have focused their attention not on determining the neural code for "odor" (which is an experience), but on determining the neural code for "odorants" (which are physical stimuli).

One outcome of this research is the concept of the **odotope.** An odotope is a group of odorants that share a specific chemical feature that determines neural firing (Mori & Yoshihara, 1995). A chemical

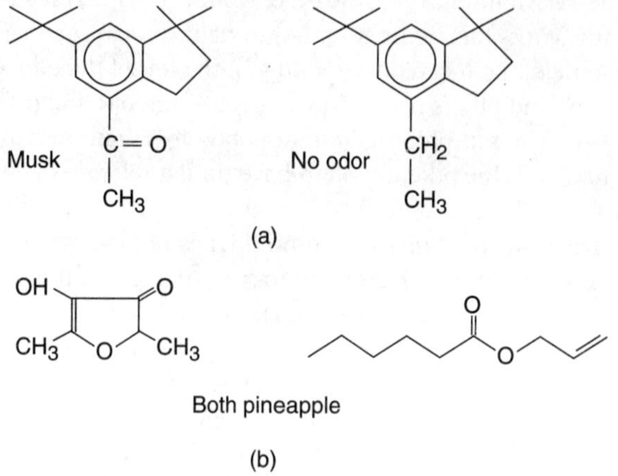

Figure 15.6
(a) Two molecules that have similar structures, but one smells like musk and the other is odorless. (b) Two molecules with different structures but similar odors.

feature can be a molecule's shape or the presence of certain chemical groups. For example, consider a particular family of odorants that all have a ring structure with a side-chain of linked carbon atoms attached. If those molecules with side chains that are between 5 and 7 carbon-atoms long all cause a particular group of neurons to fire, this group of molecules share the chemical feature of chain length that is associated with neural firing and is therefore an odotope. We will see below that neurons that fire to the same odotope are usually located near each other.

Coding at the Level of the Receptor Neurons

One approach to investigating olfactory coding at the receptor level has been to examine ways in which different odorants cause the receptor neurons to respond. Researchers have focused on how receptor neurons fire to different stimuli and how areas on the olfactory mucosa respond to different stimuli.

Olfactory Receptor Neurons Recordings from a variety of animals show that olfactory receptor neurons respond to a number of different odorants (Figure 15.7) (Blank, 1974; Holley et al., 1974; Matthews, 1972; Moulton, 1965; Sicard & Holley, 1984). By reading across this figure from left to right we can see that some of the receptors respond to just a few of the odorants, and others respond to a larger group of odorants. When a receptor neuron responds to a number of odorants, the odorants often have similar odotopes.

Areas on the Mucosa Similar types of olfactory receptor neurons are grouped in specific areas of the olfactory mucosa (Vassar, Ngia, & Axel, 1993). This grouping has been demonstrated by presenting chemicals to small areas of the mucosa and recording a response called the **electroolfactogram** that indicates the pooled activity from thousands of receptors. Figure 15.8 shows this result for two chemicals, limonene and butanol, which have very different areas of maximum sensitivity on the mucosa (MacKay-Sim & Kesteven, 1994; MacKay-Sim, Shaman, & Moulton, 1982). The difference in response of different areas of mucosa is called the **regional sensitivity effect** since different regions are sensitive to different types of chemicals.

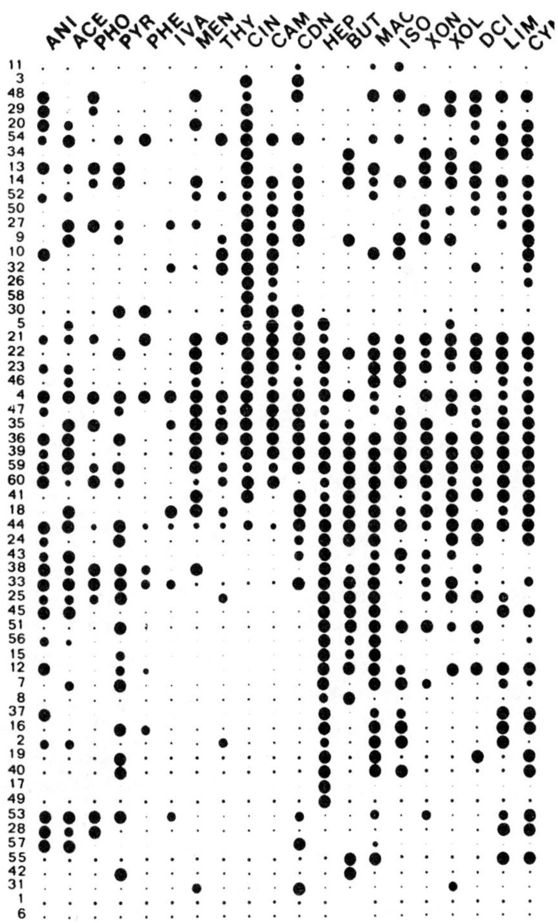

Figure 15.7
Responses of frog olfactory receptors (numbers on the left) to different compounds (letters along the top). The sizes of the spots are roughly proportional to the sizes of the responses. (From Sicard & Holley, 1984.)

Coding in the Olfactory Bulb and Olfactory Cortex

We have seen that a given olfactory receptor neuron responds to specific chemical features. Researchers

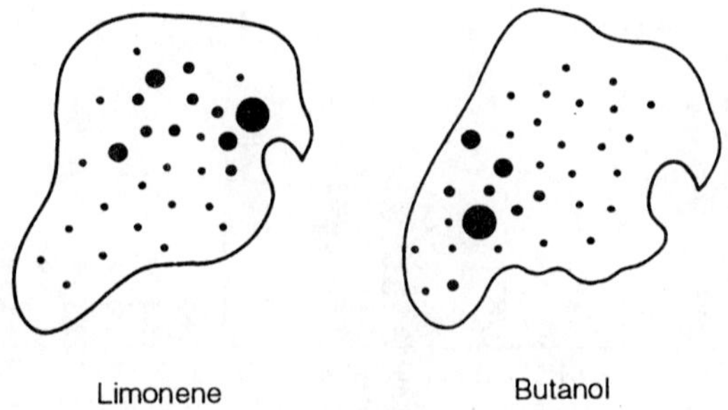

Figure 15.8
Size of the electro-olfactogram (EOG) response of the olfactory mucosa to stimulation of the mucosa by limonene and butanol. The larger the dot, the larger the size of the EOG. (From MacKay-Sim, Shaman, & Moulton, 1982.)

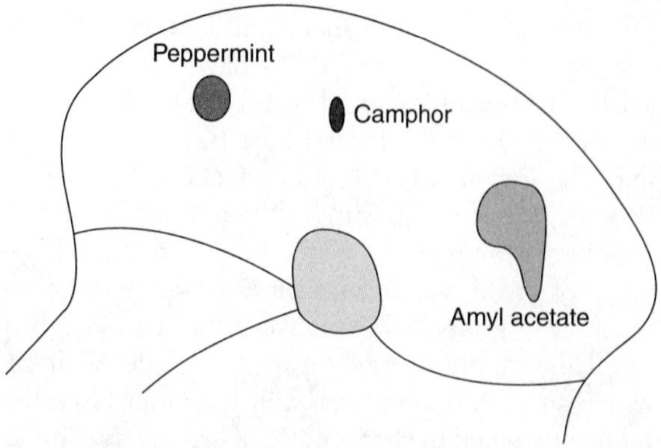

Figure 15.9
A portion of the olfactory bulb showing sites where peppermint, camphor, and amyl acetate caused buildups of radioactivity in different glomeruli. This shows that specific chemicals activate glomeruli that are located in different areas of the olfactory bulb. The result is an odotopic map on the olfactory bulb. (Adapted from Shepherd & Firestein, 1991.)

have found similar results when they have recorded from single neurons in the olfactory bulb.

Neurons in Olfactory Bulb Glomeruli Neurons in the glomeruli of the olfactory bulb respond to a range of stimuli, but a given neuron tends to respond best to molecules that have similar odotopes and neurons that respond to similar odotopes tend to be found near each other in the olfactory bulb (Mori & Yoshihara, 1995).

Areas in the Olfactory Bulb To determine how areas in the olfactory bulb respond to specific odorants, researchers have used the 2-deoxyglucose (2-DG) technique that was used in research investigating the visual system. When we first described this technique on page 90, we saw that 2-deoxyglucose has three important properties: (1) Since its structure is similar to glucose, a primary source of energy for neurons, it is taken up by neurons as though it were glucose; the more active the neuron, the more 2-DG is taken up by the neuron; (2) when 2- DG is taken up by a neuron, it accumulates inside the neuron; and (3) 2-DG can be labeled with a radioactive isotope, carbon 14. By measuring the amount of radioactivity in the various parts of a structure, we can determine which neurons are most active.

Rats injected with radioactively labeled 2-DG were exposed to different chemicals and the resulting pattern of radioactivity in the glomeruli of the olfactory bulb was measured. The results, shown in Figure 15.9, indicate that different chemicals activate glomeruli that are located in different areas (Shepherd & Firestein, 1991). Thus, odor stimuli are mapped into spatial patterns in the glomeruli in the olfactory bulb. The term **odotopic mapping** has been used to describe how odorants with different molecular features cause activity at different areas in the olfactory bulb (Shepherd, 1991, 1995).

The research we have described examining how the olfactory receptor neurons and neurons in the glomeruli of the olfactory bulb respond to various chemicals has shown that individual neurons respond to different types of odorants and that the specific odorants tend to activate specific areas in the mucosa and olfactory bulb.

According to the circuit pictured in Figure 15.4, each glomerulus in the olfactory bulb receives signals mainly from the same types of receptor neurons. There is, however, some overlap, so a particular glomerulus would respond mainly to chemicals that excite one type of receptor neuron, but will also respond to some other chemicals as well. An individual odor is, therefore, represented by strong responding in a particular glomerulus and weaker responding in a number of other glomeruli.

Olfactory Cortex T. Tanabe and coworkers (1974; Tanabe, Iino, & Takagi, 1975) have shown behaviorally that the orbitofrontal cortex (OFC), located on the underside of the frontal lobe (see Figure 15.5), may play an important role in olfaction. The behavioral experiment was simple. Two small pieces of bread were impregnated with different odors, and one piece of bread was given a bitter taste. When each piece was given to a monkey, the monkey first smelled each piece and then ate it. After determining which smell was associated with the bitter taste, the monkey avoided the bitter piece of bread, based on its smell, 81 percent of the time. Removal of the OFC, however, reduced this ability to 26 percent. This large decrease in performance did not occur with the removal of other cortical olfactory areas.

Tanabe et al.'s electrophysiological results show the degree to which eight different odorants caused neural responses in the olfactory bulb and the OFC (Figure 15.10). Each bar indicates the percentage of neurons that responded to the number of odorants indicated on the horizontal axis. Few of the cells in the olfactory bulb responded to only one odor, whereas half of the cells in the OFC responded to only one odor. Neurons in the OFC, then, are tuned to respond to much more specific odorants than are the neurons earlier in the olfactory system. Perhaps the response of these more specifically tuned OFC neurons helps us tell the difference between the large number of odorants that we are capable of smelling.

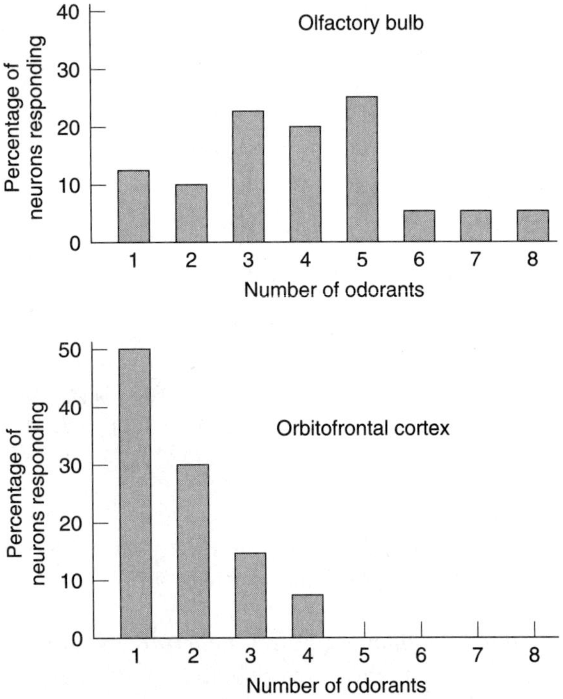

Figure 15.10
Histograms showing the percentage of neurons surveyed in the olfactory bulb and the OFC that responded to a number of odorants, indicated along the horizontal axis. (A total of eight odorants were presented.) (From Tanabe, Iino, & Takagi, 1975.)

The Perception of Flavor

Consider the following description of a dining experience, from a restaurant review:

> It is a surprise to dip your spoon into this mild-mannered soup and experience an explosion of flavor. Mushroom is at the base of the taste sensation, but it is haunted by citric tones—lemongrass, lime perhaps—and high at the top, a resonant note of sweetness. What is it? No single flavor ever dominates a dish. At first you find yourself searching for flavors in this complex tapestry, fascinated by the way they are woven together. In the end, you just give in and allow yourself to be seduced. . . . Each meal is a roller coaster of sensations. (Reichl, 1994)

My initial reaction to this review was that I wouldn't mind eating at that restaurant if only I could afford it (it is a very expensive four-star restaurant in New York City). My next reaction was that such superlatives, when applied to food, did not surprise me at all. We usually do much more than simply notice different flavors as we eat. We often evaluate them, savoring those that we find exceptionally pleasing, and dismissing others as inadequate or even disgusting.

Many of these sensory experiences are the result of the combination of taste and olfaction to create **flavor.** You can demonstrate how smell affects flavor with the following demonstration.

DEMONSTRATION

"Tasting" with and without the Nose

While holding your nostrils shut, drink a beverage with a distinctive taste, such as grape juice, cranberry juice, or coffee. Notice both the quality and the intensity of the taste as you are drinking it. (Take just one or two swallows, as swallowing with your nostrils closed can cause a build up of pressure in your ears.) After one of the swallows, open your nostrils and notice whether you perceive a flavor. Finally, just drink the beverage normally with nostrils open, and notice the flavor. You can also do this demonstration with fruits or cooked foods. ●

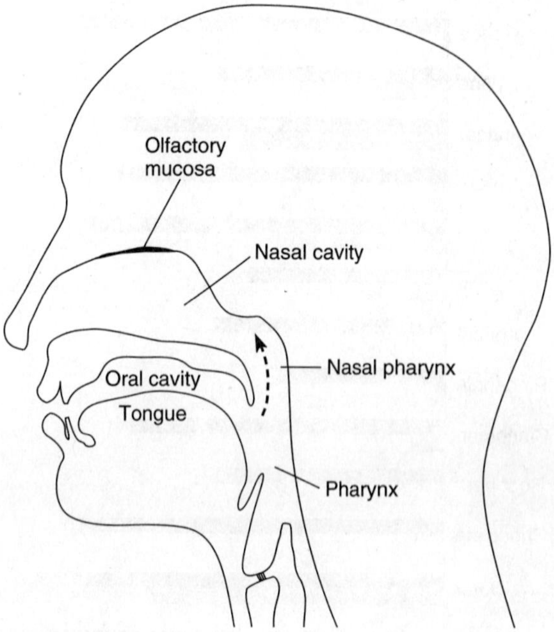

Figure 15.11
Odorant molecules released by food in the oral cavity and pharynx can travel through the nasal pharynx (dashed arrow) to the olfactory mucosa in the nasal cavity. This is the retronasal route to the olfactory receptors.

During this demonstration you probably noticed that, when your nostrils were closed, it was difficult to identify the substance you were drinking or eating, but as soon as you opened your nostrils, the flavor became obvious. This occurred because odor stimuli from the food reached the olfactory mucosa following the *retronasal route,* through the **nasal pharynx,** the passage that connects the oral and nasal cavities (Figure 15.11). Although pinching the nostrils shut does not close the nasal pharynx, it prevents vapors from reaching the olfactory receptors by eliminating the circulation of air through this channel (Murphy & Cain, 1980).

The importance of olfaction in the sensing of flavor has been demonstrated experimentally by using both chemical solutions and typical foods. For example, when Maxwell Mozell and coworkers (1969) asked subjects to identify common foods with the nostrils opened or with the nostrils pinched shut, every substance they tested was easier to identify in the nostrils-open condition (Figure 15.12). In a more recent experiment, Thomas Hettinger, Walter Myers, and Marion Frank (1990) had subjects rate the strength of various qualities experienced when solutions were applied to the tongue with the nostrils either open or clamped shut. The results for two of the chemicals, sodium oleate and ferrous sulfate, (Figure 15.13a and b) show that the oleate had a strong soapy flavor when the nostrils were open but was judged tasteless when they were closed. Similarly, the ferrous sulfate normally has a metallic flavor but was judged predominantly tasteless when the nostrils were closed. Some compounds are not influenced by olfaction. For example, monosodium glutamate (MSG) had about the same flavor whether or not the nose was clamped (Figure 15.13c). Thus, in this case, the sense of taste predominated.

The results of these experiments indicate that many of the sensations that we call taste, and that we assume are caused only by stimulation of the tongue, are greatly influenced by stimulation of the olfactory

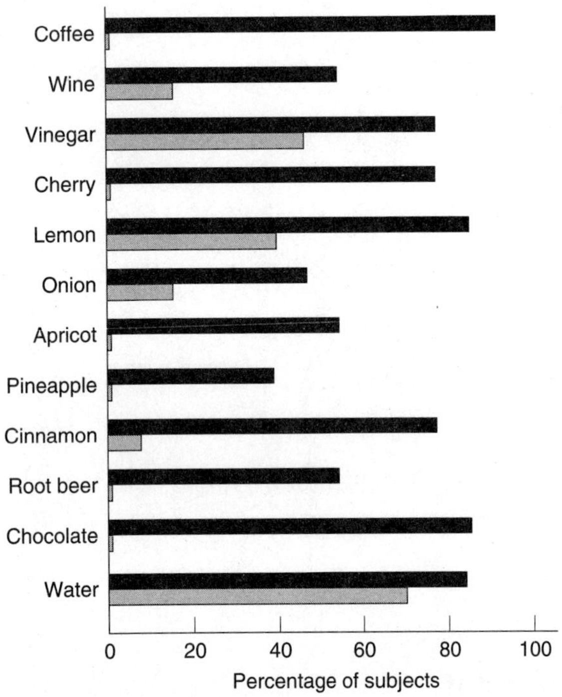

Figure 15.12
Percentage of subjects correctly identifying each flavor listed on the left, with nostrils open (solid bars) and nostrils pinched shut (shaded bars). (Adapted from Mozell et al., 1969.)

receptors. Apparently, we often mislocate the source of our sensations as being in the mouth, partially because the stimuli physically enter the mouth and partially because we experience the tactile sensations associated with chewing and swallowing (Murphy & Cain, 1980; Rozin, 1982).

Factors Influencing Food Preferences

Taste has been called the social sense because we often experience it while dining with other people (Ackerman, 1990). One thing that people do during these shared eating experiences is to share their taste experiences as they eat: "This chicken would taste better with a little more salt," "I can't stand liver," "Your apple pie is fantastic, Mom." When we share our taste experiences in this way, we are emphasizing the *affective* aspect of taste; that is, we usually label tastes as pleasant or unpleasant, and these labels affect which foods we choose to eat and which foods we avoid.

Many factors influence how foods taste to us: how much we've already eaten, our past experiences with different foods, our genetic makeup, the food

	Sodium oleate (a)		Ferrous sulfate (b)		MSG (c)	
	Clamped	Open	Clamped	Open	Clamped	Open
Sweet	x		x			
Salty	x				xxxxxxxxx	xxxxxxxx
Sour			xx	x	xxx	xxx
Bitter		x	x		xx	x
Soapy	xx	xxxxxxxxx	x	xx		
Metallic		xx	x	xxxxxxxxx		
Sulfurous				x	x	xx
Tasteless	xxxxxxxx		xxxxxx	x		
Other	x	x	x		x	xxx

Figure 15.13
How subjects described the flavors of three different compounds when they tasted them with nostrils clamped shut and with nostrils open. Each X represents the judgment of one subject. (From Hettinger, Myers, & Frank, 1990.)

we've just finished eating, and our nutritional state, among others. As we have for the other senses in this book, we want to consider the physiological workings of the sense of taste, but first, let's consider some of the factors that influence which foods we seek out and which we avoid.

Internal State

A restaurant near my house has fantastic banana cream pie. The first few forkfuls taste rich and creamy. But before I've finished just one piece of this pie, the taste just doesn't seem the same. This is a phenomenon that Cabanac (1971, 1979) calls **alliesthesia,** changed sensation. Our reaction to a taste stimulus may be positive when we first taste it, but this positive response may become negative after we've eaten for a while. To illustrate this effect, Cabanac describes an experiment in which he had people rate the pleasantness of a sugar solution. If they taste a sample and then spit it out, the sugar continues to get positive ratings over many samplings. If, however, people drink the sample each time they taste it, the originally pleasant sugar solution becomes unpleasant, and eventually the people refuse to drink any more. According to Cabanac, this experiment and many others with similar results illustrate that a given stimulus can be pleasant or unpleasant, depending on signals from inside the body.

Past Experiences

Although there is little experimental evidence that early experience with food results in permanent attachments to a particular food or flavor (Beauchamp & Maller, 1977), it is a common observation that people develop tastes for certain foods that are typically associated with their culture. Howard Moskowitz and coworkers (1975) investigated the idea that the perception of flavor can be influenced by experience by asking a group of Indian medical students and a group of Indians from the Karnataka Province to rate the pleasantness of a number of compounds. The medical students described citric acid as having an unpleasant sour taste and quinine as having an unpleasant bitter taste. However, the Karnataka Indians described both of these compounds as being pleasant-tasting.

Moskowitz felt that past experience was the most likely explanation for the Karnataka Indians' unusual preference for sour and bitter compounds. Their diet consisted of many sour foods, with the tamarind, a particularly sour fruit, making up a large portion of it. Being poor, they ate the tamarind out of necessity and, from constant exposure to this fruit, probably acquired a taste for sour foods. We don't know if the Karnataka Indians' long experience with sour and bitter compounds changed the *flavor* they experienced or simply increased their liking for sour and bitter flavors. It may be that the effect observed in the Karnataka Indians is analogous to the observation that children, who often avoid unfamiliar foods, come to prefer these foods if they are repeatedly exposed to them (Birch, 1979), if they see other children eating certain foods, such as vegetables (Birch, 1980), or if they associate eating certain foods with receiving rewards or an adult's positive attention (Birch, Zimmerman, & Hind, 1980).

Conditioned Flavor Aversion

Food preferences may be affected not only by the exposure to foods that results from long-term eating patterns, as appears to be the case for the Karnataka Indians, but also by a single pairing of food with sickness. The first experiments to illustrate this effect were done on rats (Garcia & Koelling, 1966; Garcia, Ervin, & Koelling, 1966). In a typical experiment, the researchers first determined that a rat would drink a sugar solution that tastes sweet to humans. The rats were fed sugar water and were then injected with a chemical that made them sick. After recovering from the resulting sickness, the rats would drink little or none of the sugar solution, which, before it was paired with sickness, they drank in large quantities. This avoidance of a flavor after it is paired with sickness is called **conditioned flavor aversion.** This mechanism also works in humans, as demonstrated by the observation that children made sick by chemotherapy treatments for cancer will avoid eating the ice cream they had eaten just before their chemotherapy injection (Bernstein, 1978; also see Garcia, Hawkins, & Rusiniak, 1974).

Specific Hungers

Conditioned flavor aversion has adaptive value. For example, if an animal survives after eating poison, conditioned flavor aversion prevents the animal from making the same mistake again. The adaptive value of flavor is also illustrated by built-in preferences that cause most people to like sweet foods, to dislike very bitter and very sour foods, and to like salty foods at low concentrations but to dislike them at high concentrations. There are good reasons for these built-in preferences. Sweetness usually indicates the presence of sugar, an important source of energy, whereas sourness or bitterness often indicates the presence of dangerous substances, such as poisons that result in sickness or death. Because of this, it has been suggested that the bitter taste may have evolved as a primitive poison detector (Bartoshuk & Beauchamp, 1994).

In addition to these responses to sweet, sour, and bitter tastes, there is evidence that rats and people have a **specific hunger** for sodium, a necessary component of their diets (Beauchamp, 1987). Rats deprived of sodium will increase their sodium intake to make up the deficit, and they use taste to recognize foods that contain sodium (Rozin, 1976).

A dramatic demonstration that taste regulates this hunger for sodium is an experiment by M. Nachman (1963) in which he created a need for salt in a rat by performing an adrenalectomy (removal of the adrenal gland), which caused the rat to eat large amounts of lithium chloride, even though this substance is toxic and makes the rat ill. The rat ate the lithium chloride because it tastes identical to sodium chloride, the substance the rat actually needed to correct the salt deficit created by the adrenalectomy.

Specific hunger for salt analogous to that found in Nachman's adrenalectomized rat has been reported in people who suffer from various diseases. In the 1930s, before the condition of specific salt hunger was widely recognized, a child whose adrenal cortex was diseased craved large amounts of salt. In an attempt to find out what caused this craving, the child was hospitalized, only to die after being placed on a standard hospital diet, which didn't satisfy the child's increased need for salt. Addison's disease also increases hunger for salt. A 34-year-old man with this disease was reported to routinely half-fill a glass with salt before adding tomato juice and to cover his steak with a one-inch-thick layer of salt (Liphovsky, 1977).

The Taste System

To introduce the taste system, we will first describe the anatomy of the tongue and the process of transduction that generates electrical signals from taste stimuli. We will then describe the central destinations of these signals.

The Tongue and Transduction

The process of tasting begins with the tongue (Figure 15.14a), when receptors are stimulated by taste stimuli. The surface of the tongue contains many ridges and valleys due to the presence of structures called **papillae,** of which there are four kinds: (1) filiform papillae, which are shaped like cones and are found over the entire surface of the tongue, giving it its rough appearance; (2) fungiform papillae, which are shaped like mushrooms and are found at the tip and sides of the tongue; (3) foliate papillae, which are a series of folds along the sides of the tongue; and (4) circumvallate papillae, which are shaped like flat mounds surrounded by a trench and are found at the back of the tongue (also see Figure 15.15).

All of the papillae except the filiform papillae contain taste buds (Figure 15.14b), and the whole tongue contains about 10,000 taste buds (Bartoshuk, 1971). Since the filiform papillae contain no taste buds, stimulation of the central part of the tongue,

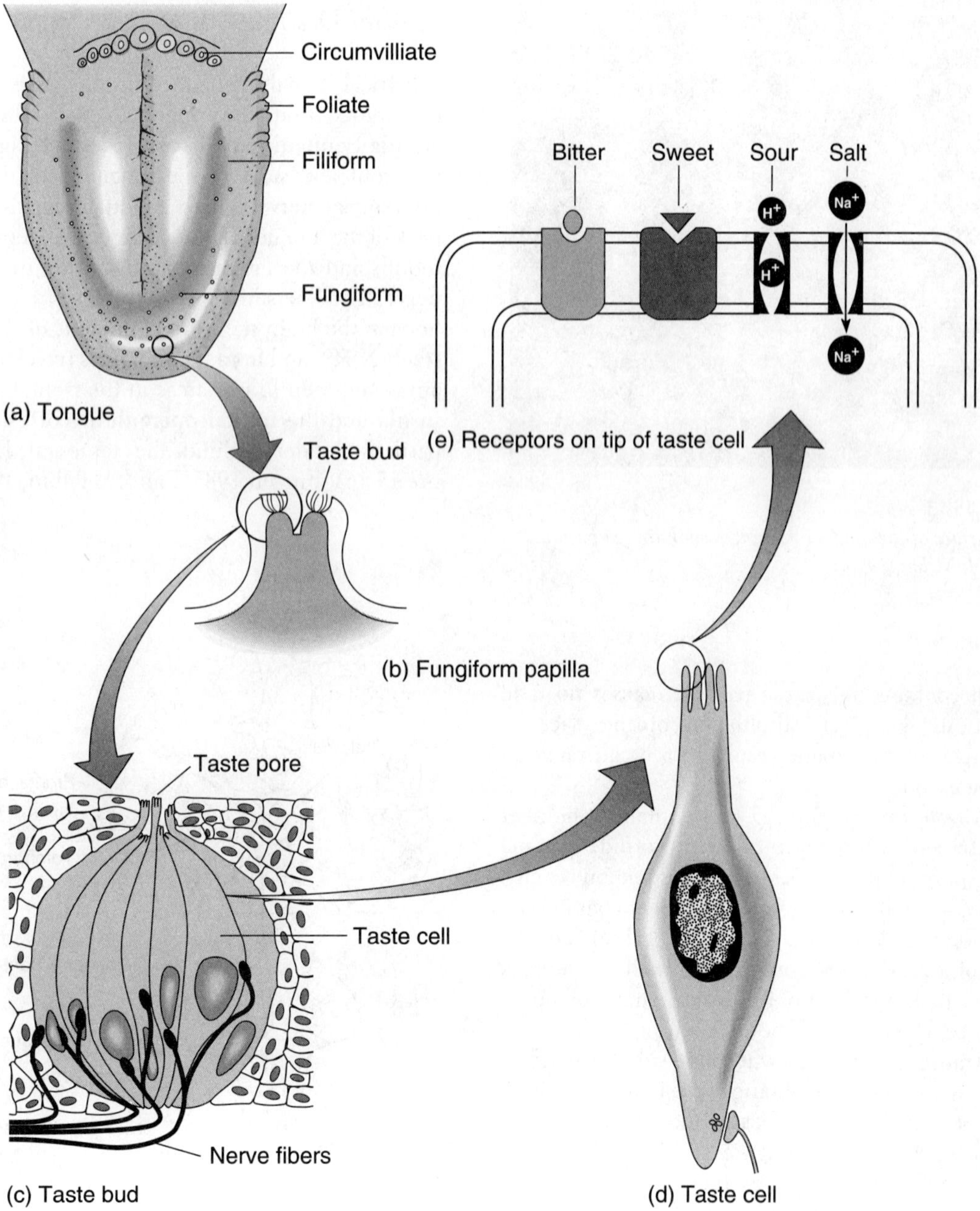

Figure 15.14

(a) The tongue, showing the four different types of papillae. (b) A fungiform papilla on the tongue; each papilla contains a number of taste buds. (c) Cross-section of a taste bud showing the taste pore where the taste stimulus enters. (d) The taste cell; the tip of the taste cell is positioned just under the pore. (e) Close-up of the membrane at the tip of the taste cell, showing the receptor sites for bitter, sour, salty, and sweet substances. Stimulation of these receptor sites, as described in the text, triggers a number of different reactions within the cell (not shown) that lead to movement of charged molecules across the membrane, which creates an electrical signal in the receptor.

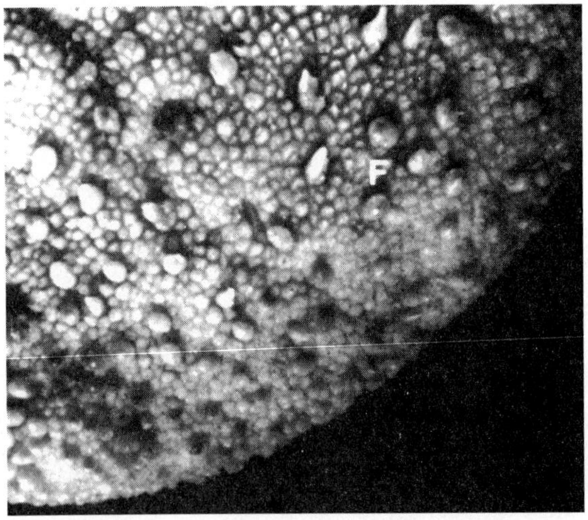

Figure 15.15
The surface of the tongue, showing fungiform (F) papillae. (From I. Miller, 1995.)

which contains only these papillae, causes no taste sensations. However, stimulation of the back or perimeter of the tongue results in a broad range of taste sensations.

A **taste bud** (Figure 15.14c) contains a number of **taste cells,** which have tips that protrude into the **taste pore** (Figure 15.14d). Transduction occurs when chemicals contact receptor sites or channels located on the tips of these taste cells (15.14e). The details of this transduction process involve complex chemical events within the taste cell (Kinnamon, 1988; Ye, Heck, & DeSimone, 1991).

Transduction occurs when taste substances affect ion flow across the membrane of the taste cell. Different types of substances affect the membrane in different ways. As shown in Figure 15.14e, molecules of bitter and sweet substances bind to receptor sites, which release other substances into the cell, whereas sour substances contain H^+ ions that block channels in the membrane, and the sodium in salty substances becomes sodium ions (Na^+) in solution that flow through membrane channels directly into the cell. Each of these mechanisms affects the cell's electrical charge by affecting the flow of ions into the cell.

Central Destinations of Taste Signals

Electrical signals generated in the taste cells are transmitted from the tongue in two pathways: the **chorda tympani nerve,** which conducts signals from the front and sides of the tongue, and the **glossopharyngeal nerve,** which conducts signals from the back of the tongue. Signals from taste receptors in the mouth and the larynx are transmitted in the **vagus nerve.** The fibers in these three nerves make connections in the brain stem in the **nucleus of the solitary tract** (NST), and from there, signals travel to the thalamus and then to two areas in the frontal lobe—the **insula** and the **frontal operculum cortex**—that are partially hidden behind the temporal lobe (Figure 15.16) (Finger, 1987; Frank & Rabin, 1989).

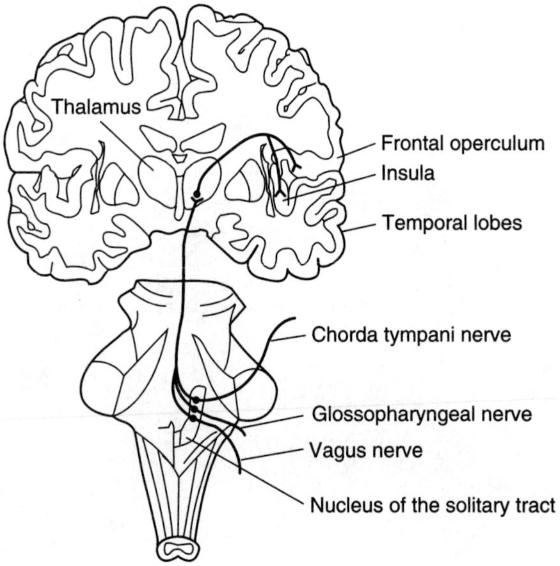

Figure 15.16
The central pathway for taste signals, showing the nucleus of the solitary tract (NST), where nerve fibers from the tongue and the mouth synapse in the medulla at the base of the brain. From the NST, these fibers synapse in the thalamus and the frontal lobe of the brain. (From Frank & Rabin, 1989.)

Taste Quality

When considering taste quality, we are in a much better position than we were for olfaction. Although we have not been able to fit the many olfactory sensations into a small number of categories or qualities, taste researchers generally describe taste quality in terms of four basic taste sensations: salty, sour, sweet, and bitter. (Although see Schiffman & Erickson, 1993, who disagree.) It has also been suggested that there is a fifth basic taste called *umami*, which has been described as meaty, brothy, or savory, and is often associated with the flavor-enhancing properties of the chemical monosodium glutamate (MSG) (Scott, 1987). We will focus on salty, sour, bitter, and sweet since most research has used these four qualities.

The Four Basic Taste Qualities

People can describe most of their taste experiences on the basis of the four basic taste qualities. For example, Donald McBurney (1969) presented taste solutions to subjects and asked them to give magnitude estimates of the intensity of each of the four taste qualities for each solution. He found that some substances have a predominant taste, and that other substances result in combinations of the four tastes. For example, sodium chloride (salty), hydrochloric acid (sour), sucrose (sweet), and quinine (bitter) are compounds that come the closest to having only one of the four basic tastes, but the compound potassium chloride (KCl) has substantial salty and bitter components (Figure 15.17). Similarly, sodium nitrate ($NaNO_3$) results in a taste consisting of a combination of salty, sour, and bitter. Subjects, therefore, can describe their taste sensations based on these four qualities. Thus, salty, sour, sweet, and bitter have been generally used by researchers to describe our taste experiences.

The Genetics of Taste Experience

Although most people describe their taste preferences in terms of four basic qualities, there are differences between people, based on genetics, that affect people's ability to sense the taste of certain substances. One of the best-documented genetic effects in taste involves people's ability to taste the bitter substance phenylthiocarbamide (PTC). Linda Bartoshuk (1980) describes the discovery of this PTC effect:

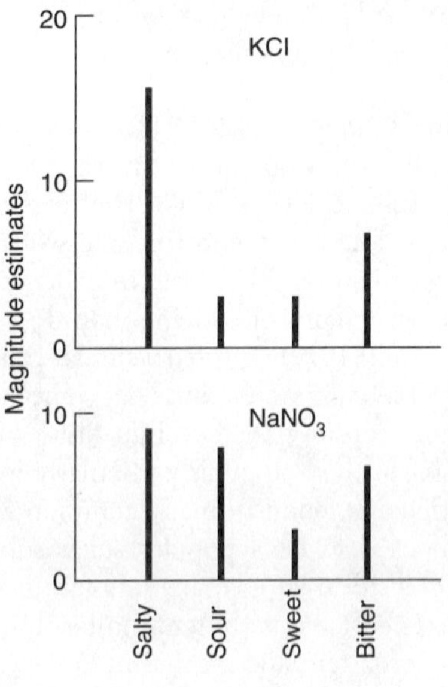

Figure 15.17
The contribution of each of the four basic tastes to the tastes of KCl and $NaNO_3$, determined by the method of magnitude estimation. The height of the line indicates the size of the magnitude estimate for each basic taste (McBurney, 1969).

> The different reactions to PTC were discovered accidentally in 1932 by Arthur L. Fox, a chemist working at the E. I. DuPont deNemours Company in Wilmington, Delaware. Fox had prepared some PTC, and when he poured the compound into a bottle, some of the dust escaped into the air. One of his colleagues complained about the bitter taste of the dust, but Fox, much closer to the material, noticed nothing. Albert F. Blakeslee, an eminent geneticist of the era, was quick to pursue this observation. At a meeting of the American Association for the Advancement of Science (AAAS) in 1934, Blakeslee prepared an exhibit that dispensed PTC crystals to 2,500 of the conferees. The results: 28 percent of

them described it as tasteless, 66 percent as bitter, and 6 percent as having some other taste. (p. 55)

People who can taste PTC are described as **tasters,** and those who cannot are called **nontasters** (or **taste-blind** to PTC). Molly Hall and coworkers (1975) have found that most people who can taste PTC also perceive a bitter taste in caffeine at much lower concentrations of caffeine than do nontasters, and Bartoshuk (1979) reported a similar result for the artificial sweetener saccharin. That some people are much more sensitive to the bitter tastes of caffeine and saccharin than others is particularly interesting, since caffeine is found in many common foods, and saccharin used to be a popular sugar substitute in foods and is still used in many fountain drinks. Caffeine makes coffee taste bitter to tasters but has little effect on nontasters, and saccharin, in the concentrations that were added to soft drinks before it was replaced by other artificial sweeteners, tastes more bitter to tasters than to nontasters.

Recently, additional experiments have been done with a substance called 6-*n*-propylthiouracil, or PROP, that has properties similar to those of PTC. Researchers have found that about one-third of people report that PROP is tasteless and that two-thirds can taste it. The people who can taste PROP (tasters) also report more bitterness in caffeine, Swiss cheese, and cheddar cheese than nontasters. This result, which is similar to that found for PTC, becomes more interesting when combined with anatomical measurements using a new technique called **video microscopy,** which by combining video technology and microscopy enables researchers to count the taste buds on people's tongues that contain the receptors for tasting.

The key result of these studies is that people who could taste the PROP had higher densities of taste buds than those who couldn't taste it (Figure 15.18) (Bartoshuk & Beauchamp, 1994). Thus, the next time you disagree with someone else about the taste of a particular food, don't automatically assume that your disagreement is simply a reflection of the fact that you prefer different tastes. It may reflect not a difference in preference (you *like* sweet things more than John does), but a difference in taste *experience* (you *experience* more intense sweet tastes than John does) that could be caused by differences in the number of taste receptors on your tongue.

This connection between the density of taste buds on the tongue and whether a person is a taster or a nontaster is an example of how receptors can affect perception. But perception also depends on the processing that occurs after the signals leave the receptors. We now consider how this processing may create a neural code for taste quality.

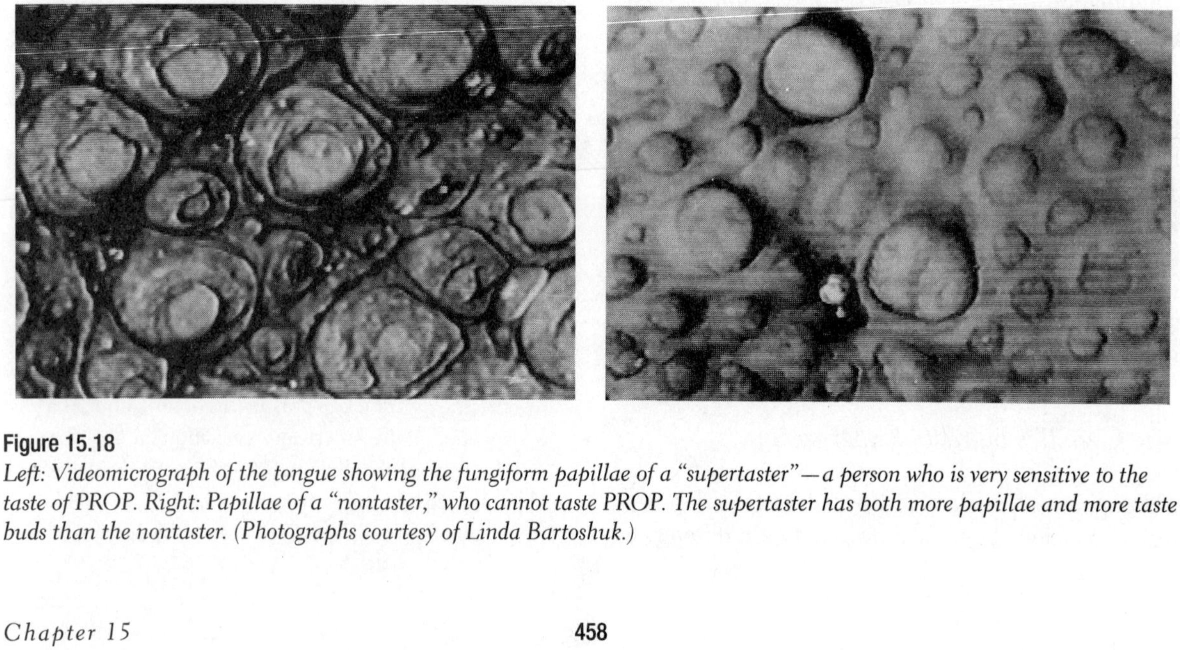

Figure 15.18
Left: Videomicrograph of the tongue showing the fungiform papillae of a "supertaster"—a person who is very sensitive to the taste of PROP. Right: Papillae of a "nontaster," who cannot taste PROP. The supertaster has both more papillae and more taste buds than the nontaster. (Photographs courtesy of Linda Bartoshuk.)

The Neural Code for Taste Quality

What is the neural code for taste quality? In Chapter 3, when we introduced the idea of sensory coding, we distinguished between *specificity coding*, the idea that quality is signaled by the activity in neurons that are tuned to respond to specific qualities, and *distributed coding*, the idea that quality is signaled by the pattern of activity distributed across many fibers. In that discussion, and in others throughout the book, we have generally favored distributed coding. The situation for taste, however, is not clear-cut, and there are good arguments in favor of both specificity and distributed coding.

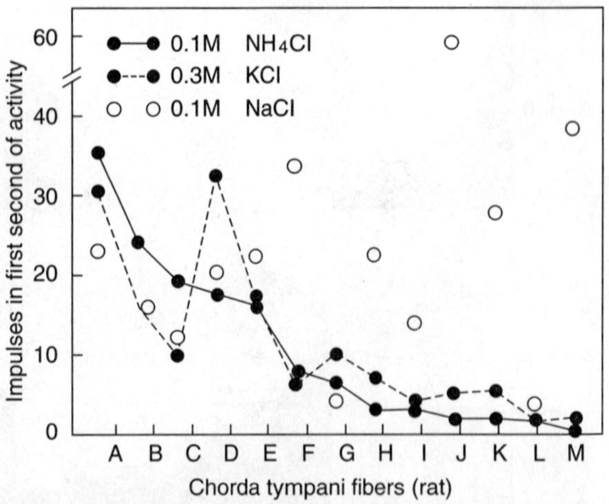

Figure 15.19
Across-fiber patterns of the response of fibers in the rat's chorda tympani nerve to three salts. Each letter on the horizontal axis indicates a different single fiber. (From Erickson, 1963.)

Distributed Coding

Let's consider some evidence for distributed coding. Robert Erickson (1963) conducted one of the first experiments that demonstrated this type of coding by presenting a number of different taste stimuli to a rat's tongue and recording the response of the chorda tympani nerve. Figure 15.19 shows how 13 nerve fibers responded to ammonium chloride (NH_4Cl), potassium chloride (KCl), and sodium chloride (NaCl). The solid and dashed lines show that the patterns of response of these 13 neurons to ammonium chloride and potassium chloride are similar to each other but are different from the pattern for sodium chloride, indicated by the open circles.

Erickson reasoned that if the rat's perception of taste quality depends on the pattern of firing of many receptors then two substances with similar patterns should taste similar. Thus, the electrophysiological results would predict that ammonium chloride and potassium chloride should taste similar and that both should taste different from sodium chloride. To test this hypothesis, Erickson shocked rats while they were drinking potassium chloride and then gave them a choice between ammonium chloride and sodium chloride. If potassium chloride and ammonium chloride taste similar, the rats should avoid the ammonium chloride when given a choice. This is exactly what they did. And when the rats were shocked for drinking ammonium chloride, they subsequently avoided the potassium chloride, as predicted by the electrophysiological results.

But what about the perception of taste in humans? When Susan Schiffman and Robert Erickson (1971) asked humans to make similarity judgments between a number of different solutions, they found that substances that were perceived to be similar were related to patterns of firing for these same substances in the rat. Solutions judged more similar psychophysically had similar patterns of firing, as distributed coding would predict.

Specificity Coding

Evidence that taste quality is coded by the activity in single neurons comes from experiments that show that there are four different types of fibers in the monkey's chorda tympani nerve (Sato, Ogawa, & Yamashita, 1994). Figure 15.20 shows how 66 fibers in the monkey's chorda tympani responded to four substances, each representing one of the basic tastes:

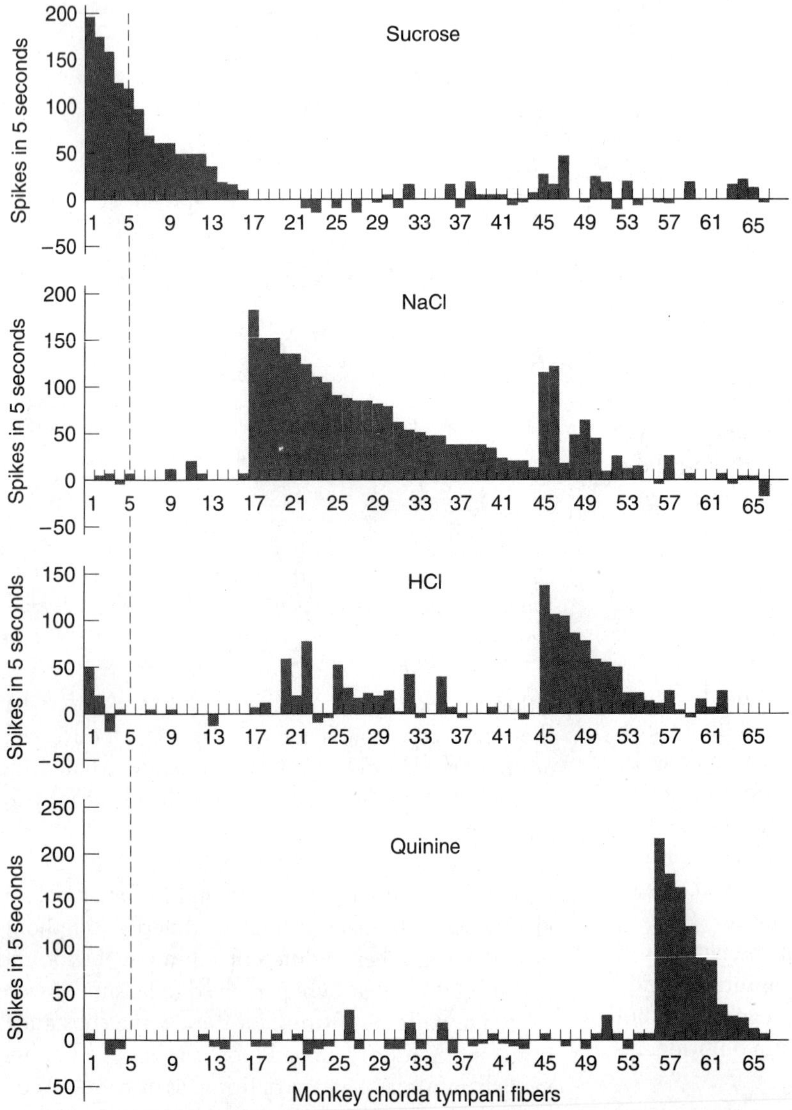

Figure 15.20
Responses of 66 different fibers in the monkey's chorda tympani nerve, showing how they responded to four types of stimuli: sucrose (sweet); sodium chloride (salty); hydrogen chloride (sour); and quinine (bitter). To determine the response of a particular fiber, pick its number and note the height of the bars for each compound. For example, fiber 5 (dashed line) fired well to sucrose but didn't fire to each of the other compounds. Fiber 5 is therefore called a sucrose-best fiber. (From Sato & Ogawa, 1994.)

sucrose (sweet); salt (NaCl, salty); hydrogen chloride (HCl, sour); and quinine (bitter). We can see that some fibers responded well to sucrose but poorly to almost all other compounds. For example, look at how fiber 5 responded to each substance by noticing the responses where the dashed line crosses the record for each substance. Fibers 1 to 16 are called *sucrose-best* since they respond best to sucrose. Figure 15.21 shows an example of the response of one of the sucrose-best fibers (Sato, Ogawa, & Yamashita, 1975). A similar situation exists for the quinine-best fibers (numbers 56–66), most of which respond only to quinine. The NaCl- and HCl-best fibers fire predominantly to one solution, but some fire to both NaCl and HCl (also see Frank, Bieber, & Smith, 1988, for similar results in the hamster).

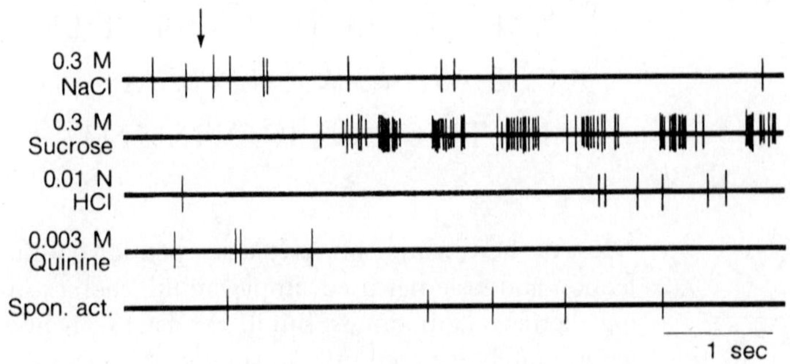

Figure 15.21
Response of a single fiber in the monkey's chorda tympani nerve to salt, sucrose, hydrochloric acid, and quinine. The bottom record indicates the rate of spontaneous activity. The arrow above the record for NaCl indicates the time of application of the stimuli (Sato, Ogawa, & Yamashita, 1975).

Another test for the operation of specificity coding was conducted by Kimberle Jacobs, Gregory Mark, and Thomas Scott (1988) who recorded from NST neurons in the rat's medulla (Figure 15.22) before and after depriving the rats of sodium. Before sodium deprivation, about 60 percent of the neurons in this area responded vigorously to sodium. However, after deprivation, these formerly sodium-active neurons fell silent. Apparently, the lack of stimulation caused by the sodium deprivation caused these neurons to become insensitive to sodium. These results are in line with specificity coding, since sodium deprivation causes only sodium-best neurons to decrease their sensitivity.

Another finding in line with specificity theory is the recently discovered transduction mechanisms, which indicate that salty, sweet, sour, and bitter substances each use different mechanisms to change the taste cell's membrane properties. Thus, the presentation of a substance called *amiloride*, which blocks sodium channels in membranes, causes a decrease in the responding of rat NST neurons that respond best to salt (Figure 15.22a) but has little effect on neurons that respond best to a combination of salty and bitter tastes (Figure 15.22b) (Scott & Giza, 1990). As we would expect from these results, applying amiloride to a human's tongue causes subjects to describe previously salty substances as "tasteless" (McCutcheon, 1992).

What does all of this evidence mean? Some experiments support distributed coding, and others support specificity coding. It is difficult to choose between the two because both can explain most of the data (Scott & Plata-Salaman, 1991). For example, David Smith and coworkers (1983) point out that, while similar-tasting compounds have highly similar across-fiber patterns, these patterns are dominated by activity in neurons that respond best to specific compounds. Thus, sweet-tasting compounds produce highly similar across-fiber patterns in the hamster, primarily because of the high firing rates contributed by the sucrose-best neurons.

Taste probably uses both specificity coding and distributed coding at the same time. Basic qualities might be identified by the firing of specific neurons, and more subtle differences between substances could be determined by the pattern of firing of larger groups of neurons (Pfaffmann, 1974; Scott & Plata-Salaman, 1991).

It is fitting to end this chapter on this note of uncertainty because it illustrates a problem common to all of the senses, which we can describe as follows: Researchers can, using their electrodes, record neural responses to various kinds of stimuli. Based on how these neurons respond, the researchers might be able to show that the firing of certain neurons is associated with a particular quality. But even after demonstrating this association between neural responding and a sensory quality, researchers are still faced with the following questions: What information is *actually being used by the brain* to determine our experience of that particular quality? Is the key information contained in individual neurons, or in the firing patterns of larger populations, or in the timing of nerve impulses? As we

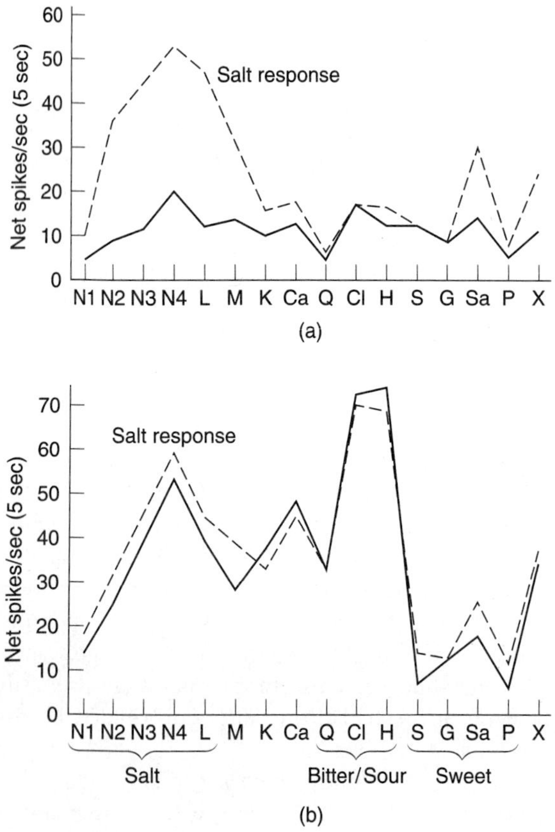

Figure 15.22

The dashed lines show how two neurons in the rat NST respond to a number of different taste stimuli (along the horizontal axis). The neuron in (a) responds strongly to compounds associated with salty tastes. The neuron in (b) responds to a wide range of compounds. The solid lines show how these two neurons fire after the sodium-blocker amiloride is applied to the tongue. This compound inhibits the responses to salt of neuron (a) but has little effect on neuron (b). (From Scott & Giza, 1990.)

have seen in this text, we are closer to answering these questions for some of the senses than for others. But even for the sensory qualities we know most about, such as perceiving color or pitch, many questions still remain to be answered by the next generation of researchers.

Something to Consider: Sensing Chemicals in the Environment

Most of the research we have described for both olfaction and taste has used simple stimuli such as single chemical compounds. But in our day-to-day lives, we are rarely exposed only to simple chemicals. We are more likely to be exposed to complex mixtures of chemicals. For example, consider a situation that might occur as you are cooking breakfast one morning and a friend comments on the smells of coffee, bacon, and toast that are emanating from your kitchen. The fact that your friend can do this may not seem particularly surprising until we recognize that the smell of coffee can arise from more than 100 different chemical constituents, and that the toast and bacon smells are also the result of a large number of different molecules that have been released into the air. Somehow, your friend's olfactory system takes this vast array of airborne chemicals, with their various physical qualities, and groups them into the three classifications: coffee, toast, and bacon (Bartoshuk, Cain, & Pfaffmann, 1985). This amazing feat of perceptual organization, which is analogous to how we separate a number of sounds coming simultaneously from a number of sources into different perceptual streams (see Bregman, 1990), is far too complex for us to understand at this time.

Because of the existence of situations like the one in the kitchen described above, researchers have begun looking at how the smell and taste systems respond to more complex stimuli. For example, Laing (1989) has found that a glomerulus in the olfactory bulb that responds strongly to propionic acid responds more weakly if another chemical, limonene, is added. Apparently, one chemical can inhibit the response generated by another chemical. Although using single chemicals has taught us a great deal about how we smell and taste, it will be necessary to use combinations of chemical stimuli if we are to understand how the chemical senses operate in our everyday environment.

Chemesthesis: A Somatosensory Component in the Nose and Mouth

If you've ever gotten a whiff of ammonia, especially in high concentrations, you probably had a negative reaction. The ammonia doesn't *smell* particularly bad, but it is very *irritating*. This irritation that you feel from breathing ammonia, as well as sensations such as the coolness of menthol, the sting of chlorine in your eyes, and the burning of hot chili peppers in your mouth are all examples of the **common chemical sense** or **chemesthesis.**

Chemesthesis, the sense responsible for detecting chemical substances that are often irritating (although the coolness of menthol is an exception), is served by the trigeminal nerve, which sends free nerve endings in the membranes of the mouth, nose, and eyes, and innervates the rest of the face as well. These free nerve endings are similar or identical to *nociceptors* that are responsible for pain perception in the skin (see Chapter 13) (Doty, 1995; Silver & Finger, 1991).

The idea that chemesthesis is a distinctly different sense than olfaction is supported not only by the fact that its signals are carried by the trigeminal nerve rather than the olfactory nerve, but also because subjects can lose their sense of smell—a condition called **anosmia**—but can still detect the irritating component of compounds (Doty, 1995).

Another difference between chemesthesis and olfaction is that chemesthetic sensations develop more slowly and last longer than olfactory sensations. They may also increase in perceived magnitude as sniff duration increases, whereas the magnitude of olfactory

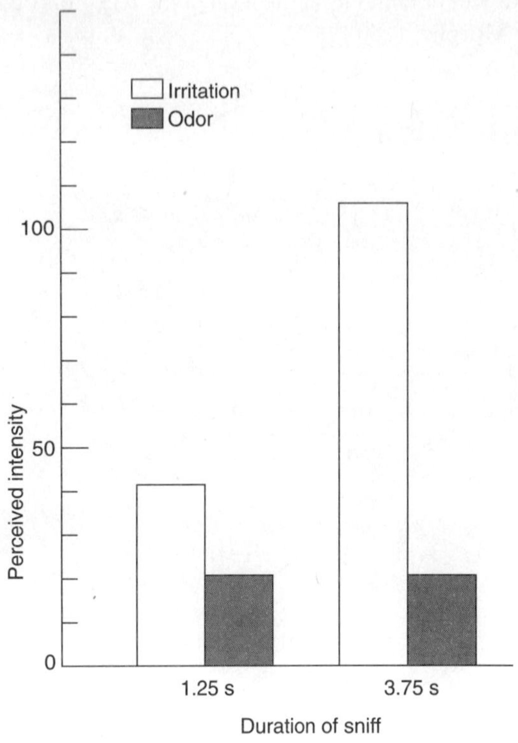

Figure 15.23
The perceived intensity of irritation caused by ammonia (open bars) increases when the sniff duration is increased from 1.25 seconds to 3.75 seconds. Notice that the perceived intensity of the odor sensation caused by the ammonia (hatched bars) is the same at both sniff durations. (Adapted from Commetto-Muniz & Cain, 1984.)

sensations stays the same (Figure 15.23). Another way to express this result is to say that constancy occurs for odors, but not for chemesthetic sensations (See Across the Senses 6: Odor constancy, page 171).

Although olfaction and chemesthesis are separate senses, they interact with one another. For example, adding CO_2, an odorless gas, to amyl buterate, which has a fruity odor and little irritation, decreases the odor of the amyl buterate. This effect appears to be central in origin, since it also occurs if the CO_2 is presented to one nostril and the amyl buterate to the other, a procedure that guarantees that these chemicals will not interact at the level of the receptors (Cain & Murphy, 1980).

Although one function of chemesthesis may be to warn us of dangerous chemicals so we can avoid them, not all chemesthesis is negative. We've already mentioned the coolness of menthol, that many people find pleasant, and chemesthesis is the basis of the "hot" or "burning" sensation of the taste of many foods that contain spices such as chili peppers, which contain the chemical irritant *capsiacin.* Although many people avoid hot foods, foods containing chili peppers are eaten by about one-quarter of adults in the world on a daily basis (Rozin, 1990). This liking for chili pepper is due both to capsiacin's ability to enhance the flavors of foods and also to the fact that many people simply like the burn!

Study Questions

Underlying Principles

Find examples of the following principles in this chapter:

- Selective receptors (459)
- Receptive fields/neural selectivity (460)
- Distributed response (459)
- Neural maps (449)
- Parallel pathways (463)
- Physiology-perception connections (458)
- Cognition-perception connection (442)
- Perceptual constancy (464)
- Perceptual grouping (462)
- Context and perception (451)

1. What are some unique properties of taste and smell compared to other senses? What is neurogenesis and why is it necessary? (439)

Olfaction: Uses and Facts

2. Define: microsmatic; macrosmatic; anosmia. (440)
3. How does the sensitivity of human olfactory receptors compare to the sensitivity of dog and cat olfactory receptors? How does the sensitivity of humans to odors compare to the sensitivity of dogs and cats to odors? Why is there a difference between human sensitivity and dog and cat sensitivity? (441)
4. Why were early measurements of the olfactory difference threshold too high? How did Cain determine that the threshold was smaller than originally reported? (441)
5. About what percentage of odors of familiar substances can humans identify? How can this percentage be improved? What is the role of memory in odor identification? (441)
6. Describe the undershirt experiment and the menstrual synchrony experiments. What is the possible mechanism for menstrual synchrony? (442)

The Olfactory System

7. Where is the olfactory mucosa located? Describe the olfactory receptor neurons. (443)
8. What is the difference between olfactory receptor neurons and olfactory receptor proteins? How is the olfactory receptor protein similar to the visual pigment molecule? (444)
9. What are two ways that odorant molecules can reach active sites on the receptor neuron? (444)
10. How many different types of receptor proteins are there? What is the relationship between receptor proteins and receptor neurons? (446)
11. How many receptor neurons are there in the olfactory system? How many different types of receptor neurons are there? How many receptor proteins are on each receptor neuron? (446)
12. Where are the glomeruli located? How many glomeruli are there? What types of receptor neurons send their signals to each glomerulus? Why are the glomeruli called information collection units? (446)
13. What neurons transmit signals from the glomeruli to more central structures? What cortical structures receive olfactory information? (446)

Odor Stimulus and Quality

14. Why would it be desirable to determine a relationship between molecular properties and smells? Has it been possible to do this? How does making changes in a molecule's structure affect its smell? (447)

The Neural Code for Odor Molecules

15. Researchers have focused on determining the neural code for ________. What is an odotope? (447)
16. How many different odorants do olfactory receptor neurons respond to, according to the results of electrophysiological recordings? (448)
17. How are receptor neurons organized on the olfactory mucosa? What is the regional sensitivity effect? (448)
18. Neurons in a particular glomerulus tend to respond best to what kinds of chemicals? (449)
19. How was the 2-deoxyglucose technique used to determine how areas in the olfactory bulb respond to specific odorants? (449)
20. What is odotopic mapping? What does odotopic mapping say about how a particular odorant will be represented in the olfactory bulb? (449)
21. Describe Tanabe's experiment that looked at the responding of neurons in the olfactory cortex. (450)

The Perception of Flavor

22. What is "flavor?" How is it related to olfaction? To taste? What is the relationship between olfaction and flavor? (450)

Factors Influencing Food Preferences

23. What is alliesthesia? What do we mean when we say that an organism's food preference can be influenced by its internal state? (453)
24. What is the evidence that past experiences with food influence food preferences? (453)
25. Describe conditioned flavor aversion. What is its adaptive significance? (453)
26. Is there any evidence for specific hungers? (454)

The Taste System

27. Describe the structure of the tongue as depicted in Figure 15.14. (454)
28. What is the difference between a taste bud, a taste cell, and a taste pore? (456)
29. Which nerves conduct signals from the tongue towards the brain? (456)
30. What are some of the central structures that receive signals from the tongue? (456)

Taste Quality

31. What are the four basic taste qualities and a possible fifth one? (457)
32. What is the relationship between genetics and taste experience? What is a taster? a nontaster? (457)
33. What is the relationship between being a taster or a non taster and the taste receptors? (458)

The Neural Code for Taste Quality

34. Describe Erickson's experiment that supports the idea of distributed coding. (459)
35. What is the evidence that distributed coding for taste might work for humans? (459)
36. What is the evidence for specificity coding in the taste system? (459)
37. What are the probable roles of distributed coding and specificity coding in taste perception? (461)

Something to Consider: Sensing Chemicals in the Environment

38. Why do we say that sensing substances in the environment is a feat of perceptual organization? (462)
39. How can the presence of one chemical affect the response to another chemical that is present at the same time? (462)

Across the Senses: Chemesthesis: A Somatosensory Component in the Nose and Mouth

40. What is the common chemical sense or chemesthesis? (463)
41. What nerve is responsible for chemesthesis? (463)
42. Why does the experience of subjects with anosmia support the idea that chemesthesis is a distinctly different senses than olfaction? (463)
43. Compare olfaction and chemesthesis in terms of how magnitude of sensation changes with increases in sniff duration. (463)
44. How do chemesthesis and olfaction interact with one another? (464)
45. Give two examples of situations in which chemesthesis is not considered negative. (464)

16

Perceptual Development

Our senses endow us with truly amazing capacities. We can see fine details and keep them in focus when an object moves from close to far away. We see something move and can follow the moving object with our eyes, keeping its image on our foveas so we can see the object clearly. We can perceive the location of a sound, transform pressure changes in the air into meaningful sentences, and create myriad tastes and smells from our molecular environment.

As adults, we can do all these things and more. But were we born with these abilities? Most 19th-century psychologists would have answered this question by saying that newborns and young infants experience a totally confusing perceptual world, in which they either perceive nothing or can make little sense of the stimulation to which they are exposed.

One of the things we will do in this chapter is to deal directly with this idea by asking what perceptual capacities are present in the newborn and very young infant. We will see that while newborns have great perceptual deficiencies compared to older children or adults, they can perceive quite a bit more than the 19th-century psychologists believed.

But our goal in this chapter goes beyond simply establishing what newborns and young infants can perceive. We will be looking at a number of the questions asked by psychologists and physiologists who are interested in perceptual development. The following are some of these questions, along with brief previews of the answers that we will expand upon in the chapter.

1. How do perceptual capacities present in the newborn develop with age?
   Most capacities develop rapidly during the first year of life.

Chapter Contents

Some Questions We Will Consider

- What can newborns perceive? (473)
- Can a newborn recognize his or her mother? (477)
- When can an infant perceive colors? (481)
- How does nearsightedness develop? (498)

2. When do new perceptual capacities emerge?
   Some capacities that aren't present at birth emerge during the first few months of life.
3. What aspects of stimuli are important to newborns and young infants?
   Movement is an example of an aspect of stimulation that helps infants perceive shapes as separated from one another.
4. What are the mechanisms that underlie perceptual development?
   Development is governed by an interaction between biological programming and the infant's perceptual experience.

Before we answer any of these questions, we must be able to determine what an infant is perceiving. This is one of the great challenges of the study of perceptual development, and one of the accomplishments of modern perceptual research has been the discovery of ways to uncover some of the characteristics of the infant's perceptual world.

Measuring Infant Perception

Why did the early psychologists think that the newborn's perceptual world was either non-existent or very confusing, whereas present-day psychologists think that newborn's have some perceptual abilities? Did infants learn to see and hear better between 1898 and 1998? Obviously not. What did happen is that psychologists learned how to measure infants' perceptual abilities that were there all along.

Problems in Measuring Infant Perception

The following statement, by a well-know researcher who studies perceptual development in 3- to 5-month-old infants, captures some of the difficulties involved in doing research on human newborns:

> I admit I've never had the courage to run a full-blown experiment with human newborns. For those who may not be aware of the difficulties involved, running such an experiment can be a formidable task: convincing hospital administrators and personnel in the neonatal nursery that the research is worth-while; setting up elaborate equipment often in cramped, temporary quarters; obtaining permission from mothers who are still recovering from their deliveries; waiting, sometimes for hours, until the infant to be tested is in a quiet, alert state; coping with the infant's inevitable changes in state after testing has begun; and interpreting the infant's responses that at one moment may seem to be nothing more than a blank stare and at another moment active involvement with the stimulus. (Cohen, 1991, p. 1)

Not only do newborns and young infants exhibit behaviors such as crying, sleeping, and not paying

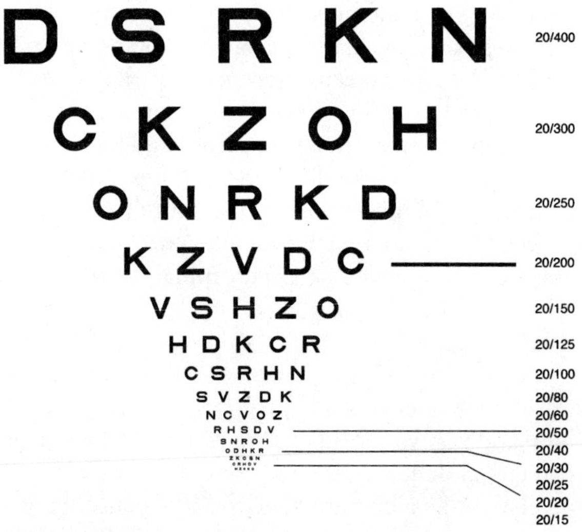

Figure 16.1
An eye chart for measuring visual acuity. This is a new version of the familiar chart with the large "E" on top. This eye chart has a number of advantages over the old one, as described on page 530 of Chapter 17. Eye charts such as this one work well for older children and adults who can answer the question "What do you see?" but does not work for infants. To measure their acuity we need to ask a different question and use a different stimulus.

attention while the experimenter is trying to test them, but the fact that they can't understand or respond to verbal instructions presents a special challenge. Even if the infant is cooperating by being quiet and paying attention, the researcher is still faced with the problem of devising methods that will make it possible to determine what the infant is perceiving.

The key to measuring infant perception is to pose the correct question. To understand what we mean by this, let's consider two questions we can ask to determine visual acuity, the ability to see details. One question we can ask is "what do you see?" This is the question that's being asked when an ophthalmologist or optometrist asks you to read the letters on an eye chart like the one in Figure 16.1. Acuity is determined using this technique by noting the smallest letters a person can accurately identify. This technique is obviously, however, not suitable for infants. To test infant acuity, we have to ask another question, and use another procedure.

Another question we can ask is "Can you tell the difference between the stimulus on the left and the one on the right?" Infants can answer this question, although not by verbally responding. For measuring visual acuity, they answer the question by where they look when presented with two stimuli like the ones in Figure 16.2. One of these stimuli is a black and white grating and the other is a homogeneous gray field that reflects the same amount of light that the grating would reflect if the dark bars were spread evenly over the whole area. To measure acuity using these stimuli we note where the infant is looking as we make the grating's bars thinner. Our goal is to determine when the infant can't tell the difference between the two fields. To accomplish this we use the *preferential looking technique.*

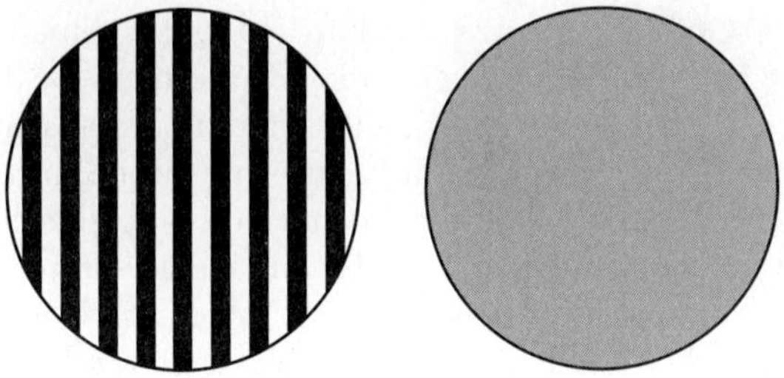

Figure 16.2
A grating stimulus and gray field of the same average intensity. This stimulus is better suited than the eye chart for measuring infant acuity, because the infants can answer the question "Can you tell me the difference between these two fields? They answer this question by where they look, and this enables us to measure their acuity.

Preferential Looking

The way infants look at stimuli in their environment provides a way to determine whether they can tell the difference between two stimuli. In the **preferential looking (PL) technique** two stimuli are presented to the infant and the experimenter watches the infant's eyes to determine where the infant is looking. If the infant looks at one stimulus more than the other, the experimenter concludes that he or she can tell the difference between them.

The reason preferential looking works is that infants have *spontaneous looking preferences;* that is, they prefer to look at certain types of stimuli. For example, to measure visual acuity, we can use the fact that infants choose to look at objects with contours over one that is homogeneous (Fantz, Ordy, & Udelf, 1962). When we present a grating with large bars and a homogeneous field, the infant can easily see the bars and therefore looks at the side with the bars, more than the side with the gray field (the grating and homogeneous field are switched randomly from side to side on each trial). By preferentially looking at the side with the bars the infant is telling us, "I see the grating" (Figure 16.3).

As we decrease the size of the bars, it becomes more difficult for the infant to tell the difference between the grating and gray stimuli, until, when they become indiscriminable, the infant looks equally at each display. We determine the infant's acuity by determining the narrowest stripe width that results in looking more to one side.

Habituation

Use of the preferential looking technique to measure acuity is based on the existence of the infant's

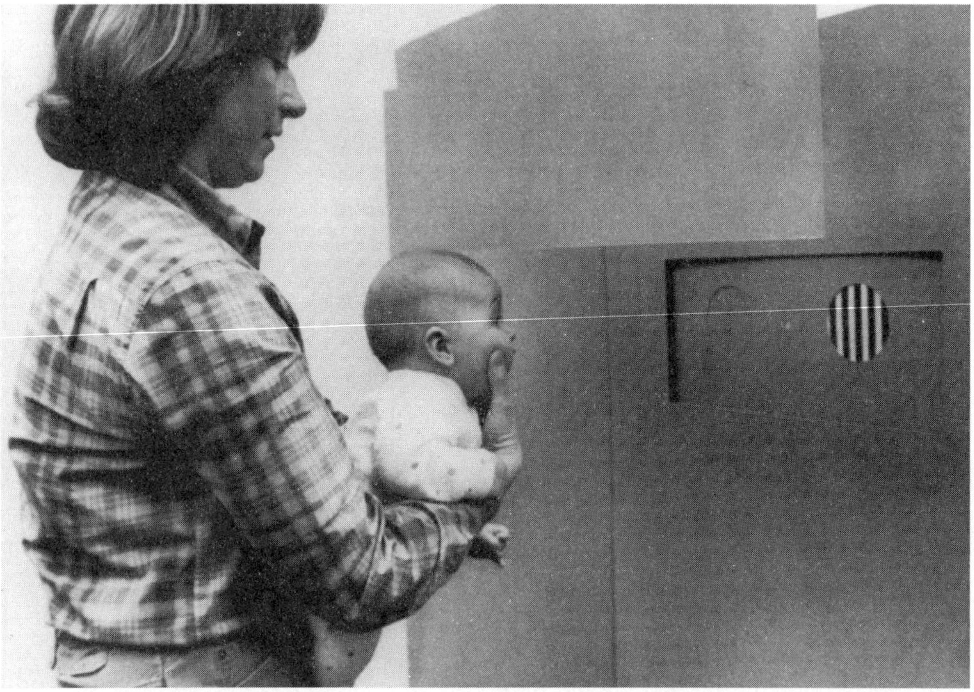

Figure 16.3

An infant being tested by the preferential looking procedure. The mother holds the infant in front of the display: a grating on the right and a homogeneous gray field on the left with the same average intensity as the grating. An experimenter, who does not know which side the grating is on in any given trial, looks through a peephole (barely visible between the grating and the gray field) and judges whether the infant is looking to the left or to the right. (Photograph courtesy of Velma Dobson.)

spontaneous looking preference for contours. But to measure other perceptual capacities, we often want to know whether the infant perceives a difference between two stimuli that the infant normally looks at equally. Researchers have solved this problem by using the following fact about infant looking behavior: When given a choice between a familiar stimulus and a novel one, an infant is more likely to look at the novel one (Fagan, 1976; Slater, Morison, & Rose, 1984).

Since infants are more likely to look at a novel stimulus, we can *create* a preference for one stimulus over another one by familiarizing the infant with one stimulus but not with the other. For this technique, which is called **habituation,** one stimulus is presented to the infant repeatedly, and the infant's looking time is measured on each presentation (Figure 16.4). As the infant becomes more familiar with the stimulus, he or she habituates to it, looking less and less on each trial.

Once the infant has habituated to this stimulus, we now determine whether the infant can tell the difference between it and another stimulus, by replacing it with a new stimulus. In Figure 16.4 this occurs on the eighth trial. If the infant can tell the difference between the habituation stimulus and the new stimulus he will exhibit **dishabituation,** an increase in looking time when the stimulus is changed, as shown by the open circles in Figure 16.4. If, however, the infant cannot tell the difference between the two stimuli he will continue to habituate to the new stimulus (since it will not be perceived as novel), as shown by the open squares in Figure 16.4.

When we report the results of habituation experiments in this chapter, we will usually use the format

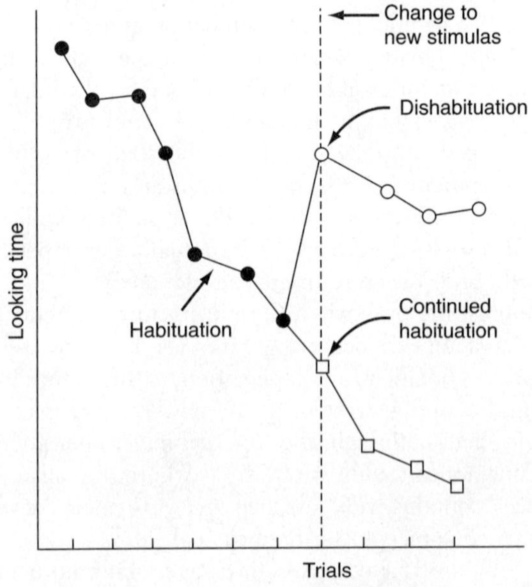

Figure 16.4
Possible results of a habituation experiment. During the initial rials the infant habituates to the stimulus, as indicated by the decrease in looking time (filled circles). At the dashed line, the stimulus is changed. If the infant can tell the difference between the original stimulus and the new one, dishabituation occurs (open circles).

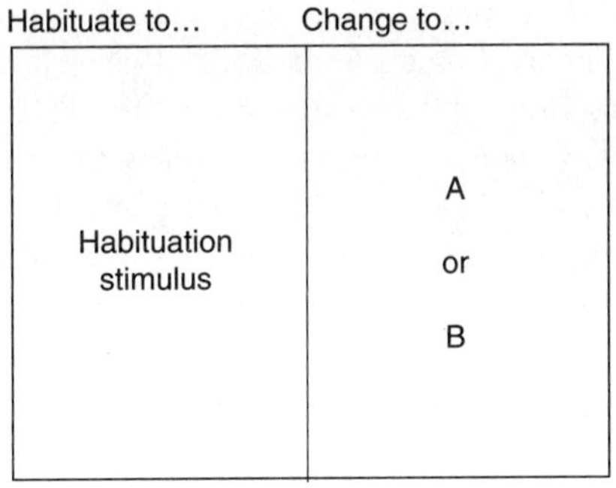

Figure 16.5
Standard format for presenting habituation results. The habituation stimulus will appear on the left and the new stimuli will appear on the right. The new stimulus that causes dishabituation is always placed on top.

shown in Figure 16.5. The stimulus to which the infant is habituated will appear on the left, and stimuli that are presented after habituation has occurred will appear on the right. The stimulus that causes dishabituation is placed on top. Thus, in this example, changing to stimulus A causes dishabituation but changing to B does not. Remember, that the occurrence of dishabituation means that the second stimulus (the one on the top right of the figure) appears different to the infant than the habituation stimulus (the one on the left).

Infant Perceptual Capacities: Vision

Now that we have described the procedures used to measure infant perception, we are ready to describe the perceptual capacities that have been discovered using these procedures. We begin by considering a number of visual capacities.

Acuity and Contrast

One of the most basic questions we can ask about infant perception is how well infants can perceive details and contrast.

Perceiving Details Visual acuity is poorly developed at birth (about 20/400 to 20/600 at 1 month),* and then rapidly increases over the first six months to just below the adult level of 20/20 (Banks & Salapatek, 1978; Dobson & Teller, 1978; Harris, Atkinson, & Braddick, 1976; Salapatek, Bechtold, & Bushnell, 1976). Acuity has been measured using the preferential looking technique (comparing gratings and homogeneous fields) and by measuring an electrical response called the **visual evoked potential (VEP),** which is recorded by disc electrodes placed on the

* The expression 20/400 means that the infant must view a stimulus from 20 feet to see the same thing that a normal adult observer can see from 400 feet. (See Chapter 13.)

back of the infant's head, over the visual cortex. The VEP is the pooled response of thousands of neurons that are near the electrode.

When using the VEP to measure acuity, the infant looks at a gray field, which is briefly replaced by either a grating or a checkerboard pattern. If the stripes or checks are large enough to be detected by the visual system, the visual cortex generates a visual evoked potential. If, however, the pattern cannot be resolved, no response is generated. Thus, the VEP provides an objective measure of the ability of the visual system to detect details. Figure 16.6 shows the acuities of a number of subjects measured using this technique. The rapid improvement of acuity until the sixth month is followed by a leveling-off period, and full adult acuity is not reached until sometime after 1 year of age.

Acuity is one of the few perceptual capacities for which we can demonstrate parallels between psychophysically measured development and physiological development. Thus, although our survey of visual capabilities will be focusing on psychophysical measurements, let's consider, for acuity, the nature of this parallel between perceptual development and physiology.

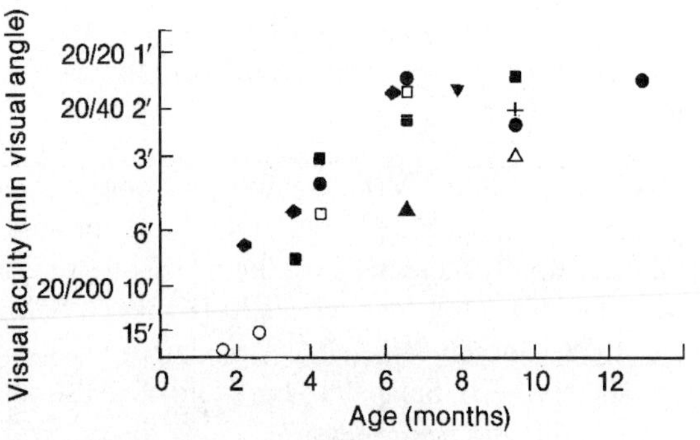

Figure 16.6
The improvement of acuity over the first year of life, as measured by the VEP technique. The numbers on the vertical axis indicate the smallest stripe width that results in a detectable evoked response. Snellen acuity values (see Chapter 17) are also indicated on this axis. The different symbols represent measurements of different subjects (Pirchio, Spinelli, Fiorientini, & Maffei, 1978).

The parallel between perception and physiology becomes obvious when we look at the state of the retina and cortex at birth. One reason for the infant's low acuity is that the infant's visual cortex is not fully developed. Figure 16.7 shows the state of cortical development at birth, at 3 months and at 6 months (Conel, 1939, 1947, 1951). These pictures indicate that the visual cortex is only partially developed at birth and becomes more developed at 3 and 6 months, the time when significant improvements in visual acuity are occurring. However, the state of the cortex is not the whole explanation for the infant's low visual acuity. If we look at the newborn's retina, we find that, although the rod-dominated peripheral retina appears adultlike in the newborn, the all-cone fovea contains widely spaced and very poorly developed cone receptors (Abramov et al., 1982).

Figure 16.8 compares the shapes of newborn and adult foveal cones. The newborn's cones have fat inner segments and very small outer segments, whereas the adult's inner and outer segments are larger and are about the same diameter (Banks & Bennett, 1988; Yuodelis & Hendrickson, 1986). These differences in shape and size have a number of consequences. The small size of the outer segment means that the newborn's cones contain less visual pigment and therefore do not absorb light as effectively as adult cones. In addition, the fat inner segment creates the coarse receptor lattice shown in Figure 16.9a, with large spaces between the outer segments. In contrast, the thin adult cones are closely packed, as in Figure 16.9b, creating a fine lattice that is well suited to detecting fine details. Martin Banks and Patrick Bennett (1988) calculated that the cone receptors' outer segments effectively cover 68 percent of the adult fovea but only 2 percent of the newborn fovea. This means that most of the light entering the newborn's fovea is lost in the spaces between the cones and is therefore not useful for vision.

Acuity is an example of a capacity we can measure at or near birth and then follow as it improves with time. We can also do this for contrast sensitivity, which as we saw in Chapter 3 provides information that goes beyond what measurements of acuity tell us. Visual acuity indicates the visual system's capacity to resolve fine details under optimum conditions. Acuity

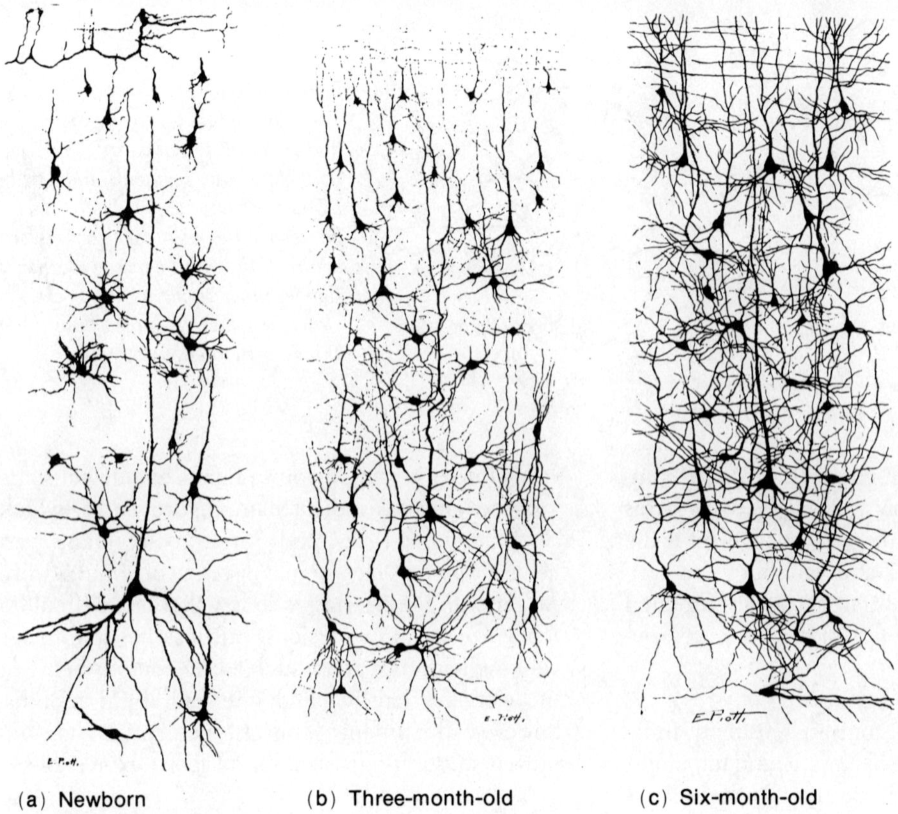

Figure 16.7
Drawings of neurons in the visual cortex of the newborn, the 3-month-old, and the 6-month-old human infant (Conel, 1939, 1947, 1951).

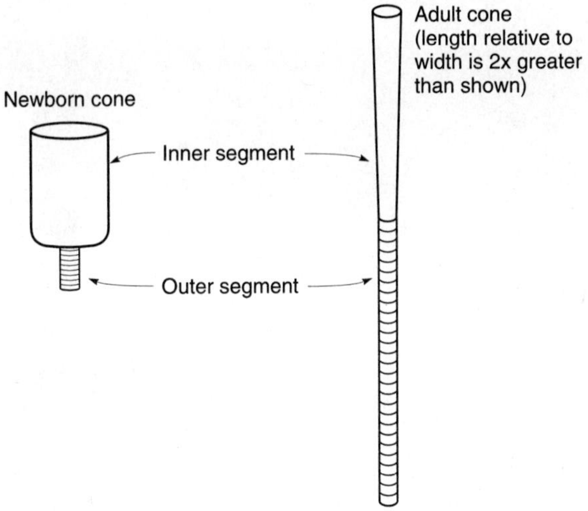

Figure 16.8
Idealized shapes of newborn and adult foveal cones. (Real cones are not so perfectly straight and cylindrical.) Foveal cones are much narrower and longer than the cones elsewhere in the retina, so these look different from the ones shown in Figures 2.11 and 2.12. The adult cone is actually twice as long as shown here. (From Banks & Bennett, 1988.)

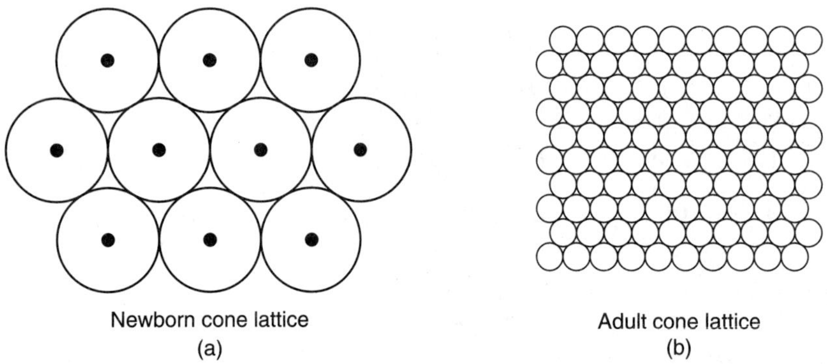

Figure 16.9
Receptor lattices for (a) newborn and (b) adult foveal cones. The newborn cone outer segments, indicated by the dark circles, are widely spaced because of the fat inner segments. In contrast, the adult cones, with their slender inner segments, are packed closely together. (Adapted from Banks & Bennett, 1988.)

tells us little, however, about how well we can see under lower contrasts and how well we can see forms that are larger than fine details. We can determine the visual system's ability to see at a wide range of contrasts, by measuring the contrast sensitivity function (CSF). (Review page 86 of Chapter 3, for a description of the CSF.)

Perceiving Contrast The contrast sensitivity functions for 1-, 2-, and 3-month-old infants and for adults, shown in Figure 16.10, indicate that (1) the infant's ability to perceive contrast is restricted to low frequencies; (2) At these low frequencies the infant's contrast sensitivity is lower than the adult's by a factor of 20 to 100; and (3) the infant can see little or nothing at frequencies above about 2 to 3 cycles/degree, the frequencies to which adults are most sensitive (Banks, 1982; Banks & Salapatek, 1978, 1981; Salapatek & Banks, 1978).

What does the young infant's depressed CSF tell us about its visual world? Clearly, infants are sensitive to only a small fraction of the pattern information available to the adult. At 1 month, infants can see no fine details and can see only relatively large objects with high contrast. The vision of infants at this age is slightly worse than adult night vision (Fiorentini & Maffei, 1973; Pirchio et al., 1978), a finding consistent with the fact that the undeveloped state of the infant's fovea forces it to see primarily with the rod-dominated peripheral retina.

We should not conclude from the young infant's poor vision, however, that it can see nothing at all. At very close distances, a young infant can detect some gross features, as indicated in Figure 16.11, which simulates how 1-, 2-, and 3-month-old infants perceive a woman's face from a distance of about 50 cm. At 1 month the contrast is so low that it is difficult to recognize facial expressions, but it is possible to see very high-contrast areas, such as the contour between the woman's hairline and forehead. By 3 months, however, the infant's contrast perception has improved so that the perception of facial expressions is

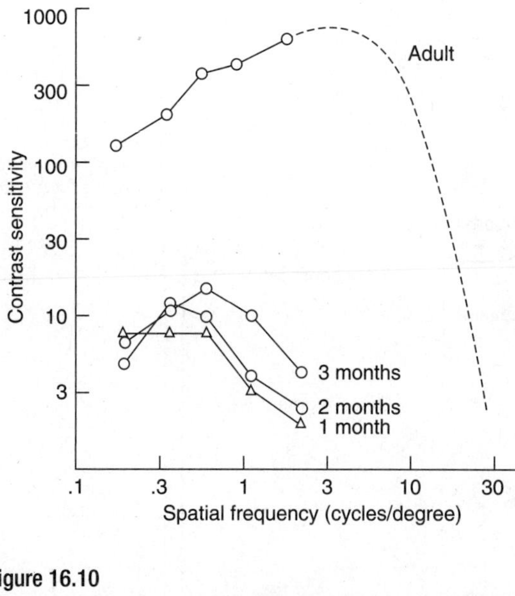

Figure 16.10
Contrast sensitivity functions for an adult and for infants tested at 1, 2, and 3 months of age.

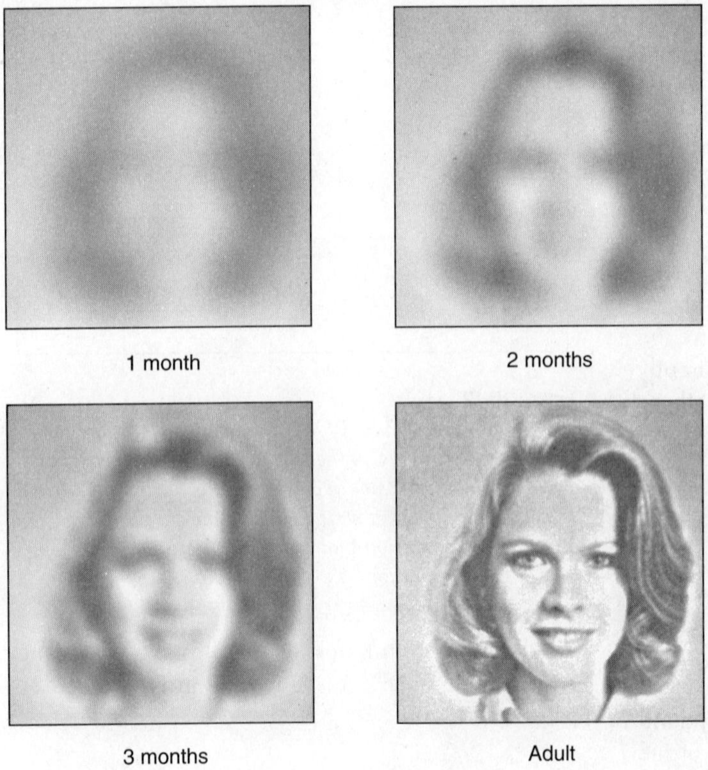

Figure 16.11
Simulations of what 1-, 2-, and 3-month-old infants see when they look at a woman's face from a distance of about 50 cm. These pictures were obtained by using a mathematical procedure that applies infant CSFs to the photograph on the right, which depicts what an adult perceives. (From Ginsburg, 1983.)

possible, and behavioral tests indicate that, by 3 to 4 months, infants can tell the difference between a face that looks happy and faces which show surprise, anger, or are neutral (LaBarbera et al., 1976; Young-Browne, Rosenfield, & Horowitz, 1977).

Infants have a very different "window on the world" from that of adults; infants see the world as if they are looking through a frosted glass that filters out the high frequencies that would enable them to see fine details, but leaves some ability to detect larger, low-frequency forms.

Perceiving Objects

The newborn's ability to use visual information exceeds what we might expect based simply on measurements of acuity or contrast sensitivity. For example, in spite of its poor acuity and contrast sensitivity, a 2- to 3-day-old infant can recognize its mother's face.

Recognizing the Mother's Face Research on the infant's ability to recognize faces provides an example of how research in perceptual development often progresses. First, an infant's ability to perceive a particular stimulus is demonstrated. Then, the result is confirmed by replicating it, perhaps also using improved procedures to rule out possible sources of bias. Finally, experiments are done to determine the information the infant is using to achieve its perception.

Using preferential looking in which 2-day-old infants were given a choice between their mother's face and a stranger's face, Bushnell, Sai, and Mullin (1989) found that infants looked at the mother about 63 percent of the time. Since this result is above the 50 percent chance level, Bushnell concluded that the 2-day-olds could recognize their mother's face. It is possible, however, that this result could have occurred because the mother was doing something to attract the infant's attention. Or perhaps the infant could detect the mother's familiar smell. Bushnell did take precautions to guard against these potential sources of bias, but just to be sure that the result was valid, Gail Walton and coworkers (1992) showed that infants still respond to the mother more than strangers when their faces are presented on videotape.

To determine what information the infants might be using to recognize the mother's face, Olivier Pascalis and coworkers (1995) showed that when the mother and stranger wore pink scarves that covered their hairline, the preference for the mother disappeared. The high-contrast border between the mother's dark hairline and light forehead apparently provides important information about the mother's physical characteristics which the infant uses to recognize its mother.

Distinguishing Figure from Ground We have considered the newborn's ability to detect the presence of visual stimuli. But detecting stimuli is just the first step in perception. To perceive objects in the environment, stimuli that are detected must become *perceptually organized.* This organization is often described in terms of figure-ground segregation—the separation of a display into a figure that is seen in front of the ground (see page 187 for more details on the differences between figure and ground).

Researchers have asked whether infants are capable of figure-ground segregation and, if they are, which aspects of the visual environment they use to achieve this separation of figure and ground. One conclusion from this research is that for infants motion is an important source of information.

Lincoln Craton and Albert Yonas (1990) used motion as a way to achieve figure-ground segregation in 5-month-old infants by using the stimulus shown in Figure 16.12. The two areas were filled with a computer-generated pattern of moving dots that created the perception that one area was covering the other area. In the example we will describe, adults saw the area on the left as the figure and the area on the right as the ground.

After the infants habituated to this stimulus, they saw either stimulus A or stimulus B. Since dishabituation occurred to Stimulus A, this means that the infant perceived the left side of the habituation stimulus as figure, just as adults did. (Remember that dishabituation occurs when a stimulus looks *different* from the habituation stimulus.) Thus, 5-month-old infants can separate areas into figure and ground based on movement.

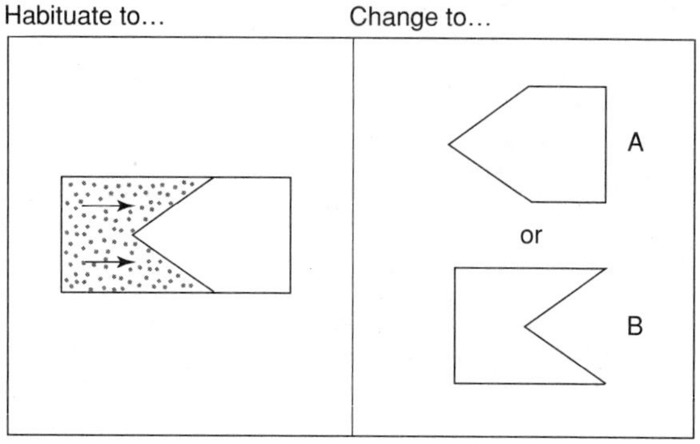

Figure 16.12
The Craton and Yonas (1990) experiment. Infants are habituated to the stimulus on the left. Dishabituation occurs to new stimulus A, but not to B. This means the infants perceived A as different from the habituation stimulus and leads to the conclusion that the infants were seeing the left side of the habituation stimulus as figure.

Grouping by Lightness Similarity To determine whether infants can perceptually group elements

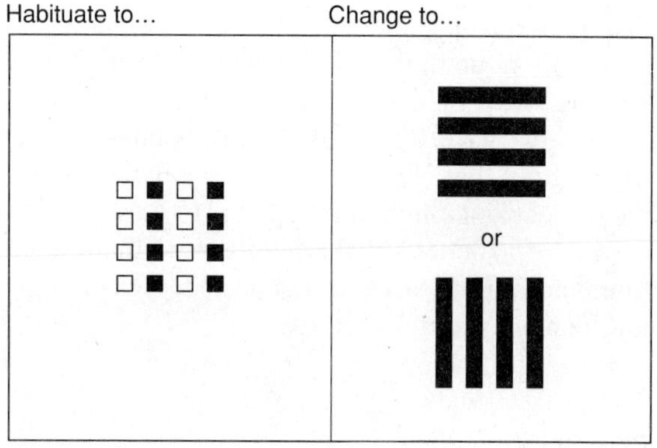

Figure 16.13
The Quinn, Burke, and Rush (1993) experiment. Infants habituated to the stimulus on the left show dishabituation to the horizontal bars. The experiment was also repeated with a habituation stimulus in which squares in horizontal rows were the same color. In that case, dishabituation occurred to the vertical bars.

based on their lightness (see the Gestalt law of similarity in Chapter 7), Paul Quinn, S. Burke, and A. Rush (1993) habituated 3-month-old infants to the pattern on the left in Figure 16.13, and then presented either horizontal bars (A) or vertical bars (B). Dishabituation occurred to the horizontal bars, indicating that the infants perceptually organized the squares into vertical columns.

Perceiving an Object as Continuing Behind an Occluder We will now describe a series of experiments that are interesting because (1) they consider a basic perceptual ability—the ability to perceive one stimulus as continuing behind an occluding stimulus—and (2) because they illustrate how researchers have zeroed in on the age at which a capacity first appears.

When adults look at the person in Figure 16.14, they perceive the man's body as continuing behind the fence. But does a young infant perceive the parts of the person that are visible as separate objects or as a single object that continues behind the fence? Philip Kellman and Elizabeth Spelke (1983) showed that movement helps infants perceive objects as continuing behind an occluding object by habituating 4-month-old infants to a rod moving back and forth behind a block (left stimulus in Figure 16.15) and then presenting either two separated rods or a single longer rod (right stimuli in Figure 16.15).

Since dishabituation occurred to the two separated rods, Kellman and Spelke concluded that 4-month-old infants perceive the partly occluded moving rod as continuing behind the block. This result does not, however, occur when the infant is habituated to a stationary rod and block display. Thus, movement provides information that a 4-month-old infant uses to infer that one object extends behind another. It appears that the 4-month-olds are making the following inference: *If the top and bottom units are moving together, then they must be part of the same object.*

If 4-month-olds perceive a moving object as continuing behind an occluding stimulus, can younger infants do this as well? When Alan Slater and coworkers (1990) repeated Kellman and Spelke's experiment for newborns, they found the opposite result. When the newborns saw the moving rod during habituation, they looked more at the single rod

Figure 16.14
An occluded person.

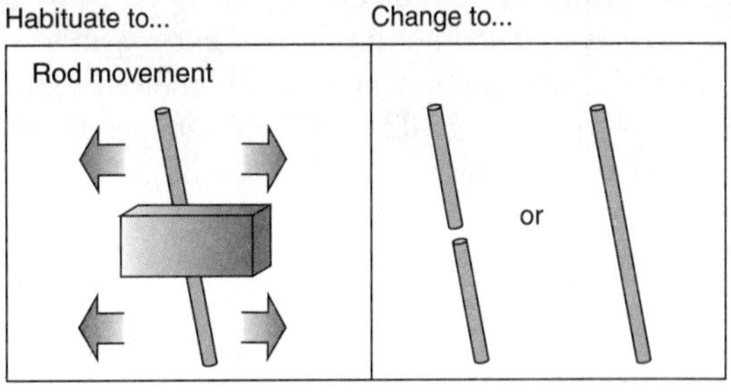

Figure 16.15
The Kellman and Spelke (1983) experiment. Infants dishabituated to the two rods on the left, but not to the longer single rod on the right. This indicates that 4-month-olds perceive the moving rod as continuing behind the block.

during dishabituation. This suggests that they saw the moving rods as two separate units, and not as a single rod extending behind the occluder. Apparently newborns do not make the inference that 4-month-olds make about the moving display.

Thus, the capacity demonstrated at 4 months does not exist (or can't be measured using this particular procedure) at birth. But when does it appear? Scott Johnson and Richard Aslin (1995) helped determine the answer to this question when they tested 2-month-olds and obtained results similar to what had previously been observed for the 4-month-olds. Apparently, the ability to use movement as a way to organize the perceptual world, develops rapidly over the first few months of life.

We have described some experiments that have looked at the infant's ability to perceive a number of different kinds of objects. Within a few days after birth, the infant can recognize its mother, apparently based on the ability to distinguish the mother's distinctive high-contrast hairline. Within the first few months of age infants can begin to perceptually organize stimuli, distinguish figure from ground, and infer the existence of stimuli that continue behind an occluder. We will now consider some experiments that used older infants as subjects. These experiments make two important points: (1) they confirm the importance of movement for organizing the perception of objects, and (2) they show that at 10 months of age the infant's ability to perceive objects is still developing.

Perceiving Adjacent Objects as Separate What characteristics or stimuli enable infants to tell that two objects that share a border are two separate objects? F. Xu and Susan Carey (1994) showed that for 10-month-old infants differences in shape or color may not be enough to signal that two objects are separate, but that movement information does help them reach this conclusion.

They habituated 10-month-old infants to a yellow toy duck sitting on top of a red toy truck (left stimulus in Figure 16.16). They then showed the infant either a hand lifting the duck and truck away from the truck (A), or a hand lifting the duck and truck together as if they were one object (B). Dishabituation occurred when the duck was lifted away from the truck (A). This result suggests that they perceived the habituation display as one object.

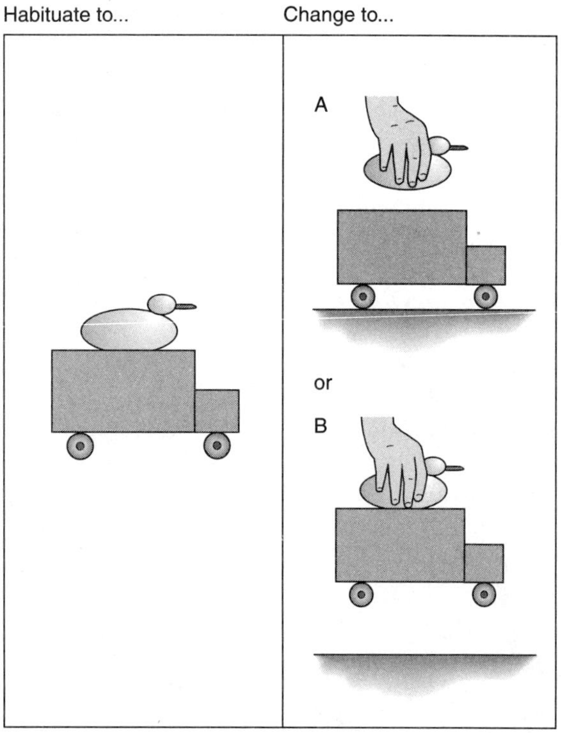

Figure 16.16
The Xu and Carey (1994) experiment in which the child is habituated to a stationary duck on top of the truck.

However, when the duck was moving back and forth on top of the truck during habituation (left stimulus in Figure 16.17), the infants looked longer when the duck and truck were lifted together (top right stimulus) suggesting that they saw the duck and truck as two separate objects. Thus, when the duck was stationary relative to the truck it did not appear separated from the truck, even though it had a different shape and color. However, when it was moving it appeared to be a separate object (Spelke, Gutheil, & Van de Walle, 1995). Apparently, 10-month-olds still lack some of the ability to differentiate one object from another that older children have, but are able to distinguish between objects when one is moving and the other is not.

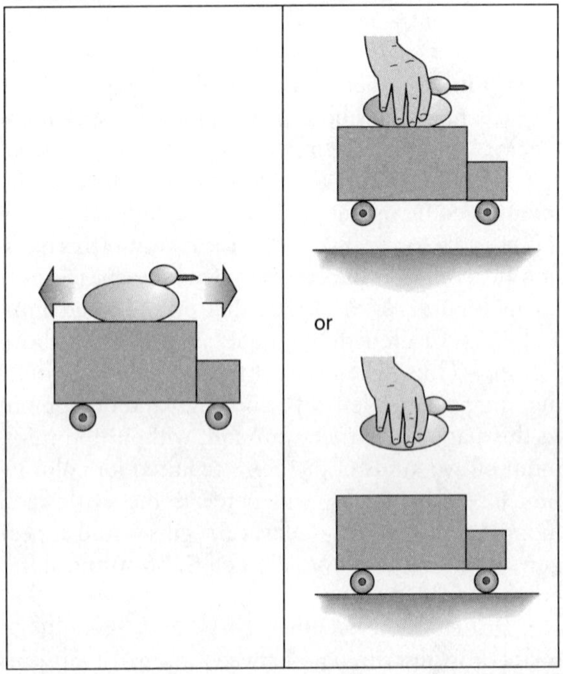

Figure 16.17
The Xu and Carey (1994) experiment in which the child is habituated to a duck that is moving on top of a stationary truck.

Our conclusion from all of these experiments is that during the early months of life infants gain the ability to perceptually organize objects in their environment. Movement is a particularly important source of information, but other information such as differences in lightness can be used as well. And by 3 to 4 months of age, infants can not only segregate some objects from one another, but are able to make discriminations between different *categories* of objects. For example, Peter Eimas and Paul Quinn (1994) showed that 3- to 4-month-old infants can tell the difference between pictures of dogs and pictures of cats. Although infants this age do not yet possess the concepts of "cat" and "dog," their ability to perceptually discriminate between them is the beginning of the process that culminates in the ability to understand categories and to use these categories to think and reason about the world.

Perceiving Color

We know that our perception of color is determined by the action of three different types of cone receptors. Since the cones are poorly developed at birth, we can guess that the newborn would not have good color vision. However, research has shown that color vision develops early and that appreciable color vision is present within the first few months of life.

One of the challenges in determining whether infants have color vision is created by the fact that a light stimulus can vary on at least two dimensions: (1) its chromatic color, and (2) its brightness. Thus, if we presented the red patch located at 12 o'clock on the color circle of Color Plate 2.3 and the yellow patch located at 3 o'clock to a totally color blind person and asked him if he could tell the difference between them, he would say *yes,* because the yellow patch is much brighter than the red one.

A way to do this experiment, if you don't have access to a color-blind person, is to use a "color-blind" black-and-white Xerox machine as your "subject." The picture you obtain by Xeroxing the color circle will tell you that even though the machine can't "see" in color, it can tell that there are differences between the two patches, based on the difference in brightness between them. This means that the stimuli used in testing for the presence of color vision should differ in wavelength, but should be the same brightness. The experiments we will now describe have done this.

Perceiving Color Categories Marc Bornstein, William Kessen, and Sally Weiskopf (1976) assessed the color vision of 4-month-old infants by asking whether they perceive the same color categories in the spectrum as adults. People with normal trichromatic vision see the spectrum as a sequence of color categories, starting with blue at the short-wavelength end, and followed by green, yellow, orange, and red, with fairly abrupt transitions between one color and the next (see spectrum of Color Plate 1.1).

Bornstein and his coworkers first habituated the infants to a 510-nm light—a wavelength that appears green to a trichromat—and then presented either a 480-nm light, which looks blue to a trichromat, or a 540-nm light, which is on the other side of the blue-green border and therefore appears green to a trichromat (Figure 16.18a). Since dishabituation occurred to the 480-nm light but not to the 540-nm light (Figure 16.18b), the 480-nm light apparently looks different than the 510-nm light and the 540-nm light looks similar to it. From this result and the results of other experiments, Bornstein concluded that 4-month-old infants categorize colors the same way trichromats do.

Bornstein and his coworkers dealt with the problem of equating brightness by setting the intensity at each wavelength so each stimulus looked equally bright to adults. This is not an ideal procedure since infants may perceive brightness differently than adults. However, as it turns out, Bornstein's result appears to be correct, since later research has shown that even younger infants have color vision.

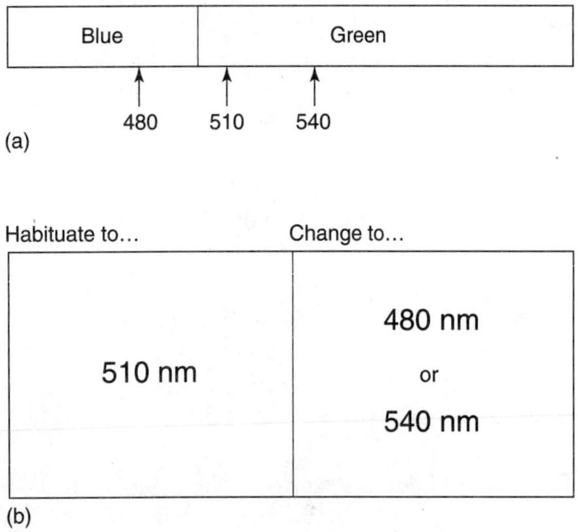

Figure 16.18
(a) The three wavelengths used in the Bornstein, Kessen, and Weiskopf (1976) experiment. The 510- and 480-nm lights are in different perceptual categories (one appears green, the other blue to adults), but the 510- and 540-nm lights are in the same perceptual category (both appear green to adults). (b) The habituation procedure and results. The infant dishabituated to 480 nm, but not to 540 nm.

Discriminating between Long-Wavelength Lights We will now describe a psychophysical experiment that was designed to answer the question, "At what age do both medium- and long-wavelength cone pigments become operational? We can understand why it is possible to use psychophysics to answer this question by looking at the cone pigment absorption spectra in Figure 16.19. Notice that only the medium- and long-wavelength pigments absorb light above 550 nm. Thus, when one of these pigments is missing, the person is left with only one kind of pigment in this part of the spectrum and, without the minimum of two kinds of pigments required for color vision (see Chapter 5), will perceive the world as a monochromat would—all wavelengths would appear gray or the same chromatic color and would differ only in brightness.

To determine whether 1-, 2-, and 3-month-old infants can discriminate between a green (550 nm) and a yellow (589 nm) with the same brightness, Russell Hamer, Kenneth Alexander, and Davida Teller (1982) used the preferential looking technique and the display in Figure 16.20. This display contains a green test square that was presented either on the left or the right side of the yellow background. If infants

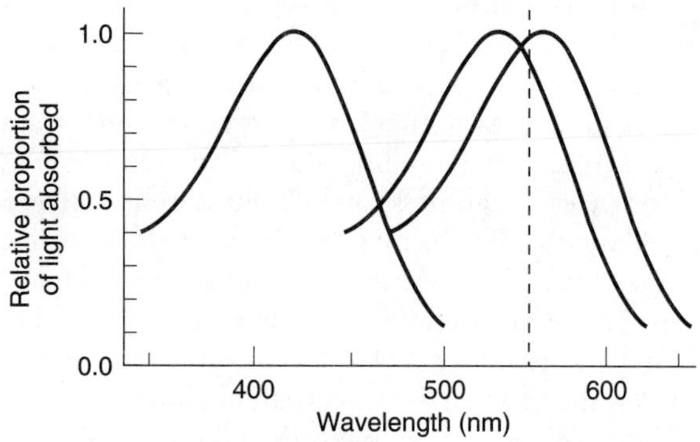

Figure 16.19
Cone absorption spectra. Notice that above the vertical line at 550 nm, only the medium- and long-wavelength pigments absorb light. (From Dartnall, Bowmaker, & Mollon, 1983.)

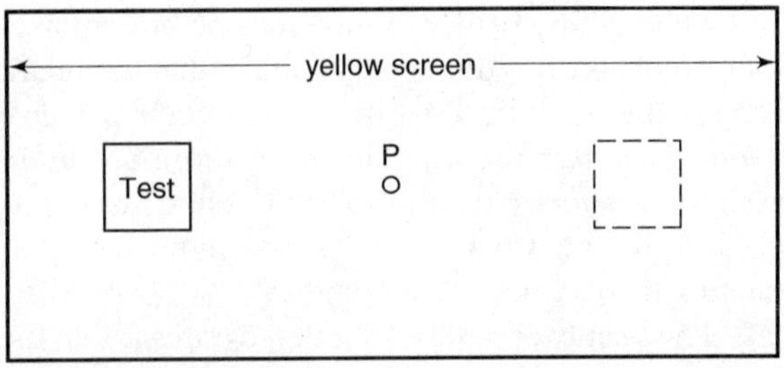

Figure 16.20
The stimulus used by Hamer, Alexander, and Teller (1982) to determine whether infants can tell the difference between two wavelengths above 550 nm that have the same brightness. A 550-nm test square that appears green to an adult is presented either on the left or on the right side of a 589-nm yellow screen. The infant's looking behavior is monitored by an observer who views the infant through the peephole, P.

can differentiate the green square from its background, they will direct their eyes to the green square.

Hamer and coworkers knew that in order to draw any conclusion about the infant's color vision they had to be sure the green square and the yellow background had the same brightness. They accomplished this by presenting the green square at a wide range of intensities on different trials, so at least one of the intensities would match the brightness of the yellow background. They reasoned that if the infant can discriminate between green and yellow based on chromatic color, they should be able to see the green square at *all* of their intensities—both the ones where the brightness would be different than the yellow background *and* the one where it would be the same.

Hamer et al. found that about one-half of the 1-month-old infants could discriminate between green and yellow at all of the intensities, and that by 3 months, almost all of the infants could make this discrimination (Figure 16.21). Based on this result, Hamer et al. concluded that some 1-month-old infants, most 2-month-old infants, and all 3-month-old infants have operational medium- and long-wavelength cone receptors.

Researchers have also asked whether infants have short-wavelength receptors. Using a procedure similar to Hamer's, D. Varner and coworkers (1985) tested infants' ability to see short-wavelength light and found that, by 2 months of age, infants have functioning short-wavelength cones. Our conclusion from the Hamer et al. and Varner et al. experiments is that all three types of cones are present by at least 2 to 3 months of age, and that some infants show evidence of three-cone vision even earlier. This infant trichromatic vision may not be identical to normal adult color vision, but it does seem likely that infants as young as 2 or 3 months old experience a wide range of colors.

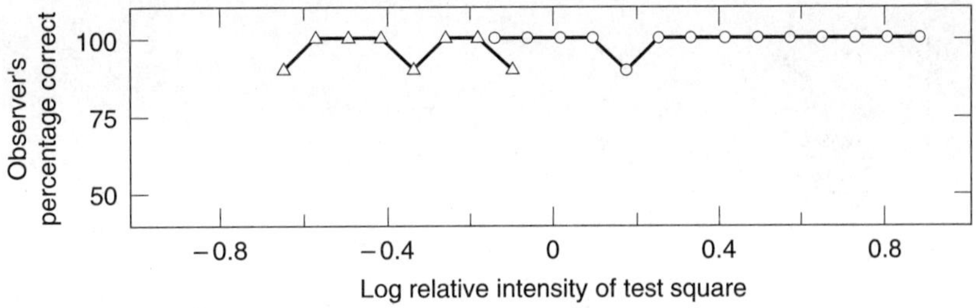

Figure 16.21
Results of the Hamer, Alexander and Teller (1982) experiment for a 4-week-old infant. The infant's ability to detect the green test square was measured at a range of intensities of the test square, indicated along the horizontal axis. The intensity marked 0 represents the intensity at which the green and the yellow have the same brightness for an adult. Since the infant's performance ranged from 80 percent to 100 percent correct at all intensities, we can infer that she was, in fact, able to distinguish the green square from the yellow background on the basis of color alone.

Perceiving Depth

When infants are born, they have poor visual acuity and little or no depth perception. At what age are infants able to use different kinds of depth information? The answer to this question is that different types of information become operative at different times, binocular disparity becoming functional early and pictorial depth cues becoming functional later.

Using Binocular Disparity One requirement for the operation of binocular disparity is that the eyes must be able to **binocularly fixate** so that the two foveas are directed to exactly the same place. Newborns have only a rudimentary ability to fixate binocularly, so their binocular fixation is imprecise, especially on objects that are changing in depth (Slater & Findlay, 1975).

Richard Aslin (1977) determined when binocular fixation develops by making some simple observations. He filmed infants' eyes while moving a target back and forth between 12 cm and 57 cm from the infant. If the infant is directing both eyes at a target, the eyes should diverge (rotate outward) as the target moves away and should converge (rotate inward) as the target moves closer (Figure 16.22). Aslin's films indicate that while some divergence and convergence does occur in 1- and 2-month-old infants, these eye movements do not reliably direct both eyes toward the target until about 3 months of age.

Although binocular fixation may be present by 3 months of age, this does not guarantee that the infant can use the resulting disparity information to perceive depth. To determine when infants can use this information to perceive depth, Robert Fox and coworkers (1980) presented random-dot stereograms to infants ranging in age from 2 to 6 months.

The beauty of random-dot stereograms is that the binocular disparity information in the stereograms results in stereopsis (the perception of depth due to binocular disparity) only (1) if the stereogram is observed with a device that presents one picture to the left eye and the other picture to the right eye, and (2) if the observer's visual system can convert this disparity information into the perception of depth. Thus, if we present a random-dot stereogram to an infant whose visual system cannot yet use disparity information, all he or she will see is a random collection of dots.

In Fox's experiment, a child wearing special viewing glasses was seated in its mother's lap in front of a television screen (Figure 16.23). The child viewed a random-dot stereogram that appeared to an observer sensitive to disparity information, as a rectangle-in-depth, moving either to the left or to the right. Fox's premise was that an infant sensitive to disparity will move his or her eyes to follow the moving rectangle. He found that infants younger than about 3 months of age would not follow the rectangle, but that infants between 3 and 6 months of age would

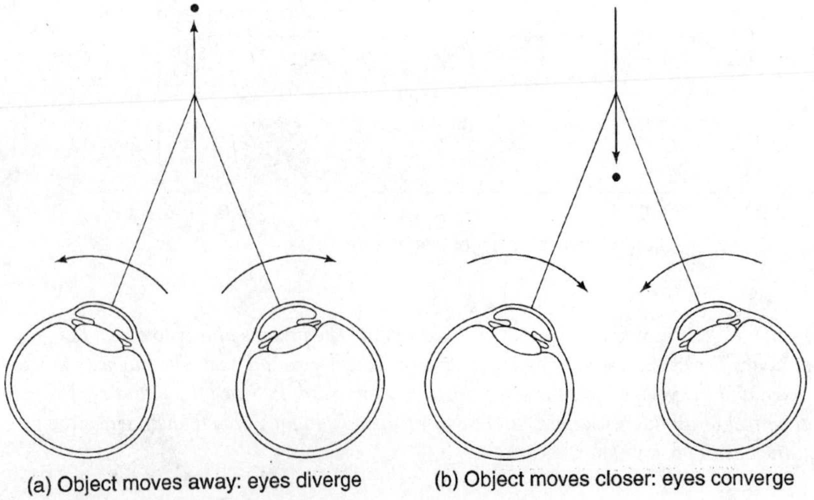

Figure 16.22
If an infant is fixating on an object that is moving, its eyes (a) diverge (rotate outward) as it follows an object that is moving away and (b) converge (rotate inward) as it follows an object that is moving closer.

Figure 16.23
The setup used by Fox et al. (1980) to test infants' ability to use binocular disparity information. If the infant can use disparity information to see depth, he or she sees a rectangle moving back and forth in front of the screen.

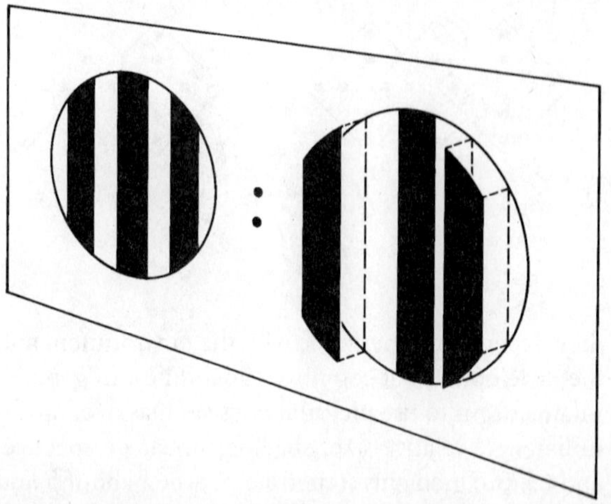

Figure 16.24
Stimuli used by Held, Birch, and Gwiazda (1980) to test stereoacuity. The pattern on the left is a two-dimensional grating. The one on the right is a stereogram that looks three-dimensional when viewed through special glasses. This three-dimensional perception occurs, however, only if the subject can perceive depth based on disparity.

follow it. He therefore concluded that the ability to use disparity information to perceive depth emerges sometime between 3½ and 6 months of age.

Richard Held, Eileen Birch, and Jane Gwiazda, 1980 showed that infants develop the ability to use disparity information by about 3½ months of age by measuring infants' **stereoacuity,** the smallest amount of disparity that results in the perception of depth. Held measured the infants' stereoacuity by having them view the display shown in Figure 16.24. One stimulus in this display was a flat picture of three black bars, and the other was a stereogram that, when viewed through special glasses, appeared to be three-dimensional to adults. This type of stereogram can create smaller differences in disparity than the random-dot stereogram and therefore provides a more sensitive measure of infants' abilities.

Using the preferential looking technique, Held determined that by about 3½ months of age, infants preferentially look at the three-dimensional stimulus. By showing the infants stereograms with a number of different disparities, Held was able to trace the development of the ability to use disparity. At 3½ months, infants are able to detect disparities of about 1 degree of visual angle, and by 4½ months, stereoacuity increases rapidly to less than 1 minute of visual angle (1 minute of visual angle = 1/60 degree). Thus, Held showed that, once the ability to detect disparity appears, infants show a rapid increase in stereoacuity to fairly good levels by between 4 and 5 months of age.

The development of the ability to use disparity to detect depth beginning just after 3 months of age is probably due to development of the physiological mechanisms involved in maintaining good binocular fixation and on the development of the neural connections necessary to create disparity-selective neurons (see page 231).

Another type of depth information, that we also discussed in Chapter 8, is the pictorial cues. These cues develop later than disparity, presumably because

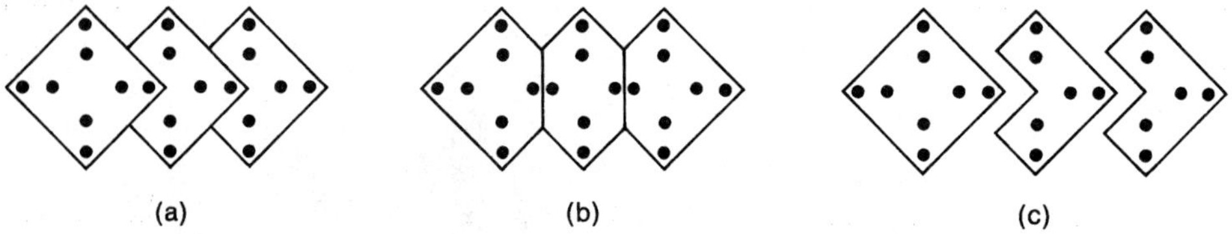

Figure 16.25
Stimuli for Granrud and Yonas's (1984) interposition experiment.

they depend on experience with the environment and the development of cognitive capabilities. In general, infants begin to use pictorial cues such as overlap, familiar size, relative size, shading, linear perspective, and texture gradients sometime between about 5 and 7 months of age (Granrud & Yonas, 1984; Granrud, Haake, & Yonas, 1985; Granrud, Yonas, & Opland, 1985; Yonas et al., 1986; Yonas, Pettersen, & Granrud, 1982). We will describe research on two of these cues—overlap and familiar size.

Depth from Overlap To test infants' ability to perceive depth from overlap, Carl Granrud and Albert Yonas (1984) showed them two-dimensional cardboard cutouts of the displays depicted in Figure 16.25. The infants viewed the cutouts with just one eye, because binocular viewing would reveal that the displays were flat and could lower the chances that the infants would respond to the pictorially-induced depth. Display (a) includes the depth cue of overlap, whereas displays (b) and (c) do not. Since infants tend to reach for objects they perceive as being nearer, they will reach more for (a) than for (b) or (c) if they are sensitive to overlap. This was the result for 7-month-olds, but not for 5-month-olds. Thus, the ability to perceive depth based on overlap appears sometime between 5 and 7 months.

Depth from Familiar Size Granrud, Haake, and Yonas (1985) conducted a two-part experiment to see if infants can use their knowledge of the sizes of objects to help them perceive depth. In the familiarization period, 7-month-old infants played with a pair of wooden objects for 10 minutes. One of these objects was large (Figure 16.26a) and one was small (Figure 16.26b). In the test period, objects (c) and (d) were presented at the same distance from the infant. The prediction was that infants sensitive to familiar size would perceive object C to be closer if they remembered, from the familiarization period, that this shape was smaller than the other one.

When tested monocularly, the 7-month-olds did reach for object C. The 5-month-olds, however, did not reach for object C, a result indicating that these infants did not use familiar size as information for depth. Thus, just as for overlap, the ability to use familiar size to perceive depth appears to develop sometime between 5 and 7 months.

This experiment is interesting not only because it indicates when the ability to use familiar size develops, but also because the infant's response in the test phase depends on a cognitive ability—the ability to *remember* the sizes of the objects that he or she played with in the familiarization phase. The 7-month-old infant's depth response in this situation is therefore based both on what is perceived *and* what is remembered.

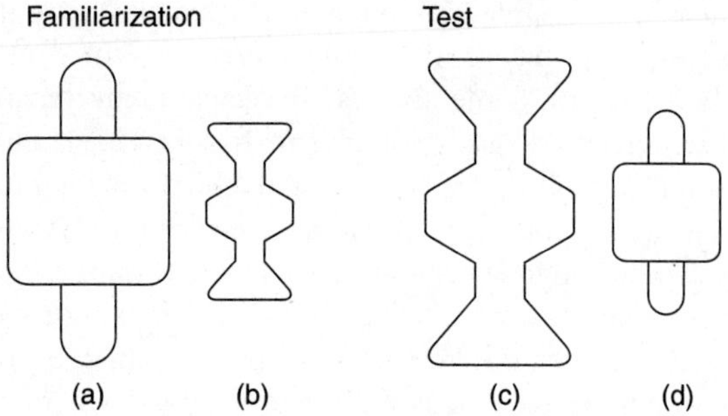

Figure 16.26
Stimuli for Granrud, Haake, and Yonas's (1985) familiar-size experiment.

Perceiving Movement

Human infants come into the world specially adapted to perceive motion, and this ability is apparent shortly after birth (Nelson & Horowitz, 1987).

Perception of a Moving Object One of the best ways to attract a young infant's attention is to move something across his or her visual field. Newborns direct their eyes at moving stimuli and follow them with a combination of head and eye movements (Haith, 1983; Kremenitzer et al., 1979). When presented with a choice between a moving stimulus and a complex three-dimensional form, the infant prefers the moving stimulus (Fantz & Nevis, 1967), and when presented with two stimuli that are identical in all respects, except movement, infants as young as 2-weeks old will look at the moving stimulus (Nelson & Horowitz, 1987).

It isn't surprising that infants begin perceiving movement at an early age. After all, movement is everywhere in an infant's environment, and it provides the infant with rich information about various characteristics of its world. But although infants perceive movement at an early age, this doesn't mean that they perceive movement in the same way as adults. For example, although infants can follow moving objects with their eyes, their eyes move in a series of short, jerky movements, called *saccades,* up to about 6 to 8 weeks of age. It isn't until about 10 to 12 weeks that infants can make smooth eye movements to follow a moving stimulus (Aslin, 1981a).

One of the characteristics of movement that we discussed in Chapters 7 and 10 and also earlier in this chapter, is that it can create perceptual organization. Two objects that are moving in the same direction at the same speed appear to belong together. One of the most interesting examples of movement creating perceptual organization is biological movement. We saw in Chapter 10 that we can create a stimulus called a *point-light walker* by placing a number of lights on a person's body (see Figure 10.33).

If we have a subject view the point-light walker in the dark, they will see the lights as individual unrelated dots when the person is stationary. However, as soon as the point-light walker begins moving, all of the lights together are suddenly perceived as a moving person. Perceiving the moving lights as a person involves perceptually organizing the individual lights into a single unit, something that infants may begin doing at around 4 months of age.

Perceiving Biological Motion Robert Fox and Cynthia McDaniel (1982) used the preferential looking technique to determine whether infants are capable of recognizing biological motion. A videotape of the lights attached to a running person was shown on one screen, and another videotape of randomly moving lights was shown on the other screen. When placed in front of the two screens, 2-month-old infants showed no preference, looking at both screens equally. But 4- and 6-month-old infants looked at the biological motion tape about 70 percent of the time. Thus, by age 4 months, infants can tell the difference between these two types of motion and prefer the biological motion.

The fact that infants are sensitive to biological motion by 4 months of age fits our earlier results, which showed that infants were capable of perceptually organizing visual stimuli by about 4 months of age. But does the fact that infants can *discriminate* between biological motion and other types of motion mean that infants *perceive* biological motion in the same way as adults? The results of an experiment by Bertenthal and coworkers (1985) suggest that the answer to this question may be *No.* In this experiment, Bertenthal et al. tested infants to determine whether they were sensitive to a property of point-light walkers that is obvious to adults—as the walker moves, certain lights are occluded from view by movement of the walker's limbs relative to other parts of the body. For example, notice in Figure 10.33 that the light on the walker's left knee is blocked from view by her right leg. As she walks, this light will become visible, then it will become occluded again, and so on.

The occlusion of some of the lights during the walker's movement is one of the properties that helps make moving point-light walker stimuli appear three-dimensional to adults. They easily recognize displays with occlusion as a walking person, but they rarely perceive a walking person when they are shown displays in which occlusion has been eliminated so that all of the lights are always visible. When Bertenthal et al. presented occluded and nonoccluded displays to infants, they found that 8-month-old infants were able to discriminate the occluded from the nonoccluded displays, but 5-month-old infants were not.

The results of this experiment suggest that although 5-month-olds can *discriminate* between the biological motion of point-light walkers and other types of point-light movement, they may not *perceive* the biological motion as a three-dimensional walking person, as adults do. Before they can achieve this perception, they need to become sensitive to occlusion, which occurs at about 8 months of age. Of course, we don't really know what 8-month-old infants perceive. All we can safely say is that their perception of point-light walkers is probably more adultlike than the 5-month-olds' perception.

Infant Perceptual Capacities: Hearing and the Chemical Senses

Hearing

What do newborn infants hear, and how does their hearing change over time? Although some early psychologists felt that newborns were functionally deaf, recent research has shown that newborns do have some auditory capacities and that this capacity improves as the child gets older (Werner & Bargones, 1992).

Recognizing the Mother's Voice One approach to determining the newborn's ability to hear is to show that they can identify sounds they have heard before. Anthony DeCasper and William Fifer (1980) demonstrated this capacity in newborns by showing that 2-day-old infants will modify their sucking on a nipple in order to hear the sound of their mother's voice. They first observed that infants usually suck on a nipple in bursts separated by pauses. They fitted infants with earphones and let the length of the pause in the infant's sucking determine whether the infant heard a recording of its mother's voice or a recording of a stranger's voice (Figure 16.27). For half of the infants, long pauses activated the tape of the mother's voice, and short pauses activated the tape of the stranger's voice. For the other half, these conditions were reversed.

DeCasper and Fifer found that the babies regulated the pauses in their sucking so that they heard their mother's voice more than the stranger's voice. This is a remarkable accomplishment for a 2-day-old, especially since most of them had been with their mothers for only a few hours between the time they were born and the time they were tested.

Why did the newborns prefer their mother's voice? DeCasper and Fifer suggested that newborns recognize their mother's voice because they heard the mother talking while they were developing in the mother's womb. This suggestion is supported by the results of another experiment, in which DeCasper and M. J. Spence (1986) had one group of pregnant women read from Dr. Seuss's book *The Cat in the Hat* and another group read the same story with the words cat and hat replaced with dog and fog. When the children were born, they regulated their sucking pattern to hear the version of the story their mother had read

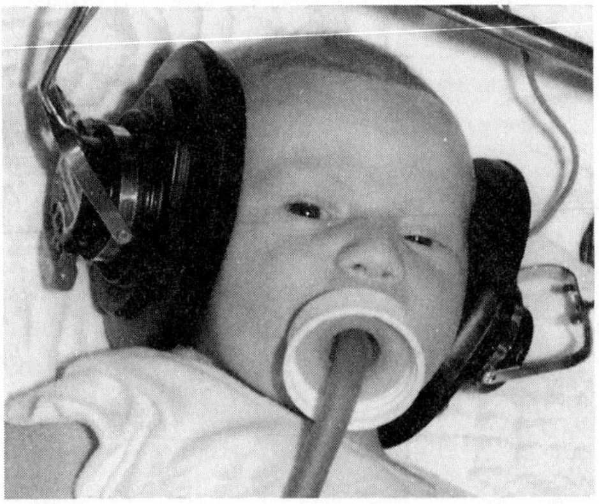

Figure 16.27
This baby, a subject in DeCasper and Fifer's (1980) study, could control whether she heard a recording of her mother's voice or a stranger's voice by the way she sucked on the nipple.

when they were in the womb. In another experiment, 2-day-old infants regulated their sucking to hear a recording of their native language rather than of a foreign language (Moon, Cooper, & Fifer, 1993). Apparently, even when in the womb, the fetus becomes familiar with the intonation and rhythm of the mother's voice, and also with the sounds of specific words. (Also see DeCasper et al., 1994.)

Thresholds for Hearing a Tone A simple way to determine whether infants can hear is to determine if they will orient toward the source of a sound. Darwin Muir and Jeffry Field (1979) presented newborn infants with a loud (80-dB) rattle sound 20 cm from either their right or their left ear and found that the infants usually turned toward the sound (Figure 16.28). Newborns can therefore hear and are capable of at least crude sound localization.

More precise measurements of infants' capacities have been achieved with older infants, who have a wider repertoire of responses to sound. Lynne Werner Olsho and her coworkers (1988) used a technique she called the *observer-based psychoacoustic procedure* to determine infants' audibility curves. This procedure works as follows: An infant is fitted with earphones and sits on the parent's lap. An observer, sitting out of view of the infant, watches the infant through a window. A light blinks on, indicating that a trial has begun, and the infant is either presented with a tone or is not. The observer's task is to decide whether or not the infant heard the tone (Olsho et al., 1987).

How can observers tell whether the infant has heard a tone? They decide by looking for responses such as eye movements, changes in facial expression, a wide-eyed look, a turn of the head, or changes in activity level. Although this determination is not an easy task for observers, we can see from the data in Figure 16.29 that it works (Olsho et al., 1988). Observers only occasionally indicated that the 3-month-old infants heard a 2,000-Hz tone that was presented at low intensities or not at all. But as the tone's intensity was increased, the observers were more likely to say that the infant had heard the tone. The infant's threshold at 2,000 Hz was determined from this curve, and the results from a number of frequencies were combined to create audibility curves, such as those in Figure 16.30. This figure, which shows curves for 3- and 6-month-olds and adults, indicates that infant and adult audibility functions look similar and that, by 6 months of age, the infant's threshold is within about 10 to 15 dB of the adult threshold.

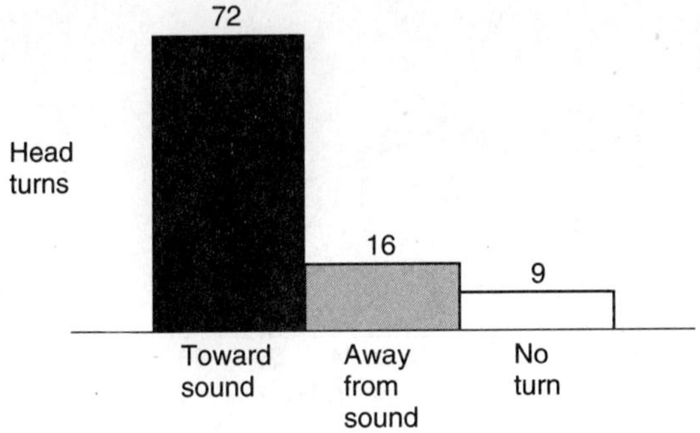

Figure 16.28
Number of head turns made by newborns in response to an 80-dB-SPL sound. Most of the turns were toward the sound, a response indicating that the infants could localize the sound. (Based on data from Muir & Field, 1979.)

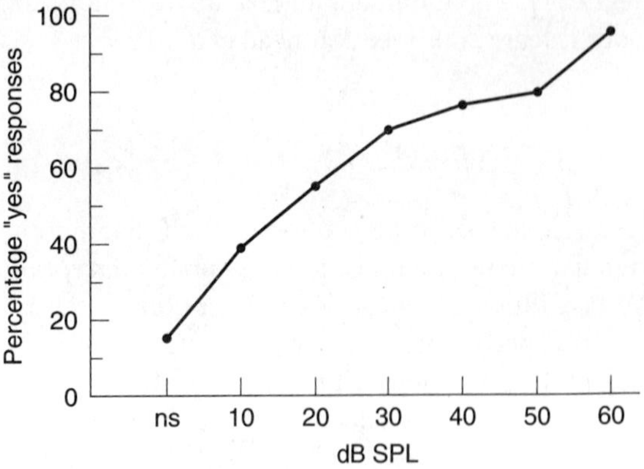

Figure 16.29
Data obtained from the observer-based psychoacoustic procedure, which indicates the percentage of trials on which the observer indicated that a 3-month-old infant heard a 2,000-Hz tone presented at different intensities. NS indicates no sound. (From Olsho et al., 1988.)

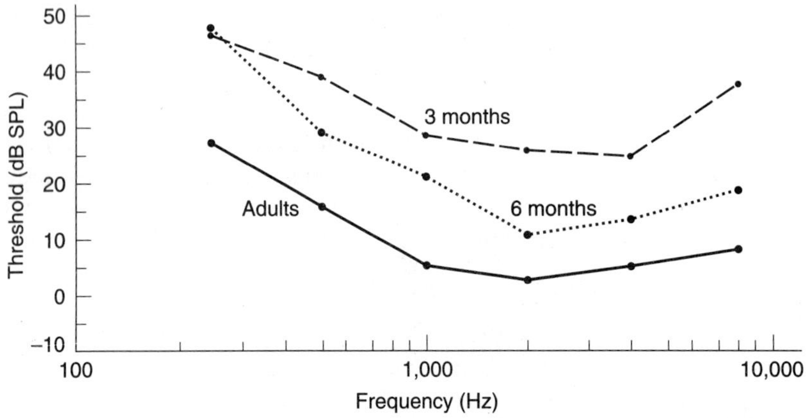

Figure 16.30
Audibility curves for 3- and 6-month-old infants determined from the observer-based psychoacoustic procedure. The curve for 12-month-olds is similar to the curve for 6-month-olds. The adult curve is shown for comparison. (Adapted from Olsho et al., 1988.)

Localizing Sounds Using a procedure similar to the one used to measure thresholds described above, Barbara Morrongiello (1988; Morrongiello, Fenwick, & Chance, 1990) measured infant's ability to locate sounds presented to their left or right. She measured the angle between two sounds that the infant could perceive—the **minimum audible angle** and found that at 8 weeks of age the minimum audible angle is 27 degrees, but by the time the child is a year and a half old, it has decreased to about 5 degrees (Figure 16.31). The minimum audible angle for adults is about 1 degree (also see Ashmead et al., 1991).

Speech Perception

Research on speech perception in adults has demonstrated a phenomenon called *categorical perception.* We can illustrate categorical perception by reviewing an experiment we described in Chapter 13. A subject is presented with a sound stimulus that sounds like "ba." A characteristic of this stimulus, called *voice onset time* (VOT), which is the time delay between the beginning of a sound and when the vocal cords start vibrating, is then systematically changed, using a computer, and the subject reports what he or she hears. (See page 390 for a more detailed description of voice onset time and categorical perception experiments.)

The main result of an experiment such as this one is that even when VOT is changed over a wide range, subjects tend to hear only two sounds. At short voice onset times they hear the sound "ba" and at long voice onset times they hear the sound "pa." There is a place between these two extremes where changing the VOT just a little causes the person's

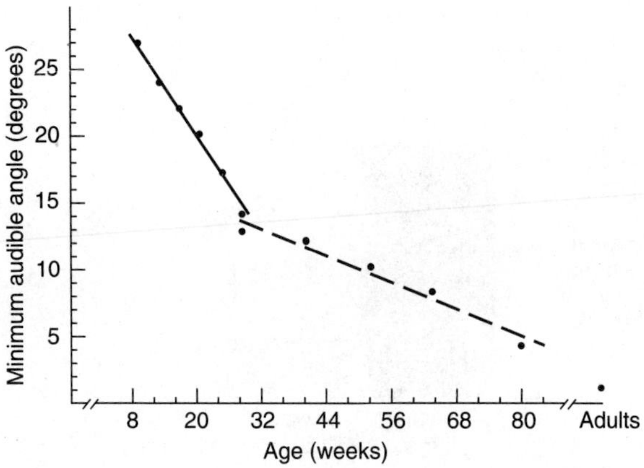

Figure 16.31
The minimum audible angle as a function of age. The infants' ability to localize sounds improves to almost adult levels over the first year and a half. (From Morrongiello, Fenwick, & Chance, 1990.)

perception to change from "ba" to "pa." This place is called the *phonetic boundary.*

The fact that subjects perceive only two sounds, "ba" and "pa," over a wide range of VOTs is categorical perception—we perceive speech sounds as being in a limited number of categories. Categorical perception was first reported for adults in 1967 (Liberman et al., 1967). In 1971 Peter Eimas and coworkers began the modern era of research on infant speech perception by showing that young infants perceive speech in categories, just as adults do.

Perceiving Speech Sounds in Categories Eimas used a habituation procedure to show that infants as young as 1 month old perform similarly to adults in categorical perception experiments. The basis of these experiments was the observation that an infant will suck on a nipple in order to hear a series of brief speech sounds, but when the same speech sounds are repeated, the infant's sucking eventually habituates to a low level. By presenting a new stimulus after the rate of sucking has decreased, Eimas determined whether the infant perceived the new stimulus as sounding the same as or different from the old one.

The results of Eimas et al.'s experiment are shown in Figure 16.32. The number of sucking responses when no sound was presented is indicated by the point at B. When a sound with voice onset time (VOT) = +20 msec (sounds like "ba" to an adult) is presented when the infant sucks, the sucking increases to a high level and then begins to decrease. When the VOT is changed to +40 msec (sounds like "pa" to an adult), sucking increases, as indicated by the points to the right of the dashed line. This result means that the infant perceives a difference between sounds with VOTs of +20 and +40 msec. The center graph, however, shows that changing the VOT from +60 to +80 msec (both sound like "pa" to an adult) has only a small effect on sucking, indicating that the infants perceive little, if any, difference between the two sounds. Finally, the results for a control group (the right graph) show that, when the sound is not changed, the number of sucking responses decreases throughout the experiment.

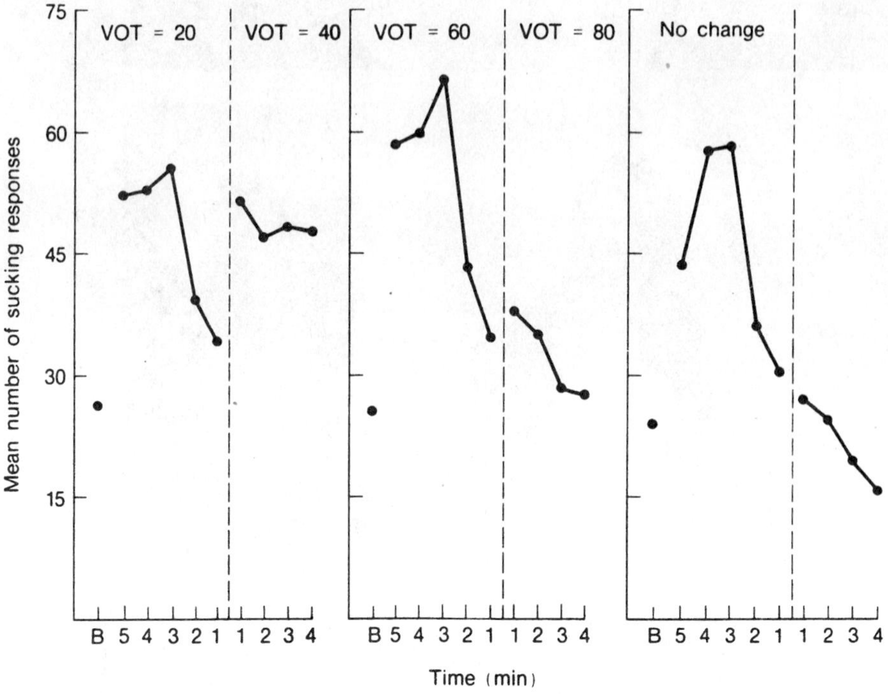

Figure 16.32
Results of a categorical perception experiment on infants, using the habituation procedure. In the left panel, VOT is changed from 20 to 40 msec (across the phonetic boundary). In the center panel, VOT is changed from 60 to 80 msec (not across the phonetic boundary). In the right panel, the VOT was not changed. See text for details.

These results show that, when the VOT is shifted across the phonetic boundary (left graph), the infants perceive a change in the sound, and when the VOT is shifted on the same side of the phonetic boundary (center graph), the infants perceive little or no change in the sound. That infants as young as 1 month old are capable of categorical perception is particularly impressive, especially since these infants have had virtually no experience in producing speech sounds and only limited experience in hearing them.

Perceiving Vowels Made by Different Speakers as Being in the Same Class Another parallel between infant and adult speech perception is Patricia Kuhl's (1983, 1989) finding that infants have an ability called **equivalence classification**—the ability to classify vowel sounds as belonging to a class, even when the speakers are different. Adults have this ability, so they can classify an /a/ sound as the vowel *a* whether it is spoken by a male or a female. By using a conditioning procedure (Figure 16.33), Patricia Kuhl (1983,

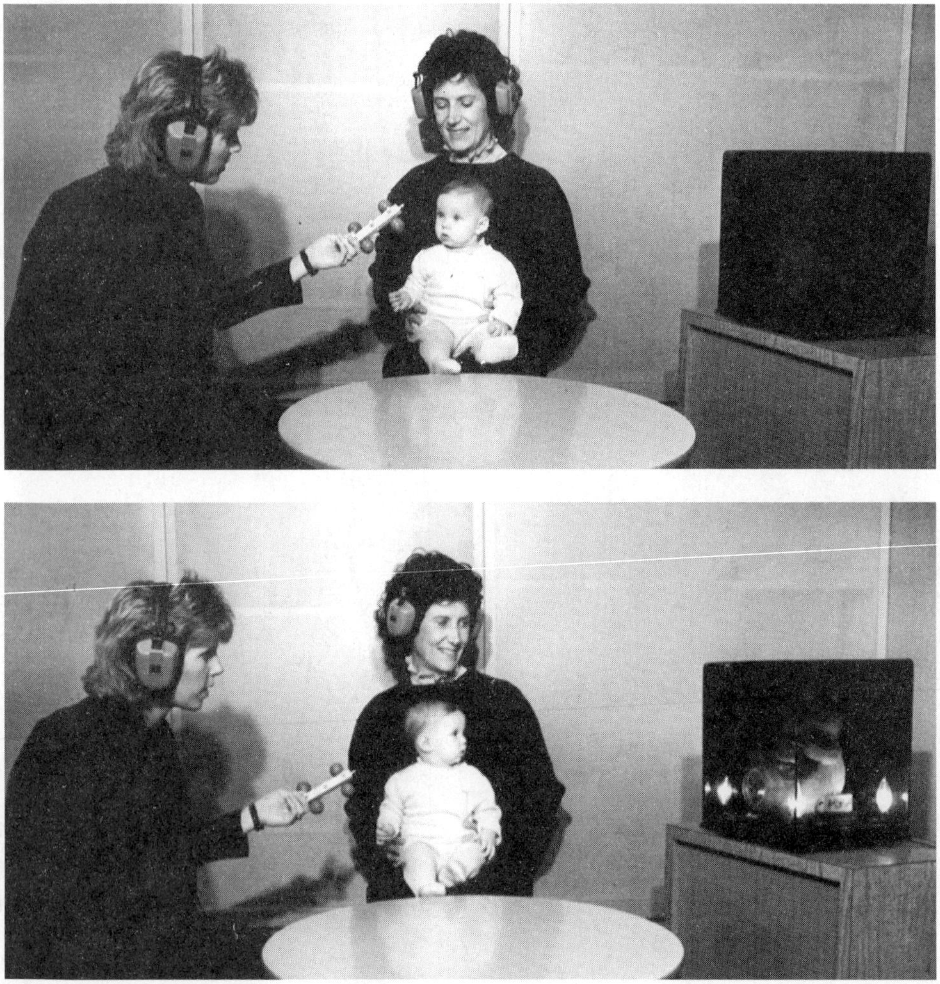

Figure 16.33
In the conditioning procedure used by Kuhl (1983, 1989), infants are trained to turn their heads toward the loudspeaker on their left when they hear a change from one speech category to another.

1989) showed that 6-month-old infants are capable of equivalence classification. The infant sits on a parent's lap and hears a speech sound such as /a/ repeated over and over. At some point, the sound changes from /a/ to /i/, and when this change happens,* a bear playing a drum is activated, and the child looks toward the bear. After this procedure is repeated a number of times, the child learns to look toward the bear anytime the sound changes from /a/ to /i/. Thus, when the child looks at the bear, the experimenter knows that the child has perceived a change.

Kuhl asked, "Does the infant perceive all /a/ sounds as belonging to the same category, even when other characteristics of the sound are changed?" She answered this question by presenting a male voice saying /a/ and then changing it to a female voice saying /a/. Even though the voice changed, no head turn occurred. However, when the stimulus was changed from a male voice saying /a/, to either a male's voice, a female's voice, or a child's voice saying /i/, head turning did occur, a result indicating that the child reacted in the same way to the /i/ stimulus no matter which voice was saying it.

From these results, Kuhl concluded that infants do achieve classification: They classify all /a/sounds as the same and all /i/ sounds as the same, no matter what the quality of the voice saying them. (Also see Marean, Werner, & Kuhl, 1992, for similar results for 2-month-olds.) Equivalence classification is important to infants because, when they eventually begin imitating adult speech, their imitations will be much higher pitched than the speech sounds made by most of the adults in their environment. They need to know that their production is equivalent to the adults' even though the pitch is different.

How Experience Affects Speech Perception We have seen that mechanisms for speech perception are in place at a very early age. However, this early speech perception ability can be affected by the child's experience with language. One example of the effects of experience is that there are some speech stimuli that infants can distinguish from each other, but that adults cannot distinguish. Thus, a Japanese infant might respond differently to /r/ and /l/, two sounds that Japanese adults have difficulty distinguishing, since they are in the same category in the Japanese language. However, by the time the children are a year old, they are no longer able to make distinctions between all pairs of sounds. Their experience in listening to other people speak has changed their speech perception so that they are sensitive only to distinctions between sounds that are important in their native language (Kuhl et al., 1992; Werker, 1991; Werker & Tees, 1984). Apparently, infants possess mechanisms for perceiving all speech sounds fairly early in their development, and during the first year of life these mechanisms become tuned to the language that the child experiences.

*The symbols /a/ and /i/ stand for the sounds "ah" (hot) and "ee" (heed), respectively.

Olfaction and Taste

Discriminating between Different Smells Do newborn infants perceive odors and tastes? Early researchers, noting that a number of olfactory stimuli elicited responses such as body movements and facial expressions from newborns, concluded that newborns can smell (Kroner, 1881; Peterson & Rainey, 1911). However, some of the stimuli used by these early researchers may have irritated the membranes of the infant's nose, so the infants may have been responding to irritation rather than to smell (Beauchamp, Cowart, & Schmidt, 1991; Doty, 1991). Modern studies using non-irritating stimuli have, however, provided evidence that newborns can smell and can discriminate between different olfactory stimuli. J. E. Steiner (1974, 1979), used non-irritating stimuli to show that infants respond to banana extract or vanilla extract with sucking and facial expressions that are similar to smiles, and that they respond to concentrated shrimp odor and an odor resembling rotten eggs with rejection or disgust responses (Figure 16.34).

Recognizing the Odor of the Mother's Breast It is perhaps not surprising that newborns would respond to strong odors such as rotten eggs. But recent research has also shown that infants can differentiate

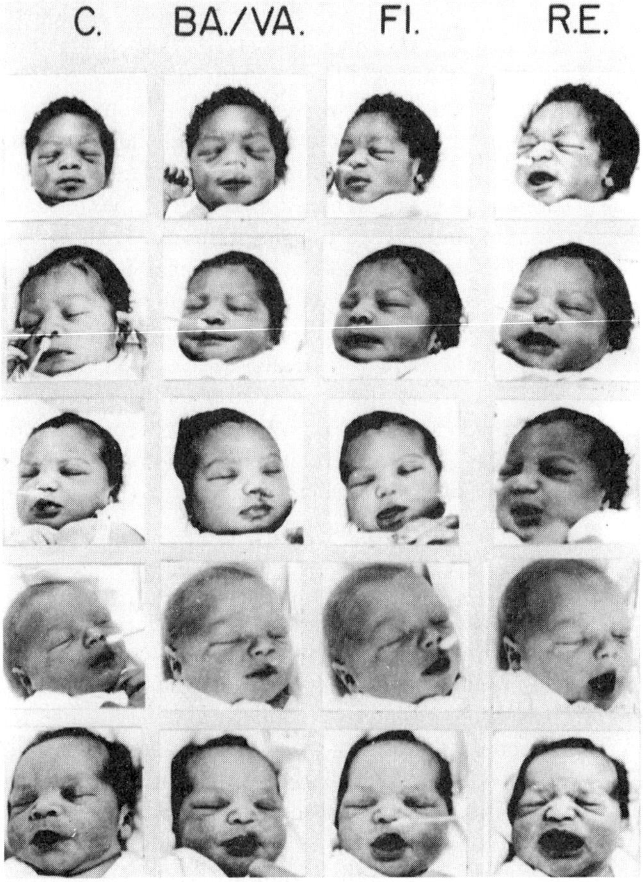

Figure 16.34
The facial expressions of 3- to 8-hour-old infants in response to some food-related odors. In each of the horizontal rows, the reactions of the same infant can be seen to the following stimulation: C = control, odorless cotton swab; BA/VA = artificial solution of banana or vanilla; FI = artificial fish or shrimp odor; R.E. = artificial rotten egg odor. The infants were tested prior to the first breast- or bottle-feeding. (Photographs courtesy of J. E. Steiner, The Hebrew University, Jerusalem.)

between subtle qualities in olfactory stimuli. These studies have shown that nursing infants can differentiate the odor of their mother's breast from the odor from the breast of another mother who is also nursing her infant. A. Macfarlane (1975) demonstrated this preference for the mother's breast odor by presenting breast pads from the mother and the other lactating female to infants in their cribs, and by noting that the infants spent significantly more time turning toward their mother's pads than toward the other woman's pad (Figure 16.35).

This preference for the mother's odor is probably learned. Jennifer Cernoch and Richard Porter (1985) demonstrated that 2-week-old breast-fed infants turn toward a pad containing their mother's axillary (armpit) odors in preference to the axillary odors of either unfamiliar lactating or nonlactating women or their father. However, bottle-fed infants did not prefer their mother's odor. Cernoch and Porter concluded that the basis for the breast-fed infants' recognition was that they had learned to recognize their mother's unique olfactory signature while feeding (also see Porter et al., 1992).

Further evidence that learning is important comes from an experiment by Rene Balogh and Richard Porter (1986), in which they exposed 1-day-old infants to either an artificial cherry odor or an artificial ginger odor in their bassinets for two days. After this exposure, the infants were tested by the presentation of two pads, one with cherry odor and the other with ginger odor, on either side of the head for two minutes. The results indicated that female

Figure 16.35
Device used to test infants' response to odorized pads. (From Porter & Schaal, 1995.)

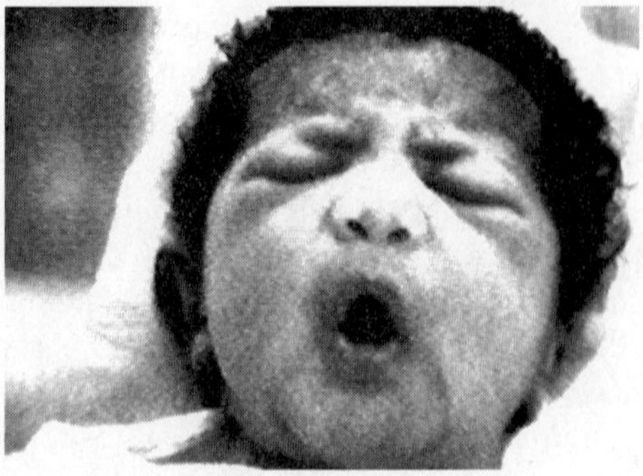

Figure 16.36
The facial expression of an infant who is less than 10 hours old to a sour taste. Specific facial expressions are also associated with bitter and sweet tastes (From Rosenstein & Oster, 1988.)

infants preferentially turned toward the odor to which they had previously been exposed. This result supports the idea that infants can perceive odors and that they can develop preferences for odors through learning.

Discriminating between Different Tastes Research investigating infants' reactions to taste has included numerous studies showing that newborns can discriminate sweet, sour, and bitter stimuli (Beauchamp, Cowart, & Schmidt, 1991). For example, newborns react with different facial expressions to sweet, sour, and bitter stimuli but show little or no response to salty stimuli (Figure 16.36) (Ganchrow, 1995; Ganchrow, Steiner, & Daher, 1983; Rosenstein & Oster, 1988).

Although responses to taste and olfaction do show some changes as the infant grows into childhood (for example, young infants are indifferent to the taste of salt but develop a response to salty stimuli as they get older; Beauchamp, Bertino, & Engelman, 1991; Beauchamp, Cowart, & Moran, 1986), we could argue that taste and olfaction are the most highly developed of all of the senses at birth.

Mechanisms of Perceptual Development: Experience or Biological Programming?

A long-standing question in psychology is whether a person's characteristics are caused by nature (innate factors focusing on built-in biological mechanisms and biologically programmed maturation) or nurture (the effect of the person's experience and the environment in which they are raised). This question has been asked about many different characteristics, including intelligence, personality, and psychological disorders, with the answer being that both nature and nurture are important. The same is true for perceptual development. Perceptual ability is both innately determined and is also determined by the person's experience in perceiving the environment.

The most accurate way to describe the roles of nature and nurture in determining perception is to say that there is an interaction between the two. One of the ways this interaction has been studied is by visual deprivation experiments in which an animal is deprived of some aspect of its normal environment.

When we introduced deprivation experiments in Chapter 8, we saw that depriving monkeys of binocular experience by monocular rearing causes a lack of binocular neurons in the visual system and a decrease in the animal's ability to perceive depth. We also saw that monocular rearing was effective in causing these changes only during an early period in the animal's life called the *sensitive period*. During this period, experience with binocular stimuli is necessary in order for the animal's physiological mechanisms for binocular vision to develop normally.

If depriving an animal of binocular experience changes the nature of their cortical neurons, what will happen if animals are deprived of other kinds of visual experience? Research using a technique called **selective rearing,** in which animals are reared in special environments during their sensitive period, show that during this early period, the cortex can be shaped by the nature of the animal's environment.

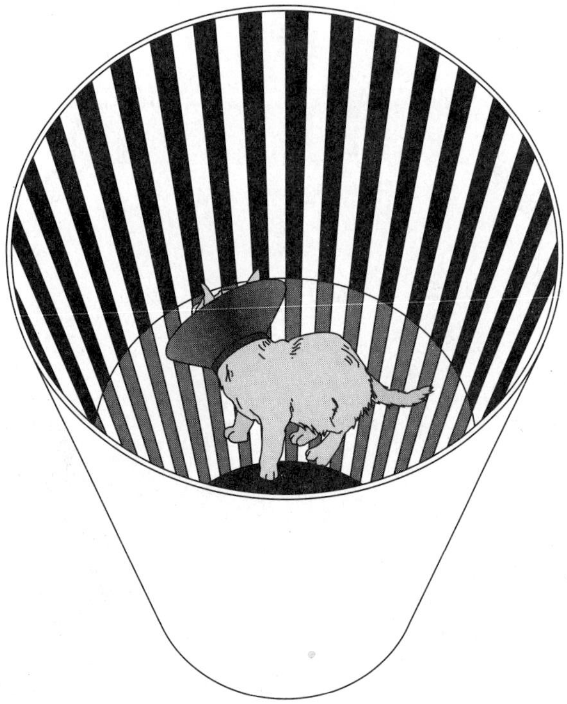

Figure 16.37
Blakemore and Cooper's (1970) striped tube. The kitten wore a black ruff to mask its body from its eyes and stood on a glass platform in the middle of the cylinder. A spotlight (not shown) illuminated the walls from above.

The Effects of Selective Rearing

The kitten's visual system is well developed early in life. Neurons that respond best to specific orientations are present within the first 6 weeks (Hubel & Wiesel, 1963; Mitchell & Timney, 1984; Sherk & Stryker, 1976). But even though kittens have orientation-selective neurons that are similar to the orientation-selective neurons of adult cats, the properties of the kittens' neurons can be changed if they are exposed to a special environment during the sensitive period. Experiments in which kittens are reared in special environments are called *selective rearing experiments*.

Selective Rearing for Orientation In one of the selective rearing experiments, kittens were exposed to either vertical or horizontal stripes. Colin Blakemore and Grahame Cooper (1970) placed kittens in striped tubes like the one in Figure 16.37. The kittens were kept in the dark from birth to 2 weeks of age, at which time they were placed in the tube for 5 hours a day; the rest of the time they remained in the dark. Since the kittens sat on a Plexiglas platform and the tube extended both above and below them, there were no visible corners or edges in their environment other than the vertical or horizontal stripes on the sides of the tube. The kittens wore neck ruffs to prevent them from turning vertical stripes into oblique or horizontal stripes by turning their heads; however, according to Blakemore and Cooper, "The kittens did not seem upset by the monotony of their surroundings and they sat for long periods inspecting the walls of the tube" (p. 477).

When the kittens' behavior was tested after 5 months of selective rearing, they seemed blind to the orientations that they hadn't seen in the tube. For example, a kitten that was reared in an environment of vertical stripes would pay attention to a vertical rod but ignored a horizontal rod. Following behavioral testing, Blakemore and Cooper recorded from cells in the visual cortex and determined the stimulus orientation

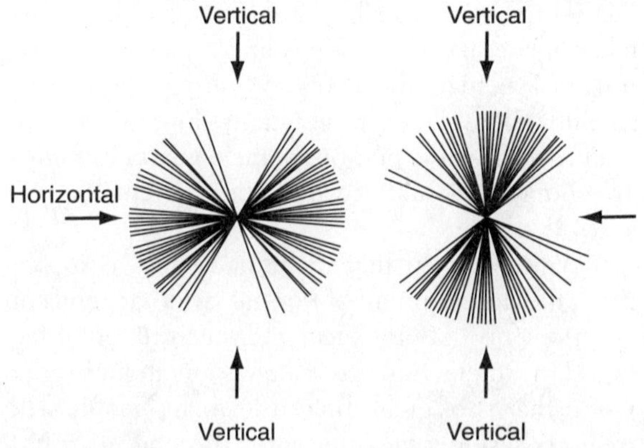

Figure 16.38
Distribution of optimal orientations for 52 cells from a horizontally experienced cat, on the left, and for 72 cells from a vertically experienced cat, on the right. (Blakemore & Cooper, 1970)

that caused the largest response from each cell. Their results indicate that many of the cells of the horizontally reared cats respond best to horizontal stimuli, but none respond to vertical stimuli (Figure 16.38).

These effects on the properties of cortical cells caused by vertical or horizontal rearing stimulated a large number of experiments in which animals were exposed to many different environments. In general, their results paralleled those of the vertical and horizontal rearing experiments: The properties of the kitten's receptive fields tended to resemble the environment to which the kitten was exposed. For example, if kittens were reared in an environment in which they see stripes that are moving in only one direction, more of their cortical cells responded to lines moving in that direction (Tretter, Cynader, & Singer, 1975).

The results of these selective rearing experiments and the results of the monocular rearing experiments described in Chapter 8, demonstrate the interaction between biology and the environment. Although biological programming creates adultlike neurons in young kittens, exposure to a normal environment is necessary in order for these neurons to develop normally. What makes these results particularly significant is that there is evidence that similar effects occur in humans.

Astigmatism in Humans We saw in Chapter 8 that we could generalize some of the results of the monocular rearing experiments to humans. Although we don't purposely deprive human infants of visual stimuli or rear them in selective environments, naturally occurring defects in an infant's optical system or eye patching following an operation has been shown to cause *amblyopia* (decreased vision in one eye) and a decrease in binocular neurons (see page 236).

A parallel with animal selective rearing experiments is produced in people who have a condition called **astigmatism.** Astigmatism, which is caused by a distortion in the shape of the cornea, results in an image that is out of focus either in the horizontal or vertical (Figure 16.39). Thus, a person who has an astigmatism at an early age is essentially exposed to an environment in which lines in one orientation are imaged sharply on the retina, but lines 90 degrees from this orientation are out of focus.

Ralph Freeman and John Pettigrew (1973) showed that cats reared with an artificial astigmatism, created by wearing a mask containing astigmatic lenses, develop cortical cells that favor whatever orientation is in sharp focus during rearing. This result

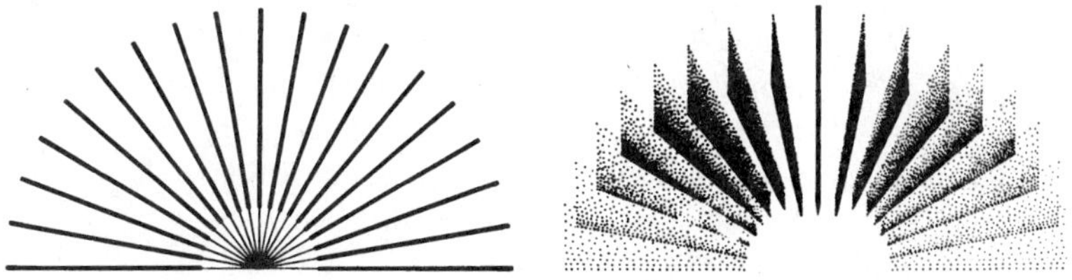

Figure 16.39
Left: astigmatic fan chart used to test for astigmatism. Right: an astigmatic patient will perceive the lines in one orientation (in this case vertical) as sharp and the lines in the other orientations as blurred. (From Trevor-Roper, 1970.)

in cats resembles a condition known as **meridional amblyopia** in humans. People with this condition often had an astigmatism at a young age that was not corrected by glasses and now, as adults, have astigmatisms that cannot be optically corrected. That is, even if these people wear glasses that compensate for their distorted corneas so that all orientations are sharply imaged on the retina, they still have impaired acuity for objects in the orientation originally blurred by their astigmatism.

To show that a person with meridional amblyopia has decreased visual acuity in one orientation, even when his or her vision is optically corrected so that the retinal image is sharp, Donald Mitchell and Frances Wilkinson (1974) carefully measured the optically corrected vision of a person with meridional amblyopia using a laser to present a sharp image to the observer's retina. This laser bypasses the observer's distorted cornea and therefore ensures that the image is focused sharply on the retina.

The results of this measurement indicate that the person's contrast sensitivity is low for horizontal orientations (Figure 16.40). Since the image on the retina is sharp, this decreased sensitivity to contrast must result not from the way the image is focused on the retina but, probably, from changes that have taken place in the observer's brain. Just as the neurons of Freeman and Pettigrew's astigmatic cats respond less well to orientations blurred by the astigmatism, so the neurons of the observer in Figure 16.40 may respond less well to lines oriented at 45° and 135 degrees.

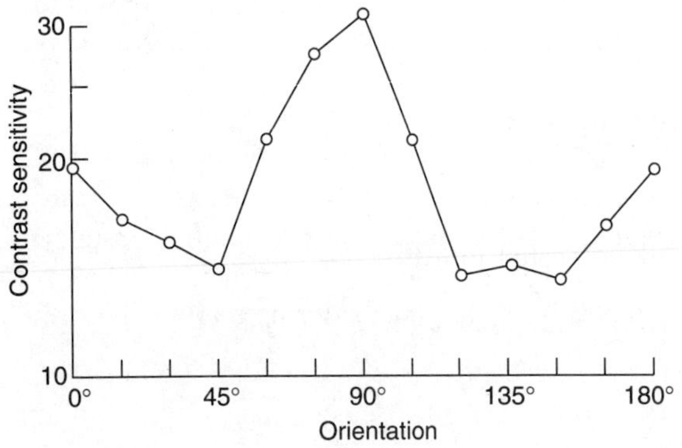

Figure 16.40
A plot of contrast sensitivity for different orientations for a person with meridional amblyopia, measured using a laser so the image was sharp on the retina. In this plot, 90° represents vertical. (From Mitchell & Wilkinson, 1974.)

We have seen that in humans, just as in animals, the development of normal vision depends on an interaction of biological and environmental factors. This interaction raises a question about human vision that is of great interest to many people who wear glasses or contact lenses: Is myopia (nearsightedness) strictly a biological problem or does visual experience such as reading play a role as well? Recent research supports the idea that both may be involved.

The Development of Myopia

In Chapter 2 we described how light is focused onto the retina by the lens and cornea. If vision is normal, the power of the eye's focusing system matches the length of the eyeball and light is focused on the retina (Figure 16.41a). This normal focusing results in **emmetropic vision** or **emmetropia.** However, if the power of the focusing system does not match the length of the eyeball, then two conditions can result: (1) The cornea and lens bend the light too much or the eyeball is too long, so the retinal image is blurred because the focus point for light is in front of the retina (Figure 16.41b). This results in **myopic vision** or **myopia** or (2) The eyeball is too short, so the retinal image is blurred because the focus point for light is behind the retina (Figure 16.41c). This results in **hyperopic vision** or **hyperopia.**

Myopia, which is also called nearsightedness, because people with myopia can only see near objects clearly, is much more prevalent than hyperopia. It affects about 25 percent of the adults in the United States (Sperduto et al., 1983), and it has been estimated that Americans with myopia spend 4.6 billion dollars annually for eye examinations, glasses, and contact lenses (Mutti et al., 1996).

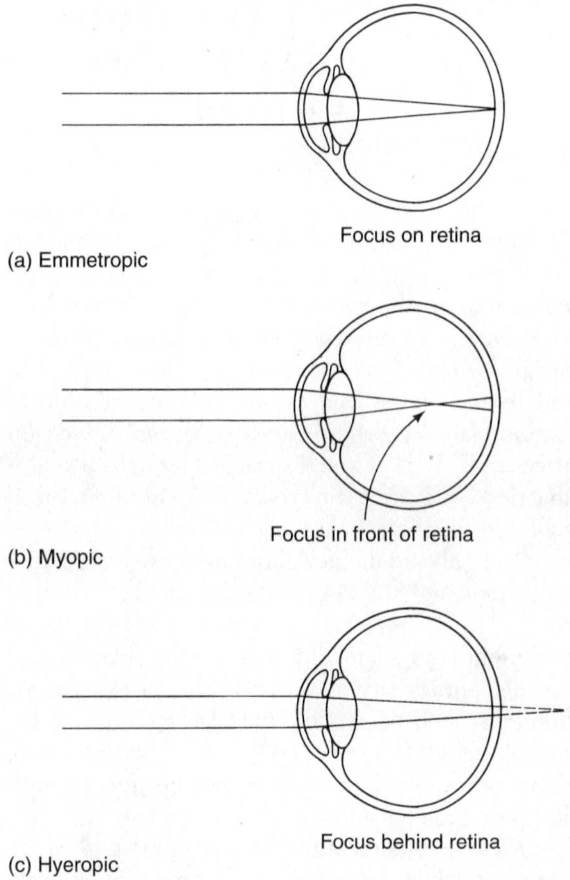

Figure 16.41
(a) Emmetropic, or normal, eye; (b) myopic eye; (c) hyperopic eye.

To understand what causes myopia we need to first consider the normal process of development. The eyes of newborns are highly hyperopic. That is, their focusing systems are not powerful enough and their eyeballs are too short (Figure 16.41c). Young infants can at least partially correct for this problem by accommodating—a process by which increasing the power of the lens brings the focus point forward toward the retina.

If development is normal, a process of **emmetropization** occurs. The eye grows larger and the optical system adjusts its power so light is focused sharply on the retina without any accommodation being necessary, thereby achieving emmetropic vision. But, in people who develop myopia, emmetropization does not fully occur. This failure of emmetropization has been linked to both genetics and the environment.

Genetic Links to Myopia Myopia runs in families. The degree of myopia is more closely related in identical twins than in non-identical (fraternal) twins, and there is a clear relationship between parents' myopia and childrens' myopia. Thirty to forty percent of children with two myopic parents have myopia, 20 to 25 percent with one myopic parent have myopia, and only 10 percent with no myopic parents have myopia (Gwiazda et al., 1993).

A particularly interesting finding about children who are at risk for myopia because they have two myopic parents, is that even before they become myopic, their eyes are longer than the eyes of children with no myopic parents (Zadnick et al., 1994). This observation that children at risk for myopia have longer eyeballs has led to the suggestion that "the 'seeds' of myopia may be sown early in life." (Mutti et al., 1996).

Environmental Links to Myopia There is also evidence that the environment can affect the likelihood of myopia. Myopia is more likely in groups that experience more education or who do more near work. For example, myopia became much more common in Eskimo children after the introduction of Western education (Mutti et al., 1996), the prevalence of myopia is as high as 70 percent in Asian children, who are subjected to a stringent educational system and high near-work demands (Au Eong, Tay, & Lum, 1993; Lin, Chen, & Hung, 1986), and myopia is more prevalent in male orthodox Jewish teenagers, who study up to 16 hours a day, compared to orthodox Jewish females, who study 8 or 9 hours a day (Zylbermann, Landau, & Berson, 1993).

The role of the environment has also been demonstrated in animal research by manipulating the animal's visual environment. Torsten Wiesel and Elio Raviola (1977) found that depriving monkeys of form vision when they are young causes them to develop myopia because their eyes become too long. Also, when just-hatched chicks are fitted with lenses that push the focus point back (so they are more hyperopic, as in Figure 16.41c), the chick's eyes grow longer to compensate (Irving, Sivak, & Callender, 1992). Similarly, if the chicks are fitted with lenses that move the focus point forward, their eyes grow shorter to compensate. These links between near work and myopia in children and environmental stimulation and eye length in animals have led to the proposal of the *visual feedback model* of emmetropization.

The Visual Feedback Model According to the **visual feedback model** of emmetropization, the growth of the eyeball that usually occurs during emmetropization is controlled by errors in the focusing of light on the retina. Thus, if there is an error in focusing, the eye grows to eliminate that error. If this process proceeds normally, the eyeball grows just the right amount to eliminate the out-of-focus condition that exists at birth. If, however, information about focus is not available, as when an animal is deprived of form vision, no image is present to indicate when the appropriate length has been reached, and elongation of the eyeball occurs. Or, if incorrect information about the eye's natural focusing power is created by fitting an animal with lenses, the length of the eyeball becomes too long or too short, as it strives to bring the lens-altered image into focus.

We still don't know exactly how this visual feedback mechanism, which is designed to achieve emmetropic vision, is misled into creating myopic vision in some people. We have seen that there is some evidence that myopia is inherited and also that in people who are susceptible to it, more visual experience is associated with greater myopia. Thus, we can describe myopia as being caused by a biological mechanism (biologically programmed visual feedback) which is affected by the environmental input it receives. What remains to be determined is how the visual feedback mechanism of people with myopic vision differs from the visual feedback mechanism of people with normal vision.

Something to Consider: The Rapid Unfolding of Perception

The research we have surveyed clearly indicates that although newborn perception is not as developed as adult perception, the newborn's perceptual abilities far surpass anything imagined by the early psychologists. Newborns can recognize some of their mother's facial features and the sound of her voice, can differentiate tastes and smells, and are capable of intermodal perception (see *Across the Senses* on pages 502–503). These capacities, as well as others that develop over the first year of life, are summarized in Table 16.1.

Not only are the newborn's perceptual capacities surprising, but the development that occurs within the first months is extremely impressive. Thus, the 4- to 5-month-old infant, although still not able to crawl, has perceptual capacities that in some cases (for example, speech perception and color vision), are approaching adult levels, and in others (visual acuity, depth perception and hearing), will be close to adult levels in just a few more months.

Why does perception develop so rapidly? As we indicated when we introduced the perceptual cycle in Chapter 1, the purpose of perception goes beyond enabling us to consciously experience the environment. The end result of perception is usually action. For infants this means things like shaking a rattle, crawling, walking, or drinking from a nipple or a cup. Thus, the answer to the question, "Why does perception develop so rapidly?" is that the infant needs its perception to be well-developed so it can support its ability to accomplish physical actions like the ones described above, and perhaps just as important, to form the foundation for the development of cognitive actions, such as learning the names of objects, learning how to talk, and learning how to interpret situations in which one event causes another event. Perception is a necessary component of all of these actions.

Table 16.1
Milestones in perceptual development. The ages indicated in this table are the youngest ages at which a particular capacity has been observed. Note that (1) these ages are subject to change, based on future research usually in the direction of younger ages for a particular capacity, and (2) just because a capacity is listed doesn't mean it is fully developed. For example, although 3-month-old infants can perceive facial expression, their perception of facial expressions is still rudimentary compared to adults.

Age	Capacity
Newborn	Recognize mother's face
	Discriminate sound of mother's voice
	Differentiate smell and taste stimuli
	Intermodal matching
2 weeks	Looks at moving stimulus
1 month	Visual acuity = 20/600. Vision slightly worse than adult night vision. Sees large objects with high contrast.
	Categorical perception of speech stimuli
2 months	Use motion information to see rod continuing behind occluder
	Short-wavelength cone present
	Minimum audible angle = 27° (Adult = 1°) (Decreases to 5 degrees by 18 months)
3 months	Grouping by lightness similarity
	Perception of facial expression
	All three types of cones present
	Binocular fixation
	Follow moving stimuli with smooth eye movement
4 months	Categorize colors like adults
	Discriminate between different categories of objects
	Perceive biological motion
	Spontaneous reaching for nearer object
	Binocular disparity (3.5–5 months)
5 months	Pictorial depth cues (5–7 months)
6 months	Visual acuity is close to adult (doesn't reach adult until after 1 year)
	Hearing thresholds are within 10–15 dB of adult
	Equivalence classification for speech
8 months	Sensitive to occlusion in biological motion
1 year	Speech perception narrows so infant is only sensitive to differences in sounds used in own language

Intermodal Perception in Infants

An adult who first feels a baseball and then sees the baseball plus a number of other objects, can easily choose the baseball as the shape he was feeling. This ability to match shapes presented in two different modalities is called **intermodal matching.** One idea about how intermodal matching ability develops is that it is based on people's experience in simultaneously seeing and feeling a variety of shapes. Another idea is that it is an inborn ability. Andrew Meltzoff and Richard Borton (1979) investigated the question of whether intermodal abilities are learned or inborn by first having 1-month-old infants suck on one of the two pacifiers shown in Figure 16.42, and then presenting the two shapes visually.

Of the 32 infants tested, 24 looked longer at the shape they had experienced when they had sucked on the pacifier. Meltzoff and Burton concluded that infants do not need to learn about correspondences between touch and vision, but that they are able to sense and store abstract information (for example, "bumpy surface" or "smooth surface") and generalize this information across senses.

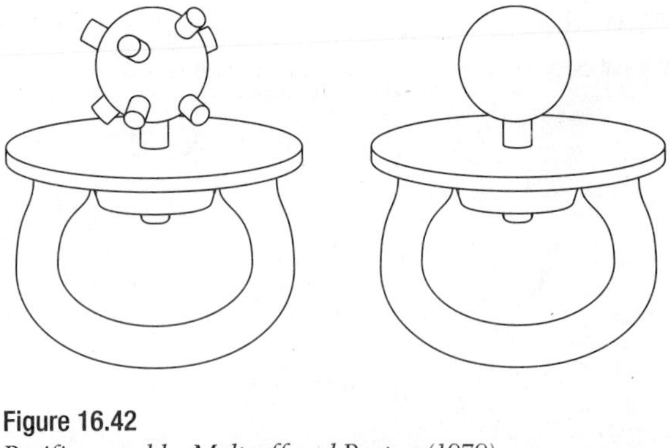

Figure 16.42
Pacifiers used by Meltzoff and Borton (1979).

Recently, another experiment, again using pacifiers as the tactual stimulus, but a different method of measurement, showed that 1-day-old newborns are capable of matching a shape they feel to a shape they can see. Kelly Kaye and T. G. R. Bower (1994) placed one of two pacifiers in the infant's mouth. When the infant began sucking, a large image of the end of one of the pacifiers appeared on a computer monitor located directly in front of the newborn (Figure 16.43). As long as the infant continued sucking, the image remained on the screen. But pausing for longer than 1 second caused the image of the other, differently shaped, pacifier to appear on the screen. Thus, the infant could determine which image appears on the screen by the way it sucked on the pacifier.

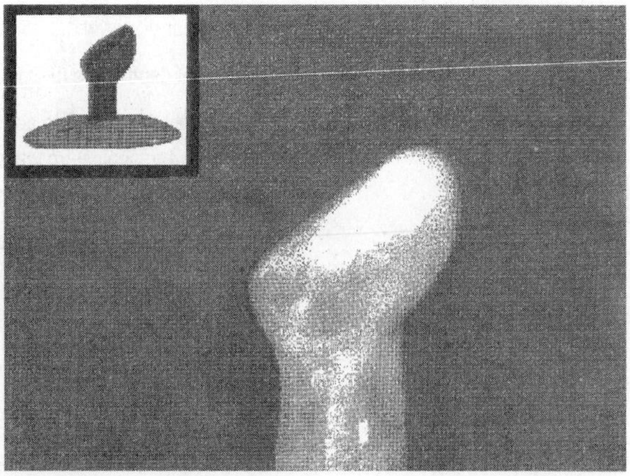

Figure 16.43
Large image: Picture of the end of the pacifier as seen by infants who were looking at a television monitor. Insert: Actual pacifier on which the infant was sucking. (From Kaye & Bower, 1994.)

The results of this experiment showed that infants controlled their sucking so that in their initial exposures to the images of the pacifiers, 11 of the 12 infants caused the image of the pacifier on which they were sucking to appear on the screen longer than the image of the other pacifier. This means that newborns are capable of sensing the shape of a pacifier in their mouths and can generalize this perception from the tactual to the visual mode.

How does the newborn achieve this feat? Clearly, it can't be due to learning because the infant is only 1-day old. Because the effect happened as soon as the infant began sucking on the pacifier, Kaye and Bower (1994) suggest that it doesn't seem likely that the infants create a tactual image of the pacifier that they compare to the visual image on the screen. Instead, they propose that the information in both tactile and visual form creates an **amodal representation**—a description that holds across more than one modality. For example, an amodal description of the pacifier in Figure 16.43 would be: "A smooth elongated object, with a rounded side and a flat side." Since this description is valid for both the visual and tactual presentations, it is amodal.

Whether or not this is the actual mechanism involved, it is clear that infants are capable of matching felt shapes and visual images from a very young age. Other experiments have demonstrated similar abilities in 11-month-old infants who are old enough to explore three-dimensional objects with their hands (Bushnell & Weinberger, 1987).

Study Questions

Underlying Principles

Find examples of the following principles in this chapter:

- Physiology-perception connection (474)
- Cognition perception connection (486)
- Perceptual constancy (493)
- Perceptual grouping (478)

Measuring Infant Perception

1. What are two questions we can ask to determine visual acuity and how would we answer each of them? Which one works for infants? (471)
2. Describe the preferential looking technique. Why does the preferential looking technique work? How would we use it to measure acuity? (471)
3. Describe the habituation technique. When would it be used instead of preferential looking? What fact about infant looking behavior is it based on? (471)

Infant Perceptual Capacities: Vision

4. What is a newborn's visual acuity and how does it increase over the first months of life? How is the visual evoked potential used to measure visual acuity? (473)
5. What are the physiological reasons for the newborn's poor visual acuity? Consider the state of both the cortex and the foveal cones in your answer. (474)
6. How does the contrast sensitivity function of infants compare to the contrast sensitivity function of adults? What does this mean about how the infant perceives the visual world? (476)
7. What kinds of things can young infants detect at close distances? (477)
8. Describe the research that has shown that newborns can recognize their mother's face. What is the experiment that indicates what information the newborn may be using to make this judgment? (477)
9. Describe Craton's experiment in which it was determined that infants can distinguish figure from ground. Be sure you understand how habituation was used to determine this. (478)
10. Describe Quinn's experiment that showed that infants can perceptually group elements by lightness similarity. (479)
11. At what age can an infant infer the existence of an object extending behind an occluder? Describe the series of three experiments that led to this conclusion. What information do infants use to make this inference? (479)
12. How did Xu and Carey use habituation to show that infants use movement to help them distinguish between two objects that are adjacent to one another? (480)
13. What is a special challenge facing anyone who wants to test for the presence of color vision? (481)
14. Describe Bornstein's experiment on color categorization. Understand how habituation was used and the principle of color categories that Bornstein used in the design of his experiment. (482)
15. What is the principle that allows us to use a psychophysical procedure to determine whether an infant has both its medium- and long-wavelength cones? (482)
16. Describe Hamer's experiment and its conclusions. How did he deal with the "special challenge" mentioned in 13, above? (483)
17. At what age do infants probably have some form of trichromatic vision? (483)
18. What is one requirement that must be met before binocular disparity can be effective? (484)
19. How did Aslin determine when infants can binocularly fixate? (484)
20. How were random-dot stereograms used to determine when infants can use binocular disparity to perceive depth? At what age are infants able to do this? (484)

21. How were stereograms used to determine infant stereoacuity? At what age is stereoacuity first measurable? How rapidly does stereoacuity develop once it appears? (485)
22. Describe the procedures that were used to determine when infants can use the depth cues of overlap and familiar size. At what age are infants first able to use this information? (486)
23. How come infants need to be older to use pictorial depth cues than to use binocular disparity? (486)
24. At what age can infants first perceive movement? How do infant eye movements compare to adults'? When are they similar to adult eye movements? (487)
25. What technique was used to determine whether infants can see biological movement? At what age can infants discriminate between the biological movement of point-light walkers and random movement? (487)
26. Does the fact that infants can discriminate between the biological movement and random movement mean that they see biological movement in the same way as adults? Explain your answer and the experiment that was done to investigate this question. (487)

Infant Perceptual Capacities: Hearing and the Chemical Senses

27. How did DeCasper and Fifer show that newborns can recognize their mother's voice? (488)
28. What does newborn head turning behavior tell us about their ability to hear a tone? (489)
29. What is the observer-based psychoacoustic procedure? What do the audibility curves determined using this procedure tell us about how infant hearing compares to adult hearing? (489)
30. What is the minimum audible angle? Has it decreased to adult levels by a year and a half of age? (490)
31. What is categorical perception in speech? How did Eimas show that infants are capable of categorical perception? (490)
32. How did Kuhl show that infants can tell that a vowel, like /a/ is the same sound even when it is spoken by different speakers? What is equivalence classification? (491)
33. How does an infant's experience with speech affect its ability to perceive speech sounds? Why can we say that infants lose the ability to differentiate sounds as they gain the ability to perceive speech? (493)
34. What is the evidence that newborns can discriminate between different smells? (493)
35. What is the evidence that newborns can recognize the odor of the mother's breast? What is the evidence that learning is involved in the infant's ability to recognize odors? (493)
36. What is the evidence that newborns can discriminate between different taste stimuli? (495)

Mechanisms of Perceptual Development: Experience or Biological Programming?

37. What is the nature-nurture problem and how has it generally been resolved in psychology? (495)
38. What is the sensitive period? What do selective rearing experiments tell us about the role of experience in perceptual development? (496)
39. How can we generalize the results of the selective rearing experiments on kittens to the development of astigmatism in humans? What is meridional amblyopia? (497)
40. Describe the process of emmetropization. (498)
41. What are some examples of genetic links to myopia? (499)
42. What are some examples of environmental links to myopia? (499)
43. What evidence led to the proposal of the visual feedback model of emmetropization? What is the relationship between this model and the development of myopia? (500)

Something to Consider: The Rapid Unfolding of Perception

44. Why is it necessary that infant perception develop rapidly during the first year of life? (500)

Across the Senses: Intermodal Perception in Infants

45. What is intermodal matching? (502)
46. Describe the Melzoff and Burton experiment on intermodal perception involving sucking on a pacifier and seeing the pacifier. (502)
47. Describe Kaye and Bower's experiment that showed that one-day old newborns are capable of matching a shape they feel to a shape they can see. (502)
48. How does the newborn accomplish the matching of shape and vision, according to Kaye and Bower? What is an amodal representation? (502)

CHAPTERS 11–16

UNDERLYING PRINCIPLES

This book has described the complexities of the deceivingly simple act we call perception. As this description of perception has unfolded throughout this book, you have seen that perception is not simple at all, and that simple perceptions are built on complex mechanisms. You have also learned a great many facts about these mechanisms. But in addition to learning about these details, you have also learned that despite the diversity of the stimuli, the receptors, the different pathways and areas of the brain, and the basic experiences associated with each of the senses, there are a great many ways in which they are similar (also see Handel, 1988; Julesz & Hirsh, 1972, Konishi, 1990; Torre et al., 1995).

SIMILARITIES WITHIN DIVERSITY

Vision and olfaction provide an example of two senses that are very different but which have some mechanisms in common. Despite the great differences in the stimuli for vision and olfaction (quanta of light vs. molecules) and the person's experience (seeing vs. smelling), the active molecules in the visual and olfactory receptors are both proteins from the same family that cross the receptor membrane seven times (Figure 16.44).

Mechanisms shared by the different senses exist not only in the receptors, but along the neural pathways to the brain and within the brain itself. A fascinating demonstration of similar mechanisms has been provided by experiments in which the nerve fibers from one sense are "rerouted" to reach the cortical areas of another sense (Frost, 1990; Sur, Garraghty, & Roe, 1988).

Anna Roe and coworkers (1992) rerouted fibers from the retina of ferrets to cells in the auditory area of the thalamus by lesioning the visual cortex of the newborn ferret and other areas that normally receive signals from the retina. Those lesions cause the lateral geniculate nucleus (the visual nucleus in the thalamus) to degenerate, and, as the ferret develops, neurons that would have gone to the LGN go instead to the nearby medial geniculate nucleus (the auditory areas of the thalamus that projects to the auditory areas of the cortex) (Figure 16.45). The result is that stimulating the eye of an adult ferret with light causes signals to reach the primary auditory cortex.

To determine how the ferrets' rewired sensory system would respond, Roe and coworkers stimulated the eye with light and recorded from neurons in the auditory cortex. They found some differences in the responding of these neurons compared to cells in the visual cortex of a normal animal: The neurons had larger receptive fields and responded more slowly and

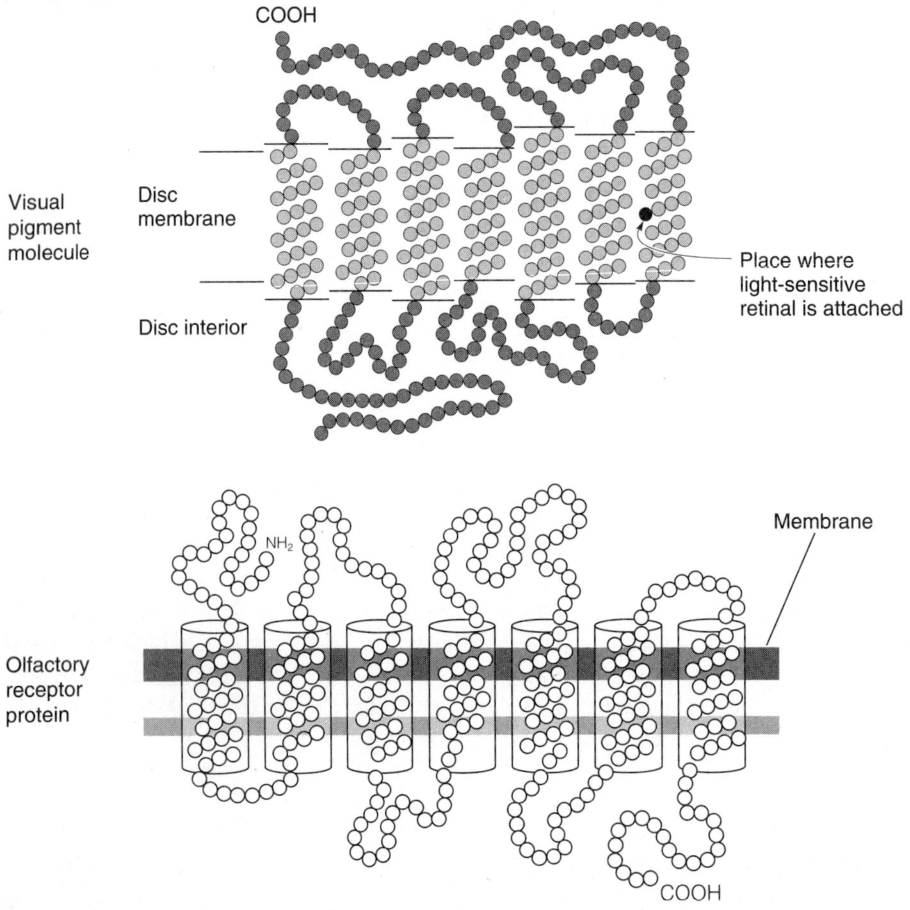

Figure 16.44
Despite the differences between vision and olfaction, the light-sensitive visual pigment molecule and the chemically-sensitive olfactory receptor protein both have the same basic structure and cross the receptor membrane seven times.

less vigorously than neurons normally would in an intact visual cortex. However, they also observed striking similarities: The receptive fields could be classified as simple or complex, just as in the visual system of the normal animal, and the neurons responded best to specific orientations and directions of movement. In other words, the wiring of the ferret's auditory cortex must be very similar to the wiring of its visual cortex, since neurons in both the auditory and visual cortices responded similarly to stimulation with light.

This remarkable rewiring experiment illustrates the existence of similar mechanisms in vision and hearing. But as dramatic as this demonstration is, it shouldn't be that surprising, because we know that the operation of all of the senses is governed by similar underlying principles.

Underlying Principles in Audition, the Cutaneous Senses, Taste, Olfaction, and Development

We introduced eight principles on pages 128–130, and showed that these principles hold across a variety

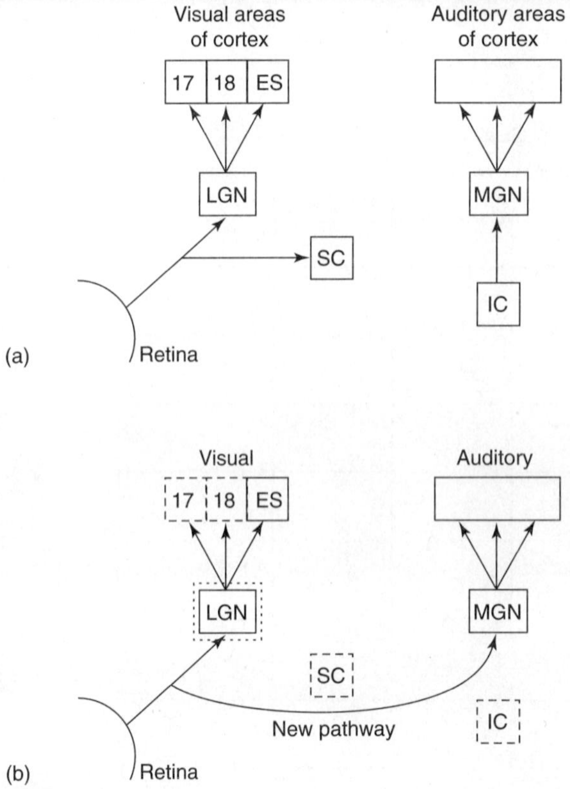

Figure 16.45
Diagram of the procedure used to reroute the signals from the ferret's retina to its auditory cortex. (a) Diagram of visual and auditory pathways in the normal ferret. In the visual system signals are transmitted from the retina to the LGN and superior colliculus (SC) and from the LGN to areas 17, 18, and other extrastriate (ES) visual areas in the cortex. In the auditory system, signals are transmitted from the inferior colliculus (IC) to the medial geniculate nucleus (MGN) to auditory areas of the cortex. (b) When areas 17, 18, the SC, and the IC are ablated (dashed lines), the LGN degenerates (dotted line) and a pathway develops from the retina to the MGN. Thus, stimulation of the retina with light causes signals to reach the auditory cortex. (Adapted from Sur, et al., 1988.)

of visual phenomena on pages 305–308. We now extend our survey of principles to the senses of audition, the cutaneous senses, the chemical senses, and perceptual development. From Table 16.2 (on page 510), which shows which of the eight principles are illustrated in Chapters 11 to 16, we can see that, with just one exception, every principle is present in each sense (columns have not been observed for the chemical senses). Specific examples of these principles are as follows:

1. **Selective Receptors** Most individual receptors respond selectively to a restricted range of stimuli.
   - Auditory hair cells respond to a narrow range of frequencies. (11)
   - Different types of mechanoreceptors respond to different stimuli. For example, the PC mechanoreceptor responds best to the onset and offset of stimulation. (14)
   - Olfactory receptor proteins and receptor neurons respond to a restricted group of chemicals. (15)

2. **Receptive Fields/Neural Selectivity** Most neurons (a) have a receptive field—an area on the receptor surface or in space which, when stimulated, influences the neuron's firing; and (b) fire selectively to a restricted range of stimuli.
   - Neurons in the cochlear nucleus and other neurons in the auditory system are tuned to respond to a narrow range of frequencies. (11)
   - Neurons in primary and secondary auditory cortex respond best to tones changing frequency in a particular direction. (11)
   - Interaural time difference detectors respond best to a specific difference in the time that sound stimuli reach the left and right ears. (12)
   - Azimuth sensitive neurons in the cat's auditory cortex respond to stimuli presented in one area in space. (12)
   - Receptive fields of neurons in the owl's MLD are located at a particular area in space and have a center-surround configuration. (12)
   - There are neurons in the somatosensory cortex that respond selectively when the skin is stimulated by an edge with a specific orientation. (14)

Table 16.2
Underlying principles in Chapters 11–16

Principle	Chapter: 11. Pitch	12. Scene	13. Speech	14. Touch	15. Chemical	16. Development
1. Selective receptors	■			■	■	
2. Receptive fields/ neural selectivity	■	■		■	■	
3. Distributed response	■	■		■	■	
4. Neural maps	■	■		■	■	
5. Columnar organization	■			■		
6. Parallel pathways	■			■	■	
7. Physiology–perception connection	■ *	■		■	■	■
8. Cognitive influences	■ *	■	■	■	■	■

■ Examples of these principles are described in the chapter (see examples above).

■ * Examples of these principles are not described in the chapter, but are relevant.

- There are neurons in somatosensory cortex that respond selectively when a monkey grasps a particular stimulus. (14)
- Neurons in the somatosensory area of the thalamus have center-surround receptive fields on the skin. (14)
- Some neurons in the olfactory cortex respond to just a few different odorants. (15)
- There are neurons in the taste system that respond best to one of the four basic taste qualities. (15)

3. **Distributed Response** A stimulus causes a specific pattern of responding across a number of neurons. This is the distributed approach to sensory coding.
   - A particular stimulus presented to the skin causes a pattern of responding in each of the types of mechanoreceptors and the pathways leading from them. (14)
   - A particular olfactory stimulus causes different amounts of responding in specific olfactory receptors and olfactory bulb neurons. Specific odors may therefore be indicated by the pattern of activity in different groups of neurons. (15)
   - The perception of taste quality may be partially determined by the pattern of responding across many different neurons. (15)

4. **Neural Maps** Neurons are arranged within a structure in an orderly way, based on a specific property.
    - There is a tonotopic map of frequencies in the cochlea. (11)
    - There is a tonotopic map of frequencies in each of the nuclei along the auditory pathway and including the auditory cortex. (11)
    - There is a map of space in the owl's MLD. (12)
    - There is a homunculus in the somatosensory cortex that is a map of the human body in which neighboring neurons represent neighboring parts of the body. The map is distorted so more space is allotted to parts of the body that are more sensitive to cutaneous stimulation. (14)
    - Odotopic maps exist in the olfactory bulb, in which odorants with specific chemical features cause activity in specific areas. The arrangement is not, however, as orderly as the maps in the visual, auditory, and cutaneous systems. (15)
5. **Columnar Organization** Neurons that respond to specific stimulus properties are arranged in columns. These columns are usually perpendicular to the surface of the structure in which the neurons are located.
    - Neurons that have the same best frequency are arranged in columns in the auditory cortex. (11)
    - Neurons in the somatosensory cortex are organized in columns based on location on the skin. (14)
6. **Parallel Pathways** There are parallel neural pathways within a sense that are specialized to process information about specific stimulus characteristics.
    - There are numerous parallel pathways that transmit auditory information from the cochlea towards the brain. (11)
    - There are efferent pathways that transmit auditory information from higher-order structures to lower-order structures. (11)
    - There are four channels of information originating from the four types of receptors in the skin. In addition, pathways transmit information from the cortex towards the receptors. (14)
    - The medial lemniscal pathway has large fibers that carry signals related to touch perception. The spinothalamic pathway has small fibers that transmit signals related to temperature and pain. (14)
    - In the olfactory system the olfactory nerve is the pathway for the transmission of information about odor quality and the trigeminal nerve is the pathway for the transmission of information about irritation. (15)
7. **Physiological Connections with Perception** Physiological processes influence what we perceive. One of the major goals of research in perception is to demonstrate the connections that exist between physiology and perception.
    - Removal of part of the auditory coretex degrades auditory localization. (12)
    - In the cutaneous system, properties of the Pacinian corpuscle causes its axon to respond best to the onset and offset of stimuli and to rapid vibration. (14)
    - The operation of the "gate control" circuit or a similar mechanism influences perception of pain stimuli. (14)
    - In the taste system the density of taste buds determines whcther a person is a "taster" or a "nontaster." (15)
    - Acuity in infants is determined by the development of foveal cones and the striate cortex. (16)
    - Myopia is determined by a lack of correspondence between the eye's focusing power and the length of the eye. (16)

8. **Cognitive Influences** The perceiver's thoughts, past experiences, and the meaning of the stimulus influence perception.
   - Melody schema: The awareness that a particular series of tones is a familiar melody facilitates the perceptual grouping of these tones. (12)
   - Speech segmentation depends on the listener's knowledge of the meanings of words. (13)
   - Phonemes and words are perceived more rapidly and accurately if they are heard within a meaningful context. (13)
   - Speech perception is more accurate for familiar speakers. (13)
   - The perception of pain can be influenced by a person's expectations, culture and past experiences. (14)
   - The ability to identify smells is influenced by our ability to access the name of the smell sensation from our memory. (15)
   - The development of the depth cue of familiar size depends on the ability to remember the sizes of previously seen objects. (16)

The existence of these examples of our eight principles for hearing, touch, taste and smell confirms the generality of these principles that we have already observed across the various visual qualities. We can also cite the following examples of the three additional principles we introduced on page 308.

1. **Perceptual Constancy** We tend to perceive the properties of objects as being constant even when the proximal stimulus changes, as when we look at an object from different distances or viewpoints.
   - Sounds which have different acoustic signals due to coarticulation can sound the same. (13)
   - Categorical perception in speech causes sounds with a wide range of acoustic signals to be perceived in just two categories. (13)
   - Odor constancy causes olfactory stimuli to be perceived to have the same magnitude even when the number or length of sniffs is varied. (6, 15)
   - Young infants perceive speech sounds categorically. This means that they perceive the same sound even though the acoustic signal is changed. (16)

2. **Perceptual Grouping** Small elements are often perceptually grouped into larger units.
   - The principles of auditory scene analysis indicate how various sounds become perceptually grouped with one another. (12)
   - Speech stimuli become perceptually segregated based on the meanings of the sounds. (13)
   - Perceptual organization occurs when the patterns of raised dots of braille are identified by touch and when objects are identified by the exploration of haptic perception. (14)
   - Hundreds of different chemicals that are simultaneously present in the air can become perceptually grouped into specific olfactory percepts, such as bacon, coffee, and toast. (15)
   - Young infants can form perceptual groups based on movement and similarity of color. (16)

3. **Context and Perception** Our perception of a stimulus often depends on the context within which the stimulus is perceived.
   - A number of the "cognitive influences" listed in Principle 8, above, are examples of how context affects perception.
   - Audio-visual speech perception: Viewing a speaker's mouth movements can influence what a listener hears. (13)
   - Vibration of the skin can decrease the magnitude of pain. (14)

Table 16.3
Across the senses summary

Chapter	Vision	Hearing	Cutaneous	Chemical
	Chapters 2–17			
2. Receptors	Rods and cone receptors	Hair cell receptors	Skin receptors	Chemical receptors
3. LGN/cortex	Maps and columns in visual cortex	Maps and columns in auditory cortex	Maps and columns in somatosensory cortex	
4. Higher–level	Neuron that responds to visual stimulation		Same neuron responds to touch (multimodal)	
5. Color	Color of foods			Color affects olfaction and taste
6. Constancy	Color, lightness, shape, & size constancy			Smell constancy
7. Objects	Sensory substitution and intersensory dominance (vision-touch)		Sensory substitution and intersensory dominance (vision-touch)	
8. Visual space	Visual space	Auditory space		
9. Size, illusions, ecology	Visual illusions		Haptic illusions	
10. Movement	Visual apparent movement		Tactile apparent movement	
11. Hearing–pitch	Cross-modality experience: seeing tones*	Cross-modality experience: hearing lights*		
12. Hearing–localization	Blindness	Improved auditory localization and cortical changes		
13. Speech		Speech stimulation	Tadoma—perceiving speech through touch	
14. Cutaneous	Drawing and visual picture perception		Perceiving tactile pictures	
15. Chemical			Chemesthesis—detecting chemical irritation	Taste and olfaction—detecting tastes and smells
16. Development	Bimodal perception—matching visual and shape stimuli		Bimodal perception—matching visual and shape stimuli	
17. Clinical	Reduced ability to attend visually	Deafness		

Unshaded squares: Similar phenomena in two senses.
Shaded squares: Interaction between two senses.
*This is also an example of interaction.

- The perception of flavor is created by stimulation of the taste receptors on the tongue combined with stimulation of the olfactory receptors in the nose. (15)

"Across the Senses" and Underlying Principles

The existence of underlying principles is one indication of the many similarities across the senses, some of which we have described in the *Across the Senses* sections at the end of each chapter (summarized in Table 16.3). These across-sense similarities fall into two categories (1) similar perceptions in two or more senses (unshaded squares in Table 16.3), such as the perception of apparent movement of both visual and tactile stimuli, and (2) interactions between the senses (shaded squares in Table 16.3), such as the way color affects the perception of smells and tastes. Remember that the examples in Table 16.3 are just a few of the connections that exist between the senses. There are many others as well, many of which reflect the fact that underlying principles are shared across the senses.

17

CLINICAL ASPECTS OF VISION AND HEARING

Although it is obvious that the man in Figure 17.1 is examining the woman's eye, most people do not understand exactly what he is seeing or what he is looking for. Even though most Americans have had their eyes and ears examined because of problems with either vision or hearing, or just as part of a routine physical examination, few people understand exactly what is going on during these examinations. One of the purposes of this chapter is to demystify what goes on during examinations of the eye and the ear.

Before we can understand what eye and ear specialists look for during an examination, we must understand the major problems that can cause impairments in vision and hearing. We therefore begin this chapter by describing a number of the most common visual problems and how they are treated to improve or restore vision. After we understand the nature of the most common causes of visual problems, we will describe how a routine eye examination detects these problems. Following our discussion of vision, we take the same approach for hearing.

CHAPTER CONTENTS

SOME QUESTIONS WE WILL CONSIDER

- What are the major causes of blindness and deafness? (516, 535)
- Can a person be legally blind but have 20/20 vision? (522)
- How can diseases of the ear and eye be treated? (521, 536)

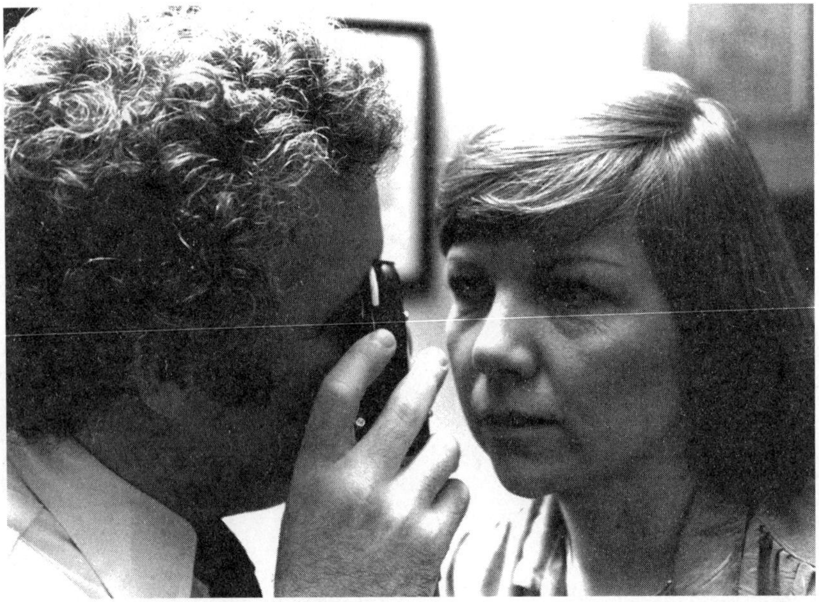

Figure 17.1
Ophthalmologist examining patient.

VISUAL IMPAIRMENT

How Can Vision Become Impaired?

Four major types of problems can cause poor vision (Figure 17.2):

1. Light is not focused clearly on the retina. Problems in focusing light can occur because the eyeball is too short or too long or because the cornea or the lens does not function properly. We will describe the following specific problems: myopia (nearsightedness), hyperopia (farsightedness), presbyopia ("old eye"), and astigmatism.
2. Light is blurred as it enters the eye. Scarring of the cornea or clouding of the lens blurs light as it enters the eye. Specific problems: corneal injury or disease, cataract.
3. There is damage to the retina. The retina can be damaged by disruption of the vessels that supply it with blood, by its separation from the blood supply, and by diseases that attack its receptors. Specific problems: macular degeneration, diabetic retinopathy, detached retina, **hereditary retinal degeneration.**
4. There is damage to the optic nerve. The optic nerve can degenerate. When this degeneration is due to a pressure buildup inside the eyeball, the cause is glaucoma. In addition, degeneration can

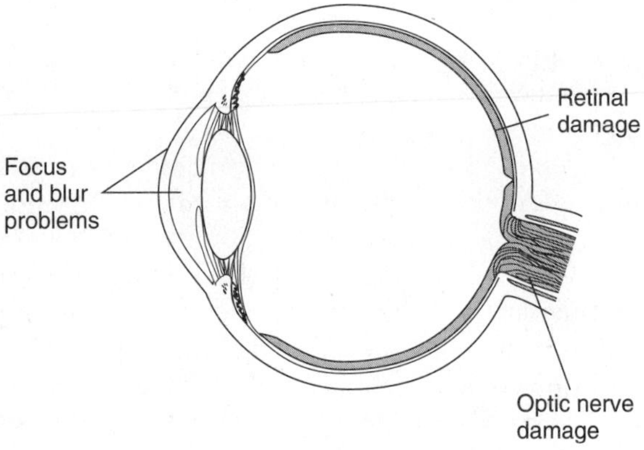

Figure 17.2
Places in the eye where visual problems can occur.

be caused by poor circulation, toxic substances, or the presence of a tumor. We will focus on glaucoma in our discussion.

We begin by considering a problem that affects more people than all the others combined: an inability to adequately focus incoming light onto the retina.

Focusing Problems

In Chapter 2, we described the optical system of the eye—the cornea and the lens—which, if everything is working properly, brings light entering the eye to a sharp focus on the retina. We also described the process of accommodation, which adjusts the focusing power of the eye to bring both near and far objects into focus.

We will now consider the conditions myopia, hyperopia, presbyopia, and astigmatism, four problems that affect a person's ability to focus an image on the retina.

Myopia

Myopia, or nearsightedness, is an inability to see distant objects clearly. The reason for this difficulty, which affects over 70 million Americans, is illustrated in Figure 17.3a: In the myopic eye, parallel rays of light are brought to a focus in front of the retina so that the image reaching the retina is blurred. This problem can be caused by either of two factors: (1) **refractive myopia,** in which the cornea and/or the lens bends the light too much, or (2) **axial myopia,** in which the eyeball is too long. Either way, light comes to a focus in front of the retina, so that the image on the retina is out of focus, and far objects look blurred. (See Chapter 16 for a discussion of how myopia develops.)

How can we deal with this problem? One way to create a focused image on the retina is to move the stimulus closer. This pushes the focus point further back (see Figure 2.10), and if we move the stimulus close enough, we can push the focus point onto the retina (Figure 17.3b). The distance at which the spot of light becomes focused on the retina is called the **far point,** and when our spot of light is at the far point, a myope can see it clearly. Although a person with myopia can see nearby objects clearly (which is why a

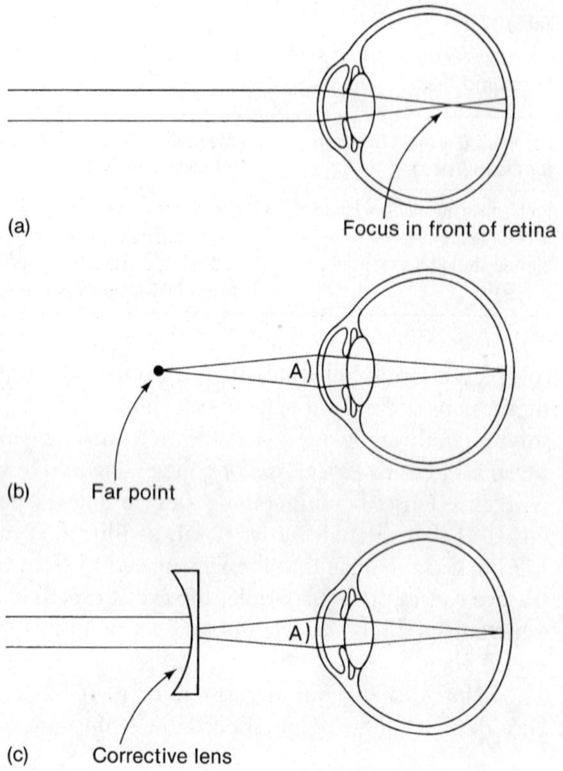

Figure 17.3
Focusing of light by the myopic (nearsighted) eye. (a) Parallel rays from a distant spot of light are brought to a focus in front of the retina, so distant objects appear blurred. (b) As the spot of light is moved closer to the eye, the focus point is pushed back until, at the far point, the rays are focused on the retina, and vision becomes clear. Vision is blurred beyond the far point. (c) A corrective lens, which bends light so that it enters the eye at the same angle as light coming from the far point, brings light to a focus on the retina. Angle A is the same in (b) and (c).

Table 17.1
Comparison of focusing problems associated with the far point and the near point

Far Point (Farthest Distance for Clear Vision)	Near Point (Closest Distance for Clear Vision)
Problem: In myopia, the far point is close to the eye, and vision is blurred beyond the far point.	Problem: In presbyopia, the near point moves away from the eye, and vision is blurred closer than the near point.

myopic person is called *nearsighted*), objects beyond the far point are still out of focus (see Table 17.1). The solution to this problem is well known to anyone with myopia: corrective eyeglasses or contact lenses. These corrective lenses bend incoming light so that it is focused as if it were at the far point, as illustrated in Figure 17.3c. Notice that the lens placed in front of the eye causes the light to enter the eye at exactly the same angle as light coming from the far point in Figure 17.3b.

Before leaving our discussion of myopia, let's consider the following question: How strong must a corrective lens be to give the myope clear far vision? To answer this question, we have to keep in mind what is required of a corrective lens: It must bend parallel rays so that light enters the eye at the same angle as a spot of light positioned at the far point. Figure 17.4 shows what this means for two different locations of the far point. When the far point is close, as in Figure 17.4a, we need a powerful corrective lens to bend the light in the large angle shown in Figure 17.4b. However, when the far point is distant, as in Figure 17.4c, we need only a weak corrective lens to bend the light in the small angle shown in Figure 17.4d. Thus, the strength of the corrective lens depends on the location of the far point: A powerful lens is needed to correct vision when the far point is close, and a weak lens is needed to correct vision when the far point is distant.

When ophthalmologists or optometrists write a prescription for corrective lenses, they specify the strength of the lens in **diopters,** using the following relationship: number of diopters = l/far point in meters. Thus, a slightly myopic person with a far point at 1 meter (100 cm) requires a 1-diopter correction

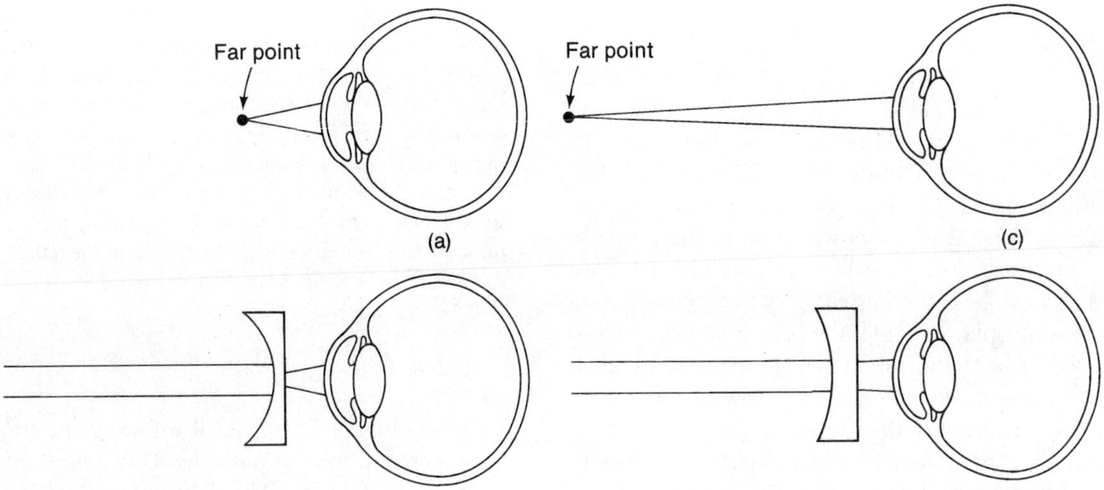

Figure 17.4
The strength of a lens required to correct myopic vision depends on the location of the far point. (a) A close far point requiring (b) a strong corrective lens. (c) A distant far point requiring (d) a weak corrective lens.

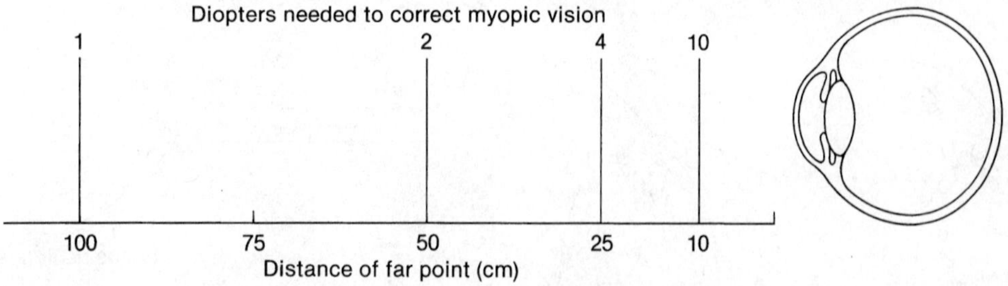

Figure 17.5
The number of diopters of lens power needed to correct myopic vision for different far points. Without a corrective lens, vision is blurred at distances greater than the far point. A far point of 10 cm represents severe myopia, and a far point of 100 cm represents mild myopia.

(diopters = 1/1 = 1.0). However, a very myopic person with a far point at 2/10 of a meter (20 cm) requires a 5-diopter correction (diopters = 1/0.2 = 5.0). This relationship between the distance of the far point and the required number of diopters of correction is shown in Figure 17.5.

Although glasses or contact lenses are the major route to clear vision for the myope, surgical procedures have recently been introduced that, for some people, may provide good vision without corrective lenses. In a procedure called **radial keratotomy,** four or eight cuts are made on the cornea (Figure 17.6a). These cuts cause the cornea to become flatter (Figure 17.6b), which reduces its power to bend light and causes the focus point of the image to move back toward the retina. Most people who have had this operation experience an improvement of vision, although sometimes their vision is either undercorrected or overcorrected, and some people's vision drifts back toward myopia over time. Because of these problems and other undesirable side effects, some ophthalmologists are cautious about recommending this operation to their patients.

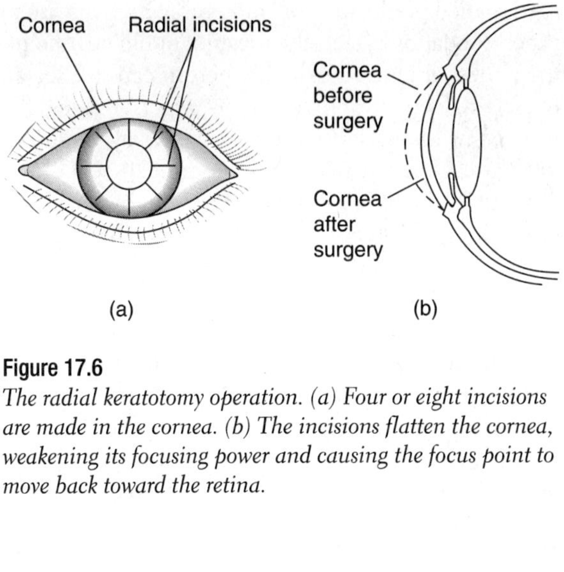

Figure 17.6
The radial keratotomy operation. (a) Four or eight incisions are made in the cornea. (b) The incisions flatten the cornea, weakening its focusing power and causing the focus point to move back toward the retina.

A newer technique, which provides more precise control over the shape of the cornea, is called **laser photorefractive keratotomy.** In this procedure, a type of laser called an *excimer laser,* which does not heat tissue, is used to sculpt the cornea to give it either less power (for myopia; Figure 17.7a) or more power (for hyperopia; Figure 17.7b). This procedure appears to be most effective for myopia.

Hyperopia

A person with hyperopia, or **farsightedness,** can see distant objects clearly but has trouble seeing nearby objects (Figure 17.8a). In the hyperopic eye, the focus point for parallel rays of light is located behind the retina, usually because the eyeball is too short. By accommodating to bring the focus point back to the retina, people with hyperopia are able to see distant objects clearly.

Nearby objects, however, are more difficult for the hyperope to deal with because moving an object

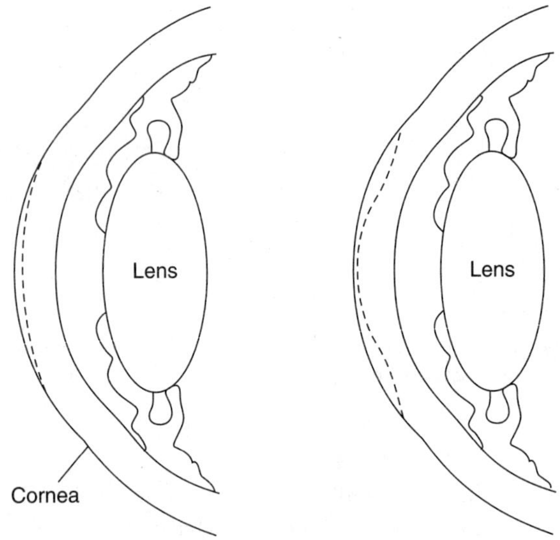

Figure 17.7
In the laser photorefractive keratotomy operation, an excimer laser is used to reshape the cornea, as shown by the dashed lines. (a) Reducing the curvature of the cornea on the myopic eye reduces the focusing power of the cornea so that the focus point moves back. (b) Increasing the curvature of the cornea in the hyperopic eye increases the focusing power of the cornea so that the focus point moves forward.

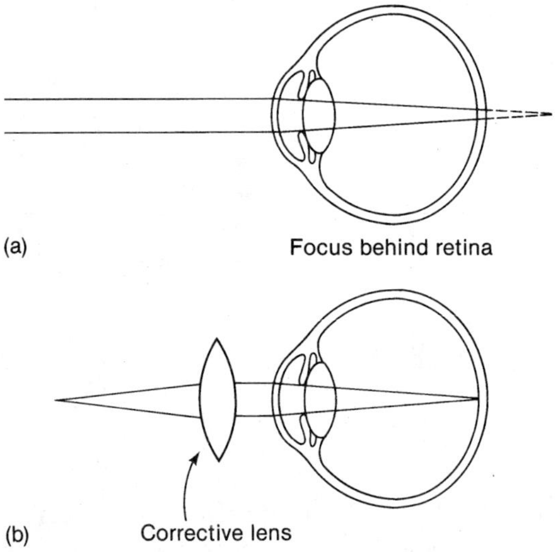

Figure 17.8
Focusing of light by the hyperopic (farsighted) eye. (a) Parallel rays from a distant spot of light are brought to a focus behind the retina, so that, without accommodation, far objects are blurred. Hyperopes can, however, achieve clear vision of distant objects by accommodating. (b) If hyperopia is severe, the constant accommodation needed for clear vision may cause eyestrain, and a corrective lens is required.

closer pushes the focus point farther back. The hyperope's focus point, which is behind the retina for far objects, is pushed even farther back for nearby objects, so the hyperope must exert a great deal of accommodation to return the focus point to the retina. The hyperope's constant need to accommodate when looking at nearby objects (as in reading or doing close-up work) results in eyestrain and, in older people, headaches. Headaches do not usually occur in young people since they can accommodate easily, but older people, who have more difficulty accommodating because of a condition called *presbyopia,* which we will describe next, are more likely to experience headaches and may therefore require a corrective lens that brings the focus point forward onto the retina (Figure 17.8b).

Presbyopia

A decrease in the ability to accommodate due to old age is called presbyopia, or "old eye." This decrease in accommodation affects the location of the near point, the closest distance at which a person can still see an object in focus (Table 17.1). As a person ages, the near point moves farther and farther away, as shown in Figure 17.9. The near point for most 20-year-olds is at about 10 cm, but it increases to 14 cm by age 30, 22 cm at 40, and 100 cm at 60. This loss in the ability to accommodate occurs because the lens hardens with age, and the ciliary muscles, which control accommodation, become weaker. These changes make it more difficult for the lens to change its shape for vision at close range. Though this gradual decrease in accommodative ability poses little problem for most people before the age of 45, at around that age the ability to accommodate begins to decrease rapidly,

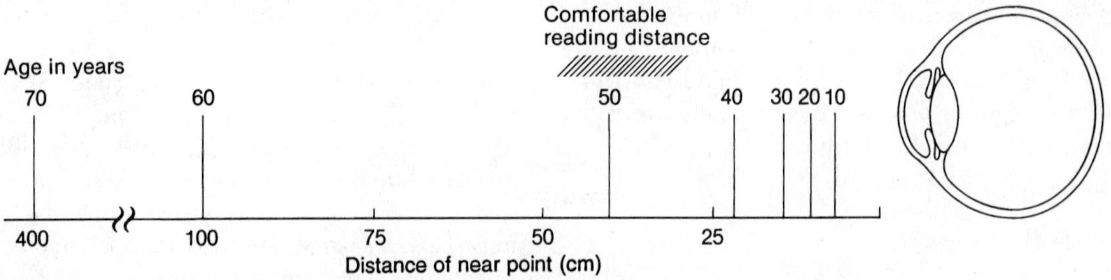

Figure 17.9
The near point as a function of age. The distance of the near point in centimeters is indicated on the scale at the bottom, and various ages are indicated by the vertical lines. Objects closer than the near point cannot be brought into focus by accommodation. Thus, as age increases, the ability to focus on nearby objects becomes poorer and poorer; eventually, past the age of about 50, reading becomes impossible without corrective lenses.

and the near point moves beyond a comfortable reading distance. This is the reason you may have observed older people holding their reading material at arm's length. But the real solution to this problem is a corrective lens that provides the necessary focusing power to bring light to a focus on the retina.

Astigmatism

Imagine what it would be like to see everything through a pane of old-fashioned wavy glass, which causes some things to be in focus and others to be blurred. This describes the experience of a person with a severe astigmatism; an astigmatic person sees through a misshapen cornea, which correctly focuses some of the light reaching the retina but distorts other light. The normal cornea is spherical, curved like a round kitchen bowl, but an astigmatic cornea is somewhat elliptical, curved like the inside of a teaspoon. Because of this elliptical curvature, a person with astigmatism will see the astigmatic fan in Figure 17.10 partially in focus and partially out of focus. As in hyperopia, eyestrain is a symptom of astigmatism, because no matter how much the person accommodates to try to achieve clear vision, something is always out of focus. Fortunately, astigmatism can be corrected with the appropriate lens.

Decreased Transmission of Light

The focusing problems described above are the most prevalent visual problems, as evidenced by the large number of people who wear glasses or contact lenses. Because these problems can usually be corrected, most people with focusing problems see normally or

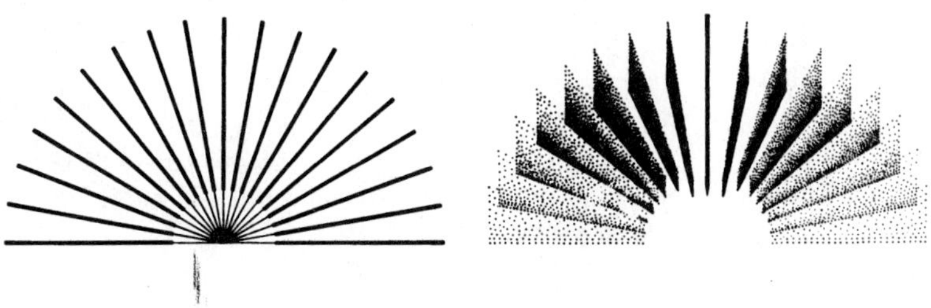

Figure 17.10
Left: Astigmatic fan chart used to test for astigmatism. Right: An astigmatic patient will perceive the lines in one orientation (in this case vertical) as sharp and the lines in the other orientation as blurred. (From Trevor-Roper, 1970.)

suffer only mild losses of vision. We will now consider situations in which disease or physical damage causes severe visual losses or, in some cases, blindness. But before we begin to discuss these problems, we will define what we mean by **blindness.**

What Is Blindness?

It is a common conception that a person who is blind lives in a world of total darkness or formless diffuse light. While this description is true for some blind people, many people who are classified as legally blind do have some vision, and many can read with the aid of a strong magnifying glass. According to the definition accepted in most states, a person is considered legally blind if, after correction with glasses or contact lenses, he or she has a visual acuity of 20/200 or less in the better eye. A visual acuity of 20/20 means that a person can see at 20 feet what a person with normal vision can see at 20 feet. However, a person with an acuity of 20/200 needs to be at a distance of 20 feet to see what a person with normal vision can see from a distance of 200 feet.

When we define blindness in terms of visual acuity, we are evaluating a person's ability to see with his or her fovea (which, as we saw in Chapter 2, is the cone-rich area of the retina that is responsible for detail vision). While poor foveal vision is the most common reason for legal blindness, a person with good foveal vision but little peripheral vision may also be considered legally blind. Thus, a person with normal (20/20) foveal vision but little or no peripheral vision may be legally blind. This situation, which is called **tunnel vision,** results from diseases that affect the retina, such as advanced glaucoma or retinitis pigmentosa (a form of retinal degeneration), which affect peripheral vision but leave the foveal cones unharmed until the final stages, when central vision can also be affected.

We begin our discussion of problems caused by disease or injury by considering some conditions that affect both peripheral and central vision because they affect the perception of light at the beginning of the visual process, as light enters the eye through the cornea and the lens.

Corneal Disease and Injury

The cornea, which is responsible for about 70 percent of the eye's focusing power (Lerman, 1966), is the window to vision because light first passes through this structure on its way to the retina. In order for a sharp image to be formed on the retina, the cornea must be transparent, but this transparency is occasionally lost when injury, infection, or allergic reactions cause the formation of scar tissue on the cornea. This scar tissue decreases visual acuity and sometimes makes lights appear to be surrounded by a halo, which looks like a shimmering rainbow. In addition, **corneal disease and injury** can also cause pain. Drugs, which often bring the cornea back to its transparent state, are the first treatment for corneal problems. If drugs fail, however, clear vision can often be restored by a **corneal transplant** operation.

The basic principle underlying a corneal transplant operation is shown in Figure 17.11. The scarred area of the cornea, usually a disk about 6–8 mm in diameter, is removed and replaced by a piece of cornea taken from a donor. For best results, this donor should be a young adult who died of an acute disease or of an injury that left the corneal tissue in good condition. In the past, a major problem with this operation was the necessity of transplanting the donor cornea within a few hours after the donor's death. Now, however,

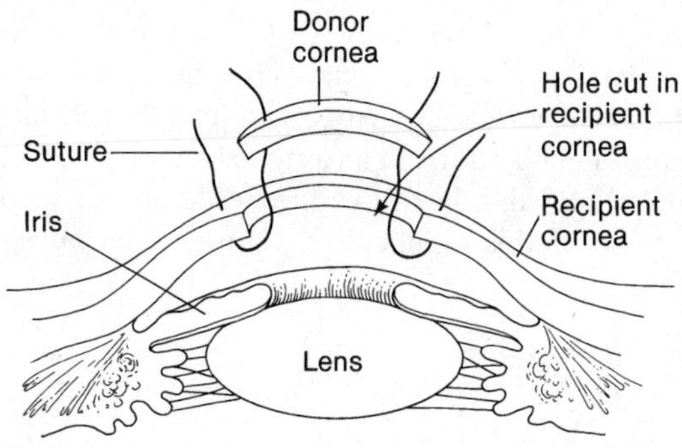

Figure 17.11
Corneal transplant operation. The scarred part of the cornea has been removed, and the donor cornea is about to be sutured in place.

donor corneas are preserved by low-temperature storage in a specially formulated solution.

Of the over 10,000 corneal transplants performed every year, about 85 percent are successful. Remember, however, that a corneal transplant operation involves only a small piece of the eye—there is no such thing as an eye transplant. Indeed, the problems involved in transplanting a whole eye are overwhelming. For one thing, the optic nerve and the retina are sensitive to lack of oxygen, so that, once the circulation is cut off, irreversible damage occurs within minutes, just as is the case for the brain. Thus, keeping the donor's eye alive presents a serious problem. And even if it were possible to keep an eye alive, there is the problem of connecting the 1 million optic nerve fibers of the donor's eye to the corresponding nerve fibers of the patient's optic nerve. At this point, whole eye transplants are purely science fiction.

Clouding of the Lens (Cataract)

Like the cornea, the lens is transparent and is important for focusing a sharp image on the retina. Clouding of the lens, which is called a **cataract**, is sometimes present at birth **(congenital cataract)**, may be caused by an eye disease **(secondary cataract)**, or may be caused by injury **(traumatic cataract)**, but the most common cause of cataract is old age **(senile cataract)**. Cataracts develop, for reasons as yet unknown, in 75 percent of people over 65 and in 95 percent of people over 85.

Although millions of people have cataracts, in only about 15 percent of the cases does the cataract interfere with a person's normal activities, and only 5 percent of cataracts are serious enough to require surgery—the only treatment. The basic principle underlying a cataract operation is illustrated in Figure 17.12a. A small opening is made in the eye, and the surgeon removes the lens while leaving in place the *capsule*, the tissue that forms a bag-like structure that helps support the lens. A method for removing the lens that has the advantage of requiring only a small incision in the eye is **phacoemulsification** (Figure 17.12b). In this procedure, a hollow tubelike instrument that emits ultrasound vibrations of up to 40,000 cycles per second is inserted through a small incision in the cornea. The vibrations break up the lens, and the resulting pieces are sucked out of the eye through the tube.

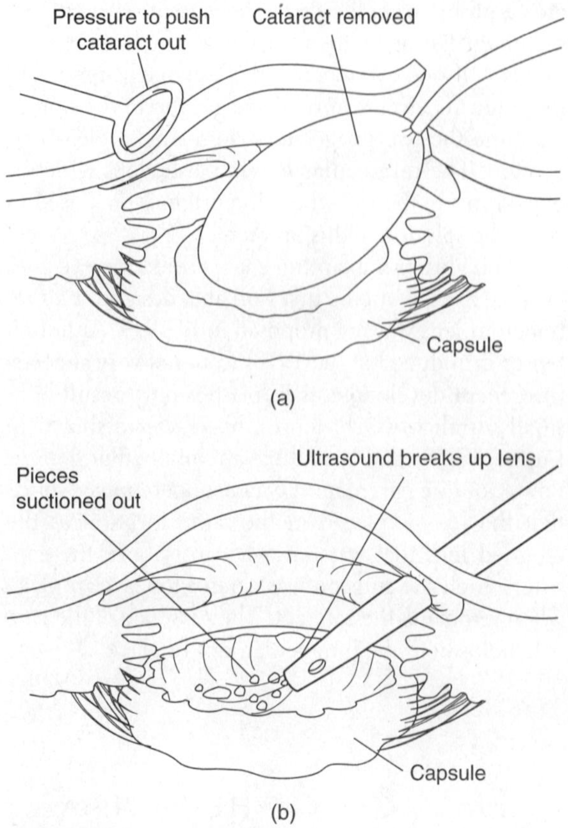

Figure 17.12
A cataract operation. (a) The cataract (the clouded lens) is removed through an incision in the cornea. (b) The phacoemulsification procedure for removing the cataract. High-frequency sound vibrations break up the lens and the pieces are sucked into the tube. After the lens is removed, an intraocular lens is inserted.

Removal of the clouded lens clears a path so that light can reach the retina unobstructed, but in removing the lens, the surgeon has also removed some of the eye's focusing power. (Remember that the cornea accounts for 70 percent of the eye's focusing power; the lens is responsible for the remaining 30 percent.) Although the patient can be fitted with glasses, these create problems of their own, because glasses enlarge the image falling on the retina by as much as 20 to 35 percent. If one eye receives this enlarged image and the other receives a normal image, the brain cannot combine the two images to form a single, clear perception. The **intraocular lens,** a plastic lens which is placed inside the eye where the original lens used to be, is the solution to this problem.

The idea of implanting a lens inside the eye goes back 200 years, but the first workable design for an intraocular lens was not proposed until 1949. Although lenses introduced in the 1950s were not very successful, recent developments in plastics have resulted in small ultralightweight lenses, like the one shown in Figure 17.13, and installing an intraocular lens is now a routine part of most cataract operations. Notice that the lens is placed in the same location as the clouded lens that was removed, just above the capsule, which the surgeon was careful to leave in place when removing the cataract. The presence of the capsule helps hold the intraocular lens in place.

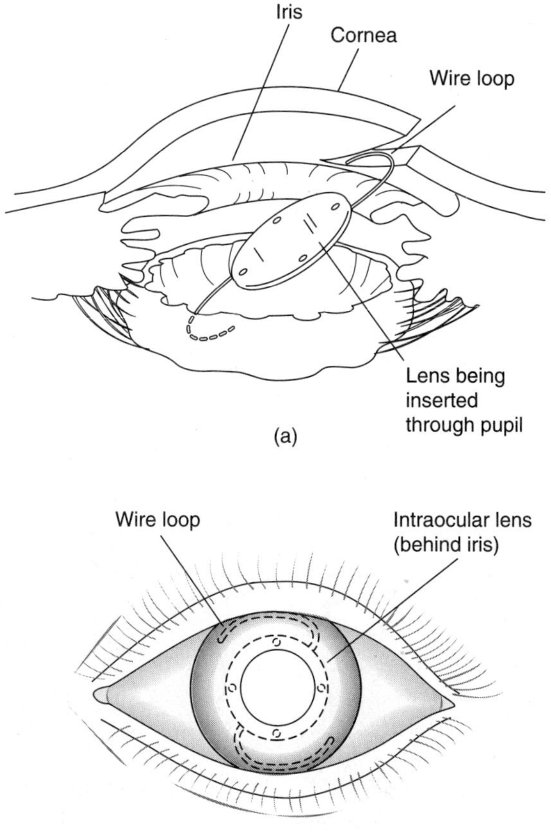

Figure 17.13
Installing an intraocular lens in the eye after the cataract has been removed. (a) The lens is inserted through an incision in the cornea. Notice that it is being inserted through the pupil so that it will be positioned where the original lens was, behind the iris and just above the capsule. (b) Frontal view, showing the lens in place behind the iris. The small wire loops hold the lens in place.

Damage to the Retina

The retina receives nourishment from the retinal circulation and from the pigment epithelium on which it rests. All four conditions described below cause a loss of vision because of their effects on the retinal circulation and on the relationship between the retina and the pigment epithelium.

Diabetic Retinopathy

Before the isolation of insulin in 1922, most people with severe **diabetes,** a condition in which the body doesn't produce enough insulin, had a life expectancy of less than 20 years. The synthesis of insulin (which won the 1923 Nobel prize for its discoverers) greatly increased the life expectancy of diabetics, but one result of this greater life expectancy has been a great increase in an eye problem called **diabetic retinopathy.** Of the 10 million diabetics in the United States, about 4 million show some signs of this problem.

Figure 17.14 shows what happens as the disease progresses. At first, the capillaries swell, and although most cases of diabetic retinopathy stop here, a large

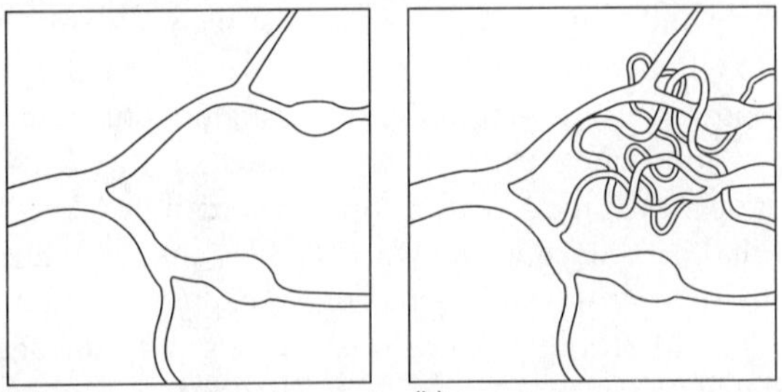

Figure 17.14
Blood vessels in diabetic retinopathy. (a) In early stages of the disease, the blood vessels swell and leak slightly. (b) In later stages, in a process called neovascularization, abnormal new blood vessels grow on the surface of the retina.

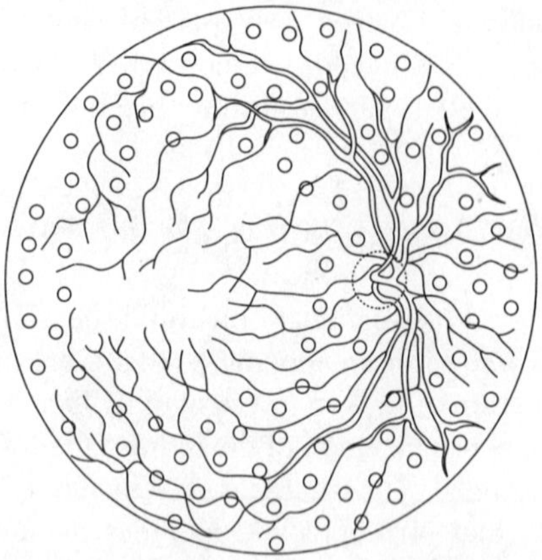

Figure 17.15
Laser photocoagulation in the treatment of diabetic retinopathy. The picture illustrates the technique of panretinal photocoagulation. Each dot represents a small laser burn on the retina.

number of diabetics suffer vision losses even when the disease stops at this point. The disease's further progression, which occurs in a small percentage of patients, involves a process called **neovascularization.** Abnormal new blood vessels are formed (Figure 17.14b), which do not supply the retina with adequate oxygen and which are fragile and so bleed into the **vitreous humor** (the jellylike substance that fills the eyeball); this bleeding interferes with the passage of light to the retina. Neovascularization can also cause scarring of the retina and retinal detachment (see below).

One technique for stopping neovascularization is called **laser photocoagulation,** in which a laser beam of high-energy light is aimed at leaking blood vessels. The laser "photocoagulates," or seals off, these vessels and stops the bleeding. A procedure called **panretinal photocoagulation** has been used with considerable success. In this technique, the laser scatters 2,000 or more tiny burns on the retina, as shown in Figure 17.15. The burns do not directly hit the leaking blood vessels, but by destroying part of the retina, they decrease the retina's need for oxygen, so that the leaking blood vessels dry up and go away.

If laser photocoagulation is not successful in stopping neovascularization, a procedure called a **vitrectomy,** shown in Figure 17.16, is used to eliminate the blood inside the eye. In this operation, which is done only as a last resort, a hollow tube containing a guillotinelike cutter takes in the vitreous humor and chops it into pieces small enough to be sucked out of the eye through the tube. When the vitreous humor

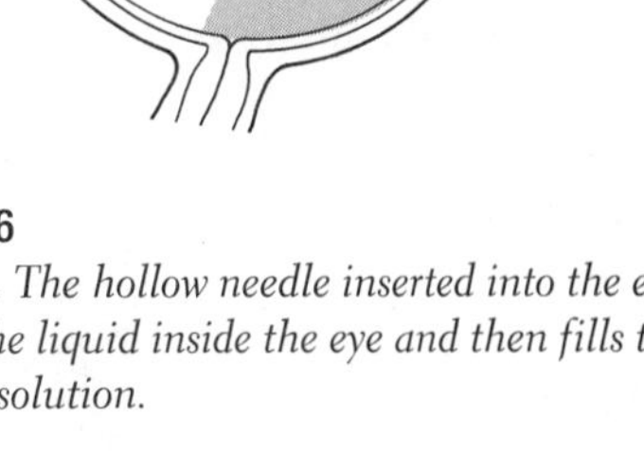

Figure 17.16
Vitrectomy. The hollow needle inserted into the eyeball first sucks out the liquid inside the eye and then fills the eyeball with a salt solution.

and blood are removed, they are replaced with a salt solution. This procedure removes the blood inside the eye and often prevents further bleeding.

Macular Degeneration

Imagine your frustration if you could see everywhere *except* where you were looking, so that every time you looked at something you lost sight of it. That is exactly what happens if a region of the retina called the **macula** is damaged. The macula is an area about 5 mm in diameter that surrounds and includes the cone-rich fovea (itself only slightly larger than one of the periods on this page). If the macula degenerates, blindness results in the center of vision (Figure 17.17). This condition is extremely debilitating because, although peripheral vision remains intact, the elimination of central vision makes reading impossible.

There are a number of forms of **macular degeneration,** but the most common is called **age-related macular degeneration** because it occurs, without obvious reason, in older people. In its mild form, there is a slight thinning of the cone receptors and the formation of small white or yellow lumps on the retina. This form of macular degeneration usually progresses slowly and may not cause serious visual problems. In 5 to 20 percent of the cases, however, small new blood vessels, similar to those in diabetic retinopathy, grow underneath the macular area of the retina. These new blood vessels form very rapidly—over a period of only one or two months—and leak fluid into the macula, killing the cone receptors.

Until recently, there was no treatment for age-related macular degeneration. However, a study by the National Eye Institute indicates that, if the problem can be caught at an early stage in some patients with the more severe form of the disease, laser photocoagulation can stop or greatly reduce leakage of the newly formed vessels.

Detached Retina

Detached retina, a condition in which the retina becomes separated from the underlying pigment epithelium (Figure 17.18), has occurred in a number of athletes because of traumatic injuries to the eye or the head. Sugar Ray Leonard, the former welterweight boxing champion, retired temporarily from boxing because of a detached retina. He returned to boxing a number of years later amid much discussion about

Figure 17.17
Macular degeneration causes a loss of central vision.

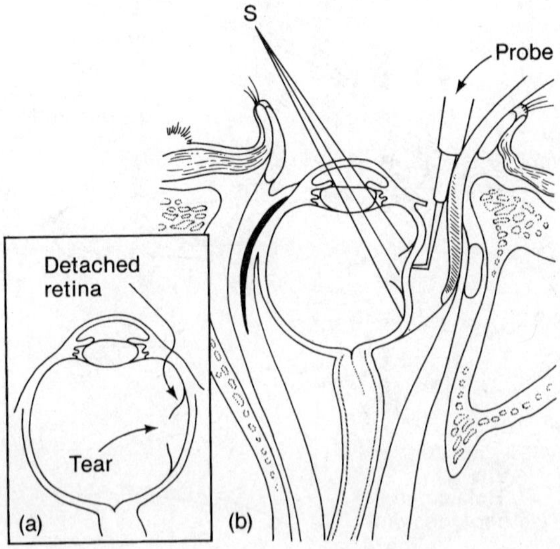

Figure 17.18
(a) A detached retina. (b) Procedure for reattaching the retina. To locate the site of detachment, a probe pushes the eyeball from outside while the surgeon, at S, looks into the eye. Once the site of the detachment is located, the outside of the eye is marked, and a cooling or heating probe is applied at the marked point.

whether returning to the ring was worth the risk of losing his sight in one eye. As it turned out, Leonard won both the fight and the gamble with his sight, apparently escaping without further damaging his eye.

A detached retina affects vision for two reasons: (1) For good image formation, the retina must lie smoothly on top of the pigment epithelium, and (2) when the retina loses contact with the pigment epithelium, the visual pigments in the detached area are separated from enzymes in the epithelium necessary for pigment regeneration. When the visual pigment can no longer regenerate, that area of the retina becomes blind.

The treatment for a detached retina is an operation to reattach it. The basic idea behind this operation is to cause the formation of scar tissue inside the eye that will attach itself to the retina and anchor it in place. This process is accomplished by applying either a cooling or a heating probe to exactly the right place on the outside of the eyeball. Figure 17.18b shows the procedure used to determine where to apply the probe. While looking into the eye with a special viewing device, the surgeon presses on the outside of the eyeball, which causes an indentation that can be seen inside the eye. The surgeon presses at a number of points, until the indentation inside the eyeball matches the location of the tear or hole in the retina, where the detachment originated.

Once the point where the detachment has occurred is located, it is marked on the outside of the eyeball, and that point is cooled or heated to create an inflammatory response. The retina must then be pushed flush with the wall of the eyeball. This is accomplished by placing a band around the outside of the eyeball that creates a dumbbell-shaped eye. Then, with the retina pressed against the wall of the eye, the inflammation causes scarring that "welds" the retina back onto the pigment epithelium. If the area of detached retina is not too big, there is a 70 to 80 percent chance that this procedure will work. In most cases, it restores vision, although vision is sometimes not restored even though the retina is successfully reattached. The larger the detached area, the less likely it is that this operation (or others, which we will not describe here) will work. Sometimes, if a retinal tear can be caught at an early stage, before fluid has gotten through it and caused the retina to detach, it is possible to prevent detachment by surrounding the tear with laser burns. This is a quick procedure that can be carried out in the ophthalmologist's office and requires no surgery.

Hereditary Retinal Degeneration

The most common form of **hereditary retinal degeneration** is a disease called **retinitis pigmentosa,** a degeneration of the retina that is passed from one generation to the next (although not always affecting everyone in a family). We know little about what actually causes the disease, although one hypothesis is that it is caused by a problem in the pigment epithelium.

A person with retinitis pigmentosa usually shows no signs of the disease until reaching adolescence. At this time, the person may begin to notice some difficulty in seeing at night, since the disease first attacks the rod receptors. As the person gets older, the disease slowly progresses, causing further losses of vision in the peripheral retina. Then, in its final stages, which may occur as early as a person's 30s or as late as the 50s or 60s (depending on the strain of the disease), retinitis pigmentosa also attacks the cones, and the result is complete blindness.

OPTIC NERVE DAMAGE

A leading cause of blindness in the United States is **glaucoma,** which causes nerve fibers in the optic nerve to degenerate and therefore prevents the nerve impulses generated by the retina from being transmitted to the brain.

Glaucoma

Although the end result of glaucoma is damage to the optic nerve, the source of the problem is at the front of the eye. We can understand how damage to the front of the eye affects the optic nerve by looking at the cross section of the eye in Figure 17.19a. Under normal conditions, the aqueous humor (the liquid found in the space between the cornea and the lens), which is continuously produced at A, passes between the iris and the lens following the path indicated by the arrows; it then drains from the eye at B. In glaucoma, the drainage of aqueous humor is partially blocked. **Closed-angle glaucoma** is a rare form of glaucoma in which a **pupillary block** (Figure 17.19b) constricts the opening between the iris and the lens and causes a pressure buildup that pushes the iris up, thereby closing the angle between the cornea and the iris and blocking the area at B where the aqueous humor leaves the eye.

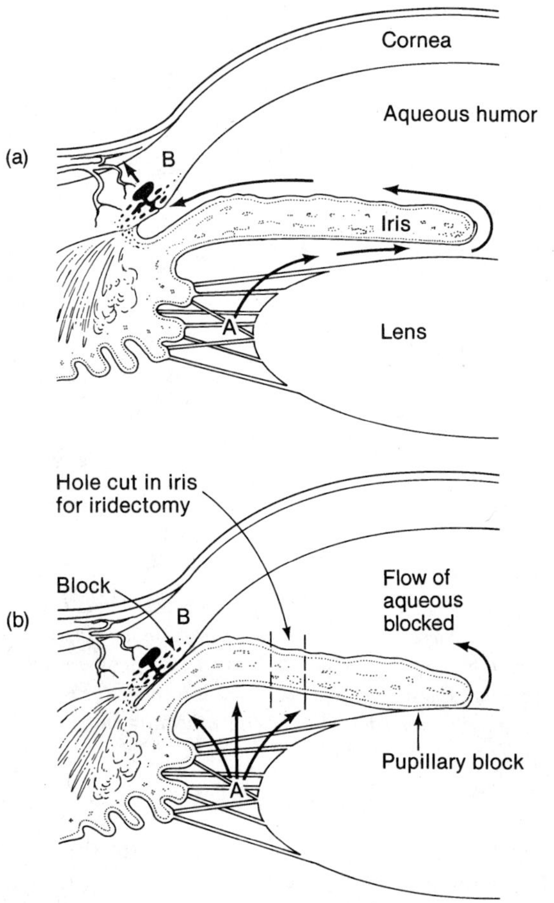

Figure 17.19
(a) Arrows indicate the flow of aqueous humor in the normal eye. The aqueous humor is produced at A and leaves the eye at B. In open-angle glaucoma, the aqueous humor cannot leave the eye because of a blockage at B. (b) In closed-angle glaucoma, the raised iris hinders the flow of aqueous humor from the eye. An iridectomy—cutting a hole in the iris—can provide a way for the aqueous humor to reach B.

In **open-angle glaucoma,** which is the most common form of the disease, the eye looks normal (Figure 17.19a), but the drainage area at B is partially blocked, so that it is more difficult for the aqueous humor to leave the eye. The blocks that occur in both closed- and open-angle glaucoma result in a large resistance to the outflow of aqueous humor, and since the aqueous humor continues to be produced inside the eye, the **intraocular pressure**—the pressure inside the eyeball—rises. This increase in intraocular pressure presses on the head of the optic nerve at the back of the eye. This pressure cuts off circulation to the head of the optic nerve, which results in the degeneration of the optic nerve fibers that causes blindness.

The increase in pressure that occurs in closed-angle glaucoma usually happens very rapidly and is accompanied by pain. The treatment for this type of glaucoma is an operation called an **iridectomy,** in which a small hole is created in the iris with a laser (Figure 17.19b). This hole opens a channel through which the aqueous humor can flow and releases the pressure on the iris. With the pressure gone, the iris flattens out and uncovers the area at B so that aqueous humor can flow out of the eye.

Intraocular pressure increases more slowly in open-angle glaucoma, so the patient may be unaware of any symptoms. In many cases, visual loss is so gradual that much of the patient's peripheral vision is gone before its loss is noticed. For that reason, ophthalmologists strongly recommend that people over 40 have their eyes checked regularly for glaucoma, since early detection greatly enhances the chances of effective treatment by medication. In 5 to 10 percent of the cases of open-angle glaucoma, medications do not decrease the pressure, and an operation becomes necessary. The goal of this operation is to cut an opening in the wall of the eyeball that creates a new route for fluid to leave the eye.

The Eye Examination

So far, we have described some of the things that can go wrong with the eye and how these problems are treated. In this part of the chapter, we will describe the procedures used to uncover some of these problems. Before describing the eye examination, we will consider who examines the eyes.

Who Examines Eyes?

Three types of professionals are involved in eye care: ophthalmologists, optometrists, and opticians.

1. An **ophthalmologist** is an M.D. who has completed undergraduate school and four years of medical school, which provide general medical training. In order to become an ophthalmologist, a person needs four or more years of training after graduation from medical school to learn how to treat eye problems medically and surgically. Some ophthalmologists receive even further training and then specialize in specific areas, such as pediatric ophthalmology (practice limited to children), diseases of the cornea, retinal diseases, or glaucoma. Most ophthalmologists, however, treat all eye problems, as well as prescribing glasses and fitting contact lenses.

2. An **optometrist** has completed undergraduate school and, after four years of additional study, has received a doctor of optometry (O.D.) degree. Optometrists can examine eyes and fit and prescribe glasses or contact lenses. In some states, optometrists have won the right to include medical treatment using drugs, for some eye conditions. Surgery, however, is still done exclusively by ophthalmologists.

3. An **optician** is trained to fabricate and fit glasses and, in some states, contact lenses, on the prescription of an ophthalmologist or an optometrist.

What Happens during an Eye Exam?

The basic aims of an eye exam are (1) to determine how well the patient can see, (2) to correct vision if it is defective, (3) to determine the causes of defective vision by examining the optics of the eye and checking for eye diseases, and (4) to diagnose diseases that the patient may not even be aware of. To accomplish these aims, an examination by an eye specialist usually includes the following:

Medical History The first step in an eye exam is to take a medical history. This history focuses on any eye problems that the patient may have had in the past, on any current eye problems, and on any general medical problems that may be related to the patient's vision.

Visual Acuity This is the familiar part of the eye exam, in which you are asked to read letters on an eye chart like the one in Figure 16.1. The old version of the eye chart, which most people are familiar with, had a large E at the top. This new version results in more accurate measurements of acuity because there are the same number of letters on each line and the spacing between the letters is proportional to the sizes of the letters. The top row of letters is the 20/400 line. This means that a person with normal vision should be able to see these letters from a distance of 400 feet. Since the eye chart is usually viewed from about 20 feet, people with normal vision see these letters easily. When asked to read the smallest line he or she can see, the patient usually picks a line that is easily read. With a little encouragement, however, most patients find that they can see lines smaller than the one they originally picked, and the examiner has the patient read smaller and smaller lines until letters are missed. The smallest line a person can read indicates his or her visual acuity, with normal vision defined as an acuity of 20/20. A person with worse than normal acuity—say, 20/40—must view a display from a distance of 20 feet to see what a person with normal acuity can see at 40 feet. A person with better than normal acuity—say, 20/10—can see from a distance of 20 feet what a person with normal vision can see only at 10 feet.

The visual acuity test described above, tests only foveal vision, since the patient looks directly at each letter, so the image of that letter falls on the fovea. Thus, as mentioned earlier, a person who scores 20/20 on a visual acuity test may still be classified as legally blind if he or she has little or no peripheral vision. Testing peripheral vision is usually not part of a routine eye exam, but when peripheral vision problems are suspected, a technique called **visual perimetry** is used, in which the patient is asked to indicate the location of small spots of light presented at different locations in the periphery. This test locates blind spots (called *scotomas*) that may be caused by retinal degeneration, detachment of the retina, or diseases such as glaucoma.

In addition to using the eye chart to test far vision, it is also customary to test near vision, especially in older patients who may be experiencing the effects of presbyopia. This testing is done by determining the smallest line of a card like the one in Figure 17.20 that the patient can see from a comfortable reading distance.

No. 1

In short-sighted persons the eye-ball is too long, and the light rays come to a focus in front of the retina,

No. 2

while in far-sighted persons the eye-ball is too short, and the focal point, therefore, falls be-

No. 3

hind the retina. In either case a blurred image is received upon the retina. In order

No. 4

to overcome this blurring, and thus correct the optical defect, the eye un-

No. 6

consciously makes an effort by which the ciliary muscle acts on

No. 8

the lens. This effort explains why eye-strain may cause

No. 10

pain and discomfort. An optical correction for

No. 12

the refractive error is found in specta-

Figure 17.20
A card for testing close vision. The patient's close vision is determined by the smallest line that he or she can read from a comfortable reading distance.

Refraction A score of 20/60 on a visual acuity test indicates worse than normal acuity but does not indicate what is causing this loss of acuity. Acuity could be decreased by one of the diseases described earlier or by a problem in focusing: myopia, hyperopia, presbyopia, or astigmatism. If the problem lies in the focusing mechanism of the eye, it is usually easily corrected by glasses or contact lenses. **Refraction** is the procedure used to determine the power of the corrective lenses needed to achieve clear vision.

The first step in refraction is a **retinoscopy exam,** an examination of the eye with a device called a *retinoscope.* This device projects a streak of light into the eye that is reflected into the eye of the examiner. The examiner moves the retinoscope back and forth and up and down across the eye, noticing what the reflected light looks like. If the patient's eye is focusing the light correctly, the examiner sees the whole pupil filled with light, and no correction is necessary (in this case, the patient will usually have tested at 20/20 or better in the visual acuity test). If, however, the patient's eye is not focusing the light correctly, the examiner sees a streak of light move back and forth across the pupil as the streak of light from the retinoscope is moved across the eye.

To determine the correction needed to bring the patient's eye to 20/20 vision, the examiner places corrective lenses in front of the eye while still moving the streak of light from the retinoscope back and forth. One way of placing these lenses in front of the eye is to use a device like the one shown in Figure 17.21. This device contains a variety of lenses that can be changed by turning a dial. The examiner's goal is to find the lens that causes the whole pupil to fill up with light when the retinoscope is moved back and forth. This lens brings light to a focus on the retina and is usually close to the one that will be prescribed to achieve 20/20 vision.

The retinoscopy exam results in a good first approximation of the correct lens to prescribe for a patient, but the ultimate test is what the patient sees.

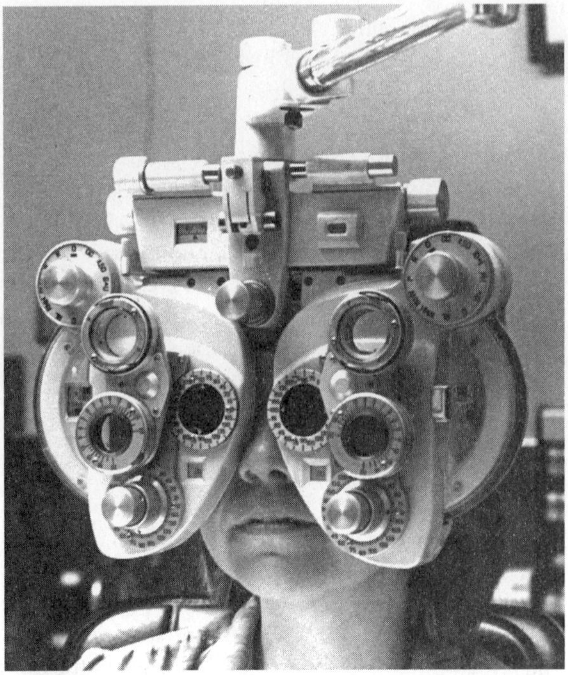

Figure 17.21
A device for placing different corrective lenses in front of the patient's eyes. Different lenses are placed in front of the eye during the retinoscopy exam and again as the patient looks at the eye chart.

To determine this, the examiner has the patient look at the eye chart, and places lenses in front of the patient's eyes to determine which one results in the clearest vision. When the examiner determines which lens results in 20/20 vision, he or she writes a prescription for glasses or contact lenses. To fit contact lenses after determining the prescription, the examiner must match the shape of the contact lens to the shape of the patient's cornea.

Refraction is used to determine the correction needed to achieve clear far vision. Using a procedure we will not describe here, the examiner also determines whether a correction is needed to achieve clear near vision. This determination is particularly important for patients over 45 years old, who may experience reading difficulties due to presbyopia.

External Eye Exam In an **external eye exam,** the examiner uses a variety of tests to check the condition of the external eye. The examiner checks pupillary reaction by shining light into the eye, to see if the pupil responds by closing when the light is presented and by opening when the light is removed. The examiner also checks the color of the eye and the surrounding tissues. "Red eye" may indicate that an inflammation is present. The movement of the eyes is checked by having the patient follow a moving target, and the alignment of the eyes is checked by having the patient look at a target. If the eyes are aligned correctly, both eyes will look directly at the target, but if the eyes are misaligned, one eye will look at the target, and the other will veer off to one side.

Slit-Lamp Examination The **slit-lamp examination** checks the condition of the cornea and the lens. The slit lamp, shown in Figure 17.22, projects a narrow slit of light into the patient's eye. This light can be precisely focused at different places inside the eye, and the examiner views this sharply focused slit of light through a binocular magnifier. This slit of light is like the sharp edge of a knife that cuts through the eye.

What does the examiner see when looking at the "cutting edge" of light from the slit lamp? By focusing the light at different levels inside the cornea and lens, the examiner can detect small imperfections—places where the cornea or the lens is not completely

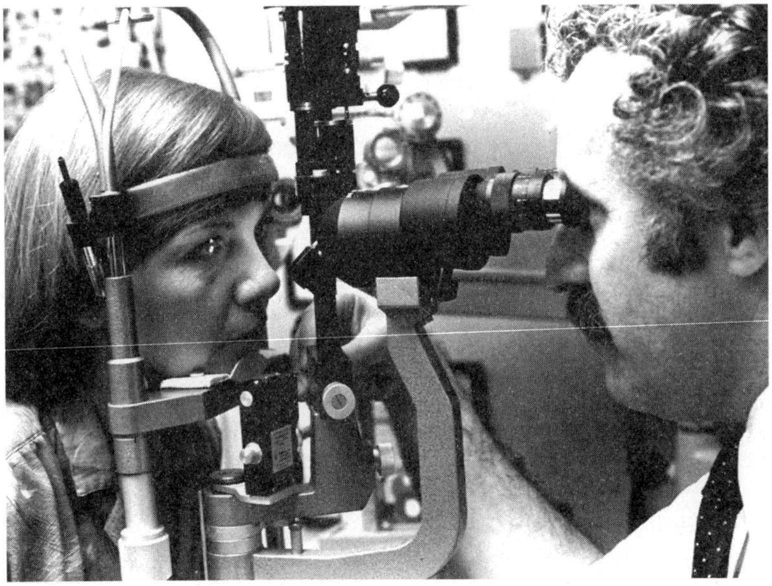

Figure 17.22
A patient being examined with a slit lamp. The examiner is checking the condition of the lens and the cornea by viewing the slit of light through a binocular magnifier.

transparent—that cannot be seen by any other method. These imperfections may indicate corneal disease or injury or the formation of a cataract.

Tonometry **Tonometry** measures intraocular pressure, the pressure inside the eye, and is therefore the test for glaucoma. Nowadays, an instrument called a **tonometer** is used to measure intraocular pressure, but before the development of this device, it was known that large increases of intraocular pressure, which accompany severe cases of glaucoma, cause the eye to become so hard that this hardness could be detected by pushing on the eyeball with a finger.

There are several types of tonometers, which measure the intraocular pressure by pushing on the cornea. The Schiotz tonometer is a hand-held device that consists of a small plunger attached to a calibrated weight. The weight pushes the plunger and indents the cornea. If the intraocular pressure is high, the plunger causes a smaller indentation than if the intraocular pressure is normal. Thus, intraocular pressure is determined by measuring the indentation of the cornea. (Though this procedure may sound rather painful, it is not, because the examiner applies a few drops of anesthetic to the cornea before applying the tonometer.)

The applanation tonometer, shown being applied to a patient's cornea in Figure 17.23, is a more sophisticated and accurate instrument than the Schiotz tonometer. After a few drops of anesthetic are applied to the cornea, the flat end of a cylindrical rod, called an **applanator,** is slowly moved against the cornea by the examiner, who watches the applanator's progress through the same magnifiers used for the slit-lamp exam (Figure 17.22). The examiner pushes the end of the applanator against the cornea until enough pressure is exerted to flatten a small area on the cornea's curved surface. The greater the force that must be exerted to flatten the cornea, the greater the intraocular pressure.

Ophthalmoscopy So far, we have looked at the outside of the eye (external eye exam), examined the lens and cornea (slit-lamp exam), and measured the intraocular pressure (tonometry), but we have yet to look at perhaps the most important structure of all: the retina. Since there is a hole (the pupil) in the front of the eye, it should be simple to see the retina; we only have to look into the hole. Unfortunately, it's not that simple; if you've ever looked into a person's pupil, you realize that it's dark in there. In order to see the retina, we must find some way to light up the

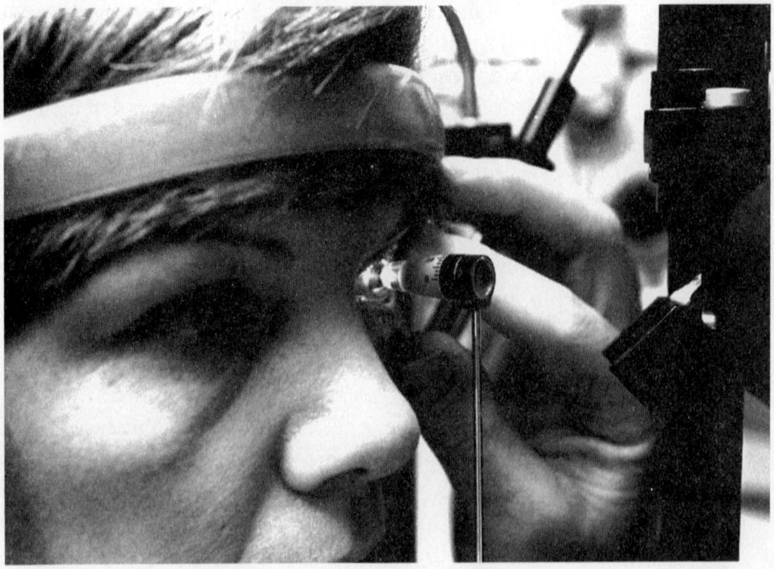

Figure 17.23
An applanation tonometer being applied to a patient's cornea.

inside of the eye. This is accomplished by the **ophthalmoscope,** which was first developed by Hermann von Helmholtz, of the Young-Helmholtz theory of color vision, in 1850.

The principle underlying Helmholtz's ophthalmoscope is shown in Figure 17.24. A light off to the side is directed into the patient's eye with a half-silvered mirror. The half-silvered mirror reflects some of the light and transmits the rest, so that an examiner positioned as shown in Figure 17.24 can see through the mirror and into the patient's eye. Actual ophthalmoscopes are much more complicated than the one diagrammed here, since they include numerous lenses, mirrors, and filters, but the basic principle remains the same as that of the original ophthalmoscope designed by Helmholtz in 1850.

Figure 17.25 is a patient's-eye view of an examination with an ophthalmoscope, although the examiner is actually very close, as shown in Figure 17.1. Figure 17.26 shows a close-up of what the ophthalmologist sees if the patient has a normal retina. (Also see the picture on the inside of the front cover.) The most prominent features of this view of the retina are the optic disk, the place where the ganglion cell fibers leave the eye to form the optic nerve, and the arteries

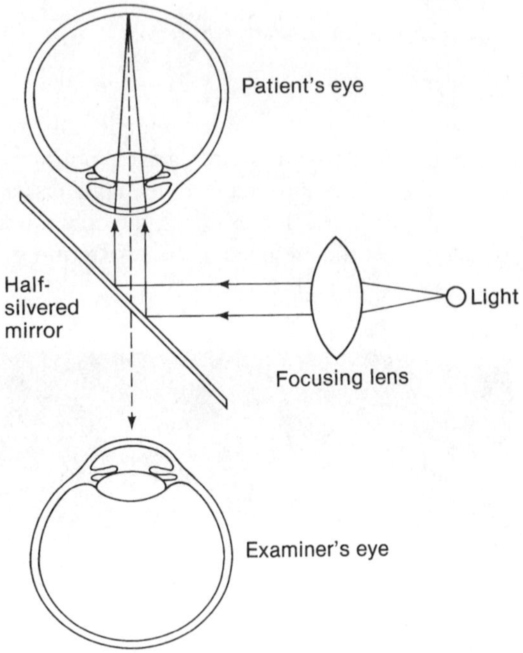

Figure 17.24
The principle behind the ophthalmoscope. Light is reflected into the patient's eye by the half-silvered mirror. Some of this light is then reflected into the examiner's eye (along the dashed line), allowing the examiner to see the inside of the patient's eye.

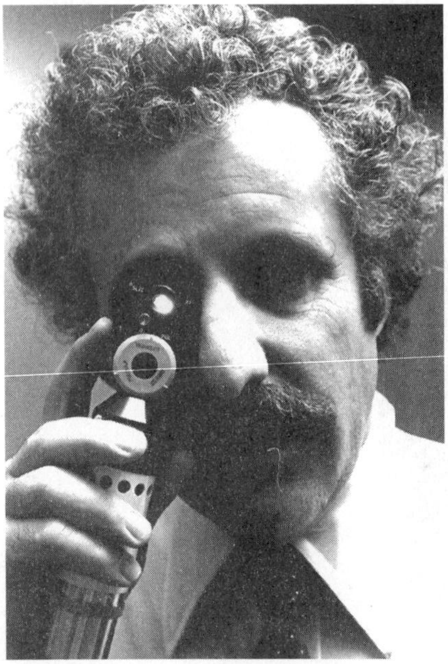

Figure 17.25
Patient's-eye view of an ophthalmoscopy exam.

and veins of the retina. In this examination, the ophthalmologist focuses on these features, noting any abnormalities in the appearance of the optic disk and the retinal circulation. For example, the ophthalmologist may detect the presence of diabetic retinopathy by noticing a number of very small blood vessels (neovascularization). In fact, all the retinal injuries and diseases described above cause some change in the appearance of the retina, which can be detected by looking at the retina with an ophthalmoscope.

Our description of an eye examination has covered most of the tests included in a routine exam. The examiner may decide to carry out other tests if a problem is suggested by the routine tests. For example, a technique called **fluorescein angiography** is used to examine more closely the retinal circulation in patients with diabetic retinopathy. A fluorescent dye is injected intravenously into the arm, and when this dye reaches the retina, it sharply outlines the retinal arteries and veins, as shown in Figure 17.27. Only by this technique can we observe the leakage of fluid that occurs in the abnormal neovascularized blood vessels that accompany diabetic retinopathy. Determining the location of the leakage identifies areas that are to be treated with photocoagulation.

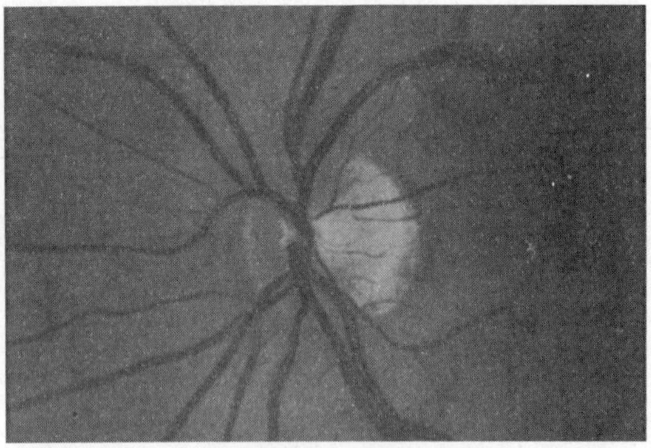

Figure 17.26
Close-up view of the head of the optic nerve and the retinal circulation as seen through an ophthalmoscope.

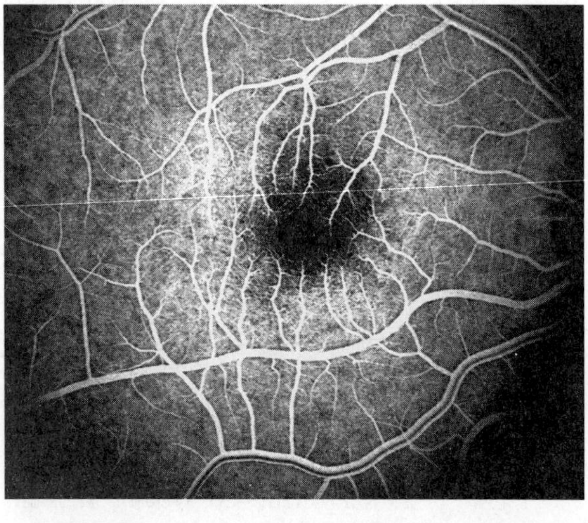

Figure 17.27
Fluorescein angiograph of a normal eye. In this view, the head of the optic nerve is on the far right, just outside the picture. The fovea is in the dark space near the middle of the picture. In the normal eye, the blood vessels stand out in sharp contrast to the background. (Photograph courtesy of Eye and Ear Hospital of Pittsburgh.)

Other tests, which we will not describe here, include the **electroretinogram,** which measures the electrical response of the rod and cone receptors and is therefore useful in diagnosing such retinal degeneration as retinitis pigmentosa, and the cortical evoked potential, which measures the electrical response of the visual cortex and is useful for diagnosing vision problems caused by head injuries or tumors.

HEARING IMPAIRMENT

In our consideration of the clinical aspects of vision, we saw that visual functioning can be impaired because of problems in delivering the stimulus to the receptors, because of damage to the receptors, and because of damage to the system that transmits signals from the receptors toward the brain. An analogous situation exists in hearing, as we will see by considering the various causes of hearing impairment.

How Can Hearing Become Impaired?

In considering the question "How can hearing become impaired?" it is important to distinguish between impairments in the auditory system and what effects these impairments have on a person's hearing. A **hearing impairment** is a deviation or change for the worse in either the structure or the functioning of the auditory system. A **hearing handicap** is the disadvantage that a hearing impairment causes in a person's ability to communicate or in the person's daily living. The distinction between an impairment and a handicap means that a hearing impairment does not always cause a large hearing handicap. For example, although a person who has lost the ability to hear all sounds above 6,000 Hz has lost a substantial portion of his or her range of hearing, this particular hearing loss has little effect on the person's ability to hear and understand speech. We can appreciate this when we realize that, even though telephones transmit frequencies only between about 500 and 3,000 Hz, most people have no trouble using the telephone for communication. Such a hearing impairment would, however, change a person's perception of music, which often contains frequencies above 6,000 Hz, and would therefore have some impact on the person's quality of life.

Problems can develop in the auditory system for the following reasons: (1) problems in delivering the sound stimulus to the receptors, (2) damage to the receptors, (3) damage to the transmission system, and (4) damage to the auditory cortex (Figure 17.28). The following is a list of the types of things that can go wrong in the auditory system within each of these categories:

1. Sound is not properly transmitted to the receptors. Problems in delivering sound to the receptors can occur because of problems such as blockage of the outer ear or damage to the system that transmits vibrations through the middle ear. These types of problems result in *conductive hearing losses.*
2. The hair cells are damaged, so they can't generate electrical signals. This problem and the one below result in *sensorineural hearing losses.*
3. There is damage to the auditory nerve or the brainstem that keeps signals that are generated from being transmitted to the auditory area of the brain. Damage at the brainstem level can interfere with the listener's ability to integrate the signals coming from the left and right ears.
4. There is damage at the auditory cortex, so when the signal reaches the cortex, it is not processed properly.

We will describe some of the major ways in which these problems occur in the auditory system, focusing on the first two categories above: conductive hearing loss and sensorineural hearing loss.

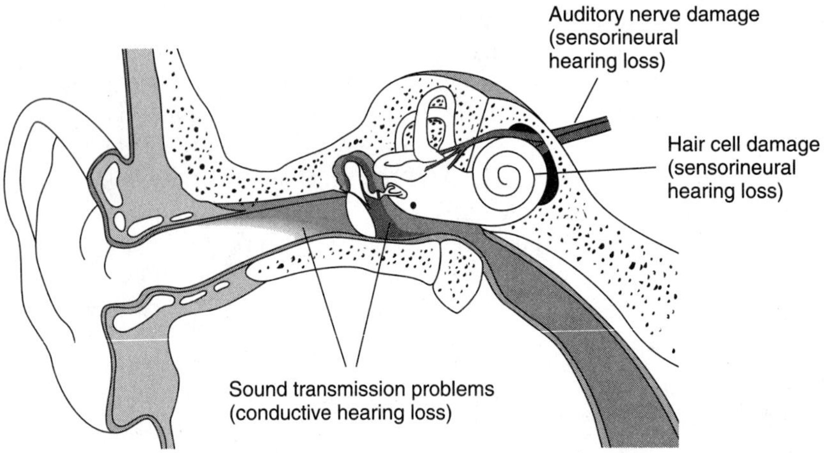

Figure 17.28
Places in the ear where hearing problems can occur.

Conductive Hearing Loss

A **conductive hearing loss** is one in which the vibrations that would normally be caused by a sound stimulus are not conducted from the outer ear into the cochlea. This kind of loss can occur in either the outer ear or the middle ear.

Outer-Ear Disorders

Sound can be blocked at the ear canal by the buildup of excessive cerumen (ear wax), or by the insertion of objects, as might occur when children decide it would be fun to put beans or wads of paper into their ears. A more serious problem occurs in children who are born with outer- or middle-ear malformations that prevent sound from traveling down the outer-ear canal and through the middle ear. Blockage may also occur because of a swelling of the canal caused by infection by microorganisms, a situation that often occurs in swimmers when water is trapped in the ear, hence the name "swimmer's ear."

Another problem occurs if the tympanic membrane at the end of the outer ear is ruptured either by a very loud noise such as an explosion or by the insertion of a sharp object too far into the ear. Such a rupture may allow microorganisms into the middle ear that may cause infection. Also, once the tympanic membrane is ruptured, it does not efficiently set the ossicles into vibration, which may cause hearing loss. Problems of the outer ear are generally treated with medication or surgery. Normal hearing is often restored after these treatments.

Middle-Ear Disorders

Most people have experienced **otitis media,** middle-ear infection, at some time. Middle-ear infections are caused by bacteria that cause swelling of the eustachian tube, the passageway that leads from the middle ear to the pharynx, which normally opens when a person swallows. This natural opening allows the pressure in the middle ear space to equalize with the pressure in the environment. However, if the eustachian tube is blocked, the pressure in the middle ear starts to decrease. With the eustachian tube closed, the bacteria have a nice, warm place to grow inside the middle ear space, and this growth eventually produces fluid in the middle ear, which prevents the tympanic membrane and the ossicles from vibrating properly.

Repeated exposure to middle-ear infections may cause a tissue buildup in the middle ear called a *cholesteatoma.* This growth interferes with the vibrations of the tympanic membrane and the ossicles and must be surgically removed. If a person does not seek treatment for a middle-ear infection, the fluid may build up until the tympanic membrane ruptures in order to release the pressure. An infection that is left untreated also may diffuse through the porous mastoid bone, which creates the middle-ear cavity. This is a very serious condition and must be treated immediately before the infection is allowed to spread to the brain. Luckily, diffusion through the mastoid bone rarely occurs if middle-ear infections are promptly treated by antibiotics.

Otosclerosis is a hereditary condition in which there is a growth of bone in the middle ear. Usually, the stapes becomes fixed in place, so it can't transmit vibrations to the inner ear. This was the condition that caused Beethoven to become so deaf that, late in his career, he was unable to hear his own music. Today, this condition can be successfully treated by a surgical procedure called *stapedectomy,* in which the stapes is replaced with an artificial strut.

Sensorineural Hearing Loss

Sensorineural hearing loss is caused by a number of factors, which have in common their site of action in the inner ear.

Presbycusis

The most common form of sensorineural hearing loss is called **presbycusis,** which means "old hearing" (remember that the equivalent term for vision is *presbyopia,* for "old eye"). This loss of sensitivity, which is greatest at higher frequencies, accompanies aging and affects males more severely than females. Figure 17.29 shows the progression of loss as a function of age. The most common complaint of people with presbycusis is that they have difficulty hearing people talking when there is noise or when other people are talking at the same time. Presbycusis is treated by the amplification provided by hearing aids and by teaching people more effective communication strategies.

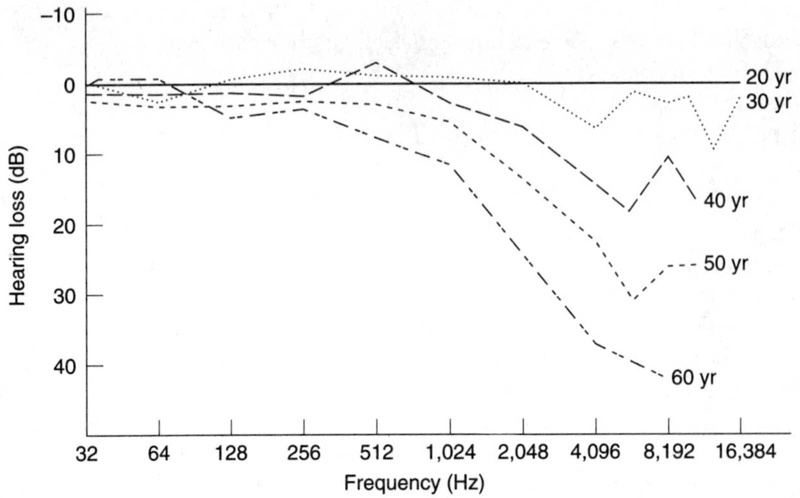

Figure 17.29
Hearing loss in presbycusis as a function of age. All of the curves are plotted relative to the 20-year curve, which is taken as the standard. (Adapted from Bunch, 1929.)

Unlike the visual problem of presbyopia, which is an inevitable consequence of aging, presbycusis is apparently caused by factors in addition to aging, since people in preindustrial cultures, who have not been exposed to the noises that accompany industrialization, or to drugs that could damage the ear, often do not experience a decrease in high- frequency hearing in old age. This may be why males, who are exposed to more workplace noise than females, as well as to noises associated with hunting and wartime, experience a greater presbycusis effect. Because of its link to environmental conditions, presbycusis is also called *sociocusis.*

Noise-Induced Hearing Loss

Noise-induced hearing loss occurs when loud noises cause degeneration of the hair cells. This degeneration has been observed in examinations of the cochleas of people who have worked in noisy environments and have willed their ear structures to medical research. Damage to the organ of Corti is often observed in these cases. For example, examination of the cochlea of a man who worked in a steel mill indicated that his organ of Corti had collapsed and no receptor cells remained (J. Miller, 1974). Apparently, this kind of damage also occurs in people who have exposed themselves to loud music for extended periods of time. Because of this exposure to loud music, rock musicians such as Steven Stills and Peter Townsend have become partially deaf and have urged musicians and concertgoers to wear earplugs (Ackerman, 1995). In fact, members of many symphony orchestras, including the Chicago Symphony, wear ear protection to preserve their hearing.

Acoustic trauma caused by implosive noises, such as explosions or machines that create a loud impact, also can result in sensorineural hearing loss. An example is a 21-year-old college student who was in the process of raiding a rival fraternity house when a firecracker exploded in his hand, 15 inches from his right ear. The result was a hearing loss of over 50 dB at frequencies above 3,000 Hz. In addition, the student also experienced a ringing sensation in his ear that was still present two years after the accident (Ward & Glorig, 1961).

Tinnitus

Ringing in the ears, which is known as **tinnitus** (ti-NYE-tus or TIN-ni-tus, from the Latin for "tinkling"), affects more than 36 million Americans, nearly 8 million of them severely. The most common cause of tinnitus is exposure to loud sounds, although this condition also can be caused by certain drugs, ear infections, or food allergies.

Whatever causes tinnitus, it is an extremely debilitating condition. According to Jack Vernon, director of the Kresge Hearing Research Laboratory at the University of Oregon, tinnitus is the third worst thing that can happen to a person, ranking only below intractable severe pain and intractable severe dizziness. In its most serious form, the constant noise of tinnitus is totally incapacitating, making it impossible for people to maintain their concentration long enough to complete a task and, in some cases, even driving people to suicide.

Is there a cure for tinnitus? Unfortunately, for most people the answer to this question is No. Some people, however, can gain relief by using a device called a **tinnitus masker.** The masker, which is worn in the ear like a hearing aid, produces noise that sounds like a waterfall. This externally produced noise masks the internal noise of tinnitus, making life bearable for some tinnitus sufferers. Also, tinnitus sufferers who use a hearing aid to compensate for a loss of hearing sometimes find that they are unaware of the tinnitus while using the hearing aid, and for several hours after taking the hearing aid off.

Meniere's Disease

Another cause of sensorineural hearing loss is **Meniere's disease,** a debilitating condition that is caused by an excessive buildup of the liquid that fills the cochlea and the semicircular canals. The symptoms of the disease include fluctuating hearing loss, tinnitus, and severe vertigo (dizziness) that is often accompanied by nausea and vomiting. By the end of the disease, the vertigo subsides, but some people are left with a sensorineural hearing loss. Physicians attempt a variety of treatments to relieve the symptoms and to treat the increase in fluid, but no one treatment is effective for all patients. The fluctuating hearing loss can be helped by a flexible hearing aid that can be reprogrammed as the hearing loss changes.

Neural Hearing Loss

All of the conditions described above have their effects primarily in the inner ear and on the hair cells. A type of sensorineural hearing loss called *neural hearing loss* may be caused by tumors on the auditory nerve along the auditory pathways in the brainstem. These tumors generally grow slowly and are benign. However, when they are surgically removed, the patient is often left with some hearing loss. In addition, neural hearing loss also can be caused by tumors or damage further along the auditory pathway.

THE EAR EXAMINATION AND HEARING EVALUATION

We begin our description of the ear examination and hearing evaluation by considering the types of professionals involved in the care of the ear and in helping people maintain their hearing.

Who Examines Ears and Evaluates Hearing?

A number of types of professionals examine the ear and test hearing. The two main categories are otorhinolaryngologists and audiologists.

1. An **otorhinolaryngologist** is an M.D. who has specialized in the treatment of diseases and disorders affecting the ear, nose, and throat, and so the name of this specialty is often abbreviated *ENT*, for "ear, nose, and throat." ENT specialists carry out physical examinations of the ear, nose, and throat and provide treatment through drugs and surgery. Some physicians with ENT training specialize in one area. For example, an **otologist** is an otorhinolaryngologist whose practice is limited to problems involving the auditory and vestibular (balance) system.
2. An **audiologist** is a professional with a master's degree or Ph.D. who measures the hearing ability of children and adults and identifies the presence and severity of any hearing problems. If a hearing loss is identified, the audiologist can fit the person with a hearing aid to make sound audible and also may work with the person on a long-term basis to teach communication strategies such as speech reading (also called *lipreading*) and other techniques for more effective communication. The audiologist may also recommend assistive devices such as telephone amplifiers and alerting systems. When hearing loss is found in children, the audiologist works with other professionals to make sure that the child develops a communication system (speech or sign language) and has access to appropriate schooling.

ENT specialists and audiologists often work together in dealing with hearing problems and the ear. For example, sometimes a person has a problem that needs medical treatment by a physician and at the same time sees an audiologist who helps the person deal with the hearing loss.

What Happens during an Ear Examination and Hearing Evaluation?

The basic aims of the ear examination and hearing evaluation are to assess hearing and to determine the cause of defective hearing so it can be treated. The basic components of the examination are the following:

Medical History The medical history focuses on hearing problems that the patient now has or may have had in the past, on general medical problems that could affect the person's hearing, on medications that may be responsible for a hearing loss and on noisy work environments or hobbies such as hunting that could affect hearing.

Otoscopy The purpose of otoscopy is to examine the tympanic membrane. To do this, the physician looks into the ear using an **otoscope,** which, much in the manner of the ophthalmoscope used to see the inside of the eye, illuminates the ear and makes it possible to view the illuminated area. The physician inspects the ear canal for foreign objects and signs of disease, notes the color of the tympanic membrane, and inspects it for evidence of tears.

Hearing Evaluation A person's hearing is typically measured in two ways: (1) by *pure-tone audiometry,* which determines an *audiogram,* the function relating hearing loss to frequency, and (2) by *speech audiometry,* which determines a person's ability to recognize words as a function of the intensity of the speech stimulus.

Pure-tone audiometry is typically measured by a device called an **audiometer,** which can present pure tone stimuli at different frequencies and intensities. The audiologist varies the intensity of the test tone and instructs the patient to indicate when he or she hears it. When the person's threshold has been determined at a number of frequencies, the audiometer

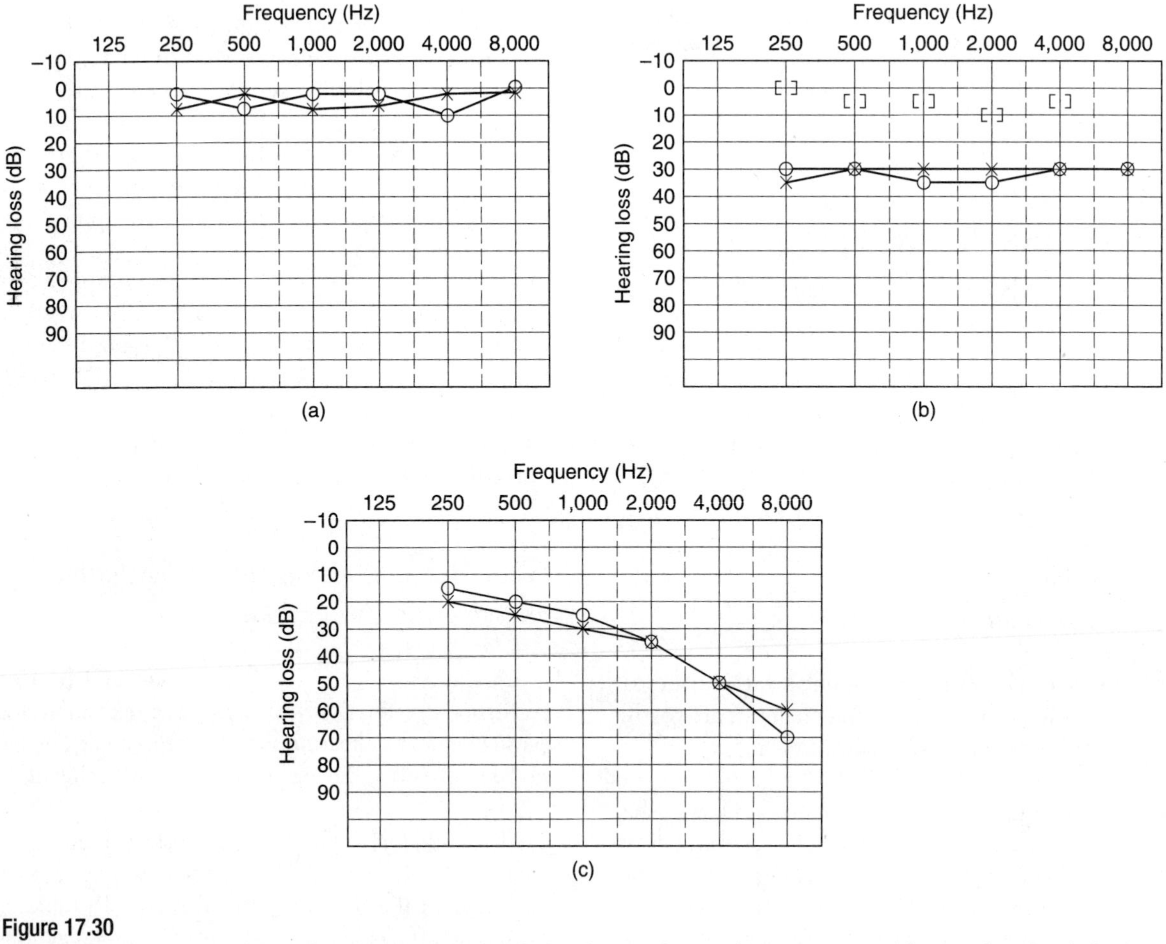

Figure 17.30
Audiograms for people with (a) normal hearing, (b) conductive hearing loss, and (c) sensorineural hearing loss. Symbols: O = right ear; X = left ear; [and] indicate bone conduction for the left and right ears for (b); The bone conduction results for (c) are not shown, but followed the same function as the person's audiogram.

creates an **audiogram,** a plot of degree of hearing loss (compared to normal) versus frequency. Figure 17.30a shows the audiogram of a patient with normal hearing, and the audiograms in Figures 17.30b and 17.30c are of a patient with about a 30-dB loss of hearing at all frequencies and a patient with high-frequency loss, respectively. Audiograms are plotted so the curve for a person with normal hearing falls between the zero line and 15 dB hearing loss for all frequencies, and any hearing loss is indicated by symbols below the 15 dB hearing loss line.

The pattern of hearing loss sometimes provides information regarding the nature of the patient's problem. For example, the audiogram in Figure 17.30b, in which the hearing loss is approximately the same across the range of hearing, is typical of a patient with a conductive hearing loss. The record in Figure 17.30c, in which hearing becomes progressively worse at high frequencies, is typical of sensorineural hearing loss. Hearing loss due to exposure to noise typically shows a maximum loss at about 4,000 Hz.

The way to differentiate between sensorineural and conductive hearing losses is to compare a person's hearing when the stimulation is presented through the air, as when sound is heard from a loudspeaker or through earphones, and when it is presented by vibrating the mastoid bone, which is located just in back of the ear. Bone conduction is measured by means of an audiometer connected to an electronic vibrator that presents vibrations of different frequencies to the mastoid. The person responds to the bone-vibrated signal in the same way as to air-conducted signals, and thresholds for bone conduction hearing are plotted on the audiogram. If air conduction hearing is worse than bone conduction hearing, this result indicates that something must be blocking sound in the outer or middle ear. If the bone conduction and air conduction results are the same, the problem must be beyond the outer and middle ear. The bracket symbols ([and]) in Figure 17.30b indicate normal bone conduction in the patient with conductive hearing loss.

Another way to measure hearing, which is particularly important in people with sensorineural loss, is to measure their word recognition ability. To do this, the audiologist presents a series of tape-recorded words at different intensities, and the patient is asked to identify the words that are spoken. The result is an **articulation function** like the one in Figure 17.31, which plots the percentage of words identified correctly versus the intensity of the sound. Patients with conductive losses tend to have articulation functions that are shifted to higher intensities, but if the intensity is high enough, they can understand the words. Patients with sensorineural loss have functions that are also shifted to higher intensities, but they often fail to reach 100 percent performance. Thus, in sensorineural hearing loss, many words cannot be consistently identified, no matter what their intensity.

Other diagnostic techniques, which we will not describe here, include **tympanometry,** in which a device called a **tympanometer** is used to measure how well the tympanic membrane and the middle-ear bones are responding to sound vibrations, and measurement of the acoustic reflex threshold. The **acoustic reflex** is the activation of the middle-ear muscles in response to high-intensity sounds. This

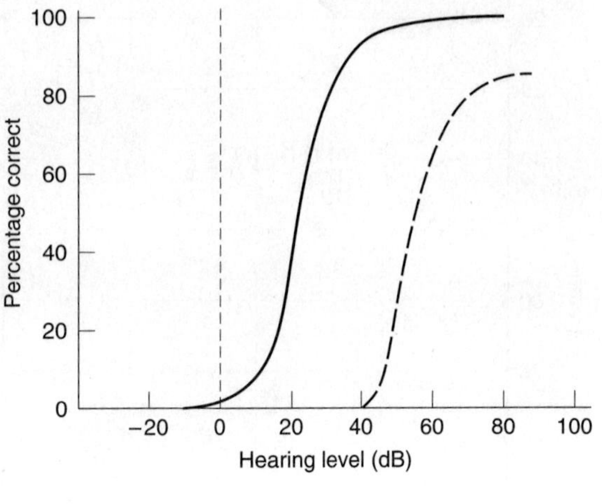

Figure 17.31
Articulation functions for a patient with conductive hearing loss (solid line) and a patient with sensorineural hearing loss (dashed line). Both curves are shifted to the right compared to normal, indicating that the patient requires greater than normal intensity to recognize the words. Also, notice that the curve for sensorineural hearing loss never reaches 100 percent, no matter what the intensity.

activation stiffens the chain of ossicles and dampens their vibration, perhaps to protect the inner ear from being overstimulated. The acoustic reflex can be measured with the tympanometer.

In addition to these diagnostic techniques that access hearing and the functioning of structures in the ear, there are also tests that measure the electrical response of the auditory nerve and the auditory cortex, which are important if there is a hearing loss even though the structures of the ear seem to be operating normally. These electrophysiological measures can therefore be useful in determining the location of sensorineural hearing loss.

Managing Hearing Loss

Hearing loss covers a very large continuum, from the individual with mild hearing loss to someone who is totally deaf and cannot make use of sound for the purpose of communication (Figure 17.32). Different individuals need different types of technology and strategies in order to communicate effectively.

The majority of individuals with conductive hearing loss receive medical treatment for their con-

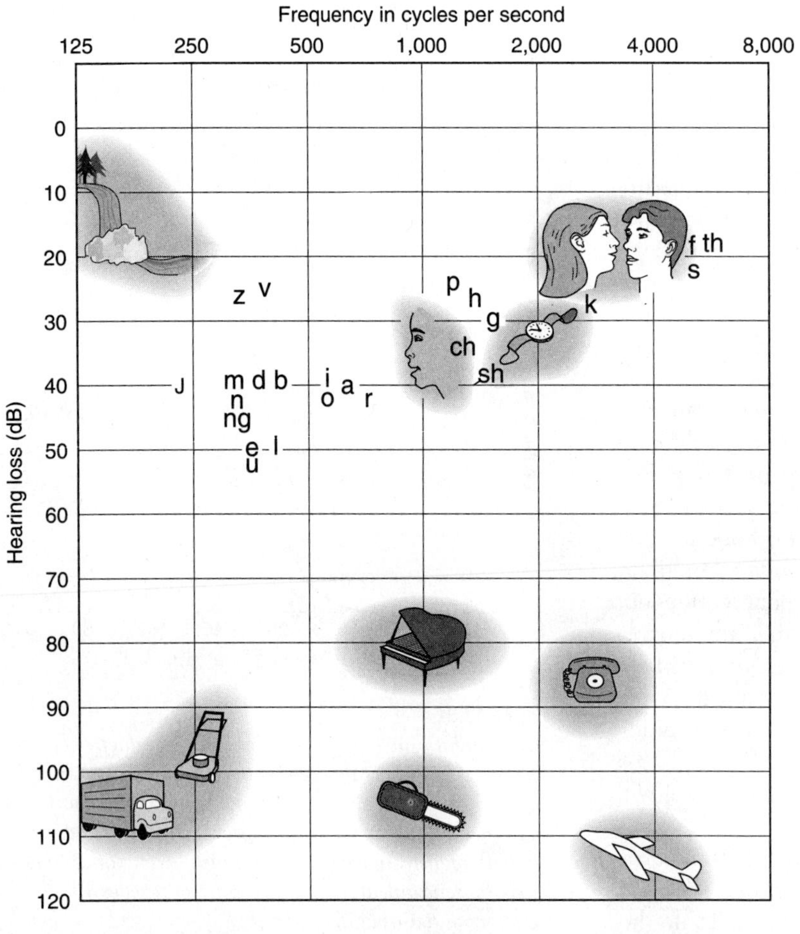

Figure 17.32
Audiogram showing the frequencies and degree of hearing loss that cause difficulties in the perception of various environmental sounds. The letters represent spoken sounds. For example, a person with a hearing loss of 100 dB around 250 Hz will not be able to hear the lawn mower. (From Northern & Downs, 1978.)

dition, and the hearing loss is eliminated as soon as the disease process is eliminated. Patients who cannot or do not choose to take advantage of surgical or medical procedures may use an amplification system such as a hearing aid to help them hear. As we noted when describing word recognition tests, as long as the sound is loud enough, these patients can hear quite well.

Individuals with sensorineural hearing loss generally use some kind of amplification. Hearing aids have changed drastically since the beginning of the 1990s, with the development of smaller hearing aids that can be automatically programmed to work effectively in different listening situations. Almost all individuals with sensorineural hearing loss can benefit from a hearing aid, which is fitted by an audiologist.

Hearing-impaired individuals also may receive training in speech reading (often called *lipreading*) and communication strategies. This type of training is often called **aural rehabilitation** and is conducted by an audiologist. Some individuals have so much hearing loss that they cannot benefit from amplification. Many of these individuals consider themselves part of the deaf culture and are happy to communicate using sign language. However, most people who lose their hearing after being able to hear for the majority of their lives wish to continue to be connected to the hearing world. For these people, a new technology called the *cochlear implant* is available.

A **cochlear implant** is a device in which electrodes are inserted in the cochlea to create hearing by electrically stimulating the auditory nerve fibers. This device offers the hope of regaining some hearing to some people who have lost their hearing because of damaged hair cells, so that hearing aids, which can amplify sound, but which can't cause that sound to be translated into electrical signals in the hair cells, are ineffective.

The cochlear implant bypasses the damaged hair cells and stimulates auditory nerve fibers directly. The following are the basic components of a cochlear implant (Figure 17.33):

- The *microphone* (1), which is worn behind the person's ear, receives the speech signal, transforms it into electrical signals, and sends these signals to the speech processor.
- The *speech processor* (2), which looks like a small transistor radio, shapes the signal generated by the microphone to emphasize the information needed for the perception of speech by splitting the range of frequencies received by the microphone into a number of frequency bands. These signals are sent, in the form of an electrical code, from the processor to the transmitter.
- The *transmitter* (3), mounted on the mastoid bone, just behind the ear, transmits the coded signals received from the processor, through the skin, to the receiver.
- The *receiver* (4) is surgically mounted on the mastoid bone, beneath the skin. It picks up the coded signals from the transmitter and converts the code into signals that are sent to electrodes implanted inside the cochlea (5).

The implant makes use of Bekesy's observation, which we described in Chapter 11, that there is a tonotopic map of frequencies on the cochlea, high frequencies being represented by activity near the base of the cochlea, and low frequencies being represented by activity at the apex of the cochlea. The most widely used implants therefore have a multichannel design, which uses a number of electrodes to stimulate the cochlea at different places along its length, depending on the frequencies in the stimuli received by the microphone. This electrical stimulation of the cochlea then causes signals to be sent to the auditory area of the cortex, and hearing results.

What does a person using this system hear? The answer to this question depends on the person. Most patients are able to recognize a few everyday sounds, such as horns honking, doors closing, and water running. In addition, many patients are able to perceive speech. In the best cases, patients can perceive speech on the telephone, but it is more common for cochlear-implant patients to use the sounds perceived from their implant in conjunction with speech reading. In one test, 24 patients scored 54 percent on a

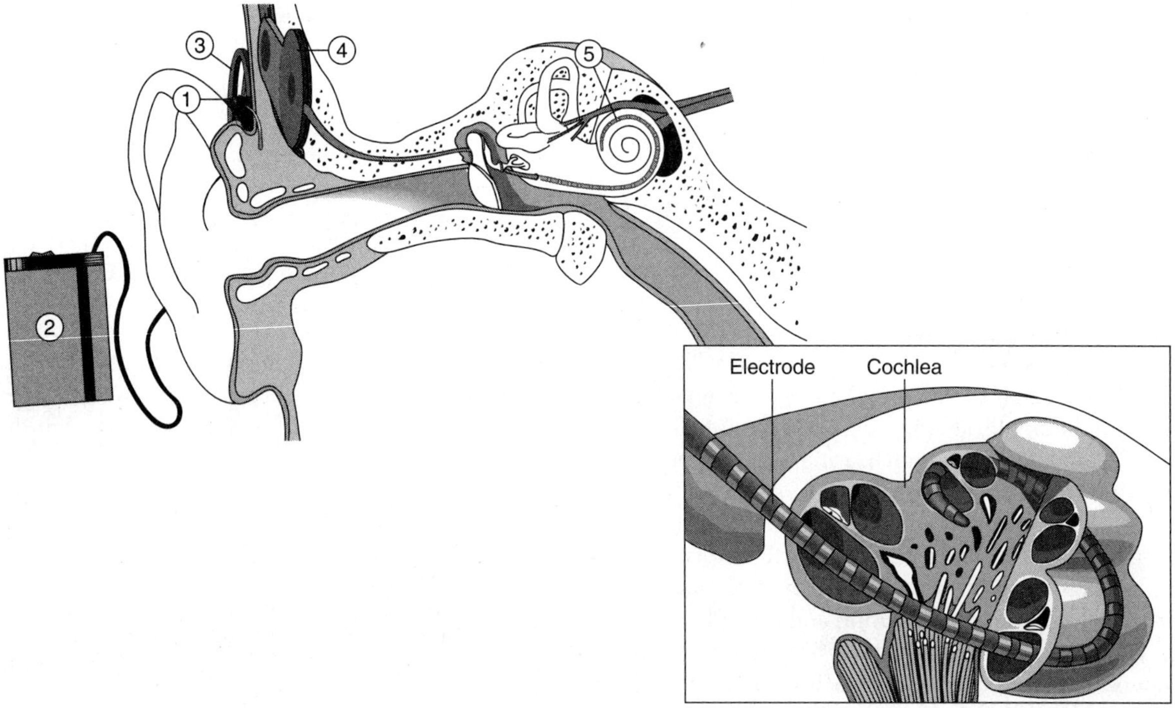

Figure 17.33
Cochlear implant device.

test of speech reading alone, and 83 percent when speech reading was combined with sound from the implant. In addition, the implant enabled patients to track speech much more rapidly—16 words per minute using speech reading alone, and 44 words per minute with speech reading plus the implant (Brown, Dowell, & Clark, 1987; Owens, 1989). In another test it was found that deaf children who received a cochlear implant before the age of 5 years were able to learn to produce speech more easily than children who received the implant when they were older (Tye-Murray, Spencer, & Woodworth, 1995).

As of 1995, over 10,000 people have cochlear implants. The best results occur for *postlingually deaf* individuals—people who were able to perceive speech before they became deaf. These people are most likely to be able to understand speech with the aid of the implant because they already know how to connect the sounds of speech with specific meanings. Thus, these people's ability to perceive speech often improves with time, as they again learn to link sounds with meanings.

To place a more human face on the effects of the cochlear implant operation, we will close this chapter, and the book, by relating the story of Gil McDougald, the standout New York Yankee infielder who played in eight World Series in the 1950s. McDougald, who in 1995 was 66 years old, had gradually gone deaf in both ears after an accident in which he was hit by a line drive during batting practice in 1955. He was almost completely deaf for about 20 years, being able to make out some sounds, but no intelligible words. His deafness cut him off from other people. He could no longer talk on the telephone, and he stopped attending "old-timers'" functions with ex-teammates like Yogi Berra and Mickey Mantle, because he was unable to communicate with them. At family functions, he would leave the table because of his frustration at not being able to hear what was going on.

McDougald heard about the implant operation and, in 1995, called implant specialist Noel Cohen at New York University Medical Center. After testing had determined that he was a good candidate for an implant, he underwent the operation. Six weeks after the operation, he went to see Betsy Bromberg, an audiologist, to have the apparatus programmed and activated (Figure 17.34). The following is an excerpt from a newspaper account of what transpired in her office (Berkow, 1995):

> In the office, McDougald sat at a desk with a computer on it. Bromberg sat across from him. His wife, Lucille, and daughter, Denise, sat within arm's length.
>
> A small microphone was set behind his ear, and a transmitter with a magnet was placed over the site of the implant. A cable was extended from the microphone to a speech processor the size of a hand calculator that can be worn on a belt or placed in a breast pocket.
>
> Then Bromberg began the test that would determine how much McDougald's hearing had improved.
>
> Bromberg covered her mouth with a sheet of paper so he could not lip read.
>
> "Tell me," she said, "what you hear."
>
> She said, "aah." He hesitated. "Aah," he answered. She went, "eeeh." He said, "eeeh."
>
> "Hello," she said. "Hello," he said. "I'm going to count to five," she said. "Do you hear me?"
>
> "Oh yeah!" he said. "Wow! This is exciting!"
>
> His wife and daughter stared, hardly moving.
>
> Bromberg wrote down four words on a pad of paper and said them: "football," "sidewalk," "cowboy," and "outside." "Now Gil," she said, "I'm going to mix up the word order and cover my mouth and you tell me the word I say."
>
> "Cowboy," she said. "Cowboy," he said. "Outside," she said. "Outside," he said. And then he began to flush. Tears welled in his eyes.
>
> "This is the first time in . . ." Lucille said and then choked up, unable to finish her sentence. "It's unbelievable."
>
> "It's a miracle," said Denise.
>
> Both began crying.
>
> Bromberg said, "It's O.K. Everybody cries at times like this." And then mother and daughter embraced. And they hugged Gil. And they hugged Bromberg, and hugged the director of the unit, Susan Waltzman, who had been observing. . . .

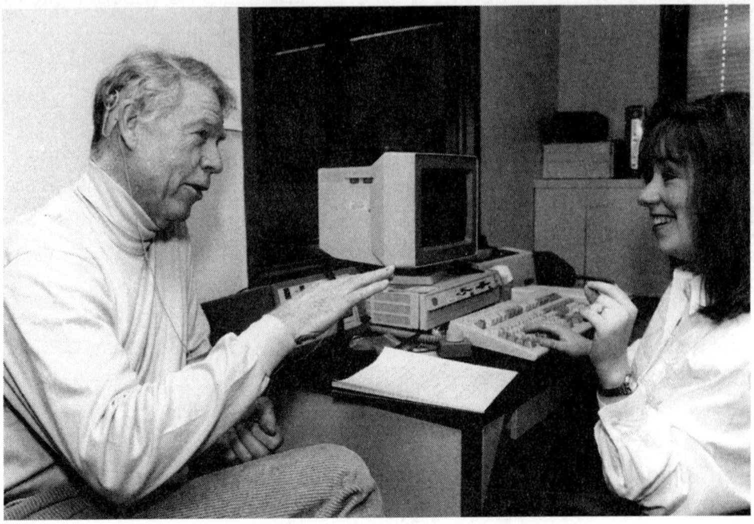

Figure 17.34
Gil McDougald trying out his cochlear implant for the first time, with audiologist Betsy Bromberg. In the office, McDougald sat at a desk with a computer on it. Bromberg sat across from him. His wife, Lucille, and daughter, Denise, sat within arm's length.

> Last night, the McDougald household was bursting with children and grandchildren. "Everyone," said Lucille McDougald, "has come to watch grandpa hear." (p. B8)

Cochlear implantation is an impressive demonstration of how basic research yields practical benefits. Advances such as this, which have proven to be effective in bringing deaf adults and children into the world of hearing (Kiefer et al., 1996; Tye-Murray, Spencer, & Woodworth, 1995), are the end result of discoveries that began in perception or physiology laboratories many years earlier. In this case, it was George von Beksey's research on how the vibration of the basilar membrane depends on the frequency of the sound that provided the knowledge about the operation of the ear that made implants possible. Systems also have been proposed for restoring vision to people who are blind, by stimulating their visual cortex (Dobelle, 1977; Dobelle et al., 1974, 1976), and for guiding blind people through the environment by applying the principles of auditory localization to the design of a "personal guidance system" (see Chapter 12, page 374).

It is clear that the study of both the psychophysics and the physiology of perception has yielded not only knowledge about how our senses operate, but also ways to apply this knowledge to create new perceptual worlds for people like Gil McDougald and countless others.

Something to Consider: The Costs of Gaining Vision in Adulthood

The story of Gil McDougald's regaining his hearing is inspiring because it describes how the implant opened a world of communication that had been lost to him for many years. But does gaining the use of a damaged sense in adulthood always result in a positive outcome?

The play *Molly Sweeney* by Brian Freil depicts the case of a young woman who, blind from birth, had learned how to function without sight and was quite happy with her life. But she got married, and her new husband, in his desire to improve her life, found out about an operation that might enable her to see. Although Molly was not enthusiastic about having this operation, since she was perfectly happy the way she was, she had it, mainly to please her husband. The operation was a success. She became able to recognize people and see well enough to get around, and at first she was quite excited about her new sight. But soon afterwards she became depressed, didn't want to leave home, and then died two years later.

While this may seem like a paradoxical outcome of gaining sight, Freil had based his play on actual cases of people who were given sight through an operation. In many of these cases the people were happy to experience sight, but then became depressed. For example, the case of S.B., reported by Richard Gregory and Jean Wallace (1963) describes a 53-year-old blind man who, after gaining sight through a corneal transplant operation, was able to recognize the faces of friends from about 15 feet away, was able to confidently cross streets, and could draw fairly detailed pictures of objects in his environment. However, by about six months after the operation, S.B., who had been a cheerful and outgoing person before the operation, became more and more depressed, eventually withdrawing from active life. He died three years after the operation.

Or consider the following diary entry of a 35-year-old man, who also gained vision through an operation:

> Paradoxically, when my sight started improving I began to feel depressed. I often experienced periods of crying, without knowing the reason, maybe because of striving so intensely for vision. In the evening I preferred to rest in a dark room. Some days I felt confused: I did not know whether to touch or to look. Often I did not remember what I had before me.
>
> Recovery of vision has been a long and hard road for me, like entering a strange world. In these moments of depression I sometimes wondered if I was happier before. . . . (from Valvo, 1968)

Why is gaining the ability to see—something that many people would think of as a precious gift—often accompanied by such negative reactions? Perhaps it is due to the reorganization of behavior that is necessary to convert from being blind to being sighted. When we consider that a person who has been dependent on the sense of touch for their entire life is thrown into the world of vision where everything is done differently, it becomes easier to understand why the result of a successful operation could lead to the patient's unhappiness.

Although these case studies are sad stories, there is also a positive message here, if we consider the people's situation *before* they had the operation. In most cases these people had adapted to their blindness and were leading happy lives. An excellent example of a person who adapted to blindness is Geerat Vermeij, the biologist who we discussed in the chapter on the cutaneous senses. Vermeij, who had both of his eyes removed at the age of four, due to a childhood eye disease, wrote an autobiography, *Privileged Hands*, in which he describes the following experience in walking through a meadow in the summer:

> The breeze blows unimpeded against my face, carrying with it the sweet smell of green grass or dry hay and quietly rustling the low plants as it sweeps by. The continuous babble of a meadowlark overhead disperses far and wide over the land without resistance from trees, or it may echo off a distant row of poplars. The sun warms the skin and brings out the sweet fragrance of a patch of chamomile or flowering white clover. I cannot appreciate the colors, the views of majestic clouds, the pastoral scenery of trees or church steeples in the distance, the cattle and sheep grazing quietly in a nearby meadow; but there is so much here to enjoy, so much to take in, such a richness of sensation, that I can hardly mourn the loss of sight. (Vermeij, 1997, p. 16)

DEAFNESS AND VISUAL ATTENTION

There is evidence supporting the idea that the senses are linked to each other during development (Smith & Katz, 1996). According to this idea, both seeing and hearing develop in tandem with one another, so that if one sense becomes deficient during development, it is possible that the other will be deficient as well. Alexandra Quittner and her coworkers (1994) tested the idea that loss of hearing causes a change in the capacity for visual attention by testing three groups of children, a deaf group, a deaf group who had received cochlear implants (see page 543), and a normal group. Subjects in each of these groups were shown a sequence of numbers presented visually, one after another, and were told to push a button every time they saw a 9 after a 1. This task, which requires that the subject pay close attention to the numbers at all times, is used to identify children with serious attentional deficits.

The results of this experiment, shown in Figure 17.35, supported the idea of a link between vision and hearing. The deaf subjects had the poorest performance, those with the cochlear implant did better, and the hearing subjects performed best of all. Thus, the better the subjects could hear, the better they performed on a task that was purely visual.

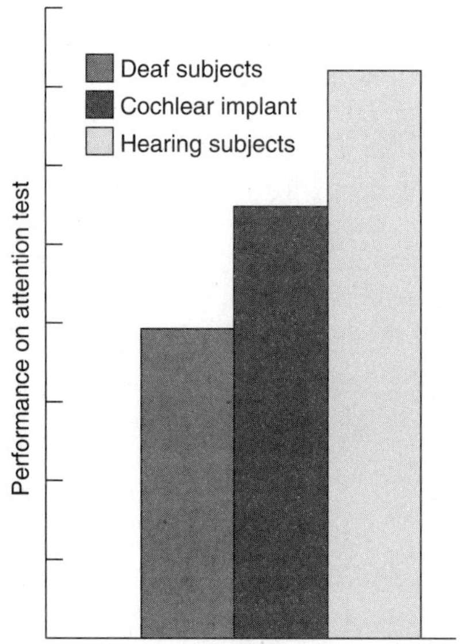

Figure 17.35
Performance of deaf subjects, subjects who had been using a cochlear implant, and hearing subjects on a visual attention tast. (Adapted from Quittner et al., 1994.)

Quittner checked this result in another way by testing the visual attention of subjects after they had been using a cochlear implant for 10 months and then testing them again at 18 months. When they compared their performance to a group of deaf subjects that was tested at the same time intervals, they found that there was no difference at 10 months, but by 18 months the cochlear implant group was less likely to commit "false alarms"—that is they were less likely to say the target (the "9") was there when it actually wasn't.

Why should deaf children be more likely to be distracted from a visual attention task than are children with normal hearing or children who have some hearing, because of a cochlear implant? Although we don't know the answer to this question, we can guess that it may have something to do with how the ability to hear might affect attention in general. A person hears a sound and turns his head towards it. A person in a crowded room that is pulsating with many conversations directs her attention to the one person she is talking with. A person sitting in a coffee house alive with conversation and music has learned to focus his attention on the book he is reading. Each of these examples involves both the focusing of attention and hearing. Because deaf people do not have any of these experiences, they are missing opportunities that might help them become better at focusing their attention. The decrement that this lack of training may be causing in a task that involves visual attention, does not, however, mean that a person who is deaf is poorer at all visual tasks. We have already seen that deaf people perform better than hearing people at detecting moving visual targets (see *Across the Senses* page 377). The importance of the present example is that it demonstrates how loss of ability in one sense might in an indirect way cause a decrease in a person's ability in another sense.

Study Questions

How Can Vision Become Impaired?

1. What are the four major types of problems that can cause poor vision? (516)

Focusing Problems

2. What is myopia? How are parallel rays of light brought to a focus in the myopic eye? What are the two possible causes for this incorrect focusing? (517)
3. How can we cause the point of focus to fall on the retina of a myopic eye without using corrective lenses? (517)
4. What is the far point? Where does the focus point fall if an object is farther from the eye than the far point? At the far point? Closer to the eye than the far point? Can a myope bring far away objects into focus by accommodation? (518)
5. How must a corrective lens bend light so that a myope can see clearly? (518)
6. What is a diopter? Be able to calculate the correction in diopters if you are given the distance of the far point. (519)
7. What are two surgical procedures that can potentially correct myopic vision? (519)
8. What is hyperopia? How are parallel rays of light brought to a focus in the hyperopic eye? How is this condition corrected? (518)
9. What is presbyopia? What is the near point? What happens to the near point as a person ages? (520)
10. What is astigmatism? What is it due to? How is this condition corrected? (521)

Decreased Transmission of Light

11. What is the legal definition of blindness? Can a person who is legally blind have 20/20 vision? (Explain your answer) (522)
12. The cornea is responsible for about ___ percent of the eye's focusing power. (522)
13. What can cause corneal diseases or injury? What is the first treatment for corneal disease or injury? If this treatment fails, what is the next alternative? (522)
14. Describe a corneal transplant operation. Exactly what is transplanted? What is the success rate of corneal transplants? (522)
15. What is a cataract? What is the most common kind of cataract and what percentage of people over the age of 65 have cataracts? What percentage of cataracts are serious enough to interfere with a person's normal activities? What percentage require surgery? (523)
16. Describe a cataract operation. (523)
17. When we remove the lens in a cataract operation, we decrease the focusing power of the eye. Why are glasses an unacceptable solution to this problem? What is the solution to this problem? (524)

Damage to the Retina

18. What is the tissue upon which the retina rests? (524)
19. Describe what happens to the retinal circulation in mild and severe cases of diabetic retinopathy. (524)
20. Describe a procedure which has been used to stop neovascularization. (525)
21. What is a vitrectomy operation? What does it accomplish? (525)
22. Describe the mild and severe types of macular degeneration. What is a treatment that can be successfully used in some patients? (526)
23. What is a detached retina? What are two reasons that a detached retina can affect vision? (526)
24. Describe the procedure used to reattach a detached retina. (527)
25. What is retinitis pigmentosa? (527)

Glaucoma

26. Describe the two forms of glaucoma. How are these two types treated? (528)

The Eye Examination

27. Describe the training and capabilities of ophthalmologists, optometrists, and opticians. (529)
28. What are the four basic aims of an eye examination? (529)
29. How is visual acuity determined? What does it mean to say that a person has 20/200 vision? (530)
30. What is visual perimetry? (530)
31. What is the purpose of the refraction part of the eye examination? What are the two steps in the refraction exam? (530)
32. What is the purpose of the external eye examination? (531)
33. What is the purpose of the slit-lamp examination? (531)
34. What does the tonometry exam measure? What disease is it a test for? What is the basic principle behind the tonometry exam? (532)
35. What is the basic principle behind an ophthalmoscope? Be able to draw a diagram of an ophthalmoscope. (532)
36. What does the examiner look for in an ophthalmoscopy exam? (532)
37. What is fluorescein angiography and what does it accomplish? (534)

How Can Hearing Become Impaired?

38. What is the difference between a hearing impairment and a hearing handicap? (535)
39. What are the four types of things that can go wrong in the auditory system? (535)

Conductive Hearing Loss

40. What is conductive hearing loss? (536)
41. Describe outer ear disorders and middle ear disorders. (536)

Sensorineural Hearing Loss

42. What is sensorineural hearing loss? (537)
43. What is the most common form of sensorineural hearing loss? Describe the role of aging and environmental exposure in causing this condition. (537)
44. Where is the main damage in noise-induced hearing loss? (538)
45. What is tinnitus? How can it be treated? (538)
46. Describe Meniere's disease. (538)
47. What is neural hearing loss? (539)

The Ear Examination and Hearing Evaluation

48. Describe the training and capabilities of otorhinolaryngologists and audiologists. (539)
49. What is the purpose of otoscopy and how is it conducted? (540)
50. Describe pure-tone audiometry. What is an audiogram? Describe how the pattern of hearing loss can provide information regarding the nature of a patient's problem. (540)
51. Describe how vibration of the mastoid bone can be used to differentiate between sensorineural hearing loss and conductive hearing loss. (541)
52. What is the articulation function? (541)
53. Describe tympanometry and the acoustic reflex. (541)

Managing Hearing Loss

54. What types of treatment are used for conductive hearing loss and sensorineural hearing loss? (543)

55. What is aural rehabilitation? (543)

56. Describe how a cochlear implant operates. How successful have cochlear implants been in restoring hearing? (543)

Something to Consider: The Costs of Gaining Vision in Adulthood

57. When blind people have had vision restored, the outcome has not always been positive. Describe what this means and why it might occur. (546)

Across the Senses: Deafness and Visual Attention

58. Describe the experiment of Quittner and coworkers that tested the idea that a loss of hearing causes a change in the capacity for visual attention. (548)

59. Describe Quittner's other experiment in which she used subjects who had been using a cochlear implant. (548)

60. What is a possible explanation for the fact that deaf children are more easily distracted from a visual attention task than children with normal hearing or children with a cochlear implant? (548)

APPENDIX

SIGNAL DETECTION: PROCEDURE AND THEORY

In Chapter 1, we surveyed various psychophysical methods that can be used to determine an observer's absolute threshold. For example, using the method of constant stimuli to randomly present tones of different intensities, we can determine the intensity to which the subject reports "I hear it" 50 percent of the time. But can the experimenter be confident that this intensity truly represents the subject's sensory threshold? For a number of reasons, which we will discuss next, the answer to this question is "Maybe not." Many researchers feel that the idea of an *absolute* measure of sensitivity, called the *threshold*, which can be measured by the classic psychophysical methods, is not valid. We will first discuss the question of whether there is an absolute threshold, and we will then describe a way of looking at this problem, called signal detection theory, that takes into account both the characteristics of the sensory system and the characteristics of the observer.

IS THERE AN ABSOLUTE THRESHOLD?

To understand the position of researchers who question the idea of an absolute threshold, let's consider a hypothetical experiment. In this experiment, we use the method of constant stimuli to measure two subjects' thresholds for hearing a tone. We pick five different tone intensities, present them in random order, and ask our subjects to say "yes" if they hear the tone and "no" if they don't hear it. Our first subject, Laurie, thinks about these instructions and decides that she wants to appear supersensitive to the tones; since she knows that tones are being presented on every trial, she will answer "yes" if there is even the slightest possibility that she hears the tone. We could call Laurie a *liberal responder*: She is more willing to say "Yes,

I hear the tone" than to report that no tone was present. Our second subject, Chris, is given the same instructions, but Chris is different from Laurie; she doesn't care about being supersensitive. In fact, Chris wants to be totally sure that she hears the tone before saying "yes." We could call Chris a *conservative responder:* She is not willing to report that she hears the tone unless it is very strong.

The results of this hypothetical experiment are shown in Figure A.1. Laurie gives many more "yes" responses than Chris and therefore ends up with a lower threshold. But given what we know about Laurie and Chris, should we conclude that Laurie is more sensitive to the tones than Chris? It could be that their actual sensitivity to the tones is exactly the same, but Laurie's apparently lower threshold is simply due to her being more willing than Chris to report that she heard a tone. A way to describe this difference between the two subjects is that each has a different **response criterion.** Laurie's response criterion is low (she says "yes" if there is the slightest chance there is a tone present), whereas Chris's response criterion is high (she says "yes" only when she is sure that she heard the tone). That factors other than the subject's sensitivity to the signal may influence the results of a psychophysical experiment has caused many researchers to doubt the validity of the absolute threshold, as determined by these psychophysical experiments, and to create new procedures based on a theory called **signal detection theory (SDT).**

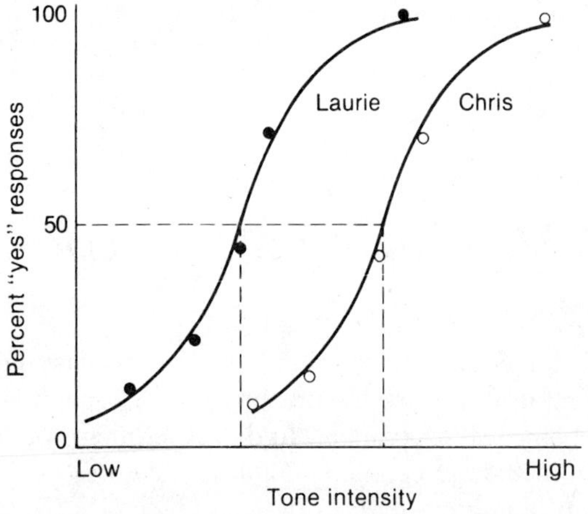

Figure A.1
Data from experiments in which the threshold for hearing a tone is determined for Laurie and Chris by means of the method of constant stimuli. These data indicate that Laurie's threshold is lower than Chris's. But is Laurie really more sensitive to the tone than Chris, or does she just appear to be more sensitive because she is a more liberal responder? Signal detection theory helps provide an answer to this question.

In the next section, we will describe the basic procedure of a signal detection experiment and will show how we can tell whether Chris and Laurie are, in fact, equally sensitive to the tone even though their response criteria are very different. After describing the signal detection experiment, we will look at the theory on which the experiment is based.

A Signal Detection Experiment

Remember that, in a psychophysical procedure such as the method of constant stimuli, at least five different tone intensities are presented, and that a stimulus is presented on every trial. In a signal detection experiment, however, we use only a single low-intensity tone that is difficult to hear, and we present this tone on some of the trials and present no tone at all on the rest of the trials. Thus, a signal detection experiment differs from a classical psychophysical experiment in two ways: In a signal detection experiment (1) only one stimulus intensity is presented, and (2) on some of the trials, no stimulus is presented. Let's consider the results of such an experiment, using Laurie as our subject. We present the tone for 100 trials and no tone for 100 trials, mixing the tone and no-tone trials at random. Laurie's results are as follows:

When the tone is presented, Laurie

- Says "yes" on 90 trials. This correct response—saying "yes" when a stimulus is present—is called a **hit** in signal detection terminology.

- Says "no" on 10 trials. This incorrect response—saying "no" when a stimulus is present—is called a **miss.**

When no tone is presented, Laurie

- Says "yes" on 40 trials. This incorrect response—saying "yes" when there is no stimulus—is called a **false alarm.**
- Says "no" on 60 trials. This correct response—saying "no" when there is no stimulus—is called a **correct rejection.**

These results are not very surprising, given that we know Laurie has a low criterion and likes to say "yes" a lot. This gives her a high hit rate of 90 percent but also causes her to say "yes" on many trials when no tone is presented at all, so her 90 percent hit rate is accompanied by a 40 percent false-alarm rate. If we do a similar experiment on Chris, who has a higher criterion and therefore says "yes" much less often, we find that she has a lower hit rate (say, 60 percent) but also a lower false-alarm rate (say, 10 percent). Note that, although Laurie and Chris say "yes" on numerous trials on which no stimulus is presented, that result would not be predicted by classical threshold theory. Classical theory would say "no stimulus—no response," but that is clearly not the case here.

By adding a new wrinkle to our signal detection experiment, we can obtain another result that would not be predicted by classical threshold theory. Without changing the tone's intensity at all, we can cause Laurie and Chris to change their percentages of hits and false alarms. We do this by manipulating each subject's motivation by means of **payoffs.** Let's look at how payoffs might influence Chris's responding. Remember that Chris is a conservative responder who is hesitant to say "yes." But being clever experimenters, we can make Chris say "yes" more frequently by adding some financial inducements to the experiment. "Chris," we say, "we are going to reward you for making correct responses and are going to penalize you for making incorrect responses by using the following payoff scale:

Hit:	Win $100
Correct rejection:	Win $10
False alarm:	Lose $10
Miss:	Lose $10

What would you do if you were in Chris's position? Being smart, you analyze the payoffs and realize that the way to make money is to say "yes" more. You can lose $10 if a "yes" response results in a false alarm, but this small loss is more than counterbalanced by the $100 you can win for a hit. While you don't decide to say "yes" on every trial—after all, you want to be honest with the experimenter about whether or not you heard the tone—you do decide to stop being so conservative. *You decide to change your criterion for saying "yes."* The results of this experiment are interesting. Chris becomes a more liberal responder and says "yes" a lot more, responding with 98 percent hits and 90 percent false alarms.

This result is plotted as data point L (for "liberal" response) in Figure A.2, a plot of the percentage of hits versus the percentage of false alarms. The solid curve going through point L is called a **receiver**

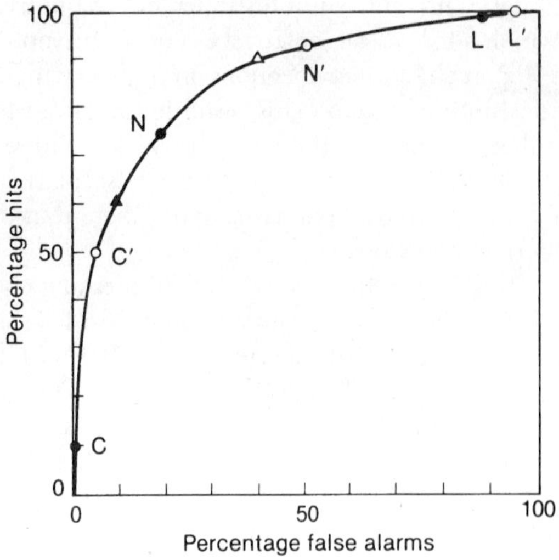

Figure A.2
A receiver operating characteristic (ROC curve). The fact that Chris's and Laurie's data points all fall on this curve means that they have the same sensitivity to the tone.

operating characteristic (ROC curve). We will see why the ROC curve is important in a moment, but first let's see how we determine the other points on the curve. Determining the other points on the ROC curve is simple: All we have to do is to change the payoffs. We can make Chris raise her criterion and therefore respond more conservatively by means of the following payoffs:

Hit:	Win $10
Correct rejection:	Win $100
False alarm:	Lose $10
Miss:	Lose $10

This schedule of payoffs offers a great inducement to respond conservatively since there is a big reward for saying "no" when no tone is presented. Chris's criterion is therefore shifted to a much higher level, so Chris now returns to her conservative ways and says "yes" only if she is quite certain that a tone is presented; otherwise she says "no." The result of this new-found conservatism is a hit rate of only 10 percent and a minuscule false-alarm rate of 1 percent, indicated by point C (for "conservative" response) on the ROC curve. We should note that, although Chris hits on only 10 percent of the trials in which a tone is presented, she scores a phenomenal 99 percent correct rejections on trials in which a tone is not presented. (This result follows from the fact that, if there are 100 trials in which no tone is presented, then correct rejections + false alarms = 100. Since there was one false alarm, there must be 99 correct rejections.)

Chris, by this time, is rich and decides to go buy the Miata she's been dreaming about. (So far she's won $8,980 in the first experiment and $9,090 in the second experiment, for a total of $18,070! To be sure you understand how the payoff system works, check this calculation yourself. Remember that the signal was presented on 100 trials and was not presented on 100 trials.) However, we point out that she may need a little extra cash to have a CD player installed in her car, so she agrees to stick around for one more experiment. We now use the following neutral schedule of payoffs:

Hit:	Win $10
Correct rejection:	Win $10
False alarm:	Lose $10
Miss:	Lose $10

and obtain point N on the ROC curve: 15 percent hits and 20 percent false alarms. Chris wins $1,000 more and becomes the proud owner of a Miata with a CD player, and we are the proud owners of the world's most expensive ROC curve. (Do not, at this point, go to the psychology department in search of the nearest signal detection experiment. In real life, the payoffs are quite a bit less than in our hypothetical example.)

Chris's ROC curve shows that factors other than sensitivity to the stimulus determine the subject's response. Remember that in all of our experiments the intensity of the tone has remained constant. The only thing we have changed is the subject's criterion. However, in doing this, we have succeeded in drastically changing the subject's responses.

What does the ROC curve tell us in addition to demonstrating that subjects will change how they respond to an unchanging stimulus? Remember, at the beginning of this discussion, we said that a signal detection experiment can tell us whether or not Chris and Laurie are equally sensitive to the tone. The beauty of signal detection theory is that the subject's sensitivity is indicated by the *shape* of the ROC curve, so if experiments on two subjects result in identical ROC curves, their sensitivities must be equal. (This conclusion is not obvious from our discussion so far. We will explain below why the shape of the ROC curve is related to the subject's sensitivity.) If we repeat the above experiments on Laurie, we get the following results (data points L′, N′, and C′ in Figure A.2):

Liberal payoff:
Hits = 99 percent
False alarms = 95 percent

Neutral payoff:
Hits = 92 percent
False alarms = 50 percent

Conservative payoff:
Hits = 50 percent
False alarms = 6 percent

The data points for Laurie's results are shown by the open circles in Figure A.2. Note that although these points are different from Chris's, they fall on the same ROC curve as do Chris's. We have also plotted the data points for the first experiments we did on Laurie (open triangle) and Chris (filled triangle) before we introduced payoffs. These points also fall on the ROC curve.

That Chris's and Laurie's data both fall on the same ROC curve indicates their equal sensitivity to the tones, thus confirming our suspicion that the method of constant stimuli misled us into thinking that Laurie is more sensitive, when the real reason for her apparently greater sensitivity is her lower criterion for saying "yes."

Before we leave our signal detection experiment, it is important to note that signal detection procedures can be used without the elaborate payoffs that we described for Chris and Laurie. Much briefer procedures, which we will describe below, can be used to determine whether differences in the responses of different subjects are due to differences in threshold or to differences in the subjects' response criteria.

What does signal detection theory tell us about functions such as the spectral sensitivity curves (Figure 2.25) and the audibility function (Figure 12.2), which were determined by one of the classical psychophysical methods? When the classical methods are used to determine functions such as the spectral sensitivity curve and the audibility function, it is usually assumed that the subject's criterion remains constant throughout the experiment, so that the function measured is due not to changes in the subject's criterion but to changes in the wavelength or some other physical property of the stimulus. This is a good assumption, since changing the wavelength of the stimulus probably has little or no effect on factors such as motivation, which would shift the subject's criterion. Furthermore, experiments such as the one for determining the spectral sensitivity curve usually use highly practiced subjects who are trained to give stable results. Thus, even though the idea of an "absolute threshold" may not be strictly correct, classical psychophysical experiments run under well-controlled conditions have remained an important tool for measuring the relationship between stimuli and perception.

Signal Detection Theory

We will now discuss the theoretical basis for the signal detection experiments we have just described. Our purpose is to explain the theoretical bases underlying two ideas: (1) The percentage of hits and false alarms depends on the subject's criterion, and (2) a subject's sensitivity to a stimulus is indicated by the shape of the subject's ROC curve. We will begin by describing two of the key concepts of signal detection theory (SDT): signal and noise. (See Swets, 1964.)

Signal and Noise

The **signal** is the stimulus presented to the subject. Thus, in the signal detection experiment we described above, the signal is the tone. The **noise** is all the other stimuli in the environment, and since the signal is usually very faint, noise can sometimes be mistaken for the signal. Seeing what appears to be a flash of light in a completely dark room is an example of visual noise. Seeing a flash of light when there is none is what we have been calling a false alarm, according to signal detection theory. False alarms are caused by the noise. In the experiment we described above, hearing a tone on a trial in which no tone was presented is an example of auditory noise.

Let's now consider a typical signal detection experiment, in which a signal is presented on some trials and no signal is presented on the other trials. Signal detection theory describes this procedure not in terms of presenting a signal or no signal, but in terms of presenting signal plus noise (S + N) or noise

(N). That is, the noise is always present, and on some trials, we add a signal. Either condition can result in the perceptual effect of hearing a tone. A false alarm occurs if the subject says "yes" on a noise trial, and a hit occurs if the subject says "yes" on a signal-plus-noise trial. Now that we have defined signal and noise, we introduce the idea of probability distributions for noise and signal plus noise.

Probability Distributions

Figure A.3 shows two probability distributions. The probability distribution on the left represents the probability that a given perceptual effect will be caused by noise (N), and the one on the right represents the probability that a given perceptual effect will be caused by signal plus noise (S + N). The key to understanding these distributions is to realize that the value labeled "Perceptual effect" on the horizontal axis is what the subject experiences on each trial. Thus, in an experiment in which the subject is asked to indicate whether or not a tone is present, the perceptual effect is the perceived loudness of the tone.

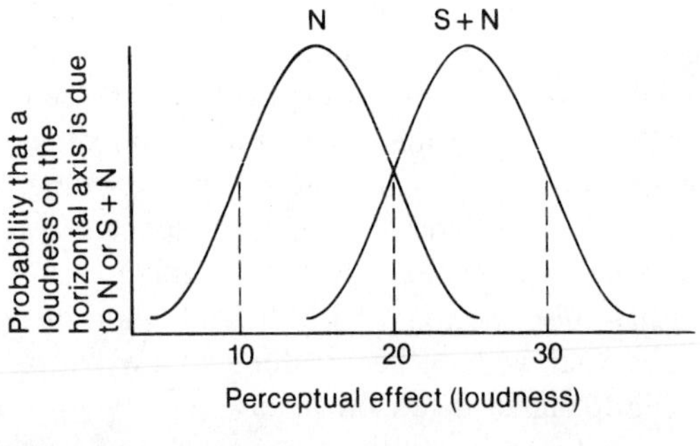

Figure A.3
Probability distributions for noise alone (N), on the left, and for signal plus noise (S + N), on the right. The probability that any given perceptual effect is caused by the noise (no signal is presented) or by the signal plus noise (signal is presented) can be determined by finding the value of the perceptual effect on the horizontal axis and extending a vertical line up from that value. The place where that line intersects the (N) and (S + N) distributions indicates the probability that the perceptual effect was caused by (N) or by (S + N).

Remember that in an SDT experiment the tone always has the same intensity. The loudness of the tone, however, can vary from trial to trial. The subject perceives different loudnesses on different trials, because of either trial-to-trial changes in attention or changes in the state of the subject's auditory system.

The probability distributions tell us what the chances are that a given loudness of tone is due to (N) or to (S + N). For example, let's assume that a subject hears a tone with a loudness of 10 on one of the trials of a signal detection experiment. By extending a vertical dashed line up from 10 on the "Perceptual effect" axis in Figure A.3, we see that the probability that a loudness of 10 is due to (S + N) is extremely low, since the distribution for (S + N) is essentially zero at this loudness. There is, however, a fairly high probability that a loudness of 10 is due to (N), since the (N) distribution is fairly high at this point.

Let's now assume that, on another trial, the subject perceives a loudness of 20. The probability distributions indicate that, when the tone's loudness is 20, it is equally probable that this loudness is due to (N) or to (S + N). We can also see from Figure A.3 that a tone with a perceived loudness of 30 would have a high probability of being caused by (S + N) and only a small probability of being caused by (N).

Now that we understand the curves of Figure A.3, we can appreciate the problem confronting the subject. On each trial, she has to decide whether no tone (N) was present or whether a tone (S + N) was present. However, the overlap in the probability distributions for (N) and (S + N) means that for some perceptual effects this judgment will be difficult. As we saw above, it is equally probable that a tone with a loudness of 20 is due to (N) or to (S + N). So, on a trial in which the subject hears a tone with a loudness of 20, how does she decide whether or not the signal was presented? According to signal detection theory, the subject's decision depends on the location of her criterion.

The Criterion

We can see how the criterion affects the subject's response by looking at Figure A.4. In this figure, we

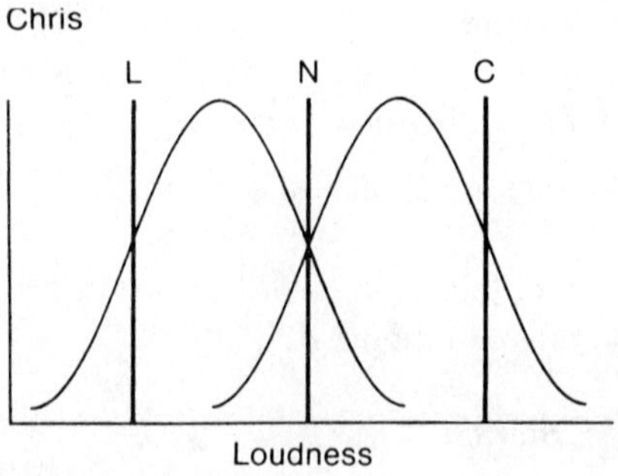

Figure A.4
The same probability distributions from Figure A.3, showing three criteria: liberal (L), neutral (N), and conservative (C). When a subject adopts a criterion, he or she uses the following decision rule: Respond "yes" ("I detect the stimulus") if the perceptual effect is greater than the criterion. Respond "no" ("I do not detect a stimulus") if the perceptual effect is less than the criterion.

have labeled three different criteria: liberal (L), neutral (N), and conservative (C). Remember that we can cause subjects to adopt these different criteria by means of different payoffs. According to signal detection theory, once the subject adopts a criterion, he or she uses the following rule to decide how to respond on a given trial: If the perceptual effect is greater than (to the right of) the criterion, say, "Yes, the tone was present"; if the perceptual effect is less than (to the left of) the criterion, say, "No, the tone was not present." Let's consider how different criteria influence the subject's hits and false alarms.

Liberal Criterion To determine how criterion L will affect the subject's hits and false alarms, let's consider what happens when we present (N) and when we present (S + N):

1. Present (N): Since most of the probability distribution for (N) falls to the right of the criterion, the chances are good that presenting (N) will result in a loudness to the right of the criterion. This means that the probability of saying "yes" when (N) is presented is high; therefore, the probability of a false alarm is high.
2. Present (S + N): Since the entire probability distribution for (S + N) falls to the right of the criterion, the chances are excellent that presenting (S + N) will result in a loudness to the right of the criterion. Thus, the probability of saying "yes" when the signal is presented is high; therefore, the probability of a hit is high. Since criterion L results in high false alarms and high hits, adopting that criterion will result in point L on the ROC curve in Figure A.5.

Neutral Criterion

1. Present (N): The subject will answer "yes" only rarely when (N) is presented, since only a small portion of the (N) distribution falls to the right of the criterion. The false-alarm rate, therefore, will be fairly low.
2. Present (S + N): The subject will answer "yes" frequently when (S + N) is presented, since most of the (S + N) distribution falls to the right of the criterion. The hit rate, therefore, will be fairly high (but not as high as for the L criterion). Criterion N results in point N on the ROC curve in Figure A.5.

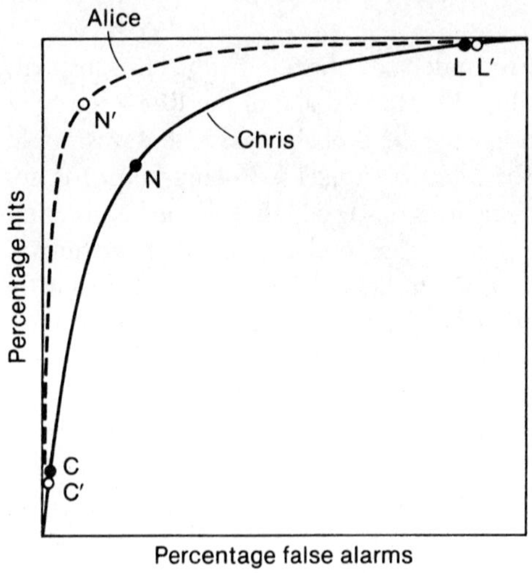

Figure A.5
ROC curves for Chris (solid) and Alice (dashed).

Conservative Criterion

1. Present (N): False alarms will be very low, since none of the (N) curve falls to the right of the criterion.
2. Present (S + N): Hits will also be low, since only a small portion of the (S + N) curve falls to the right of the criterion. Criterion C results in point C on the ROC curve in Figure A.5.

You can see that applying different criteria to the probability distributions generates the ROC curve in Figure A.5. But why are these probability distributions necessary? After all, when we described the experiment with Chris and Laurie, we determined the ROC curve simply by plotting the results of the experiment. The reason the (N) and (S + N) distributions are important is that, according to signal detection theory, the subject's sensitivity to a stimulus is indicated by the distance (d′) between the peaks of the (N) and (S + N) distributions and this distance affects the shape of the ROC curve. We will now consider how the subject's sensitivity to a stimulus affects the shape of the ROC curve.

The Effect of Sensitivity on the ROC Curve

We can understand how the subject's sensitivity to a stimulus affects the shape of the ROC curve by considering what the probability distributions would look like for Alice, a subject with supersensitive hearing. Alice's hearing is so good that a tone barely audible to Chris sounds very loud to Alice. If presenting (S + N) causes Alice to hear a loud tone, this means that Alice's (S + N) distribution should be far to the right, as shown in Figure A.6. In signal detection terms, we would say that Alice's high sensitivity is indicated by the large separation (d′) between the (N) and the (S + N) probability distributions. To see how this greater separation between the probability distributions will affect Alice's ROC curve, let's see how she would respond when adopting liberal, neutral, and conservative criteria.

Liberal Criterion

1. Present (N): high false alarms.
2. Present (S + N): high hits.

The liberal criterion, therefore, results in point L′ on the ROC curve of Figure A.5.

Neutral Criterion

1. Present (N): low false alarms. It is important to note that Alice's false alarms for the neutral criterion will be lower than Chris's false alarms for the neutral criterion, because only a small portion of Alice's (N) distribution falls to the right of the criterion, whereas some of Chris's (N) distribution falls to the right of the neutral criterion (Figure A.4).
2. Present (S + N): high hits. In this case Alice's hits will be higher than Chris's, because all of Alice's (S + N) distribution falls to the right of the neutral criterion, whereas not all of Chris's does (Figure A.4). The neutral criterion, therefore, results in point N′ on the ROC curve in Figure A.5.

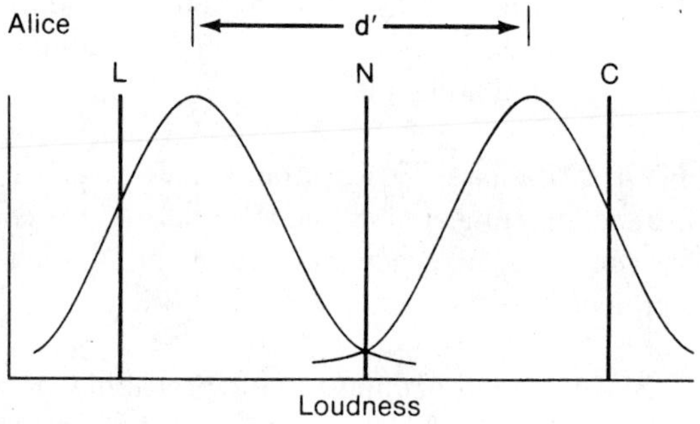

Figure A.6
Probability distributions for Alice, a subject who is extremely sensitive to the signal. The noise distribution remains the same, but the (S + N) distribution moves to the right.

Conservative Criterion

1. Present (N): low false alarms.
2. Present (S + N): low hits. The conservative criterion, therefore, results in point C′ on the ROC curve.

The difference between the two ROC curves in Figure A.5 is obvious, since Alice's curve is more "bowed." But before you conclude that the difference between these two ROC curves has anything to do with where we positioned Alice's L, N, and C criteria, see if you can get an ROC curve like Alice's from the two probability distributions of Figure E.4. You will find that, no matter where you position the criteria, there is no way that you can get a point like point N′ (with very high hits and very low false alarms) from the curves of Figure A.4. In order to achieve very high hits and very low false alarms, the two probability distributions must be spaced far apart, as in Figure A.6.

Thus, increasing the distance (d′) between the (N) and the (S + N) probability distributions changes the shape of the ROC curve. When the subject's sensitivity (d′) is high, the ROC curve is more bowed. In practice, d′ can be determined by comparing the experimentally determined ROC curve to standard ROC curves (see Gescheider, 1976), or d′ can be calculated from the proportions of hits and false alarms that occur in an experiment, by means of a mathematical procedure we will not discuss here. This mathematical procedure for calculating d′ enables us to determine a subject's sensitivity by determining only one data point on an ROC curve. Thus, this mathematical procedure makes it possible to use the signal detection procedure without running a large number of trials.

GLOSSARY

The number in parentheses after each item indicates the chapter in which the term is introduced. When more than one chapter is indicated, this means that the term is also discussed at length in the second chapter.

Absolute threshold. See Threshold, absolute.

Absorption spectrum. A plot of the amount of light absorbed by a visual pigment versus the wavelength of light. (2)

Accommodation (depth cue). A depth cue. Muscular sensations that occur when the eye accommodates to bring objects at different distances into focus may provide information regarding the distance of that object. (8)

Accommodation (focus). The eye's ability to bring objects located at different distances into focus by changing the shape of the lens. (2)

Accretion. The uncovering of the farther of two surfaces due to observer movement. (8)

Achromatic color. Colors without hue; white, black, and all the grays between these two extremes are achromatic colors. (5)

Acoustic cues. The sound energy associated with a particular phoneme. (13)

Acoustic reflex. Activating of the middle ear muscles in response to high-intensity sounds. (17)

Acoustic shadow. Shadow created by the head that blocks high-frequency sounds from getting to the opposite side of the head. (12)

Acoustic signal. The pattern of frequencies and intensities of the sound stimulus. (13)

Acoustic stimulus. Physical pressure changes in the air that potentially can cause the perception of sound. (11)

Acoustic trauma. Damage to the inner ear caused by implosive noises such as those created by explosions or machines. (17)

Action potential. Rapid increase in positive charge in a nerve fiber that is propagated down the fiber. Also called a nerve impulse. (1)

Active touch. Touch in which the observer plays an active role in touching and exploring an object, usually with his or her hands. (14)

Acupuncture. A procedure in which fine needles are inserted into the skin at specific points. Twirling these needles or passing electrical current through them can cause analgesia. (14)

Adapting field. A field of light presented to adapt the receptors. (2)

Additive color mixture. See Color mixture, additive. (5)

Adjustment, method of. A psychophysical method in which the experimenter or the observer slowly changes the stimulus until the observer detects the stimulus. (1)

Aerial perspective. See Atmospheric perspective. (8)

Afterimage. An image that is perceived after the original source of stimulation is removed. A visual afterimage usually occurs after one views a high-contrast stimulus for 30 to 60 seconds. (5)

Age-related macular degeneration. Degeneration of the macular area of the retina associated with old age. (17)

Albedo. The percentage of light reflected from an object. (6)

Alberti's window. A transparent surface on which an artist traces the scene viewed through the surface in order to draw a picture in linear perspective. (8)

Alliesthesia. "Changed sensation." The change in reaction to a stimulus, which may be positive when we first experience it but, after repeated presentations, becomes more negative. (15)

All-or-none response. The nerve impulse either fires or it doesn't. When it does fire, it has just one size no matter what the intensity of the stimulus that generated the response. (1)

Amacrine cell. A neuron that transmits signals laterally in the retina. Amacrine cells synapse with bipolar cells and ganglion cells. (2)

Amblyopia. A large reduction in the acuity in one eye. (16, 17)

Ames room. A distorted room, first built by Adelbert Ames, that creates an erroneous perception of the sizes of people in the room. The room is constructed so that two people at the far wall of the room appear to stand at the same distance from an observer. In actuality, one of the people is much farther away than the other. (9)

Amodal representation. An internal description of a stimulus that holds across more than one modality. (16)

Amplitude. In the case of a repeating sound wave, such as the sine wave of a pure tone, amplitude represents the pressure difference between atmospheric pressure and the maximum pressure of the wave. (11)

Analgesia. The elimination of pain without loss of consciousness. (14)

Angle of disparity. The visual angle between the images of an object on the two retinas. If the images of an object fall on corresponding points, the angle of disparity is zero. If the images fall on noncorresponding points, the angle of disparity indicates the degree of noncorrespondence. (8)

Angular expansion, rate of. The rate at which a moving object's visual angle expands as it gets closer to an observer. (10)

Angular size-contrast theory. An explanation of the moon illusion that states that the perceived size of the moon is determined by the sizes of the objects that surround it. According to this idea, the moon appears small when it is surrounded by large objects, such as the expanse of the sky when the moon is overhead. (9)

Anomalous trichromat. A person who needs to mix a minimum of three wavelengths to match any other wavelength in the spectrum but mixes these wavelengths in different proportions from a trichromat. (5)

Anosmia. Loss of the ability to smell due to injury or infection. (15)

Apex of the basilar membrane. The end of the basilar membrane farthest from the middle ear. (11)

Aphasia. Difficulties in speaking or understanding speech due to brain damage. (13)

Apparent distance theory. An explanation of the moon illusion that is based on the idea that the horizon moon, which is viewed across the filled space of the terrain, should appear farther away than the zenith moon, which is viewed through the empty space of the sky. This theory states that, since the horizon and zenith moons have the same visual angle, the farther-appearing horizon moon should appear larger. (9)

Apparent movement (or stroboscopic movement). An illusion of movement that occurs between two objects separated in space when the objects are flashed rapidly on and off, one after another, separated by a brief time interval. (7, 10)

Applanator. The part of an applanation tonometer that is pushed against the patient's cornea to determine the intraocular pressure. (17)

Area centralis. The horizontal area of high receptor density found in some animals, such as the turtle. (9)

Articulation function. A plot of the percentage of words identified correctly versus the intensity of the words. (17)

Articulators. Structures involved in speech production, such as the tongue, lips, teeth, jaw, and soft palate. (13)

Astigmatism. A condition in which vision is blurred in some orientations because of a misshapen cornea. (17)

Atmospheric perspective. A depth cue. Objects that are farther away look more blurred and bluer than objects that are closer, because we must look through more air and particles to see them. (8)

Attack. The buildup of sound at the beginning of a tone. (12)

Attention. The process of seeking out stimuli that are of interest. (4)

Audibility curve. A curve that indicates the sound pressure level (SPL) at threshold for frequencies across the audible spectrum. (12)

Audiogram. A plot of the threshold for hearing pure tones versus the frequencies of the tones. Threshold in an audiogram is plotted relative to "normal threshold," which is set at "0." Thus, normal hearing would be a horizontal line at "0" threshold. (17)

Audiologist. A professional with a master's or doctoral degree who measures the hearing ability of children and adults to identify the presence and severity of any hearing problems. Audiologists also fit hearing-impaired people with hearing aids and teach them strategies for more effective communication. (17)

Audiometer. A device for measuring an audiogram. (17)

Audio-visual speech perception. A perception of speech that is affected by both auditory and visual stimulation, as when a person sees a tape of someone saying /ga/with the sound /ba/ substituted and perceives /da/. (13)

Auditory canal. The canal through which air vibrations travel from the environment to the tympanic membrane. (11)

Auditory localization. The perception of the location of a sound source. (12)

Auditory masking. A psychophysical technique in which one sound is presented that decreases (masks) a person's ability to hear another sound. (11)

Auditory receiving area. The area of the cortex, located in the temporal lobe, that is the primary receiving area for hearing. (11)

Auditory response area. The psychophysically measured area that defines the frequencies and sound pressure levels over which hearing functions. This area extends between the audibility curve and the curve for the threshold of feeling. (12)

Auditory scene. The sound environment, which includes the locations and qualities of individual sound sources. (12)

Auditory scene analysis. The process by which listeners sort superimposed vibrations into separate sounds. (12)

Auditory stream segregation. The effect that occurs when a series of tones that differ in pitch are played so that the high- and low-pitched tones alternate so rapidly, that the high and low pitches become perceptually separated into simultaneously occurring independent streams of sound. (12)

Aural rehabilitation. Training for hearing-impaired people that consists of training in speech reading and other communication strategies. (17)

Axial myopia. See Myopia, axial. (17)

Axon. The part of the neuron that conducts nerve impulses over distances. Also called the nerve fiber. (1)

Azimuth-sensitive neurons. Neurons in the auditory cortex that respond best to a sound's left-right position in space. (12)

Base of the basilar membrane. The part of the basilar membrane nearest the middle ear. (11)

Basilar membrane. A membrane that stretches the length of the cochlea and controls the vibration of the cochlear partition. (11)

Behavioral approach to perception. The approach that focuses on the relationship between the physical properties of stimuli and the perceptual response (the stimulus-perception relationship). (1)

Bimodal neurons. Neurons that responds to stimulation of two senses. For example, a neuron that responds to both visual and tactile stimulation. (4)

Binaural cells. Neurons in the auditory system that receive inputs from both ears. (12)

Binaural cues. Sound localization cues that involve both ears. (12)

Binding problem. The problem of how neural activity in many separated areas in the brain is combined to create a perception of a coherent object. (4)

Binocular deprivation. Depriving an animal of vision in both eyes during some portion of their development. (12)

Binocular depth cell. A neuron in the visual cortex that responds best to stimuli that fall on points separated by a specific degree of disparity on the two retinas. (8)

Binocular depth cue. A depth cue that requires the participation of both eyes. Binocular disparity is the major binocular depth cue. (8)

Binocular disparity. The result when the retinal images of an object fall on disparate points on the two retinas. (8)

Binocular fixation. Simultaneous direction of the foveas of both eyes at an object. (16)

Binocular rivalry. The situation that occurs when two different images are presented to the left and right eyes and perception alternates back and forth between the two images. (4)

Biological movement. Motion produced by biological organisms. Most of the experiments on biological motion have used walking humans with lights attached to their joints and limbs as stimuli. (10)

Bipolar cell. A neuron that is stimulated by the visual receptors and sends electrical signals to the retinal ganglion cells. (2)

Blindness. A visual acuity of 20/200 or less after correction or little peripheral vision (the legal definition of blindness). (17)

Blindsight. A situation in which a person can't see a light at a particular place in the visual field but can indicate that a stimulus is at that location by pointing or by other means. (2)

Blind spot. The small area where the optic nerve leaves the back of the eye; there are no visual receptors in this area so small images falling directly on the blind spot can't be seen. (2)

Blobs. Cells found in areas of the visual cortex that take up a stain that selectively colors areas that contain the enzyme cytochromeoxidase. Many of these cells have double color-opponent receptive fields. (5)

Body-centered neurons. Neurons that have visual receptive fields that respond when a visual stimulus is presented near a particular part of the body. (4)

Bottom-up processing. Processing in which a person constructs a perception by first analyzing small units such as primitives. Treisman's preattentive stage of processing, in which a stimulus is analyzed into parts, is an example of bottom-up processing. (1)

Cataract. A lens that is clouded. (17)

Cataract, congenital. A cataract present at birth. (17)

Cataract, secondary. A cataract caused by another eye disease. (17)

Cataract, senile. A cataract due to old age. This is the most common form of cataract. (17)

Cataract, traumatic. A cataract caused by injury. (17)

Categorical perception. In speech perception, perceiving one sound at short voice onset times and another sound at longer voice onset times. The listener perceives only two categories across the whole range of voice onset times. (13)

Cell assembly. A group of neurons that fire together in response to a particular stimulus. (4)

Cell body. The part of a neuron that contains the neuron's metabolic machinery and that receives stimulation from other neurons. (1)

Center frequency. The frequency positioned midway between the lower and upper frequencies in a complex sound stimulus such as noise. (12)

Center-surround antagonism. The competition between the center and surround regions of a center-surround receptive field. (2)

Center-surround receptive field. A receptive field that consists of a roughly circular excitatory area surrounded by an inhibitory area, or a circular inhibitory center surrounded by an excitatory surround. (2)

Central pitch processor. A hypothetical central mechanism that analyzes the pattern of a tone's harmonics and selects the fundamental frequency that is most likely to have been part of that pattern. (11)

Cerebral cortex. Thin layer of neurons that covers the surface of the brain, which is responsible for higher functions such as perception and thinking. (1)

Characteristic frequency. The frequency at which a neuron in the auditory system has its lowest threshold. (11)

Chemesthesis. The sense responsible for detecting chemical substances that are irritating or which have a tactile component. Also called the Common Chemical Sense. (15)

Chorda tympani nerve. A nerve that transmits signals from receptors on the front and sides of the tongue. (15)

Chromatic adaptation. The adaptation of the eye to chromatic light. Chromatic adaptation is selective adaptation to wavelengths in a particular region of the visible spectrum. (5)

Chromatic color. Colors with hue, such as blue, yellow, red, and green. (5)

Cilia. Fine hairs that protrude from the inner and outer hair cells of the auditory system. Bending the cilia of the inner hair cells leads to transduction. (11)

Classical psychophysical methods. The methods of limits, adjustment, and constant stimuli, described by Fechner for measuring thresholds. (1)

Coarticulation. The overlapping articulation of different phonemes. (13)

Cochlea. The snail-shaped, liquid-filled structure that contains the structures of the inner ear, the most important of which are the basilar membrane, the tectorial membrane, and the hair cells. (11)

Cochlear implant. A device in which electrodes are inserted into the cochlea to create hearing by electrically stimulating the auditory nerve fibers. This device is used to restore hearing in people who have lost their hearing because of damaged hair cells. (17)

Cochlear nucleus. The nucleus where nerve fibers from the cochlea first synapse. (11)

Cochlear partition. A partition in the cochlea, extending almost its full length, that separates the scala tympani and the scala vestibuli. (11)

Cold fiber. A nerve fiber that responds to decreases in temperature or to steady low temperatures. (14)

Color. A perceptual response to objects and lights that causes them to possess qualities such as redness, greenness, whiteness, and grayness. (5)

Color, achromatic. See Achromatic color. (5)

Color, chromatic. See Chromatic color. (5)

Color constancy. The effect in which the perception of an object's hue remains constant even when the wavelength distribution of the illumination is changed. Approximate color constancy means that our perception of hue usually changes a little when the illumination changes, though not as much as we might expect from the change in the wavelengths of light reaching the eye. (6)

Color deficiency. People with color deficiency (sometimes incorrectly called color blindness) see fewer colors than people with normal color vision and need to mix fewer wavelengths to match any other wavelength in the spectrum. (5)

Color-matching experiment. A procedure in which observers are asked to match the color in one field by mixing two or more lights in another field. (5)

Color mixing. Combining two or more different colors to create a new color (see Color mixture, additive, and Color mixture, subtractive). (5)

Color mixture, additive. The result when lights of different colors are superimposed. (5)

Color mixture, subtractive. The result when paints of different colors are mixed together. (5)

Color-opponent cells, type 1. Cortical cell which has a center-surround receptive field that is inhibited by one band of wavelengths presented to the surround, and excited by another band presented to the center (or visa versa). (5)

Color-opponent cell, double. A cell with a center-surround receptive field that responds in an opponent manner to stimulation of the field's center with a reversed opponent response to stimulation of the surround. For example, if the center response is R+G- the surround response will be R-G+. (5)

Columnar arrangement. The arrangement of neurons with similar properties in columns perpendicular to the surface of the cortex. For example, there are location, orientation, and ocular dominance columns in the visual system and frequency columns in the auditory system. (3)

Common chemical sense. See Chemesthesis. (15)

Common fate, law of. Gestalt law: Things that are moving in the same direction appear to be grouped together. (7)

Comparator. A structure hypothesized by the corollary discharge theory of movement perception. The corollary discharge signal and the sensory movement signal meet at the comparator. (10)

Complex cell. A neuron in the visual cortex that responds best to moving bars with a particular orientation. (3)

Componential recovery, principle of. A principle stating that, if an object's geons can be identified, then the object can be rapidly and correctly recognized. (7)

Computational approach. An approach to explaining object perception that treats perception as the end result of a mathematical analysis of the retinal image. (7)

Conditioned flavor aversion. Avoidance of a flavor after it has been paired with sickness. (15)

Conductive hearing loss. Hearing loss that occurs when the vibrations of a sound stimulus are not conducted normally from the outer ear into the cochlea. (17)

Cones. Cone-shaped receptors in the retina that are primarily responsible for vision in high levels of illumination, and for color vision and detail vision. (2)

Conflicting cues theory. A theory of visual illusions proposed by R. H. Day, which states that our perception of the length of lines depends on an integration of the actual length of lines and the overall length of the figure. (9)

Congenital cataract. See Cataract, congenital. (17)

Constant stimuli, method of. A psychophysical method in which a number of stimuli with different intensities are presented repeatedly in a random order. (1)

Contralateral eye. The eye on the opposite side of the head from a particular structure. (2)

Contrast. The difference in light intensity between two areas. For a visual grating stimulus, the contrast is the amplitude of the grating divided by its mean intensity. (7)

Contrast sensitivity. Sensitivity to the difference in the light intensities in two adjacent areas. Contrast sensitivity is usually measured by taking the reciprocal of the minimum intensity difference between two bars of a grating necessary to see the bars. (3)

Contrast sensitivity function (CSF). A plot of contrast sensitivity versus the spatial frequency of a grating stimulus. (3)

Convergence angle. The angle between the two eyes as they fixate on an object. (8)

Convergence (depth cue). A depth cue. Muscular sensations that occur when the eyes move inward (convergence) or outward (divergence) to view objects at different distances may provide information regarding the depth of that object. (8)

Convergence (neural). The process of many neurons synapsing onto fewer neurons. (2)

Cornea. The transparent focusing element of the eye that is the first structure through which light passes as it enters the eye and that is the eye's major focusing element. (2)

Corneal disease and injury. Any disease or injury that damages the cornea, causing a loss of transparency. (17)

Corneal transplant. The replacement of a damaged piece of cornea with a piece of healthy cornea taken from a donor. (17)

Corollary discharge signal (CDS). A copy of the signal sent from the motor area of the brain to the eye muscles. The corollary discharge signal is sent not to the eye muscles, but to the hypothetical comparator of corollary discharge theory. (10)

Corollary discharge theory. According to the corollary discharge theory of motion perception, the corollary discharge signal is sent to a structure called the comparator, where the information in the corollary discharge is compared to the sensory movement signal. If the corollary discharge signal and the sensory movement signal do not cancel each other, movement is perceived. (10)

Correct rejection. In a signal detection experiment, saying, "No, I don't detect a stimulus" on a trial in which the stimulus is not presented (a correct response). (Appendix)

Correspondence problem. The visual system's matching of points on one image with similar points on the other image in order to determine binocular disparity. (8)

Corresponding retinal points. The points on each retina that would overlap if one retina were slid on top of the other. Receptors at corresponding points send their signals to the same location in the brain. (8)

Cortical malleability. The ability of neurons in the visual cortex to change their properties in response to environmental changes. (8)

Covert awareness. An awareness of a stimulus that appears to happen "under the surface" of conscious perception. Blindsight is an example of covert awareness. (4)

Crossed disparity. Binocular disparity in which objects are located in front of the horopter (see Uncrossed disparity). (8)

Cross-modality matching. A subject is presented with a stimulus of one modality and is asked to adjust a stimulus in another modality to match its magnitude. (11)

Cue theory. The approach to depth perception that focuses on identifying information in the retinal image that is correlated with depth in the world. (8)

Cutaneous sensations. Sensations based on the stimulation of receptors in the skin. (14)

Dark adaptation. Visual adaptation that occurs in the dark, during which the sensitivity to light increases. (2)

Dark adaptation curve. The function that traces the time course of the increase in visual sensitivity that occurs during dark adaptation. (2)

Dark adapted sensitivity. The sensitivity of the eye after it has completely adapted to the dark. (2)

Decay. The decrease in sound at the end of a tone. (12)

Decibel (dB). A unit that indicates the presence of a tone relative to a reference pressure: $dB = 20 \log (p/p_o)$ where p is the pressure of the tone and P_o is the reference pressure. (11)

Deletion. The covering of the farther of two surfaces due to observer movement. This provides information for depth. (8)

Dendrites. Nerve processes on the cell body that receive stimulation from other neurons. (1)

Depth cues. Two-dimensional information on the retina that is correlated with depth in the scene. (8)

Dermis. The inner layer of skin that contains nerve endings and receptors. (14)

Detached retina. A condition in which the retina is detached from the back of the eye. (17)

Deuteranopia. A form of red-green color dichromatism caused by lack of the middle-wavelength cone pigment. (5)

Diabetes. A condition in which the body doesn't produce enough insulin. One side effect of diabetes is a loss of vision due to diabetic retinopathy. (17)

Diabetic retinopathy. Damage to the retina that is a side effect of diabetes. This condition causes neovascularization—the formation of abnormal blood vessels that do not supply the retina with adequate oxygen and that bleed into the vitreous humor. (17)

Dichromat. A person who has a form of color deficiency. Dichromats can match any wavelength in the spectrum by mixing two other wavelengths. Deuteranopes, protanopes, and tritanopes are all dichromats. (5)

Diopter. The strength of a lens. Diopters = 1/far point in meters. (17)

Directionally-sensitive neurons. Neurons in auditory cortex that respond to the direction in which a sound stimulus is moving. (12)

Direct perception. J. J. Gibson's idea that we pick up the information provided by invariants directly and that perceptions result from this information without the need of any further processing. (8)

Direct sound. Sound that is transmitted to the ears directly from a sound source. (11)

Dishabituation. An increase in looking time that occurs when a stimulus is changed. This response is used in testing infants to see if they can differentiate two stimuli. (16)

Disparate points. See Noncorresponding points. (8)

Disparity detectors. Neurons that respond best to stimuli that fall on retinal points separated by a specific angle of disparity. Also called binocular depth cells. (8)

Dissociation. A situation that occurs as a result of brain damage when one function is present and another is absent.

Dissociation, double. In brain damage, when function A is present and function B is absent, and, in another person, when function A is absent and function B is present. Presence of a double dissociation means that the two functions involve different mechanisms and operate independently of one another. (4)

Dissociation, single. When, as a result of brain damage, one function is present and another is absent. Existence of a single dissociation indicates that the two functions involve different mechanisms, but may not be totally independent of one another. (4)

Distal stimulus. The stimulus in the environment (usually at a distance from the observer.) (1)

Distributed coding. Type of neural code in which different perceptions are signaled by the pattern of activity that is distributed across many neurons (see Specificity coding). (3)

Doctrine of specific nerve energies. A principle stating that the brain receives environmental information from sensory nerves and that the brain distinguishes between the different senses by monitoring the activity in these sensory nerves. (1)

Dorsal pathway. Pathway that conducts signals from the striate cortex to the parietal lobe. This has been called the "where" or the "how" pathway. (2, 4)

Dorsal root. The pathway through which fibers from the skin enter the spinal cord. (14)

Double color-opponent cell. See Color-opponent cell, double. (5)

Double dissociation. See Dissociation, double. (4)

Duplex perception. The result when one stimulus causes a person to hear both speech and nonspeech sounds simultaneously. (13)

Duplicity theory of vision. The idea that the rod and cone receptors in the retina operate under different conditions and have different properties. (2)

Eardrum. Another term for the tympanic membrane, the membrane located at the end of the auditory canal that vibrates in response to sound. (11)

Echolocation. Locating objects by sending out high-frequency pulses and sensing the echo created when these pulses are reflected from objects in the environment. Echolocation is used by bats and dolphins. (8)

Ecological approach. The approach to perception that emphasizes studying perception as it occurs in natural settings, particularly emphasizing the role of observer movement. (9)

Effect of the missing fundamental. See Periodicity pitch. (12)

Efferent feedback. Signals that travel from higher levels toward the periphery. An example of efferent feedback in the auditory system is a signal that is transmitted from the superior olivary nucleus to the hair cells. (11)

Efferent fibers. Fibers carrying signals from the brain toward the periphery. (14)

Elaborate cells. Neurons in the IT cortex that respond best to complex stimuli such as specific shapes or shapes combined with a color or texture. (See Primary cells). (4)

Electromagnetic energy. Energy radiated as waves that are produced by electric charges. The electromagnetic spectrum is a continuum of electromagnetic energy. (2)

Electromagnetic spectrum. Continuum of electromagnetic energy that extends from very short wavelength gamma rays to long-wavelength radio waves. Visible light is a narrow band within this spectrum. (2)

Electro-olfactogram. An electrical response recorded from the pooled activity of thousands of receptors in the olfactory mucosa. (15)

Electroretinogram. An electrical response of the visual receptors that is used in diagnosing retinal degenerations. (17)

Emmert's law. A law stating that the size of an afterimage depends on the distance of the surface against which the afterimage is viewed. The farther away the surface against which an afterimage is viewed, the larger the afterimage appears. (8)

Emmetropia. The condition in which the eye brings the images of objects into accurate focus on the retina. (16)

Emmetropic vision. See Emmetropia. (16)

Endorphins. Chemicals that are naturally produced in the brain and that cause analgesia. (14)

End-stopped cell. A cortical neuron that responds best to lines of a specific length that are moving in a particular direction. (3)

Envelope of the traveling wave. A curve that indicates the maximum displacement at each point along the basilar membrane caused by a traveling wave. (11)

Enzyme cascade. Sequence of reactions triggered by an activated visual pigment molecule that results in transduction. (2)

Epidermis. The outer layers of the skin, including a layer of dead skin cells. (14)

Equal loudness curve. A curve that indicates the sound pressure levels that result in a perception of the same loudness at frequencies across the audible spectrum. (12)

Equivalence classification. In speech perception, the ability to classify vowel sounds as belonging to the same class, even if the speakers are different. (13)

Everyday listening. Listening that focuses on events such as an air conditioner blowing or a chair squeaking (see Musical listening). (12)

Evoked potential. See Visual evoked potential. (16)

Excitation. A condition that facilitates the generation of nerve impulses. (1)

Excitatory. Referring to the type of neurotransmitter associated with increases in the rate of nerve firing. Can also refer to neural responses that are associated with increases in firing rate. (1)

Excitatory-center-inhibitory-surround receptive field. A center-surround receptive field in which stimulation of the center area causes an excitatory response and stimulation of the surround causes an inhibitory response. (2)

Excitatory response. The response of a nerve fiber in which the firing rate increases. (1)

Exploratory procedures (EPs). People's movements of their hands and fingers while they are identifying three-dimensional objects by touch. (14)

External eye exam. Examination of the condition of the outer eye. This exam includes, among other things, examination of the reaction of the pupil to light, the color of the eye, and the alignment of the eyes. (17)

Extrastriate cortex. Areas in the cerebral cortex outside the striate cortex. (2, 4)

Extrastriate visual areas. Areas in the cortex that are activated by visual stimuli but are outside the striate cortex. (2, 4)

False alarm. In a signal detection experiment, saying, "Yes, I detect the stimulus" on a trial in which the stimulus is not presented (an incorrect response). (Appendix)

Familiarity, law of. Gestalt law: Things are more likely to form groups if the groups appear familiar or meaningful. (7)

Familiar size. A depth cue. Our knowledge of an object's actual size sometimes influences our perception of an object's distance. (8)

Far point. The distance at which the rays from a spot of light are focused on the retina of the unaccommodated eye. For a person with normal vision, the far point is at infinity. For a person with myopic vision, the spot must be moved closer to the eye to bring the rays to a focus on the retina. (17)

Farsightedness. See Hyperopia. (17)

Feature detector. A neuron that responds selectively to a specific feature of the stimulus. (3)

Feature integration approach. The idea that object perception occurs through a sequence of steps that begins with the identification of basic features called primitives. (7)

Feature integration theory. A sequence of steps proposed by Treisman to explain how objects are broken down into primitives and how these primitives are recombined to result in a perception of the object. (7)

Flavor. The perception that occurs from the combination of taste and olfaction. (15)

Flow pattern. Pattern of visual stimulation that is created as elements in the environment flow past an observer due to observer motion. (10)

Fluorescein angiography. A technique in which a fluorescent dye is injected into a person's circulation. The outline of the retinal arteries and veins produced by this dye gives information about the condition of the retinal circulation. (17)

Focused-attention stage of processing. The stage of processing in which the primitives are combined. This stage requires conscious attention. (7)

Focusing power. The degree to which a structure such as the lens or the cornea bends light. The greater the focusing power, the more the light passing through the structure is bent. (2)

Focus of expansion (F. O. E.). The point in the flow pattern caused by observer movement in which there is no expansion. According to Gibson, the focus of expansion always remains centered on the observer's destination. (10)

Formants. Horizontal bands of energy in the speech spectrogram that are associated with vowels. (13)

Formant transitions. In the speech stimulus, the rapid shifts in frequency that precede formants. (13)

Fourier analysis. A mathematical technique that analyzes complex periodic waveforms into a number of sine-wave components. (5, 8)

Fourier spectrum. The sine-wave components that make up a periodic waveform. Fourier spectra are usually depicted by a line for each sine-wave frequency, the height of the line indicating the amount of energy at that frequency. (8)

Fovea. A small area in the human retina that contains only cone receptors. The fovea is located on the line of sight, so that when a person looks at an object, its image falls on the fovea. (2)

Frequency. In the case of a sound wave that repeats itself like the sine wave of a pure tone, frequency is the number of times per second that the wave repeats itself. (11)

Frequency sweep detector. A neuron in the auditory cortex that fires only when frequencies are smoothly increased or decreased. (11)

Frequency tuning curve. Curve relating the threshold intensity for stimulating an auditory neuron and frequency. (11)

Frontal eyes. Eyes located in front of the head, so the views of the two eyes overlap. (8)

Frontal operculum cortex. An area in the frontal lobe of the cortex that receives signals from the taste system. (15)

Fundamental frequency. Usually the lowest frequency in the Fourier spectrum of a complex tone. The tone's other components, called harmonics, have frequencies that are multiples of the fundamental frequency. (11)

Ganglion cell. A neuron in the retina that receives inputs from bipolar and amacrine cells. The axons of the ganglion cells are the fibers that travel toward the lateral geniculate nucleus of the thalamus in the optic nerve. (2)

Gas chromatograph. A device that accurately measures the concentration of the vapor given off by a chemical stimulus. (15)

Gate control theory. Melzak and Wall's idea that our perception of pain is controlled by a neural circuit that takes into account the relative amount of activity in large (L) fibers and small (S) fibers. (14)

Geon. "Geometric ion"; Volumetric primitives proposed by Biederman. (7)

Gestalt psychology. A school of psychology that has focused on developing principles of perceptual organization, proposing that "the whole is different from the sum of its parts." (7)

Glaucoma. A disease of the eye that usually results in an increase in intraocular pressure. (17)

Glaucoma, closed-angle. A rare form of glaucoma in which the iris is pushed up so that it closes the angle between the iris and the cornea and blocks the area through which the aqueous humor normally drains out of the eye. (17)

Glaucoma, open-angle. A form of glaucoma in which the area through which the aqueous humor normally drains out of the eye is blocked. In this form of glaucoma, the iris remains in its normal position so that the angle between the iris and the cornea remains open. (17)

Global optical flow. Information for movement that occurs when all elements in a scene move. (10)

Glossopharyngeal nerve. A nerve that transmits signals from receptors located at the back of the tongue. (15)

Good continuation, law of. Gestalt law: Points that, when connected, result in straight or smoothly curving lines are seen as belonging together, and lines tend to be seen in such a way as to follow the smoothest path. (7)

Good figure, law of. Gestalt law: Every stimulus pattern is seen so that the resulting structure is as simple as possible. (7)

Gradient of flow. In a flow pattern a gradient is created by movement of an observer through the environment. The speed of movement is rapid in the foreground and becomes slower as distance from the observer increases. (9)

Grating. A stimulus pattern consisting of alternating bars with different lightnesses or colors. (3)

Habituation. The result when the same stimulus is presented repeatedly. For example, infants look at a stimulus less and less on each succeeding trial. (16)

Hair cells. Neurons in the cochlea that contain small hairs, or cilia, that are displaced by vibration of the basilar membrane and fluids inside the inner ear. There are two kinds of hair cells: inner and outer. (11)

Hair cells, inner. Auditory receptor cells in the inner ear that are primarily responsible for auditory transduction and the perception of pitch. (11)

Hair cells, outer. Auditory receptor cells in the inner ear that amplify the responce of the inner hair cells (see motile response). (11)

Haptic perception. The perception of three-dimensional objects by touch. (14)

Harmonics. Fourier components of a complex tone with frequencies that are multiples of the fundamental frequency. (11)

Hearing handicap. The disadvantage that a hearing impairment causes in a person's ability to communicate or in the person's daily living. (17)

Hearing impairment. A deviation or change for the worse in either the structure or the functioning of the auditory system (see Hearing handicap). (17)

Hereditary retinal degeneration. A degeneration of the retina that is inherited. Retinitis pigmentosa is an example of a hereditary retinal degeneration. (17)

Hertz (Hz). The unit for designating the frequency of a tone. One Hertz equals one cycle per second. (11)

Hit. In a signal detection experiment, saying, "Yes, I detect astimulus" on a trial in which the stimulus is present (a correct response). (Appendix)

Homunculus. "Little man," a term referring to the map of the body in the somatosensory cortex. (14)

Horizon ratio. The proportion of an object that is above the horizon divided by the proportion that is below the horizon. (9)

Horizon ratio principle. A principle stating that, if a person is standing on flat terrain, a point on an object that intersects the horizon will be one eye-height above the ground, and that if two objects that are in contact with the ground are the same size, the proportions of the objects above and below the horizon will be the same. (9)

Horizontal cell. A neuron that transmits signals laterally across the retina. Horizontal cells synapse with receptors and bipolar cells. (2)

Horopter. An imaginary surface that passes through the point of fixation. Objects falling on this surface result in images that fall on corresponding points on the two retinas. (8)

Hue. The experience of a chromatic color such as red, green, yellow, or blue or combinations of these colors. (5)

Hypercolumn. A column of cortex about 1 mm on a side that contains a location column for a particular area of the retina, left and right ocular dominance columns, and a complete set of orientation columns. A hypercolumn can be thought of as a processing module for a particular location on the retina. (3)

Hyperopia (farsightedness). The inability to see near objects clearly because the focus point for parallel rays of light is behind the retina. (17)

Hypothesis testing. The idea that sensory stimulation provides data for hypotheses about the world. According to this idea, perceiving involves testing different hypotheses about what is causing the stimulation. (7)

Illusion. A situation in which an observer's perception of a stimulus does not correspond to the physical properties of the stimulus. For example, in the Muller-Lyer illusion, two lines of equal length are perceived to be of different lengths. (9)

Illusions of movement. The perception of movement in situations in which there is actually no movement in the physical stimulus. Examples of illusions of movement are the waterfall illusion, induced movement, and stroboscopic movement. (10)

Illusory conjunctions. Illusory combinations of primitives that are perceived when stimuli containing a number of primitives are presented briefly. (7)

Illusory contours. Contours that are perceived even though they are not present in the physical stimulus. (7)

Image movement signal. In corollary discharge theory, the signal that occurs when an image stimulates the receptors by moving across them. (10)

Impossible object. An "object" that can be represented by a two-dimensional picture but cannot exist in three-dimensional space. (7)

Incus. The second of the three ossicles of the middle ear. It transmits vibrations from the malleus to the stapes. (11)

Indexical characteristics. Characteristics of the speech stimulus that indicate information about things such as the speaker's age, gender, and emotional state. (13)

Indirect sound. Sound that reaches the ears after being reflected from a surface such as a room's walls. (12)

Induced movement. The illusory movement of one object that is caused by the movement of another object that is nearby. (10)

Inferior colliculus. A nucleus in the hearing system along the pathway from the cochlea to the auditory cortex. The inferior colliculus receives inputs from the superior olivary nucleus. (11)

Inhibition. A condition that decreases the likelihood that nerve impulses will be generated. (1)

Inhibitory-center-excitatory-surround receptive field. A center-surround receptive field in which stimulation of the center causes an inhibitory response and stimulation of the surround causes an excitatory response. (2)

Inhibitory response. The response of a nerve fiber in which the firing rate decreases due to inhibition from another neuron. (1)

Inner ear. The innermost division of the ear, containing the cochlea and the receptors for hearing. (11)

Inner hair cells. See Hair cells, inner.

Insula. An area in the frontal lobe of the cortex that receives signals from the taste system. (15)

Interaural differences. Differences in the stimuli reaching the left and right ears, especially the intensity and frequency of the stimuli. (12)

Interaural intensity difference. The greater intensity of a sound at the closer ear when a sound source is positioned closer to one ear than to the other. This effect is most pronounced for high-frequency tones. (12)

Interaural time difference. The effect that, when a sound source is positioned closer to one ear than to the other, the sound reaches the close ear slightly before reaching the far ear. (12)

Interaural time difference detector. A neuron that fires only when a stimulus is presented first to one ear and then to the other, with a specific delay between the stimulation of the two ears. (12)

Intermodal matching. Ability to match shapes presented in two different modalities. (16)

Interocular transfer. The aftereffect in one eye when an adaptation stimulus is presented to the other eye. (7)

Intersensory dominance. When stimulation of one sense controls perception when placed in conflict with stimulation of another sense. (7)

Interstimulus interval (ISI). The time interval between two flashes of light in an apparent movement display. (10)

Intraocular lens. A plastic or silicone lens that is inserted into the eye after the removal of a cataract. This lens partially compensates for the loss of focusing power caused by removal of the patient's lens. (17)

Intraocular pressure. Pressure inside the eyeball. (17)

Invariant acoustic cues. In speech perception, aspects of an auditory signal that remain constant even in different contexts. (13)

Invariant information. Environmental properties that do not change as the observer moves. For example, the spacing, or texture, of the elements in a texture gradient does not change as the observer moves on the gradient. The texture of the gradient therefore supplies invariant information for depth perception. (9)

Ions. Charged molecules found floating in the water that surrounds nerve fibers. (1)

Ipsilateral eye. The eye on the same side of the head of the structure to which the eye sends inputs. (2)

Iridectomy. A procedure used to treat closed-angle glaucoma, in which a small hole is cut in the iris. This hole opens a channel through which aqueous humor can flow out of the eye. (17)

Ishihara plate. A display made up of colored dots used to test for the presence of color deficiency. The dots are colored so that people with normal (trichromatic) color vision can perceive numbers in the plate, but people with color deficiency cannot perceive these numbers or perceive different numbers from someone with trichromatic vision. (5)

Isomerization. Change in shape of the retinal part of the visual pigment molecule that occurs when the molecule absorbs a quantum of light. (2)

Just noticeable difference (JND). The smallest difference in intensity that results in a noticeable difference between two stimuli. (1)

Kinesthesis. The sense that enables us to feel the motions and positions of the limbs and body. (14)

Kinetic depth effect. Occurs when a stimulus's three-dimensional structure becomes apparent from viewing a two-dimensional image of the stimulus as it rotates. (10)

Labeled lines. An application of specificity coding to taste that suggests that different taste qualities are signaled by activity in specific nerve fibers. (15)

Large-diameter fiber (L-fiber). According to gate control theory, activity in L-fibers closes the gate control mechanism and therefore decreases the perception of pain. (14)

Laser photocoagulation. A procedure in which a laser beam is aimed at blood vessels that are leaking because of neovascularization. This laser beam photocoagulates—seals off—the blood vessels and stops the leaking. (17)

Laser photo refractive keratotomy. A surgical procedure in which an excimer laser is used to change the shape of the cornea to improve the vision of people with myopia or hyperopia. (17)

Lateral eyes. Eyes located on opposite sides of an animal's head, so the views of the two eyes do not overlap or overlap only slightly, as in the pigeon and rabbit. (8)

Lateral geniculate nucleus (LN). The nucleus in the thalamus that receives inputs from the optic nerve and sends fibers to the cortical receiving area for vision. (2)

Lateral inhibition. Inhibition that is spread laterally across a nerve circuit. In the retina, lateral inhibition is spread by the horizontal and amacrine cells. (2)

Lateral plexus. A structure that transmits nerve impulses laterally in the limulus eye. (2)

Laws of perceptual organization. See Perceptual organization, laws of. (7)

Lens. The transparent focusing element of the eye through which light passes after passing through the cornea and the aqueous humor. The lens's change in shape to focus at different distances is called accommodation. (2)

Light adapted sensitivity. The sensitivity of the light adapted eye. (2)

Lightness. Perception of reflectance. The perception of lightness is usually associated with the achromatic colors: white, gray, and black. (5)

Lightness constancy. The constancy of our perception of an object's lightness under different intensities of illumination. (6)

Likelihood principle. A principle proposed by Helmholtz stating that we will perceive the object that is most likely to be the cause of our sensory stimulation. (7)

Limits, method of. A psychophysical method for measuring threshold in which the experimenter presents stimuli in alternating ascending and descending series. (1)

Linear perspective (depth cue). The visual effect that parallel lines (like railroad tracks) converge as they get farther away. This convergence of parallel lines is a depth cue, with greater convergence indicating greater distance. (8)

Linear perspective (drawing system). A method of representing three-dimensional space on a two-dimensional surface. (8)

Local depth information. Information at a localized place on a figure that indicates depth. (7)

Localization. See Auditory localization. (12)

Localization cues. Information that is used to locate sound sources. (12)

Localization of function. The principle that specific areas of the brain serve specific functions. (1)

Local movement signal. Information for movement that occurs when one object moves in an otherwise stationary field. (10)

Location column. A column in the visual cortex that contains neurons with the same receptive field locations on the retina. (3)

Location-invariant neurons. Neurons that respond to a stimulus over large areas of the retina. (4)

Locomotor flow line. The flow line that passes directly under a moving observer. (10)

Long-wavelength pigment. A cone visual pigment that absorbs light maximally at the long-wavelength end of the spectrum. In humans, this pigment absorbs maximally at 558 nm. (2)

Loudness. The quality of sound that ranges from soft to loud. For a tone of a particular frequency, loudness usually increases with increasing decibels. (12)

Mach bands. A perceptual effect that causes a thin dark band on the dark side of a light-dark border and a thin light band on the light side of the border even though corresponding intensity changes do not exist. (2)

Macrosmatic. Having a keen sense of smell that is important to an animal's survival. (15)

Macula. An area about 5 mm in diameter, that surrounds and includes the fovea. (17)

Macular degeneration. A degeneration of the macula area of the retina. (17)

Macular degeneration, age related. The most common form of macular degeneration, occurring in older people. (17)

Magnification factor. The apportioning of proportionally more space on the cortex to the representation of specific areas of sensory receptors. For example, a small area on the retina in or near the fovea receives more space on the cortex than the same area of peripheral retina. Similarly, the fingertips receive more space on the somatosensory cortex than the forearm or leg. (3, 14)

Magnitude estimation. A psychophysical method in which the subject assigns numbers to a stimulus that are proportional to the subjective magnitude of the stimulus. (1)

Magnocellular (or magno). Neurons in layers 1 and 2 of the lateral geniculate nucleus that receive inputs from the M ganglion cells. (3)

Malleus. The first of the ossicles of the middle ear. Receives vibrations from the tympanic membrane and transmits these vibrations to the incus. (11)

Manner of articulation. The mechanical means by which consonants are produced and the way air is pushed through openings in the vocal tract. (13)

Masking. See Auditory masking. (11)

M-cells. Retinal ganglion cells that have medium-sized cell bodies and which respond with sustained firing. M-cells synapse in the magnocellular layer of the LGN. (3)

McGurk effect. See Audio-visual speech perception. (13)

Mechanoreceptor fibers. Fibers that respond to mechanical displacements of the skin. There are two types of mechanoreceptive fibers, rapidly adapting fibers (the two main kinds being RA1 and PC), and slowly adapting fibers (the two main kinds being SAI and SAII). (14)

Medial geniculate nucleus. A nucleus in the auditory system along the pathway from the cochlea to the auditory cortex. The medial geniculate nucleus receives inputs from the inferior colliculus. (11)

Medial lemniscal pathway. A pathway in the spinal cord that transmits signals from the skin toward the thalamus. (14)

Medium-wavelength pigment. A cone visual pigment that absorbs light maximally in the middle of the spectrum. In humans, this pigment absorbs maximally at 531 nm. (2)

Meissner corpuscle. A receptor in the skin, associated with RA I mechanoreceptors, that responds best to taps on the skin. (14)

Melodic channeling. See Scale illusion. (12)

Melody schema. A representation of a familiar melody that is stored in a person's memory. (12)

Memory color. The idea that an object's characteristic color influences our perception of that object's color. (6)

Meniere's disease. A form of sensorineural hearing loss caused by an excessive buildup of the liquid that fills the cochlea and the semicircular canals. (17)

Menstrual synchrony. Women who live together experience menstrual periods that begin at approximately the same time. (15)

Meridional amblyopia. A condition in which a person has an astigmatism that cannot be optically corrected. (16)

Merkel receptor. A disk-shaped receptor in the skin associated with slowly adapting fibers, small receptive fields, and the perception of pressure. (14)

Merkel receptors. Receptors in the skin, associated with SA I mechanoreceptors, that respond best to light pressure and are sensitive to details. (14)

Metamers. Two lights that have different wavelength distributions but are perceptually identical. (5)

Method of adjustment. See Adjustment, method of. (1)

Method of constant stimuli. See Constant stimuli, method of. (1)

Method of limits. See Limits, method of. (1)

Microelectrode. A thin piece of wire or glass that is small enough to record electrical signals from single nerve fibers. (1)

Microneurography. A procedure for recording the activity of single neurons in the skin of awake humans. (14)

Microsmatic. Having a weak sense of smell that is not crucial to an animal's survival. (15)

Microspectrophotometry. A procedure for determining pigment absorption spectra that involves shining light through single receptors or through small numbers of receptors. (2)

Middle ear. The small air-filled space between the auditory canal and the cochlea that contains the ossicles. (11)

Middle-ear muscles. Muscles attached to the ossicles in the middle ear. The smallest skeletal muscles in the body, they contract in response to very intense sounds and dampen the vibration of the ossicles. (11)

Mind-body problem. The problem of how physical processes such as nerve impulses cause mental processes such as perceptual experience. (1)

Minimum audible angle. The smallest angle between two sound sources that results in the perception of two separate sounds. (16)

Misapplied size constancy. A principle, proposed by Gregory, that when mechanisms that help maintain size constancy in the three-dimensional world are applied to two-dimensional pictures, an illusion of size sometimes results. (9)

Miss. In a signal detection experiment, saying, "No, I don't detect a stimulus" on a trial in which the stimulus is present (an incorrect response). (Appendix)

Missing fundamental, effect of. See Periodicity pitch. (12)

Modularity. Specialization of the brain in which specific cortical areas processes information about specific perceptual qualities. (4)

Modular organization. The organization of specific functions into specific brain structures. (1)

Module. A structure that processes information about a specific behavior or perceptual quality. Often identified as a structure that contains a large proportion of neurons that respond selectively to a particular quality.

Monaural localization cue. Information for sound localization that reaches only one ear. (12)

Monochromat. A person who is completely color-blind and therefore sees everything as black, white, or shades of gray. A monochromat can match any wavelength in the spectrum by adjusting the intensity of any other wavelength. (2, 5)

Monochromatic light. Light which contains only a single wavelength. (2)

Monocular depth cues. Depth cues, such as overlap, relative size, relative height, familiar size, linear perspective, movement parallax, and accommodation that work if we use only one eye. (8)

Monocular rearing. Rearing an animal so it has use of only one eye. When done at a young age this rearing affects development of binocular neurons in the cortex. (8)

Moon illusion. An illusion in which the moon appears to be larger when it is on or near the horizon than when it is high in the sky. (9)

Motile response. A response to sound of the outer hair cells in which the cells move. The cells tilt and get slightly longer, which amplifies basilar membrane vibration and therefore amplifies the response of the inner hair cells. (11)

Motion agnosia. An effect of brain damage in which the ability to perceive motion is disrupted. (10)

Motion parallax. A depth cue. As an observer moves, nearby objects appear to move rapidly whereas far objects appear to move slowly. (8)

Motor signal (MS). In corollary discharge theory, the signal that is sent to the eye muscles when the observer moves or tries to move his or her eyes. (10)

Movement aftereffect. An illusion of movement that occurs after a person views an inducing stimulus such as a waterfall. (10)

Movement-produced cues. Cues that create the impression of depth from movement. The movement-produced cues are motion parallax and deletion and accretion. (8)

Muller-Lyer illusion. An illusion consisting of two lines of equal length that appear to be different lengths because of the addition of "fins" to the ends of the lines. (9)

Multimodal neurons. Neurons that respond to stimulation of two or more senses. (4)

Musical listening. Listening that focuses on the perceptual qualities of a sound—things such as a sound's pitch or timbre (see Everday listening). (12)

Myopia (nearsightedness). The inability to see distant objects clearly because parallel rays of light are brought to a focus in front of the retina. (17)

Myopia, axial. Myopia caused by an elongated eyeball. (17)

Myopia, refractive. Myopia that occurs when the cornea and the lens bend light too much (they have too much focusing power). (17)

Naloxone. A substance that inhibits the activity of opiates. It is hypothesized that naloxone also inhibits the activity of endorphins. (14)

Nasal pharynx. A passageway that connects the mouth cavity and the nasal cavity. (15)

Natural constraints. Basic properties of the environment, such as the fact that intensity usually changes gradually at the borders of shadows. According to some theories of object perception, our perceptual system takes these properties into account as part of the process of object perception. (7)

Near point. The distance at which the lens can no longer accommodate enough to bring close objects into focus. Objects nearer than the near point can be brought into focus only by corrective lenses. (2)

Neovascularization. The formation of abnormal small blood vessels that occurs in patients with diabetic retinopathy. (17)

Nerve. A group of nerve fibers traveling together. (1)

Nerve fiber. In most sensory neurons, the long part of the neuron that transmits electrical impulses from one point to another. Also called the axon. (1)

Neural circuit. A number of neurons that are connected by synapses. (2)

Neural plasticity. The fact that the anatomy and functionality of the nervous system can change in response to experience. Examples are how early visual experience can change the proportion of binocular neurons in the visual cortex, and how tactile experience can change the sizes of areas in the cortex that represent different parts of the body. (14)

Neural processing. Operations that transform electrical signals within a network of neurons, or which transforms the response of individual neurons. (1)

Neurogenesis. The cycle of birth, development, and death of a neuron. This process occurs for the receptors for olfaction and taste. (15)

Neuron. A cell in the nervous system that generates and transmits electrical impulses. (1)

Neuropsychology. The study of how brain damage affects a person's behavior. (4)

Neurotransmitter. A chemical stored in synaptic vesicles that is released in response to a nerve impulse and has an excitatory or inhibitory effect on another neuron. (1)

Neutral point. The wavelength at which a dichromat perceives gray. (5)

Nociceptor. A fiber that responds to stimuli that are damaging to the skin. (14)

Noise. All stimuli in the environment other than the signal. Noise can also be generated within a person's nervous system. The subject's perception of noise in a signal detection experiment sometimes causes the subject to think mistakenly that a signal has been presented. (Appendix)

Noise-induced hearing loss. A form of sensorineural hearing loss that occurs when loud noises cause degeneration of the hair cells. (17)

Noncorresponding (disparate) points. Two points, one on each retina, that would not overlap if the retinas were slid onto each other. (8)

Nontasters. People who cannot taste the compound phenylthiocarbamide (PTC). (15)

Nuclei. Small areas in the nervous system at which many synapses occur. (1)

Nucleus of the solitary tract (NST). The nucleus in the brain stem that receives signals from the tongue, the mouth, and the larynx transmitted by the chorda tympani, glossopharyngeal, and vagus nerves. (15)

Occipital lobe. A lobe at the back of the cortex that is the site of the cortical receiving area for vision. (1)

Occlusion. Depth cue in which one object hides or partially hides another object from view, causing the hidden object to be perceived as being farther away. (8)

Octave. Tones that have frequencies that are binary multiples of each other($\times 2$, $\times 4$, etc.). For example, an 800-Hz tone is one octave above a 400-Hz tone. (11)

Ocular dominance. The degree to which a neuron is influenced by stimulation of each eye. A neuron has a large amount of ocular dominance if it responds only to stimulation of one eye. There is no ocular dominance if the neuron responds equally to stimulation of both eyes. (3)

Ocular dominance column. A column in the visual cortex that contains neurons with the same ocular dominance. (3)

Ocular dominance histogram. A histogram that indicates the degree of ocular dominance of a large population of neurons. (8)

Oculomotor cues. Depth cues that depend on our ability to sense the position of our eyes and the tension in our eye muscles. Accommodation and convergence are oculomotor cues. (8)

Odotope. A group of odorants that share a specific chemical feature that determines neural firing. (15)

Odotopic mapping. The way different odors cause activity in different areas of the olfactory bulb. (15)

Off-response. A burst of firing when a stimulus is turned off. (2)

Olfactometer. A device that presents olfactory stimuli with great precision. (15)

Olfactory binding proteins. Proteins contained in the olfactory mucosa that are secreted into the nasal cavity, bind to olfactory stimuli and transport them to active sites on the olfactory receptors. (15)

Olfactory bulb. The structure that receives signals directly from the olfactory receptors. (15)

Olfactory cortex. A small area under the temporal lobe of the cortex that receives signals that originate in the olfactory receptors. (15)

Olfactory mucosa. The region inside the nose that contains the receptors for the sense of smell. (15)

Olfactory receptor neurons. Neurons in the olfactory mucosa that contain the olfactory receptor proteins that respond to odor stimuli. (15)

Olfactory receptor proteins. Active sites for olfaction on the olfactory cilia of the olfactory receptor neurons. (15)

Ommatidium. A structure in the eye of the Limulus that contains a small lens, located directly over a visual receptor. The Limulus eye is made up of hundreds of these ommatidia. (2)

On response. The response of a nerve fiber in which there is an increase in the firing rate when the stimulus is turned on; the same as an excitatory response. (2)

Ophthalmologist. A person who has specialized in the medical treatment of the eye by completing four or more years of training after receiving the M. D. degree. (17)

Ophthalmoscope. A device that enables an examiner to see the retina and the retinal circulation inside the eye. (17)

Ophthalmoscopy. The use of an ophthalmoscope to visualize the retina and the retinal circulation. (17)

Opponent cell. A neuron that has an excitatory response to wavelengths in one part of the spectrum and an inhibitory response to wavelengths in the other part of the spectrum (see Color opponent cell). (5)

Opponent-process theory of color vision. A theory stating that our perception of color is determined by the activity of two opponent mechanisms: a blue-yellow mechanism and a red-green mechanism. The responses to the two colors in each mechanism oppose each other, one being an excitatory response and the other an inhibitory response. (This theory also includes a black-white mechanism, which is concerned with the perception of brightness.) (5)

Opsin. The protein part of the visual pigment molecule, to which the light-sensitive retinal molecule is attached. (2)

Optacon. A portable system that transforms printed letters or graphic images into patterns of vibration that can be sensed through the fingers. (7)

Optic array. The way the light of the environment is structured by the presence of objects, surfaces, and textures. (2)

Optic disk. The disk-shaped area at the back of the eye where the optic nerve leaves the eye. (2)

Optic flow pattern. The flow pattern that occurs when an observer moves relative to the environment. Forward movement causes an expanding optic flow pattern, whereas backward movement causes a contracting optic flow pattern. The term optic flow field is used by some researchers to refer to this flow pattern. (10)

Optician. A person who is trained to fit glasses and, in some cases, contact lenses. (17)

Optic nerve. Bundle of nerve fibers that carry impulses from the retina to the lateral geniculate nucleus and other structures. Each optic nerve contains about 1 million ganglion cell fibers. (2)

Optometrist. A person who has received the doctor of optometry (O. D.) degree by completing four years of postgraduate study in optometry school. (17)

Orbitofrontal cortex. An area in the frontal lobe, near the eyes, that receives signals originating in the olfactory receptors. (15)

Organization, laws of. See Perceptual organization, laws of. (7)

Organ of Corti. The major structure of the cochlear partition, containing the basilar membrane, the tectorial membrane, and the receptors for hearing. (11)

Orientation. The angle of a stimulus relative to vertical. (3)

Orientation column. A column in the visual cortex that contains neurons with the same orientation preference. (3)

Orientation tuning curve. A function relating the firing rate of a neuron to the orientation of the stimulus. (3)

Ossicles. Three small bones in the middle ear that transmit vibrations from the outer to the inner ear. (11)

Otitis media. An infection of the middle ear. (17)

Otologist. An otorhinolaryngologist whose practice is limited to problems involving the auditory and vestibular systems. (17)

Otorhinolaryngologist. A medical doctor who has specialized in the treatment of diseases and disorders affecting the ear, nose, and throat. More commonly known as an ENT (ear, nose, and throat) specialist. (17)

Otosclerosis. A hereditary condition in which there is a growth of bone in the middle ear. (17)

Otoscope. A device used to see the tympanic membrane. (17)

Outer ear. The pinna and the external auditory meatus. (11)

Outer hair cells. See Hair cells, outer. (11)

Oval window. A small membrane-covered hole in the cochlea that receives vibrations from the stapes. (11)

Overlap. A depth cue. If object A covers object B, then object A is seen as being in front of object B. (8)

Pacinian corpuscle. A receptor with a distinctive elliptical shape associated with RA II mechanoreceptors. It transmits pressure to the nerve fiber inside it only at the beginning or end of a pressure stimulus. (14)

Panoramic neuron. A neuron in the auditory system that fires to sounds originating in any direction and which indicates each location by its temporal pattern of firing. (12)

Panretinal photocoagulation. A procedure in which a laser is used to create many small burns on the retina.

This procedure has been successful in treating the neovascularization associated with diabetic retinopathy. (17)

Papillae. Ridges and valleys on the tongue, some of which contain taste buds. There are four types of papillae: filiform, fungiform, foliate, and circumvallate. (15)

Parietal lobe. A lobe at the top of the cortex that is the site of the cortical receiving area for touch. (2)

Parvocellular (or parvo). Neurons in layers 3, 4, 5, and 6 of the lateral geniculate nucleus. These neurons receive inputs from the P ganglion cells. (3)

Payoffs. A system of rewards and punishments used to influence a subject's motivation in a signal detection experiment. (Appendix)

P-cells. Retinal ganglion cells that have larger cell bodies than the M-cells and which respond with brief bursts of firing. P-cells synapse in the parvocellular area of the LGN. (3)

Penumbra. The fuzzy border at the edge of a shadow. (6)

Perceptual constancy. The perception of a particular stimulus property, such as size, shape, or color, as remaining the same even when the conditions of stimulation are changed. (6)

Perceptual organization, laws of. Series of rules proposed by the Gestalt psychologists that specify how we organize small parts into wholes. (7)

Perceptual processing. Mental or neural processing that occurs during the process of perception. (7)

Perceptual segregation. Perceptual organization in which one object is seen as separate from other objects. (5)

Perimetry. A technique in which a small spot of light is presented to different areas of the visual field, to determine areas in which subjects can and cannot perceive the spot. Used to determine the location and extent of scotomas. (4)

Periodicity. The repetition of a sound wave's pattern. (11)

Periodicity pitch. The effect in which a complex tone's pitch remains the same even if we eliminate the fundamental frequency. This is also called the effect of the missing fundamental. (12)

Peripheral retina. All of the retina except the fovea and a small area surrounding the fovea. (2)

Permeability. A property of a membrane that refers to the ability of molecules to pass through the membrane. If the permeability to a molecule is high, the molecule can easily pass through the membrane. (1)

Phacoemulsification. A technique for removing a cataract by breaking up the lens with ultrasonic vibrations and then sucking the pieces of lens out of the eye through a hollow needle. (17)

Phantom limb. A person's continued perception of a limb, such as an arm or a leg, even though that limb has been amputated. (14)

Phase locking. Auditory neurons' firing in synchrony with the phase of an auditory stimulus. (8)

Phenomenological method. Method of determining the relationship between stimuli and perception in which the experimenter asks the subject to describe what he or she perceives. (1)

Phoneme. The shortest segment of speech that, if changed, would change the meaning of a word. (13)

Phonemic restoration effect. An effect that occurs in speech perception when listeners perceive a phoneme in a word even though the acoustic signal of that phoneme is obscured by another sound, such as white noise or a cough. (13)

Phonetic boundary. The voice onset time when perception changes from one speech category to another in a categorical perception experiment. (13)

Physiological approach to perception. As used in this book, this term refers to explanations of perceptual processes based on the relationship between physiological processes and perception. Related to the physiological approach to perception is the study of "pure" physiology, in which physiological processes of sensory systems are studied but are not directly related to perception. (1)

Physiology-perception relationship. The relationship between physiological activity in the nervous system and perception. (1)

Pictorial cues. Depth cues, such as overlap, relative height, and relative size, that can be depicted in pictures. (8)

Pigment bleaching. The process that begins when a visual pigment molecule absorbs light. The molecule changes shape, and the color of the rod visual pigment changes from red to transparent. Sometimes, early in this process, visual transduction takes place. (2)

Pigment epithelium. A layer of cells that lines the inside of the eyeball under the retina. (2)

Pigment regeneration. The reconstruction of the visual pigment molecule from its bleached state to its original unbleached state. (2)

Pinna. The part of the ear that is visible on the outside of the head. (11)

Pitch. The quality of sound, ranging from low to high, that is most closely associated with the frequency of a tone. (11)

Placebo. A substance that a person believes will relieve symptoms such as pain but that contains no chemicals that actually act on these symptoms. (14)

Place code for frequency. The idea that the frequency of a tone is signaled by the place in the auditory system that is maximally stimulated. (11)

Place of articulation. The place where the airstream is obstructed during the production of a sound. (13)

Ponzo illusion. An illusion of size in which two rectangles of equal length that are drawn between two converging lines appear to be different in length. Also called the railroad track illusion. (9)

Pop-out boundaries. Boundaries between areas in a display that are seen almost immediately because they "pop out." (7)

Positron emission tomography. A technique that can be used in aware human subjects to determine which brain areas are activated by various tasks. (4)

Postsynaptic neuron. A neuron on the receiving side of a synapse that receives neurotransmitter from the presynaptic neuron. (1)

Power function. A mathematical function of the form $P = KS^n$, where P is perceived magnitude, K is a constant, S is the stimulus intensity, and n is an exponent. (1)

Pragnanz, law of. A Gestalt law that is also called the law of good figure or the law of simplicity. It states that every stimulus pattern is seen in such a way that the resulting structure is as simple as possible. (7)

Preattentive stage of processing. An automatic and rapid stage of processing, during which a stimulus is decomposed into small units called primitives. (7)

Precedence effect. The effect that occurs when two identical or very similar sounds reach a listener's ears separated by a time interval of less than about 50–100 msec, and the listener hears the sound that reaches his or her ears first. (12)

Preferential looking (PL) technique. A technique used to measure perception in infants. Two stimuli are presented, and the infant's looking behavior is monitored for the amount of time the infant spends viewing each stimulus. (16)

Presbycusis. A form of sensorineural hearing loss that occurs as a function of age and is usually associated with a decrease in the ability to hear high frequencies. Since this loss also appears to be related to exposure to environmental sounds, it is also called sociocusis. (17)

Presbyopia ("old eye"). The inability of the eye to accommodate due to the hardening of the lens and a weakening of the ciliary muscles. It occurs as people get older. (17)

Presynaptic neuron. A neuron on the sending side of the synapse, which releases neurotransmitter onto the postsynaptic neuron. (1)

Primary cells. Neurons in the IT cortex that respond best to simple stimuli like slits, spots, ellipses, and squares. (See Elaborate cells). (4)

Primary receiving area. The area of the cerebral cortex that first receives most of the signals initiated by a sense's receptors. (1)

Primitives. Basic stimuli that are the "building blocks" of more complex stimuli. For example, Treisman proposed primitives such as color, line tilt, and curvature. Biederman's primitives are volumetric shapes. (7)

Principle of componential recovery. Biederman's principle stating that we can identify an object if we can perceive its individual geons. (7)

Problem of sensory coding. The problem that involves determining how the firing of neurons represents various characteristics of the environment. (See Distributed coding, Specificity coding). (3)

Processing module. A term used in Chapter 3 to refer to hypercolumns, each of which processes information from a small area of the retina. (3)

Propagated response. A response, such as a nerve impulse, that travels all the way down the nerve fiber without decreasing in amplitude. (1)

Proprioception. The sensing of the position of the limbs. (14)

Prosopagnosia. A form of visual agnosia in which the person can't recognize faces. (4)

Protanopia. A form of red-green dichromatism caused by a lack of the long-wavelength cone pigment. (5)

Proximal stimulus. Stimulus that stimulates the receptors. For example, the image on the retina is a proximal stimulus to the retina. (1)

Proximity, law of. Gestalt law: Things that are near to each other appear to be grouped together. Also called the law of nearness. (7)

Psychophysical tuning curve. A function that indicates the intensity of masking tones of different frequencies that cause a low-intensity pure tone to become just barely detectable. (11)

Psychophysics. Methods for quantitatively measuring the relationship between properties of the stimulus and the subject's experience. (1)

Pupil. The small opening at the front of the eye. (2)

Pupillary block. A blockage that constricts the opening between the iris and the lens of the eye, making it difficult for aqueous humor to leave the eye. It is caused by the pushed-up iris characteristic of closed-angle glaucoma. (17)

Pure tone. A tone with pressure changes that can be described by a single sine wave. (11)

Pure-tone audiometry. Measurement of the threshold for hearing as a function of the frequency of a pure tone. (17)

Purkinje shift. The shift from cone spectral sensitivity to rod spectral sensitivity that takes place during dark adaptation. (2)

Radial keratotomy. A surgical procedure in which four to eight cuts are placed radially around the cornea. When successful, this operation decreases the focusing power of the cornea and improves the vision of people with myopia. (17)

Random-dot stereogram. A stereogram in which the stimuli are pictures of random dots. If one section of this pattern is shifted slightly in one direction, the resulting disparity causes the perception of depth when the patterns are viewed in a stereoscope. (8)

Rapidly adapting (RA) fiber. A mechanoreceptive fiber that adapts rapidly to continuous stimulation of the skin. Rapidly adapting fibers are associated with Meissner corpuscle and Pacinian corpuscle receptors. (14)

Rate of angular expansion. See Angular expansion, rate of. (10)

Ratio principle. A principle stating that two areas that reflect different amounts of light will look the same if the ratios of their intensities to the intensities of their surrounds are the same. (6)

Rat-man demonstration. The demonstration in which presentation of a "ratlike" or "manlike" picture influences an observer's perception of a second picture, which can be interpreted either as a rat or as a man. (1)

Raw Primal sketch. In Marr's computational approach to object perception, a rough sketch of the object that basically overlaps the light and dark areas of an image and which consists of an object's primitives and its edges. The raw primal sketch occurs at an early stage of image processing and is not available to consciousness. (7)

Rayleigh scattering. The scattering of sunlight by small particles in the earth's atmosphere, the amount of scatter being inversely proportional to the fourth power of the light's wavelength. This means that short-wavelength light is scattered more than long-wavelength light and is why we see the sky as blue. (8)

Real movement. The physical movement of a stimulus. (10)

Receiver-operating-characteristic (ROC) curve. A graph in which the results of a signal detection experiment are plotted as the proportion of hits versus the proportion of false alarms for a number of different response criteria. (Appendix)

Receptive field. A neuron's receptive field is the area on the receptor surface (the retina, for vision; the skin, for touch) that, when stimulated, affects the firing of that neuron. There are some exceptions, however, such as receptive fields for auditory space perception in the owl. In this case, the receptive fields are locations in space rather than areas on the receptor surface. (2)

Receptor. A sensory receptor is a neuron sensitive to environmental energy that changes this energy into electrical signals in the nervous system. (1)

Receptor sites. Small areas on the postsynaptic neuron that are sensitive to specific neurotransmitters. (1)

Recognition. The ability to place an object in a category that gives it meaning. For example, recognizing a particular red object as a tomato. (1)

Recognition by components (RBC). A mechanism of object perception proposed by Biederman, in which we recognize objects by decomposing them into volumetric primitives called geons. (7)

Recording electrode. A small shaft of metal or glass that, when connected to appropriate electronic equipment, records electrical activity in nerves or nerve fibers. (1)

Reflectance. The percentage of light reflected from a surface. (5)

Reflectance curve. A plot showing the percentage of light reflected from an object versus wavelength. (5)

Refraction. A procedure used to determine the power of the corrective lenses needed to achieve clear vision. (17)

Refractive myopia. See Myopia, refractive. (17)

Refractory period. The time period of about 1/1,000 second that a nerve fiber needs to recover from conducting a nerve impulse. No new nerve impulses can be generated in the fiber until the refractory period is over. (1)

Regional sensitivity effect. In the olfactory system, the fact that different areas on the mucosa are sensitive to some odorants and are not as sensitive to others. (15)

Relative height. A depth cue. Objects that have bases below the horizon appear to be farther away if they are higher in the field of view. If the object's bases are above the horizon, they appear to be farther away if they are lower in the field of view. (8)

Relative size. A cue for depth perception. If two objects are of equal size, the one that is farther away will take up less of the field of view. (8)

Resonance. A mechanism that enhances the intensity of certain frequencies because of the reflection of sound waves in a closed tube. Resonance occurs in the auditory canal. (11)

Resonance theory. Helmholtz's theory of pitch perception, which proposed that the basilar membrane is made up of a series of transverse fibers, each tuned to resonate to a specific frequency. (11)

Resonant frequency. The frequency that is most strongly enhanced by resonance. The resonance frequency of a closed tube is determined by the length of the tube. (11)

Response compression. The result when doubling the physical intensity of a stimulus less than doubles the subjective magnitude of the stimulus. (1)

Response criterion. In a signal detection experiment, the subjective magnitude of a stimulus above which the subject will indicate that the stimulus is present. (Appendix)

Response expansion. The result when doubling the physical intensity of a stimulus more than doubles the subjective magnitude of the stimulus. (1)

Resting potential. The difference in charge between the inside and the outside of the nerve fiber when the fiber is not conducting electrical signals. (1)

Retina. A complex network of cells that covers the inside back of the eye. These cells include the receptors, which generate an electrical signal in response to light, as well as the horizontal, bipolar, amacrine, and ganglion cells. (2)

Retinal. The light-sensitive part of the visual pigment molecule. (2)

Retinal size. The size of an image on the retina. (8)

Retinitis pigmentosa. A retinal disease that causes a gradual loss of vision. (17)

Retinoscopy exam. Examination with a device called a retinoscope that indicates the power of the corrective lenses needed to achieve normal vision. (17)

Retinotopic map. A map on a structure in the visual system, such as the lateral geniculate nucleus or the cortex, that indicates locations on the structure that correspond to locations on the retina. In retinotopic maps, locations adjacent to each other on the retina are usually represented by locations that are adjacent to each other on the structure. (3)

Reverberation time. The time it takes for a sound produced in an enclosed space to decrease to 1/1000 of its original pressure. (12)

Reversible figure-ground. A figure-ground pattern that perceptually reverses as it is viewed, so that the figure becomes the ground and the ground becomes the figure. (7)

Rod monochromat. A person who has a retina in which the only functioning receptors are rods. (2)

Rod spectral sensitivity curve. A graph showing the rod system's sensitivity to light as a function of the light's wavelength. (2)

Rod-cone break. The point on the dark adaptation curve at which vision shifts from cone vision to rod vision. (2)

Rods. Rod-shaped receptors in the retina that are primarily responsible for vision at low levels of illumination. The rod system is extremely sensitive in the dark but cannot resolve fine details. (2)

Round window. A small membrane-covered opening at the end of the scala tympani in the cochlea of the ear. (11)

Ruffini cylinder. A receptor structure in the skin associated with slowly adapting fibers, large receptive fields, and the perception of "buzzing," stretching of the skin, and limb movements. (14)

Ruffini ending. A receptor in the skin, associated with SA II mechanoreceptors. (14)

Running spectral display. A way of representing the speech stimulus in which a number of short-term spectra are arranged to show how the frequencies in the speech stimulus change as time progresses. (13)

Saturation (color). The relative amount of whiteness in a chromatic color. The less whiteness a color contains, the more saturated it is. (5)

Saturation (nerve firing). The intensity at which a nerve fiber reaches its maximum response. Once the fiber is saturated, further increases in intensity cause no further increase in the fiber's firing rate. (11)

Scale illusion. An illusion that occurs when successive notes of a scale are presented alternately to the left and the right ears. Even though each ear receives notes that jump up and down in frequency, smoothly ascending or descending scales are heard in each ear. (12)

Scotoma. An area of blindness in the visual field, usually caused by retinal or cortical damage. (4)

Secondary auditory cortex. Auditory area A2, located next to the primary auditory area (A1). (11)

Secondary cataract. See Cataract, secondary.

Secondary somatosensory receiving area (S II). The area in the parietal lobe next to the primary somatosensory area (S I) that processes neural signals related to touch, temperature, and pain. (14)

Selective adaptation. A procedure in which a person or animal is selectively exposed to one stimulus and then the effect of this exposure is assessed by testing with a wide range of stimuli. Exposing a person to vertical bars and then testing a person's sensitivity to bars of all orientations is an example of selective adaptation to orientation. Selective adaptation can also be carried out for spatial frequency, wavelength, and speech sounds. (3)

Selective rearing. A technique in which animals are reared in special environments, usually during their sensitive period. (16)

Selective reflection. When an object reflects some wavelengths of the spectrum more than others. (5)

Semantics. A system that specifies whether it is appropriate to use a word in a sentence based on its meaning. (13)

Senile cataract. See Cataract, senile. (17)

Sensitive period. A period of time, usually early in an organism's life, during which changes in the environment have a large effect on the organism's physiology or behavior. (8)

Sensitivity. 1.0 divided by the threshold for detecting a stimulus. Thus, lower thresholds correspond to higher sensitivities. (2)

Sensory coding, problem of. See Problem of sensory coding.

Sensory movement signal. The electrical signal generated by the movement of an image across the retina. This is one of the signals that plays a role in the corollary discharge theory of movement perception. (10)

Sensory substitution. Substituting one sense for the function served by another, as when touch is substituted for vision. (7)

Shadowing. Subjects' repetition aloud of what they hear as they are hearing it. (13)

Shape constancy. The constancy of the perception of an object's shape that is maintained even when the object is viewed from different angles. (6)

Shortest-path constraint. The principle that apparent movement occurs along the shortest path between two stimuli that cause apparent movement when flashed on and off with the appropriate timing. (10)

Short-term spectrum. A plot that indicates the frequencies in a sound stimulus during a short period, usually at the beginning of the stimulus. (13)

Short-wavelength pigment. The cone visual pigment that absorbs maximally at short wavelengths. In the human, this pigment absorbs maximally at about 419 nm. (2)

Signal. The stimulus presented to a subject. A concept in signal detection theory. (Appendix)

Signal detection theory (SDT). A theory stating that the detection of a stimulus depends both on the subject's sensitivity to the stimulus and on the subject's response criterion. (Appendix)

Similarity, law of. A Gestalt law stating that similar things appear to be grouped together. (7)

Simple cortical cell. A neuron in the visual cortex that responds best to bars of a particular orientation. (3)

Simplicity, law of. See Good figure, law of. (7)

Simultaneous contrast. The effect that occurs when surrounding one color with another changes the appearance of the surrounded color. (2)

Simultaneous lightness contrast. Effect that occurs when one area is surrounded by another area that is either lighter or darker. The surrounding area changes the lightness of the area that is surrounded. (2)

Sine-wave grating. A grating stimulus with a sine-wave intensity distribution. (3)

Single dissociation. See Dissociation, single. (4)

Size constancy. The constancy of the perception of the size of a stimulus that is maintained even when the object is viewed from different distances. (6, 9)

Size cues. Cues such as familiar size and relative size that help us determine the sizes of objects. (9)

Size-distance scaling. A hypothesized mechanism that helps maintain size constancy by taking an object's distance into account. (9)

Size-invariant neurons. Neurons that respond equally well to stimuli of various sizes. (4)

Slit lamp examination. An examination that checks the condition of the cornea and lens. (17)

Slowly adapting (SA) fiber. A mechanoreceptive fiber in the skin that adapts slowly to continuous stimulation of the skin. Slowly adapting fibers are associated with Merkel receptors and Ruffini cylinders. (14)

Small-diameter fiber (S-fiber). According to gate control theory, activity in S-fibers opens the gate control mechanism and therefore increases the perception of pain. (14)

Somatosensory receiving area (SI). An area in the parietal lobe of the cortex that receives inputs from the skin and the viscera that are associated with somatic senses such as touch, temperature, and pain (see Secondary somatosensory receiving area). (14)

Somatosensory system. The system that includes the cutaneous senses (senses involving the skin), proprioception (the sense of position of the limbs), and kinesthesis (sense of movement of the limbs). (14)

Somatotopic map. A map created on the somatosensory area of the brain by the arrangement of neurons so that neurons that respond to adjacent parts of the body are found next to each other on the brain. (3)

Sone. Unit of loudness. One sone is the loudness of a 1,000-Hz tone at 40dB. (12)

Sound. The experience of hearing. Sound also refers to the physical stimulus for hearing. To avoid confusion, the term acoustic stimulus or sound stimulus can be used to denote the physical sound stimulus. (11)

Sound pressure level (SPL). A designation used to indicate that the reference pressure used for calculating a tone's decibel rating is set at 2×10^{-5} micropascals, near the threshold in the most sensitive frequency range for hearing. (11)

Sound spectrogram. A plot showing the pattern of intensities and frequencies of a speech stimulus. (13)

Sound source. Anything that creates sound stimuli. (12)

Sound stimulus. See Acoustic stimulus. (11)

Sound waves. Pressure changes in a medium. Most of the sounds we hear are due to pressure changes in the air. (11)

Spatial event plots. Plots showing the pattern of response generated by a neuron to a touch stimulus. (14)

Spatial frequency. For a grating stimulus, spatial frequency refers to the frequency with which the grating repeats itself per degree of visual angle. For more natural stimuli, high spatial frequencies are associated with fine details, and low spatial frequencies are associated with grosser features. (3)

Spatial frequency channels. Hypothesized channels in the visual system that are sensitive to narrow ranges of spatial frequencies. (3)

Spatial summation. The summation, or accumulation, of the effect of stimulation over a large area. (2)

Specific hunger. A genetically programmed taste preference that helps organisms seek out food that meets specific nutritional needs. (15)

Specificity coding. Type of neural code in which different perceptions are signaled by activity in specific neurons (see Distributed coding). (3)

Spectral sensitivity. The sensitivity of visual receptors to different parts of the visible spectrum (see Spectral sensitivity curve). (2)

Spectral sensitivity curve. The function relating a subject's sensitivity to light to the wavelength of the light. (2)

Spectrophotometer. A device that measures the amount of light absorbed by a substance as a function of wavelength. For vision, spectrophotometers are used to measure the amount of light absorbed by visual pigments. (2)

Spinothalamic pathway. One of the nerve pathways in the spinal cord that conducts nerve impulses from the skin to the somatosensory area of the thalamus. (14)

Spontaneous activity. Nerve firing that occurs in the absence of environmental stimulation. (1)

S-potential. A slow electrical response recorded from neurons in the fish retina that have opponent properties (see Opponent cell). (5)

Square-wave grating. A grating stimulus with a square-wave intensity distribution. (3)

Stapes. The last of the three ossicles in the middle ear. It receives vibrations from the incus and transmits these vibrations to the oval window of the inner ear. (11)

Stereoacuity. The ability to resolve small differences in disparity. (16)

Stereopsis. The impression of depth that results from differences in the images on the retinas of the two eyes. (8)

Stereoscope. A device that presents pictures to the left and the right eyes so that the binocular disparity a person would experience when viewing an actual scene is duplicated. The result is a convincing illusion of depth. (8)

Stevens's power law. A law concerning the relationship between the physical intensity of a stimulus and the perception of the subjective magnitude of the stimulus. The law states that $P = KS^n$, where P is perceived magnitude, K is a constant, S is the stimulus intensity, and n is an exponent. (1)

Stimulation-produced analgesia (SPA). Brain stimulation that eliminates or strongly decreases the perception of pain. (14)

Stimulus deprivation amblyopia. Amblyopia due to early closure of one eye. (8)

Stimulus-perception relationship. The relationship between physical stimuli in the world and what an organism perceives. (1)

Stimulus-physiology relationship. The relationship between the stimulus and the physiological response to the stimulus. (1)

Strabismus. A condition in which an imbalance in the eye muscles upsets the coordination between the two eyes. (8)

Stress-induced analgesia. Analgesia that occurs when an organism experiences a stressful situation. (14)

Striate cortex. The visual receiving area of the cortex, located in the occipital lobe. (2)

Stroboscopic movement. See Apparent movement. (10)

Structuralism. The approach to psychology, prominent in the late 19th and early 20th centuries, that postulated that perceptions result from the summation of many elementary sensations. (7)

Subjective contour. See Illusory contour. (7)

Substantia gelatinosa. A nucleus in the spinal cord that, according to gate control theory, receives inputs from S-fibers and L-fibers and sends inhibition to the T-cell. (14)

Subtractive color mixture. See Color mixture, subtractive. (5)

Superior colliculus. A structure at the base of the brain that is important in controlling eye movements. A small proportion of the nerve fibers in the optic nerve synapse in the superior colliculus. (2)

Superior olivary nucleus. A nucleus along the auditory pathway from the cochlea to the auditory cortex. The superior olivary nucleus receives inputs from the cochlear nucleus. (11)

Synapse. A small space between the end of one neuron and the cell body of another neuron. (1)

Synesthesia. Occurs when stimulation of one modality leads to perceptual experience in another modality, as when hearing sounds results in the perception of colors. (11)

Tadoma. A method of tactile speech perception in which a person identifies speech sounds by feeling the vibrations of a speaker's vocal cords.

Taste-blind. A person who is taste-blind cannot taste phenylthiocarbamide (PTC) and also tends to be less sensitive to certain other tastes than someone who is not taste-blind. (15)

Taste bud. A structure located within papillae on the tongue that contains the taste cells. (15)

Taste cells. Cells located in taste buds that cause the transduction of chemical to electrical energy when chemicals contact receptor sites or channels located at the tips of these cells. (15)

Taste pore. An opening in the taste bud through which the tips of taste cells protrude. When chemicals enter a taste pore, they stimulate the taste cells and result in transduction. (15)

Tasters. People who can taste the compound phenylthiocarbamide (PTC). (15)

Tectorial membrane. A membrane that stretches the length of the cochlea and is located directly over the hair cells. Vibrations of the cochlear partition cause the tectorial membrane to stimulate the hair cells by rubbing against them. (11)

Temporal lobe. A lobe on the side of the cortex that is the site of the cortical receiving area for hearing. (1)

Texture gradient. The pattern formed by a regularly textured surface that extends away from the observer. The elements in a texture gradient appear smaller as distance from the observer increases. (8)

Texture segregation. The perceptual separation of fields with different textures. (7)

Thalamus. A nucleus in the brain where neurons from all of the senses, except smell, synapse on their way to their cortical receiving areas. (2)

Thermoreceptor. Receptors in the skin that respond to specific temperatures or changes in temperature. (14)

3-D representation. The end result of Marr's computational process; the perception of the three-dimensional stimulus. (7)

Threshold, absolute. The minimum stimulus energy necessary for an observer to detect a stimulus. (1)

Threshold, difference. The minimal detectable difference between two stimuli. (1)

Threshold, relative. The amount of stimulus energy that can just be detected, expressed relative to another threshold. For example, "The amount of energy needed to detect a 500-nm light is twice as high as the amount of energy needed to detect a 540-nm light." (2)

Tilt aftereffect. The result when staring at an adapting field of tilted lines and then looking at vertical lines causes the vertical lines to appear to be tilted in a direction opposite to the tilt of the adapting field. (8)

Timbre. The quality of a tone. Different musical instruments have different timbres, so when we play the same note on different instruments, the notes have the same pitch but sound different. (8)

Timing code of frequency. The sensory code for the frequency of an auditory stimulus in which stimulus frequency is signaled by the timing of nerve impulses in nerve fibers or groups of nerve fibers. (11)

Tinnitus. A condition caused by damage in the inner ear in which a person experiences ringing in the ears. (17)

Tinnitus masker. A unit that generates white noise to mask the ringing in the ears associated with tinnitus. (17)

Tone chroma. The perceptual similarity of notes separated by one or more octaves. (11)

Tone height. The increase in pitch that occurs as frequency is increased. (11)

Tonometer. A device for measuring the eye's intraocular pressure. (17)

Tonometry. An examination that determines the pressure inside the eye. (17)

Tonotopic map. The frequency map that is formed on an auditory structure when neurons with the same characteristic frequency are grouped together and neurons with nearby characteristic frequencies are found near each other. (11)

Top-down processing. Processing that starts with the analysis of high-level information, such as the context in which a stimulus is seen. (1)

Transduction. In the senses, the transformation of environmental energy into electrical energy. For example, the retinal receptors transduce light energy into electrical energy. (2)

Transmission cell (T-cell). According to gate control theory, the cell that receives input from the L- and S-fibers. Activity in the T-cell determines the perception of pain. (14)

Traumatic cataract. See Cataract, traumatic.

Traveling wave. In the auditory system, vibration of the basilar membrane in which the peak of the vibration travels from the base of the membrane to its apex. (11)

Trichromat. A person with normal color vision. Trichromats can match any wavelength in the spectrum by mixing three other wavelengths in various proportions. (5)

Trichromatic theory of color vision. A theory postulating that our perception of color is determined by the ratio of activity in three cone receptor mechanisms with different spectral sensitivities. (5)

Tritanopia. A form of dichromatism thought to be caused by a lack of the short-wavelength cone pigment. (5)

Tungsten light. Light produced by a tungsten filament. Tungsten light has a wavelength distribution that has relatively more intensity at long wavelengths than at short wavelengths. (5)

Tuning curve, frequency. See Frequency tuning curve. (11)

Tuning curve, orientation. See Orientation tuning curve. (3)

Tunnel vision. Vision that results when there is little peripheral vision. (17)

2½-D sketch. The second stage of Marr's computational process. This stage is the result of processing the primitives. The resulting 2½-D sketch is then transformed into the 3-D representation. (7)

Two-color threshold method. A method used by Stiles in which the thresholds for different wavelengths are measured with a test flash that is superimposed on an adapting field. (2)

2-Deoxyglucose technique. An anatomical technique that makes it possible to see which neurons in a structure have been activated. For example, this technique was used to visualize the orientation columns in the visual cortex. (3)

Two-point threshold. The smallest separation between two points on the skin that is perceived as two points; a measure of acuity on the skin. (14)

Tympanic membrane (eardrum). A membrane at the end of the auditory canal that vibrates in response to vibrations of the air and transmits these vibrations to the ossicles in the middle ear. (11)

Tympanometer. A device for measuring how well the tympanic membrane and the middle-ear bones respond to sound vibrations. (17)

Tympanometry. Procedure for measuring how well the tympanic membrane and middle ear bones are responding to sound vibrations. (17)

Uncrossed disparity. Binocular disparity that occurs when objects are located beyond the horopter (see Crossed disparity). (8)

Unilateral dichromat. A person who has dichromatic vision in one eye and trichromatic vision in the other eye. (5)

Vagus nerve. A nerve that conducts signals from taste receptors in the mouth and larynx. (15)

Ventral pathway. Pathway that conducts signals from the striate cortex to the temporal lobe. This has also been called the "what" pathway. (2, 4)

Ventral posterior nucleus. A nucleus in the thalamus that receives inputs from the somatosensory system, primarily from the spinothalamic and lemniscal pathways. (14)

Ventriloquism effect. See Visual capture. (8)

Veridical perception. Perception that matches the actual physical situation. (9)

Video microscopy. A technique that has been used to take pictures of papillae and taste buds on the tongue. (15)

View invariant. Shapes that have properties that don't change when viewed from different angles. The geons in the RBC theory of object perception are view invariant. (7)

View-invariant cells. Neurons that respond equally well to different views of an object. View-invariant cells for faces have been found in IT cortex.(See View-specific cells). (4)

View-specific cells. Neurons that respond best to specific views of a stimulus. View-specific cells that respond best to specific views of faces have been found in IT cortex. (See View-invariant cells). (4)

Visible light. Band of electromagnetic energy that can be perceived with the visual system. For humans, visible light has wavelengths between 400 and 700 nanometers. (2)

Visual acuity. The ability to resolve small details. (2)

Visual angle. The angle between two lines that extend from the observer's eye, one line extending to one end of an object and the second to the other end of the object. An object's visual angle is always determined relative to an observer; therefore, an object's visual angle changes as the distance between the object and the observer changes. (7)

Visual capture. When sound is heard coming from its seen location, even though it is actually originating somewhere else. Also called the ventriloquism effect. (8)

Visual evoked potential (VEP). An electrical response to visual stimulation recorded by the placement of disk electrodes on the back of the head. This potential reflects the activity of a large population of neurons in the visual cortex. (16)

Visual feedback model. Explanation for the development of emmetropia which states that the growth of the eyeball that occurs during this development is controlled by errors in the focusing of light on the retina. Thus, if there is an error in focusing, the eye grows to eliminate this error. (16)

Visual from agnosia. A condition in which a person can see clearly but has difficulty recognizing what he or she sees. This condition, which is often caused by brain injuries, makes it difficult for people to synthesize parts of an object into an integrated whole. (7)

Visual perimetry. A procedure for testing vision that tests a person's ability to detect small spot stimuli presented at various locations in the person's visual field. (17)

Visual pigment. A light-sensitive molecule contained in the rod and cone outer segments. The reaction of this molecule to light results in the generation of an electrical response in the receptors. (2)

Visual receiving area (or visual cortex). The area in the occipital lobe, also called the striate cortex, that receives inputs from the lateral geniculate nucleus. (2)

Visual search. A procedure in which a subject's task is to find a particular element in a display that contains a number of elements. (7)

Visual transduction. Transformation of light energy into electrical energy that occurs in the rod and cone receptors in the retina. (2)

Vitrectomy. A procedure in which a needle placed inside the eye removes vitreous humor and replaces it with a salt solution. This procedure is used if the vitreous humor is filled with blood, usually because of neovascularization. (17)

Vitreous humor. The jellylike substance that fills the eyeball. (17)

Voice onset time. In speech production, the time delay between the beginning of a sound and the beginning of the vibration of the vocal chords. (13)

Volley principle. Wever's idea that groups of nerve fibers fire in volleys, some fibers firing while others are refractory. In this way, groups of fibers can effect high rates of nerve firing. (11)

Volumetric primitives. Primitives proposed in the recognition-by-components theory of recognition that are three-dimensional shapes that roughly correspond to an object's parts. (7)

Warm fiber. A nerve fiber that responds to increases in temperature or to steady high temperatures. (14)

Waterfall illusion. An aftereffect of movement that occurs after viewing a stimulus moving in one direction, such as a waterfall. Viewing the waterfall creates other objects to appear to move in the opposite direction. (10)

Waveform. A waveform describes functions in which stimulus intensity or amplitude is plotted versus time or space. For example, we can describe the waveform of a pure tone stimulus (a plot of pressure change vs. time) as a sine wave, or we can refer to the waveform of a grating stimulus (a plot of light intensity vs. distance) as a sine wave or a square wave. (3)

Wavelength. For light energy, the distance between one peak of a light wave and the next peak. (2)

Wavelength distribution. The amount of energy in a light at each of the wavelengths in the spectrum. (5)

Weber's law. A law stating that the just noticeable difference (JND) equals a constant (K), called the Weber fraction, times the size of the stimulus (S). This law is usually expressed in the form $K = JND/S$. (1)

Wernike's aphasia. An inability to comprehend words or arrange sounds into coherent speech. (13)

White light. Light that contains an equal intensity of each of the visible wavelengths. (5)

White noise. An auditory stimulus that creates an band of frequencies with equal sound pressure at each frequency. (11)

Young-Helmholtz theory of color vision. See Trichromatic theory of color vision. (5)

REFERENCES

Abeles, M., & Goldstein, M. H. (1970). Functional architecture in cat primary auditory cortex: Columnar organization and organization according to depth. *Journal of Neurophysiology*, 33, 172–187.

Abramov, I., & Gordon, J. (1994). Color appearance: On seeing red, or yellow, or green, or blue. *Annual Review of Psychology*, 45, 451–485.

Abramov, I., Gordon, J., Hendrickson, A., Hainline, L., Dobson, V., & LaBossiere, E. (1982). The retina of the newborn human infant. *Science*, 217, 265–267.

Ache, B. W. (1991). Phylogeny of smell and taste. In T. V. Getchell, R. L. Doty, L. M. Bartoshuk, & J. B. Snow (Eds.), *Smell and taste in health and disease* (pp. 3–18). New York: Raven Press.

Ackerman, D. (1990). *A natural history of the senses.* New York: Vintage Books.

Ackerman, D. (1995). *Mystery of the senses: Taste.* Boston: WGBH-TV and Washington, DC: WETA-TV.

Adelson, E. H. (1993). Perceptual organization and the judgment of brightness. *Science*, 262, 2042–2044.

Adrian, E. D. (1928). *The basis of sensation.* New York: Norton.

Adrian, E. D. (1932). *The mechanism of nervous action.* Philadelphia: University of Pennsylvania Press.

Ahissar, M., Ahissar, E., Bergman, H., & Vaadia, E. (1992). Encoding of sound-source location and movement: Activity of single neurons and interactions between adjacent neurons in the monkey auditory cortex. *Journal of Neurophysiology*, 67, 203–215.

Aitkin, L. (1990). *The auditory cortex.* London: Chapman & Hall.

Albrecht, D. G., DeValois, R. L., & Thorell, L. G. (1980). Visual cortical neurons: Are bars or gratings the optimal stimuli? *Science*, 207, 88–90.

Ali, M. A., & Klyne, M. A. (1985). *Vision in vertebrates.* New York: Plenum Press.

Allison, T., Ginter, H., McCarthy, G., Nobre, A., Puce, A., Luby, M., & Spencer, D. D. (1994). Face recognition in human extrastriate cortex. *Journal of Neurophysiology*, 71, 821–825.

Alpern, M., Kitahara, K., & Krantz, D. H. (1983). Perception of color in unilateral tritanopia. *Journal of Physiology*, 335, 683–697.

American Foundation for the Blind. (1969). *Understanding braille.* [Pamphlet]. New York.

Ammons, C. H., Worchel, P., & Dallenbach, K. M. (1953). Facial vision: The perception of obstacles out of doors by blindfolded and blindfolded-deafened subjects. *American Journal of Psychology*, 66, 519–553.

Arnheim, R. (1974). *Art and visual perception* (2nd ed.). Berkeley: University of California Press.

Ashmead, D. H., Davis, D. L., Whalen, T., & Odom, R. (1991). Sound localization and sensitivity to interaural time differences in human infants. *Child Development*, 62, 1211–1226.

Ashmead, D. H., DeFord, L., & Odom, R. D. (1990). Perception of relative distances of nearby sound sources. *Perception and Psychophysics*, 47, 326–331.

Aslin, R. N. (1977). Development of binocular fixation in human infants. *Journal of Experimental Child Psychology*, 23, 133–150.

Aslin, R. N. (1981a). Development of smooth pursuit in infants. In D. F. Fisher, R. A. Monty, & J. W. Senders (Eds.), *Eye movements: Cognition and visual perception*. Hillsdale, NJ: Erlbaum.

Aslin, R. N. (1981b). Experiential influences and sensitive periods of perceptual development: A unified model. In R. N. Aslin, J. Alberts, & M. J. Petersen (Eds.), *Development of perception* (Vol. 2, pp. 45–93). New York: Academic Press.

Aslin, R. N., & Banks, M. S. (1978). Early experience in humans: Evidence for a critical period in the development of binocular vision. In S. Sten-Schneider, H. Liebowitz, H. Pick, & H. Stevenson (Eds.), *Psychology: From basic research to practice*. New York: Plenum Press.

Aubert, H. (1886). Die Bewegungsempfindung. *Archiv für die gesamte Physiologie des Menschen und der Tiere*, 39, 347–370.

Au Eong, K. G., Tay, T. H., & Lim, M. K. (1993). Race, culture and myopia in 110,236 young Singaporean males. *Singapore Medical Journal*, 34, 29–32.

Awaya, S., Miyake, Y., Imayuni, Y., Shiose, Y., Kanda, T., & Komuro, K. (1973). Amblyopia in man, suggestive of stimulus deprivation amblyopia. *Japanese Journal of Ophthalmology*, 17, 69–82.

Axel, R. (1995, April). The molecular logic of smell. *Scientific American* 273, 154–159.

Azzopardi, P., & Cowey, A. (1993). Preferential representation of the fovea in the primary visual cortex. *Nature*, 361, 719–721.

Bach-y-Rita, P. (1972). *Brain mechanisms in sensory substitution*. New York: Academic Press.

Bach-y-Rita, P., Collins, C. C., Saunders, F., White, B., & Scadden, L. (1969). Vision substitution by tactile image projection. *Nature*, 221, 963–964.

Bach-y-Rita, P., Collins, C. C., Scadden, C., Holmlund, G. W., & Hart, B. K. (1970). Display techniques in a tactile vision substitution system. *Medical and Biological Illustration*, 20, 6–12.

Backus, J. (1977). *The acoustical foundations of music* (2nd ed.). New York: Norton.

Baird, J. C., Wagner, M., & Fuld, K. (1990). A simple but powerful theory of the moon illusion. *Journal of Experimental Psychology: Human Perception and Performance*, 16, 675–677.

Balogh, R. D., & Porter, R. H. (1986). Olfactory preferences resulting from mere exposure in human neonates. *Infant Behavior and Development*, 9, 395–401.

Banks, M. S. (1982). The development of spatial and temporal contrast sensitivity. *Current Eye Research*, 2, 191–198.

Banks, M. S. (1992). Optics, receptors, and spatial vision in human infants. In L. A. Werner & E. W. Rubel (Eds.), *Developmental psychoacoustics*. Washington, DC: American Psychological Association.

Banks, M. S., Aslin, R. N., & Letson, R. D. (1975). Sensitive period for the development of human binocular vision. *Science*, 190, 675–677.

Banks, M. S., & Bennett, P. J. (1988). Optical and photoreceptor immaturities limit the spatial and chromatic vision of human neonates. *Journal of the Optical Society of America*, A5, 2059–2079.

Banks, M. S., & Salapatek, P. (1978). Acuity and contrast sensitivity in 1-, 2-, and 3-month-old human infants. *Investigative Ophthalmology and Visual Science*, 17, 361–365.

Banks, M. S., & Salapatek, P. (1981). Infant pattern vision: A new approach based on the contrast sensitivity function. *Journal of Experimental Child Psychology*, 31, 1–45.

Barinaga, M. (1994). Neurons tap out a code that may help locate sounds. *Science*, 264, 775.

Barlow, H. B. (1972). Single units and sensation: A neuron doctrine for perceptual psychology? *Perception*, 1, 371–394.

Barlow, H. B., Blakemore, C., & Pettigrew, J. D. (1967). The neural mechanism of binocular depth discrimination. *Journal of Physiology, 193,* 327–342.

Barlow, H. B., & Mollon, J. D. (Eds.). (1982). *The senses.* Cambridge, England: University of Cambridge Press.

Barrow, H. G., & Tannenbaum, J. M. (1986). Computational approaches to vision. In K. R. Boff, L. Kaufman, & J. P. Thomas (Eds.), *Handbook of perception and human performance* (Chapter 35). New York: Wiley.

Bartoshuk, L. M. (1971). The chemical senses: I. Taste. In J. W. Kling & L. A. Riggs (Eds.), *Experimental psychology* (3rd ed.). New York: Holt, Rinehart and Winston.

Bartoshuk, L. M. (1979). Bitter taste of saccharin: Related to the genetic ability to taste the bitter substance propylthioural (PROP). *Science, 205,* 934–935.

Bartoshuk, L. M. (1980, September). Separate worlds of taste. *Psychology Today, 243,* 48–56.

Bartoshuk, L. M., & Beauchamp, G. K. (1994). Chemical senses. *Annual Review of Psychology, 45,* 419–449.

Bartoshuk, L. M., Cain, W. S., & Pfaffmann, C. (1985). Taste and olfaction. In G. A. Kimble & K. Schlesinger (Eds.), *Topics in the history of psychology* (Vol. 1, pp. 221–260). Hillsdale, NJ: Erlbaum.

Battaglini, P. P., Galletti, C., & Fattori, P. (1996). Cortical mechanisms for visual perception of object motion and position in space. *Behavioural Brain Research, 76,* 143–154.

Batteau, D. W. (1967). The role of the pinna in human localization. *Proceedings of the Royal Society of London, 168B,* 158–180.

Bauer, R. M. (1984). Autonomic recognition of names and faces in prosopagnosia: A neuropsychological application of the guilty knowledge test. *Neuropsychologia, 22,* 457–469.

Baylis, G. C., & Driver, J. (1995). One-sided edge assignment in vision: 1. Figure-ground segmentation and attention to objects. *Current Directions in Psychological Science, 4,* 140–146.

Baylor, D. (1992). Transduction in retinal photoreceptor cells. In P. Corey & S. D. Roper (Eds.), *Sensory transduction* (pp. 151–174). New York: Rockefeller University Press.

Beauchamp, G. K. (1987). The human preference for excess salt. *American Scientist, 75,* 27–33.

Beauchamp, G. K., Bertino, M., & Engelman, K. (1991). Human salt appetite. In M. I. Friedman, M. G. Tordoff, & M. R. Kare (Eds.), *Chemical senses* (Vol. 4, pp. 85–108). New York: Marcel Dekker.

Beauchamp, G. K., Cowart, B. J., & Moran, M. (1986). Developmental changes in salt acceptability in human infants. *Developmental Psychobiology, 19,* 17–25.

Beauchamp, G. K., Cowart, B. J., & Schmidt, H. J. (1991). Development of chemosensory sensitivity and preference. In T. V. Getchell, R. L. Doty, L. M. Bartoshuk, & J. B. Snow (Eds.), *Smell and taste in health and disease* (pp. 405–416). New York: Raven Press.

Beauchamp, G. K., & Maller, O. (1977). The development of flavor preferences in humans: A review. In M. R. Kare & O. Maller (Eds.), *Chemical senses and nutrition* (pp. 291–311). New York: Academic Press.

Beck, J. (1982). Textural segmentation. In J. Beck (Ed.), *Organization and representation in perception.* Hillsdale, NJ: Erlbaum.

Beck, J. (1993). The British aerospace lecture: Visual processing in texture segregation. In D. Brogan, A. Gale, & K. Carr (Eds.), *Visual search* (Vol. 2, pp. 1–35). London: Taylor & Francis.

Beck, J., Hope, B., & Rosenfeld, A. (Eds.). (1983). *Human and machine vision.* New York: Academic Press.

Beck, P. W., Handwerker, H. O., & Zimmerman, M. (1974). Nervous outflow from the cat's foot during noxious radiant heat stimulation. *Brain Research, 67,* 373–386.

Beecher, H. K. (1972). The placebo effect as a nonspecific force surrounding disease and the treatment of disease. In R. Janzen, W. D. Kerdel, A. Herz, C. Steichele, J. P. Payne, & A. P. Burt (Eds.), *Pain: Basic principles, pharmacology, and therapy.* Stuttgart, West Germany: Georg Thiene.

Beets, M. G. J. (1978). Odor and stimulant structure. In E. C. Carterette & M. P. Friedman (Eds.), *Handbook of perception* (Vol. 6A, pp. 245–255). New York: Academic Press.

Beets, M. G. J. (1982). Odor and stimulant structure. In E. T. Theimer (Ed.), *Fragrance chemistry: The science of the sense of smell* (pp. 77–122). New York: Academic Press.

Békésy, G. von (1960). *Experiments in hearing.* New York: McGraw-Hill.

Berger, K. W. (1964). Some factors in the recognition of timbre. *Journal of the Acoustical Society of America, 36,* 1881–1891.

Berkow, I. (1995, January 5). The sweetest sound of all. *New York Times,* p. B8.

Berlin, B., & Kay, P. (1969). *Basic color terms: Their universality and evolution.* Berkeley: University of California Press.

Bernstein, I. (1978). Learned taste aversions in children receiving chemotherapy. *Science, 200,* 1302–1303.

Bertenthal, B. I., & Bai, D. L. (1989). Infants' sensitivity to optical flow for controlling posture. *Developmental Psychology, 25,* 936–945.

Bertenthal, B. I., Proffitt, D. R., Spetner, N. B., & Thomas, M. A. (1985). The development of infant sensitivity to biomechanical motions. *Child Development, 56,* 531–543.

Biederman, I. (1981). On the semantics of a glance at a scene. In M. Kubovy & J. Pomerantz (Eds.), *Perceptual organization.* Hillsdale, NJ: Erlbaum.

Biederman, I. (1987). Recognition-by-components: A theory of human image understanding. *Psychological Review, 94,* 115–147.

Biederman, I., & Cooper, E. E. (1991). Priming contour-deleted images: Evidence for intermediate representations in visual object recognition. *Cognitive Psychology, 23,* 393–419.

Biederman, I., Cooper, E. E., Hummel, J. E., & Fiser, J. (1993). Geon theory as an account of shape recognition in mind, brain, and machine. In J. Illingworth (Ed.), *Proceedings of the Fourth British Machine Vision Conference* (pp. 175–186). Guildford, Surrey, U.K.: BMVA Press.

Birch, L. L. (1979). Dimensions of preschool children's food preferences. *Journal of Nutrition Education, 11,* 77–80.

Birch, L. L. (1980). Effects of peer model's food choices and eating behaviors on preschooler's food preferences. *Child Development, 51,* 489–496.

Birch, L. L., Zimmerman, S. I., & Hind, H. (1980). The influence of social-affective context on the formation of children's food preferences. *Child Development, 51,* 856–861.

Blake, R., & Hirsch, H. V. B. (1975). Deficits in binocular depth perception in cats after alternating monocular deprivation. *Science, 190,* 1114–1116.

Blake, R., & Wilson, H. R. (1991). Neural models of stereoscopic vision. *Trends in Neuroscience, 14,* 445–452.

Blakemore, C., & Cooper, G. G. (1970). Development of the brain depends on the visual environment. *Nature, 228,* 477–478.

Blakemore, C., & Tobin, E. A. (1972). Lateral inhibition between orientation detectors in the cat's visual cortex. *Experimental Brain Research, 15,* 439–440.

Blank, D. L. (1974). Mechanism underlying the analysis of odorant quality at the level of the olfactory mucosa: II. Receptor selective sensitivity. *Annals of the New York Academy of Sciences, 237,* 91–101.

Bloom, F., Lazerson, A., & Hofstadter, L. (1985). *Brain, mind, and behavior.* New York: Freeman.

Blumstein, S. E., & Stevens, K. N. (1979). Acoustic invariance in speech production: Evidence from measurements of the spectral characteristics of stop consonants. *Journal of the Acoustical Society of America, 66,* 1001–1007.

Bolanowski, S. J., Gescheider, G. A., & Verrillo, R. T. (1994). Hairy skin: Psychophysical channels and their physiological substrates. *Somatosensory and Motor Research, 11,* 279–290.

Bolanowski, S. J., Gescheider, G. A., Verrillo, R. T., & Checkosky, C. M. (1988). Four channels mediate the mechanical aspects of touch. *Journal of the Acoustical Society of America, 84,* 1680–1694.

Bonda, E., Petrides, M., Ostry, D., & Evans, A. (1996). Specific involvement of human parietal systems and the amygdala in the perception of biological motion. *Journal of Neuroscience, 161,* 3737–3744.

Borg, G., Diamant, H., Strom, C., & Zotterman, Y. (1967). The relation between neural and perceptual intensity: A comparative study of neural and psychophysical responses to taste stimuli. *Journal of Physiology, 192,* 13–20.

Bornstein, M. H., Kessen, W., & Weiskopf, S. (1976). Color vision and hue categorization in young human infants. *Journal of Experimental Psychology: Human Perception and Performance,* 2, 115–119.

Boussourd, D., Ungerleider, L. G., & Desimone, R. (1990). Pathways for motion analysis: Cortical connections of the medial superior temporal and fundus of the superior temporal visual areas in the macaque. *Journal of Comparative Neurology,* 296, 462–495.

Bowmaker, J. K., & Dartnall, H. J. A. (1980). Visual pigments of rods and cones in a human retina. *Journal of Physiology,* 298, 501–511.

Boynton, R. M. (1979). *Human color vision.* New York: Holt, Rinehart and Winston.

Boynton, R. M., & Olson, C. X. (1987). Locating basic colors in the OSA space. *Color Research Applications, 12,* 94–105.

Boynton, R. M., & Olson, C. X. (1990). Salience of basic chromatic color terms confirmed by three measures. *Vision Research, 30,* 1311–1317.

Bradley, D. R., & Petry, H. M. (1977). Organizational determinants of subjective contour: The subjective Necker cube. *American Journal of Psychology,* 90, 253–262.

Brainard, D. H., & Wandell, B. A. (1986). Analysis of the retinex theory of color vision. *Journal of the Optical Society of America,* A3, 1651–1661.

Brainard, D. H., & Wandell, B. A. (1992). Asymmetric color matching: How color appearance depends on the illuminant. *Journal of the Optical Society of America,* A9, 1433–1448.

Bregman, A. S. (1990). *Auditory scene analysis.* Cambridge: MIT Press.

Bregman, A. S. (1993). Auditory scene analysis: Hearing in complex environments. In S. McAdams & E. Bigand (Eds.), *Thinking in sound: The cognitive psychology of human audition* (pp. 10–36). Oxford, England: Oxford University Press.

Bregman, A. S., & Campbell, J. (1971). Primary auditory stream segregation and perception of order in rapid sequence of tones. *Journal of Experimental Psychology, 89,* 244–249.

Bregman, A. S., & Pinker, S. (1978). Auditory streaming and the building of timbre. *Canadian Journal of Psychology, 32,* 19–31.

Bregman, A. S., & Rudnicky, A. I. (1975). Auditory segregation: Stream or streams? *Journal of Experimental Psychology: Human Perception and Performance, 1,* 263–267.

Brich, L. L. (1980). Effects of peer model's food choices and eating behaviors on preschooler's food preferences. *Child Development, 51,* 489–496.

Brich, L. L., Zimmerman, S. I., & Hind, H. (1980). The influence of social-affective context on the formation of children's food preferences. *Child Development, 51,* 856–861.

Bridgeman, B., & Stark, L. (1991). Ocular proprioception and efference copy in registering visual direction. *Vision Research, 31,* 1903–1913.

Britten, K. H., Shadlen, M. N., Newsome, W. T., & Movshon, J. A. (1993). Responses of neurons in macaque MT to stochastic motion signals. *Visual Neuroscience, 10,* 1157–1169.

Brosch, M., Bauer, R., & Eckhorn, R. (1997). Stimulus-dependent modulations of correlated high-frequency oscillations in cat visual cortex. *Cerebral Cortex, 7,* 70–76.

Brown, A. A., Dowell, R. C., & Clark, G. M. (1987). Clinical results for postlingually deaf patients implanted with multichannel cochlear prosthetics. *Annals of Otology, Rhinology, and Laryngology,* 96(Suppl. 128), 127–128.

Brown, C. M. (1984). Computer vision and natural constraints. *Science, 224,* 1299–1305.

Brown, C. M., & Nuttall, A. L. (1984). Efferent control of cochlear inner hair cell responses in the guinea-pig. *Journal of Physiology, 354,* 625–646.

Brown, K. T. (1969). A linear *area centralis* extending across the turtle retina and stabilized to the horizon by non-visual cues. *Vision Research, 9*, 1053–1062.

Brown, P. K., & Wald, G. (1964). Visual pigments in single rods and cones of the human retina. *Science, 144*, 45–52.

Brownell, W. E., Bader, C. R., Bertrand, D., & Ribaupierre, Y. D. (1985). Evoked mechanical responses of isolated cochlear outer hair cells. *Science, 227*, 194–196.

Bruce, C., Desimone, R., & Gross, C. G. (1981). Visual properties of neurons in a polysensory area in the superior temporal sulcus of the macaque. *Journal of Neurophysiology, 46*, 369–384.

Brugge, J. F., & Merzenich, M. M. (1973). Responses of neurons in auditory cortex of the macaque monkey to monaural and binaural stimulation. *Journal of Neurophysiology, 36*, 1138–1158.

Brugge, J. F., & Reale, R. A. (1985). Auditory cortex. In A. Peters & E. G. Jones (Eds.), *Cerebral cortex: Vol. 4. Association and auditory cortices* (pp. 229–271). New York: Plenum Press.

Brugge, J. F., Reale, R. A., & Hind, J. E. (1996). The structure of spatial receptive fields of neurons in primary auditory cortex of the cat. *Journal of Neuroscience, 16*, 4420–4437.

Bruno, N., & Cutting, J. E. (1988). Minimodularity and the perception of layout. *Journal of Experimental Psychology: General, 117*, 161–170.

Buchsbaum, G., & Gottschalk, A. (1983). Trichromacy, opponent colours coding and optimum colour information transmission in the retina. *Proceedings of the Royal Society of London, B220*, 89–110.

Buck, L., & Axel, R. (1991). A novel multigene family may encode odorant receptors: A molecular basis for odor recognition. *Cell, 65*, 175–187.

Bugelski, B. R., & Alampay, D. A. (1961). The role of frequency in developing perceptual sets. *Canadian Journal of Psychology, 15*, 205–211.

Bunch, C. C. (1929). Age variations in auditory acuity. *Archives of Otolaryngology, 9*, 625–626.

Burton, A. M., Young, A. W., Bruce, V., Johnston, R. A., & Ellis, A. W. (1991). Understanding covert recognition. *Cognition, 39*, 129–166.

Bushnell, E. W., & Boudreau, J. P. (1993). Motor development and the mind: The potential role of motor abilities as a determinant of aspects of perceptual development. *Child Development, 64*, 1005–1021.

Bushnell, E. W., & Weinberger, N. (1987). Infants' detection of visual-tactual discrepancies: Asymmetries that indicate a directive role of visual information. *Journal of Experimental Psychology: Human Perception and Performance, 13*, 601–608.

Bushnell, I. W. R., Sai, F., & Mullin, J. T. (1989). Neonatal recognition of the mother's face. *British Journal of Developmental Psychology, 7*, 3–15.

Butler, R. A., & Belendiuk, K. (1977). Spectral cues utilized in the localization of sound in the median sagittal plane. *Journal of the Acoustical Society of America, 61*, 1264–1269.

Butler, R. A., & Humanski, R. A. (1992). Localization of sound in the vertical plane with and without high-frequency spectral cues. *Perception and Psychophysics, 51*, 182–186.

Cabanac, M. (1971). Physiological role of pleasure. *Science, 173*, 1103–1107.

Cabanac, M. (1979). Sensory pleasure. *Quarterly Review of Biology, 54*, 1–29.

Cain, W. S. (1977). Differential sensitivity for smell: "Noise" at the nose. *Science, 195*, 796–798.

Cain, W. S. (1979). To know with the nose: Keys to odor identification. *Science, 203*, 467–470.

Cain, W. S. (1980). *Sensory attributes of cigarette smoking* (Branbury Report: 3. A safe cigarette?, pp. 239–249). Cold Spring Harbor, NY: Cold Spring Harbor Laboratory.

Cain, W. S. (1988). Olfaction. In R. A. Atkinson, R. J. Herrnstein, G. Lindzey, & R. D. Luce (Eds.), *Stevens' handbook of experimental psychology: Vol. 1. Perception and motivation* (Rev. ed., pp. 409–459). New York: Wiley.

Cain, W. S., & Murphy, C. L. (1980). Interaction between chemoreceptive modalities of odor and irritation. *Nature, 284*, 255–257.

Campbell, F. W., & Robson, J. G. (1968). Application of Fourier analysis to the visibility of gratings. *Journal of Physiology, 197,* 551–566.

Casagrande, V. A. (1994). A third parallel visual pathway to primate area V1. *Trends in Neuroscience, 17,* 305–310.

Casagrande, V. A., & Norton, T. T. (1991). Lateral geniculate nucleus: A review of its physiology and function. In J. R. Coonley-Dillon (Vol. Ed.) & A. G. Leventhal (Ed.), *Vision and visual dysfunction: The neural basis of visual function* (Vol. 4, pp. 41–84). London: Macmillan.

Cernoch, J. M., & Porter, R. H. (1985). Recognition of maternal axillary odors by infants. *Child Development, 56,* 1593–1598.

Chatterjee, S. H., Freyd, J. J., & Shiffrar, M. (1996). Configural processing in the perception of apparent biological meotion. *Journal of Experimental Psychology: Human Perception and Performance, 22,* 916–929.

Churchland, P. S., & Ramachandran, V. S. (1996). Filling in: Why Dennett is wrong. In K. Atkins (Ed.), *Perception.* Oxford, England: Oxford University Press.

Cinelli, A. R. (1993). Review of "Science of olfaction." *Trends in Neurosciences, 16,* 123–124.

Clark, W. C., & Clark, S. B. (1980). Pain responses in Nepalese porter. *Science, 209,* 410–412.

Clulow, F. W. (1972). *Color: Its principles and their applications.* New York: Morgan & Morgan.

Colby, C. L., Duhamel, J.-R, Goldberg, M. E. (1995). Oculocentric spatial representation in parietal cortex. *Cerebral Cortex, 5,* 470–481.

Cohen, L. B. (1991). Infant attention: An information processing approach. In M. J. Weiss & P. R. Zelazo (Eds.), *Newborn attention: Biological constraints and the influence of experience* (pp. 1–21). Norwood, NJ: ABLEX.

Collett, T. S. (1978). Peering—A locust behavior pattern for obtaining motion parallax information. *Journal of Experimental Biology, 76,* 237–241.

Collett, T. S., & Harkness, L. I. K. (1982). Depth vision in animals. In D. J. Ingle, M. A. Goodale, & R. J. W. Mansfield (Eds.), *Analysis of visual behavior* (pp. 111–176). Cambridge, MA: MIT Press.

Coltheart, M. (1970). The effect of verbal size information upon visual judgments of absolute distance. *Perception and Psychophysics, 9,* 222–223.

Comel, M. (1953). *Fisiologia normale e patologica della cute umana.* Milan: Fratelli Treves Editori.

Cometto-Muniz, J. E., & Cain, W. S. (1984). Temporal integration of pungency. *Chemical Senses, 8,* 315–327.

Conel, J. L. (1939). *The postnatal development of the cerebral cortex* (Vol. 1). Cambridge: Harvard University Press.

Conel, J. L. (1947). *The postnatal development of the cerebral cortex* (Vol. 2). Cambridge: Harvard University Press.

Conel, J. L. (1951). *The postnatal development of the cerebral cortex* (Vol. 3). Cambridge: Harvard University Press.

Connolly, M., & Van Essen, D. (1984). The representation of the visual field in parvocellular and magnocellular layers of the lateral geniculate nucleus in the macaque monkey. *Journal of Comparative Neurology, 226,* 544–565.

Costanzo, R. M., & Gardner, E. B. (1980). A quantitative analysis of responses of direction-sensitive neurons in somatosensory cortex of awake monkeys. *Journal of Neurophysiology, 43,* 1319–1341.

Cowey, A., & Stoerig, P. (1991). The neurobiology of blindsight. *Trends in Neuroscience, 14,* 140–145.

Craton, L. G., & Yonas, A. (1990). The role of motion in infants' perception of occlusion. In J. T. Enns (Ed.), *The development of attention: Research and theory* (pp. 21 –46). London: Elsevier.

Crawford, M. L. J., Smith, E. L., Hawerth, R. S., & von Noorden, G. K. (1984). Stereoblind monkeys have few binocular neurons. *Investigative Ophthalmology and Visual Science, 25,* 779–781.

Crawford, M. L. J., & von Noorden, G. K. (1980). Optically induced concomitant strabismus in monkey. *Investigative Ophthalmology and Visual Science, 19,* 1105–1109.

Crick, F., & Koch, C. (1995). Are we aware of neural activity in primary visual cortex? *Nature, 375,* 121–123.

Culler, E. A., Coakley, J. D., Lowy, K., & Gross, N. (1943). A revised frequency-map of the guinea-pig cochlea. *American Journal of Psychology, 56,* 475–500.

Cutting, J. E. (1986). *Perception with an eye for motion.* Cambridge, MA: MIT Press.

Cutting, J. E., & Vishton, P. M. (1995). Perceiving layout and knowing distances: The integration, relative potency, and contextual use of different information about depth. In W. Epstein & S. Rogers (Eds.), *Handbook of perception and cognition: Perception of space and motion* (pp. 69–117). New York: Academic Press.

Cynader, M., Timney, B. N., & Mitchell, D. E. (1980). Period of susceptibility of kitten visual cortex to the effects of monocular deprivation extends beyond six months of age. *Brain Research, 191,* 545–550.

Dallos, P. (1996). Overview: Cochlear neurobiology. In P. Dallos, A. N. Popper, & R. R. Fay (Eds.), *The cochlea* (pp. 1–43). New York: Springer.

Dalton, J. (1948). Extraordinary facts relating to the vision of colour: With observations. In W. Dennis (Ed.), *Readings in the history of psychology* (pp. 102–111). New York: Appleton-Century-Crofts. (Original work published 1798)

Damasio, A. R., Tranel, D., & Damasio, H. (1990). Face agnosia and the neural substrates of memory. *Annual Review of Neuroscience, 13,* 89–109.

Dartnall, H. J. A., Bowmaker, J. K., & Mollon, J. D. (1983). Human visual pigments: Microspectrophotometric results from the eyes of seven persons. *Proceedings of the Royal Society of London, 220B,* 115–130.

Davis, R. G. (1981). The role of nonolfactory context cues in odor identification. *Perception and Psychophysics, 30,* 83–89.

Day, R. H. (1989). Natural and artificial cues, perceptual compromise and the basis of veridical and illusory perception. In D. Vickers & P. L. Smith (Eds.), *Human information processing: Measures and mechanisms* (pp. 107–129). North Holland, The Netherlands: Elsevier Science.

Day, R. H. (1990). The Bourdon illusion in haptic space. *Perception and Psychophysics, 47,* 400–404.

Dear, S. P., Simmons, J. A., & Fritz, J. (1993). A possible neuronal basis for representation of acoustic scenes in auditory cortex of the big brown bat. *Nature, 364,* 620–623.

DeCasper, A. J., & Fifer, W. P. (1980). Of human bonding: Newborns prefer their mothers' voices. *Science, 208,* 1174–1176.

DeCasper, A. J., & Spence, M. J. (1986). Prenatal maternal speech influences newborn's perception of speech sounds. *Infant Behavior and Development, 9,* 133–150.

DeCasper, A. J., Lecanuet, J.-P., Busnel, M.-C., Deferre-Granier, C., & Maugeais, R. (1994). Fetal reactions to recurrent maternal speech. *Infant Behavior and Development, 17,* 159–164.

DeHaan, E. H. F., Young, A. W., & Newcombe, F. (1987). Face recognition without awareness. *Cognitive Neuropsychology, 4,* 385–415.

Delgutte, B., & Kiang, N. Y. S. (1984a). Speech coding in the auditory nerve: 1. Vowel-like sounds. *Journal of the Acoustical Society of America, 75,* 887–896.

Delgutte, B., & Kiang, N. Y. S. (1984b). Speech coding in the auditory nerve: 3. Voiceless fricative consonants. *Journal of the Acoustical Society of America, 75,* 887–896.

Delk, J. L., & Fillenbaum, S. (1965). Differences in perceived color as a function of characteristic color. *American Journal of Psychology, 78,* 290–293.

DeLucia, P., & Hochberg, J. (1985). Illusions in the real world and in the mind's eye [Abstract]. *Proceedings of the Eastern Psychological Association, 56,* 38.

DeLucia, P., & Hochberg, J. (1986). Real-world geometrical illusions: Theoretical and practical implications [Abstract]. *Proceedings of the Eastern Psychological Association, 57,* 62.

DeLucia, P., & Hochberg, J. (1991). Geometrical illusions in solid objects under ordinary viewing conditions. *Perception and Psychophysics, 50,* 547–554.

Denes, P. B., & Pinson, E. N. (1993). *The speech chain* (2nd ed.). New York: Freeman.

Derrington, A. M., Lennie, P., & Krauskopf, J. (1983). Chromatic response properties of parvocellular neurons in the macaque LGN. In J. D. Mollon & L. T. Sharpe (Eds.), *Colour vision* (pp. 245–251). London: Academic Press.

Desor, J. A., & Beauchamp, G. K. (1974). The human capacity to transmit olfactory information. *Perception and Psychophysics, 13,* 271–275.

Deutsch, D. (1975). Two-channel listening to musical scales. *Journal of the Acoustical Society of America, 57,* 1156–1160.

Deutsch, D. (1996). The perception of auditory patterns. In W. Prinz & B. Bridgeman (Eds.), *Handbook of perception and action* (Vol. 1, pp. 253–296). San Diego, CA: Academic Press.

DeValois, K. K., DeValois, R. L., & Yund, E. W. (1979). Responses of striate cortex cells to gratings and checkerboard patterns. *Journal of Physiology, 291,* 483–505.

DeValois, R. L. (1960). Color vision mechanisms in monkey. *Journal of General Physiology, 43,* 115–128.

DeValois, R. L., & DeValois, K. K. (1993). A multistage color model. *Vision Research, 33,* 1053–1065.

DeValois, R. L., & Jacobs, G. H. (1968). Primate color vision. *Science, 162,* 533–540.

DeValois, R. L., & Jacobs, G. H. (1984). Neural mechanisms of color vision. In J. M. Brookhart & V. B. Mountcastle (Eds.), *Handbook of physiology: 3. The nervous system* (pp. 425–456). Bethesda, MD: American Physiological Society.

deVries, H., & Stuiver, M. (1961). The absolute sensitivity of the human sense of smell. In W. A. Rosenblith (Ed.), *Sensory communication.* Cambridge, MA: MIT Press.

Dobelle, W. H. (1977). Current status of research on providing sight to the blind by electrical stimulation of the brain. *Journal of Visual Impairment and Blindness, 71,* 290–297.

Dobelle, W. H., Mladejovsky, M. G., Evans, J. R., Roberts, T. S., & Girvin, J. P. (1976). "Braille" reading by a blind volunteer by visual cortex stimulation. *Nature, 259,* 111–112.

Dobelle, W. H., Mladejovsky, M. G., & Girvin, J. P. (1974). Artificial vision for the blind: Electrical stimulation of visual cortex offers hope for a functional prosthesis. *Science, 183,* 440–444.

Dobson, V., & Teller, D. (1978). Visual acuity in human infants: Review and comparison of behavioral and electrophysiological studies. *Vision Research, 18,* 1469–1483.

Dodd, G. G., & Squirrell, D. J. (1980). Structure and mechanism in the mammalian olfactory system. *Symposium of the Zoology Society of London, 45,* 35–56.

Dodd, J., & Castellucci, V. F. (1991). Smell and taste: The chemical senses. In E. R. Kandel, J. H. Schwartz, & T. M. Jessell (Eds.), *Principles of neural science* (3rd ed., pp. 512–529). New York: Elsevier.

Dong, W. K., Chudler, E. H., Sugiyama, K., Roberts, V. J., & Hayashi, T. (1994). Somatosensory, multisensory, and task-related neurons in cortical area 7b (PF) of unanesthetized monkeys. *Journal of Neurophysiology, 72,* 542–564.

Doty, R. L. (Ed.). (1976). *Mammalian olfaction, reproductive processes and behavior.* New York: Academic Press.

Doty, R. L. (1991). Olfactory system. In T. V. Getchell, R. L. Doty, L. M. Bartoshuk, & J. B. Snow (Eds.), *Smell and taste in health and disease* (pp. 175–203). New York: Raven Press.

Doty, R. L. (1995). Intranasal trigeminal chemoreception. In R. L. Doty (Ed.), *Handbook of olfaction and gustation* (pp. 821–833). New York: Marcel Dekker.

Doty, R. L., Green, P. A., Ram, C., & Yankell, S. L. (1982). Communication of gender from human breath odors: Relationship to perceived intensity and pleasantness. *Hormones and Behavior, 16,* 13–22.

Dowling, J. E., & Boycott, B. B. (1966). Organization of the primate retina. *Proceedings of the Royal Society of London, 166B,* 80–111.

Dowling, W. J. (1973). The perception of interleaved melodies. *Cognitive Psychology, 5,* 322–337.

Dowling, W. J., & Harwood, D. L. (1986). *Music cognition.* New York: Academic Press.

DuBose, C. N., Cardello, A. V., & Maller, O. (1980). Effects of colorants and flavorants on identification, perceived flavor intensity, and hedonic quality of fruit-flavored beverages and cake. *Journal of Food Science, 45,* 1393–1400.

Duclaux, R., & Kenshalo, D. R. (1980). Response characteristics of cutaneous warm fibers in the monkey. *Journal of Neurophysiology, 43,* 1–15.

Duffy, C. J., & Wurtz, R. H. (1991). Sensitivity of MST neurons to optic flow stimuli: 2. Mechanisms of response selectivity revealed by small-field stimuli. *Journal of Neurophysiology, 65,* 1346–1359.

Durlach, N. I., & Colburn, H. S. (1978). Binaural phenomena. In E. C. Carterette & M. P. Friedman (Eds.), *Handbook of perception* (Vol. 4, pp. 365–466). New York: Academic Press.

Durrant, J., & Lovrinic, J. (1977). *Bases of hearing science.* Baltimore: Williams & Wilkins.

Edin, B. B., Essick, G. K., Truisson, M., & Olsson, K. A. (1995). Receptor encoding of moving tactile stimuli in humans: I. Temporal pattern of discharge of individual low-threshold mechanoreceptors. *Journal of Neuroscience, 15,* 830–847.

Edwards, M. H. (1996). Animal models of myopia. *Acta Ophthalmologica Scandinavica, 74,* 213–219.

Egan, J. P., & Hake, H. W. (1950). On the masking pattern of a simple auditory stimulus. *Journal of the Acoustical Society of America, 22,* 622–630.

Eimas, P. D., & Corbit, J. D. (1973). Selective adaptation of linguistic feature detectors. *Cognitive Psychology, 4,* 99–109.

Eimas, P. D., & Quinn, P. C. (1994). Studies on the formation of perceptually based basic-level categories in young infants. *Child Development, 65,* 903–917.

Eimas, P. D., Siqueland, E. R., Jusczyk, P., & Vigorito, J. (1971). Speech perception in infants. *Science, 171,* 303–306.

Emmert, E. (1881). Grossenverhaltnisse der Nachbilder. *Klinische Monatsblaetter fuer Augenheilkunde, 19,* 443–450.

Engel, A. K., Konig, P., Kreiter, A. K., Schillen, T. B., & Singer, W. (1992). Temporal coding in the visual cortex: New vistas on integration in the nervous system. *Trends in Neurosciences, 15,* 218–226.

Engel, A. K., Konig, P., Kreiter, A. K., & Singer, W. (1991). Interhemispheric synchronization of oscillatory neuronal responses in cat visual cortex. *Science, 252,* 1177–1179.

Engel, A. K., Konig, P., & Singer, W. (1991). Direct physiological evidence for scene segmentation by temporal coding. *Proceedings of the National Academy of Sciences, 88,* 9136–9140.

Engen, T. (1972). Psychophysics. In J. W. Kling & L. A. Riggs (Eds.), *Experimental psychology* (3rd ed., pp. 1–46). New York: Holt, Rinehart and Winston.

Engen, T., & Pfaffmann, C. (1960). Absolute judgments of odor quality. *Journal of Experimental Psychology, 59,* 214–219.

Epstein, W. (1965). Nonrelational judgments of size and distance. *American Journal of Psychology, 78,* 120–123.

Epstein, W. (1977). What are the prospects for a higher-order stimulus theory of perception? *Scandinavian Journal of Psychology, 18,* 164–171.

Erickson, R. (1975). *Sound structure in music.* Berkeley: University of California Press.

Erickson, R. P. (1963). Sensory neural patterns and gustation. In Y. Zotterman (Ed.), *Olfaction and taste* (Vol. 1, pp. 205–213). Oxford, England: Pergamon Press.

Erickson, R. P. (1984). On the neural bases of behavior. *American Scientist, 72,* 233–241.

Essick, G. K., & Edin, B. B. (1995). Receptor encoding of moving tactile stimuli in humans: II. The mean response of individual low-threshold mechanoreceptors to motion across the receptive field. *Journal of Neuroscience, 15,* 848–864.

Evans, E. F. (1978). Place and time coding of frequency in the peripheral auditory system: Some physiological pros and cons. *Audiology, 17,* 369–420.

Fagan, J. F. (1976). Infant's recognition of invariant features of faces. *Child Development, 47,* 627–638.

Fantz, R. L. (1965). Visual perception from birth as shown by pattern selectivity. *Annals of the New York Academy of Sciences, 118,* 793–814.

Fantz, R. L., & Nevis, S. (1967). Pattern preferences and perceptual-cognitive development in early infancy. *Merrill-Palmer Quarterly, 13,* 77–108.

Fantz, R. L., Ordy, J. M., & Udelf, M. S. (1962). Maturation of pattern vision in infants during the first six months. *Journal of Comparative and Physiological Psychology, 55,* 907–917.

Farah, M. J. (1990). *Visual agnosia: Disorders of object recognition and what they tell us about normal vision.* Cambridge, MA: MIT Press.

Farah, M. J. (1992). Is an object an object an object? Cognitive and neuropsychological investigations of domain specificity in visual object recognition. *Current Directions in Psychological Science, 1,* 164–169.

Feddersen, W. E., Sandel, T. T., Teas, D. C., & Jeffress, L. A. (1957). Localization of high frequency tones. *Journal of the Acoustical Society of America, 5,* 82–108.

Felleman, D. J., & Van Essen, D. C. (1991). Distributed hierarchical processing in the primate cerebral cortex. *Cerebral Cortex, 1,* 1–47.

Finger, T. E. (1987). Gustatory nuclei and pathways in the central nervous system. In T. E. Finger & W. L. Silver (Eds.), *Neurobiology of taste and smell* (pp. 331–353). New York: Wiley.

Fiorentini, A., & Maffei, L. (1973). Contrast in night vision. *Vision Research, 13,* 73–80.

Firestein, S. (1992). Physiology of transduction in the single olfactory sensory neuron. In D. P. Corey & S. D. Roper (Eds.), *Sensory transduction* (pp. 61–71). New York: Rockefeller University Press.

Fletcher, H., & Munson, W. A. (1933). Loudness: Its definition, measurement, and calculation. *Journal of the Acoustical Society of America, 5,* 82–108.

Fodor, J. A. (1984). *The modularity of mind.* Cambridge, MA: MIT Press.

Fodor, J. A., & Pylyshyn, Z. W. (1981). How direct is visual perception? Some reflections of Gibson's "ecological approach." *Cognition, 9,* 139–196.

Foulke, E. (1991). Braille. In M. A. Heller & W. Schiff (Eds.), *The psychology of touch* (pp. 219–223). Hillsdale, NJ: Erlbaum.

Fowler, C. A., & Rosenblum, L. D. (1990). Duplex perception: A comparison of monosyllables and slamming doors. *Journal of Experimental Psychology: Human Perception and Performance, 16,* 742–754.

Fox, C. R. (1990). Some visual influences on human postural equilibrium: Binocular versus monocular fixation. *Perception and Psychophysics, 47,* 409–422.

Fox, R., Aslin, R. N., Shea, S. L., & Dumais, S. T. (1980). Stereopsis in human infants. *Science, 207,* 323–324.

Fox, R., Lehmukuhle, S. W., & Westendorf, D. H. (1976). Falcon visual acuity. *Science, 192,* 263–265.

Fox, R., & McDaniel, C. (1982). The perception of biological motion by human infants. *Science, 218,* 486–487.

Frank, M. E., Bieber, S. L., & Smith, D. V. (1988). The organization of taste sensibilities in hamster chorda tympani nerve fibers. *Journal of General Physiology, 91,* 861–896.

Frank, M. E., & Rabin, M. D. (1989). Chemosensory neuroanatomy and physiology. *Ear, Nose and Throat Journal, 68,* 291–292, 295–296.

Freeman, R. D., & Pettigrew, J. D. (1973). Alterations of visual cortex from environmental asymmetries. *Nature, 246,* 359–360.

Friedman, M. B. (1975). Visual control of head movements during avian locomotion. *Nature, 225,* 67–69.

Frost, D. O. (1990). Sensory processing by novel, experimentally induced cross-modal circuits. *Annals of the New York Academy of Sciences, 608,* 93–112.

Fujita, I., Tanaka, K., Ito, M., & Cheng, K. (1992). Columns for visual features of objects in monkey inferotemporal cortex. *Nature, 360,* 343–346.

Fuld, K., Wooten, B. R., & Whalen, J. J. (1981). Elemental hues of short-wave and spectral lights. *Perception and Psychophysics, 29,* 317–322.

Fuzessery, Z. M., & Feng, A. S. (1983). Mating call selectivity in the thalamus and midbrain of the leopard frog *(Rana p. pipiens):* Single and multiunit analyses. *Journal of Comparative Physiology, 150A,* 333–344.

Galletti, C., Battaglini, P. P., & Fattori, P. (1990). "Real-motion" cells in area V3A of macaque visual cortex. *Experimental Brain Research, 82,* 67–76.

Galletti, C., Battaglini, P. P., & Fattori, P. (1993). Parietal neurons encoding spatial locations in craniotopic coordinates. *Experimental Brain Research,* 96, 221–229.

Galletti, C., Battaglini, P. P., & Fattori, P. (1995). Eye position influence on the parieto-occipital area PO (V6) of the macaque monkey. *European Journal of Neuroscience,* 7, 2486–2501.

Gamble, A. E. McC. (1898). The applicability of Weber's law to smell. *American Journal of Psychology,* 10, 82–142.

Ganchrow, J. R. (1995). Ontogeny of human taste perception. In R. L. Doty (Ed.), *Handbook of olfaction and gustation* (pp. 715–729). New York: Marcel Dekker.

Ganchrow, J. R., Steiner, J. E., & Daher, M. (1983). Neonatal facial expressions in response to different qualities and intensities of gustatory stimuli. *Infant Behavior and Development,* 6, 473–484.

Garbin, C. P. (1988). Visual-haptic perceptual nonequivalence for shape information and its impact upon cross-modal performance. *Journal of Experimental Psychology: Human Perception and Performance,* 14, 547–553.

Garcia, J., Ervin, F. R., & Koelling, R. A. (1966). Learning with prolonged delay of reinforcement. *Psychonomic Science,* 5, 121–122.

Garcia, J., Hawkins, W. G., & Rusiniak, K. W. (1974). Behavioral regulation of the milieu interne in man and rat. *Science,* 185, 824–831.

Garcia, J., & Koelling, R. A. (1966). A relation of cue to consequence in avoidance learning. *Psychonomic Science,* 4, 123–124.

Gardner, E. P., & Costanzo, R. M. (1980). Neuronal mechanisms underlying direction sensitivity of somatosensory cortical neurons in awake monkeys. *Journal of Neurophysiology,* 43, 1342–1354.

Gardner, E. P., Palmer, C. I., Hamalainen, H. A., & Warren, S. (1992). Simulation of motion on the skin: V. Effect of stimulus temporal frequency on the representation of moving bar patterns in primary somatosensory cortex of monkeys. *Journal of Neurophysiology,* 67, 37–63.

Gardner, M. B., & Gardner, R. S. (1973). Problem of localization in the median plane: Effect of pinnae cavity occlusion. *Journal of the Acoustical Society of America,* 53, 400–408.

Gaver, W. W. (1993a). How do we hear in the world?: Explorations in ecological acoustics. *Ecological Psychology,* 5, 285–313.

Gaver, W. W. (1993b). What in the world do we hear? An ecological approach to auditory event perception. *Ecological Psychology,* 5, 1–29.

Gelb, A. (1929). Die "Farbenkoinstanz" der Sehding. *Handbook norm. path. Phys.,* 12, 594–678.

Gescheider, G. A. (1976). *Psychophysics: Method and theory.* Hillsdale, NJ: Erlbaum.

Geschwind, N. (1979, September). Specializations of the human brain. *Scientific American,* 241, 108–119.

Getty, D. J., & Howard, J. H. (Eds.). (1981). *Auditory and visual pattern recognition.* Hillsdale, NJ: Erlbaum.

Gibson, J. J. (1950). *The perception of the visual world.* Boston: Houghton Mifflin.

Gibson, J. J. (1962). Observations on active touch. *Psychological Review,* 69, 477–491.

Gibson, J. J. (1966). *The senses considered as perceptual systems.* Boston: Houghton Mifflin.

Gibson, J. J. (1979). *The ecological approach to visual perception.* Boston: Houghton Mifflin.

Gilbert, C. D., & Wiesel, T. N. (1989). Columnar specificity of intrinsic horizontal and corticocortical connections in cat visual cortex. *Journal of Neuroscience,* 9, 2432–2442.

Gillam, B. (1995). The perception of spatial layout from static optical information. In W. Epstein & S. Rogers (Eds.), *Handbook of perception and cognition: Perception of space and motion* (pp. 23–67). New York: Academic Press.

Ginsburg, A. (1983). *Contrast perception in the human infant.* Unpublished manuscript.

Glickstein, M. (1988, September). The discovery of the visual cortex. *Scientific American,* 259, 118–127.

Goldstein, E. B. (1998). When does visual processing become cognitive? *Contemporary Psychology,* 43, 127–129.

Goldstein, E. B., & Fink, S. I. (1981). Selective attention in vision: Recognition memory for superimposed line drawings. *Journal of Experimental*

Psychology: Human Perception and Performance, 7, 954–967.

Goldstein, J. L. (1978). Mechanisms of signal analysis and pattern perception in periodicity pitch. *Audiology, 17*, 421–445.

Goodale, M. A., & Milner, A. D. (1992). Separate visual pathways for perception and action. *Trends in Neurosciences, 15*, 20–25.

Goodale, M. A., Milner, A. D., Jakobsen, L. S., & Carey, D. P. (1991). A neurological dissociation between perceiving objects and grasping them. *Nature, 349*, 154–156.

Gordon, J., & Abramov, I. (1988). Scaling procedures for specifying color appearance. *Color Research Applications, 13*, 146–152.

Gouras, P. (1991a). Color vision. In E. R. Kandel, J. H. Schwartz, & T. M. Jessell (Eds.), *Principles of neural science* (3rd ed., pp. 467–480). New York: Elsevier.

Gouras, P. (1991b). Cortical mechanisms of colour vision. In P. Gouras (Ed.), *Vision and visual dysfunction* (Vol. 6, pp. 179–197). London: Macmillan.

Gouras, P. (1991c). Precortical physiology of colour vision. In P. Gouras (Ed.), *Vision and visual dysfunction* (Vol. 6, pp. 163–178). London: Macmillan.

Graham, C. H. (1965). Perception of movement. In C. Graham (Ed.), *Vision and visual perception* (pp. 575–588). New York: Wiley.

Graham, C. H., Sperling, H. G., Hsia, Y., & Coulson, A. H. (1961). The determination of some visual functions of a unilaterally color-blind subject: Methods and results. *Journal of Psychology, 51*, 3–32.

Graham, N. (1992). Breaking the visual stimulus into parts. *Current Directions in Psychological Science, 1*, 55–61.

Graham, N., Beck, J., & Sutter, A. (1992). Nonlinear processes in spatial-frequency channel models of perceived texture segregation: Effects of sign and amount of contrast. *Vision Research, 32*, 719–743.

Granrud, C. E., Haake, R. J., & Yonas, A. (1985). Infants' sensitivity to familiar size: The effect of memory on spatial perception. *Perception and Psychophysics, 37*, 459–466.

Granrud, C. E., & Yonas, A. (1984). Infants' perception of pictorially specified interposition. *Journal of Experimental Child Psychology, 37*, 500–511.

Granrud, C. E., Yonas, A., & Opland, E. A. (1985). Infants' sensitivity to the depth cue of shading. *Perception and Psychophysics, 37*, 415–419.

Gray, C. M., & Singer, W. (1989). Stimulus specific neuronal oscillations in orientation columns of cat visual cortex. *Proceedings of the National Academy of Sciences, 86*, 1698–1702.

Graziadei, P. P. C. (1976). Functional anatomy of the mammalian chemoreceptor system. In D. Muller-Schearze & M. Mozell (Eds.), *Chemical signals in vertebrates* (pp. 435–454). New York: Plenum Press.

Graziano, M. S. A., Andersen, R. A., & Snowden, R. J. (1994). Tuning of MST neurons to spiral motions. *Journal of Neuroscience, 14*, 54–67.

Graziano, M. S. A., & Gross, C. G. (1995). The representation of extrapersonal space: A possible role for bimodal, visual-tactile neurons. In M. S. Gazzaniga (Ed.), *The cognitive neurosciences* (pp. 1021–1034).Cambridge, MA: MIT Press.

Green, D. M. (1976). *An introduction to hearing.* Hillsdale, NJ: Erlbaum.

Gregory, R. L. (1966). *Eye and brain.* New York: McGraw-Hill.

Gregory, R. L. (1973). *Eye and brain* (2nd ed.). New York: McGraw-Hill.

Gregory, R. L., & Wallace, J. G. (1963). Recovery from early blindness: A case study. *Experimental Psychology Society Monograph*, 2.

Grimes, J. (1996). On the failure to detect changes in scenes across saccades. In K. Akins (Ed.), *Perception* (pp. 89–110). New York: Oxford University Press.

Gross, C. G. (1992). Representation of visual stimuli in inferior temporal cortex. *Transactions of the Royal Society of London, B335*, 3–10.

Gross, C. G. (1994). How inferior temporal cortex became a visual area. *Cerebral Cortex, 5*, 455–469.

Gross, C. G., Bender, D. B., & Rocha-Miranda, C. E. (1969). Visual receptive fields of neurons in inferotemporal cortex of the monkey. *Science, 166,* 1303–1306.

Gross, C. G., & Mishkin, M. (1977). The neural basis of stimulus equivalence across retinal translation. In S. Harnad, R. Doty, J. Jaynes, L. Goldstein, & G. Krauthamer (Eds.), *Lateralization in the nervous system* (pp. 109–122). New York: Academic Press.

Gross, C. G., Rocha-Miranda, C. E., & Bender, D. B. (1972). Visual properties of neurons in inferotemporal cortex of the macaque. *Journal of Neurophysiology, 35,* 96–111.

Grunwald, A. P. (1965). A braille reading machine. *Science, 154,* 144–146.

Guinan, J. J. (1996). Physiology of olivocochlear efferents. In P. Dallos, A. N. Popper, & R. R. Fay (Eds.), *The cochlea* (pp. 435 –502). New York: Springer.

Gulick, W. L. (1971). *Hearing.* New York: Oxford University Press.

Gulick, W. L., Gescheider, G. A., & Frisina, R. D. (1989). *Hearing.* New York: Oxford University Press.

Gwiazda, J., Thorn, F., Bauer, J., & Held, R. (1993). Emmetropization and the progression of manifest refraction in children followed from infancy to puberty. *Clinical Visual Science, 8,* 337–344.

Gyr, J. W. (1972). Is a theory of direct perception adequate? *Psychological Bulletin, 77,* 246–261.

Hagen, M. A. (Ed.). (1979). *The perception of pictures* (Vols. 1, 2). New York: Academic Press.

Hagen, M. A. (1986). *Varieties of realism.* Cambridge, England: Cambridge University Press.

Hagins, W. A., Penn, R. D., & Yoshikami, S. (1970). Dark current and photocurrent in retinal rods. *Biophysical Journal, 10,* 380–409.

Haith, M. M. (1983). Spatially determined visual activity in early infancy. In A. Hein & M. Jeannerod (Eds.), *Spatially oriented behavior.* New York: Springer.

Hall, E. G., & Davies, S. (1991). Gender differences in perceived intensity and affect of pain between athletes and nonathletes. *Perceptual and Motor Skills, 73,* 779–786.

Hall, J. L. (1965). Binaural interaction in the accessory superior-olivary nucleus of the cat. *Journal of the Acoustical Society of America, 37,* 814–823.

Hall, M. D., & Pastore, R. E. (1992). Musical duplex perception: Perception of figurally good chords with subliminal distinguishing tones. *Journal of Experimental Psychology: Human Perception and Performance, 18,* 752–762.

Hall, M. J., Bartoshuk, L. M., Cain, W. S., & Stevens, J. C. (1975). PTC taste blindness and the taste of caffeine. *Nature, 253,* 442–443.

Halpern, D. L., Blake, R., & Hillenbrand, J. (1986). Psychoacoustics of a chilling sound. *Perception and Psychophysics, 39,* 77–80.

Hamer, R. D., Alexander, K. R., & Teller, D. Y. (1982). Rayleigh discriminations in young human infants. *Vision Research, 22,* 575–587.

Handel, S. (1988). Space is to time as vision is to auditory: Seductive but misleading. *Journal of Experimental Psychology: Human Perception and Performance, 14,* 315–317.

Handel, S. (1995). Timbre perception and auditory object identification. In B. C. J. Moore (Ed.), *Hearing* (pp. 425–461). San Diego, CA: Academic Press.

Hanson, A. R., & Riseman, E. M. (1978). *Computer vision systems.* New York: Academic Press.

Harris, L., Atkinson, J., & Braddick, O. (1976). Visual contrast sensitivity of a 6-month-old infant measured by the evoked potential. *Nature, 246,* 570–571.

Hartline, H. K., Wagner, H. G., & Ratliff, F. (1956). Inhibition in the eye of *Limulus. Journal of General Physiology, 39,* 651–673.

Haxby, J. V., Grady, C. L., Horwitz, B., Ungerleider, L. G., Mishkin, M., Carson, R. E., Hersovitch, P., Schapiro, M. B., & Rapoport, S. I. (1991). Dissociation of object and spatial visual processing pathways in human extrastriate cortex. *Proceedings of the National Academy of Sciences, 88,* 1621–1625.

He, S., Cavanagh, P., & Intriligator, J. (1997). Attentional resolution. *Trends in Cognitive Sciences, 1,* 115–121.

Hecaen, H., & Angelerques, R. (1962). Agnosia for faces (prosopagnosia). *Archives of Neurology, 7,* 92–100.

Hecht, S., Shlaer, S., & Pirenne, M. H. (1942). Energy, quanta, and vision. *Journal of General Physiology, 25,* 819–840.

Heffner, H. E. (1983). Hearing in large and small dogs. Absolute thresholds and size of the tympanic membrane. *Behavioral Neuroscience, 97,* 310–318.

Heffner, H. E., & Masterton, R. B. (1980). Hering in glires: Domestic rabbit, cotton rat, feral house mouse, and kangaroo rat. *Journal of the Acoustical Society of America, 68,* 1584–1599.

Heffner, R. S., & Heffner, H. E. (1980). Hearing in the elephant (Elephas maximus). *Science, 208,* 518–520.

Heffner, R. S., & Heffner, H. E. (1985). Hearing in mammals: The least weasel. *Journal of Mammalogy, 66,* 745–755.

Heise, G. A., & Miller, G. A. (1951). An experimental study of auditory patterns. *American Journal of Psychology, 57,* 243–249.

Held, R., Birch, E. E., & Gwiazda, J. (1980). Stereoacuity of human infants. *Proceedings of the National Academy of Sciences, 77,* 5572–5574.

Heller, M. A. (1986). Active and passive tactile braille recognition. *Bulletin of the Psychonomic Society, 24,* 201–202.

Heller, M. A. (1989). Picture and pattern perception in the sighted and the blind: The advantage of the late blind. *Perception, 18,* 379–389.

Helmholtz, H. von. (1852). On the theory of compound colors. *Philosophical Magazine, 4,* 519–534.

Helmholtz, H. von. (1911). *Treatise on physiological optics* (J. P. Southall, Ed. & Trans.) (3rd ed., Vols. 2 & 3). Rochester, NY: Optical Society of America. (Original work published 1866)

Helmholtz, H. von. (1954). *Die Lehr von den Tonenpfindungen als physiologische Grundlege für die Theorie der Musik* [On the sensations of tone as a physiological basis for the theory of music] (A. J. Ellis, Trans.). New York: Dover. (Original work published 1863)

Helson, H. (1933). The fundamental propositions of Gestalt psychology. *Psychological Review, 40,* 13–32.

Helson, H., Judd, D. B., & Wilson, M. (1956). Color rendition with fluorescent sources of illumination. *Illuminating Engineering, 51,* 329–346.

Hering, E. (1878). *Zur Lehre vom Lichtsinn.* Vienna: Gerold.

Hering, E. (1905). Grundzuge der Lehre vom Lichtsinn. In *Handbuch der gesamter Augenheilkunde* (Vol. 3, Chap. 13). Berlin.

Hering, E. (1964). *Outlines of a theory of the light sense* (L. M. Hurvich & D. Jameson, Trans.). Cambridge, MA: Harvard University Press.

Hershenson, M. (Ed.). (1989). *The moon illusion.* Hillsdale, NJ: Erlbaum.

Hettinger, T. P., Myers, W. E., & Frank, M. E. (1990). Role of olfaction in perception of nontraditional "taste" stimuli. *Chemical Senses, 15,* 755–760.

Heywood, C. A., Cowey, A., & Newcombe, F. (1991). Chromatic discrimination in a cortically colour blind observer. *European Journal of Neuroscience, 3,* 802–812.

Hildreth, E. C. (1990). The neural computation of the velocity field. In B. Cohen & I. Bodis-Wollner (Eds.), *Vision and the brain* (pp. 139–164). New York: Raven Press.

Hiris, E., & Blake, R. (1992). Another perspective on the visual motion aftereffect. *Proceedings of the National Academy of Sciences, 89,* 9025–9028.

Hochberg, J. E. (1970). Attention, organization, and consciousness. In D. I. Mostofsky (Ed.), *Attention: Contemporary theory and analysis* (pp. 99–124). New York: Appleton-Century-Crofts.

Hochberg, J. E. (1971). Perception. In J. W. Kling & L. A. Riggs (Eds.), *Experimental psychology* (3rd ed., pp. 396–550). New York: Holt, Rinehart and Winston.

Hochberg, J. E. (1987). Machines should not see as people do, but must know how people see.

Computer Vision, Graphics and Image Processing, 39, 221–237.

Hohmann, A., & Creutzfeldt, O. D. (1975). Squint and the development of binocularity in humans. *Nature*, 254, 613–614.

Holley, A. (1991). Neural coding of olfactory information. In T. V. Getchell, R. L. Doty, L. M. Bartoshuk, & J. B. Snow (Eds.), *Smell and taste in health and disease* (pp. 329–343). New York: Raven Press.

Holley, A., Duchamp, A., Revial, M. F., Juge, A., & Macleod, P. (1974). Qualitative and quantitative discrimination in the frog olfactory receptors: Analysis from electrophysiological data. *Annals of the New York Academy of Sciences*, 237, 102–114.

Holway, A. H., & Boring, E. G. (1941). Determinants of apparent visual size with distance variant. *American Journal of Psychology*, 54, 21–37.

Houtsma, A. J. M., & Goldstein, J. L. (1972). Perception of musical intervals: Evidence for the central origin of the pitch of complex tones. *Journal of the Optical Society of America*, 51, 520–529.

Hsiao, S. S., Johnson, K. O., Twombly, A., & DiCarlo, J. (1996). Form processing and attention effects in the somatosensory system. In O. Franzen, R. Johannson, & L. Terenius (Eds.), *Somesthesis and the neurobiology of the somatosensory cortex* (pp. 229–247). Basel: Biorkhauser Verlag.

Hsiao, S. S., O'Shaughnessy, D. M., & Johnson, K. O. (1993). Effects of selective attention on spatial form processing in monkey primary and secondary somatosensory cortex. *Journal of Neurophysiology*, 70, 444–447.

Hubel, D. H. (1982). Exploration of the primary visual cortex, 1955–1978. *Nature*, 299, 515–524.

Hubel, D. H., & Wiesel, T. N. (1959). Receptive fields of single neurons in the cat's striate cortex. *Journal of Physiology*, 148, 574–591.

Hubel, D. H., & Wiesel, T. N. (1961). Integrative action in the cat's lateral geniculate body. *Journal of Physiology*, 155, 385–398.

Hubel, D. H., & Wiesel, T. N. (1963). Receptive fields of cells in striate cortex of very young, visually inexperienced kittens. *Journal of Neurophysiology*, 26, 994–1002.

Hubel, D. H., & Wiesel, T. N. (1965a). Receptive fields and functional architecture in two nonstriate visual areas (18 and 19) of the cat. *Journal of Neurophysiology*, 28, 229–289.

Hubel, D. H., & Wiesel, T. N. (1965b). Binocular interaction in striate cortex of kittens reared with artificial squint. *Journal of Neurophysiology*, 28, 1041–1059.

Hubel, D. H., & Wiesel, T. N. (1970). Cells sensitive to binocular depth in area 18 of the macaque monkey cortex. *Nature*, 225, 41–42.

Hubel, D. H., & Wiesel, T. N. (1974). Uniformity of monkey striate cortex: A parallel relationship between field size, scatter, and magnification factor. *Journal of Comparative Neurology*, 158, 295–306.

Hubel, D. H., & Wiesel, T. N. (1977). Functional architecture of macaque monkey cortex. *Proceedings of the Royal Society of London*, 198, 1–59.

Hubel, D. H., Wiesel, T. N., & Stryker, M. P. (1978). Anatomical demonstration of orientation columns in macaque monkey. *Journal of Comparative Neurology*, 177, 361–379.

Hubel, D. H., & Livingstone, M. (1990). Color puzzles. *Cold Spring Harbor Symposia on Quantitative Biology*, 60, 643–649.

Hudspeth, A. J. (1983). The hair cells of the inner ear. *Scientific American*, 248(1), 54–64.

Hudspeth, A. J. (1989). How the ear's works work. *Nature*, 341, 397–404.

Humphrey, A. L., & Saul, A. B. (1994). The temporal transformation of retinal signals in the lateral geniculate nucleus of the cat: Implications for cortical function. In D. Minciacchi, M. Molinari, G. Macchi, & E. G. Jones (Eds.), *Thalamic networks for relay and modulation* (pp. 81–89). New York: Pergamon Press.

Humphreys, G. W., & Riddoch, M. J. (1987). *To see but not to see: A case of visual agnosia.* London: Erlbaum.

Hurvich, L. (1981). *Color vision.* Sunderland, MA: Sinauer Associates.

Hyman, A. (1983). The influence of color on the taste perception of carbonated water preparations. *Bulletin of the Psychonomic Society, 21,* 145–148.

Hyvarinin, J., & Poranen, A. (1978). Movement-sensitive and direction and orientation-selective cutaneous receptive fields in the hand area of the postcentral gyrus in monkeys. *Journal of Physiology, 283,* 523–537.

Ilg, U. J., Bridgeman, B., & Hoffmann, K. P. (1989). Influence of mechanical disturbance on oculomotor behavior. *Vision Research, 29,* 545–551.

Irving, E. L., Sivak, J. G., & Callender, M. G. (1992). Refractive plasticity of the developing chick eye. *Ophthalmology and Physiological Optics, 12,* 448–456.

Ito, M., Tamura, H., Fujita, I., & Tanaka, K. (1995). Size and position invariance of neuronal responses in monkey inferotemporal cortex. *Journal of Neurophysiology, 73,* 218–226.

Ittleson, W. H. (1952). *The Ames demonstrations in perception.* Princeton, NJ: Princeton University Press.

Jacobs, K. M., Mark, G. P., & Scott, T. R. (1988). Taste responses in the nucleus tractus solitarius of sodium-deprived rats. *Journal of Physiology, 406,* 393–410.

Jacobson, A., & Gilchrist, A. (1988). The ratio principle holds over a million-to-one range of illumination. *Perception and Psychophysics, 43,* 1–6.

James, W. (1890/1981). *The principles of psychology* (Rev. ed.). Cambridge, MA: Harvard University Press. (Original work published 1890)

Jameson, D. (1985). Opponent-colors theory in light of physiological findings. In D. Ottoson & S. Zeki (Eds.), *Central and peripheral mechanisms of color vision* (pp. 8–102). New York: Macmillan.

Jenkins, W. M., & Merzenich, M. M. (1984). Role of cat primary auditory cortex for sound-localization behavior. *Journal of Neurophysiology, 52,* 819–847.

Jenkins, W. M., & Merzenich, M. M. (1987). Reorganization of neocortical representations after brain injury: A neurophysiological model of the bases of recovery from stroke. *Progress in Brain Research, 71,* 249–266.

Jessell, T. M., & Kelly, D. D. (1991). Pain and analgesia. In E. R. Kandel, J. H. Schwartz, & T. M. Jessell (Eds.), *Principles of neural science* (3rd ed., pp. 385–399). New York: Elsevier.

Johansson, G. (1975). Visual motion perception. *Scientific American, 232,* 76–89.

Johnson, K. O., & Lamb, G. D. (1981). Neural mechanisms of spatial tactile discrimination: Neural patterns evoked by braille-like dot patterns in the monkey. *Journal of Physiology, 310,* 117–144.

Johnson, S. P., & Aslin, R. N. (1995). Perception of object unity in 2-month-old infants. *Developmental Psychology, 31,* 739–745.

Johnstone, B. M., & Boyle, A. J. F. (1967). Basilar membrane vibrations examined with the Mossbauer technique. *Science, 158,* 390–391.

Johnstone, B. M., Patuzzi, R., & Yates, G. K. (1986). Basilar membrane measurements and the traveling wave. *Hearing Research, 22,* 147–153.

Jones, K. R., Spear, P., & Tong, L. (1984). Critical periods for effects of monocular deprivation differences between striate and extrastriate cortex. *Journal of Neuroscience, 4,* 2543–2552.

Jones, L. A. (1988). Motor illusions: What do they reveal about proprioception? *Psychological Bulletin, 103,* 72–86.

Jones, M. R., & Yee, W. (1993). Attending to auditory events: The role of temporal organization. In S. McAdams & E. Bigand (Eds.), *Thinking in sound: The cognitive psychology of human audition* (pp. 69–112). Oxford, England: Oxford University Press.

Judd, D. B., & Kelly, K. L. (1965). *The ISCC-NBS method of designating colors and a dictionary of color names* (2nd ed.) (U.S. National Bureau of Standards Circular 553). Washington, DC: U.S. Government Printing Office.

Judd, D. B., MacAdam, D. L., & Wyszecki, G. (1964). Spectral distribution of typical daylight as a function of correlated color temperature. *Journal of the Optical Society of America, 54,* 1031–1040.

Julesz, B. (1971). *Foundations of cyclopean perception.* Chicago: University of Chicago Press.

Julesz, B. (1981). Textons, the elements of texture perception, and their interactions. *Nature, 290,* 91–97.

Julesz, B. (1984). A brief outline of the texton theory of human vision. *Trends in Neuroscience, 7,* 41–45.

Julesz, B., & Hirsh, I. J. (1972). Visual and auditory perception –an essay of comparison. In E. E. David & P. B. Denes (Eds.), *Human communication: A unified view* (pp. 283–340). New York: McGraw-Hill.

Kaas, J. H. (1991). Plasticity of sensory and motor maps in adult mammals. *Annual Review of Neuroscience, 14,* 137–167.

Kaas, J. H., Merzenich, M. J., & Killackey, H. P. (1983). The reorganization of somatosensory cortex following peripheral nerve damage in adult and developing mammals. *Annual Review of Neuroscience, 6,* 325–356.

Kaas, J. H., & Pons, T. P. (1988). The somatosensory system of primates. In H. D. Steklis & J. Erwin (Eds.), *Comparative primate biology* (Vol. 4, pp. 421–468). New York: Liss.

Kandel, E. R., & Jessell, T. M. (1991). Touch. In E. R. Kandel, J. H. Schwartz, & T. M. Jessell (Eds.), *Principles of neural science* (3rd ed., pp. 367–384). New York: Elsevier.

Kanizsa, G. (1979). *Organization in vision.* New York: Praeger.

Kaplan, E., Mukherjee, P., & Shapley, R. (1993). Information filtering in the lateral geniculate nucleus. In R. Shapley & D. Man-Kit Lam (Eds.), *Contrast sensitivity* (Vol. 5). Cambridge, MA: MIT Press.

Kaplan, G. (1969). Kinetic disruption of optical texture: The perception of depth at an edge. *Perception and Psychophysics, 6,* 193–198.

Kauer, J. S. (1987). Coding in the olfactory system. In T. E. Finger & W. C. Silver (Eds.), *Neurobiology of taste and smell* (pp. 205–231). New York: Wiley.

Kaufman, L., & Rock, I. (1962a). The moon illusion. *Science, 136,* 953–961.

Kaufman, L., & Rock, I. (1962b). The moon illusion. *Scientific American, 207,* 120–132.

Kawase, T., Delgutte, B., & Liberman, M. C. (1993). Anti-masking effects of the olivocochlear reflex: II. Enhancement of auditory-nerve response to masked tones. *Journal of Neurophysiology, 70,* 2533–2549.

Kaye, K. L., & Bower, T. G. R. (1994). Learning and intermodal transfer of information in newborns. *Psychological Science, 5,* 286–288.

Kellman, P., & Spelke, E. (1983). Perception of partly occluded objects in infancy. *Cognitive Psychology, 15,* 483–524.

Kellogg, W. N. (1962). Sonar system of the blind. *Science, 137,* 399–404.

Kelly, J. P. (1991). Hearing. In E. R. Kandel, J. H. Schwartz, & T. M. Jessell (Eds.), *Principles of neural science* (3rd ed., pp. 481–499). New York: Elsevier.

Kennedy, J. M. (1993). *Drawing and the blind.* New Haven, CT: Yale University Press.

Kennedy, J. M. (1997, January). How the blind draw. *Scientific American,* 76–81.

Kenshalo, D. R. (1976). Correlations of temperature sensitivity in man and monkey, a first approximation. In Y. Zotterman (Ed.), *Sensory functions of the skin in primates, with special reference to man* (pp. 305–330). New York: Pergamon Press.

Kewley-Port, D. (1983). Time-varying features as correlates of place of articulation in stop consonants. *Journal of the Acoustical Society of America, 73,* 322–335.

Kewley-Port, D., & Luce, P. A. (1984). Time-varying features of initial stop consonants in auditory running spectra: A first report. *Perception and Psychophysics, 35,* 353–360.

Khanna, S. M., & Leonard, D. G. B. (1982). Basilar membrane tuning in the cat cochlea. *Science, 215,* 305–306.

Kimura, D. (1961). Cerebral dominance and the perception of verbal stimuli. *Canadian Journal of Psychology, 15,* 166–171.

King, W. L., & Gruber, H. E. (1962). Moon illusion and Emmert's law. *Science, 135,* 1125–1126.

Kinnamon, S. C. (1988). Taste treanduction: A diversity of mechanisms. *Trends in Neurosciences, 11,* 491–496.

Kirman, J. H. (1974). Tactile apparent movement: The effects of interstimulus onset interval and stimulus duration. *Perception and Psychophysics, 15,* 1–6.

Klatzky, R. L., Lederman, S. J., & Metzger, V. A. (1985). Identifying objects by touch: An "expert system." *Perception and Psychophysics, 37,* 299–302.

Knill, D. C., & Kersten, D. (1991). Apparent surface curvature affects lightness perception. *Nature, 351,* 228–230.

Knudsen, E. I., & Konishi, M. (1978a). Center-surround organization of auditory receptive fields in the owl. *Science, 202,* 778–780.

Knudsen, E. I., & Konishi, M. (1978b). A neural map of auditory space in the owl. *Science, 200,* 795–797.

Kobatake, E., & Tanaka, K. (1994). Neuronal selectivities to complex object features in the ventral visual pathway of the macaque cerebral cortex. *Journal of Neurophysiology, 71,* 856–867.

Kolb, B., & Whishaw, I. Q. (1985). *Fundamentals of human neuropsychology* (2nd ed.). New York: Freeman.

Kolers, P. S. (1964). The illusion of movement. *Scientific American, 211,* 98–106.

Konishi, M. (1984). Spatial receptive fields in the auditory system. In L. Bolis, R. D. Keynes, & S. H. Maddrell (Eds.), *Comparative physiology of sensory systems* (pp. 103–113). Cambridge, England: Cambridge University Press.

Konishi, M. (1990). Similar algorithms in different sensory systems and animals. *Cold Spring Harbor Symposium on Quantitative Biology, 55,* 575–584.

Korte, M., & Rauschecker, J. P. (1993). Auditory spatial tuning of cortical neurons is sharpened in cats with early blindness. *Journal of Neurophysiology, 70,* 1717–1721.

Kosambi, D. D. (1967). Living prehistory in India. *Scientific American, 216,* 105.

Kozlowski, L., & Cutting, J. (1977). Recognizing the sex of a walker from a dynamic point-light display. *Perception and Psychophysics, 21,* 575–580.

Kreithen, M. L., & Quine, D. B. (1979). Infrasound detection by the homing pigeon: A behavioral audiogram. *Journal of Comparative Physiology, 129,* 1–4.

Kremenitzer, J. P., Vaughn, H. G., Kurtzberg, D., & Dowling, K. (1979). Smooth-pursuit eye movements in the newborn infant. *Child Development, 50,* 442–448.

Kris, J. von. (1896). Uber die Funktion der Netzhautstabhen. *Zeitschrift fuer Psychologie, 9,* 81.

Kroner, T. (1881). Über die Sinnesempfindungen der Neugeborenen. *Breslauer aerzliche Zeitschrift.* (Cited in Peterson, F., & Rainey, L. H. (1910–1911). The beginnings of mind in the newborn. *Bulletin of the Lying-In Hospital, 7,* 99–122.

Kruger, L. E. (1970). David Katz: Der Aufbau der Tastwelt [The world of touch: A synopsis]. *Perception and Psychophysics, 7,* 337–341.

Kruger, L. E. (1982). A word-superiority effect with print and braille characters. *Perception and Psychophysics, 31,* 345–352.

Kubovy, M. (1986). *The psychology of perspective and Renaissance art.* Cambridge, England: Cambridge University Press.

Kuffler, S. W. (1953). Discharge patterns and functional organization of mammalian retina. *Journal of Neurophysiology, 16,* 37–68.

Kuhl, P. K. (1983). Perception of auditory equivalence classes for speech in early infancy. *Infant Behavior and Development, 6,* 263–285.

Kuhl, P. K. (1989). On babies, birds, modules, and mechanisms: A comparative approach to the acquisition of vocal communication. In R. J. Dooling & S. H. Hulse (Eds.), *Comparative psychology of audition* (pp. 379–419). Hillsdale, NJ: Erlbaum.

Kuhl, P. K., Williams, K. A., Lacerda, F., Stevens, K. N., & Lindblom, B. (1992). Linguistic experience alters phonetic perception in infants by 6 months of age. *Science, 255,* 606–608.

Kunnapas, T. (1957). Experiments on figural dominance. *Journal of Experimental Psychology, 53,* 31–39.

LaBarbera, J. D., Izard, C. E., Vietze, P., & Parisi, S. A. (1976). Four- and six-month-old infants' visual responses to joy, anger, and neutral expressions. *Child Development, 47,* 535–538.

Laing, D. D., Doty, R. L., & Breipohl, W. (Eds.). (1991). *The human sense of smell.* New York: Springer.

Laing, D. G. (1985). Optimum perception of odor intensity by humans. *Physiology and Behavior, 34,* 569–574.

Laing, D. G. (1989). The role of physiochemical and neural factors in the perception of odor mixtures. In D. G. Laing, W. S. Cain, R. L. McBride, & B. W. Ache (Eds.), *Perception of complex smells and tastes* (pp. 189–204). San Diego, CA: Academic Press.

Laing, D. G. (1995). Perception of odor mixtures. In R. L. Doty (Ed.), *Handbook of olfaction and gustation* (pp. 283–298). New York: Marcel Dekker.

Lancet, D. (1992). Olfactory reception: From transduction to human genetics. In D. P. Corey & S. D. Roper (Eds.), *Sensory transduction* (pp. 73–91). New York: Rockefeller University Press.

Land, E. H. (1983). Recent advances in retinex theory and some implications for cortical computations: Color vision and the natural image. *Proceedings of the National Academy of Sciences, USA, 80,* 5163–5169.

Land, E. H. (1986). Recent advances in retinex theory. *Vision Research, 26,* 7–21.

Land, E. H., & McCann, J. J. (1971). Lightness and retinex theory. *Journal of the Optical Society of America, 61,* 1–11.

Land, M. F., & Lee, D. N. (1994). Where we look when we steer. *Nature, 369,* 742–744.

Landy, M. S., Maloney, L. T., Johnston, E. B., & Young, M. (1995). Measurement and modeling of depth cue combination: In defense of weak fusion. *Vision Research, 35,* 389–412.

Lederman, S. J., & Abbott, S. G. (1981). Texture perception: Studies of intersensory organization using a discrepancy paradigm, and visual versus tactual psychophysics. *Journal of Experimental Psychology: Human Perception and Performance, 7,* 902–915.

Lederman, S. J., & Klatzky, R. L. (1987). Hand movements: A window into haptic object recognition. *Cognitive Psychology, 19,* 342–368.

Lederman, S. J., & Klatzky, R. L. (1990). Haptic classification of common objects: Knowledge-driven exploration. *Cognitive Psychology, 22,* 421–459.

Lee, D. N. (1974). Visual information during locomotion. In R. B. MacLeod & H. L. Pick, Jr. (Eds.), *Perception: Essays in honor of J. J. Gibson* (pp. 250–267). Ithaca, NY: Cornell University Press.

Lee, D. N. (1976). A theory of visual control of braking based on information about time to collision. *Perception, 5,* 437–459.

Lee, D. N. (1980). The optic flow field: The foundation of vision. *Transactions of the Royal Society, 290B,* 169–179.

Lee, D. N., & Aronson, E. (1974). Visual proprioceptive control of standing in human infants. *Perception and Psychophysics, 15,* 529–532.

LeGrand, Y. (1957). *Light, color and vision.* London: Chapman & Hall.

Lehrer, M., Srinivasan, M. V., Zhang, S. W., & Horridge, G. A. (1988). Motion cues provide the bee's visual world with a third dimension. *Nature, 332,* 356–357.

Leopold, D. A., & Logothetis, N. K. (1996). Activity changes in early visual cortex reflect monkeys' percepts during binocular rivalry. *Nature, 379,* 549–553.

Lerman, S. (1966). *Basic ophthalmology.* New York: McGraw-Hill.

LeVay, S., & Voigt, T. (1988). Ocular dominance and disparity coding in cat visual cortex. *Visual Neuroscience, 1,* 395–414.

Levin, D. & Simons, D. (1997). Failure to detect changes in attended objects in motion pictures. *Psychonomic Bulletin and Review,* in press.

Lewis, E. R., Zeevi, Y. Y., & Werblin, F. S. (1969). Scanning electron microscopy of vertebrate visual receptors. *Brain Research, 15,* 559–562.

Li, S., Logan, R., & Pastore, R. (1991). Perception of acoustic source characteristics: Walking sounds. *Journal of the Acoustical Society of America, 90*, 3036–3049.

Liberman, A. M., Cooper, F. S., Shankweiler, D. P., & Studdert-Kennedy, M. (1967). Perception of the speech code. *Psychological Review, 74*, 431–461.

Liberman, A. M., & Mattingly, I. G. (1989). A specialization for speech perception. *Science, 243*, 489–494.

Lieberman, M. C. (1978). Auditory-nerve response from cats raised in a low-noise chamber. *Journal of the Acoustical Society of America, 63*, 442–455.

Liebowitz, H. W., Shina, K., & Hennessy, H. R. (1972). Oculomotor adjustments and size constancy. *Perception and Psychophysics, 12*, 497–500.

Lim, D. J. (1986). Functional structure of the organ of Corti: A review. *Hearing Research, 22*, 117–146.

Lin, L. L., Chen, C. J., Hung, P. T., & Ko, L. S. (1988). Nation-wide survey of myopia among school-children in Taiwan. *Acta Ophthalmol, 185*(Suppl.), 29–33.

Lindsay, P. H., & Norman, D. A. (1977). *Human information processing* (2nd ed.). New York: Academic Press.

Liphovsky, S. (1977). The role of the chemical senses in nutrition. In M. R. Kare & O. Muller (Eds.), *The chemical senses and nutrition* (pp. 413–428). New York: Academic Press.

Livingstone, M. S., & Hubel, D. H. (1984). Anatomy and physiology of a color system in the primate visual cortex. *Journal of Neuroscience, 4*, 309–356.

Livingstone, M. S., & Hubel, D. H. (1987). Psychophysical evidence for separate channels for the perception of form, color, movement, and depth. *Journal of Neuroscience, 7*, 3416–3468.

Livingstone, M. S., & Hubel, D. H. (1988). Segregation of form, color, movement, and depth: Anatomy, physiology, and perception. *Science, 240*, 740–749.

Logothetis, N. K., & Pauls, J. (1995). Psychophysical and physiological evidence for viewer-centered object representations in the primate. *Cerebral Cortex, 5*, 270–288.

Logothetis, N. K., Pauls, J., Bulthoff, H. H., & Poggio, T. (1994). View-dependent object recognition by monkeys. *Current Biology, 4*, 401–414.

Logothetis, N. K., Pauls, J., & Poggio, T. (1995). Shape representation in the inferior temporal cortex of monkeys. *Current Biology, 5*, 552–563.

Logothetis, N. K., & Schall, J. D. (1989). Neuronal correlates of subjective visual perception. *Science, 245*, 761–763.

Loomis, J. M., Golledge, R. G., Klatzky, R. L., Speigle, J. M., & Tietz, J. (1994). *Personal guidance system for the visually impaired.* Proceedings of the First Annual International ACM/SIGCAPH Conference on Assistive Technologies, Marina del Rey, CA.

Loomis, J. M., Hebert, C., & Cicinelli, J. G. (1990). Active localization of virtual sounds. *Journal of the Acoustical Society of America, 88*, 1757–1764.

Lorig, T. S. (1992). Cognitive and non-cognitive effects of odour exposure: Electrophysiological and behavioral evidence. In S. von Toller & G. H. Dodd (Eds.), *Fragrance: The psychology and biology of perfume* (p. 161). London: Elsevier.

Lowenstein, W. R. (1960). Biological transducers. *Scientific American, 203*, 98–108.

Lowenstein, W. R., & Skalak, R. (1966). Mechanical transmission in a Pacinian corpuscle: An analysis and a theory. *Journal of Physiology, 182*, 346–378.

Lueschow, A., Miller, E. K., & Desimone, R. (1994). Inferior temporal mechanisms for invariant object recognition. *Cerebral Cortex, 4*, 523–531.

Luria, A. R. (1968). *The mind of a mnemonist.* New York: Basic Books.

Lythgoe, J. N., & Partridge, J. C. (1989). Visual pigments and the acquisition of visual information. *Journal of Experimental Biology, 146*, 1–20.

Macfarlane, A. (1975). Olfaction in the development of social preferences in the human neonate. In A. Macfarlane (Ed.), *Ciba Foundation Symposium, 33*, 103–117.

Mach, E. (1959). *The analysis of sensations.* New York: Dover. (Original work published 1914)

MacKay-Sim, A., & Kesteven, S. (1994). Topographic patterns of responsiveness to odorants in the rat olfactory epithelium. *Journal of Neurophysiology, 71*, 150–160.

MacKay-Sim, A., Shaman, P., & Moulton, D. (1982). Topographic coding of olfactory quality: Odorant-specific patterns of epithelial responsivity in the salamander. *Journal of Neurophysiology, 48*, 548–596.

Maffei, L., & Fiorentini, A. (1973). The visual cortex as a spatial frequency analyzer. *Vision Research, 13*, 1255–1267.

Makous, J. C., & Middlebrooks, J. C. (1990). Two-dimensional sound localization by human listeners. *Journal of the Acoustical Society of America, 87*, 2188–2200.

Marean, G. C., Werner, L. A., & Kuhl, P. K. (1992). Vowel categorization by very young infants. *Developmental Psychology, 28*, 396–405.

Margoliash, D. (1983). Acoustic parameters underlying the responses of song-specific neurons in the white-crowned sparrow. *Journal of Neuroscience, 3*, 1029–1057.

Markowtiz, J. A. (1996). *Using speech recognition.* Upper Saddle River, NJ: Prentice-Hall.

Marks, L. E. (1974). On associations of light and sound: The mediation of brightness, pitch, and loudness. *American Journal of Psychology, 87*, 173–188.

Marks, L. E. (1975). On colored-hearing synesthesia: Cross-modal translations of sensory dimensions. *Psychological Bulletin, 82*, 303–331.

Marks, W. B., Dobelle, W. H., & MacNichol, E. F. (1964). Visual pigments of single primate cones. *Science, 143*, 1181–1183.

Marr, D. (1976). Early processing of visual information. *Transactions of the Royal Society of London, 275B*, 483–524.

Marr, D. (1982). *Vision.* San Francisco: Freeman.

Marr, D., & Hildreth, E. (1980). Theory of edge detection. *Proceedings of the Royal Society of London, 207B*, 187–207.

Marr, D., & Nishihara, H. K. (1978). Representation and recognition of the spatial organization of three-dimensional shapes. *Proceedings of the Royal Society of London, 200B*, 269–294.

Martin, J. H. (1991). Coding and processing of sensory information. In E. R. Kandel, J. H. Schwartz, & T. M. Jessell (Eds.), *Principles of neural science* (3rd ed., pp. 339–352). Norwalk, CT: Appleton & Lange.

Martin, J. H., & Jessell, T. M. (1991). Modality coding in the somatic sensory system. In E. R. Kandel, J. H. Schwartz, & T. M. Jessell (Eds.), *Principles of neural science* (3rd ed., pp. 339–352). Norwalk, CT: Appleton & Lange.

Masland, R. H. (1988). Amacrine cells. *Trends in Neuroscience, 9*, 405–410.

Matin, L., Picoult, E., Stevens, J., Edwards, M., & MacArthur, R. (1982). Oculoparalytic illusion: Visual-field dependent spatial mislocations by humans partially paralyzed with curare. *Science, 216*, 198–201.

Matthews, D. F. (1972). Response patterns of single neurons in the tortoise olfactory epithelium and olfactory bulb. *Journal of General Physiology, 60*, 166–180.

Mattingly, I., & Studdert-Kennedy, M. (Eds.). (1991). *Modularity and the motor theory of speech perception.* Hillsdale, NJ: Erlbaum.

Maunsell, J. H. R., Nealey, T. A., & DePriest, D. D. (1990). Magnocellular and parvocellular contributions to responses in the middle temporal visual area (MT) of the macaque monkey. *Journal of Neuroscience, 10*, 363–401.

Maunsell, J. H. R., & Newsome, W. T. (1987). Visual processing in monkey extrastriate cortex. *Annual Review of Neuroscience, 10*, 363–401.

Mayer, D. J. (1979). Endogenous analgesia systems: Neural and behavioral mechanisms. In J. J. Bonica (Ed.), *Advances in pain research and therapy* (Vol. 3, pp. 385–410). New York: Raven Press.

McAdams, S. (1993). Recognition of sound sources and events. In S. McAdams & E. Bigand (Eds.), *Thinking in sound: The cognitive psychology of human audition* (pp. 146–198). Oxford, England: Oxford University Press.

McArthur, D. J. (1982). Computer vision and perceptual psychology. *Psychological Bulletin, 92*, 283–309.

McBeath, M. K., Shaffer, D. M., & Kaiser, M. K. (1995). How baseball outfielders determine where to run to catch fly balls. *Science, 268,* 569–573.

McBurney, D. H. (1969). Effects of adaptation on human taste function. In C. Pfaffmann (Ed.), *Olfaction and taste* (pp. 407–419). New York: Rockefeller University Press.

McBurney, D. H., Levine, J. M., & Cavanaugh, P. H. (1977). Psychophysical and social ratings of human body odor. *Personality and Social Psychology Bulletin, 3,* 135–138.

McClintock, M. K. (1971). Menstrual synchrony and suppression. *Nature, 229,* 244–245.

McCutcheon, N. B. (1992). Human psychophysical studies of saltiness suppression by amiloride. *Physiology and Behavior, 51,* 1069–1074.

McFadden, S. A. (1987). The binocular depth stereoacuity of the pigeon and its relation to the anatomical resolving power of the eye. *Vision Research, 27,* 1967–1980.

McFadden, S. A., & Wild, J. M. (1986). Binocular depth perception in the pigeon. *Journal of the Experimental Analysis of Behavior, 45,* 149–160.

McGurk, H., & MacDonald, T. (1976). Hearing lips and seeing voices. *Nature, 264,* 746–748.

McKenna, T. M., Weinberger, N. M., & Diamond, D. M. (1989). Responses of single auditory cortical neurons to tone sequences. *Brain Research, 481,* 142–153.

McKenzie, D. (1923). *Aromatics and the soul:* A *study of smells.* New York: Hoeber.

McLean, J. H., & Shipley, M. T. (1992). Neuroanatomical substrates of olfaction. In M. J. Serby & K. L. Chobor (Eds.), *Science of olfaction* (pp. 126–171). New York: Springer-Verlag.

McLeod, R. W., & Ross, H. E. (1983). Optic-flow and cognitive factors in time-to-collision estimates. *Perception, 12,* 417–423.

McNeil, J. E., & Warrington, E. K. (1993). Prosopagnosia: A face-specific disorder. *Quarterly Journal of Experimental Psychology, 46A,* 1–10.

Meddis, R., & Hewitt, M. J. (1991). Virtual pitch and phase sensitivity of a computer model of the auditory periphery: I. Pitch identification. *Journal of the Acoustical Society of America, 89,* 2866–2882.

Mehler, J. (1981). The role of syllables in speech processing: Infant and adult data. *Transactions of the Royal Society of London, B295,* 333–352.

Meltzoff, A. N., & Borton, R. W. (1979). Intermodal matching by human neonates. *Nature,* 282, 403–404.

Melzack, R. (1973). *The puzzle of pain.* New York: Basic Books.

Melzack, R. (1992). Phantom limbs. *Scientific American, 266,* 121–126.

Melzack, R., & Wall, P. D. (1965). Pain mechanisms: A new theory. *Science, 150,* 971–979.

Melzack, R., & Wall, P. D. (1983). *The challenge of pain.* New York: Basic Books.

Melzack, R., & Wall, P. D. (1988). *The challenge of pain* (Rev. ed.). New York: Penguin Books.

Mendelson, J. R., & Cynader, M. S. (1985). Sensitivity of cat primary auditory cortex (A1) neurons to the direction and rate of frequency modulation. *Brain Research, 327,* 331–335.

Menzel, R., & Backhaus, W. (1989). Color vision in honey bees: Phenomena and physiological mechanisms. In D. G. Stavenga & R. C. Hardie (Eds.), *Facets of vision* (pp. 281–297). Berlin: Springer-Verlag.

Menzel, R., Ventura, D. F., Hertel, H., deSouza, J., & Greggers, U. (1986). Spectral sensitivity of photoreceptors in insect compound eyes: Comparison of species and methods. *Journal of Comparative Physiology, 158A,* 165–177.

Merigan, W. H., & Maunsell, J. H. R. (1993). How parallel are the primate visual pathways? *Annual Review of Neuroscience, 16,* 369–402.

Mershon, D. H., & Bowers, J. N. (1979). Absolute and relative cues for the auditory perception of egocentric distance. *Perception, 8,* 311–322.

Merzenich, M. M., Recanzone, G., Jenkins, W. M., Allard, T. T., & Nudo, R. J. (1988). Cortical representational plasticity. In P. Rakic & W. Singer (Eds.), *Neurobiology of neocortex* (pp. 42–67). Berlin: Wiley.

Michael, C. R. (1986). *Functional and morphological identification of double and single opponent color cells in layer IVCb of the monkey's striate* *cortex.* Paper presented at the meeting of the Society for Neuroscience.

Middlebrooks, J. C., Clock, A. E., Xu, L., & Green, D. M. (1994). A panoramic code for sound location by cortical neurons. *Science, 264,* 842–844.

Middlebrooks, J. C., & Green, D. M. (1991). Sound localization by human listeners. *Annual Review of Psychology, 42,* 135–159.

Middlebrooks, J. C., & Pettigrew, J. D. (1981). Functional classes of neurons in primary auditory cortex of the cat distinguished by sensitivity to sound location. *Journal of Neuroscience, 1,* 107–120.

Mikami, A., Newsome, W. T., & Wurtz, R. H. (1986). Motion selectivity in macaque visual cortex: I. Mechanisms of direction and speed selectivity in extrastriate area MT. *Journal of Neurophysiology, 55,* 1308–1327.

Miller, G. A., & Heise, G. A. (1950). The trill threshold. *Journal of the Acoustical Society of America, 22,* 637–683.

Miller, G. A., & Isard, S. (1963). Some perceptual consequences of linguistic rules. *Journal of Verbal Learning and Verbal Behavior, 2,* 212–228.

Miller, I. J. (1995). Anatomy of the peripheral taste system. In R. L. Doty (Ed.), *Handbook of olfaction and gustation* (pp. 521–548). New York: Marcel Dekker.

Miller, J. D. (1974). Effects of noise on people. *Journal of the Acoustical Society of America, 56,* 729–764.

Milner, A. D., & Goodale, M. A. (1995). *The visual brain in action.* New York: Oxford University Press.

Mishkin, M. (1986, January 24). *Two visual systems.* Talk presented at Western Psychiatric Institute and Clinic, Pittsburgh.

Mishkin, M., Ungerleider, L. G., & Macko, K. A. (1983). Object vision and spatial vision: Two central pathways. *Trends in Neuroscience, 6,* 414–417.

Mitchell, D. E., & Timney, B. (1984). Postnatal development of function in the mammalian visual system. In J. M. Brookhart & V. B. Mountcastle (Eds.), *Handbook of physiology: The nervous system III* (pp. 507–555). Bethesda, MD: American Physiological Society.

Mitchell, D. E., & Wilkinson, F. (1974). The effect of early astigmatism on the visual resolution of gratings. *Journal of Physiology, 243,* 739–756.

Mollon, J. D. (1989). "Tho' she kneel'd in that place where they grew . . ." *Journal of Experimental Biology, 146,* 21–38.

Mollon, J. D. (1990). The club-sandwich mystery. *Nature, 343,* 16–17.

Mollon, J. D. (1992). Signac's secret. *Nature, 358,* 379–380.

Mollon, J. D. (1993). Mixing genes and mixing colours. *Current Biology, 3,* 82–85.

Montagna, W., & Parakkal, P. F. (1974). *The structure and function of skin* (3rd ed.). New York: Academic Press.

Moon, C., Cooper, R. P., & Fifer, W. P. (1993). Two-day-olds prefer their native language. *Infant Behavior and Development, 16,* 495–500.

Moran, J., & Desimone, R. (1985). Selective attention gates visual processing in the extrastriate cortex. *Science, 229,* 782–784.

Mori, K., & Yoshihara, Y. (1995). Molecular recognition and olfactory processing in the mammalian olfactory system. *Progress in Neurobiology, 45,* 585–619.

Morrison, E. E., & Moran, D. T. (1995). Anatomy and ultrastructure of the human olfactory neuroepithelium. In R. L. Doty (Ed.), *Handbook of olfaction and gustation* (pp. 75–101). New York: Marcel Dekker.

Morrongiello, B. A. (1988). Infants' localization of sounds along the horizontal axis: Estimates of minimum audible angle. *Developmental Psychology, 24,* 8–13.

Morrongiello, B. A., Fenwick, K. D., & Chance, G. (1990). Sound localization acuity in very young infants: An observer-based testing procedure. *Developmental Psychology, 26,* 75–84.

Moskowitz, H. R., Kumriach, V., Sharma, H., Jacobs, L., & Sharma, S. D. (1975). Cross-cultural differences in simple taste preference. *Science, 190,* 1217–1218.

Moulton, D. G. (1965). Differential sensitivity to odors. *Cold Spring Harbor Symposium on Quantitative Biology, 30,* 201–206.

Moulton, D. G. (1977). Minimum odorant concentrations detectable by the dog and their implications for olfactory receptor sensitivity. In D. Miller-Schwarze & M. M. Mozell (Eds.), *Chemical signals in vertebrates* (pp. 455–464). New York: Plenum Press.

Mountcastle, V. B., & Powell, T. P. S. (1959). Neural mechanisms subserving cutaneous sensibility, with special reference to the role of afferent inhibition in sensory perception and discrimination. *Bulletin of the Johns Hopkins Hospital, 105,* 201–232.

Movshon, J. A., & Newsome, W. T. (1992). Neural foundations of visual motion perception. *Current Directions in Psychological Science, 1,* 35–39.

Mozell, M. M., Smith, B. P., Smith, P. E., Sullivan, R. L., & Swender, P. (1969). Nasal chemoreception in flavor identification. *Archives of Otolaryngology, 90,* 131–137.

Muir, D., & Field, J. (1979). Newborn infants orient to sounds. *Child Development, 50,* 431–436.

Muller, J. (1842). *Elements of physiology* (W. Baly, Trans.). London: Tayler & Walton.

Murphy, C., & Cain, W. S. (1980). Taste and olfaction: Independence vs. interaction. *Physiology and Behavior, 24,* 601–606.

Mutti, D. O., Zadnik, K., & Adams, A. J. (1996). Myopia: The nature versus nurture debate goes on. *Investigative Ophthalmology and Visual Science, 37,* 952–957.

Nachman, M. (1963). Taste preferences for sodium salts by adrenalectomized rats. *Journal of Comparative and Physiological Psychology, 55,* 1124–1129.

Nakamura, H., Gattass, R., Desimone, R., & Ungerleider, L. G. (1993). The modular organization of projections from areas V1 and V2 to areas V4 and TEO in macaques. *Journal of Neuroscience, 13,* 3681–3691.

Nakayama, K. (1994). James J. Gibson—An appreciation. *Psychological Review, 101,* 329–335.

Nathan, P. W. (1976). The gate control theory of pain. *Brain, 99,* 123–158.

Nathans, J., Thomas, D., & Hogness, D. S. (1986). Molecular genetics of human color vision: The genes encoding blue, green, and red pigments. *Science, 232,* 193–202.

Neitz, J., Neitz, M., & Jacobs, G. H. (1993). More than three different cone pigments among people with normal color vision. *Vision Research, 33,* 117–122.

Neitz, M., Neitz, J., & Jacobs, G. H. (1991). Spectral tuning of pigments underlying red-green color vision. *Science, 252,* 971–974.

Nelson, C. A., & Horowitz, F. D. (1987). Visual motion perception in infancy: A review and synthesis. In P. Salapatek & L. Cohen (Eds.), *Handbook of infant perception* (Vol. 2, pp. 123–153). New York: Academic Press.

Nelson, M. E., & Bower, J. M. (1990). Brain maps and parallel computers. *Trends in Neuroscience, 13,* 403–408.

Nelson, P. G., Erulkar, S. D., & Bryan, S. S. (1966). Responses of units of the inferior colliculus to time-varying acoustic stimuli. *Journal of Neurophysiology, 29,* 834–860.

Nelson, R. J., Sur, M., Felleman, D. J., & Kaas, J. H. (1980). Representations of the body surface in postcentral parietal cortex of *Macaca fasicularis. Journal of Comparative Neurology, 192,* 611–643.

Neuenschwander, S., & Singer, W. (1996). Long-range synchronization of oscillatory light responses in the cat retina and lateral geniculate nucleus. *Nature, 379,* 728–733.

Neville, H. J. (1990). Intermodal competition and compensation in development. *Annals New York Academy of Science, 608,* 71–91.

Newman, E. R., & Hartline, P. H. (1982, March). The infrared "vision" of snakes. *Scientific American, 246,* 116–127.

Newsome, W. T., Britten, K. H., & Movshon, J. A. (1989). Neuronal correlates of a perceptual decision. *Nature, 341,* 52–54.

Newsome, W. T., Mikami, A., & Wurtz, R. H. (1986). Motion selectivity in macaque visual cortex: III. Psychophysics and physiology of apparent motion. *Journal of Neurophysiology, 55,* 1340–1351.

Newsome, W. T., & Pare, E. B. (1988). A selective impairment of motion perception following lesions of the middle temporal visual area (MT). *Journal of Neuroscience, 8,* 2201–2211.

Newsome, W. T., Shadlen, M. N., Zohary, E., Britten, K. H., & Movshon, J. A. (1995). Visual motion: Linking neuronal activity to psychophysical performance. In M. S. Gazzaniga (Ed.), *The cognitive neurosciences* (pp. 401–414). Cambridge, MA: MIT Press.

Newton, I. (1704). *Optiks*. London: Smith and Walford.

Nordby, K. (1990). Vision in a complete achromat: A personal account. In R. F. Hess, L. T. Sharpe, & K. Nordby (Eds.), *Night vision* (pp. 290–315). Cambridge, England: Cambridge University Press.

Northern, J., & Downs, M. (1978). *Hearing in children* (2nd ed.). Baltimore, MA: Williams & Wilkins.

Norton, S. J., Schultz, M. C., Reed, C. M., Briada, L. D., Durlach, N. L., & Rabinowitz, W. M. (1977). Analytic study of the Tadoma method: Background and preliminary results. *Journal of Speech and Hearing Research, 20*, 574–595.

Nothdurft, H. C. (1990). Texton segregation by associated differences in global and local luminance distribution. *Proceedings of the Royal Society of London, B239*, 295–320.

Nygaard, L. C., & Pisoni, D. B. (1995). Speech perception: New directions in research and theory. In J. L. Miller & P. D. Eimas (Eds.), *Speech, language, and communication* (pp. 63–97). San Diego, CA: Academic Press.

Nygaard, L. C., Sommers, M. S., & Pisoni, D. B. (1994). Speech perception as a talker-contingent process. *Psychological Science, 5*, 42–46.

Oldfield, S. R., & Parker, S. P. A. (1984). Acuity of sound localization: A topography of auditory space: 2. Pinna cues absent. *Perception, 13*, 601–617.

Olsen, J. F., & Suga, N. (1991a). Combination sensory neurons in the medial geniculate body of the mustache bat: Encoding of relative velocity information. *Journal of Neurophysiology, 65*, 1254–1273.

Olsen, J. F., & Suga, N. (1991b). Combination sensory neurons in the medial geniculate body of the mustache bat: Encoding of target range information. *Journal of Neurophysiology, 65*, 1275–1296.

Olsho, L. W., Koch, E. G., Carter, E. A., Halpin, C. F., & Spetner, N. B. (1988). Pure-tone sensitivity of human infants. *Journal of the Acoustical Society of America, 84*, 1316–1324.

Olsho, L. W., Koch, E. G., Halpin, C. F., & Carter, E. A. (1987). An observer-based psychoacoustic procedure for use with young infants. *Developmental Psychology, 23*, 627–640.

Olson, C. R., & Freeman, R. D. (1980). Profile of the sensitive period for monocular deprivation in kittens. *Experimental Brain Research, 39*, 17–21.

Olson, H. (1967). *Music, physics, and engineering* (2nd ed.). New York: Dover.

Oram, M. W., & Perrett, D. I. (1994). Responses of anterior superior temporal polysensory (STPa) neurons to "biological motion" stimuli. *Journal of Cognitive Neuroscience, 6*, 99–116.

Orban, G. A., Lagae, L., Verri, A., Raiguel, S., Xiao, D., Maes, H., & Torre, V. (1992). First-order analysis of optical flow in monkey brain. *Proceedings of the National Academy of Sciences, 89*, 2595–2599.

O'Shea, R. P. (1991). Thumb's rule tested: Visual angle of thumb's width is about 2 deg. *Perception, 20*, 415–418.

Owens, E. (1989). Present status of adults with cochlear implants. In E. Owens & D. K. Kessler (Eds.), *Cochlear implants in young deaf children* (pp. 25–52). Boston: Little, Brown.

Owens, M. (1994, June 6). Designers discover the sweet smell of success. *New York Times.*

Oxford American Dictionary. (1980). New York: Oxford University Press.

Oyama, T. (1960). Figure-ground dominance as a function of sector angle, brightness, hue, and orientation. *Journal of Experimental Psychology, 60*, 299–305.

Palmer, A. R., & Evans, E. F. (1979). On the peripheral coding of the level of individual frequency components of complex sounds at high sound levels. In O. Creutzfeldt, H. Scheich, & C. Schreiner (Eds.), *Hearing mechanisms and speech.* Berlin: Springer-Verlag.

Palmer, S. E. (1975). The effects of contextual scenes on the identification of objects. *Memory and Cognition*, 3, 519–526.

Palmeri, T. J., Goldinger, S. D., & Pisoni, D. B. (1993). Episodic encoding of voice attributes and recognition memory for spoken words. *Journal of Experimental Psychology: Learning Memory and Cognition*, 19, 309–328.

Parkin, A. J. (1996). *Explorations in cognitive neuropsychology.* Oxford, England: Blackwell.

Pascalis, O., deSchonen, S., Morton, J., Deruelle, C., & Fabre-Grenet, M. (1995). Mother's face recognition by neonates: A replication and an extension. *Infant Behavior and Development*, 18, 79–85.

Pasternak, T. (1990). Vision following loss of cortical directional selectivity. In M. A. Berkley & W. C. Stebbins (Eds.), *Comparative perception* (Vol. 1, pp. 407–428). New York: Wiley.

Pasternak, T., & Merigan, E. H. (1994). Motion perception following lesions of the superior temporal sulcus in the monkey. *Cerebral Cortex*, 4, 247–259.

Patuzzi, R. (1996). Cochlear micromechanics and macromechanics. In P. Dallos, A. N. Popper, & R. R. Fay (Eds.), *The cochlea* (pp. 186 –257). New York: Springer.

Paulesu, E., Harrison, J., Baron-Cohen, S., Watson, J. D. G., Goldstein, L., Heather, J., Frackowiak, R. S. J., & Frith, C. D. (1995). The physiology of colored hearing. *Brain*, 118, 661–676.

Pauls, J. (1995). Psychophysical and physiological evidence for viewer-centered object representations in the primate. *Cerebral Cortex*, 5, 270–288.

Penfield, W., & Rasmussen, T. (1950). *The cerebral cortex of man.* New York: Macmillan.

Perl, E. R., & Kruger, L. (1996). In L. Kruger (Ed.), *Pain and touch* (pp. 179–221). San Diego, CA: Academic Press.

Perrett, D. I., Harries, M. H., Benson, P. J., Chitty, A. J., & Mistlin, A. J. (1990). Retrieval of structure from rigid and biological motion: An analysis of the visual responses of neurones in the macaque temporal cortex. In A. Blake & T. Troscianko (Eds.), *AI and the eye* (pp. 181–200). New York: Wiley.

Perrett, D. I., Hietanen, J. K., Oram, M. W., & Benson, P. J. (1992). Organization and function of cells responsive to faces in the temporal cortex. *Transactions of the Royal Society of London*, B225, 23–30.

Perrett, D. I., & Oram, M. W. (1993). Neurophysiology of shape processing. *Image and visual computing*, 11, 317–333.

Peterson, F., & Rainey, L. H. (1911). The beginnings of mind in the newborn. *Bulletin of the Lying-In Hospital*, 7, 99–122.

Peterson, M. A. (1994). Object recognition processes can and do operate before figure-ground organization. *Current Directions in Psychological Science*, 3, 105–111.

Pettit, M. J., & Schwark, H. D. (1993). Receptive field reorganization in dorsal column nuclei during temporary denervation. *Science*, 262, 2054–2056.

Pevsner, J., Hou, V., Snowman, A. M., & Snyder, S. H. (1990). Odorant-binding protein: Characterization of ligand binding. *Journal of Biological Chemistry*, 265, 6118–6125.

Pevsner, J., Trifletti, R. R., Strittmatter, S. M., & Snyder, S. H. (1985). Isolation and characterization of an olfactory protein for odorant pyrazines. *Proceedings of the National Academy of Sciences*, 82, 3050–3054.

Pfaffmann, C. (1974). Specificity of the sweet receptors of the squirrel monkey. *Chemical Senses*, 1, 61–67.

Pfeiffer, C. A., & Johnston, R. E. (1994). Hormonal and behavioral responses of male hamsters to females and female odors: Roles of olfaction, the vemeronasal system, and sexual experience. *Physiology and Behavior*, 55, 129–138.

Phillips, D. P., Mendelson, J. R., Cynader, M. S., & Douglas, R. M. (1985). Responses of single neurons in cat auditory cortex to time-varying stimuli: Frequency-modulated tones of narrow excursion. *Experimental Brain Research*, 58, 443–454.

Pick, A. D., Thomas, M. L., & Pick, H. L. (1966). The role of grapheme-phoneme correspondences in the perception of braille. *Journal of Verbal Learning and Verbal Behavior*, 5, 298–300.

Pickles, J. O. (1988). *An introduction to the physiology of hearing.* San Diego, CA: Academic Press.

Pirchio, M., Spinelli, D., Fiorentini, A., & Maffei, L. (1978). Infant contrast sensitivity evaluated by evoked potentials. *Brain Research, 141,* 179–184.

Pizlo, Z., Salach-Golyska, M., & Rosenfeld, A. (1997). Curve detection in a noisy image. *Vision Research,* 37, 1217–1241.

Plack, C. J., & Carlyon, R. P. (1995). Loudness perception and intensity coding. In B. C. J. Moore (Ed.), *Hearing* (pp. 123–160). San Diego: Academic Press.

Plug, C., & Ross, H. E. (1994). The natural moon illusion: A multifactor account. *Perception, 23,* 321–333.

Poggio, G. F. (1990). Cortical neural mechanisms of stereopsis studied with dynamic random-dot stereograms. *Cold Spring Harbor Symposia on Quantitative Biology,* 55, 749–758.

Poggio, T. (1984, April). Vision by man and machine. *Scientific American,* 106–116.

Pokorny, J., Shevell, S. K., & Smith, V. C. (1991). Color appearance and color constancy. In P. Gouras (Ed.), *The perception of color: Vol. 6. Vision and visual dysfunction* (pp. 43–61). Boca Raton, FL: CRC Press.

Pollak, G. D., & Casseday, J. H. (1989). *The neural basis of echolocation in bats.* New York: Springer-Verlag.

Pomerantz, J. R. (1981). Perceptual organization in information processing. In M. Kubovy & J. Pomerantz (Eds.), *Perceptual organization.* Hillsdale, NJ: Erlbaum.

Pomerantz, J. R., & Lockhead, G. R. (1991). Perception of structure: An overview. In G. R. Lockhead & J. R. Pomerantz (Eds.), *Perception of structure* (pp. 1–20). Washington, DC: American Psychological Association.

Pons, T. P., Garraghty, P. E., Ommaya, A. K., Kaas, J. H., Taub, E., & Mishkin, M. (1991). Massive cortical reorganization after sensory deafferentation in adult macaques. *Science,* 252, 1857–1860.

Porter, R. H., Makin, J. W., Davis, L. B., & Christensen, K. M. (1992). Breast-fed infants respond to olfactory cues from their own mother and unfamiliar lactating females. *Infant Behavior and Development, 15,* 85–93.

Porter, R. H., & Schaal, B. (1995). Olfaction and development of social preferences in neonatal organisms. In R. L. Doty (Ed.), *Handbook of olfaction and gustation* (pp. 299–321). New York: Marcel Dekker.

Power, R. (1981). The dominance of touch by vision: Occurs with familiar objects. *Perception, 10,* 29–33.

Preti, G., Cutler, W. B., Garcia, C. R., Huggins, G. R., & Lawley, H. J. (1986). Human axillary secretions influence women's menstrual cycles: The role of donor extract from females. *Hormones and Behavior,* 20, 474–482.

Price, J. L., Carmichael, S. T., Carnes, K. M., Clugnet, M. C., Kuroda, M., & Ray, J. P. (1991). Olfactory output to the prefrontal cortex. In J. L. Davis & H. Eichenbaum (Eds.), *Olfaction: A model system for computational neuroscience* (pp. 101–120). Cambridge, MA: MIT Press.

Proffitt, D. R., & Kaiser, M. K. (1995). Perceiving events. In W. Epstein & S. Rogers (Eds.), *Perception of space and motion* (pp. 227–261). San Diego, CA: Academic Press.

Purkinje, J. E. (1825). *Neurre Beitrage zur Kenntniss des Sehens in subjectiver Hinsicht.* Berlin: Reimer.

Quinn, P. C., Burke, S., & Rush, A. (1993). Part-whole perception in early infancy: Evidence for perceptual grouping produced by lightness similarity. *Infant Behavior and Development, 16,* 19–42.

Quinn, P. C., & Eimas, P. D. (1996). Perceptual organization and categorization in young infants. In L. Lipsitt & C. Rovee-Collier (Eds.), *Advances in infancy research* (Vol. 10). New York: ABLEX.

Quinn, P. C., Rosano, J. L., & Wooten, B. R. (1988). Evidence that brown is not an elemental color. *Perception and Psychophysics,* 43, 156–164.

Quittner, A. L., Smith, L. B., Osberger, M. J., Mitchell, T. V., & Katz, D. B. (1994). The impact of audition on the development of visual attention. *Psychological Science,* 5, 347–353.

Rafal, R., & Robertson, L. (1995). The neurology of visual attention. In M. S. Gazzaniga (Ed.), *The cognitive neurosciences* (pp. 625–648). Cambridge, MA: MIT Press.

Ramachandran, V. S. (1992, May). Blind spots. *Scientific American*, 86–91.

Ramachandran, V. S., & Anstis, S. M. (1986, May). The perception of apparent motion. *Scientific American*, 102–109.

Ranganathan, R., Harris, W. A., & Zuker, C. S. (1991). The molecular genetics of invertebrate phototransduction. *Trends in Neurosciences, 14*, 486–493.

Ratliff, F. (1965). *Mach bands: Quantitative studies on neural networks in the retina.* New York: Holden-Day.

Rauschecker, J. P. (1995). Compensatory plasticity and sensory substitution in the cerebral cortex. *Trends in Neurosciences, 18*, 36–43.

Rauschecker, J. P., & Korte, M. (1993). Auditory compensation for early blindness in cat cerebral cortex. *Journal of Neuroscience, 13*, 4538–4548.

Rauschecker, J. P., Tian, B., & Hauser, M. (1995). Processing of complex sounds in the macaque nonprimary auditory cortex. *Science, 268*, 111–114.

Raviola, E., & Wiesel, T. N. (1985). An animal model of myopia. *New England Journal of Medicine, 312*, 1609–1615.

Rayleigh, L. (1881). Experiments on colour. *Nature, 25*, 64–66.

Reale, R. A., & Imig, T. J. (1980). Tonotopic organization in auditory cortex of the cat. *Journal of Comparative Neurology, 192*, 265–291.

Reddy, D. R. (1976). Speech recognition by machine: A review. *Proceedings of the Institute of Electrical and Electronic Engineers, 64*, 501–531.

Reed, C. M., Durlach, N. I., Braida, L. D., & Schultz, M. C. (1982). Analytic study of the tadoma method: Identification of consonants and vowels by an experienced Tadoma user. *Journal of Speech and Hearing Research, 25*, 108–116.

Reed, R. R., Bakalyar, H. A., Cunningham, A. M., & Levy, N. S. (1992). The molecular basis of signal transduction in olfactory sensory neurons. In D. P. Corey & S. D. Roper (Eds.), *Sensory transduction* (pp. 53–60). New York: Rockefeller University Press.

Regan, D. (1986). Luminance contrast: Vernier discrimination. *Spatial Vision, 1*, 305–318.

Regan, D., & Cynader, M. (1979). Neurons in area 18 of cat visual cortex selectively sensitive to changing size: Nonlinear interactions between responses to two edges. *Vision Research, 19*, 699–711.

Rehn, T. (1978). Perceived odor intensity as a function of air flow through the nose. *Sensory Processes, 2*, 198–205.

Reichardt, W. (1961). Autocorrelation, a principle for the evaluation of sensory information by the central nervous system. In W. A. Rosenblith (Ed.), *Sensory communication* (pp. 303–318). New York: Wiley.

Reichl, R. (1994, March 11). Dining in New York. *New York Times.*

Rensink, R. A., O'Regan, J. K., & Clark, J. J. (1995). Image flicker is as good as saccades in making large scene changes invisible. *Perception*, 24(Suppl.), 26–27.

Rensick, R. A., O'Regan, J. K., & Clark, J. J. (1996). To see or not to see: The need for attention to perceive changes in scenes. *Investigative Opthalmology and Visual Science, 37*, S215.

Restle, F. (1970). Moon illusion explained on the basis of relative size. *Science, 167*, 1092–1096.

Reymond, L. (1985). Spatial visual acuity of the eagle *Aquila audax:* A behavioral, optical and anatomical investigation. *Vision Research, 25*, 1477–1491.

Reynolds, D. V. (1969). Surgery in the rat during electrical analgesia induced by focal brain stimulation. *Science, 164*, 444–445.

Ribaupierre, F. de. (1997). Acoustical information processing in the auditory thalamus and cerebral cortex. In G. Ehret & R. Romand (Eds.), *The central auditory system* (pp. 317–398). New York: Oxford University Press.

Rice, C. E. (1967). Human echolocation. *Science, 155*, 656–664.

Riggs, L. A. (1965). Visual acuity. In C. Graham (Ed.), *Vision and visual perception.* New York: Wiley.

Risset, J. C., & Mathews, M. W. (1969). Analysis of musical instrument tones. *Physics Today, 22,* 23–30.

Robinson, D. L., & Wurtz, R. (1976). Use of an extra-retinal signal by monkey superior colliculus neurons to distinguish real from self-induced stimulus movement. *Journal of Neurophysiology,* 39, 852–870.

Robson, J. G., Tolhurst, D. J., Freeman, R. D., & Ohzawa, I. (1988). Simple cells in the visual cortex of the cat can be narrowly tuned for spatial frequency. *Visual Neuroscience, 1,* 415–419.

Rock, I., & Gutman, D. (1981). The effect of inattention on form perception. *Journal of Experimental Psychology: Human Perception and Performance, 7,* 275–285.

Rock, I., & Kaufman, L. (1962). The moon illusion: Part 2. *Science, 136,* 1023–1031.

Rock, I., & Palmer, S. (1990, December). The legacy of Gestalt psychology. *Scientific American,* 84–90.

Rock, I., & Victor, J. (1964). Vision and touch: An experimentally created conflict between the senses. *Science, 143,* 594–596.

Rodman, H. R., Scalaidhe, S. P. O., & Gross, C. (1993). Response properties of neurons in temporal cortical visual areas of infant monkeys. *Journal of Neurophysiology, 70,* 1115–1136.

Roe, A. W., Pallas, S. L., Kwon, Y. H., & Sur, M. (1992). Visual projections routed to the auditory pathway in ferrets: Receptive fields of visual neurons in primary auditory cortex. *Journal of Neuroscience, 12,* 3651–3664.

Roland, P. (1992). Cortical representation of pain. *Trends in Neuroscience, 15,* 3–5.

Rollman, G. B. (1991). Pain responsiveness. In M. A. Heller & W. Schiff (Eds.), *The psychology of touch* (pp. 91–114). Hillsdale, NJ: Erlbaum.

Rolls, E. T. (1992). Neurophysiological mechanisms underlying face processing within and beyond the temporal cortical visual areas. *Transactions of the Royal Society of London, B335,* 11–21.

Rolls, E. T., & Tovee, M. J. (1995). Sparseness of the neuronal representation of stimuli in the primate temporal visual cortex. *Journal of Neurophysiology, 73,* 713–726.

Rose, J. E., Brugge, J. F., Anderson, D. J., & Hind, J. E. (1967). Phase locked response to low frequency tones in single auditory nerve fibers of the squirrel monkey. *Journal of Neurophysiology,* 30, 769–793.

Rosenstein, D., & Oster, H. (1988). Differential facial responses to four basic tastes in newborns. *Child Development, 59,* 1555–1568.

Rosenthal, E. (1992, December 29). Chronic pain fells many yet lacks clear cause. *New York Times,* pp. B5, B6.

Rosowski, J. J. (1996). Models of external–and middle-ear function. In H. Hawkins, T. A. McMullen, A. N. Popper, & R. R. Fay (Eds.), *Auditory computation* (pp. 15–61). New York: Springer-Verlag.

Rouiller, E. M. (1997). Functional organization of the auditory pathways. In G. Ehret & R. Romand (Eds.), *The central auditory system* (pp. 3–96). Oxford, England: Oxford University Press.

Royden, C. S., Banks, M. S., & Crowell, J. A. (1992). The perception of heading during eye movements. *Nature, 360,* 583–585.

Rozin, P. (1976). The selection of foods by rats, humans, and other animals. In J. S. Rosenblatt, R. A. Hinde, & C. Beer (Eds.), *Advances in the study of behavior.* New York: Academic Press.

Rozin, P. (1982). "Taste-smell confusions" and the duality of the olfactory sense. *Perception and Psychophysics, 31,* 397–401.

Rozin, P. (1990). Development in the food domain. *Developmental Psychology, 26,* 555–562.

Rubin, E. (1915). *Synoplevde Figurer.* Copenhagen: Gyldendalske.

Rubin, P., Turvey, M. T., & Van Gelder, P. (1976). Initial phoneme are detected faster in spoken words than in spoken nonwords. *Perception and Psychophysics, 19,* 394–398.

Rudel, R. G., & Teuber, H.-L. (1963). Decrement of visual and haptic Muller-Lyer illusion on repeated trials: A study of crossmodal transfer. *Quarterly Journal of Experimental Psychology, 15,* 125–131.

Runeson, S. (1977). On the possibility of "smart" perceptual mechanisms. *Scandinavian Journal of Psychology, 18*, 172–179.

Rushton, W. A. H. (1961). Rhodopsin measurement and dark adaptation in a subject deficient in cone vision. *Journal of Physiology, 156*, 193–205.

Rushton, W. A. H. (1964). Color blindness and cone pigments. *American Journal of Optometry and Archives of the American Academy of Optometry, 41*, 265–282.

Russell, I. J., & Sellick, P. M. (1977). Tuning properties of cochlear hair cells. *Nature, 267*, 858–860.

Russell, M. J. (1976). Human olfactory communication. *Nature, 260*, 520–522.

Russell, M. J., Switz, G. M., & Thompson, K. (1980). Olfactory influence on the human menstrual cycle. *Pharmacology, Biochemistry and Behavior, 13*, 737–738.

Rutherford, W. (1886). A new theory of hearing. *Journal of Anatomy and Physiology, 21*, 166–168.

Ryan, A., & Dallos, P. (1975). Absence of cochlear outer hair cells: Effect on behavioral auditory threshold. *Nature, 253*, 44–46.

Sachs, M. B., Young, E. D., & Miller, M. I. (1981). Encoding of speech features in the auditory nerve. In R. Carson & B. Grandstrom (Eds.), *The representation of speech in the peripheral auditory system* (pp. 115–139). New York: Elsevier.

Sacks, O. (1985). *The man who mistook his wife for a hat.* London: Duckworth.

Sakata, H., & Iwamura, Y. (1978). Cortical processing of tactile information in the first somatosensory and parietal association areas in the monkey. In G. Gordon (Ed.), *Active touch* (pp. 55–72). Elmsford, NY: Pergamon Press.

Sakata, H., Taira, M., Mine, S., & Murata, A. (1992). Hand-movement-related neurons of the posterior parietal cortex of the monkey: Their role in visual guidance of hand movements. In R. Caminiti, P. B. Johnson, & Y. Burnod (Eds.), *Control of arm movement in space: Neurophysiological and computational approaches* (pp. 185–198). Berlin: Springer-Verlag.

Salapatek, P., & Banks, M. S. (1978). Infant sensory assessment: Vision. In F. D. Minifie & L. L. Lloyd (Eds.), *Communicative and cognitive abilities: Early behavioral assessment* (pp. 61–106). Baltimore: University Park Press.

Salapatek, P., Bechtold, A. G., & Bushnell, E. W. (1976). Infant visual acuity as a function of viewing distance. *Child Development, 47*, 860–863.

Salasoo, A., & Pisoni, D. B. (1985). Interaction of knowledge sources in spoken word identification. *Journal of Memory and Language 24*, 210–231.

Samuel, A. G. (1981). Phonemic restoration: Insights from a new methodology. *Journal of Experimental Psychology: General, 110*, 474–494.

Samuel, A. G. (1990). Using perceptual-restoration effects to explore the architecture of perception. In G. T. M. Altmann (Ed.), *Cognitive models of speech processing* (pp. 295–314). Cambridge, MA: MIT Press.

Sato, M., & Ogawa, H. (1994). Neural coding of taste in macaque monkeys. In K. Kurihara, N. Suzuki, & H. Ogawa (Eds.), *Olfaction and taste* (Vol. 11, pp. 388–392). Tokyo: Springer-Verlag.

Sato, M., Ogawa, H., & Yamashita, S. (1975). Response properties of macaque monkey chorda tympani fibers. *Journal of General Physiology, 66*, 781–810.

Sato, M., Ogawa, H., & Yamashita, S. (1994). Gustatory responsiveness of chorda tympani fibers in the cynomolgus monkey. *Chemical Senses, 19*, 381–400.

Scharf, B. (1975). Audition. In B. Scharf (Ed.), *Experimental sensory psychology* (pp. 112–149). Glenview, IL: Scott, Foresman.

Scheich, H., Langner, G., Tidemann, C., Coles, R. B., & Guppy, A. (1986). Electroception and electrolocation in platypus. *Nature, 319*, 401–402.

Schiff, W. (1980). *Perception: An applied approach.* Boston: Houghton Mifflin.

Schiff, W., & Detwiler, M. L. (1979). Information used in judging impending collision. *Perception, 8*, 647–658.

Schiffman, H. R. (1967). Size-estimation of familiar objects under informative and reduced conditions of viewing. *American Journal of Psychology, 80,* 229–235.

Schiffman, S. S., & Erickson, R. P. (1971). A psychophysical model for gustatory quality. *Physiology and Behavior, 7,* 617–633.

Schiffman, S. S., & Erickson, R. P. (1993). Psychophysics: Insights into transduction mechanisms and neural coding. In S. A. Simon & S. D. Roper (Eds.), *Mechanisms of taste transduction* (pp. 395–424). Boca Raton, FL: CRC Press.

Schiller, P. H. (1992). The ON and OFF channels of the visual system. *Trends in Neurosciences, 15,* 86–92.

Schiller, P. H., Logothetis, N. K., & Charles, E. R. (1990). Functions of the colour-opponent and broad-band channels of the visual system. *Nature, 343,* 68–70.

Schnapf, J. L., Kraft, T. W., & Baylor, D. A. (1987). Spectral sensitivity of human cone photoreceptors. *Nature, 325,* 439–441.

Schreiner, C. H., & Mendelson, J. R. (1990). Functional topography of cat primary auditory cortex: Distribution of integrated excitation. *Journal of Neurophysiology, 64,* 1442–1459.

Schubert, E. D. (1980). *Hearing: Its function and dysfunction.* Wien: Springer-Verlag.

Schwartz, A. S., Perez, A. J., & Azulaz, A. (1975). Further analysis of active and passive touch in pattern discrimination. *Bulletin of the Psychonomic Society, 6,* 7–9.

Schwind, R. (1978). Visual system of Notonecta glaucia: A neuron sensitive to movement in the binocular visual field. *Journal of Comparative Physiology, 123,* 315–328.

Scott, T. R. (1987). Coding in the gustatory system. In T. E. Finger & W. L. Silver (Eds.), *Neurobiology of taste and smell* (pp. 355–378). New York: Wiley.

Scott, T. R., & Giza, B. K. (1990). Coding channels in the taste system of the rat. *Science, 249,* 1585–1587.

Scott, T. R., & Giza, B. K. (1995). Theories of gustatory neural coding. In R. L. Doty (Ed.), *Handbook of olfaction and gustation* (pp. 611–633). New York: Marcel Dekker.

Scott, T. R., & Plata-Salaman, C. R. (1991). Coding of taste quality. In T. V. Getchell, R. L. Doty, L. M. Bartoshuk, & J. B. Snow (Eds.), *Smell and taste in health and disease* (pp. 345–368). New York: Raven Press.

Searle, C. L., Jacobson, J. Z., & Rayment, S. G. (1979). Stop consonant discrimination based on human audition. *Journal of the Acoustical Society of America, 65,* 799–809.

Sedgwick, H. A. (1973). The visible horizon: A potential source of visual information for the perception of size and distance. *Dissertation Abstracts International, 34,* 1301B–1302B.

Sedgwick, H. A. (1983). Environment-centered representation of spatial layout: Available visual information from texture and perspective. In A. Rosenthal & J. Beck (Eds.), *Human and machine vision* (pp. 425–458). New York: Academic Press.

Sedgwick, H. A. (1986). Space perception. In K. R. Boff, L. Kaufman, & J. P. Thomas (Eds.), *Handbook of perception and human performance* (Chapter 21). New York: Wiley.

Segui, J. (1984). The syllable: A basic perceptual unit in speech processing? In H. Bouma & D. G. Gouwhuis (Eds.), *Attention and performance X* (pp. 165–181). Hillsdale, NJ: Erlbaum.

Shapley, R. (1995). Parallel neural pathways and visual function. In M. S. Gazzaniga (Ed.), *The cognitive neurosciences* (pp. 315–324). Cambridge, MA: MIT Press.

Shepherd, G. M. (1991). Sensory transduction: Entering the mainstream of membrane signaling. *Cell, 67,* 845–851.

Shepherd, G. M. (1992a). Modules for molecules. *Nature, 358,* 457–458.

Shepherd, G. M. (1992b). Toward a consensus working model for olfactory transduction. In D. P. Corey & S. D. Roper (Eds.), *Sensory transduction* (pp. 19–37). New York: Rockefeller University Press.

Shepherd, G. M. (1994). Discrimination of molecular signals by the olfactory receptor neuron. *Neuron, 13,* 771–790.

Shepherd, G. M. (1995). Toward a molecular basis for sensory perception. In M. S. Gazzaniga (Ed.), *The cognitive neurosciences* (pp. 105–118). Cambridge, MA: MIT Press.

Shepherd, G. M., & Firestein, S. (1991). Making scents of olfactory transduction. *Current Biology, 1,* 204–206.

Sherk, H., & Stryker, M. P. (1976). Quantitative study of cortical orientation selectivity in visually inexperienced kittens. *Journal of Neurophysiology, 39,* 63–70.

Sherman, S. M., & Koch, C. (1986). The control of retinogeniculate transmission in the mammalian lateral geniculate nucleus. *Experimental Brain Research, 63,* 1 –20.

Sherrick, C. E. (1968). Bilateral apparent haptic movement. *Perception and Psychophysics, 4,* 159–160.

Sherrick, C. E., & Rogers, R. (1966). Apparent haptic movement. *Perception and Psychophysics, 1,* 175–180.

Shiffrar, M. (1994). When what meets where. *Current Directions in Psychological Science, 3,* 96–100.

Shiffrar, M., & Freyd, J. J. (1990). Apparent motion of the human body. *Psychological Science, 1,* 257–264.

Shiffrar, M., & Freyd, J. J. (1993). Timing and apparent motion path choice with human body photographs. *Psychological Science, 4,* 379–384.

Shih, G., & Kessell, R. (1982). *Living images.* Boston: Jones and Bartlett.

Sicard, G., & Holley, A. (1984). Receptor cell responses to odorants: Similarities and differences among odorants. *Brain Research, 292,* 283–296.

Silver, W. L., & Finger, T. E. (1991). The trigeminal system. In T. V. Getchell, R. L. Doty, L. M. Bartoshuk, & J. B. Snow (Eds.), *Smell and taste in health and disease* (pp. 97–108). New York: Raven Press.

Simons, D. J. (1996). In sight, out of mind: When object representations fail. *Psychological Science, 7,* 301–305.

Singer, W., Artola, A., Engel, A. K., Konig, P., Kreiter, A. K., Lowel, S., & Schillen, T. B. (1993). Neuronal representations and temporal codes. In T. A. Poggio & D. A. Glaser (Eds.), *Exploring brain functions: Models in neuroscience* (pp. 179–194). New York: Wiley.

Sivak, J. G. (1976). Optics of the eye of the "four-eyed" fish *Anableps anableps. Vision Research, 16,* 513–516.

Slater, A. M., & Findlay, J. M. (1975). Binocular fixation in the newborn baby. *Journal of Experimental Child Psychology, 20,* 248–273.

Slater, A. M., Morison, V., & Rose, D. (1984). Habituation in the newborn. *Infant Behavior and Development, 7,* 183–200.

Slater, A. M., Morison, V., Somers, M., Mattock, A., Brown, E., & Taylor, D. (1990). Newborn and older infants' perception of partly occluded objects. *Infant Behavior and Development, 13,* 33–49.

Sloan, L. L., & Wollach, L. (1948). A case of unilateral deuteranopia. *Journal of the Optical Society of America, 38,* 502–509.

Smith, D., Van Buskirk, R. L., Travers, J. B., & Bieber, S. L. (1983). Coding of taste stimuli by hamster brain stem neurons. *Journal of Neurophysiology, 50,* 541–558.

Smith, L. B., & Katz, D. B. (1996). Activity-dependent processes in perceptual and cognitive development. In R. Gelman (Ed.), *Perceptual and cognitive development* (pp. 413–445). San Diego, CA: Academic Press.

Spelke, E. S., Gutheil, G., & Van de Walle, G. (1995). The development of object perception. In S. M. Kosslyn & D. N. Osherson (Eds.), *Visual cognition* (pp. 297–330). Cambridge, MA: MIT Press.

Sperduto, R. D., Siegel, D., Roberts, J., & Rowland, M. (1983). Prevalence of myopia in the United States. *Archives of Ophthalmology, 101,* 405–407.

Srulovicz, P., & Goldstein, J. L. (1983). A central spectrum model: A synthesis of auditory-nerve timing and place cues in monaural communication of frequency spectrum. *Journal of the Acoustical Society of America, 73,* 1266–1276.

Stark, L., & Bridgeman, B. (1983). Role of corollary discharge in space constancy. *Perception and Psychophysics, 34,* 371–380.

Steiner, J. E. (1974). Innate, discriminative human facial expressions to taste and smell stimulation. *Annals of the New York Academy of Sciences, 237*, 229–233.

Steiner, J. E. (1979). Human facial expressions in response to taste and smell stimulation. *Advances in Child Development and Behavior, 13*, 257–295.

Stevens, J. K., Emerson, R. C., Gerstein, G. L., Kallos, T., Neufeld, G. R., Nichols, C. W., & Rosenquist, A. C. (1976). Paralysis of the awake human: Visual perceptions. *Vision Research, 16*, 93–98.

Stevens, K. N., & Blumstein, S. (1978). Invariant cues for place of articulation in stop consonants. *Journal of the Acoustical Society of America, 64*, 1358–1368.

Stevens, K. N., & Blumstein, S. (1981). The search for invariant acoustic correlates of phonetic features. In P. D. Eimas & L. L. Miller (Eds.), *Perspectives on the study of speech.* Hillsdale, NJ: Erlbaum.

Stevens, S. S. (1957). On the psychophysical law. *Psychological Review, 64*, 153–181.

Stevens, S. S. (1961). To honor Fechner and repeal his law. *Science, 133*, 80–86.

Stevens, S. S. (1962). The surprising simplicity of sensory metrics. *American Psychologist, 17*, 29–39.

Stiles, W. S. (1953). Further studies of visual mechanisms by the two-color threshold method. Coloquio sobre problemas opticos de la vision. Madrid: *Union Internationale de Physique Pure et Appliqué, 1*, 65.

Stone, H., & Bosley, J. J. (1965). Olfactory discrimination and Weber's law. *Perceptual and Motor Skills, 20*, 657–665.

Stone, J. (1965). A quantitative analysis of the distribution of ganglion cells in the cat's retina. *Journal of Comparative Neurology, 124*, 277–352.

Stryer, L. (1986). Cyclic GMP cascade of vision. *Annual Review of Neuroscience, 9*, 87–119.

Stryker, M. P. (1989). Is grandmother an oscillation? *Nature, 338*, 297–298.

Suga, N. (1990, June). Biosonar and neural computation in bats. *Scientific American*, 60–68.

Sur, M., Garraghty, P. E., & Roe, A. W. (1988). Experimentally induced projections into auditory thalamus and cortex. *Science, 242*, 1437–1441.

Sussman, H. M., Hoemeke, K. A., & Ahmed, F. S. (1993). A cross-linguistic investigation of locus equations as a phonetic descriptor for place of articulation. *Journal of the Acoustical Society of America, 94*, 1256–1268.

Sussman, H. M., McCaffrey, H. A., & Matthews, S. A. (1991). An investigation of locus equations as a source of relational variance for stop place categorization. *Journal of the Acoustical Society of America, 90*, 1309–1325.

Svaetichin, G. (1956). Spectral response curves from single cones. *Acta Physiologica Scandinavica Supplementum, 134*, 17–46.

Swets, J. A. (1964). *Signal detection and recognition by human observers.* New York: Wiley.

Taira, M., Mine, S., Georgopoulos, A. P., Murata, A., & Sakata, H. (1990). Parietal cortex neurons of the monkey related to the visual guidance of hand movement. *Experimental Brain Research, 83*, 29–36.

Takagi, S. F. (1980). Dual nervous systems for olfactory functions in mammals. In H. Van der Starre (Ed.), *Olfaction and taste* (Vol. 7, pp. 275–278). London: IRC Press.

Tanabe, T., Iino, M., & Takagi, S. F. (1975). Discrimination of odors in olfactory bulb, pyriform-amygdaloid areas and orbito-frontal cortex of the monkey. *Journal of Neurophysiology, 38*, 1284–1296.

Tanabe, T., Iino, M., Oshima, Y., & Takagi, S. F. (1974). An olfactory area in the prefrontal lobe. *Brain Research, 80*, 127–130.

Tanaka, K. (1993). Neuronal mechanisms of object recognition. *Science, 262*, 684–688.

Tanaka, K., Siato, H.-A., Fukada, Y., & Moriya, M. (1991). Coding visual images of objects in inferotemporal cortex of the Macaque monkey. *Journal of Neurophysiology, 66*, 170–189.

Tarr, M. J. (1994). Visual representation. In V. Ramachandran (Ed.), *Encyclopedia of human* *behavior* (Vol. 4, pp. 503–512). New York: Academic Press.

Taylor, M. M., Lederman, S. J., & Gibson, R. H. (1973). Tactual perception of texture. In E. C. Carterette & M. P. Friedman (Eds.), *Handbook of perception* (Vol. 3). New York: Academic Press.

Teghtsoonian, R., Teghtsoonian, M., Berglund, B., & Berglund, U. (1978). Invariance of odor strength with sniff vigor: An olfactory analogue to size constancy. *Journal of Experimental Psychology: Human Perception and Performance, 4,* 144–152.

Teller, D. Y. (1990). The domain of visual science. In L. Spellman & J. S. Werner (Eds.), *Visual perception: The neurophysiological foundations* (pp. 11–21). San Diego, CA: Academic Press.

Terwogt, M. M., & Hoeksma, J. B. (1994). Colors and emotions: Preferences and combinations. *Journal of General Psychology, 122,* 5–17.

Tessier-Lavigne, M. (1991). Phototransduction and information processing in the retina. In E. R. Kandel, J. H. Schwartz, & T. M. Jessell (Eds.), *Principles of neural science* (3rd ed., pp. 400–417). New York: Elsevier.

Teuber, H. L. (1960). Perception. In J. Field, H. W. Magoun, & V. E. Hall (Eds.), *Handbook of physiology* (Sect. 1, Vol. 3). Washington, DC: American Physiological Society.

Thouless, R. H. (1931). Phenomenal regression to the real object I. *British Journal of Psychology, 21,* 339–359.

Tittle, J. S., & Braunstein, M. L. (1993). Recovery of depth from binocular disparity and structure from motion. *Perception and Psychophysics, 54,* 509–523.

Todd, J. T. (1981). Visual information about moving objects. *Journal of Experimental Psychology: Human Perception and Performance, 7,* 795–810.

Todd, J. T., & Norman, J. F. (1991). The visual perception of smoothly curved surfaces from minimal apparent motion sequences. *Perception and Psychophysics, 50,* 509–523.

Tonndorf, J. (1960). Shearing motion in scala media of cochlear models. *Journal of the Acoustical Society of America, 44,* 1546–1554.

Tonndorf, J., & Khanna, S. M. (1968). Submicroscopic displacement amplitudes of the tympanic membrane (cat) measured by laser interferometer. *Journal of the Acoustical Society of America, 44,* 1546–1554.

Tovee, M. J. (1995). Face recognition: What are faces for? *Current Biology, 5,* 480–482.

Tovee, M. J. (1996). *An introduction to the visual system.* Cambridge, England: Cambridge University Press.

Tovee, M. J., Rolls, E. T., & Azzopardi, P. (1994). Translation invariance in the responses to faces of single neurons in the temporal visual cortex areas of the alert macaque. *Journal of Neurophysiology, 72,* 1049–1060.

Tranel, D., & Damasio, A. R. (1985). Knowledge without awareness: An autonomic index of facial recognition by prosopagnosics. *Science, 228,* 1453–1454.

Tranel, D., & Damasio, A. R. (1988). Nonconscious face recognition in patients with face agnosia. *Behavioral Brain Research, 30,* 235–249.

Treisman, A. (1986). Features and objects in visual processing. *Scientific American, 255,* 114B–125B.

Treisman, A. (1987). Properties, parts, and objects. In K. R. Boff, L. Kaufman, & F. P. Thomas (Eds.), *Handbook of perception and human performance* (Chapter 35). New York: Wiley.

Treisman, A. (1993). The perception of features and objects. In A. Baddeley & L. Weiskrantz (Eds.), *Attention: Selection, awareness, and control* (pp. 5–34). Oxford, England: Clarendon Press.

Tretter, F., Cynader, M., & Singer, V. (1975). Modification of directional selectivity of neurons in the visual cortex of kittens. *Brain Research, 84,* 143–149.

Trevor-Roper, P. (1970). *The world through blunted sight.* Indianapolis, IN: Bobbs-Merrill.

Trotter, Y., Celebrini, S., Stricanne, B., Thorpe, S., & Imbert, M. (1992). Modulation of neural stereoscopic processing in primate area V1 by the viewing distance. *Science, 257,* 1279–1281.

Truax, B. (1984). *Acoustic communication.* Norwood, NJ: ABLEX.

Ts'o, D. Y. (1989). The functional organization and connectivity of color processing. In D. M.-K. Lam & C. Gilbert (Eds.), *Neural mechanisms of visual perception* (pp. 87–115). Woodlands, TX: Portfolio.

Tyler, C. W. (1990). A stereoscopic view of visual processing streams. *Vision Research, 30,* 1877–1895.

Tyler, C. W. (1994). The birth of computer stereograms for unaided stereovision. In S. Horibuchi (Ed.), *Stereogram* (pp. 83–89). San Francisco: Cadence.

Tyler, C. W. (1997a). Analysis of human receptor density. In V. Lakshminarayanan (Ed.), *Basic and clinical applications of vision science* (pp. 63–71). Norwell, MA: Kluwer Academic.

Tyler, C. W. (1997b). *Human cone densities: Do you know where all your cones are?* Unpublished manuscript.

Tye-Murray, N., Spencer, L., & Woodworth, G. G. (1995). Acquisition of speech by children who have prolonged cochlear implant experience. *Journal of Speech and Hearing Research, 38,* 327–337.

Uchikawa, K., Uchikawa, H., & Boynton, R. M. (1989). Partial color constancy of isolated surface colors examined by a color-naming method. *Perception, 18,* 83–91.

Ullman, S. (1980). Against direct perception. *Behavioral and Brain Sciences, 3,* 373–415.

Ungerleider, L. G., & Haxby, J. V. (1994). "What" and "where" in the human brain. *Current Opinion in Neurobiology, 4,* 157–165.

Ungerleider, L. G., & Mishkin, M. (1982). Two cortical visual systems. In D. J. Ingle, M. A. Goodale, & R. J. Mansfield (Eds.), *Analysis of visual behavior* (pp. 549–580). Cambridge, MA: MIT Press.

Valdez, P., & Mehribian, A. (1994). Effect of color on emotions. *Journal of Experimental Psychology: General, 123,* 394–409.

Vallbo, A. B., & Hagbarth, K. E. (1967). Impulses recorded with microelectrodes in human muscle nerves during stimulation of mechanoreceptors and voluntary contractions. *Electroencephalography and Clinical Neurophysiology, 23,* 392.

Vallbo, A. B., & Johansson, R. S. (1978). The tactile sensory innervation of the glabrous skin of the human hand. In G. Gordon (Ed.), *Active touch* (pp. 29–54). New York: Oxford University Press.

Vallvo, A. (1968). Behavioral patterns and visual rehabilitation after early and long lasting blindness. *American Journal of Ophthalmology, 65,* 19–23.

Van Essen, D. C., & DeYoe, E. A. (1995). Concurrent processing in primate visual cortex. In M. S. Gazzaniga (Ed.), *The cognitive neurosciences* (pp. 383–400). Cambridge, MA: MIT Press.

Varner, D., Cook, J. E., Schneck, M. E., McDonald, M., & Teller, D. Y. (1985). Tritan discriminations by 1- and 2-month-old human infants. *Vision Research, 25,* 821–831.

Vassar, R., Ngia, J., & Axel, R. (1993). Spatial segregation of odorant receptor expression in the mammalian olfactory epithelium. *Cell, 74,* 309–318.

Vega-Bermudez, F., Johnson, K. O., & Hsiao, S. S. (1991). Human tactile pattern recognition: Active versus passive touch, velocity effects, and patterns of confusion. *Journal of Neurophysiology, 65,* 531–546.

Vermeij, G. (1997). *Privileged hands: A scientific life.* New York: Freeman.

von Holst, E. (1954). Relations between the central nervous system and the peripheral organs. *British Journal of Animal Behaviour, 2,* 89–94.

von Noorden, G. K., & Maumanee, A. E. (1968). Clinical observations on stimulus deprivation amblyopia (amblyopia ex anopsia). *American Journal of Ophthalmology, 65,* 220–224.

Wachmuth, E., Oram, M. W., & Perrett, D. I. (1994). Recognition of objects and their component parts: Responses of single units in the temporal cortex of the macaque. *Cerebral Cortex, 4,* 509–522.

Walcott, C., Gould, J. L., & Kirschvink, J. L. (1979). Pigeons have magnets. *Science, 205,* 1027–1028.

Wald, G. (1964). The receptors of human color vision. *Science, 145,* 1007–1017.

Wald, G., & Brown, P. K. (1958). Human rhodopsin. *Science, 127,* 222–226.

Wald, G., & Brown, P. K. (1965). Human color vision and color blindness. *Cold Spring Harbor Symposia on Quantitative Biology, 30,* 345–359.

Waldrop, M. M. (1988). A landmark in speech recognition. *Science, 240,* 1615.

Wall, P. D., & Melzack, R. (Eds.). (1994). *Textbook of pain* (3rd ed.). Edinburgh, England: Churchill Livingstone.

Wallace, M. A. (1994). Implicit perception in visual neglect: Implications for theories of attention. In M. J. Farah & G. Ratcliff (Eds.), *Neuropsychology of high level vision* (pp. 359–370). Hillsdale, NJ: Erlbaum.

Wallach, H. (1963). The perception of neutral colors. *Scientific American, 208*(1), 107–116.

Wallach, H., Newman, E. B., & Rosenzweig, M. R. (1949). The precedence effect in sound localization. *American Journal of Psychology, 62,* 315–336.

Wallach, H., & O'Connell, D. N. (1953). The kinetic depth effect. *Journal of Experimental Psychology, 45,* 205–217.

Walls, G. L. (1942). *The vertebrate eye.* New York: Hafner. (Reprinted in 1967)

Walls, G. L. (1953). *The lateral geniculate nucleus and visual histophysiology.* Berkeley: University of California Press.

Walton, G. E., Bower, N. J. A., & Power, T. G. R. (1992). Recognition of familiar faces by newborns. *Infant Behavior and Development, 15,* 265–269.

Ward, W. D., & Glorig, A. (1961). A case of firecracker induced hearing loss. *Laryngoscope, 71,* 1590–1596.

Ware, C., & Mitchell, D. E. (1974). On interocular transfer of various visual aftereffects in normal and stereoblind observers. *Vision Research, 14,* 731–735.

Warren, D. H., & Rossano, M. J. (1991). Intermodality relations: Vision and touch. In M. A. Heller & W. Shiff (Eds.), *The psychology of touch* (pp. 119–137). Hillsdale, NJ: Erlbaum.

Warren, R. M. (1970). Perceptual restoration of missing speech sounds. *Science, 167,* 392–393.

Warren, R. M., Obuseck, C. J., & Acroff, J. M. (1972). Auditory induction of absent sounds. *Science, 176,* 1149.

Warren, S., Hamalainen, H., & Gardner, E. P. (1986). Objective classification of motion- and direction-sensitive neurons in primary somatosensory cortex of awake monkeys. *Journal of Neurophysiology, 56,* 598–622.

Warren, W. H. (1995). Self-motion: Visual perception and visual control. In W. Epstein & S. Rogers (Eds.), *Handbook of perception and cognition: Perception of space and motion* (pp. 263–323). New York: Academic Press.

Warren, W. H., Mestre, D. R., Blackwell, A. W., & Morris, M. (1991). Perception of circular heading from optical flow. *Journal of Experimental Psychology: Human Perception and Performance, 17,* 28–43.

Warren, W. H., Morris, M. W., & Kalish, M. (1988). Perception of translational heading from optical flow. *Journal of Experimental Psychology: Human Perception and Performance, 14,* 646–660.

Wassle, H., Grunert, U., Rohrenbeck, J., & Boycott, B. B. (1990). Retinal ganglion cell density and cortical magnification factor in the primate. *Vision Research, 30,* 1897–1911.

Watkins, C. R., & Mayer, D. J. (1982). Organization of endogenous opiate and nonopiate pain control system. *Science, 176,* 1149.

***Webster's new collegiate dictionary.* (1956).** Springfield, MA: Merriam.

Weinstein, S. (1968). Intensive and extensive aspects of tactile sensitivity as a function of body part, sex, and laterality. In D. R. Kenshalo (Ed.), *The skin senses* (pp. 195–218). Springfield, IL: Thomas.

Weisenberg, M. (1977). Pain and pain control. *Psychological Bulletin, 84,* 1008–1044.

Weiskrantz, L. (1986). *Blindsight: A case study and implications.* Oxford, England: Oxford University Press.

Weiskrantz, L. (1987). Residual vision in a scotoma. *Brain, 110,* 77–92.

Weiskrantz, L., Warrington, E. K., Sanders, M. D., & Marshall, J. (1974). Visual capacity in the hemianopic field following a restricted occipital ablation. *Brain*, 97, 709–728.

Weisstein, N., & Wong, E. (1986). Figure-ground organization and the spatial and temporal responses of the visual system. In E. C. Schwab & H. C. Nusbaum (Eds.), *Pattern recognition by humans and machines* (Vol. 2). New York: Academic Press.

Werker, J. (1991). The ontogenty of speech perception. In I. G. Mattingly & M. Studdert-Kennedy (Eds.), *Modularity and the motor theory of speech perception* (pp. 91–109). Hillsdale, NJ: Erlbaum.

Werker, J. F., & Tees, R. C. (1984). Cross-language speech perception: Evidence for perceptual reorganization during the first year of life. *Infant Behavior and Development*, 7, 49–63.

Werker, J. F., & Tees, R. C. (1992). The organization and reorganization of human speech perception. *Annual Review of Neuroscience*, 15, 377–402.

Werner, L. A., & Bargones, J. Y. (1992). Psychoacoustic development of human infants. In C. Rovee-Collier & L. Lipsett (Eds.), *Advances in infancy research* (Vol. 7, pp. 103–145). Norwood, NJ: ABLEX.

Wertheimer, M. (1912). Experimentelle Stuidien uber das Sehen von Beuegung. *Zeitchrift fuer Psychologie*, 61, 161–265.

Wessel, D. L. (1979). Timbre space as a musical control structure. *Computer Music Journal*, 3, 45–52.

Wever, E. G. (1949). *Theory of hearing.* New York: Wiley.

Wever, E. G., & Bray, C. W. (1937). The perception of low tones and the resonance-volley theory. *Journal of Psychology*, 3, 101–114.

Whalen, D. H., & Liberman, A. M. (1987). Speech perception takes precedence over nonspeech perception. *Science*, *237, 169–171.*

White, J. (1968). *The birth and rebirth of pictorial space* (2nd ed.). London: Faber & Faber.

Whitfield, I. C., & Evans, E. F. (1965). Responses of auditory neurons to stimuli of changing frequency. *Journal of Neurophysiology*, 28, 655–672.

Whitsel, B. L., Roppolo, J. R., & Werner, G. (1972). Cortical information processing of stimulus motion on primate skin. *Journal of Neurophysiology*, 35, 691–717.

Wiesel, T. N., & Hubel, D. H. (1963). Single cell responses in striate cortex of kittens deprived of vision in one eye. *Journal of Neurophysiology*, 26, 1003–1017.

Wiesel, T. N., & Raviola, E. (1977). Myopia and eye enlargement after neonatal lid fusion in monkeys. *Nature*, 266, 66–68.

Wightman, F. L. (1973). Pitch and stimulus fine structure. *Journal of the Acoustical Society of America*, 54, 397–406.

Wightman, F. L., & Jenison, R. (1995). Auditory spatial layout. In W. Epstein & S. Rogers (Eds.), *Perception of space and motion* (pp. 365–400). San Diego, CA: Academic Press.

Wightman, F. L., & Kistler, D. J. (1993). Sound localization. In W. Yost, R. R. Fay, & A. N. Popper (Eds.), *Human psychophysics* (pp. 155–192) New York: Springer-Verlag.

Wildsoet, C. F. (1997). Active emmetropization–evidence for its existence and ramifications for clinical practice. *Ophthalmology and Physiological Optics*, 17, 279–290.

Wilson, J. R., Friedlander, M. J., & Sherman, M. S. (1984). Ultrastructural morphology of identified X- and Y-cells in the cat's lateral geniculate nucleus. *Proceedings of the Royal Society*, *B211*, 411–436.

Winston, P. H. (1975). *The psychology of computer vision.* New York: McGraw-Hill.

Wittreich, W. J. (1959). Visual perception and personality. *Scientific American*, 200(4), 56–60.

Wolfe, J. M. (1997). Inattentional amnesia. In V. Goltheart (Ed.), *Fleeting memories.* Cambridge, MA: MIT Press.

Xu, F., & Carey, S. (1994, June). *Infants' ability to individuate and trace the identity of objects.* Paper presented at the International Conference on Infant Studies, Paris.

Ye, Q., Heck, G., & DeSimone, J. A. (1991). The anion paradox in sodium taste reception: Resolution by voltage-clamp studies. *Science*, 254, 724–726.

Yonas, A., Granrud, C. E., Arterberry, M. E., & Hanson, B. L. (1986). Infant's distance from linear perspective and texture gradients. *Infant Behavior and Development*, 9, 247–256.

Yonas, A., Pettersen, L., & Granrud, C. E. (1982). Infant's sensitivity to familiar size as information for distance. *Child Development*, 53, 1285–1290.

Yost, W. A., & Guzman, S. J. (1996). Auditory processing of sound sources: Is there an echo in here? *Current Directions in Psychological Science*, 5, 125–131.

Yost, W. A., & Sheft, S. (1993). Auditory processing. In W. A. Yost, A. N. Popper, & R. R. Fay (Eds.), *Handbook of auditory research* (Vol. 3). New York: Springer-Verlag.

Young, M. P. (1995). Open questions about the neural mechanisms of visual pattern recognition. In M. S. Gazzaniga (Ed.), *The cognitive neurosciences* (pp. 463–474). Cambridge, MA: MIT Press.

Young, M. P., & Yamane, S. (1992). Sparse population coding of faces in e inferotemporal cortex. *Science*, 256, 1327–1331.

Young, R. S. L., Fishman, G. A., & Chen, F. (1980). Traumatically acquired color vision defect. *Investigative Ophthalmology and Visual Science*, 19, 545–549.

Young, T. (1802). On the theory of light and colours. *Transactions of the Royal Society of London*, 92, 12–48.

Young-Browne, G., Rosenfield, H. M., & Horowitz, F. D. (1977). Infant discrimination of facial expression. *Child Development*, 48, 555–562.

Yuodelis, C., & Hendrickson, A. (1986). A qualitative and quantitative analysis of the human fovea during development. *Vision Research*, 26, 847–855.

Zadnik, K., Satariano, W. A., Mutti, D. O., Sholtz, R. I., & Adama, A. J. (1994). The effect of parental history of myopia on children's eye size. *Journal of the American Medical Association*, 271, 1323–1327.

Zatorre, R. J. (1988). Pitch perception of complex tones and human temporal-lobe function. *Journal of the Acoustical Society of America*, 84, 566–572.

Zatorre, R. J., Evans, A. C., & Meyer, E. (1994). Neural mechanisms underlying melodic perception and memory for pitch. *Journal of Neuroscience*, 14, 1908–1919.

Zatorre, R. J., Evans, A. C., Meyer, E., & Gjedde, A. (1992). Lateralization of phonetic and pitch discrimination in speech processing. *Science*, 256, 846–849.

Zeki, S. (1980). A century of cerebral achromatopsia. *Brain*, 113, 1721–1777.

Zeki, S. (1983a). Color coding in the cerebral cortex: The responses of wavelength-selective and color coded cells in monkey visual cortex to changes in wavelength composition. *Neuroscience*, 9, 767–781.

Zeki, S. (1983b). Color coding in the cerebral cortex: The reaction of cells in monkey visual cortex to wavelengths and colours. *Neuroscience*, 9, 741–765.

Zeki, S. (1984). The construction of colours by the cerebral cortex. *Proceedings of the Royal Institute of Great Britain*, 56, 231–257.

Zeki, S., Watson, J. D. G., Lueck, C. J., Friston, K. J., Kennard, C., & Frackowiak, R. S. J. (1991). A direct demonstration of functional specialization in human visual cortex. *Journal of Neuroscience*, 11, 641–649.

Zellner, D. A., Bartoli, A. M., & Eckard, R. (1991). Influence of color on odor identification and liking ratings. *American Journal of Psychology*, 104, 547–561.

Zenner, H. P. (1986). Motile responses in outer hair cells. *Hearing Research*, 22, 83–90.

Zihl, J., von Cramon, D., & Mai, N. (1983). Selective disturbance of movement vision after bilateral brain damage. *Brain*, 106, 313–340.

Zihl, J., von Cramon, D., Mai, N., & Schmid, C. (1991). Disturbance of movement vision after bilateral posterior brain damage. *Brain*, 114, 2235–2252.

Zimmerman, M. (1979). Peripheral and central nervous mechanisms of nociception, pain, and pain therapy: Facts and hypotheses. In J. J. Bonica, J. D. Liebeskind, & D. G. Albe-Fessard (Eds.), *Advances in pain research and therapy* (Vol. 3, pp. 3–32). New York: Raven Press.

Zrenner, E., Abramov, I., Akita, M., Cowey, A., Livingston, M., & Valberg, A. (1990). Color perception. In L. Spillmann & J. S. Werner (Eds.), *Visual perception: The neurophysiological foundations* (pp. 163–204). San Diego: Academic Press.

Zwicker, E. (1974). On the psychoacoustic equivalent of tuning curves. In E. Zwicker & E. Ternhardt (Eds.), *Facts and models in hearing* (pp. 132–141). Berlin: Springer-Verlag.

Zylbermann, R., Landau, D., & Berson, D. (1993). The influence of study habits on myopia in Jewish teenagers. *Journal of Pediatric Ophthalmology and Strabismus, 30*, 319–322.

Author Index

Subject Index

Credits

This page constitutes an extension of the copyright page. We have made every effort to trace the ownership of all copyrighted material and to secure permission from copyright holders. In the event of any question arising as to the use of any material, we will be pleased to make the necessary corrections in future printings. Thanks are due to the following authors, publishers, and agents for permission to use the material included.

Illustration and Text Credits

About the cover artist: The cover painting is by Damir Polić, a young artist born in Sarajvo who, since arriving in the United States a few years ago, has won numerous awards for his work. He is continuing his studies in the United States and Europe.

Chapter One: **7:** Figure 1.07, Adapted from "The Role of Frequency in Developing Perceptual Sets," by B. R. Bugelski and D. A. Alampay, 1961, *Canadian Journal of Psychology, 15,* 205–211. Copyright © 1961 by the Canadian Psychological Association. Reprinted with permission. **8:** Figure 1.08, From "The Effects of Contextual Scenes on the Identification of Objects," by S. E. Palmer, 1975, *Memory and Cognition,* 3, 519–526, figure 1. Copyright © 1975 by The Psychonomic Society. Reprinted by permission. **11:** Figure 1.13, Adapted from "The Role of Frequency in Developing Perceptual Sets," by B. R. Bugelski and D. A. Alampay, 1961, *Canadian Journal of Psychology, 15,* 205–211. Copyright © 1961 by the Canadian Psychological Association. Reprinted with permission. **12:** Figure 1.14, Adapted from "The Surprising Simplicity of Sensory Metrics," by S. S. Stevens,1962, *American Psychologist, 17,* pp. 29–39. Copyright © 1962 by American Psychological Association. **13:** Figure 1.15, Adapted from "The Surprising Simplicity of Sensory Metrics," by S. S. Stevens, 1962, *American Psychologist, 17,* pp. 29–39. Copyright © 1962 by American Psychological Association. **26:** Figure 1.27, From "Object Recognition Processes Can and Do Operate Before Figure-Ground Orientation," by M. A. Peterson, 1994, *Current Directions in Psychological Science,* 3, 105–111. Copyright © 1994 by Cambridge University Press.

Chapter Two: **32:** Figure 2.04, Adapted from "Organization of the Primate Retina," by J. E. Dowling and B. B. Boycott, 1966. *Proceedings of the Royal Society of London, 16,* Series B., 80–111. Copyright © 1966 by The Royal Society. Adapted by permission. **33:** Figure 2.06, Adapted from *Human Information Processing,* by P. Lindsay and D. A. Norman, 1977, 2nd ed., p. 126. Copyright © 1977 Academic Press, Inc. Adapted by permission. **37:** Figure 2.12, From "Scanning Electron Microscopy of Vertebrate Visual Receptors," by E. R. Lewis, Y. Y. Zeevi, & F. S. Werblin, 1969, *Brain Research, 15,* 559–562. Copyright © 1969 Elsevier Science Publishers, B.V. Reprinted by permission. **37:** Figure 2.13, Adapted from *Human Information Processing,* by P. Lindsay and D. A. Norman, 1977, 2nd ed., p. 126. Copyright © 1977 Academic Press, Inc. Adapted by permission. **39:** Figure 2.17, From a figure by Johnny Johnson on page 88 of "Blind Spots," by Vilaynaur S. Ramachandran, *Scientific American,* May 1992. Reprinted with permission. Copyright © 1992 by Scientific American, Inc. All rights reserved. **44:** Figure 2.23, Partial data from "Rhodopsin Measurement and Dark Adaptation in a Subject Deficient in Cone Vision," by W. A. H. Ruston, 1961, *Journal of Physiology, 156,* 193–205. Copyright © 1961 by the Physiological Society, Cambridge University Press. **46:** Figure 2.24, Adapted from "The Receptors of Human Color Vision," by E. Wald, 1964, *Science, 145,* pp. 1009 and 1011. Copyright © 1964 by the American Association for the Advancement of Science. Adapted by permission. **47:** Figure 2.25, From "Human Rhodopsin," by G. Wald and P. K. Brown, 1958, *Science, 127,* pp. 222–226, figure 6, and "The Receptors of Human Color Vision," by G. Wald, 1964, *Science, 145,* pp. 1007–1017. Copyright © 1964 by the American Association for the Advancement of Science. Reprinted by permission. **51:** Figure 2.32, From "Amacrine Cells," by R. H. Masland, 1988, *Trends in Neuroscience, 11*(9), 405–410, figure 2. Copyright © 1988 by Elsevier Science Ltd. Reprinted by permission. **53:** Figure 2.36, From "Integrative Action in the Cat's Lateral Geniculate Body," by D. H. Hubel and T. N. Wiesel, 1961, *Journal of Physiology, 155*, 385–398, figure 1. Copyright © 1961 by The Physiological Society, Cambridge University Press. Reprinted by permission. **56:** Figure 2.39, From "Visual Acuity," by L. A. Riggs, 1965. In C. Graham, Ed., *Vision and Visual Perception*, figure 11.4, page 324. Copyright © 1965 by John Wiley & Sons., Inc. Reprinted by permission of John Wiley & Sons. **59:** Figure 2.43, From *Mach Bands: Quantitative Studies on Neural Networks in the Retina*, by F. Ratliff, 1965, figure 3.25, p. 107. Copyright © 1965 Holden-Day, Inc. Reprinted by permission

Chapter Three: **73:** Figure 3.03, From "Segregation of Form, Color, Movement and Depth: Anatomy, Physiology and Perception," by M. Livingston and D. H. Hubel, 1988, *Science, 240*, 740–749. Copyright © 1988 by the American Association for the Advancement of Science. Reprinted by permission of M. Livingston. **75:** Figure 3.05, Reprinted with permission from *Nature*, " Functions of the Colour-Opponent and Broad-Band Channels of the Visual System," by P. H. Schiller, N. K. Logthetis & E. R. Charles, 1990, 343, p. 68, figure 1a &b. Copyright © 1990 by Macmillan Magazines, Ltd. **76:** Figure 3.06, From "Functional Architecture of Macaque Monkey Cortex," by D. H. Hubel and T. N. Wiesel, 1977, *Proceedings of the Royal Society of London, 198*, 1–59. Copyright © 1977 by the Royal Society. Reprinted by permission of D. H. Hubel. **77:** Figure 3.08, From "Receptive Fields of Single Neurons in the Cat's Straite Cortex," by D. H. Hubel and T. N. Wiesel, 1959, *Journal of Physiology, 148*, 574–591, figure 2. Copyright © 1959 by The Physiological Society, Cambridge University Press. Reprinted by permission. **78:** Figure 3.10, From "Receptive Fields of Single Neurons in the Cat's Straite Cortex," by D. H. Hubel and T. N. Wiesel, 1959, *Journal of Physiology, 148*, 574–591, figure 8. Copyright © 1959 by The Physiological Society, Cambridge University Press. Reprinted by permission. **82:** Figure 3.15, From "Size Adaptation: A New Aftereffect," by C. Blakemore and P. Sutton, 1969, *Science, 166*, 245–247, figure 1. Copyright © 1969 by the American Association for the Advancement of Science. Reprinted by permission. **86:** Figure 3.22, From "Application of Fourier Analysis to the Visibility of Gratings," by F. W. Campbell and J. G. Robson, 1968, *Journal of Physiology, 197*, 551–556, figure 2. Copyright © 1968 Physiological Society, Cambridge University Press. Reprinted by permission. **86:** Figure 3.21, From "The Visual Cortex as a Spatial Frequency Analyzer," by L. Maffei and A. Fiorentini, 1973, *Vision Research, 13*, 1255–1267, figure 3. Copyright © 1973 with kind permission from Elsevier Science Ltd, The Boulevard, Langford Land, Kidlington 0X5 1GB, UK.

Chapter Four: **104:** Figure 4.01, From "Object Vision and Spatial Vision: Two Central Pathways," by M. Mishkin, L. G. Ungerleider & K. A. Makco, 1983, *Trends in Neuroscience, 6*, 414–417, figure 1. Copyright © 1983 Elsevier Science Publishers B.V. Reprinted by permission. **108:** Figure 4.06, From *The Visual Brain in Action* by A. D. Milner and M. A. Goodale. Copyright © 1995 by Oxford University Press. Reprinted by permission. **109:** Figure 4.07, From *The Visual Brain in Action* by A. D. Milner and M. A. Goodale. Copyright © 1995 by Oxford University Press. Reprinted by permission. **110:** Figure 4.10, From "A Selective Impairment of Motion Perception Following Lesions of the Middle Temporal Visual Area (MT)," by W. T. Newsome and E. B. Pare, 1988, *Journal of Neuroscience*, 8(6), 2201–2211, figure 1. Copyright © 1988 by Society for Neuroscience. Reprinted by permission of Oxford University Press. **111:** Figure 4.11, From "Coding Visual Images of Objects in Interotemporal Cortex of the Macaque Monkey," by K. Tanaka, H-A. Siato, Y. Fukada, and M. Moriya, 1991, *Journal of Neurophysiology, 66*, 170–189. Copyright © 1981 by The American Physiological Society. Reprinted by permission. **112:** Figure 4.13, From "Visual Properties of Neurons in a Polysensory Area in the Superior Temporal Sulcus of the Macque," by C. Bruce, R. Desimone & C. G. Gross, 1981, *Journal of Neurophysiology, 46*, 369–384, figure 7. Copyright © 1981 by The American Physiological Society. Reprinted by permission. **112:** Figure 4.12, From "Open Questions About the Neural Mechanisms of Visual Pattern Recognition," by M. P. Young in *The Cognitive Neurosciences*, edited by M. S. Gazzaniga. Copyright © 1995 by MIT Press. Reprinted by permission. **113:** Figure 4.14, From "Recognition of Objects and Their Component Parts: Responses of Single Units in the Temporal Cortex of the Macaque," by E. Washmuth, M. W. Oram, and D. I. Perrett, 1994, *Cerebral Cortex, 4*, Copyright © 1994 by Oxford University Press. **113:** Figure 4.15, From "Coding Visual Images of Objects in Interotemporal Cortex of the Macaque Monkey," by K. Tanaka, H-A. Siato, Y. Fukada, and M. Moriya, 1991, *Journal of Neurophysiology, 66*, 170–189. Copyright © 1981 by The American Physiological Society. Reprinted by permission. **114:** Figure 4.17, From "Psychophysical and Physiological Evidence for Viewer-Centered Object Representations in the Primate," by N. K. Logothetis and J. Pauls, 1995, *Cerebral Cortex*, 5. Copyright © 1995 by Oxford University Press. **114:** Figure 4.18, From "Psychophysical and Physiological Evidence for Viewer-Centered Object Representations in the Primate," by N. K. Logothetis and J. Pauls, 1995, *Cerebral Cortex*, 5. Copyright © 1995 by Oxford University Press. **115:** Figure 4.19, From "Residual Vision in a Scotoma," by L. Weiskrantz, 1987, *Brain, 110*, Copyright © 1987 by Oxford University Press. **116:** Figure 4.21, From "Visual Capacity in the Hemianopic Field Following a Restricted Occipital Ablation," by L. Weiskrantz, E. K. Warrington, M. D. Sanders, and J. Marshall, 1974, *Brain*, 97, Copyright ©

1974 by Oxford University Press. Reprinted by permission. **117:** Figure 4.22, From *To See But Not To See* by G. W. Humphreys and M. J. Riddoch. Copyright © 1987 by Lawrence Erlbaum. **119:** Figure 4.24, Adapted by permission from "Selective Attention Gates Visual Processing in the Extrastriate Cortex," by J. Moran and R. Desimone, 1985, *Science*, 229, 782–784. Copyright © 1985 by the American Association for the Advancement of Science. **119:** Figure 4.23, From "The Effect of Inattention on Form Perception," by I. Rock and D. Gutman, 1981, *Journal of Experimental Psychology: Human Perception and Performance*, 7, 275–285. Copyright © 1981 Academic Press. Reprinted by permission. **120:** Figure 4.25, From "Oculocentric Spatial Representation in Parietal Cortex," by C. L. Colby, J-R. Duhamel, and M. E. Goldberg, 1995, *Cerebral Cortex*, 5. Copyright © 1995 by Oxford University Press. Reprinted by permission. **121:** Figure 4.26, Adapted from "Temporal Coding in the Visual Cortex: New Vistas on Integration in the Nervous System," by A. K. Engel, P. Konig, A. K. Kreiter, T. B. Schillen & W. Singer, 1992, *Trends in Neuroscience*,*15*, 218–226, figure 1. Copyright © 1992 by Elsevier Science Ltd. Adapted by permission. **124:** Figure 4.28, From "The Representation of Extrapersonal Space: A Possible Role for Bimodal, Visual-Tactile Neurons," by M. S. A. Graziano and C. G. Gross in *The Cognitive Neurosciences*, edited by M. S. Gazzaniga. Copyright © 1995 by MIT Press. Reprinted by permission. **125:** Figure 4.29, From "The Representation of Extrapersonal Space: A Possible Role for Bimodal, Visual-Tactile Neurons," by M. S. A. Graziano and C. G. Gross in *The Cognitive Neurosciences*, edited by M. S. Gazzaniga. Copyright © 1995 by MIT Press. Reprinted by permission.

Chapter Five: **134:** Figure 5.01, From *Color Vision*, by Leo M. Hurvich, 1981. Reprinted by permission of Dr. Leo M. Hurvich. **136:** Figure 5.04, Based on data from "Spectral Distribution of Typical Daylight as a Function of Correlated Color Temperature," by D. B. Judd, D. L. MacAdam & G. Wyszecki, 1964, *Journal of the Optical Society of America*, *54*, 1031–1040. **136:** Figure 5.05, Adapted from *Color: Its Principles and Their Applications*, by F. W. Clulow, 1972, Morgan and Morgan. Copyright © 1972 by F. W. Clulow. Used by permission of the author. **137:** Figure 5.06, Adapted from *Color: Its Principles and Their Applications*, by F. W. Clulow, 1972, Morgan and Morgan. Copyright © 1972 by F. W. Clulow. Used by permission of the author. **141:** Figure 5.10, From "Color Appearance: On Seeing Red, or Yellow, or Green, or Blue," by I. Abramov and J. Gordon, 1994. Reproduced,with permission, from *Annual Review of Psychology*, *45*, 451–485, figure 1a. Copyright © 1994 by Annual Reviews, Inc. **144:** Figure 5.15, From "Spectral Response Curves from Single Cones," by G. Svaetichin, 1956, *Acta Physiologica Scandanavica, Suppl 134*, 17–46, figure 1. Copyright © 1956 Karolinska Institutet. Reprinted by permission. **145:** Figure 5.16, From "Primate Color Vision," by R. L. DeValois and G. H. Jacobs, 1968, *Science*, *162*, 533–540, figure 5. Copyright © 1968 by the American Association for the Advancement of Science. Reprinted by permission. **146:** Figure 5.18, From "Anatomy and Physiology of a Color System in the Primate Visual Cortex," by M. S. Livingstone and D. H. Hubel, 1984, *Journal of Neuroscience*, *4*(1), 309–356, figure 34. Copyright © 1984 Society for Neuroscience. Reprinted by permission of Oxford University Press. **151:** Figure 5.23, From "Color Vision Honey Bees: Phenomena and Physiological Mechanisms," by R. Menzel and W. Backhaus, 1989. In Stavenga and Hardie (Eds.) *Facets of Vision*, p. 283. Copyright © 1989 Springer-Verlag BV, Berlin. Reprinted by permission.

Chapter Six: **160:** Figure 6.04, From "Partial Color Constancy of Isolated Surface Colors Examined by a Color-Naming Method," by K. Uchikawa, H. Uchikara, and R. M. Boynton, 1989, *Perception*, *18*, 83–91. Copyright © 1989 by Pion Ltd., London. Reprinted by permission. **164:** Figure 6.09, Adapted from "Perception" by Julian Hochberg: Figure from *Woodworth & Schlosberg's Experimental Psychology*, Third Edition by J. W. Kling and Lorrin A. Riggs, copyright © 1971 by Holt, Rinehart & Winston. Reproduced by permission of the publisher.

Chapter Seven: **179:** Figure 7.08, From *Art and Visual Perception*, by R. Arnheim, 1974, p. 27. Copyright © 1974 University of California Press, Berkeley. Reprinted by permission. **188:** Figure 7.25, From "Perception," by Julian Hochberg: Figure from *Woodworth & Schlosberg's Experiment Psychology*, Third Edition by J. W. Kling and Lorrin A. Riggs, copyright © 1971 by Holt, Rinehart & Winston. Reproduced by permission of the publisher. **192:** Figure 7.34, Reprinted with permission from "Neuronal Mechanisms of Object Recognition," by K. Tanaka, 1993, *Science*, *262*, 646–688, figure 2. Copyright © 1993 by the American Association for the Advancement of Science. **193:** Figure 7.35, From "Sparseness of the Neuronal Representation of Stimuli in the Primate Temporal Visual Cortex," by E. T. Rolls and M. J. Tovee, 1995, *Journal of Neurophysiology*, 73, 713–726. Copyright © 1995 by The American Physiological Society. Reprinted by permission. **194:** Figure 7.36, From "Sparseness of the Neuronal Representation of Stimuli in the Primate Temporal Visual Cortex," by E. T. Rolls and M. J. Tovee, 1995, *Journal of Neurophysiology*, 73, 713–726. Copyright © 1995 by The American Physiological Society. Reprinted by permission.**196:** Figure 7.39, From "Texton Segregation by Associated Differences in Global and Local Luminance Distribution," by H. C. Nothdurft, 1990, *Proceedings of the Royal Society of London*, *B239*, 296–320. Reprinted by permission of The Royal Society.**203:** Figure 7.48, From "Recognition-by-Components: A Theory of Human Image Understanding," by I. Biederman, 1985, *Computer Vision*,

Graphics and Image Processing, 32, 29–73. Copyright © 1985 Academic Press. Reprinted by permission. **204:** Figure 7.49, From "Recognition-by-Components: A Theory of Human Image Understanding," by I. Biederman, 1985, *Computer Vision, Graphics and Image Processing,* 32, 29–73. Copyright © 1985 Academic Press. Reprinted by permission. **204:** Figure 7.50, From "Recognition-by-Components: A Theory of Human Image Understanding," by I. Biederman, 1985, *Computer Vision, Graphics and Image Processing,* 32, 29–73. Copyright © 1985 Academic Press. Reprinted by permission. **206:** Figure 7.52, From "On Semantics of a Glance at a Scene," by I. Biederman, 1981. In M. Kubovy and J. Pomerantz (Eds.) *Perceptual Organization,* figure 8.1, p. 218. Copyright © 1981 by Lawrence Erlbaum Associates, Inc. Reprinted by permission. **206:** Figure 7.53, From "Perception of Structure: An Overview," by J. R. Pomerantz and G. R. Lockhead in *Perception of Structure* edited by R. Lockhead an J. R. Pomerantz, pp. 1–20. Copyright © 1991 by The American Psychological Association. Reprinted by permission.

Chapter Eight: **227:** Figure 8.17, From "The Perception of Spatial Layout from Static Optical Information," by B. Gilliam in *Handbook of Perception and Cognition: Perception of Space and Motion* edited by W. Epstein and Rogers, pp. 23–67. Copyright © 1995 by Academic Press. Reprinted by permission. **230:** Figure 8.22, Figure from *Foundations of Cyclopean Perception,* by B. Julesz, 1971, figures 2.4-1 and 2.4-3. Copyright © 1971 University of Chicago Press. Reprinted by permission. **232:** Figure 8.24, From "Cells Sensitive to Binocular Depth in Area 18 of the Macaque Monkey Cortex," by D. H. Hubel and T. Wiesel, 1970, *Nature,* 225, 41–42, figure 1. Copyright © 1970 by Macmillan Magazines, Ltd.. Reprinted by permission. **234:** Figure 8.26, From "Single Cell Responses in Striate Cortex of Kittens Deprived of Vision in One Eye," by T. N. Wisel and D. H. Hubel, 1963, *Journal of Neurophysiology,* 26, 1002–1017, figures 1 and 3. Copyright © 1963 by The American Physiological Society. Reprinted by permission. **237:** Figure 8.31, From "Sensitive Period for the Development of Human Binocular Vision," by M. S. Banks, R. N. Aslin & R. D. Letson, 1975, *Science, 190,* 675–677, figure 1C. Copyright © 1975 by the American Association for the Advancement of Science. Reprinted by permission.

Chapter Nine: **248:** Figure 9.04, From "Determinants of Apparent Visual Size with Distance Variant," by A. H. Holway and E. G. Boring, 1941, *American Journal of Psychology,* 54, 21–34, figure 2. University of Illinois Press. **249:** Figure 9.06, From "Determinants of Apparent Visual Size with Distance Variant," by A. H. Holway and E. G. Boring, 1941, *American Journal of Psychology,* 54, 21–34, figure 22. University of Illinois Press. **260:** Figure 9.22, Reprinted from *Vision Research,* 16, p. 534, "Optics of the Eye of the 'Four-Eyed Fish' (Anableps Anableps)," by J. G. Sivak, 1976. Copyright © 1976 with kind permission from Elsevier Science Ltd. The Boulevard, Langford Lane, Kidlington OX5 1GB, UK. **268:** Figure 9.33, From "The Bourdon Illusion in Haptic Space," by R. H. Day, 1990, *Perception & Psychophysics,* 47, pp. 400–404. Copyright © 1990 by Psychonomic Society, Inc. Reprinted by permission. **268:** Figure 9.34, From "The Bourdon Illusion in Haptic Space," by R. H. Day, 1990, *Perception & Psychophysics,* 47, pp. 400–404. Copyright © 1990 by Psychonomic Society, Inc. Reprinted by permission

Chapter Ten: **278:** Figure 10.07, Courtesy of Mark Friedman, Pittsburgh, PA. **283:** Figure 10.15, From "Lateral Inhibition Between Orientation Detectors in the Cat's Visual Cortex," by C. Blakemore and E. A. Tobin, 1972, *Experimental Brain Research, 15,* 439–440, figure 1. Copyright © 1972 Springer-Verlag Publishers. Reprinted by permission. **283:** Figure 10.16, From "A Selective Impairment of Motion Perception Following Lesions of the Middle Temporal Visual Area (MT)," by W. T. Newsome and E. B. Pare, 1988, *Journal of Neuroscience,* 8(6), 2201–2211, figure 1. Copyright © 1988 by Society for Neuroscience. Reprinted by permission of Oxford University Press. **285:** Figure 10.18, From "Perception," by H. L. Teuber, 1960. In J. Field, H. W. Magoun & V. E. Hall (Eds.) *Handbook of Physiology, Section 1, Neurophysiology,* Vol. 3, pp. 1595–1668, figure 31. Copyright © 1960 by the American Physiological Society. Reprinted by permission. **87:** Figure 10.22, From "'Real Motion' Cells in Area V3A of Macaque Visual Cortez," by C. Galletti, P. P. Battaglini, and P. Fattori, 1990, *Experimental Brain Research,* 82, 67–76, figure 1. Copyright © 1990 Springer-Verlag Publishers. Reprinted by permission. **292:** Figure 10.30, From "Retrieval of Structure from Rigid and Biological Motion: An Analysis of the Visual Responses of Neurones in the Macaque Temporal Cortex" by D. I. Perrett, M. H. Harries, P. J. Bensen, A. J. Chitty & A. J. Mistlin, 1990. In A. Blake and T. Troscianko, *AI and the Eye,* 181–200, figure 2. Copyright © 1990 by John Wiley & Sons Ltd. Reprinted by permission of D. I. Perrett and John Wiley & Sons, Ltd. **295:** Figure 10.35, Adapted from "Responses of Anterior Superior Emporal Polysensory (STPa) Neurons to 'Biological Motion' Stimuli," by M. W. Oram and D. I. Perrett, 1994, *Journal of Cognitive Neuroscience, 6,* 99–116. Copyright © 1994 by Massachusetts Institute of Technology. **298:** Figure 10.40, Based on figure from "Visual Proprioceptive Control of Standing in Human Infants," by D. N. Lee and E. Aronson, 1974, *Perception and Psychophysics, 15,* 529–532, figure 2. Psychonomics Society Publications. **302:** Figure 10.44, From "Tactile Apparent Movement: The Effects of Interstimulus Onset Interval and Stimulus Duration," by J. H. Kiman, 1974, *Perception & Psychophysics, 15,* pp. 1–6. Copyright © 1974 by Psychonomic Society, Inc. Reprinted by permission

Chapter Eleven: **315:** Figure 11.06, Reprinted with permission of C.G. Conn Ltd, Hatfield Herts, England. **319:** Figure 11.10, Redrawn by permission from *Human Information Processing,* by P. H. Lindsay and D. A. Norman, 2nd ed., 1977, p. 229. Copyright © 1977 by Academic Press, Inc. **320:** Figure 11.13, From "Hearing: Its Function and Dysfunction," by E. D. Schubert, 1980, *Disorders of Human Communication, Vol 1.* pp. 15 and 18. Copyright © 1980 Springer-Verlag, Wien-New York. Reprinted by permission. **325:** Figure 11.19, Adapted from *Hearing: Physiology and Psychophysics,* by W. Lawrence Gulick. Copyright © 1971 by Oxford University Press, Inc. **326:** Figure 11.22, From *An Introduction to the Physiology of Hearing,* 2/e by James O. Pickles. Copyright © 1988 by Academic Press. Reprinted by permission of the publisher Academic Press Limited, London. **328:** Figure 11.25, From "Shearing Motion in Scala Media of Cochlear Models," by J. Tonndorf, 1960, *Journal of the Acoustical Society of America,* 32, 238–244, figure 7b. Copyright © 1960 by the American Institute of Physics. Reprinted by permission. **328:** Figure 11.27, From *Experiments in Hearing,* by G. von Bekesy, 1960, figures 11.43. Copyright © 1960 by McGraw-Hill Book Company, New York. Reprinted by permission. **328:** Figure 11.26, From "Hearing: Its Function and Dysfunction," by E. D. Schubert, 1980, *Disorders of Human Communication, Vol 1.* pp. 15 and 18. Copyright © 1980 Springer-Verlag, Wien-New York. Reprinted by permission. **329:** Figure 11.28, From *Experiments in Hearing,* by G. von Bekesy, 1960, figures 11.59 . Copyright © 1960 by McGraw-Hill Book Company, New York. Reprinted by permission. **330:** Figure 11.29, From "A Revised Frequency Map of the Guinea Pig Cochlea," by E. A. Culler, J. D. Coakley, K. Lowy & N. Gross, 1943, *American Journal of Psychology,* 56, 475–500, figure 11. Copyright © 1943 by the Board of Trustees of the University of Illinois. Used with the permission of the University of Illinois Press. **330:** Figure 11.30, Data from "The Tuning Properties of Cochlea Hair Cells—Addendum" by I. J. Russell, and P. M. Selleck, 1977. In E. F. Evans and J. P. Wilson, *Psychophysics and Physiology of Hearing,* p. 81. **331:** Figure 11.31, Adapted from "Stimulus Representation in the Discharge Patterns of Auditory Neurons," by N. Y. S. Kiang, 1975. In E. L. Eagles, (Ed.) *The Nervous System Vol.* 3, pp. 81–96. Copyright © 1975 by Raven Press. Adapted by permission. **332:** Figure 11.33, Adapted from "On the Masking Pattern of a Simple Auditory Stimulus," by J. P. Egan and H. W. Hake, 1950, *Journal of the Acoustical Society of America,* 22, 622–630. Copyright © 1950 by the American Institute of Physics. Adapted by permission. **340:** Figure 11.45, From "Processing of Complex Sounds in the Macaque Nonprimary Auditory Cortex," by J. P. Rauschecker, B. Tian, M. Hauser, 1995, *Science,* 268, 111. Copyright © 1995 by American Association for the Advancement of Science. Reprinted by permission. **343:** Figure 11.46, From "On Associations of Light and Sound: The Mediation of Brightness, Pitch, and Loudness," by L. E. Marks, 1974, *American Journal of Psychology,* 87, 173–188. Copyright © 1975 American Psychological Association. Reprinted by permission. **344:** Figure 11.47, From "On Associations of Light and Sound: The Mediation of Brightness, Pitch, and Loudness," by L. E. Marks, 1974, *American Journal of Psychology,* 87, 173–188. Copyright © 1975 American Psychological Association. Reprinted by permission.

Chapter Twelve: **351:** Figure 12.02, From "Loudness: Its Definition, Measurement and Calculation," by H. Flectcher and W. A. Munson, 1933, *Journal of the Acoustical Society of America,* 5, 82–108, figure 4. Copyright © 1993 by the American Institute of Physics. Reprinted by permission. **355:** Figure 12.06, From *Music, Physics and Engineering,* 2nd ed. by H. F. Olson, 1967. Copyright © 1967 by Dover Publications, Inc. Reprinted by permission. **355:** Figure 12.07, From *Music, Physics and Engineering,* 2nd ed. by H. F. Olson, 1967. Copyright © 1967 by Dover Publications, Inc. Reprinted by permission. **362:** Figure 12.14, From "Two-Channel Listening to Musical Scales," by D. Deutsch, 1975, *Journal of the Acoustical Society of America,* 57. Copyright © 1975 by the American Institute of Physics. Reprinted by permission. **365:** Figure 12.18, From "Sound Localization by Human Listeners," by J. C. Middlebrooks & David M. Green, 1991, *Annual Review of Psychology,* 42, 135–159, figure 1. Copyright © 1991 Annual Reviews, Inc. Reprinted by permission. **70:** Figure 12.25, From "Encoding of Sound-source Location and Movement: Activity of Single Neurons and Ineractions between Adjacent Neurons in the Monkey Auditory Cortex," by M. Ahissar, E. Bergman, and E. Vaadia, 1992, *Journal of Neurophysiology,* 67, 203–215. Copyright © 1992 by The American Physiological Society. Reprinted by permission. **370:** Figure 12.26, From "Encoding of Sound-Source Location and Movement: Activity of Single Neurons and Ineractions between Adjacent Neurons in the Monkey Auditory Cortex," by M. Ahissar, E. Bergman, and E. Vaadia, 1992, *Journal of Neurophysiology,* 67, 203–215. Copyright © 1992 by The American Physiological Society. Reprinted by permission. **371:** Figure 12.28, From "Space and Frequency are Represented Separately in Auditory Midbrain of the Owl," by E. I. Knudsen and M. Konishi, 1978, *Journal of Neurophysiology,* 41, 870–883, figure 1. Copyright © 1978 by The American Physiological Society. Reprinted by permission. **371:** Figure 12.27, Adapted from " A Panoramic Code for Sound Location by Cortical Neurons," by J. C. Middlebrooks, A. E. Clock, L. Xu & D. M. Green, 1994, *Science,* 264, 842–844. Copyright © 1994 by the American Association for the Advancement of Science. Adapted by permission. **372:** Figure 12.29, From "A Neural Map of Auditory Space in the Owl," by E. I. Knudsen and M. Konishi, 1978, *Science,* 200, 795–797, figure 1. Copyright © 1978 by the American Association for the Advancement of Science. Reprinted by permission.

377: Figure 12.33, From "Role of Cat Primary Cortex for Sound-Localization Behavior," by M. W. Jenkins and M. M. Merzeich, 1984, *Journal of Neurophysiology*, 52, 819. Copyright © 1984 by The American Physiological Society. Reprinted by permission. **378:** Figure 12.34, From "Compensatory Plasticity and Sensory Substitution in the Cerebral Cortex," by J. P. Rauschecker, 1995, *Trends in Neuroscience, 18*, 36–43. Copyright © 1995 Elsevier Science Ltd. Reprinted by permission.

Chapter Thirteen: **386:** Figure 13.06, From "Perception of the Speech Code," by A. M. Liberman, 1967, *Psychological Review, 74*, 431–461, figure 1. Copyright © 1967 by the American Psychological Association. Reprinted by permission of the author. **389:** Figure 13.09, From "Time-Varying Features of Initial Stop Consonants in Auditory Running Spectra: A First Report," by D. Kewley-Port and P. A. Luce, 1984, *Perception and Psychophysics, 35*, 353–360, figure 1. Copyright © 1984 by Psychonomic Society Publications. Reprinted by permission. **390:** Figure 13.11, From "Selective Adaptation of Linguistic Feature Detectors," by P. Eimas and J. D.Corbit, 1973, *Cognitive Psychology, 4*, 99–109, figure 2. Copyright © Academic Press, Inc. Reprinted by permission. **397:** Figure 13.18, From "Encoding of Speech Features in the Auditory Nerve," by M. B. Sachs, E. D. Young & M. I. Miller, 1981. In R. Carlson and B. Granstrom (Eds.) *The Representation of Speech in the Peripheral Auditory System*, pp. 115–130. Copyright © 1981 by Elsevier Science Publishing, New York. Reprinted by permission. **399:** Figure 13.20, Adapted from "Speech Perception Takes Precedence Over Nonspeech Perception," by D. H. Whalen and A. M. Liberman, 1987, *Science, 237*, 169–171, 10 July 1987, figure 1. Copyright © 1987 by the American Association for the Advancement of Science. Adapted by permission .

Chapter Fourteen: **413:** Figure 14.08, From "Biological Transducers," by W. R. Lowenstein, 1960, p. 103. Copyright © 1960 by Scientific American, Inc. All rights reserved. **413:** Figure 14.09, From "Modality Coding in the Somatic Sensory System," by J. H. Martin and T. M. Jessell, 1991. In E. R. Kandel, J. H. Schwartz & T. M. Jessell (Eds.) *Principle of Neural Science*, 3rd ed., figure 24.10. Copyright © 1991 by Appleton & Lange, Norwalk, CT. **414:** Figure 14.10, Adapted from "Neural Mechanisms of Spatial Tactile Discrimination: Neural Patterns Evoked by Braille-Like Dot Patterns in the Monkey," by K. O. Johnson and G. D. Lamb, 1981, *Journal of Physiology, 310*, 117–144. Copyright © 1981 by The Physiological Society, Oxford. Adapted by permission. **414:** Figure 14.11, From " Human Tactile Pattern Recognition: Active Versus Passive Touch, Velocity Effects, and Patterns of Confusion," by F. Vega-Bermudez, K. O. Johnson & S. S. Hsiao, 1991, *Journal of Neurophysiology, 65*, 531–546, figure 12. Copyright © 1991 by The American Physiological Society. Reprinted by permission. **415:** Figure 14.12, From "Response Characteristics of Cutaneous Warm Fibers in the Monkey," by R. Duclaux and D. R. Kenshalo, 1980, *Journal of Neurophysiology, 43*, 1–15, figure 3. Copyright © 1980 by The American Physiological Society. Reprinted by permission. **416:** Figure 14.13, From "Correlations of Temperature Sensitivity in Man and Monkey, A First Approximation," by D. R. Kenshalo, 1976. In Y. Zotterman (Ed.) *Sensory Functions in the Skin of Primates*, p. 309. Copyright © 1976 by Plenum Publishing Group. Reprinted by permission. **417:** Figure 14.14, From "Intensive and Extensive Aspects of Tactile Sensitivity as a Function of Body Part, Sex, and Laterality," by S. Weinstein, 1968. In D. R. Kenshalo (Ed.)*The Skin Senses*, pp. 206, 207. Copyright © 1968 b Charles C. Thomas. Courtesy of Charles C. Thomas, Publishers, Springfield, IL. **418:** Figure 14.16, From "The Tactile Sensory Innervation of the Glabrous Skin of the Human Hand," by A. B. Ballbo and R. S. Johansson, 1978. In G. Gordon (Ed.) *Active Touch*, figure 1, p. 45. Copyright © 1978 by Pergamon Press Ltd. Reprinted by permission. **419:** Figure 14.18, Reprinted with permission of Simon & Schuster, Inc. from *The Cerebral Cortex of Man*, by Wilder Penfield and Theodore Rasmussen, 1950, p. 214. Copyright © 1950 by Macmillan Publishing Co., renewed 1978 by Theodore Rasmussen. **420:** Figure 14.19, From "Cortical Representational Plasticity," by M. M. Merzenich, G. Reconzone, W. M. Jenkins, T. T. Allard & R. J. Nudo, 1988. In P. Rakic and W. Singer (Eds.) *Neurobiology of Neocortex*, pp. 42–67, figure 1. Copyright © 1988 John Wiley & Sons. Reproduced by permission of M. M. Merzenich. **421:** Figure 14.21, From "Movement-Sensitive and Direction and Orientation Selective Cutaneous Receptive Fields in the Hand Area of the Postcentral Gyrus in Monkeys," by L. Hyvarinen and A. Poranen, 1978, *Journal of Physiology, 283*, 523–537, figure 3. Copyright © 1978 by The Physiological Society, UK. Reprinted by permission. **421:** Figure 14.22, From "Movement-Sensitive and Direction and Orientation Selective Cutaneous Receptive Fields in the Hand Area of the Postcentral Gyrus in Monkeys," by L. Hyvarinen and A. Poranen, 1978, *Journal of Physiology, 283*, 523–537, figure 7. Copyright © 1978 by The Physiological Society, UK. Reprinted by permission. **422:** Figure 14.24, From "Cortical Processing of Tactile Information in the First Somatosensory and Parietal Association Areas in the Monkey," by H. Sakata and Y. Iwamura, 1978. In G. Gordon (Ed.) *Active Touch*, p. 61. Copyright © 1978 by Pergamon Press Ltd. Reprinted by permission. **422:** Figure 14.23, From "Effects of Selective Attention on Spatial Form Processing in Monkey Primary and Secondary Somatosensory Cortex," by S. S. Hsiao, D. M. O'Shaughnessy, and K. O. Johnson, 1993, *Journal of europhysiology, 70*, 444–447. Copyright © 1993 by The American Physiological Society. Reprinted by permission. **425:** Figure 14.26, From "Hand Movements: A Window into Haptic

Object Recognition," by S. J. Lederman and R. L. Klatzky, 1987, *Cognitive Psychology, 19*, 342–368, figure 1. Academic Press, Inc. **425:** Figure 14.27, Data from "Hand Movements: A Window into Haptic Object Recognition," by S. J. Lederman and R. L. Klatzky, 1987, *Cognitive Psychology, 19*, 342–368. Academic Press, Inc. **426:** Figure 14.28, From "Nervous Outflow From the Cat's Foot During Noxious Radiant Heat Stimulation," by P. W. Beck, H. O. Handwerker & M. Zimmerman, 1974, *Brain Research, 67*, 373–386, figure 3A. Copyright © 1974 by Elsevier Biomedical Press, B.V. Reprinted by permission. **427:** Figure 14.30, Adapted from "Living Prehistory in India," by D. D. Kosambi, *Scientific American*, February 1967, figures on pp. 210–211. **427:** Figure 14.29, From "Somatosensory, Multisensory, and Task-Related Neurons in Cortical Area 7b (PF) of Unanesthetized Monkeys," by W. K. Dong, E. H. Chudler, K. Sugiyama, and T. Hayashi, 1994, *Journal of Neurophysiology, 72*, 542–564. Copyright © 1994 by The American Physiological Society. Reprinted by permission. **433:** Figure 14.33, From "Picture and Pattern Perception in the Sighted and the Blind: The Advantage of the Late Blind," by M. A. Heller, 1989, *Perception, 18*, 379–389. Copyright © 1989 by Pion Ltd., London. Reprinted by permission. **434:** Figure 14.35, From "How the Blind Draw," by J. M. Kennedy, January 1997, 76–81, *Scientific American*, p. 103. Copyright © 1997 by Scientific American,Inc. All rights reserved.

Chapter Fifteen: **448:** Figure 15.07, From "Receptor Cell Responses to Odorants: Similarities and Differences Among Odorants," by G. Sicard and A. Holley, 1984, *Brain Research*, 292, 283–296, figure 4. Copyright © 1984 by Elsevier Science Publishing. Reprinted by permission. **449:** Figure 15.08, Adapted from "Topographic Coding of Olfactory Quality. Ordorant-Specific Patterns of Epithelial Responsivity in the Salamander," by A. MacKay-Sim, P. Shaman & D. Moulton, 1982, *Journal of Neurophysiology, 48*, 584–596, figure 4. Copyright © 1982 by the American Physiological Society. Adapted by permission. **450:** Figure 15.10, Adapted from "Discrimination of Odors in Olfactory Bulb, Pyriformamygdaloid Areas and Orbito-Frontal Cortex of the Monkey," by T. Tanabe, M. Iino & S. F. Takagi, 1975, *Journal of Neurophysiology*, 38, 1284–1296. Copyright © 1975 by The American Physiological Society. Reprinted by permission. **452:** Figure 15.12, Adapted from Nasal Chemorecption in Flavor Identification," by M. M. Mozell, B. P. Smith, P. E. Smith, R. L. Sullivan & P. Swender, 1969, *Archives of Otolaryngology, 90*, 367–373, figure 3. Copyright © 1969 by the American Medical Association. Adapted by permission of M. M. Mozell. **452:** Figure 15.13, Adapted from "Role of Olfaction in Perception of Non-Traditional 'Taste' Stimuli," by T. P. Hettinger, W. E. Myers & M. E. Frank, 1990, *Chemical Senses, 15*, 755–760, figure 2. Copyright © 1990 by Oxford University Press. Adapted by permission of Oxford University Press, UK. **459:** Figure 15.19, From "Sensory Neural Patterns and Gustation," by R. Erickson, 1963. In Y. Zotterman (Ed.) *Olfaction and Taste*, Vol. 1, pp. 205–213, figure 4. Copyright © 1963 by Pergamon Press, Ltd. Reprinted by permission. **460:** Figure 15.20, Adapted from "Neural Coding of Taste in Maccaque Monkeys," by M. Sato and H. Ogawa, 1993. In K. Kurihara, N. Suzuki & H. Ogawa (Eds.), *Olfaction and Taste XI*, p. 398. Copyright © 1993 by Springer-Verlag. Adapted by permission. **461:** Figure 15.21, Reproduced from " Response Properties of Macaque Monkey Chorda Tympani Fibers," by M. Sato, H. Ogawa & S. Yamashita, 1975, *The Journal of General Physiology, 66*, 781–810, figure 4, by copyright © 1975 permission of The Rockefeller University Press. **462:** Figure 15.22, Adapted from "Coding Channels in the Taste System of the Rat," by T. R. Scott and B. K. Giza, 1990, *Science, 249*, 1585–1587, figure 1. Copyright © 1990 by the American Association for the Advancement of Science. Adapted by permission.

Chapter Sixteen: **474:** Figure 16.06, From "Infant Contrast Sensitivity Evaluated by Evoked Potentials," by M. Pirchio, D. Spinelli, A. Fiorentini & L. Maffei, 1978, *Brain Research, 141*, 179–184, figure 3C. Copyright © 1978 Elsevier Biomedical Press B.V. Reprinted by permission. **475:** Figure 16.07, From *The Postnatal Development of the Cerebral Cortex*, Vol. 1, 1939 and Vol. 3, 1947, and *The Postnatal Development of the Human Cerebral Cortex*, Vol. 4, 1951, by J. L. Conel, plates LVIII, LXIV and LXIV. Copyright © 1939, 1947, 1951 by Harvard University Press. Reprinted by permission of the publisher. **478:** Figure 16.15, From "Perception of Partly Occluded Objects in Infancy," by P. J. Kellman and E. S. Spelke, 1983, *Cognitive Psychology, 15*, 483–524, figure 3. Copyright © 1983 by Academic Press. Reprinted by permission. **478:** Figure 16.13, From "Part-whole Perception in Early Infancy: Evidence for Perceptual Grouping Produced by Lightness Similarity," by P. C. Quinn S. Burke and A. Rush, 1993, *Infant Behavior and Development, 16*, 19–42. Copyright © 1993 by Ablex Publishing Corporation. Reprinted by permission of the author. **485:** Figure 16.23, From "Assessment of Stereopsis in Human Infants," by S. L. Shea, R. Fox, R. Aslin & S. T. Dumais, 1980, *Investigative Ophthalmology and Visual Science, 19*, 1440–1404, figure 1. Copyright © 1980 C.V. Mosby Company, St. Louis MO. Reprinted by permission. **486:** Figure 16.25, From "Infants' Perception of Pictorially Specified Interposition," by C. E. Granrud and A. Yonas, 1984, *Journal of Experimental Child Psychology*, 27, 500–511, figure 1 b and d. Copyright © 1984 Academic Press, Inc. Reprinted by permission. **486:** Figure 16.26, From "Infants' Sensitivity to Familiar Size: The Effect of Memory on Spatial Perception," by C. E. Granrud, R. J. Haake & A. Yonas, 1985, *Perception and Psychophysics*, 37, 459–466. Copyright © 1985 Psychonomic Society Publications. Reprinted by permission. **489:** Figure 16.29, Adapted from "Pure-Tone Sensitivity of Human Infants," by L. W. Olsho, E. G. Koch, E. A. Carter, C. F. Halpin & N. B. Spetner, 1988, *Journal of the Acoustical Society of America, 84*, 1316–1324. American Institute of Physics. **490:** Figure 16.30, Adapted from "Pure-Tone Sensitivity of Human Infants," by L. W. Olsho, E. G. Koch, E. A. Carter, C. F. Halpin & N. B. Spetner, 1988, *Journal of the Acoustical Society of America, 84*, 1316–1324, figure 5. Copyright © 1988 by the American Institute of Physics. Reprinted by permission. **502:** Figure 16.42, From "Intermodal Matching by Human Neonates," by A. N. Meltzoff and R. W. Borton, 1979, *Nature*, 282, 403–404. Copyright © 1979 by Macmillan Journals Ltd. Reprinted by permission.

Chapter Seventeen: **536:** Figure 17.28, Adapted from *Human Information Processing*, 2nd ed., by Peter Lindsay and Donald Norman, 1977. Copyright © Academic Press, Inc. Adapted by permission. **537:** Figure 17.29, Adapted from "Age Variations in Auditory Acuity," by C. C. Bunch, 1929, *Archives of Otolaryngology*, 9, 625–636. Copyright © 1929 by American Medical Association. Adapted by permission. **542:** Figure 17.32, Based on a figure in *Hearing in Children*, 2nd ed. by J. Northern and M. Downs, 1978. Williams & Wilkins. **548:** Figure 17.35, From "The Impact of Audition on the Development of Visual Attention," by A. L. Quittner, L. B. Smith, M. J. Osberger, T. V. Mitchell and D. B. Katz, 1994, *Psychological Science*, 5, 347–353. Copyright © 1994 by American Psychological Society. Reprinted by permission.

Photo Credits

About the Author: Christopher Baker.

Chapter One: **24,** George Hall/Corbis; **25,** Edward Hopper, Yale University Art Gallery, New Haven, CT.

Chapter Two: **37,** From "Scanning Electron Microscopy of Vertebrate Visual Receptors," by E. R. Lewis, Y. Y. Zeevi, and F. S. Werblin, 1969, *Brain Research, 15*, 559–562, © 1969 Elsevier Science Publishers, B. V. Reprinted by permission; **67,** Breck P. Kent.

Chapter Three: **73,** From "Segregation of Form, Color, Movement and Depth: Anatomy, Physiology and Perception," by M. Livingston and D. H. Hubel, 1988, *Science, 240*, 740–749, © 1988 by the American Association for the Advancement of Science. Reprinted by permission; **76,** From "Functional Architecture of Macaque Monkey Cortex," by D. H. Hubel and T. N. Wiesel, 1977, *Proceedings of the Royal Society of London, 198*, 1–59, © 1977 by the Royal Society. Reprinted by permission; **101,** Hubel, Wiesel, and Stryker, 1978.

Chapter Four: **106,** Grant LeDuc/Monkmeyer Press.

Chapter Five: **135,** Bodlein Library, MSWC 361 Vol. 2.

Chapter Seven: **176,** R. C. James; **177,** Courtesy of Thomas Macaulay; **181,** Photograph by Randy Choura courtesy of the Pittsburgh Ballet Theater; **182,** Courtesy of the Pittsburgh Ballet Theater; **183,** Museum of Art, Carnegie Institute, Pittsburgh, PA; **193,** From "Sparseness of the Neuronal Representation of Stimuli in the Primate Temporal Visual Cortex," by E. T. Rolls and M. J. Tovee, 1995, *Journal of Neurophysiology*, 73, 713–716; **200,** From "Failure to Detect Changes in Attended Objects in Motion Pictures," by D. Levin and D. Simons, 1997, *Psychonomic Bulletin and Review;* **209,** Courtesy of Telesensory Corporation.

Chapter Eight: **218,** The Carnegie Museum of Art, Pittsburgh, PA; Acquired through the generosity of the Sarah Mellon Scaife family, 66.24.2; **220,** Photograph by Ansel Adams. Copyright © by the Trustees of the Ansel Adams Publishing Rights Trust; **222,** The Carnegie Museum of Art, Pittsburgh, PA; **225,** Mike Chikiris/Pittsburgh Stereogram Company, Pittsburgh, PA, 1990; **226,** UPI/Corbis-Bettman.

Chapter Nine: **255, bottom,** Baron Wolman/Woodfin Camp & Associates; **262,** W. Perry Conway/Corbis; **263,** Albright-Knox Gallery, Buffalo, NY. Gift of Seymour H. Knox, 1969.

Chapter Ten: **277,** From Edwin S. Porter's *The Great Train Robbery*, 1903; **278,** Charles Mauzy/Corbis; **291,** Photographs courtesy of Maggie Shiffrar.

Chapter Thirteen: **384,** Courtesy of Kerry Green; **385, top,** Courtesy of Kerry Green; **385, bottom,** Courtesy of David Pisoni; **387,** Courtesy of David Pisoni; **388,** Courtesy of James Sawusch; **390,** Courtesy of Ron Cole.

Chapter Fourteen: **407,** Shih and Kessell, 1982.

Chapter Fifteen: **444,** Morrison and Moran, 1995; **456,** Courtesy of Inglis Miller; **458,** Courtesy of Linda Bartoshuk.

Chapter Sixteen: **472,** Courtesy of Velma Dobson; **488,** Walter Salinger/Photo property of Anthony DeCasper; **492,** Kuhl, 1989; **494,** Courtesy of J. E. Steiner, Hebrew University, Jerusalem; **495,** From "Differential Facial Responses to Four Basic Tastes in Newborns," by D. S. Rosenstein and H. Oster, 1988, *Child Development,* 59; **502,** From "Learning and Intermodal Transfer of Information in Newborns," by K. L. Kaye and T. G. R. Bower, 1994, *Psychological Science,* 5, 286–288.

Chapter Seventeen: **534,** Courtesy of Eye and Ear Hospital of Pittsburgh; **545,** Chester Higgins Jr./NYT Pictures.

Color Essays: **Plate 1.3,** Courtesy of Mitchell Glickstein; **Plate 1.4a and b,** F. De Monasterio et al., 1981; **Plate 2.1a and b,** Phil Degginger/Tony Stone; **Plate 2.2a and b,** Ruth Dixon/Stock, Boston; **Plate 3.8,** The Carnegie Museum of Art, Pittsburgh, PA; Acquired through the generosity of the Sarah Mellon Scaife family, 66.24.2.

TO THE OWNER OF THIS BOOK:

I hope that you have found *Sensation and Perception*, Fifth Edition, useful. So that this book can be improved in a future edition, would you take the time to complete this sheet and return it? Thank you.

School and address: ______________________________

Department: ______________________________

Instructor's name: ______________________________

1. What I like most about this book is: ______________________________

____

____

2. What I like least about this book is: ______________________________

____

____

3. My general reaction to this book is: ______________________________

____

4. The name of the course in which I used this book is: ______________________________

____

5. Were all of the chapters of the book assigned for you to read? ______________________________

If not, which ones weren't? ______________________________

6. In the space below, or on a separate sheet of paper, please write specific suggestions for improving this book and anything else you'd care to share about your experience in using the book.

____

____

____

____

____

Optional:

Your name: ______________________________ Date: ______________________________

May Brooks/Cole quote you, either in promotion for *Sensation and Perception*, Fifth Edition, or in future publishing ventures?

Yes: __________ No: _________

Sincerely,

Bruce Goldstein

FOLD HERE

NO POSTAGE NECESSARY IF MAILED IN THE UNITED STATES

BUSINESS REPLY MAIL

FIRST CLASS PERMIT NO. 358 PACIFIC GROVE, CA

POSTAGE WILL BE PAID BY ADDRESSEE

ATT: *Bruce Goldstein*

Brooks/Cole Publishing Company
511 Forest Lodge Road
Pacific Grove, California 93950-5098

FOLD HERE